ENCYCLOPEDIA OF AFRICA

ENCYCLOPEDIA OF

Africa

EDITORS

KWAME ANTHONY APPIAH

HENRY LOUIS GATES, JR.

VOLUME 1 Abacha, Sani–Kilimanjaro

OXFORD
UNIVERSITY PRESS
2010

OXFORD
UNIVERSITY PRESS

Oxford University Press, Inc., publishes works that further
Oxford University's objective of excellence
in research, scholarship, and education.

Oxford   New York

Auckland   Cape Town   Dar es Salaam   Hong Kong   Karachi
Kuala Lumpur   Madrid   Melbourne   Mexico City   Nairobi
New Delhi   Shanghai   Taipei   Toronto

With offices in

Argentina Austria Brazil Chile Czech Republic France Greece
Guatemala Hungary Italy Japan Poland Portugal Singapore
South Korea Switzerland Thailand Turkey Ukraine Vietnam

Published by Oxford University Press, Inc.
198 Madison Avenue, New York, NY 10016

www.oup.com

Oxford is a registered trademark of Oxford University Press

The Library of Congress Cataloging-in-Publication Data
Encyclopedia of Africa / editors, Kwame Anthony Appiah, Henry
Louis Gates, Jr.
p.   cm.
Includes bibliographical references and index.
Summary: "The Encyclopedia of Africa focuses on African history
and culture with articles that cover prominent individuals, events,
trends, places, political movements, art forms, business and trade,
religions, ethnic groups, organizations, and countries throughout
Africa"—Provided by publisher.
ISBN 978-0-19-533770-9 (hard cover: acid-free paper)
1. Africa—Encyclopedias.   I. Appiah, Anthony.   II. Gates,
Henry Louis.
DT3.E53 2010
960.03—dc22
2009038184

1 3 5 7 9 8 6 4 2

Printed in the United States of America
on acid-free paper

Editorial and Production Staff

Contents

List of Maps, Charts, and Tables

Introduction

In the first decade of the twentieth century when W. E. B. Du Bois first imagined an Encyclopedia Africana, he was inspired by the thought that educating others about black people would help in the fight against racism. As the century wore on, he became increasingly convinced that racism wasn't a matter of ignorance. Rather, he thought (inspired by Marxist theories of ideology) that racism served the interests of capitalists by stopping workers of different races from banding together to fight for better wages and conditions. But Du Bois was one of the first scholars to have a profound knowledge of the lives and the works of black people in Africa and her Diaspora, and he never gave up on the dream of creating an encyclopedia that reflected the truth about black people. Regardless of whether or not an encyclopedia of the black world would help in the struggles against racism, it would be a marvelous scholarly accomplishment. Along with fascinating information, it could assemble a magnificent record of black achievement, much of it unknown not just to non-Africans but also to most people of African descent; a record that could provide a rebuttal to centuries of contempt and misrepresentation.

It was Du Bois's vision that several decades ago led Wole Soyinka, Henry Louis Gates, Jr., and I to begin to plan our own Africana encyclopedia. By the time we assembled the resources to create such an encyclopedia, the world Du Bois faced had disappeared. The study of Africa, and of the lives of people of African descent, exploded in the latter part of the twentieth century; Du Bois's project required much original research, while ours could build on a vast new library of knowledge about Africa. Racism, which was still ascendant both in and outside Africa when he began his work, was on the retreat. The world of encyclopedia publishing was also undergoing rapid change, with the invention of the digital encyclopedia, first on CD-ROM and then online.

And so, when we began our work at the end of the twentieth century, we were able to create the first multimedia encyclopedia of the African Diaspora grounded in this new scholarship—Africana (1999). But we are people of the book. We wanted our encyclopedia to live not only in the digital world, but also in the world of print. We wanted it to evolve, as encyclopedias naturally do, with the growth of knowledge and the expansion of scholarship. Our partnership with Oxford University Press in the second edition of Africana (2005) allowed us to realize our goal.

The five-volume Africana covers the experience of people within Africa and of people of African descent. But embedded in it, of course, are many articles that focus on the continent of Africa itself, the homeland in which the African Diaspora finds its roots. We recently realized that we could create out of the larger work a new encyclopedia focused solely on Africa, one that would allow those who were looking for information and insight about the continent to find it in a single source. The two-volume Encyclopedia of Africa is the result. It does for the continent what Du Bois originally aimed to do for the Diaspora: it enlarges the knowledge and understanding of Africa for people of all races—informing, fascinating, and perhaps even inspiring them.

The response in the Diaspora to Africana was immensely rewarding, in part because it seemed to inspire people to learn about the rich world of creativity in Africa and the places where her children have settled. People in the Diaspora wanted to add the book to their collection so they and their families could learn about the history and achievements of African Americans, as well as reflect on the problems and challenges they face. The Encyclopedia of Africa will allow anyone with an interest in Africa to do the same. It covers the great diversity of the people of this multiracial continent over the millennia, and it updates articles from Africana to reflect recent events such as the election of Ellen Johnson-Sirleaf as president of Liberia in 2006 (the first female elected head of state in Africa), the 2008 charges brought by the International Criminal Court against Sudanese President Omar Hassan al-Bashir for crimes against humanity in the Darfur genocide, controversial elections in Nigeria (2007) and Zimbabwe (2008), and President Barack Obama's visit to Africa in 2009.

Whether you want to understand the history of the independence movements in West Africa, the rise and fall of apartheid in South Africa, or the musical traditions of the Maghreb, these volumes will allow you to find the people, the places, the objects, the institutions, and the ideas that you need to answer your questions. And even if you come to the Encyclopedia of Africa with only your curiosity about African life, you will find something to interest and engage you on any page you choose to begin your journey.

Kwame Anthony Appiah
Henry Louis Gates, Jr.
September 1, 2009

Acknowledgments

Building an encyclopedia requires the labor and support of hundreds of individuals and many institutions. In addition to the contributors, who are acknowledged elsewhere in this book, the editors wish to express their profound gratitude to the following persons who, in a variety of ways, contributed to the collection of entries upon which this encyclopedia is based:

Sharon Adams, Kofi Agawu, Rachel Antell, Bennett Ashley, Robbie Bach, Tim Bartlett, Craig Bartholomew, John Blassingame, Sara S. Berry, Suzanne Preston Blier, Lawrence Bobo, William G. Bowen, Peggy Cooper Cafritz, Elizabeth Carduff, Albert Carnesale, Jamie Carter, Sheldon Cheek, Chin-lien Chen, Frederick Cooper, Moore Crossey, Selwyn R. Cudjoe, Jacques dAdesky, Coureton C. Dalton, Karen C. C. Dalton, the late Charles T. Davis, Rafael de la Dehesa, Howard Dodson, Anani Dzidzienyo, John Donatich, David Du Bois, Joseph Duffy, Olawale Edun, Richard Ekman, David Eltis, Lynn Faitelson, Amy Finch, Henry Finder, Lisa Finder, Kerry Fishback, Susanne Freidberg, Elaikne Froehlich, Paul Gilroy, Tony Gleaton, Peter Glenshaw, Lisa Goldberg, Matthew Goldberg, Jaman Greene, Jane Guyer, Martin Hall, Stuart Hall, Holly Hartman, Evelyn Brooks Higginbotham, Pete Higgins, Jessica Hochman, Chihiro Hosoe, Paulin J. Hountondji, John Hunwick, Abiola Irele, Pat Jalbert, Mary Janisch, Miriam Jiménez-Roman, Quincy Jones, Paul Kahn, Randall Kennedy, Leyla Keough, Jamaica Kincaid, Jeremy Knowles, Joanne Kendull, Harry Lasker, Todd Lee, Krzysztof Lenk, Marvín Lewis, Erroll McDonald, Jack McKeown, Della R. Mancuso, J. Lorand Matory, Nancy Maull, Ali A. Mazrui, Sonny Mehta, Joel W. Motley III, Lucia Nagib, Richard Newman, Peter Norton, Mark OMalley, Jennifer Oppenheimer, Francisco Ortega, Nell Irvin Painter, Hans Panofsky, Orlando Patterson, Martin Payson, Frank Pearl, Ben Penglase, Kevin Rabener, Arnold Rampersad, Toni Rosenberg, Daryl Roth, Michael Roy, Neil Rudenstine, Kelefa Sanneh, Carrie Seglin, Keith Senzel, Bill Smith, Thomas E. Skidmore, Werner Sollors, Doris Sommer, Wole Soyinka, Claude Steele, Patti Stonesifer, Patricia Sullivan, Carol Thompson, Larry Thompson, Lucy Tinkcombe, Kate Tuttle, Charles Van Doren, Robert Vare, Michael Vazquez, Alberto Vitale, Sarah Von Dreele, Philippe Wamba, Carrie Mae Weems, Cornel West, William Julius Wilson, and X Bonnie Woods.

The editors would also like to thank Robert Arlt and Jason Miller for diligently reviewing and updating the entries in this collection.

Chronology of Selected Events

Dates	Events	Dates	Events
4–2.5 million years B.C.E.	Two major groups of hominids emerge in East Africa.	c. 1350 B.C.	Pharoah Akhenaton, regarded by some historians as the first monotheist, rules Egypt from 1350 to 1334.
c. 3400 B.C.E.	Egyptians adopt a special symbol for the number ten. Around the same time other symbols are adopted: a spiral for 100 and a lotus blossom for 1,000.	c. 1000 B.C.E.– 350 C.E.	Kingdom of Nubia flourishes.
		c. 920 B.C.E.– 250 C.E.	Nok culture thrives in central Nigeria.
c. 3200 B.C.E.	Egyptian writing (hieroglyphics) is invented.	c. 800– 146 B.C.E.	Carthage dominates the western Mediterranean region; Phoenician trade flourishes.
c. 3100– 2258 B.C.E.	Egypt's Old Kingdom thrives until famine and Bedouins attack the borders and the civilization falls into decline.	525 B.C.E.	Under the leadership of Cambyses II, Persia conquers Egypt; camels are introduced into Egypt.
c. 2800 B.C.E.	Papyrus, a plant found along the banks of the Nile, is made into writing material by the Egyptians.	332 B.C.E.	Greek presence in Africa begins with the entry of Alexander the Great into Egypt.
c. 2680– 2565 B.C.E.	The first stone pyramid—and the oldest surviving example of an architectural monument—is built for the pharaoh Zoser.	305 B.C.E.	Ptolemy, a Macedonian general, establishes the Ptolemaic dynasty in Egypt.
c. 2134–1668 B.C.E.	Egypt's Middle Kingdom thrives. During this time, the pharaohs establish a standing army and extend Egypt's influence toward Libya, Palestine, and into Nubia.	146 B.C.E.	After the destruction of Carthage, Rome acquires its first territory in Africa—a province of about 5,000 square miles roughly corresponding to the boundaries of present-day Tunisia.
1730–1580 B.C.E.	Kingdom of Kush controls Nubia south of the Elephantine.	60–30 B.C.E.	Cleopatra, the last Ptolemaic ruler of Egypt, forms alliances with Rome's most important leaders, Julius Caesar and Mark Antony.
1567– 1085 B.C.E.	Egyptians drive foreigners from their land and establish the New Kingdom. Tutankhamen ascends the throne at the age of nine and dies at age eighteen.	First century C.E.	Camels are introduced into the Sahara. By the 300s or 400s C. E., camels are transporting gold and salt across the desert. The use of camels increases the mobility of individuals and groups as well as the potential for nomads to attack Roman territories.
1504 B.C.E.	Hatshepsut becomes regent and rules for her infant nephew Thutmose III.	c. 50–900s C.E.	Aksum Kingdom flourishes in Ethiopia.

Dates	Events	Dates	Events
c. 106 C.E.	Egyptian merchant compiles *Periplus Maris Erythraei* (The periplus of the Eritrean sea), a book that describes trade of the Red Sea, eastern Africa, and South Arabia with India and China.	c. 900–present	Kingdom of Benin and its capital, Benin City, is founded on a sandy plain in the middle of the tropical rain forest of western Nigeria. The original inhabitants of Benin called themselves, their capital, and their language Edo, as their descendants do today.
354 C.E.	Saint Augustine is born in North Africa to a pagan father and Christian mother. He is considered to be one the "Doctors of the Church," a title bestowed during the Middle Ages to particularly influential and saintly theologians.	969–1171	Fatimids, an expansionist military power and fervent evangelists for the Shiite branch of Islam, arrive in Egypt from the west and establish a dynasty.
400–1076	Kingdom of Ghana, the first large sub-Saharan state, flourishes.	1000s	Shona on the Zimbabwe plateau begin to export gold and build the stone structures that become Great Zimbabwe, which flourishes until its decline in the 1500s.
640–1500s	Islam, which had its beginnings among Arabs who inhabited the desert of present-day Saudi Arabia, spreads in Africa through trade, missionary activity, and conquest. By the beginning of the eleventh century, Muslim sultanates exist throughout the region.	1056–1147	Almoravids, a confederation of Saharan Berbers, rule northwestern Africa and Muslim Spain.
700s–1400s	Swahili civilization develops along the eastern coast of Africa.	1147–1269	Almohads displace the Almoravids and establish a dynasty ruling North Africa and Spain from Marrakesh in Morocco.
784	Kingdom of Kanem-Bornu is founded between Lake Chad and the southern end of the Saharan trade route known as the Bahr al-Ghazal, providing the most direct line between the Lake Chad region and the Mediterranean.	1169–1252	Under the Ayyubid dynasty Egypt becomes the most important center of Arabic civilization.
800s–1500s	Ife, the urban center in southern Nigeria and homeland (according to oral traditions) of the Yoruba, is founded and flourishes. Yoruba kings claim descent from Ife ancestors, and most states on the Bight of Benin regard Ife as the source of Divine Kingship.	c.1200	Lalibela, the king of Ethiopia, creates a ceremonial center in the Lasta province of Roha, which is now known as Lalibela.
		1240–1400	Kingdom of Mali, founded by Sundiata Keita, flourishes.
		1260–1517	Mamluks, former slaves of Turkish descent, rule Egypt for almost three centuries.

Dates	Events	Dates	Events
1300s– early 1700s	Nimi Lukeni establishes the kingdom of Kongo, which is later ruled by Nzinga Mbemba (also known as Afonso I). Afonso opens the country to Portugal and makes Christianity the state religion.	1517	Sultan Selim I defeats the Mamluk army and brings Ottoman rule to Egypt.
1324	Mansa Musa, ruler of Mali, makes a pilgrimage to Mecca and returns with Muslim scholars and artisans. Musa reportedly ascended the throne when his predecessor left the region with 2,000 ships to explore the other side of the Atlantic Ocean.	1554	Sa'adi dynasty begins with the taking of Fès in Morocco, which is followed by four decades of struggle against colonizing Europeans.
		c. 1570	A ship carrying slaves from Guinea to Panama is wrecked off the coast of Ecuador. The escaped Africans, or maroons, establish the Republic of Esmeraldas.
1441	First black slaves and gold dust from West Africa arrive in Portugal.	1605–1694	The *quilombo* (community of escaped slaves) of Palmares is established in Pernambuco in Brazil. The largest and best organized of the quilombos, Palmares flourishes for nearly a century.
1444	Portuguese captain Dinis Dias finds the Senegal River, the first great tropical river to be seen by Europeans. In the *Chronicle of the Discovery and Conquest of Guinea*, Gomes Eanes de Zurara recounts how 235 African slaves were brought to Portugal and sold.	1619	A Dutch frigate discharges twenty Africans at Jamestown, Virginia. According to surviving documents, these were the first Africans to arrive in North America. They were classified as indentured servants, not slaves.
1460–1591	Founded by fishermen from Dendi, the Songhai empire dominates the land along the right bank of the Niger River. Weakened by epidemic diseases and struggles within the royal family, the empire eventually falls to Moroccan invaders.	1624–1663	Baptized Dona Ana de Souza by the Portuguese, Njinga Mbande rules Matamba as regent from 1624 until her brother's death two years later and then as queen. Allied with the Dutch, she eventually defeats the Portuguese in Angola.
1481	To protect their monopoly of the gold trade, the Portuguese erect a stone fort at Elmina on the coast of Ghana.	1625– early 1800s	Kingdom of Dahomey flourishes in the southern region of present-day Benin, becoming a major force in the region.
1510	Transatlantic slave trade begins with Spain and Portugal bringing an estimated 367,000 Africans to the New World during the 1500s. By the 1860s an estimated 12 million men, women, and children will have been shipped to a life of slavery in the Americas.	1652	Dutch send a contingent to build a fort near the Cape of Good Hope as a stopover for Dutch ships sailing between the Netherlands and Java. By 1707 the fort is a Dutch colony consisting of nearly 1,800 free men, women, and children and more than 1,100 slaves.

Dates	Events	Dates	Events
1660–present	Second Sa'adi dynasty (Alawites) rules Morocco.	1815	Paul Cuffe, merchant-mariner, philanthropist, and promoter of African American colonization of Africa, transports thirty-eight black people to Sierra Leone at his own expense.
1668	Group of independent English merchants establish the Gambia Adventurers Company to exploit the slave trade on the Gambia, Sierra Leone, and Sherbro rivers; replaced by the Royal African Company in 1672.	1816–1884	Zulu kingdom emerges among the northern Nguni chiefdoms of southeastern Africa during a period of change and coincides with the era known as *mfecane* ("time of trouble"), when local populations grew rapidly and were overtaxing the land and water supplies.
1670s	Four empires—Aowin, Denkyira, Akwamu, and Asante—vie for primacy on the lower Guinea coast. By the mid-1700s, the Asante consolidate power over the others, forming a confederation of states.	1839	Cinque, a West African, leads other slaves in a mutiny aboard the Spanish ship *La Amistad*. The subsequent trials, culminating before the U.S. Supreme Court, eventually free the surviving rebels and allow them to return to Africa.
1788–1890s	Europeans, including Sir Joseph Banks, Sir Richard Burton, John Hanning Speke, David Livingstone, and Heinrich Barth, explore the interior of the African continent.	1876–1960s	European countries stake claims to land in Africa: Portugal annexes Mozambique and Angola; Berlin Conference begins the Scramble for Africa, the "legal" portioning of the continent by European countries.
1789	Olaudah Equiano's autobiography, published in 1789, tells of his boyhood in West Africa, his capture and enslavement, his experience during the infamous Middle Passage, and his eventual purchase of his own freedom.	1880–1881	Afrikaners rebel against Britain in the First Boer War; British withdraw from Transvaal in southern Africa.
1795	To prevent the French from seizing the Cape peninsula of South Africa and attacking British ships en route to India, Britain sends an expedition to take possession of the region. Although the Cape would revert to the Dutch between 1803 and 1806, by 1814 British sovereignty over the tip of southern Africa is reaffirmed.	1896	Army of Ethiopian emperor Menelik II wins a decisive victory over the Italian army at the Battle of Adwa. Ethiopia was the only African country to maintain its independence from colonial domination.
1807	Great Britain and the United States abolish the slave trade, effective January 1, 1807.	1899–1901	British defeat the Afrikaners in the Second Boer War.
		1910	Union of South Africa is established.

Dates	Events	Dates	Events
1914–1918	World War I rages; French and British troops capture German Togo; Africans fight in the armies of various colonial powers.	1963	Jomo Kenyatta becomes head of state in independent Kenya; Zanzibar gains its independence; FRELIMO begins an armed struggle for the liberation of Mozambique; Organization of African Unity is established.
1922	Egypt gains its independence.		
1935	Italy invades Ethiopia.		
1936	Union Party in South Africa revokes the voting rights of blacks.	1964	Nelson Mandela is tried and convicted in South Africa; Tanganyika and Zanzibar join to form Tanzania; Malawi and Zambia become independent; Hutus overthrow Tutsi rule in Burundi.
1939–1945	World War II battles are fought in North Africa; Africans in British and French colonies are drafted to fight in Europe and Asia.		
1940s	Nationalist parties form in western Africa.	1965	Rhodesia declares its independence under Ian Smith; Mobutu Sese Seko takes power in Congo-Kinshasa and renames the country Zaire; King Hassan reestablishes the monarchy in Morocco; Gambia gains its independence.
1945	Arab League is formed in Cairo.		
1948	Apartheid policy is established in South Africa.		
1951	Libya becomes an independent monarchy under Idris I.		
1956	Sudan, Morocco, and Tunisia gain their independence.	1966	Lesotho and Botswana gain their independence.
1957	Ghana gains its independence, becoming the first independent black state on the continent; Kwame Nkrumah becomes president.	1967–1970	Biafra attempts to secede from Nigeria; Swaziland becomes independent; Muammar al Qaddafi seizes power in Libya.
1958	Guinea becomes independent. Things Fall Apart, a novel by the Nigerian Chinua Achebe, is published.	1970s	Civil and ethnic wars erupt across the African continent.
		1974–1975	Guinea, Cape Verde, Angola, and Mozambique become independent.
1960	Independence is won in Cameroon, Chad, Congo, Dahomey (Benin), Gabon, Côte d'Ivoire, Madagascar, Mali, Mauritania, Niger, Nigeria, Senegal, Somalia, Togo, Upper Volta (Burkina Faso), and Zaire.	1976	Residents of Soweto and other black townships begin violent protests against apartheid.
1961	Rwanda, Sierra Leone, and Tanganyika gain their independence.	1977	Alex Haley publishes Roots, the half fact, half fiction epic that traces his maternal lineage back to an enslaved West African ancestor named Kunta Kinte; the book is later turned into a successful television miniseries. Somalia invades Ethiopia's Ogaden region, but are soon driven out.
1962	Algeria, Burundi, and Uganda become independent.		

Dates	Events	Dates	Events
1980	Zimbabwe becomes independent.	2000	Paul Kagame becomes the first Tutsi president of Rwanda. An International AIDS conference is held in Africa, the first time that such a conference has been held on the continent.
1988	Somalia and Ethiopia sign a peace accord.		
1990	Nelson Mandela is released from prison; Namibia becomes independent.		
		2001	Joseph Kabila becomes president of Congo-Kinshasa after the assassination of his father. The African Union replaces the Organization of African Unity. Some 4.1 million South Africans are believed to be HIV positive.
1992	U.N. forces are dispatched to Somalia as part of an international peacekeeping mission following the collapse of the government and the rise of rival warlord factions. U.S. Marines arrive in Mogadishu to help in the humanitarian effort.		
		2003	With support from the United Nations, the United States, and several African countries, opposition groups succeed in removing Charles Taylor from the presidency of Liberia. Rebel groups in the Darfur region of Sudan demand power-sharing from the Arab-controlled government, which responds by attacking civilian populations in rebel areas.
1993	Apartheid ends in South Africa.		
1994	Nelson Mandela becomes the first black president of South Africa. A genocide of Tutsis and Hutu in Rwanda—with a death toll estimated as high as 1 million—breaks out; President Juvénal Habyarimana is assassinated during the violence. The United States abandons its mission in Somalia following the deaths of seventeen U.S. Army rangers.		
		2004	Thousands of Sudanese refugees flee to neighboring Chad to avoid attacks by government supported Janjaweed militias; Kofi Annan (secretary-general of the UN) and Colin Powell (U.S. secretary of state) travel to Sudan to focus world attention on the dire humanitarian crisis in Darfur.
1995	Deadly outbreak of Ebola virus kills thousands in Africa. The United Nations abandons its mission in Somalia.		
1996	The South African Supreme Court orders South African public schools to begin admitting black students.		
		2005	The United Nations agrees to dispatch some 10,000 peacekeepers to southern Sudan. However, the killing in Darfur continues.
1997	Laurent Kabila takes power in Zaire and renames the country the Democratic Republic of Congo (Kinshasa).		
		2007	Former Liberian president Charles Taylor is brought before the Hague, charged for his part in inciting crimes against humanity during the violence in Sierra Leone.
1999	Nelson Mandela steps down as president of South Africa. He is succeeded by Thabo Mbeki. Nigeria transitions from a military government to a civilian authority.		

Dates	Events	Dates	Events
2008	Ethiopian soldiers leave Somalia. A government is established but quickly comes under attack by rebel factions. Madagascar begins producing crude oil after a sixty-year stoppage. The International Criminal Court at the Hague charges Sudanese president Omar Hassan al-Bashir for crimes against humanity in the Darfur genocide. Somali pirates seize the Saudi Arabian oil tanker *Sirius Star*.	2009	U.S. President Barack Obama visits Africa, making stops in Kenya, Sudan, and Congo. The president's father was a native Kenyan.

ENCYCLOPEDIA OF AFRICA

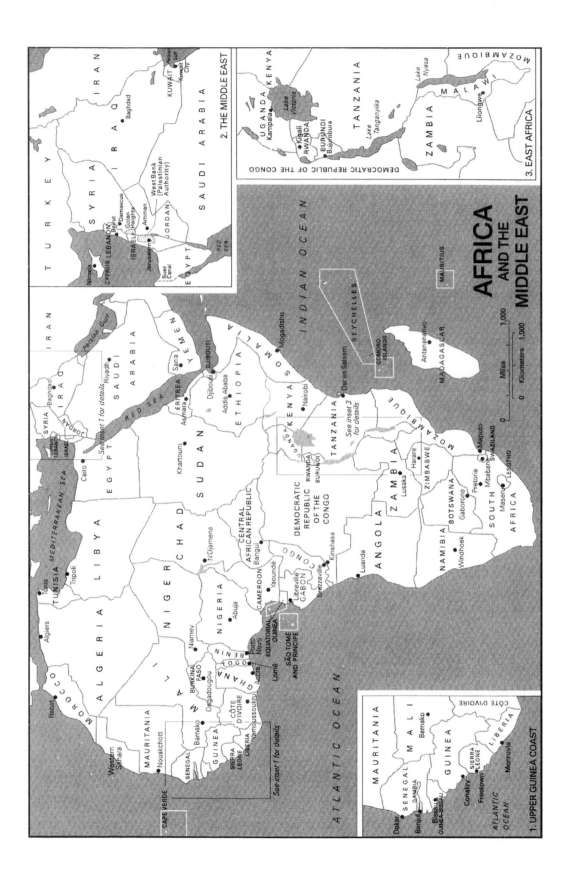

AFRICA AND THE MIDDLE EAST

2. THE MIDDLE EAST

3. EAST AFRICA

1. UPPER GUINEA COAST

A

Abacha, Sani
1943–1998
Military president of Nigeria.

Sani Abacha attended primary and secondary school in his home state of KANO and then joined the army in 1962. As a soldier he attended the Nigerian Military Training College in Kaduna State (1962–1963) and then went to England for further military schooling. Abacha achieved steady promotions as a soldier and by the mid-1980s had entered Nigeria's military elite. In 1983 he was among those who overthrew Shehu Shagari, leader of the Second Republic, in a coup that led to the military rule of Muhammadu Buhari. In 1985 Abacha participated in a second coup, which replaced Buhari with General Ibrahim BABANGIDA, who appointed Abacha minister of defense in 1990. As head of state, Babangida announced that free elections would be held in the early 1990s. In 1993, however, after Babangida nullified the results of these belated free elections, Abacha staged a third coup and ousted his former ally. Once in power, Abacha dissolved all of Nigeria's democratic institutions, from local governments to the national assembly and the constitution. He replaced state governors with military officers and banned the country's two political parties. Abacha also began imprisoning and executing most of his opposition. Among the long list of people imprisoned under him were Olusegun OBASANJO, a former Nigerian head of state; Moshood K. O. ABIOLA, the presumed winner of the 1993 elections; numerous human rights lobbyists; and several journalists. Obasanjo's vice president, Shehu Musa Yar'Adua, died in prison in 1997, and environmental activist and writer Ken SARO-WIWA was jailed and then executed in 1995. Abacha even imprisoned his own second-in-command, Oladipo Diya, in December 1997. In addition to maintaining a large personal guard, Abacha employed plainclothes policemen to flush out dissenters. Although his image was plastered everywhere, Abacha himself rarely appeared in public. Abacha scheduled elections for August 1998, but months beforehand all five legal parties nominated him as their "consensus candidate." As the election approached, Abacha used the military and police to break up pro-democracy demonstrations. Sani Abacha died unexpectedly of a heart attack in June 1998.

See also COLONIAL RULE; NIGERIA.

ERIC BENNETT

Abd Allah ibn Yasin
died 1059?
Islamic scholar and one of the founders of the Almoravids movement; also known as Abdullah b. Yasin al-Gazuli and Abdallah ibn Rasin.

The ALMORAVIDS movement of Abd Allah ibn Yasin conquered parts of northwestern Africa and later Spain during the eleventh and twelfth centuries and converted the defeated populations to Malekite (Maliki) Sunni Islam. Little is known of Abd Allah ibn Yasin's life prior to 1035, when as a student he was visited by a Sanhadja BERBER chieftain and invited to return home with him to teach his people the true faith of Islam. A devout Muslim, Abd Allah ibn Yasin was scandalized by the lax and immoral practices of the Sanhadja Berbers. He encouraged them to convert to Malekite Sunni Islam, imposing a strict interpretation of Qur'anic law. Eventually he even restructured the Berber's military to conduct jihads (holy wars) in accordance with the Qur'an. By 1041, however, the Berber chieftains resented the religious scholar's rule and sent him away. Abd Allah ibn Yasin and a group of followers spent a year at a coastal ribat (religious retreat) and then returned and launched a series of attacks on Berber communities, marking the beginning of the Almoravid movement. Under Abd Allah ibn Yasin, the Almoravids conquered the Gadala, Lemtuna, and Messufa Berber clans in the southern part of present-day MOROCCO and brought Islam to the kingdom of Ghana. They also captured several important Saharan market towns, such as Aoudaghost and Sijilmasa. In 1059 Abd Allah ibn Yasin died in a battle against Gadala Berbers. He was succeeded by Abu Bakr ibn Omar and his cousin Yousuf ibn Tasfin, who led the movement throughout Morocco and into northern Spain.

See also GHANA, EARLY KINGDOM OF; SAHARA.

ELIZABETH HEATH

Abd al-Qadir

1807–1883

Algerian religious and military leader, credited with unifying the Algerian territory through his campaign against French colonization.

Considered a hero of anticolonial resistance by many contemporary Algerians, Abd al-Qadir created an Arab-Berber alliance to oppose French expansion in North Africa in the 1830s and 1840s. He also organized an Islamic state that, at one point, controlled the western two-thirds of the inhabited land in ALGERIA. Abd al-Qadir owed his ability to unite Arabs and Berbers, who had been enemies for centuries, in part to the legacy of his father, head of the Hashim tribe in Mousakar (Mascara) and leader of a Sufi Muslim brotherhood. In 1826 Abd al-Qadir and his father made a pilgrimage, or hajj, to Mecca in Saudi Arabia, the birthplace of the prophet Muhammad, founder of Islam. When he returned in 1828, Abd al-Qadir's own reputation as an Islamic religious and cultural leader grew, and both Arabs and Berbers looked to him to lead the resistance against the French, who had invaded ALGIERS in 1830. The French expanded westward, and in 1832 Abd al-Qadir led attacks on French-occupied Oran, taking the city within six months. He signed a treaty with France in 1834 that permitted French occupation of western coastal cities, but resumed fighting after a new French military leader attempted to organize tribal resistance against him. Through military and diplomatic triumphs over both the French and rival local groups, Abd al-Qadir expanded and consolidated his rule over the territory in the surrounding Oran province. As emir, he governed a hierarchical, theocratic state integrating tribal traditions and promoted commerce and education. In 1837 France signed the Treaty of Tafna with Abd al-Qadir, acknowledging his sovereign authority over an area encompassing two-thirds of Algeria. The French abandoned the policy of limited occupation when General Thomas-Robert Bugeaud came to power. Using scorched-earth tactics, the French systemically destroyed the means of the Algerians' livelihood, including razing and destroying villages, crops, livestock, and forests. The French also reportedly trapped surrendering Muslims in caves and burned them alive. In 1843 the emir was forced into exile in MOROCCO, but when former allies there turned on him, he returned to Algeria to lead resistance efforts. His last retreat to Morocco in July 1846 ended in complete loss of Moroccan support, and in 1847 he returned to Algeria and surrendered to French authorities. The French broke promises of safe conduct and imprisoned him for four years in France, until Emperor Napoleon III released him to permanent exile. In 1852 Abd al-Qadir went to Damascus, in present-day Syria, where he wrote about politics and studied science.

During the anti-Christian riots of 1860 in Damascus and Lebanon, he gathered several hundred followers to rescue thousands of Christians from their attackers. Napoleon III awarded him the Grand Cross of the Legion of Honor. In Algeria, Abd al-Qadir's legacy remained an inspiration through the War of Independence (1954–1962). In 1968 the newly independent nation erected a monument to Abd al-Qadir in the place where a French monument to General Bugeaud had stood and took up his green and white standard as its flag.

MARIAN AGUIAR

Abé

Ethnic group of the Côte d'Ivoire, also known as the Abbe or Abbey.

The Abé, numbering around 200,000, mostly live in the Agboville region of CÔTE D'IVOIRE. One of some five dozen ethnic groups in the region, the Abé speak a Niger-Congo language. Linguistically and culturally, they belong to the AKAN group.

See also LANGUAGES, AFRICAN: AN OVERVIEW.

ARI NAVE

Abeokuta, Nigeria

Capital of Ogun State, in southwestern Nigeria.

The EGBA leader Sodeke founded Abeokuta around 1830 as a settlement for a group of refugees from the collapse of the Oyo Kingdom. Abeokuta translates as "under the rocks," or "refuge among rocks," and refers to the city's location on the craggy east bank of the Ogun River. The early city comprised four Egba subgroups, the Ake, Gbagura, Oke-Ona, and Owu, each in a separate ward. (The Egba are themselves a subgroup of the YORUBA.) In the 1840s missionaries and freed Egba slaves introduced CHRISTIANITY and secular European influences to Abeokuta. The subsequent arrival of SIERRA LEONE Creoles further diversified the town.

In the mid-nineteenth century, Abeokutans warred with the neighboring kingdom of Dahomey (in present-day BENIN) and then with IBADAN. Abeokuta maintained an alliance with Great Britain during this war and the later Yoruba civil wars (1877–1893). Consequently, when Great Britain asserted its control over the region in 1893, it granted Abeokuta and the surrounding Egba region a degree of autonomy. Abeokutans protested their city's incorporation into British NIGERIA in 1914.

Today Abeokuta serves as a market town for the surrounding agricultural region, which produces staple crops, fresh produce, cotton, and palm products. It lies on the main rail line from LAGOS to Ibadan and the interior, and highways link it to surrounding cities, including Ketou in

Benin. Abeokutans are known for their traditional adire, cotton cloth dyed with locally grown indigo. Small-scale local industries include fruit canning, brewing, saw milling, and the manufacture of plastic and aluminum products. In 1984 the University of Lagos established an Abeokuta campus, which focuses on science, technology, and agriculture. The National Universities Commission declared the University of Agriculture Abeokuta (UNAAB) Nigeria's best university for the year 2000. The city's population is 593,140 (2005 estimate).

See also DAHOMEY, EARLY KINGDOM OF; OYO, EARLY KINGDOM OF.

ERIC BENNETT

Abidjan, Côte d'Ivoire
Largest city and chief seaport in Côte d'Ivoire, located in the southeastern part of the country.

The cultural and economic center of the CÔTE D'IVOIRE, Abidjan surrounds the Ébrié Lagoon on the Atlantic Ocean's Gulf of GUINEA. Historians are not sure when people first inhabited the area, but modern settlement dates from the early sixteenth century. Later in the century the Ébrié people selected the area as the site for three fishing villages Locodjo, Anoumabo, and Cocody. Portuguese traders explored the area for a brief period in the seventeenth century, but Europeans largely ignored it until French COLONIAL RULE in the late nineteenth and early twentieth centuries. In 1903 the French chose the settlement as the endpoint for a railway connecting Upper Volta (now BURKINA FASO) to the coast, and a small town soon developed around the train station. The lack of a viable port, however, initially stifled the town's growth.

In 1934, shortly after the completion of the rail link to the Upper Volta city of BOBO-DIOULASSO, the French moved the colonial capital from nearby Bingerville to Abidjan and began building a series of bridges between the mainland and the lagoon islands. The completion of the Vridi Canal in 1950, followed by the construction of a port on the barrier island of Petit-Bassam, made Abidjan the colony's center of industry and shipping. The opening of the port also dramatically increased the city's wealth and population, and Abidjan has since become the most populous city in the Côte d'Ivoire. As of 2006 the population was an estimated 3.7 million, a fact that prompted the government of President Félix HOUPHOUËT-BOIGNY to begin planning to move the capital to Houphouët-Boigny's hometown, YAMOUSSOUKRO, in 1983. These plans, however, were suspended after his death in 1993. In 2001 President Laurent Gbagbo announced that the transfer of political power to Yamoussoukro would be completed. A year later, the city was officially combined with a number of outlying regions to form the District of Abidjan, though the city itself (now officially dissolved and known as Abidjan Ville) continues to function as the country's administrative, executive, legislative, and judicial center, as well as serving as the de facto capital.

A series of islands centered on a business center called the Plateau, Abidjan is considered one of the most cosmopolitan (and expensive) African cities, sometimes referred to as "the Petit Paris of Africa." Its glass-walled skyscrapers house the headquarters of numerous international firms and agencies, and shopping centers and French restaurants cater to a sizeable population of European expatriates. Most of the city's African residents—many of whom are migrants from Burkina Faso, Mali, and other West African countries—live in neighborhoods such as Treichville and Adjamé, both centered on huge outdoor markets. The city boasts a museum of traditional Ivorian art, a national library, a university, and several agricultural and scientific research institutes.

Abidjan is home to the country's largest port as well as to factories that process the country's main exports—cocoa, coffee, and palm oil. Although these industries have contributed to the city's prosperity, its population is still sharply divided economically, and many of the neighborhoods beyond the Plateau are extremely poor, crowded, and inadequately serviced. In recent years the government has attempted to counteract urban poverty by training the unemployed as farmers and then giving them land in the country's interior. Although some of these "back to the land" programs have had a measure of success, overpopulation and underemployment remain significant problems in Abidjan.

ELIZABETH HEATH

Abiola, Moshood Kashimawo Olawale
1937–1998
Nigerian businessman, presidential candidate, and political prisoner.

On June 12, 1993, the popular businessman Moshood Kashimawo Olawale Abiola won a long-awaited presidential election in NIGERIA, only to have the country's military leader, Ibrahim BABANGIDA, annul the election results. When Abiola declared himself the country's legitimate leader a year later, Babangida's successor, General Sani ABACHA, jailed him for treason. As a political prisoner, Abiola became the rallying symbol for Nigerians' democratic aspirations.

Abiola was born into a poor, polygamous household of YORUBA-speaking Muslims in the ancient town of ABEOKUTA. None of his parents' first twenty-two children had survived past infancy, so Abiola, the twenty-third, was given the middle name Kashimawo, meaning "Let's see if he will survive." He began his education at the Islamic Nawar Ud-Deen School and then transferred to the Christian-run African Central School. As an indigent student at the Baptist Boys' High School, Abiola sold firewood to pay for his books. He was so poor that he could not afford an egg until he was nineteen years old. He organized a traveling orchestra that performed at public events, often for food. Abiola spoke with a slight stammer, and although he had questionable musical talent, he had tremendous determination.

After leaving high school, Abiola worked briefly as a bank clerk and a civil servant and then received a scholarship to Glasgow University to study accounting. A bright student, he graduated with several awards in 1965. Returning to Nigeria, he worked as an accountant for the LAGOS University Teaching Hospital. He soon became divisional controller for Pfizer Products, a pharmaceutical company. In 1968 he joined International Telephone and Telegraph (ITT), a corporation that was owed a considerable debt by the Nigerian army. After securing the repayment of the debt, Abiola was named the company's chairman in Nigeria and its vice president for Africa and the Middle East.

In 1974 Abiola launched his own company, Radio Communications of Nigeria. He rapidly became a wealthy man. At his death, Abiola's business interests spanned 60 countries and included firms engaged in banking, shipping, oil prospecting, agriculture, publishing, air transportation, and entertainment. His Nigerian companies alone employed close to 20,000 workers.

Abiola's philanthropy was famous throughout Nigeria. He supported education, sports, and numerous social and political causes. He called for reparations from the West to compensate African peoples for the transatlantic slave trade. He married at least five wives and, by some accounts, fathered more than fifty children.

Abiola's public life contained many paradoxes. As a businessman, he received large contracts from his military friends, yet he became an outspoken opponent of the military dictatorship. Abiola's political career was cut short by two such friends: Babangida, who annulled Abiola's presidential victory, and Abacha, who had him imprisoned.

Abiola was the first presidential candidate from the southern part of the country who won a majority of votes even in the predominantly HAUSA north. Hopes for his release from prison soared after Sani Abacha died suddenly in June 1998 and his successor, General Abdulsalam Abubakar, announced the release of many other political prisoners. However, Abiola, who had suffered from heart problems for several years, fell ill on July 7, 1998, while meeting with United States diplomats to discuss the terms of his release. He died several hours later, apparently of a heart attack. Abiola's death in detention sparked anger and violence in parts of Nigeria.

OKEY NDIBE

Abrahams, Peter
1919–
Expatriate South African novelist.

The son of an Ethiopian father and a mother of French and African descent, Peter Abrahams was considered "Coloured" in the South African racial classification scheme. He grew up outside Johannesburg and began working at the age of nine, never having attended school. He later enrolled, however, after he was inspired by hearing *Othello* read to him by a coworker. As a teenager Abrahams discovered works by African American writers such as W. E. B. Du Bois, Countee Cullen, Langston Hughes, Claude McKay, and Jean Toomer in the library at the Bantu Men's Social Centre.

Abrahams began publishing his own poems in local newspapers while studying at a teachers' training college. While enrolled at St. Peter's Secondary School—a fertile political environment—Abrahams became a member of the Communist Party of South Africa (later renamed the SOUTH AFRICAN COMMUNIST PARTY). After his failed attempt to start a school for poor African children in CAPE TOWN, Abrahams left SOUTH AFRICA in 1939, taking a job as a stoker on a steamship. Two years later he settled in England.

Though he never again lived in South Africa, Abrahams wrote six of his seven novels about his home country. *Song of the City* (1945) and *Mine Boy* (1946) explore the racial injustices of a rapidly industrializing and urbanizing South Africa. Abrahams also wrote a historical novel about South Africa's Afrikaners, *Wild Conquest* (1950), and another about African/Indian solidarity, *A Night of Their Own* (1965).

In the 1950s Abrahams wrote for the London *Observer* and the New York *Herald Tribune*; an assignment in Jamaica led him to move his family there in 1956. *This Island Now* (1966) deals with political struggles in a fictional Caribbean setting. Abrahams worked as a radio journalist and eventually became chairman of Radio Jamaica, but he resigned in 1964 to concentrate on writing. His historical novel *The View From Coyaba* (1985) is a sweeping examination of the relationship between blacks and whites in Africa, the Caribbean, and North America. In 2000, Abrahams published the autobiographical/historical work, *The Black Experience in the 20th Century: An Autobiography and Meditation.*

Abrahams is known as a novelist of ideas whom some critics considered didactic, but in whom many readers found provocative and idealistic theories. Abraham's travel books, which include *Jamaica: An Island Mosaic* (1957), and the two memoirs, *Return to Goli* (1953) and *Tell Freedom* (1954), are among his most widely praised works.

See also JOHANNESBURG, SOUTH AFRICA; SOUTH AFRICA.

KATE TUTTLE

Abron

Ethnic group of West Africa, also known as Abrong, Bron, Brong, Bono, and Tchaman.

The Abron inhabit the borderlands of CÔTE D'IVOIRE, GHANA, and BURKINA FASO. They speak a Niger-Congo language and are part of the larger AKAN cultural and linguistic group. Their ancestors, the Bono, founded the first known Akan kingdom during the fourteenth century. As of 2003 some 1,181,000 people identify themselves as Abron.

DAVID P. JOHNSON, JR.

Abuja, Nigeria

Official capital of Nigeria.

The town of Abuja was founded by the HAUSA Zazzua dynasty and conquered by the FULANI during their early eighteenth-century jihad (holy war). Abuja is also home to numerous smaller ethnic groups, making it one of the more ethnically "neutral" cities in NIGERIA. The 2006 census set the population at 778,567.

Relative ethnic parity was one of several reasons that the Nigerian government chose Abuja as the capital. Other factors included its central location—almost exactly in the middle of the country—and its comfortable climate, low population density, and potential for expansion. Abuja is located on the grassy, rolling Chukuku Hills, at an elevation of 360 meters (1,180 feet).

Plans for Abuja's development were drafted in 1976, and construction, slowed by Nigeria's debt, took place over several years. In 1991 Abuja officially replaced congested Lagos as the capital. The city's central zone contains government buildings, including the National Assembly, as well as cultural institutes; residential and commercial areas lie at the periphery. The Federal Capital Territory Ministry has recently begun demolishing houses and buildings as part of a development plan to sanitize Abuja.

Electricity from Shiroro Dam, seventy-four kilometers (forty-six miles) to the southwest on the NIGER RIVER, powers Abuja. Expressways connect the city to other parts of the country, and an airport services international flights.

See also URBANISM AND URBANIZATION IN AFRICA.

ERIC BENNETT

Accra, Ghana

Capital, transportation hub, and largest city of Ghana.

The political, economic, and cultural center of GHANA, Accra occupies a flat, level plain on the Atlantic coast. Originally the site of several villages of the GA people, Accra developed after the Europeans established three fortified trading posts in the vicinity. In 1650 the Dutch built Fort Crevecoeur, which was later renamed Ussher Fort. The Danes constructed Christiansborg Castle in 1661 at nearby Osu, while the British erected Fort James in 1673. Three towns, Danish Christiansborg (or Osu), the Dutch Accra (or Ussher Town), and the British Accra (or James Town), developed around the forts as trade increased. Gradually the entire area became known as Accra, a corruption of nkran, the AKAN word for the black ants common in the area. Accra quickly became an important center in the gold and slave trades. During the eighteenth century traders from ASANTE traveled to Accra to deal with Ga and European coastal traders. The region developed a distinctive urban and mercantile—and predominantly Ga—culture.

In 1850 the Danish relinquished their GOLD COAST possessions, including Christiansborg, to the British. The Dutch left in 1872. Accra became the capital of the British Gold Coast crown colony in 1877. The Accra Town Council was formed in 1898. During the 1920s, after workers completed a rail line linking Accra to KUMASI and interior cocoa-growing regions, the city's commercial economy expanded. By the 1930s Accra boasted polo fields and a number of British colonial governmental buildings. On March 6, 1957, the Gold Coast became the independent nation of Ghana, with Accra its capital. Ghana's first president, Kwame NKRUMAH, declared Accra a city in 1961.

Today Accra is a sprawling metropolis with a population of some three million. Migrants from rural areas continue to pour into Accra looking for work. If growth remains unchecked, the World Bank predicts Accra's population will soar to over four million by 2020. Unplanned population growth has clogged streets and increased water pollution and sanitation problems. Since many people are unable to find employment, more than half of Accra's residents live below the World Bank's absolute poverty threshold. Impoverished shantytowns contrast with the skyscrapers of the city's commercial center. Subsistence farming makes up the most substantial part—some 36 percent of the GDP—of the local economy.

One-third of Ghana's manufacturing takes place in or near Accra. Industries include auto assembly plants, food-processing facilities, distilleries, breweries, textile manufacturing, lumber exporting, and aluminum plants. A hydroelectric dam nearby provides electricity. Three major markets provide food and other goods. Accra has an international airport, while railroads and paved roads link it with Ghana's interior. The city is also home to many technology companies. Experts believe that if the government and business community provide enough infrastructure support, Accra could become the information and communication technology center of Africa.

Christiansborg Castle, sometimes called Osu Castle after the section of Accra it is located in, is now the seat of government. Pan-African leaders W. E. B. Du Bois and

George PADMORE are buried there. Other notable Accra institutions include the Kwame Nkrumah Conference Centre, National Archives, National Museum, Korle Bu General Hospital, Ghana Medical School, and University of Ghana. A variety of clubs, bars, and theaters provide for a vibrant nightlife.

See also GOLD TRADE; SLAVERY IN AFRICA; URBANISM AND URBANIZATION IN AFRICA.

DAVID P. JOHNSON, JR.

Achebe, Chinua

1930–

Nigerian author, whose novel *Things Fall Apart* (1958) is one of the most widely read and discussed works of African fiction.

Chinua Achebe once described his writing as an attempt to set the historical record straight by showing "that African people did not hear of culture for the first time from Europeans; that their societies were not mindless but frequently had a philosophy of great depth and value and beauty, that they had poetry and, above all, they had dignity." Achebe's works portray Nigeria's communities as they pass through the trauma of colonization into a troubled nationhood. In bringing together the political and the literary, he neither romanticizes the culture of the indigenous nor apologizes for the colonial.

Achebe's own upbringing spanned the indigenous and colonial worlds. Born Albert Chinualumogu Achebe to an IGBO family active in the Christian church, he grew up in the rural village of Ogidi, in eastern NIGERIA. At a young age, he received a coveted scholarship to Government College in Umuahia, where he studied alongside some of Nigeria's future political and cultural leaders. After receiving a bachelor's degree from University College of Ibadan (now University of Ibadan), he worked for the Nigerian Broadcasting Corporation, ultimately acting as director of the radio program *Voice of Nigeria* in Lagos.

Achebe moved to London, England, in 1957 to attend the British Broadcasting Corporation (BBC) staff school. There he decided to publish the fiction he had been writing for several years. He was inspired, in part, by a need to respond to the racist portrayals of Africa in the work of prominent European writers. In his first novel, *Things Fall Apart*, Achebe retells the history of colonization from the point of view of the colonized. The novel depicts the first contact between the Igbo people and European missionaries and administrators. Since its publication, *Things Fall Apart* has generated a wealth of literary criticism grappling with Achebe's unsentimental representations of tradition, religion, manhood, and the colonial experience. Immediately successful, the novel secured Achebe's

position both in Nigeria and in the West as a preeminent voice among Africans writing in English.

Achebe subsequently wrote several novels that spanned more than a century of African history. Although most of these works deal specifically with Nigeria, they are also emblematic of what Achebe calls the "metaphysical landscape" of Africa, "a view of the world and of the whole cosmos perceived from a particular position." *No Longer at Ease* (1960) tells the story of a young man sent by his village to study overseas who then returns to a government job in Nigeria only to find himself in a culturally fragmented world. As the young man sinks into materialism and corruption, Achebe represents a new generation caught in a moral and spiritual conflict between the modern and the traditional. *Arrow of God* (1964) returns to the colonial period of 1920s Nigeria. In this novel, Achebe focuses on a theme that underscores all of his work: the wielding of power and its deployment for the good or harm of a community. *A Man of the People* (1966), a work Achebe has characterized as "an indictment of independent Africa," is set in the context of the emerging African nation-state. Representing a nation thought to be based on Nigeria, Achebe portrays the vacuum of true leadership left by the destruction of the governance provided by the traditional village. Achebe's critical political commentary continues in *Anthills of the Savannah* (1987), in which he uses a complex mythical structure to depict an African nation passing into the shadow of a military dictatorship.

During the twenty-year gap between *A Man of the People* and *Anthills of the Savannah*, Achebe was a prolific writer and speaker. He helped found a publishing company in Nigeria with poet Christopher OKIGBO and in 1971 was a founding editor for the prominent African literary magazine *Okike*. In addition, he published children's books and award-winning poetry collections.

After the start of the Nigerian civil war (1967–1970), Achebe traveled throughout Europe and North America on behalf of the Biafra state, which had split off from Nigeria. After the war, he taught literature at the University of Nigeria at Nsukka. During this period, Nigeria was shaken by a series of military coups. Many of his lectures and essays from the 1960s and 1970s were published in *Morning Yet on Creation Day* (1975), *The Trouble with Nigeria* (1983), and *Hopes and Impediments* (1988). In addition to discussing the war and the political situation in Nigeria, Achebe's nonfiction works address topics such as the role of the writer in the postcolonial African nation, literary depictions of Africa, and the debate over language choice by African writers. Responding to critics such as NGUGI WA THIONG'O, who point to the political and cultural implications of writing in the colonial language, Achebe has defended his use of English, asserting that as a "medium of international exchange," the language is a lingua franca (common language) that will connect the communities of Africa.

"Art is man's constant effort to create for himself a different order of reality from that which is given to him," Achebe wrote in his essay "The Truth of Fiction." Achebe, a professor emeritus at the University of Nigeria at Nsukka, has used his position as one of the most widely read African writers to comment on the crisis situation in contemporary Nigeria. Since the 1970s, he has taught at several American universities. Three lectures he gave at Harvard University in 1998 on the emergence of a native African literature were combined into the semi-biographical volume, *Home and Exile* (2000). As of 2008 he was serving as Charles P. Stevenson Professor of Languages and Literature at Bard College, New York.

In 1990 Achebe was involved in an automobile accident that left him paralyzed from the waist down and forced him to rely on a wheelchair. Neither accident nor advancing age, however, stopped his productivity. In 2005 he was at work on a novella based on ancient African myth. Two years later he was awarded the Man Booker International Prize for his contribution to world literature. It is fiction, as ever, that provides for Achebe "the weapon for coping with [threats to integrity], whether they are found within our problematic and incoherent selves or in the world around us."

See also CHRISTIANITY: MISSIONARIES IN AFRICA; COLONIAL RULE; FICTION, ENGLISH-LANGUAGE, IN AFRICA.

BIBLIOGRAPHY

Achebe, Chinua. *Hopes and Impediments*. Heinemann, 1988.

Lindfors, Bernth. *Conversations with Chinua Achebe*. University of Mississippi, 1997.

Petersen, Kirsten Holst, and Anna Rutherford. *Chinua Achebe: A Celebration*. Heinemann, 1991.

MARIAN AGUIAR

Acholi

Ethnic group living primarily along the border of Uganda and Sudan; also called Acoli, Gang, or Shuli.

The Acholi people live mostly in the Acholi district of Uganda, an 18,000-sq-km (11,000-sq-mi) savanna plateau. While 43 percent of Acholi clans trace descent from Nilo-Saharan-speaking LUO groups that migrated from present-day Sudan during the sixteenth and seventeenth centuries, others trace descent from the LANGO, Karamojong, Mandi, and Bari ethnic groups. Thus the Acholi represent an emergent ethnic identity, forged among a number of distinct groups who have come to share a homeland as well as a language and certain cultural traditions. Recent census figures put the number of Acholi in Uganda at nearly 750,000, with another 45,000 living in Sudan.

Most Acholi live in small hamlets organized into patrilineal clans. Several clans make up a chiefdom, or *kaka mandit*. The Acholi distinguish between "royal" lineages, most of which claim to be of Luo origin, and "commoners," but they have not historically recognized a centralized political authority. Like many neighboring groups, the Acholi have traditionally farmed (staple foods include millet, sorghum, maize, and various legumes) as well as raised livestock; cattle are particularly valued as a symbol of wealth.

Precolonial Acholi chiefdoms often raided each other for cattle. With the arrival of Arab traders in the area during the nineteenth century, they also began raiding neighboring groups for slaves. Exchanging captives and ivory for firearms, some clan leaders were able to acquire considerable wealth and regional political power.

Although British colonization during the late nineteenth century put an end to the most powerful Acholi chiefs' expansionistic ambitions, it otherwise had relatively little initial impact on Acholi society. Colonial administrators perceived the Acholi as excellent warriors and recruited them into the colonial army and police force, but showed little interest in the Acholi region, which had neither great strategic importance nor especially valuable natural resources. In addition, the Acholi's relatively decentralized political organization appeared less threatening to colonial authority than kingdoms such as Buganda. The colonial regime only began to intervene seriously in the Acholi region in the early twentieth century, when it imposed a poll tax, confiscated weapons, and altered the spheres of control of some chiefs. It also strongly encouraged cotton cultivation, which many households undertook in order to pay their taxes.

The colonial administration's official designation of the Acholi as a "tribe" contributed to the development of a distinct Acholi identity, as did missionary efforts to transcribe the Acholi language and create a written version of their history. After Uganda achieved independence in 1963, such categories came to shape political alliances and conflicts. While the Bantu-speaking Baganda of southern Uganda were the largest ethnic group, the Acholi and their traditional enemies, the Lango, both northerners, dominated the military. When the first Ugandan prime minister, Milton OBOTE, was ousted by Idi AMIN in 1971, soldiers and civilians from both groups faced severe persecution, including summary execution and torture. When Amin in turn was forced from office in 1979, Acholi members of the army and security forces sought retribution, killing many people of Amin's ethnic group, the Kawka. Obote later relied heavily on Acholi soldiers to fight Yoweri MUSEVENI's National Resistance Army (NRA) during the early 1980s.

After Museveni came to power in 1986, the Acholi again found themselves out of favor with the Ugandan government, which has concentrated economic development efforts in the south of the country. The impoverished Acholi region provided fertile soil for the rise of the insurgent "Holy Spirit" group in 1986, led by self-proclaimed prophet Alice Lakwena, who guaranteed her followers magical protection against bullets when combating the NRA. Museveni's troops, whose bullets failed to turn to water in response to Lakwena's magic, imposed heavy casualties on the Acholi. Betty Bigombe, an Acholi member of Museveni's government, has begun to make some headway in improving the conditions of the Acholi in recent years.

See also HOLY SPIRIT MOVEMENT; IVORY TRADE; SLAVERY IN AFRICA; SUDAN; UGANDA.

ARI NAVE

Acquired Immunodeficiency Syndrome in Africa: An Interpretation

Acquired immunodeficiency syndrome (AIDS) is a fatal disease caused by the slow-acting human immunodeficiency virus (HIV). The virus multiplies in the body until it causes immune system damage, leading to diseases of the AIDS syndrome. HIV emerged in Africa in the 1960s and traveled to the United States and Europe the following decade. In the 1980s it spread silently across the globe until it became pandemic, or widespread. Some areas of the world were already significantly affected by AIDS, while in others the epidemic was just beginning. The virus is transmitted mainly via sexual fluids, but also by blood, from mother to child in the womb, and during delivery or breastfeeding. AIDS first was identified in the United States and France in 1981, principally among homosexual men. Then in 1982 and 1983, heterosexual Africans also were diagnosed. Today, AIDS poses a threat to the survival of millions, especially where health and social infrastructures have been weakened by prolonged economic crises. Ninety percent of the more than 65 million people who contracted HIV/AIDS by 2003 lived in less developed countries. More than two-thirds of the total, some 35 million, were Africans, of whom 15 million already have died. In 2007 some 1.5 million died from AIDS in sub-Saharan Africa.

In the countries of sub-Saharan Africa most affected, AIDS has raised death rates and lowered life expectancy among adults between the ages of 20 and 49 by about twenty years. AIDS has wreaked havoc among people from all walks of life—teachers, health workers, business executives and government officials, and among workers in agriculture, mining, transportation, and other vital industries. AIDS disrupts seasonal labor-intensive agriculture and food processing. The recent prolonged drought in Southern Africa has combined with labor shortages and policy measures that prevented accumulation of food supplies, with millions suffering from hunger as a result.

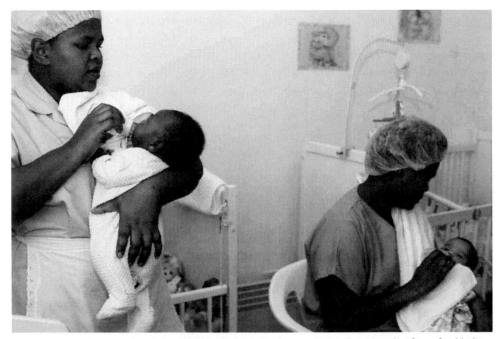

THE IMPACT OF AIDS. Midwives at Shepherds Keep Orphanage in Durban, South Africa, feed babies orphaned by AIDS. (*Themba Hadebe/AP Images*)

The prolonged disease process is extremely painful in its later stages, and the sick require extensive nursing care. Much of the burden of care falls on poor women who may be sick themselves, or elderly, and without resources. Deaths of potentially productive adults leave orphaned children and isolated elders who had once depended on the now-deceased individuals. UNICEF estimates that there are now 11 million AIDS orphans under the age of fifteen and expects the number to reach to 20 million by 2010. With many people becoming ill and others over-worked and demoralized by so much death around them, the impact on social life in the affected areas is severe. Families that care for loved ones, and are unable to hide the nature of the illness, may find themselves isolated. AIDS orphans may be shunned and left to roam the streets, where they are particularly vulnerable to HIV infection. Blaming others allows people to deny the risk and to avoid taking realistic steps toward protecting themselves and others. Where people believe that AIDS is caused by "polluted" women or by unseen forces, scapegoating, witch-hunts, and social unrest compound socioeconomic disruption.

Globally, the epidemic spreads with gathering speed. More than 5 million people became infected in 2003, some 3.5 million in Africa. AIDS now is described as "a major disaster," a "humanitarian catastrophe," even a "holocaust." At the outset, however, the international community and many African governments were slow to recognize the epidemic's potential and slow to respond. Negative ethnocentric representations of African sexuality in Western popular and medical literature created resistance and contributed to the denial of the AIDS threat by both political leaders and ordinary people. Many epidemiologists underestimated the potential magnitude of HIV and AIDS in Africa.

In the late 1980s, international development agencies regarded AIDS control as a technical medical problem rather than one involving all areas of economic and social life. Because public health authorities perceived AIDS to be an urban phenomenon associated with prostitution, they believed that the majority of Africans who lived in "traditional" rural areas would be spared. They believed that the heterosexual epidemic could be contained by focusing prevention efforts on persuading the so-called core transmitters—people such as sex workers and truck drivers, known to have multiple sex partners—to use condoms. Risky sexual behaviors were seen as matters of individual choice, rather than inherent in social relations of unequal power. These factors retarded prevention campaigns in many countries for more than a decade.

Social scientists and epidemiologists who view epidemics as social phenomena, however, foresaw the coming catastrophe. Many viewed AIDS as a development issue, linked to Africa's poverty and exploitation; a few linked gender inequality and underdevelopment. AIDS is not just another disease; the HIV virus is not just one among many new microorganisms affecting humans. A number of biological and social factors make HIV infection exceedingly difficult to control. Neither a cure nor an effective vaccine is likely to emerge in the near future, leaving prevention and treatment of HIV as the only means of controlling the pandemic. Yet both prevention and treatment are exceedingly complex.

Today, several economic and political processes propel the spread of the epidemic. These include a global economy that relegates Africa to production of a few agricultural and mineral exports and unbalanced domestic economies inherited from colonialism. These circumstances resulted in unfavorable terms of trade, massive foreign debt, landlessness, and unemployment, and widening disparities in wealth exacerbated by repressive politicians who siphon wealth from public funds. Economic hardships have fueled the epidemic by increasing the number of vulnerable young people.

Since the mid-1970s, increasingly millions of Africans have lived in abject poverty, their survival precarious, their youth deprived of education, jobs, and hope for the future. Poor people's survival strategies include migration in search of paid work, trading goods over long distances to urban markets, smuggling, and trading sex for food and shelter. The struggle to survive has divided families and changed behavioral standards in both rural and urban areas. Mines, plantations, trading towns, fishing camps, and ports attract job seekers in large numbers. Most are youths and men who come without their families, while adolescent girls, divorced women, and widows also provide low-cost migrant labor and are vulnerable to sexual exploitation.

In the 1980s, deepening economic crisis and the "reforms" imposed by Structural Adjustment Programs (SAPs) to spur debt reimbursement fell hardest on the poor. Peasant incomes and wages declined sharply; government job cuts and de-industrialization raised unemployment levels. Governments reduced funding for public services, including education and health care. The harshest conditions were visited on women and girls who struggle to feed families in the face of overwhelming odds. Their health status deteriorated as economic crisis and SAPs left health systems in shambles. In the 1990s, burdensome debt service continued, while new foreign investments took place mainly in minerals' extraction, chiefly in oil, and in the bribes and military spending needed to win and protect these investments.

Pervasive poverty, norms of gender inequality, lack of education, and economic autonomy make it especially difficult for girls and women to avoid sexual risk. Poor women have few income-earning opportunities that pay as well as sex. Lack of access to effective treatment raises levels of untreated "classic" sexually transmitted diseases (STDs) that multiply the risk of acquiring HIV. The prevalence patterns bear this out. More than half of those infected are young females. Adolescent girls are especially vulnerable, biologically and socially, to sexual infection. Girls socialized for subservience to men find it difficult to refuse sex to men who seek young sexual partners, believing them to be free of infection. Three to six times more adolescent females are infected than males of the same age, while young women in the next age groups are at even higher risk. Few people anywhere have only a single lifetime sex partner, and rural areas are neither isolated nor unchanging. As infection prevalence rates rise, the chance that any one partner will be free of HIV infection decreases. Over time, this puts spouses and other regular partners at risk. For most women, poor, middle class, or wealthy, the major risk factor is marriage to, or co-habitation with, a seropositive man. Their own fidelity does not protect them.

As in many other areas of the world, many men derive prestige from control over many sex partners. Some men's alcohol abuse and violence against women, often associated with unemployment, poverty, and hopelessness—factors that increase the risk of HIV infection—also constitute major social risks. Competition for resources has led to power struggles in which protagonists foment ethnic violence to mobilize followers. Unemployed young men with limited prospects for the future are prime targets of hate propaganda and the promise of booty. Civil wars, ethnic conflict, mass population displacement, and military occupation lead to civilian deaths, hunger, and rape. The numbers who succumb to AIDS as a result eventually may be higher than those killed immediately by violence or hunger. Together, these desperate conditions help to explain high rates of HIV transmission.

Thus, economic and gender inequalities must be addressed across a broad spectrum of social institutions to bring about the changes that reduce HIV risk. This does not mean that HIV risk cannot be reduced until poverty and inequality have been eliminated. Nevertheless, numerous cognitive, emotional, and cultural obstacles must be recognized and overcome. The biological processes involved are difficult for lay people, including political leaders, to understand. Relatively few in Africa have had secondary education, let alone training in contemporary biology. Linked to reproduction and death, AIDS in Africa carries a heavy emotional and symbolic charge. Fear often breeds denial and stigma.

The syndrome's multiple diseases offer a broad cultural field for reinterpretation in keeping with old, widespread concepts of disease causation. Because the infection is sexually transmitted and incurable, some may blame AIDS on moral transgressions and unseen forces. Not surprisingly, across the continent, many men think of AIDS as "a disease of women," and a wife may be blamed for a man's infection. Some religious leaders proclaim that AIDS is divine punishment for the "sins" of fornication and debauchery, but that the "innocent" are protected. Such views not only stigmatize the afflicted; they give false reassurance to women who have remained faithful to husbands who have multiple partners. Because the period between infection with HIV and the onset of disease symptoms is lengthy and varies among individuals, AIDS appears to strike arbitrarily. Temporary remissions allow some people to claim healing powers, as well as to identify mystical causes.

Effective prevention involves enabling large numbers of people to change sexual practices that are widely considered to be natural, essential to health, and a sign of masculine power. A major challenge for prevention is to encourage people to make realistic personal risk assessments. People who carry the virus may appear and feel healthy for some years and HIV testing is not widely available. Few know when they are infected and can transmit the infection; fewer of those infected use protection consistently. People who have had multiple partners in the past should accept the possibility that they may be infected and use condoms to protect to all sexual partners, including spouses and other steady partners. If condom use is inconsistent, the infection progresses and the infected partner is likely to transmit HIV to others.

Another major challenge is to persuade young people to delay sexual activity, to use condoms from the time they begin having sex, to remain faithful to a single partner over time, and to continue using condoms until they both can be tested for the virus. While many young men are able to make such choices once they understand their risks, others live in circumstances that discourage protection, such as single-sex migrant hostels and war. Even if inexpensive condoms are made widely and readily available, a variety of political, social, and cultural obstacles discourage their use. Condoms are not popular among men, many of whom employ a double standard to rationalize their relations with numerous, often much younger, sex partners, while they strictly control the sexuality of wives and girlfriends. Few women, married or single, can refuse sex to a steady partner, even if they suspect that he may be infected, nor can most suggest condom protection. Penalties for doing so may include beatings, rape, or abandonment. Condoms have been widely stigmatized by association with prostitutes and STDs. Even men who wish to use condoms may fear that their lover will berate them with accusations of mistrust or infidelity, and so they may avoid the subject. AIDS often provokes fear and hostility toward the afflicted. Husbands may abandon HIV-positive wives who were tested at prenatal clinics, even though they themselves may have been the source of the wife's infection. Alternatively, not understanding that AIDS takes years to develop, they may accuse the wife of infidelity, when in fact she may have acquired the infection from a previous partner years before.

In many countries, powerful interest groups have treated AIDS, like other STDs, as a moral issue rather than as a health issue, making it difficult for some governments to conduct rational prevention campaigns. Many conservative religious leaders who oppose condoms have spread disinformation to discourage their use. They have spread rumors that condoms do not protect, that they spread HIV, or that they render women sterile. Many adults are convinced that sex education and condoms will increase sexual activity among youth, although research carried out in numerous settings shows that this is not the case. Many men believe that access to condoms will lead wives to become unfaithful. Most married women who become infected, however, are infected by their husbands. Where national, community, and nongovernmental organization leaders share a moralistic perspective, their stance often inhibits effective prevention campaigns.

To date, no person with HIV has recovered a healthy immune system. The new highly active antiretroviral therapies (HAART) can suppress viral replication and delay disease onset, thus prolonging healthy lives. In the West, HAART drugs have transformed AIDS into a chronic disease for many of those with access to adequate health care. Effective treatment is costly and even pain medications are inaccessible to the poor majority in Africa. The treatment requires enormous resources in money, trained personnel, and effective public health delivery systems. Treatment must be lifelong, and most may be expected to progress to AIDS eventually. Yet treatment can serve as an incentive to learn one's status. News that HIV is not an immediate death sentence gives people hope and may increase their desire to protect others. In addition, a treatable chronic disease may carry less stigma and enhance the reputation of biomedicine, thereby deflecting the effects of belief in witchcraft and unseen forces. Thus, treatment and prevention can be mutually reinforcing.

International activism has succeeded in forcing several transnational pharmaceutical companies to lower prices for brand name drugs. A few Third World firms now produce less expensive generics, including a single-dose combination pill, which the World Health Organization (WHO) recommended in its "3 x 5" program to bring treatment to three million sufferers by the year 2005. One pill per day is more patient-friendly than the multiple single-drug doses required by the brand name products. The United Nations' Global Fund to combat AIDS, tuberculosis, and malaria that will strengthen public health systems and train practitioners to use the drugs effectively is sorely underfunded. Some countries began treatment with demonstration projects by research projects and philanthropic organizations; some will scale up free medications in the near future. Thus far, however, HAART is accessible chiefly to urban elites and their families, while even middle class households have to choose who among their members will get the drugs. Further reductions in drug prices and newer HAART drug combinations pose major challenges to the international community, as well as to African nations. At present, the United States government prefers to expend the bulk of its promised AIDS funds to support its own pharmaceutical manufacturers and consultants.

Prevention must continue as the first line of defense, but it must incorporate much more than public health messages with advice to abstain, to be faithful, or use condoms, the so-called ABCs of prevention. Both prevention and treatment require political commitment to provide equitable access to public services and willingness to embark on sociocultural change, especially to institute changes in power relations that determine how individuals interact with one another sexually and socially. Not least among the power relations that must be changed are inequalities of class, gender, generation, and ethnicity in local, national, and international arenas.

There is also good news from Africa, with the prevalence of HIV/AIDS declining in some countries and low, stable rates in others. In Uganda, Tanzania, and Senegal campaigns began in 1986, but strong resistance to ABC prevention by some religious leaders and community elders continued into the early 1990s. Alarmed governments, nevertheless, did not stop at advising men to avoid prostitutes, women to stay faithful to current partners, and young people to abstain from sex before marriage. They also instituted safer-sex education in the army and in schools and made STD treatment and condoms widely available.

Uganda's story is the most remarkable, demonstrating the importance of strong government commitment, flexibility, vigorous civic activity, and donor support. The campaign began in 1986 as the restoration of peace brought renewed hope and economic betterment to many in the country. Incidence of new infections may have begun to fall from that time. Researchers documented the reduction in the southwest from 1992. National HIV prevalence fell from about 15 percent in 1992 to 5 percent in 2002. Virtually everyone has lost relatives and friends, so that most people know that AIDS is real and deadly, people talk about prevention, and many have reduced the number of sexual partners they have. Dialogue about sexual relations and condoms has become acceptable to many, especially among educated young people, many of whom delay having sex until the later teen years. Free primary education brought many more girls to school. An educated young woman can tell her partner that she wants him to use condoms. Girls who have not completed primary school, however, are less likely to be able to delay sexual activity or to negotiate condom use. Along with these changes, advocacy by women professionals for social and legal changes has lessened the oppression of women.

Still certain risks remain. Violence in northern Uganda, with abductions, mass population displacement, and extreme poverty, creates a large zone of increased risk. Multiple partners are still common among wealthy men, poor single women, and men who travel for employment and trade. Many people need to be tested and to learn their results. This means increasing the number of testing facilities, training counselors, holding out realistic possibility of treatment, reducing the stigma and fear of AIDS, as well as passing and vigorously upholding laws against sexual violence and gender discrimination. Political leaders need to speak out in favor of change rather than hiding behind "tradition."

Even in countries that have reduced the prevalence of HIV, prevention requires constant vigilance. Elsewhere, the virus continues to spread rapidly, not only in cities where the epidemic was well established in the 1980s, but also to rural areas and to countries that once had very low levels or were free of HIV.

Recently, several U.S. writers have suggested logical-sounding measures that, in view of actual conditions, are little more than wishful thinking. One is the utterly unfounded notion that abstinence-only education can protect young people from HIV. Another is that sexually active adults are going to have only one uninfected lifetime partner. Neither of these is realistic for the majority, in Africa or in the United States. Condemning condom distribution can only make the situation worse. A third is the call to make HIV testing and counseling mandatory for anyone seeking a marriage license or health care, including assistance in childbirth. The advocates of this plan apparently assume that those who know their status will then practice safer sex. They acknowledge certain drawbacks, such as lack of confidentiality, loss of jobs, and for women, the threat of violence and the loss home and family, but then ignore them. Culture and societies unfortunately do not respond so easily to advice requiring changes in complexly motivated human behaviors.

In sum, an epidemic such as AIDS is an essentially social process, the spread of a microorganism shaped by political, economic, and cultural factors. Limiting sexual transmission requires empowering substantial numbers of people to change highly valued behaviors or to cease activities that enhance people's short-term survival. HIV and AIDS prevention requires alleviating the problems faced by people at risk, rather than simply relaying prevention instructions or messages. Empowerment strategies that incorporate a deep understanding of local cultures and social group dynamics have the potential to bring about changes in sexual behavior and in the social environment in which sex occurs. Dialogue in community groups can identify problems faced by vulnerable populations. Creative mass media communications can enhance their impact. Male dominance can be examined, gender oppression understood, and more egalitarian behaviors modeled. Problem-posing methods can not only overcome obstacles to condom use, but also can attempt to address broader issues of poverty and inequality within a context of social action in support of democracy and development. This potential for social change makes many government leaders reluctant to initiate programs of community-based consciousness-raising to prevent AIDS. The method requires trained professionals and support personnel, which makes it expensive, although it is cheap in comparison to the existing alternatives: drugs for a lifetime and/or death.

Responses to AIDS have political dimensions in Africa, as elsewhere. Public health action takes place in an environment in which differences in understanding and unequal power relationships prevail. Because social structures limit the choices people make, stopping AIDS requires eliminating the barriers that deprive women of control over their sexual interactions and deprive poor people of control over their lives. Changes on the interpersonal level are insufficient, and to be sustained they must be supported by broader institutional, economic, and political change.

The components of sustainable development, which must incorporate both long-term economic growth and social justice, are well known. Sustainable development must include an agrarian strategy that supports food production by small farmers instead of large export-oriented farms and corporations. Sustainable development also requires support for rural nonfarm production, for development of viable regional import substitution industries, and for export diversification. Finally, sustainability entails the development of human capacities through broad access to education and training. The international community must help provide the conditions necessary for this development, including debt forgiveness, increased aid for human needs, and policies that avoid the illusion that market capitalism by itself, without social programs, can create bright futures for the poor. National leaders must accept responsibility for reducing corruption and redirecting funds to reducing inequality. Policymakers have not generally accepted the understanding on which this perspective is based or the need for global redistribution of power and wealth that follow. Instead, they tend to seek simple solutions—limited interventions that appear to offer a hope of interrupting the epidemic without threatening vested interests.

Africa is the first but not the only continent to experience the effects of prolonged and complex crisis. A major new center of HIV infection lies in South and Southeast Asia, home to well over a billion people. Despite its rapid industrial development, economic crisis in Southeast and East Asia is expected to increase the spread of the AIDS pandemic, already rampant in the sex "industry," among the military and among intravenous drug users. Within the United States, new infections are disproportionately concentrated among poor people of color. While the burdens of care for the sick and orphaned mount, wealthy nations may become complacent and efforts to stem the pandemic may slacken. This was the case in the recent past with more easily preventable and treatable diseases such as tuberculosis, malaria, cholera, and STDs such as syphilis and gonorrhea that are now pandemic. Unless policies address the underlying struggles of millions to survive the consequences of poverty, powerlessness, and hopelessness, HIV infection will continue to spread among the world's poor.

See also HEALTH CARE IN AFRICA; STRUCTURAL ADJUSTMENT IN AFRICA.

BIBLIOGRAPHY

Barnett, Tony, and Allan Whiteside, eds. *AIDS in the Twenty-first Century: Disease and Globalization*. Palgrave Macmillan, 2003.

Farmer, Paul. *Pathologies of Power: Health, Human Rights and the New War on the Poor*. University of California Press, 2003.

Grown, Caren, Geeta Rao Gupta, and Zahia Kahn. "Promises to Keep: Achieving Gender Equality and the Empowerment of Women". Millennium Project Task Force on Education and Gender Equality, 2003.

Irwin, Alexander, Joyce Millen, and Dorothy Fallows. *Global AIDS, Myths and Facts: Tools for Fighting the AIDS Pandemic*. South End Press, 2003.

Kalipeni, Henry, Susan Crawford, et al., eds. *AIDS in Africa: Beyond Epidemiology*. Blackwell Publishers, 2004.

Kim, Jim Yong, Joyce V. Millen, Alec Irwin et al., eds. *Dying for Growth: Global Inequality and the Health of the Poor*. Common Courage Press, 2000.

Schoepf, Brooke G. *Women, Sex and Power: A Multisited Ethnography of AIDS in Africa*. Blackwell Publishers, 2004.

World Health Report, 2003. Chapter 3: "HIV/AIDS: Confronting a Killer." World Health Organization, 2003.

BROOKE GRUNDFEST SCHOEPF

Adangbe
Ethnic group of southeastern Ghana; also known as the Adangme, Adampa, Dangme, and Krobo.
The Adangbe live primarily along Ghana's coast and in the hills of the Accra Plain. They speak a Niger-Congo language closely related to GA. Approximately 600,000 people identify themselves as Adangbe.

See also LANGUAGES, AFRICAN: AN OVERVIEW.

Addis Ababa, Ethiopia
Capital and largest city in Ethiopia.
Addis Ababa is Ethiopia's political, commercial, manufacturing, and cultural center. Located at the approximate geographical center of ETHIOPIA, it is the hub of the country's highway network and contains its international airport and the inland terminus of its only railroad. Its manufacturing sector produces consumer goods and building materials. In addition, the city houses Addis Ababa University and other cultural institutions. Addis Ababa is also the headquarters of the ORGANIZATION OF AFRICAN UNITY (now called the African Union) and the United Nations Economic Commission for Africa, both of which are located in Africa Hall.

While Emperor Menelik II was away on a military campaign in 1886, his wife, Empress Taitu, founded Addis Ababa, Amharic for "New Flower," on the site of hot springs. The center of the early city was the royal palace and the surrounding aristocratic residences and military encampments. A French firm completed a railroad linking the city to the Red Sea port of DJIBOUTI in 1917. The rail link promoted trade and population growth. The government planted Australian acacia trees around the city as a source of firewood, and many remain today to provide shade and greenery along the streets of the city. Between 1935 and 1941, officials of the Italian occupation oversaw a program of modernization, including paved roads, a modern water supply, a hydroelectric plant, and a central district, known as the Piazza, built using European-style architecture. The Italians relocated the Mercato, one of the largest open-air markets in Africa, outside the city center. The city has continued to grow rapidly in recent decades, as rural refugees have fled Ethiopia's war and famine-ravaged countryside in search of jobs and security. According to the 2007 census, Addis Ababa is home to some 2,738,248 people.

See also UNITED NATIONS IN AFRICA; URBANISM AND URBANIZATION IN AFRICA.

ROBERT FAY

Ade, King Sunny

1946–

Popular Nigerian vocalist and guitarist; innovator of juju music.

Sunday Anthony Ishola Adeniyi Adegeye, known internationally to African music fans as King Sunny Ade, was raised in a home where Christian and YORUBA religious and cultural perspectives were thoroughly intermingled. Ade's father was a church organist. Ade attended missionary schools, then dropped out of college in the 1960s to pursue a career as a drummer in JUJU bands. Juju, a form of Nigerian pop music first developed by Yoruba musicians in the 1920s, was just beginning to gain an international audience. Ade's chief musical inspiration was I. K. Dairo, though Ade's later song lyrics drew more inspiration from his Christian education.

The early 1970s marked the birth of Ade's reputation as an African superstar with an international audience. Ade deviated from the Dairo legacy through a series of innovations. He expanded the juju band lineup from a single electric guitarist to as many as six, played with at least that number of drummers, and introduced both the pedal steel guitar (previously identified with American country music) and the synthesizer. This augmented instrumentation creates a massive and complex soundscape, made all the more imposing through the recording studio technology that Ade utilized. Studio effects included altering the sounds of his band's instruments through the intensive use of echo and reverb, a technique known as "dub" in Jamaican reggae. Another of Ade's innovations, one known only to concert-goers, was his choreography dramatizing his soft vocals, perhaps a borrowing from American rhythm and blues and soul entertainers. As Ade's electric guitar playing is an extension of his singing, so are his stage dances.

Ade's recordings—over 120 currently—also broke new ground in two arenas. Juju music lyrics before Ade relied almost entirely upon Yoruba folkloric sayings. Ade's first hit recording in NIGERIA, by way of contrast, was a newsy account of soccer. Although vocals, guitar lines, and drum patterns were still based on traditional Yoruba speech, proverbs, and metaphors, Ade's song topics included local and world politics, the dishonest nature of the music industry, and a Christian interpretation of the world's end. Ade's other innovation involved song length. Ade expanded the length of songs to a half-hour or more, turning them into intricately layered drum and guitar jams.

However imposing his number of recordings, Ade gained renown with international music fans primarily through a single album, *Juju Music* (1982), released on the Island label. This was intended to become the first juju music recording to win the genre an international audience, and it did exactly that. Although some Nigerian music critics find the recording a dilution of Ade's talent, there is no question that African music fans outside Africa find the recording to be a revelation. Heavily laced with studio dub effects and emotionally expressive pedal steel guitar colors, the studio recording replicates the feel of a live Nigerian party. No Ade recording since has achieved such international sales and acclaim, though *Seven Degrees North* (2000) impressed some reviewers as comparable to *Juju Music*.

In 1996 Ade joined with a number of other well-known Nigerian musicians to form the Way Forward touring group. Following the terrorist attacks on New York and Washington, DC, in 2001, however, travel to the United States became rather more difficult than before. More stringent visa restrictions led to the cancellation of a planned 2003 tour. Despite these frustrations, Ade—who serves as the president of Nigeria's Musical Copyright Society—continues an active schedule of international touring and recording with an eighteen-piece band.

See also MUSIC, AFRICAN.

BIBLIOGRAPHY

Waterman, Christopher A. *Juju: A Social History and Ethnography of an African Popular Music.* University of Chicago Press, 1990.

NORMAN WEINSTEIN

Adja

Ethnic group of West Africa, also known as Aja.

The Adja primarily inhabit southern BENIN and TOGO. They speak a Niger-Congo language. The western Adja belong to the EWE cultural and linguistic group. Approximately 740,000 people identify themselves Adja Ewe. "Adja" is sometimes also used as an umbrella term to include all Ewe- and FON-speaking peoples.

See also LANGUAGES, AFRICAN: AN OVERVIEW.

Afar

Ethnic group found in parts of Djibouti, Eritrea, and Ethiopia, also known as Danakil, Denakil, and Adal.

Approximately 1.5 million people belong to the Afar ethnic group, mostly in the Denakil plain, which includes parts of northern ETHIOPIA, ERITREA, and DJIBOUTI. Apart from the Aussa oasis and the Djibouti coastline, the territory of the Afar is among the most arid on the continent. The Afar speak Safo, an Afro-Asiatic language (part of the Eastern

Cushitic language group). The first known written references to the Afar appeared in the 13th century in the work of Arabic geographer Ibn Said. He called them the Danakil, a name that the Afar now consider offensive but one that is still used widely by neighboring Arab groups. The Somali people mostly use the term Adal or Udali. The Afar have traditionally lived as pastoral nomads, raising sheep, goats, camels, and cattle. Some work as salt miners on the Denakil plain, where temperatures regularly reach 50° C (120° F). Most Afar are Sunni Muslim, although some practice Sufism, an Islamic religion that emphasizes mysticism. Some—especially the nomads—adhere to traditional beliefs.

Little is known about the origins of the Afar. They are generally believed to have migrated from the higher elevations of southern Ethiopia to the desert regions that most now inhabit. Historically, the Afar political structure rested on a system of sultanates, a type of centralized rule found in some Muslim countries. Each sultanate was subdivided into federations ruled by local chiefs. Of the sultanates, the most powerful was probably the Aussa, which dominated the Awash River region (in what is now eastern Ethiopia) starting in the sixteenth century. The sultanate retained its independence until it fell to Abyssinia (now Ethiopia) in 1944, after more than fifty years of Italian colonial support.

Considered by their neighbors and early European explorers to be violent and warlike, the Afar have a complex social system that distinguishes between the Asaimara, or red men, and the Adoimara, or white men. Asaimara families hold nobility status and receive tributes from the Adoimara, who are considered lower-class tenants on Afar land. The family structure is patrilineal, meaning that ancestral descent is traced through male family members. Afar tradition allows multiple marriages. With their nomadic lifestyle only slightly affected by colonialism, the Afar have maintained many of their traditions into the postcolonial era.

Afonso I

c. 1460–1543

King of the Kongo kingdom, the first Kongo king to embrace Catholicism and European trade relations.

Born Nzinga Mbemba, Afonso I ascended the throne in 1506 after the death of his father, Nzinga a Nkuwu. Unlike his father, who had rejected Catholicism and limited contact with the Portuguese explorers, Afonso had been baptized as a Christian when the KONGO court converted in 1491. During his time as governor of Kongo's Nsundi province, Afonso entertained Portuguese priests and gained a reputation for Christian piety. When his father died, around 1590, Afonso returned to Mbanza Kongo, the capital, to seek the throne. His half brother, Mpanzu

Kitima, raised a provincial army to remove Afonso from the capital. Afonso characterized the struggle as being between Christian and anti-Christian forces and later maintained that the Christians had won through the intervention of Saint James.

From the beginning of his reign, Afonso sought to Christianize Kongo, creating a financial base, a school system, a parish organization, and a "naturalized" form of Christianity for his country. He took a personal interest in theological matters and sent a number of Kongo children, including his son Henrique, to study in Portugal. He proclaimed Catholicism the state religion and established a strong trade alliance with the Portuguese crown.

Eager to acquire European goods and to educate and Christianize his people, Afonso asked King Manuel of Portugal to send him priests, craftsmen, and military supplies. In return, Afonso supplied the monarch with ivory and slaves, two things for which the Portuguese seemed to have an unlimited appetite. This demand ultimately strained relations between Portugal and Kongo, and Portuguese traders soon sidestepped Afonso's authority and acquired ivory and slaves from Kongo villagers. Realizing the threat to his power, Afonso asked Manuel to send a representative to enforce his kingdom's laws. In 1515 the representative arrived with a plan to recreate the kingdom on the Portuguese model, a service that the Portuguese would render in return for large amounts of slaves, ivory, and copper. Afonso rejected the offer.

In order to reestablish his authority, Afonso tried to limit slave trading in the Kongo kingdom. But he could do little to stop the Portuguese, who were determined to procure not only slaves, but also the kingdom's alleged mineral wealth. Tensions escalated as Afonso tried to control the traders and denied the existence of the mythical gold mines, but even after the Portuguese attempt to assassinate the Kongo king in 1540, he maintained relations with the Europeans in the hope that they would eventually send more missionaries. By the time of his death in 1545, however, no missionaries had arrived. Although some Kongolese later claimed that Afonso's contacts with the Portuguese ultimately led to the breakup of the kingdom, others, such as the famous prophetess Dona Beatrice, looked back at Afonso's reign as the golden age of the Kongo.

African City: An Interpretation

Examination of major themes in African urban history.

In Africa, as elsewhere, urbanization was above all a spatial process, bringing, as geographer Akin Mabogunje has put it, relatively large numbers of people into a relatively small space. But it was also a social process that created ethnic, linguistic, professional, and class distinctions.

If one were to pick a single defining feature of urbanization, it would not be the use of writing (as historians of the West have proposed), but the fact that, in the economic space of a city, not all people make their living from agriculture. What results is a diverse population, and a society engaged in various forms of commerce with the outside world, including the exchange of manufactured goods for necessary foodstuffs.

The concept of the "colonial city" has been widely used for many years but is itself "colonial" in its Eurocentrism. Its inventors, most of them Westerners, are heavily influenced by the urban model derived from their culture, education, and worldview. To quote just one example, archaeologist Anthony Whitty's insistence in his writings about ruined stone towns in southern Africa, that "[n]either ZIMBABWE nor Inyanga reached a stage of development approaching 'true urbanization'" is questionable, to say the least. Such writers create a biased picture in which the colonial city is perceived as "modern"—that is, Western in its design—and "white." However, if we take a closer look at a classic colonial city—NAIROBI, KENYA—the capital of what was supposed to be a settlement colony founded by white people at the turn of the century, we find that in 1933 only 7.5 percent of the total population of Nairobi consisted of European colonists (the figure was around 7,500, or nearly half—48 percent—of the European population in Kenya). Needless to say, the proportion of Western-style houses in Nairobi was similar.

Our notion of a colonial city needs to be revised. We can start by examining four major themes. First, cities in Africa predated the colonial period. In addition to the diverse examples of cities in precolonial Africa, recent archaeological discoveries have shown that urbanization occurred in Africa even before the arrival of influences from the Islamic Arab world. As happened elsewhere, urbanization began with the development of agricultural settlements by the first millennium B.C.E. The DJENNÉ-JENO site in the loop of the NIGER, which flourished between 250 B.C.E. and the ninth century C.E. and disappeared at the time of the Islamic invasion, most likely as a result of it, is a stunning example. Thus African cities were not merely European or Arab imports. There is no question that during the course of history, many influences have come into play in their development. But these influences—Arab-Muslim, Swahili, Portuguese, and more generally European (after the arrival of the Portuguese in the sixteenth century)—which were cumulative and combined, were woven into a variety of indigenous African contributions. Cities, then, have been poles of attraction for multiple converging influences.

That said, it is true that the arrival and ascendance of Western capitalism changed the course of precolonial urban development. Between the mid-eighteenth and the mid-nineteenth centuries, most African cities became more or less integrated into the prevailing Western economic system. From this perspective, colonial urban history was a crucial turning point and a new beginning, although grafted onto older urban elements whose cumulative heritage needs to be appreciated.

Second, cities, in Africa and elsewhere, have always been vehicles of colonization. Because they are places where different cultures are forced into contact with one another—as well as living organisms in constant evolution—cities have had great importance as social melting pots and vectors of cultural change and have had a defining impact on the territories under their control. Their power has varied from being coercive and brutal at one extreme, as in the case of conquering cities or colonial cities in the strict sense, to the progressive and alluring cultural resplendence (religious, artistic, and technological) of a city such as medieval DJENNÉ, whose architectural forms spread throughout the western SUDAN. However, the results have been the same: as the central city grows, it disrupts the surrounding region and reorganizes it to its own advantage, crisscrossing it with a hierarchical urban network in which it becomes the dominant force. The DYULA merchants helped in this process.

Why does such a process occur? Unlike the countryside, where a subsistence economy prevails, a city by definition cannot exist independently, because at least a portion of its inhabitants do not earn a living directly from agriculture. For it to survive, a city must effectively manage the economic and political processes of production and exchange and maintain an openness to the exterior. Cities require an agricultural surplus to feed nonproducers, such as rulers, chiefs, craftspeople, and bureaucrats. Before the technological revolution and the development of international transportation, cities had to control the food-producing land around them in order to produce such a surplus. This required the presence of a political force to impose control and to establish the rules regulating the movement of goods. In other words, trade is essential to cities. In Africa it is possible to find a market without a city, but never a city without a market; traders and merchants are crucial intermediaries, both within the city and in its relations with the outside environment. In conclusion, a city is by definition open and accessible, as well as being ethnically, professionally, socially, and culturally heterogeneous. Cities are cultural crucibles, places where memories are cross-fertilized.

The city dwellers who control the surrounding region are settlers recently arrived from the countryside, from another city, or from abroad. Cities therefore create symbioses between multiple civilizations, especially between the civilizations of the original inhabitants and those of the conquerors. This symbiosis likely occurred in the case of the YORUBA towns. The creation of these towns was almost certainly the result of the gradual migration toward the south, between the seventh and tenth centuries, of the peoples who had founded the parent town of IFE. Their desire to dominate and exploit the still scattered local populations derived in large part from their mastery of ironwork (which was already practiced by the local populations) and from their wish to act as a commercial crossroads between the Chadian region (Kanem-Bornu) and the southern lands that they had recently settled. Existing sources provide no concrete evidence that a hierarchical urban network developed before the nineteenth century. But such a network must have been in place long before then: Sahelian influences date back to the HAUSA and NUPE caravans, and Atlantic influences had made their mark as early as the sixteenth century. Cities provided their inhabitants with protection and allowed for a concentration of administrative and commercial activity. Many hamlets were forced to consolidate into larger settlements, a trend that increased in the nineteenth century as a result of the "Yoruba wars," which pitted towns against their neighbors and against the FULANI invaders. From that time on, towns served as fortresses, grouping together rural populations in a thirty-mile radius. Still, the Yoruba towns were perceived more as living communities than as artificially constructed entities, and they adopted and exploited religious traditions in order to legitimize and give historical embellishment to their political domination and economic control over their regions.

The ASANTE settlements are another example: the expansion of urban centers of control and trade such as KUMASI, Salaga, and Bonduku was also a colonization process in which a new set of political and economic values was imposed on, and diffused through, a subordinate and dependent local environment. From this perspective, the city of Begho (to the north of the future Asante lands) can be seen as a bridgehead of the civilization of the middle Niger, a MANDE colony with easy access to the gold- and kola-producing forests. Of course, as in the Yoruba lands, influences from the north were mingled with contributions from the Atlantic. Several centuries later, Kumasi, by then a crossroads lying astride major trade routes, would in turn become the cultural base of a conquering civilization. In the eighteenth and nineteenth centuries, the Swahili city-states on the Indian Ocean played the same role, generating similar cultural and economic syntheses.

The purpose here is not to minimize the importance of the colonial period but to emphasize that the colonial cities of the nineteenth and twentieth centuries were merely an extreme example of all-embracing coercive power,

although they were actually satellites of other metropolitan centers that held the real power. Despite our characterizations, white authorities in colonial cities did not have any more cultural power over "the excluded middle" than in the precolonial examples. Indeed, the proportion of indigenous African inhabitants in the cities was larger than in previous centuries, and the urban cultural crucible was working at full strength.

Third, colonial cities in Africa were not white cities. The notion that colonial cities were primarily white is misleading and stems from the fact that cities became quintessential expressions of white power. Whereas a subsistence economy could, if necessary, function without cities (as was largely true until the sixteenth century in Central Africa), for the colonial regime they were indispensable. Military garrisons at first, then administrative centers, they provided natural homes for Western companies: banks; branches of import-export companies that set up small factories in the interior settlements; the first mining companies; and, later, industrial firms. Cities were also focal points of the labor market, not because they were places of production, but because, besides employing sizable administrative staffs such as interpreters, clerks in the public and private sectors, municipal employees, post office workers, junior doctors, and all kinds of unskilled laborers, they controlled both the demand and supply of labor. Their role was to organize the movement of workers, leaving most of the responsibility for the reproduction of the work force to the countryside. This is why, more and more, cities not only consumed the produce of the countryside, but also drew its people. In turn, migrants eagerly took back to their homelands all that they had discovered and absorbed in the cities.

Fourth, cities were places of cultural crystallization. Colonial cities were "colonization spaces" above all else, in the cultural sense in which "modernization" has been equated with openness to colonization. They were the key facilitators of the process by which what we know as conventional values (that is, those that were implanted earlier) combined and synthesized with the dominating Western values, undergoing modification in the process. Thus, the dichotomy commonly drawn between "traditional" and "modern" is a false one. On the contrary, with varying degrees of success, people combined the old with the new, integrating the heritage of the past with the need for change.

The labor market enabled everyone in a city to find a niche in a shared social space. All those working with the colonial administration, whether they were independent, self-motivated businesspeople or simply common people, acted, consciously or not, as brokers of technology and culture. The idea, still voiced occasionally, that Africans from the beginning felt themselves "strangers to the city" is a Eurocentric misconception. It is true that the colonial regime imposed a brutal dislocation between the city—the headquarters of white power—and the uprooted migrant workers used as cheap labor in mining or in railroad or highway construction. But at the same time the migrants refashioned the urban environment, and they did this much more quickly than the whites liked to think. Wherever whites sought to admit only those whose labor they could directly control, Africans out of necessity developed their own varied patterns of settlement and irregular employment. The result was the early appearance of indigenous economic institutions; these have been poorly understood and wrongly labeled with the vague designation "informal," which in reality means everything not controlled by the central authorities.

Forced to improvise and innovate in a new environment, Africans were inspired by the construction methods, work habits, and communitarianism that they had brought with them from the countryside. On the other hand, living in today's megacities of several thousand or even several million inhabitants is a far cry from living in villages with between fifty and five hundred inhabitants.

Africans are not products of cities, but rather their makers, and we must see African cities not as adaptations to a Western model, but as examples of synthesis and creativity. They are neither a good nor a bad thing; they are a fact of contemporary life, the places where the future of African societies will play itself out. The formation of classes, of associations, the development of languages, artistic forms, and ideas—all these processes will be strongly affected by Western influences, but these influences will have been domesticated, assimilated, and reworked by urban populations.

A city is forged by a given society, but it also reflects that society. African cities are neither "traditional"—an absurd term, because a tradition is only an accumulation of older, preexisting things—nor "modern" (a misapplied and ambiguous term used to mean either "colonial" or "Western" in a more general sense). They are entities, in a constant state of flux, that correspond to complex and specific economic and social realities. More than ever, African cities are centers of power—social and political construction sites. By 2020 more than 50 percent of Africans will live in urban areas; therefore, it is in these areas that the policies and politics of the future will take shape and are already taking shape. It is time we shed the mental reflexes instilled in us by a century of actual or cultural colonialism: the tendencies to demonize the city, idealize rural Africa, and oppose tradition and modernity. These habits cause us to recirculate a set of prejudices without stopping to examine their historical origins. If only out of convenience, we continue to use terms such as "ethnic group," "rural community," "colonial [white] city," "dichotomy," "tradition," and "modernity," all terms that carry burdensome intellectual baggage. We realize this only when we reread the seminal texts—all written during the colonial period—that are the source of these ideas. It is vital that we reexamine and reinvestigate the history of cities so that we have the necessary tools to understand new realities.

See also COLONIAL RULE; ISLAM IN AFRICA; SWAHILI CIVILIZATION; URBANISM AND URBANIZATION IN AFRICA.

CATHERINE COQUERY-VIDROVITCH

African Condition in the Shadow of Globalization

In its broadest meaning globalization consists of all the forces that are leading the world toward becoming a global village. Globalization is thus the "villagization" of the world. In its narrower meaning globalization is the maturation of global capitalism and its interdependencies, alongside a new network of the information superhighway.

Although the word globalization is relatively new, the process itself has been going on for generations. In the experience of black people, this process gave birth to the concept of PAN-AFRICANISM (the unity of black people throughout the world) and, more recently, the concept of Global Africa (meaning the links between Africa and its diaspora). These concepts were connected with forces leading toward a global village.

Long before the world and the human condition were alerted to the crisis of the nation-state everywhere, Pan-Africanism as a movement was in itself a challenge to the nation-state. As the twentieth century came to a close, and in the wake of globalization, the nation-state as a system of political organization was threatened by two contradictory forces. On the one hand there is the trend toward enlargement of economic and political scale, as in the evolution of the European Union (EU). Individual members of the EU have been in the process of giving up more and more areas of jurisdiction that were once regarded as inseparable from national sovereignty. Chastened by the experience of two world wars, Europe wants to defuse the excesses of nationalism. And the North Atlantic Treaty Organization (NATO) has been trying to become the lion-tamer of the beast of nationalism in Bosnia, Serbia, and the Balkans more generally.

What the EU has achieved is a dream whose realization has long eluded Pan-Africanists in their own separate continent of Africa. That Pan-Africanist dream was a challenge to the nation-state precisely because it sought continental unity. Sometimes the Pan-Africanist dream envisioned the creation of a racial commonwealth of black people that defied both continental and national boundaries. It would be a commonwealth that would embrace the children of Kwame Nkrumah of GHANA as well as those of Michael Manley of Jamaica, the solemnity of Archbishop Desmond Tutu as well as the passions of O. J. Simpson.

But at the dawn of the twenty-first century the nation-state is also being challenged at the micro level. This is the level below the state, the level that includes ethnicity, sectarianism, and sacred and secular fundamentalism, all of which have been challenging either nationhood (shared identity) or statehood (shared authoritative control) in different parts of the world. Is Pan-Africanism an ally of these subnational passions, or is it threatened by them?

We hope to demonstrate that in Africa ethnicity provides an additional case for Pan-Africanism, partly because it denies legitimacy to the colonial boundaries of African states.

Large-scale unification is almost always inspired by a past (or present) nightmare, on the one hand, and a future dream on the other. European unification was inspired by the past experience of Europe at war with itself and the dream of a future when war between western European countries would be inconceivable. Pan-Africanism was inspired by the nightmare of colonialism and humiliation and the dream of a truly empowered Africa. Western political analysts are already arguing that mature democracies like those of the West do not go to war against each other.

As a role model for Africa's political union, many Pan-Africanists have looked to the American federation, going back to the efforts of the original thirteen colonies. On the other hand, the role model for Africa's economic union has been the record of European continental integration. The United States is an example of effective political union. Western Europe is an example of effective economic union. Both later became the vanguard of globalization.

There were times when African leaders such as Kwame Nkrumah and Nnamdi AZIKIWE of NIGERIA were profoundly and emotionally inspired by the American founding fathers and their federalist ambitions in pursuit of liberty. The dream of a United States of Africa was a direct echo of the American experience. Americans had once been inspired by their own past nightmare of British imperialism and their future dream of American liberties.

Nkrumah viewed European economic unification with some suspicion. He feared that the European giant emerging after the 1958 Treaty of Rome might be an ominous force for the exploitation and marginalization of Africa, rather than a model that Africa might emulate. In reality the EU served both functions in Africa's experience. Its success impressed Africa with the potentialities of greater unity as a source of strength. But Europe's success also alarmed Africa as an emerging new Euro-threat capable of subjecting Africa to a new experience of marginalization.

This Euro-paradox collided with other contradictions in the aftermath of the Cold War and globalization. Here we are dealing with layers of contradictions, a kind of dialectic of layers of social geology. The United States—long admired as a role model for political union—has now become so hegemonic and all-powerful that it too has helped to marginalize Africa, especially since the end of the Cold War and the emergence of globalization.

In the concluding decade of the twentieth century, major trends were discernible in Africa's historical change. We should not let the isolated catastrophes like Rwanda, however monumental, obscure the larger picture. Some of these trends have continued to be paradoxical. The African people even in Nigeria have been increasing their influence on their governments, but at a time when the African governments have been losing their influence in world affairs. The African state has seemed to be moving deeper into the global periphery, while the African people have been moving closer to the national center. With some important exceptions, Africa experienced in the 1990s internal democratization and external marginalization at the same time. The African state has been receding into the global shadows; the African people have been emerging into the national light. Let us took at these parallel trends of the 1990s more closely.

In parts of Africa, hegemonic presidentialism, the absolutism of the head of state, is on the decline, while parliamentary influence is beginning to reassert itself. In many parts of Africa, the executive branch is on the defensive while the legislative branch seeks to share power after thirty years of presidential monopoly. Francophone Africa has from time to time also experimented with prolonged and often passionate national dialogues on constitutional engineering.

But perhaps a more fundamental paradox of the 1990s was this: within two-thirds of the African countries, the people indeed were trying to assert greater control over their governments, at exactly the time when African governments were losing influence on world events. While African people were getting empowered, African states were getting enfeebled. Is this process symptomatic of the human condition? Globalization is partially relevant for the popular empowerment; it is fully relevant for the enfeeblement of the African state. New systems of information have helped democratic forces in Africa; new economic and political alignments abroad have weakened the leverage of the African state.

TOWARD REDEMOCRATIZING AFRICA

The forces of democratization in Africa vary in their success from country to country. But almost everywhere, even African dictators know that they are on notice and under siege. One or two have been resisting calls for their resignation as president, but political forces in their countries are now strong enough to cause sleepless nights. The human condition cannot endlessly endure the burdens of tyranny. Computers and the Internet are beginning to weaken the tyrant's monopoly of information.

Since 1990 more than twenty countries have taken steps toward democracy, steps such as legalizing political opposition. Pluralism is respectable again in large parts of Africa. Was this process aided by the triumph of pro-democracy movements in Eastern Europe and Latin America?

Pro-democracy tendencies in Africa have taken a variety of forms. First, there have been those pro-democracy movements that have resulted in changing one-party states into pluralistic multiparty systems. Countries that were transformed in this way in the concluding decade of the twentieth century include TANZANIA, CÔTE D'IVOIRE, KENYA, ZAMBIA, and MALAWI.

Partly related have been pro-democracy movements that have led to the electoral defeat of long-standing presidential founding fathers. Particularly sensational were the electoral defeat of Kenneth KAUNDA in Zambia in 1991 and the defeat of Hastings BANDA in Malawi in 1994. In 1992 President Daniel arap MOI of Kenya could have been similarly defeated had the opposition parties agreed on putting forward a single rival candidate. But the Kenyan opposition—unlike that of Zambia and Malawi—was too fractured and divided.

There has also been democratization via recivilianization—pro-democracy movements that have forced a military ruler either to return to the barracks or to run for elections as a civilian candidate. The most impressive case was that of Flight Lieutenant Jerry RAWLINGS of Ghana, who was freely elected in 1991 and reelected in 1996 in contests that were internationally supervised. In 1999 General Olusegun OBASANJO, who had been military ruler of Nigeria in the 1970s, was democratically elected president of Nigeria's Third Republic.

The 1980s and 1990s also witnessed the phenomenon of the voluntary retirement of major African political leaders. There was the voluntary retirement of Léopold Sédar SENGHOR as president of SENEGAL in 1981, setting a very impressive precedent. This was followed by the more hesitant retirement of Ahmadou AHIDJO of CAMEROON in 1982. President Julius K. NYERERE of Tanzania retired in installments from 1985 onward.

As for a military ruler handing over power to a freely elected civilian administration, one precedent was indeed that of General Obasanjo when he handed over power to Alhaji Shehu Shagari in Nigeria in 1979. In 1985 General 'Abd ar-Rahman Siwar ad-Dahab of the SUDAN handed over power to the elected civilian prime minister Sadiq al-Mahdi. Neither Nigeria nor Sudan, however, has managed to keep the soldiers out of politics for very long.

Africa since the 1980s has also experienced pro-democracy wars. War is of course a dangerous method of seeking democracy, but it has sometimes been the ultimate resort. The most successful pro-democracy war was waged by Yoweri Museveni when he created his own army to fight the government of Milton Obote in UGANDA. After half a decade, Museveni's private army defeated the official army of the state. Museveni started the reconstruction of Uganda, which had been devastated by more than twenty years of tyranny and conflict. The country moved toward democratization. It became more peaceful (though not in the north) and more politically transparent. Economic development was impressively revived at last. Uganda seemed to be one African beneficiary of the economic side of globalization.

But there are risks when opposition to tyranny takes a military form. The ensuing civil war could get out of hand. This has been the problem in Algeria since the pro-Islamic elections were aborted in 1992. This was true of Somalia's struggle against the dictatorship of Mohamed Siad Barre, who had been in power since 1969. The dictatorship was indeed overthrown in 1991, but what followed were anarchy, starvation, and persistent conflict. The Cold War rivalry between the superpowers had poured too many weapons into Somalia. The post–Cold War era turned those weapons against the Somali people themselves.

The Liberian civil war also started as military opposition to the brutal dictatorship of Sergeant Samuel K. DOE. While Doe himself was in the end tortured and killed, the country was for a while plunged into the depths of anarchy and conflict. Democratization through armed struggle may sometimes be necessary (as it was during the American Revolution), but it is an extremely risky route to take toward democracy. In the post–Cold War era, Liberia suffered for a while from international indifference to its fate. Few major powers cared enough early enough. The end of the Cold War sometimes created cruelty by neglect. But the military forces of West African States (ECOMOG) led by Nigeria later intervened and, soon with assistance from the United Nations (UN), helped to bring relative peace and elections to Liberia.

The Sudanese People's Liberation Army (SPLA) was also fighting a war for political freedom and religious tolerance in Sudan, but the human costs in the 1990s have been heavy. Has southern Sudan also suffered from international indifference in the post–Cold War era? Negotiations with the government in Khartoum for a possible referendum in the south have made progress.

A happier story is that of Namibia, where armed struggle did finally result in ending South Africa's racist control of the country. Namibia became an independent multiparty country in 1990. A rapprochement between the United States and the Union of Soviet Socialist Republics contributed to finding a UN solution in Namibia.

A more distinctive experiment in democratization is that of Ethiopia since the overthrow in 1991 of the military Marxist-Leninist regime of Mengistu Haile Mariam. The old regime collapsed as it was being abandoned by its Soviet patrons. The new Ethiopian government attempted to construct a federation of cultures, decentralizing power substantially to regions and ethnic alliances. A thousand years of centralized government in Ethiopia appeared to be in the process of being replaced by a confederation of tribes and nationalities. Power was, in this special sense, being returned to the grassroots. There was also the remarkable case of Eritrea attaining independence in 1992 after thirty years of war against the central forces of Ethiopia. When independence for Eritrea finally came, it was with the blessing of Addis Ababa. Unfortunately the two countries did not finalize the border between them before the separation. Conflict broke out between Ethiopia and Eritrea in 1998 and 1999.

Will post-apartheid South Africa too be forced eventually to become a federation of ethnic and racial regions after dismantling the centralized power? That is certainly the scenario favored by KwaZulu-Natal, by Chief Mangosutho BUTHELEZI, the Zulu leader, and by sections of conservative white opinion. But the new constitution approved in 1996 was more unitarist than that and yet was nevertheless one of the most liberal constitutions in human history. Liberalism returns power to individuals rather than to "the people" in the collective sense.

EROSION OF INTERNATIONAL INFLUENCE

But while Africa was a more open continent in the 1990s than it was in the 1980s, it was at the same time a less influential continent in the 1990s than it was at the beginning of the 1980s. The momentous international changes that have occurred as a result of globalization and the end of the Cold War have, on the whole, marginalized Africa to some extent. While the rest of the world was experiencing globalization, was Africa being disglobalized?

Western attention has been diverted to the former republics of the Soviet Union and to the former members of the Warsaw Pact. With the possible exception of Serbia, former enemies in Europe have politically become much more valuable to the United States than former friends in Africa. Is Africa being disglobalized? We define disglobalization as creeping irrelevance to global concerns.

Africa's influence in the UN has also declined despite the fact that Boutros BOUTROS-GHALI of Egypt became its first African secretary general and was followed in that role by Kofi ANNAN of Ghana. The former members of the Warsaw Pact as a socialist voting bloc used to be on the side of African aspirations on most issues in international forums. The end of the Cold War has deprived Africa of major socialist allies in world affairs. These days Hungary, Poland, the Czech Republic, and Russia are, on most issues, more anxious to please Washington than to support the aspirations of the Third World.

Africa's influence has also declined because of the changing composition of the world body. In the 1980s the African states were almost one-third of the total membership of the UN. Since then some twenty additional countries have become members of the UN, but only two of them are African—NAMIBIA and ERITREA. The others include the two Koreas, the Baltic states, the other former republics of the Soviet Union, and the republics of the former Yugoslavia. The percentage of Africa's voting power in the UN has declined.

In terms of Western aid and investment, the new rivals for Western resources are not only in Europe but also in Asia. The end of the Cold War has revalidated pro-market ideologies. India (with a population of nearly a billion people) has begun to liberalize and to encourage Western investment. The People's Republic of China has adopted a policy of "market Marxism" and is at last responsive to Western investment. Even Vietnam has opened its economic doors, after being boycotted by the United States since the end of the Vietnam War. Before long American businesspeople were bound to be cultivating Vietnam as a more promising market than any African country. (The population of Vietnam is more than 86 million, larger than that of any African country except Nigeria.) Capitalism has no permanent enemies and no permanent friends, only a permanent profit motive! Americans and Vietnamese seemed destined to be close business partners.

Yet another factor that has deepened Africa's marginality is Nigeria's inability to emerge as a world power. A population of more than 100 million people, with important oil resources, Nigerians have kept shooting themselves in the foot. Former president Ibrahim BABANGIDA was on his way toward making heroic history as a military leader who constructed a new democratic constitution for his country, supervised its elections, and then stepped down voluntarily. It did not happen that way. He did oversee a transition plan to democracy over three years, stage by stage, from local government to state government to federal. He stood a chance of being remembered as Nigeria's Charles de Gaulle (the French president and general who was the architect of the present-day Fifth Republic of France).

Unfortunately, by June 1993 President Babangida suffered from a failure of will at the last stage of his own transition program. The soldiers refused to hand over power to the man who was, by most accounts, popularly elected under their own scheme. Chief Moshood K. O. Abiola won the June 12 presidential elections in 1993, but the results were never officially confirmed. Instead an interim government was established to prepare for another election in February 1994. That interim government was itself subsequently overthrown by yet another military change of the guard. Chief Abiola died on the eve of being released from prison in 1998. In 1999 Nigeria held another presidential election. As indicated, this time a former soldier won, General Obasanjo. In turn, Obasanjo was defeated in 2007 by Umaru Yar'Adua of the People's Democratic Party in a highly controversial and bitterly contested election.

When Nigeria does succeed in putting its house in order, and when South Africa consolidates its new system under majority rule without having to lean on the stature of Nelson MANDELA, Africa as a whole will have two clear leaders on the world stage. Sometimes a continent needs some of its members to be "more equal than others" if leadership is to be sustained. The Republic of South Africa has the credentials of mineral resources, a large middle class, industrialization, and a people hardened by struggle. Nigeria has the resources of a large population, the endowment of oil, and a creative people in the process of learning new disciplines.

The rise of democratic forces in Africa in the 1990s, with all their imperfections, is a matter for celebration. The marginalization of the continent after the Cold War is a cause for serious concern. Leadership is needed to close the gap between the happy news of greater freedom at home and the sad news of diminishing influence abroad. In the twenty-first century, Nigeria and post-apartheid South Africa will have to provide some of that leadership toward an African transformation in the wake of globalization.

In the final analysis, the end of the Cold War is only part of the explanation for the rise of democratic forces in Africa, but it is a central cause of the marginalization of Africa in the international community. Is Africa being disglobalized?

Also contributing to the marginalization of Africa is the declining commitment of France to Africa in the wake of new opportunities in eastern and central Europe. Following the death of Félix HOUPHOUËT-BOIGNY in 1993, France could at last be more pragmatic about the limits of its support to the monetary systems of its former colonies. The CFA franc was devalued almost as a symbol of France's partial disengagement from Africa.

Also symbolic of the marginalization of Africa in the 1990s is the relative shortage of towering African personalities in power, capable of being regarded as world figures. Nelson Mandela is almost in a class by himself. This contrasts sharply with the early 1960s when African leaders like Kwame Nkrumah, Gamal Abdel NASSER, Jomo KENYATTA, Emperor Haile Selassie I, Habib IBN ALI BOURGUIBA, and Félix Houphouët-Boigny were each "bestriding this narrow world like a colossus." Julius K. NYERERE survived as president into the 1980s but is now in partial retirement.

Also marginalizing for Africa was the partial diffusion of the Arab-Israeli rivalry in the Middle East. When Arabs and Israelis were bitter enemies, African governments were important to each side as potential allies in international bodies and as potential economic partners. Arabs and Israelis vied with each other in African capitals, trying to win friends and influence people. African votes were crucial at the UN.

The good news in the 1990s was that the Arabs and the Israelis were not quite as bitterly divided as they were in the 1960s, although they were still far from being friends. The bad news for Africa was that it lost its strategic value in the Arab-Israeli equation. Neither the Arabs nor the Israelis need African support quite as much as they once did.

Also marginalizing for Africa has been the impact of the Newly Industrializing Countries (NICs) of Asia despite the economic slowdown since 1997. Some of these have not only outstripped Africa in economic performance more generally, they are outstripping Africa in the production of some of the very commodities in which Africa had once been preeminent. For example, Malaysia has outstripped West African countries in the production of palm oil and cocoa. Indeed, Malaysia is, from time to time, affluent enough to be investing in African countries, such as Zimbabwe and Ghana.

Is Islamic militancy causing further marginalization of Africa? Certainly Sudan and Libya have been threatened by the West, although Libya is more Arab nationalist than Islamist. Libya has been subjected to UN sanctions. Is Islamic militancy likely to lead to the deeper isolation of parts of Africa? Or is that militancy the first sign of Africa's rebellion against global marginalization and Western hegemony? Is Islamic "fundamentalism" a clarion call for resistance against this sentence of marginalization?

The facts are still ambiguous, but there are signs of Africa's dismarginalization through other causes. In other words, Africa is indeed fighting back against marginalization, and some reversals of the trend are under way. Perhaps the human spirit is capable of periodic bursts of reinvigoration. Is the dismarginalization of Africa on the horizon?

To begin with, some African economies have begun to demonstrate that recovery can be much faster than some economic observers ever thought possible. When Museveni captured power in Uganda in 1986, he was inheriting an economy that had been so brutally damaged that some people thought that it would take a generation to mend. And yet within a decade Uganda's economy was transformed to growth rates that left next door Kenya looking sluggish. In the mid-1980s the Ghanaian infrastructure was in shambles, from roads with huge potholes to buses without wheels and a quite unreliable electricity supply nationwide. Within a decade the economic infrastructure of Ghana was improved to three times its previous quality. What all this means is that even when Africa is way down, there is every reason to believe that it can rise again. Africa's marginalization can indeed be reversed, and some of that reversal is already under way.

At a more symbolic level, Africa entered the 1980s with only one Nobel Prize to its credit, the Prize for Peace that was won by Albert LUTHULI of South Africa in 1960. Since the beginning of the 1980s, Africa has added the following heroes among its laureates: Desmond Tutu (1984 Peace Prize), Wole SOYINKA (1986 Literature Prize), Naguib MAHFOUZ (1988 Literature Prize), Nadine GORDIMER (1991 Literature Prize), Nelson Mandela and F. W. DE KLERK (1993 Peace Prize). Five of the seven Nobel laureates in Africa were South Africans, the last African country to be liberated.

The dismarginalization of Africa has continued in other areas as well. Let us now turn more fully to these paradoxical tendencies.

IN SEARCH OF AFRICA'S REGLOBALIZATION

Is international marginalization a necessary intermediate stage before Africa can be forced to learn the skills of self-reliance? One area of self-reliance is self-pacification and self-stabilization. This is the crux of Pan-Africanism. It could be a step toward reglobalization.

It was not until the 1990s that the Organization of African Unity (OAU) seriously discussed ways of intervening in internal conflicts, beginning with the approval of a mechanism for such conflict resolution passed at the summit meeting of the OAU in Cairo in 1993. Although many members of the OAU have reservations about a military African interventionist force in situations of political collapse, the idea was discussed more seriously in the 1990s than at any time since the OAU was formed in 1963.

The administration of U.S. President Bill Clinton joined the debate about a possible Rapid Crisis Response Initiative for Africa and the United States is now helping to train African troops for such a force. Where the Clinton administration differed from African versions hinges on accountability. The Clinton administration wanted the Rapid Response Initiative to be answerable to the United Nations Security Council, ultimately controlled by the West. Many Africans preferred that the initiative answer to a special African Security Council, under a reformed OAU.

Readiness to impose sanctions against the present military government of Burundi is another area in which Africa appears to be more ready to handle its own crises and take strong action. The East African sanctions in 1996 were intended to force the Burundi regime to start discussion with all political parties with a view to the restoration of democracy. Improvement in the performance of Burundi eased the sanctions in 1999.

Another part of the dismarginalization is the story of the Republic of South Africa. Although economic apartheid in South Africa is still substantially intact, political apartheid has been substantially dismantled. The wealth of the society is still maldistributed along racial lines. The whites said to the blacks "You have the crown; we shall keep the jewels." The best land, the best jobs, the best mines are disproportionately in white hands.

But there is no doubt about the political achievements against apartheid, the moral authority of Nelson Mandela, the prospects of a peaceful post-Mandela transition, and the ratification of what is perhaps the most liberal constitution in the world. South Africa's international influence is a partial dismarginalization of Africa as a whole.

Yet another part of the dismarginalization is the fact that the UN now has its first black African secretary general, that the worldwide body is beginning the twenty-first century partly under the African leadership of Annan. Is this Africa's reglobalization?

In other organizations, Africa no longer occupies the director generalship of United Nations Educational, Scientific, and Cultural Organization (UNESCO) in Paris, following the ouster of Amadou-Mahtar M'bow by Anglo-American pressure. But throughout the 1990s Africa retained the secretary generalship of the Commonwealth of Nations from Marlborough House in London.

With regard to Africa's dismarginalization and reglobalization within the World Bank and the International Monetary Fund (IMF), the question arises whether the World Bank staff from Africa are rising to policy-making positions. We know from experience that sometimes North Africa blazes the trail and that sub-Saharan Africa takes advantage of the new opportunities that open up.

Most North African countries became independent long before sub-Saharan nations.

In the history of Pan-African nonalignment, Egypt's Gamal Abdel Nasser blazed a trail in the 1950s, and other African leaders south of the Sahara followed suit. In the UN Boutros-Ghali of Egypt blazed a trail as secretary general, and now Annan of Ghana has followed him with a Pan-African trail.

And within the World Bank, Egypt's Ismail Serageldin has become a vice president and a special commissioner on problems of poverty. Black Africa has followed suit with another vice president, Callisto Madivo. People like Dunstan Wai from southern Sudan had considerable policy input at the World Bank from the early 1980s until the mid-1990s.

From 1987 to 1999 the World Bank had a Council of African Advisors, independent of both African governments and African central banks. When I was a member of the council, the council met twice a year with the most senior members of the World Bank working on Africa under the chair of the vice president for the African region.

The quest for regional integration is part of the process of the dismarginalization of Africa. Regional integration in the military field included ECOMOG's efforts toward pacifying Liberia, a kind of military arm of ECOWAS (the Economic Organization of West Africa States). ECOMOG in Liberia has not been an unqualified success, but it has been an important precedent in Pax Africana. Nigeria on behalf of ECOMOG also intervened in Sierra Leone to end a military coup and restore a democratically elected government.

Regional Pan-African integration in the economic field includes the Southern African Development Community (SADEC). Also in the economic field is the revival of interest in East African integration. Uganda, the most parochial East African country in the 1960s, became the most Pan-East African in the 1990s.

Who gained as a result of the dethronement of Boutros-Ghali and the succession of Annan of Ghana in his place? The immediate triumph was that of the United States, which had vetoed the reelection of Boutros-Ghali on the grounds that most countries regarded it as inspired more by the domestic politics of the United States than by any fair criticism of Boutros-Ghali's performance. In the final analysis, Africa also gained by the final outcome of the whole dispute. Now Africa has had two secretaries general "for the price of one"—two appointees representing very different parts of the continent. Was this a kind of reglobalization of Africa? If Boutros-Ghali had served his two full terms, there would have been no black African secretary-general for at least another thirty years.

What is an "African?" There are two main types: those who are African in a continental sense (such as Egyptians and Algerians) and those who are African in a racial sense (such as Nigerians, Ugandans, and Senegalese). Egyptians and Algerians are Africa's children of the soil. Sub-Saharan blacks are Africa's children of the blood.

In reality all those who are Pan-African natives of Africa are children of the soil (called wana-nchl in the Swahili language). But sub-Saharan blacks are in addition Africa's children by racial blood. Boutros-Ghali is a continental African of the soil. Annan is an African in both the continental and the racial sense, both son of the soil and son of Africa's racial blood. In the position of secretary general, Africa has been enriched to have had both types of Africans.

There is a lot of work to be done in Africa, not just by the UN but also by Africans themselves and by the international community at large. Central to Africa's political problems are issues of identity, both ethnic and national, and the fragility of territorial integrity.

While the world's attention is often focused on African refugees, their movements and their human needs, the underlying causes of Africa's problems are not addressed. Just because the media spotlight in 1994 sometimes turned on eastern Zaire (now the Democratic Republic of Congo) or on the resettlement of refugees from Rwanda did not mean that the crisis in Burundi had gone away. Nor did the 1996 disarray of the HUTU Interahamwe militia in what was then Zaire necessarily mean that they would not regroup and start conspiring for a future Hutu invasion of Rwanda.

The crisis that broke out in eastern Zaire in 1996 and the tensions between Zaire and its neighbors from 1996 to 1999 posed the greatest challenge yet to the artificial borders that European imperial powers had drawn at the turn of the century to create the present African so-called nation-states. Of course, Africa and the international community have to deal with more immediate problems of refugees and the threats of starvation, disease, and ongoing conflicts. But the region in the 1990s as a whole was being forced to reexamine more compellingly whether the present borders are viable in the long run. It has taken a Tutsi trigger to spark an agonizing reappraisal.

Zaire is now the Democratic Republic of Congo. On the negative side was the danger of the disintegration of Congo, the largest and richest French-speaking country in Africa and, since its independence, the most unruly. Would it break up into three or more separate countries under the weight of its chronic instability, aggravated by the Tutsi rebellion in the east and the continuing weakness of the central government in KINSHASA? Would all this be symbolic of the fragility of the territorial integrity of most postcolonial states?

Also on the negative side was the possibility of escalating conflict between forces in Congo and Rwanda, with the potential of engulfing Burundi and Uganda as well and sending forth hundreds of thousands of new refugees all over southern and eastern Africa.

On the positive side, the continuing crisis in the Great Lakes area provided an opportunity for long-term Pan-African planning about African security and Pan-African peacekeeping. Long before the Clinton administration started championing an African rapid response initiative to deal with African political collapses, others in African diplomatic circles and the OAU had been recommending the establishment of a Pan-African emergency force specially trained to intervene in crises such as those of Liberia, Somalia, Rwanda, Burundi, and now eastern Congo. Some had argued that if a modestly trained African army of a poor country like Tanzania could successfully intervene in Uganda in 1979 and end the tyranny and chaos created by President Idi AMIN, fifty African countries among themselves could create a more specially trained interventionist force for situations of political collapse. External friends of Africa could help with some of that training and with resources for logistical support.

The main difference between such a Pan-African proposal and that of the Clinton administration lay as previously indicated, in accountability. While the Pan-African proposal envisaged that such an army would be answerable to an African Security Council specially created under the OAU, we have referred to the Clinton administration's preference for accountability to the UN, and therefore indirectly to the Western powers who dominate the Security Council in New York, regardless of who is secretary general of the UN.

Another possible scenario that was emerging from the crisis in eastern Congo and the clash between Congo and Rwanda and their respective allies was the gradual redefining of the boundaries between Congo, Rwanda, and Burundi. Each one of those three countries had Hutu and Tutsi of its own, indigenous to its own borders. The European partition of Africa in the nineteenth and twentieth centuries made no attempt to make the borders of countries coincide with the borders of ethnic groups.

In the mid-1990s the Tutsi found themselves with the upper hand in Burundi, Rwanda, and then for a while Congo, after fluctuating fortunes. Was this the moment for making ethnic boundaries coincide with national boundaries? Were we seeing the tumultuous process of creating a Tutsi "Israel"—an independent homeland for the Tutsi? Was a Tutsi-stan being born?

Until the mid-1980s the Tutsis seemed to be the Kurds of eastern Africa—a marginalized minority in Rwanda, Zaire, and under a different name (the Hima) in Uganda.

Temporarily they clung desperately and brutally to power in Burundi. But as a minority they seemed to be up against history. It was thought that in time they would become the marginalized Kurds of Burundi also.

In the early 1970s Frank Kalimuzo was accused by President Amin of Uganda of being a disloyal Rwandese masquerading as a Ugandan. Kalimuzo was vice chancellor (president) of Makerere University at the time. In reality he was a Ugandan by birth and ancestry, but he came from an ethnic group in Uganda that was related to the Rwandese. In broad daylight Kalimuzo was arrested in 1972 by Amin's soldiers from his home on campus, never to be seen again. He must have been murdered soon after his arrest. Did he die partly because his ethnic group of Ankole district was linked to Rwanda? (His murder shook many intellectuals so deeply that some left Uganda for refuge in the Western world.)

It was not until 1986 that the tide turned when Museveni, ethnically linked to Kalimuzo and to the people of Rwanda, captured power in Uganda. The Tutsi and the Hima of Uganda were ethnic cousins. After Museveni's successful consolidation of his political base in Uganda, he turned to his "pay back" obligation to the Rwandans. Museveni helped to train the Rwanda Patriotic Front.

In 1994 the Rwanda Patriotic Front staged a successful "Bay of Pigs" operation from the Ugandan border. Like the Cuban exiles under U.S. presidents Dwight D. Eisenhower and John F. Kennedy, the Rwandan exiles had been trained by a neighboring country for a major military penetration of their own country. But unlike the Cuban effort of 1961, the 1994 Rwanda operation was indeed completely successful in capturing power. The Rwandan exiles from Uganda routed the Hutu and established an alternative government in Kigali.

This operation created a situation in which Hutu refugees in Congo started plotting and training for a counteroffensive, with secret support from Kinshasa itself and possibly from Kenya and France. To make matters worse, the Congolese security forces started picking on Congolese Tutsi who had been part of Congo since before the partition of Africa in the nineteenth century.

When Congolese Tutsi were threatened with expulsion from their Congolese homeland by Congolese armed forces, the Tutsi decided to resist. They formed an army of resistance, secretly supported by Rwanda, and turned out to be more than a match for the thoroughly inefficient Congolese security forces. In their resistance they in fact threatened the integrity of the entire Congolese state. If Tutsi rebels could get away with their resistance in one part of the country, what was to stop political emulation (or the copycat syndrome) in other parts of Congo? Moreover, were we witnessing a Tutsi-stan in the making—a homeland of the kind which has so far eluded the Kurds' dream of Kurdistan?

But what are the Tutsi going to do with their Hutu neighbors? The exchange of populations to create a separate Hutu state may be a prescription for future interstate wars, as the Arabs and Israelis, and as the Indians and Pakistanis, have found to their cost.

A more viable longer term Pan-African solution is arguably the federation of Rwanda, Burundi, and Tanzania. Out of the anguish of a nightmare comes a future dream. The armies of Rwanda and Burundi would be pensioned off. In this larger political community the Hutu and Tutsi would discover how much they have in common culturally. They might learn to be on the same political side on many issues in the enlarged Tanzania, just as their ethnic cousins in Uganda, the Hima and the Iru, have often voted on the same side against other groups in the larger national context of Uganda.

Unless the Hutu and Tutsi are either partitioned into separate countries or federated into a larger, stable, and democratic political community, they are likely to turn against each other in a genocidal frenzy every few years. In 1994 exiled Tutsi invaded Rwanda from Uganda; a few years from now, exiled Hutu could counter-invade Rwanda or Burundi from Congo. The international community, perhaps through the UN, should put together a large package of inducements and incentives to persuade the three countries of Rwanda, Burundi, and Tanzania to create the United States of Central Africa. Regional integration of this kind is necessary for dismarginalization and reglobalization. Whether parts of Congo will one day break off and seek admission into the new federation is entirely feasible. The redrawing of colonial boundaries need not mean smaller and smaller African states. It could simply mean more rational and more viable Pan-African political communities.

Another long-term project toward dismarginalization and victim-oriented globalization is the emerging debate about reparations to Africa and the black world for centuries of servitude, exploitation, and colonization. Precedents from the experience of other people include reparations for Jews from Germany for the Holocaust; for Gypsies demanded from Germany for the Holocaust and now championed by Jews in England; for Koreans from Japan for brutal colonization; for Korean women who were exploited as prostitutes for Japanese soldiers; for Kuwait from Iraq for the military annexation of 1990 and 1991.

But what kinds of back reparations would go toward dismarginalization? Potential forms of reparations include capital transfer (a kind of Marshall Plan for the black world); skill transfer to mend the damage to Africa's capacity for helping itself; and power sharing, giving Africans an extra say in institutions with power over Africa, such as the World Bank, the IMF, and a permanent seat on the United Nations Security Council.

At its summit meeting in Dakar in 1992, the OAU appointed a Group of Eminent Persons (GEP) to study the logistics and modalities of a campaign for reparations for Africa's enslavement, colonization, and centuries of exploitation. The GEP elected Chief M.K.O. Abiola of Nigeria as a chairman, Professor Amadou-Mahtar M'Bow of Senegal as co-chair, and Ambassador Dudley Thompson of Jamaica as rapporteur general. A number of publications by members of GEP have appeared on the issue of reparations since then. But Chief Abiola, the chair, has died, and this has weakened the African movement. On the other hand, the reparations crusade in the United States became stronger in the 1990s.

Curiously enough, the EU is still the role model for economic aspirations; the United States is the role model for ultimate political ambitions. The paradoxes persist as the struggle continues. Reparations has a leading champion in the British House of Commons, Bernie Grant, M.P. (Labour). In the Congress of the United States, the leading champion of reparations is Congressman John Conyers of Michigan. Yes, the struggle continues.

CONCLUSION

The twentieth century ended with the forces of globalization at work, seeking to turn planet Earth into a global village. But Africa has fluctuated between globalization and disglobalization.

The most powerful trends in Africa in the concluding years of the twentieth century include a domestic tendency toward democratization and an external tendency toward marginality. The African state has, at the global level, receded deeper into the shadows of the periphery. But in two-thirds of the continent, the African people have, at the national level, emerged more openly into the center. While the African state has become globally enfeebled, the African people are getting nationally more empowered.

However, we have noted that the real picture is not as neat and tidy as all that. Nigeria, one of Africa's leaders, is still struggling to find the right balance between sovereignty and human rights. South Africa, another African leader, is still struggling to add victory over economic apartheid to the triumph over political apartheid.

Africa's marginalization is not in any case irreversible. We have attempted to demonstrate that the dismarginalization and reglobalization of Africa are indeed already under way. The struggle continues to find the right equilibrium between popular empowerment and adequate African involvement in world affairs. As the twentieth century ended, Africa had made some progress toward expanding political participation within Africa itself. The

Pan-African struggle continues toward enhancing regional integration and African participation at the global level. The dialectic between past nightmares and future dreams continues to unfold. The pains of yesterday and the plans of tomorrow intersect in Africa's political experience.

ALI MAZRUI

African Cup of Nations
Biennial tournament among African national football (soccer) teams.

The African Cup of Nations was founded to be not only a sporting event, but also a means of promoting African sovereignty and unity. Despite religious and linguistic differences among member nations and periods of political instability, both the number and quality of competitors in the African Cup have steadily increased since its founding nearly fifty years ago. Because of their skill exhibited at the tournaments, African soccer players are now highly sought by leagues throughout the world.

The African Cup of Nations began in February 1957 when representatives from SUDAN, EGYPT, ETHIOPIA, and SOUTH AFRICA met in the Sudanese capital of KHARTOUM to form the governing body of African football, the Confédération Africaine de Football (CAF), and to plan a continental international football tournament. Newly independent Sudan was picked to host the first tournament, in which only three teams competed—Sudan, Ethiopia, and Egypt, the eventual winner. After winning in 1998, Egypt tied GHANA for the most cups won—four. Winning the tournament is a source of national pride. Some national leaders have been known to offer houses to their players in exchange for a victory. By 2003 the Fédération Internationale de Football Association (FIFA) had ranked the fifty participating countries, of which only sixteen would make it to the tournament finals in 2004 in TUNISIA.

The history of the African Cup of Nations has been marred by political conflict on several occasions. South Africa, which refused to allow its white players to play with black players, was disqualified from the inaugural African Cup, leaving just three participants, Egypt, Ethiopia, and Sudan. While Ghana, NIGERIA, and UGANDA had achieved independence and had become CAF members by 1959, they declined to participate, leaving the same three teams to compete in the second tournament. In 1961, the African Cup was delayed for a year because of political instability in many newly independent nations.

More recently, criticism by former South African president Nelson MANDELA regarding Nigerian leader, General Sani ABACHA, led to Nigeria's withdrawal from the 1998 African Cup. Although Nigeria claimed it feared for its players' safety while traveling in a "hostile country,"

the CAF responded by banning the Nigerian national team from cup competition for two years.

Monetary problems have also plagued some of the event's hosts and participants. KENYA once declined the opportunity to host the tournament for lack of funds. Burkina Faso, a country much poorer than Kenya, managed to find the resources to run the 1998 African Cup. Many people believed that money problems were behind the withdrawal of the national teams from CHAD and COMOROS. By 2008 the tournament's schedule was somewhat in flux, as a number of European teams argued that the winter program forced them to go without some of their key players during their own domestic seasons. However, any rearrangement was complicated by Africa's unpredictable (often wet) summer weather.

Nevertheless, supporters of the African Cup—including Mandela—still consider the tournament to be the continent's premier sporting event and a showcase for its growing number of talented athletes. Scouts from European professional leagues attend the tournament regularly, hoping to discover the latest African talent.

BIBLIOGRAPHY

Murray, Bill. *The World's Game: A History of Soccer.* University of Illinois Press, 1996.

ROBERT FAY

African National Congress
Ruling South African political party, which once led the struggle against apartheid in that country.

In the history of SOUTH AFRICA, no group is more identified with the struggle against APARTHEID—the system of racial segregation instituted by the country's former white-minority government—than the African National Congress (ANC). Many groups participated in the country's ANTIAPARTHEID MOVEMENT, but it was the ANC's Nelson MANDELA who, through negotiations with the ruling NATIONAL PARTY, finally brought about apartheid's demise. In South Africa's first free elections in 1994, the ANC won the majority of legislative seats and the presidency. From its founding in 1912 by middle-class, college-educated black South Africans, the ANC has grown from an interest group to a protest movement and finally to the instrument of freedom for South Africa's black majority. Although the organization has undergone periods of considerable internal dissent, it has proven capable of compromise and growth and has consistently embraced a vision of equality for people of all races.

By the time the ANC was established, South Africa had long been stratified by race. The 1910 formation of the Union of South Africa, a dominion of Great Britain, further institutionalized the "color bar." In response, a group of mostly foreign-educated Africans, including Pixley ka Izaka Seme, Solomon PLAATJE, and John DUBE, formed the South African Native National Congress (renamed the African National Congress in 1923). The leaders hoped to win increased economic and political rights for Africans and to eliminate an ever-growing list of discriminatory laws. Seme's speech to the founding convention, in which he addressed "chiefs of royal blood and gentlemen of our race," suggested the aristocratic nature of the group's original, mostly middle-class leadership.

The ANC initially fought the color bar through legal and constitutional means—mostly petitions, speeches, and publicity drives. These efforts accomplished relatively little, but for several years the ANC membership resisted a more radical approach. In 1930 it did not reelect its president, Josiah Gumede, because he advocated cooperation with the Communist Party of South Africa (later renamed the SOUTH AFRICAN COMMUNIST PARTY). More an intellectual movement than a mass political movement, the ANC was almost completely inactive for the next decade.

During the 1940s a period of unprecedented trade union activism in South Africa helped revive the ANC. Its new president, Alfred XUMA, worked to draft a set of demands, including full political rights for Africans. He also organized protests against the hated PASS LAWS, restrictions that sharply curtailed the freedom of movement of non-whites, especially Africans. But Xuma's overall caution disappointed a new generation of activists. In 1944 young ANC members, including Anton LEMBEDE, Nelson Mandela, Oliver TAMBO, and Walter SISULU, formed the ANC Youth League (ANCYL). Lembede died in 1947, but Mandela, Tambo, Sisulu, and other young leaders eventually made the ANC into the single most powerful political force in South Africa.

In 1949, a year after the newly elected National Party government began implementing its apartheid policies, the ANCYL took over the ANC leadership. Influenced by the principles of nonviolent action and passive resistance pioneered by Indian nationalist leader Mohandas K. Gandhi, in 1952 the ANC and other groups organized the "Defiance Campaign against Unjust Laws." The campaign's acts of civil disobedience did not result in any legislative reforms, but they did help swell ANC membership from about 7,000 to 100,000 members within a few months. In addition, the campaign ushered in a new era of cooperation with antiapartheid groups representing other racial constituencies, such as the Coloured People's Congress, the South African Indian Congress, and the white Congress of Democrats.

These groups, together with the ANC, formed the Congress Alliance, which convened a large "Congress of the People" that adopted the FREEDOM CHARTER on June 26, 1955. The charter called for an end to racial discrimination, economic equality, and full democratic rights for all South Africans. The ANC adopted the Freedom Charter as its official policy in 1956. Even as the ANC's membership and alliances grew, however, the organization faced new challenges. Increased harassment by the government resulted in treason charges against 156 persons. The ANC sometimes appeared indecisive in confronting the government's heavy-handed tactics, and this vacillation led several ANC leaders to break away and found the more militant Pan-Africanist Congress (PAC) in 1959.

The struggle against apartheid intensified after March 21, 1960, when police opened fire on a group of unarmed protesters at an anti-pass demonstration organized by the PAC in SHARPEVILLE, a black township south of JOHANNESBURG. Sixty-nine people were killed, shot in the back as they fled. Protest marches, strikes, and scattered uprisings followed, and the government banned both the PAC and the ANC. In May 1961, operating underground, Mandela and other ANC leaders concluded that the time had come to meet government violence with armed resistance. Mandela, Tambo, and longtime ANC associate and Communist Party leader Joe SLOVO informed ANC President Albert Luthuli of their plan to form a separate paramilitary organization. The ANC officially formed the new group Umkhonto we Sizwe ("Spear of the Nation," commonly abbreviated as MK) in December 1961.

At first, MK primarily committed acts of sabotage against South African infrastructure and against symbols of apartheid such as the Bantu Administration offices. In 1962, however, its leaders began planning a guerrilla war, hoping to inspire a popular uprising that would topple the apartheid government. These plans were foiled when police raided MK's South African headquarters, at Rivonia. Evidence found there was used to convict Mandela and others of treason. Mandela, already in prison for inciting strikes, was given a life sentence and sent to the maximum-security prison on ROBBEN ISLAND. Slovo, out of the country at the time of the raid, went into exile.

With most of its leaders either exiled or imprisoned, the ANC entered a period of internal turmoil in the 1960s. Factions disagreed over whether to emphasize political or economic objectives. Beginning in the 1970s, however, the ANC, now led by Oliver Tambo, was re-energized by both the student-led BLACK CONSCIOUSNESS movement and South Africa's increasingly militant labor unions. The SOWETO uprising of 1976—sparked by a police massacre of protesting students—marked the revival of mass resistance, which had been largely dormant during the 1960s. Hundreds of township youths fled the country to join MK, and the organization slowly managed to reassert a presence within South Africa. At the same time, the defeat of white-ruled regimes in ANGOLA and MOZAMBIQUE brought new hope that the battle against apartheid could be won.

The government responded to the ANC's growing strength with harassment, detentions, torture, and assassination. But the crackdown only solidified the ANC's standing as the most viable alternative to apartheid rule. As international pressure grew in the 1980s, the South African government began secretly negotiating with Mandela and others. When F. W. DE KLERK succeeded P. W. BOTHA as president in 1989, he freed Mandela from his twenty-eight-year imprisonment and lifted the ban on the ANC.

Three years later, talks among more than 20 organizations—but dominated by the ANC and the ruling National Party—led to a transitional government, a new interim constitution, and plans for the country's first democratic election in April 1994. The electoral power of black South Africans, exercised for the first time, swept the ANC into a commanding legislative majority and Nelson Mandela into the presidency.

Since becoming the nation's ruling party, the ANC has sought to retain its mass appeal while also building ties with business interests in order to ensure economic growth. Under the leadership of Nelson Mandela, the ANC crafted an image of pragmatism over militancy, which has appealed to business constituencies without alienating the ANC's core support base of labor unions, socialists, and women's groups. Even potentially damaging testimony about MK activities before the TRUTH AND RECONCILIATION COMMISSION, which was created to investigate South Africa's apartheid-era crimes, has not significantly eroded the ANC's popularity. To the surprise of few analysts, the party won a decisive victory in the 1999 elections, improving on its performance in the 1994 elections. The new parliament selected ANC President Thabo MBEKI, the successor to Nelson Mandela, as South Africa's new president. In 2007 Jacob Zuma—who had faced allegations of official corruption just two years earlier—defeated Mbeki and seized the ANC presidency. In some quarters, this was an unpopular outcome, but any hopes that the charges hanging over the controversial Zuma's head might upend his bid for the presidency of South Africa were dashed just a year later when Zuma successfully petitioned the court to dismiss the charges brought by the National Directorate of Public Prosecutions on a technicality. As a result of Zuma's ascendancy, a number of members—Mosiuoa Lekota and Mbhazima Shilowa among them—split away to form the Congress of the People, which hoped to contest the 2009 elections.

The ANC faces several significant challenges at the beginning of the twenty-first century. A great deal of racial tension and bitterness, left over from the long years of apartheid, still divides many South Africans. Most ANC supporters are black, while whites and "coloreds" typically support the white-led opposition party, the Democratic Alliance. In addition, poor black South Africans are becoming increasingly frustrated with the failure of the ANC to fulfill its promises of economic improvement. Although the ANC took power on the pledge of equality for all South Africans, the richest third of the population (both black and white) still controls almost 90 percent of the nation's wealth. Building a truly inclusive South Africa in the land their predecessors freed from apartheid will be the main task facing the current generation of ANC leaders.

See also SHARPEVILLE MASSACRE.

BIBLIOGRAPHY

Davis, Stephen M. *Apartheid's Rebels: Inside South Africa's Hidden War.* Yale University Press, 1987.

Holland, Heidi. *The Struggle: A History of the African National Congress.* Grafton Books, 1989.

Mandela, Nelson Rolihlahla. *Long Walk to Freedom.* Little, Brown, 1994.

KATE TUTTLE

African Oral Literature
Styles and forms of oral artistic expression in Africa.

Artistic forms of expression are deeply ingrained in the black cultural experience and in the lives of African peoples, providing a forum for participation in the community and for exploring the mysteries of humanity. The artistic forms exert a huge impact on Africa's cultural realities, institutions, the system of values, and her vision for the future in a global context. The oral art forms are the best examples of the African imaginative expression; and their deployment in performance has become a rallying point for a call to an African renaissance and rejuvenation

A STORYTELLER IN THE DESERT. An Arab weaves a tale for his rapt listeners in a mural celebrating the oral tradition of African storytelling. (*Prints and Photographs Division, Library of Congress*)

VILLAGE STORYTELLERS. U.S. President Bill Clinton and first lady Hillary Rodham Clinton listen to tradtional storytellers in the Dal Diam village in Senegal, 1998. (*Greg Gibson/AP Images*)

throughout the continent. Although African societies have developed writing traditions, Africans are primarily an oral people, and it is that tradition that has dominated their cultural norms. The term orature, which means "the artistic use of language in oral performance," refers to something that is passed on through the spoken word and, because it is based on the spoken language, orature comes to life only in a living community. Where community life fades away, orality loses its function and dies. It needs people in a living social setting, it needs life itself. Orature grows out of tradition and keeps tradition alive.

Because orature has a social and political function in society, oral texts can only be understood and interpreted within their wider political and social contexts. By its very nature, orality tends to simplify the structure of leadership in society and by doing so manages to present issues to the audience in a very powerful way. Folktales are popular stories, memories that are centuries old and testify to a core of truth handed down orally from generation to generation. Women dominate the artistic mastering of language during courting, wedding, and folktale and storytelling when the grandmother becomes the immediate teacher in the use of carefully chosen language. The art of storytelling is such an important aspect of African life that

most societies have an animal character as the designated teller of tales. In some parts of West Africa, for example, it is anansi (the spider), in Central Africa nadzikambe (the chameleon), and in South Africa fudukazi (the tortoise), hence the popularity of these animal characters even in modern literary writing. Tales are important because they give useful insights in psychological understanding of the communities that produced them, they are a manifestation of the human condition (predicament) and human imagination, and much of modern literature (and thinking) is based on them. Themes of folktales may range from the creation, peoples' relationship with the universe, the origin of disease, witchcraft, marriage and family, and human relationship with animals.

POWER OF THE SPOKEN WORD

Orality is, by definition, performance, and only in performance can the performer hope to engage his audience and be engaged by them in direct dialogue. Orature is a strategic communal tool for nonliterate societies in their consolidation and socialization processes, and its spoken nature guarantees its widest circulation. Furthermore, oral performance and its flexibility in a multimedia setting, and the power of the spoken word in a largely illiterate society, are frequently utilized to political advantage by exploiting their potential for mass communication and multiple interpretations. In this regard it is a form of social control since it is performed in a public space, shouted out for all to hear. It is at once a form of socialization and a way of legitimating power, telling all what is permissible and what is not. Orality, therefore, promotes social cohesion, conserves and transmits social consciousness, while simultaneously entertaining the audience.

African orature is a development of a complex literary genre that demands the establishment of its own aesthetics for its interpretation and evaluation. Unlike written literature, orature has unfixed boundaries, which gives it greater freedom in its execution and interpretation—it can thus be used to praise and criticize those in power. The principal execution of orature is by performance, which combines sound, action, and meaning. Oral performance brings to the fore and concretizes the interaction among the principals of text, medium, performer, and audience so that an utterance can most adequately be interpreted and evaluated within the context of the total performance. African oral forms include ritual, divining/healing, folktales, myths, legends, mimes, narratives, and song and dance.

African oral traditions can be divided stylistically into those transmitted in a stereotypical way and those transmitted freely, changing with differences of time, place, and individual speakers. The first category includes traditions that function in ritual and cult, such as invocations, incantations, funeral songs, and praise songs. Language in this category is highly stylized, and cadence, meter, and rhythm are more important than conceptual coherence because in traditional society every word is charged with a particular force. The second category includes stories, legends of the origin of human institutions, as well as stories told for didactic purposes and for entertainment. Myths and legends are concepts and beliefs about the early history of a race, or explanations of natural events, such as the seasons, handed down from ancient times. They are humankind's search for meaning: concepts of the human mind, creations of man invented to give meaning and purpose to the enigma that is called "life" on earth and to explain the phenomena of nature, events, and human behavior. Thus myths are burdened with all that cannot be explained except by divine intervention; they reconcile man to the human condition and reveal the conditions and problems, social and personal, that people face in life.

PERFORMANCE STYLE

In African societies cultural production and aesthetics become associated with specific oral performers, such as the griot as oral historian among the Mandika in West Africa and the *imbongi* as praise poet among the NGUNI in southern Africa. In all these cultural practices, initiates are trained, within their cultural environment, by more experienced performers who provide the model and supervise the rehearsals. A potential performer may be recognized as such from early childhood and may then be entrusted to an experienced performer from whom he learns the traditional way of presenting the art form. The initiate and experienced performer may train and rehearse in relative seclusion before the trainee can perform in public. During training the trainee learns the appropriate voice qualities and movements for effective performance, learns how to posture, what language to use, and what costume to wear at what occasion. The careful training of the performers and the close supervision of the performance by elders of the culture ensure that variation in texts from different periods and by different performers is limited. The presence of and supervision by elders also gives the performance prestige and stability. Sex and age of the performer may determine the style of the performance; younger performers tend to be more vigorous than older ones. Thus the fact that the performer belongs to a particular sex, age, and social group influences his or her performance and its reception by the audience.

Oral performance involves public rendition because the most memorable performances are done at large events before a substantial audience. The performer is usually given enough space at the performance site to allow movement and interaction with the audience and other participants, whether it is within a fireside circle or an open public arena where the performer may be required to walk around. The language is usually in a highly stylized poetic form rendered in chant rather than ordinary speaking voice and accompanied by rhythmic body movements, thus enabling words and action to compliment each other. The power of the oral narrator is his or her ability to describe the events in a way that makes the audience feel satisfied that they understand what happened and why it happened. But narration of the events can never be neutral, and the narrator selects and orders the events in an attempt to influence their interpretation.

Text forms part of the poet's training and refers to the verbal content, which the performer memorizes, and upon which he improvises. In oral performances specific texts are recited, although only a few individuals may know the actual words in the text, and the style and manner of the recitation of the text may differ with individual performer and occasion. Because performance styles vary, no two oral performances and their narratives ever contain exactly the same material, and this may result in textual variation of the "ultimate version" of an oral text. For this reason, the manner of performance is often more important than the content, and the audience's focus is on the manner of delivery, not just on content. Although performance is inseparable from its context of use, verbal art can be treated as self-contained, bounded objects separable from their social and cultural contexts of production and reception, and decontextualized and recontextualized. Since many participants usually perform an oral text, it has a public audience, and integrates text, performer, and audience, and thus brings community together in the public arena in an interactive way.

SONG AND SINGERS

Song, as another example of African orature, has always been the most basic and dynamic form of cultural production of the African literary landscape, and it is considered a mode of performance profoundly embedded in its historical context and social environment. African folklore is full of instances where the song enchants a ferocious lion or snake and enables the victim to escape from danger. Song enables a kidnapped victim not only to fly to safety but also to know the right way home. Song is an elaborate form of language set to music, composed, and transmitted entirely through the oral medium. Song performance consists of repetition in various configurations, ranging from one word to a fairly lengthy line, and it can also occur in cyclic fashion where the whole structure is repeated. The fluidity of its structure, unfixed and flexible, renders song more suited to improvisation than a written text. Just as the structure and genre boundaries of song are fluid and unfixed, so too is the audience, as people at a public performance may come and go as they wish. When people come back the performance cannot be "rewound" to where it was when they left! Song performance also implies accompaniments, whether by dance or musical instruments or both.

There is a close and intense interaction between song, singer, and audience, actualized in call-and-response technique, ululation, and body movement. In the traditional multipart organization of voices, the call-and-response aesthetic relationship is also manifested in clapping hands, snapping fingers, whistling, stomping feet and other body movements. In song performance, the chorus is divided into two voice parts, each of which recites a different text. The temporal relationship between these parts is governed by the principle of nonsimultaneous entry, in such a way that the chorus "response" follows the narrator's "calling" phrase—the two voices alternating throughout the performance. The voice of the lead singer who introduces the song is allowed to intermingle with the melody provided by the chorus, thus foregrounding the melodious nature of the lyric that dominates the rhythm of the song. The employment of melodious language enables listeners themselves to work through the words of the song to attain the meaning behind them. Thus the African oral aesthetic event brings the principle of creation into play in a variety of forms: in the antiphonal patterns of sound

between leader and chorus, and in the audio-visual integration of music and dance. Through call-and-response, the spontaneous interaction of the audio and the visual, the oral-aesthetic event becomes a creative transition that takes place within each person participating and among the group as a whole. Call-and-response also establishes and reinforces social and political order within the community since each member contributes a note or phrase at predetermined points in a performance, reflecting their decentralized system of consensus and the interdependence that is necessary for group success. Call-and-response is not just an opening and closing device; it is also meant to enlist audience participation in the performance.

POEMS OF PRAISE

Praise poems are another example of African oral literary genres. A professional bard usually recites a praise poem. Expressed in carefully selected language, the poem defines and names an individual in bold imagery, comprising a cumulative series of praises and epithets that contain concise allusions to historical events and memorable achievements, from childhood onward, interspersed with narrative passages or comments. There are several types of praise poems: birth praises, wedding praises, dirge type praises, beer party praises, worker praises, war praises, love praises, political praises, topical praises, heroic praises, and hortatory praises, among others. Praise poems differ from eulogies, odes, and epics because, although they attempt to present their subjects in a favorable light, they also incorporate some negative characteristics. Furthermore, odes are inclined to have a reflection on philosophy and philosophical theory, while as praise poetry is based on social theory and action.

African societies treasure praise poetry as the loftiest and most excellent examples of their traditional heritage of literary imaginative expression. What makes praise poetry a fascinating piece of creative imagination is, among other things, the consistency and cohesiveness of form and content, the linguistic as well as the aesthetic values portrayed, the socio-historical referentiality, the artist's intentionality, the impact and effectiveness of the transmitted experience on the audience, and the universality of a given text. In terms of its linguistic features, praise poetry is recognizable through stylized language of imagery, metaphor, rhythm, rhyme, harmony and tone patterns, enhanced through the vocal mode of delivery. These features are intended specifically to intensify the effect of language and set it apart from everyday communication. They regulate departures from the normal register of everyday speech, and thus help language draw attention to itself— to give pleasure and assume an aesthetic rather than a purely communicative function. These distinctive linguistic features enable the society to construct an extensive repertoire of culture heritage. Thus, key to the cohesive force of oral literature is the peoples' pride in their language and history, and hence the language achieves an extraordinary sense of cultural identity.

Because they deal with contemporary events in and around the individual being praised or criticized, praise poems are documentary and help people to remember their past. They are collection points of insights to the transformations in society and the lives of people; they serve as a record of the peoples' histories, beliefs, and values and the changes that have taken place. They chronicle genealogies that link the present generation to their ancestors. They thus strengthen the common culture and legitimize the claim to power of those in authority. In this regard, praise poetry is the central local language of politics and is recognized as an important medium of political discourse that reflects the current political atmosphere in the community.

The main themes in praise poetry and other oral literary forms are morally instructive, but never prescriptive in the narrow sense. They encompass the whole spectrum of life drawn from peoples' everyday existence. Male poet performers tend to focus on themes of honor, devotion, character, loyalty, courage, and manhood. The themes of female poets usually concern domestic and more basic social matters: womanhood, filial relationships, charity, generosity, jealousy, peace, justice, courtesy and etiquette, agricultural chores, and the futility of war. Oral literary forms are thus a socially acceptable way of giving public expression to personal emotion, and the text and experience are naturalized because they are contextualized in family, circle of friends, acquaintances, and clan members. This familiarity between oral literature and community means that language now is left to be employed as a tool in the struggle for cohesion in society and for the integration of the culture with those who otherwise might feel left out, particularly women and the young.

HEROIC TALES AS LESSONS

Epics, as an example of legends, are poetic accounts of the deeds of great heroes and heroines, or of a nation's past history orally transmitted as well as performed in a ceremonial context. The epic is a reservoir of social and ecological knowledge, such as genealogy, relationships between clans, the seasons, names of the fauna, and the origin of things. The epic explains the origin of some traditions and teaches a traditional code of behavior, respect for customs, courtesy, and hospitality to strangers. The epic also gives a lesson in honor and courage. It condemns cowardice, fear, treason, lies, flight in front of the enemy, acceptance of bondage, and respects bravery, chivalry, and loyalty to one's country and companions in arms. The recounting of an epic entertains the public, but it also serves simultaneously as an act of celebration, as education for the younger generation, as an enforcer of group identity, and as a way of keeping alive the lore—historical, biological, zoological, sociological, religious, and geographical. The most frequently cited examples of African epics are *Sunjata* in West Africa, SHAKA in South Africa, *Mwindo* in Central Africa, and *Liongo* in East Africa. The *Sunjata* epic is about the history of the great Mali ruler, Sunjata Keita, and is performed during the septennial Kamabolon ceremony in Kingaba, Mali. The site for the ceremony is the Kamanolon sanctuary—a traditional hut with colorful paintings on which a new roof has been restored on the previous night. The occasion determines the length of the performance, some allowing elaborate embellishment of the text, and others, more formal ones, being more restrictive under the assumption that the stories are already known to the audience. *Sunjata* and *Mwindo* ceremonies may last for several days and may be regarded as a recreation of society because they have the function of inaugurating a new generation, because it is the young people who are responsible for most of the ritual labor, such as restoring the walls of the sanctuary.

African oral epic forms seem to have fairly recurring common themes, such as sibling rivalry, exile and the prodigal son, corruption at court, return of exile, restoration of order, kindness and generosity, respect for elderly parents, mysterious birth, and orphanage. The distinctive organizing motifs in the African epic include journey, departure, moral decay, corruption of home, obstacle and triumph, return, restoration, and others. Genealogy or the mention of a list of ancestors from whom the hero descends is a very important part of oral histories. Specialized language is used to communicate experiences and concerns, life events, human struggles that orature articulates, and such language exhibits artistic beauty in content, and draws its power from specific linguistic features, such as alliteration, repetition, rhyme, rhythm, mnemonics, ideophones, antithesis, parallelism, assonance, allegory, euphemism, and synecdoche. These devices not only make the expression unusual, but also make it appealing, and therefore easily remembered. Where there is a combination of form and content, the artistic expression is born and literature is created.

MUSIC AND DANCE

Apart from folktales, songs, praise poems, epics, and legends, music and dance comprise a distinctive feature of African orality, and African musical culture and its fusion with various modern forms, such as jazz, choral, and gospel singing has produced a unique sound and a major export for the continent. The musical event provides a useful departure point for a discussion of other African art forms such as instrument design, masks, and costume that are part of dance performance. In African practice there is no division between music and dance because music and movement constitute an integrated form of expression. Dance also bridges the divide between spirit and flesh, and even between the present and the eternal. Thus the funeral dirges and dances will often range from expressions of grief to joyous sounds and fertility dances, thus transforming the trauma of confronting death into a celebration of life for the benefit of those still living. Dance performance is not only a facilitator in the duality of communication to the body and soul, but also an important dimension of culture as well as an indicator of how knowledge about culture is produced and utilized. It is the primary site for the production of knowledge, and the place where multiple and often simultaneous discourses are employed. It is a means by which society reflects on its current condition, on the members' relationships with one another and with their environment. It enables people to define or reinvent themselves and their society and to either reinforce, resist, or subvert prevailing social orders. In music and dance performance subversion and legitimization can emerge in the same utterance or act.

Music mirrors a culture's social and political arrangements and protocols, and it provides the accompaniment for an individual's rites of passage throughout life. Because histories are kept and recited by specialist performers, people throughout Africa maintain and transmit fundamentally similar values in their expressions of the oral aesthetic. The size of the continent means that Africa is a land of diversity of cultures in many forms, sometimes related, sometimes diametrically opposed. Thus, in contrast to the highly rhythmic instrumental music from Central and West Africa, Southern Africa has vocal music that, under the influence of missionary-taught hymns, has taken on the form of simple Western harmony. The social dynamics have resulted in both the flourishing of some music and the struggle of others to survive.

MIME AND NARRATIVE

In addition to music and dance, African orature performance forms also include mimic and narrative. Mime is the use of facial expressions and gestures to tell a story. For example, the hunter who slew the beast may pantomime: sighting the animal, creeping after it, and aiming his arrows or spear, or whatever weapon he used to kill the beast. Typical of the African oral tradition, episode by episode, the hunter narrates his exploits in song, and while singing and narrating, he dances, mimes, and dramatically represents the main developments of the story.

The encounter between the beast and the slayer symbolizes the attitude of the hunters toward beasts with whom they are constantly engaged in a relationship of reciprocal adversary as they both prey on the same game. The pantomiming of the hunt and the mimicking of both the hunter's and the animal's movement is thus a celebration of the animal's submission to man. But this dance is also part of the hunt, and without its performance the hunt would be incomplete. To the people participating, therefore, this dance is not only a ritual but also a meaningful activity. In narrative, the element of narration, of addressing an audience directly, interspersed with mime of significant episodes from the narrative, is a central element of this category of performance, particularly to a largely illiterate and rural audience where orality is the principal means of communication. Narrative is the representation of an event or sequence of events, real or fictitious, by means of language.

As opposed to earlier studies that were from a structuralist paradigm, current oral studies approach oral performance as an agency for social and political action. This presupposes three things: 1) text; 2) the agency (i.e., space, medium); and 3) resistance or opposition (i.e., performance). A functional framework situates performance, like all forms of cultural work, in an embedded resistance mode, replacing aesthetics as the primary concern. Orality and performance have to be approached from a balanced perspective that avoids projecting orality as a fossilized artifact or the performer and audience as passive, disengaged bystanders. Performance, viewed from a process perspective, is temporal, participatory, and interactive. Thus by focusing on the specific performers, there is also a shift from structure to process, from the narrative timeless to the time-centered, particular and historically situated. The African creative process reveals a multidimensional nature of oral literature, founded on the interplay between the forces of narrative, rhythm, and dance. Performances of song lyrics, for example, are subtly variable in nuance and style, sensitive to content and occasion, and intimately dependent on the performer's rapport with his/her audience. In this sense, oral performance is a collective enterprise rather than an individualistic one.

FUNCTION IN SOCIETY

Performance is also generated through, participated in, and shaped by the community and its needs. Apart from providing entertainment for the community, the performances of the various oral forms have a specific social purpose. Weddings, for example, are performed to elaborate the continuation of the community, while epic and praise poetry are performed to record the history of the community and to urge courage and endurance. However, while the epic boasts of complete historical records, the praise poem deals with current and partially historical events. Oral performance may also play a religious function—the praise poet may evoke genealogy as a way of invoking the ancestors to bear witness to the occasion. In this way orality becomes a medium of communication between the living and the dead, an intermediary between the ancestors and the people present, a facilitator in the interplay between spirit and flesh. But oral performance is also for entertainment; even in healing, the performance goes beyond the call to cure the invalid of his or her ailment, and entertains the village audience in attendance. Because the healer is also an entertainer, in interpreting the text the whole social context of the performance must be understood because the actor is performing within the confines of space, time, and social context that determine the form of performance and gives it its meaning. Therefore, although it is true that oral performance is meant as a link to the absent ancestors and to symbolic time, it is also performed for the contemporary village audience, with emphasis on its relevance to their current situation and experience, indicated by the accompanying lyrics.

African oral literature is not only a way of expressing public opinion; it also provides an effective means of social control for the recitations are in the public arena. This function of oral literature and its performance in the legitimation of power in the constant power struggles involving ruleship explains the logic of its organization, the material justification of each situation, and why some performances are peculiarly male or female. The structure and function of the oral literature institution is highly flexible and adaptable, and the performer's qualities include the ability to adapt to the immediate socio-political environment. Since oral literature performance can be used for social maintenance, social identity, and re-creation of society with the corroboration of the political content it can easily be abused by those with money and power, creating tension for the artists and raising a serious question about their credibility. The artist's position in the community relies on his or her ability to gauge the political current in that community and the power structure, to extemporize and compose, and to use the aesthetics of persuasion to sway audiences with his or her performance. Oral performance is also an important instrument in the educational system for not only does it act as an incentive to and reward for socially approved actions, but also its recital reminds all present what qualities and conduct is laudable and what is condemnable. It reestablishes communal values and discourages individual tendencies by keeping the oral tradition not only a "secret" known to the few initiated, but also a group "heritage," communally owned. Focus in oral literature is on the collective, on group action, and the performer is always surrounded, encouraged, prompted, and accompanied—the performer is never alone on the stage.

See also ORAL TRADITIONS IN AFRICA; SUNDIATA KEITA.

BIBLIOGRAPHY
Biebuyck, D., and Kahombo C. Mateene. Mwindo Epic. University of California Press, 1969.
Cope, Trevor. Izibongo Zulu Praise Poems. Oxford University Press, 1968.
Hale, Thomas. Scribe, Griot, & Novelist. University of Florida Press, 1990.
Kunene, Mazisi. Emperor Shaka the Great: A Zulu Epic. Heinemann, 1979.
Niane, D. T. Sundiata: An Epic of Old Mali. Longman, 1960.
Okpewho, Isidore. The Epic in Africa. Columbia University Press, 1979.
Okpewho, Isidore. African Oral Literature. Indiana University Press, 1992.

LUPENGA MPHANDE

African Origins of Humanity
Discussion of the evidence for humanity's recent common origins in Africa.

It has been several decades since the man from Kibish made his appearance before the world of science. Strongly built, stained in hues of blue and brown from his lengthy immersion in the soil, the fragments of his skull, jaw, and skeleton had been disinterred from their resting place on the banks of the River Kibish in ETHIOPIA in 1967.

Researchers did not realize it at the time, but scrutiny of those few bone fragments would prove to be crucial in a fundamental rethinking about the evolution of our species.

KIBISH ENIGMA
This reappraisal has since formed part of an entirely new hypothesis, developed in the past fifteen years, about the origin of modern humans and about the source of what are commonly called racial differences. This new theory has, in turn, triggered one of the fiercest, most bitter debates about our origins—a considerable achievement for a field already infamous for the polemical divisions and open rivalry that it generates.

The man from Kibish (the skeleton's features suggest it was male) died before the last Ice Age, long before the last of the Neanderthals, that mysterious, sturdy lineage of human precursors that had lived, died, and been buried in the caves of Europe. But the Kibish man was different; he still had a powerful physique compared with an average modern male, with a noticeable brow ridge over his eyes and a rather broad and receding forehead. He had a higher and rounder skull and a bigger chin than any Neanderthal and his skeleton suggests his was a taller and lighter frame than we find in those archetypal cavepeople.

In short, the man from Kibish was quite different from Neanderthals—and that is because he was a member of our own species, *Homo sapiens*. Give or take some fragmentary bones from other parts of Africa, he is the most ancient direct kin for which fossils have been discovered. His bones were found by an expedition led by Richard Leakey, whose later research around LAKE TURKANA, in his native KENYA, a few hundred kilometers over the border from the Kibish region, made him one of the world's most successful "fossil hunters."

No volcanic rocks, which often supply important geological and chronological data, were found around the site. However, samples of shells collected from well above the level of the Kibish dig were dated to around 40,000 years ago, indicating that the bones, which were found far below this sequence of beds, must be far older. In addition, shells from the same level as the Kibish site were dated—using a special technique known as uranium-series dating—to around 130,000 years old.

At the time, by the standards of other African finds, this seemed an unremarkable date for a supposedly primitive human being. However, after proper studies had been carried out, researchers found that the ancient skull and skeleton of Kibish man resembled those of modern humans in a number of ways. It was then that the importance of the find began to be appreciated, as Leakey recalls in *One Life*.

Geological investigations and dating have shown that the two skulls are about 130,000 years old, yet despite their antiquity they are both clearly identifiable as *Homo sapiens*, our own species. At the time of their discovery, scientists generally believed that our species had only emerged in the last 60,000 years and many considered the famous Neanderthal Man to be the immediate precursor to ourselves. The Omo fossils thus provided important evidence that this was not so.

Richard Leakey's work at Omo-Kibish provided scientists with a fresh start in their study of *Homo sapiens'* origins. Indeed his finds gave them two new beginnings. First, they led a few researchers in the 1970s to conclude that the Kibish man was a far more likely ancestor for the Cro-Magnons, a race of early Europeans who thrived about 25,000 years ago, than their immediate predecessors in Europe, the heavyset Neanderthals. Then in the 1980s, a new reconstruction and study of the Kibish man revealed an even more startling possibility—that he was a far better candidate as the forbear, not just for the Cro-Magnons but for every one of us alive today, not just Europeans but all

the other peoples of the world, from the Eskimos of Greenland to the TWA people of Africa, and from Australian aborigines to Native Americans. In other words, the Kibish man acted as pathfinder for a new genesis for the human species.

In the past few years, many paleontologists, anthropologists, and geneticists have come to agree that this ancient resident of the riverbanks of Ethiopia and all his Kibish kin—both far and near—could indeed be among our ancestors. However, it has also become clear that the evolutionary pathway of these fledgling modern humans was not an easy one. At one stage, according to genetic data, our species became as endangered as the mountain gorilla is today, its population reduced to only about 10,000 adults. Restricted to one region of Africa, but tempered in the flames of near extinction, this population went on to make a remarkable comeback. It then spread across Africa until—by about 100,000 years ago—it had colonized much of the continent's savannas and woodlands. We see the imprint of this spread in biological studies that have revealed that races within Africa are genetically the most disparate on the planet, indicating that modern humans have existed there in larger numbers for a longer time than anywhere else.

We can also observe intriguing clues about our African origins in other less obvious but equally exciting arenas. One example comes from Congo-Kinshasa. This huge tropical African country has never assumed much importance in the field of paleoanthropology, the branch of anthropology that is concerned with the investigation of ancient humans. Unlike the countries to the east, Ethiopia, Kenya, and TANZANIA, Congo-Kinshasa has provided few exciting fossil sites—until recently.

In the neglected western branch of the African RIFT VALLEY, that giant geological slash that has played such a pivotal role in human evolution, the Semliki River runs northward between two large lakes, and its waters eventually form the source of the Nile. Along its banks, sediments are being exposed that were laid down 90,000 years ago, just as *Homo sapiens* was making its mark across Africa.

At the town of Katanda this erosion has produced an archaeological treasure trove: thousands of artifacts, mostly stone tools, plus a few bone implements that quite astonished the archaeologists, led by the husband-and-wife team of John Yellen, of the National Science Foundation, Washington, and Alison Brooks, of George Washington University. Among the wonders they have uncovered are sophisticated bone harpoons and knives. Previously it was thought that the Cro-Magnons were the first humans to develop such delicate carving skills—50,000 years later. Yet this very much older group of *Homo sapiens*, living in the heartland of Africa, displayed the same extraordinary skills as crafts workers. It was as if, said one observer, a prototype Pontiac car had been found in the attic of Leonardo da Vinci.

There were other surprises for researchers, however. Apart from the finely carved implements, they found fish bones, including some from two-meter-long catfish. It seems the Katanda people were efficiently and repeatedly catching catfish during their spawning season, indicating that systematic fishing is quite an ancient human skill and not some relatively recently acquired expertise, as many archaeologists had previously thought. In addition, the team found evidence that one of the Katanda sites had at least two separate but similar clusters of stones and debris that looked like the residue of two distinct neighboring groupings, signs of the possible impact of the nuclear family on society, a phenomenon that now defines the fabric of our lives.

Clearly, our African forbears were sophisticated people. Bands of them, armed with new proficiencies, like those men and women who had flourished on the banks of the Semliki, began an exodus from their African homeland. Slowly they trickled northward, and into the Levant, the region bordering the eastern Mediterranean. Then, by about 80,000 years ago, small groups began spreading across the globe, via the Middle East, planting the seeds of modern humanity in Asia and later on in Europe and Australia.

Today men and women conduct themselves in highly complex ways: some are uncovering the strange, indeterminate nature of matter, with its building blocks of quarks and leptons; some are probing the first few seconds of the origins of the universe fifteen billion years ago; while others are trying to develop artificial brains capable of staggering feats of calculation. Yet the intellectual tools that allow us to investigate the deepest secrets of our world are the ones that were forged during our fight for survival, in a very different set of circumstances from those that prevail today. How on earth could an animal that struggled for survival like any other creature, and whose time was absorbed in a constant search for meat, nuts, and tubers, and who had to maintain constant vigilance against predators, develop the mental hardwiring needed by a nuclear physicist or an astronomer? This is a vexing issue that takes us to the very heart of our African exodus, to the journey that brought us from precarious survival on a single continent to global control.

If we can ever hope to understand the special attributes that delineate a modern human being we have to attempt to solve such puzzles. How was the Kibish man different from his Neanderthal cousins in Europe, and what evolutionary pressures led the Katanda people to develop in such crucially different ways—ironically in the heart of a continent that has for far too long been stigmatized as backward?

MOTHER OF ALL HUMANS?

Picture this simple scene. A group of lowland gorillas—a male, six females, and their offspring—ambles through a forest in Central Africa. Moving on all fours, their knuckles bearing the weight of their powerful upper bodies, the animals pluck at the occasional shoot, rummage for berries, and gnaw at bits of vegetation. Then they stumble into a clearing, where they are confronted by another gorilla group, similarly led by a dominant silverback. The two males stare at each other. Then they start to display. They roar, throw leaves in the air, beat their chests, and finally begin running sideways, tearing up bushes and plants and banging their fists on the ground. The demonstration proves too much for the leader of the first group. He turns, and, with his females and children in tow, scrambles back into the forest.

There is one striking feature about these two groups (and about all other gorillas in our forest) that sheds a great deal of light not upon our primate cousins but upon ourselves. If one took specimens of a special type of genetic material, known as mitochondrial DNA, from those two squabbling males, and then compared them with samples from an Eskimo and an Australian aborigine, one would uncover a surprising fact: the latter pair (the humans) are more genetically alike than the former (the gorillas). Yet the Eskimo and aborigine live half a world away from each other in dramatically contrasting environments. Our two gorilla combatants share the same forest. Nevertheless, there is more variation in their genetic constitutions than in the most distantly related members of *Homo sapiens*. When it comes to genes, "humans are less different … even than lowland gorillas living in a restricted geographic area of west Africa," states a team of Harvard University anthropologists, led by Professor Maryellen Ruvolo, in a paper in the Proceedings of the National Academy of Sciences in 1994. Nor is this phenomenon restricted to *Homo sapiens* and *Gorilla gorilla gorilla* (as the lowland gorilla is imaginatively classified). The Harvard team's research on Chimpanzee and orangutan mitochondrial DNA has also revealed that these species are considerably more diverse than *Homo sapiens*.

It is not the gorilla, nor the chimpanzee, nor the orangutan, that is unusual, however. Each enjoys a normal spectrum of biological variability. It is the human race that is odd. We display remarkable geographical diversity, and yet astonishing genetic unity. This dichotomy is perhaps one of the greatest ironies of our evolution. Our nearest primate relations may be much more differentiated with regard to their genes but today are consigned to a band of land across Central Africa and to the islands of Borneo and Sumatra. We, who are stunningly similar, have conquered the world.

This revelation has provided the unraveling of our African origins with one of its most controversial chapters, and it is not hard to see why. The realization that humans are biologically highly homogeneous has one straightforward implication: that humankind has only recently evolved from one tight little group of ancestors. We simply have not had time to evolve significantly different patterns of genes. Human beings may look dissimilar, but beneath the separate hues of our skins, our various types of hair, and our disparate physiques, our basic biological constitutions are fairly unvarying. We are all members of a very young species, and our genes betray this secret.

It is not this relative genetic conformity per se that has caused the fuss but the results of subsequent calculations that have shown that the common ancestor who gave rise to our tight mitochondrial DNA lineage must have lived about 200,000 years ago. This date, of course, perfectly accords with the idea of a separate recent evolution of Homo sapiens shortly before it began its African exodus about 100,000 years ago. In other words, one small group of Homo sapiens living roughly 200 millennia ago must have been the source of all our present, only slightly mutated mitochondrial DNA samples—and must therefore be the fount of all humanity. Equally, the studies refute the multiregional hypothesis—the notion that modern humans have spent the last one million years quietly evolving from Homo erectus ancestors in different parts of the globe toward their present status. Our DNA is too uniform for that to be a realistic concept. As Professor Ruvolo's team points out, their research places a common human ancestor "at 222,000 years, significantly different from one million years (the presumed time of [a] Homo erectus emergence from Africa). The data ... therefore do not support the multiregional hypothesis for the emergence of modern humans." In fact, Professor Ruvolo puts it more emphatically when not constrained by the normal, dry academic prose required of a scientific journal: "No way does any of this information support the idea there was a common human ancestor living as long ago as one million years," she says. "In fact, when I wrote that paper in late 1993, I assumed a date of one million years before present for the emergence of Homo erectus from Africa. But now that date has been pushed back to at least 1.8 million years ago following those new dates of the Homo erectus skeletons in Java. Our research therefore rejects the multiregional hypothesis even more strongly." On the other hand, the Harvard team's work is entirely consistent with the "Out of Africa" theory that proposes the separate recent evolution

of Homo sapiens in Africa roughly 200,000 years ago. "It is a comparative way of showing you how humans are all very, very alike—and that similarity translates into one thing: the recency of the origin of our common ancestor," adds Professor Ruvolo.

Unraveling the history of human migration from our current genetic condition is not an easy business, of course. It is a bit like trying to compile a family tree with only an untitled photograph album. Nevertheless, biologists are beginning to make a telling impact in unraveling this biological plot and in understanding Homo sapiens' African exodus. And they have done this thanks to the development of some extraordinarily powerful techniques for splitting up our genes, which are made of strands of DNA (deoxyribonucleic acid) and which control the process of biological inheritance.

"The most golden of molecules," DNA is found in two different places within our bodies. There is mitochondrial DNA, and there is nuclear DNA. The latter makes up the genes that control the development of the growing embryo and that determine whether we will be short or tall, blue- or brown-eyed, and much else. This type of DNA is found in the nucleus of every cell in our body (hence the "nuclear" adjective) and is bundled together into chromosomes, along which are ranged those genes for brown eyes, height, and other attributes.

When a cell divides, so does its DNA. Its double helical strands of complementary chains of individual chemical bases—adenine (A), cytosine (C), guanine (G), and thymine (T)—separate, and each grows a new second chain, with the result that an exact copy of the originator's genetic script is created. This duplicate DNA migrates to the freshly created cell, where it renews the business of directing the manufacture of proteins, the biological building blocks from which our bodies are constructed. We shall examine the importance of nuclear DNA research in the unraveling of our history later in this essay. Before we do, however, let us look at the far more controversial role played by the other form—mitochondrial DNA.

This second type of genetic material is found outside the nucleus, but inside the cell, in objects called mitochondria organelles, which act as cells' microscopic power packs, and which have their own genetic blueprint: mitochondrial DNA. However, mitochondrial DNA differs from nuclear DNA in one important aspect. Unlike the latter, bequeathed as a fifty-fifty mixture from both our parents, the former is inherited solely from our mothers, because our fathers' sperm does not contribute mitochondria to the fertilized egg from which the embryo grows.

Having an unbroken biological bond with our past is clearly a source of important information. However, we should not assume we have exactly the same mitochondrial

DNA as our great-grandmother twenty times removed. The thread, although not broken, is frayed very slightly over the millennia because it accumulates occasional mutations. Imagine a DNA sequence made up of a long stretch of those four A, C, G, and T bases mentioned earlier. Sometimes a mistake in replication occurs, and a C replaces a G, or an A is substituted for a T. It is a well-understood phenomenon that, in the nucleus, is usually spotted and put right by special biological repair molecules. In the mitochondria, the mechanism for reconditioning old DNA is much less effective, so mutations accrue at a more rapid rate.

This apparent evolutionary oversight is good news for biologists. Thanks to the development of highly specific techniques for studying DNA, they can examine bases along a particular stretch of mitochondrial DNA in different people, from different races, and count those bases that are shared and those that are not. And the greater the number of unshared bases, the greater the number of accumulated mutations, and the longer it has been since the two individuals (and presumably the populations they represent) shared a common ancestor. The fewer the number of mitochondrial DNA differences, the greater the similarity, and the more recent must have been the date that they shared a forbear. In this way, scientists realized they could study the relatedness of the world's dispersed peoples.

And this is exactly what Allan Wilson, Rebecca Cann, and Mark Stoneking did in 1987 at the University of California at Berkeley. They took specimens from placentas of 147 women from various ethnic groups and analyzed the mitochondrial DNA of each. By comparing these in order of affinity, they assembled a giant tree, a vast family network, a sort of chronological chart for humankind, which linked up all the various samples, and therefore the world's races, in a grand, global genealogy.

The study produced three conclusions. First, it revealed that very few mutational differences exist between the mitochondrial DNA of human beings, be they Vietnamese, New Guineans, Scandinavians, or Nigerians. Second, when the researchers put their data in a computer and asked it to produce the most likely set of linkages between the different people, graded according to the similarity of their mitochondrial DNA, it created a tree with two main branches. One consisted solely of Africans. The other contained the remaining people of African origin, and everyone else in the world. The limb that connected these two main branches must therefore have been rooted in Africa, the researchers concluded. Finally, the study showed that African people had slightly more mitochondrial DNA mutations compared to non-Africans, implying their roots are a little older. In total,

these results seemed to provide overwhelming support for the idea that humankind arose in Africa, and, according to the researchers' data, very recently. Their arithmetic placed the common ancestor as living between 142,500 and 285,000 years ago, probably about 200,000 years ago. These figures show that the appearance of "modern forms of Homo sapiens occurred first in Africa" around this time and "that all present day humans are descendants of that African population," stated Wilson and his team.

The Berkeley paper outlining these findings was published in the journal Nature in January 1987 and made headlines around the world, which is not surprising given that Wilson pushed the study's implications right to the limit. He argued that his mitochondrial tree could be traced back, not just to a small group of Homo sapiens, but to one woman, a single mother who gave birth to the entire human race. The notion of an alluring fertile female strolling across the grasslands of East Africa nourishing our forbears was too much for newspapers and television. She was dubbed "African Eve"—though this one was found not in scripture but in DNA. (The honor of so naming this genetic mother figure is generally accorded to Charles Petit, the distinguished science writer of the San Francisco Chronicle. Wilson claimed he disliked the title, preferring instead "Mother of us all" or "One lucky mother.")

The image of this mitochondrial matriarch may seem eccentric, but it at least raises the question of how small a number of Homo sapiens might have existed 200,000 years ago. In fact, there must have been thousands of women alive at that time. The planet's six billion inhabitants today are descendants of many of these individuals (and their male partners), not just one single supermother. As we have said, we humans get our main physical and mental characteristics from our nuclear genes, which are a mosaic of contributions from a myriad ancestors. We appear to get our mitochondrial genes from only one woman, but that does not mean she is the only mother of all humans.

"Think of it as the female equivalent of passing on family surnames," states Sir Walter Bodmer, the British geneticist. "When women marry they usually lose their surname, and assume their husband's. Now if a man has two children, there is a 25 per cent chance both will be daughters. When they marry, they too will change their name, and his surname will disappear. After twenty generations, 90 per cent of surnames will vanish this way, and within 10,000 generations—which would take us from the time of 'African Eve' to the present day—there would only be one left." An observer might assume that this vast, single-named clan bore a disproportionately high level of its originator's genes. In fact, it would contain a fairly complete blend of all human genes. And the same effect is true for mitochondrial DNA (except of course it is the man who is "cut out"). The people of the world therefore seem to have basically only one mitochondrial "name." Nevertheless, they carry a mix of all the human genes that must have emanated from that original founding group of *Homo sapiens*. It is a point that Wilson tried, belatedly, to make himself. "She wasn't the literal mother of us all, just the female from whom all our mitochondrial DNA derives."

But there were other criticisms in store for the Berkeley team. For a start, of the 147 individuals who had been used to supply the raw data, 98 had been found in American hospitals, and in particular, of the 20 "Africans," only 2 were actually born there. The other 18 were African Americans, though they were classified as Africans for the study. Given that so much had been made of its African results, the failure to sample directly from people who actually lived on the continent appeared a little remiss. For their part, the researchers pointed out that technological constraints forced this local arrangement upon them. "The techniques that we had to use then required a great deal of mitochondrial DNA and we could only get that from placentas," recalls Mark Stoneking. "There was not enough in a normal blood sample. Indeed, we would have bled our subjects dry fulfilling our needs." So the team had to restrict themselves to using placentas from the San Francisco Bay area. In any case, added the researchers, this geographical inexactitude made little difference. Until very recently, male African Americans did not often produce children with white women. Interracial breeding was almost exclusively between black women and white men. The African origins of the resulting children's mitochondrial DNA (from their mothers) would therefore have been preserved.

These complaints about Wilson's survey could not be ignored so easily. So the Berkeley team repeated its research, with several changes in methodology, and in 1991 published two key papers (in Proceedings of the National Academy of Sciences, or PNAS, and second in Science) shortly before Wilson's death from leukemia. The research used a more reliable ethnic mix as a source of samples. Again their work produced those two branches that place humankind's birthplace firmly, and recently, in Africa. "Our study provides the strongest support yet for the placement of our common mitochondrial DNA ancestor in Africa some 200,000 years ago," they announced.

Given the absence of ancient mitochondrial DNA in people today, the study showed our ancestors must have emerged out of Africa and completely supplanted, without any interbreeding, existing populations of other human lines, an extreme form of replacement that was not an essential of the original African exodus model put forward by scientists like Chris Stringer and Günter Bräuer. This earlier model allowed some limited interbreeding. There was not a single sign of that in the genetic data, however.

Everything seemed nicely settled—until scientists began to look more closely at the statistics used by Wilson, Cann, and Stoneking. Then one or two of them became uneasy. For example, Maryellen Ruvolo noticed that there were actually two versions of the African tree created in the Berkeley team's later work. In the 1991 PNAS paper, the !Kung, a San group from southern Africa, were found at the base of the two main branches, suggesting their ancestors could actually be the progenitors of all humanity. In the second 1991 paper, the Twa were promoted to this hallowed position. "You couldn't have it both ways on the same set of data," recalls Ruvolo.

By contrast, Alan Templeton, a geneticist at Washington University, St. Louis, was far more outspoken in his criticisms, which he outlined in brief in Science in 1992, and then in full in American Anthropologist in 1993. He denounced the very concept of assuming that a gene tree was the same as a population tree. The former reflects the evolutionary history of a particular piece of DNA, he said; the latter indicated the movements of entire groups of individuals, and all the genes these groups carry.

But far more damning than this qualitative critique was Templeton's quantitative attack on the Berkeley team's computing methods. The researchers used a program called Phylogenetic Analysis Using Parsimony (PAUP). They put in their data, and out popped the tree. "As a result of analyzing just one run, they fooled themselves into thinking they had a well-resolved evolutionary tree," adds Templeton. "In fact, there are thousands of equally good but different trees that can be made from the Berkeley data."

This point is acknowledged by Ruvolo, who accepts that the research is flawed, but unlike Templeton does not believe that "Eve is officially dead." She admits thousands of different trees can be grown from the data, but points out that nearly all these mitochondrial bushes are only trivially different from one another. "In fact, we found three groups of trees—although there may be more if one searched further. Two had their roots in Africa, while the third's origins are unclear. So there is still evidence of an African origin, but it is not proof."

OUT OF AFRICA
However, the Out of Africa model, developed by Stringer, Bräuer, and others based on fossil evidence, retains a ruddy sheen of intellectual good health, for it does not depend on the work of Wilson, Cann, and Stoneking. In any case, Eve had by no means been expelled from her mitochondrial Paradise. "To paraphrase Mark Twain," says Roger Lewin,

in The Origin of Modern Humans, "reports of Eve's death have been greatly exaggerated." There was much in the two Berkeley studies that still suggested, but did not prove, that we had only emerged from our African homeland a short time ago on our road to world domination. For one thing, establishing the fact that most Africans are mitochondrially more disparate than the rest of the world's population is highly significant. Nor have the Berkeley teams been the only ones to demonstrate such diversity. A large-scale mitochondrial analysis of more than 3,000 people, carried out by Andrew Merriwether of Pittsburgh University, Douglas Wallace of Emory University, in Atlanta, and a group of other geneticists, revealed, in 1991, that "the native African populations have the greatest diversity. [This,] consistent with evidence from a variety of sources, suggests an African origin for our species."

More to the point, the question of mapping the roots of our African exodus is not actually the most important when considering modern humankind's origins. We know we come from Africa. The dispute is about whether we did so very recently, within the last 100,000 years, and about whether we replaced all other forms of hominids in the process, or whether different races today have far more ancient antecedents. "It is not really a question of where our ancestor arose," Stoneking acknowledges. "Even if we are able to prove beyond any statistical doubt that there was an African origin, it would not distinguish between the two competing hypotheses. The question is: when did we arise?"

In 1995 Satoshi Horai, of Japan's National Institute of Genetics, produced even more striking backing for the Out of Africa theory. He and his colleagues sequenced all 16,500 bases of the mitochondrial genomes of three humans—one each from Africa, Europe, and Japan—as well as four apes: an orangutan, a gorilla, a pygmy, and a common chimpanzee. This was an extraordinarily powerful and complete set of data, and it produced a correspondingly dramatic result. Horai used the ape mitochondrial sequences to get a highly accurate fix on mutation rates among primate populations. Then he applied those rates to the three human lineages and produced a figure that indicated they shared a common ancestor 143,000 years ago. As the African lineage was found to have the most diversity, Horai concluded that the last common ancestor lived there.

The evidence from our mitochondria may therefore seem conclusive: our cellular power packs were recently made in Africa, and, by inference, so must Homo sapiens have been. But there is still that critique of Templeton to consider: that our veneration of mitochondrial DNA blinds us to a broader picture. One little piece of DNA might have a singular source, but that is not necessarily true for the rest of our genome. A gene tree traces back the history of only one fragment of DNA (such as our mitochondrial DNA) but a population tree does not. It, in effect, is an average of many gene trees. So one gene tree may have its roots in Africa, but do the rest? It is a crucial question. So can geneticists resolve it?

The answer is yes—by studying the other, far more common form of genetic material that we encountered earlier in this essay: nuclear DNA. This, of course, is made up of tens of thousands of different genes, not just one small piece of DNA. So if we can trace all their roots, we will be able to unravel each gene's ancestry and should therefore be able to establish without doubt that we have an immediate African pedigree. The trouble is that we inherit our nuclear genes from both parents, in a manner that involves much random shuffling and makes it impossible for researchers to create exact long lineages with connected branches. This genealogical miasma has not stopped researchers from implementing some highly effective pieces of research, however. Some of this is statistical, but nevertheless illuminating. The rest is highly specific, concentrating, as it does, on particulate pieces of nuclear DNA. Both avenues confirm that we are recent African interlopers, with one of the most dramatic examples of the latter approach being provided by Professor Ken Kidd and Sarah Tishkoff at Yale University's department of genetics.

They have been searching for variations in nuclear DNA that define populations and their relations with each other, and the combination that they have found on chromosome 12 has turned out to be an eye opener. They focused on genetic material called polymorphisms, which often serve no function—like so much of our DNA. Our genes, which direct the manufacture of proteins, are, in fact, a few oases of sense in a desert of nonsense. Over the past few decades, geneticists have found to their surprise that most DNA is junk, long lists of repetitions and meaningless strings of bases uninvolved in protein manufacture. However, these bits and pieces of genetic flotsam often come in several forms. Some of us inherit one kind, others a different type, and this variation can be exploited. In the case of the Yale study, the researchers aimed at two sections that lie close together on chromosome 12 and found that some people lack a long piece of DNA containing 250 of those A, C, G, and T bases. This missing section of genetic material is known as a deletion. Other individuals possess this section, however. And in their other genetic target, people have been found to possess a variable number of repetitions of a little section of five bases, CTTTT. (There are a total of three billion bases that make up the six-foot-length gossamer strands of DNA that are coiled inside a single cell.) Some people have between four and 15 copies of this little genetic stammer. Again, this variation has no bearing on a person's genetic well-being.

When one looks at people living in Sub-Saharan Africa, one finds that individuals have every variety of deletion or non deletion along with any variety of number of CTTTT repeats. For example, one person may have a chromosome containing the CTTTT sequence repeated eight times as well as a deletion, and another person may have a chromosome with the CTTTT sequence repeated 12 times with no deletion. There are many combinations of numbers of repeats and deletions and nondeletions in Sub-Saharan Africa. Outside this region—in other words, throughout the rest of the world—one sees something very different. Chromosomes with deletions have only one pattern of CTTTT repeats, a sixfold one, while nondeletion chromosomes only have CTTTTs reiterated five or ten times. In other words, Africa shows complete variability. The rest of the world does not. And there is only one feasible explanation: that the small wave of settlers who set off from their African home to conquer the world was made up of a tribe or group of African *Homo sapiens* among whom only those who possessed a chromosome 12 had a sixfold CTTTT repetition. They carried this combination out to the world 100,000 years ago, and now scientists have picked up its signal like a discarded genetic calling card.

If the association of the chromosome 12 deletion and the six-unit repeat were old, they too would have been reshuffled and would no longer always be linked with each other—as is the situation in Africa. But they are not reshuffled, and to judge from the very few cases where there has been recombination across the globe, fairly simple genetic calculations produce a figure that ranges between 90,000 and 140,000 years for the appearance of these special chromosome 12s, the genetic cargo of the first, and only, wave of modern humans who were then on their way to take over the world.

The question is: What does this discovery do for the multiregional hypothesis? "I could be polite about this, and say it poses some serious problems," says Professor Kidd. "If I was being truthfully blunt, however, I would have to say our work blows the theory right out of the water. It is utterly incompatible with the facts that we have uncovered."

Professor Luca Cavalli-Sforza, of Stanford University, has been studying the different genetic constitutions of races for two decades, a process that he inaugurated when he began analyzing and differentiating among blood groups (and later other proteins) and their underlying genes. Then he started to draw trees and timetables that tracked the unfolding of our species' racial diversification, a decades-long project that culminated in 1994 in the publication of his massive work *The History and Geography of Human Genes*, co-authored with Paolo Menozzi and Alberto Piazza. More than 70,000 frequencies of various gene types in nearly 7,000 human population types are included, combined with anatomical, linguistic, and anthropological studies. It is an august body of work that comes down fairly and squarely on the side of the Out of Africa theory. "We conclude a definite preference for the rapid replacement model," states Cavalli-Sforza.

Much of Cavalli-Sforza's study is concerned with genetic distances between populations, a concept that measures the relatedness of one group or tribe with another. "One can estimate degrees of relatedness by subtracting the percentage of rhesus negative individuals among, say, the English (16 percent) from that among the Basques (25 percent) to find a difference of nine percentage points," states Cavalli-Sforza. "But between the English and the East Asians its comes to sixteen points—a greater distance that perhaps implies a more ancient separation. There is thus nothing formidable in the concept of genetic distance."

This concept allows scientists to calculate when two populations—say the English and the Germans—split from their original founding population and began their own separate existences: "When other matters are equal, genetic distance increases simply and regularly over time. The longer two populations are separated, the greater their genetic distance should be." So Cavalli-Sforza and his collaborators analyzed all the various genetic distances for all the different peoples of the world and revealed a picture that is exactly "what one would expect if the African separation was the first and oldest in the human family tree." The researchers found that the genetic distance between Africans and non-Africans is roughly twice that between Australians and Asians, and the latter is about twice that between Europeans and Asians. And these ratios parallel those produced by the Out of Africa theory: 100,000 years for the separation between Africans and Asians, 50,000 years for that between Asians and Australians, and 30,000 years for that between Asians and Europeans. "In these cases, at least, our distances serve as a fair clock," adds Cavalli-Sforza.

More specifically, Cavalli-Sforza looked at certain sequences on two human chromosomes—numbers 13 and 15—and discovered that there was more variety within the African versions of these "microsatellites" than those from other parts of the world. And when he used that diversity to calculate how much time has passed since Africans separated from other populations, he got a figure of 112,000 years. Sounds familiar, doesn't it?

As this essay has made clear, there is little evidence to support the multiregional model of human origins. *Homo sapiens* is not the child of an entire planet, but a creature, like any other, that has its roots in one place and period—in this case with a small group of Africans for whom "time and chance" has only just arrived. In 2001 a team of researchers discovered what appears to be even earlier evidence of human origins in Africa—a skull, jawbone, and teeth between six and seven million years old. The discovery in Chad of the specimen named Toumai, meaning "hope of life" in the Goran language, is expected to provide new information about a period in human evolution that is virtually unknown. In describing Toumai's characteristics, scientists noted that it has traits of both apes and humans and have assigned it a new genus and species. Studies of the Chadian fossil over the next few years should add to the mounting evidence that permits proper self-evaluation and provides an understanding of the gulf we are crossing from a clever ape to a hominid that can shape a planet to its requirements—if only it could work out what these are.

Indeed, a more recent study, this one led by Andrea Manica, a geneticist, examined the skulls of some 6,000 specimens in an attempt to unravel the puzzle of humanity's place of origin. The results, published in a 2007 edition of *Nature*, suggest that genetic variations among humans tended to diminish the farther the specimens were from Africa. Though Manica's findings are not conclusive, they do nevertheless offer yet more proof for the Out of Africa model.

CHRIS STRINGER

African Religions: An Interpretation

African peoples have created hundreds of distinct religions that, despite centuries of contact with Islam and Christianity, remain important both in Africa itself and to followers in the Americas and in Europe. Approximately half of Africa's current population identify themselves as

SHAMANS OF MASAI. This group of young shamans was photographed in the Masai region of Kenya sometime between 1920 and 1930. (*Prints and Photographs Division, Library of Congress*)

Muslim. A smaller number identify themselves as Christian or as followers of indigenous African religions, and small groups (under one million each) identify themselves as Jewish or Hindu. This essay focuses on those religions created by African peoples south of the Sahara. While there is considerable diversity in African religions, this essay will emphasize their commonalities.

WESTERN VIEWS OF AFRICAN RELIGIONS

Any discussion of African religions must consider the way in which Western observers have described them. It is fair to say that African religions have been subjected to the most negative stereotyping of any of the world's religious traditions. Beginning in the sixteenth century, Westerners attempted to justify the enslavement of African peoples by claiming that Africans lacked a sense of both history and religion. In the nineteenth century this alleged deficiency was used to justify the colonization of the African continent. Europeans initially claimed that the slave trade and then colonization would bring Africans into history and, through missionary activity, into religion. Europeans assumed that religious activity occurred in buildings and in reference to sacred scriptures. Such categories excluded Africa.

Beginning in the late nineteenth century, European administrators, travelers, missionaries, and anthropologists became increasingly aware that African cultures possessed something that corresponded to what Europeans regarded as religion. Still, they could take comfort in the general absence of sacred written texts and what appeared to be a lack of focus on a supreme being, both of which stood in sharp contrast to the three major monotheistic traditions—Christianity, Judaism, and Islam. African religions became relegated to a special category, labeled at various times as primitive, animist, fetishist, oral, traditional, and so on—essentially as living museums for a distant religious past. When missionaries sought to preach in African communities and to translate prayers and scriptures into African languages, they realized that most African religions have a term for the supreme being. Still, they insisted that this was not an active god, like that of Western religions. It was a god who began the act of creation and then stepped back. It became what they called a deus otiotus, a remote god, rarely invoked in African religions, which focused their attention on lesser spirits and ancestors and the rituals designed to supplicate them.

Western scholars have also characterized African societies as resistant to change. This view has even been accepted by some of the leading African scholars of religion who argued that African religious change prior to colonial conquest was so slow as to be imperceptible. As John Mbiti has described it: "Human life is relatively stable and almost static. A rhythm of life is the norm and any radical change is either unknown, resented or so slow that it is hardly noticed."

While it is true that Africans do not have a word equivalent to the term religion, there are a number of terms in African languages that describe activities, practices, and a system of thought that corresponds with what most Westerners mean by religion. African religions are often closely associated with African peoples' concepts of ethnic identity, language, and culture. They are not limited to beliefs in supernatural beings or to ritual acts of worship, but govern all aspects of life, from farming to hunting, from travel to courtship. Like most religious systems, African religions focus on the eternal question of what it means to be human: What is the meaning of life, and what are the correct relations between humans, between humans and spiritual powers, and with the natural world? African religious systems seek to explain the persistence of evil and suffering, and they seek to portray the world as operating with some degree of order and predictability. They uphold certain types of ethical behavior, which their followers see as influencing their status in the afterlife. These ideas are expressed in sacred oral traditions, handed down from generation to generation through the performance of rituals, and through intensive periods of education, including RITES OF PASSAGE AND TRANSITION.

SUPREME BEINGS

While every African religious tradition has an idea of a supreme being who began the process of creating the universe and who created lesser spirits, they vary as to how they worship these supreme beings and how they perceive their involvement in people's daily lives. Most Western scholars see African supreme beings as somewhat remote, based on the relative lack of shrines devoted to such beings; on the fact that African ritual life typically focuses on lesser spirits; and also on the many African myths describing a supreme being who was active in the initial stages of world history, but then withdrew.

For example, the DINKA of SUDAN describe a time when the supreme being hovered just over the earth and provided humans with a grain of millet each day, which was sufficient for all their nutritional needs. According to one version of this myth, one day a woman decided to plant more than the one grain allotted to her. When she raised her hoe in the air to plant it, she poked the supreme being, Nhialic, in the eye. Nhialic withdrew into the sky, and death and hardship became forces in Dinka life. Nhialic withdrew because of the woman's greed, and because she had invented agriculture, a task for the supreme being. One could argue, however, that the supreme being was simply

too close, and humans needed some distance to carve out an area for their own initiative. A proverb told by the IGBO of southeastern NIGERIA also illustrates this sense of distance and the belief that the supreme being should be approached only on matters of major importance: "God is like a rich man. You approach him through his servants." According to this view, the supreme being remains in charge of major concerns, such as rain, but is relatively uninvolved in the minor events of daily life.

These images of a remote supreme being, however, do not tell the whole story. Among the Igbo and also the SHONA of ZIMBABWE, the supreme being is said to speak to humans through spiritual mediums when they enter a state of possession. These mediums are usually women, though it is men who interpret the supreme being's message. Among the JOLA of SENEGAL, fifty men and women have claimed to be prophets of the supreme being. They spread their teachings throughout their communities on such topics as warfare between neighboring villages, the introduction of new forms of rain rituals, and the introduction of a day of rest for the land. Among the AKAN-speaking peoples of GHANA and CÔTE D'IVOIRE, daily rituals are performed to honor the supreme being, Nyame. In most African religions, the supreme being is both the giver of life and the judge of human conduct after death. Thus, for the YORUBA of Nigeria and BENIN, Olorun breathes life into a newborn and gives it a destiny. When a person dies, it is Olorun who decides whether that person will become an ancestor and will eventually be reborn, or whether it will go to the place of broken pots, where those who led destructive lives rest for all eternity. It is a hot place, heated not with fire but with West African peppers. These are not the actions of a remote deity, but one who plays a vital role in African views of the universe.

LESSER SPIRITS

As the Igbo proverb suggests, the supreme being has assistants who help humans to resolve particular concerns. Among the Yoruba of Nigeria and Benin, these lesser spirits are known as orishas. There are said to be 401 orishas, each with a distinct character, special powers, and appropriate rituals. The most important of these include Obatalá, who was sent by Olorun to create the universe, but became inebriated on palm wine before he could finish creating human beings; Oduduwa, who completed Olorun's task and descended to earth to become the first king (oni) of IFE; Changó, the god of thunder; OSHÚN, a goddess associated with the rivers and with feminine ideals of beauty; and Ifa, the god of divination. These deities are also worshiped in the African-inspired religious traditions of Vodou, Santería, and Candomblé in the Americas.

Among the peoples of east, central, and southern Africa, many of the lesser spirits once lived as human beings, often as kings. This is especially true of the BUGANDA of UGANDA and the Shona. Elsewhere, the lesser spirits are associated with particular forces of nature or human activities. In other cases, the lesser spirits do not have such elaborate biographies, but are associated with particular forces of nature or with particular types of issues. Thus, among the DOGON of MALI, the Nommo are associated with the life-giving properties of water. The Jola have lesser spirits associated with rain, fishing, blacksmithing, community governance, women's fertility, and male initiation, among other things. It is not uncommon to have lesser spirits associated with rivers, the ocean, particular caves or springs, and other places in the natural world.

In all of these cases, however, the lesser spirits derive their powers from the supreme being. Much as Yoruba kings are said to reign rather than to rule (they delegate their authority to various types of councils and advisers at their courts), so Olorun delegates much of his power to the orisha. This is equally true of the NUER and Dinka of Sudan, who regard most of the spirits as creations of the supreme being. In some parts of Africa, these lesser spirits make their presence known through spirit possession. Among the FON of Benin and the Yoruba, the spirit enters into the body of the devotee and is said to ride him or her like a horse. The possessed person speaks and moves in the manner of the spirit and communicates its desires to an assembled congregation. In other areas of Africa, lesser spirits communicate through dreams and visions but do not possess their devotees. Spirits who fail to communicate with their devotees or to respond to their prayers are abandoned, and their cults forgotten.

In a separate, but closely related category, are the spirits of the ancestors. In some cases, such as the Yoruba and the Jola, this category is limited to spirits of people who led benevolent lives. They continue to help the living by appearing to their descendants in dreams and visions and providing them with advice and warnings. In southern and central Africa, the ancestors are not necessarily benevolent. They often seize people with illnesses, to punish them for neglecting ritual obligations or obligations to the extended family.

Finally, African religions recognize powers that circulate in the universe and originated from the supreme being. The Dogon, for example, worship a supreme being called Amma, whose vital force, which circulates throughout the universe, is known as nyama. For the Igbo of southeastern Nigeria, the supreme being is known as Chiukwu or Chineke, and the life force that circulates in the world and governs people's destiny is known as chi.

African religions' lesser spirits show clearly how the religions themselves have changed. For example, in the Yoruba creation myth about Oduduwa's completing the making of human beings after Obatalá became drunk on palm wine, historians see a symbolic account of the rise of Ife and its god Oduduwa, who conquers or displaces the indigenous population who worshiped Obatalá. Both orishas find their way into a Yoruba pantheon, even though Obatalá's origins may not be Yoruba. With the growing importance of agriculture in Africa over the last 8,000 years, one can trace the development of earth goddess cults like Ala among the Igbo and Asase Ya among the ASANTE. The increasing importance of cults associated with iron, like that of Ogun among the Yoruba, may well have reflected the growing importance of iron. Among the Kongo and related peoples of central Africa and among the Jola of Senegal, new cults of lesser spirits emerged in relation to the development of the Transatlantic Slave Trade. Similarly, the European conquest of Africa catalyzed a variety of new religious movements, which aimed to interpret the religious experience of conquest and offer a solution to the challenges of COLONIAL RULE. Like most religious systems, African religions have been influenced by disruptive events such as conquest, famines, droughts, and epidemics, all of which challenge their ability to explain the world and reassure adherents of its predictability and order.

AFRICAN RELIGIOUS EXPRESSION AND INSTRUCTION
African religious belief is expressed through the recitation of myth and oral traditions and through discussion both among elders and between generations. It is also expressed through ritual, which often involves making offerings in order to attract a spirit's power or win its benevolence. One reason that ritual offerings are seldom made to the supreme being, according to many traditions, is that the supreme being already owns everything in the world. Ritual offerings are often accompanied by libations of palm wine, millet beer, or water, which are seen to increase the power of the spoken word. Animal sacrifice may be used in order to release the life force of the animal, which combines with the force of the libation and of the spoken word, and thus further increases the ritual's power. Usually, a ritual's participants consume the meat of the sacrifice and the beverage of the libations, thereby binding the congregation, its priest, and the spirit being supplicated to work toward the fulfillment of their prayers.

Many African art forms are used primarily in religious ritual. In most of Africa, masks and costumes are used to impersonate the lesser spirits. Among the Yoruba, Igbo, Fon, and EWE of West Africa, wearing a mask and costume invites the presence of a god in one's body. Such masking traditions and impersonations are never done for the supreme being, whose physical image is also not represented in statuary. In most African religions lesser spirits are represented in statues, but these are not idols; they are intended only to symbolize or attract the spirits portrayed.

Dance is also an important part of ritual activity. Dances invite the presence of particular spirits, depict the history of particular cults, or honor the dead. Among the Kung of southern Africa, dance is a particularly important part of healing rituals. The dance itself ignites a spiritual power within the dancer, enabling him or her to enter an altered state of consciousness and heal other people. Dance is also a powerful means of prayer, both to the supreme being and to lesser spirits.

While several African countries, including Nigeria and the DEMOCRATIC REPUBLIC OF THE CONGO, have established formal schools devoted to African healing systems and African religions, most forms of religious instruction are not officially chartered. Much of it occurs within the family and between elders and children. More formal occasions for religious instruction are often associated with rites of passage. Boys often endure an initiation school just before or after puberty, during which they are taught about their religious and social responsibilities as men. Such initiations into manhood may or may not be accompanied by circumcision, though usually some sort of physical ordeal is involved. Girls are often initiated around the age of menarche. In some cases they receive instruction in small groups, from their mothers; in other cases female initiation is more formal, with a period of ritual seclusion comparable to that of male initiation.

RELIGIOUS VIEWS OF EVIL AND SUFFERING

African explanations of evil and suffering focus on disruptive spirits, often called tricksters, and on humans who use life-destroying powers for personal gain or to harm others. One trickster among the Yoruba is the messenger god Exú, who dislikes an overly orderly world. Exú often changes messages offered in prayer to see how events will unfold. While mistakenly identified as the Devil by early missionaries, Exú does not work to advance evil, but fully embraces life's incertitude, passion, and beauty. For the Dogon, the trickster figure—variously identified as the Pale Fox or as the Jackal—is a solitary figure who creates chaos in his efforts to find his natural companion. In both cases, these trickster gods make communication with the supreme being and with lesser spirits an uncertain enterprise and help to explain the failure of even the most carefully prepared ritual.

But supernatural beings are not the only cause of suffering. Some humans are said to be able to separate their souls from their bodies and send them in the night to attack other people or other people's goods. These attacks are said to be the source of many illnesses, deaths, and other calamities. In troubled times, societies have often blamed witchcraft and undertaken elaborate witch-finding rituals. But identifying witches is particularly difficult because their activities, occurring entirely in the spiritual realm, are not visible to ordinary people. Sorcerers, on the other hand, use medicines and rituals for personal gain or to harm others. They also cause human suffering, but their use of material objects makes them more readily identifiable than witches. Witchcraft accusations greatly increased in number and frequency during the European conquest of Africa, as people searched for the spiritual significance of their loss of freedom.

While the overwhelming majority of North Africans as well as substantial minorities in East and West Africa now embrace Islam, African religions continue to command a substantial following in most of sub-Saharan Africa. Despite nearly a thousand years of contact with Islam, and nearly five centuries of contact with Christianity, African religions continue to address the spiritual needs of their adherents. They have also influenced the practice of Islam and Christianity in Africa itself. In addition, African religions are practiced by communities across the Americas, as well as in Europe. It appears that African religions will continue to play an important role in Africa and in the West in the twenty-first century.

See also ANTHROPOLOGY IN AFRICA; CHRISTIANITY: MISSIONARIES IN AFRICA; COLONIAL RULE; FEMALE CIRCUMCISION IN AFRICA; ISLAM IN AFRICA; JEWISH COMMUNITIES IN NORTH AFRICA.

ROBERT BAUM

African Socialism

Political philosophy popular in Africa from the 1950s through the 1970s, proposed as an African alternative to both Western capitalism and European and Chinese socialism.

During the independence era, some of Africa's most prominent statesmen supported a political philosophy that they labeled African socialism. Among the proponents of this philosophy were Léopold SENGHOR of Senegal, Sékou TOURÉ of Guinea, Julius NYERERE of Tanzania, Kwame NKRUMAH of Ghana, and Modibo KEITA of Mali. These leaders advocated African socialism as a means of promoting rapid economic development in independent Africa without generating the inequality and injustice characteristic of Western capitalism.

PRINCIPLES OF AFRICAN SOCIALISM

The term African socialism actually encompassed a range of different views and approaches to economic and political development. African socialism lacked a basic theoretical work, such as *Das Capital* by Karl Marx, which helped to define European socialism. Instead, the principles of different forms of African socialism appeared in the writings and speeches of its proponents. Most forms of African socialism started from the idea that precolonial African lineages, or extended families—traditionally the basic social unit—were, in effect, socialist collectives with in which all members shared the burdens of providing food, shelter, and clothing. African socialists argued that through cooperation and a commitment to the common good, precolonial African lineages prospered and all members' needs were met. African socialism aimed to revive these traditions in the modern context in order to achieve prosperity, secure economic independence from colonialist powers, and build a sense of nationhood.

Proponents of African socialism claimed that it was distinct from European socialism because it derived from ancient, uniquely African traditions. In addition, some adherents of African socialism claimed that unlike European socialism, it was not a response to class conflict, which they believed was basically absent within modern African societies. Instead, African socialism was an attempt to modernize traditional collectivism and apply it to contemporary society. Nkrumah, the former president of Ghana, frequently argued that Africans possess an innate sense of inward dignity, integrity, and value. For Nkrumah, these attributes formed the basis for a cooperative society in which able-bodied members willingly provided for those who could not support themselves, including orphans, the elderly, and the sick. Many saw communal ownership of land in precolonial African societies as a further sign of traditional collectivism. As Kenyan Tom MBOYA argued, "We are all sons and daughters of the soil."

AFRICAN SOCIALISM IN ACTION

During the first three decades of African independence, from the mid-1950s through the mid-1980s, African leaders made several attempts to implement African socialism in the context of modern nation-states. These attempts shared a variety of common features. Usually governments nationalized the major industries and thereby assumed control over industrial production and management. African socialists also tried to improve the quality of life by improving access to education and health care. Frequently, socialist states provided incentives to students by guaranteeing them employment after graduation from high school or college, or both. In several cases, governments strove to increase agricultural production by introducing new farming methods and tools and by implementing national land reform policies. Governments

hoped to use the profits from agriculture to invest in the industrial sector.

In 1967 Nyerere initiated one of the best-known socialist experiments in Africa in Tanzania. The program, outlined in Nyerere's famous Arusha Declaration, attempted to develop the Tanzanian economy through rural land-reform and development projects, including the creation of collective farm villages, based on the principle of ujamaa, or familyhood. Nyerere believed that moving peasants from scattered homesteads (until then the prevailing settlement pattern in rural Tanzania) into larger villages would give the population better access to government services and agricultural assistance. At the same time, he believed, the collective organization would help prevent the emergence of poverty or profit-driven greed among individuals. Nyerere argued that these villages and farms would provide an engine for economic and social development and at the same time build a self-sufficient, debt-free, and classless society.

Between 1969 and 1980, the Tanzanian government forced millions of peasants to abandon their rural homesteads and move into ujamaa villages. By 1977 more than 80 percent of the population had been settled in the villages. Although the program did improve the quality of life in some ways—rural populations had better access to clean water, health care, and schools—it caused considerable human hardship and failed to increase agricultural productivity. In fact, agricultural production decreased during this period because the surrounding lands could not support the large numbers of farmers in the villages using intensive farming practices. By the late 1970s, it was evident that ujamaa had failed, and Tanzania, like many other nations that experimented with socialist programs, had to borrow heavily from foreign lenders in order to support the failing economy.

CRITICISMS OF AFRICAN SOCIALISM

African socialism has faced several major criticisms. Many observers have questioned the claim that socialism is an African tradition. Critics, including African scholars and some who sympathize with the goals of African socialism, have argued that few precolonial African societies really exhibited the broad-based equality and solidarity claimed by proponents of African socialism. Precolonial African societies, particularly those ruled by centralized states, critics argue, possessed both social classes and a concept of private property. According to critics' arguments, even those societies that once might have been more egalitarian had invariably lost these qualities as a result of colonialism and incorporation into global markets. Thus, virtually all modern African societies already incorporate class divisions and capitalist market values. Some critics have urged African leaders to define African socialism less as a return to doubtful traditions and more as a response to European capitalist imperialism. Finally, some critics argue that African socialism should embrace the influence of Marxist European socialism, particularly in its humanist and liberatory ideals.

The most biting critique of African socialism, however, stems from the fact that no African state has been able to develop a sustainable economy based on African socialist ideals. Although numerous countries, including Tanzania, Benin, Ethiopia, Mali, Ghana, Liberia, and Mauritania, experimented with socialism at some time between 1960 and 1990, none did so successfully. In almost every case, socialist regimes undermined their countries' economies and eventually had to borrow heavily from foreign lenders. Ultimately, these countries were forced to seek assistance from the International Monetary Fund (IMF), which granted loans on the condition that their governments undertake STRUCTURAL ADJUSTMENT reforms—particularly economic liberalization and privatization of national industries—that reversed African socialist policies. By the mid-1980s, almost every African state that had implemented a socialist program had to abandon it.

See also ECONOMIC DEVELOPMENT IN AFRICA.

ELIZABETH HEATH

Afrikaner

South African ethnic group whose 3.4 million members claim descent from seventeenth-century Dutch settlers.
In 1652 the Dutch East India Company established a colony on the Cape of Good Hope, intended primarily to provision company ships sailing between Europe and Asia. The colony's first Dutch settlers built CAPE TOWN and farmed in the surrounding countryside. Over the next several decades Germans and Huguenots arrived—many of them fleeing religious persecution in Europe—and intermarried with the Dutch settlers. The descendants of this population forged the Afrikaner ethnic identity, characterized by adherence to Calvinism and the Afrikaans language, which is closely related to Dutch.

From its early years the Cape Colony relied on slaves imported from India, Indonesia, MADAGASCAR, and later, MOZAMBIQUE. The colonialists imported slaves largely because they considered the local KHOIKHOI pastoralists an unsuitable labor force. Attempts of Afrikaner farmers (also known as Boers) to take over land occupied by the Khoikhoi led to two wars (1659–1660 and 1673–1677). The Boers' firepower, combined with an 1813 smallpox epidemic, nearly wiped out the Khoikhoi population.

In 1806 the British took over the Cape Colony, principally to protect trade ships passing the Cape of Good Hope en route to India. The Afrikaners resented the imposition of the English language and culture and above all the abolition of slavery in 1834. In response, over 12,000 Boers (approximately one-tenth of the colony's white population) began what Afrikaners later called their Great Trek out of the Cape Colony in 1835. As their ox-drawn wagons moved inland, the trekkers clashed with Zulu and NDEBELE groups. A trekker community would often draw its wagons into a circle, or laager; later the laager became a metaphor for Afrikaners' sense of persecution and the need for community cohesion. After two years the Afrikaners had traveled beyond the Orange River, where they established the Orange Free State, also known as the South African Republic.

Afrikaner political independence did not last long. The 1867 discovery of diamonds near the Orange River sparked an expansionist drive by the British Cape Colony which, despite the claims made by the Orange Free State, annexed the diamond mine area in 1871, calling it Griqualand West. The British also took over the South African Republic in 1877, but then relinquished it after an Afrikaner rebellion in 1881, at which point the republic was renamed the TRANSVAAL. The discovery of gold at Witwatersrand in 1886, however, ultimately brought an end to Transvaal independence. Thousands of immigrant prospectors, mainly British, began to arrive in search of fortune. Soon Uitlanders, or foreigners, outnumbered Afrikaners in the goldmining region. When the British sent troops to protect Uitlander interests in 1899, the Transvaal declared war. The Anglo-Boer War, as it was called, lasted less than three years and was followed by the British takeover of the Afrikaner colonies. In 1910 these colonies joined the CAPE COLONY and Natal in the Union of South Africa.

As South Africa underwent rapid industrialization and urbanization during the early twentieth century, many rural Afrikaners migrated to cities such as JOHANNESBURG and PRETORIA, where they typically took low-paying manual labor or civil service jobs. In the countryside, Afrikaners whose farms depended on cheap African labor were among those who sought restrictions on Africans' access to land. This demand, as well as demands for racial segregation in general, became part of the platform of the NATIONAL PARTY, formed in 1914. In 1948 the National Party came to power and instituted the APARTHEID policies that endured in South Africa until the 1990s. Since the election in 1994 of Nelson MANDELA and a government dominated by the AFRICAN NATIONAL CONGRESS, however, the National Party has lost even many of its former white supporters, and relatively few civil service jobs now go to Afrikaners. Some Afrikaners (who altogether account for about 7 percent of the national population) have joined up with Afrikaner nationalist groups such as Afrikaner Volksfront, who continue to call for a separate Afrikaner state. Most, however, are in the process of adjusting to life in a major-ity-controlled South Africa where they are frequently iden-tified with the brutal oppression of the apartheid years.

BIBLIOGRAPHY

Giliomee, Hermann Buhr. *The Afrikaners: Biography of a People.* University of Virginia, 2003.

Middleton, John, ed. *Peoples of Africa.* Arco Pub. Co., 1978.

Moodie, T. D. *The Ride of Afrikanerdom: Power, Apartheid, and the Afrikaner Civil Religion.* University of California Press, 1975.

Thompson, L. *A History of South Africa.* Yale University Press, 1995.

ARI NAVE

Afro-Atlantic Culture: On the Live Dialogue Between Africa and the Americas

When Africa is regarded as part of the cultural and political history of the African diaspora, it is usually recognized only as an origin—as a past to the African American present, as a source of survival in the Americas, as the roots of African American branches and leaves, or, at the most dialectical, as a concept conjured up by New World blacks as a trope of racial unity.

Yet, in truth, the cultures of both Africa and the Americas have shaped each other through a live dialogue that continued beyond the end of the slave trade. In ways easily documented since the eighteenth century, travel by free Africans and African Americans (by which I mean people of African descent throughout the Americas) has continued to shape political identities and cultural prac-tices in North and South America, the Caribbean, and Africa.

Since the eighteenth century, enslaved or free black seamen have woven a living web of links among the most diverse points around the Atlantic perimeter, transporting ideas, practices, and people between diaspora and home-land and among diaspora locales. Black seamen were especially cosmopolitan in their reflections on the black experience, which they freely spread among Providence, New York, Charleston, New Orleans, Havana, Kingston, Port-au-Prince, Rio de Janeiro, London, and LAGOS. So, it is no accident that, for example, seamen wrote the first six autobiographies published in English by blacks, all before 1800, or that Denmark Vesey used his network of black sailors to spread his revolutionary doctrine. Massachusetts shipper Paul Cuffe (1759–1817) is considered by some to be the father of Black nationalism. Through such black mar-iners, the inhabitants of Lagos and Cape Town were never far removed from political and cultural developments sur-rounding Port-au-Prince and New York. Nor were the inhabitants of Rio and Havana out of touch with develop-ments in Lagos or FREETOWN, SIERRA LEONE. Likewise, for centuries, free and slave sailors made Rio and LUANDA

into twin cities, while CAPE VERDE seamen and ship-owners linked networks of kin stretching from Rhode Island and Massachusetts to GUINEA-BISSAU, ANGOLA, and MOZAMBIQUE.

Hence, not all of these transatlantic links were transitory. Many were kin networks or the foundations of international political movements. For example, thou-sands of English-speaking blacks from Jamaica, the United States, and Canada immigrated to Freetown in the late eighteenth and nineteenth centuries, while thousands from the United States immigrated to LIBERIA in the nine-teenth century. Similarly, from the 1700s to the late 1800s, thousands of Spanish- or Portuguese-speaking blacks emi-grated from Cuba and Brazil to the Gulf of Guinea coast, between Lagos, in what is now NIGERIA, and ACCRA, now in GHANA. Hence, from MONROVIA to Lagos, returnees formed a culturally hybrid bourgeoisie with extensive inter-national links, on the basis of which they also established the cultural and the ideological foundations of the nation-states that would later emerge in coastal West Africa. Many Afro-Latin returnees continued to travel back and forth, trading in slaves and other merchandise between the Guinea coast and Bahia, Brazil. They tended to maintain ties among relatives, former owners, slaves, and friends on multiple continents.

As we shall see, Afro-Latin travelers such as Martiniano do Bonfim of Bahia and Adechina of Cuba profoundly influenced African American religiosity through the ideas they bore among Afro-Atlantic locales. While English-speaking travelers like the Saint Thomas–born Edward Wilmot Blyden revolutionized black political thought not only in the United States, the greater West Indies, and West Africa but, through Afro-Latin travelers in Lagos, in Bahia, as well. Over the past century these religious and political streams have converged in various YORUBA-affiliated poli-tico-religious movements in Nigeria, Brazil, Cuba, and the United States.

Missionaries, traveling entertainers, and audio record-ings from the African diaspora have also profoundly reshaped African popular culture and politics. In turn, free Africans who immigrated to the Americas have deeply influenced African American popular cultures. Some Africans who had never been slaves chose freely to immi-grate to Brazil or the Caribbean in the 19th century. Indeed, some of the founding figures in the Afro-Brazilian Candomblé religion are said to have entered Brazil as free persons. King Christophe is said to have recruited 4,000 free Dahomeans into the police force of postrevolutionary Haiti, and over 15,000 free West and Central Africans, some of them rescued from slave ships by the British Royal Navy, were settled in the British West Indies after abolition in 1834. One such immigrant built an important temple to the Dahomean Vodun gods on the Caribbean island of Trinidad. A few of these immigrants returned to Africa in the 1840s, sharing their berths with freed Afro-Cubans, also en route to the ancestral motherland. These examples illustrate the antiquity and scope of a live dialogue that continues to constitute both African homeland and diaspora well into the early 21st century.

Neither then nor now has the effect of this dialogue always been harmony or unity. Returnees from the African diaspora regularly organized themselves socially, economically, and politically as a distinct class of intermediaries between Africans and Europeans. In the most shocking case, the Americo-Liberians set themselves up as a distinct and oppressive caste, unapologetically dominating the indigenous peoples of Liberia for a century and a half. More recently, African immigrants to the United States in the late 20th and early 21st centuries have, in turn, tended to emphasize their distinctness from native-born African Americans, lest they be treated like members of a native-born caste regularly despised by the dominant group in North American society. Yet African merchants and hair-dressers in the United States often take advantage of their comparative advantage in the sale of the symbols of Afrocentric identity, such as African clothing and hairstyles. By contrast, the nineteenth-century Afro-Latin returnees to Lagos have been integrated seamlessly into Lagosian society and, although contemporary African American residents of South Africa are sometimes resented as interlopers, black South African education, politics, and culture generally are deeply influenced by black North American models that were warmly embraced from the 1890s to the 1920s. Thus, this live dialogue between Africa and its American diaspora has produced, if not always harmony, then a set of new, hybrid discourses of self-expression and identity. This article is intended to illustrate the historical and ongoing influence of this dialogue on the political identities, cultural practices, and, in particular, the religious practices of Africans and African Americans.

TRANSATLANTIC DIALOGUES OVER POLITICAL IDENTITY

Since the 1800s, free Africans and African Americans have interacted in ways less notable for their large numbers than for their momentous influence on subsequent political developments at and around the sites of that interaction. The circumstances and outcomes of such interactions have varied, but all have been affected by the emergence of the idea of territorial nationalism in eighteenth-century France and its subsequent imitation all over the globe. Moreover, this black Atlantic dialogue has occurred amid the specific rise of the British, French, and U.S. empires over their Portuguese and Spanish predecessors, as well as the peculiar racial ideas and policies propagated by Great Britain, France, and the United States.

Twentieth-century Africa has hosted several major settler colonies, including ALGERIA, KENYA and the former Rhodesia (present-day ZIMBABWE). Better integrated into the Atlantic system, the other three major settler colonies have also lasted much longer. SIERRA LEONE, LIBERIA, and SOUTH AFRICA border on the Atlantic and have been characterized by pivotal, long-running, and mutually transformative dialogues with the African diaspora. Sierra Leone and Liberia were first colonized by diasporic blacks seeking political independence from white oppression. These returnees thus founded novel creole societies held together by alliance, patronage, oppression, commerce, and reciprocal emulation between Africans and Westernized black settlers. South Africa's geographical location and its mineral wealth made it a major commercial hub of the Atlantic world. Most of South Africa's colonial settlers were white, creating a racially hierarchical system akin to, and regularly in dialogue with, those in the Americas. Thus, all three of these settler colonies have long hosted influential missionaries, scholars, sailors, diplomats, and entertainers from the diaspora, while sending numerous students and other visitors in return. Moreover, Africa's Atlantic settler colonies have been an important theme in African Americans' reflections on their own political identity and potentials, just as the activities and writings of African Americans have powerfully shaped Liberian, Sierra Leonean, and South African politics.

Recently freed people from England, called the Black Poor, first colonized Sierra Leone in 1787. These overseas returnees were joined by another sizeable group of ex-captives. Over the next decade and a half, they were joined by 1,190 Nova Scotian blacks (British Loyalists who had fled slavery in the rebellious 13 colonies) and 550 maroons, former fugitive slaves from Jamaica. As part of Britain's efforts to enforce legislation against the slave trade, the Royal Navy rescued over 50,000 Africans from slave ships over the next seven decades and settled them in Freetown, the future capital of Sierra Leone. Many of these so-called recaptives had come from the Oya kingdom in what is now Yorubaland, in Nigeria.

Though a British divide-and-conquer strategy initially sowed dissent among these groups, their intermarriage and embrace of missionary education welded them into a community known as Creole, or in their own hybrid language Krio. Their equally hybrid culture reflected both their Western education and their diverse African and diasporic origins. Not only did the Krios provide the core of what would become the national language, culture, and early leadership of Sierra Leone, but they exported their

Creole culture. Oya-born missionaries trained in Sierra Leone combined Oya language with a variety of neighboring dialects and coinages from the diaspora, giving form for the first time to the language that came to be called standard Yoruba. They then reduced this composite to writing. While missionizing the hinterland of Lagos, they introduced standard Yoruba and its texts, including a translation of the Bible, which became foundations of an emergent Yoruba identity and of the fame that followed its progressive reinterpretation in the African-inspired religions of Brazil, Cuba, Trinidad, and the United States.

The Yoruba identity is not the only one in Africa that appears to have postdated the dispersion of its would-be bearers. Many of the black ethnic groups, or nations, to which the slaves of Cuba, Brazil, Trinidad, and Haiti belonged—and the religious nations, or denominations to which many of their descendants still belong—had not existed in ancient Africa but were instead labels imposed by slave traders. These ethnic labels reflected the captives' African port of embarkation more often than they did any cultural, linguistic, or political category recognized by Africans in the homeland. However, labels such as Rada in Haiti, Lucumí in Cuba, Mina in Louisiana, and Jeje in Brazil were often embraced and institutionalized through American religious brotherhoods, denominations, secret societies, work crews, and rebel armies.

Much as the Yoruba identity was confabulated by Western-educated exiles in Sierra Leone and only then introduced into the Lagos hinterland to refer collectively to a score of disparate linguistic and political units, the Jeje identity was constructed and labeled as such in Brazil, and only then introduced as an identity into the African ancestral home of its Brazilian bearers. Even though the speakers of the sometimes mutually comprehensible EWE, Gen, Aja, and FON language varieties were exported to Brazil in the greatest numbers before 1800, I have found no written mention of the name Jeje in the Gulf of Guinea region before 1864, after the effective end of the slave trade. On the other hand, the term Jeje appears in Brazilian documents as early as 1739, around 125 years earlier than its first appearance in Africa. In Brazil, the origin of this ethnonym is subject to much speculation, but the leading lexicographer of Fon, Segurola, denies that the term originates in that language, even though the Fon people were once among its primary referents. The term may have had some prior referent in West Africa now lost to memory, but it could not have referred to the entire Ewe-Gen-Aja-Fon dialect cluster and then gone unnoticed by the scores of European and American travelers who published accounts of their visits to the Gulf of Benin between the seventeenth and nineteenth centuries. In sum,

Brazil, it's slave-traders, and its former slaves are the most likely sources of the Jeje ethnonym in Africa.

However obscure the origins of this term, its use in Africa after 1864 reveals much about the transatlantic history of African ethnicity and nationality. From the middle third of the nineteenth century onward, hundreds and perhaps thousands of Brazilian Jejes returned to the Gulf of Benin—to Lagos, PORTO-NOVO, Ouidah, Grand-Popo, Petit-Popo, Agoué, and Porto-Seguro (this last having been founded by the returnees themselves). It was evidently these travelers who applied the name Jeje to all the Africans whom they considered their compatriots, despite the fact that these compatriots had probably never previously identified themselves in these terms.

We know of these developments through the writings of the priests of the Society of African Missions—a French organization that, as guests of the prosperous Afro-Brazilian returnees, missionized this region at the end of the nineteenth century. The priests of this society were the first Europeans to designate Ewe, Gen, Aja, and Fon as the same language and the first Europeans to call this language and all its speakers Jeje. Though after 1889 this ethnic label described only the speakers of these language varieties in the city of Porto-Novo, the term continued to be used until the 1930s to distinguish the alleged natives of colonial southern Dahomey (now Benin Republic) from the Yoruba, whose British commercial and cultural connections made them threatening to French colonialists. Ignoring the reality that ancestors of the Yoruba had lived in this land for centuries, the French thereby implied that the British-influenced Yoruba were foreigners to French territory. Hence, not only did the British prepare the ground on which Yoruba became a major African ethnic identity but the French, in an effort to naturalize and secure their domain against British influence, subsidized the Jeje identity introduced by the Brazilian returnees. Eventually, the Jeje identity in West Africa gave way to such categories as Fon and GOUN. Nonetheless, what remains clear is the powerful role of the European-dominated Atlantic political economy in creating the conditions of the black Atlantic dialogue over collective identity.

The changing political conditions of Anglo-America propelled North American and Anglophone West Indian blacks headlong into this transatlantic dialogue as well. Since the time of the American Revolution, black North American leaders reflected on blacks' exclusion from the rights of citizenship in the new republic. The many who had lost hope in the United States dreamt of immigration to Africa, Haiti, Brazil, or elsewhere as places to form a community and live out their collective black identity as a territorial nation. The West African nation of Liberia resulted from the most successful emigrationist project in U.S. history.

Though advocacy by the white-dominated American Colonization Society put off many potential emigrants, about 16,000 U.S. blacks and 400 Afro-West Indians settled in Liberia between 1822 and 1900. By 1846 the Americo-Liberian repatriates had achieved their own political and commercial independence from the American Colonization Society, well in advance of Sierra Leone's liberation from the British colonizers in 1961. Much like the rulers of Haiti, the Americo-Liberians barred whites from citizenship and land ownership in their black republic.

In the nineteenth and early twentieth centuries, some of the most quoted figures in black North American debates over collective identity and political strategy—such as Martin R. Delaney, Edward Wilmot Blyden, and W. E. B. Du Bois—were equally often quoted in Liberian, Sierra Leonean, and Lagosian debates over the proper shape of their own emergent national societies. Many returnees to Liberia had envisioned themselves not only achieving freedom for themselves but enlightening a benighted, heathen Africa. In their ambivalent regard for Africa, however, they often behaved oppressively toward indigenous Liberians. There are doubts about accusations that the Americo-Liberians enslaved their African neighbors, but, if they are true, Americo-Liberians would join the company of the many Sierra Leonean settlers and Afro-Latin returnees on the Gulf of Benin coast who did undoubtedly capture and sell African slaves during the decades after the British had outlawed the trade. Many of these repatriates from the African diaspora indeed modeled their lifestyles on those of their Euro-American former masters. In turn, the Creole cultures they produced, including the forms of transatlantic racial identity that they propagated, became objects of both resentment and imitation by their indigenous neighbors around the Gulf of Guinea.

It is well known that important leaders of West African independence movements in the 1950s and 1960s, such as Nnamdi AZIKIWE of Nigeria and Kwame NKRUMAH of Ghana, had reversed the direction of African American return and gone to the United States for training in historically black colleges. Nkrumah, for example, studied at the historically black Lincoln University during the 1930s and joined the Beta Sigma fraternity, the same fraternity to which Alain Locke, Booker T. Washington, James Weldon Johnson, George Washington Carver, and future president of Liberia William TUBMAN belonged. Nkrumah also studied the writings of Jamaican-American emigrationist and Pan-Africanist Marcus Garvey. Nkrumah subsequently became not only the first president of Ghana, but also the most committed Pan-Africanist head of state in Africa's history. It is difficult to avoid the conclusion that these leaders' experience of Jim Crow and of black North Americans' ideology of racial unity and struggle helped to shape their later resolve to struggle against British colonialism.

What is less often recognized is the age of African Americans' dialogue with black South Africa's political leadership and the centrality of its enduring effects. For example, in the early 1890s a small group of African Americans and Africans in Port Elizabeth, South Africa, established an interregional economic union, the goal of which was job creation, management training for black-owned businesses, and the promotion of black unity and racial uplift. They hoped to use a capitalist economic base to gain political power locally. John DUBE, president of the South African National Congress, which was the forerunner of Nelson MANDELA's African National Congress (ANC), had been influenced profoundly by Booker T. Washington and had even visited Tuskegee Institute. Therefore, during the first third of the twentieth century, he was known as the Booker Washington of South Africa. At the turn of the century, as black South African churches sought independence from white missionary denominations, they hosted a visit from Henry McNeal Turner, bishop of the black North American African Methodist Episcopal Church (AME). His visit also inspired future ANC president James Thaele to seek training at Wilberforce University, another historically black college in the United States. Thaele was, in turn, responsible for introducing Garveyism to the ANC. Both Garveyism and the ideas of W. E. B. Du Bois were well known in South Africa from the 1920s to the 1940s. Another ANC president, Alfred Bitini XUMA, who served until 1949, visited the United States, married a black North American, and endorsed the National Association for the Advancement of Colored People (NAACP) as a model for the ANC. The Black Consciousness Movement of the 1970s, which is best known for the martyrdom of its spokesman Stephen BIKO, embraced the influence of Eldridge Cleaver's Soul on Ice (1967), Alex Haley's The Autobiography of Malcolm X (1965), Charles Hamilton's and Stokely Carmichael's Black Power (1967), the theology of James Cone, and Frantz FANON's The Wretched of the Earth (1963). Hence, both its place in the Atlantic economy and its political commonalities with the American settler colonies have placed South Africa in sustained dialogue with the black Americas.

In the 1980s as black North Americans seemed more besieged and less unified than they had in decades, one issue that appeared to invite no controversy in the divided black political class was the Free South Africa movement. The persistence and success of Randall Robinson's trans-Africa lobby is a rare example of African American success at shaping U.S. foreign policy in the interest of black people globally. In the democratic South Africa of the 1990s, African American immigrants and businesspeople have perhaps sentimentalized this history and overestimated the degree to which black South Africans would welcome their arrival. Whereas many African Americans expect to be welcomed home, many South Africans regard them as interlopers, too anxious to claim the credit for South Africa's democratization and too ready to take corporate jobs that black South Africans feel rightfully belong to them. In South Africa, as in many parts of the continent, African American visitors, with their varied complexions and Western ways, are hardly recognized as black, much less as long-lost African brothers and sisters. Such identifications have repeatedly been negotiated and renegotiated over time according to the circumstances—no less in the Americas—(where, for example, light-skinned people have not everywhere and always been considered black)—than in Africa. And the dialogue continues.

Indeed, African immigrants often report that they had not indentified themselves as black until they immigrated to the United States or Britain. Few Africans in Africa outside Kenya, Zimbabwe, and South Africa had had any reason to do so. In the daily lives of most Africans, blackness constitutes neither a barrier nor an admission pass to any particular social rights, and it signals no salient political or cultural identity. In the Americas, the social stigma attached to blackness and the rebellious conduct identified with black Americans in fact become a reason for African immigrants to demand recognition as different from the native blacks. In the United States, this option has become more possible for all immigrant groups of African descent since the official desegregation of housing and educational institutions in the 1950s, 1960s, and 1970s.

On the other hand, some African immigrants to the United States have been leaders in the articulation of Pan-African identity. First, though they are often ill-informed about Africans of other national origins, many Africans in the United States vocalize a sense of cultural unity and social camaraderie with the entire community of immigrants from Africa. For example, many North American universities host an African students' organization. Second, not only African merchants and hairdressers but African priests and professors profitably supply the goods and information that many African Americans have, in the past 20 years, come to embrace as signs of their ancestral roots. Thus, peddlers of kente cloth, itinerant diviners, and scholars of African art have a vested interest in Pan-Africanist and culturally nationalist forms of black identity.

Several factors have combined to make Lagos and New York City into international epicenters of black identity-formation and reaction to racism. First, these were prosperous cities that beckoned black immigrants from far and wide. Black-led rebellions were crushed in Brazil in 1835 and in Cuba in 1844, leading to deportations and general

oppression. Many of the black victims fled to Lagos, where they enjoyed British protection from reenslavement and from the expropriation of their belongings by African rulers. Beginning in the 1860s and 1870s, whites in the United States South reacted violently to the civil rights gains of blacks during reconstruction, thus accelerating the flight of blacks to Harlem, New York, and other northern cities, as well as the eastward immigration of smaller numbers to Liberia. New York City's prosperity and temporarily liberal U.S. immigration laws also drew numerous West Indians and black Latin Americans, as well as a small but influential coterie of Africans, into the city in the 1900s and 1910s.

Lagos emerged as a capital of black identity for a second reason as well. Late-nineteenth-century U.S. racism had its parallel in British West Africa. Since the early nineteenth century Western-educated Africans (including those who had returned from servitude in England or the Americas and those rescued from slave ships by the British Royal Navy) enjoyed, by and large, the respect and cooperation of British colonialists and missionaries. However, racial discrimination against the black bourgeoisie of British West Africa appeared to increase sharply in the 1880s and 1890s, when improvements in tropical medicine enabled increasing numbers of whites to immigrate and compete with blacks for the best jobs. Subject to a sudden upsurge in racial discrimination, these highly Western-educated Africans who had thoroughly identified with the British colonial project felt compelled to turn the tools of their rescuers in their own defense. Culturally Creole Lagos became the hotbed of an ingenious cultural nationalism.

These multiregional and multicultural convergences of privileged and elite blacks in prosperous cities, unified by the shared experience of racial marginality but relatively safe from the coordinated violence suffered by their kin elsewhere, inspired lively literary and cultural movements in both Lagos and New York City. In the 1890s Lagos hosted a cultural renaissance that at once opposed British racism, endorsed the virtue of black racial purity, and canonized an emergent, internationally inspired Yoruba culture as the paramount exemplar of black racial dignity. The elites of Lagos thus produced a black literary and cultural explosion without parallel in its day. Both in the texts they produced and in person, they influenced generations of Afro-Latin Americans and Afro-Latin Americanists, who have judged the Yoruba superior to other Africans. Where Afro-Latin Americans in Cuba and Brazil have embraced the value of cultural and racial purity, they appear to do so under the influence of the Lagosian cultural renaissance of the 1890s.

From around 1914 to 1920 Jamaican immigrant Marcus Garvey led the largest mass organization in black North American history, boasting an estimated eight million members at its height. Though headquartered in New York City, Garvey's Universal Negro Improvement Association had branches all over the black world. His plan to repatriate blacks to Africa failed, but hardly any subsequent black nationalist movement has escaped the influence of his ideology and iconography. In the 1920s the culturally diverse immigrants who converged on Harlem produced another culturally and racially nationalist explosion of political, literary, and musical creativity—namely the Harlem Renaissance. Together, Garveyism and the Harlem Renaissance made black New York the inspiration, epicenter, and model for similarly racially nationalist cultural movements all around the Atlantic perimeter in the 1920s and 1930s, including the Afrocubanismo of Nicolás Guillén and others, the Haitian cultural nationalism of Jean Price-Mars and François Duvalier, and the Négritude that, through Martinique's Aimé CÉSAIRE and SENEGAL's Léopold SENGHOR, captivated the whole black Francophone world. In turn, the ideas and the vocabulary of Négritude have lately been taken up in the Spanish- and Portuguese-speaking Americas, while the influence of the North American Black Power Movement of the 1960s, in many ways the successor to the Harlem Renaissance, has been felt in Trinidad's Black Power Movement and South Africa's Black Consciousness Movement in the 1970s as well.

It can be no accident that these most influential cultural renaissance movements arose in cities where cosmopolitan, culturally diverse, and culturally hybrid populations were compelled by racism to articulate and rationalize a cultural basis for their political unity. Nor is it an accident, in an age of increasing Anglo-Saxon military and economic dominance, that the most influential sites of such movements were Anglophone. Over the two centuries under consideration, the English language and the English-language publishing industry have afforded unparalleled media access to black Atlantic leaders who could write, record, or broadcast in English.

In general, both African Americans' experience of racially marked oppression in the lands of their birth and contemporary Africans' sojourns outside the continent have sparked unprecedented reflections on the collective nature of black experience and political identity. It is no surprise, then, that the best-documented and most influential Pan-Africanist dialogues have taken place in European or Euro-American metropolises, where the diverse black subjects of Britain, France, and the United States in particular have conferred over their shared values and conditions of struggle. From 1900 to 1945 a sequence of PAN-AFRICAN CONGRESSES brought together the leading intellectuals and politicians of the black Atlantic world in London, Paris, Lisbon, New York, and Manchester. Thus, in the formative years of the African and West

Indian independence movements, North Americans like W. E. B. Du Bois and William Monroe Trotter came to know the Senegalese Blaise DIAGNE, while Ghana's Kwame Nkrumah and Nigeria's Nnamdi Azikiwe came to know the likes of Trinidad's George PADMORE and Kenya's Jomo KENYATTA. Far more than the African American emigration and colonization movements of the nineteenth century, the Pan-African congresses of the 20th century occasioned a dialogue among far-flung peers and a novel consensus among the elites of the Afro-Atlantic world that their constituencies shared a common spirit, political interest, and destiny. Though Pan-Africanism had begun in the Americas, this series of congresses demonstrated that, by 1945, it was no longer the dream of African Americans alone. In contrast to the paternalistic missionary aspirations of the nineteenth-century emigrationists, the new Pan-Africanists of the 1945 congress condemned Christianity for its exploitation of West African peoples. The diverse black peoples of the Atlantic perimeter surely shared numerous traditions, conventions, and political aspirations before the nineteenth- and twentieth-century dialogue among such free people began, but the changing investments of the black Atlantic political and intellectual classes shaped new and powerfully centripetal standards of Afro-Atlantic education, entertainment, worship, and other cultural symbolism. These are the subject of the next section.

TRANSATLANTIC DIALOGUES OVER CULTURAL PRACTICES

Education and popular culture around the black Atlantic clearly share deep ancestral roots, but they have also been transformed over the past two centuries of transoceanic dialogue and debate among free Africans and African Americans. In the nineteenth century black North American missionaries in Africa inspired generations of young Africans to seek higher education in the United States, very often at predominantly black, church-related institutions. Booker T. Washington and his successors at Tuskegee Institute initiated various agricultural, educational, and economic development projects in Liberia, German TOGO, and British West Africa during the first half of the 20th century and found powerful advocates in educator Dr. James Aggrey of Gold Coast/Ghana and Harry THUKU of Kenya, as well as European colonial governments themselves. The ideas of W. E. B. Du Bois were also known and debated in West Africa during the first third of the century. This transoceanic dialogue thus helped to inspire the founding of both Tuskegee-style industrial-training institutes and liberal arts colleges in Africa. In turn, Robert R. Moton, the president of Tuskegee Institute from 1915 to 1935, acquired fame as a spokesperson for African affairs and integrated the aim of acquainting black North American students with African affairs into the Tuskegee project. This dialogue on education is imbued with the history and the ambiguous motives of African Americans' 19th-century project to "uplift" Africa, which was premised on a degree of accommodation to Western and white dominance and, by and large, on a sense of African cultural inferiority. However, the dialogue with those who had been most brutally enslaved by the West ultimately provided Africans with models of resistance to cultural assimilation and political domination as well. As we have seen, a number of the West African protagonists in this dialogue led their own countries to independence.

Black South African cultural leaders in the late nineteenth and twentieth centuries found these models similarly attractive. A major secessionist movement swept through the black churches of South Africa between 1892 and 1894, when Reverend Magena M. Mokone left the white-dominated Wesleyan Methodist denomination and founded the Ethiopian Church. The movement of cultural, political, educational, and religious autonomy that he inspired thus came to be known as Ethiopianism. Soon thereafter, in 1896, Bishop Henry McNeal Turner of the U.S.-based AME Church visited South Africa, whereupon many Ethiopian churches in South Africa attached themselves to this African American denomination. Many leaders of the Ethiopianist movement traveled to the United States to study in historically black colleges, until the Ethiopian churches themselves founded the University of Fort Hare in South Africa in 1916.

Simultaneously, in the realm of entertainment, missionized South African Christians were creating an urban identity modeled on British colonial high society, which, in South Africa, had itself embraced American-style blackface minstrelsy as the dominant form of musical and theatrical entertainment. By the 1850s, soon after the first minstrel shows were performed in New York, they became popular among South African whites and, like those in New York, regularly featured made-up white performers. Black South Africans much more readily embraced performances by visiting African American sailors, adventurers, and professional performers who arrived late in the century. Coloured performers in Cape Town were particularly impressed with the music and dance styles of visiting black North Americans and West Indians. In the 1890s Cape Coloureds and the nascent African middle class witnessed performances of the Fisk Jubilee Singers and McAdoo's Jubilee Singers, who inspired much local imitation. Thereafter, local minstrel shows increasingly featured black religious music from the southern United States. Visiting African American performers helped black

South African performers to recognize the commercial potential of their own musical creativity, through which a richly hybrid South African musical style has emerged and been reexported by such contemporary groups as LADYSMITH BLACK MAMBAZO. Yet Ladysmith Black Mambazo is not the first African group to speak back to America. In the mid-1890s a black South African minstrel troupe called the African Native Choir toured the United States. When the troupe ran out of funds in the midwestern United States, the African Methodist Episcopal Church stepped in and offered educational opportunities, whereby eight members of the troupe eventually earned bachelor's degrees at historically black Wilberforce and Lincoln Universities. Their own cultural work continued when they returned to urban South Africa, imbued with black North American ideas about education and racial progress. For example, during and after their tour, African Native Choir member Charlotte Manye continued to cultivate contacts between the African Methodist Episcopal Church and the growing number of independent African clergymen.

Thus, at the turn of the century music, religion, and education dovetailed in the genesis of urban black South African identity just as they did in the genesis of black North American identity. The Fisk Jubilee Singers, for example, sang the sacred music of African American slaves in a manner adapted to the concert hall. Their project was both a statement about the dignity of African Americans in an age of Jim Crow and a fund-raising venture for black higher education. The consequence has been a permanent and widespread transformation of black North American musical tradition. The songs now honored as Negro spirituals are far closer to the adaptations of the Fisk Jubilee Singers than they are to the antecedent improvisational folk genre of the same name. It is understandable, then, that music played such an important and enduring role in the emergence of black South African identity during the same period and that African American performers found such a willing interlocutor in black South Africa. Yet, in the first half of this century, the colonial Gold Coast (now Ghana, West Africa) also hosted a tradition of blackface minstrelsy, African American spirituals, and humorous plantation songs. Its continued influence in Ghana is, however, less evident.

Yet West Africa engaged actively in the transoceanic musical dialogue in other ways. Since the early nineteenth century Afro-Latin returnees to the Gulf of Benin coast and the troops of the British West India regiments were introducing urban West Africa to the syncretic musical styles of the African diaspora, and Brazilian returnees to Lagos exercised a particularly profound influence on the popular music of Lagos. Moreover, in the early 20th century European firms began importing gramophone discs into West Africa. The most influential of these were recordings of Afro-Cuban groups such as Septeto Habanero and Trio Matamoros. The importation of Afro-Cuban recordings and instruments, such as maracas, congas, and bongos, grew lively after World War II, further inspiring the growth of highlife music, which integrated the influence of black North American vaudeville and Trinidadian calypso as well. "As incredible as it may seem to Africans today," writes Wolfgang Bender, "the gradual re-Africanization [of urban African music] proceeded in a roundabout way via Afro-American percussion instruments." Bender makes a similar point about the fabulous growth of Afro-Cuban-inspired rumba music in Zaire (now the DEMOCRATIC REPUBLIC OF THE CONGO, or Congo-Kinshasa) since the 1950s and its re-Africanization (i.e., the increase in rhythmic elements) under the influence of recordings by black North Americans like James Brown and Aretha Franklin in the mid-1960s. Since the 1950s hardly any region of western Africa—from Senegal to Congo-Kinshasa—has been exempt from the influence of Afro-Cuban music or, since the 1960s, from the influence of soul, reggae, and disco.

As in the case of Afro-Atlantic music, much of the shared vocabulary of Afro-Atlantic dance is a shared ancestral legacy. However, some African dance performances, such as Bumba-Meu-Boi, were introduced to the Gulf of Benin coast by Afro-Brazilian returnees, and some Brazilian dance performances, such as that of the Egungun masquerade, are said to have been introduced to Brazil by free immigrants from West Africa.

Not all cultural legacies are continuous and none is primordial. Anthropologist Melville Herskovits, I think, correctly intuited the endurance of certain intergenerationally learned African bodily habitus among the peoples of the African diaspora. However, the meanings given to them and the performances in which they are structured sometimes follow patterns that are hardly reducible to passive cultural inheritance. And, most importantly for the present argument, Africans and African Americans share many forms of movement and meaning, but many of them are products of a recent, transoceanic dialogue.

In fact, the politically inspired and government-sponsored dialogue between Africans and African Americans has played an important role in creating a number of national dance traditions on the Atlantic perimeter. Since the 1940s, Trinidadian Pearl Primus and black North Americans Katherine Dunham, Alvin Ailey, and Judith Jamison—perhaps the most famous dance professionals in the black Atlantic world—have all traveled extensively in contemporary Africa, with the support of the U.S. government or foundations, and have collaborated with African governments and artists to establish an unprecedented tradition of Afro-Atlantic concert dance.

Katherine Dunham and Pearl Primus were the founders of black North American concert dance as we know it, and, as long as we have known it, its roots have been cosmopolitan. Primus, choreographer and anthropologist, combined African and West Indian ritual, music, and movement in her dance compositions and introduced these into black North American concert dance. In 1949 she received a Rosenwald Fellowship to make the first of several journeys to Africa—this time, for eighteen months in Gold Coast/Ghana, Angola, CAMEROON, Liberia, Senegal, and the Belgian Congo/Congo-Kinshasa. In 1959 President William Tubman of Liberia, himself an Americo-Liberian, appointed Dunham director of the National Dance Company of Liberia and head of the African Performing Arts Center in Monrovia.

Dance anthropologist Katherine Dunham traveled and performed many times in Africa, after similar stints in Jamaica and Haiti. Her choreographic style integrates African and Afro-Caribbean myths and dance techniques with modern dance. By her efforts, not only African dance but Haitian dance has become canonical in the black North American concert dance. During her first audience with Senegalese president Léopold Senghor, she was told that her work "had caused a cultural revolution" and that various sub-Saharan African heads-of-state "had been encouraged by her formula and format. ... [Dunham's presence] in Africa thus opened a new vista for blacks [and] aided in spearheading Africa's cultural revolution." Senghor appointed her a technical and cultural adviser and teacher at Senegal's National Ballet.

In the 1960s and 1970s Alvin Ailey and Judith Jamison also traveled extensively in Africa (under U.S. government sponsorship), collaborated with African artists, and integrated urban African dances they saw into their choreography. In particular, Ailey collaborated with South African jazz trumpeter Hugh MASEKELA, himself a frequent sojourner in the United States, in a work that was ostensibly about South African apartheid but, according to one of Ailey's dancers, was intended to evoke the U.S. South as well. "Cry," one of Ailey's most highly praised works, dramatizes the auctioning off of an African American slave woman and, according to Judith Jamison, features dance moves that Jamison and Ailey had seen in Zaire. Jamison recounts that one night, in a club, she and Ailey had seen movements that would eventually become the last steps in "Cry."

It should not be forgotten that their travels placed Ailey and Jamison in direct dialogue with anthropologist, cultural nationalist, and Kenyan president Jomo Kenyatta, as well as Négritude poet, romanticist of black dance, and Senegalese president Léopold Senghor. As the successive directors of the most popular black dance company in the

United States, Ailey and Jamison have done more than any other artists to establish the Pan-African character of black North American concert dance. Yet, in this tradition, they are disciples of Primus and Dunham. By the appointment of early African presidents, aesthetic Pan-Africanists Primus and Dunham have even participated in setting the standards of national dance performance in a number of African countries. Hence, by their efforts, the folklorics that are now staged as representations of emergent African national identities and those staged to represent the Pan-African identity of Anglophone New World blacks have emerged from a set of choreographers in close communication with each other. The New-World Anglophone choreographers have not only borrowed models of folkloric dance from the black Francophone world (e.g., Congo-Kinshasa, Haiti, and Sengal) but demonstrated influential forms of cultural nationalism resistant to Francophone black elites' usual drift toward European aesthetic models.

Perhaps the most famous cultural nationalism of the black Atlantic world is Négritude, which had its very beginnings in a transatlantic dialogue and, like the dialogue concerning dance, bridged the gap between Francophone and Anglophone in the Atlantic world. Long before he became the president of Senegal, Léopold Sédar Senghor was a student in Paris, where, in 1931, he met Martinican poet, eventual mayor of Fort-de-France, and deputy to the French national legislature, Aimé Césaire. At this early stage in their careers, both men had begun to feel dissatisfied with their total immersion in French culture and had grown curious about Africa. Through the numerous African American intellectuals who sojourned in Paris, Senghor and Césaire learned about the Harlem Renaissance, a cultural and literary movement in the 1920s that celebrated and scrutinized black culture worldwide. Under this inspiration, the Francophone Antilleans and Africans who founded La Revue du Monde Noir published articles on the black world, including extensive commentaries on blacks in the United States, Tuskegee Institute, the black colonizers of Liberia, the poetry of Afro-North American Langston Hughes, and Jamaican-American Claude McKay. In the 1930s Senghor read the work of other African American poets, as well as that of W. E. B. Du Bois and Carter G. Woodson. He read journals such as the NAACP's The Crisis and the Urban League's Opportunity, and Alain Locke's famous edited volume The New Negro (1925)—a book that also deeply influenced Nigerian nationalist politician Nnamdi Azikiwe. The title of Locke's volume so impressed Senghor that he used its translation, le nègre nouveau, to identify the new man and the new attitudes he hoped to see in French-speaking blacks. Through the hybrid cultural and literary movement they founded, Césaire and

Senghor endeavored to recognize and validate the shared spirit of the world's black cultures and thereby redeem it from the image of inferiority and undermine the contempt that so often divided Africans from France's black Antillean subjects. These were the transatlantic and cross-linguistic roots of Négritude, the most enduring literary expression of Pan-Africanism in Atlantic history.

Yet the forms of unity envisaged in political Pan-Africanism and of spiritual commonality imagined in Négritude are seldom fully realized where Africans and African Americans meet in person. For the most seemingly common of experiences sometimes evoke profoundly different meanings for the two groups. For example, African American visits to the coastal slave forts have, in recent decades, become an increasingly important dimension of tourism in West African countries such as Ghana and Senegal. Though no other sites better typify the African American link to Africa, they are the foci of clashing interpretations. For African American tourists, filmmakers, tour guides, and other culture brokers, Ghana's Elmina Castle, to give one example, is a somber place—"sacred ground not to be desecrated." Ghanaians, however, have a much more complex relationship with the fort that extends beyond its uses as a slave market. Hence, Ghanaian visitors, merchants, and government officials envisage a redeveloped Elmina as a festive place and often regard the African American tourists as too emotional. Hence, rather than preserving the fort as it is, Ghanaian planners wish to convert it into a bustling commercial center. These differences of thought and feeling reinforce the sense that African Americans, not unlike their white counterparts, are foreigners to Africa, even as those African Americans understand themselves to be coming home.

On the other hand, Kwame Nkrumah's prime ministership (1960–1966) has cast a long shadow over public opinion in Ghana, where, perhaps more than in any other African country, African Americans are publicly recognized as Pan-African brothers and sisters. Even if slave fort tourism has not yet created an interpretive consensus, it has enhanced Ghanaians' interest in their own cultural history and linked diverse black Atlantic populations in projects of local West African development and in the movement to secure reparations for the descendants of those victimized by the slave trade. Among the greatest sponsors of the reparations movement has been the late president-elect of Nigeria, Moshood ABIOLA. The Gambian government, for its part, has made moves to develop Alex Haley's ancestral town, Juffure, in order to attract African American tourists. A representative of The Gambia's National Council for Art and Culture even presented the outlines of this effort for discussion at a North American conference on diaspora research. Though relatively few black North Americans' ancestors may have embarked from Elmina or any Nigerian coastal site, Ghanaians and Nigerians have now joined Senegalese and African Americans in forging new political alliances and validating new focal symbols of their shared cultural history.

Under many circumstances, the will to unity has inspired many Africans and African Americans to undo their differences and search for the terms of similarity. Throughout the history of black North Americanist anthropology and folklore studies, both foes and advocates of African American dignity have looked for African survivals in black North American lifeways. "Should some weird, archaic, Negro doctrine be brought to his attention," writes Newbell Niles Puckett of one common interpretive error, the average white man "considers it a 'relic of African heathenism,' though in four cases out of five it is a European dogma from which only centuries of patient education could wean even his own ancestors."

Melville J. Herskovits led many subsequent generations of scholars and other culture brokers, such as dancer Katherine Dunham, in the study of Africa's positive contributions to African American cultures, though many equally well-intentioned scholars, such as E. Franklin Frazier, have preferred to attribute any cultural differences between black and white North Americans to the effects of oppression and deprivation on the blacks. The Gullah people of the Georgia Sea Coast Islands have long been the focus of scholarly investigation into what remains culturally African about black North Americans, despite what all agree is their generally high degree of acculturation in Western ways. Geographical isolation long kept the speech and lifeway of the Sea Coast Islanders somewhat distinctive. Various scholars have sought to explain that distinctiveness as a debt to the cultures of what are now Sierra Leone and Liberia. In the second half of the eighteenth century, the rice farmers of the Sea Coast Islands drew many of their workers from the rice-growing regions of Sierra Leone and Liberia, and the term Gullah might derive from the ethnonym of Sierra Leone's Gola people. On the other hand, African captives had come to these islands from many other regions as well, and students of the local creole language, known as Gullah or Geechee, have identified an extremely diverse set of African origins in its lexicon and in its justly famous basket-making tradition. Indeed, some identify the term Angola as the more likely source of the term Gullah.

As African Americans have grown more willing to embrace Africa as a cultural model and emblem of collective identity, the decline of Gullah language and crafts has been reversed. Indeed, the Africanness of Gullah basketry has become its major selling point and a means of livelihood for many craftswomen in coastal South Carolina. However, it was the intervention of Joseph Opala, anthropologist and former member of the Peace Corps in Sierra Leone, that established the local conviction that Sierra Leone in particular was the source of the islanders' Africanness and the appropriate target of their return to the motherland. Indeed, the interest in this ahistorically specific tie was reciprocal. President Joseph Saidu Momoh of Sierra Leone paid a highly public visit to the Sea Coast Islands in 1986 and encouraged the islanders to visit their ancestral homeland, which a score of them did in 1989. President Momo continued the American tradition of attributing the islanders' linguistic distinctiveness to their African roots and identified Gullah's similarities to Sierra Leonean Krio, or creole, as proof. In fact, both language varieties are predominantly English in their lexicon, since Krio resulted largely from the interaction of African American returnees, British-educated recaptives, British administrators, and Anglophone missionaries in Freetown. Thus, the similarity of condition between Gullah and Krio is highly ambiguous evidence of the Gullah people's African roots. Yet a complex, politically, economically, and academically shaped dialogue made the highly creolized Gullah dialect into the grounds of a powerful new kinship—of a so-called family across the sea.

Contemporary New York City is the site of an equally complex and identity-transforming dialogue. Whereas the Harlem Renaissance of the 1920s and the Black Power Movement of the 1960s extensively involved Afro-Caribbean immigrants in the reformulation of African American collective identity, the more recent Yoruba renaissance and Afrocentrism have, since the 1980s, increasingly involved African priests, scholars, and merchants as well. Itinerant African priests, such as Wande Abimbola, Afolabi Epega, and Sikiru Salami, have begun initiating Yoruba priests in the New World and have introduced a new standard of authenticity into already-well-established American religions like Brazilian Candomblé, Cuban Santería, and Trinidadian Shango. As African civilization has come to be regarded as the classical origin of African American cultures, African academics have become increasingly prominent interpreters of that classical legacy in art history and Afro-American studies departments. Finally, African hairstylists and merchants of cloth, leatherware, and sculpture are now the chief suppliers of the African blazonry of popular Afrocentrism in the United States. African clothing, jewelry, wood carvings, and braids are now found in virtually every black North American home. Much to these merchants' profit, they have integrated not only wares from African ethnic groups far beyond their own but also imagery of American origin, such as Malcolm X t-shirts.

The role of African merchants in cobbling together and supplying a Pan-African imagery of black North American identity has not, however, created a Pan-African uniformity of political opinion. For example, when New York City officials forcibly removed Harlem's "African Market" from its existing location in 1992, African American merchants tended to blame the eviction on white racism, while African merchants tended to blame a plot by the black Muslims.

TRANSATLANTIC DIALOGUE OVER RELIGIOUS PRACTICES

A staple of the Herskovitsian literature on Haiti, Suriname, Brazil, and the United States, as well as that of Brazilian and Cuban folklore studies generally, has been the "survival" of African religious forms in the Americas. On the other hand, African American missionaries and others imbued with the missionary zeal to redeem Africa have played significant roles in Africa's cultural history, above all in West Africa and South Africa. Since the mid-1970s, when reggae music became popular in English-speaking West Africa, some young West African Christians have adopted Rastafarian ideals and symbols, such as ganja-smoking, dreadlocks, and dread speak. The influence of this religion has increased at the hands of Jamaican and Anglo-Jamaican missionaries, who set up communities in West Africa in the 1970s, and of West African travelers who met Jamaican Rastas in London and Amsterdam.

Much American religious culture that is thought to have survived slavery was in fact introduced, sustained, or deeply modified by free migrants from Africa to the Americas. The Brazilian Candomblé, for example, is often identified as an exemplary, if not the most exemplary, survival of African culture in the Americas. Yet the oral history identifies many of the founders of its leading institutions as voluntary immigrants from Africa. For example, Otampê Ojarô, founder of the Alakêtu temple; Marcos Pimentel, a nineteenth-century chief priest of the Mocambo temple on the island of Itaparica; and, most importantly, Iya Naso, founder of the ancient Casa Branca temple, are all identified as free immigrants from Africa. Iya Naso's mother is said to have secured her own manumission in Bahia and returned to Africa but voluntarily moved to Bahia to found this first of the three most famous Candomblé temples in Brazil. Her successor, Marcelina, is said to have gone from Africa to Bahia, Brazil, voluntarily, and then returned to Africa for an extended sojourn before returning finally to Bahia to assume the leadership of the Casa Branca temple. Verger reports that it was Marcelina who first brought to Bahia the famous Bamgbose—the *babalawo* diviner from Oya and founder of Brazil's most illustrious line of male priests.

Similarly, in Cuba, the famous African-born Adechina is said to have been enslaved in Cuba but to have returned to Africa for initiation as a babalawo diviner, later returning to Cuba. The oral history also identifies a free-born African woman named Efunche (also Efunsetan or La Funche) who traveled as a free person to Cuba and there reformed Afro-Cuban religion in the 19th century.

These reports are made largely credible by archives documenting the return of thousands of Afro-Brazilians and Afro-Cubans to the West African coast. Moreover, in the lamentably incomplete Bahian archives of return voyages from Lagos, I have counted dozens of ships and hundreds of free Africans traveling from Lagos to Bahia or through Bahia to Rio or the State of Pernambuco, Brazil, between 1855 and 1898. Journalistic, epistolary, and ethnographic evidence reveals repeated journeys of another score of African-Brazilian travelers up to the 1930s. Many of them carried British passports, and most appear to have engaged in commerce, selling ethnically marked Brazilian merchandise (such as salted meat and Afro-Brazilian religious paraphernalia) to returnees in West Africa and authentically African merchandise (such as the kola nuts and woven cloth used in the Candomblé) to their black customers in Brazil. Thus, under British protection and motivated by their own commercial interests, a generation of back-and-forth travelers consolidated a set of novel, religiously based, and transnational identities unprecedented before the slave trade and as yet fragmentary before the 19th-century return of Afro-Brazilians and Afro-Cubans to Africa. These were the Yoruba and Jeje identities.

As these identities blossomed in early 1900s Brazil, they displayed not only the memory of religious icons, myths, and practices from the Africa that preceded the slave trade but the effects of the radical ideological transformations of late-nineteenth-century Yoruba ethnogenesis, which occurred primarily after the end of the slave trade. The interaction of Westernized African recaptives and returnees in Sierra Leone and Lagos in the 19th century had produced, for the first time, a self-ascribed Yoruba identity that embraced the diverse peoples of Oya, Xangô—in what is still described as Brazil's most purely African Candomblé temple, Ilê Axé Opô Afonjá.

Ironically, beyond the marked prestige and pursuit of purity articulated in this transatlantic religious culture, a most persistent set of its shared institutions and motifs derives from a British institution—Freemasonry. Freemasonry took its modern form as a male fraternal order and speculative philosophy, rather than an association of craftsmen, in the early 1700s. Over the next two centuries, it spread beyond England to other parts of Europe and to Europe's overseas colonies, where membership often became a highly prestigious marker of bourgeois status or an equally prestigious context of conspiracy against European rule, as it became in the British North American colonies. Avowedly based on pre-Christian philosophical and religious principles and parallel to many Afro-Atlantic religions in it fraternal secrecy, Freemasonry and its iconography have proved inviting to numerous West Africans, Afro-Brazilians, Afro-Cubans, Haitians, and black North Americans. Thus, tens of thousands of black men around the Atlantic perimeter are united by their shared membership in this British-founded fraternity.

Moreover, Freemasonry has inspired several neo-traditional spin-off organizations, such as the Reformed Ogboni Fraternity and the Aborigine Ogboni Fraternity of Nigeria, while the Masonic compass, the All-Seeing Eye, and the secret handshakes turn up in the apparently "traditional" religions of Nigerian villages, Haitian Vodou temples, the Afro-Cuban Palo Mayombe order, and at least one Afro-Brazilian diviner's office.

And there is a further irony. Americans have helped to re-Africanize religious policies of African nation states through bank, civil service, and school holidays. On the one hand, West African nation-states in the 20th century have tended to marginalize non-Christian and non-Islamic religions. For example, only Christian and Islamic religious holidays tend to be recognized through civil service and school vacations. On the other hand, the West African–inspired religions of the African diaspora have grown exponentially in wealth and membership since the 1960s. In Brazil, Cuba, Trinidad, and the Cuban-American and African American communities of the United States— not to mention Haiti, where it occurred well before the 1960s—these religions have become emblems of national identity. In Brazil, military dictators and democratic politicians alike have sought popular support through the temples of Afro-Brazilian religion.

During the past forty years, the Brazilian government, the United Nations (UNESCO), and various U.S. corporate foundations have repeatedly sponsored Brazil's exchange of priests, professors, and museum exhibitions with state institutions in Nigeria and the People's Republic of Benin. These exchanges have highlighted the Yoruba and Ewe-Gen-Aja-Fon religious legacy that Brazil shares with Africa. Brazil's official support appears to be motivated partly by its desire for political and commercial leadership in the nonaligned world. Whatever Brazil's public relations motives might be, the Brazilian government established African-diaspora religion as a medium of transatlantic diplomacy and helped pave the way for numerous subsequent transoceanic priestly exchanges, involving Haitians, U.S. Latinos, Trinidadians, and black North Americans as well. Thus, New World governments, foundations, and

priests have now inspired changes in the official cultural policies of at least one African government. The Beninese government has now reversed the pattern among African states and established an official and annual holiday for the Vodun gods, on January 10.

Hence, the cultural history that unites African and African American religions consists of much more than pre-slave trade African origins and American survivals. Much that appears to be primordial in so-called African traditional religion is in fact the product of a live Afro-Atlantic dialogue, and much that appears to survive of African religion in the Americas is in fact shaped by an African cultural politics that long postdated the slave trade. No less than the dialogue over political identity, the dialogue that has produced the most African of Afro-Atlantic religions is often mediated through European languages, colonial and postcolonial capitals, European institutions, and texts published in Roman script. For example, in the 20th century, texts such as Col. A. B. Ellis's *The Yoruba-Speaking Peoples of the Slave Coast of West Africa* (1890), Samuel Johnson's *The History of the Yorubas* (1921), Melville J. Herskovits's *The Myth of the Negro Past* (1941), and Robert Farris Thompson's *Flash of the Spirit* (1983), have all exercised a momentous influence on African Americans' conception of their religion and cultural identities generally. Even more importantly, these transatlantic cultural politics demonstrate the overwhelming role of black volition in reshaping inherited and imposed cultural realities.

CONCLUSION

Melville J. Herskovitz is correct in observing that intergenerational learning of belief, practice, and bodily habits continues to link contemporary African Americans to the African cultures of their ancestors. On the other hand, Paul Gilroy (author of *The Black Atlantic*, 1993) is also correct in observing the numerous discontinuous forms of communication by which locales in the African diaspora have influenced each others' culture and politics. This essay is intended to illustrate the further point that the diaspora and Africa itself are united by discontinuous and mutually influential dialogue that has continued long beyond the end of the slave trade. The dialogue between Africans and African Americans has not always produced the harmony and unity dreamt of by Pan-Africanists, but they have produced significant transformations of political identity, religious practice, and culture generally in both Africa and its diaspora. Thus, the conventional narrations of cultural history that identify the roots of African American culture in Africa and trace their survival, syncretization, or gradual dissolution in the Americas tell only part of the story. Not unlike other diasporas and their homelands—Jewish, Chinese, Irish, South Asian, and Lebanese—the African diaspora in the Americas reflects the effects of an enduring dialogue and a dialectic of mutual transformation over time.

See also DAHOMEY, EARLY KINGDOM OF; LANGUAGE, AFRICAN: AN OVERVIEW; PAN-AFRICANISM.

J. LORAND MATORY

Afro-Beat
Genre of contemporary African music.

The Nigerian musicians Fela Anikulapo KUTI, popularly known as Fela, and Orlando Julius Ekemode both claim to have coined the term Afro-Beat to describe their fusion of highlife, soul, jazz, and traditional Nigerian musical styles, including JUJU and fuji, during the late 1960s and early 1970s. The music of James Brown and other African American artists contributed heavily to the Afro-Beat style. While the early recordings of Ekemode, such as his hit "Juagua Nana," show the elements of Afro-Beat, most recognize Fela's band, Africa 70, as the definitive Afro-Beat band. Their 1971 recording "Why Black Men Dey Suffer," defined the Afro-Beat style, incorporating call-and-response vocals with a unique beat and tempo.

Afro-Beat's popularity stemmed, in part, from Fela's courageous stance against political corruption and economic injustice in Nigeria. This made him a role model for the Nigerian urban underclass and intelligentsia. Writing lyrics in "pidgin" English rather than YORUBA to reach the urban masses throughout Anglophone Africa, he recounted stories of police brutality and government persecution. The 1978 album *Coffin for Head of State*, for example, blames Nigeria's leader at the time, Olusegun OBASANJO, for the death of Fela's mother. His eighty-two-year-old mother died of injuries sustained when the army and police raided Fela's compound and threw her from a window.

Africa 70 was an entourage of talented musicians playing drum, electric bass, rhythm guitar, congas, percussion sticks, gourd rattlers, tenor sax, baritone sax, and two trumpets, as well as twenty backup singers. In the 1980s Fela began to experiment with longer and more complex compositions, including elements of polytonality, when he expanded his band, renamed Egypt 80. Despite his death, in 1997, he is still the recognized king of Afro-Beat.

ARI NAVE

Afro-Brazilian Emigration to Africa

The phenomenon of African former slaves returning to their original homes has thus far not received the attention it deserves. Pierre Verger has done much work on the relationship between Brazil and West Africa, and several others have written on the subject. More needs to be done,

however, to clarify the motivations and the influences that determined the former slaves' attitudes and reactions on returning to their home areas.

This essay examines the attitudes, occupations, and contributions of Brazilian returnees to West Africa in the nineteenth century. Their stay in Brazil so affected them that they behaved more like Brazilians than Africans on the West African coast. For this reason, in this essay they are called "Brazilians."

The term, however, is not completely accurate because the "Brazilian" communities included people of different origins, some having had little or no connection with Brazil. Some were men who had been former officials at Portuguese forts and factories, who had remained on the coast, and had children by local women. Others were Brazilian, Portuguese, and even Spanish slave-ship crewmen who were left on the coast after their ships had been seized and destroyed by British patrols. By far the most numerous, however, were the former slaves who returned to West Africa when they secured their freedom or were deported from Bahia (in Brazil) because of their supposed involvement in the slave revolt of 1835. Other West Africans who had never left Africa have become identified with the group because they were slaves and servants to some wealthy Brazilian colonizers in West Africa.

ARRIVAL IN AFRICA

Some Brazilians came to West Africa even before the nineteenth century. They usually arrived at Whydah, where the Portuguese had built a fort in 1721. But their growth as a separate and numerically important group dates from the early nineteenth century. Despite the expulsion of the governor of the Portuguese fort and its abandonment at the end of the eighteenth century, the slave coast continued to attract large numbers of Portuguese and Brazilian ships and nationals. Some minor officials of the fort indeed chose to remain after the expulsion and engaged in trade. These and other Brazilian traders who came and settled on the coast became the nucleus of the Brazilian community in the nineteenth century. Newcomers attached themselves to this group. One of the more famous of this early group was Francisco Felix de Souza, known as "Xaxa," a minor Brazilian official of the Portuguese fort who stayed and became a rich, independent slave trader.

Significant numbers of Brazilians arrived in West Africa during the first decades of the nineteenth century. In 1835, an uprising of the black population—slave and free—in Salvador, Bahia, shocked the authorities so much that they forced many former slaves to leave for West Africa. Local authorities placed severe restrictions on people of African descent, including fines and deportations of those who in any way were "suspected of trying to provoke slaves into insurrection." Under these restrictions, many freed Africans left, seeking a more congenial life elsewhere. Many eventually came to West Africa, which they regarded as home. Thus, the Brazilian community in ACCRA, GHANA, after which a street is named (Brazil Street) in James Town, dates its arrival to this period (1836).

Throughout the nineteenth century, more immigrants continued to arrive as they acquired their freedom and the money to pay for their passage. The final abolition of slavery, which occurred in Brazil in 1888, provided another impetus for former slaves to migrate to West Africa. Many of those who had been taken to Brazil as young people nurtured the memories of their homes in Africa and longed to return. The total abolition of slavery opened the way for them to attempt to fulfill this longing. Many boarded ships bound for the West African coast in the period immediately following 1888, and even later. They risked the uncertainties of the voyage and reception to come to LAGOS, Whydah, Badagry, and other port cities of West Africa. The most recent estimates put the number that left Brazil at approximately 3,000 for the whole of the nineteenth century.

The arrival date in West Africa significantly affected the fortune of many returnees. Those who arrived in the period before 1851 seem to have had better outcomes than those who arrived later. Some of the earlier arrivals, such as de Souza, José Domingos Martins, and Joaquim d'Almeida, established powerful and wealthy independent commercial houses and exercised great political and social influence. Later arrivals seemed to have less commercial, political, and social success in the nineteenth century, mostly because the Europeans were more active as traders or representatives of their governments after 1851. The establishment of the British in Lagos in 1851 and the French in PORTO-NOVO, BENIN, soon after meant that the incoming Brazilians were at a disadvantage if they sought to establish commercial enterprises. In addition, many of those Brazilians of the earlier period became rich because they had engaged in the slave trade to Brazil that allowed Africans to be imported until 1850, even though legally the trade had been abolished in 1831 in Brazil. As a result, to this day the families established by the pre-1851 arrivals enjoy a higher social standing in the Brazilian communities than those of the post-1850 immigrants.

RETURN TO WEST AFRICA

In Brazil the former slaves and other Brazilians of African descent had left their mark on Brazil's culture and society. They also took with them vestiges of their stay, which were revealed in their views, their social aspirations, and their economic activities in West Africa. They came as "Brazilians of African origin" who saw West Africa as the home to which they wanted to return, at least to die. For a long time they remained as a separate, alien group in West African societies—belonging to two places and to none.

The influence of this group's time in Brazil showed particularly in their attitude toward land ownership. Many aspired to own land on a large scale, setting up a plantation to produce a cash crop with a large house, many servants, and slaves. Those who were economically successful in West Africa set up palm oil plantations, built large houses, owned slaves and servants, and had many children and dependents, emulating the pattern of a Brazilian patriarchal plantation owner. However, these immigrants built their wealth through trade—something the Brazilian landowners never bothered with, depending instead on the labor of the slaves and servants on their lands.

"Xaxa" Francisco Felix de Souza exemplified the Brazilian patriarchy in West Africa. He owned land in Whydah that he developed into a palm oil plantation, with numerous slaves and servants. He also owned several large houses built on the model of the Brazilian sobrados, urban townhouses in the cities along the coast in which the master lived regally. José Domingo Martins, another Brazilian trader, similarly established plantations and built "big houses" along the coast. So did Joaquim d'Almeida, a returned former slave. These Brazilians, even the former slaves, willingly enslaved others. Following patterns established in nineteenth-century Brazil, they enjoyed being the masters and members of an elite society.

Indeed, these people rarely forgot the Brazil they had left. According to John Duncan, those who were deported to West Africa looked to Brazil as "a place where they had spent their happiest days." After the end of slavery in Brazil, some even returned to live in Brazil. Others traveled between Brazil and the West African coast and sent their children to be educated in Bahia and sometimes to settle there.

Their stay in Brazil also influenced the kinds of economic activities they pursued when they returned to West Africa. The most important occupation was trading, which came almost naturally to the Brazilians. In Brazil, little opportunity existed for the former slaves who had few skills and no money to invest in land or other enterprises. Thus, many had taken to petty trading, retailing small items that they obtained on credit from large firms. Many others sold food items they made themselves. Still others sold fruits, vegetables, and corn that they raised on small rented plots near the cities. This kind of trading became a common way for many of the returnees to make a living. New arrivals generally sold small items for others at first, but soon acquired goods on credit from European trading firms along the coast. Eventually some returnees became wealthy and owned stores from which they sold or supplied goods to small retailers. Antonio Olinto portrays this well in his book *Casa d'Agua*, a historical novel based on the experiences of some returnees to Lagos.

Some of the free Africans in Brazil engaged in the intercontinental trade in bulk goods—an experience several carried to West Africa. Michael Turner tells of a number of merchants who engaged in trade between Bahia and the West African coast. Two of these Africans, Antonio de Costa and João Monteiro, chartered a British ship—the *Nimrod*—to transport 160 freedpeople to West Africa despite the restrictions and persecutions of the community conducted by the local authorities following the 1835 revolt. Such merchants did profitable business, bringing tobacco, sugar, and salted beef to West Africa and carrying back palm oil, kola nuts, drums, Yoruba cloth, pepper, beads, and other items.

In the period immediately before and after 1851, British, French, and German firms installed agents in the coastal towns to act as suppliers of European goods and buyers of local export products. The greater involvement of the agents of the European firms, such as Victor Regis, Thomas Hutton, Oswald and Company, and the Banner Brothers, in local commerce challenged and in the end eliminated the position of the Brazilians as large-scale merchants and middlemen. The ability of these firms to control the sources of the European trade goods, their ownership of the means of transportation (ships), and their home governments' political presence or influence gradually pushed out the Brazilians. The Brazilian traders were reduced to taking goods from these firms or to becoming agents for them if they wanted to maintain their trading activities. A few, however, continued to trade with Bahia on their own, an activity that diminished after the effective abolition of the slave trade in Brazil in 1851.

The next most important occupation of the Brazilians was artisanship—the practice of various trades that had been learned in Brazil. Many former slaves were apprenticed to master carpenters, masons, goldsmiths, blacksmiths, bakers, shoemakers, tailors, and others. With the skills they acquired, they were able to earn more money than they would otherwise have made for their masters and themselves. Many freed themselves by what they earned through such skilled work and continued the same work as freedpeople. Those who were unskilled when they were freed often apprenticed themselves to others to learn a trade. Thus, in Brazil in 1872, there were 40,766 seamstresses, 13,196 textile workers, 5,599 carpenters, 2,163 shoemakers, 1,379 tailors, 1,858 artists, and 808,401 plantation hands. The skilled slaves had great market value, which masters proudly advertised whenever they wanted to sell them. For example, newspaper advertisements in nineteenth-century Brazil might read "For sale: a mulatto of

twenty-two years of age, a good tailor and a good herdsman; also a black of the same age; there is also a young girl who cooks very well and bakes, too. Her conduct is very good. There is another black woman twenty-two years old who is a very good cook. Location: Livramento street No. 4"; and, "A very young slave girl, with a beautiful figure is for sale. She knows how to cook and starch and iron clothes. She is a perfect dressmaker, ideal for any seamstress. Location: The dispensary of Joaquim Ignacio Ribeiro Jnr. on Boa Vista Square."

Many of those who returned to the West African coast had skills with which they could earn a living. Opportunities for large-scale trade were limited and retail trade and hawking were unattractive to most people. Farming was not feasible because the system of landholding in West African societies made it difficult for outsiders to obtain land. Many, therefore, had to rely on their skills. José Paraiso, for example, the founder of the Paraiso family of Porto-Novo and Agoue, arrived around 1850 and served as a barber to the established slave trader and compatriot José Domingos Martins.

Marcus Augusto José Cardoso, skilled in carpentry and joinery, arrived in Lagos with his father in 1869. He built several religious and educational facilities in Lagos, COTONOU, IBADAN, and Ebutemetta. He became famous in the region for his leadership in various undertakings, including the construction of the first Roman Catholic cathedral in the area, the Holy Cross of Lagos. Another former slave, Martiano do Bomfin, worked as a carpenter and brick mason on the same cathedral, earning the respectable wage of two shillings and sixpence a day. He later returned to Bahia. Another, Paulo Freitas, worked as a carpenter in Nigeria for twenty years—from 1890 to 1910—and then returned to Bahia, where he died in 1918.

The skills of the former slaves had special value during the second half of the nineteenth century in West Africa. The Europeans had begun to establish themselves, but not well enough to have trained the necessary artisans for constructing the various government and trade buildings they needed. The carpenters, masons, joiners, tailors, and barbers arriving from Brazil were welcome additions, and the Europeans recognized this. A French official at Porto-Novo urged his government to establish a French protectorate there because "although there was not a sizable European population resident in the town, the presence of this Creole community with its links to western civilization should encourage the French to act." Similarly, J. Chapman, one of the Christian missionaries in Lagos, wrote to his counterpart in Sierra Leone that "the influx of [the Brazilians], all of whom must have something of European civilization among them (though doubtless alloyed with European vices and much error for many of them are Roman Catholics) together with the return of so many from Sierra Leone, must have a most important influence for good upon the interior of Africa." A British resident in Lagos observed that the Brazilians had among them "master masons, carpenters, painters, cabinet makers and mastersmiths. . . . On the women's side proficiency in bakery . . . laundry and dressmaking distinguished the Agudas."

The value of the skills of the returnees was reflected in good wages, especially in Lagos, where the Europeans were more numerous. Thus, even as early as 1845 the missionary Charles A. Gollmar warned his group from Lagos that "we must be prepared for a greater expense . . . than I anticipated." He blamed the Portuguese slave traders for the fact that "carpenter work is paid 300 percent higher than at Badagry." But the obvious explanation was that the many different groups—missionaries, British government officials, various trading company representatives—all placed a high demand on the few artisans available. Demand continued to grow in the coastal towns like Lagos and Porto-Novo throughout the nineteenth century. The wages of a carpenter (two shillings and sixpence a day) in the 1880s were very good, considering that in the 1890s a Nigerian official of the Prisons Department, who had years of experience and overseas training, earned about four shillings a day. In Accra, Brazilians were greatly respected for their building, tailoring, and farming skills.

The Brazilian immigrants also affected agriculture in West Africa. Most of them had abandoned the hope of reaching the Brazilian ideal of a lordly life when they came to West Africa. Yet some managed to acquire land, either through gifts by local rulers or through purchase. Xaxa de Souza, for example, received a land grant from King Guezo of DAHOMEY for a plantation. On part of this land he built a luxurious two-story house for his descendants, but also established a plantation of palm trees on which his many slaves and servants worked. The father of the Bahian Maxwell Porferia Assumpção Alakija bought land soon after his arrival in ABEOKUTA, NIGERIA. He was the first person in that city to own a cotton gin for processing the cotton he had planted. José Domingos Martins also owned a number of palm oil plantations as well as other farms, near Porto-Novo, on which he raised cattle.

Other immigrants had small pieces of land, often given to them by their wealthier compatriots, such as Xaxa de Souza. They raised crops to supply their own needs and those of their community. These small farmers became more easily absorbed into the local community, and greater interchanges of ideas took place as a result. John Duncan commented on the knowledge of agriculture that the former slaves had and that they used in cultivating "several very fine farms about six or seven miles from Whydah." He added that the cultivation of crops "in drills" in places beyond Abomey had resulted from "the instruction of returned slaves from the Brazils." The Brazilians in Accra received parcels of land on which they planted gardens of mangoes, coconuts, many varieties of beans, and manioc.

The farming skills of the Brazilian returnees came not only from their experiences on plantations, but also from traditional practices in Africa. On many plantations in Brazil the owners allotted small plots of land to the slaves, where in their free time, they raised food crops to supplement their meager daily allowance, and to sell in order to raise money to purchase goods and, in some cases, their own freedom. Subsistence farming was not new to these people, who had been farming in West Africa long before the Europeans arrived in the fifteenth century. But plantation agriculture—raising cash crops—represented new experiences for the slaves and freedpeople in Brazil. Plantation farming suited a country preoccupied with supplying the demands of foreign countries for raw materials.

Experiences with Brazilian agriculture were useful in nineteenth-century West Africa, where Europeans similarly had begun to demand more and more raw materials. West Africans had concentrated on producing cash crops for domestic use and so the Brazilians' experience was helpful. The palm oil plantations of the wealthier Brazilians in Porto-Novo, Whydah, and other places were geared toward meeting the European demands. Speculation exists to suggest that the Dahomeans began cultivating palm oil on plantations as a result of the influence of the Brazilians who had such direct experience.

The Brazilians also exerted influence in the area of education. They had seen in Brazil that education could raise one's social status and earning power. Some had acquired education in parochial schools or in the homes of their masters. However, not many schools existed for the education of the population as a whole. At independence in 1822, few schools existed, and the educational system had not recovered from the expulsion of the Jesuits in 1759. Under the empire (1822–1889), primary education came under local and municipal authorities who had little interest in the spread of education to the populace. In fact, even in Europe, popular education began to interest politicians only in the second half of the nineteenth century.

Thus, only the children of the landed aristocratic families, rich merchants, and professionals received any measure of education. The vast majority of the population—80 percent, by C. H. Haring's estimate, which included almost all the Africans—remained illiterate. According to another estimate, out of a slave population of 1.5 million in 1872, only 1,403 (or 0.09 percent) had some education.

In West Africa, however, the Brazilians sought to educate their children so that they could improve their status. They knew the advantages that Western education could give a person in the increasingly European-dominated society of nineteenth-century coastal West Africa. Indeed, those who had some education became scribes, interpreters, and advisers to local chiefs, and acquired an important place in the society. Moreover, those who took to trading had an opportunity to use their education to advantage in their dealings with the Europeans (Portuguese was for a long time the trade language along the coast). In the period of greater European presence (from 1851 on), those with education served as interpreters, negotiators, and advisers to both local rulers and the Europeans, especially in the inevitable clashes that occurred between the two. Under colonial administrations, educated people had both job security and social standing. In Dahomey, the French relied heavily on the Brazilians, and in Lagos the British used their services.

The first European schools in Dahomey opened in the abandoned Portuguese fort in Whydah and in Brazilians' homes. Before that the Brazilians had sent their children to the mission schools established by the French and British. In fact, they had demanded schools from the missionaries, organizing and actually building the schools, as Marcos Cardoso did in Dahomey and Nigeria in the late 1800s. Recognizing the advantages of education and seizing the opportunities offered by the European officials and missionaries enabled the Brazilians to gain disproportionate prominence among the elite of the West African coastal states Togo, Benin, and Nigeria.

The contributions the returnees made to architecture in West Africa also reflected the Brazilian influence. The masons, carpenters, joiners, and others used their skills to construct private and public buildings in the coastal cities and inland. José Cardoso worked as a carpenter and joiner in the construction of various chapels, school buildings, and cathedrals. Others contributed their skills as masons. Having learned their skills in Brazil, they naturally copied the architectural styles of the buildings in Brazil.

When the wealthy Brazilians built individual houses in West Africa, they modeled them after those they had seen in Brazil. Many such houses still stand in the areas where the Brazilian communities lived in the various towns in West Africa. As the Reverend G. K. Nelson, himself a descendant of Brazilian immigrants, wrote in 1963, "Some houses which the Brazilians constructed are still standing, some of those having served, until recently, as residences (palaces) of some tribal chiefs of Accra." In 1962, the newspaper Brazilian Report carried a picture of a neoclassic building in Salvador, Bahia, with an explanation that the houses of the Brazilians in Lagos and other places resembled buildings in Bahia. A more detailed scholarly study of the buildings on the two sides of the Atlantic would clarify such Brazilian influences on West African architecture.

Finally, in the area of religion, the Brazilians helped spread Christianity and Islam in West Africa. All slaves had to receive baptism before setting foot on Brazilian soil. The slave traders usually performed a mass baptism before loading their human cargo onto the ships. Once in Brazil, however, each slave owner had to provide for the Roman Catholic religious education of his slaves. Many plantations had their own chapels, with resident chaplains. Morning and evening prayers for all the residents of a plantation took place daily. In theory, all were Roman Catholics; and in practice, many became committed to Catholicism. At least they became, like most Latin Americans, attached to the external forms and ceremonials of that religion.

Many African slaves retained their traditional beliefs and practices, however, often disguising these under Roman Catholic worship and forms. Others kept their Islamic faith despite the hostility they faced in the strongly Catholic country. Indeed, those who came to Bahia in the first half of the nineteenth century had such a zealous attachment to Islam that they converted others to their religion there. According to Michael Turner, they even set up an imamate in Salvador and had qadis (Islamic judges) in the provinces. They are reputed to have provided the leadership for various revolts in Bahia, culminating in the famous one of 1835, which historians have considered an extension of the jihads of West Africa.

Most Brazilians, however, professed Roman Catholicism when they returned to West Africa, which helped to distinguish them. As Michael Turner shows, they welcomed the first Roman Catholic missionaries to the area, provided the first congregations, contributed to the needs of the missions, and helped to build the first churches and schools. Their enthusiasm arose from the desire for material things (such as schools) and a desire to maintain the cultural inheritance from Brazil that helped them forge a separate identity as a community. But they proved to be generally poor Catholics in the eyes of the missionaries because they tended to be more observant of the outward ceremonials and festivals (especially those they had celebrated in Brazil) while they showed indifference toward Roman Catholic rituals and personal morality. These factors earned them the censure of the European missionaries, whose initial enthusiasm toward them quickly waned. But the Brazilians supplied a ready congregation and the support and encouragement for the mission. Their contribution to the building of churches and schools and the zeal of some helped establish Roman Catholicism in many places in West Africa.

The Muslims among them also continued in their beliefs and practices. They joined Muslim communities in the coastal towns and other places. Some even became occasional spokespersons. For example, the French lieutenant governor of Dahomey in 1902 chose Ignacio Paraiso to be a Muslim representative to his central Committee of Public Instruction. Others, such as Saidon of Ague and Abdullahi Alechou of Whydah, served as imams for the Muslim communities where they lived. The influence these Muslims exercised was somewhat limited. Islam had been in West Africa far longer than in Brazil, and leaders for the local communities generally came from the indigenous groups. In addition, under the French and British COLONIAL RULE, they found little opportunity for leadership in the Westernized atmosphere that favored their Roman Catholic counterparts.

CONCLUSION

Socially and economically, the roles the Brazilians played in West Africa, in large measure, came from their experiences and training in Brazil. Most had left Brazil because the society was hostile to them, and they thought it offered them fewer opportunities for attaining a respectable place, economically or socially.

By the time they reached West Africa, many Brazilians had abandoned their high goals, and some were disappointed. But on the whole, the Brazilians did well for themselves. Through diligence and experiences and skills they had acquired in Brazil, they achieved a reasonable standard of living and, in some cases, great wealth. Socially, although an alien group in what they had regarded as "home" while they were in Brazil, they achieved the respectability they had previous been denied. Indeed, although sometimes regarded as only partially European, the measure of European culture and skills they possessed gave them an advantage over those who had never left the coast of West Africa, which may explain the high positions they rose to in colonial and postcolonial West Africa.

See also ART AND ARCHITECTURE, AFRICAN; ISLAM IN AFRICA; ISLAM AND TRADITION: AN INTERPRETATION.

S. Y. BOADI-SIAW

Afrocentricity

Afrocentricity is an intellectual perspective deriving its name from the centrality of African people and phenomena in the interpretation of data. Maulana Karenga, a major figure in the Afrocentric Movement, says, "It is a quality of thought that is rooted in the cultural image and human interest of African people."

ORIGINS AND ORIENTATIONS

The Afrocentric school was founded by Molefi Kete Asante in the late twentieth century with the launching of the book Afrocentricity, in which theory and practice were merged as necessary elements in a rise to consciousness. Among the early influences were Kariamu Welsh, Abu Abarry, C. T. Keto, Linda James Myers, J. A. Sofola, and others. Afrocentricity examined some of the same issues that confronted a group calling themselves the Black Psychologists, who argued along lines established by Bobby Wright, Amos Wilson, Na'im Akbar, Kobi Kambon, Wade Nobles, Patricia Newton, and several others. African American scholars who were trained in political science and sociology, such as Leonard Jeffries, Tony Martin, Vivian Gordon, Kwame Nantambu, Barbara Wheeler, James Turner, and Charshee McIntyre, were greatly influenced by the works of Yosef Ben-Jochannon and John Henrik Clarke and had already begun the process of seeking a non-European way to conceptualize the African experience prior to the development of Afrocentric theory. On the other hand, Afrocentricity finds its inspirational source in the Kawaida philosophy's long-standing concern that the cultural crisis is a defining characteristic of twentieth-century African reality in the diaspora just as the nationality crisis is the principal issue on the African continent. (Developed by Karenga, professor and chair of the Department of Black Studies at California State University, Long Beach, Kawaida is defined briefly as "an ongoing synthesis of the best of African thought and practice in constant exchange with the world.") Afrocentricity sought to address these crises by repositioning the African person and African reality from the margins of European thought, attitude, and doctrines to a centered, therefore positively *located*, place within the realms of science and culture. Afrocentricity finds its grounding in the intellectual and activist precursors who first suggested culture as a critical corrective to a displaced agency among Africans. Recognizing that Africans in the diaspora had been deliberately deculturalized and made to accept the conqueror's codes of conduct and modes of behavior, the Afrocentrist discovered that the interpretative and theoretical grounds had also been moved. Thus, synthesizing the best of Alexander Crummel, Martin Robison Delany, Edward Wilmot Blyden, Marcus Garvey, Paul Robeson, Anna Julia Cooper, Ida B. Wells-Barnett, Larry Neal, Carter G. Woodson, Willie Abraham, Frantz FANON, Malcolm X, Cheikh Anta DIOP, and W. E. B. Du Bois in his later writings, Afrocentricity projects an innovation in criticism and interpretation. It is therefore in some sense a paradigm, a framework, and a dynamic. However, it is not a worldview and should not be confused with Africanity, which is essentially the way African people, any African people, live according to the customs, traditions, and mores of their society. One can be born in Africa, follow African styles and modes of living, and practice an African religion and not be Afrocentric. To be Afrocentric one has to have a self-conscious awareness of the need for centering. Thus, those individuals who live in Africa and recognize the decentering of their minds because of European colonization may self-consciously choose to be demonstratively in tune with their own agency. If so, this becomes a revolutionary act of will that cannot be achieved merely by wearing African clothes or having an African name.

SCHOOL OF THOUGHT

Among contemporaries the works of Karenga, Abarry, Nantambu, Chinweizu, Ngugi wa Thiong'o, J. A. Sofola, Ama Mazama, Aboubacry Moussa Lam, Terry Kershaw, Walter Rodney, Leachim Semaj, Danjuma Modupe, Errol Henderson, Runoko Rashidi, Charles Finch, Nah Dove, Marimba Ani, Aisha Blackshire-Belay, Theophile Obenga, and Oba T'shaka have been inspiring in defining the nature of the principal Afrocentric school of thought. The principal motive behind their intellectual works seems to have been the use of knowledge for the cultural, social, political, and economic transformation of African people by suggesting the necessity for a recentering of African minds, in a way that brings about a liberating consciousness. Indeed, Afrocentricity contends that there could be no social or economic struggle that would make sense if African people remained enamored of the philosophical and intellectual positions of white hegemonic nationalism as it relates to Africa and African people. At base, therefore, the work of the Afrocentric school of thought is a political one in the sense that all social knowledge has a political purpose. No one constructs or writes about repositioning and recentering merely for the sake of self-indulgence; none could afford to do so because the African dispossession appears so great and the displacing myths so pervasive that simply to watch the process of African peripheralization without taking any correction action is to acquiesce in African decentering. The Afrocentrist contends that passion can never be a substitute for argument as argument should not be a substitute for passion. Afrocentric intellectuals may disagree over the finer points of interpretation and some facts, but the overall project of relocation and reorientation of African action and data has been the rational constant in all Afrocentric work. Interest in African people is not sufficient for one's work to be called Afrocentric. Indeed, Afrocentricity is not merely the discussion of African and African American issues, history, politics, or consciousness; any one may discuss these issues and yet not be an Afrocentrist. Further, it is not a perspective based on skin color or biology and should not be confused with melanist theories, which existed before Afrocentricity and whose emphasis tends to be on biological determinism. Modupe of Hunter College has posited agency, centeredness, psychic integrity, and cultural fidelity as the minimum four theoretical constructs that are necessary for a work to be called Afrocentric. Thus, what is clear is that neither a discussion of the Nile Valley civilizations or of developing economic productivity in African American communities, nor an argument against white racial hierarchy, is sufficient for a discourse to be considered Afrocentric. Operations that involve the Afrocentric framework, identified by the four theoretical constructs put forward by Modupe, represent an Afrocentric methodology. As in every other case, the presentation of theory and methodological considerations implies avenues for criticism. Those criticizing Afrocentricity have been taken more seriously when the criticism has been derived from the definitions established by the proponents of Afrocentricity themselves. At other times criticism has devolved into low-level intellectual sniping at points considered irrelevant by most Afrocentrists. For example, the debate over extraneous issues such as whether Aristotle or Cleopatra were black has nothing at all do with Afrocentricity. What is more relevant for the Afrocentrist is the question, "What is the location of the person asking such questions or the location of the person needing to answer them?"

EMERGENCE OF A THEORY

Although a number of writers and community activists growing out of the Black Power Movement had increasingly seen the need for a response to marginality, Afrocentricity did not emerge as a critical theory and a literary practice until the appearance of two small books by the Amuleti Publishing Company in Buffalo, New York. The press published Welsh's Textured Women, Cowrie Shells, Cowbells, and Beetlesticks in 1978 and Molefi Kete Asante's book Afrocentricity in 1980. These were the first self-conscious markings along the intellectual path of Afrocentricity, that is, where the authors, using their own activism and community organizing, consciously set out to explain a theory and a practice of social and economic liberation by reinvesting African agency as the fundamental core of African sanity. Welsh's book was a literary practice growing out of her choreographic method/technique, umfundalai, which had been projected in her dances at the Center for Positive Thought, which she directed. On the other hand, the book Afrocentricity was the first time that the theory of Afrocentricity had been launched as an intellectual idea. The book was written from observations and textual analyses of what intellectual activists such as Welsh, Karenga, and Haki Madhubuti were doing with social transformation in community organizations. Rather than use political organization for the sake of organization, they had articulated a cultural base for the organizing principle. This had a more telling effect on and a more compelling attraction for African people. Based in the lived experiences of African people in the diaspora and the African continent, the Afrocentric idea had to be concerned with nothing less than the relocation of subject-place in the African world after hundreds of years of living on the imposed and ungrounded terms of Europe. Unlike the Négritude Movement, to which the Afrocentric Movement is often compared, Afrocentricity has not been limited to asking artistic questions. Indeed the cultural question as constructed by the Afrocentrists involves not only literature, art, music, and dance, but the entire process by which Africans are socialized to live in the modern world. Thus, economics is a cultural question as much as religion and science in the construction of the Afrocentrists. This is why Afrocentrists tend to pose three sets of questions: How do we see ourselves and how have others seen us? What can we do to regain our own accountability and to move beyond the intellectual and cultural plantation that constrains our economic, political, and scientific development? What allied theories and methods may be used to rescue those African ideas and ideals that are marginalized by Europe and thus in the African's mind as well? These have become the crucial questions that have aggravated our social and political worlds and agitated the brains of the Afrocentrists.

FIVE DISTINGUISHING CHARACTERISTICS
As a cultural configuration, the Afrocentric idea is distinguished by five characteristics: (1) an intense interest in psychological location as determined by symbols, motifs, rituals, and signs; (2) a commitment to finding the subject-place of Africans in any social, political, economic, architectural, literary, or religious phenomenon with implications for questions of sex, gender, and class; (3) a defense of African cultural elements as historically valid in the context of art, music, education, science, and literature; (4) a celebration of centeredness and agency and a commitment to lexical refinement that eliminates pejoratives about Africans or other people; (5) a powerful imperative from historical sources to revise the collective text of African people.

Essentially, these have remained the principal features of the Afrocentric theory since its inception in the late 1970s. While numerous writers have augmented the central tendency of the Afrocentric theory, it has remained concerned with resolving the cultural crisis as a way of achieving economic, political, and social liberation. A group of thinkers, including Mazama, Abarry, Modupe, Asante,

Aisha Blackshire-Relay, Kariamu Welsh-Asante, Clenora Hudson-Weems, Miriam Maat Ka Re Monges, Katherine Bankole, Cynthia Lehman, Ayi Kwei Armah, Terry Kershaw, Clovis Semmes, Nilgun Anadolu Okur, C. T. Keto, and their students located the terms of Afrocentricity in the vital areas of linguistic, historical, sociological, and dramatic interpretations of phenomena. This tendency has been called the Temple Circle of Afrocentricity. For example, Abarry has examined orature and libation oratory in African cultural history in connective ways, thus avoiding the disconnected discourses usually found concerning Africa. Others, such as Mekada Graham and Jerome Schiele, have concentrated on the social transformative aspects of centrality, believing that it is possible to change the conditions of the socially marginalized by teaching them to see their own centrality and thus empower themselves to confront their existential and material situations. Afrocentrists believe that there is a serious difference between commentary on the activities of Europeans, past and present, and the revolutionary thrust of gaining empowerment through the reorientation of African interests. There is no rush to discover in Europe the answers for the problems that Europe created for the African condition, psychologically, morally, and economically. Afrocentrists do not shun answers that may emerge in the study of Europe, but what Europeans have thought and how Europeans have conceived their reality all too often lead to further imprisonment of the African mind. Thus, Afrocentrists call for the liberation of the mind from any notion that Europe is teacher and Africa is pupil; one must contest every space and locate in that space the freedom for Africa to express its own truths. This is not a biologically determined position, it is a culturally and theoretically determined one. That is why there are now Afrocentrists who are European and Asian while simultaneously one can find Africans who are not Afrocentric. The new work on Du Bois by the Chinese Afrocentrist Ji Yuan, and the work of Lehman on the Egyptian texts are examples of non-Africans exploring the various dimensions of centeredness in their analyses of African phenomena. It is consciousness, not biology, that decides how one is to apprehend the intellectual data, because the key to the Afrocentric idea is orientation to data, not data themselves. Where do you stand when you seek to locate, that is, interrogate, a text, phenomenon, or person?

OBJECTIVITY-SUBJECTIVITY
The rise of the Afrocentric idea has coincided at a time when Eurocentric scholars seemed to have lost their way in a dense forest of deconstructionist and postmodernist concepts that are challenging the prevailing orthodoxies of the

Eurocentric paradigm. Perhaps because of this we have found a deluge of challenges to the Afrocentric idea as a reaction to postmodernity. But it should be clear that the Afrocentrists, too, have recognized the inherent problems in structuralism, patriarchy, capitalism, and Marxism with their emphasis on received interpretations of phenomena as different as the welfare state and the poetry of e.e. cummings. Yet the issues of objectivity and subject-object duality, central pieces of the Eurocentric project in interpretation, have been shown to represent hierarchies rooted in the European construction of the political world. Afrocentrists claim that the aim of the objectivity argument is always to protect the status quo because the status quo is never called upon to prove its objectivity; only the challengers to the status quo are asked to explain their objectivity. In a society where white supremacy has been a major component of the social, cultural, and political culture, the African will always be in the position of challenging the white racial privileged status quo, unless, of course, he or she is co-opted into defending the economic, literary, critical, political, social, or cultural status quo. In each case the person will be defending the reality created by Eurocentrists. It is the subversion of that configuration that is necessary to establish a level playing field. But to claim that those who take the speaker or the subject position vis-à-vis others counted as audiences and objects are on the same footing as these others is to engage in intellectual subterfuge without precedent. On the other hand, it is possible, as the Afrocentrists claim, to create community when one speaks of subject-subject, speaker-speaker, audience-audience relationships. This allows pluralism without hierarchy. As applied to race and racism, this formulation is equally clear in its emphasis on subject-subject relationships. Of course, this subject-subject relationship is almost impossible in a racist system, or in the benign acceptance of a racist construction of human relationships as may be found in the American society. White supremacy cannot be accommodated in a normal society, and therefore when a writer or scholar or politician refuses to recognize or ignores the African's agency, he or she allows for the default position, white supremacy, to operate without challenge and thus participates in a destructive mode for human personality. If African people are not given subject place, then we remain objects without agency, intellectual beggars without a place to stand. There is nothing essentially different between this enslavement and the previous historical enslavement except our inability to recognize the bondage. Thus, you have a white-subject and black-object relationship expressed in sociology, anthropology, philosophy, political science, literature, and history rather than a subject-subject reality. It is this marginality that is rejected in the writings of Afrocentrists.

DIOPIAN INFLUENCE

The late Cheikh Anta Diop did more than anyone else to reintroduce the African as a subject in the context of African history and culture. It was Diop's singular ambition as a scholar to reorder the history of Africa and to reposition the African in the center of her own story. This was a major advance during the time when so many African writers and scholars were rushing after Europe to prove Europe's own point of view about the rest of the world. Diop was confident that the history of Africa could not be written without throwing off the falsifications of Europe, falsifications that had justified the enslavement and colonization of Africans. Doing this was not only politically and professionally dangerous, but it was considered to be impossible, given the hundreds of years of accumulated information in the libraries of the West. To begin with, Diop had to challenge the leading scholars of Europe, meet them in their intellectual home arena, defeat their arguments with science, and establish Africa's own road to its history. The fact that Diop achieved his purpose has meant that the scholars who have declared themselves to be Afrocentrists have done so with the example of Diop marching before in splendor. His key contention was that the ancient Egyptians laid the basis of African and European civilization and that the ancient Egyptians were not Arabs or Europeans, but, as Diop would say "Black Africans," to emphasize that there should be no mistake. These "Black Africans" of the Nile Valley gave the world astronomy, geometry, law, architecture, art, mathematics, medicine, and philosophy. The ancient African Egyptian term seba, first found in an inscription on the tomb of Antef I from 2052 B.C.E., had as its core meaning in the Medu Neter, the "reasoning style of the people." Beginning with Homer in 800 B.C.E., Greeks came to Egypt, Kemet, the Black Country, to study. Thus, Thales, Isocrates, Democritus, Eudoxus, Anaximander, Anaxigoras, Pythagoras, and many other Greek authors were students of the Africans during the eight hundred years before Jesus Christ. What Diop taught his students and readers was that Europe pronounced itself the categorical superior culture, and therefore its reasoning often served the bureaucratic functions of "locking" Africans in a conceptual cocoon that seems, at first glance, harmless enough. Nevertheless, the prevailing positions, often anti-African, were supported by this bureaucratic logic. How can an African liberate himself or herself from these racist mental structures? Afrocentrists take the position that this is possible, and indeed, essential, but can happen only if we search for answers in the time-space categories that are antihegemonic. These are categories that place Africa at the center of analysis of African issues and African people as agents in our own contexts. Otherwise, how can we ever raise practical questions of improving our situation in the world? The Jews of the Old Testament asked, How can you sing a new song in a strange land? The Afrocentrists ask, How can the African create a liberational philosophy from the icons of mental enslavement?

AFROCENTRICITY AS A CORRECTIVE AND CRITIQUE

There are certainly political implications here, because the issue of African politics throughout the world becomes one of securing a place from which to stand, unimpeded by the interventions of a decaying Europe that has lost its own moral way in its reach to enslave and dispossess other people. This is not to say that all of Europe is bad and all of Africa is good. To even think of or pose the issue in that manner is to miss the point I am making. For Africans and Native Americans, Europe has been dangerous; it is a five-hundred-years' dangerousness and I am not now speaking of physical or economic danger, though that history is severe enough, but of psychological and cultural danger, the danger that kills the soul of a people. One knows, I surmise, that a people's soul is dead when it can no longer breathe its own air or speak its own language and when the air of another culture seems to smell sweeter. Following Frantz Fanon, the Afrocentrists argue that it is the assimiladoes, the educated elite, whose identities and affiliations are often killed first. Fortunately, their death does not mean that the people are doomed; it only means that they can no longer be trusted to speak what the people know because they are dead to the culture, to the human project. Therefore, Afrocentricity stands as both a corrective and a critique. Whenever African people, who collectively suffer the experience of dislocation, are relocated in a centered place, that is, with agency and accountability, we have a corrective. By recentering the African person as an agent, we deny the hegemony of European domination in thought and behavior, and then Afrocentricity becomes a critique. On the one hand, we seek to correct the sense of place of the African, and on the other hand, we make a critique of the process and extent of the dislocation caused by the European cultural, economic, and political domination of Africa and African peoples. It is possible to make an exploration of this critical dimension by observing the way European writers have defined Africa and Africans in history, political science, anthropology, and sociology. To condone the definition of Africans as marginal and fringe people in the historical processes of the world, including the African world, is to abandon all hope of reversing the degradation of the oppressed. Thus, the aims of Afrocentricity as regards the cultural idea are not hegemonic. Afrocentrists have expressed no interest in one race or culture dominating another; they express an ardent belief in the possibility of diverse populations living on the same earth without giving up their fundamental traditions, except where those traditions invade other peoples' space. This is precisely why the Afrocentric idea is essential to human harmony. The Afrocentric idea represents a possibility of intellectual maturity, a way of viewing reality that opens new doors toward human understanding. I do not object to viewing it as a form of historical consciousness, but more than that, it is an attitude, a location, an orientation. To be centered is to stand someplace and to come from someplace; the Afrocentrist seeks for the African person the contentment of subject, active, agent place.

PRINCIPAL CONCEPTS

Afrocentricity represents a reaction against several tendencies. It spurns the limited analysis of Africans in the Americas as Europeans as well as the notion that Africans in the Americas are not Africans. Rather it concentrates on what Modupe calls the condition-effects-alleviation complex and the global formation. Modupe contends that the communal cognitive will is activated by cultural fidelity to that will and that cultural fidelity to that will is also fidelity to Afrocentricity itself. He is one of the leading proponents of the view that Afrocentric consciousness is necessary for psychological liberation and cultural reclamation. There are four areas of inquiry in Afrocentricity: cosmological, epistemological, axiological, and aesthetics. Accordingly, the Afrocentrist places all phenomena within one of these categories. Cosmological refers to the myths, legends, literatures, and oratures that interact at a mythological or primordial level with how African people respond to the cosmos. How are racial or cultural classifications developed? How do we distinguish between Yoruba and African Brazilian? How do gender, class, and culture interact at the intersection of science? The epistemological issues are those that deal with language, myth, dance, and music as they confront the question of knowledge and proof of truth. What is the rational structure of Ebonics as an African language, and how does it present itself in the African American's behavior and culture? Axiology refers to the good and the beautiful as well as to the combination that gives us right conduct within the context of African culture. This is a value issue. Since Afrocentricity is a transgenerational and transcontinental idea, as understood by Winston Van Horne of the University of Wisconsin-Milwaukee, it utilizes aspects of the philosophies of numerous African cultures to arrive at its ideal. "Beauty is as beauty does" is considered an African American adage, but similar proverbs, statements, and sayings are found throughout the African world, where beauty and goodness are often equated. Aesthetics as an area of inquiry is closely related to the issue of value.

Afrocentrists, however, have isolated, such as in the work of Welsh-Asante, seven senses of the Afrocentric approach to aesthetics: polyrhythm, dimensionality and texture, polycentrism, repetition, curvilinearity, epic memory, and wholism. Welsh-Asante contends that these elements are the leading aspects of any inquiry into African plastic art, sculpture, dance, music, and drama. A number of Afrocentric scholars have delved into a discussion of ontology, the study of beingness, as another issue of inquiry. This should not be confused with the idea of personalism in the original Afrocentric construction of philosophical approaches to Afrocentric cultural theory (critical methodology) and Afrocentric methodology (interpretative methodology). In earlier writings on Afrocentricity, I contended that the European and Asian worlds might be considered materialistic and spiritualistic, whereas the dominant emphasis in the African world was personalism. This was not to limit any cultural sphere but to suggest the most prominent ways in which large cultural communities respond to their environments. Karenga has identified seven areas of culture. These cultural elements are frequently used by Afrocentrists as well as practitioners of Kawaida when conceptualizing areas of intellectual organization. They are history, mythology, motif, ethos, political organization, social organization, and economic organization. Used most often in the critical analysis of culture, these organizing principles are applied to the social, communication, historical, cultural, economic, political and psychological fields of study whenever a student wants to determine the relationship between culture and a given discipline.

DISCIPLINE OF AFRICOLOGY

Finally the Afrocentrists have determined that a new discipline, Africology, emerges from the various treatments of data from the Afrocentric perspective. Africology is defined as the Afrocentric study of African phenomena. It has three major divisions: cultural/aesthetics, social/behavioral, and policy/action. Under cultural/aesthetics the scholar can consider at a minimum three key epistemic, scientific, and artistic dimensions. In terms of epistemic dimensions, the Afrocentrist examines ethics, politics, psychology, and other modes of behavior. The scientific dimensions include history, linguistics, economics, and other methods of investigation. The artistic dimension involves icons, art, motifs, symbols, and other types of presentation.

BIBLIOGRAPHY
Asante, Molefi Kete. The Afrocentric Idea. Temple University Press, 1998.
Asante, Molefi Kete. Kemet, Afrocentricity, and Knowledge. Africa World, 1990.
Asante, Molefi Kete. Malcolm X as Cultural Hero and Other Afrocentric Essays Africa World, 1993.
Asante, Molefi Kete. The Painful Demise of Eurocentrism: An Afrocentric Response to Critics. Africa World, 1999.
Asante, Molefi Kete, and Abu Abarry. The African Intellectual Heritage. Temple University Press, 1996.
Diop, Cheikh Anta. Civilization or Barbarism: An Authentic Anthropology. Trans. Yaa-Lengi Meema Ngemi. Lawrence Hill, 1991.
Karenga, Maulana. Introduction to Black Studies. University of Sankore Press, 1993.
Monges, Ma'at Ka Re Miriam. Kush: The Jewel of Nubia. Reconnecting the Root System of African Civilization. Africa World, 1997.
Nascimento, Abdias do. Orixás: Os Deuses Vivos da África Orishas; The Living Gods of Africa in Brazil. IPEAFRO/Afrodiaspora, 1995. Dual language edition.
Welsh-Asante, Kariamu ed. The African Aesthetic: Keeper of the Traditions. Greenwood, 1994.

ROBERT FAY

Afusari

The Afusari, an ethnic group of NIGERIA, are also known as Afusare, Izere, Jari, Jarawa, Feserek, Afizarek, Fezere, Jarawan Dutse and Fizere. The Afusari primarily inhabit the Kadima, Plateau, and Bauchi States of Nigeria. They speak a Niger-Congo language. Approximately 275,000 people consider themselves Afusari.

Afwerki, Isaias
1945–
Leader of Eritrean fight for independence from Ethiopia and president of Eritrea since 1993.

As a leader of the largest rebel force in Eritrea's independence struggle, Isaias Afwerki strove to unify peoples of diverse cultures and religious beliefs. Since assuming office, he has been widely praised for his pragmatism and modesty and for maintaining a regime free of corruption. Like Rwanda's Paul KAGAME, Uganda's Yoweri MUSEVENI, and Ethiopia's Meles ZENAWI, Afwerki belongs to what has been called Africa's "new generation" of leaders, all of whom are known for their military backgrounds and for their tactical rather than ideological approach to leadership.

Isaias Afwerki was born in Asmara, Eritrea, at a time when the fate of the former Italian colony was in limbo. By the time he graduated from the elite Prince Makonnen Secondary School in Asmara in 1965, Ethiopia had annexed Eritrea, and Eritrean opponents to the despotic rule of Emperor Haile SELASSIE were preparing for all-out warfare. But like many TIGRINYA youth, Afwerki still went to Haile Selassie University in Addis Ababa, Ethiopia, where he studied engineering. After only a year, however, he was gripped by the revolutionary fervor sweeping through the Eritrean student body, and he quit school to join the Eritrean Liberation Front (ELF).

Afwerki rose through the ranks to become a deputy division commander for the ELF but soon clashed with the organization's Muslim-dominated leadership. A few years later he helped found the Eritrean People's Liberation Front (EPLF). Like the ELF, the EPLF described itself as a Marxist organization, and Afwerki was among those who went to China for training in guerrilla warfare. By the time the Ethiopian regime fell in 1991, the EPLF had moderated its previous positions, and Afwerki was the clear choice to become independent Eritrea's first leader. He served as acting president until the country gained official independence on May 24, 1993, and was formally elected president by the National Assembly shortly thereafter. The Assembly has not held a presidential election since Afwerki first won the office. Despite a struggling national economy, exacerbated by a destructive Ethiopian invasion in 2000, Afwerki enjoyed broad popular support in Eritrea.

Though the country had enjoyed a fairly warm relationship with the United States—and had been part of the so-called Coalition of the Willing, which abetted the 2003 invasion of Iraq—the relationship began to fray around 2006–2007. Afwerki accused the Bush administration of meddling in the border demarcation process following the Eritrean-Ethiopian war. The U.S. State Department accused the Afwerki government of aiding terrorists—specifically, of arming Islamic extremists in Somalia—and threatened to put Eritrea on its list of state sponsors of terrorism. Afwerki denied the charges.

See also ADDIS ABABA, ETHIOPIA; ASMARA, ERITREA.

DAVID P. JOHNSON, JR.

Agadez, Niger
City in northern Niger.

Today an important tourist and commercial center at the edge of the SAHARA, Agadez was once the center of the Agadez sultanate, a loose TUAREG confederacy. The town, whose original name may have been Takadest (Arabic for "place of congregation of visitors"), was founded in 1430 by Alissaoua, the sultan of Aãr, who made it his capital. In theory, Alissaoua ruled over the Tuareg; but because he was descended from the slave of an Ottoman ruler, he in fact had little status, and little power beyond the arbitration of disputes between clans. As a result, Agadez never became the capital of a centralized Tuareg kingdom.

Nevertheless, Agadez quickly attracted trans-Saharan trade caravans because of its central position between TOMBOUCTOU and Gao to the west, ZINDER and the HAUSA STATES to the south, the Tibesti to the east, and Tamanrasset and the Mediterranean to the north. By the sixteenth century the town had become one of the biggest trading centers in the region and a major slave market, factors that contributed to the sultan's wealth and enabled him to build an elaborate mosque in the center of Agadez. By 1850, however, the town had lost much of its business to other towns, such as Iférouane, and its population had declined. Agadez remained fairly small until the 1960s, when the discovery of uranium nearby prompted the migration of thousands of people seeking mining jobs. According to the 2001 census, Agadez and its surrounding region was home to some 321,639 inhabitants, with the city itself accounting for nearly 90,000.

Since NIGER achieved independence in 1960, the economy of Agadez has depended on uranium revenues and tourists who come to see the elaborate architecture remaining from the Agadez sultanate. During times of drought, the town has also been a place of refuge for nomads seeking food and housing. Throughout the early 1990s, however, Agadez's economy, particularly its tourist trade, fell victim to the raids of Tuareg rebels. Many of these raids targeted tourists traveling on the roads to NIAMEY and Zinder, but safety concerns also prevented transport of the town's main product—uranium. The attacks subsided after the Tuareg rebels and Nigerien government concluded peace treaties in the mid-1990s. By the early 2000s, the tourist industry was strong again in Agadez.

See also DROUGHT AND DESERTIFICATION; MINERALS AND MINING IN AFRICA; SLAVERY IN AFRICA; TOURISM IN AFRICA.

ELIZABETH HEATH

Agaja
1673–1740
King of Dahomey.

The third ruler of the Dahomey Kingdom, Agaja succeeded his brother, Akaba, in 1708. Agaja was a shrewd and powerful king, expanding the kingdom and making it one of the most powerful in West Africa. He spent much of his early reign instituting administrative reforms that centralized and strengthened the kingdom: he created an elite corps of female guards, enlarged the royal army, and employed a group of military spies who acquired information about neighboring groups. These innovations proved crucial to his victorious conquest of the Allada and Whydah Kingdoms in the 1720s. The acquisition of these coastal kingdoms gave the previously landlocked Dahomey access to the sea and, consequently, European trade.

Agaja's ambition to control the transatlantic slave trade that flowed through these ports brought him into rivalry with the neighboring YORUBA kingdom of OYO, whose attacks on Dahomey forced Agaja to surrender in 1730 and agree to pay tribute. Some believe that Agaja had hoped to replace the Transatlantic Slave Trade with a domestic slave economy so that his kingdom could reap the economic benefits of slave labor, but Europeans showed little interest in his invitation to establish slave plantations in Dahomey. Instead the kingdom, seeking to finance the purchase of firearms and other goods from the Europeans, became one of the biggest slave suppliers on the Slave Coast (present-day BIGHT OF BENIN). Agaja essentially attempted to monopolize the slave trade, angering independent Dahomean slave traders, and by 1735 his kingdom faced serious internal unrest. Two years later Agaja acquiesced to the independent traders' demands for access to the lucrative slave trade. Nevertheless, the kingdom of Dahomey reemerged as a dominant supplier of slaves after the death of Agaja in 1740. His conquests and internal reforms buttressed Dahomey's strength and prosperity, which endured for more than a century.

See also DAHOMEY, EARLY KINGDOM OF; SLAVERY IN AFRICA.

BIBLIOGRAPHY

Akinjagbin, I. A. *Dahomey and Its Neighbors, 1708—1818.* Cambridge University Press, 1967.

Law, Robin. "King Agaja of Dahomey, the Slave Trade and the Question of West African Plantations: the Embassy of Bulfinch Lambe and Adomo Tomo to England, 1726–32". *Journal of Imperial and Commonwealth History* 19, no. 2: 137–163. F. Cass, 1991.

ELIZABETH HEATH

Agaw
Ethnic group of the Horn of Africa, also known as the Agau and Agew.

The Agaw primarily inhabit central and northern ETHIOPIA and ERITREA. They speak an Afro-Asiatic language in the Cushitic cluster, suggesting that their ancestors lived in the region for thousands of years before the arrival of speakers of Semitic languages, such as the AMHARA and TIGRE. Approximately 200,000 people identify themselves as Agaw.

Ahanta
Ethnic group of Ghana.

The Ahanta primarily inhabit the coast of western GHANA. They speak a Niger-Congo language and are considered part of the larger AKAN ethnolinguistic group. Some 160,000 people identify themselves as Ahanta.

Ahidjo, El Hajj Ahmadou
1924–1989
Nationalist leader and president of Cameroon from 1960 to 1982.

Born and raised as a Muslim in the northern administrative center of Garoua, Ahmadou Ahidjo attended secondary school and college in Yaoundé. After working for several years as a radio operator, Ahidjo turned to politics. His 1949 election to the Cameroon representative assembly was followed by election in the 1950s to the territorial and union assemblies. He built a strong power base among the northern elite, composed of Fulbé notables and HAUSA merchants. As head of the northern Union Camerounaise (UC), Ahidjo became vice prime minister in the pre-independence coalition government with the Union of the Population of Cameroun (UPC). When the coalition collapsed in 1958, Ahidjo formed a new government, calling for immediate independence while reassuring France that close ties would be maintained.

On the first day of 1960, CAMEROON became independent, with Ahidjo as president. He ruled Cameroon for the next twenty-two years. Realizing the divisiveness of ethnic, regional, religious, and linguistic identities, Ahidjo focused on building national unity. Through a 1961 plebiscite Ahidjo reunified British Cameroons and French Cameroon. He also capitalized on his popular appeal as the "father" of the nation to carry out authoritarian measures. Ahidjo centralized the government and incorporated associations representing women, youth, and labor into the sole legal party, the Cameroon National Union (CNU). Security forces, with French assistance, suppressed the vestiges of political opposition, particularly the UPC, which continued to wage a low-level insurgency war. The media was heavily censored.

Infrastructure projects both encouraged economic growth and centralized authority in the capital, Yaoundé. By the time Ahidjo replaced the federation with a republic in 1972, he faced no significant political opposition. He further solidified his control by balancing ethnic representation in the cabinet and national assembly and by dispensing patronage to supporters in the government bureaucracy, the military, and the business community. This created a situation in which, as one Cameroonian saying goes, "the politics of the belly" predominated. Ahidjo's tight control over the economy and close relations with France made it possible for him to maintain an apparently stable, if fairly repressive regime, and to assure Cameroonians a fairly high national standard of living.

On November 4, 1982, Ahidjo resigned, claiming exhaustion, and handed over power to Paul BIYA, his chosen successor and then prime minister. Ahidjo did not, however, leave the political scene altogether, and as head of the CNU he tried to run the country from behind the scenes. Biya resisted, and conflicts between the two men led Ahidjo Loyalists in the Republican Guard to mount a bloody uprising. But the uprising failed and Ahidjo retired to France where, in absentia, he was tried, convicted, and condemned to death in 1984. President Biya commuted the death sentence, and Ahidjo spent time primarily in Senegal and France until his death in 1989.

See also YAOUNDÉ, CAMEROON.

ERIC YOUNG

Ahmad Baba
1556–1627
Islamic scholar, writer, and jurist.

Ahmad Baba was one of the best-known Islamic scholars and writers of his time. Born into the prestigious Aqit family near TOMBOUCTOU (Timbuktu) in 1556, he was educated in Islamic theology and law. After completing his studies, he began writing books and treatises on theology, Islamic jurisprudence, history, and Arabic grammar. Over the course of his life he wrote more than fifty-six works. More than half of these are still in existence, and several are still used by West African ulama (scholars). Ahmad Baba also was a great collector of books; he amassed a library containing thousands of volumes. At this time, Tombouctou, ruled by the SONGHAI EMPIRE, was renowned throughout the Islamic world as a center of learning.

In 1591 the sultan of MOROCCO invaded Tombouctou. Ahmad Baba and other scholars refused to serve the Moroccan rulers and, by some accounts, instigated a 1593 rebellion against the invaders. Because of their resistance, the Moroccans arrested Ahmad Baba and other prominent literati and deported them to MARRAKECH in 1594. The Moroccans also confiscated several of the scholars' private libraries. Ahmad Baba reportedly lost nearly 1,600 volumes.

In Morocco, Ahmad Baba continued to write and was even allowed to teach and practice law. During this period he wrote the famous *Kifayat al-Muktaj*, a biographical dictionary of Maliki legal scholars and jurists. After the death of the Moroccan sultan in 1607, he was allowed to return to Tombouctou. Upon his return, he wrote a catalog of Islamic and pagan peoples of the Sudan. This text was later used by Usuman dan Fodio. Ahmad Baba also wrote a text on Arabic grammar, which is still used in some areas of northern Nigeria.

ELIZABETH HEATH

Aidid, Mohamed Farah
1934–1996
Leader of the Somali organization that overthrew President Mohamed Siad Barre.

Mohamed Farah Aidid was born in Italian Somaliland and trained in the military in Rome and Moscow. After returning to independent SOMALIA, Aidid served in the army under General Mohamed Siad Barre. When Siad Barre assumed the presidency in 1969, he appointed Aidid chief of staff of the army. Later that year, however, he began to suspect Aidid's loyalties and imprisoned him without trial for seven years on charges of treasonous conspiracy.

In 1977 Siad Barre released Aidid and welcomed him back to the administration, no doubt seeking his help for the ongoing border war against ETHIOPIA. The loyalties of Aidid to his former jailer are unclear, but he served Siad Barre's military administration until the late 1980s. In 1989 Aidid broke with Siad Barre and joined the United Somali Congress (USC), an organization dominated by the Hawiye clan. The USC was one of several groups seeking the overthrow of the government. Aidid headed the USC capture of MOGADISHU, a key victory that led to the ultimate ouster of Siad Barre. Shortly afterward, a rift within the USC between Aidid and Ali Mahdi Mohamed, who had been appointed interim president, turned into a full-scale war between subclans. The country, already suffering from the violence of the military regime, was thrown into complete civil war, with paramilitary groups fighting each other for whatever resources remained.

Both men were declared president by their supporters within the Hawiye clan. In the ensuing power struggle, the factions not only destroyed much of Mogadishu but impeded the distribution of famine relief during one of the worst droughts in Somalia's history. The United Nations sent peacekeeping troops, at first to deliver food aid but later to try to end the war. The United States viewed the "warlord" Aidid as the primary threat to peace, particularly after he was accused of inciting riots against foreign intervention and ambushes that killed 24 Pakistani soldiers and wounded 59. After an unsuccessful attempt by U.S. soldiers to capture Aidid left 300 Somali and 18 Americans dead, the United States withdrew in 1994, and the United Nations left a year later.

Aidid took the town of Baidoa in 1995, holding international aid workers hostage for several days and confiscating their equipment. A coalition fought against Aidid for power in southern Mogadishu, but he held onto power until his death in August 1996 of complications from a bullet wound. His son Hussein Mohammed, a former U.S. marine, succeeded him as head of the clan's faction and in 1998 controlled part of Mogadishu.

See also UNITED NATIONS IN AFRICA.

MARIAN AGUIAR

Aidoo, Ama Ata

1942–

Ghanaian writer whose plays, novels, and poetry examine the traditional roles assigned to African women.

Christina Ama Ata Aidoo was born in Abeadzi Kyiakor, GHANA, into a FANTE family she once characterized as "a long line of fighters." Encouraged by her liberal-minded father, Aidoo pursued an English degree at the University of Ghana in Legon. As a student, she won a short-story prize, but her interests centered on drama as a means of bringing to life the rich oral traditions of the Fante. She worked closely with leading Ghanaian dramatist Efua Sutherland and became familiar with a Fante dramatic style that blossomed in the 1930s.

Aidoo's first play, *The Dilemma of a Ghost*, was staged in 1964 by the Student's Theatre at the University of Ghana. With this play, Aidoo earned her lasting reputation as a writer who examines the traditional African roles of wife and mother. The play, like many of her later works, also demonstrated her willingness to grapple with complex and controversial issues. *The Dilemma of a Ghost* tells the story of an African man who returns to his village from abroad with his African American wife. While the young wife struggles as an outsider among the village women, her Westernized husband attempts to reconcile his inherited traditions with his adopted views. Ultimately, the wife bears the brunt of the couple's decisions, particularly the decision not to have children. Critics of the play noted Aidoo's compelling portrayal of relationships between women.

After receiving a creative writing fellowship at Stanford University in California, Aidoo spent two years traveling. Her next play, *Anowa* (1970), reworked a traditional legend she had learned as a song from her mother. Set in the late nineteenth century, *Anowa* tells the story of a strong-willed woman who refuses an arranged marriage and instead marries a man of her choice who later makes her miserable. As Anowa's husband becomes a slaveholder, the play also confronts the fact of African participation in the transatlantic slave trade. Speaking about *Anowa* in an interview, Aidoo cited the importance of dealing with the uncomfortable history of African slavery as a key to resolving Africa's future.

Aidoo's next work, *No Sweetness Here* (1970), is a collection of short stories that undertook a number of complicated themes, including the divide between men and women and between rural and urban societies. In these stories, Aidoo brought a sense of the oral to the written word through the use of elements such as African idioms.

Aidoo described her *Our Sister Killjoy; or Reflections from a Black-Eyed Squint* (1977) as fiction in four episodes. In this dense work, Aidoo used an experimental form, interspersing the prose narrative with poetry. The story follows a young African woman as she travels from Africa to Europe in the late 1960s, reflecting on the different yet intertwined histories of the two continents. In *Our Sister Killjoy*, which examines underdevelopment, racism, and the exoticizing of Africans and includes a scene in which the main character rejects the sexual advances of a white woman, Aidoo again showed a willingness to deal with controversial issues.

In 1982 Aidoo was appointed Ghana's minister of education. She left the country a year later for Zimbabwe, where she continued to teach as well as write poems, which were published in the collection *Someone Talking to Sometime* (1985), and two children's books.

The 1991 novel *Changes* explores the possibilities of self-determination for contemporary women. The story narrates a woman's experience of a polygamous marriage and her ultimate decision to leave her husband. For Aidoo, who once proclaimed that, given the seriousness of Africa's political problems, she could not imagine herself writing something so frivolous as an African love story, the novel was a realization that "love or the workings of love is also political." It later won her the Commonwealth Writers Prize for African writers. She followed this novel with a second volume of poetry, *An Angry Letter in January* (1992), and a short-story collection, *The Girl Who Can and Other Stories* (1997). In 2005 she was given the Millenium Award for Literary Excellence by Ghana's Excellence Awards Foundation. During the late 2000s, Aidoo served as visiting professor of Africana studies and creative writing at Brown University.

See also FICTION, ENGLISH-LANGUAGE, IN AFRICA; POETRY, AFRICAN.

BIBLIOGRAPHY

James, Adeola. *In Their Own Voices: African Women Writers Talk.* J. Currey, 1990.

Wilentz, Gay Alden. *Binding Cultures: Black Women Writers in Africa and the Diaspora.* Indiana University Press, 1992.

MARIAN AGUIAR

Akan

Cluster of ethnic groups living in southern Ghana and adjacent parts of Côte d'Ivoire and Togo.

The broad Akan grouping includes a number of separate ethnic groups. The Akan speak a group of closely related languages belonging to the Kwa branch of the Niger-Congo family. The Akan peoples share several cultural traits, but each has its own history and customs. In modern Ghana, the term Akan also refers to the country's most widely spoken indigenous language—also known as Twi—which is shared by the ASANTE, the FANTE, and several other Ghanaian peoples. However, the "Akan" language of

GHANA is but one of several languages in the larger Akan grouping. The main Akan ethnicities include the Akyem, Akwamu, Asante, Brong, Denkyira, Fante, Nzima, Sefwi, and Wassa of Ghana, and the BAULE and ANYI of CÔTE D'IVOIRE. Linguistic and archaeological evidence suggests that ancestors of the Akan have inhabited a heartland in south central Ghana for at least 2,000 years. However, migrants from the north, including MANDE merchants who arrived as early as the eleventh century, may have intermarried with the Akan and contributed to the development of Akan kingdoms.

The early Akan lived in agricultural villages raising yams, plantains in forest regions, and millet and sorghum in the north. Many Akan also hunted, worked metals such as iron and gold, and wove baskets and cloth. In ancient times, headmen governed rural villages, although some scholars say that even small units had queen mothers and kings who ruled with the assistance of a council of elders.

Traditionally, Akan societies trace descent, including inheritance, kinship ties, and succession, matrilineally, or through the mother's line, though spiritual attributes and certain offices may pass patrilineally, or through the father's line. All Akan societies comprise seven or eight matrilineal clans, or abusua. Patrilineal groupings, the ntoro, also control certain taboos and rituals. Traditionally, Akan peoples worship a supreme being, Nyame. His children or creations form a secondary group of lesser deities, abosom, which inhabit everyday objects. Priests derive their power from the third level of supernatural entities, the talismans.

During the fourteenth century, the Brong were the first Akan people to form a powerful kingdom, known as Bono. Bono grew rich by controlling the GOLD TRADE with the north. Bono introduced standard gold weights made of brass, later adopted by other Akan nations, for use in the gold trade. By 1500 trade in gold and nuts probably fostered the development of larger Akan kingdoms throughout the Akan heartland.

With the arrival of Portuguese on the coast during the late fifteenth century, Akan groups began to expand south toward the coast to trade directly with the Europeans. The period of major state formation, 1650 to 1750, also marked the rise of the slave trade. The Akwamu, Denkyira, and the Fante federation traded gold and slaves in exchange for guns and other products from the Europeans. However, it was the Asante who built the strongest Akan state, which dominated most of what is now Ghana from about 1700 until the British finally conquered it in 1900. The Baule ruled much of modern Côte d'Ivoire from about 1750 until the French conquest around 1900.

The British policy of indirect rule left power in the hands of Akan chiefs and lineage heads. For instance, the exiled Asante king was allowed to return in 1924. Christian missionaries arrived in greater numbers after the French and British imposed colonial rule over the Akan. Although many Akan today retain traditional beliefs, CHRISTIANITY is a major force in Akan society, especially in the south. Muslim influence is stronger in the north. Under colonial rule, gold extraction continued in Akan lands, but many Akan turned to the production of cash crops, especially cocoa, to purchase manufactured goods and meet colonial tax obligations.

A population report issued in 2007 puts the number of Akan peoples at more than eighteen million, almost half of Ghana's population, and one of the larger groupings in Côte d'Ivoire. They are primarily agriculturalists, farming cash crops such as cocoa and coffee along with subsistence crops such as yams and plantains. They have occupied prominent political offices in both countries. Ghana's first president, Kwame NKRUMAH, was an Akan of Nzima origin, and Côte d'Ivoire's independence leader, Félix HOUPHOUËT-BOIGNY, was a Baule.

See also COLONIAL RULE; LANGUAGES, AFRICAN: AN OVERVIEW; METALWORKING IN AFRICA.

DAVID P. JOHNSON, JR.

Akposo

Ethnic group of West Africa, also known as the Akposso.
The Akposo primarily inhabit central TOGO and adjacent eastern GHANA. They speak a Niger-Congo language and are believed to have been among the indigenous population of Togo before EWE speakers migrated into the area from the east. Approximately 184,000 people living in Togo consider themselves Akposo, though a few thousand also live elsewhere.

Aksum

Ancient kingdom that ruled parts of present-day Ethiopia and Eritrea from the first to the tenth century C.E.
"Pride of the entire universe and jewel of kings," Aksum ruled an ancient Ethiopian kingdom in a time remembered as a golden age of African civilization. This was true in a very literal sense: Aksumite kings issued a splendid gold coinage at a time when few other economies needed such a sophisticated currency or could have afforded it. The kings also marked their tombs with magnificent stone pillars, or stelae. The tallest of these stelae were the largest stone monuments erected in the ancient world, surpassing in height even the obelisks of the Egyptian pharaohs.

The site of Aksum offered access to important international trade routes, as well as to the basic essentials of water and agricultural land. The city rose to power by using wealth gained from the control of trade to conquer other peoples who lived on the Ethiopian plateau, as far as the seacoast in ERITREA. By the end of the first century C.E., when Aksum first appears in the historical record, the state was the most powerful in the region. The system of government was imperial, with the negusa nagast (the king of kings) ruling over a number of subordinate states whose rulers paid tribute. Royal inscriptions from the fourth century C.E. describe Aksumite campaigns against "rebels" in various parts of the country and across the Red Sea in South Arabia (present-day Yemen) as well. One Aksumite expedition conquered the Nubian kingdom of Meroe in present-day SUDAN. The titles of the kings indicate claims to rule over Saba and Himyar, two important Arabian kingdoms, as well as over the Beja, Kasu, and Noba in Africa. The last two names refer to Kush and NUBIA.

The inscriptions of the kings, their coinage, and the occasional mention of Aksum in Greek, Latin, and Arabic texts preserve only a limited amount of information. However, two kings stand out as exceptional. Scholars have often described Ezana, who ruled in the middle of the fourth century, as "the Constantine of Ethiopia" after his contemporary, the powerful Roman emperor who made Christianity the imperial religion. His inscriptions and coins record that he converted to Christianity from the traditional worship of the gods Astar, Beher, Meder, and Mahrem. One of his inscriptions refers to the Father, the Son, and the Holy Spirit, and during his reign, the Christian cross replaced the disk and crescent of the old religion. He was the first Christian king to employ the cross in this way, before even the emperors of Rome. The Latin church historian Rufinus corroborates the evidence of Ezana's coins and inscriptions by recording that the patriarch of ALEXANDRIA appointed the first Ethiopian metropolitan bishop at this time. There is no indication that Ezana or his successors ever returned to pre-Christian religions.

During the sixth century, the Aksumite king Kaleb led a military expedition to South Arabia to crush a Jewish king who had killed the Christian community at Najran. This event caused a sensation throughout the Christian world, and is consequently well documented. Kaleb defeated the Jewish king Dhu Nuwas and installed a viceroy, but after a short time an Aksumite named Abreha deposed the viceroy. Abreha began to govern Yemen in defiance of Kaleb and refused to pay tribute to the king of kings. In Sura 105 of the Qu'ran (Koran), there is an account of Abreha leading an expedition against Mecca in what is called "the Year of the Elephant," perhaps a reference to the use of African elephants in battle. Early Islamic historians also record that disciples of the Prophet, including his wife Umm Habiba, took refuge in Aksum when Muhammad was being persecuted in Arabia.

With the rise of Islamic power in Arabia during the seventh century, the kings of Aksum began to retreat from the Red Sea. There may also have been changes in climate, and the land around the city of Aksum may have been farmed too intensively to support its people, but once Arabians took control of the Red Sea trade, Aksum began to decline. Aksum suffered its final defeat at the hands of rebels during the tenth century.

In addition to the stelae and the coinage, accomplished styles of pottery making, ivory carving, and glassware production, and metalwork in gold, silver, bronze, and iron all attest to the skill of Aksumite craftsmen and the luxury and sophistication of their capital. The remains of palaces and royal tombs confirm the complete mastery of granite by Aksumite masons, whose decorative motifs were copied on the famous churches at LALIBELA.

See also ANCIENT AFRICAN CIVILIZATIONS; ETHIOPIA; ETHIOPIAN ORTHODOX CHURCH.

STUART MUNRO-HAY

Akuapem
Ethnic group of Ghana, also known as Akwapim.
The Akuapem inhabit primarily the eastern region of GHANA. They speak a Niger-Congo language and belong to the larger AKAN cultural and linguistic group. According to a 2004 population estimate, some 555,000 people consider themselves Akuapem.

Akunakuna
Ethnic group of West Africa.
The Akunakuna inhabit primarily the Cross River State of NIGERIA and western CAMEROON. They speak a Bantu language and are related to the EFIK and IBIBIO, also of Nigeria. Approximately 350,000 people consider themselves Akunakuna.

Akwamu
For a period of fifty years (1680–1730) the Akwamu polity, under the rule of the Abrade dynasty, was a powerful, forest-based political-military system. It was a product of the military revolution that swept across the forest hinterland of the Gold Coast in the seventeenth century. The revolution introduced mass conscription, new forms of military organization, new battlefield tactics and strategies, and a new technology (firearms). The imperial history of Akwamu can be conveniently divided into two periods.

MILITARY PERIOD
The imperial period began with the Akwamu conquest of the Great Accra kingdom, Akwamu's erstwhile overlord, and the destruction of its capital Great Accra. From the

1680s until 1710 Akwamu armies were engaged in military conquests and territorial expansion. Armies of musketeers, numbering up to 25,000 or more, were led by officers who carried such titles as owurafram (master of muskets) and obrafo (war hero). Akwamu rulers—Ansa Sasraku II (d. 1689), Ado (1689–1702), and Akwanno (1702–1725)—conducted successful campaigns over a wide area. Polities located on the eastern Gold Coast and the western Slave Coast and in their hinterlands came under their jurisdiction and suzerainty. From 1710 until 1730, the authority of the Akwamuhene, or king, extended along the coast for a distance of more than 200 miles and into the interior for more than one hundred miles. Imperial expansion was tied to a wealth accumulation regime based on the acquisition of territory, war booty, and the collection of tribute and other levies. The profits of long-distance trade were also an important revenue source.

Imperial Akwamu exercised authority over a heterogeneous population of Akan-, Adãnme-, Gã-, Guan-, and Ewe-speaking peoples. A late seventeenth-century Danish report mentions nine occupations: agriculture, fishing, salt making, hunting, crafts, animal husbandry, trade, priestly activities, and warfare. Between 1703 and 1730 ten to fifteen tribute-paying districts constituted Greater Akwamu. Each had an Akwamu governor, who was appointed by the king. Most governors lived in or near the capital, Nyanawase. Their duties included the collecting of tribute, taxes, gifts, and fines, the settling of disputes, the promotion of trade, and the maintenance of law and order.

The export of enslaved persons from Akwamu-dominated ports to the markets of the Americas assumed growing importance in the 1690s, its value being roughly equivalent to the export value of gold and ivory. The export of enslaved captives, debtors, and so on continued to increase substantially into the 1720s. Each of the European trading stations in the three main Accra ports—Little Accra (Crevecoeur Fort: Dutch), Osu (Christiansborg Castle: Danish), and Soko (James Fort: English)—paid a monthly ground-rent to the Akwamuhene and they were also obliged to send regular gifts to him, his court, and his high-ranking officeholders. Each fort had a chief broker, appointed by the king, who was also a senior Akwamu official. Between 1700 and 1726, the Danish, Dutch, and English trading companies established new trading stations along Akwamu-dominated coast. Cowrie shells began to circulate as a currency on a greater scale in the early eighteenth century, alongside gold, and Akwamu and its Accra ports played an important mercantile role in the Lower Guinea Coast's cowrie-gold currency zones.

Two late seventeenth-century descriptions provide information about the Akwamu heartland, which lay in the Middle Densu Valley basin. There, the capital and twenty-two large and small towns were located. Together they could mobilize around 7,000 musketeers for war. The capital was divided into several large wards, which were separated from each other by tree-lined, thirty-foot-wide streets. The principal street was one hundred and sixty feet wide and stretched for a distance of between seven and nine miles. It was lined with trees and houses along its entire length. The palace of the king was located in the center of the main street and the heir apparent's palace was situated about a mile away. Between the two was a complex of buildings: council buildings, the judicial court, stool houses, and the shrines of the state deities. The royal court was rich in gold and included six hundred officers and numerous soldiers. In the immediate environs of the capital were large royal plantations worked by unfree labor.

PARAMILITARY PERIOD

During this period territorial conquests ended and the dominant mode of wealth accumulation was linked to a royal credit system, judicial fines, and confiscation of property. Military predation and long distance trade ceased to be major sources of wealth for the ruling class. The royal court was the organizing center of this mode of appropriation. Between 1705 and 1710, Akwamuhene Akwanno created a special paramilitary unit, known as the sika den, which was responsible for collecting fines, apprehending debtors for nonpayment of their loans, and confiscating property, both within Akwamu's territorial limits and beyond. During the reign of Ansaku, or Akonno (1725–1730), the paramilitary unit confined its operations to Akwamu. Persons unable or unwilling to pay their fines and debtors who could not settle their debt obligations with royal creditors were sold at the European forts and factories. Consisting of "clever young men," as one source calls them, the royal sika den acquired a reputation of notoriety. Through the seizures and confiscations of the sika den, the akwamuhene and his principal men, mainly officials of the royal court, engaged in a substantial trade with the forts and factories. They also traded with merchants from the FANTE polity, one of the wealthiest and most powerful states on the Gold Coast. The collection of tribute and taxes continued; however, the social relations of trade changed. In the 1710s and 1720s Akwamu merchants were primarily engaged in the fish, salt, produce, and livestock trade and, compared to earlier decades, were less involved in the export slave, ivory, and gold trade. Merchants from the coastal Fante town of Anomabo acquired the right of free trade in Akwamu as a result of the 1715 treaty between the Nyanawase and Anomabo governments. From this time, they controlled a significant portion of Akwamu's export slave-gold trade.

INVASION

In 1728–1729 a rural and town revolt against the Akwamu government broke out. Initially, the rebels achieved military success, however, the Akwamu counteroffensive put them on the defensive and they were compelled to seek assistance from the rulers of the neighboring, inland Akyem kingdoms. The Akyem kings organized a broad political coalition of forces, drawn from much of the Gold Coast and its hinterland. The Akyem-led coalition invaded Akwamu in 1730, destroyed its capital, and occupied its heartland and western provinces. Remnants of the ruling dynasty and senior officeholders were able to flee to the eastern provinces where they established a smaller polity on the banks of the Volta River in the early 1730s.

See also GHANA; SALT TRADE.

BIBLIOGRAPHY

Ajyai, J. F. Ade, and Michael Crowder, eds. History of West Africa. Columbia University Press, 1985.

Anquandah, James, Rediscovering Ghana's Past. Longman Group Ltd., 1982.

Davidson, Basil, The Growth of African Civilization: A History of West Africa, 1000–1800. New ed. Longman Group Ltd., 1990.

Kea, Ray A. Settlements, Trade and Polities on the Seventeenth Century Gold Coast. The Johns Hopkins University Press, 1982.

Ogot, B. A., ed. General History of Africa V. Africa from the Sixteenth to the Eighteenth Century. University of California Press, 1992.

Ward, W. E. F. A History of Ghana. George Allen and Unwin Ltd., 1959.

Wilks, Ivor. Akwamu 1640–1750. A Study of the Rise and Fall of a West African Empire. Norwegian University of Science and Technology, 2001.

RAY A. KEA

Akyem

Ethnic group of Ghana; also known as Akem.

The Akyem primarily inhabit the eastern region of GHANA. They comprise three major subgroups: the Abuakwa, the Bosume, and the Kotoku. They speak a Niger-Congo language and belong to the AKAN cultural and linguistic group. Approximately one million people consider themselves Akyem.

Aladura Churches

Group of religious movements founded as independent African expressions of Christianity.

Aladura is a YORUBA word for "People of Prayer." The name describes an informal religious movement that began during the first half of the twentieth century in West Africa, particularly NIGERIA. The movement has grown steadily since. Aladura began mostly among members of mainline churches, such as the Anglican, Methodist, or Baptist churches. These members usually followed a charismatic man or woman (or both) who felt called to lead their members as prophets. Some of the earliest such movements or churches were the Church of the Lord (Aladura), Christ Apostolic Church, the Garrick Braide movement, and the Cherubim and Seraphim. The most popular and fastest growing of the Aladura churches in the 1990s included the Celestial Church of Christ and the Brotherhood of the Cross and Star, which, though established in Nigeria, grew to include churches in Europe and the United States. The members formed prayer groups (thus, the term people of prayer)—often during social or spiritual crises, such as epidemics or economic depressions. Josiah Ositelu belonged to the Anglican Church before founding the Church of the Lord (Aladura). After a series of visions, he came to believe that witches haunted him. A Christian prophet, with whom Ositelu went to study, helped him to exorcise the witches through prayer and fasting. His visions continued, however; Ositelu claimed to have experienced more than 10,000 in one nine-year period. In 1929 Ositelu joined the Faith Tabernacle, for which he began to preach. Ositelu's popularity and unorthodox practices—including his use of a secret script he said had been divinely revealed, and his claim that a list of divinely revealed names could cause miracles—led to a split between Ositelu and the leaders of the Faith Tabernacle. Like the Precious Stone Church, the Cherubim and Seraphim began as a prayer group among members of the Anglican Church. Moses Orimolade and Christiana Abiodun Akinsowon led the Cherubim and Seraphim. By 1928 the Cherubim and Seraphim was an independent church. It featured a rejection of witches and traditional Yoruba religious practices. In time, some of its members left to form their own churches. Aladura churches vary in size, but they are generally small local bodies. Some churches have fewer than one hundred members while others boast thousands of members. Also, because of their local nature, church organizations vary widely. They do not recognize a formal hierarchy. In addition, in most Aladura churches the authority lies with the founder. As a result, few have as well-defined or highly regimented doctrine as the missionary churches. Members generally see the founder as someone who has been divinely inspired or received divine information, most of it infallible. Aladura prophetic churches generally feature more creative worship than their missionary counterparts, and draw upon African religious traditions, such as African dance and the performance of African music on instruments such as drums, gongs, and flutes. Some use biblical references to support polygyny.

BIBLIOGRAPHY

Kalu, Ogbu, ed. *Christianity in West Africa: The Nigerian Story.* Daystar Press, 1978.

Peel, J. D. Y. *Aladura: A Religious Movement among the Yoruba.* Oxford University Press, 1968.

ROBERT FAY

Alassane, Mousstapha

1942–

Nigerois film director; one of the few African film directors to produce animated films.

Mousstapha Alassane, one of Niger's first filmmakers, excels in animation, a genre of film typically ignored in Africa. His work aims to preserve and revalue his African cultural heritage and to provide biting social commentary on Niger's postcolonial bourgeoisie.

Alassane was born in N'Jougou, Benin. He moved with his family to NIGER in 1953. While in primary school, he began to develop the film style he would later polish as an adult. Alassane entertained his relatives and friends with shadow shows and makeshift cartoons drawn on translucent wrappings and shown through a projector he built. Throughout his teenage years, he refined his animation technique and at the age of twenty, he produced two short animated films—*Le Piroguier* (The Canoe-Paddler) and *La Pileuse de mil* (Woman Pounding Millet). While working at the Institut Fondamental d'Afrique Noire, Alassane had the opportunity to show these films to French ethnologist and filmmaker Jean Rouche, who was so impressed with Alassane's work that he hired him. While working on Rouche's film crew, Alassane acquired the basic techniques of filmmaking and produced his first film, *Aouré* (1962), which won the Bronze Medal for short films at the 1962 Cannes Film Festival. Under Rouche's direction, Alassane enrolled in the training program at the National Film Board of Canada in Montréal in 1963.

After studying animation and hand-painting film in Montréal, Alassane returned to Niger and began work on a series of short animated works. Although animated films are often thought to be less "serious" than other forms of film, Alassane's productions reveal his struggle to create artistically—as well as socially and politically—sophisticated animation that provides contemporary social commentary by means of African folklore traditions. Alassane urges other African filmmakers to take up this struggle as well.

Two of his most popular animated films are *La Mort de Gandji* (1965; Gandji's Death) and *Bon voyage Sim* (1966), both satires of postcolonial politics in Niger. *La Mort de Gandji* criticizes the patronage system through a story of a king toad and his sycophantic courtesan toads. *Bon voyage Sim* mocks the pompousness of official state visits by contemporary African presidents.

In addition to animated work, Alassane has also produced a number of nonanimated fiction films. His first full-length feature film, *Le retour de l'aventurier* (1966; The Adventurer's Return), explored a concern common to many filmmakers in the mid-1960s—the role of Western cinema in the cultural alienation of African youth. Although the film was criticized for technical flaws, its plot was praised for its witty parody.

In 1972 Alassane produced *F.V.V.A. (Femmes, Villa, Voiture, Argent)* (Wives, Villa, Car, Money), a story of a young man, Ali, who changes from an honest but modest clerk to a flamboyant criminal. The film examines arranged marriages, the exploitative power of MARABOUTS (Islamic religious authorities), and the abuses of family solidarity, but its chief target is the greed and corruption of the postcolonial bourgeoisie.

Since 1972 Alassane has produced two other full-length feature films, *Toula ou le Génie des Eaux* (1974; Toula or the Water Spirit) and *Kankamba* (1982), in addition to several animated projects and documentaries for the Nigerian government. He has also focused on his own movie theater in Tahoua, Niger, and participated in activities of the Fédération Panafricaine des Cinéastes (FEPACI). In 2003 at FESPACO, Africa's largest film festival, Alassane's animated film *Kokoa* (2001) was recognized for its creativity.

See also FILM, AFRICAN.

ELIZABETH HEATH

Alcohol in Africa

Alcoholic beverages have played an important role in the religious, political, economic, and social history of sub-Saharan Africa. As early as the eleventh century C.E., historical records mention the presence of alcoholic drinks in the Sahelian kingdom of GHANA. Alcohol is a cultural artifact, a ritual object, an economic good, and a social marker. As a cultural artifact, its production, distribution, and consumption were circumscribed by rules in the precolonial era. Perceived as a sacred fluid in many cultures, it facilitated communication among the living, the ancestors, and the gods. Through the ritual of libation—the pouring of an alcoholic drink on the ground accompanied by prayer—alcohol played a key role in RITES OF PASSAGE AND TRANSITION and festivals. It was a valuable commodity, and its possession conferred status and wealth. Alcoholic drinks were coveted, and male elders monopolized the consumption of alcohol. As a marker of inclusion and exclusion, control over alcohol informed age, gender, and status conflicts. It is then not surprising that alcohol would become a major item in the trade among Europe, the Americas, and Africa. European missionary societies condemned this liquor traffic to Africa, and they hoped

European COLONIAL RULE would end the slave trade and liquor traffic. Indeed, colonial rule did eventually abolish the slave trade, but colonial governments found liquor revenues too valuable to abrogate the liquor trade. In postcolonial Africa, breweries and distilleries often have been the cornerstone of industrialization projects.

INDIGENOUS BEERS IN SUB-SAHARAN AFRICA

Indigenous beers have been prepared for generations in African societies from malted sorghum, millet, or maize. The resultant opaque beer was brownish in color with an alcoholic content of between 3 and 5 percent per volume. It had a heavy body because of the large quantities of particles and yeast suspended in it. Referred to as *dolo* or *pito* in parts of West Africa and as *utshwala* in SOUTH AFRICA, it was an important dietary component. Women brewed beer as an extension of domestic chores. A fermented banana drink was popular among BANTU speakers in East Africa. Palm wine has been obtained from the oil palm and the raffia palm in forested regions of sub-Saharan Africa and from the coconut palm along the African coast. Although young men may have tapped the wine, they had little control over its consumption.

The economic value of these cereals, bananas, and palm trees made them indices of wealth controlled by male elders. Among the Akan of Ghana, it was taboo for a woman to climb an oil palm tree. This appears to have been an attempt to ensure male control over the valuable oil palm. Among the Giriama of KENYA, wine and copra prepared from coconuts have been central to accumulation and social mobility in the twentieth century. All these indigenous beers have a short shelf life and must be consumed in a day or two. This meant that drinking was irregular, but large amounts may have been drunk at a time.

ALCOHOL, RITUAL, AND SOCIALIZATION IN PRECOLONIAL AFRICA

Alcohol's intoxicating quality seems to have infused it with some element of spirituality. Akan folktales about the first experience with palm wine emphasize the puzzling sequence of intoxication, deep slumber, and reawakening, comparing it with a journey to the land of the dead and back. Palm wine was used in naming, marriage, and funeral rites among the Akan. Akan perception of family and society encompassed the ancestors, the living, and those yet unborn. Any gathering important to the visible and invisible members of the family or community warranted the use of alcohol in libation. It bound the family or community and cemented their relations with the supernatural world of spirits. In preliterate African societies, the exchange of drinks and the pouring of libation served as a seal in legal transactions. Alcohol was also crucial to

social life, and the beer party was the spice of rural life. Among the Kofyar of NIGERIA, the beer-brewing cycle even determined the structure of the week. The meaning and importance of beer were central to the philosophy of the ITESO of UGANDA and Kenya.

The European liquor traffic was inserted into this cultural context. Before the transatlantic trade in the fifteenth century, distilled spirits were virtually unknown in subSaharan Africa. Dutch and German traders monopolized the trade in gin and schnapps, while New England traders brought rum to West Africa. Brandy and whiskey were popular among Europeans in West Africa but not with the West Africans. Among the Akan, rum was incorporated into ritual by the seventeenth century. The higher cost and potency of European liquor made it a valuable offering to the ancestors and gods. In southern Nigeria, cases of gin were in use as currency in the nineteenth century. Trade spirits were attractively packaged, had an unlimited shelf life, and were in great demand. Gin fulfilled the functions of money. Individuals and social groups that profited from the Euro-African trade viewed the consumption of European liquor as a mark of their social distinction. For young men who had migrated from villages to participate in European coastal commerce, liquor was the symbol of their new independence from the control of rural elders.

Mention must be made of the West African savanna belt and the SWAHILI COAST, where Islamic influence has been growing since the eighth century C.E. Islam proscribes alcohol for believers. European missionaries denounced the havoc European liquor wreaked on the "less-civilized" peoples of Africa. In the 1880s, the Native Races and Liquor Traffic United Committee would emerge among missionary interests in England to champion the abolition of liquor traffic to Africa.

ALCOHOL IN COLONIAL AFRICA

European trade extended the purview of European influence even before the formal onset of colonialism. Gifts of alcoholic drinks featured prominently in Euro-African protocol. European merchants used liquor and other European goods to induce some African chiefs to sign treaties of protection. These agreements would become important when the BERLIN CONFERENCE OF 1884–1885 required treaties as evidence of protectorate relations and the basis of colonial rule. European missionaries assumed that colonialism would end liquor traffic. Indeed, this assumption had motivated their support for colonial imposition. But colonies were designed to benefit colonial powers, and economic self-sufficiency was the minimum requirement of colonies. Liquor revenues and liquor legislation became crucial to colonial policy. In West Africa, where European settlement was minimal because of the mosquito and tsetse fly, colonial powers exploited the existing demand for liquor as a source of revenue. Import tariffs were imposed on liquor imports, enabling colonial governments to circumvent direct taxation in the early years of colonial rule. Between 1892 and 1903, import duties on liquor contributed over 55 percent of the total revenue of the colony of LAGOS. The corresponding figure for the Gold Coast between 1910 and 1913 was 38 percent. Missionary interests felt betrayed and refused to be pacified by the findings of the Liquor Commissions of Inquiry in Southern Nigeria (1909) and the Gold Coast (1930) that these colonies had no liquor problems. Sometimes in partnership with African chiefs, missionary interests forged temperance organizations in African colonies.

In East and South Africa, strict liquor laws regulated even the consumption of indigenous beer to protect white settlers. These liquor laws reflected the insecurities of early colonial rule and were repealed or modified—as in the case of Kenya—with the consolidation of colonial rule. The discovery in South Africa of diamonds in Kimberley in the 1870s and gold on the Witwatersrand in the 1880s, and the subsequent transformations in race relations, bequeathed a complex legacy to the social history of alcohol. Alcohol became entwined in labor issues, as it constituted bait in the attraction of migrant labor. The strategy posed problems, however, for a drinking labor force is potentially unproductive. Mine owners on the Witwatersrand successfully lobbied for prohibition at the beginning of this century, but the failure of prohibition foreshadowed the American experiment in the 1930s.

For migrant male workers in African cities, drinking was an important social activity. Male migrants often perceived migration as temporary and thus migrated as individuals. Bereft of family and kinship networks, they forged new social networks in the drinking bars and shebeens (neighborhood taverns) of South Africa. The indispensability of alcohol to town life encouraged municipalities in South Africa to establish beer halls for migrant workers. The proceeds would finance APARTHEID. Migrant labor weakened rural economies, making rural families dependent on remittances from migrant workers. The brunt of rural production fell on women, and overburdened widows, divorcees, and abandoned wives gradually made their way into the towns. Deprived of economic opportunities in the male-oriented colonial economy, women commercialized beer brewing and inserted an old domestic chore into the urban economy.

INTERNATIONAL LIQUOR CONVENTIONS AND AFRICA

Missionary pressure was partly responsible for securing the implementation of international liquor conventions to regulate the European liquor traffic to Africa. In 1890 an international convention in Brussels prohibited European liquor from areas in Africa without a previous history of liquor consumption. A wide belt in the interior of Africa, between latitudes 20 degrees north and 22 degrees south, was subject to this potential ban on European liquor. The next significant convention was passed at Saint Germain-en-Laye (France) in September 1919. This convention banned the traffic in "trade spirits" in Africa, defined loosely as cheap spirits imported clearly for African consumption. An import duty of 800 francs (about 80 pounds sterling in the early 1920s) was imposed on every hectoliter (about 22 gallons) of pure alcohol, and the distillation of spirits was explicitly forbidden in colonial Africa. These stipulations would come under nationalist attack during the general assault on colonial rule.

ALCOHOL AND NATIONALIST POLITICS

Liquor revenues and liquor legislation became contested arenas as African nationalists challenged the legitimacy of colonial rule from the 1930s on. To criticize liquor revenue was to assail the edifice of colonial rule. Liquor legislation, and colonial law in general, underscored the loss of African independence. The emergence of popular culture in African towns in the early twentieth century—drinking bars, dance bands, popular music, comic opera, "dressing up," soccer, romance—elevated the relevance of alcohol. Popular culture provided an antiestablishment ideology, and drinking bars in particular became the forum for political discussion. In southern Rhodesia (present-day ZIMBABWE), educated Africans agitated for the repeal of legislation that forbade European wine and spirits to Africans. Decolonization, and the introduction of general elections through universal adult suffrage, emphasized the importance of popular culture, as the African political elite needed mass support. Politicians promised to abolish restrictive liquor legislation. Political parties adopted specific brands of beer and extended patronage to particular drinking establishments. It may have sounded incongruous on the eve of independence for African politicians to be discussing access to alcohol, but alcohol was central to the culture of power in African societies, and it could not be disassociated from the processes of colonization and decolonization.

ALCOHOL IN INDEPENDENT AFRICA

Independent African governments quickly came to appreciate the value of alcohol revenues and the use of alcohol as a form of social control. Independence was achieved mostly in the 1950s and 1960s, and every African country yearned to modernize its economy. Breweries and distilleries would be part of this endeavor. Corporate Western capital entered the southern African market, developing the sorghum beer technology of South Africa for mass manufacture in the subregion. In West Africa, international giants such as Heineken, Holstein, and Guinness have established breweries and partnerships in Ghana, Nigeria, and CAMEROON. Dividends, excise duties, and sales taxes from the alcohol industry contributed to government coffers. The importance of the alcohol industry increased for African governments as world market prices for African exports—unprocessed cash crops and minerals—declined in the decades after independence. The *Washington Post* reported on July 14, 1991, that alcohol generated between 7 and 15 percent of government revenue in many Third World countries, including Kenya, TANZANIA, and Zimbabwe.

As dictatorial governments became the norm and economies declined in Africa in the 1970s and 1980s, governments ensured an abundance of alcoholic drinks internally to distract attention from political and economic failure and to divide the nation by gender and class conflicts. South African youth attacked beer halls during the SOWETO riots of 1976 because, in their view, the elders, with their alcohol-soaked minds, had become politically quiescent, and the proceeds from the beer halls built the migrant-labor hostels that perpetuated apartheid. As ZAMBIA's economy declined with the collapse of the price for copper, the trucks that delivered beer became the major symbol of government presence in some rural areas. In 1980 the government of Kenneth KAUNDA admitted the existence of an alcohol problem in Zambia, and a program was implemented in conjunction with the World Health Organization to redress the situation. For many independent African governments, the challenge for the twenty-first century is to find a balance between the economic desirability of alcohol revenues and the social costs of alcoholism.

Alcohol's multiple uses, its ability to bridge the gap between the physical and supernatural worlds, and its place in the culture of power explains its endurance over the centuries of Africa's history. In contemporary Africa, old uses and meanings of alcohol persist in new contexts. A wealthy Akan would still consider the two bottles of schnapps as essential to his daughter's marriage rites, but would specify that they be J. H. Henkes (imported from Holland) and not a local manufacture. The presence of the youth in drinking bars also underscores the changing face of alcohol.

See also ISLAM IN AFRICA; MARRIAGE, AFRICAN CUSTOMS OF; SAHEL.

BIBLIOGRAPHY

Akyeampong, Emmanuel. *Drink, Power, and Cultural Change: A Social History of Alcohol in Ghana, c.1800 to Recent Times.* Heinemann, 1996.

Colson, Elizabeth, and Thayer Scudder. *For Prayer and Profit: The Ritual, Economic, and Social Importance of Beer in the Gwembe District, Zambia, 1950—1982.* Stanford University Press, 1988.

Crush, Jonathan, and Charles Ambler, eds. *Liquor and Labor in Southern Africa.* Ohio University Press, 1992.

Pan, Lynn. *Alcohol in Colonial Africa.* Scandinavian Institute of African Studies, 1975.

Parkin, David J. *Palms, Wine, and Witnesses: Public Spirit and Private Gain in an African Community.* Waveland Press, 1994.

EMMANUEL AKYEAMPONG

Alexandria, Egypt

The main port and second-largest city in Egypt.

Occupying more than 40 kilometers (about 25 miles) of the NILE Delta's western edge on the Mediterranean Sea, the city of Alexandria is one of modern EGYPT's most important economic and industrial centers. A 2006 census put the city's population at 4.1 million. Now overshadowed by the Egyptian capital of CAIRO, 183 kilometers (114 miles) away, Alexandria dates back more than 2,000 years, and was once considered the Western world's greatest city. Intending it to be a naval base and the capital of his Egyptian province, Alexander the Great founded Alexandria in 332 B.C.E. He entrusted its planning and construction to his personal architect, Dinocrates, and he left Egypt under the command of a general named Ptolemy Soter. But Alexander never saw his city completed, and when he died in 323 B.C.E., his empire disintegrated.

Ptolemy Soter built an empire based at Alexandria, and under his descendants, the Greek-speaking Ptolemies, the city reached what many consider to be its golden age. A network of canals linking it to the Nile and the Red Sea made the city a major commercial center. It was also a center of scholarship and science, boasting such residents as Euclid, Archimedes, Plotinus, and Ptolemy and Eratosthenes, who studied at the Mouseion, a center of higher learning. Some believe that Jewish scholars translated the Hebrew Bible into Greek in Alexandria. The city's famous library had the largest collection in the ancient world.

The Roman Empire gained control of the city in 30 B.C.E. and Alexandria became the capital of the Roman province of Egypt. Under Roman rule, Alexandria became important to the development of CHRISTIANITY. Saint Mark, the attributed author of the second canonic Christian Gospel, is said to have preached in Alexandria in the mid-first century C.E. The city also played a key role in theological debates. Many Alexandrians embraced Monophysite Christianity, the doctrine that Jesus had a single divine nature. The Western Church (including the forerunners of the present-day Eastern Orthodox, Catholic, and Protestant Churches) rejected this doctrine and insisted on the dual human and divine nature of Jesus at the Council of Chalcedon in 451 C.E. Alexandrians and other Egyptian Christians (along with the Christians of ETHIOPIA) subsequently broke with the Western Church to form the Coptic Orthodox Church, still a substantial minority in modern Egypt.

Alexandria suffered a number of setbacks under Roman rule. The Romans massacred the city's Jewish population in 116 C.E. and its male population in 215 C.E. for opposing Roman rule. In the fourth century, Constantinople, the new capital of the Eastern Roman Empire (later known as the Byzantine Empire), eclipsed Alexandria as the political, economic, and cultural center of the eastern Mediterranean.

The decline of the Byzantine Empire, which had succeeded Rome in Egypt, left Alexandria vulnerable to the Arabs, who met no opposition when they sacked the city during the 640s. The Arabs established their Egyptian capital at al-Fustat, today a part of Cairo. Alexandria remained important as a naval base and commercial center, especially for the lucrative spice trade, which the Egyptians dominated until the sixteenth century, when Europeans discovered a route to Asia around southern Africa. After the Ottoman Turks took control of Egypt in 1517, Alexandria's importance dwindled further. The canal linking it with the Nile filled with silt, and the city became only a minor port.

In 1805, as part of his effort to modernize Egypt, Pasha Muhammad 'Ali ordered the al-Mahmudiyah Canal built to restore the city's access to the Nile. Cotton became a principal export and source of wealth, particularly during the cotton shortage caused by the United States Civil War in the 1860s. The opening of the SUEZ CANAL in 1869 furthered Alexandria's prosperity, but also attracted greater interest in the region from British colonialists. After the British bombarded Alexandria in 1882, the city surrendered to British forces; thus began the British occupation of Egypt.

Although the city never recaptured the cultural luster it once had, it remains a center of cultural significance. The opening of the Bibliotheca Alexandria in 2002 and the Alexandria National Museum in 2003 attracted international attention. Alexandria has also remained an important commercial center. The city now accounts for one-third of Egypt's industrial output. Its economic activities include banking, shipping, warehousing, and textile manufacturing. The majority of Egypt's foreign trade travels through Alexandria, particularly its modern Western port, including all cotton and oil exports. The city is also Egypt's most cosmopolitan, with large communities of expatriates from European and other Middle Eastern countries.

See also ALEXANDRIA AND GRECIAN AFRICA: AN INTERPRETATION; CHRISTIANITY, AFRICAN: AN OVERVIEW; ISLAM IN AFRICA; JEWISH COMMUNITIES IN NORTH AFRICA; ROMAN AFRICA: AN INTERPRETATION.

BIBLIOGRAPHY

Forster, E. M. *Alexandria: A History and a Guide.* Overlook Press, 1974.

Steen, Gareth L., ed. *Alexandria: The Site and the History.* New York University Press, 1993.

ROBERT FAY

Alexandria and Grecian Africa: An Interpretation
On the city of the Ptolemies and the fate of their Egyptian empire.

Alexandria flourished for more than a thousand years as the intellectual and cultural center and the greatest city of the ancient Mediterranean world. It was the prime conduit for the passage of African images and ideas into Europe and European images and ideas into Africa. This article deals primarily with the role of Alexandria in the development of Grecian Africa in ancient times. (For a history of the city up to modern times, see the entry on ALEXANDRIA.)

ANCIENT EGYPT

For the early Greeks, Egypt was the oldest, the wisest, and the richest of all nations. The Greeks were new to civilization; when they first visited Egypt they discovered a civilization that was already more than 2,000 years old. Temples and monuments loomed in the desert, their origins lost in the mists of time. The Great Sphinx looked down upon the newcomers with its benign, unfathomable gaze, as it had for twenty centuries or more. Confronted by the splendors of the Egyptian past, Greeks like the historian Herodotus (who visited Egypt in the middle of the fifth century B.C.E.) were overcome with a kind of religious awe.

Egyptian civilization was not only the oldest in the world, it was also astonishingly stable, at least when compared to every other nation known to the early Greeks. The concept of ma'at, or social order, ruled every aspect of Egyptian life. Greeks were iconoclasts; they constantly tested their laws and traditions, always seeking improvement, or at least novelty. Egyptians clung to their unimaginably ancient traditions; in their eyes, change was always dangerous and never desirable, as it was to the Greeks, for its own sake.

The agricultural economy of Egypt was based on the annual floods of their great river. Each year, in late summer, the river rose, bringing with it a flux of mud and silt that spread over the lands of the **Nile** Delta like a blanket of rich

ANCIENT EGYPT. Bas reliefs depict the Sobek and Ptolemy VI Philometor on the Temple of Sobek and Haroeris built at Kom Ombo by the Ptolemies. (*Giraudon/Bridgeman Art Library International Ltd.*)

fertilizer. Farmers planted their fields, and the harvest was nearly always bountiful. A portion of the wealth brought by the river went to the king, or pharaoh, and to the priests who supported him and interpreted his will and that of the gods. But almost always there was enough for all, and over the centuries the national wealth had also become unimaginable.

For more than two millennia, from about 3500 to about 1500 B.C.E., Egypt was content with the unchanging existence it had chosen. In the second millennium B.C.E. it began to reach out, north into Palestine, Lebanon, and Syria, east into Arabia, south into NUBIA and present-day SUDAN. During the fifteenth century B.C.E., under Thutmose III, an Egyptian empire expanded over most of northeastern Africa and much of the Near East as well. Inevitably, these aggressive moves provoked a response. Slowly at first and then more rapidly, the nation was forced back within its ancient borders. A time of troubles ensued, with frequent revolts and rival claimants to the throne. Always there was the threat of Persia and other Asiatic powers. Vast wealth

and innumerable artistic treasures remained, but when Alexander arrived with his army in 330 B.C.E. he was able to conquer the Old Kingdom without a battle. He was proclaimed pharaoh and king, and as a symbol of his triumph, in 332 B.C.E., he established a new city near the west branch of the Nile Delta and named it after himself.

ALEXANDER THE GREAT

Alexander was born in 365 B.C.E. in a small country in northern Greece called Macedonia, of which his father, Philip, was the king. From ages thirteen to sixteen, the philosopher Aristotle, who was brought from Athens by Philip, tutored him. Alexander was more interested in warfare than in philosophy. Philip was assassinated in 336 B.C.E., and the Macedonian nobles and army accepted Alexander as their new king.

Philip had defeated a large force of allied Greek city-states before his death; now Alexander set about confirming Macedonian power in Greece. This took less than two years, whereupon he embarked on the adventure he had dreamed of since a child, namely, the conquest of Greece's perennial enemy, the Persian Empire. By now, Persia was the largest and richest nation in the world; its military prowess was legendary, its wealth almost mythical, its size and population many times greater than Greece, to say nothing of little Macedonia. Undaunted, Alexander set out on the Persian expedition in the spring of 334 B.C.E. with an army of 30,000 men and 5,000 cavalry, plus at least an equal number of surveyors, engineers, architects, scientists, court officials, historians, and of course, women. He let it be known that he intended to conquer not only Persia but the entire world.

He headed east, stopped at Troy to pay his respects to Achilles, and then turned south along the eastern coast of the Mediterranean Sea, defeating every Persian and other army that stood in his way. In Gordium, a city in Asia Minor, he was shown a famous knot that no one had ever untied; the man who could untie it, he was told, was fated to be the ruler of Asia. Alexander said nothing but drew his sword and cut the Gordian knot in twain. Within three years he was the undisputed lord of Asia, having conquered all of Persia and having been acclaimed as the Great King. He was then twenty-five years old.

Alexander founded half a dozen Alexandrias in various parts of Asia and India, but the Egyptian city was always his favorite. Choosing the site carefully, he endowed the new town with riches gleaned from his victories. He departed after two years to complete his conquest of the entire world as he knew it, but it seems he always intended to return. He did so, but only after his death, which occurred in Babylon in his thirty-third year. His body was carried to Alexandria and buried in a coffin of solid gold that has long been sought but never found.

THE PTOLEMIES

After his death, Alexander's vast empire, which he had hoped to unify and make permanent, was soon broken up and shared among his generals. One of the most capable of these was Ptolemy Soter, who had been left in charge of the Egyptian city. Ptolemy, who founded a dynasty that bore his name, was a man of parts. A brilliant military strategist and a cunning politician (cunning being an indispensable virtue of the times), he was also deeply curious and a true Greek, tolerant of new ideas.

Eleven different Ptolemies in the direct line ruled Egypt from the death of Alexander to the conquest of the country by Rome, in 30 B.C.E., but of these only the first three, Ptolemy I Soter (ruled 323–282 B.C.E.), Ptolemy II Philadelphus (282–246 B.C.E.), and Ptolemy III Euergetes (246–221 B.C.E.), were enlightened and effective monarchs. Father, son, and grandson, they ruled their city for a difficult one hundred years, maintaining it as the center of a commercial and cultural sphere of influence extending from the Straits of Gibraltar to the shores of India.

The ups and downs of Egyptian political and military power during this period are too complex to discuss here; in any case, the achievements of the first Ptolemies in other realms were more important and enduring. At the head of these were two great institutions. Intended to rival and surpass Plato's Academy and Aristotle's Lyceum at Athens, the Mouseion (or Museum) was founded around 300 B.C.E. as a kind of research university and institute for advanced study. It occupied a large site near the king's palace on which were erected a number of structures, connected to one another by colonnades winding among beautiful gardens, each of which was devoted to the study of a different branch of knowledge. A faculty of experts in every field was paid by the king (later by the Roman emperors), who also funded scholarships that brought prominent poets, historians, and scientists from all over the Hellenic world to Alexandria, which soon became universally recognized as the place to live and work.

Among the famous scholars who studied and wrote in Alexandria's Mouseion during those halcyon years were Euclid, Archimedes, Aristarchus the astronomer, and Hipparchus, all famous mathematicians and physicists, and, in later years, Strabo the geographer, and Ptolemy (not a member of the royal family) the astronomer. Ptolemy's geocentric theory of the universe prevailed for over 1,000 years before it was displaced by the heliocentric theory of Copernicus, Galileo, and Newton. (Ironically, Aristarchus the astronomer, while at Alexandria, had also proposed a heliocentric theory.)

Among the poets were Callimachus and Theocritus. The former was, after Homer, the most oft-cited poet of the later classical world. The latter had even greater influence, for his delicate, lovely verses about nature and country things were the foundation of the pastoral school of poetry, among whose practitioners were Virgil, Milton, Wordsworth, and Robert Frost, as well as a host of others.

The other renowned Ptolemaic institution was a library, the largest in the ancient world and one of the most important in history. Founded by Ptolemy I Soter as part of the Mouseion, it provided employment as well as a place to work for many scholars. At its most extensive, around the time of Christ, it was said to contain more than 500,000 volumes. Tragically, this magnificent source of knowledge and scholarship did not survive the tumultuous years of the early first millennium C.E. Often desecrated, the great library of Alexandria was finally burned toward the end of the third century C.E.; nothing is known definitely to have survived. Not a single classical scholar of the last five hundred years has failed to bemoan this terrible loss, perhaps the greatest in Western intellectual history.

The Ptolemies were Greeks; they spoke, read, and wrote Greek and looked to the land of their ancestors as the ultimate source of scientific and artistic ideas. But they were also Egyptians, and as such, also Africans. Ptolemy I Soter was aware of the need to be, or at least to seem to be, Egyptian, especially in religion, and he established a new cult of the god Sarapis that combined Greek and Egyptian religious elements. Based in the ancient Egyptian capital city of Memphis, the cult spread all over the Mediterranean world and influenced Greek religious practices in Athens and other cities.

CLEOPATRA AND ANTONY

Julius Caesar was assassinated in the Roman Senate on the Ides of March (March 15) in the year 44 B.C.E. After Caesar's death the fierce final phase ensued to the civil war that had been brewing for nearly a century. The two main factions were led by Octavian, named Caesar's successor in his will, and Mark Antony, who had been the dead man's closest associate. Octavian was a brilliant, handsome, and ruthlessly cold young man; he was eighteen when Caesar died. Antony was a violent and passionate man of thirty-six who was adored by his soldiers and by many women.

One woman adored him more than any other, and he adored her with a passion that endured until their deaths. She was CLEOPATRA, queen of Egypt, who had seduced Caesar when he had visited her country a few years before and now undertook to seduce the man she assumed would

CLEOPATRA'S NEEDLE. Soaring above its humble surroundings, the so-called Cleopatra's Needle was photographed between 1856 and 1860. (*Prints and Photographs Division, Library of Congress*)

succeed him. How she did so is, thanks to Plutarch and Shakespeare, the stuff of legend. In Shakespeare's play (act 2, scene 2), Enobarbus, Antony's lieutenant, tells his friend Agrippa how "when she first met Mark Antony, she pursed up his heart, upon the river of Cydnus." Agrippa is astounded by the splendor of this famous meeting; nevertheless, he declares, Antony must leave Cleopatra if he is to succeed. Enobarbus replies:

> Never; he will not. Age cannot wither her, nor custom stale
> Her infinite variety. Other women cloy
> The appetites they feed, but she makes hungry
> Where most she satisfies. (II, ii, 239)

And so it was. Antony divorced his wife (who happened to be Octavian's sister) to marry Cleopatra. Spending too little time in Rome, he spent too much in Alexandria. He was generous and open, but his gifts were interpreted by the calculating Octavian as the excesses of a wastrel and a slave to love. Such a man, Octavian whispered, was not worthy to be the ruler of all Rome.

In the end, love and spectacle could not prevail over hard, practical politics. Too many Romans, even Antony's followers, believed Octavian was right. The last battle of the long civil war was fought at Actium, on the coast of Greece. The combined fleets of Antony and Cleopatra were soundly beaten and the lovers fled to Alexandria, where,

abandoned and alone, they committed suicide. Octavian, henceforth unopposed and supported by all the Roman armies, became the man we know as Augustus, the first Roman emperor.

WHAT IF ANTONY AND CLEOPATRA HAD WON THE BATTLE OF ACTIUM?

It's a good question, although there can be no certain answer. Paris and London are monopole cities; they are the artistic, intellectual, financial, and political capitals of their countries. Italy today has two capitals: Milan for business and finance, Rome for political administration. The artistic and financial capital of the United States is New York, while the national government is based in Washington, D.C. Both systems work, though in different ways.

After Actium, Alexandria continued for centuries as the center of artistic and intellectual life of the Mediterranean, and one of the most important financial centers as well. But it had no political power beyond its minor role as the capital of the Roman province of Egypt. Lacking power, it was spared the political tumult that made life in Rome so dangerous. At the same time, Alexandria was starved for support, although the emperors made efforts to support the Mouseion and its library. Augustus was a Roman and a northern Italian; he had little interest in Africa. Alexandria continued to be a conduit for African products, men, and ideas under his rule, but the stream did not flow so richly as it had under the Ptolemies.

Mark Antony was a Roman, but he was the son and grandson of soldiers and had lived all over the world. His first allegiance was probably to Greece, not Rome; he tried for years to institute a Greco-Roman alliance that would include Egypt in an alliance of countries of the eastern Mediterranean. And he loved Cleopatra.

Augustus proclaimed, after spending millions of his people's money, that he had "found Rome brick and left it marble." The diversion of revenues from outlying provinces had made this possible. If Antony had won, the funds that rebuilt Rome might have rebuilt the ancient cities of the Nile and made of Alexandria a glittering and better fortified imperial capital that might, because of its position on the African coast, have held off the barbarian invasions that inaugurated the Dark Ages.

Antony, Greek in spirit, was curious about new ideas. As emperor, he would have sought them out, even in that relatively unknown world beyond and below the Sahara. Under Augustus, the Roman Empire tended steadily northwest and east. Under Antony, guided by Cleopatra, it could have moved south and west. That difference would have changed almost everything.

As one example of what might have happened, note that slavery was rare in Egypt; it was endemic in Italy and Greece. The classical world was founded on the economic institution of slavery, without which, most Romans agreed, society could not endure. Aristotle had observed that if machines could do the work of men, then slaves would not be needed. A certain Greek, Hero of Alexandria, invented the steam engine, but the Augustans ignored its possibilities; the Antonians might have seen how to exploit it to replace slave labor. Taking these and other things into account, is it possible that Antony and Cleopatra, if they had won, might have established another kind of empire, based on the ideas of human equality instead of inequality, and freedom instead of slavery? And if so, might the Roman Empire, instead of being destroyed by Christianity (as Gibbon wrote), have made an early peace with it that changed not only the empire but Christianity as well?

CLEOPATRAS NOSE

These speculations may seem absurd, or at the least misguided and illegitimate. Indeed, there is some truth in that judgment. Whatever happened in the past was the result of a long line of causes, not just one, and thus was more or less inevitable; at any rate, a single event could not be said to have determined the entire future. Thus the great changes that were occurring around the end of the first millennium B.C.E.—the collapse of the Roman Republic and its replacement by something like the Roman Empire, the advent of Christianity, and, later, the gradual movement of the center of Western civilization from the shores of the Mediterranean north and west, to Germany, to France, to Great Britain (to use the modern names for those parts of Europe)—were probably going to occur anyway, whatever the outcome of a single battle.

We may remember, however, that famous remark of a great philosopher, Blaise Pascal, a remark that has teased schoolboys, if not professional historians, for three hundred years. "Cleopatra's nose," he wrote, "if it had been shorter, the whole course of history would have changed." Presumably, if her nose had been shorter, she would not have been so beautiful, Mark Antony would not have fallen in love with her, he and Octavian would have reached some sort of reconciliation, and . . .

We should remember something else. History is always written by the winners. The bad character of Mark Antony, the irresponsibility of Cleopatra, are at least in part the creation of the Augustans. They had good reason to sully the reputations of their defeated foes, and they did so.

Perhaps it is not misguided or illegitimate, then, to imagine a past that was different than it actually was and a present that is consequently different from what it actually is. At the least, if Antony and Cleopatra had won, the role played by Africa in the history of the last 2,000 years would have been different. And the world we live in might be a good deal better than it is.

See also EGYPT, ANCIENT KINGDOM OF.

CHARLES VAN DOREN

Algeria

Republic of western North Africa; bounded on the north by the Mediterranean Sea; on the east by Tunisia and Libya; on the south by Niger, Mali, and Mauritania; and on the west by Morocco.

To many outside observers, Algeria has been a preeminent symbol of postcolonial independence, a nation that waged a highly visible war against a European colonial power, France, in the mid-twentieth century, and won an independent secular state. The electoral success during the early 1990s of the Islamic Salvation Front (FIS), considered by many to be an Islamic fundamentalist group, was all the more startling. This apparent inconsistency revealed a complexity that stems from the fact that Algeria spans the traditions of the BERBER, Arab, and European worlds. For the people of Algeria, Islam has been central to the culture

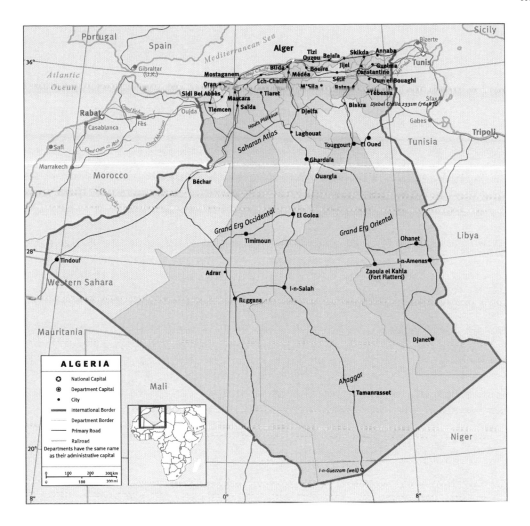

since the seventh century. Within its history are many other strands as well, including the uneasy integration of Berber-dominated territories, the experience of women at the forefront of the independence struggle, the socialist strategies of the newly independent state, and the capitalist vision of economic development that supplanted it.

EARLY HISTORY

The Berber people, who call themselves Imazighen, or "free men," historically have made up the majority of the population in the area that later became Algeria. From 208 to 148 B.C.E. the North African coastal kingdom Numidia encompassed portions of this region. After the destruction of CARTHAGE (146 B.C.E.), Rome colonized the territory, transforming the vassal-state into a major provider of grain for the empire and bringing Christianity to parts of the region. Later conquerors included the Vandals in the fifth century and a coastal presence of the Byzantine Empire in the sixth century. Certain areas, however, historically

remained under independent Berber confederacies, particularly the Aurès and Kabylia, maintaining a distinct cultural status within the region that would become Algeria.

Islam spread through North Africa in the seventh century, brought at first by raids and later by the immigration of Arabs to the area of northwest Africa known as the Maghreb, or "the land of the setting sun." The Berber population gradually converted to Islam, despite militant resistance in strongholds of Berber political rule. The extent to which the Berber culture and language was Arabized during this time in Algeria is a question still debated by historians. A series of Islamic dynasties spread over the Maghreb for the next few centuries, encompassing the area of present-day Algeria. The rule of the Berber Dynasty ALMOHADS brought the region into a prosperous alliance with the rest of the Maghreb and Muslim Spain. These dynasties marked the region culturally as well as politically, linking it to a heterogeneous Islamic world and facilitating the influx of peoples displaced by the Christian reconquest, including the Andalusian Muslims and Jews. Cities such as Constantine, TLEMCEN, Annaba (Bône), Bejaïa (Bouie), and ALGIERS flourished as centers of learning and commerce.

The sixteenth century brought Spain to North Africa in a military campaign that was both a crusade against Muslim power in North Africa and an attempt to dominate the Mediterranean region. The Algerian coastal cities, including Algiers and Oran, were taken as strategic locations for the lucrative occupations of sea trade and piracy. After the death of the Spanish king, Ferdinand of Castile, in 1516, the Turkish "Barbarossa" brothers Aruj and KHAYR AD-DIN intervened. They ostensibly put the region under the protection of an Islamic power—the Ottoman sultan—but also served their own ambitions for trade and piracy in the Mediterranean region. Some scholars mark this intervention as the origin of Algeria as a political entity.

After the Spanish withdrew in 1541, Algeria entered the period known as the Regency. Historians have described the political state as an "Algerian Ottoman Republic," operating autonomously despite official allegiance to the Ottoman Empire. With a fertile countryside, thriving artisan trade communities, and an economy enriched by piracy, the area around Algiers developed over the next few centuries into a viable cosmopolitan center that was highly attractive to the French.

FRENCH COLONIZATION

By the nineteenth century, France was trading extensively with merchants in the Algiers region, but the Bourbon government's refusal to honor a debt owed to an Algerian exporting firm signaled a shift toward more confrontational relations. In 1827 French king Charles X ordered a blockade, ostensibly because an Algerian official slapped the French consul with a flywhisk, but also to display his military clout in a time of waning French support for his regime. On June 14, 1830, General Louis de Bourmont landed at Sidi Fredj, west of Algiers. Within a month, the French had captured Algiers, defeating Turkish and allied Berber forces. Charles's successor, Louis-Philippe, saw in colonization an opportunity to capture new markets and strategic military sites as well as to expand the reach of French civilization. He helped secure the French position by invading Constantine in 1837.

The population actively and persistently resisted French colonial occupation. Islam provided one nexus for an anti-colonial alliance. One of the most prominent early anti-colonial leaders was ABD AL-QADIR, who organized an Islamic state in the west that at one point controlled two-thirds of Algeria's inhabited land. Considered a strategic genius, Abd al-Qadir consolidated his position as leader of

Berber confederacies and attempted to gain diplomatic recognition from England and Spain. France did grant the influential leader territorial autonomy by signing the Treaty of Tafna in 1837. But when land ambitions conflicted, the French army, under a new leader, General Bugeaud, used massacres and "scorched earth" tactics—burning surrendering enemies alive and systematically destroying Algerian villages, crops, livestock, and forests—to defeat Abd al-Qadir ten years later. Some historians have argued that Abd al-Qadir planted the first seeds of nationalism by uniting the Berbers and Arabs against "infidel" invaders.

The conquest was completed when the French defeated the independent Berber confederacies in the Kabylia in 1857. The French military paved the way for an influx of European settlers, a population originally only half French and mostly poor. The interests of the settlers and the military-dominated administration were not always harmonious. The European settlers' political power grew as their population swelled, from 10,000 settlers in 1834 to more than one million shortly before independence in 1962. They benefited from the confiscation of Algerian land, especially after the unsuccessful Kabylia Revolt in 1871. From 1830 to 1940, more than eight million acres were taken over. During this period settlers campaigned for civilian rule and then colonial autonomy and even waged an insurrection in 1898. Two years later, the settlers secured nominal administrative and financial autonomy from France, but maintained a governor general office.

As settlers took over the countryside, the region's peasant-based agrarian economy shifted to settler-owned, large-scale agricultural and industrial enterprises. Large expanses of the cereal producing lands were transformed into vineyards for wine export. The effects were devastating for the indigenous population: warfare, famine, and a series of plagues reduced a population of three million to one million within forty years of the conquest. The traditional economy was no longer viable. With war and poverty undermining original tribal relationships, Algerians turned to a vision of national resistance to colonization.

STRUGGLE FOR NATIONAL INDEPENDENCE

During the early twentieth century, Algerian intellectuals spoke out against the inequity of the colonial relationship and proposed reforms to equalize French and Muslim status. Those who protested French policies included the Young Algerians, or évolués, educated at European universities, and Algerians holding official positions, such as Emir Khalid, a captain in the Algerian army and grandson of Abd al-Kadir. Algerian sacrifices during World War I had won them a degree of respect in France, and following the war Premier Georges Clemenceau introduced measures to ensure full citizenship for Muslims. Settler groups violently opposed these measures, creating a rift in the alliance between the settler population and its military and civil foundation, the colonial government. Settler opposition to reform created a fissure between France and European Algerians that would tear open during the struggle for Algerian independence.

As settlers resisted early reform efforts and France capitulated, more of the indigenous population turned toward a goal of national liberation. During the 1930s a nationalist alliance emerged, bringing together anti-colonialist leaders, such as Ferhat Abbas and Messali Hadj, and Islamic leaders, notably Shaykh abd al-Hamid ibn Badis (Ben Badis). In the 1943 Manifesto of the Algerian People, Ferhat Abbas called for an independent Algeria, and a year later organized the Association des Amis de la Manifest (AML). The first congress of the AML elected Messali as its leader and made clear that French leader Charles de Gaulle's appeasing gesture, the Ordinance of March 1944, did not meet their demands for autonomy. When Messali was then quickly deported, the Algerian people demonstrated their outrage with riots in Sétif and Guelma.

Nationalists formed the outlawed Organisation Speciale (OS), which was succeeded by the Comté Révolutionnaire pour l'Unité et l'Action (CRUA) and later the Front de Libération Nationale (FLN). The FLN became the force of the revolution, aiming, as its 1954 statement said, for "national independence through the restoration of the Algerian state, sovereign, democratic and social, within the framework of the principles of Islam." Its leaders, such as Ahmed BEN BELLA, Mohamed Boudiaf, Rabah Bitat, and Hocine Ait Ahmed, would become synonymous with the struggle for independence. Political theorist Frantz FANON's writings about the struggle captured the world's attention as well as the support of prominent European intellectuals such as Jean-Paul Sartre. The nationalist army, Armée de Libération (ALN), waged a fierce guerrilla campaign for decolonization, while the French army responded with equally ruthless counterinsurgency tactics, including torture. Settlers organized the vigilante army Organisation de l'Armée Secrète (OAS).

The Soummam Conference of FLN members still within Algeria marked a decisive point in the coalition of nationalist forces, as the FLN developed a framework for a future state and accelerated the urban guerrilla campaign. The campaign catapulted Algerian women into key roles in the struggle as weapons couriers and spies in French quarters. In 1958 the FLN formed the Provisional Government of the Algerian Republic (GPRA). As France under Charles de Gaulle began preparing for decolonization, a faction of the army joined the settler OAS to resist, targeting the French as well as the Algerians with bombs.

INDEPENDENT ALGERIA
In March 1962 a cease-fire was finally arranged between government and FLN representatives at Evian, France. In the long-awaited referendum, held the following July, Algeria voted overwhelmingly for independence. The settlers began a mass evacuation; before the end of the year most of them had left the country.

A number of different groups had come forward to take leadership positions during the war for independence, often filling the void as other organizations were forced to disband or leaders were sent into exile. As Algeria began the task of building a new nation, the euphoria of independence gave way to a bitter struggle for leadership between the FLN and GPRA, and within GPRA itself. In September 1962, after fratricidal battles, an elected Algerian Assembly appointed Ferhat Abbas as president and Ahmed Ben Bella as prime minister. Once in office, Ben Bella outlawed opposition parties, making the FLN the only legal party. Bella's power-mongering tactics furthered the divisiveness between former leaders of the nationalist struggle.

Bella's regime chose a socialist path to rebuild a society ravaged by years of violent war and the massive repatriation of Europeans with wealth and professional skills. Algeria maintained tenuous links with France, bargaining military sites for technical and educational services.

After a bloodless coup d'état in 1965, Houari BOUMEDIENNE assumed the leadership of Algeria, filling a new governing body, the Council of the Revolution, with civilian technocrats and military supporters. Under Boumedienne, Algeria gained a reputation as a socialist nation determined to sidestep the pitfalls of foreign dependence. Concentrating his power through the suppression of political rivals, Boumedienne attempted to build an economically independent Algerian state through "super industrialization," inaugurating a four-year plan to subsidize Algerian development through hydrocarbons export. After Boumedienne's death in 1978, Chadli BENJEDID assumed power, reversing the socialist strategies of his predecessors by privatizing state-held agricultural land and opening the country to foreign investment.

Despite these moves, during the 1980s Algeria faced a rising Islamic populism, Berber unrest, and a severe shortage of consumer goods. In addition, intellectuals, proponents of women's rights, and advocates of free speech attacked the government for its repressive political and social constraints. These conditions prompted massive

INDEPENDENCE DAY. Algerians march through the streets of Oran on July 3, 1962, celebrating their independence after 132 years of French rule. (*AP Images*)

riots in October 1988. In an attempt to save the FLN from its deteriorating reputation as a front for corrupt politicians, Chadli implemented a series of reforms. In July 1989 the FLN legalized opposition parties, including the Islamic Salvation Front (FIS), lifted press restrictions, and scheduled Algeria's first free multiparty elections for the following year.

In June 1990 the FIS party won the majority of first-round local elections. Some observers have read this victory as an Algerian mandate for Islamic fundamentalism, others as a sign of disillusionment with Chadli's government. Declaring Algeria to be under a state of siege, President Chadli halted the elections and in January 1992 dissolved the National People's Assembly. The new High Council of State forced Chadli's removal, and Mohamed Boudiaf, along with a group of military leaders, assumed control of the country.

Boudiaf was assassinated in June 1992, and Algeria declared a state of emergency. With massacres and random killings leaving tens of thousands dead, Algeria once again became a battlefield. The Islamic movement splintered, producing various factions of Islamic nationalists. Many attribute the terrorist attacks to the Groupes Islamiques Armés (GIA) because the banned FIS distanced itself from the violence—in September 1997 the FIS called for its followers to lay down their arms. During this time, the military-backed government under President Liamine Zeroual created internment camps and made massive arrests, reportedly using torture to flush out suspected FIS members and sympathizers. Some communities, wary of the violence that followed in the wake of military patrols, formed independent groups to keep twenty-four-hour watch over towns.

The progovernment National Democratic Rally party won national elections in 1997, but opposition groups alleged widespread electoral fraud. Two years later, similar charges led six opposition candidates to boycott the national presidential election at the last minute. Abdelaziz Bouteflika, who ran unopposed, won with over 70 percent of the vote. Bouteflika made some progress in reducing the level of violence. In January 2000 the armed wing of the FIS (known as the Islamic Salvation Army) and members of other militant groups laid down their weapons as part of a government amnesty program.

Violence persisted, however, with small, armed bands targeting government forces and carrying out isolated terror attacks. The killing of a civilian protestor by Algerian police led to riots in Kabylia in April 2001 and sparked a movement in the region to mobilize political activity among local youth. This movement, known as the "Coordinations," has made various demands on the government, including withdrawal of government troops from Kabylia and recognition of Berber as an official language. In 2002, however, a general amnesty was offered to the various rebel factions throughout the country, a gesture most of them decided to accept.

See also ISLAM IN AFRICA.

Algeria (At a Glance)

OFFICIAL NAME:
People's Democratic Republic of Algeria

AREA:
2,381,740 sq km (919,595 sq mi)

LOCATION:
Northern Africa; bordering the Mediterranean Sea, Morocco, Tunisia, Libya, Mali, Mauritania, Niger, and the Western Sahara

CAPITAL:
Algiers (population 1.5 million; 2007 estimate)

OTHER MAJOR CITIES:
Oran (population 683,250), Constantine (462,167)

POPULATION:
34,178,188 (2009 estimate)

POPULATION DENSITY:
14 persons per sq km (about 37 persons per sq mi)

POPULATION BELOW AGE 15:
25.4 percent (male 4,436,591; female 4,259,729; 2009 estimate)

POPULATION GROWTH RATE:
1.196 percent (2009 estimate)

TOTAL FERTILITY RATE:
1.79 children born per woman (2009 estimate)

LIFE EXPECTANCY AT BIRTH:
Total population: 74.02 years (male 72.35 years; female 75.77 years [2009 estimate])

INFANT MORTALITY RATE:
27.73 deaths per 1000 live births (2009 estimate)

LITERACY RATE (AGE 15 AND OVER WHO CAN READ AND WRITE):
Total population: 70 percent (male 78.8 percent; female 61 percent; 2003 estimate)

EDUCATION:
Primary education is free and compulsory for all children between the ages of six and 15. In the early 1990s some 5.8 million pupils attended primary schools, 2.3 million were enrolled in secondary schools, and another 147,418 attended vocational schools. By the mid-1990s nearly 300,000 were pursuing higher education.

LANGUAGES:
Arabic is the official language and is spoken by about 83 percent of the population; most of the remainder speak Berber. French, the colonial language, is still widely read and spoken by many educated Algerians.

ETHNIC GROUPS:
Arabs, Berbers, or people of mixed Arab-Berber ancestry make up 99 percent of the population; Europeans constitute less than 1 percent.

RELIGIONS:
Sunni Islam is the state religion and is practiced by 99 percent of the population; 1 percent of the population are Christians or Jews

CLIMATE:
The Tell region in the north has warm, dry summers and mild, rainy winters, with an annual rainfall of between 400 and 1000 mm (16 to 39 in). During the summer an exceedingly hot, dry dust and sand-filled wind, the *sirocco* (known locally as the *Chehili*), blows north from the Sahara. To the south the climate becomes increasingly dry, with an annual rainfall in the High Plateau and Saharan Atlas from about 200 to 400 mm (about 8 to 16 in). The Sahara is a region of daily temperature extremes, wind, and great aridity; annual rainfall is less than 130 mm (5 in) in all places.

LAND, PLANTS, AND ANIMALS:
The Tell region, between the northern Mediterranean coast and the mountainous Tell Atlas area, contains most of Algeria's arable land. The country's principal river, the Chelif (725 km/450 mi long), flows from the Tell Atlas to the Mediterranean Sea. Lying to the south and southwest is the High Plateau, a level, sparsely vegetated highland region. During rainy periods, basins collect water, forming large, shallow lakes that become salt flats, called *chotts*, or *shotts*, during dry seasons. The mountains of the Saharan Atlas lie south of this region. More than 90 percent of the country's total area lies in the Algerian Sahara, covered mostly by gravel with vast regions of sand dunes. Rising above the desert to the south are the Ahaggar Mountains, with Mount Tahat (3,003 m/9,852 ft), the highest peak in Algeria.

Remnants of forests exist in a few areas of the higher Tell and Saharan Atlas. Scattered plant life in the Sahara consists of drought-resistant grasses, acacia, and jujube trees. Wildlife includes scavengers, such as jackals, hyenas, and vultures, as well as antelope, hares, gazelles, and reptiles.

NATURAL RESOURCES:
Petroleum, natural gas, iron ore, phosphates, uranium, lead, zinc

CURRENCY:
The Algerian dinar

GROSS DOMESTIC PRODUCT (GDP):
$171.3 billion (2008 estimate)

GDP PER CAPITA:
$7,000 (2008 estimate)

GDP REAL GROWTH RATE:
3 percent (2008 estimate)

PRIMARY ECONOMIC ACTIVITIES:
Mineral production (primarily crude petroleum and natural gas), agriculture, fishing. Since the late 1960s the government has instituted major industrialization programs.

PRIMARY CROPS:
Wheat, barley, oats, melons, grapes, dates, olives, citrus

INDUSTRIES:
Petroleum, light industries, natural gas, mining, electricity production, petrochemical, food processing

PRIMARY EXPORTS:
Petroleum and natural gas make up 97 percent of export revenues. Other exports include iron ore, vegetables, phosphates, fruit, cork, and hides.

PRIMARY IMPORTS:
Machinery, textiles, sugar, cereals, iron and steel, coal, gasoline

PRIMARY TRADE PARTNERS:
Italy, France, United States, Germany, Spain, Japan

GOVERNMENT:
Under its constitution, revised in November 1996, Algeria is a socialist republic with a president who is elected to a five-year term by universal adult suffrage. A prime minister, appointed by the president, serves as head of government. Abdelaziz Bouteflika has served as president since his election in April 1999. Ahmed Ouyahi was appointed prime minister in May 2003. A bicameral parliament consists of a National People's Assembly of 389 members and a 144-seat Council of Nations. Members of the National People's Assembly are popularly elected and serve five-year terms. One-third of the Council of Nations' members are appointed by the president; the remainder are indirectly elected. The constitution requires that half of its members be renewed every three years. The most recent elections for the assembly were held in May 2002; the last council elections took place in 2003.

Marian Aguiar

BIBLIOGRAPHY

Naylor, Phillip, and Heggoy Alf Andrew. *Historical Dictionary of Algeria.* Scarecrow Press, 1994.

Ruedy, John. *Modern Algeria: The Origins and Development of a Nation.* Indiana University Press, 1992.

MARIAN AGUIAR

Algiers, Algeria

Capital city of Algeria, located on the northern coast of the country along the Mediterranean Sea.

Algiers was built through multiple conquests, and layers of different cultures can be found in its architecture and social character. Legend has it that the ancient city of Icosium, founded by twenty companions of Hercules, lies beneath the foundations of the modern city. Romans, BERBERS, Vandals, Byzantines, and Arabs all left their mark on the site, but it was not until the mid-tenth century that the Berber emir Bulkkin, built the harbor town into an important North African trading center, al-Jaza'ir.

For several hundred years a series of Islamic Maghreb rulers claimed the city as their seat of power. For the most part, the region operated as an independent city-state under dynastic rule, but at several points, al-Jaza'ir was governed by its own citizens. During the early sixteenth century, the city also became home to persecuted Andalusian Muslims, or Moors, and Jews, displaced by Christian reconquests in southern Europe. Spain followed closely on the heels of the fleeing Muslims and Jews, taking the islet Peñón in the bay of Algiers in 1511 as a base. For the next five years, Spaniards vied with the residents of the Ottoman Empire, founded by Turks, for control of the city, considered a prime location for lucrative sea trade and piracy.

After the Turkish Barbarossa brothers Aruj and Khayr ad-Din gained control of the city in 1516, Algiers thrived as a relatively independent city under the nominal control of the Ottoman Empire. The Ottomans and the Turkish-Algerian rulers who succeeded them transformed the city's architectural character, constructing mosques similar to those in Asia Minor and erecting the famous whitewashed military fortification, the Casbah.

Epidemics, famine, and declining trade undermined the vitality of the city during the early nineteenth century. France took Algiers in 1830, using it as a base for colonial occupation. Over the next 132 years, the French colonial administration developed the port, built wide boulevards, and constructed an opera house and several cathedrals. The city served as a military base during World War II (1939–1945) and briefly as the provisional capital of France. By the mid-1950s, nearly half of the population was European.

Algiers was also home to many prominent Algerian intellectual and political figures, and it became a center for the anti-colonial movement and eventually for the guerrilla campaigns of the National Liberation Army (ALN). As Algerians planted bombs in European neighborhoods and French soldiers scoured the streets for revolutionaries, the city suffered ten years of urban warfare known as the Battle of Algiers.

Since independence in 1962, the capital city of Algiers has grown into the most important Mediterranean shipping center of northwest Africa. A 2007 estimate put the population of Algiers at over two million inhabitants, while a 2008 projection had the number above three million. The city has, at times, found it difficult to develop infrastructure sufficient to keep pace with such rapid population growth.

Algiers remains a center of ongoing political and social upheaval. In October 1988 residents of Algiers rioted to protest the scarcity of basic necessities. Violence filled the streets again after the 1991 elections were cancelled to forestall a potential victory by the ISLAMIC SALVATION FRONT (FIS) party. Since then, terrorist attacks and military reprisals waged as part of the conflict between the military-backed government and militant Islamic groups have repeatedly struck Algiers and its suburbs. In November 2001, riots broke out after floods killed over 500 residents in one of Algiers' poorest neighborhoods. Residents faulted the government for its failure to respond quickly to the disaster. Some also blamed the high death toll on police actions that they claim exposed residents of the area to greater risks from the flooding. More recently, the city has fallen victim to a number of terror attacks. A string of car bombings in April and December 2007—targeting the offices of the prime minister, a UN building, and the city's Constitution Court—left at least sixty people dead and more than 300 wounded. Islamic radicals took credit for the attacks.

See also CORSAIRS; JEWISH COMMUNITIES IN NORTH AFRICA.

BIBLIOGRAPHY

Naylor, Phillip, and Heggoy Alf Andrew. *Historical Dictionary of Algeria.* Scarecrow Press, 1994.

MARIAN AGUIAR

Almohads

Arabic al-muwahhid, meaning "who proclaim the unity of God"; Berber Muslim reform movement and dynasty established in North Africa and Spain during the twelfth and thirteenth centuries.

The origin of the movement is traced to Muhammad ibn Tumart, an Arab reformer in MOROCCO who preached moral reform and the doctrine of the unity of divine being. He gathered a large following of Arabs and BERBERS and in 1121 was proclaimed Al Mahdi ("The Rightly Guided"). The founder of the dynasty was the Berber Abd al-Mumin, who succeeded Ibn Tumart and took the title of caliph. He conquered Morocco (1140–1147) and other parts of North Africa, thus putting an end to the previous dynasty of the ALMORAVIDS. By 1154 he also ruled Islamic Spain and part of Portugal. Notable among successive Almohad rulers was Yakub al-Mansur, who ruled in Spain from 1184 until his death. He aided the sultan Saladin against the crusaders and was responsible for the construction of numerous architectural monuments such as the the Hassan Tower (a 55-m/180-ft minaret) in Rabat, Morocco.

The Almohads incorporated Berber traditions of rule, such as representative government and tribal councils, into their centralized Islamic theocracy. They fostered a Renaissance of Islamic scholarship in Andalusian (Southern) Spain and Northwestern Africa, sponsoring philosophers and scientists such as Ibn Bajja (Avempace), Ibn Tufayl, Ibn Rushd, (Averroës), as well as the great explorer IBN BATTUTAH. The Almohad Dynasty flourished until 1212, when the united kings of Castile, Aragón, and Navarre defeated the Almohad forces in the Battle of Navas de Tolosa. After that defeat, the power of the Almohads declined and finally came to an end in Spain in 1232 and in Africa in 1269.

See also CRUSADES.

BIBLIOGRAPHY

Park, Thomas K. *Historical Dictionary of Morocco.* Scarecrow Press, 1996.

Almoravids
Berber dynasty that ruled in Africa and Spain in the eleventh and twelfth centuries C.E.

Between 1053 and 1061, a large part of northwestern Africa was under the rule of a dynasty that began as an Islamic religious movement espousing a return to a more ascetic form of Islam. Leadership of the movement in the western Maghreb passed to Yusuf ibn Tashfin, a Berber chieftain. After enlarging their domain in northwestern Africa, the Almoravids invaded Spain in 1086. During the next four years, they conquered the area between the Tagus (Tajo) and Ebro rivers and set up viceroys in Seville and Granada. Upon returning from Spain, Yusuf ibn Tashfin was declared emir by councils of the east and western regions of the dynasty. In 1146 the dynasty was overthrown by the ALMOHADS, another Muslim reform movement.

BIBLIOGRAPHY

Park, Thomas K. *Historical Dictionary of Morocco* Scarecrow Press, 1996.

Alur
Ethnic group of East Africa.

The Alur primarily inhabit the northern shores of Lake Albert, both in western UGANDA and northeastern Congo-Kinshasa. They speak a Nilo-Saharan language and belong to the Western Nilotic cultural and linguistic cluster. Though precise numbers are difficult to come by, more than 500,000 people consider themselves Alur.

Amadi, Elechi
1934–
Nigerian novelist whose works describe the folklore and spirituality of traditional village life.

A member of the IGBO ethnic group, Elechi Amadi was born in a small southeastern Nigerian village near Port Harcourt. In 1959 he graduated with a degree in physics and mathematics from the University College of Ibadan, a prestigious college attended by other well-known Nigerian writers, such as Chinua ACHEBE, John Pepper CLARK, Christopher OKIGBO, and Wole SOYINKA. After working as a land surveyor, Amadi taught science for three years at missionary schools in Ahoada and Oba. In 1963 he joined the Nigerian Army; he taught the Ikwerri dialect of Igbo at a military school in Zaria.

His first book, *The Concubine*, blended acute psychological detail and precise observation to tell the story of a young village woman's battle with spiritual forces. The book's publication in 1966 coincided with the proclamation of an independent state—Biafra—in Igbo-dominated southeastern NIGERIA. Amadi's allegiance to the Federal side in the conflict put him virtually alone among Igbo writers. Steadfastly refusing to write political novels, which he called "a prostitution of literature," Amadi did not detail his wartime experiences until 1973, when he published *Sunset in Biafra: A Civil War Diary*. His novels *The Great Ponds* (1969) and *The Slave* (1978) completed what is thought of as Amadi's trilogy of the mythical in village life.

After the war, Amadi became dean of arts at the Rivers State College of Education (1985–1986) and, later, commissioner for education in Rivers State (1988–1989). In 1986 he published *Estrangement*, a departure from his earlier work in both its urban setting and its exploration of the effects of the war on Nigeria's survivors. In addition, Amadi has published four plays: *Isiburu* (1973), *Peppersoup* (1973), *The Road to Ibadan* (1973), and *Dancer of Johannesburg* (1979), and a scholarly work, *Ethics in Nigerian Culture* (1982).

See also FICTION, ENGLISH-LANGUAGE, IN AFRICA.

KATE TUTTLE

Amazon
A division of the precolonial Dahomean army that was composed solely of women soldiers.

While the term Amazon most commonly refers to a female warrior society described in Greek mythology, it is also applied to an army of female soldiers in the precolonial Early KINGDOM OF DAHOMEY. Originally called the ahosi, or "king's wives," the female troops were first called Amazons by Europeans and then by the Dahomeans themselves.

Although the origins of the Amazons are uncertain, European explorers such as Sir Richard BURTON, who visited the Dahomean king AGAJA in 1720, reported that the king employed a small troop of women as nighttime palace guards. Recruited from the king's harems and wives, these women enabled Agaja to maintain his security while adhering to the royal dictate that "no man [shall] sleep within the wall of any of [my palaces] after sunset but myself." Amazons also participated in select activities outside the palace, such as ceremonial parades, but it is unlikely that they were employed as a branch of the regular army until the reign of King Ghezo (1818–1859).

Ghezo came to power in a coup d'état and immediately increased the size of the Amazon forces in an effort to prevent his own overthrow. Later in his reign, the imperialistic Ghezo began training Amazons as soldiers. According to Dahomean histories, nearly 8,000 women served in the Amazon forces, and they played a crucial role in many important battles against the YORUBA as well as in the victorious war against the Mahi in 1847. European accounts from explorers such as John Duncan attest to the Amazons' bravery and skill: "They are far superior to the men in every thing—in appearance, dress, in figure, in activity, in their performances as soldiers, and in bravery." But there is also evidence that the Amazons consistently suffered the heaviest battlefield fatalities, and by the time of the first Franco-Dahomean war in 1890, the Amazon division was only half its original size. The force was essentially destroyed during the 1890 war; this loss contributed to the defeat of the Dahomean army during their second war against the French in 1892.

ELIZABETH HEATH

Amhara
Ethnic group of Ethiopia.
The Amhara, one of the two largest ethnic groups of Ethiopia, occupy central and western Ethiopia. Traditionally, the Amhara have been the country's dominant people—all but one of the Ethiopian emperors were Amhara—and their language, Amharic, a Semitic language like Hebrew or Arabic, has been the country's official language. Amhara's political dominance has created tensions between them and other ethnic groups, including the TIGRE and the OROMO. Historically, the Amhara belonged to the ETHIOPIAN ORTHODOX CHURCH, which was the Ethiopian state religion until the overthrow of emperor Haile Selassie in 1974. Many Amhara, especially in rural areas, still regard church rules as law.

The origins and early history of the Amhara remain the subject of some speculation. Archaeological evidence suggests that sometime before 500 B.C.E. a Semitic-speaking people, from whom the Amhara are descended, migrated from present-day Yemen to the area of northern Ethiopia that would become AKSUM. These Himyarites, as they have come to be called, intermarried with indigenous speakers of Cushitic languages, such as AGAW, and gradually spread south into the present-day homeland of the Amhara. Their descendants spoke Ge'ez, an ancient Semitic tongue that is no longer spoken but remains the official language of the Ethiopian Orthodox Church. They developed a civilization that made use of dams, cisterns (one of which was still operating in the 1950s) and other irrigation techniques, stone houses, and a unique form of writing. According to the traditional account contained in the national epic *Kebra Negast* (Ge'ez for "The Glory of the Kings"), the Amhara and related groups such as the TIGRINYA are descended from the Israelite King Solomon and the QUEEN OF SHEBA. Therefore, each Ethiopian emperor held the title "Lion of Judah." Christianity spread to Ethiopia during the fourth century C.E., and religion played a central role in shaping Amharic society.

The Amhara created a highly stratified feudal society. At the top sat the emperor, who was considered the head of the state, the army, and the church. Under the emperor was a class of landed nobility and clergy. Below this class were various classes of farmers and merchants and lower-class peddlers, merchants, and weavers. Slaves were considered beneath this class structure entirely. Status was tied to land ownership. The more land a man owned, the more important he was. A wealthy man who owned no land had little status among the Amhara. Under the imperial system, the emperor granted nobles titles to lands in exchange for military service. Tenants farmed the land and paid the owner tribute.

For many Amhara, the Ethiopian Orthodox Church defines their identity. They tend to look down on surrounding Muslim peoples. Traditionally, the Amhara have considered many of the church's tenets laws; this remains true in the rural areas where roughly 90 percent of Amhara still live. Priests serve as examples by their holy lives, offer spiritual guidance to families, and recite the Ge'ez liturgy, but typically they do not preach.

Most Amhara base their livelihood on subsistence agriculture. The most important crop is teff, a cereal unique to the Ethiopian highlands that is grown as a staple food. They also grow maize (known as corn in the United States), wheat, and other grains, as well as a variety of legumes and vegetables. Many Amhara raise cattle, sheep, chickens, and other livestock. Coffee is the major cash crop. The Amhara trace descent along both the father's and mother's lines, though most scholars agree that the father's line was traditionally considered more important. KINSHIP AND

DESCENT IN AFRICA historically provided the basis for land inheritance. Extended families, the descendants of a common ancestor along with their spouses, lived in their own hamlets, farmed their own land, and acknowledged the authority of a council of elders.

The Amhara imperial dynasty lasted from roughly 1270 to 1974, when a military council overthrew the regime of emperor Haile Selassie I and a Marxist government, led by HAILE MARIAM MENGISTU, took power. The Mengistu regime revolutionized traditional Amhara society by eliminating the feudal hierarchy and landholding patterns and by ending Amhara political dominance. Amhara still predominated in civil service and university teaching positions, however. In 1993 a long-running Tigrean rebellion against the Mengistu regime, led by Meles Zenawi, overthrew Mengistu. Tigreans (mostly members of the Tigrinya ethnic group) began to occupy prominent government positions, a situation that many Amhara resented. A new constitution established a federal structure and divided the country into ethnically defined regions. It permitted regions to secede, and ERITREA declared its independence in 1993. Many Amhara believed that the new constitution was put in place to ensure Tigrean ascendancy, and tensions persisted during the late 1990s. Population estimates in the early twenty-first century put the number of Amhara at more than twenty million.

See also ETHIOPIC SCRIPT AND LANGUAGE.

ROBERT FAY

Amin, Idi

1925–2003
President of Uganda (1971–1979), also known as Idi Amin Dada.

Self-titled "His Excellency President for Life Field Marshal Al Hadji Dr. Idi Amin, VC, DSO, MC, Lord of All the Beasts of the Earth and Fishes of the Sea and Conqueror of the British Empire in Africa in General and Uganda in Particular," Idi Amin also made a name for himself as one of modern Africa's most tyrannical and brutal rulers. A member of the KAKWA ethnic group, Idi Amin was born to Muslim parents near Koboko in northern UGANDA when that part of Africa was under British control. After receiving a missionary school education, Amin joined the King's African Rifles (KAR), the African unit of the British Armed Forces, in 1946. He served in SOMALIA, Uganda, and KENYA while British authorities there suppressed an African uprising called the MAU MAU REBELLION, earning a reputation as a skilled and eager soldier. But early in his career he revealed his excessive tendencies—one commanding officer described him as "overzealous" during a campaign against cattle thieves in northern Uganda. Also combative off the battlefield, Amin won his country's light

AMIN'S EXILE. Former Ugandan President Idi Amin and his eight-year-old son Muzammel, during an interview with the Associated Press in Jidda, Saudi Arabia. (*Aly Mahmoud/AP Images*)

heavyweight boxing championship in 1951 and retained the title for nine years.

When Uganda achieved independence in 1962, Amin was one of only two African officers in the Ugandan armed forces. Amin had been an early political supporter of Milton OBOTE, the first prime minister of independent Uganda. The two were accused of selling smuggled gold and ivory out of the DEMOCRATIC REPUBLIC OF THE CONGO during the early 1960s, gold intended to purchase arms for Congolese revolutionary Patrice LUMUMBA. The cabinet suspended Amin from his position as colonel until the charges could be investigated, but Obote had five cabinet ministers arrested. He then suspended the 1962 constitution, declaring himself executive president.

In 1968 Obote promoted Amin to major general and commander of the armed forces. Soon afterward the president began to lose control over Amin, who was supplying arms to rebels in southern SUDAN and cultivating ties with British and Israeli agents. Shortly after an assassination attempt on Obote, Amin's rival, Brigadier Pierino Okoya, was murdered. A suspicious Obote placed Amin under house arrest in 1970.

In January of the following year, Amin took control of Uganda in a coup while President Obote was in Singapore. At first the Ugandan people, disillusioned with the corrupt Obote, welcomed Amin, as did the international community. But the new president's brutality quickly dampened his popularity within Uganda.

Among Amin's first targets were the ACHOLI and LANGO ethnic groups, who dominated the Ugandan army and had supported Obote. Amin began killing them and replacing them with ethnic Kakwa and soldiers from Sudan and the Democratic Republic of the Congo (then known as ZAIRE). After Obote attempted an unsuccessful counter-coup in 1972 from TANZANIA, Amin retaliated by bombing Tanzanian towns and stepping up his campaign to terrorize Acholi and Lango, killing civilians as well as soldiers.

Amin dealt a severe blow to the Ugandan economy. In 1972 he declared an "Economic War" on the country's large Asian population, which dominated trade and manufacturing and also played an essential role in the civil service. After giving the 70,000 holders of British passports three months to leave the country, Amin turned thousands of their abandoned businesses over to his friends and supporters. In addition, he claimed that Uganda now owned all British companies in the country—some eighty-five firms—after Great Britain cut diplomatic ties with Uganda.

Suspicious and temperamental, Amin frequently reorganized his army and security forces as well as his diplomatic alliances. For example, at first he had close ties to Israel, where he had once received paratrooper training. Later, however, he turned to LIBYA and Russia (then known as the Soviet Union) for political and military support. After expelling Israeli diplomats from Uganda in 1972, he invited the Palestine Liberation Organization (PLO) to occupy the former Israeli embassy, and he reportedly sent a cable to Israeli leader Golda Meir claiming to be sorry that German dictator Adolf Hitler had failed to exterminate the Jews. Amin is also believed to have invited hijackers to force an Air France plane full of Israelis to land at Entebbe in 1976. The hostages were freed by Israeli paratroopers, who at the same time killed the hijackers and Ugandan troops and destroyed Amin's fleet of fighter jets.

Amin is thought to have arranged the murders of numerous prominent Ugandans, including the Anglican Archbishop of Uganda, the chief justice, the chancellor of Makerere College, and the governor of the Bank of Uganda. Tens of thousands of lesser-known Ugandans were abducted, tortured, and killed by the notorious State Research Bureau and Public Safety Unit. Not even Amin's family members escaped the violence. His first wife, Kay Amin, left him—she was later arrested, released, and ultimately found murdered. After his second wife, Mama Miriam, was also arrested and fined, Amin divorced his third wife, Nora, and battered his fourth, Madina, sending her to the hospital with a broken jaw. A brother-in-law who served briefly as foreign minister was found dead and mutilated on the banks of the NILE RIVER two weeks after being dismissed from his post.

Rumored to have engaged in cannibalism as well as traditional Kakwa blood rituals, Amin came to be viewed by many as both sadistic and irrational. Some have attributed Amin's behavior to hypomania, a form of manic-depression characterized by erratic emotional outbursts and extremely rapid thinking. At the same time, the president's charisma and humorous antics in front of the international press helped him to develop a foreign image as a man-of-the-people leader who defied the remnants of colonialism and other outside forces trying to control African destiny.

In 1978 Amin's ambition led to his fall from power. In October he tried to take control of the Kagera Salient, part of Tanzania. Tanzanian president Julius NYERERE responded by sending troops into Uganda. Supported by Ugandan rebel forces, the Tanzanian army captured the capital city of KAMPALA in April 1979. Shortly afterward, Amin fled to exile in Libya. There he remained until 1989, when used a false passport to leave Libya and enter Zaire, where he announced plans to return to power in Uganda. Authorities in Uganda, however, declared that if Amin returned he would be arrested and tried. Several other countries refused to offer refuge to Amin, but finally Saudi Arabia took him. Amin spent the rest of his life in exile in Riyadh, Saudia Arabia. He died of kidney failure on August 16, 2003.

See also GOLD TRADE; INDIAN COMMUNITIES IN AFRICA; IVORY TRADE.

ARI NAVE

Amistad Mutiny
Rebellion of Africans held captive aboard the slave ship La Amistad that occurred in July 1839 off the northern coast of Cuba.

Although England and Spain had signed a treaty in 1817 prohibiting the transatlantic slave trade, a group of African MENDE were captured in an area near Sierra Leone in April 1839 and forced onto a Portuguese slave ship bound for Havana, Cuba. To avoid prosecution for breaking international law, the captives were smuggled onto the island at night when the ship reached Cuba. While in Havana, fifty-three Africans (forty-nine adult males, three girls, and one boy) were sold to two Spaniards, José Ruiz and Pedro Montes, who intended to use them as slaves on Cuban plantations. On June 28, 1839, the Africans were loaded aboard the Spanish schooner La Amistad as it set sail along the Cuban coast for Puerto Príncipe. On La Amistad's fourth day at sea, a few of the captives were allowed to come on deck for exercise. One of them, Joseph CINQUE, found a nail and smuggled it back below with him. Using the nail to force open their chains and shackles, Cinque and his comrades seized cane knives and initiated the rebellion.

Along with the ship's captain and cook, ten Africans were killed. Ruiz and Montes were captured and, with translation provided by a slave cabin boy named Antonio, instructed to sail the ship back to Africa. Cinque and the others were able to use the rising sun to ensure that the ship headed eastward during the day. However, unable to navigate by the stars, the Africans were tricked by Ruiz and Montes into sailing northwest at night. La Amistad zigzagged through the waters for two months, finally landing near Culloden Point, Long Island, New York, on August 24, 1839. When Cinque sent a group to find water and food on shore, Lieutenant Thomas R. Gedney of the United States Navy seized the ship and arrested the Africans for murder and piracy. Three New York abolitionists, Lewis Tappan, Joshua Leavitt, and Simeon Jocelyn, formed a committee called Friends of the Amistad to help defend the African captives. On March 9, 1841, the Supreme Court of the United States ruled that President Martin Van Buren did not have the right to return the Africans to Cuba and that the Africans were never slaves under international law and should be granted their freedom. Despite their victory in court, only thirty-five of the original fifty-three Africans survived to board the ship *Gentleman* that set sail for Africa on November 27, 1841. Arriving in Sierra Leone in January 1842, almost three years after their capture, these Africans regained their freedom.

BIBLIOGRAPHY

Jones, Howard. *Mutiny on the Amistad.* Oxford University Press, 1987.

ALONFORD JAMES ROBINSON, JR.

Ana

Ethnic group of West Africa, also known as Atakpamé.

The Ana primarily inhabit central TOGO and neighboring regions of BENIN. They speak a Niger-Congo language and are considered part of the YORUBA peoples. Approximately 150,000 people consider themselves Ana.

Anang

Ethnic group of Nigeria, also known as the Anaang and the Annang.

The Anang primarily inhabit the Cross River State of NIGERIA. They speak a Niger-Congo language and are closely related to the IBIBIO people. More than 800,000 people consider themselves Anang.

Ancient African Civilizations

Societies that flourished in Africa before the arrival of European colonial powers.

The great chiefdoms, states, and empires of Africa were some of the last great civilizations of antiquity to come to the attention of the Western world. Before the fifteenth century, when the coasts of Africa fell increasingly within the European trading sphere, the states of the African interior were known in Europe only through frail rumors received at one remove from the Arabic world. By the time

Europeans finally achieved the interior vastness of the continent in the nineteenth century, many of its great polities had been reduced by internal dissension or had withered away, leaving only their ruins. Oral traditions also remained, but for many years they went unheard or uncredited by the ear of the colonizer. Since the last few decades of the colonial era, much has been reconstructed about the vanished African past through the use of oral traditions, a few textual sources (mostly in Arabic), historical linguistics, and—most of all—by archaeological research.

Virtually every new program of field research provides alterations to the status quo of African prehistory. However, outside of southeastern Africa, interdisciplinary studies incorporating oral histories, linguistics, and comparative ethnography are still very rare. Thus, it must be remembered that any synthesis in this rapidly changing field is imminently liable to augmentation. Despite this, it is possible to highlight the salient features of our current knowledge of the first African states.

In their distribution, the ancient complex societies of Africa cluster around the great water bodies of the continent. The NIGER and Nile river basins have both figured prominently in the rise of African states, as have the CONGO RIVER and the shores of the Red Sea and the Indian Ocean. It will be observed in the earliest state formations of Saharan and sub-Saharan Africa that two factors played central roles: livestock wealth and interregional trade, with the latter eclipsing the former in importance over time. Although much was made in first postcolonial African histories of the role of external trade in the formation of African states, archaeological research has indicated that extensive internal, rather than external, trade webs formed the principal impetus for the formation of African complex societies.

AFRICA AND EGYPT

Much has been written in recent years about the connections of Egypt and the African interior. Whether concerning Egypt in Africa or Africa in Egypt, the fountainhead of this new literature was the work of the late Cheikh Anta Diop. Embraced by the public and uncomfortably ignored by professional scholars, Diop's radical tenets posited that all original early Holocene (c. 10,000–4000 B.C.E.) inhabitants of North Africa were black and that they alone were responsible for the predynastic culture of Egypt and for all of the early dynasties. During the Old Kingdom it was thought that small-scale Caucasoid incursions from the Levant lightened the skin tone of the original Egyptians, with subsequent "invasions" from Persia, Greece, and Rome further transforming the physical characteristics of the Egyptians. Needless to say, this in-mixing of foreigners was thought to be linked to the decline of Egypt, with the best of Egyptian ideas being responsible for the grandeur of Greece and

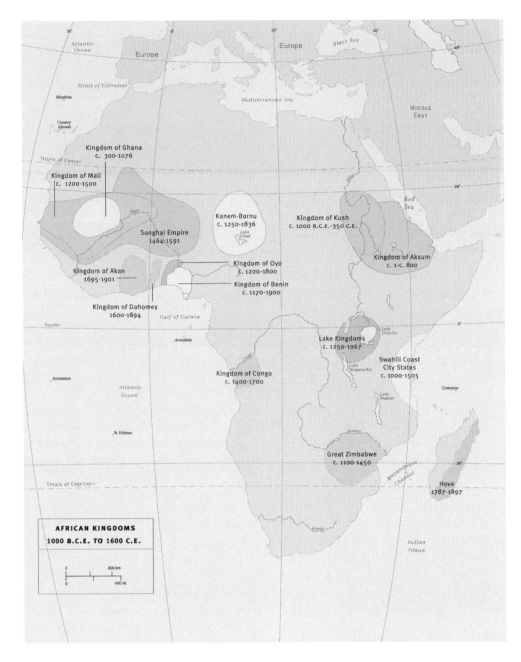

subsequent European civilization. This is not the place to enter into a point-by-point debate on Diop's claims and those of his numerous intellectual descendants. At their best they do much to redress the anti-African bias inherent in early Egyptology; at their worst they recreate in reverse the oblique racism inherent in the hyperdiffusionistic school of Grafton Elliot-Smith in the 1930s. Modern consensus sees Egypt, from its beginnings, as a multiracial civilization, with African cultural aspects particularly coming from Egypt's NUBIAN corridor to Africa.

The great civilization of Egypt developed between Mediterranean and African spheres of influence out of a long tradition of incipient stratified social systems, already boasting well-organized agro-pastoral economies, ceremonial architecture, and sailing craft (the predynastic, 5500–

3100 B.C.E.). Between 3100 and 331 B.C.E., Egyptian dynasties would profoundly influence socioeconomic developments in northeast Africa and southwest Asia, and forever alter the landscape of Egypt with some of the most impressive monuments known to humanity. Throughout this time Egypt's neighbors in NUBIA possessed their own unique cultural institutions and political structures. These southern polities sometimes cooperated and sometimes contested the power of their northern neighbor.

Kerma, potentially the first Nubian state, prospered between the third and fourth cataracts of the Nile from roughly 2500 to 1500 B.C.E. During Kerma's earliest development, its cultural influences were undoubtedly from the African SAHEL, manifested in round dwellings and ceremonial structures, as well as distinctive burial practices and circular tumuli featuring livestock sacrifices. Over time, however, the cultural proximity of Egypt becomes increasingly visible in linear-walled, fired mud-brick architecture; more elaborate burial practices; and prestige goods imported from the lower Nile (Middle to Final Kerma, c. 2050–1500 B.C.E.). Kerma's economy appears to have been based upon external trade in ivory, diorite, and to the north, with its subsistence base founded upon pastoralism and an as yet unverified grain component. From 1550 B.C.E. onward, Egypt began a period of violent conflict with Kerma, which culminated in the fall and burning of Kerma sometime around 1500 B.C.E.

After the collapse of Kerma, following a period of Egyptian domination, other Nubian states would arise in the same region. The most notable of these were Napata (c. 860–270 B.C.E.) and Meroe (c. 270 B.C.E.–350 C.E.). Napata formed around a reemergent upper Nubian elite, with a heartland situated south of Kerma, during a time of dissension in Egypt. Its first rulers were buried in a monumental cemetery at Kurru, with later rulers being inhumed near Napata. With Egypt fragmented into approximately eleven competing polities in the early first millennium B.C.E., Napata was able to push its influence northward, ruling Egypt as a pharaonic dynasty from 750 to 660 B.C.E. Egypt then reunited under an indigenous dynasty, and Napata's sphere of influence contracted to its original center.

From the declining Napatan state, Meroe arose and endured for more than five hundred years (c. 270 B.C.E.–350 C.E.). Its center was the royal court at Meroe, although it was eventually to stretch as a mercantile empire into lower Nubia and the frontiers of Ptolemaic Egypt. William Adams, the first great synthesist of Nubian archaeology, wrote that both Ptolemaic Egypt and Meroe were "provincial expressions of a world civilization." In other words, they were both cultural outposts of Hellenistic Greece. Even the most fervent Africanists would be hard-pressed to argue against this sentiment. From Classic Kerma onward there is a progressive cultural trend in Nubia of looking away from Africa and toward the Mediterranean world.

However, Meroe did retain some of its own gods—most notably the lion-headed Apedemack. Meroe also developed its own hieroglyphic-derived script, which unfortunately is as yet untranslatable. Meroe is also famed for its massive iron production, the first large-scale industry of its kind in the Nile Valley. But the technology of this industry is essentially Roman, rather than sub-Saharan. Indeed, although sub-Saharan animals, both as living circus animals or as animal products, continued to flow through Nubia, the region had by this time become more of a cul-de-sac and less of a corridor, seeking its luxuries and ideals from the Greco-Roman world.

ANCIENT AFRICAN CIVILIZATIONS. A Colossus of the Nubian Pharoah Aspelto who ruled Egypt and Nubia from 600 and 580 B.C.E. The cobras on his forehead were symbols of royalty. (*Museum of Fine Arts, Boston/Harvard University—Boston Museum of Fine Arts Expedition, 23.730/Bridgeman Art Library International Ltd.*)

CATTLE AS CAPITAL: EARLY COMPLEX SOCIETIES OF THE SAHARA AND SAHEL

By the third millennium B.C.E., a broad swath of cultures economically dominated by pastoralism stretched across the African Sahel, from modern SUDAN to MAURITANIA. At that time the SAHARA was much moister than it is today, being carpeted with grasslands and crisscrossed by seasonally filled waterways and ponds. Its vast expanse was also populated with linguistically and culturally diverse groups that had both pastoral and hunter-gatherer ways of life. The small stone and earthen tumuli and monuments left in the wake of the early pastoral cultures attest to a degree of social ranking in the former—probably based around the accumulation of livestock and widely traded polished stone objects (beads, arm rings, axes, etc.). The origins of these mobile complex societies extend almost to the beginnings of cattle-keeping in Africa, whose origins may be as early as 7000 B.C.E. in the northeastern corner of the continent. From a relatively early date, they were constructing small stone monuments of a communal nature, including a circle of standing stones (built between 5000 and 4000 B.C.E., near Nabta Playa, Egypt), and small tumuli for cattle "sacrifices" or lineage bulls (c. 5000 B.C.E., NIGER and CHAD). Soon, however, monuments of a more individualistic nature would appear across the central Sahara. Stone tumuli, alignments, and burial complexes, singling out the elites of these societies for special treatment, are well documented from 4000 B.C.E. until the virtual abandonment of the gradually desiccating region during the first millennium B.C.E.. In two places, environmental and external social factors crystallized these mobile societies into more sedentary and complex polities, such as those known from Kerma (see the section on Africa and Egypt) and Dhar Tichitt.

Around 1500 B.C.E., far in the west of the continent, the first substantial masonry structures in Africa outside the Nile Valley were being built. Along the escarpments of Dhar Tichitt and Dhar Oualata, in modern Mauritania, a pristine chiefdom developed in a deteriorating environment where arable land and pasturage were at a premium. Remote sensing has revealed a four-tier settlement hierarchy, with the largest regional centers exceeding 90 hectares (220 acres) in area. The evolution of Tichitt-Oualata society remains unclear, with competing hypotheses of long-term local development, rapid evolution, or immigration from elsewhere being obscured by thin stratigraphy at deflated settlement sites. By the mid-second millennium B.C.E., however, it is clear that pastoral peoples living in this zone had started to become more sedentary, building dry-stone masonry structures and cultivating millet. From this time onward, the presence of large stone-walled corral areas and numerous granary foundations points to the importance of mixed farming, with definite evidence present for domestic millet, cattle, sheep, and goats. Inorganic wealth resided in the same objects valued by contemporary Sahelian pastoral cultures: carnelian and amazonite beads, polished stone bracelets, and a plethora of ax types, from large functional varieties to miniature tokens. Unfortunately, none of this region's many tumuli have yet been excavated. It would appear that the collapse of Tichitt-Oualata between 800 and 500 B.C.E. was brought about both by continually shrinking local ponds and grasslands, as well as increasing harassment from BERBER interlopers from farther north.

THE EMPIRES OF GHANA AND MALI

During the first millennium B.C.E. the advent of metallurgy added further impetus to the growth of complex societies south of the Sahara. Indeed, gold would play a key role in international trade between West Africa and the Mediterranean world throughout the late first and early second Millennia C.E. At a more regional level, iron and copper figured as crucial sources for both practical

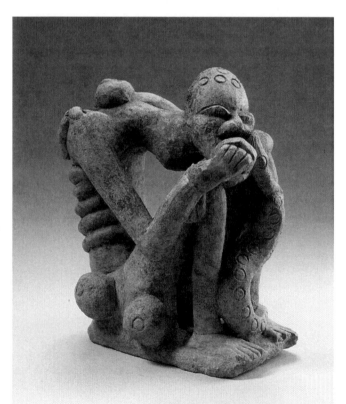

ANCIENT AFRICAN CIVILIZATIONS. The ancient urban center of Djenne-Djeno developed a tradition of pottery scupture. This terracotta figure probably dates from between the eleventh and sixteenth centuries. (*Private Collection/Heini Schneebeli/ Bridgeman Art Library International Ltd.*)

and prestige objects. Coupled with ivory and the slave trade, the control of metallurgical commodities supplanted mere subsistence as the power basis of African elites from the beginning of the first millennium C.E.

By the time Arab geographers began to write of West Africa in the eighth century C.E., the empire of GHANA—described as a "land of gold"—was already in existence. The origins of Ghana, and even its precise extent, remain unclear. But we do know that it was situated within the modern states of Mauritania and MALI. It should be noted that the modern state of Ghana was named after the empire because of possible historical connections, even though geographically there is no relation.

It was not until the tenth and eleventh centuries C.E. that travelers and compilers of travelers' tales began to assemble a more complete written record of Ghana—an empire reaching the end of its existence by that time. Most notable among them were Ibn Hawkal, a late-tenth-century traveler; and the great geographical synthesist al-Bakri, whose masterwork was completed in 1068 C.E. Only eight years after this, the ALMORAVIDS Berbers completed their invasion of Ghana and captured its current capital (Koumbi Saleh). It would appear that this act laid waste to the power structure of the state and marked its effective dissolution.

In their writings, Ibn Hawkal and al-Bakri paint a picture of a powerful and wealthy state able to "put 200,000 warriors in the field, more than 40,000 of them being armed with bow and arrow." The king, it was said, controlled the traffic of all gold out of his kingdom to the north and the flow of salt from the Sahara to the south.

The ruins of Ghana's last capital, Kumbi Saleh, lie in southeastern Mauritania, yet the most substantive settlement clusters known from the first millennium C.E. rest within the bounds of the middle Niger in the neighboring Republic of Mali. Earlier scholarly thought placed Ghana as a puppet state founded by Arab traders, but recent research has emphasized the indigenous development of regional trade webs by the SONINKÉ people, long before the Arab conquest of North Africa (c. 750 C.E.).

There is thus an unknown Ghana, the Ghana that existed before the first written accounts. There is a tantalizing reference in the Tarikh as-Sudan, a compilation of oral traditions written in TOMBOUCTOU about 1650 C.E. It states that there were twenty-one kings of Ghana before the beginning of the Muslim era (622 C.E.) and twenty-one kings after that. If we accept this as anything more than an exercise in symmetry, then it would seem to place the origins of Ghana sometime before 300 C.E.

Archaeologically, if we move the center of gravity southward toward the inland Niger Delta, much evidence exists to support this claim. The substantial settlements that have been excavated along the middle Niger were all in existence by this time. At some sites, such as Tongo Maaré Diabal, permanent mud architecture is present from 250 C.E. Certainly the high point of middle Niger civilization in terms of maximum settlement growth would date to the period between 400 and 800 C.E., well before the textually recorded Ghana. Was this the early Ghana eluded to in the Tarikh as-Sudan? On current evidence, it would appear likely. It is expected that future work will confirm the view that the heart of the empire of Ghana, like that of the MANDINKA empire of Mali, lay not in its trade entrepôts in the Sahara, but closer to the resource centers of the middle Niger.

The inland Niger Delta's best-excavated sequence is that of DJENNÉ-JENO (250 B.C.E. to 1400 C.E.), a 33-hectare (82-acre) mud-brick settlement mound. From its foundation, the inhabitants of the site fished, cultivated rice and sorghum, and had domestic livestock. Trade with adjoining regions brought in commodities such as copper, iron, and sandstone. By 450 C.E., local craft specialization, the building of a monumental city wall, and a regional site hierarchy centered on Djenné-Jeno point to an urban status for the site. It must be stressed, however, that Djenné-Jeno is only one of more than a dozen settlements of comparable size now known from the middle Niger, and—if one were to consider smaller settlement mounds—only one of thousands. The occupation of such sites continued through the time of Ghana's Islamic successor states, the empire of Mali (1250–1600 C.E.) and the empire of SONGHAI (1375–1600).

With the conquest of Ghana by the Islamic Almoravid movement, and the subsequent rapid disintegration of this movement, there came a brief period of small feudal states in this region of West Africa. These successor kingdoms included those of Soso, in the north of ancient Ghana; and Kangaba, located in the modern Mali/GUINEA frontier zone. Kangaba had developed out of a grouping of local Mandinka chiefdoms and stateless societies, probably as a response to slave raiding during the time of the late empire of Ghana.

In the early thirteenth century, animistic Soso, under the rule of Sumanguru Kante, began to expand. It raided the territories of the Mandinka and blocked their way to commerce in the north. Around 1240, Sundiata Keita, or Mari-Diata, the young ruler of Kangaba, defeated the army of Sumanguru, conquered the north, and gained total control of the West African gold trade routes. With this conquest, Keita founded the empire later known as Mali. Mali was to become the first great Muslim empire of West Africa, eventually controlling much of modern SENEGAL, Mauritania, Guinea, and Mali. By 1312, Mali's greatest ruler, Mansa Musa, took the throne. He ruled for twenty-five years, making an elaborate pilgrimage to Mecca in 1324, during which the gold he lavished on CAIRO was to have the effect of ruining the local gold standard. During his reign several monumental mosques were constructed within the territory of modern Mali. However, Mali did not last as long as Ghana, enduring as an empire for less than two hundred years. Its short life may have been due to the instability created by its rapid expansion through conquest and its consequent ethnic diversity and potential for internal dissension.

Unfortunately, archaeologically we know very little about Mali. Excavations at its putative capital of Niani (in modern Guinea) showed substantial occupations dating to before and after the time of Mali, but very little during its epoch. It is likely that Mali had many capitals, with the capital moving with each new successor to the throne. Much archaeology remains to be done in the Mali/Guinea border region, both to understand better the origins of the Sundiata's power base and to locate the later centers of Malian rule.

IGBO-UKWU, IFE, AND BENIN: GRANDEUR IN THE WEST AFRICAN FOREST

The first complex societies of the West African forest probably took root sometime in the first millennium C.E. Limited excavations during the late first millennium have only begun to hint at the political organization of these societies, but their richness and artistic expertise have been well demonstrated at the site of Igbo-Ukwu (NIGERIA), dated to about 900. From this site, a regal burial and a storehouse of regalia have been excavated, both holding superb brass castings made by the lost wax method and thousands of glass trade beads. The presence of such wealth hints at a well-organized system of trade, craft specialists, and a wealthy elite; but we know little of settlements in the region until the emergence of the state of IFE around 1100.

The tropical West African state of Ife does not benefit from the weight of textual records available for its contemporaries in the savanna and Sahel. However, a good deal of effort has been put into its archaeology, which is a compensating factor. Initial archaeological inquiries at Ife began as long ago as 1910, when the German anthropologist Leo Frobenius visited a shrine at the living holy city of Ife and there acquired a series of naturalistic bronze and terracotta busts for £6 and some alcohol. He was later apprehended by the colonial authorities and the bronzes returned, but seven terracottas found their way into European museums. As a result there was much speculation as to who could have created this magnificent lifelike sculpture. Frobenius, on stylistic grounds, asserted that ancient Ife was a lost Greek colony founded around 1300 B.C.E. and abandoned by 800 B.C.E. We now know that this is not even remotely true. The ancient art of Ife was entirely African in its origin and dated instead to the earlier part of the second millennium C.E. The YORUBA city of Ife

is itself an object of wonder. It is surrounded by high earthworks arranged in rings around the town, with the outer ring being 11.6 km (7.2 mi) in circumference. The date of these earthworks is not yet precisely known, but it is assumed that at least some of them correspond with the apogee of Ife as a political center.

Archaeological work at Ife and other sites in its vicinity has been driven primarily by accidental discoveries during building activities, as much of its ancient expanse remains covered with habitations, businesses, and public buildings. Excavations have generated a series of radiocarbon dates that allow the reconstruction of a rudimentary cultural sequence. Finds from between 500 and 950 C.E. are mainly of poor grave pits concentrated near the center of the town. For the period dating from 950 to 1300, however, there are rich graves, numerous ritual structures, and a distribution of finds throughout, and even beyond, the vast area enclosed by the earthworks. Most of the terracotta portrait busts have been thermoluminescence dated to c. 1200–1300 C.E. In some sculptures, personages are depicted richly adorned in ceremonial regalia. Shrines featuring such depictions may point to a form of divine kingship that is known to have existed historically in the region.

Perched at the edge of Nigeria's tropical forest, Ife is thought to have come to prominence by the control of local products (ivory, gold, pepper, kola nuts, and slaves) in the external trade to Niger River civilizations. By 1300 its walled capital was at the peak of its wealth, with many shrines featuring elaborate potsherd pavements and sculptures scattered throughout the city. To support this large elite and artisanal population, Ife's subsistence base appears to have been yams, oil-palm products, and small livestock. Surrounding Ife there was likely to have been a continuous hinterland of farmsteads. Around 1500 the city of Ife declined, and the region's center of power shifted to BENIN, without any appreciable break in cultural tradition, despite the fact that Benin City was founded by a different ethnic group (Edo instead of Yoruba).

The rise of Benin and its eclipse of Ife (fifteenth century C.E.) corresponds to the beginning of contacts with the Portuguese and a shift to coastal rather than riverine trade. The first of the great kings of Benin was Oba Euware (1440 C.E.). He is said in oral traditions to have captured 201 towns and made them render regular tribute to him. He is also said to have been the builder of the walls and ditches of Benin, as well as external road networks. From the time of Oba Euware on, there were further innovations in bronze (or more properly brass) casting, with the advent of brass plaques showing the exploits of kings, and with brass pendant plaques being worn by local rulers and functionaries as badges of rank. The walls of Benin are even more spectacular than those of Ife, earning a spot in the *Guinness Book of World Records* as the world's largest earthwork. Benin City continued to flourish until the advent of the colonial era, when a British punitive expedition sacked the capital in 1897.

PRE-AKSUMITE AND AKSUMITE CIVILIZATION IN ETHIOPIA

Like Meroe, which was more linked to Egypt than Africa, we find in AKSUM another outwardly looking state, wedded to the trading sphere of the Red Sea and southern Arabia rather than the African interior. Although there has been some debate concerning the cultural origins of Aksum, it is most likely that there was in fact an undifferentiated Ethiopian/South Arabian cultural sphere from the late first millennium B.C.E. into the first millennium C.E. Unfortunately the epoch most likely to shed important light on this matter, the pre-Aksumite period (500 B.C.E.–100 C.E.), has barely been studied. Indeed, little has been well documented save several religious and funerary shrines bearing South Arabian inscriptions. The best preserved of these are known from the site of Yeha, where there is a pre-Aksumite temple dedicated to the South Arabian moon god Alouqah. In addition, it can be noted that the distribution of pre-Aksumite material culture more or less equates to that of later Aksum: the northern Ethiopian/Eritrean highlands. Thus, Aksum has been viewed as the successor to this earlier complex society. The last few centuries of the pre-Aksumite period are sometimes referred to as the Intermediate Period. During this time inscriptions in South Arabian script decline, being replaced by a local script based upon the Ge'ez language.

Classic Aksumite civilization prospered between 100 and 600 C.E. The first textual mentions of Aksum may be found in the *Periplus of the Erythraean Sea*, an Alexandrian Greek trading guide published in the late first century C.E. The guide makes reference to a metropolis called "Axomite." There is also a mention in Ptolemy's *Geography* that would lead us to expect a city and a king's palace at Aksum in the mid-second century. Archaeologically, during this early Aksumite period, the first stellae are known to have been installed in the funerary park of the city of Aksum. Textual records from South Arabian temples indicate that by the third century, Aksumite armies were fighting with success in southern Arabia, allied with local rulers, and being led in person by the Aksumite king Gadarat. By 270 Aksum was minting its own coinage, marked with a distinctive disk and crescent symbol and the head of the ruler (in the first case, King Endybis). Between 200 and 330, Aksum's greatest monuments were erected. These include the underground chambered tombs of Nefas Mawcha and the Tomb of the Brick Arches, as well as the great stellae of Aksum (the

largest being 30 m, or 98 ft, in height, and weighing 517 tons). These stellae were carved from single blocks of stone, with low-relief sculpture on their surfaces representing multistoried structures with doors, windows, and beams. By this time we know that Aksum was supplying African luxury goods (particularly ivory and animal skins) to the Red Sea trade, receiving in return precious metals, glass, cloth, wine, and spices.

Aksum's most celebrated king, Ezana, came to power around 330. During his reign Aksum was sovereign over ETHIOPIA as well as parts of Yemen and SUDAN. Ezana converted to Christianity in 333. There followed a trend toward simpler burial traditions and the replacement of the disk and crescent with the cross on Aksumite coinage.

From 600 onward, Aksum began to decline. Aksum ceased to be the state's capital in 619. At this time the kingdom also lost its one seaport of Adulis, as a result of internal dissension. One of the world's first Christian states, Aksum's successors were to retain their religion in the wake of the Islamic expansion of the late first millennium.

THE SWAHILI COAST AND THE EAST AFRICAN INTERIOR

Along the East African littoral, during the first millennium C.E., coastal trade was to play an important role in the elaboration of local social hierarchies, just as trans-Saharan trade was doing in the west. Likewise, for many years the SWAHILI CIVILIZATION—a chain of semiautonomous city-states dotting the East African coast—was thought to be the direct result of Arabian colonization. Its cities were viewed as the very edge of the Islamic world—wealthy trading posts perched on the edge of a foreboding interior from which trade goods would "appear" in exchange for cloth and beads. However, the past few decades of research have exposed the indigenous African roots of the Swahili culture and their eventual synergy with incoming Arabian/Islamic culture.

Although the guide written in the late first century C.E., *Periplus of the Erythraean Sea* (see the section on the Aksumite civilization), cites the presence of a trading city (Rhapta) along the coast of KENYA or TANZANIA, little substantial archaeological evidence exists for East African trading societies until the ninth century. However, there is some encouraging recent evidence from the site of Unjuja Ukuu (situated at the southern tip of the island of ZANZIBAR, Tanzania). There, local ceramics have been found in stratigraphy with fragments of Egypto-Roman pottery, with the whole assemblage radiocarbon dated to 400–550 C.E. This at least attests to coastal trade with Roman Egypt by that time and hints that Rhapta may not be a myth.

By 800 Swahili trading cities dotted the East African coast, fusing Islamic religion and architecture with indigenous sociopolitical organization and commercial acumen. Trading settlements, of which 170 are known, eventually extended from southern SOMALIA to MOZAMBIQUE. From these towns the Indian Ocean acted as a trade corridor to the Far East, with lateen and square-rigged dhows stocking the menageries of Chinese emperors and carrying silks and porcelain to Swahili merchants and their sultans. At an incipient level, it is now apparent that Swahili civilization arose out of coastal agro-pastoral societies, whose gradual mastery of the sea lanes made them ideal intermediaries with foreign mariners. At the well-studied site of Shanga (Tanzania), mud and thatch indigenous architecture in the eighth and ninth centuries gives way to a local mutation of Islamic mortar and stone buildings in the tenth century, with evidence for long-distance trade being present throughout the site's sequence. At its apex, however, the Swahili coast packed a lavish Islamic veneer, with impressive palaces and mosques distributed among sites such as Kilwa and Gedi. Indeed, by 1331 the great traveler IBN BATTUTAH would write "Kilwa is one of the most beautiful and well-constructed towns in the world." The eventual downfall of the Swahili trading network and its days of glory was brought about by the arrival of Portuguese mariners in the first years of the sixteenth century. They sacked Kilwa in 1505 and rapidly constructed a chain of stone and wood forts along the eastern seaboard, and the east coast trade soon lost its efficiency. The Portuguese, unlike the Arab traders, did not integrate well into the existing trading community.

During the time of the Swahili civilization, numerous complex societies and states grew in the interior, often as trade-item consolidators for the coastal trade. Farthest from the coast were the wealthy societies of the DEMOCRATIC REPUBLIC OF THE CONGO's Upemba Depression, the neighboring Kisalian and Katotian polities (c. 700–1300). Both are known for their sumptuous graves, with those of the Kisalian suggesting wealth deriving from an intra-African trade (copper, iron, and ivory) and those from the Katotian suggesting firmer links with Indian ocean commerce (cowries, conus shells, glass beads). The successor to the Kisalian polity was the historic kingdom of LUBA.

GREAT ZIMBABWE (AND ITS PREDECESSOR MAPUNGUBWE)

Farther to the south, trading states developed where Bantu agro-pastoralists had already established transient chiefdoms based upon the manipulation of livestock wealth. The first of these states, Mapungubwe (c. 1000–1200), grew up in the South African Limpopo River basin. Here, an intermediary role in the coastal trade fossilized existing, and otherwise transient, social hierarchies based upon cattle wealth. Glass trade beads, cowries, and copper

ingots came in from the coast to the Mapungubwe hill settlement in exchange for ivory, animal skins, and locally mined gold. From 1075 it is apparent that artisanal specialists existed at the site, including metal, ivory, and bone workers, as well as spinners of cotton thread. These items would have been of use in both local and external trade.

A further elaboration of such hierarchies, but over a greater zone of influence, can be seen in the state of GREAT ZIMBABWE (c. 1100–1450). Famed for the towering, dry-stone masonry architecture of its impressive central settlement, the Great Zimbabwe tradition like Mapungubwe consolidated the gold and animal product wealth of its hinterland as a powerful bargaining chip in the competitive coastal trade.

It is interesting to note that Great Zimbabwe, like Ife, was once perceived by colonialists as an outpost of peoples foreign to the African continent. Great Zimbabwe first became known to Europeans through Portuguese contacts. By 1506 there were rumors of a King Mwene Motapa, who ruled a series of lands ranging from the Kalahari Desert to the Indian Ocean. However, in the seventeenth century, Portuguese missionaries and historians, who by now had seen the abandoned ruins of the interior, began to cast doubt upon their African origins—interpreting them instead as the remains of the vanished Christian kingdom of Prester John, or King Solomon's mines. The first archaeological investigations at the site in the late nineteenth century set out merely to determine the nature of Great Zimbabwe's external origins. Such work was supported by Cecil Rhodes, who saw in Great Zimbabwe an ancient Phoenician trading settlement, mirroring the then current British marine hegemony. At this time, treasure hunters mined much of the site for its valuables. As the twentieth

ANCIENT AFRICAN CIVILIZATIONS. Built around 1200 C.E., the walls of Great Zimbabwe were constructed from granite blocks without the use of mortar and rise approximately 36 feet. (*World Religions Photo Library/Bridgeman Art Library International Ltd.*)

century dawned, a series of professional archaeologists, including Keith Robinson and Gertrude Caton-Thompson, demonstrated through excavations that there was no evidence for a foreign presence at the site, with local (proto-SHONA) pottery, art, and architectural styles present throughout. Despite this, wrangles over the site's origins would continue until a comparatively recent period, with the site figuring as an important propaganda tool in the Zimbabwean struggle for independence.

The site of Great Zimbabwe is only one of over fifty other masonry settlements of its type scattered throughout ZIMBABWE and northern BOTSWANA, although it is without doubt the most grandiose. It is now known that Great Zimbabwe was founded in the eleventh century C.E. as a relatively small-scale trading and herding center, consisting only of Daga (mud) dwellings dotting the local hills and valleys. But from 1085 C.E. on, profound changes began to take place. First the labyrinthine Hill Ruin was constructed. This high-walled multiroom structure is accessed only by a precipitous stone stairway winding along the side of the hill. It has been interpreted as royal residence and a spiritual/ritual center. Later, the Valley Ruin, with its much-photographed cyclopean Elliptical Building, was constructed. With its narrow, three-story-tall entrance passageway, and central court featuring two circular stone towers, it has been interpreted by some as a later king's residence and by others as women's area, perhaps a dwelling for the king's wives or a noblewomen's initiation center. From 1085 to 1450 Daga huts continued to dot the plains around the stone complexes, taking in almost 100 hectares (250 acres) in area. At its height in the thirteenth century, Great Zimbabwe's capital was home to as many as 18,000 people. Subsistence to support such population concentrations remained crucial, and it is likely that cattle and agricultural surplus continued to play a highly visible role in the maintenance of power.

Contemporary with Great Zimbabwe there is evidence for regional centers subordinate to the central site. The best documented of these is Ingombe Ilede on the ZAMBEZI RIVER. There, the fifteenth-century graves of local rulers have been excavated. They were adorned with necklaces of local gold and imported glass beads and wrapped in fine cloth burial shrouds, of which traces remain. As was the case elsewhere in Africa, these local nodes of power served to consolidate goods for the external trading center of Great Zimbabwe (for example, ivory, rhinoceros horn, animal skins, gold, and slaves). Undoubtedly Great Zimbabwe owed much of its wealth to international trade, but it was also part of a long-term internal development, with its power based as much upon cattle wealth and military power as foreign riches.

The collapse of the Great Zimbabwe occupation is dated to the mid- to late-fifteenth century, when most of the site was abandoned. Reasons posited for Great Zimbabwe's collapse have included the possible exhaustion of local gold, arable land, or water resources, and the disruption of the Indian Ocean trading sphere by the Portuguese. Majestic successor states such as Khami, located farther in the interior, soon sprang up, but none ever achieved the power of Great Zimbabwe.

See also BANTU: DISPERSION AND SETTLEMENT; EGYPT, ANCIENT KINGDOM OF; GOLD TRADE; IVORY TRADE; SALT TRADE.

KEVIN MACDONALD

Andrianampoinimerina
mid-1700s–1810?
Ruler (born Ramboàsalàma) of the Merina Empire of Madagascar from 1795 to 1810.
Oral traditions recorded by Jesuit missionaries in the late eighteenth century suggest that Andriambélomàsina, ruler of the Imerina (the territory of the Merina ethnic group) from 1730 to 1770, directed that his eldest son Andrianjàfy succeed him, followed by his grandson Ramboàsalàma, son of his eldest daughter. Andrianjàfy, however, intended for his own son to take his place and plotted to kill Ramboàsalàma, who, fearing for his life, fled to the north. Supported by a dozen Merina chiefs, Ramboàsalàma returned in 1787, overtaking the city of Ambohimànga and exiling his uncle, who was later killed.

Ramboàsalàma was crowned Andrianampoinimerina, "the prince in the heart of Imerina." After consolidating power through treaties and marriage alliances and establishing a capital at Antananarivo in about 1795, Andrianampoinimerina, also known as Nampoina, began to expand the Merina Empire. Eventually he controlled much of the island, conquering and consolidating the Betsileo, Sihanaka, and Bezanozano kingdoms.

During his reign, Nampoina developed a legal system, instituted corvée, or forced labor, to complete public works, established extensive trading networks, and constructed irrigation channels in the rice paddies that fed his growing army. Andrianampoinimerina also established relations with Europeans, particularly French merchants trading weapons for slaves. As many as eighteen hundred slaves were exported annually, most of whom were sent to Ile de France (now MAURITIUS) and Bourbon (RÉUNION). Barthélemy Hugon, one such European trader, wrote of Nampoina in 1808, "He is without doubt the richest, the most feared, the most enlightened, and has the largest kingdom, of all the kings of Madagascar."

On his death, Nampoina was buried in a silver canoe. Although he never conquered Madagascar in its entirety, Andrianampoinimerina's dreams would be largely fulfilled by his son, RADAMA I, to whom Nampoina proclaimed while dying, "Imerina has been gathered into one, but behold the sea is the border of my rice-fields, O Radama."

BIBLIOGRAPHY
Allen, Philip M. *Madagascar: Conflicts of Authority in the Great Island.* Westview Press, 1995.

ARI NAVE

Anga

Ethnic group of Nigeria; also known as Nnga and Kerang.
The Anga primarily inhabit the Plateau State of NIGERIA. They speak an Afro-Asiatic language belonging to the Chadic group. Approximately 400,000 people consider themselves Anga.

See also LANGUAGES, AFRICAN: AN OVERVIEW.

Angola

Country on the southwest coast of Africa bordering the South Atlantic Ocean, between Namibia and the Democratic Republic of the Congo.
Few African countries have seen their natural and human potential as underutilized and thoroughly ravaged by violence as Angola. Precolonial southern Africa was home to some of the continent's richest kingdoms, which welcomed European merchants and missionaries in the fifteenth century, only to be corrupted and ultimately destroyed by the transatlantic slave trade in the sixteenth century. The abolition of the trade—a politically and economically destabilizing event—was followed by the repressive taxation and forced labor regimes of Portuguese colonialism. Although much of the rest of the continent underwent rapid decolonization in the 1960s, the armed struggle for independence in Angola took nearly fifteen years and perpetuated internal divisions that turned into a decades-long, ongoing civil war. Although Angola's vast natural resources hold great promise, immense obstacles to development remain, particularly landmines and a shattered infrastructure.

PRECOLONIAL KINGDOMS AND THE SLAVE TRADE

Small groups of hunter-gatherer KHOIKHOI people were the first to inhabit the region of present-day Angola. Late in the first millennium Bantu-speaking people migrated to the area from the north, pushing some Khoikhoi farther south and incorporating others. The Bantu speakers brought with them iron-smelting skills, agricultural practices, and cattle, all of which they used to establish some of the largest and most centralized kingdoms in Central Africa. In the mid-thirteenth or fourteenth century, KONGO kings organized the mostly matrilineal agricultural settlements surrounding the mouth of the CONGO RIVER into provinces, collected taxes, and established an official currency of shells. South of the Kongo, in the early sixteenth century, the centralized Ndongo controlled the trade in salt and iron. Later in the century the LUNDA formed a kingdom in the grasslands of the upper Kasai River.

Ironwork, weaving, and extensive trade took place in these and other inland kingdoms, especially the MATAMBA and Kasanje to the east, the Bié, Bailundu, and Ciyanda on the eastern plateau, and the Kwanhama in the south. Most of the kings held divine powers. The coastal kingdoms tended to be centralized and agricultural, capturing slaves and extracting people and natural resources, including ivory and gold, from the interior. The interior kingdoms, by contrast, were less centralized, more heterogeneous, and supported themselves through hunting and fishing. Over time, patterns of migration among the kingdoms produced the major ethnolinguistic groups of Angola—including the Bakongo, MBUNDU, and OVIMBUNDU—as well as smaller groups such as the Nganguela, Lunda-Chokwe, HERERO, Nyaneka-Humbe, and Ambo.

Portuguese explorer Diogo Cam (also spelled Cão), the first European to visit the region, sailed into the mouth of the Congo River in 1482. Portuguese missionaries soon followed and some kingdoms, including the Kongo, adopted Catholicism as the official religion. The Portuguese initially maintained peaceful relations with the Kongo, trading goods with such leaders as King Afonso I in exchange for slaves. But as they moved farther south into the Ndongo kingdom, Portuguese slave-traders became more intrusive and violent, while Africans, such as Queen Nzinga, resisted. When they began to meet resistance from the Bakongo—many of whom considered the trade contradictory to Christianity—the Portuguese monarchy sent troops to Angola.

During the first major military campaign (1574–1594), *conquistadores* established forts and a system of vassalage, setting a pattern that would be replicated throughout the region. The Portuguese recognized African chiefs, or sobas, in exchange for their subservience. In their effort to move into the interior of Angola, the Portuguese found tropical diseases, African hostility, and land unsuitable for agriculture. It was not until the middle of the seventeenth century that the major coastal kingdoms had been subjugated. Portuguese officials taxed the African kings in the use of porters and ivory, but predominately in slaves.

Slavery and a local trade in slaves existed in some form in most of Angola's kingdoms. The transatlantic slave trade, however, was unsurpassed in scale and impact. It

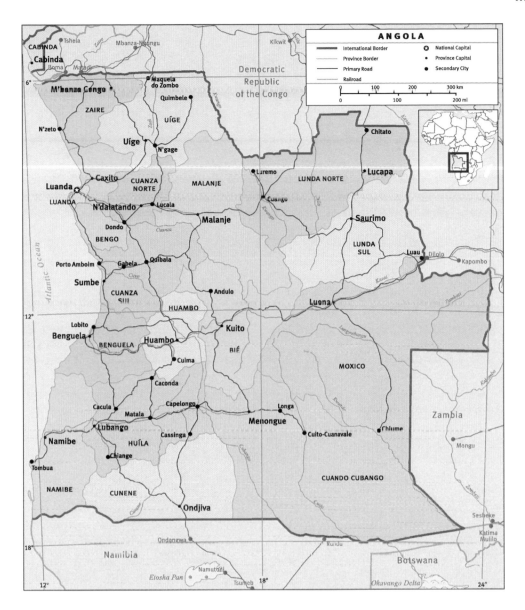

is estimated that between the late sixteenth century and 1836, when Portugal officially abolished slave trafficking, four million people from the region were captured for the slave trade. Only about two million of these people survived the march to the coast, confinement, and the journey across the Atlantic. As many as one million slaves were transported to Brazil, and the rest went to plantations in the Caribbean. Slave trading agents, or pombeiros—some Portuguese, most African or Afro-Portuguese (mestiços)—bought slaves from local chiefs in exchange for cloth, guns, and other European goods.

The slave trade made some chiefs enormously wealthy, but it ultimately undermined local economies and political stability as villages' vital labor forces were shipped overseas and slave raids and civil wars became commonplace. Demand for slaves was slowed, but not stopped, by the

official ban on the trade. The transatlantic trade had made slavery an integral part of the economy and social structure in Angola that continued after Portugal abolished slavery there in 1858. Portuguese settlers in Angola sustained labor laws that forced Africans to work on agricultural estates.

PORTUGUESE SETTLERS AND THE OVERSEAS PROVINCE

After the official slave trade ended, Portugal sought other means to exact revenue and labor from Angola. In addition to raising port customs and imposing a higher hut tax, beginning in the 1830s Portugal launched a military expansion into the Angolan interior. These costly campaigns met opposition from both Africans and other European powers, especially the British and AFRIKANERS. Eventually the Portuguese retreated to their coastal settlements at LUANDA and Benguela, where they mixed with the local African population, creating a class of *mestiços*. Although there was little racial segregation, whites clearly dominated the social and economic hierarchy, despite the fact that many of these Portuguese emigrants were social outcasts, deserters, and criminals.

Portuguese plantation owners had perennial problems retaining African workers, even with the imposition of labor conscription laws. Laws passed in 1878 and 1899 upheld the status of liberto, or freed slave, but introduced vagrancy laws that enabled Portuguese officials to force Africans to work on government projects and plantations in need of labor. Despite a growth in agriculture production—particularly of coffee, sugar, and, later, rubber—that generated significant revenue, Angola's economy stagnated from a lack of capital to develop the infrastructure. For most Africans, the Sertanejo, or trader, was the most visible evidence of Portuguese presence. In the latter half of the nineteenth century, however, the European expansionism that preceded the BERLIN CONFERENCE OF 1884–1885 led Portugal to occupy more of Angola. Portuguese soldiers and settlers, unsuccessful in acquiring the Shire River highlands (in present-day MALAWI) and the south bank of the Congo River, did retain Cabinda, a small enclave on the north bank of the river. At the turn of the century Portugal occupied one-tenth of the land that today comprises Angola.

Throughout the nineteenth century and until the military campaigns ended in 1930, many sectors of Angolan society resisted domination by the Portuguese monarchy. Kings, especially the well-educated leaders of the Kongo, invoked historical treaties to resist Portuguese dictates. Protestant and Catholic missionaries often sided with Africans against the Portuguese governor general in Angola. European settlers, soldiers, and businessmen periodically took advantage of the weak government in Lisbon to attempt secession from Portugal or unification with Brazil. Other vocal critics of Portuguese rule included assimilados—those Africans who had assimilated Portuguese education and culture—and *mestiços*, many of whom held positions in the civil service and military.

The introduction of the Estado Novo, or New State, to Portugal in 1926 led to the suppression of indigenous Angolan resistance and institutionalized Angola's social stratification. New legislation made *assimilado* a legal rather than social status and suppressed many rights of Africans, with the claim that they were not "advanced" and had to be "civilized" through education and religion. In 1950, thirty-one thousand out of four million Angolans held *assimilado* status. The Estado Novo also changed the status of Angola itself from a colony to an even less autonomous "overseas province." The economy of the province boomed after World War II, when the completion of the

Benguela Railway linked the fertile, mineral-rich Belgian Congo to the coast. Diamond mining and coffee production expanded rapidly, and the Portuguese government encouraged emigration to Angola and the purchase of land. But this new prosperity was fragile, dependent on a cheap and increasingly volatile African labor force.

AFRICAN NATIONALISM AND THE WAR FOR INDEPENDENCE

The postwar era saw an explosion of nationalist political activity. Although heavily censored by colonial authorities, more than sixty parties and associations formed in the 1940s and 1950s to protest Portuguese policies. These groups represented a variety of interests, including the old *assimilado* associations, militant Africans, ethnic separatists, and Europeans. Many cultural associations, prophets, and separatist religious groups also opposed Portuguese colonialism, but little unity existed among them. Resentment of assimilation policies and white immigration, especially in urban centers, led to the creation of several nationalist political parties, though they remained divided by ethnicity and class. In 1953 urban intellectuals formed the Party of the United Struggle of Africans of Angola, which later joined with other organizations to form the MOVIMENTO POPULAR DE LIBERTAÇÃO DE ANGOLA, or MPLA, under the leadership of Agostinho NETO. Meanwhile, Bakongo nationalists formed the Union of Angolan People, or UPA, which later became the National Front for the Liberation of Angola, or FNLA.

In 1961 rebellions in the north were joined by MPLA actions in Luanda. Colonial policemen crushed the rebellions, massacring thousands of civilians: in response, UPA insurgents in the north massacred settlers and *mestiços*. These atrocities roused the opposition groups, but did not unite them. Throughout the early and mid-1960s, the FNLA and MPLA disagreed over ideology, strategy, and leadership. Because both movements faced overwhelming Portuguese military superiority, each concentrated on building their fighting forces in camps in neighboring countries. Instability in the Congo reinvigorated the war as the superpowers competed for influence in the region. The Eastern Bloc supported the Mbundu-dominated and socialist-leaning MPLA. The West backed the Bakongo-dominated and populist FNLA. China, and later the United States and South Africa, supported the Ovimbundu-dominated National Union for the Total Independence of Angola (UNITA), a breakaway faction led by Jonas SAVIMBI that professed little coherent ideology.

The war for independence continued until 1975. It became increasingly conventional as the militaries grew, but the nationalist groups fought each other as much as they did the Portuguese, while the civilian population suffered. Ultimately it was the effort of simultaneously fighting three insurgency wars—in MOZAMBIQUE and GUINEA-BISSAU, as well as in Angola—that sapped the strength of the Portuguese military and helped precipitate the overthrow of the Caetano government in Lisbon in April 1974. A month before Angolan independence, SOUTH AFRICA invaded on the pretext of assisting the FNLA-UNITA, and in response the MPLA received additional military aid from the Soviet Union and assistance from Cuba. This international involvement did not, however, produce a clear victor, and on November 11, 1975, Portugal ceded independence to the people of Angola. The MPLA declared victory and the MPLA leader became president, though in fact the party controlled little of the country and fighting between the factions continued.

CIVIL WAR AND A FRAGILE PEACE

The South African invasion, Cuban intervention, and Soviet and American assistance internationalized the Angolan conflict. The FNLA and UNITA allied to form an alternative government based in the southern town of Huambo. Although the FNLA ceased to exist in 1976, UNITA, benefiting from extensive South African military assistance as well as United States aid and a lucrative diamond smuggling industry, built a formidable fighting force of around 40,000 soldiers.

The MPLA, a Marxist-Leninist vanguard party since 1977, expanded educational opportunities and the health care system, and nationalized industries deserted by Portuguese settlers and foreign corporations. But its state-owned farms and inefficient bureaucracies only made life more difficult in the countryside, where roads deteriorated and small farmers were left without access to markets or agricultural inputs. President Neto and José Eduardo DOS SANTOS, who succeeded Neto in 1979, both pursued pragmatic economic policies, permitting private ownership and cooperating with western oil companies in exploiting Angola's rich reserves off the coast of Cabinda. The enclave had in fact become one of the largest oil-producing regions in Africa, and Cabinda separatists continue to fight the Angolan government for their independence. Much—if not all—of the $400 million annual oil revenues were spent on the war effort, as defense accounted for 40 percent of annual government expenditures.

Not until the end of the Cold War were genuine international efforts made to stop the fighting in Angola. In 1988 negotiations between the warring factions and their international sponsors resulted in the withdrawal of Cuban and South African troops from Angola. This slow and uneven peace process culminated in a ceasefire, in 1991, and the outline of a plan for military demobilization and elections. Refusing to participate in runoff elections,

Savimbi and UNITA withdrew from the peace process, and fighting resumed. In 1994 the international community pressured Savimbi into a second peace accord that resulted in UNITA representatives assuming several posts and parliamentary seats in a government of national unity. In 1997 the Angolan military supported Laurent-Désiré KABILA in the Democratic Republic of the Congo and Denis Sassou-Nguesso in the Republic of the Congo and may have backed a coup attempt in Zambia.

Angola, a country devastated by war, desperately needed economic recovery in the 1990s. The country needed to rebuild its infrastructure to benefit from its rich natural resources, including gold, diamonds, timber, fish, and agricultural products. More than 100,000 active landmines hidden throughout the countryside, however, continued to impede economic development. Angola also faced the burden of rehabilitating the approximately 70,000 landmine victims.

In September 1998 UNITA representatives were expelled from the Angolan unity government on the grounds that UNITA had not disarmed, as required by the 1994 peace accords. By the end of 1998 escalating political and military tension between the Angolan government and UNITA erupted into a full-scale resumption of civil war. UNITA's alliance with Tutsi-led rebels seeking to oust President Laurent-Désiré Kabila of the Democratic Republic of the Congo prompted the Angolan government to intervene in support of Kabila. Meanwhile, there was consensus building within the fourteen-nation Southern African Development Community (SADC) that UNITA posed a threat to regional stability and should be crushed. The Angolan military launched a major offensive in 1999 that destroyed UNITA's conventional military power and recaptured the cities held by UNITA forces. Savimbi then resumed guerrilla warfare against the government, but fighting ended after he died in combat in February 2002.

In April 2002, the government and UNITA signed a formal cease-fire, and in August UNITA demobilized all of its military personnel. On November 21, 2002, the two sides declared that all outstanding issues between them had been resolved and that both parties agreed to accept the conditions laid out in the 1994 peace accords. National elections were at last held in September 2008—sixteen years after the most recent—with the promise of a presidential election in 2009. The major challenges facing Angola at this time are healing the divisions created during the long civil war and resettling some four million Angolans displaced by the decades of conflict.

See also COLONIAL RULE; DECOLONIZATION IN AFRICA: AN INTERPRETATION; SLAVERY IN AFRICA.

Angola (At a Glance)

OFFICIAL NAME:
Republic of Angola

FORMER NAME:
People's Republic of Angola

AREA:
1,246,700 sq km (498,680 sq mi)

LOCATION:
Southern Africa, bordering the South Atlantic Ocean, between Namibia and the Democratic Republic of the Congo

CAPITAL:
Luanda (population 4.8 million; 2007 estimate)

OTHER MAJOR CITIES:
Huambo (population 822,000), Benguela (600,000) (2008 estimates)

POPULATION:
12,531,357 (2008 estimate)

POPULATION DENSITY:
11 persons per sq km (about 25 persons per sq mi)

POPULATION BELOW AGE 15:
43.6 percent (male 2,760,264; female 2,707,665; 2008 estimate)

POPULATION GROWTH RATE:
1.97 percent (2003 estimate)

TOTAL FERTILITY RATE:
6.2 children born per woman (2008 estimate)

LIFE EXPECTANCY AT BIRTH:
Total population: 37.92 years (male 36.99 years; female 38.9 years; 2008 estimate)

INFANT MORTALITY RATE:
182.31 deaths per 1000 live births (2008 estimate)

LITERACY RATE (AGE 15 AND OVER WHO CAN READ AND WRITE):
67.4 percent (male 82.9 percent; female 54.2 percent; 2001 estimate)

EDUCATION:
Officially compulsory for children age 7 to 15, but the majority of the population is rural and poor. Educational reforms enacted in the 1990s have produced an increase in primary school enrollment to 1.3 million students in 1993. Angola's only university is Agostinho Neto University, founded in 1976 in Luanda.

LANGUAGES:
Portuguese is the official language. More than 90 percent of the population speaks Bantu languages. The most commonly spoken include Kimbundu, Umbundu, and Kikongo.

ETHNIC GROUPS:
Ovimbundu 37 percent, Kimbundu 25 percent, Bakongo 13 percent, mestiào (of indigenous and European descent) 2 percent, European 1 percent, other 22 percent

RELIGIONS:
Indigenous beliefs 47 percent, Roman Catholic 38 percent, Protestant 15 percent

CLIMATE:
Angola is a tropical country. It is semiarid in the south and along the coast to Luanda; the north has a cool, dry season (May to October) and hot, rainy season (November to April). Annual rainfall ranges from 50 mm (about 2 in) near the Namibe desert to 1,500 mm (about 60 in) in the central plateau.

LAND, PLANTS, AND ANIMALS:
Angola is the seventh largest country in Africa. The majority of the land comprises meadows, pastures, forests, and woodlands. Less than 3 percent of the land is arable. The primary rivers, the Cuanza and Cunene, drain to the Atlantic Ocean. Angola has no major lakes.

NATURAL RESOURCES:
Petroleum, diamonds, iron ore, phosphates, copper, feldspar, gold, bauxite, uranium, manganese

CURRENCY:
The new kwanza

GROSS DOMESTIC PRODUCT (GDP):
$95.46 billion (2007 estimate)

GDP PER CAPITA:
$7,800 (2007 estimate)

GDP REAL GROWTH RATE:
16.7 percent (2007 estimate)

PRIMARY ECONOMIC ACTIVITIES:
Subsistence agriculture is the main livelihood for 80 to 90 percent of the population but accounts for less than 15 percent of GDP. Oil production and the supporting activities contribute about 45 percent of GDP and make up over half of all exports.

PRIMARY CROPS:
Coffee, cassava, bananas, sugar cane, sisal, corn, cotton, manioc (tapioca), tobacco

INDUSTRIES:
Mining of petroleum, diamonds, iron ore, phosphates, feldspar, bauxite, uranium, gold; fish processing; food processing; brewing; tobacco processing; sugar; textiles; cement; basic metal products

PRIMARY EXPORTS:
Oil, diamonds, refined petroleum products, gas, coffee, sisal, fish and fish products, timber, cotton

PRIMARY IMPORTS:
Capital equipment (machinery and electrical equipment), food, vehicles and spare parts, textiles and clothing, medicines, substantial military deliveries

PRIMARY TRADE PARTNERS:
United States, European Union (Portugal especially), Brazil

GOVERNMENT:
Angola currently has a transitional government and is nominally a multiparty democracy with a strong presidential system. Universal suffrage begins at age 18. The legislative branch is unicameral, and the National Assembly (Assembleia Nacional) seats 220. The president appoints the judges of the Supreme Court (Tribunal da Relaàão) and the Council of Ministers. Major political parties include the Popular Movement for the Liberation of Angola (MPLA) and the National Union for the Total Independence of Angola (UNITA). National independence was achieved on November 11, 1975 (from Portugal). President Jose Eduardo Dos Santos (since September 21, 1979) was originally elected without opposition under a one-party system and stood for election in Angola's first multiparty elections on September 29±30, 1992. He received 49.6 percent of the total vote, making a runoff election necessary between him and second-place Jonas Savimbi; the runoff was not held and Savimbi's UNITA party disputed the results of the first election; the civil war was resumed. A national unity government took power in 1997, but fighting resumed in late 1998. The death of UNITA leader Jonas Savimbi in 2002 led to a ceasefire that raised hopes for a peaceful future. In 2007, after twenty-seven years and as many as 1.5 million dead, the civil war at last came to an end, and the country began to rebuild both its economic and physical infrastructure.

Alonford James Robinson, Jr. and Eric Young

Annan, Kofi

1938–

Secretary-general of the United Nations.

A lifelong diplomat, Annan assumed the top post of the UNITED NATIONS (UN) in January 1997 to serve a term lasting through 2001. In 2001 the UN General Assembly unanimously elected him to a second term running from 2002 through 2006. That same year Annan and the United Nations shared the 2001 Nobel Peace Prize, awarded to the secretary-general for "bringing new life to the organization" and to the UN in recognition of its role in promoting "global peace and cooperation." Two years later, however, Annan faced the challenging task of piloting the UN through one of the biggest crises in its history, the United States war against Iraq.

Kofi Annan is the first head of the UN to come from Africa south of the SAHARA Desert. He is also the first secretary-general to have risen through the UN ranks. Annan had impressed the international diplomatic community while serving as the UN's undersecretary-general for peacekeeping, a job in which he coordinated efforts to help such tortured areas as RWANDA, SOMALIA, and the former Yugoslavia. He began his term as secretary-general under pressure to reform the large and economically troubled UN bureaucracy. Following his appointment, Annan pledged to improve UN programs in poor countries, saying, "economic development is not merely a matter of projects and statistics. It is, above all, a matter of people—real people with basic needs: food, clothing, shelter, and medical care."

Annan was born into a prominent family in Kumsai, GOLD COAST (now the nation of GHANA). His father was both a hereditary chief of the FANTE people and a high-ranking civil servant. Annan took advantage of the educational opportunities available to him. After studying science and technology in Ghana, he traveled to the United States in 1959 to study at Macalester College in St. Paul, Minnesota. "It was an exciting period," says Annan. Two years earlier, Ghana had claimed its independence, and in America the Civil Rights Movement was gaining momentum. Annan graduated from Macalester in 1961 with a degree in economics, saying that his American years had taught him that "you [should] never walk into a situation and believe that you know better than the natives."

It was a lesson Annan would apply often during his diplomatic career. After graduate studies in economics in Geneva, Switzerland, Annan took his first UN job at the World Health Organization (WHO). After more than a decade of diplomatic work, he took a break to serve from 1974 to 1976 as director of the Ghana Tourist Development Company. Four years later, he received his first high-level UN post, as deputy director of administration and head of personnel at the office of the UN high commissioner for refugees. In 1983 he became budget director in the office of financial services. By 1990 he had risen to the office of assistant secretary-general for program planning, budget, and finance.

Annan's 1993 appointment to the head of peacekeeping operations made him one of the UN's most visible and potentially controversial leaders. UN peacekeeping missions in Somalia and Bosnia (part of the former Yugoslavia) had drawn widespread criticism and raised doubts about the agency's future. Annan acted decisively in 1995, giving UN permission for the North Atlantic Treaty Organization (NATO) to bomb Serbian forces fighting in the former Yugoslavia—an act that forced the Serbs to negotiate for an end to the war. According to an American official quoted in the *New York Times*, Annan was "the only top official of the UN who came out of the Bosnia experience with dignity and without having harmed the organization or relations with any one of the great powers. That's what a great diplomat's about." Annan gained an international reputation not only for shrewd diplomacy, but also for honesty and charm. When the United States publicly campaigned against a second term for then-secretary-general Boutros BOUTROS-GHALI, the UN turned to Annan.

Annan was expected to shrink the UN administration at the same time as making the organization more responsive to member nations. In light of these opposing expectations, it is not surprising that he faced criticism in the early years of his secretariat. By favoring agreement-building and compromise over quick decision-making, Annan irritated some in the U.S. government, whose support—and repayment of its massive UN debt—was seen by many as crucial for Annan's success. At the same time, other member nations accused Annan of currying favor with the United States, to which he replied that he would "devote the same attention to any country that pays 25 percent of the dues and owes $1.3 billion." Annan's skillful handling of his first major diplomatic test as UN leader silenced many of his critics. In February 1998 he negotiated with Iraqi president Saddam Hussein. The Iraqi leader's agreement to allow UN weapons inspectors into the country prevented a possible war, adding to Annan's reputation as a peacemaker.

Annan achieved another victory in 2000, when the General Assembly agreed to overhaul the UN's system of financing and substantially lower U.S. dues. In return, the U.S. government agreed to pay the UN nearly $1 billion in past debts. The compromise removed a major source of tension between the UN and the United States. He issued the Millennium Report, urging UN members to commit themselves to plans for ending violence, poverty, and environmental decay. As secretary-general, Annan has reformed the management of the UN and recommitted the ogranization to its goals of economic development, social justice, and international peace. He has also worked to improve human rights worldwide and to end the epidemic of ACQUIRED IMMUNODEFICIENCY SYNDROME (AIDS). His reelection as secretary general in 2001 was uncontested, reflecting his popularity among both developing and industrialized nations.

The September 11, 2001, terrorist attack on New York City and Washington, D.C., had far-reaching consequences for the UN and for Annan. Partly as a result of that attack, the United States became increasingly determined to end Hussein's rule in Iraq, claiming that Hussein supported terrorism. Annan's earlier success with Saddam Hussein now backfired on the secretary-general, as it became clear that Hussein had not kept his agreement. The American movement toward war in early 2003 became a showdown with the UN when the UN Security Council failed to approve military action in Iraq. The United States went ahead without UN approval—an act that seemed to say to Americans and many others around the world that the UN had become meaningless and powerless. Later in 2003, months after the official end of the war in Iraq, Annan confronted the difficult task of restoring UN prestige, defining a possible role for the UN in postwar Iraq, and keeping the organization moving forward in other important areas, such as fighting AIDS. Some observers declared that the very survival of the UN could be at stake. One former American UN official was quoted in the *New York Times* as saying, "The future of the institution depends upon how [Annan] responds to the challenge."

Annan's tenure as secretary general was marked by a number of serious attempts at organizational reform and a dedication to strengthening the role of the UN in world affairs. Annan remained in his role as secretary general until December 2006, at which point he returned to Ghana. He was named chairperson of the United Nations Foundation, a charitable organization. In 2008 he was named chancellor of the University of Ghana.

See also TOURISM IN AFRICA; UNITED NATIONS IN AFRICA.

BIBLIOGRAPHY

Crossette, Barbara. "Salesman for Unity Kofi Atta Annan." *New York Times* (Dec. 14, 1996): 7.

Meisler, Stanley. *Kofi Annan: A Man of Peace in a World of War.* Wiley, 2008.

KATE TUTTLE

Antaisaka
Ethnic group of Madagascar, also known as the Taisaka and the Tesaki.

The Antaisaka primarily inhabit southeastern MADAGASCAR, around the city of Farafangana. They speak a Malayo-Polynesian language and belong to the MALAGASY cultural and linguistic group. Approximately 650,000 people consider themselves Antaisaka.

Antananarivo, Madagascar
Capital city of Madagascar.

Antananarivo is located in the central highland province of the same name. According to a 2001 census, approximately 1,403,449 people inhabit the city, and although the province is dominated by the MERINA—the largest ethnic group—Antananarivo, popularly referred to as Tana, is ethnically diverse.

Antananarivo was founded in the seventeenth century by Merina king Andrianjaka. Originally named Analamànga (the Blue Forest), the high plateau site was selected for its defensive character and proximity to nearby wetlands, where rice could be cultivated. The settlement quickly grew into the largest city in the Merina territory.

In a campaign to consolidate Merina fiefdoms, Andrianampoinimerina, the king of nearby Ambohimanga, took control of Antananarivo in 1794, overthrowing his uncle after several previous attempts. As the Merina Empire grew under the tenure of Andrianampoinimerina's son RADAMA I, so did the city, becoming the capital of Imerina (the territory of the Merina people). An estimated 15,000 people inhabited the city by the close of the eighteenth century.

When the French colonized MADAGASCAR in 1895, they named the city Tananarive. By this time the city's population had grown to between 50,000 and 75,000, the majority of whom were slaves. European influence can be found in the urban architecture, particularly the many two-story brick buildings. Antananarivo gained a reputation in Europe as an exquisitely beautiful city.

Today 10 percent of the country's entire population inhabits the capital, which spans a dozen steep hills, crowned by the Rova, the royal palace. The city's population is larger than the population of the five province capitals combined, and continual urban migration only amplifies the domination of Antananarivo.

Although Madagascar remains a predominately agrarian society, the country's main industries, which constitute 13.1 percent of the country's gross domestic product (GDP) and employ 5.5 percent of the work force, are centered in Antananarivo. These include food and tobacco processing, brewing, and soap production, as well as textile and leather manufacturing. Economic stagnation has hit residents of Antananarivo particularly hard, since they are more dependent on market forces than are subsistence farmers in rural areas. The number of jobs has declined while the number of job seekers has risen. Austerity measures introduced as part of a structural adjustment program that started in the mid-1990s also caused a significant decline in the standard of living for urban dwellers, increasing inflation and taxes while eliminating subsidies. In 2002, Antananarivo's economy was further disrupted when the city was blockaded during a six-month civil war.

See also COLONIAL RULE; SLAVERY IN AFRICA; STRUCTURAL ADJUSTMENT IN AFRICA; URBANISM AND URBANIZATION IN AFRICA.

BIBLIOGRAPHY

Allen, Philip M. *Madagascar: Conflicts of Authority in the Great Island.* Westview Press, 1995.

Brown, Mervyn. *Madagascar Rediscovered.* Damien Tunnacliffe, 1978.

ARI NAVE

Antandroy

Ethnic group of Madagascar, also known as the Tandroy or Tandruy.

The Antandroy primarily inhabit southern MADAGASCAR between the Mandrare and Menara rivers. They speak a Malayo-Polynesian language and belong to the larger MALAGASY cultural and linguistic group. More than 600,000 people consider themselves Antandroy, over half of them members of the Antanosy subgroup.

Anthropology in Africa

What was known about Africa before there were serious academic studies was sparse and variable in credibility. Anthropology, as a formal academic subject, was a late-nineteenth-century Anglo-Euro-American academic invention. It began as the comparative study of little-known non-Western societies, but very soon broadened into the study of all human societies. After some tentative starts, by the 1920s Africa had become a major area of serious research. Colonial administration made access easy, and the objective of achieving a greater understanding of the peoples of Africa attracted scholars, missionaries, and officials alike.

Inevitably, the first project was to identify who the peoples of Africa were, where they were situated geographically, and what their way of life might be. The task of information gathering was daunting. Hundreds of LANGUAGES and dialects were spoken by as many groups of people, each of which identified itself as having a distinct history and culture. There also were numerous

communities where a plurality of peoples were intermixed. Since there was no indigenous African form of writing, the absence of written records made recovering local history very difficult. The contemporary picture was obviously complex, and the past remained to be reconstructed.

FIELDWORK: THE ANTHROPOLOGICAL METHOD OF RESEARCH

From the 1920s on, social anthropology became committed to the method of research that has characterized it ever since. Information is collected through fieldwork, the close study of a group of people and the context of their lives through firsthand contact. From the 1930s into the 1950s and beyond, British social anthropologists were dominant in African studies. They produced the major ethnographic and comparative work during that era. They approached this work with a basic theoretical presupposition. They assumed that there was an underlying coherent logic in the customs and ideas of each African society in their sociocultural structure. The anthropologist's job, as they saw it, was to figure out what that logic was and explain it. No doubt, the British colonial policy of indirect rule, the policy of governing through indigenous institutions, stimulated an emphasis on political structure, but it could scarcely account for the passionate broader interest anthropologists had in everything from kinship to ritual.

The fieldwork standard of these British anthropologists was set by Bronislaw Malinowski, who became a prominent teacher in the field. He showed that the method of study he developed while living in a Trobriand village (in the Pacific) for two years could be applied anywhere. His detailed picture of everyday life in the Trobriands also carried a theoretical message. The thesis, which he called functionalism, argued that preindustrial society was in all its facets—economy, religion, kinship, politics, and law—a single integrated system in which every element of cultural practice had a function that complemented and reinforced the others.

Many Africanists, including Jomo KENYATTA, later to become president of KENYA, attended Malinowski's seminars at the London School of Economics and were deeply influenced by him. Malinowski wrote the introduction to Kenyatta's ethnography of the KIKUYU, *Facing Mount Kenya* (1938). Many Africans studied in England in that period, and their presence enhanced the interest in Africanist anthropology. Major monographs resulted. These provided a high level of detailed description about local affairs.

As anthropologists collected information on more and more particular peoples, they realized that there was a bewildering range of variation among them in KINSHIP organization, in other features of culture, in economy, and in politics.

There were sophisticated kingdoms and ruler-less nomadic groups. There were herders and agriculturalists. As the monographs accumulated, the possibility of broad comparative analysis opened. The need to classify became an imperative of the field, to make order in the aggregation of diverse information culled from fieldwork, and to understand the logic of similarities and differences.

COMPARISON OF RECONSTRUCTED TRADITIONAL SYSTEMS

One of the first anthropological classifiers of African societies was an American, Melville Herskovits, who was ultimately to become the doyen of African studies in the United States. He founded a center for African studies at Northwestern University, and in 1957 was one of the founders of the African Studies Association in the United States. In 1938 he published a history of the kingdom of DAHOMEY. But more than a decade before that, in his dissertation (1926), he applied to Africa a mode of classification that had been used by Clark Wissler to map the cultures of the indigenous peoples of the Americas, namely the culture area. Herskovits divided Africa into six areas, classifying them into two categories: the dominantly pastoral and the dominantly agricultural.

Although this simplification omitted important matters, it was a significant step forward. Firmly grounded on known economic criteria, it was a departure from nineteenth-century tendencies to classify societies in terms of some unsteady yardstick of evolutionary advancement or later efforts to explain the differences and similarities among societies in terms of geographical diffusion of cultural traits by conjecturing where particular cultural ideas and practices originated and where they spread.

From its outset the French research method and criteria of classification were very different from the British and American methods. Marcel Griaule, the leading French Africanist of the 1930s, based his categories on the different modes of thought of different peoples. He worked in West Africa among the DOGON people in what is now MALI and studied their modes of thought through the information given him by a learned Dogon who explicated local philosophical precepts, myths, and rituals in elaborate detail. This use of a single informant who was interrogated largely about philosophical and symbolic matters was very different from the direct observation of daily life.

Generalizing very broadly from the Dogon material, and making a few comparisons, Griaule expanded his ideas to the point where he constructed his own version of the African, a generic personage having a philosophical outlook distinct from the Christian European, but who was his philosophical equal. On the basis of very limited comparative data regarding distributions of symbols, myths and rituals, technologies and aesthetics, he constructed a geographical typology of three variants, characterized by three African epistemological fields, three forms of knowledge.

Parallel in time to Herskovits and Griaule, with their work extending over several decades, was the group of British social anthropologists alluded to earlier. They worked in an entirely different manner, living among the people, observing and discussing mundane life, in all its facets, as it unfolded from day to day. They assembled very careful and vivid descriptions of work, of politics, of kinship and ritual, and of the life cycle of individuals and groups. On their return from Africa, they often met at seminars and symposia, heard each other's papers, read each other's books, and compared their approaches and findings.

This ready-made audience enriched the whole enterprise, so that by the time Malinowski left the scene and was replaced as a theoretical leader in 1937 by A. R. Radcliffe-Brown, at Oxford, their intellectual circle was well established. Radcliffe-Brown had also not worked in Africa, but rather in Australia. His principal contribution to African studies was to produce an elaborated theoretical framework, structural functionalism, that went beyond Malinowski's simple, functional notions of institutional and societal coherence.

Radcliffe-Brown posed specific questions about the way in which particular practices were related to each other, customs which on first sight did not seem at all connected. He wanted to turn anthropology into a general science of social laws. To do any such thing, even to approach such an ambition, he needed detailed ethnographies he could compare. At that time, the Africanists were able to supply the information required by such an approach. Under his aegis a major comparative volume was edited by E. E. Evans-Pritchard and Meyer Fortes called *African Political Systems* (1940). It classified the political systems of Africa into two kinds, polities with a centralized form of rule and headless systems. In the acephalous systems the political order depended on the competitions and balances between groups, between segmentary lineages, not on the rule of chiefs or kings. This was a major step toward understanding how different types of political structure worked and that the same patterns of political structure could appear in very different cultural milieus that had no connection with one another. Another major contribution was *African Systems of Kinship and Marriage*, published in 1950, edited by Radcliffe-Brown and Daryll Forde. In that volume Radcliffe-Brown tried to produce general laws regarding the logic of kinship nomenclatures (terms for relatives) and practices. Needless to say, there have been subsequent critiques and refinements of many of the contentions in these volumes, but these were the ones that broke the ground.

In all of these early theoretical works, the units of comparison were indigenous systems, whole societies and the way they functioned. Comparisons were made, typologies were developed. The theorizing was about the way these societies operated in the precolonial period, a reconstruction of the past that edited out colonial changes. The colonial period was not theoretically interesting at that stage. Only the great variety of reconstructed but putatively authentic and pure African cultures were useful for the kind of theorizing that was done at the time.

CHANGING ANTHROPOLOGY OF A CHANGING AFRICA

Traditional African systems the way they "must have been" in precolonial times were reconstructions from observed evidence. But this kind of holistic, tradition-oriented structural functional anthropology was carried on at the same time as anthropologists were actually seeing and experiencing an Africa that was deeply affected by colonial rule and changing rapidly. Anthropologists not only took note of this; they wrote about it. Thus, parallel to the academic concern with reconstructed past structures, there was a strong practical interest in what was going on in Africa at the time. The same anthropologists who wrote monographs about the traditional reported on current matters in very different papers and books. They wrote on rural economies and the effects of cash cropping. They wrote on labor migration. They were interested in the changes in political organization and law effectuated by the colonial authorities. At first, these matters were not treated as a serious object of theorizing. They were treated as reports of current history.

Thus there were two Africanist anthropologies in the British high period, one concerning the reconstructed past and all that remained of it, particularly in the countryside, and the other anthropology, which was occupied with change itself, with the new cities and the mix of migrants from many ethnic groups who peopled them. The anthropology of change included the study of the mining townships and the commercial towns and the altered countryside from which out-migration took place and into which cash cropping was installed and to which missionaries and teachers and medical personnel and agricultural and veterinary officers sometimes came.

As long as structural functionalism prevailed, changing Africa was not the object of any theorizing subtlety in anthropology. Crude contrasts between traditional society and modern were the elements of the basic model. Africa was seen as caught between the two,

neither traditional nor modern, in transition, its holistic traditions disrupted but its intimations of a coherent modernity not fully realized.

But from midcentury on new forms of research were appearing to which the old techniques and totalizing concepts could not be applied, and gradually those were abandoned. Studies of urban situations in which Africans from many different ethnic groups were living and working next to each other did not lend themselves to the old methods. Network studies of the connections of individuals to other individuals emerged, with labor organization and neighborhood and ethnicity and kinship all in the mix. Extended case studies followed unfolding situations. Some were microhistories of conflicts; others noted changing patterns of marriage and divorce and still others the formation of ethnic ties without kinship ties underpinning them.

The change in perspective marked by these studies in Africa was of major theoretical significance to anthropology. Not only were the elements of time, history, and change incorporated into the anthropological canon but individual agency was a decisive feature of these accounts. Africa was now being treated as part of the historical time of those who were observing it.

TOPICALLY SPECIALIZED ANTHROPOLOGY: PRESENT AWARENESS AND THE HISTORICAL MOMENT

Many new theoretical initiatives followed those of the midcentury. Two major influences in French anthropology had wide international influence in the 1960s and 1970s: 1) Marxist interpretations of African society and 2) studies of systems of symbolic patterning, using the ideas of Claude Lévi-Strauss about a grammar of culture. But other themes were also focal. Thus, with the advent of independence and the primacy of the nation-building project in Africa, the political importance of ethnic pluralism became the object of anthropological study and debate. In the 1970s a rich international literature accumulated on the new RELIGIONS of Africa, the indigenized and re-imagined versions of world religions. There also were studies of ethnic and class-specific religious practices, and the political meanings of these, most notably in South Africa. Studies of African elites and class differences appeared, studies of African servants, and, of course, studies of African commerce and class. Medical anthropology emerged, with its focus on indigenous theories of disease and curing. The studies of women's lives increased in number and kind. Feminist studies emerged. An interest in African law that began in the colonial period was carried forward in new dimensions, including national legal institutions, international human rights, and local customary practices.

It is obvious that the intellectual approaches of anthropology changed radically in the late colonial period and thereafter. This was partly a response to changes in the world, not the least in Africa itself, but partly because the questions with which anthropology became preoccupied were very different from those of earlier generations of scholars. Once differentiated only by their interests in particular geographical regions and ethnic groups, social anthropologists further divided themselves into numerous large thematic subspecialties, economic, political, semiotic-symbolic, historical, and others. Within these frameworks, specialized monographs are now written on such varied topics as economic development projects, ideas and practices relating to illness, law, human rights, music, art, agriculture, environment, land tenure, popular culture, religion, education, gender, refugees, colonial history, film, and numerous others.

Once an Anglo-Euro-American monopoly, Africanist anthropology is now completely internationalized, with professional specialists found all over the world, scattered everywhere from Japan to Africa itself. Today there are enough African anthropologists for a Pan-African Association of Anthropologists to have been established, and many African social scientists also contribute to the publications of CODESRIA, the Council for the Development of Social Science Research in Africa, whose headquarters are in Dakar. Still, as some anthropologists have noted, the challenges associated with ground-level field work in Africa—among them the prevalence of certain health risks and continued civil turmoil throughout much of the continent—remain a serious consideration and potential impediment to future expansion.

As one of the first and one of the most active academic disciplines concerned with studying African affairs, anthropology has had much to do with dispelling the mythic notions of an Africa that did not exist except in the minds of outsiders. There remains much to learn about Africa's ever-changing present, both in its local and national forms and in its global connections. The old ethnographies are now read critically, but they remain valued for their content as close observations of a time long gone. The focus of anthropological interest has changed as Africa has changed. But the basic methodological commitment to fieldwork continues. There is no substitute for the firsthand observations of a trained researcher and for the way he or she hears what it all means from African people themselves.

See also CHRISTIANITY: INDEPENDENT AND CHARISMATIC CHURCHES IN AFRICA; ETHNICITY AND IDENTITY IN AFRICA: AN INTERPRETATION; GLOBALIZATION AND AFRICA: AN INTERPRETATION; HUMAN RIGHTS IN AFRICA; ISLAM AND TRADITION: AN INTERPRETATION; PASTORALISM.

SALLY FALK MOORE

Antiapartheid Movement
The people and organizations who fought to end apartheid in South Africa.

In 1990 the South African government reversed its long ban on various black organizations, such as the African National Congress (ANC), the Pan-Africanist Congress (PAC), and the South African Communist Party (SACP). It also freed Nelson MANDELA, the ANC leader who had been imprisoned since 1962, and began negotiations that eventually replaced white minority rule with electoral democracy and equal rights for all South Africans. As dramatic as these events were, they represented not a sudden reversal but rather the results of a long, complicated history of many individuals and groups that fought against South Africa's official policy of APARTHEID. Apartheid—the name comes from the Dutch word expressing "apartness"—refers to the vast web of laws and regulations which restricted the rights and opportunities of South Africa's black majority, as well as its "nonwhite" minorities. It was imposed in the years after the NATIONAL PARTY first came to power in South Africa in 1948. All South Africans were subjected to racial classification and designated as white, "Coloured" (people of mixed ethnic background), Asian (which included people of Indian descent), or black (people of African descent, also called native, Bantu, or—offensively—kaffir). Under apartheid, blacks were denied the right to vote, own land, and even live outside of strictly regulated rural "bantustans" or urban "locations" or townships. They were treated as second-class citizens whose inferior educational and occupational opportunities doomed them to lives of poverty and powerlessness. Asians and "Coloured" South Africans faced similar, but less severe, forms of discrimination. Although apartheid was only officially imposed in the mid-twentieth century, racial inequality had been part of South Africa's history since the arrival of Europeans nearly three centuries earlier. Africans had long fought white domination, but some of the earliest modern resistance to segregation and other racist policies came from the Indian community. Founded in 1894 by Mohandas K. Gandhi—who would later lead India to independence—the Natal Indian Congress pioneered strategies of mass demonstrations, civil disobedience, and passive resistance to arrest. These nonviolent tactics would be employed by a variety of groups in the early history of the antiapartheid movement. The African National Congress, which would become the most powerful of these groups, was founded in 1912 as the South African Native National Congress. Initially it was fairly limited in size and scope—composed mostly of educated, bourgeois blacks intent on seeking reform through petitions and other legal channels. Its vision of a multiracial resistance movement was an important first step. The Communist Party of South Africa (later renamed the South African Communist Party), founded in 1921, eventually became a close though controversial ally of the ANC. The Communists saw segregation and later full-scale apartheid in the context of a capitalist system that exploited all workers, but black workers most of all. They sought to fight this racist system with a multiracial, class-based movement. Black workers were excluded from trade unions during South Africa's industrial revolution at the turn of the century, but after the 1920 formation of the Industrial and Commercial Workers' Union of Africa (ICU), labor demands and actions became a central part of the resistance movement. Although the ICU itself was short-lived, black unions in the 1940s waged repeated strikes to protest labor policies which subjected African workers to the most dangerous, unhealthy, and poorly paid jobs. The African Mine Workers' Union was one of several unions that helped the antiapartheid movement grow beyond its bourgeois roots. The 1940s were also a fertile time for the ANC, especially after the young lawyers Nelson Mandela and Oliver TAMBO helped found the ANC's Youth League in 1944. The Youth League rejected the ANC's traditionally tame tactics and instead called for strikes, demonstrations, and mass civil disobedience campaigns. By the late 1940s, membership rose to nearly 100,000 and the ANC was soon cooperating with a wide range of groups. In 1955 the Congress Alliance—consisting of the ANC, South African Indian Congress, Coloured Peoples' Congress, and the Congress of Democrats (a white organization)—drafted the FREEDOM CHARTER, which called for self-government, legal equality, human rights, and economic justice. The postwar era was also an important time for the role of women in the fight against racial inequality. Black women had demonstrated against the hated PASS LAWS—which required blacks to carry identification proving they had legal rights to reside and work in the city—as early as the second decade of the twentieth century. But sexual discrimination kept women in general, and black women in particular, from exerting much political power during the first half of the century. At the time of its founding, women were excluded from the ANC and relegated to the Bantu Women's League, a group that initially did little more than cater the men's meetings. Other early women's groups, such as the National Council of African Women, concerned themselves mostly with social welfare and charity work. Many of the most active women in the antiapartheid movement came out of the Communist Party or the trade unions. Communist Party members included middle-class white women such as Ruth FIRST. During World War II increasing numbers of black women joined both the industrial work force and the labor movement. The Federation of South African Women (FSAW) was founded in 1954 by a multiracial group of women active in the Congress Alliance. Its campaigns against pass laws and in favor of racial and sexual equality attracted attention, and government intimidation, throughout the 1950s.

During this period, the National Party government not only passed apartheid legislation, but also increasingly harassed those who opposed it. In 1956 Mandela and SACP leader Joe SLOVO, along with 156 antiapartheid activists, were charged with treason; after a four-year trial they were finally acquitted. In response to the government's increasing repression, more militant antiapartheid activists formed new groups, among them the Pan-Africanist Congress, founded in 1959 by Robert SOBUKWE and others. The PAC saw the fight against apartheid in terms of Black Nationalism, not class struggle, and sought to win an "Afrika for Africans." A demonstration against pass laws, sponsored by the PAC, led to a police massacre in SHARPEVILLE in which sixty-nine protesters were killed. In the wake of rioting that followed Sharpeville, the South African government banned both the PAC and ANC (the Communist Party was already outlawed, and many antiapartheid leaders were already imprisoned, exiled, or banned from political activity), arrested more than 2,000 activists, and declared martial law. The increased government repression ushered in a new era of antiapartheid activism. Rejecting the nonviolence they had embraced for so long, the ANC and SACP jointly founded Umkhonto we Sizwe ("the Spear of the Nation," often abbreviated as MK), an armed paramilitary wing. Overseen by exiled leaders such as Slovo and Tambo, MK carried out acts of sabotage against selected government targets such as military bases and pass offices. As the struggle intensified in the 1960s and 1970s, new antiapartheid groups emerged, including many inspired by the Black Consciousness Movement. The South African Students' Organization (SASO), founded in 1968 by Stephen BIKO and others, grew out of the National Union of South African Students, a multiracial students' group. Influenced by independence movements throughout Africa, the philosophy of Négritude, and the Black Power Movement in the United States, Black Consciousness groups sought to empower black people to escape the "slave mentality" caused by centuries of oppression. The South African Students' Movement, an independent group of primary and secondary students, helped launch the school boycotts and protests that led to the 1976 uprisings in SOWETO, the country's largest black township. As in Sharpeville, mostly peaceful protests led to massive police violence, ending in 575 deaths. Divisions among antiapartheid groups had always been present: some felt apartheid was a class-based evil best fought by multiracial solidarity; others believed that it was primarily a racial matter in which blacks needed to reject the aid of concerned white liberals and forge their own victory. But after Soweto, conflicts within the antiapartheid movement multiplied. The South African government increasingly exploited political rivalries in an attempt both to weaken the opposition and to portray the urban violence as "tribal" warfare. Some groups that had initially fought apartheid, such as Gatsha BUTHELEZI's Inkatha movement, were accused of helping the government undermine the ANC. Murders of suspected government collaborators and informants grew common, as did violence at the increasingly frequent funerals of antiapartheid activists who were killed in police custody or under mysterious circumstances. Yet the 1983 founding of the United Democratic Front brought together some 575 different organizations, including women's and students' groups as well as less political bodies such as sports clubs, into an allied fight against apartheid. By the early 1980s the situation in South Africa was attracting massive international attention. Antiapartheid demonstrations on college campuses and in cities around the world pressured businesses to divest their South African investments and called on governments to tighten economic sanctions against the country. Already banned from international sports competitions and boycotted by most foreign entertainers, South Africa was becoming a pariah nation. In the mid-1980s President P. W. BOTHA instituted small reforms, but succeeded only in alienating his right-wing constituency. Soon after replacing Botha in 1989, President F. W. DE KLERK released Mandela (who had been imprisoned since 1962) and removed the ban on major antiapartheid organizations. Long and difficult negotiations produced a transitional government and a new constitution that dismantled apartheid. Following South Africa's first free elections in 1994, many of the leaders of the antiapartheid movement won offices in President Nelson Mandela's government.

See also INKATHA FREEDOM PARTY; SHARPEVILLE MASSACRE; SOUTH AFRICA.

KATE TUTTLE

Anuak

Ethnic group of Sudan and Ethiopia; also known as the Anyuak or the Annuak.

The Anuak primarily inhabit a stretch of the BLUE NILE River in western ETHIOPIA and eastern SUDAN. They speak a Nilo-Saharan language and are closely related to the SHILLUK people. Approximately 130,000 people consider themselves Anuak.

In 2003 Ethiopian soldiers allegedly massacred some 400 Anuak in Gambella for what were ostensibly antigovernment activities.

Anyi

Ethnic group of West Africa, also known as the Agni, the Bini, the Kotoko, and the Ton.

The Anyi inhabit primarily southeastern CÔTE D'IVOIRE and southwestern GHANA. They speak a Niger-Congo language and belong to the AKAN cultural and linguistic group. Approximately 800,000 people consider themselves Anyi.

See also LANGUAGES, AFRICAN: AN OVERVIEW.

Apartheid

Social and political policy of racial segregation and discrimination enforced by the white minority government in South Africa from 1948 until the early 1990s.

The term apartheid (Afrikaans for "apartness") was coined in the 1930s and used as a political slogan of the NATIONAL PARTY in the early 1940s, but the practice of segregation in South Africa extends to the beginning of white settlement in South Africa in 1652. After the Afrikaner-dominated National Party came to power in 1948, regionally varied practices of racial segregation were intensified and made into a uniform set of national laws. Scholars disagree over why apartheid was adopted in South Africa. Some argue that apartheid was at its root a policy that served businesses by creating a large pool of low-cost labor. Other scholars dispute this, claiming that apartheid was adopted because

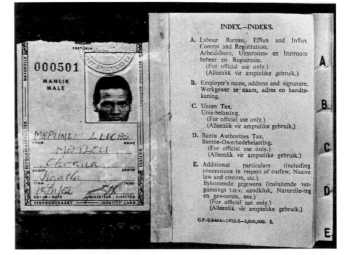

FOR OFFICIAL USE ONLY. An example of the type of pass that African blacks were forced to carry at all times during the apartheid era in South Africa, 1960. (*AP Images*)

of deep racism among most white South Africans and that the policy actually damaged the economy.

MAJOR ELEMENTS

The implementation of the apartheid policy, later referred to as "separate development," was made possible by the Population Registration Act of 1950, which put all South Africans into three racial categories: Bantu (black African), white, or Coloured (of mixed race). A fourth category, Asian (including Indians, Pakistanis, and Chinese), was added later. The system of apartheid was further elaborated by a series of laws in the 1950s: The Group Areas Act of 1950 assigned races to different residential and business sections in urban areas, and the Land Acts of 1954 and 1955 restricted nonwhite residence to specific areas. These laws further restricted the already limited right of black Africans to own land, entrenching the white minority's control of over 80 percent of South African land. One of the most repressive apartheid restrictions was the law requiring that blacks and other nonwhites carry a "pass book" stating their legal residence and workplace. Those without the proper papers could be stopped by police and summarily expelled to the countryside. In 1952 the government passed the Natives (Abolition of Passes and Coordination of Documents) Act. The new law tightened pass regulations, renamed the passes "reference books," and required women to carry them for the first time.

Other laws prohibited most social contacts between the races. The Prohibition of Mixed Marriages Act of 1949 barred interracial marriage, and the Immorality Act of 1950 prohibited sexual relations between different races. The 1953 Reservation of Separate Amenities Act permitted the systematic segregation of train stations, buses, movie theaters, hotels, and virtually all other public facilities and barred the courts from overturning such restrictions. Opponents of apartheid referred to these rules as "petty apartheid." The Bantu Education Act of 1953 closed private schools for Africans and forced them to attend a separate, inferior education system. Labor regulations in the 1950s all but outlawed the formation of trade unions except by whites and reserved most skilled occupations for whites. The Promotion of Bantu Self-Government Act of 1959 furthered geographic divisions between the races by creating ten so-called homelands or bantustans for the black population.

The government continued to implement new apartheid regulations in the 1960s, 1970s, and 1980s. The Bantu Laws Amendment Act of 1964, for example, gave the government complete authority to banish blacks from any urban area and from white agricultural areas. During the 1970s the government stripped thousands of blacks of their South African citizenship when it granted nominal independence to their homelands. Most of the homelands had few natural resources, were not economically viable, and being both small and fragmented, lacked the autonomy of independent states. In the 1980s the government eased some apartheid regulations such as pass laws, but then ordered more systematic enforcement of restrictions on squatting, which had the same effect of restricting black residence in the cities.

Apartheid extracted a huge human cost. In its efforts to create completely segregated residential areas, the South African government destroyed thousands of houses in racially mixed areas. With their homes destroyed, tens of thousands of people were forced into small, substandard houses located in bleak townships and neighborhoods with poor services. Limits on black residence in urban areas also broke apart families in cases where one parent obtained a residence permit but the other did not. Restrictions on the size and location of black businesses squelched the economic aspirations of many blacks, preventing them from competing effectively with white-owned businesses. Apartheid educational policies condemned black South Africans to a severely overcrowded school system with educational policies designed to limit achievement. Indians and Coloureds had somewhat better schools and business opportunities, but they still lagged behind whites.

RESISTANCE AND THE DEMISE OF MINORITY RULE

The implementation and enforcement of many elements of apartheid was accomplished through a widespread use of force. The brutality of apartheid elicited nearly continual resistance within South Africa. Black political groups, sometimes supported by small numbers of sympathetic whites, opposed apartheid using a variety of tactics. Antiapartheid groups such as the African National Congress (ANC), Pan-Africanist Congress (PAC), and the United Democratic Front relied on tactics such as strikes, demonstrations, sabotage, and other forms of violence. Resistance often resulted in severe reprisals by the government. The international community denounced apartheid. In 1961 South Africa was forced to withdraw from the British Commonwealth by member states that were critical of the apartheid system. In 1974 South Africa was expelled from the United Nations General Assembly, and in 1977 the United Nations imposed an arms embargo on South Africa. In the late 1970s many countries began imposing their own sanctions against the apartheid regime. In 1985 the widespread international sanctions campaign culminated with severe new sanctions imposed by the governments of the United States and the United Kingdom.

As antiapartheid pressure mounted within and outside South Africa, the South African government, led by President F. W. DE KLERK, began to dismantle the apartheid system in the early 1990s. It legalized black opposition groups such as the ANC and the PAC and ordered the

SIGNS OF APARTHEID. A bus in Johannesburg, South Africa, clearly advertising the racial segregation of the time with a sign reading "Non-Europeans Only" 1973. (AP Images)

release of some political prisoners, such as ANC leader Nelson MANDELA. In 1994 a new interim constitution was adopted and free general elections were held for the first time in South Africa's history. The constitution prohibited racial and other forms of discrimination and established limits on government power to prevent abuses such as those that occurred under apartheid. With Mandela's election as South Africa's first black president, the last vestiges of the apartheid system were finally eliminated.

ASSESSMENT

Although the apartheid system was abolished, it left a painful legacy in South Africa. Many analysts regard it as unlikely that South Africans, especially blacks, will be eager to forget the homes that were razed, the families divided, the children who were killed, and the many other injustices of apartheid. Apartheid also created massive social and economic inequalities along racial lines, and it is likely that it will take generations to put the races on a more equal footing. In addition, apartheid bequeathed to

all South Africans a preoccupation with race that is likely to diminish only slowly. Apartheid encouraged fears and suspicions between whites, blacks, Coloureds, and Indians, and these present a formidable barrier to constructing a new society.

BIBLIOGRAPHY

Christopher, A. J.. The Atlas of Apartheid. Routledge, 1994.
Ormond, Roger. The Apartheid Handbook: A Guide to South Africa's Everyday Racial Policies. Viking Penguin, 1985.

ALONFORD JAMES ROBINSON, JR.

Appiah, Joseph
1918–1990
Ghanaian politician and diplomat, known for his close association with Ghanaian political leader Kwame Nkrumah and later for his opposition to Nkrumahs undemocratic rule.

Joseph Appiah was born in Kumasi, the capital of the Ashanti region in the British colony of Gold Coast (present-day GHANA). His father, an expert in ASANTE law, served at the court of the Asantehene, the traditional Asante ruler. As a boy, Appiah attended primary school in Kumasi and secondary school in Cape Coast. After graduation he worked at the United Africa Company, the largest British trading firm in West and Central Africa. He then traveled to Great Britain in 1943 to study law at the Middle Temple, a prestigious center for legal education. While in Britain, Appiah developed a close friendship with future Ghanaian president Kwame NKRUMAH and became involved in the Ghanaian independence movement. When Nkrumah returned to Ghana after the formation of the Convention People's Party (CPP), Appiah served as his representative in Britain. He returned to Ghana in 1954 after becoming a member of the Ghanaian bar (a lawyer licensed to practice law in Ghana). Although Appiah did not win high elective office during his political career, he played an important role in pushing Ghana toward democracy by serving as an opposition figure. In 1955, objecting to what he believed were the CPP's corrupt and authoritarian practices, Appiah resigned from the party and joined the Asante-based National Liberation Movement (which was later absorbed by the United Nationalist Party). Appiah won a seat in the legislative assembly in 1956. Ghana officially won its independence from Britain in 1957. Not long after independence, Appiah became known as an outspoken critic of Nkrumah's CPP, especially of restrictive measures such as the 1958 Preventive Detention Act, which allowed the government to detain dissidents without trial. Appiah's strong opposition led to his fifteen-month imprisonment under the act from 1961 to 1962. After his release, Appiah practiced law, defending many opponents of the Nkrumah regime. He finally returned to politics after a military coup ousted Nkrumah in 1966, joining a committee charged with restoring civilian rule. In response to his disapproval of the leadership style of party leader Kofi Busia, Appiah formed his own United Nationalist Party. However, the party fared poorly in the elections of 1969, and he soon joined the Justice Party, serving as its leader outside of parliament. Ghanaian politics once again convulsed in the early 1970s, resulting in another military takeover, this time led by Colonel Ignatius Acheampong in 1972. Appiah became a roving ambassador in Acheampong's regime, but left his post early, before Acheampong was forced to resign in 1978. Appiah was once again imprisoned, and his political career effectively ended. After his release he returned to Kumasi, where he lived until his death. His memoir, *Autobiography of an African Patriot* (1990), was published shortly after his death.

Appiah, Kwame Anthony
1954–
Anglo-Ghanaian writer and professor of philosophy and African and African American studies.

"My first memories," writes Kwame Anthony Appiah in the preface to In My Father's House: Africa in the Philosophy of Culture (1992), "are of a place called 'Mbrom,' a small neighborhood in Kumasi, capital of Asante, as that kingdom turned from being part of the British Gold Coast colony to being a region of the Republic of Ghana." Raised in a country at the dawn of its independence, Appiah developed an early consciousness that straddled not only the colonial and the postcolonial, but also, as the son of a Ghanaian father and an English mother, the African and the European. Not surprisingly, questions of identity, culture, and race occupy a central role in Appiah's work as a philosopher and writer. Anthony Appiah was born in London, England. After attending elementary school in Kumasi, he was sent back to England to live with his grandmother and attend boarding school, returning to GHANA for most school holidays. The decision to send him to England was based partially on the political climate in Ghana at the time. His father, Joseph APPIAH, had once been a friend and colleague of Ghana's first president, Kwame NKRUMAH, but had since fallen out of favor with Nkrumah and faced government harassment. Appiah began his university studies at Cambridge, first as a medical student, then taking a degree in philosophy. While at Cambridge, Appiah met the American graduate student Henry Louis Gates, Jr., who became his academic colleague and a longtime collaborator on several significant literary projects. After graduating Cambridge, Appiah taught philosophy at the University of Ghana, Legon, for a year before

returning to Cambridge for graduate studies. In 1982 Anthony Appiah became the first person of African descent to receive a Ph.D. in philosophy from Cambridge University. Soon after receiving his doctoral degree, Appiah joined the faculty of Yale University, where he was a member of both the philosophy and African and Afro-American studies departments. While his early published work, including the monographs "Assertion and Conditionals" (1985) and "For Truth in Semantics" (1986), dealt primarily with the philosophical fields of logic and language, Appiah increasingly turned his attention to questions of race, culture, and identity. Together with Gates, then his colleague at Yale, Appiah edited a collection of early African American writing and launched a series of books examining African American literary figures. Appiah left Yale for Cornell University in 1986 and then moved to Duke in 1990. After only a year at Duke, he joined Gates at Harvard University, where Gates had been appointed chair of the Afro-American studies department. Appiah moved to Princeton University in 2002. He and Gates continue to work together, coediting TRANSITION, a literary and political journal; The Dictionary of Global Culture (1997); and Encarta Africana (1999), a CD-ROM encyclopedia. In addition, Appiah co-authored Color Conscious: The Political Morality of Race (1996) with Amy Gutmann and has written mystery novels. Perhaps his most influential work, however, is the collection of essays titled In My Father's House, which won the 1993 Herskovits Prize of the African Studies Association.

RICHARD NEWMAN

Armah, Ayi Kwei
1939–
Ghanaian novelist and journalist.

Ayi Kwei Armah has pursued his career as writer and teacher on three continents. In a 1985 article Armah described himself as not simply a member of the EWE people, a Ghanian, and a West African, but "most significantly as an African." His writings explore the meaning of Africa's past in the lives of its present-day people.

Born in the western region of Ghana, Armah attended local schools and Achimota College near ACCRA. In 1959 he went to the United States, where he attended Harvard University, from which he received a degree in sociology. Shortly afterward, he moved to ALGIERS, where he worked as a translator for the weekly paper Révolution Africaine (African Revolution). After a period in his home country, teaching English and writing for Ghana Television, Armah enrolled in 1967 in the Graduate Writing Program at New York City's Columbia University. Later he joined the staff of Jeune Afrique (Young Africa), published in Paris, but he left France in 1968 for professorships in the United States and later in TANZANIA. Armah has spent much of his later life in SENEGAL and has gained much attention through venomous attacks on Ghanaian leaders of Ghana, particularly Kwame NKRUMAH, for continuing what Armah saw as the corrupt and abusive practices of the colonial governments. An author of poetry, short stories, and novels, Armah is best known for the three novels *The Beautyful* (sic) *Ones Are Not Yet Born* (1968), *Fragments* (1970), and *Why Are We So Blest?* (1971). In these works Armah critically examines the political and social consequences of colonialism in Ghana, leaving readers with little hope of for future change. Armah's later novels, *Two Thousand Seasons* (1973) and *The Healers* (1978), make greater use of allegory and less use of realistic detail, a noticeable shift from his earlier work. *Osiris Rising* (1995) uses the ancient Egyptian myth of the god Osiris to tell a modern African story.

Aro

Ethnic group of Nigeria.

The Aro of NIGERIA speak a Niger-Congo language and are one of the IGBO peoples. As many as a million people consider themselves Aro.

See also LANGUAGES, AFRICAN: AN OVERVIEW.

Art and Architecture, African

In general, those works created by historical or contemporary African artists living south of the Sahara.

Although the immense Sahara serves as a natural barrier within the African continent, evidence has shown a considerable dissemination of influences through trade routes that traversed the continent from early times. Today, for example, many Islamic art and architectural forms of North African inspiration appear among cultures south of the Sahara. In addition, research has pointed to concurrent influences of sub-Saharan African arts and cultures on northern African areas closer to the Mediterranean Sea. Egypt, one of the most resplendent of African civilizations, can also be seen as having important ancient artistic and cultural parallels with sub-Saharan African civilizations.

The arts of Africa illuminate the rich histories, philosophies, religions, and societies of the inhabitants of this vast continent. African artworks, in addition to their inherent significance to the peoples who produced them, have inspired some of the most important artistic traditions emerging in Europe and the Americas in the modern era. Western artists of the twentieth century have admired both the African artists' emphasis on abstraction and their freedom from naturalism (a style of art that emphasizes precise, literal depictions of subjects).

OVERVIEW

Described in the seventeenth and eighteenth centuries as a place of powerful kings and lavish courts, Africa came to be looked on far less favorably in the second half of the nineteenth century, at the brink of the colonial period. At the conclusion of the period of colonial conquest in the early 1900s, the continent was redefined in maps, scholarly texts, and exhibitions as a place primarily of "tribal" entities that were assumed to lack sophisticated political and economic institutions. Related works of African art generally were referred to as tribal art.

Today scholars no longer use the term *tribe* in discussions of Africa's cultures and arts. The word is avoided partly because it is regarded as a highly negative term that would not be used in Western contexts. Few people would speak of the Scottish or Irish as members of a tribe, for example. The term is also avoided because the idea of tribe carries with it suggestions of sealed stylistic borders within which little, if anything, changes over time. This notion of each culture having its own distinctive, monolithic style runs counter to current scholarly views of African culture, history, and the arts. As with the term *tribal art*, the label primitive art—employed to describe African art until recently—is also rejected because of its negative connotations and because it is a distinctively Western invention.

African art was first displayed in natural history museums in Europe and the United States, long before it was viewed as acceptable to collect and exhibit these works in fine arts museums. Until recently, many of the best collections of African art open to the public were those displayed in anthropological and natural science museums. The categorization of African art as natural history rested on the now antiquated notion that African people and the art they created were an organic product of the African environment, scarcely different from a zebra or a mangrove tree.

Early practices of African art collecting often dovetailed with colonialism. Scientists from the American Museum of Natural History in New York City, for example, collected more than 49 metric tons of materials during a five-year expedition to the Mangbetu court (in what is now the northeastern Democratic Republic of the Congo, or DRC) beginning in 1909. These materials included not only artworks and decorative objects, but also flora and fauna specimens. Although the United States did not colonize the region, this sort of plundering was very much a part of colonial-era assumptions that Africa and Africans could be exploited without limit. Mangbetu arts—as with those of many other African cultures—thus came to be linked to Western concerns with global dominance and colonial identity. Today African art is no longer relegated to natural history museums; both fine art museums and

APPROACHING "THE STEP." Step Pyramid constructed during Egypt's Third Dynasty around the twenty-seventh century B.C.E. (*Prints and Photographs Division, Library of Congress*)

anthropological museums around the world have important collections and displays of African art.

Although works created by African artists are now viewed in the West as legitimate works of art, African art still faces barriers to acceptance in the West on its own terms. People in the West tend to see art as something beautiful or visually compelling but devoid of function. Such a definition is problematic because it would expunge from the category of art all early and late European religious art, works of art commissioned for political purposes, and modern architecture. For the same reason that such a narrow definition of European art would not be useful, African art is defined broadly to include both functional and purely decorative items.

In Africa, as in Europe before the Renaissance (roughly fourteenth to sixteenth centuries), a number of words for "art" exist. But as with many of the European examples, the African terms are less concerned with quality as such than they are with the question of skill or know-how. The Fon of contemporary Benin use the word alonuzo ("something made by hand") to designate art. The nearby Ewe of Togo employ the term adanu (accomplishment, skill, or value) to indicate art, technique, and ornamentation. These terms share essential conceptual similarities with ars, the Latin word for art, which has its origins in artus, meaning "to join or fit together." Both the Italian word arte and the German term Kunst (derived from the verb können, "to know") are also linked to the idea of practical activity, trade, and know-how.

The history of art in Africa covers many centuries. Among the most ancient of these arts are the rock paintings and engravings from Tassili and Ennedi in the Sahara, dating from 6000 B.C.E. to the first century C.E. Many other examples of early arts come from what is now Nigeria, including the terra-cotta sculptures created by artists from the NOK civilization (dating from at least the fifth century B.C.E. to the second century C.E.), the decorative bronze works found at Igbo-Ukwu (ninth to tenth century C.E.), and the extraordinary bronze and terra-cotta sculptures from the city of Ife (twelfth to fifteenth century C.E.). The technical expertise and naturalistic qualities of these latter arts led early viewers to assume erroneously that they must have been of classical Greek inspiration. Today rich African traditions continue, with artists working both within the traditional modes of expression and in nontraditional genres.

AFRICAN ARTISTIC HERITAGE

African artists have developed diverse traditions of sculpture (figures and masks), architecture (principally domestic structures), furniture, pottery, textiles, and jewelry. In addition, body decoration (coiffure and cicatrization, or decorative scarring) and painting (on building, textile, and the human body) are part of the African artistic heritage.

Materials

The most commonly employed materials include wood, fiber, metal (especially bronze, iron, and gold), ivory, clay, earth, and stone. The forms of representation within each medium vary from relative naturalism to general abstraction, with art styles conforming to the aesthetic tradition established within a particular cultural area. In African art, considerable concern is given both to the maintenance of traditional artistic forms within a culture and to the encouragement of creativity and innovation within the parameters of each artistic tradition.

Artists

African artists have generally worked as specialists, receiving their training from established artists living in the community or wider area. In some old kingships, such as that of Benin in Nigeria, active guild systems controlled the training of young artists. Among the nearby YORUBA, important schools of artists were developed at local family compound centers. Often the artistic profession was seen as hereditary, with talent being passed from generation to generation, and with creativity and success often linked to a divine ancestral endowment. For this reason, among the DOGON and BAMBARA (or Bamana) of Mali, sculptors were all selected

ANCIENT BAS RELIEF. The art of ancient Africa produced much of the world's most enduring and recognizable images. These hieroglyphs under the watchful eyes of the god Horus were captured on film sometime around 1900. (*Prints and Photographs Division, Library of Congress*)

from an ancient endogamous group of blacksmiths. The place of work and the materials employed were also important to the artist during the creative process. Often these were controlled by religious proscriptions.

Aesthetics

Community criticism has been an essential part of artistic traditions in many African cultures. Studies of the aesthetic canons followed by artists and critics in Africa indicate a deliberate concern for abstraction in the design process. Thus, for example, among the Yoruba of Nigeria, the criteria for sculptural beauty consist of a number of specifically nonrepresentational elements. These include visibility, even if this necessitates proportional distortion; straightness, which implies youth and good health; symmetry, to the exclusion of more natural poses or postures;

ephebism, the depiction of each person at an idealized youthful age; smoothness, suggesting again youth and health without natural body imperfections; and hypermimesis, an emphasis on general resemblance rather than on exact representation.

In some African cultures, correct aesthetic canons have been intentionally distorted in order to portray characters whose behavior was antisocial. The IGBO (Ibo) and Ibibio of Nigeria, for example, carve masks with diseased, horrific, monstrous, or asymmetrical features to represent characters who were unruly, evil, or dangerous. In Igbo and Ibibio masquerade performances, such masks are often contrasted with other, more beautifully featured and aesthetically pleasing masks that are worn to portray persons who were orderly, good, or peaceful.

Patronage

Patronage, like aesthetics, has played an important role in the creation of African artworks. Kings and their courts are of particular significance in this regard because of their artistic requirements for the mounting of state pageants, the performance of religious ceremonies, and the manufacture of elaborate homages to royalty. In architecture, the most elaborately and richly decorated structures were usually the palaces of precolonial kings, such as those of the Yoruba (in present-day Nigeria), the AKAN (in present-day Ghana), the Bamiléké and the Bamum (in present-day Cameroon), the Mangbetu and Quba (in present-day Democratic Republic of the Congo), and in the kingdom of Benin. The expensive materials available to these rulers included ivory, bronze, gold, glass beads, and plush raffia velours. Such decorative materials are amply displayed in the arts produced at these royal courts. Important types of art made for such regal patronage include staffs of office, thrones, state swords, crowns, royal memorial sculptures, drinking vessels, and serving containers.

Difference in social status often found expression in royal arts. Status was indicated through variations in media (precious metals versus wood, for example), artistic scale (throne height or building size), genre typologies (portraiture exemplars and complex pipe forms), and subject matter (themes of dominance or class difference). Initiation into a range of religious, political, and age grade associations played an important role as well, and art was often commissioned by these institutions. As part of the coronation rituals in the kingdom of Benin, for example, each new king established an altar to his father and commissioned beautiful cast metal heads and other sculptural forms to decorate the shrine. Running along the altar's front periphery were various bells. Rung without interruption throughout royal ceremonies, the bells' continuing sound gave evidence of ongoing ancestral presence.

Other important sources of art patronage in Africa included the various associations of men and women formed within many communities for social and political, as well as religious, control. The still-active Poro men's associations of the Dan and their neighbors in Liberia and Côte d'Ivoire are characteristic examples of this type of patronage association. Poro members commissioned many of the masks and figural sculptures found in this region.

Associations that united community members by age and occupation were also important African art patrons. Examples of artworks commissioned by such associations are found among the Bambara and among the Igbo and Ejagham (both in Nigeria), among others. Often each age group or occupationally linked section of the association had its own distinctive representations or masquerade themes. Among the Ejagham, animal forms characterized the masks of hunting societies, and themes of human deformity were often found in conjunction with warfare masks. Images of women were commonly employed for the headdresses of the women's clubs or ancestral associations.

Traditional religious and cult organizations were also important as sources of art patronage in Africa. Artworks were not only a central component of many traditional shrines and chapels but also played a critical role in the diverse religious pageants. Among the Yoruba of Nigeria, cults linked with the principal deities—Shango (thunder), Obá (creativity), Oshún (water), Ifa (knowledge), Yemoja (sorcery), Eshu (examination), and Odudua (earth)—had a vast array of associated art forms, including figures, masks, pottery, textiles, and jewelry. Here, as elsewhere in Africa, the artworks used in conjunction with each particular cult were often identifiable through their iconography, materials, styles, and modes of manufacture.

ART IN AFRICAN SOCIETY

The multiple roles that art plays in African communities are as diverse as the forms of patronage. These include social, political, economic, historical, and therapeutic functions.

Social Role

One of the most important functions of African art is distinctly social. In fulfilling this role, African art frequently depicts women as mothers, usually nursing or cradling their young. Men, on the other hand, are often presented both as elders—the traditional community leaders—and as successful warriors, appearing on horseback or with armaments. Social themes are prevalent in many African masquerade performances as well. In these masquerades, animal and human characters, in appropriate masks and garb, assume a variety of roles in demonstrating proper and improper forms of societal behavior. Performances of the Ijo and southern Igbo of Nigeria include diverse antisocial characters, such as the miser, the greedy person, the prostitute, the incompetent physician, and the unscrupulous lawyer. In the Egungun performances of the nearby Yoruba, the gossip, the glutton, and the strange-mannered foreigner have key parts as negative social models.

Political Role

Political control is another major concern displayed through art in Africa. Among the Dan (Liberia), Kota (Gabon), Pende (DRC), and others, special masks are worn by persons serving as community judges and policemen. The Gon maskers of Gabon are a particularly good example of this type of masked community official. Because of their anonymity and perceived special powers, these Gon masked figures are able to break normal societal codes and proscriptions as a means of redistributing scarce food and animals at times of great community need. A different type of social control is achieved by certain African figures and architectural motifs. The reliquary figures of the Kota, Sogo, and FANG of Gabon, for example, are used as guardian images to protect the sacred ancestral relics of the community from theft or harm. The Dogon of Mali and the SENUFO of Côte d'Ivoire carve elaborate doors that ritually protect the community food supplies and sacred objects.

Economic Role

Art in Africa fulfills an important economic role. The elegant wooden Chi Wara antelope headdresses of the Bambara of Mali are worn in planting and harvest ceremonies. Chi Wara, the mythical Bambara inventor of agriculture, is said to have buried himself in the earth as an act of self-sacrifice. The dance of the Chi Wara maskers on the agricultural fields (Chi Wara's grave) serves to honor this great being and to remind the young Bambara farmers of Chi Wara's sacrifice that they in turn must make each year. Among the Senufo of Côte d'Ivoire, delicately carved figures are used in a similar way to encourage farmers in their difficult work. The Senufo secure *daleu* staffs in the ground at the end of cultivation rows; these staffs use bird or female imagery and serve as goals, markers, and trophies for the field-planting competitions.

Historical Role

African art fulfills an important historical role through its memorialization of important persons and events of the past. With this in mind, the Dogon of Mali have carved numerous images of their legendary ancestors, the Nommo, who descended from the sky at the beginning of time. Such Nommo figures occupy important places on granary doors, in cave paintings, and on sacred architectural supports. Some of these figures have upraised hands pointing to the sky and their village of origin.

In the powerful kingdom of Benin in Nigeria, elaborate relief plaques cast in bronze similarly carried images of important persons and events of the past. The images represent the meetings of foreign dignitaries, battle scenes, court pageants, nobles in state dress, religious ceremonies, musicians, and other historical figures and events.

Therapeutic Role

Some traditional African therapies have required special forms of art. Divination—the means by which problems and their potential resolutions could be determined—was particularly important in the production of artworks. Yoruba (Nigeria) Ifa diviners used elaborately sculpted divination boards, bowls, and other items as an essential part of their ritual equipment. Similarly, the BAULE of Côte d'Ivoire used elaborate divination vessels for oracular purposes. Among the KONGO of the Democratic Republic of the Congo, powerful wooden fetish figures stuck through with iron nails were employed therapeutically as a means of repelling personal danger and trauma.

REGIONAL DISTINCTIONS

The widely differing cultures of sub-Saharan Africa are more readily comprehended if grouped by geographic regions, in view of the diversity in climate, topography, and social organization within this vast area. Although some of these cultures have vanished, much of their art remains; other cultures have survived and continue to produce their traditional art.

Western Savanna

Among the best known of the traditional western savanna arts are those of the Dogon, Bambara, MOSSI, BOBO, and Tamberma. These groups live in the dry, grassy plains of the West African interior. The Dogon are one of the most isolated of these peoples, but their arts have been especially well researched. The Dogon have a rich and complex philosophical foundation on which their arts are based. The Dogon village plan, for example, is seen to have the form of a human; this form represents the Nommo, the first humans created by the Dogon sun and creator god. Important parts of the Dogon village physiognomy include its head (the smithy and men's house), chest (the houses of lineage leaders), hands (women's houses), genitals (an altar and a heavy grinding bowl), and feet (shrines). Dogon masks, carved for the men's association, Awa, represent in their totality the Dogon image of the world, including the animals and people that inhabit it. The antelope, the bird, the hare, Fulani women, and Samana men are some of the characters who appear in the funerary performances of this association. Other masks presented at such times depict more abstract philosophical concepts. One mask, the 9-m (30-ft) serpentine Great Mother mask, recalls the origin of death. The roughly cruciform Kanaga mask is worn by a dancer whose motions recreate the origin of the world.

Farther east, among the linguistically related Tamberma of Togo, house architecture has reached an apex of beauty and symbolic complexity. The two-story earthen "castles" of these people serve not only as their homes but also as their fortresses, cathedrals, theaters, and cosmological diagrams. The name that these people call themselves, Batammariba, or the "people who are the architects," bears out the importance of architecture among this group. Like the Dogon village, each Tamberma house is said to be distinctly human. Accordingly, its outer surfaces are scarified with the same patterns that are incised on women. Appropriate body parts are also found in the house, for example, the door "mouth," the window "eyes," the grinding stone "teeth," and so on.

Western Forests

The great forested West Atlantic coast—often called the Guinea Coast—incorporates the diverse cultures and arts of Guinea, Sierra Leone, Liberia, and Côte d'Ivoire on the west and Ghana, Togo, Benin, and Nigeria on the east. In the western coastal forests, the dominant art patrons are associations of men and women, such as Sandé and Poro. The women's Sandé society of the MENDE (Sierra Leone) people has a particularly important masquerade tradition. Sandé masks, which are polished a deep black to reflect the richness and beauty of the sea, are worn by female association leaders during the ceremonies that initiate young women in the community. In their form, the most beautiful of these masks reflect the features that the Mende admire in themselves: a high, smooth forehead; an elaborate coiffure; and an elegant, strong neck.

Poro, the parallel men's association, has elaborate masking traditions as well. In their association performances, Dan, Kran, and Guere Poro members from Liberia and nearby Côte d'Ivoire present a diverse cast of players. These include the judge, the singer, and the runner. Elegance of form, shiny black facial surfaces, and complex woven coiffures are featured in these masks. When not being worn, the masks are secured in a special sacred go (ge) house under the guardianship of the go-master. The wife of this important man has her own special art form: a decorated spoon that she displays in feasts for the community.

Some of the most important aristocratic arts of Africa are from the eastern region of the Atlantic coast that encompasses the countries of Ghana, Togo, Benin, and Nigeria. Perhaps the most famous of the kingships is the Benin dynasty in Nigeria. The royal city of Benin (not to be confused with the recently named neighboring country of Benin) was at its height in the seventeenth and eighteenth centuries; travelers compared it to the great contemporaneous cities of The Netherlands. The palace of the king, or oba as he was called, was especially impressive. At one time its walls were covered with beautiful cast bronze plaques that were said to shimmer like gold. The three main buildings at the palace were each surmounted by immense turrets supporting giant bronze birds and pythons. On the royal palace altars, bronze memorial heads and sculptures were displayed for private and state festivities.

Palaces of the kings of the nearby Yoruba people were massive structures with open interior courtyards, often with a large cistern to collect rainwater. The more important of these palace courtyards were covered by roofs with intricate support columns that were often sculpted with themes of royal status and power. These roof supports are characterized by their monumental size, their polychrome (many-colored) surfaces, and their integration of local aesthetic values such as clarity of form, balance, youthfulness, and character. Prominent themes for palace roof supports included the king, who was often shown on horseback; his first wife; and members of the powerful military forces that once protected local monarchies. Depictions of royal women also appear prominently in the carvings on Yoruba palace roof supports. One of the most important women in the court was the king's senior wife, who was often a subject of these sculptures. Not only did she have the responsibility for placing the crown on the newly designated king's head; she also oversaw the state treasury and harem. Often her breasts were shown bare, a reference to her critical role in bearing and nurturing the royal children and to the power of women more generally in Yoruba society.

Many Akan arts, especially those of Asante royalty in Ghana, emphasize themes of governmental authority and prerogative. Ceremonial stools that symbolize the possession of power are known as chieftaincy stools. Historically, these were commissioned by the king, or for him by loyal subjects. In the twentieth century, stools of this sort also began to be available on the open market for nonroyal individuals. Carved of wood and covered with precious metal, the stools vary in size as well as in other decorative features that once served to distinguish the owner's rank, occupation, and identity. Decorative patterns were also important. A typical design might include the silhouette of a stool, evoking political legitimacy. Another design would feature a bird with its head turned toward the back, suggesting the harm that can come to the young if their mother—and rulers—are not vigilant. Special brass vessels known as kuduo were used to hold gifts for Akan royalty and offerings for associated ancestors. Reflecting their ritual importance, most royal kuduo were kept near the royal ancestral stools. Kuduo visual sources are complex, revealing a mixture of indigenous, Islamic, and European inspirations. A kuduo scene might show a leopard attacking a goat, an image that referred to the striking power differences in the kingdom between rulers and those they ruled.

Central, Southern, and East Africa.

Still other artistic forms are emphasized in the thick equatorial forests and drier savanna regions that run from Gabon through the Republic of the Congo, the Democratic Republic of the Congo, and various countries to the east and south. In

IVORY CARVINGS. A detail of a carved tusk from the Republic of the Congo. Tusks depicted the people of Congo in everyday situations. (*Bridgeman Art Library International Ltd.*)

the matrilineal cultures of southern Democratic Republic of the Congo, female figures are particularly important. The Pende chief's house, for example, often bears a full-scale image of a woman at the peak of the roof. This figure sometimes holds a child (a symbol of the family line and future heirs) and an ax (a symbol of power).

In the late nineteenth and early twentieth centuries many African courts, including that of the Mangbetu kingdom, used special forms of musical instruments, vessels, and weapons. These were luxury goods and a means to convey ideas of royal identity and institutional power. Mangbetu royal weapons symbolize the potency of rulership through the complex and beautiful shapes of their deadly blade parts. Court harps and vessels integrate key features of the human body. Their elegant form affirms the key role that individual court men and women played in palace life.

Kongo artists (in what is now the western DRC) created royal guardian sculptures called mintadi that served as surrogates for rulers who journeyed away from the palace. Such sculptures helped guard the royal family during his absence. After the ruler died, the sculptures were placed on the royal burial grounds to represent the deceased and his attendants. The soft stone used in these works alludes to the permanence of the chieftaincy; after his death, the ruler was said to be embodied in stone. Many mintadi show the ruler wearing the royal crown, its corners surmounted by the four inward curving claws of a leopard. Images of mothers and children appear prominently in royal funeral-related rituals in recognition of the critical role women play in establishing new lineages.

KUBA kings (in what is now the central DRC) underwent complex initiation rites. These rites provided insight into environmental, historical, and religious concerns essential to the identity of the king, who was a member of the ruling elite from the dominant Bushong group. After the king's initiation, he supervised the initiation of the youth of the capital, appearing himself in an elephant-shaped mask called moshambwooy. This character was intended to represent not only the first human and the founder of the dynasty, but also a forest spirit, or ngesh. This moshambwooy mask and two other royal masks form a performance triptych (a work in three parts), and together they act out the ancient royal story of power, deception, and conflict. In related performances, the Mboom mask personifies several characters at once: the king's younger brother, a pygmy, and commoners who fight the king for the affections of the king's sister—known as the *Ngady aMaash*. In addition to this royal masquerade triad, other types of Kuba masks appeared in royal and nonroyal funerals, initiations, and festivals.

LUBA stools (from what is now the southern DRC) played an important role in investiture (conferring of authority) ceremonies and other royal events. Such stools were so politically potent that ownership alone sometimes served to signify legitimacy. The political importance of royal Luba women is reflected in the prominent depiction of these women in stools and related royal arts. One caryatid (column carved in the shape of a draped female figure) shows a woman kneeling calmly, her fingers resting on the seat of the stool. This depiction underscores the critical role that Luba women play as chieftaincy founders; it also indicates their role as contemporary political players such as royal counselors, healers, diviners, guardians of royal relics, and ambassadors.

Among the relatively isolated Gato, Bongo, and Konso of Sudan and Ethiopia, memorial figures of wood were set up in prominent positions in the village to survey its entrance and the tombs of its important ancestors. In most other East African cultures, monumental sculpture has historically been rare. Instead, body decoration became an important focus of the arts. The MAASAI of Kenya and the ZULU of South Africa are particularly noted for their beaded jewelry. Circular forms such as those in the jewelry of the Maasai are also emphasized in Bantu village planning in this area. The great elliptical stone building built about 1200 C.E., of the ancient Monomotapa culture near Fort Victoria in Zimbabwe, is conceptually part of this tradition in circular design and architecture.

CONTEMPORARY AFRICAN ART

Many of the so-called traditional arts of Africa are still actively being commissioned, carved, and used in traditional contexts. As in all art periods, important innovations coexist with significant elements of established styles and modes of expression. In recent years, with the changes in transportation and mass communications within the continent, a number of art forms have been disseminated widely among diverse African cultures. For example, today some Nigerian-style masks are being used in Ghanaian and other coastal centers on the eastern Guinea Coast.

In addition to distinctly African influences, a number of changes also have originated from the outside. For example, Islamic architecture and design motifs are evident in many of the arts of the northern regions of Nigeria, Mali, Burkina Faso, and Niger. East Indian print motifs have similarly found their way into sculptures and masks of the Ibibio and Efik artists living along the southern coast of Nigeria. Some contemporary artists have taken up Christian themes in their designs for panels, doors, and baptismal fonts for Africa's Christian churches and cathedrals. In recent years, artists have also found important sources of patronage for various art forms in the banks, commercial establishments, government offices, and other official institutions of some nations. Tourists have been responsible for still other art demands, particularly for decorative masks and ornamental African sculptures made of ebony or ivory.

The development of schools of art and architecture in sub-Saharan African cities has pushed artists to work in new mediums such as cement, oil and other paints, ink, stone, aluminum, and a variety of graphic modes. The images and designs they have created reflect a vibrant union of African and contemporary Western traditions. Artists such as TWINS SEVEN-SEVEN and Ashira Olatunde of Nigeria, Nicholas Mukomberanwa of Zimbabwe, and Chéri SAMBA of the DRC are among the most successful practitioners of these novel creative forms.

See also ROCK ART, AFRICAN.

SUZANNE PRESTON BLIER

Art Market in Africa
See COMMODIFICATION OF AFRICAN ART: AN INTERPRETATION.

Artists, African
Visual artists from Africa.
For information on African art in general: See ART AND ARCHITECTURE, AFRICAN; COMMODIFICATION OF AFRICAN ART: AN INTERPRETATION. Motion pictures and filmmakers: See ALASSANE, Mousstapha; CINEMA, AFRICAN; CISSÉ, Souleymane; FAYE, Safi; FÉDÉRATION PANAFRICAINE DES CINÉASTES; GERIMA, Haile; HONDO, ABID MOHAMED MEDOUN (MED); OUÉDRAOGO, Idrissa; THIRD CINEMA; VIEYRA, Paulin. Painters: See BOUABRÉ, Frédéric-Bruly; SAMBA, Chéri; SEVEN-SEVEN, TWINS; WOMEN ARTISTS, AFRICAN: AN INTERPRETATION. Photography and photographers: See KEITA, Seydou; PHOTOGRAPHY, AFRICAN. Sculptors: See GUTSA, Tapfuma; KWEI, Kane; MUKOMBERANWA, Nicholas; MUNYARADZI, Henry; SEGOGELA, Johannes; WOMEN ARTISTS, AFRICAN: AN INTERPRETATION.

Arusha
Ethnic group of Tanzania, also known as the Warusha.
The Arusha primarily inhabit the region adjacent to the Burka River in TANZANIA. They speak a Nilo-Saharan language and are closely related, both linguistically and culturally, to the MAASAI. Approximately 120,000 people consider themselves Arusha.

Arusha, Tanzania
City in northeastern Tanzania, at the foot of Mount Meru, that is an important center for tourism and trade and that has been the site of some important political events.
Surrounded by farmlands of the MERU and ARUSHA peoples, Arusha began as a small market town that marked the

halfway point between Cairo, Egypt, and Cape Town, South Africa, on the Great Northern Road. It has since become a major manufacturing city and the terminus for a railroad to the port cities of Tanga, Tanzania, and Mombasa, Kenya. As the country's largest processing center of pyrethrum (a source of insecticide), sisal, and coffee, Arusha is also home to factories producing plastics, radios, and meerschaum pipes. In addition, the city caters to a thriving tourist industry by serving as a gateway to nearby SERENGETI NATIONAL PARK and Arusha and Tarangire national parks, as well as Ngorongoro Crater, Mount KILIMANJARO, and Olduvai Gorge. In politics, Arusha has hosted a number of important events in Tanzania, such as the 1967 Arusha Declaration by former Tanzanian president Julius K. NYERERE, in which he outlined his vision of African socialism. Arusha is estimated to have a population of approximately 270,000 people, with an annual growth rate of 11 percent.

Beginning in the mid-1990s Arusha received worldwide attention for housing the International Criminal Tribunal for RWANDA to try people responsible for mass killings there. Chosen for its neutral location by the United Nations Security Council and deemed suitable because it had previously hosted East African regional conferences and peace talks, Arusha has since been criticized for its inaccessibility, lack of adequate building space for the tribunal courts, and unreliable communication and electrical systems. As the tribunal has proceeded, however, Arusha officials have received funding to improve facilities and services.

ELIZABETH HEATH

Arusi

Ethnic group of Ethiopia, also known as the Arisi, the Arssi, and the Arsi.

The Arusi primarily inhabit Bale Province in ETHIOPIA. They speak an Afro-Asiatic language and belong to the OROMO cultural and linguistic group. Approximately 300,000 people consider themselves Arusi.

Asante

Dominant ethnic group of a powerful nineteenth-century empire and today one of the leading ethnic groups of Ghana.

The Asante are members of the AKAN cluster of ethnic groups. Their language, variously known as Asante or Twi, is also often called Akan, but is actually one of a number of separate Akan languages, all of which belong to the Kwa subgroup of the Niger-Congo language family. The Asante are often considered the custodians of the nation's culture because of the power, artistic splendor, and duration of their empire, which covered nearly all of present-day GHANA by 1800. Today the

Asante number more than five million, or some 28 percent of the total population of Ghana.

Asante oral accounts of the group's origin vary. According to one account, their ancestors are descended from the rulers of the ancient GHANA empire, far to the north in present-day Mali and Mauritania. This account forms the basis for the name of the modern nation. Other accounts claim that their ancestors emerged from the ground in their present homeland. Linguistic and archaeological evidence suggests that ancestors of the Asante have lived in their present homeland for at least 2,000 years. With the expansion of gold production and trade in the fourteenth and fifteenth centuries, kingships began to emerge among the Akan. The further expansion of trade in the sixteenth and seventeenth centuries, following the arrival of Europeans along the coast, spurred the development of powerful states in the Asante region. By the early seventeenth century, the Denkyira kingdom had conquered the independent Asante clans.

The political, military, and spiritual foundations of the Asante nation date to the first Asante king, OSEI TUTU. He forged the Asante Union by bringing together several subgroups from roughly 1670 to the 1690s. He also built a capital, KUMASI, created the legend of the GOLDEN STOOL to legitimize his rule, and began celebrating the Odwira, or yam festival, as a symbol of national unity. From 1698 to 1701, the united Asante army defeated the Denkyira people. Over the course of the eighteenth century, Asante conquered most of the surrounding peoples, including the DAGOMBA.

By the early nineteenth century, Asante territory covered nearly all of present-day Ghana, including the coast, where the Asante could trade directly with the British. In exchange for guns and other European goods, the Asante sold gold and slaves, usually either captured in war or accepted as tribute from conquered peoples. As they prospered, Asante culture flourished. They became famous for gold and brass craftsmanship, wood carving, furniture, and brightly colored woven cloth, called kente. Although the Asante maintained traditional beliefs, Muslim traders and Christian missionaries won some converts among them to their respective religions.

During the nineteenth century, Asante fought several wars with the British, who sought to eliminate the slave trade and expand their control in the region. A series of defeats at the hands of the British gradually weakened and reduced the territory of the Asante kingdom. After nearly a century of resistance to British power, Asante was finally declared a crown colony in 1902 following the uprising known as the Third British-Asante War, or the Yaa Asantewa War.

Before long, however, Asante reemerged to contribute to the nationalist movement that would help shape modern

Ghana. The exiled Asante king was allowed to return to Kumasi in 1924, and the British recognized the Asante Confederacy as a political entity in 1935. Today, most Asante live in the Asante Region of Ghana. They are primarily farmers, growing cocoa for export and yams, plantains, and other produce for local consumption. The Golden Stool, the Asante imperial palace, and artifacts at the Museum of National Culture in Kumasi have become enduring symbols of Ghana's illustrious past.

See also GHANA, EARLY KINGDOM OF; LANGUAGES, AFRICAN: AN OVERVIEW.

DAVID P. JOHNSON, JR.

Asantewa, Yaa
1850?–1921
Heroine who led the Asante in the British-Asante War.

An indomitable aristocrat who led her people's last stand against incorporation into the British Empire in 1900, Yaa Asantewa is a much-loved figure in Asante history. In 1896 the British occupied the Asante capital, KUMASI, and sent King Prempeh I and several chiefs and elders to exile in the SEYCHELLES Islands in the Indian Ocean. Among them was Yaa Asantewa's grandson, Kwasi Afrane II, chief of Edweso, one of the states in the Asante Union. As queen mother of Edweso, Yaa Asantewa used her position to organize Asante leaders behind an attack on the British.

In April 1900 the British governor Sir Frederick Hodgson outraged the Asante by demanding the GOLDEN STOOL, the sacred symbol of Asante nationhood. Hodgson also announced that the exiled king would be assessed interest payments on his war indemnity and never be allowed to return. The Asante leaders, led by Yaa Asantewa, responded by demanding Prempeh's return, a restoration of the slave trade, an end to conscript labor, and the expulsion of foreigners from Kumasi.

Yaa Asantewa commanded the rebellion that broke out in April, an uprising often remembered as the Yaa Asantewa War. The siege of the British garrison trapped Hodgson and his wife until they escaped in June. The British broke the siege in July, but some resistance continued into 1901. Yaa Asantewa and other leaders were sent to join Prempeh in exile. She died in the Seychelles in 1921. The British annexed the Asante kingdom in 1902; it is today part of the Republic of GHANA.

DAVID P. JOHNSON, JR.

Askia Muhammad
?–1538
King of Songhai from 1493 to 1528.

A governor under Ali, Muhammad rebelled against Ali's son and successor and in 1493 ascended the throne. Two years later he went on a prolonged pilgrimage to Mecca that became legendary both in Europe and the Middle East for its pomp and ostentation. On his return, Muhammad set out not only to enlarge his empire, but also to transform the previously African state into an Islamic kingdom. Although he failed in that effort, he restored TOMBOUCTOU as a center of faith and learning and favored Muslim scholars with grants of land and high posts in government. Refining the administrative machinery inherited from Ali, he established directorial positions—similar to those of modern cabinet ministers—for finance, justice, agriculture, and other affairs. Although more a statesman than a warrior, he added vast territories to his realm, extending his influence as far west as the Atlantic Ocean. In 1528 Muhammad was overthrown by his son, and he spent most of his remaining years in banishment on an island in the NIGER RIVER.

Asmara, Eritrea
Capital and largest city of Eritrea.

Asmara is located in a highland region of ERITREA that was settled roughly 700 years ago. It is believed to have been the site of four small, feuding villages, which, under pressure from the villages' women inhabitants, finally made peace and united around 1515. The name Asmara comes from Arbate Asmara, which in the TIGRINYA language means "the four villages of those [women] who brought harmony." Sixteenth-century Italian sources describe Asmara as a caravan trading center.

Shortly afterward Asmara was sacked by Islamic warriors and went into decline. Few historical records even mention Asmara again until the late nineteenth century, when the Italians began their colonial conquest of the region. After occupying Aseb in 1882 and Massawa in 1885, the Italians pushed into the highlands, where they encountered resistance. However, in exchange for weapons Ethiopian Emperor Menelik II signed a treaty in 1889 acquiescing to Italian control of the highlands. Asmara became the colonial capital of Eritrea in 1900. It grew rapidly during the 1930s, as rural Eritreans and immigrant Italians alike sought work in new industries, among them textiles and food processing. Residential areas in Asmara at this time were strictly segregated.

In 1941 British troops occupied Asmara. The city slumped following Eritrea's federation with ETHIOPIA in 1951. No longer an administrative capital, Asmara soon lost its industrial base as well. Ethiopian Emperor Haile Selassie had factories dismantled and moved to ADDIS ABABA.

During Eritrea's thirty-year war for independence, from 1963 to 1993, Asmara's residents suffered through periods of siege, but the city itself emerged relatively undamaged.

Since 1993 Asmara has been the national capital. With a population of approximately 400,000 (according to a 2005 estimate), it is a city known for its Italian architecture, tiled sidewalks, cafés, cleanness and neatness, and mild climate. The University of Asmara and the National Museum are located in Asmara, as are most of the nation's industries. The city has an international airport, and rail links to the port city of MASSAWA are being rebuilt.

See also COLONIAL RULE; URBANISM AND URBANIZATION IN AFRICA.

DAVID P. JOHNSON, JR.

Assin

Ethnic group of Ghana, also known as the Asen.

The Assin inhabit primarily the central region of GHANA. They speak a Niger-Congo language and belong to the AKAN cultural and linguistic group. Some 147,000 people consider themselves Assin.

Astronomy, African

Modern, cultural, and traditional astronomy in Africa.

Astronomy on the African continent includes a long history of observations of the night sky done without the aid of telescopes, as well as modern observatories with impressive instruments. Africa is home to several world-class observing facilities, mostly in SOUTH AFRICA—Boyden Observatory (1927), Hartebeesthoek Radio Astronomy Observatory (1961), Hermanus Magnetic Observatory (1941), and the South African Astronomical Observatory (1820); and NAMIBIA houses the High Energy Stereoscopic System (2002), a gamma-ray observatory. Many African countries have astronomy societies, planetariums, or small observatories associated with universities that have telescopes suitable for teaching and public viewing. These include Algeria, Egypt, Ethiopia, Gabon, Mauritius, Morocco, Tunisia, and Zimbabwe. The Working Group on Space Sciences in Africa is a continent-wide organization that promotes the development of astronomy, concerning itself with astronomy education, public outreach, fund-raising, international collaborations, and the development of observation sites throughout Africa. Modern astronomy has a strong presence in Africa and will continue to grow as more observing facilities are completed, including the South African Large Telescope (SALT), which will be one of the world's largest when completed in 2004. Indigenous, traditional, or cultural astronomy focuses on the many ways that people and cultures interact with celestial bodies. Cultural astronomy also includes the study of how the science developed in Africa, how observatories are funded and built, and how resources are distributed among astronomers in Africa, but typically excludes the collection and analysis of modern astronomical observations. Traditional astronomy is more widely practiced in the general populace. Africa is home to many long-standing cultural traditions that include beliefs, practices, and observations relating to the sky. African traditional astronomy is rich with mythic figures, cosmology and cosmogony, divination methods that utilize observations of celestial bodies, and many other sky-related beliefs and traditions. The names that Africans have given to celestial bodies reveal myths, societal structures, physical environments, and seasonal activities. The names can be categorized in terms of physical characteristics, such as the bright star Canopus being named U-Canzibe (brilliant) by the XHOSA of South Africa. Names can also reflect the appearance of certain stars and constellations coinciding with agricultural or animal activities, such as the Pleiades having names associated with rain, planting, or fertility by the Bantu, the Batammaliba of Benin, the Sotho-Twana and ZULU of South Africa, and the MAASAI of Kenya, and with the Belt of Orion that is the Sotho's Makolobe stars (wild pigs) appearing at sunset during the time that bush pigs give birth. Numerous ethnic groups associate celestial bodies with myth and legend clusters, such as sun/predator/king and moon/female/wife. Venus is often associated with women, marriage, and the initiation of young girls. The connection between Venus and women may relate to the 263-day cycle where it appears alternately as a morning star or evening star, which is close to the human gestation period of 270 days. Africans have a continuing tradition of artistic representations of celestial objects in recognizable forms such as stars, constellations, the moon, the sun, and eclipses like in the designs of the Bahima of Uganda, the Egyptians, and the rock paintings of the San of southern Africa. Other representations are culturally encoded symbols and images that on first inspection do not reveal their connection to astronomy, such as the masks and memory boards of the Luba of Congo, and the symbols of the Bamana of Mali and the Batammaliba. Cosmological concepts and astronomical imagery are apparent in the art of the MAMBILA of Cameroon, the DOGON of Mali, and the Swazi of Swaziland. The layout of buildings, compounds, villages, and towns are aligned for prime viewing of celestial events: The Batammaliba, Bamana, and Swazi have structures positioned in relation to the annual north-south motion of the Sun on the horizon either marking the winter solstice, summer solstice, or equinox positions. As it does for people everywhere, the night sky served as a source of inspiration and provoked fascination, but was also utilized for practical purposes. Observations were useful for navigating at night, timekeeping and establishing an accurate calendar, and noting menses and fertility cycles. The TUAREG of the Sahara, the SWAHILI of East

Africa, and the AFAR of Eritrea and Djibouti are among the Africans noted for their skill at navigating by the stars. African calendars cannot be classified into one type. Some cultures utilize observations of the moon, the sun, the stars, or combinations thereof; others such as the AKAN of Ghana have established mathematically based calendars that do not rely on celestial observations. The accuracy of these calendars is typically within a half day to several days of the true 365.25-day year. Women throughout Africa observe the moon to keep track of their menses and regulate their fertility, since the 29.5-day lunar cycle is close to the 28-day menstruation cycle. This may be the reason that the moon is often regarded as female or is associated with women in many cultures around the world. Of major concern is how the cultural astronomical traditions of Africa are being impacted by the processes of modernization; some knowledge and practices are thriving while others are disappearing as the elders die and youths move into urban areas. This lends a sense of urgency to study and record traditional African astronomy that is in increasing danger of passing into African history.

J.C. HOLBROOK

Aswan High Dam

Dam in southern Egypt that impounds the waters of the Nile River in Lake Nasser, the worlds second-largest artificial lake.

Located near the city of Aswan, the Aswan High Dam provoked controversy even before it was constructed. The United States had promised funds to Egyptian leader Gamal Abdel NASSER to underwrite the construction of the dam. Egypt claimed nonalignment during the Cold War—that is, it allied with neither the Union of Soviet Socialist Republics (USSR) nor the United States. However, while seeking funding for the dam, EGYPT completed an arms deal with the USSR In retaliation, the United States withdrew the funding offer, whereupon Nasser nationalized the SUEZ CANAL, claiming that revenue from the canal would offset the dam's construction costs. This provoked an international conflict over control of the canal. Nasser, meanwhile, secured funds from the USSR for one-third of the dam's construction costs, the total of which exceeded $1 billion. The dam was an important part of Nasser's vision for Egypt. He sought it to provide inexpensive power and irrigation to the Nile Valley, even in times of drought. Although construction lasted from 1960 to 1970, by 1964 the dam was storing water, and it produced hydroelectric power by 1968. The dam was formally inaugurated in 1971. It was an impressive engineering feat. The dam is 111 m (364 ft) tall and 3,600 m (11,800 ft) long. This massive barrier created Lake Nasser—90 m (300 ft) deep, 16 km (10 mi)

wide, and with a holding capacity of 168,900,000,000 cubic m (about 136,927,000 acre-ft), or the volume of the Nile's entire flow for roughly two years. The Aswan High Dam has provided economic benefits to Egypt. The lake has brought an additional 324,000 hectares (about 800,000 acres) under cultivation and converted 283,000 hectares (700,000 acres) from flooded land to useful farmland. A treaty grants Egypt's southern neighbor, Sudan, one-third of the water impounded, while Egypt has rights to the remaining two-thirds. (In fact, economic difficulties have prevented SUDAN from claiming its full share, and Egypt has consumed more than its share.) The annual Nile flood is now controlled, the dam provides hydroelectric power, and Lake Nasser supports a fishing industry. The dam has caused a number of problems, however. The creation of Lake Nasser forced the Egyptian government to relocate an ancient Egyptian temple at Abu Simbel that would have otherwise been submerged and destroyed. Other archaeological sites were lost. Egypt also had to relocate 90,000 Egyptians and Nubians, including some in Sudan, from lands that were flooded or submerged. In addition, massive amounts of water evaporate from Lake Nasser, which is surrounded by a hot and arid desert. This reduces the amount of water available for irrigation or the generation of electricity, and it increases the river's salinity. The dam has severely reduced the deposits of fertile silt that the floodwaters once brought to the valley floodplain and Nile Delta. Consequently, Egyptian farmers have had to increase the use of chemical fertilizers. Meanwhile sediment accumulates at the bottom of the reservoir, which gradually reduces the reservoir's volume. The lack of sedimentation downstream from the dam has had other harmful effects, such as erosion of the riverbanks. More ominously, with the loss of the silt that once regenerated the delta, erosion has led to flooding in the delta caused by the encroachment of salty seawater. A projected rise in global sea levels could submerge large areas of the delta, the site of two-thirds of Egypt's crowded farmland. The loss of silt has also damaged the ecology of the eastern Mediterranean Sea. This silt once nourished algae and plankton that in turn fed sardines, shrimp, and other sea creatures. Since the opening of the Aswan High Dam, the fish and shrimp catches have declined significantly.

ROBERT FAY

Athletes, African, Abroad

African athletes who compete in soccer, running, basketball, boxing, and other sports around the world.

Africa has a long tradition of competitive sports, particularly in wrestling, athletics, and canoe racing. During the colonial era, European missionaries and educators encouraged a variety of sports in Africa to promote discipline. Since independence, African countries have participated in the Olympic Games, World Championships, Commonwealth Games, and other major international sporting events, while individuals have competed at both the professional and amateur levels throughout the world. Foreign universities and sports clubs often recruit young athletes from secondary schools and clubs in major African cities. Soccer, by far the most popular sport in contemporary Africa, is also one in which Africans have excelled abroad. Africans have played soccer overseas since the 1920s, and some have recently ranked among the world's top international players, including George WEAH of LIBERIA, Abedi Pele of GHANA, Roger Milla of CAMEROON, and Glory Alozie of NIGERIA. Approximately 350 Africans play on professional teams in Asia, Europe, the Middle East, and North and South America. In Europe, African players charged other players with using racist epithets during competitions in the sport in the mid-1990s. Africans have also won international recognition in track and field events. Since the 1960s African runners, particularly Kenyans and Ethiopians, have trained and raced in Europe and the United States. Runners such as Said Abouita of MOROCCO, Kipchogo KEINO of KENYA, and Haile GEBRSELASSIE of ETHIOPIA have dominated the middle-distance events, while Kenyans Moses Tanui and Tegla LOROUPE and Ethiopians Fatima Roba and Abebe BIKILA have taken top prizes in long-distance races. More recently, sprinters such as Maria Mutola of MOZAMBIQUE and Frankie FREDERICKS of NAMIBIA have also performed well. In the late 1990s, many of Africa's top-finishing professional roadrunners—especially Kenyans—faced a backlash from American race officials, who were seeking to restrict winnings available to Africans and other international athletes. By the end of the twentieth century it was more common for Africans to participate in professional sports in the United States. Players such as Hakeem OLAJUWON and Dikembe Mutombo made tremendous impacts in the National Basketball League (NBA). African athletes also made a mark in the National Football League (NFL). Nigerian born Christian Okoye, who played for the Kansas City Chiefs during the 1980s, set many team rushing records. Africans have boxed at the international level since the colonial era, when in 1922 Louis Faal of Senegal became the first African to win a world title. Other Africans to win boxing titles abroad include Nigerian Dick IHETU, in the 1940s, and Ghanaian Azumah Nelson, in the 1980s and 1990s. African countries have also produced top international athletes and teams in golf (Ernie Els, Gary PLAYER, and Nick Price), rugby (SOUTH AFRICA), tennis (ZIMBABWE), field hockey (Kenya), cricket (Kenya, Zimbabwe, and South Africa), handball (Kenya and TANZANIA), and swimming (South Africa). Many of these,

as well as various white South African athletes, lived and competed abroad during the APARTHEID years.

See also CAMEROON LIONS.

ERIC YOUNG

Attié

Ethnic group of Côte d'Ivoire; also known as the Atié, Akié and the Akyé.

The Attié primarily inhabit the area directly north of ABIDJAN, CÔTE D'IVOIRE. They speak a Niger-Congo language and belong to the AKAN cultural and linguistic group. Approximately 380,000 people consider themselves Attié.

See also LANGUAGES, AFRICAN: AN OVERVIEW.

Attitudes toward Blacks in the Ancient Mediterranean World

Who were "blacks" in the ancient Mediterranean world and where did they live? Ancient written and artistic (iconographical) evidence provides copious information about people with physical types that closely resemble Africans and peoples of African descent in the modern world. These ancient people, known in common and historical usage as Negroes or blacks, inhabited the NILE RIVER valley south of EGYPT (often called KUSH in Egyptian records and ETHIOPIA or NUBIA in Greco-Roman documents) as well as the southern fringes of northwest Africa (roughly from at least present-day Fezzan, LIBYA, and the oases of southern TUNISIA to the Atlantic coast of MOROCCO). For the most part, blacks who found their way to areas outside Africa came from regions of the Nile Valley and also, to some extent, from northwest Africa.

EGYPTIAN EVIDENCE

The earliest iconographic evidence comes from Egyptian artists who realistically portrayed the features of their southern neighbors, whom they often called Kushites, in countless paintings, sculptures, and other pieces. These Egyptian artifacts clearly depict the black skin and woolly or tightly curled hair of the Kushites, which differed markedly from the portrayal of these features of Egyptians in Egyptian art. On this point Egyptologist David O'Connor has observed: "Thousands of sculpted and painted representations from Egypt as well as hundreds of well-preserved bodies from cemeteries show that the typical physical type was neither 'Negro' nor 'Negroid.'" Egyptian art points to the presence of blacks in Egypt as early as the Old Kingdom (about 2755–2255 B.C.E.). A limestone head from about 2600 B.C.E. clearly delineates the rather broad nose and thick lips of a wife of an Egyptian prince from the court of Memphis. Although black women are depicted in early Egyptian art, the artists of that time primarily used black men—soldiers, mercenaries, and captives—as subjects. Examples include the limestone heads of prisoners found at the temples of Pepi I and II, built sometime between 2423 and 2200 B.C.E. at Saqqara, southwest of Cairo. These blacks were of a pronounced Negroid type—broad noses, thick lips, and hair arranged in parallel rows of tightly coiled braids. Stelae (carved or inscribed stone slabs or pillars) of black mercenaries and their wives, sometimes Egyptian, attest to the presence of blacks at Gebelein, near the ancient Egyptian capital of Thebes, sometime between 2180 and 2040 B.C.E. Wooden models of archers point to the presence of black-skinned recruits farther north at Assiut about 2000 B.C.E. The much more frequent appearance of blacks in the art of the New Kingdom (1570–1070 B.C.E.) reflects increased Egyptian activity in Kush during this period. The sculptures of the Twenty-fifth Dynasty (about 761–671 B.C.E.)—whose rulers were from Kush and were called Ethiopians in Greek documents—clearly portray the Negroid features of the kings of this dynasty, such as Kashta, Shabaka, and Taharqa. In short, long before Greek and Roman writers described the physical characteristics of Kush in accurate detail for the first time in the ancient world, important iconographic documents from Egypt had provided clear portraits of the black skin and woolly or tightly coiled hair of the Kushites.

GRECO-ROMAN EVIDENCE

Egyptians, having been well acquainted with their black neighbors from earliest times, saw nothing unusual in the differences between Egyptian physical features and those of the black southerners. The Greeks and Romans, however, as the first Europeans to encounter blacks, were struck by the physical characteristics of people so markedly different from themselves. Hence, Greek and Roman literature contains the most detailed descriptions in the ancient world of the observable physical traits of blacks. Xenophanes, a Greek philosopher-poet who lived during the sixth and fifth centuries B.C.E., described Ethiopians as black and flat nosed. In the first century B.C.E. the Greek historian Diodorus Siculus described Ethiopians who lived near the Nile as black, flat nosed, and woolly haired. The fact that Ethiopians were the blackest people known in the Roman world was illustrated by a familiar "color scheme" succinctly stated in the first century C.E. by the Roman poet Manilius in his didactic poem on astrology. In that poem, known as Astronomica, he classified dark and dark-skinned peoples as follows: Ethiopians, the blackest; Indians, less sunburned; Egyptians, mildly dark; and Moors, the lightest. The idea that a white man could pass for an Ethiopian merely by blackening his body was

ridiculous, the Roman satirist Petronius Arbiter pointed out, because color alone does not make an Ethiopian. A complete Ethiopian disguise, he argued, required several modifications in the white man's makeup—hair, lips, and facial scarification. It is important to emphasize that the Greeks and Romans clearly saw black-skinned Africans as a separate group of people. This was highlighted in the Greek word Aithiops, meaning, literally, a dark-skinned person. The word was applied only to some Ethiopians and to certain other dark and black-skinned Africans. With a few poetical exceptions, it was not applied to Egyptians or to inhabitants of northwest Africa, such as Carthaginians, Numidians, or Moors. The understanding of Egyptians as distinct from their southern neighbors is also clear in the ancient iconographic and written evidence. The evidence also shows that the physical type of the Ethiopian inhabitants of the Nile Valley south of Egypt, not the Egyptians, most clearly resembled that of Africans and peoples of African descent described in the modern world as Negroes or blacks.

FIRST ENCOUNTERS WITH BLACKS

Differences in black-white relations in the ancient and modern worlds are striking. In the first place, in the ancient world prolonged contacts between blacks and whites occurred from early times. These contacts frequently involved soldiers or mercenaries, not so-called savages. Egyptians, Greeks, and Romans perceived the area south of Egypt as an independent country, rich in coveted resources and inhabited by the blackest people in their experience. The abilities of these blacks, skilled in archery and able to defend themselves from foreign exploitation, earned them the respect of their enemies. In fact, in about 750 B.C.E.—after almost 500 years of Egyptian occupation—blacks came north, turned the tables on their former conquerors, and ruled Egypt until they were driven out by a superior Assyrian war machine in 664 B.C.E. Black military power also won the respect of the Ptolemies, and later, the Romans. The Romans decided that the most effective way to prevent attacks on the Roman southern boundary in Egypt was not by arms but by diplomacy. For example, the Roman emperor Augustus granted Ethiopian ambassadors everything they pleaded for, including remission of the tribute he had imposed.

EXPLAINING THE DIFFERENCES

Despite Egypt's centuries-old conflict with its black southern neighbors, the Great Hymn to Aten, a hymn to the sun god or solar disk, looked impartially on differences in skin color. In the hymn all peoples, whether from the lands of Khor (the Egyptian name for Syria), Kush, or Egypt, are viewed as creations of Aten (Aton). Nubians and Syrians were examples of "the other" in the Egyptian mind. Greeks and Romans selected the fair, straight-haired Scythians of the distant north in south Russia (the area between the Dnieper and the Don rivers, according to the Greek historian Herodotus) and the black, woolly-haired Ethiopians of the deep south as examples of ethnic types differing from themselves. These two peoples became favorite illustrations of a Greco-Roman environmental theory in the first century B.C.E. Diodorus, for example, wrote in Bibliotheca Historica, his world history in forty books, that in view of the vast differences between Scythia and Ethiopia, it is not at all surprising that "both the fare and manner of life as well as the bodies of inhabitants of both regions should be very different from those that prevail among us." The relevance of the environmental theory to an unbiased view of blacks is seen in the fact that the north-south, Scythian-Ethiopian contrast was also chosen by Greek and Roman advocates of the view that color is of no importance in evaluating the worth of Scythians and Ethiopians. These northern and southern peoples exemplified the broad scale of human potentiality. Menander, the fourth-century B.C.E. Greek writer of comedy, emphasized this when he wrote that it makes no difference whether one is as physically different from a Greek as a Scythian or Ethiopian; it is merit, not color that counts. Later, these same north and south peoples also figured prominently in a highly spiritual Christian imagery.

OPPORTUNITIES IN ALIEN LANDS

The color of blacks presented no obstacles that excluded them from opportunities available to others living in Egypt, Greece, or Italy. Ancient slavery was color-blind. Both blacks and whites were kept as slaves, and the ancient world never developed a concept of the equivalence of slave and black or Negro, nor did it create theories to prove that blacks were more fit than whites for slavery. The majority of slaves were white, not black, and although enslaved prisoners of war undoubtedly accounted for a substantial number of black slaves, the advantages of cosmopolitan centers, such as Alexandria and Rome, were as attractive to blacks as to Jews or Syrians. As did other slaves and free people, blacks often engaged in occupations at the lower end of the economic scale, but blacks with special abilities found places for their talent and skill. In Egypt blacks had long found a career in the military to be a means of achieving positions of security and prestige. Roman imperial armies included Ethiopians, such as those in the numerus Maurorum (unit of Moors) of the Emperor Septimius Severus depicted in a scene on a third-century C.E. sarcophagus. (Like the others, this unit was apparently a member of the emperor's elite bodyguard.) In the Roman world some blacks were popular in the theater.

A famous black animal fighter was praised by the poet Luxorius in the fifth century C.E. in these words: "The fame of your renown will live long after you and Carthage will always remember your name." Included among the distinguished followers of the Greek philosopher Epicurus was a black from Alexandria named Ptolemaeus. A black known as Memnon was one of the celebrated disciples of Herodes Atticus, the well-known Greek scholar and patron of the arts who lived in the second century C.E.

RACIAL MIXTURE

Racial mixture in the ancient world between blacks and whites gave rise to nothing resembling modern strictures against miscegenation. Intermarriage between blacks and Egyptians was common and dated back at least to the Fourth Dynasty (about 2600 B.C.E.), as attested by the limestone heads of a prince from the court of Memphis and his black wife. Greeks and Romans, like many black and whites then and now, used their own physical traits as a yardstick in their aesthetic preferences, forming what H. Hoetink has referred to as a "somatic norm image." This he defined in Two Variants in Caribbean Race Relations: A Contribution to the Sociology of Segmented Societies (1967) as the "complete physical (somatic) characteristics accepted by a group as its norms and ideal," pointing out that each group considers itself aesthetically superior to others. Some scholars have read a nonexistent antiblack sentiment into the Greco-Roman expressions of preference for their own physical traits. Such distortions of the classical view of the Ethiopians' color have overlooked the fact that there were those who emphasized the subjectivity of their criteria, others who extolled the beauty of blackness, and still others who preferred blacks and did not hesitate to say so. Herodotus, the first European to express an opinion about the physical appearance of Ethiopians, described them as the most handsome of men. One of the love poems of Philodemus, written sometime in the first or second century B.C.E. to a certain Philaenion, short, black, with hair more curled than parsley and skin more tender than down, concluded: "May I love such a Philaenion, golden Cypris, until I find another more perfect." Greek and Roman writers (such as Aristotle and Plutarch) and others who had occasion to refer to interracial marriages or to mention black and white racial mixture as illustrations of the transmission of inherited physical characteristics, as evidence of adultery, or for any other reason, developed no theories of "white purity" and nothing resembling later strictures on miscegenation. In other words, like other peoples, white and black alike, Greeks and Romans used their own physical traits in statements of aesthetic preferences. And it should be noted that realistic portrayals of mulattos and other clearly mixed black and white types by Greco-Roman artists vividly illustrate the results of black and white racial mixture. At the same time, they point to the physical assimilation of blacks into the predominantly white population.

BLACKS IN RELIGIONS OF THE ANCIENT WORLD

Religion knew no color bar. Blacks and whites worshiped Isis—a national deity of Egypt and a leading goddess elsewhere in the Mediterranean world—at the same shrines as other worshipers and played an influential role in the spread of Isiac worship in Egypt, Greece, and Italy. Frescoes from Herculaneum (near Naples, Italy) depict Isiac cultists, black and white, men and women. In one fresco a black choirmaster is seen directing a chorus of the faithful of both sexes, and in another a central black figure is executing a dance with the eyes of most worshipers focused upon him. Black devotees of Isis, though often far from their homeland, may have been strangers to temples in Greece or Italy but were at home in the Isiac faith. The strong bond that had united blacks and whites in the common worship of Isis was reinforced by Christianity. Scythians and especially Ethiopians figured prominently in the imagery of the early Christian credo. When Origen, the theologian from Alexandria in Egypt, declared in the third century C.E. that all whom God created He created equal and alike, whether they were born among Hebrews, Greeks, Ethiopians, Scythians, or Taurians, he was adapting a formula well known in classical thought that left no doubt as to its meaning and comprehensiveness. Saint Augustine, the bishop of Hippo in North Africa who lived in the fourth and fifth centuries C.E., stated that the Catholic Church was not to be limited to a particular region of the earth, but would reach even the Ethiopians, the remotest and the blackest of men. Augustine was not only recalling Homer's distant Ethiopians (inhabiting the Nile River valley south of Egypt), he no doubt also had in mind those Ethiopians on the southernmost fringes of his own bishopric in northwest Africa. Man's common descent and his common human nature were recognized by early Christians in these words of Augustine's De civitate Dei: "Whoever is born anywhere as a human being ... however strange he may appear to our senses in bodily form or color ... or in any faculty, part or quality of his nature whatsoever, let no true believer have any doubt that such an individual is descended from the one man who was first created."

The baptism of the Ethiopian queen's minister by Philip the Evangelist described in the Bible in Acts of the Apostles 8:26–40 was a landmark in proclaiming that considerations of color were to be of no significance in determining membership in the Christian church. Blacks were not only humble converts but influential figures, such as Saint Menas (sometimes portrayed as a Negro), a national saint

of Egypt sometime in the third or fourth century C.E. A black Ethiopian, Abba Moses, a patriarch of the Egyptian desert, was frequently cited as a model of the monastic life, as an excellent teacher, and as a "Father's Father." He left about seventy disciples when he died late in the fourth or early in the fifth century C.E.

SUMMARY

In the entire corpus of evidence relating to the Egyptian, Greco-Roman, and early Christian world, only a few concepts, such as the classical somatic norm image, have been cited as so-called evidence of antiblack sentiment. These misinterpretations and similar misreadings of the ancient evidence, however, are examples of modern, not ancient prejudices. As H. C. Baldry observed in his Unity of Mankind in Greek Thought (1965): "In treating a subject which is so alive today, nothing is easier than to read back twentieth-century ideas into documents which in reality have quite another meaning." And this is precisely what some modern scholars have done. Misled by modern sentiments, they have seen color prejudice where none existed. Some have argued that color prejudice is "human" or "natural," and many disagree as to the precise stage in the history of black and white relations that color acquired the importance it has assumed in the modern world. One point, however, is certain: The onus of intense color prejudice cannot be placed upon the shoulders of the Egyptians, Greeks, Romans, or Christians of the ancient Mediterranean world.

BIBLIOGRAPHY

Snowden, Frank M., Jr. Before Color Prejudice: The Ancient View of Blacks. Harvard University Press, 1983.

Snowden, Frank M., Jr. Blacks in Antiquity: Ethiopians in the Greco-Roman Experience. Harvard University Press, 1970.

Snowden, Frank M., Jr. "Blacks, Early Christianity and". In The Interpreter's Dictionary of the Bible. Supplementary edition. Abingdon, 1976.

Snowden, Frank M., Jr. "Bernal's 'Blacks' and the Afrocentrists". In Black Athena Revisited, ed. by Mary R. Lefkowitz and Guy MacLean Rogers. University of North Carolina Press, 1996.

Vercoutter, Jean, Frank M. Snowden, Jr., et al. The Image of the Black in Western Art. Vol. 1: From the Pharaohs to the Fall of the Roman Empire. William Morrow, 1976.

FRANK M. SNOWDEN, JR.

Augustine, Saint

354–430
Catholic thelogian from North Africa and major influence on subsequent Christian theology.

One of the most famous theologians of his time, Augustine was raised in a mixed household: his mother was Christian but his father, an official of the Roman empire, was pagan. He spent his early years in what is today called Souk-Ahras, in ALGERIA. Despite the piety of his mother, Augustine abandoned Christianity at an early age, attracted instead by Manichaeism, a system of material dualism that claimed the human soul was like light imprisoned by darkness. A precocious learner, Augustine considered Christian scripture intellectually crude. Inspired by Hortensius, a now-lost text by Cicero, he mastered rhetoric and, while still in his teens, held a professional chair of rhetoric in Carthage. Ever questioning the nature of things, Augustine discarded Manichaeism for Academic Skepticism, and, later, Neoplatonism. At the age of twnenty-eight, he left Carthage for the Roman capital of Milan in search of better-disciplined students. In Milan, Augustine was profoundly impressed by Saint Ambrose, the preeminent Roman churchman of the time, and converted to Christianity. Saint Ambrose baptized Augustine, who thereafter returned to Africa and passed the remainder of his life deep in Christian thought. In contrast to his youthful agnosticism, the repentant Augustine decided that faith was the first and most essential step toward wisdom. He was ordained as an assistant priest in Hippo Regius in 391 and became the bishop of Roman Africa five years later. Augustine's famous autobiography, The Confessions, showcases the tormented self-deprecation that underpins Augustine's theology and that flavored 1,500 years of Christian faith. Augustine's most influential works include his philosophy of creation and of time, his philosophy of history, and his theory of salvation. In contrast to Greek notions of eternal substance, Augustine believed that, as the Bible said, God created the world from absolute nothingness. Augustine also claimed that God was outside of time, existing always, and always the same. He posited that past and future were constructs of the human mind, ever-present sensations of memory and expectation. In The City of God, Augustine created what was perhaps the first philosophy of history. Here he proclaimed that two cities—that of earth and that of heaven—are combined in this world. At the end of this world, however, these cities shall be divided into their true forms: the elect and the reprobate, the saved and the damned, heaven and hell. Augustine claimed that the Church was the only means by which people could attempt to enter the City of God. By doing this, he set the stage for the struggle between emperors and popes that characterized Western European history until the Protestant Reformation. Although his work affected Western Europe more than it did Africa, Augustine was part of an imperial order that suppressed the Donatists, African Christians who often contested the Catholic establishment for economic and social as well as religious reasons. Augustine died on August 28, 430, as Vandals were besieging the city of Hippo; August 28 has since become the day on which Catholics honor him.

ERIC BENNETT

Aushi

Ethnic group of south central Africa; also known as Ushi.
The Aushi primarily inhabit the southeastern tip of Congo-Kinshasa and northern ZAMBIA. They speak a BANTU language and belong to the BEMBA cultural and linguistic group. Approximately 400,000 people consider themselves Aushi.

See also CONGO, DEMOCRATIC REPUBLIC OF THE; LANGUAGES, AFRICAN: AN OVERVIEW.

Awolowo, Obafemi
1909–1987
Nigerian statesman and Yoruba chief; prominent political leader in the years surrounding Nigerian independence.
Born in Ikenne, the son of a farmer, Obafemi Awolowo was educated at great cost to his family. He studied at local mission schools, training to be a teacher after his father's death. But Awolowo soon became involved in Nigerian commerce. He founded the Nigerian Produce Traders Association, and in the late 1930s he assumed the position of secretary of the Nigerian Motor Transport Traders Association. In 1943 Awolowo organized the Trades Union Congress of Nigeria, and the following year he traveled to London, England, to study law. There he established a YORUBA cultural and political group, the Egbe Omo Oduduwa, and published Path to Nigerian Freedom (1947), in which he argued for a federated government.

Law degree in hand, Awolowo returned to Nigeria in 1947 and was appointed general secretary of Egbe Omo Oduduwa in 1948. Awolowo helped found the Action Group, a political party identified with the Yoruba people, and led the government of the Western Region in the period leading to independence from Britain in 1960. In the next few years the Action Group, originally moderate and pro-Western, turned hard left under the influence of younger, more radical party members. Late in 1962, in the wake of a bitter party split, Awolowo and several associates were charged with treason. Sentenced to fifteen years in Calabar Prison, Awolowo wrote Thoughts on the Nigerian Constitution (1967). He was freed by a new military government in 1966 and reentered the political scene as leader of the Yoruba-dominated Western Region of Nigeria. In 1967 he was appointed minister of finance, a post he held until 1971. His publications include Awo: The Autobiography of Chief Obafemi Awolowo (1960; republished in 1968 as My Early Life), The People's Republic (1968), and The Strategy and Tactics of the People's Republic of Nigeria (1970).

Awoonor, Kofi

1935–

Ghanaian poet and novelist.

Kofi Awoonor's works in English focus on life in GHANA following independence from Great Britain in 1957, but they also draw heavily from the traditional literature of the EWE culture in which he grew up. He published his first work under the name George Awoonor-Williams but has used his birth name since the late 1960s.

Awoonor was born in the coastal town of Wheta. In 1960 he received a B.A. degree in English from the University of Ghana at Legon, near ACCRA. He then served as managing editor of the Ghana Film Corporation. In 1968 Awoonor went to the United States, where he earned a Ph.D. degree in comparative literature from the State University of New York at Stony Brook in 1972. He later taught there and at the University of Texas at Austin. Awoonor returned to Ghana in 1975 to teach in the English department at the University of Cape Coast. His opposition to the military government led to his arrest and imprisonment. Pardoned and released in 1976, he returned to the university. Beginning in the 1980s, Awoonor held a number of diplomatic positions, most notably as Ghana's ambassador to the United Nations in the early 1990s.

Awoonor has established himself as one of the most significant contemporary African writers, primarily through his poetry. His poems are lyrical but strongly involved with political and cultural concerns. Awoonor's first two books of verse, *Rediscovery* (1964) and *Night of My Blood* (1971), move from fascination with his African roots to a blend of traditional and Western ideas. His first novel, *This Earth, My Brother . . . : An Allegorical Tale of Africa* (1971), remains his most widely read work. It tells of a young lawyer's coming to terms with postcolonial West African society. As in his early poetry, Awoonor employs rhythms and motifs from traditional Ewe funeral songs to express the alienation and anguish that demand a restructuring, refocusing, and revitalizing of individual and communal order in contemporary Africa. *The Breast of the Earth: A Critical Survey of Africa's Literature, Culture, and History* (1975), an introduction to African culture and artists, became one of Awoonor's best-known books.

The poetry collection *Ride Me, Memory* (1973) reflects on Awnoor's sojourn in America, often following the patterns of traditional African praise and abuse poetry. The title of his next collection, *The House by the Sea* (1978), refers to the place where he was imprisoned, and the poems turn his personal experience of imprisonment into a collective statement about his people. The novel *Comes the Voyager at Last* (1991) examines an African American who comes to Africa to find his roots. *The Latin American and Caribbean Notebook, Volume I* (1992) is a collection of poems reflecting

on global relations during Awoonor's years as an ambassador. In *The Ghana Revolution: A Background Account from a Personal Perspective* (1984) and *Ghana: A Political History from Pre-European to Modern Times* (1990), Awoonor presented his views on history and politics.

Axum

See AKSUM.

Azande

Major ethnic group of southern Sudan, northeastern Congo-Kinshasa, and the southeastern Central African Republic.

In the early nineteenth century the Bandia people formed kingdoms that ruled over the Vungara, whose language they adopted, in the savannas of what is today the southeastern CENTRAL AFRICAN REPUBLIC. The two groups merged to form the Azande people. Each Azande king directly administered the central province of his kingdom and delegated authority in outlying areas to his sons, nobles, or occasionally to particularly talented commoners. Each province had a court that served as an administrative as well as a social center, and each provincial governor collected tribute on behalf of the king.

With the king's death, however, a power struggle began that did not end until one of the king's sons came to dominate the bulk of his father's territory. The sons who lost their authority in this struggle frequently sought to establish kingdoms of their own in neighboring regions. By this means, the Azande expanded rapidly eastward and northward during the early nineteenth century toward the Bahr al-Ghazal and NILE rivers; their subjects, though, included many non-Azande. Because the Azande were divided in rival kingdoms, they could not develop a united front against foreign invaders. The raids of northern Sudanese slave traders checked the northward expansion of the group in the mid-nineteenth century.

Since precolonial times, Azande have resolved disputes by consulting oracles with the guidance of ritual specialists. The community often considered misfortune, disease, and disaster to be the result of witchcraft. (The Azande believed that witches attacked the spiritual essence of their victims, not with medicines or charms, but through the ability of the witches' souls to attack other people at night.) Sorcery, which was also practiced in Azande communities, involved the ritual manipulation of objects, medicines, or the spoken word to achieve the perpetrator's personal goals.

During the scramble for Africa, France, Belgium, and the Anglo-Egyptian SUDAN each claimed a portion of the Azande homeland, and the Azande have remained divided among three different states since then. Although the

Anglo-Egyptian administration left the Azande hierarchy intact by imposing a system of indirect rule through the aristocracy, the wealth of the royal and provincial courts fell sharply when the government hindered their ability to collect tribute. In fact, impoverished conditions have been common to the Azande in Sudan, Congo-Kinshasa, and the Central African Republic.

After World War II (1939–1945), the British developed a project known as the Zande Scheme to promote cotton cultivation in southern Sudan in a last-minute effort to bring that region's level of development up to that of northern Sudan. This effort largely failed. Because their homeland is so isolated—far from ports and in regions lacking good transportation infrastructure—the Azande's opportunities for trade have been limited, and an ongoing civil war in Sudan has compounded the difficulties of the Azande in that country. To compensate for their isolation many Azande who once lived in dispersed homesteads have migrated to towns along major roads in all three countries, often at the prompting of government authorities, to improve their economic chances. Since precolonial times, the Azande have hunted and farmed millet, sorghum, and corn. They also once produced considerable amounts of cotton cloth. Today the Azande farm cassava and peanuts as cash crops. Though reliable numbers are difficult to come by, it is estimated that between one million and four million people consider themselves Azande.

See also CONGO, DEMOCRATIC REPUBLIC OF THE.

Azania

Name used during the era of apartheid, or forced segregation, in South Africa in reference to a country of the future, independent and ruled by blacks.

The term azania, meaning "the land of the blacks," was the name Arab traders gave the eastern coast of Africa beginning in the first century B.C.E. In the 1970s Azania was adopted by militant black South Africans, including the Pan-Africanist Congress (PAC), as a more authentic name for their country.

Organizations that were part of the Black Consciousness Movement also used the name. The South African government banned Black Consciousness organizations in 1977, but in 1978 the Azanian People's Organization (AZAPO) was founded. Like the Black Consciousness organizations, AZAPO advocated a liberated Azania under black rule. The AFRICAN NATIONAL CONGRESS (ANC), on the other hand, never supported Azania as a future name for South Africa.

In 1990 the South African government lifted its ban on antiapartheid groups. Black Consciousness organizations put forward the Azanian Manifesto in June 1993 in opposition to the ANC's statement of purpose, called the FREEDOM CHARTER. The manifesto stood as an alternative to nonracial strategies like those of the ANC and discouraged any collaboration with the former white oppressors. The ANC, however, had been holding negotiations with the ruling National Party, and in 1994 South Africa held its first multiracial, democratic, national elections. The ANC won a majority of the vote and formed a new government. The term Azania fell out of use after South Africa achieved majority rule.

Azikiwe, Nnamdi
1905–1996
First president of independent Nigeria.

A member of the IGBO people of western NIGERIA, Nnamdi Azikiwe was educated at mission schools in the city of LAGOS. He worked briefly as a clerk for the national treasury at Lagos, but in 1925 he left Nigeria in 1925, a stowaway on a ship bound for the United States. There, he studied history and political science while supporting himself as a coal miner, casual laborer, dishwasher, and boxer. As a graduate student at the University of Pennsylvania, Azikiwe became familiar with black activist Marcus **Garvey** and the Back to Africa movement.

In 1934 Azikiwe moved to GHANA, became editor of the Africa Morning Post, and published Liberia in World Affairs, a book about another West African nation. He published Renascent Africa in 1937. That same year he returned to Nigeria, where he joined the executive committee of the Nigerian Youth Movement and started a chain of newspapers, including the West African Pilot and four other journals. Azikiwe was appointed secretary-general of the National Council of Nigeria and the Cameroons in 1944. He took a leading role in the rise of Nationalism in Africa as a political movement, and in 1954 he became premier of Nigeria's Igbo-dominated Eastern Region, a post he held for five years. When Nigeria gained its independence in 1960, Azikiwe became governor-general. Three years later the country became a republic, and Azkikiwe was unanimously elected its first president. Three years after that, however, a military coup removed him from office. Later Azikiwe returned to Nigeria, where he served as chancellor of the University of Lagos. He died in 1996 after a lengthy illness.

B

Bâ, Amadou Hampaté
1901–1991
Malian writer, storyteller, historian, and Islamic theologian who transcribed African oral epics into French and is known for coining the phrase "In Africa, when an old person dies, it is a library that burns down."

Amadou Hampaté Bâ was born in the town of Bandiagara, approximately 500 km (300 mi) northeast of BAMAKO, MALI, and belonged to an important family of MARABOUTS (Muslim religious leaders). Bâ's father died when he was two years old, and he was adopted and raised by a chief in the region. Educated at French schools in Bandiagara and Djenné, about 200 km (124 mi) from Bandiagara, Bâ nonetheless managed to continue his traditional Islamic education with famed Islamic teacher Tierno Bokar, a man whose wisdom Bâ later immortalized in Vie et enseignement de Tierno Bokar (The Life and Teachings of Tierno Bokar, 1980). It was also at this time that Bâ encountered Kullel, a storyteller and traditional educator who gave Bâ his first lessons in the African oral tradition. Bâ later earned the nickname Amkullel ("Little Kullel"), and he honored his teacher by titling the first volume of his autobiography Amkoullel, l'enfant peul (Amkullel, the Fulani Child, 1991).

While serving as a clerk in the French colonial administration during the 1920s and 1930s, Bâ was assigned the task of collecting and transcribing African tales and fables. Throughout the 1940s and 1950s, Bâ traveled in the French Sudan (now MALI) and Upper Volta (now BURKINA FASO), accumulating African folktales and epics. He traveled to France for the first time in 1951 on a scholarship from the United Nations Educational, Scientific, and Cultural Organization (UNESCO). In 1962 he returned to Paris to serve on the executive council of UNESCO, a post he held until 1971.

While working at UNESCO, Bâ published African tales and epics in French, including Koumen (1961), a young man's coming-of-age story, and Kaïdara (1969), a traditional Fulani oral account of a man's quest for spiritual knowledge. During his years at UNESCO Bâ became widely known as a committed defender of the African oral tradition, advocating for the preservation of African oral culture by transcribing the oral literature. After he left UNESCO, Bâ returned to Mali but soon retired in ABIDJAN, CÔTE D'IVOIRE, where he continued his writing career.

In subsequent years Bâ published numerous transcriptions of oral texts. Among these was L'Étrange destin de Wangrin (1974; trans. The Fortunes of Wangrin, 1987), a story about a cunning African man who tricks colonial authorities into helping him while at the same time convincing them that he is subservient, and L'Éclat de la grande étoile (The Brilliance of the Great Star, 1976), a sequel to Kaïdara. In the same period he produced works of a more sociological nature, including Aspects de la civilisation africaine (Aspects of African Civilization, 1972) and Jésus vu par un musulman (Jesus as Seen by a Muslim, 1993).

The most remarkable aspect of Bâ's work is not simply that he managed to preserve important parts of the African oral tradition, but that he created a new form in doing so. His best-known work, L'Étrange destin de Wangrin, has been cited as an example of a text that modifies the Western narrative form in a way that makes it appropriate for the oral tradition. In this way, L'Étrange destin de Wangrin and other works by Bâ function as powerful symbols of the contact between Africa and the West, as well as of the conflict between African tradition and modern culture.

See also ORAL TRADITIONS IN AFRICA.

Bâ, Mariama
1929–1981
Senegalese writer whose work highlighted the social inequities facing women.

Mariama Bâ, the daughter of SENEGAL's first minister of health, was born into a highly educated Muslim family. Bâ's father had a strong belief in the value of education and, ignoring traditional prohibitions, insisted that his daughter pursue higher education. Bâ attended a prestigious French boarding school near DAKAR, passing the entrance examination with the highest marks of all candidates in West Africa that year.

While still a student, Bâ began writing essays for local journals and newspapers. Her writing revealed her as an articulate and political young woman: one essay, for example, attacked assimilation, a French policy encouraging Africans to adopt French identity and culture. An active participant in women's organizations, the young Bâ found her voice as a spokesperson for African women facing new troubles in the traditional institution of marriage. Bâ would later confront these difficulties in her own life, when, as a mother of nine, her marriage to a Senegalese politician ended in divorce.

Bâ's first and best-known novel, *Une Si Longue Lettre* (So Long a Letter, 1980), articulated the social inequities facing women in contemporary Senegalese society, particularly the practice of polygamy. The Noma Prize-winning novel takes the form of a letter from Ramatoulaye, whose husband has just died, to her friend Aïssatou. Both women have suffered from their marriages and the fact that they are highly educated and married for love does not protect them from the oppression experienced by their mothers. In her letter, Ramatoulaye tells the story of how both marriages unravel as their husbands take other, younger brides. The story of a third woman, Jaqueline, unfolds around the challenge of a cross-cultural relationship between a Muslim Senegalese man and a Christian woman from CÔTE D'IVOIRE. By showing the conflict between individual desires and obligations to the extended family, the novel renders the oppression of women without apology or sentimentalism. Abiola Irele characterized *Une Si Longue Lettre* as "the most deeply felt presentation of the female condition in African fiction."

Bâ followed the success of her first novel with *Le Chant Écarlate* (Scarlet Song, 1981), also an examination of cross-cultural relationships. The novel traces how a marriage between a white French woman and a Senegalese man collapses under the strain of conflicting worldviews and pressures from the extended family. But the story also depicts another, successful interracial relationship, leaving open the possibility of transcending a cultural gap through compromise and sacrifice. The novel was Bâ's final work; she died shortly before its publication.

See also FEMINISM IN AFRICA: AN INTERPRETATION; MARRIAGE, AFRICAN CUSTOMS OF.

MARIAN AGUIAR

Babangida, Ibrahim Gbadamosi

1941-

President of Nigeria.

Ibrahim Gbadamosi Babangida, born to Muslim parents in northern NIGERIA, received an education that eventually placed him among the country's military elite. After primary school Babangida studied at the government college in Bida (1957–1962) and the Nigerian Military Training College in Kaduna (1962–1963). He traveled abroad to study with the Indian Military Academy (1964), the Royal Armoured Center in Great Britain (1966–1967), and the U.S. Army (1972). Back in Nigeria, his military studies continued at the Command and Staff College in Jaji (1977) and the Nigerian Institute for Policy and Strategic Studies in Kuru (1979–1980). Long before his education was complete, however, Babangida began active military duty.

Babangida was a lieutenant by 1966. During Nigeria's Biafran War (1967–1970) he commanded the Forty-fourth Infantry Battalion, called The Rangers, and won recognition as a capable leader. In 1974 the army promoted him to lieutenant colonel; the next year he became head of the armored corps. In 1976 Babangida led forces that successfully resisted a coup attempt to overthrow the government. By the early 1980s he had established himself as a leader.

Having prevented one coup, Babangida led another in 1983, after being promoted to major general and named chief of army staff. His coup overthrew Shehu Shagari, the civilian leader of Nigeria's Second Republic (1979–1983). The coup placed Muhammadu Buhari in control of the country, but two years later Babangida forced Buhari out of office, claiming that he had failed to revive Nigerias ailing economy. Inside observers suggested that a truer motive might have been political conflict between Buhari and a majority of the Supreme Military Council (SMC), which Babangida dominated.

Babangida had taken over a troubled office. Nigeria's economy was debt-ridden, and Muslims and Christians were fighting in the north. Babangida tried to reassure the public on the day of his coup by appearing on television. He announced plans to liberalize the economy, grant greater freedom to the press, and protect human rights. His rule, however, was at least as repressive as those of earlier dictators, and he largely failed to provide economic growth and stability. The International Monetary Fund (IMF) recommended economic reforms for Nigeria. At first Babangida refused to accept them, but he did introduce measures that caused high inflation and widespread hardship. When students and labor unions protested these measures in 1988, Babangida closed the universities and dissolved the executive committee of the National Labour Council.

Early in his term Babangida announced that the shift from military to civilian rule would be completed by October 1990, a date he then pushed back to 1992, and later delayed again until 1993. The two-party democracy he described would exclude military leaders who had held office in earlier regimes, including himself. But Babangida then proceeded to crush free speech, and he chose the two presidential candidates himself, banning all other contenders. His less favored pick was businessman Moshood ABIOLA. When Abiola won the election, Babangida canceled the result of the vote and installed a temporary government. This move made Nigerians angry enough that General Sani ABACHA, Babangida's chief of staff, was easily able to overthrow Babangida in a coup three months later. Babangida made the news again after Olugesun OBASANJO became president of Nigeria in 1999. Human-rights groups criticized Obasanjo for not bringing Babangida—from whom he had received support and campaign contributions—before the country's Human Rights Violations Investigation Commission. Activists accused Babangida of having been involved in numerous human-rights abuses during his presidency, including the murder by bomb of a journalist who had been investigating the president. A human rights commission appointed by President Olusegun Obasanjo in 1999 failed to force Babangida to testify but did suggest that Babangida was responsible for the journalist's murder and recommended further investigation into the matter. More recently, Babangida has demonstrated his continuing political ambitions, and it is widely believed that he will again seek the Nigerian presidency in the 2011 election cycle.

See also HUMAN RIGHTS IN AFRICA.

ERIC BENNETT

Babimbi

Ethnic group of Cameroon.

The Babimbi primarily inhabit southern CAMEROON. They speak a BANTU language and are related to the BASSA and BAKOKO. Approximately 150,000 people consider themselves Babimbi.

See also BASSA OF CAMEROON; LANGUAGES, AFRICAN: AN OVERVIEW.

Bade

Ethnic group of West Africa; also known as the Bede and the Bedde.

The Bade primarily inhabit southeastern BURKINA FASO, southwestern NIGER, northwestern NIGERIA, and northern BENIN. They speak an Afro-Asiatic language belonging to the Chadic group. Approximately 380,000 people consider themselves Bade.

See also LANGUAGES, AFRICAN: AN OVERVIEW.

Baga

Ethnic group of Guinea.

The Baga primarily inhabit coastal GUINEA between Rio Nunez and CONAKRY. They traditionally spoke a Niger-Congo language belonging to the Senegambian cluster of Western Atlantic languages, though today many Baga speak SOSO. Approximately 60,000 people consider themselves Baga.

See also LANGUAGES, AFRICAN: AN OVERVIEW.

Baganda

Major ethnic group in Uganda; also known as Ganda Baganda.

With a population of approximately five million, the Baganda are the dominant ethnic group in UGANDA, both in numbers and influence. Some Baganda also live in KENYA and the DEMOCRATIC REPUBLIC OF THE CONGO. They speak Luganda, a BANTU language of the Benue-Congo group, and are thought to be the descendants of settlers who arrived in southern and central Uganda around the thirteenth century. Together with Nilotic-speaking pastoralists who came from the north, the Baganda formed Buganda, one of pre colonial Africa's most powerful states.

Baganda history and mythology converge on one name: Kintu. According to the Baganda legend, Kintu was the first man on earth. After taking for his bride a woman from heaven, he endured the wrath of her family and countered the problem by fathering enough children to conquer his supernatural enemies and populate a nation. In the late fourteenth century, the first king to unite the disparate clans called himself Kato Kintu in an apparent bid to win the loyalty and devotion of the Baganda people. Over the next four centuries, the kingdom of Buganda consolidated its power, slowly winning territory from the neighboring Bunyoro Kitara kingdom. Recognized as the political, judicial, and spiritual leader, the kabaka, or king, ruled over the Baganda people. These people worked in agriculture, lived in small villages, and were organized into a system of clans. Baganda society was based on patrilineal family ties, in which ancestry was traced through the male family line. For Baganda royalty, however, succession was matrilineal. This difference caused complex and at times contentious transitions from one king to the next.

Before the advent of European colonization, Arab traders visited the kingdom of Buganda. The traders brought guns and gunpowder, taking away slaves and ivory. Arab visitors also brought the Islamic faith to the Baganda. It was not until the late nineteenth century that Christian missionaries arrived in great numbers, on the heels of famed British explorers John Hanning SPEKE and Henry Morton Stanley, who explored the region in the early 1860s. Hoping that European ties would help protect his kingdom from invasion from powerful EGYPT, Kabaka Mutesa I (who ruled from 1856 to 1884) gave the missionaries a privileged position in his court. Although Mutesa himself did not convert to Christianity, many Baganda did adopt the new religion. (Today, nearly 60 percent of Baganda practice Christianity.) In the waning decades of the nineteenth century, the British began to take control of Buganda. Kabaka Mwanga (1884–1899), who had executed many prominent Baganda Catholics, resisted British control, but the kingdom of Buganda fell in 1900 when the Buganda Agreement established British sovereignty over the region.

When the country of Uganda won its independence in 1963, the government initially allowed the state of Buganda to retain regional autonomy within the new nation. In 1966, however, Prime Minister Milton OBOTE abolished the monarchy and expelled the king, Kabaka Mutesa II. It was not until 1993, when Yoweri MUSEVENI took over as president, that the Bugandan monarchy was restored. Since then, the king has held a ceremonial position in the government. The Baganda, who claim about 20 percent of Uganda's population, continue to play an important role in the country's affairs. They are particularly prominent in the country's capital, KAMPALA, which was also the capital of ancient Buganda. Among the rural Baganda, traditional work continues to center on farming plantains, cotton, and coffee, as well as on making baskets, weavings, and other handcrafts.

See also BUGANDA, EARLY KINGDOM OF; CONGO, DEMOCRATIC REPUBLIC OF THE.

Bagaza, Jean-Baptiste
1946–
Senior army officer and president of Burundi.

Jean-Baptiste Bagaza held power in the Central African nation of BURUNDI during years when conflict between the HUTU AND TUTSI ethnic groups erupted in mass violence. Bagaza was born into a family of the ethnic Tutsi-Hima people in southern Urundi, now Burundi. After attending a local Roman Catholic school, he entered the army. Following Burundi's independence in 1962, Bagaza went to an officer school and military school in Belgium. He returned to Burundi in 1971 to become assistant to the army chief of staff. Bagaza was related to President Michel MICOMBERO—a connection that gave him access to high positions in government and the

military. In 1972 Bagaza was placed in charge of logistics as the Tutsi-dominated army carried out genocide throughout the country, killing between 100,000 and 200,000 Hutu. His particular role in the genocide is unclear, but when it ended he was promoted to colonel and chief of staff of the military.

In November 1976, with dissatisfaction growing in the military, Colonel Bagaza overthrew President Micombero in a bloodless coup, claiming that "clans of self-interested politicians" used their positions for personal gain. He established a Supreme Revolutionary Council of military officers, although he promised to return Burundi to civilian rule. At first he also promised to heal the terrible divisions that had torn Burundi, and he introduced farm reforms and a new constitution. In 1984 he held election—which he won with 99.63 percent of the vote. Bagaza forbade politicians to use the terms "Tutsi" and "Hutu," fearing the ethnic terms would lead to new outbreaks of violence, and peace prevailed during his term in office. But for unknown reasons Bagaza launched a campaign against the Roman Catholic Church, forcing foreign missionaries to leave, closing church-run schools, and banning church activities. His heavyhanded style of personal rule upset Burundi's military, among other factions, and in September 1987 Major Pierre BUYOYA overthrew Bagaza, who fled to Belgium and later to exile in LIBYA. While in Libya he was accused of taking part in a coup that overthrew Burundi's elected president Melchoir Ndadaye, though he denied the charges. In 1996, with the return to power of Pierre Buyoya, Bagaza became the leader of hard-line Tutsi groups who opposed democratic change and negotiations with Hutu rebels. In 1997 he was arrested for stockpiling weapons to overthrow Buyoya.

ERIC YOUNG

Baggara
Ethnic group of Sudan; also known as the Seleim, the Mesiriya, the Ta'aisha, and the Rashaida.

The Baggara primarily inhabit the DARFUR and Kordofan regions of SUDAN. They speak Arabic and one of the Juhayna Arab languages. More than one million people consider themselves Baggara.

See also LANGUAGES, AFRICAN: AN OVERVIEW.

Baghio'o, Jean Louis
1910–1994
Guadeloupean novelist and poet.

Jean Louis Baghio'o is the pen name of Jean-Louis Victor, a native of the Caribbean island of Guadeloupe, once colonized by France. His novels and poems deal with the complex racial and cultural legacy of French colonialism in the Caribbean.

Unlike the more revolutionary works of his friends and fellow writers Léon-Gontran Damas, Léopold Sédar SENGHOR, and Jacques Rabemananjara, Baghio'o's writings explore the lives of the mulatto, or mixed-race, middle class. His most important work, *Le Flamboyant à fleurs bleues* (The Blue-Flame Tree, 1973), describes four centuries of such a family's life on Guadeloupe, focusing on the nineteenth century, when the family acquires land and enters into direct rivalry with the white plantation owners who were formerly its masters. Baghio'o uses this family, with its mixture of Africans, East Indians, Carib Indians, and Europeans, as a metaphor for the Creoles of Guadeloupe, who must fight to preserve their complex cultural identity. In *Choutoumounou* (1995), Baghio'o continues the story of the same family, placing the action and characters in present-day Paris. The difficulties encountered by the two main characters, twins named Choutoumounou and Pampou, illustrate the alienation of the Guadeloupean "of color" in Paris today.

Baghio'o's island narratives have been criticized for pandering to readers' taste for the "exotic," but his serious approach to the history of the French-speaking Caribbean islands has earned him the respect of many, including fellow Guadeloupean novelist Maryse Condé, who wrote a preface to the second edition of *Le Flamboyant à fleurs bleues*.

Baghio'o has also published the novel *Le Colibri blanc* (1980) and a collection of poems, *Les Jeux du soleil* (1960).

RICHARD WATTS

Baha'i Faith
Persian faith, popular in Africa and South America, that emphasizes the unity and equality of humankind.
Mirza Husayn Ali, an Iranian who believed that he was a messenger of God, founded the Baha'i faith in Persia in 1863. After seceding from the Bab sect of Islam, Husayn Ali took the name Baha Ullah. The Islamic government of the Ottoman Empire eventually imprisoned Baha Ullah for blasphemy, and during his time in prison he wrote the principal body of Baha'i scriptures.

Baha'i is centered on social and ethical reform and teaches the unity of humankind. The sexes are equal, and all racial, religious, and political prejudices are shunned. Private prayer, an annual fasting period, pilgrimage to various Baha'i holy sites, and monetary contributions are among the key rituals of the Baha'i faith. Baha'i is strongly pacifist and envisions world peace through its message of unity and equality. In Baha'i, God is an unknowable being, and immortality is assured. The faith eschews ceremonial leaders.

Baha'i spread from its spiritual center in Acre, Palestine, through significant missionary work. Its message of social reform reached America around 1894. Baha'i followers spread knowledge of the religion throughout the rural American South, adding thousands of African Americans to its corps of believers. Many converts responded to Baha'i's mission to end racism and to heal ethnic divisions within society. Since the 1960s Baha'i has gained popularity in less developed countries, especially in sub-Saharan Africa, India, and South America. In the late 1990s the Baha'i faith claimed 130,000 members in the United States, a third of whom were reported to be African American. Some observers dispute these figures, claiming the total U.S. membership to be less than 30,000.

Baka
Ethnic group of north Central Africa.
The Baka primarily inhabit southwestern SUDAN, the eastern CENTRAL AFRICAN REPUBLIC, and northern UGANDA. They speak a Nilo-Saharan language and belong to the MADI cultural and linguistic group. Though reliable numbers are difficult to come by, estimates of the number of Baka people range from the low thousands to some 30,000.

See also LANGUAGES, AFRICAN: AN OVERVIEW.

Bakèlè
Ethnic group of Gabon and Equatorial Guinea; also known as Kalai, Akèlè, Bongom, or Bougom.
The Bakèlè speak an Equatorial BANTU language. Although they call themselves the Bongom or Bougom, outsiders have generally followed their Myènè-speaking neighbors in calling them the Bakèlè. Historians are unsure when the Bakèlè arrived in the north-central area of the country presently known as GABON. Historically they have maintained amicable relations with the Babongo pygmies, who probably preceded them in the region. Traditionally, the Bakèlè were farmers and hunters, traveling widely in search of elephants and other game. The Bakèlè participated in the regional expansion of trade during the nineteenth century. They obtained goods such as ivory from the FANG, which they traded to coastal groups such as the MPONGWE, who in turn traded with the Europeans. On the Ogooué and other rivers they controlled trade more directly by taxing passing traders.

To meet the increasing demand for slaves from the mid-eighteenth to the mid-nineteenth century, the Bakèlè became prominent slave raiders and slave traders. They undertook large raids to obtain slaves from their neighbors, and they also sold their own village outcasts as slaves. The Bakèlè prospered in the trade. As the slave trade came to an end, the migrating Fang gradually drove the Bakèlè south toward the Gabon Estuary and the Ogooué Valley, where the Bakèlè engaged in the rubber, ivory, and dyewood trades.

The Bakèlè's seminomadic lifestyle and lack of hierarchy hindered French colonization and American missionary efforts in the late 1800s. The Bakèlè have played only a minor role in the early French colonial administration and in the later national politics since independence. Today, the Bakèlè number around 40,000 in Gabon and EQUATORIAL GUINEA.

See also COLONIAL RULE; PYGMY; SLAVERY IN AFRICA.

ERIC YOUNG

Bakoko

Ethnic group of Cameroon.

The Bakoko primarily inhabit southern CAMEROON. They speak a BANTU language and are related to the BASSA and BABIMBI, also of southern Cameroon. Approximately 100,000 people consider themselves Bakoko.

See also BANTU: DISPERSION AND SETTLEMENT; BASSA OF CAMEROON; LANGUAGES, AFRICAN: AN OVERVIEW.

Bakossi

Ethnic group of Cameroon; also known as Kossi.

The Bakossi primarily inhabit western CAMEROON. They speak a BANTU language and belong to the Bassa-Bokoko cultural and linguistic group. Approximately 60,000 people consider themselves Bakossi.

See also BAKOKO; BANTU: DISPERSION AND SETTLEMENT; BASSA OF CAMEROON; LANGUAGES, African: AN OVERVIEW.

Bakota

Ethnic group of northeastern Gabon and northwestern Republic of the Congo.

With nearly 125,000 members, the BANTU-speaking Bakota are one of the largest ethnic groups of GABON. The Bakota migrated to the region from the northwest during the nineteenth century, fleeing a Bakouélé invasion known as the War of Poupou. The Bakouélé themselves were fleeing the FANG expansion farther north. The Bakota finally settled near the confluence of the Ivindo and Ogooué Rivers, where they were able to ward off additional Bakouélé invasions. The powerful Fang eventually divided the Bakota into two groups, one in the east and one in the west. The eastern group became known for their ironwork, including the high-quality weapons they used to defend themselves.

The Bakota earned their livelihood from farming and trade, exchanging ivory and rubber with the Europeans for weapons and cloth. In the 1890s a French concessionary company took control of the area and expanded the rubber and ivory trade by forcing Bakota to labor as porters. The settlement of Booué subsequently became the commercial center for the Bakota region. But the Bakota benefited little from the colonial and missionary educational systems, which remained concentrated outside their territory on the coast. As a result, the Bakota played a minor role in the colonial administration and remained largely outside of the formal political structures of independent Gabon and the REPUBLIC OF THE CONGO. Today, many Bakota work in the iron ore mines of the region.

See also COLONIAL RULE; CONGO, DEMOCRATIC REPUBLIC OF THE; IRON IN AFRICA; IVORY TRADE.

ERIC YOUNG

Bakweri

Ethnic group of Cameroon; also known as the Bakwere and the Bakwiri.

The Bakweri live on the slopes of Cameroon Mountain and surrounding regions of South West Province. They speak a BANTU language and comprise several subgroups, including the Isuwu, the Kpe, the Moboko, and the Wovea. According to the last available census, the Bakweri number some 32,000.

See also BANTU: DISPERSION AND SETTLEMENT.

Balanta

Ethnic group of Guinea-Bissau and Senegal.

The Balanta, literally "those who resist," are the largest ethnic group of GUINEA-BISSAU, representing more than one-quarter of the population, some 440,000 people. But despite their numbers, they have remained outside the colonial and postcolonial state because of their social organization. The Balanta can be divided into four subgroups, the largest of which are the Balanta Brassa.

Archaeologists believe that the people who became the Balanta migrated to northern present-day Guinea-Bissau in small groups between the tenth and fourteenth century C.E. During the nineteenth century they spread throughout the area that is presently Guinea-Bissau and southern SENEGAL in order to resist the expansion of the KAABU kingdom.

Chiefs occasionally governed some Balanta groups, but in general egalitarianism prevailed among these rice-cultivating peoples. Consequently, the Portuguese colonialists found it difficult to govern the Balanta. In the late nineteenth and early twentieth centuries, Portugal mounted "pacification" campaigns against the resistant Balanta, and subjected them to appointed Fulbe chiefs. Because of this Portuguese repression, the Balanta enlisted in great numbers as soldiers in the nationalist struggle during the 1960s and 1970s. When the nationalists assumed power after independence, however, they found it difficult to establish village committees and other organizations among the Balanta because of their decentralized social organization. Many Balanta resented their exclusion from the government; their prominence in the military spurred a series of Balanta-led coup attempts in the 1980s.

See also COLONIAL RULE; GUINEA-BISSAU; SENEGAL.

ERIC YOUNG

Balewa, Abubakar Tafawa

1912–1966

First prime minister of independent Nigeria.

Unlike other members of the northern Nigerian elite that he was to join, Alhaji Abubakar Tafawa Balewa was born into a low-status, non-Fulani family. He attended primary and secondary school in Bauchi State and then enrolled at Katsina Higher College. In 1933 he became a schoolmaster, and in 1934 he published *Shaihu Umar*, a novel.

Balewa's political career began in 1943 when he cofounded the Bauchi General Improvement Union, a group that promoted modernization and criticized British colonialism in NIGERIA. Less radical than his cohorts, Balewa won election in 1946 to the northern legislature and became vice president of the Northern People's Congress (NPC). The government appointed him minister of works in 1952 and minister of transport in 1954. In September 1957 Balewa became the prime minister of Nigeria under British control, a position he held until 1959. He was knighted by Queen Elizabeth II of England the following year.

When Nigeria gained its independence in 1960, Balewa served a second term as prime minister. Although he could act independently, Balewa's power depended on the support of a stronger politician, Ahmadu BELLO, a traditional leader of northern Nigeria in Sokoto. Presiding over a new, volatile, and deeply divided political landscape, Balewa's moderate positions probably saved Nigeria from disintegration during its early years. Despite his diligence and integrity, Balewa was assassinated on January 15, 1966, during a coup.

See also FULANI.

ERIC BENNETT

Bamako, Mali

Capital and largest city of Mali.

The administrative, economic, and cultural center of MALI, Bamako lies on the left bank of the NIGER RIVER in the southwestern part of the country. Little is known about Bamako before the eleventh century, when it achieved prominence as a center of Islamic scholarship in the MALI EMPIRE. After the fall of Mali in the sixteenth century, the BAMBARA occupied the town, which became a fishing and trading center. In 1806 Scottish explorer Mungo Park estimated Bamako's population to be less than 6,000. By 1880 the town had fallen under the domination of the MANDINKA warrior Samory TOURÉ, whose kingdom covered an expanse of territory to the south.

In 1883 French Lieutenant Colonel Gustave Borgnis-Desbordes occupied Bamako and used it as a base for military campaigns against Touré. Bamako took on new importance under the French, who valued the town's position on the navigable portion of the Niger River—an asset that had long facilitated Bamako's trade with other towns along the river. The French planned a railroad to connect the town with the navigable section of the SENEGAL RIVER and DAKAR. After securing the region, the French completed the railroad as far as Kayes in 1904. In 1908 the French moved the capital of FRENCH SUDAN from Kayes to Bamako.

Since the colonial era Bamako has served as a regional crossroads; it connects many of the country's smaller towns with the Atlantic coast and Dakar. Roads fan out from the city to every province of Mali, and also to the ports of CONAKRY, GUINEA, and MONROVIA, LIBERIA. Bamako is an also an important trade center for the gold mined in the west and the kola nuts and rice crops of the south and east. It is Mali's primary shipping port for its major exports—cotton, peanuts, livestock, and fish—and it is the country's main financial and administrative center. The economy of Bamako includes manufacturing plants that produce motor vehicles, textiles, and pharmaceuticals.

In recent years the city's prosperity has attracted many migrants from rural areas. As a result, the city has been expanding to accommodate the influx and has recently absorbed some of the small villages on the right bank of the Niger River. Despite the influences of colonialism, Bamako has retained much of its precolonial structure. It is distinct among West African capitals for the mud-brick architecture of its residential areas. According to a 2006 estimate, Bamako had a population of approximately 1,690,471.

See also COLONIAL RULE; EXPLORERS IN AFRICA SINCE 1800; GOLD TRADE.

BIBLIOGRAPHY

Imperato, Pascal James. *Historical Dictionary of Mali.* Scarecrow Press, 1996.

Lawder, Donald. *Fishing in the Sky.* Permanent Press, 1997.

ELIZABETH HEATH

Bamba, Ahmadou
ca. 1851–1927
Senegalese Muslim scholar.

In his lifetime Ahmadou Bamba acquired a following of disciples who would become known after his death as the Muridiyya, a Muslim Sufi way. SUFISM is an esoteric dimension of Muslim practice and thought in which disciples seek the path to divine union in this life. The Senegalese historian Cheikh Anta Babou suggests that at the time of Bamba's death in 1927, estimates of Murid disciples totaled about 100,000. The Murid path is founded on the teachings of Bamba, who is said to have produced over seven tons of scholarship, which is now housed in the Murid library in Tuba, SENEGAL. During his lifetime Bamba demonstrated qualities of waliyat (saintliness) and developed considerable spiritual authority. Bamba was a student of the Qur'anic sciences, which he studied with his maternal uncles. Local qadis (Qur'anic scholars) recognized that he was a master scholar. Bamba's biography, *Les Bienfaits de l'eternal,* written in Arabic by Serigne Bachir Mbacke and translated into French by Khadim Mbacke, supports his status as a wali (saint) by drawing out his genealogical ties, establishing his inheritance of the wird (litanies) and sufficient baraka (spiritual grace) as can be read from the miraculous episodes he experienced during his exile from Senegal imposed by French colonial authorities. Initially, Bamba was sent to GABON for seven years, from 1895 to 1902. Later, Bamba was exiled for four years in Mauritania from 1903 to 1907, where he became widely recognized among the Qadiriyya as a master scholar. Cheikh Sidya, a Mauritanian linked to the Kunta of Timbuktu, initiated Bamba into the Qadiriyya way. On his return to Senegal, Bamba was kept under house arrest in an isolated area of Jolof from 1907 to 1912. Bamba's exile led to the strengthening of his authority, as his exile is believed to be a reenactment of the hijra—the flight of the Prophet Muhammad from Mecca to Medina in 622 (year 1 in the Muslim calendar). In Muslim societies across Sudanic Africa, scholars survived on the alms of the community. In addition to alms, which were usually made in cash or kind, shaykhs of the Tijani and Kadiri orders in Senegal also accepted agricultural labor in exchange for lessons in the Qur'an. Bamba not only accepted labor in exchange for Qur'anic lessons, he promulgated a practical form of Sufism in which the masses could participate. On agricultural communes organized by Murid shaykhs, disciples cultivated peanuts, and in exchange shaykhs offered guardianship of their salvation. Although Sufism posits that salvation is achieved through asceticism, usually in the form of prayer, Bamba suggested a soteriology, a doctrine of salvation, whereby labor in a calling—as a form of ascetic practice equal to prayer—would lead to salvation. Bamba's early communes, in the rural hinterland on the Ferlo fringe of the WOLOF kingdom of Kayor, were organized into those who would be scholars and those who would be laborers, each meeting the needs of the other. The emphasis on work as it relates to salvation is unique to the Murid way.

See also COLONIAL RULE.

BIBLIOGRAPHY

Babou, Cheikh Anta. "Brotherhood Solidarity, Education and Migration: The Role of the Dahiras among the Murid Muslim Community of New York." *African Affairs* 101: 151–170, 2002.

Mbacke, Serigne Bachir. *Les bienfaits de leternel ou la biographie de Cheikh Ahmadou Bamba MBacke.* Translated by Khadim Mbacke. IFAN, 1995.

Roberts, Allen. "The Ironies of System D." In *Recycled, Reseen: Folk Art from the Global Scrap Heap.* Eds. C. Cerny and S. Seriff. Harry Abrams for The Museum of International Folk Art, Santa Fe, 1996.

Robinson, David. "Beyond Resistance and Collaboration: Amadu Bamba and the Murids of Senegal." *Journal of Religion in Africa* 21 (2): 149–169, 1991.

BETH ANN BUGGENHAGEN

Bambara
African ethnolinguistic group.

The nearly three million or so Bambara (sometimes called Bamana), who speak languages of the MANDE group, live primarily in MALI along the NIGER RIVER but can also be found in BURKINA FASO and SENEGAL, among other countries. They are descendants of the people of the ancient Mali empire, who founded the kingdoms of Segu and Kaarta. Bambara means "unbeliever" or "infidel"; the group acquired the name because it resisted Islam after the religion was introduced in 1854 by TUKULOR conqueror Umar Tal. Religion and agriculture for the Bambara are intertwined. For example, the high god of the Bambara is represented as a grain from which the whole of creation is born. The Bambara recognize one god, known as Bemba or Ngala, as the creator of all things. This god is a being who cannot be perceived by humans through the usual senses but whose existence is manifested as an immaterial force, often as a whirlwind or a thought. Many of their religious beliefs are symbolized in their masks and carvings, which often feature the antelope; the Bambara believe that the antelope taught humans to grow crops. Although many present-day Bambara are Muslim, they still make masks, mostly to sell to tourists.

The traditional social organization of the Bambara is the large united clan, a group of families descended from a common ancestor. Family heads are obligated to obey the village chief, who not only organizes the village for religious activities but also acts as mediator for the chief of the earth spirits. Although clan links the Bambara, there has long been a great deal of intermingling among ethnic groups in this region, and there is no strong centralized Bambara political authority.

Traditionally cultivators of millet and Guinea corn, the Bambara now also grow crops such as peanuts, rice, and cotton. Many Bambara now live in Bamako, Mali, and some migrate seasonally to work on the cocoa and coffee plantations of GHANA and CÔTE D'IVOIRE.

Bamiléké

A term commonly used to refer to several ethnic groups of Cameroon.

The name Bamiléké comes from the phrase mba lekeo, or "the people who live over there," which was used by people of the western grasslands of CAMEROON to describe their neighbors to the east. European travelers to the region corrupted the word into "Bamiléké" and used it to describe the people of the eastern highlands, including such Bantu-speaking groups as the Babadju, Bafoussam, Bagam, Baham, Banjoun, and Bangu. At the end of the nineteenth century, the population of the Bamiléké was estimated at 1.8 million. The number now appears to be closer to two million, though estimates vary due to a lack of reliable census data. The Bamiléké were not indigenous to the eastern grasslands, but fled there from the north, primarily during the eighteenth century, to escape the slave raids of the FULANI. They mixed with the indigenous inhabitants of the area and reestablished highly stratified dynasties, loosely based on a conception of divine kingship that had been adopted from various Sudanese empires. Sub-chiefs often formed their own chiefdoms.

The Bamiléké chiefdoms did not share a unified ethnic or national identity, though many Bamiléké groups have similar social structures and cultural practices. Historically, most have been agrarian peoples, cultivating maize and peanuts, though in contemporary Cameroon they have excelled in business as well. They are also accomplished carvers of wood and ivory; their elaborate masks are used in the elephant masquerades held by men's societies, and in public ceremonies and funerals. Customary political structures revolve around kinship, which the Bamiléké define by dual descent—patrilineal ties typically determine village residence and rights to land, but matrilineal ties define ritual obligations and the inheritance of movable property. Although Islam penetrated some Bamiléké groups, most of the people have retained their traditional religious beliefs.

Although the grasslands had long held high population densities, since the colonial era many Bamiléké have migrated to urban centers, especially DOUALA, as a result of both their business aspirations and increasing pressures for land. After Cameroon was divided between the French and British colonial mandates, many Bamiléké began working on French-owned agricultural plantations, but over time they came to own their own land and be involved in commerce and transportation. Some scholars discern the emergence of a rural bourgeoisie in this process, though many Bamiléké were also recruited into the colonial administration and banking. They formed agricultural cooperatives, and after World War II they supported the leading, though ultimately unsuccessful nationalist party, the Union of the Peoples of Cameroon (UPC). During the anticolonial insurgency the Bamiléké area was the site of much of the violence, which was exacerbated by resentment of their economic success. The hopes of many Bamiléké to benefit politically and economically from independence have been fulfilled only rarely, and anti Bamiléké sentiments have often flared. At the same time, the Bamiléké, because of their migration between east and west, have come to symbolize the unification of southern Cameroon with the rest of the country.

See also BANTU: DISPERSION AND SETTLEMENT; CAMEROON.

ERIC YOUNG

Banda

The largest ethnic group of the Central African Republic; they also occupy adjacent parts of Cameroon and the Democratic Republic of the Congo.

The Banda number nearly 1.3 million. They are the largest ethnic group in the CENTRAL AFRICAN REPUBLIC and inhabit the central part of that country. The Banda speak a Niger-Congo language. Though they have a tradition of migration in the early 1800s from the DARFUR in the SUDAN to their present homeland, their language suggests a longer presence in the region. During the nineteenth century the Banda resisted slave raids from the kingdoms of Wadai and Darfur and later resisted conquest by RABIH AL-ZUBAYR.

The Banda traditionally worked iron and grew crops such as peanuts, corn, and sweet potatoes. Women traditionally gathered wild foods and farmed, while men hunted and fished on the many rivers of the area. Families could be polygamous, and marriage required payment of a bride price, often in the form of iron tools. They lived in dispersed homesteads loosely governed by a headman. During times of crisis, such as slave raids and warfare, the people would select a war chief.

In addition to food crops, the Banda cultivate cotton as a cash crop. They are perhaps best known for their craftsmanship, especially their large slit drums, typically carved in the shape of animals. Historically, people in homesteads and villages used the drums in order to communicate in times of crisis and celebration. The demands of a market economy and modern life have brought an end to many Banda traditions, such as polygamy.

See also LANGUAGES, AFRICAN: AN OVERVIEW; MARRIAGE, AFRICAN CUSTOMS OF; SLAVERY IN AFRICA.

BIBLIOGRAPHY

Kalck, Pierre. Histoire de la République Centrafricaine. Editions Berger-Levrault, 1974.

O'Toole, Thomas. The Central African Republic: The Continents Hidden Heart. Westview Press, 1986.

ERIC YOUNG

Banda, Ngwazi Hastings Kamuzu
1906?–1997
First prime minister (1964–1966) and president (1966–1994) of Malawi.

Known as the "Lion of Malawi," Ngwazi Hastings Kamuzu Banda was also known as the dictator who showed so little appreciation for his country's people and culture that he was sometimes suspected of being an American impostor. Kamuzu Banda was born to Chewa peasants in a village near Kasunugu, NYASALAND (present-day MALAWI). No birth records were kept at the time; while his official year of birth is 1906, other sources cite 1898. As a child Banda left the household of his maternal grandmother and entered a newly established school built by Church of Scotland missionaries. Influenced by his uncle, Hanock Phiri, Banda converted to Christianity and adopted the surname of missionary John Hastings.

Shortly after completing primary school, Banda traveled with his uncle to SOUTH AFRICA (supposedly walking the 1667 km [1000 mi]), where they initially worked in a coal mine in Dundee, Natal. Upon reaching JOHANNESBURG, he again worked as a clerk for a mining company and continued his secondary schooling in the evenings. Banda joined the black separatist African Methodist Episcopal Church, which arranged for him to continue his education at the church-sponsored Wilberforce University in Ohio. He later attended Indiana University, transferred to the University of Chicago and completed a degree in history and political science in 1931, and then attended medical school at Meharry Medical College in Nashville, Tennessee.

In 1937 Banda traveled to Scotland, intending to qualify as a physician so he could return to Nyasaland to practice medicine. But both the Church of Scotland and the colonial administration refused to allow Banda to practice medicine in Nyasaland, reportedly because he was black, so he opened a general practice in Liverpool. After World War II (1939–1945) he moved his practice to London, where he met African nationalist leaders Jomo KENYATTA and Kwame NKRUMAH. Despite his geographical distance from Malawi, Banda kept in contact with members of the nationalist Nyasaland African Congress (NAC) and used earnings from his thriving medical practice to provide the NAC with financial support.

In 1953 Kwame Nkrumah asked Banda to come to the GOLD COAST (present-day GHANA), and Banda agreed, settling in KUMASI. For unknown reasons, the Ghanaian Ministry of Health suspended Banda from his medical practice in 1957. Although his suspension was ultimately reversed, Banda abandoned his practice and returned to Nyasaland, where he had been invited to lead the NAC's struggle for independence.

Banda's maturity, education, and professionalism earned him great respect among the colony's young nationalists. As the newly elected NAC president, he immediately embarked on a program of Fabian resistance to the colonial authorities, instigating a movement that became increasingly violent and demanding, resulting in his arrest in March 1959, along with the banning of the NAC. After thirteen months in prison, Banda was released, only to take charge of the newly formed Malawi Congress Party (MCP), which replaced the NAC. By then Britain had agreed to the country's independence, and, in the general elections held in 1963, Banda became Malawi's first prime minister. In 1966 he was elected president.

Banda's ruthless authoritarianism became apparent at an early date. His primary political challenge had originally come from opposition leader Dunduza Chisiza, who died in 1962 in a suspicious car accident. Once in power, Banda moved quickly to eradicate any remaining political opposition. Many dissidents fled the country while others mysteriously disappeared or died. Within his own government ranks, Banda relied heavily on expatriate experts and bureaucrats, who posed less of a challenge to his power than Malawian intellectuals. Toward Malawian citizens, Banda adopted an overtly paternalistic attitude, referring to them as his "children" and dictating laws on everything from skirt length to hairstyle. He banned the Simon and Garfunkel song "Cecilia" in deference to Malawi's "Official

Hostess," Mama Cecelia Kadzamira, with whom he had been living for over thirty years.

Even while Banda denounced Western miniskirts and pop songs as immoral, he himself preferred Western culture, and his economic policies were staunchly pro-Western and anticommunist. His foreign policy was equally paradoxical; officially nonaligned, he maintained relations with South Africa despite international sanctions, but he supported the anticolonial struggle of the FRONT FOR THE LIBERATION OF MOZAMBIQUE (FRELIMO), by allowing resistance fighters to enter Malawi.

Despite his dictatorial governance and disregard for human rights, Banda nurtured bonds with international financial institutions such as the World Bank and the International Monetary Fund, and he encouraged foreign investment. Consequently, Malawi developed a high credit rating in the international finance sector. Despite this, the country has developed little industry. Malawi also has extreme disparities between the poor masses and the rich elite. Banda himself accounted for much of this disparity; "as trustee for the nation" he owned Press Holdings, an investment corporation composed of companies that earned 40 percent of the entire country's gross domestic product.

Rumors have circulated that the real Kamuzu Banda died in the United States and that Malawi's ruler was in fact an imposter, perhaps one Richard Armstrong, a roommate of Banda's during medical school. As evidence, subscribers of this theory point out that Banda could not speak his native Nayanja. In fact he could speak the language, although his fluency had diminished and he used out-of-date phrases because he had been gone from the country for so long. Nevertheless, this rumor reflected the alienation that many Malawians felt toward their leader, who was so distant and so completely "Europeanized" in his taste for homburgs (formal continental-style hats) and his distaste for Malawian food that he seemed indistinguishable from the colonial administrators he replaced.

Pressured by international human rights monitoring organizations and newly emerging opposition parties, in 1992 Banda agreed to hold a referendum on the reinstatement of multiparty politics. When the electorate returned an overwhelming vote in favor of multiparty elections, Banda acquiesced. Banda was reportedly becoming increasingly senile. In 1993 he underwent brain surgery after he suffered a cranial hemorrhage. During the following year he was deposed in the first multiparty elections. Later he was tried and acquitted of the murders of three cabinet members and a parliament member. He died of pneumonia in a South African hospital in 1997 and was given a state funeral.

ARI NAVE

Bangui, Central African Republic
Capital and largest city of the Central African Republic.

Sited on the northwest bank of the UBANGI RIVER, Bangui is both a major trading center and the national capital. The French first established a military post nearby in 1889, at the confluence of the Ubangi and Mpoko rivers. Two years later they moved the post upstream to the present site of Bangui, at the base of several rapids on the Ubangi. Local inhabitants initially resisted the French presence and killed two chiefs-of-post. In 1906 the post became the administrative center of the Ubangi-Chari territory of FRENCH EQUATORIAL AFRICA. It grew slowly as an administrative and trading center, fanning northwest from its administrative hub, bounded by a large hill to the east and the river to the south, until World War II. As the country's economy boomed during the war, the city expanded rapidly.

As the capital of the independent CENTRAL AFRICAN REPUBLIC (CAR), Bangui has witnessed the coronation of Jean-Bédel BOKASSA as emperor in 1977, the demonstrations and bloody massacre that led to his downfall two years later, and, more recently, the widespread crime that followed the overthrow of president Ange-Félix PATASSÉ in March 2003. The city has a soap-making factory, breweries, and other light industries, but is primarily a commercial and trading center. A network of roads connects the city with most parts of the Central African Republic. Bangui's docks ship cotton, timber, coffee, and sisal downriver to BRAZZAVILLE, where a rail line provides connections to oceangoing commerce. A ferry runs to Zongo, across the river in the DEMOCRATIC REPUBLIC OF THE CONGO.

Today Bangui has an aggregate population of more than 800,000, divided between the expatriate and elite, who live in the center, and the majority, who live in sprawling suburbs, or kodros, to the north and west, most of which are ethnically homogeneous. According to a 2003 census, the city proper is home to some 531,000 people. The most important and vibrant kodro is Kilométre Cinq, which houses a vast marketplace, bars, and dance halls as well as the city's largest mosque. After a decade of continuing unrest, unemployment remains above 20 percent and the government often does not have enough money to pay its civil servants. The city continued to fair poorly in international estimates of livability. A 2003 report named Bangui one of the 215 worst cities in the world, due in no small part to the continuing violence and political unrest that afflict its streets.

ERIC YOUNG

Banjul, Gambia
Capital and largest city of the Republic of Gambia.

Shortly after Britain outlawed the transatlantic slave trade in 1804, it began seeking a means of patrolling illegal slave trading in the coastal areas of SENEGAMBIA. Rather than rebuild the port at James Island, which had been destroyed by the French in the early 1780s, the British decided to establish a new settlement on a small, strategically located island near the mouth of the GAMBIA RIVER. In 1816 Captain Alexander Grant purchased the island, which was known by its MANDINKA name of Banjul, and named it after Lord Henry Bathurst, who was then Britain's secretary of state. WOLOF traders settled in Bathurst in the 1820s and 1830s, and were soon joined by small groups of Jola, Mandinka, and Aku (liberated slaves and their descendants from SIERRA LEONE). Throughout the colonial period Bathurst served as the GAMBIA's administrative center, maritime port, and military base, though epidemics of yellow fever, cholera, and other diseases slowed the growth of the city, earning one particularly hard-hit neighborhood the nickname "Half Die." By 1850 the city had become the center of the colony's peanut and palm oil trades. In the early twentieth century it became home to a small peanut-shelling and peanut-oil-processing industry, as well as to most of the colony's few schools.

In 1965 The Gambia achieved independence, and eight years later Bathurst was officially given the name Banjul, which had long been used by local Mandinka and other African communities. Although Banjul remains the administrative and maritime capital of the Gambia, it has outgrown the two square kilometers of land (1.24 miles) it once occupied, and much of its commercial activity has been moved to the nearby towns of Serrekunda, Bakau, and Fajara. A 2003 census recorded Banjul's population as 357,000.

See also DISEASE AND AFRICAN HISTORY; SENEGAMBIA, CONFEDERATION OF; URBANISM AND URBANIZATION IN AFRICA.

ROBERT BAUM

Bankole, Ayo
1935–1976
Nigerian composer of art music who played a key role in the development of a Nigerian musical style that combines elements of classical European and traditional Yoruba music.

Since the 1960s Ayo Bankole has gained popularity in NIGERIA as a composer who successfully fused West African traditional music with stylistic traits of European art music. According to music scholar Olabode F. Omojola, Bankole was "constantly aware of the sacred bonds between a musician and society in traditional Nigerian communities ... [and his] works often highlight bold experiments characterized by a synthesis of opposing styles and techniques." Nowhere is this more evident than in Bankole's Festac cantata (1974), a work that applies a

European harmonic language to YORUBA ceremonial music and employs both European and traditional African instruments.

Bankole grew up in LAGOS, NIGERIA, where Anglican and Catholic missionaries had introduced European-based musical education in the mid-nineteenth century. Nigerian musicians trained in missionary schools include Ekundayo Phillips and Dayo Dedeke, both masters of indigenous hymnody as well as the stylistic paradigms on which Nigeria's modern art music is based. Bankole himself wrote a wealth of popular Nigerian hymns (often in the Yoruba language) and religious works for Nigeria's amateur choirs.

Bankole was encouraged to study music by his father, a church organist in Lagos, and his mother, who taught music at a West Nigerian secondary school. As a boy he joined the choir at Lagos's Christ Church, directed by Ekundayo Phillips. He received additional musical training at the Baptist Academy Secondary School. In 1954 he studied organ with Fela SOWANDE, Nigeria's best-known composer of contemporary art music. Deeply influenced by Sowande's use of Nigerian folk music in his works, Bankole decided to pursue a musical career and in 1957 left for London to study at the Guildhall School of Music and Drama.

In 1961 Bankole won a scholarship to Cambridge University, where he continued to study both European classical music and Yoruba traditional music. Inspired by Nigerian melodies and rhythms, he composed such works as the cantata Baba se we lomo rere (Father, Make us Good Children) and Three Yoruba Songs (for baritone and piano). The first song, Ojo maaro, as noted by Omojola, "is set to a popular traditional Yoruba prayer for abundant rainfall."

After graduating with a B.A. degree in 1964, Bankole studied ethnomusicology at the University of California, Los Angeles. He continued to experiment with African traditional instruments, dance rhythms, and improvisational styles. His work Ethnophony (1964), for example, was composed for traditional instruments and based on Yoruba drum rhythms.

In 1966 Bankole returned to Lagos, where he became a senior music producer for the Nigerian Broadcasting Corporation and taught music at the University of Lagos. Realizing how foreign classical music seemed to most Nigerians, he initiated educational programs and concerts for school children. He also formed, directed, and composed music for several amateur choral groups. Bankole died in 1976 at the age of forty-one, but Nigerian concert halls continue to feature regular performances of his works.

See also MUSIC, AFRICAN.

ROANNE EDWARDS

Bantu: Dispersion and Settlement
Spread of Bantu-speaking peoples across sub-Saharan Africa.

Analysis of linguistic and genetic evidence suggests that groups of Bantu speakers, who originated in present-day eastern NIGERIA and adjoining areas of CAMEROON, spread across a vast area of central, southern, and eastern Africa over the course of 3,000 years. In the past, researchers associated the dispersion of Bantu speakers with the spread of iron working, agriculture, and a unique pottery style, collectively known as the Early Iron Age Complex.

Agriculture and the use of iron do seem to have disseminated together, but recent linguistic analysis confidently places the initial wave of Bantu expansion well before the Early Iron Age.

BANTU ORIGINS

The Bantu language is a member of the Benue-Congo branch of the Niger-Congo family of languages spoken widely across West Africa and as far east as southern SUDAN. Speakers of the Benue-Congo branch of this family live almost exclusively within eastern Nigeria and

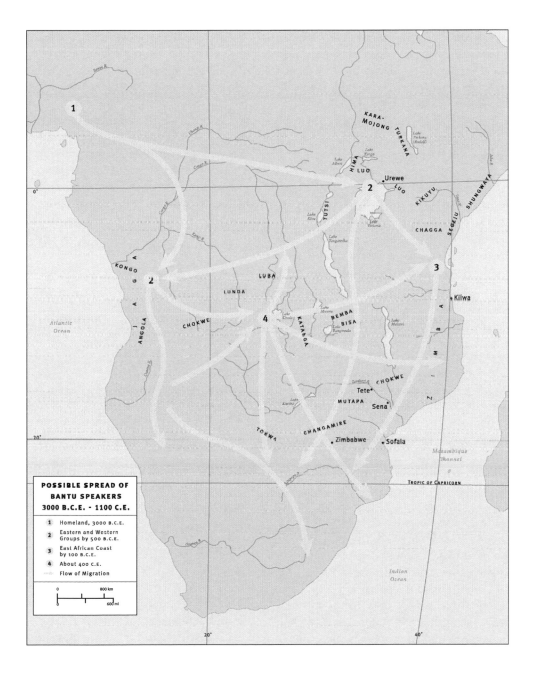

POSSIBLE SPREAD OF
BANTU SPEAKERS
3000 B.C.E. - 1100 C.E.

1 Homeland, 3000 B.C.E.
2 Eastern and Western Groups by 500 B.C.E.
3 East African Coast by 100 B.C.E.
4 About 400 C.E.
   Flow of Migration

0   800 km
0   600 mi

adjoining areas of southern Cameroon—with the exception of the expansive Bantu. The word bantu, literally translated, means "people." Using a technique known as glottochronology to estimate how long it would take Bantu languages to separate from a common ancestor, linguists suggest that proto-Bantu speakers began to spread throughout the tropical rain forests and the adjoining savanna margins that straddle the equator approximately 4,000 years ago. The proto-Bantu were probably shifting cultivators of yams and oil palms, as well as riverine fishers, given the antiquity of related Bantu words. In contrast, the proto-Bantu had no words for iron or iron working, as one would expect if the invention predated their dispersion. However, eastern and western branches of Bantu languages do share related words that refer to iron forging. Thus iron technologies were probably adapted after the proto-Bantu had dispersed throughout the tropical rain forest but before the secondary dispersion further east and south.

BANTU EXPANSION

As early as 1500 B.C.E. the proto-Bantu speakers had settled on the GABON coast. Linguistic patterns suggest that from there they migrated along two distinct routes beginning around 1000 B.C.E. One cluster moved south to ANGOLA, forming the Western Bantu group. The Eastern Bantu group expanded to the east and southeast. Initially researchers believed that iron working led to the sudden rapid expansion east and south. Revisionist theories, however, place more emphasis on the adaptation of new crops, such as the grain millet, a practice that likely diffused from Sudanic and Cushitic-speaking peoples with whom the Bantu came into contact as they moved eastward into more arid regions. The exact reasons for the Bantu expansion, however, remain unclear. By the time the Eastern Bantu reached Urewe in the Great Lakes region during the last millennium B.C.E., words for iron working were widespread. From Urewe the Bantu spread rapidly to the south and further to the east, reaching the east coast by the second century B.C.E. Likewise the Western Bantu had moved as far as the Democratic Republic of the Congo by about 400 B.C.E. Genetic and linguistic evidence suggests that as the Eastern Bantu moved south and west of Lake Tanganyika, they came into contact with already established Western Bantu, leading to the intermixing of both people and ideas.

No single element can explain the rapid Bantu drive southward and eastward, although a number of possibilities have been suggested. Much of the early Bantu migration may simply have resulted from agriculturists encroaching on the lands of hunter-gatherers who were more mobile and lived at lower population densities, pushing populations of Khoisan-speakers into increasingly marginal environments. Other scholars have suggested that the continued desiccation of the SAHARA until the middle of the third millennium B.C.E. resulted in the loss of wooded savanna and rain forest, aggravating the need to clear new tracts of forest. However, the Bantu expansion proceeded in a number of fits and starts, suggesting that multiple forces influenced the dispersion. For example, the introduction or invention of iron may have enabled them to more readily clear land for agriculture as well as provided more effective weapons, contributing to the more rapid expansion of Bantu speakers after the first millennium B.C.E. The diffusion of bananas and Asian yams has also been posited as a factor leading to the Bantu dispersion in moister climates.

Although Bantu-speaking peoples spread into areas of low population density, these areas were not altogether devoid of people either. Bantu populations absorbed Nilo-Saharan speakers as they moved east and south. By between 500 and 1000 C.E. the majority of the Bantu dispersion had taken place. Through intermarriage and diffusion, however, the Bantu language and culture continues to spread, assimilating people in other populations, such as among the Khoikoi speakers in southern Africa and Dahalo speakers in East Africa. Today Bantu speakers live in a wide range of ecosystems and have adapted numerous subsistence strategies, from sedentary agriculture to fishing.

See also: IRON IN AFRICA; LANGUAGES, AFRICAN: AN OVERVIEW.

BIBLIOGRAPHY

Chigwedere, A. S. *Birth of Bantu Africa*. Books for Africa, 1982.

Ehret, C., and M. Posnansky. *The Archaeological and Linguistic Reconstruction of African History*. University of California Press, 1982.

Mimanyara, Alfred M. *The Restatement of Bantu Origin and Meru History*. Longman Kenya, 1992.

Vansina, Jan. *Paths in the Rainforests: Toward a History of Political Tradition in Equatorial Africa*. University of Wisconsin Press, 1990.

ARI NAVE

Bantu Educational Cinema Experiment

Project conducted by the British government to explore the possible educational uses of film in African colonies. In 1935 the Colonial Office of the British Film Institute assigned British director Leslie Alan Notcutt to lead an experimental mission to test the uses of film in Africa. The British hoped that the mission, called the Bantu Educational Cinema Experiment (BECE), could accomplish several important tasks at once. The first was to form a monopoly control over films shown to African audiences. British colonial administrators believed that commercial American and European films depicted whites unfavorably and feared these images could jeopardize

British colonial authority in Africa. As Notcutt noted in his field report, *The African and the Cinema*, the British assumed Africans were unable to distinguish fact from fiction: "Reflection will convince any unprejudiced person that, with backward peoples unable to distinguish between truth and falsehood, it is surely our wisdom, if not our obvious duty, to prevent, so far as it is possible, the dissemination of wrong ideas. Should we stand by and see a distorted presentation of the life of the white races accepted by millions of Africans when we have it in our power to show them the truth?" The second goal was to use film as a supplement to classroom education and to help adult Africans understand and adapt to new conditions. Finally, the British hoped to continue their "civilizing mission." They believed that film could help Africans "to conserve what is best in African traditions and culture by representing these in their proper setting as stages in racial development and as an inheritance to be cherished with pride." Arriving in TANGANYIKA (Tanzania) in 1935, Notcutt and his crew spent the next two years producing thirty-five short educational films with brief dialogues in English, SWAHILI, SUKUMA, KIKUYU, LUO, BAGANDA, NYANJA, BEMBA, and TUMBUKA. Working under the assumption that Africans were intellectually limited, Notcutt wrote slow moving films with simple plots and minimal dialogue. He also made the movies no more than twenty minutes long, believing his audience could not absorb much information at once. A classic example of the BECE films is *Post Office Savings Bank*, one of Notcutt's earliest and (according to him) most successful efforts. Filmed in KENYA, the movie tells the story of two African plantation workers, one who deposits his wages in the Post Office Savings Bank, and one who buries his beneath his hut, where a thief steals it. The moral of the story is simple: after the thief is apprehended, the second worker gets his money back and quickly deposits it in the Post Office Savings Bank. After producing a number of such films, Notcutt sought ways to establish a permanent and cost-effective film company in the colonies. He trained Africans to do the menial technical tasks on the project, after he realized that they were competent and could be paid less than British workers. In addition, he suggested that the British build a central production facility in Africa. In 1939 the British colonial government established the Colonial Film Unit with several branches throughout the African colonies and a central office in London. Notcutt completed the BECE project confident that he had successfully created a style of educational movies fitted to Africans' intelligence and capabilities. In fact, this style ensured the BECE's failure to monopolize cinema in Anglophone Africa. The European and American movies were more technically sophisticated and proved much

more popular; Africans ultimately were not interested in the clumsy, boring, and paternalistic movies made by the BECE that, in many ways, reflected the British colonial government's own erroneous stereotypes of Africans. Unfortunately, the BECE and the Colonial Film Unit set a negative precedent for film in Anglophone Africa, where, without viable film schools or infrastructure, an independent film industry has not been established

See also CINEMA, AFRICAN; COLONIAL RULE.

BIBLIOGRAPHY

Notcutt, L. A., and G. C. Lantham. *The African and the Cinema: An Account of the Bantu Educational Cinema Experiment during the Period March 1935 to May 1937*. Edinburgh House Press, 1937.
ELIZABETH HEATH

Bantu Migrations in Sub-Saharan Africa
See BANTU: DISPERSION AND SETTLEMENT.

Banu Hilal and Banu Sulaim
Bedouin ethnic groups that migrated into North Africa.
In the eleventh century the Banu Hilal and the Banu Sulaim, Arabic-speaking nomadic tribes originally from the central Arabian plateau, began to migrate westward from Upper EGYPT to the land called Ifriqiya (present-day TUNISIA and eastern ALGERIA). They settled in the regions now comprising LIBYA, Algeria, TUNISIA, and later, MOROCCO. Historians mark the movement of the "Hilalians," as they were collectively known, as a critical moment in the "Arabization" of North Africa. The migration of around 200,000 Bedouin herders reached places that had maintained distinct Berber identities even during the period of Roman rule, transforming the people, the language, and the land.

Arabic historical accounts place the Hilalian migration in the context of an eleventh-century power struggle between the Fatimids, then based in Egypt, and the Berber Zirid Dynasty. The Fatimids had left the Zirids in power over their western holdings in Ifriqiya, and when the Zirids claimed autonomy, the Fatimids sent the Banu Hilal to invade the West—or, at least, the Fatimids allowed the Hilalians to pass beyond the NILE without challenge.

Historians disagree on the impact of the Hilalian's westward migration. Until recently, it was portrayed as a pillaging, destructive "invasion" of the Berber countryside. This account is based partly on the Arabic historian IBN KHALDUN's description of the Banu Hilal as a swarm of locusts who sacked villages, burned farms, and filled wells. However, some historians have now challenged the opposition between the Hilalians as destructive nomads and the Berbers as civilized settlers. These historians point out that the region had a long history of intra-Berber conflict between sedentary and nomadic groups. In any case, the Hilalians occupied the land in huge numbers—the Banu Sulaim migration stopping for some time in Libya, and the Banu Hilal continuing west, settling Algeria, Tunisia and, by the mid-twelfth century, Morocco. Some Berber groups fled into remote mountainous regions, where they maintained a distinct Berber identity and language.

Two hundred years later another large Hilalian migration moved west through North Africa. In the thirteenth century the Banu Sulaim traveled from the regions of Tripolitania and Cyrenaica in present-day Libya to Tunisia. They were encouraged by the Tunisian Hafsid Dynasty, which sought to undermine growing Banu Hilal power. Using incentives such as land rewards and official positions, the Hafsids placed the Banu Sulaim in bureaucratic and military positions over the Banu Hilal.

Although Islam had already made its mark in North Africa, Arab culture had for the most part remained the culture of the urban elite, communicated through the classical Arabic language and literary traditions. Both the Banu Hilal and the Banu Sulaim, however, brought Arab culture to the countryside, including the colloquial Arabic language of their oral traditions.

The definition of *Arab* is tricky in North Africa—after all, the Banu Hilal and Banu Sulaim had left the central Arabian plateau at the beginning of the eleventh century, and the migration lasted through the thirteenth century. The migration produced a hybrid culture, and the historical observer may characterize the change brought by this migration as either the Arabization of the Berber population or the assimilation of new North African traditions into the Berber identity.

See also BEDOUIN; BERBER.

MARIAN AGUIAR

Bara
Ethnic group of Madagascar.
The Bara primarily inhabit the southern highlands of MADAGASCAR. They speak MALAGASY, a Malayo-Polynesian language, and are made up of several subgroups, including the Barobe and the Imamono. According to a 2000 survey, some 520,000 people consider themselves Bara.

Barghash ibn Sa'id
1834–1888
Sultan of the east African island of Zanzibar during the height of its prosperity; he ultimately saw his realm humbled and partitioned by European colonialists.
After his father, Sayyid Sa'id ibn Sultan, died in 1856, Barghash tried to usurp the throne from his older brother, Majid ibn Sa'id. His attempt failed, however, and Barghash

was exiled to Bombay. He returned to ZANZIBAR two years later and ascended the throne peacefully after his brother's death in 1870.

In 1872 a hurricane destroyed Zanzibar's navy and many of the island's valuable clove and coconut plantations. In order to recover from this disaster, Barghash allied himself with British forces in the region and signed antislavery treaties in exchange for funding and military equipment. This support enabled Barghash to consolidate his hold on the coastal mainland. By the late 1870s the tariffs and tributes he collected from mainland possessions substantially increased his revenue and compensated for the loss of the slave trade. Although his power never extended far inland, agreements with Arab/Swahili traders such as Tippu Tip enabled the sultan to acquire valuable goods—ivory and rubber—which he sold to Europeans. By 1882 the Europeans, however, particularly the Germans, began to challenge Barghash's territorial claims. The sultan believed his British allies would help defend his territory, but he was mistaken. In 1886 the British secretly met with the Germans and divided the sultanate's possessions between themselves. Thereafter, the sultanate consisted solely of the island of Zanzibar, which became a British protectorate after the death of Barghash in 1888.

BIBLIOGRAPHY

Ayany, S. G. *A History of Zanzibar.* East African Literature Bureau, 1970.

Bennett, Norman. *Arab versus European: Diplomacy and War in Nineteenth-Century East Central Africa.* Africana Publishing, 1986.

ELIZABETH HEATH

Bari
Ethnic group of north Central Africa.
The Bari primarily inhabit the region just east of the NILE in southern SUDAN and northern UGANDA. They speak a Nilo-Saharan language. Population estimates for this group vary widely, with some sources placing the number as high as 70,000.

See also LANGUAGES, AFRICAN: AN OVERVIEW.

Bariba
Ethnic group of West Africa; also known as the Borgawa, the Bargu, and the Batonun.
The Bariba primarily inhabit northern BENIN, southeastern BURKINA FASO, northeastern NIGERIA, and northern TOGO. They speak a Niger-Congo language belonging to the Voltaic group and are made up of two distinct groups: the Busa of Nigeria and the Nikki of Benin. Approximately one million people consider themselves Bariba.

See also LANGUAGES, AFRICAN: AN OVERVIEW.

Barth, Heinrich
1821–1865
German explorer of western and northern Africa.

During the mid-nineteenth century, Heinrich Barth traveled widely in northern Africa and the central SUDAN and authored some of the earliest and most comprehensive works on North and West African history. The son of a German businessman, Barth earned a degree in classics and linguistics at the University of Berlin. He completed his studies in 1845 and subsequently spent two years traveling in northern Africa, where he perfected his Arabic and kept a detailed diary of his trip. After a disappointing experience teaching in Germany, he accepted an offer to join a British expedition to the central Sudan. At first led by James Richardson, the expedition left TRIPOLI in 1850. Within a year, however, Richardson died and Barth assumed command. During the next four years, Barth led the group through present-day CHAD, CAMEROON, NIGERIA, NIGER, and MALI and visited all of the major towns, including ZINDER, Sokoto, TOMBOUCTOU, and KANO. The group returned to England in 1855, where Barth recorded his memoirs of the journey. This work provided the basis for a five-volume series—Travels and Discoveries in North and Central Africa—chronicling the history and linguistics of the areas he visited. Although some of his remarks on the SOKOTO CALIPHATE have recently been challenged, Barth's work remains an invaluable resource for African scholars.

ELIZABETH HEATH

Bassa of Cameroon
Ethnic group of Cameroon.

The Bassa primarily inhabit southern CAMEROON. They speak a BANTU language and are related to both the BAKOKO and BABIMBI, also of Cameroon. Some 230,000 people consider themselves Bassa.

See also BANTU: DISPERSION AND SETTLEMENT.

Bassa of Liberia
Ethnic group of Liberia; also known as the Basa, the Basso, and the Gbasa.

The Bassa primarily inhabit Grand Bassa County, LIBERIA. They speak a Niger-Congo language belonging to the KRU group and are divided into several distinct subgroups. Approximately 350,000 people consider themselves Bassa.

See also LANGUAGES, AFRICAN: AN OVERVIEW.

Basutoland
Former name of Lesotho.

See LESOTHO.

Baule
The largest ethnic group in the Côte d'Ivoire.

According to oral tradition, the Baule were originally part of the powerful ASANTE Confederation, based in what is present-day GHANA, but a violent succession struggle forced the group to break from the confederation. Led by Queen Aura Pokou, the sister of one of the slain contenders, the Baule migrated west in the late eighteenth century. During the journey they absorbed members of the many smaller DYULA, KRU, and Voltaic groups they encountered, and also established profitable trade connections with several of the larger groups with whom they traded the luxurious cloth produced by Baule women for guns, salt, and grain. They eventually settled in the valley between the Comoé and Bandama rivers, in the central region of what is now the CÔTE D'IVOIRE, and established trade connections between the coastal and savanna peoples. By the mid-nineteenth century, the Baule had become prosperous from a lucrative north-south trade in gold, cloth, palm oil, and slaves.

Originally a highly centralized and hierarchical society, the Baule's experience of migration and relocation gradually undermined their authority structures. By the time France attempted to colonize the Côte d'Ivoire in the late nineteenth century, the Baule state had broken into decentralized village clusters, bound only by kinship and commerce. Although village chiefs typically led these groups, successful traders with connections to other powerful clusters occasionally seized control. Internal rivalries, however, were fairly rare, and generally were limited to trade groups vying for commercial profits. It is this antagonism that the French attempted to exploit during the early twentieth century in their efforts to subdue the Baule populations.

Although the Baule welcomed commercial relations with the French, they were much less receptive to French troops passing through their homeland en route to conquests farther north, especially because the French demanded the use of Baule slaves as porters. In 1893 their attacks on French troops delayed a military campaign against the warrior-chief Samory Touré. In the following years they accumulated guns and ammunition; when the French finally defeated Touré in 1898, they found the Baule stronger than before and just as unwilling to accept COLONIAL RULE.

In 1900 the French began a series of military campaigns against the Baule, but they proved no match for the Baule's guerrilla warfare tactics. Attempts to tax Baule merchants' trade also met with strong resistance. In 1908 the governor of the Côte d'Ivoire, Gabriel Angoulvant, announced a campaign of "pacification," ordering colonial troops to "search and destroy" all rebels, as well as their crops and villages. The French administration also attempted to play rival trade groups off each other. Although these tactics were at first only partially successful, the destruction of crops caused famines that, by 1911, ultimately destroyed organized Baule resistance.

Throughout the colonial era the Baule remained wary of the French, though many were educated at missionary schools and went on to become high-ranking civil servants and wealthy plantation owners. Consequently, the Baule exercised considerable influence within the colonial Côte d'Ivoire, helping Ivoirians vocalize their demands for decolonization in the 1940s. The Baule's most famous nationalist leader, Félix HOUPHOUËT-BOIGNY, led the country to independence in 1960. Houphouët-Boigny ruled the country for the next thirty years, during which the Baule became the most influential and richest ethnic group in the Côte d'Ivoire. In 1993 he was succeeded by another Baule, Henri-Konan BÉDIÉ, whose administration continued to promote the concerns of Baule plantation owners until Bédié was overthrown in a 1999 coup. Today, some 400,000 people consider themselves Baule, though estimates range as high as one million.

BIBLIOGRAPHY
Guerry, Vincent. *Life with the Baoule.* Translated by Nora Hodges. Three Continents Press, 1975.
Weiskel, Timothy. *French Colonial Rule and the Baule Peoples: Resistance and Collaboration, 1889–1911.* Clarendon Press, 1980.

ELIZABETH HEATH

BCM
See BLACK CONSCIOUSNESS IN AFRICA.

Beatrice, Dona
1682?–1706
Seventeenth-century prophet who preached the reunification of the Kongo kingdom.

Dona Beatrice was born Kimpa Vita in the KONGO kingdom (present-day DEMOCRATIC REPUBLIC OF THE CONGO, or Congo Kinshasa). As a young woman, Vita (later baptized Beatrice and known as Dona Beatrice) led a religious movement to restore the empire to its former glory during a period of instability and fragmentation within the Kongo kingdom. Beatrice began her movement, later called Antonianism, in 1704, when she claimed to have had a near-death vision of Saint Anthony. She said the popular Portuguese saint appeared to her as an African, after which she died and came back to life as the saint. Soon afterward she began preaching a religious message that combined an anti-Catholic Christianity with Kongo culture, through which she hoped to reunite the Kongo kingdom.

Within months Beatrice established a church in the Kongo capital of São Salvador. Although based on Christian theology, Beatrice preached that the founders of Christianity were Africans, Kongo was the Holy Land, and that Christ had been born in São Salvador. She later tried to reenact the beginnings of Christianity by giving birth to a son she claimed was immaculately conceived. In addition, Beatrice renounced fetishes (including the cross, because it was the instrument of Christ's death), witchcraft, and European clothing. According to Beatrice, these were the correct tenets of Christianity, and through their adherence, the Kongo people would redeem themselves before God and pave the way for heaven on earth—the reformation of the Kongo kingdom as it was during the rule of former king AFONSO I.

As Beatrice gained followers, however, Catholic missionaries tried to find ways to discredit her. At the same time, Pedro IV, ruler of the Kimbangu clan, was looking to solidify his power over the Kongo kingdom. Claiming Beatrice to be the supporter of a rival clan, the missionaries convinced Pedro to arrest her, which he did in 1706 after the questionable birth of her son. She was tried before the royal council and sentenced to death. On July 12, 1706, Beatrice and her son were burned at the stake as heretics.

See also CHRISTIANITY, AFRICAN: AN OVERVIEW.

ELIZABETH HEATH

Bechuanaland
See BOTSWANA.

Bédié, Henri-Konan
1934–
President of Côte d'Ivoire.

Henri-Konan Bédié was born in Dadiékro, in central CÔTE D'IVOIRE. A member of the BAULE ethnic group, which has dominated the nation's politics and cocoa interests since independence, he attended schools in Côte d'Ivoire and France before completing a doctoral degree in economics from the University of Poitiers in France. He entered the Côte d'Ivoire civil service in 1960 during the Côte d'Ivoire's final months as a French colony, serving as diplomatic counselor at the French Embassy in the United States. From 1961 to 1966 he was Côte d'Ivoire's first ambassador to the United States. In January 1966 he returned home to accept appointment as minister delegate for financial affairs. He was soon promoted to minister of economy and finance. At the same time he acted as a governor of the International Monetary Fund and administrator for the International

Bank for Reconstruction and Development (also known as the World Bank). In June 1977, after being dismissed from his ministry following the bankruptcy of six state-owned sugar factories, Bédié became special adviser for African affairs to the president of the International Finance Corporation of the World Bank in Washington, D.C. Returning home in December 1980, Bédié, a member of the Democratic Party of Côte d'Ivoire, was elected president of the new National Assembly. Having been reelected assembly president in 1986, he became acting president of Côte d'Ivoire in 1993, following the death of President Félix HOUPHOUËT-BOIGNY. In October 1995 Bédié won election to a five-year term as president. He was credited with reducing violent crime in Côte d'Ivoire but was accused of persecuting journalists who criticized him. In December 1999 Bédié was overthrown in Côte d'Ivoire's first successful military coup since independence. He fled to TOGO and then to Paris, where he attempted to rebuild his political career from afar. Returning to Côte d'Ivoire in 2001, he regained control of his party and vowed to run for president in the elections presumptively scheduled for sometime in early 2009.

Bedouin

Arabs who live in the deserts of the Middle East and North Africa and who have traditionally practiced nomadic pastoralism.

The Bedouin are Arab nomads who traditionally controlled caravan trade routes through the Arabian and Saharan deserts and played a substantial role in the politics and economy of the Middle East and North Africa. Proud of their strict ethical codes and their nomadic lifestyle, the Bedouin helped introduce Islam to Africa.

The Bedouin originated in the Arabian Peninsula, where their ancestors lived in a number of distinct tribes before the emergence of Islam during the seventh century. The Bedouin have remained divided into numerous tribal groups and, with one brief exception, never formed a coherent state. The Bedouin unified briefly under the leadership of the prophet Muhammad and his successors during the mid-seventh century to embrace Islam. Indeed, the first Muslims were primarily the Bedouin. By 642, Muslim—largely Bedouin—armies conquered much of the Middle East, including EGYPT. During the late seventh and eighth centuries Bedouin armies brought Islam to the remainder of North Africa. They initially settled in garrison cities, which then served as bases for further Arab expansion.

Throughout the following centuries the Bedouin competed with BERBER nomads such as the TUAREG for control of the Saharan trade routes. The Bedouin were important figures in the Arabization of North Africa. Throughout the eleventh and thirteenth centuries the Bedouin tribes of BANU HILAL AND BANU SULAIM migrated west from Egypt and LIBYA, respectively, bringing Arab culture, language, and traditions to ALGERIA, TUNISIA, and MOROCCO.

The traditional Bedouin economy centered on animal husbandry and trade. Most North African Bedouin groups raised camels, while some raised horses, donkeys, sheep, goats, and cattle. Living in tents, the Bedouin migrated seasonally in search of pasture. In summer they often settled in camps near villages where they exchanged animal products for manufactured goods and some foods. They also acted as transporters of products between the countryside and towns. Bedouins provided caravans passing through their desert oasis camps with shelter, animals, guides, and guards. Caravans that refused to pay tolls to the Bedouin were sometimes subject to raiding.

Because of the harsh desert conditions in which they lived, the erratic nature of their nomadic lifestyle, and their economic dependence on raiding, the Bedouin have developed a culture defined by disciplined group solidarity and loyalty. Traditionally Bedouins have valued courage and bravery and maintained rigorous codes of honor, revenge, loyalty, and hospitality. Their customary organization has been in tribes made up of several clans or extended families that are strictly patriarchal, led by a *shaykh* and a group of male leaders. Clans have traditionally migrated together, shared pastures, and united to defend or avenge their members.

The Bedouin in Africa continued to fulfill a vital role in trans-Saharan trade until the late nineteenth century. The Bedouins' independence, however, and their resistance to the boundaries, taxes, and trade restrictions imposed by modern states made them an obstacle to colonialism during this period. During the early twentieth century British and French colonialists sought to force the Bedouin to settle by converting their chiefs into landlords, and building trains and roadways across the SAHARA to render camels obsolete. In the early part of the twentieth century Italians colonized Libya, where they attempted to seize Bedouin land. But the Bedouin of Libya—largely united in the reformist and purist Sufi sect, the Sanusiya—resisted Italian rule, and Libya gained independence in 1951.

During the twentieth century the Bedouin lost control of the desert. Modern-day national borders have blocked the Bedouins' traditional freedom of movement and trade, government wells have violated tribal rights to water preserves in the desert, and cars, trucks, and planes have reduced the value of camels as a form of transportation. While a few North African Bedouin struggle to maintain their traditional lifestyle despite these obstacles, many have turned to wage labor even though Bedouin culture has historically looked down on the dependence entailed in working for a wage. Today many Bedouin drive trucks rather than camels, or work in North Africa's oil industry. Nevertheless, the romantic ideal of the traditional Bedouin lifestyle, symbolic of the purest Arab values, persists— Bedouin poetry, glorifying great journeys, martyrs of love and war, and proud and honorable deeds, remains popular among Arabs both of the desert and city. Though, almost by definition, it is impossible to provide an exact population for the Bedouin, between one million and four million live in North Africa, including MAURITANIA, WESTERN SAHARA, Morocco, Algeria, MALI, Libya, Tunisia, CHAD, Egypt, and SUDAN. A few million more live in Saudi Arabia and surrounding countries.

See also ISLAM AND TRADITION: AN INTERPRETATION; SLAVERY IN AFRICA; SUFISM.

LEYLA KEOUGH

Beira, Mozambique

Major city of central Mozambique.

Named after a former Portuguese province, Beira is the second largest city in MOZAMBIQUE. Beira is located at the mouth of the Pungue and Buzi rivers on the Indian Ocean. Although the Portuguese explorer Pero da Covilhã anchored near present-day Beira in 1487, it was not until 1891 that the Mozambique Company founded Beira as its headquarters. In 1941 the colonial state of PORTUGUESE EAST AFRICA acquired Beira from the company. Under company and colonial control, Beira served as a major port for Indian Ocean trade. Beira became a busy international commercial entrepôt during the colonial period due to the construction of road and rail links to present-day MALAWI, ZIMBABWE, ZAMBIA, and the DEMOCRATIC REPUBLIC OF THE CONGO.

Portuguese colonialists exported agricultural products from Beira and built a light-manufacturing sector in the city. After Mozambique's independence in 1975 the government pursued a policy of rapid industrialization, some of which took place in Beira's suburbs. The city suffered, however, in the 1980s as a result of the war between the government of Mozambique and the Mozambican National Resistance (RENAMO) insurgents. Today the port at Beira provides a vital outlet to the sea for Malawi and Zimbabwe. The road and rail route to Zimbabwe, called the Beira Corridor, has recently attracted considerable investment to the region. In recent years, however, AIDS has taken a heavy toll on the truckers who drive this route. Beira has few amenities for tourists, although there are beautiful beaches nearby and the town provides access to the Gorongosa National Park. According to a 2007 estimate, the city has a population of 436,240.

See also ACQUIRED IMMUNODEFICIENCY SYNDROME IN AFRICA: AN INTERPRETATION; COLONIAL RULE.

BIBLIOGRAPHY

Newitt, M. A History of Mozambique. Hurst and Co., 1995.

ERIC YOUNG

Beja

Ethnic group comprising several smaller subgroups of people who live mostly in Sudan, Eritrea, western Ethiopia, and southern Egypt; also known as Bega or Bujah.

Inhabiting the area between the Nile River and the Red Sea, the Beja are one of the largest non-Arabic ethnic groups in SUDAN. Although exact numbers are difficult to ascertain, most experts estimate the Beja population at about three million people, approximately 10 percent of Sudan's population. They are thought to descend from people who lived in the area from the fourth century B.C.E. The Beja mostly speak Bedawiyi, part of the Northern Cushitic language group. Many also speak Arabic as a second language. One Beja subgroup, the BENI AMER, speaks Tigré, an Ethio-Semitic language. Some still live as pastoral nomads, traveling with portable tents and living on the meat and milk of their cattle and camels. Many Beja, however, have settled into villages and raise sorghum and cotton.

Historians believe the Beja were Christians during the sixth century, but Islam has been the dominant religion within the population since about the thirteenth century. As with other nomadic pastoralists in the region, such as the AFAR, the Beja combine their Muslim beliefs with traditional religious practices. Beja social structure is based upon patrilineal family ties, meaning that ancestral descent is traced through the male line of the family. Multiple marriages for men are permitted, but the expense of supporting two households makes this practice rare.

Regional conflicts over Eritrean independence in the 1970s and 1980s drove many Eritrean Beja into Sudan. This led to major lifestyle changes, including some migration into urban areas such as Port Sudan and KHARTOUM, where Beja often work in the railroad and port industries. Still, fewer than 10 percent of the Beja live in cities. Perhaps a greater modern influence on the Beja has been governmental demand for tax payment, forcing even the nomadic

Beja to enter the cash economy. In the late twentieth century, the increasingly settled Beja of the Sudan called for an independent nation—Bejaland—and formed a political entity, the Beja Congress.

See also ERITREA; LANGUAGES, AFRICAN: AN OVERVIEW.

Belgian Congo
See CONGO, DEMOCRATIC REPUBLIC OF THE.

Bell, Rudolph Douala Manga
1873–1914
Chief of the Duala and early nationalist leader in Cameroon.

Like many early nationalist leaders in Africa, Rudolph Douala Manga Bell was from a chiefly lineage and initially collaborated with the colonial authorities before ultimately turning against them. Born in the commercial port town of Douala, Bell was the eldest son of DUALA king Manga Ndumbe, who had signed an annexation treaty ceding large tracts of land to the Germans. At the age of twelve he traveled to Germany to attend the gymnasium at Ulm and university in Bonn. In 1896 Bell returned to then-German Kamerun to work as a civil servant. When his father died in 1908 Bell became the paramount chief of the Duala. He soon disagreed with the colonial authorities about what he considered their contravention of an 1884 treaty that his father had signed concerning Duala rights on the Jos Plateau. The Germans had effectively attempted to break the Duala trade monopoly for good. Because of his objections, the Germans stripped Bell of his chieftaincy in 1913. Bell also organized resistance to German segregation policies in Douala that threatened to dispossess the Duala of their primary source of income—the land. Although unsuccessful in this protest, Bell was at the forefront of the Duala's growing political activism. He sought support from the British, and encouraged other chiefs and civil servants, such as Martin-Paul Samba, to become involved in the planned rebellion. When the Germans uncovered the plot on the eve of World War I, Bell was charged with treason and hanged in Douala.

ERIC YOUNG

Bello, Ahmadu
1910–1966
Traditional Islamic leader and Nigerian regional premier and power broker during the first years of independence.

Ahmadu Bello was a descendant of royal blood: his grandfather, Atiku na Rabah, was the seventh sultan of Sokoto in the years 1873–1877; his great-great-grandfather, Usuman dan Fodio (1754–1817), founded and ruled the SOKOTO

CALIPHATE. Throughout his life, Bello relied on his illustrious ancestry as a source of political power.

Bello studied at the Sokoto provincial school and then trained as a teacher at Katsina College. He received less Western education than did other prominent Nigerian politicians. Nevertheless, his status and family connections smoothed his ascent to power. Although his cousin Abubakar beat him out for the highest traditional position, the sultanate of Sokoto, Abubakar granted Bello the high position of sardauna, or military commander of the caliphate.

As regional administrator and sardauna, Bello achieved considerable power during the 1940s. His most significant advance, however, came with his membership in the Northern People's Congress (NPC) in 1951. Shortly after its founding, the NPC became the dominant power in Nigerian politics. By rising through its ranks, Bello advanced in the national power structure; by assuming the position of premier of the Northern Region, as he did in 1954, Bello became the virtual leader of NIGERIA.

Although Bello was Nigeria's preeminent politician until 1966, his primary interest lay in the Northern Region. By lauding his ancestors, remaining in the northern city of Kaduna (unlike other regional premiers, who frequented LAGOS), and allowing Abubakar Tafawa BALEWA of the NPC to become prime minister, Bello revealed his commitment to customary rule, which is based on tradition rather than on written law or contract.

Bello focused on advancing the interests of the Northern Region. Aware that southerners tended to be better educated, he established programs to train his constituency for public service and the armed forces. Bello also implemented rules that made it difficult for southerners to receive civil service jobs, extending preference to northerners first, to Europeans second, and only then to workers from the south. This spurred southern resentment, as did Bello's Islamic zealotry, because he proselytized among followers of indigenous religions and supported a foreign policy that denigrated Israel.

Bello's policies won him passionate support in the north and considerable animosity in the south. He was assassinated in the 1966 coup. His death was mourned in the north and celebrated in some parts of the south.

ERIC BENNETT

Bello, Muhammad
1781–1837
Military leader and ruler of the Sokoto caliphate.

Muhammad Bello was born in Gobir, in what is now NIGER. He helped his father, Usuman dan Fodio, overthrow the HAUSA STATES and build the powerful SOKOTO CALIPHATE, which ruled over the northern half of present-day NIGERIA. In the early nineteenth century Bello's father, a FULANI Muslim religious leader, called on the rulers of the Hausa states to abandon their corrupt ways. He organized a popular movement among the Fulani and among Hausa peasants and merchants, advocating a purer form of Islam and the application of the Shari'a, or Islamic law. Usuman first tried peaceful means, but his peaceful movement only provoked repression from the Hausa rulers. In 1804 Usuman and his followers called for a jihad, or holy war, to overthrow resistant rulers. Among those who led the military campaign was Usuman's 23-year-old son, Muhammad Bello. A capable military leader and administrator, Bello was crucial to the defeat of the states of Gobir, Kebbi, Zamfara, Zaria, Katsina, and Kano, which later became emirates within a single large Islamic empire—the Sokoto caliphate.

In 1812, after most of the fighting had subsided, Usuman divided the caliphate between Bello and Bello's uncle, Abdullahi, and retired to religious life. Bello oversaw the eastern emirates and built the new capital of Sokoto for the caliphate. Upon his father's death in 1817, Bello assumed overall leadership of the caliphate as "commander of the faithful." During his reign Bello consolidated the empire and soothed internal conflicts between the Hausa and the Fulani leadership by constructing an impartial justice system, reinstating some Hausa leaders, and improving access to education. Bello also commissioned a network of fortresses for the caliphate's defense along the border with the Kanem-Bornu empire. Under Bello, Sokoto's forces raided and enslaved peoples to the south. These slaves provided the agricultural labor that generated much of the caliphate's revenue. The resolution of internal conflict enabled Bello to extend the empire to include NUPE and YORUBA territory. Sokoto's power and stability under Bello supported a thriving economy. By the time of Bello's death the Sokoto caliphate was the largest state in sub-Saharan Africa, with a population of almost ten million. When Bello died in 1837, his brother Abubakar Atiku succeeded him.

See also SLAVERY IN AFRICA.

ELIZABETH HEATH

Bemba
The dominant ethnic group in Zambia.
The Bemba are a Central Bantu-speaking people, numbering roughly 1.7 million, or more than 14 percent of Zambia's population in 2005. However, more than one-third of ZAMBIA's population speaks the Bemba language, Cibemba (or chiBemba), which is the prevailing language in Zambia's populous Copperbelt and, increasingly, the lingua franca for the country as a whole. Though many

have migrated to the Copperbelt and other parts of Zambia, the Bemba homeland lies in Zambia's Northern and Luapula provinces. Additionally, more than 120,000 Bemba live in the DEMOCRATIC REPUBLIC OF THE CONGO, and 39,000 inhabit TANZANIA.

The exact origins of the Bemba are unclear. Oral histories record that during the eighteenth century, LUBA migrants from the Congo Basin arrived in what is now northeastern Zambia. They settled along the banks of the Kalungu River among a group (probably of earlier Bantu-speaking immigrants) known as the Bemba. The newcomers adopted Bemba cultural traits but maintained the Luba institution of chiefship. Over time the two groups fused into a single ethnic group. Although multiple distinct chiefdoms existed, all leaders deferred to a senior chief called the Chitimukulu, after the great leader, Chiti. The Chitimukulu were believed to possess divine powers, though they had little real power over the various chiefs. Members of a matrilineal royal lineage filled the more powerful chiefships.

A highly centralized Bemba kingdom emerged in the nineteenth century. The Bemba preyed upon more loosely organized neighbors, including the BISA, whom the Bemba absorbed and raided to acquire slaves for trade. Traditionally, the Bemba were considered excellent hunters and fierce warriors. In the past their ability to hunt elephants and harvest ivory for trade formed the basis of their wealth, as did their military proficiency. Under the leadership of two great Chitimukulus, Chileshye and Chitapankwa, the Bemba expanded their sphere of influence to control the commodities important in the Indian Ocean trade, namely slaves, ivory, and copper. This expansion resulted in the wide adoption of the Cibemba language and Bemba culture by other ethnic groups. Although native Cibemba speakers, known as Babemba, share a high degree of cultural homogeneity, eighteen different Babemba ethnic groups can be differentiated, only one of which is the "Bemba proper."

Major demographic changes came when the British occupied Central Africa, ended the slave trade, and developed copper mines in the Copperbelt. Large numbers of Bemba, forced to pay a "hut tax" to the colonial government, migrated to the Copperbelt and sought employment in the mines to earn currency. Consequently, within the cities and towns of Zambia—particularly those of the Copperbelt—Cibemba emerged as the lingua franca. The Babemba continue to dominate the NORTHERN PROVINCE, where they mainly practice shifting cultivation of finger millet and manioc. Because of the prevalence of the tsetse fly in this region, there is no tradition of cattle herding. Poor soils still spur the Babemba to migrate to Zambia's cities.

The Bemba took a central role in the African labor movement, beginning in the 1930s, and in the nationalist movements that led to Zambian independence. Nationalist leaders such as Vice President Simon Kapwepwe hailed from the Bemba ethnic group. Today the Babemba continue to dominate the politics of Zambia. Although President Kenneth Kaunda's parents are Malawian, he is also a native Cibemba speaker, having been raised at Lubwe. Cibemba speakers hold the majority of seats in the national legislature.

See also IVORY TRADE; LANGUAGES, AFRICAN: AN OVERVIEW; SLAVERY IN AFRICA.

ARI NAVE

Bembeya Jazz National
A flamboyant and renowned Guinean band.

The Bembeya Jazz National band formed in 1961 in Beyla, a forested region of southeastern GUINEA. At the time, the musicians were amateurs who had acquired their instruments from the Sékou TOURÉ government under its policy of *authenticité*, which promoted indigenous forms of cultural expression. The group fused Latin-style horns and percussion, particularly Cuban Rumba, with traditional MANDINKA, FULANI, and SOSO musical forms, including griot and jali praise singing, to create a brand of dance music where the guitar was central. The celebrated lead guitarist, Sékou "Diamond Fingers" Diabaté, helped define the Guinean style, in which frequently alternating cords accompany a steady melody. This "Hendrix of Africa" used the guitar to mimic the music of the kora, a traditional twenty-one-string instrument, and the hardwood xylophone. Initially, Bembeya Jazz National also played non-Guinean musical styles, including Congolese. However, in accordance with authenticité, the band had to abandon foreign styles in favor of more traditional Guinean music.

In 1964 the group won the competition at the national music festival. Subsequently, they were chosen to represent Africa at the Tri-Continental festival, held in Cuba in 1965. In 1966 Bembeya Jazz National was named the national orchestra of Guinea, and designated to represent the nation at international contests. The group grew in popularity and traveled throughout Africa. But in 1973 the band suffered a serious setback when its charismatic lead vocalist, songwriter, and central figure, Aboubacar Demba Camara, was killed in a car accident. For three years after his death the band neither recorded nor performed. The band was further demoralized in 1977 when the bass player, Mory Kouyate II, died shortly after returning to music and touring in Moscow. Despite these tragedies the group reorganized in 1985 and renamed itself Bembeya International, with five original members and ten new ones. Bembeya International went on to tour Europe and to release a number of hits in the tradition of Bembeya Jazz National.

See also MUSIC, AFRICAN.

BIBLIOGRAPHY

Graham, Ronnie. *Sterns Guide to Contemporary African Music*. Off the Record Press, 1989.

Stapleton, C., and C. May. *African Rock: The Pop Music of a Continent*. Belisk, 1990.

ARI NAVE

Ben Bella, Ahmed
1919–
Founding member of an Algerian national independence revolutionary organization and first president of Algeria (1963–1965).

Ahmed Ben Bella was born in Maghnia, ALGERIA. After fighting for the French during World War II, Ben Bella returned home to witness the colonial administration's crackdown on the Algerian population. During the crackdown, the French bombed Islamic villages and killed thousands of Muslims in response to the 1945 anticolonial riots in the Sétif region. Inspired to join the growing Algerian independence movement, Ben Bella worked with several illegal revolutionary groups until he was arrested and imprisoned by the French in 1950.

After escaping from prison in 1952, Ben Bella joined other exiled anticolonial leaders, including Mohamed Boudiaf and Hocine Aït Ahmed, in CAIRO, EGYPT. Together they helped found the main revolutionary party, the Algerian National Liberation Front (FRONT DE LIBÉRATION NATIONALE, or FLN). Ben Bella was an arms procurer for the FLN in 1956 when he was captured aboard a plane and imprisoned in France.

Ben Bella was released from prison at the end of the war of independence, only to find his position as preeminent revolutionary leader assumed by others who had stayed in Algeria throughout the struggle. He fought his way into his home country, joining up with military commander Houari BOUMEDIENNE to defeat his political rival Yusuf Ben Kheddha for leadership of the newly independent Algeria.

As Algeria's first prime minister from 1962 to 1963 and as the first elected president of the Algerian Republic from 1963 to 1965, Ben Bella charted a socialist path for the new country. Algeria had suffered severe economic losses from the war and the subsequent flight of colonial resources. Under the leadership of Ben Bella and Vice President Boumedienne, Algeria gained a reputation as a self-reliant nation and a proponent of Third World anticolonial struggles. At home,

Ben Bella used strong-arm tactics to secure his power and suppress dissent.

In 1965 Vice President Boumedienne overthrew Ben Bella and placed him under house arrest for the next fourteen years. Upon release in 1980 Ben Bella left for France, where he formed an opposition party calling for a multiparty democratic Algerian government. He returned to Algeria ten years later and ran for president in 1991. When Algeria fell into a state of civil war a year later, Ben Bella took part in peace talks, held in Rome in 1995. However, in 1997, new restrictions on political movements forced the dissolution of his own party, Mouvement pour la Démocratie en Algérie (MDA).

See also AFRICAN SOCIALISM.

MARIAN AGUIAR

Bena
Ethnic group of Tanzania.
The Bena primarily inhabit the Iringa Plateau and the Ulanga Plains of south central TANZANIA. They speak a Bantu language. The Sowe and the Vemba, also of Tanzania, are sometimes considered Bena subgroups. A 2001 estimate put the number of Bena at some 670,000.

See also BANTU: DISPERSION AND SETTLEMENT.

Benedict of Palermo, Saint
1526–1589
Franciscan lay brother who was the first African to be canonized in the Roman Catholic Church and who is known as the patron saint of the blacks of North America.
Benedetto, or as he became known, Saint Benedict the Moor, was born in San Fratello, on the Italian island of Sicily, to Christopher and Diane Manasseri. His parents had been transported as slaves from Africa to Sicily, where they converted to Christianity. Benedetto worked on a farm until he gained his freedom as a teen.

Benedetto continued to work as a laborer. Sharing his wages with the poor and healing the sick, he became known as "the black saint." He joined a group of hermits who chose Benedetto as their leader. In 1562 he became a lay brother. Stories began to circulate about his saintliness and miraculous deeds; he is said to have resurrected a young boy. Church accounts report that people of all classes in Sicily sought his prayers and his counsel. In 1578, though he was neither a priest nor literate, he was chosen to lead a Palermo friary. Under his charge the monastery became famous and prosperous. Toward the end of his life he requested leave from his duties at the friary to work as a cook. According to church accounts, he died of a severe illness at the exact hour he had predicted.

Upon his death, a cult arose around him. He became very popular in Brazil, particularly among Afro-Brazilians. The Church canonized Benedetto in 1807, and church sources refer to him as "the patron saint of the Negroes of North America."

LEYLA KEOUGH

Benga
Popular music style that dominated the Kenyan music scene in the early 1970s.
Benga, which emerged in the late 1950s, is a guitar-centered adaptation of the dance music of the LUO people, which is traditionally played on acoustic string instruments. Other musical styles played a part in its development as well. Benga is characterized by a driving rhythmic pattern supported by a steady bass drum pulse. Over this rhythmic base, short melodic phrases played on guitar interact with a syncopated bass line.

Benga has its roots in the 1940s, when the establishment of a powerful radio station in NAIROBI spurred the expansion of the recording industry. In the late 1940s and 1950s, European-style dance bands and small ensembles with one or two guitarists accompanied by bottle tapping were prevalent. This music, Congolese rumba, and other music from nearby Belgian Congo (now DEMOCRATIC REPUBLIC OF THE CONGO) were broadcast regionally on the Nairobi radio station. An innovative guitar-playing style began to be heard over the airwaves, performed by Congolese guitarists Jean-Bosco Mwenda and Edouard Massengo. The groundwork for benga was established when well-known Kenyan guitarists such as Fundi Konde adopted the new finger-picking technique of Bosco and began to synthesize a new type of music from indigenous musical styles. Bosco eventually moved to Nairobi in the late 1950s, further encouraging this trend. Record sales soared as the innovative guitar style gained in popularity.

In the late 1950s Nairobi musicians such as Ojwang Ogara, Festo Ochuka, Keri Were, and Adero Onani began incorporating Luo dance music into popular styles based on Congolese rumba and Kenyan guitar and bottle music. The Luo music was rooted in the dance rhythms associated with two traditional Luo string instruments—the nyatiti, an eight-string lyre-like instrument, and the orutu, a one-string violin. The instrumental playing of the nyatiti was adapted to the acoustic guitar, forming a contemporary version of the traditional Luo dance music. This became the acoustic form of benga. Musicians of the KIKUYU and KAMBA ethnic groups also played derivations of the new style. Well-known Kikuyu musicians who played benga include Joseph Kamaru, Francis Rugwati, and Daniel Kamau. Kamba groups, including

Kilimambogo Boys, Peter Mwambi and his Kyanganga Boys, and the Katitu Boys, also gained popularity with variants of the style.

D. O. Misiani, who was born in Tanganyika (now TANZANIA), gradually emerged as one of the most prominent benga performers. In the late 1960s Misiani, with his group Shirati Jazz, and Ochieng Nelly of the Victoria Kings were the first to transfer the older acoustic guitar styles and what was emerging as the benga sound to electric instruments. The two groups, working independently, also added a light but driving percussion beat and two-part singing. Later known as the "King of Benga," Misiani and Shirati Jazz had a number of hits over many years. The Luo flavor of the music was so much in demand during the 1970s that even bands consisting of non-Luo musicians would occasionally invite a Luo guitarist or even a Luo nyatiti musician to join the ensemble for select performances. In KENYA throughout the 1970s, benga outsold even the regionally popular Congolese rumba and other styles of East and Central African popular music.

The lyrics of early benga music were based on the praise-singing tradition, in which performers sing poetic praises, jokes, and other commentaries about an individual, family, or clan. In later versions of benga, contemporary political and social topics and personal songs of love became common.

The Kenyan government decreed in 1980 that primarily Kenyan music should dominate the national radio station airwaves. Despite this decree, other international styles such as Congolese SOUKOUS continued to grow in popularity. Still, because of its distinctive traditional Kenyan roots, in the 1990s benga remained the most recognizable Kenyan popular music.

See also MUSIC, AFRICAN.

Beni Amer

Ethnic group of northeastern Africa; also known simply as Amer and Nabtab.

The Beni Amer primarily inhabit eastern SUDAN and northwestern ETHIOPIA. They speak an Afro-Asiatic language and are one of the BEJA peoples. Some 300,000 people consider themselves Beni Amer.

See also LANGUAGES, AFRICAN: AN OVERVIEW.

Benin

West African country bordered by Togo, Burkina Faso, Niger, Nigeria, and the Atlantic Ocean.

Benin, formerly DAHOMEY, is a country better known by its past than its present. Along its narrow tropical coast, precolonial kingdoms grew wealthy through participation in the transatlantic slave trade. They developed rich religious traditions, such as Vodou, and built formidable armies, which for years resisted French conquest. During the colonial era, Dahomey—a small palm oil exporter known for frequent uprisings—found itself on the periphery of France's West African empire. In the years that followed independence in 1960, Dahomey maintained its reputation for political volatility while doing little to invigorate an economy still heavily dependent on palm oil exports. Since democratic reforms in the early 1990s, however, Benin's political climate and economy have both improved considerably. Observers are now waiting to see if this progress continues after the 2001 reelection of former dictator Mathieu KÉRÉKOU.

PRECOLONIAL HISTORY

The early histories of northern and southern Benin are markedly different. Although powerful kingdoms controlled both regions, north and south had little interaction until the period of European colonialism that began in the 1890s. The northern region was inhabited primarily by the BARIBA. Little is known about the precolonial Bariba, except that they were reputed to have killed every European explorer who crossed their borders. According to oral histories, the Bariba Kingdom was founded by a Persian warrior, Kisra, during the seventh century. She led the group from what is now SUDAN to the present-day Borgou province, where they settled between the NIGER RIVER and the Atacora Mountains. The kingdom divided into four main states—Bussa, Illo, Nikki, and Wawa—and a number of smaller semiautonomous states. Bussa was the ruling state, but Nikki was the largest and possessed the strongest army. The smaller states such as Bikki, Kani, Kouande, and Parakou formed the base of the kingdom's hierarchy. In each the landed nobility, called wasangari, ruled over FULANI herdsmen and gando, slaves who had been acquired through conquests and slave raids. The Bariba's economy was based primarily on agriculture and trade, mostly with trans-Saharan merchants and neighboring HAUSA and Fulani states, including the SOKOTO CALIPHATE. Although some trade occurred with the southern kingdom of Dahomey during the eighteenth century, it was relatively infrequent and limited to slave trading.

The history of southern Benin, home of the Dahomey, Allada, Houéda, and Gun Kingdoms, is much better recorded. These kingdoms were founded by ADJA peoples who migrated to the area from Tado (in present-day TOGO) during the fifteenth and sixteenth centuries. By the late sixteenth century the FON (or Agadja) had created the Dahomey Kingdom near Abomey in the southern interior. The Allada, Houéda, and Gun established their kingdoms closer to the Atlantic coast, where they built ports at COTONOU, Ouidah (or Wydah), and PORTO-NOVO. All

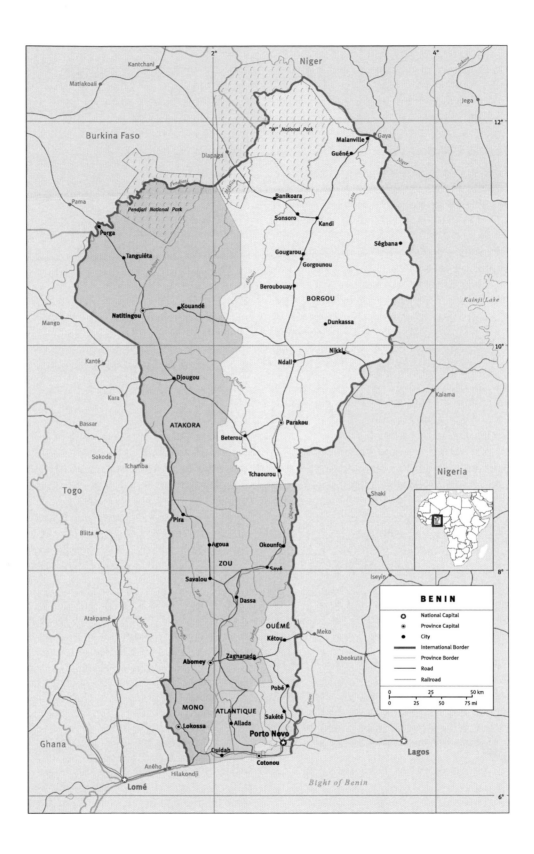

Kantchani

Matiakoali

Niger

Jega

Sokoto

2°   4°

Burkina Faso   12°

Diapaga   "W" National Park   Malanville   Gaya

                                                   Guéné

Pama   Pendjari   Niger

              Pendjari National Park   Banikoara

Porga   Sonsoro   Kandi

         Tanguiéta   Ségbana

                                      Gougarou

Mango   Kouandé   Gorgounou   Kainji Lake

              Natitingou   Beroubouay   BORGOU

Kanté   Dunkassa

                                                              10°

                         Djougou   Nikkl

Kara   Ndali   Kaiama

Bassar   ATAKORA

                                          Parakou

Sokode   Beterou

Tchamba   Nigeria

                                   Tchaourou

Togo   Shaki

                                                              8°

                         Pira   Iseyin

Bliita   Agoua   Okounfo

                         ZOU   Savé

                    Savalou

Atakpamé   Dassa   Meko

                              OUÉMÉ

                         Kétou   Abeokuta

                    Zagnanado

              Abomey   Pobé

         MONO   ATLANTIQUE   Sakété

              Lokossa   Allada

Ghana   Ouidah   Porto Novo   Lagos

    Aného   Cotonou

       Hilakondji

Lomé   Bight of Benin

                                                              6°

BENIN

⊛ National Capital

◉ Province Capital

● City

━━ International Border

── Province Border

── Road

···· Railroad

0   25   50 km
0   25   50   75 mi

168

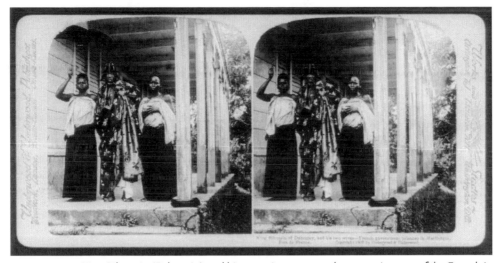

PRISONERS. King Bihuazin (Behanzin) and his two wives are seen here as prisoners of the French in this stereo card from 1902. (*Prints and Photographs Division, Library of Congress*)

paid tribute to the more powerful YORUBA Oyo Empire. In the late seventeenth century these kingdoms began to use their ports to trade slaves for firearms with European merchants, particularly the Portuguese and French. In the 1720s, this lucrative trade came almost entirely under the control of King Agaja of Dahomey, after he conquered the Allada and Houéda.

The participation of the Dahomey Kingdom in the transatlantic slave trade dramatically transformed the region's economy and political relations. Dahomean armies had always raided neighboring peoples for slaves to be used in the royal court, on the king's plantations, and as sacrificial victims in the Annual Custom religious ceremonies. However, the booming European demand for slaves led Dahomean rulers to devote more time and people to raids and wars of conquest. The firearms they obtained from the Europeans facilitated their military exploits, but many historians argue that Dahomean reliance on the slave trade ultimately weakened the kingdom. On the other hand, Dahomey managed to cast off Oyo domination in 1818, and successfully weathered the Europeans' formal abolition of the transatlantic slave trade in the early 1800s by switching the kingdom's economic focus to palm oil. Produced on the king's plantations by the king's slaves, palm oil had a fairly stable market in France but generated smaller profits than slave trading. In the 1860s and 1870s, the Dahomean king Ghezo attempted to earn additional revenue by leasing ports such as Cotonou to the French. But as the European conquest of the continent gained momentum, France used these leases to gain a foothold in coastal West Africa. Ultimately it was disputes between the French and the Dahomean leadership, rather than the economic loss of the slave trade, that led to the defeat of the kingdom and its subsequent colonization by France.

FRANCO-DAHOMEAN WARS AND THE FALL OF THE KINGDOM OF DAHOMEY

Relations between Dahomey and France began to sour in 1889, when Ghezo's successor, Glele, refused the proposal by the lieutenant governor of French West Africa, Jean Bayol, to allow France to improve the Cotonou port and recoup the costs by imposing its own tariffs on all goods shipped through it. Glele died shortly thereafter, and his successor, Behanzin, declared all previous treaties regarding the port illegal and sent Bayol a long list of complaints about French behavior on Dahomean soil. The French government urged Bayol to resolve the dispute quickly, while French missionaries, citing the use of human sacrifice in Dahomean Annual Customs, claimed the Fon were barbarous heathens who needed to be Christianized and "civilized." The king of Porto-Novo, himself seeking respite from Dahomean attacks, also beseeched Bayol to take decisive action. In early 1890 the lieutenant governor did just that: he blockaded the coastline and declared war on Dahomey.

Behanzin mobilized his army, including the fierce Amazon troops, and for more than a year deflected the attacks. By the end of 1891, the French appeared resigned to Dahomean sovereignty. But Behanzin, seeking to prepare his army for future attacks, arranged to exchange slaves for firearms with German and Portuguese merchants, who would then ship the slaves to the colonies of the Congo Free State (present-day DEMOCRATIC REPUBLIC OF THE CONGO), Kamerun (present-day CAMEROON), and SÃO TOMÉ AND PRÍNCIPE. The deals ultimately strained the Dahomey Kingdom, which was suffering a severe drought. The king's subjects were reluctant to export slaves when their labor was desperately needed not only to tend to the king's palm plantations, but also to counteract the crop failures that were threatening the kingdom's food supply. In addition, the deals forced the Dahomey to raid neighboring peoples, such as the Gun, who had by then established close connections with the French. Finally, French missionaries used reports of these slave raids to rally French popular opinion in support of retaliation against the kingdom.

Retaliation came in 1892 after the Dahomey raided the Whéme valley, by then a French protectorate. It took two years for French troops to capture Dahomey's capital, Abomey, but Behanzin escaped into the bush; from there he led an armed resistance movement for another two years. In 1894 the French finally captured Behanzin and forced him to sign a peace treaty, ceding the Dahomean coastline and roads and abolishing the kingdom's custom of human sacrifice, before allowing him to leave for exile in Martinique. The French installed a successor, Agboli-Agbo, but within six years they had deposed him as well. Soon afterward the French conquered the Bariba kingdoms in the north and by 1900 had formal control of the colony of Dahomey.

FRENCH COLONIAL RULE

Although united under a single administration, northern and southern Dahomey experienced colonialism very differently. In the southern region, the transition to French COLONIAL RULE was fairly smooth. There the French had a limited military presence and took full advantage of the Dahomean administrative structure, delegating the duties of tax collection and labor recruitment to local chiefs.

In the north, however, the French faced a much greater challenge. The Bariba Kingdom had essentially disintegrated when the French abolished domestic slavery. The ruling *wasangaris* lost their primary source of income and status, and the former *gandos* formed "freedom" villages, where their small farms produced barely enough for subsistence, much less for trade. Hostilities between the two groups were soon superseded by resentment toward the heavy taxes and compulsory labor service imposed by the colonial administration. These resentments escalated during World War I, when forced military conscription became known in Dahomey as the "blood tax." During this time resistance leaders such as Bio Guera and Gaba mobilized popular discontent to wage strikes and revolts throughout the region. The French managed to subdue the north after World War I, but by then unrest was spreading throughout the south.

In 1923 major demonstrations broke out in Porto-Novo and neighboring areas. The French authorities blamed Islamic religious leaders, as well as intellectuals such as Louis HUNKANRIN, but these figures had simply articulated the underlying causes of popular discontent: poverty compounded by harsh taxes. Even while Dahomey suffered depressed commodity prices after World War I, the administration of FRENCH WEST AFRICA funneled much of the colony's revenue to its seat in DAKAR, where it was used to support France's less profitable colonies in Central Africa. What little revenue remained in Dahomey was used primarily to run the administration and support the colony's French businesses. During World War II, the Dahomey colonial administration used land and conscripted labor, previously devoted to the palm oil industry, to produce maize and other crops for export to France. After the war ended, Dahomey's export sector was in disarray, and the colony grew increasingly dependent on aid from France.

While war undermined the economy, it also sparked new political initiative among army veterans and mission-educated intellectuals in Dahomey, many of whom joined the nationalist organization Union Progressiste Dahoméene (UPD). Under pressure from the UPD and other groups, in 1946 France granted Dahomey direct representation in the French National Assembly as well as its own territorial council. Because voting rights initially had been limited to French citizens and a handful of African civil servants, few formal political parties formed until 1956. In that year the French enacted the Loi Cadre, which universalized the franchise only weeks before territorial assembly elections.

Faced with little time to develop either a platform or a base of supporters, candidates for these elections resorted to clientelism, a strategy employed by the emerging political classes throughout decolonizing Africa. Candidates promised goods and services, such as a new school or pay increase, in return for votes from large groups such as labor unions, merchant communities, and ethnic and regional coalitions. In Dahomey, the most successful politicians were members of major ethnic groups, such as Fon politician Tometin Justin Ahomadegbe; civil servants in influential positions, such as former teacher Hubert Maga; and candidates from major cities, such as Sorou-Migan Apithy from Porto-Novo, who also gained the support of preexisting national organizations, including the UPD. After Dahomey won internal self-rule in 1958, the government's new members sought to secure their positions by offering supporters valuable state resources, such as civil service employment. By the time France formally granted Dahomey independence in 1960, clientelism was firmly ingrained in Dahomean politics.

INDEPENDENCE

For the first three years after independence, President Hubert Maga and his team of French advisers appeared to have firm control over the government, despite outspoken criticism from his opponents Apithy and Ahomadegbe. In October 1963, however, news that a National Assembly delegate had evaded a trial on murder charges provoked massive protests from student and civil servant unions throughout the southern region. Dahomeans saw the so-called "Bohiki Affair" as evidence of their leadership's corruption and lack of accountability. With the purported aim of restoring peace to the riot torn country, General Christophe Soglo seized control of the government. His coup d'état would be the first of many: during the next nine years Dahomey went through six military coups and twelve different governments.

In 1972 a group of junior army officers with broad popular support, especially from students, overthrew the government of Ahomadegbe. One of the officers, Major Mathieu Kérékou, moved quickly to the forefront. Within a year he had restructured the army and dismissed senior army officers over the age of forty, imprisoned the three former presidents—Maga, Apithy, and Ahomadegbe—and channeled his student support into one "official" student organization. In 1973 Kérékou named himself president and began guiding Dahomey on a radically different course.

THE PEOPLE'S REPUBLIC OF BENIN
In 1974 Kérékou declared Marxist-Leninism the official state ideology and renamed the country the People's Republic of Benin. Shortly thereafter he strengthened diplomatic relations with China, North Korea, and Russia, and threatened to cut ties with France. In addition, Kérékou took steps to consolidate his power by weakening potential opposition in the country side. Kérékou disguised his intentions as a campaign to remove "traditional rulers" such as village chiefs, who Kérékou claimed were taking cuts from local taxes. Toward this goal, he installed "revolutionary committees" in each village and town to take responsibility for local administration and taxation. He later announced an "anti-feudalism" campaign, barring many landowners from holding local government positions. When these programs failed to sufficiently reduce the influence of rural chiefs, Kérékou tried a more radical policy: a crusade to eliminate witchcraft.

Because many chiefs were also vodun priests, Kérékou believed that he could unseat them by declaring witchcraft illegal. At first, all went smoothly—only village headmen and chiefs that Kérékou wanted eliminated were named sorcerers. Within weeks, however, the accusations increased exponentially. Villagers began using the campaign to accuse their enemies and avenge vendettas. Public confessions, many of which were coerced by the military, aggravated the situation. During the next few months, accusations divided villages and families. Many innocent people were executed or imprisoned, and others fled the country in fear. Although Kérékou ended the campaign in 1975 after its devastating effects became apparent, in many areas it took years to recover from the divisions that remained.

At this point Kérékou turned his attention to economic reforms, beginning with a program to collectivize agriculture. Villagers were required to join cooperatives and work on collective fields, while the state took over the trade in agricultural commodities. Yet despite support from foreign donors, Kérékou's rural development programs did not make farming a more attractive livelihood to many of the Beninese who enrolled in school with the hope of obtaining employment in the burgeoning state bureaucracies.

Benin's already fragile economy was devastated by the end of Nigeria's oil boom in the global recession of the early 1980s. NIGERIA expelled almost 100,000 migrant workers and closed its borders. The effects for Benin were overwhelming; not only did Nigeria end all trade between the two countries, it sent thousands of laid-off Beninese and other migrant laborers across the border to Benin, where there were few jobs to be found. In 1985 the debt-ridden government of Benin stopped regular salary payments to its employees; two years later, state-owned banks began to collapse. In 1988 international donors, concerned that Benin would default on its loans, pressured Kérékou to adopt new austerity measures. The government enacted social service and payroll cuts that immediately provoked student and union protests. Kérékou, fearing a coup d'état, agreed to demands for democratic reforms, including a new constitution and free elections. In 1991, economist and former director of the International Bank for Reconstruction and Development Nicéphore SOGLO received 67 percent of the vote and became president of Benin.

At first Soglo enjoyed broad support both in the National Assembly and among the public. His determination to adhere to the conditions of World Bank STRUCTURAL ADJUSTMENT measures, however, provoked another wave of widespread demonstrations in 1992, which Soglo met with a military crackdown. As unrest continued, foreign firms, whose investments in manufacturing and construction were vital to Soglo's plans to reinvigorate and diversify the national economy, began to pull out of the country. In 1996 Kérékou returned to power, winning reelection in 2001 and leaving office in 2006. He was succeeded by Thomas Yayi Boni, a political independent and reformer.

See also AFRICAN SOCIALISM; DECOLONIZATION IN AFRICA: AN INTERPRETATION; FRENCH DAHOMEY.

ELIZABETH HEATH

Benin (At a Glance)

OFFICIAL NAME:
Republic of Benin

FORMER NAME:
Dahomey

AREA:
112,622 sq km (43,483 sq mi)

LOCATION:
West Africa, bordering the Atlantic Ocean, Burkina Faso, Nigeria, Niger, and Togo

CAPITAL:
Porto-Novo (population 237,100; 2003 estimate)

OTHER MAJOR CITIES:
Cotonou (population 650,660), Parakou (144,627) (2003 estimates)

POPULATION:
8,294,941 (2008 estimate)

POPULATION DENSITY:
75 persons per sq km (about 194 persons per sq mi)

POPULATION BELOW AGE 15:
45.5 percent (2008 estimate)

POPULATION GROWTH RATE:
3.01 percent (2008 estimate)

TOTAL FERTILITY RATE:
5.58 children born per woman (2008 estimate)

LIFE EXPECTANCY AT BIRTH:
Total population: 58.56 years (male 57.42 years; female 59.76 years; 2008 estimate)

INFANT MORTALITY RATE:
66.2 deaths per 1,000 live births (2008 estimate)

LITERACY RATE (AGE 15 AND OVER WHO CAN READ AND WRITE):
Total population 34.7 percent (male 47.9 percent; female 23.3 percent; 2002 estimate)

EDUCATION:
In 1975 Benin made education free and compulsory. Although total literacy rates in the country remain below 40 percent, great gains have been made in school enrollment. According to data from 2004, some 96 percent of all primary-school-age children are enrolled in schools.

LANGUAGES:
French is the official language, but most people speak an African language. Yoruba and Fon are the most common languages in the south, and at least six major languages are spoken in the north.

ETHNIC GROUPS:
At least 42 different ethnic groups are represented in Benin's population. The Fon, or the Dahomeans, and the closely related Adja group account for at least 59 percent of the total population, and they are the major ethnic groups in the south. In the north the Bariba and Somba (together about 15 percent of the total population) are the largest ethnic groups. The Yoruba (9 percent of the total population) predominate in the southeast.

RELIGIONS:
About 50 percent of the population adhere to indigenous beliefs. Christians account for about 30 percent of the population; Muslims make up about 20 percent.

CLIMATE:
Tropical in the south, semi-arid in the north. The south receives about 1,300 mm (about 51 in) of rainfall a year, mostly between March and July and between October and November. The average temperatures in the south range from 20° C (68° F) to 34° C (93° F). The temperatures in the north are nearly the same. In the north the rainy season occurs between May and September and annual rainfall averages 890 mm (about 35 in).

LAND, PLANTS, AND ANIMALS:
Benin is mostly flat to undulating plains, with some hills and low mountains. At one time dense tropical forest covered much of the land near Benin's coast. Most of this forest has been cleared, except near the rivers. Palm trees now dominate the south. Central Benin is covered by woodlands, and northern Benin is savanna. Animals found in Benin include elephants, buffalo, antelope, panthers, monkeys, crocodiles, and wild ducks.

NATURAL RESOURCES:
Offshore oil deposits, limestone, marble, and timber

CURRENCY:
The CFA franc

GROSS DOMESTIC PRODUCT (GDP):
$12 billion (2007 estimate)

GDP PER CAPITA:
$1,400 (2007 estimate)

GDP REAL GROWTH RATE:
4.5 percent (2007 estimate)

PRIMARY ECONOMIC ACTIVITIES:
Agriculture employs 60 percent of the labor force. The remainder are engaged mostly in small-scale trade and manufacturing.

PRIMARY AGRICULTURAL PRODUCTS:
Corn, sorghum, cassava (tapioca), yams, beans, rice, cotton, palm oil, peanuts, and livestock

INDUSTRIES:
Textiles, cigarettes, beverages, food, construction materials, and petroleum

PRIMARY EXPORTS:
Cotton, crude oil, palm products, and cocoa

PRIMARY IMPORTS:
Foodstuffs, beverages, tobacco, petroleum products, capital goods, and light consumer goods

PRIMARY TRADE PARTNERS:
France, Thailand, India, the United States, and China

GOVERNMENT:
Benin is a republic under multiparty democratic rule. The executive branch is led by President Thomas Yayi Boni and the Executive Council, which he appoints. The legislative branch is the elected 83-member National Assembly.

Elizabeth Heath

Benin, Art of the Early Kingdom of

Full-scale portraits, sculpted heads, statues of people and animals, small devotional objects, and bas-relief (raised-design) plaques from the Kingdom of Benin, which are among the most prized examples of African art.

Among the best known of the Benin works are the strikingly beautiful metal heads. These heads once sat on the royal altar, which functioned simultaneously as the king's tomb, memorial, and symbolic source of sacred authority. The heads increased in size and weight from the fifteenth to the nineteenth century, reflecting in part the greater availability of imported metal. Later the heads served as bases to support richly carved tusks of ivory. Heads of the queen mother display tall coiffures curving slightly toward the front, a reference to the hairstyle worn by royal women. Raised marks, known as ikharo, along the brow line of the heads also serve as important markers of identity. Sculptures depicting women and foreigners have four such marks, and those of Edo men have three.

During the rites of coronation a new king's head was modeled of clay and used as the core for a cast head of the ruler. While the earliest of the metal heads are thought to portray defeated enemies, those produced from the late sixteenth through the nineteenth century are assumed to represent Benin monarchs exclusively. Unlike Benin royalty, lower-level authorities, such as chiefs, were memorialized with wooden heads, wood being a far less expensive material, signifying their lesser status. High-ranking commoners and foreigners were identified with heads of rams, antelopes, or bullocks. Terra-cotta heads distinguish the altars of families of the first dynasty, the Ogiso, which lasted from the early tenth century to the second half of the thirteenth century.

Incorporated into the design features of most such heads—regardless of status or material—are rows of stylized coral beads, which represented the red oblong beads that feature prominently in the crown and robe that the king wore on certain ceremonial occasions. Chiefs and others who were allied with the king wore one or more such beads in recognition of their ties to the palace. These coral beads were re-sanctified at yearly ceremonies in the capital.

Other important symbols of royal power included the leopard, and rulers are said to have once kept live leopards in the palace. A 1668 engraving by a Dutch compiler of African geography and culture shows the Benin king on horseback in front of the palace, accompanied by musicians, priests, soldiers, and others. Near the front of the royal group, two leopards on leashes are depicted. A number of portrayals of leopards appear among the body of art from the Benin kingdom. One of the most beautiful is a pair of leopards carved of ivory and affixed with metal spots. A beaded waistband of coral encircles the haunches. These leopards are now in the collection of the Queen of England.

Much of Benin's finest art was taken as booty from the kingdom and is now held in collections outside of Africa. In 1897 British troops entered the capital of the Benin kingdom, arrested the king, and absconded with the royal treasury—much of it in the form of art. The British troops brought home many objects, including fragments of gigantic metal pythons that had been positioned vertically down the palace roof turrets, a reference to the king's vast power and wealth. Sculptures representing gigantic birds with long legs and broad wingspans were positioned at the top of each turret. Facing north, the direction associated with the Benin god of lightning and death, the palace, with its lightning-like downward zigzagging pythons, also underscored the vast physical and metaphysical power of the king. Stone axes or celts—known locally as thunderbolts—were placed on the royal altar underneath the open mouth of a python sculpture in the centermost turret, extending down into the royal palace.

The most numerous of the Benin arts, which unfortunately are also held mostly in Western collections, are cast

BENIN ARTS. The Oba (king) of Benin depicted in a high relief bronze plaque. Dating from the 16th century, the plaque was originally displayed on a palace column. (*British Museum, London/Bridgeman Art Library International Ltd.*)

metal plaques showing elaborate scenes of court life and lore dating from the sixteenth to the eighteenth century. Said originally to have decorated the walls or pillars of the palace, these works were used by Benin court authorities as visual references to Benin history long after they had been removed from their original palace locations. These plaques contain important insights into traditional forms of costuming and ritual, and they have played a role in refashioning the ancient kingship in the contemporary era.

SUZANNE PRESTON BLIER

Benin, Early Kingdom of
Medieval African empire centered in the Edo state of contemporary Nigeria.

The early kingdom of Benin gained prominence in the fifteenth century under the rule of the Oba or king, Ewuare. Ewuare established the empire's political organization and consolidated its territory by conquering YORUBA territory to the west and IGBO land to the east. Despite the arrival of Portuguese merchants in the late fifteenth century, the kingdom maintained independence from European control. Under Oba Ewuare, as well as under the next two obas, relationships between the people of Benin and the Portuguese were largely peaceful and cooperative.

The empire grew in the sixteenth century under the rule of Oba Esigie. Like many of the great African empires, Benin was intimately involved in the slave trade; various border conflicts and civil disturbances were exploited to send large numbers of non-Benin Africans to the Americas. The empire's power waned throughout the eighteenth and nineteenth centuries as neighboring Yoruba states, especially the Oyo kingdom, gained prominence. In 1897 the British took the city of Benin, forcing Oba Ovonramwen into exile and effectively ending Benin's independence. In 1900 Benin was incorporated into British colonial administration within the Protectorate of Southern Nigeria. Although the position of oba is not obsolete, the present-day Benin oba has only an advisory role in the government. The story of the defeat of the Benin empire is told in *Ovonramwen Nogbaisi* (1973), a tragic drama by the Nigerian playwright and director Olawale Rotimi.

Benin Bronzes
See BENIN, ART OF THE EARLY KINGDOM OF.

Benjedid, Chadli
1929–
Third president of Algeria.

Chadli Benjedid grew up in the Annaba region of colonial ALGERIA, then joined the military wing of the national liberation group, the FRONT DE LIBÉRATION NATIONALE (FLN). Moving quickly through the ranks, he became a rebel commander in 1960. After Algeria's independence he helped oversee the withdrawal of French troops.

While in the rebel army, Benjedid earned the trust of chief of staff Houari BOUMEDIENNE, whom he later supported in the 1965 coup d'état against President Ahmed BEN BELLA. Under President Boumedienne, Benjedid held high positions in the military and served on the ruling Revolutionary Council.

Within the FLN Benjedid gained a reputation as an evenhanded leader, and for this reason he was sought as the presidential candidate to heal divisions within the party after Boumedienne's death. In 1979 Benjedid was elected and began a tenure that lasted through two reelections. During his thirteen years as president, he took steps to liberalize the state-controlled economy and to develop regional relations.

In the 1980s Benjedid faced increasing pressure from groups critical of the FLN's exclusive hold on power. Hoping to appease pro-Islamic groups, Benjedid signed the National Charter, which affirmed Algeria's Arab and socialist identity. Despite these gestures, Benjedid continued to draw criticism, particularly as the national economy floundered in the late 1980s. In 1988 the military killed more than 500 civilians following a riot over food shortages. In the aftermath of this incident, popular outrage forced Benjedid to make concessions such as the legalization of the ISLAMIC SALVATION FRONT (FIS) and other banned parties.

Although Benjedid was reelected president in 1989, the Islamic Salvation Front won municipal elections in 1990. In 1991 Benjedid resigned as the head of the FLN as support for the FIS grew. Shortly thereafter, he was deposed by a coup and placed under house arrest. More than a decade of violent unrest would follow, mostly involving Islamic groups in opposition to government forces. Some 150,000 people were killed before the fighting largely came to an end in 2002.

See also ISLAMIC FUNDAMENTALISM: AN INTERPRETATION.

MARIAN AGUIAR

Berber
Large and widely dispersed ethnic group in North and West Africa.

The origins of the name Berber are uncertain. Some historians claim the word means "outcast," or "barbarian," or "those from the land of Ber" (the son of biblical figure Ham). The word refers to several disparate groups who speak related languages and share certain historical experiences. Berbers have lived in North Africa since at least 3000 B.C.E.; today the largest populations of the estimated fifteen million people (though some estimates

ALGERIAN BERBER. Photographed in Algeria sometime between 1860 and 1890. (*Prints and Photographs Division, Library of Congress*)

exceed twenty million) of Berber heritage are found in ALGERIA and MOROCCO, but significant populations also exist in TUNISIA, LIBYA, EGYPT, MAURITANIA, MALI, BURKINA FASO, NIGERIA, and NIGER. Many Berbers call themselves the Imazinghan, the free people, and indeed in North Africa the Carthaginians, Romans, Vandals, Byzantines, Arabs, and French all encountered Berber resistance. Famous Berbers include Goliath, Septimius Severus, and Saint Augustine.

Some of the larger Berber groups include the nomadic TUAREG, Rif, KABYLIA, Shawia, HARATINE, Shluh, and Beraber. Although their languages are distinct, all belong to the Berber branch of the Afro-Asiatic language family, and some also employ a writing system called tifinagh, which is based on an ancient Libyan script. In addition to linguistic variations, historians have typically distinguished between Berber groups according to whether they are nomadic or sedentary, urban or rural.

Centuries of migration, assimilation, and Islamization in North and West Africa have both broadened and blurred the borders of Berber identity. Many Berber confederacies in North Africa resisted Arab rule; the revolt led by the Berber queen KAHINA in the seventh century was just one of the best known. Other Berber confederacies entered semiautonomous alliances with Islamic rulers, maintaining a decentralized tradition of rule. The mass migrations through the region of Arabs (particularly the BANU HILAL), which began in the ninth century, led to the gradual conversion of most Berbers to Islam. Many Berbers also began to speak Arabic. Although Berber groups' experiences with Islam have varied widely, it may be said that Berber tradition remade Islam in North Africa as Islam remade the Berbers. North African Islamic dynasties, including the ALMORAVIDS, the ALMOHADS, and the Marinids, were led by Berbers, and some incorporated elements of Berber confederate leadership, such as succession based on female kinship. As these Islamic empires conquered portions of southern Spain, Berber influence traveled throughout the Mediterranean.

In the nineteenth century many Berber confederacies resisted the French presence in North Africa, but tensions between them played into the hands of the French. One of the more formidable Berber opponents to French colonial rule was Abd el-Krim, who in the early twentieth century founded the RIF REPUBLIC, a Berber state on the northeast edge of Morocco. Given the Berbers' long history in North Africa, the French viewed them as anti-Arab and created a cultural stereotype of a Berber race, a somewhat contradictory characterization of Berbers as honest, free, non-black, and friendly, but also shifty and xenophobic. The French institutionalized their vision of the Berbers as potential allies against Islamic resistance under the Berber Policy, particularly after they began conquering predominantly Berber areas in 1913. Like many of the colonial-era native policies implemented south of the SAHARA, this policy endorsed Berber customary law while calling for a vigorous Christianizing campaign. French rule had a profound impact on Berber self-identity, as well as on the conception of the Berbers by the outside world. The tensions that developed between groups who identified as Berber and those who identified more closely with Islam continue to be felt today.

Following independence, Berbers in North Africa became increasingly integrated into Arabic-speaking, mixed-ancestry national populations. Some of the nomadic Berber groups living in the Sahara and the SAHEL, such as the Tuareg, have maintained relatively distinct identities. Most Berbers identify themselves as Islamic, but some continue to honor pre-Islamic religious traditions, such as the traditional ritual of the King of the Devils.

Although many North African Berbers live in mountainous rural areas or in the desert, they are also a significant presence in cities, and migrant laborers have carried Berber traditions into Europe.

Political protests, such as a 1994 strike in Algeria for official recognition of the Berber Tamazight language, show that in some locations the distinctive Berber identity remains vital. In 2001, tensions between Algerian Berbers and the government erupted into rioting after a Berber high school student died while in police custody. Algeria is not the only place where Berbers feel marginalized, however. In Morocco, where one-third of the population is Berber, the Berber script Tifinagh is banned and parents may not give their children Berber names. Moroccan Berbers have recently organized to fight the takeover of tribal lands by the government, as well as to obtain a share of the profits from oil companies operating on Berber lands.

See also COLONIAL RULE; ETHNICITY AND IDENTITY IN AFRICA: AN INTERPRETATION; LANGUAGES, AFRICAN: AN OVERVIEW; LAW IN AFRICA: COLONIAL AND CONTEMPORARY.

MARIAN AGUIAR

Bérenger, Paul

1945–

Secretary general of the Mouvement Militant Mauricien (MMM) and prominent Mauritian politician.

Born in Quatre Bornes, Mauritius, Paul Bérenger was raised in a Franco-Mauritian family. He became interested in Marxist politics while studying philosophy, French, and journalism in Wales and in Paris, France. Upon returning to Mauritius, he immediately became involved in the independence movement. Finding the politics of the Mauritius Labour Party (MLP) too conservative, he created the left-wing Club des Étudiants Militants and began organizing demonstrations against the MLP and allied parties. He also became a union organizer, leading a series of strikes.

Bérenger envisioned a country unified by a common language and culture rather than divided by ethnic tensions. In 1969 he founded a new political party, the Mouvement Militant Mauricien (MMM), together with Dev Virahsawmy, a Telegu, and Jooneed Jeerooburkhan, a Muslim. The party's socialist platform and nonethnic orientation appealed to the large working class, particularly dockhands, plantation workers, and unemployed youth.

In response to Bérenger's disruptive strikes, Mauritian Prime Minister Seewoosagur RAMGOOLAM declared a state of emergency in 1971, suspending trade unions, banning political meetings, and shutting down *Le Militant*, the MMM paper. That same year Bérenger survived an assassination attempt only to be arrested, along with other MMM leaders, and jailed for a year without charges.

Ramgoolam's actions only helped legitimize Bérenger's strategies and increase MMM support. Even after he was elected to parliament in 1976, Bérenger continued to organize strikes. By the 1982 elections, the MMM had gathered enough popular support to win control of the government, and Bérenger became minister of finance while Anerood JUGNAUTH became prime minister. As Bérenger gained experience in public life, his politics evolved and his staunch Marxist orientation gave way to more moderate and pragmatic policies. When left in charge of improving the country's economy, Bérenger in fact adhered to unpopular International Monetary Fund (IMF) and World Bank strategies. Consequently, he came into conflict with Jugnauth and resigned from the ministry. The government fell apart, and new elections were called in 1983. Bérenger was defeated but still gained an appointed seat in the parliament and became leader of the opposition, a position he retained until 1987.

Bérenger's aspirations to lead the country have been derailed by Mauritian ethnic politics and the demand for a Hindu prime minister. In 1987, and again in 1990, he unsuccessfully attempted to make Mauritius a republic and to make himself president. Despite these failures, he served as minister of finance under Jugnauth from 1990 until his dismissal in 1993. Following the 1995 elections, Bérenger took the posts of deputy prime minister and minister of foreign relations. In Mauritian tradition, disagreements among government leaders led Bérenger to resign his post in 1996, when he again became leader of the opposition. A coalition of the Mauritian Socialist Movement and MMM swept the September 2000 legislative elections, and Bérenger was again appointed deputy prime minister. He ran again in 2005 but was defeated.

BIBLIOGRAPHY

Oodiah, Malenn. *Mouvement Militant Mauritien: 20 Ans dHistoire (1969–1989)*. Electronic Graphic Systems, 1989.

Bowman, Larry W. *Mauritius: Democracy and Development in the Indian Ocean*. Westview Press, 1991.

ARI NAVE

Beri

Ethnic group of north Central Africa; also known as Kige and Pari.

The Beri primarily inhabit western SUDAN and eastern CHAD. They speak a Nilo-Saharan language and consist of two major subgroups: the ZAGHAWA and the Bideyat. More than 350,000 people consider themselves Beri.

See also LANGUAGES, AFRICAN: AN OVERVIEW.

Berlin Conference of 1884–1885

Meeting at which the major European powers negotiated and formalized claims to territory in Africa; also called the Berlin West Africa Conference.

The Berlin Conference of 1884–1885 marked the climax of the European competition for territory in Africa, a process commonly known as the SCRAMBLE FOR AFRICA. During the 1870s and early 1880s European nations such as Great Britain, France, and Germany began looking to Africa for natural resources for their growing industrial sectors as well as a potential market for the goods these factories produced. As a result, these governments sought to safeguard their commercial interests in Africa and began sending scouts to the continent to secure treaties from indigenous peoples or their supposed representatives. Similarly, Belgium's King Leopold II, who aspired to increase his personal wealth by acquiring African territory, hired agents to lay claim to vast tracts of land in central Africa. To protect Germany's commercial interests, German Chancellor Otto von Bismarck, who was otherwise uninterested in Africa, felt compelled to stake claims to African land.

Inevitably, the scramble for territory led to conflict among European powers, particularly between the British and French in West Africa; EGYPT, the Portuguese, and British in East Africa; and the French and King Leopold II in central Africa. Rivalry between Great Britain and France led Bismarck to intervene, and in late 1884 he called a meeting of European powers in Berlin. In the subsequent meetings, Great Britain, France, Germany, Portugal, and King Leopold II negotiated their claims to African territory, which were then formalized and mapped. During the conference the leaders also agreed to allow free trade among the colonies and established a framework for negotiating future European claims in Africa. Neither the Berlin Conference itself nor the framework for future negotiations provided any say for the peoples of Africa over the partitioning of their homelands.

The Berlin Conference did not initiate European colonization of Africa, but it did legitimate and formalize the process. In addition, it sparked new interest in Africa. Following the close of the conference, European powers expanded their claims in Africa such that by 1900, European states had claimed nearly 90 percent of African territory.

ELIZABETH HEATH

Berti

Ethnic group of north Central Africa.

The Berti inhabit primarily DARFUR Province, SUDAN. They once spoke a Nilo-Saharan language, although today they speak Arabic. Some ethnologists consider the Berti part of the larger SHILLUK ethnic cluster. More than 200,000 people consider themselves Berti.

See also LANGUAGES, AFRICAN: AN OVERVIEW.

Bété

Ethnic group of Côte d'Ivoire.

One of the largest groups of KRU speakers, the Bété number more than 600,000 people, the majority of whom live near the cities of Daloa, Soubre, and Gagnoa in southwestern CÔTE D'IVOIRE. According to Bété history, the group migrated to the area in the seventeenth century after warfare (perhaps connected with the expansion of the MALI empire) drove them out of their home in the savanna to the northwest. They displaced the Gagu, Dida, and Guro people who formerly occupied the region and practiced hunting and gathering. The Bété fiercely resisted French COLONIAL RULE into the early twentieth century. After a final rebellion in 1906 the French army incorporated Bété territory into the Côte d'Ivoire colony.

Surprisingly, the group quickly embraced both Christianity and cash crop farming—the mainstay of the colonial economy—and soon constituted one of the largest groups of plantation workers in the colony. According to some historians, the term Bété took on a pejorative meaning during the colonial era because of their affiliation with plantation work, which was considered degrading, and at times the term was indiscriminately used to refer to any plantation worker. Since independence in 1960, however, members of the Bété group have made a concerted effort to redefine Bété ethnicity and to affirm their own cultural importance. Today the Bété constitute a substantial percentage of coffee and cocoa farmers in the southern regions of the Côte d'Ivoire, though many have also migrated to the capital of ABIDJAN.

BIBLIOGRAPHY

Mundt, Robert. *Historical Dictionary of the Côte dIvoire*. Scarecrow Press, 1997.

Paulme, Denise. *Une société de Côte dIvoire; Les Bétés*. Mouton, 1962.

ELIZABETH HEATH

Beti

Ethnic group of Cameroon, considered by most anthropologists to be a subgroup of the Fang people.

The Beti live primarily in central CAMEROON. They probably migrated from the upper NILE region with other FANG subgroups, such as the BULU, to the northern reaches of present-day Cameroon in the seventh or eighth century. Their movement farther south in the nineteenth century was probably a result of pressure from the expansion of the FULANI. Known by their neighbors as fierce warriors, the Beti settled mostly as farmers.

The Beti number some three million people (though estimates vary) and are themselves often divided into subgroups, including the Yaunde and the Eton. All Beti speak a Fang language, which is part of the larger Bantu language family. Along with French, Yaunde is one of the dominant languages in Yaoundé, Cameroon, the capital city. Many Beti are Roman Catholic and live an urbanized lifestyle as a result of their close association with the French during the colonial era. Those who continue to live and work in a rural setting grow corn, cassava, yams, and plantains as staple crops; cash crops include peanuts and cacao.

Beti society, especially among the rural Beti, revolves around both family groups (determined by the father's line) and the grouping of same-age people into similar roles within the community. Family groups tend to live in close proximity but not in tightly structured villages. Along with the other changes brought by European influence, most of the traditional Beti arts and crafts, such as ironworking and woodworking, have nearly disappeared. Perhaps the best-known member of the Beti people is MONGO BETI, a writer and political philosopher.

Beti, Mongo

1932–2001

Cameroonian novelist and political essayist whose works examine Africa's transition from a traditional to a modern society, with specific attention to the ongoing effects of colonial policies in his country.

Born Alexandre Biyidi-Awala in Mbalmayo, a town near YAOUNDÉ, he adopted the pen name Eza Bota with his first work and thereafter used the pseudonym Mongo Beti. Educated in Catholic mission schools and then at a French lycée in Yaoundé, Cameroon, Beti went to France in 1951 to study literature at the University of Aix-en-Provence. He published his first novel, Ville cruelle, in 1954. This work introduces the major themes of his early writing: the social disorientation caused by colonialism, and the African's revolt against traditional village life, especially its patriarchy.

With his second novel, Le pauvre Christ de Bomba (1956; The Poor Christ of Bomba, 1971), Beti established himself as an important Francophone (French-language) writer. The novel was banned in Cameroon, however, because it presumes a complicity between missionaries and the government in maintaining colonialism. Written in the form of a diary, it traces the journey of a naive young man as he follows a European priest on his missionary circuit and learns how destructive missionaries can be despite good intentions. Mission Terminée (1957; Mission to Kala, 1958) tells of a young man who has just failed the baccalaureate examination. He returns home to be greeted as a hero

because of the Western education his people believe he has. He subsequently learns that he can adapt neither to the colonial order nor to the traditional society.

Beti put aside his writing for more than a decade but returned to his craft in the 1970s with a political book, Main basse sur le Cameroun (Rape of Cameroon, 1972). This work clearly marked a new phase in his writing in which he denounced the government of Cameroon for neocolonial policies that allowed France to maintain its influence. His first novel of this period, Perpétue et l'habitude du malheur (1974; Perpetua and the Habit of Unhappiness, 1978), is an allegory in which a woman represents both an Africa conquered by European nations and the victims of neocolonialism. Les Deux Mères de Guillaume Ismaël Dzewatama, futur camionneur (The Two Mothers of Guillaume Ismaël Dzewatama, Future Truck Driver, 1982) tells of a mixed marriage between a French woman and a Cameroonian man.

Beti remained in France after completing his education and taught literature at a lycée in Rouen beginning in the late 1950s. In the early 1990s he returned to Cameroon and ran a bookstore.

Betsileo

Ethnic group of Madagascar.

The Betsileo primarily inhabit the Central Highlands of MADAGASCAR. They speak MALAGASY, a Malayo-Polynesian language, and consist of four subgroups: the Arindrano, the Halangina, the Isandra, and the Manadriana. Approximately 1.5 million people consider themselves Betsileo.

See also MADAGASCAR, ETHNICITY IN.

Betsimisaraka

Ethnic group of Madagascar.

The Betsimisaraka primarily inhabit the east coast of MADAGASCAR. They speak MALGASY, a Malayo-Polynesian language. Approximately 1.8 million people consider themselves Betsimisaraka, including members of the Betanmena subgroup.

See also MADAGASCAR, ETHNICITY IN.

Biafra, Republic of

Secessionist state in West Africa from 1967 to 1970.

The name Biafra, the alternative name for the Republic of Biafra, has been used to designate the secessionist eastern region of NIGERIA, which, under the leadership of Lieutenant Colonel Emeka Odumegwu OJUKWU (the former military governor of the region), waged a three-year war with Nigeria in the late 1960s. The secessionist state was named after a bay in the Atlantic—the Bight of Biafra—located in the curve at the easternmost coastline of West Africa, adjacent to southeastern Nigeria. During the Nigeria-Biafra war, Biafran sovereignty was recognized by five nations: GABON, Haiti, CÔTE D'IVOIRE, TANZANIA, and ZAMBIA.

The Biafran secession and resultant war were caused by a very unpleasant chain of events. One of those unfortunate incidents was the bloody Nigerian military coup of January 15, 1966, which was seen by many natives of northern and western Nigeria as an IGBO coup because it was masterminded by Major Chukwuma Kaduna Nzeogwu, an Igbo military officer. Moreover, almost all the Nigerian dignitaries killed in that abortive coup were non-Igbos. They included four Northern senior army officers, two YORUBA senior military officers, and three top-ranking government officials—Samuel Ladoke Akintola, Abubakar Tafawa BALEWA, and Ahmadu BELLO.

In revenge for the killing of the high officials, some northern military officers (mostly Muslims) carried out a countercoup during a special meeting in IBADAN on July 29, 1966, killing Nigeria's highest military officer, General Aguiyi Ironsi (an Igbo) and his host, Colonel Francis Adekunle Fajuyi. This was followed by the killing of several hundred Igbo army officers in LAGOS, ABEOKUTA, and elsewhere. Thereafter, an alarmingly large number of easterners, estimated at around 30,000 civilians, mainly Igbos, were killed in northern Nigeria, with the result that nearly two million surviving eastern migrants in the north fled, causing an unprecedented influx of refugees in eastern Nigeria.

Another event that escalated the Nigerian crisis was the peace meeting held at Aburi, GHANA, in January 1967, between Ojukwu and the Nigerian head of state, Lieutenant Colonel Yakubu Gowon. Rehabilitating the refugees in the east was one of the chief concerns of Ojukwu during the Aburi conference. After the meeting, when there was some evidence of default from Gowon's side, the easterners, over their radio at Enugu, starting chanting "On Aburi we stand. On Aburi we stand," and Ojukwu insisted that only a faithful implementation of the agreement reached at Aburi would be the basis for national reconcialtion.

On March 31, 1967, Ojukwu promulgated a Revenue Collection Edict that authorized his officers to place all the federal revenue collected from eastern Nigeria into the regional treasury so that he could manage the refugee problem in light of the provisions of the Aburi agreement, which had been neglected by the federal government. In the view of the Nigerian government, however, Ojukwu had another motive for issuing the Revenue Collection Edict, namely that he wanted to deprive other Nigerians from their share of the revenue from the rich oilfields in the eastern region. In addition, Gowon argued that Ojukwu

had no right to implement the Aburi agreement unilaterally. Gowon retaliated by blocking some federal services to the east; and on May 27, 1967, he proclaimed the division of Nigeria into twelve states, splitting the eastern region into three: East Central State, Rivers State, and South East State. Because of that announcement, Ojukwu, with the mandate of the Eastern Consultative Assembly, declared on May 30, 1967, the independence and sovereignty of eastern Nigeria, which he renamed the Republic of Biafra.

War became inevitable; Gowon immediately mobilized the federal forces to crush the secession. On July 6, 1967, the Nigerian Army sent troops from the northern front to Biafra in an attack described by Gowon as a "police action, not civil war." In response, Biafran soldiers launched their own offensive against the western part of Nigeria, capturing a number of towns, including Benin City. They moved swiftly towards Lagos, capturing Ore and Okitipapa about 100 miles from Lagos, which was then the federal capital. However, owing to a powerful counterattack from federal troops, the Biafrans eventually withdrew from the west and mid-west. By the end of 1967 the Nigerian Army had captured several important Biafran cities, including Nsukka, Enugu, Calabar, and Bonny.

In 1968 and 1969 both the federal government and Biafra experienced a number of setbacks. On March 31, 1968, for example, in a Biafran town of Abagana, almost all of the Nigerian 2 Division perished as its motorcade, consisting of scores of trailers and war vehicles loaded with ammunition, caught fire in a mysterious ambush. While this devastating incident boosted Biafrans' determination to continue fighting, it had a very demoralizing effect on the Nigerian military, as did the recognition of Biafra as a sovereign and independent state announced by Tanzania on April 13, Gabon on May 8, Côte d'Ivoire on May 14, and Zambia on May 20—all in 1968. Nevertheless, Biafra also suffered a series of disheartening setbacks. In addition to capturing Biafra's main food-producing regions, Nigeria imposed a total land, sea, and air blockade against the state, and finally forbade the Red Cross and other American and European relief agencies from bringing food, clothing, and medicines to the Biafran refugees, who had been ravaged by famine, malnutrition, and diseases.

The Biafran condition continued to deteriorate until the beginning of 1970, when Ojukwu, after conferring with his cabinet and his chief of staff, boarded the last plane flying from Biafra and escaped to Côte d'Ivoire on January 11, 1970. The following day General Phillip Effiong announced the surrender of Biafra; and on January 15 he formally renounced the secession. Gowon welcomed the surrender in good faith, and did not use any punitive measure against the suffering ex-Biafran people. A movement to again secede was defeated in 2005 by the government of Nigeria.

EDDIE ENYEOBI OKAFOR

Bidima, Jean-Godefroy
1958–
Cameroonian philosopher and writer.

Jean-Godefroy Bidima's primary training is in philosophy, but his published work extends over a wide range that includes not only the related field of cultural anthropology, but also literature and art history. His first published work, titled *Théorie critique et modernité africaine* (1993), based on his doctoral thesis at the Sorbonne, draws on theoretical concepts and methodological approaches from these various disciplines, in a sustained reflection on the implications of the African encounter with Europe and the process of transition in African society set in motion by this encounter, in the specific historical and cultural contexts in which it occurred. The reference to "critical theory" associated with the Frankfurt school may suggest a simple application of the models and ideas of this school. In fact, Bidima reaches back to a tradition of German sociology, including notably the work of Karl Marx and Max Weber, on which the so-called critical theory itself is grounded, in order to reconceptualize its concepts and to examine their relevance to the African experience. The central preoccupation that emerges from Bidima's work is that of modernity as an existential project in Africa.

Bidima's next book, *La philosophie négro-africaine* (1995), is a survey of the various currents that have emerged in the development of a modern African philosophical discourse. Bidima is at pains to outline a new approach to African philosophical reflection through an emphasis on ethics as the essential foundation of thought. Furthermore, he foresees the emergence of a new mode of African aesthetic consciousness that derives from and at the same time transcends the paradigms associated with African art in western manuals.

The description of this mode forms the subject of *L'art négro-africain* (1995). The book departs from the standard model of an academic presentation of African art conceived as a distinctive form, developing rather as an exploration of the rich variousness of expressive means in evidence across the continent. For Bidima, African art is not so much a monolithic category as the convergence of several traditions in constant evolution. Bidima's approach, avowedly governed by the reception theory of Wolfgang Iser, is appropriately dynamic: each artistic tradition, each specific work that he identifies is interpreted in terms not only of the cultural background from which it derives a primary meaning, but also of the potential it offers for symbolic

resonance. It is safe to say that this is one of the most original works on African art.

La palabre: une juridiction de la parole, published in 1997, is arguably Bidima's most accomplished work. His scholarship is at its most precise and trenchant in this book, in which he cites ethnographic evidence from a wide range of relevant studies in order to demonstrate the existence of rules of procedure in the judicial systems of African traditional societies. He shows that these rules are based on clearly conceived ethical principles and governed by an implicit rationality that he undertakes to uncover. Bidima's analytical effort in the book is driven by a conviction determined in the first place by his cultural location and confirmed by the empirical facts he summons in support of his position, namely, that orality represents a viable support of indigenous legal systems in Africa. It is significant to note that Bidima's position runs counter to that advocated by western anthropologists such as Jack Goody and Walter Ong, who deny the potential of oral discourse to formulate abstract ideas. Thus, apart from the wide range of its references, Bidima's work assumes a considerable theoretical significance, in the way it extends the range of studies devoted to the phenomenon of orality not only as a mode of imaginative and symbolic expression, but also as an effective mediation of forms of social practice and conceptual systems. There is indeed a sense in which Bidima pursues in this work the intuitions underlying Levi-Strauss's structuralist method to their ultimate consequences.

Bidima's preoccupation with modernity as an existential project in Africa is best exemplified by his essay entitled "Esquisses philosophiques sur les devenirs africains" published in *Diogène* in 1998. The title suggests that he is returning to the critical project begun in his doctoral dissertation, in a comprehensive re-appraisal of an African modernity predicated uneasily but inescapably on the western paradigm. In this essay, Bidima examines various areas of contemporary African experience and the modes of discourses by which they have been apprehended. He seeks to go beyond what he calls the Manichean analysis (*l'analyse manichéenne*) of the African situation that prevails in current debates, the tendency to set up sharp polarities where a more critical awareness of the multiple tensions by which African experience has been traversed would have provided a more adequate response. His discussion of the problem of identity that has haunted contemporary thought in Africa is especially illuminating in this regard. He is concerned not so much with the definition of an original African identity—in opposition to an acquired cultural baggage imposed on the assimilated westernized elite—as with exploring the interactions that animate contemporary African life at every level, from the intimate and personal to the institutional. Bidima asserts that the real interest of African philosophy is a critical reflection on the constant renewal of African life entailed by the dialectic of tradition and modernity. African history can thus be comprehended as a process of self-projection in what he calls a "tension vers le futur."

As the title suggests, the essay represents the outline (esquisse) of a philosophical investigation of the possibilities of a meaningful accession to modernity in Africa. In other words, it offers the lineaments of a meditation on the subject of an African "becoming" in our time. Bidima's work can thus be seen to revolve around issues affecting some of the most fundamental concerns of African intellectual endeavor at this time—concerns which find their most forceful imaginative expression in the literature of Francophone African writers—and to carry forward intellectual reflection on the African condition to a point of critical interrogation.

F. ABIOLA IRELE

Bight of Benin
Bay in West Africa that forms the western part of the Gulf of Guinea.

The Bight of Benin extends from the mouth of the Volta River to the mouth of the NIGER RIVER and measures about 720 km (about 450 mi) long. It is fed by the Mono, Donga, Ogun, and Benin rivers. Principal ports include ACCRA, GHANA; LOMÉ, TOGO; PORTO-NOVO and COTONOU, BENIN; and LAGOS, NIGERIA. The coast is characterized by rough surf and low offshore islands that protect shallow anchorages. Throughout the eighteenth century the Bight of Benin was known as the Slave Coast, when Badagri (in Nigeria) and Ouidah (in Benin) were major slaving ports. Between 1711 and 1810 about one million people were captured along the Bight of Benin, most of them from the YORUBA ethnic group in southwest Nigeria and some from the HAUSA and NUPE groups living north of the Niger.

Bijagó
Ethnic group of Guinea-Bissau.

The Bijagó people inhabit the GUINEA-BISSAU archipelago of the same name. For years they fiercely resisted foreign domination. Anthropologists believe the Bijagó are related to mainland ethnic groups such as the Papeis and Nalus, who migrated to the region between the tenth and fourteenth centuries. Retaining their animist religious beliefs, the Bijagó lived in small chiefdoms. They fished, cultivated a variety of crops (especially rice), produced palm wine, and built canoes that were able to hold up to seventy people.

The Bijagó's canoes enabled raids on slave traders and trading outposts that were involved in the transatlantic slave trade. Many Bijagó also participated in the transatlantic trade. During the early nineteenth century, Portugal tried unsuccessfully to suppress the Bijagó. Successive Portuguese military campaigns finally suppressed the Bijagó in 1936. COLONIAL RULE on the islands was harsh because of past Bijagó resistance and isolation from mainland scrutiny. Portuguese-appointed chiefs, or regulos, collected young men for forced labor on palm oil plantations. Many Bijagó evaded forced labor and taxes, and the Portuguese collectively punished these Bijagó's family members.

Many Bijagó participated in the independence war, but the war on the islands was one-sided from the start because of the lack of a Portuguese presence. There are approximately 16,000 Bijagó (some estimates are as high as 30,000), many of who are involved in palm oil production and fishing. International nongovernmental organizations have been working with the Bijagó to create a national park in the archipelago.

BIBLIOGRAPHY

Forrest, Joshua. Guinea-Bissau: Power, Conflict, and Renewal in a West African Nation. Westview Press, 1992.

Scantamburlo, Luigi. Etnologia dos Bijagos da Ilha de Bubaque. Instituto de Investigacao Científica Tropical, Instituto Nacional de Estudos e Pesquisa, 1991.

ERIC YOUNG

Bikila, Abebe
1932–1973
Ethiopian runner who won two Olympic gold medals in the marathon.

Abebe Bikila was born in Mout, Ethiopia. Before competing as a runner he was a member of the imperial bodyguard of HAILE SELASSIE I, the Ethiopian emperor. The marathon at the 1960 Olympic Games in Rome, Italy was only Bikila's third race at this distance, but he set a new world best time of 2 hours 15 minutes 16.2 seconds. The designation world best is used instead of record because marathon courses differ greatly and comparison of finish times is difficult. Bikila also attracted attention by running barefoot.

At the 1964 Olympic Games in Tokyo, Japan, Bikila, no longer competing barefoot, became the first runner to win the Olympic marathon twice. He finished with a new world best time of 2 hours 12 minutes 11.2 seconds. His previous mark had been broken several times between the Olympic games. Bikila competed in the marathon at the 1968 Olympic Games in Mexico City, but he dropped out after about 16 km (about 10 mi) because of an injury. His Ethiopian teammate Mamo Wolde went on to win the race. In 1969 an automobile accident left Bikila paralyzed below the waist, and he died of a brain hemorrhage four years later. During his career Bikila won twelve of the fifteen marathons he entered, an outstanding accomplishment. Since then many Ethiopian distance runners have followed in Bikila's record-breaking footsteps, including Fatima Roba, who in 1996 became the first Ethiopian woman to win a gold medal in the Olympic marathon event. Bikila's career marked the beginning of a period of excellence by Ethiopian runners at longer distances.

BIBLIOGRAPHY

Lovett, Charles C. *Olympic Marathon: A Centennial History of the Games Most Storied Race.* Praeger, 1997.

ROBERT FAY

Biko, Stephen

1946–1977
Founder of the South African Students' Organization and leader of the Black Consciousness Movement.

Stephen Biko's death at the age of thirty robbed SOUTH AFRICA of one of its most popular and effective antiapartheid activists and gave the movement its most famous martyr. Memorialized in the 1987 film *Cry Freedom*, Biko became an international symbol of the brutal repression facing those who fought racial injustice in South Africa.

The third of four children, Stephen Biko grew up in the all-black Ginsberg area of King William's Town, in the EASTERN CAPE. He was only four when his father, a policeman, died. When Biko was sixteen the town raised money to send him to the Lovedale Institution, the school that his older brother Khaya attended. Shortly after Biko arrived, Khaya was arrested on suspicion of belonging to the banned PAN-AFRICANIST CONGRESS (PAC). Although Khaya was later acquitted,

FUNERAL FOR BIKO. Priests and ministers lead a funeral procession for slain Black Consciousness Movement leader Stephen Biko on Sepember 25, 1977. Biko was beaten to death two weeks earlier while in police custody. (*Matt Franjola/AP Images*)

both brothers were expelled from the school. Biko completed his studies in 1965 at St. Francis' College, a Catholic boarding school in Natal Province.

The following year Biko entered the University of Natal to study medicine. There he joined the National Union of South African Students (NUSAS), a multiracial antiapartheid student group. By 1967 international events led Biko to question his commitment to a nonracial approach. Much of Africa had only recently gained independence from years of white colonial rule, and in the United States the Black Power Movement was growing.

Resolving that it was time to reject the help of white liberals and establish an all-black antiapartheid organization, Biko and other members of NUSAS and the University Christian Movement (UCM) founded the South African Students' Organisation (SASO) in 1968. As SASO's first president, Biko traveled throughout South Africa training students to lead their own SASO chapters. In his SASO newsletter column "I Write What I Like," he expressed his views on BLACK CONSCIOUSNESS, the belief that black South Africans could overcome injustice only by first defeating the mentality of oppression. Even after stepping down as president in 1970 (SASO's bylaws provided for a new president every year), he continued to function as the organization's heart and soul. His studies suffered, and in 1972 Biko left the university before completing his medical degree.

Biko went to work for the newly formed Black Community Programmes (BCP), helping to organize youth groups aimed at building skills and self-esteem among its members. He also continued to serve as publicity director for SASO, and began a correspondence course in law. In addition, Biko helped found the Black Peoples' Convention (BPC), which sought to expand SASO's work beyond the student population. In 1973 the South African government issued orders banning the activities of Biko and seven other SASO leaders. Confined to King William's Town, Biko established and led an Eastern Cape branch of the BCP until 1975.

By that time Stephen Biko was looking to increase SASO and BPC cooperation with the banned African National Congress (ANC) and PAC. But after the student uprising in SOWETO in 1976, the government intensified its harassment of Biko, one of the few leading figures in the antiapartheid movement who had not been imprisoned or exiled. He was detained twice under the Terrorist Act, and then on August 18, 1977, he was once again taken into police custody, where he was stripped naked and beaten for refusing to cooperate. Less than a month later, his lifeless, naked, and manacled body was found in a PRETORIA jail cell.

An official investigation into Biko's death cleared the police, and in October 1977 the government banned all Black Consciousness Movement organizations. For years the South African police denied responsibility for his death, first claiming that he had starved while on a hunger strike, and then that he had smashed his own head into a wall, fatally fracturing his skull. In 1997 testimony before the TRUTH AND RECONCILIATION COMMISSION and the public, including Biko's widow Nontsikelelo, the officers involved finally admitted to torturing and murdering Biko two decades earlier. In 2003 *The New York Times* reported that the five policeman accused of his killing would not be prosecuted due to a lack of sufficient evidence and, because the incident had occurred in 1997, the time frame for prosecution had expired.

BIBLIOGRAPHY

Biko, Steve. *I Write What I Like*. Bowerdean Press, 1978.

Woods, Donald. *Biko*. Henry Holt, 1991.

KATE TUTTLE

Bilin

Ethnic group of the Horn of Africa, also known as Bilen, Belen, Bogo, and Gabra Tarqwe Qur.

The Bilin primarily inhabit western ERITREA and the Tigray Province of ETHIOPIA. Large numbers of Bilin refugees also settled in SUDAN during the Eritrean secession wars of the 1970s and 1980s. They speak an Afro-Asiatic language and are one of the AGAW peoples. Approximately 250,000 people consider themselves Bilin.

See also LANGUAGES, AFRICAN: AN OVERVIEW.

Bimoba

Ethnic group of West Africa; also known as Bimawba, B'Moba, Moab, and Moba.

The Bimoba inhabit primarily northern GHANA and northern TOGO. They speak a Niger-Congo language and belong to the GURMA cultural and linguistic group. Approximately 133,000 people consider themselves Bimoba.

See also LANGUAGES, AFRICAN: AN OVERVIEW.

Biogeography of Africa

Distribution of plant and animal life on the continent of Africa.

Due to its tectonic history, weather patterns, and sheer longitudinal sprawl—7,918 km (4,920 mi)—from TUNIS, TUNISIA to CAPE TOWN, SOUTH AFRICA), Africa contains an extraordinary variety of habitats. As a result, measurements of species diversity, average biomass, and "primary productivity" (amount of energy plants photosynthesize) vary immensely. In addition, the flora and fauna of Africa have evolved and adapted according to specific local and regional conditions, which have, in turn, been influenced by global patterns and epochal changes. Thus the CLIMATE and GEOMORPHOLOGY of Africa play primary roles in the determination of biological diversity. Although the complexity of life in Africa limits the use of simple categories, the continent may be roughly classified into a small number of biomes, or ecological types. Scientists use biomes to classify large regions of relative uniformity, where soil, plants, animals, and weather suggest a continuity of condition. A biome most often takes the name of the predominant vegetation within it. Biomes in Africa appear to radiate concentrically from the equator, as those to the south mirror those to the north. Biogeographers often divide Africa into at least seven biomes, but main variations may be characterized in five. Tropical rain forests cut the middle of the continent, savannas spread outward from these, deserts emerge from the savanna at higher latitudes, and Mediterranean conditions prevail on the southern tip as well as the northern coast of the continent. In addition, mountainous regions, also called Afromontane biomes, are scattered throughout.

TROPICAL RAIN FOREST

In Africa, four distinct rain forest regions exist, all close to the equator: the Congolian Rain Forest belt, which sprawls across GABON, Republic of the Congo, Democratic Republic of the Congo, and western TANZANIA; the smaller Upper Guinean belt, which extends from GUINEA to GHANA; and two narrow coastal strips, one abutting the ocean in MOZAMBIQUE, Tanzania, and KENYA, and the other covering east MADAGASCAR. The Congolian and Guinean belts display numerous biotic similarities, including year-round high temperatures and rainfall—at least 1,400 mm (55 in) annually (and over 5,000 mm [200 in] in some areas), and rich species diversity. Together they are thought to contain more than 8,000 plant species, most of them native to the region. The forests on the east coast and Madagascar receive less rain and host fewer species of flora.

Rain forest flora commonly assume a three-level structure—a few exceptionally tall trees of up to 50 m (165 ft), a denser middle canopy of interlocking treetops that range from 25 to 35 m (80 to 115 ft), and a bottom tier of small trees that are about 15 m (50 ft) tall. In its most developed form, the rain forest allows little forest-floor vegetation, since the middle canopy blocks out much of the sunlight. Where trees have fallen or been cut or burned, undergrowth may proliferate on the exposed patches. Broad-leafed evergreen trees, including palms, predominate in African rain forests, especially in the wetter regions. In drier, semideciduous belts, such as those of the east coast, the canopy is thinner and the undergrowth typically more dense. A great variety of bird species populate Africa's rain forests, along with many higher primates. Despite the upper-strata richness of life

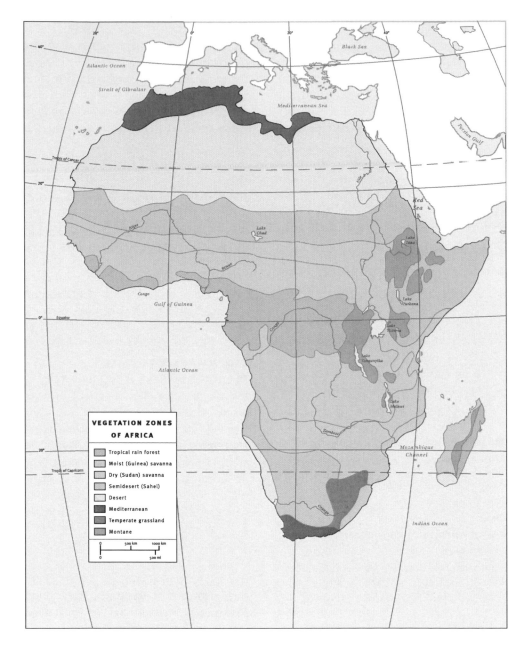

VEGETATION ZONES
OF AFRICA

Tropical rain forest
Moist (Guinea) savanna
Dry (Sudan) savanna
Semidesert (Sahel)
Desert
Mediterranean
Temperate grassland
Montane

in these regions, however, rain forest soil contains little organic matter, in part because of rapid bacterial breakdown. Farmers in rain forest regions typically practice shifting cultivation, in which they relocate their plots every two or three years, thereby allowing tired soils to regain fertility. Although rain forests cover only about 7 percent of sub-Saharan Africa, they contain more than 50 percent of Africa's native species. Within the biome, biologists have identified at least eight distinct subcategories according to moisture, soil, and elevation. Compared with the rain forests of Asia and the Amazon, however, African rain forests lack biodiversity.

They do, however, face similar threats, especially from logging companies that export high-value tropical hardwoods.

SAVANNA

Savannas stretch across Africa, both to the north and to the south of the Congolian and Guinean rain forest belts. The Sudanian savanna in the Northern Hemisphere and the Zambezian savanna in the Southern Hemisphere are the largest savanna biomes. The term savanna connotes grassland, but can also refer to regions with abundant trees. So-called moist or Guinea savannas, in fact, contain large woodland areas. Compared to the grasslands in Australia and South America, the savannas of Africa include a high number of trees and tree species. Unlike the rain forest regions, the African savannas have distinct dry and rainy seasons, which influence patterns of plant growth and animal migration. In the drier zones many grasses and trees, such as baobabs and acacias, have evolved to resist fire and drought. Africa's famous large fauna, such as lions and zebras, African elephants and rhinoceroses, roam the savannas in migratory patterns that reflect the seasonal rains.

DESERT AND SEMI-DESERT

Savanna vegetation dwindles on the edges of Africa's deserts. The largest of these are the SAHARA, in the north; the KALAHARI, primarily in BOTSWANA; and the NAMIB, which lies along the southwestern coast. In the semiarid regions bordering the deserts, such as the SAHEL, immediately south of the Sahara, plants tend to be perennials and succulents, and all animal life is sparse. Many of the people living in these regions practice nomadic PASTORALISM and migrate throughout the year to find adequate water and fodder for their livestock.

Like the savannas, transitional desert regions exhibit numerous variations. The border areas of the Namib, for instance, display a far wider diversity of flora than the Sahel. In all three deserts, patches of vegetation grow around oases or sprout after occasional torrential rains. In general, biological proliferation is an "event-driven" affair in arid regions. Life happens when rain falls. Sometimes deserts receive as little as 20 mm (1 in) of rain annually, and even semiarid regions seldom get more than 500 mm (20 in). Although aridity is typically accompanied by extremely high daytime temperatures, sometimes over 40° C (104° F), at night temperatures can drop precipitously, often to near 0° C (32° F).

MEDITERRANEAN

Because of the moderating effect of the South Atlantic Ocean, a zone of Mediterranean-like conditions exists on the southern tip of Africa as well as along the Mediterranean Sea. Warm dry summers and cool rainy winters characterize both regions, though rainfall averages often resemble those of semiarid zones. Floral diversity far exceeds faunal diversity in the Mediterranean biomes. Native plant species display drought-resistant adaptations, such as long periods of dormancy and thick spiny leaves. The relatively temperate climate of these regions also supports diverse forms of agricultural production, ranging in South Africa, for example, from grain and yam farming to vineyards and orchards.

AFROMONTANE

Afromontane vegetation occurs in high-altitude areas throughout the continent, including the CAMEROON and Guinea highlands of West Africa, the Ethiopian, Kenyan, Tanzanian, and Albertine Rift highlands of East Africa, and the Drakensberg highlands in the Southeast. Vegetation in such regions often occurs in vertical belts, reflecting gradients in temperature and precipitation. Montane forests cover the lower areas, 1,200 to 2,500 m (3,900 to 8,200 ft), and at higher levels, 3,000 m (10,000 ft) and above, vegetation thins out, due to the great fluctuation between daytime and nighttime temperatures. Mountain forests in the equatorial zone are noted for their towering heath and heath-like flora. Elsewhere, evergreens predominate.

In the Afromontane biomes, windward slopes often catch precipitation that leeward slopes miss, causing mountains to develop lopsided patterns of vegetation. Precipitation often freezes at the highest elevations, as evinced by the snows of KILIMANJARO and MOUNT KENYA. Because highland regions tend to have relatively fertile soils, they are among the most intensively farmed areas of Africa.

ERIC BENNETT

Birifor

Ethnic group of West Africa; also known as Birifo and Malba.

The Birifor primarily inhabit northern GHANA, southern BURKINA FASO, and northern CÔTE D'IVOIRE. They speak a Niger-Congo language and belong to the Mole-Dagbane linguistic and cultural group. Approximately 147,000 people consider themselves Birifor.

See also LANGUAGES, AFRICAN: AN OVERVIEW.

Birom

Ethnic group of Nigeria; also known as Berum, Borom, Kibo, Gbang, Afango, and Kibyen.

The Birom primarily inhabit the Jos Plateau of NIGERIA. They speak a Niger-Congo language and consist of three distinct subgroups: Western Birom, Southern Birom, and Eastern Birom. More than 400,000 people consider themselves Birom.

See also LANGUAGES, AFRICAN: AN OVERVIEW.

Bisa

Ethnic group of Zambia.

The Bisa primarily inhabit eastern ZAMBIA. They speak a Bantu language and belong to the larger BEMBA cultural and linguistic group. Approximately 140,000 people consider themselves Bisa.

See also BANTU: DISPERSION AND SETTLEMENT; LANGUAGES, AFRICAN: AN OVERVIEW.

Bisharin

Ethnic group of Sudan and Eritrea.

The Bisharin inhabit northeastern SUDAN and neighboring ERITREA. They speak an Afro-Asiatic language and are one of the larger BEJA peoples. Some 40,000 people consider themselves Bisharin.

See also LANGUAGES, AFRICAN: AN OVERVIEW.

Bissau, Guinea-Bissau

Capital of Guinea-Bissau and major port city.

When Portuguese explorers first anchored in the Geba River estuary, on the central coast of present-day GUINEA-BISSAU, in the late 1450s, they found the Papei people living on its shores. European influence in the region remained limited, and it was Afro-Portuguese slave traders who first established a base at Bissau in the late fifteenth century, on an island that has since become a peninsula in the river. With the intensification of the transatlantic slave trade in the seventeenth century, European activity on the island increased. Its economic importance was second to CACHEU, and Portugal's hold was tenuous. In 1753, after abandoning the island for several years, the Portuguese, alarmed at French inroads into the area, returned in force to build a fortress at Bissau. The Papei occasionally attacked the Portuguese, although the Portuguese paid the Papei for the right to remain in the area.

The end of the slave trade in the early 1800s nearly destroyed Bissau's economy, but slowly the town recovered, and in 1869 it became a district capital, with a population of 573. Until the mid-twentieth century, Bissau remained a minor colonial town, subject to disease and continued resistance from the Papei. In 1941, however, Bissau became the capital of PORTUGUESE GUINEA, and Africans began to migrate to the city. In 1959 the killing of Bissau dockworkers helped spark Guinea-Bissau's war for independence, which drove refugees into the city and increased the population from 25,000 to 80,000.

Guinea-Bissau became independent in 1974, with Bissau as its capital. In 2005 the population of Bissau was 407,424, nearly 26 percent of the country's population. Bissau remains the economic hub of the country, but Guinea-Bissau's poverty has stunted Bissau's development since independence, despite the city's rapid population growth.

See also COLONIAL RULE; URBANISM AND URBANIZATION IN AFRICA.

ERIC YOUNG

Biya, Paul

1933–

President of Cameroon since 1982.

Paul Biya was born to poor parents of the BULU ethnic group in southern French CAMEROON. After his primary education, Biya briefly entered the seminary, but ultimately attended a French secondary school in YAOUNDÉ. Later he studied in France at the Sorbonne, the Institut des études politiques, and the Institut des Hautes études d'Outre Mer. Returning to Cameroon in 1962, he began serving in administrative positions in the office of the presidency. Biya held a variety of administrative and cabinet posts until President Ahmadou AHIDJO appointed him minister of state in 1970. Five years later, Ahidjo named him prime minister.

In November 1982 Ahidjo resigned and Biya became the second president of Cameroon. Ahidjo, however, retained his position of head of the sole legal party. Conflict ensued as Biya moved away from the autocratic style of his predecessor, but in 1983 Biya prevailed. He later formed a new party, seeking to further distinguish himself from Ahidjo.

Biya outlined his philosophical principles in his book *Communal Liberalism* (1987), in which he called for greater "rigor" and "moralization" in politics and society. In Biya's conception, communal liberalism would allow for personal freedom and democracy, but emphasize national unity above all. This scenario, Biya claimed, would require a strong party and state to avoid regional, ethnic, and religious fragmentation. But progress toward such goals was slow and Biya's rule was marked by authoritarianism, even after he held and narrowly won elections in 1992. In the 1997 elections Biya ran unopposed and won another seven-year term.

ERIC YOUNG

Black-Asian Relations

Because Northeast Africa is adjacent to the Middle East and Southwest Asia, contacts between black Africans and Asians in the area have occurred since prehistoric times. Although these contacts have been known, contacts between East Asians and blacks have been less frequent and not adequately known, even to academics. This is partly due to a general lack of interest in this topic and partly because of the limited availability of records. Furthermore, historical studies of Africa or the African diaspora have tended to be treated within the context of national histories or relations with Western countries. This article, therefore, will focus first on the relations chiefly between East Asians and Africans and then the former's contacts with African Americans.

BEFORE THE TWENTIETH CENTURY

Contacts between Africans and South or East Asians can be traced back to the ancient period. Archaeological and historical studies, for instance, have revealed African influence and presence in the Indus Valley civilization. After the rise and spread of Islam in the seventh century, black Muslims visited China's great cosmopolitan capital at

Changan during the Tang dynasty (618–907). Japanese envoys also visited the city during the same period. Many East Africans had their first close encounter with the Chinese when a fleet, led by the well-known Muslim navigator Zeng He (Cheng Ho), sailed from China and reached East Africa in 1418. Portuguese maritime activities in Asia since the sixteenth century created numerous opportunities for Africans and Asians to interact with each other. Africans were brought to Portuguese trading and military outposts in South Asia, Southeast Asia, China, and even to Japan. The Portuguese kidnapped some Japanese people and sold them as slaves abroad. In Macao in the sixteenth and early seventeenth century, even Africans and Malays, who themselves were slaves of Portuguese, possessed Japanese slaves who had been sold by Portuguese. In 1613 a Chinese official reportedly questioned a Portuguese counterpart about why he kept Japanese slaves while Portuguese were using black slaves on a large scale. A Dutch report, issued ten years later, says that the forts of Macao were staffed by black soldiers. Black sailors and slaves also visited East Asian ports on Dutch ships and some spent time in such ports as Melaka, Jakarta, and Nagasaki, Japan, from the seventeenth to the early nineteenth century. Around the turn of the eighteenth to the nineteenth century, African Americans began to visit East Asia for the first time on U.S. vessels and whaling ships. The first American vessels to reach Japans shore were the *Lady Washington* and the *Grace*, arriving in 1791 during Japans 250-year period of isolation. These two ships anchored off the small town of Kushimoto on the main island, but were not allowed to deal in furs and guns, as they intended. According to a Japanese record, some fifty Westerners, some twenty blacks and about five Chinese were on board the *Lady Washington*. In the mid-nineteenth century, African American contacts with Asians increased in East Asia. Many of them were on whaling ships. The *Manhattan* saved more than twenty Japanese castaways, and Pyrrhus Concer, a former slave who became a skilled helmsman on the ship, played a significant role in the development of early friendly Japan-U.S. relations in 1845, eight years before Commodore Matthew Perry forced Japan to open its door to foreign nations. A few high officials of the Japanese mission of 1860 to the United States were invited to a concert at which a blind black pianist performed. Some members of the mission had witnessed slavery in the United States and had observed the slave trade in a port on the West African coast as they made their way back to Japan. Masumizu Kuninosuke, one of the earliest Japanese emigrants to the United States, settled in Sacramento, California. In 1869 he married Carrie Wilson, the daughter of a former slave from Missouri. Their four mixed blood children thus became

the first Nisei, the second generation of Japanese Americans. The Fisk Jubilee Singers, who had made a few European tours to raise funds, sailed home in 1878 by way of Asia. During the voyage, they visited and performed in several Asian cities, including three port cities of Japan. From the 1880s, students from East Asia, mostly Chinese, Japanese, and Koreans, began to attend black educational institutions, such as Hampton Normal and Agricultural Institute (now Hampton University) and Howard University. Some Asians also studied at Oberlin College, which was the first college in the United States to admit students without respect to color. In the photograph titled Hamptons Girdle Around the World-1890, there are eight people dressed in their ethnic costumes including a Native American and students from Turkey, China, Japan, and West Africa. Howard University admitted three Chinese students in 1870 and six Koreans in 1896. A few Japanese were enrolled in the 1890s.

TWENTIETH CENTURY AND ONWARD

W. E. B. Du Bois, a staunch believer in PAN-AFRICANISM, advocated the need for cooperation and solidarity between blacks and Asians. As he foresaw in *The Souls of Black Folk* (1903), the problem of the twentieth century was indeed "the problem of the color-line—the relation of the darker to the lighter races of men in Asia and Africa, in America and the islands of the sea." Against Western colonialism, he thought, darker people in Africa and Asia were to mutually constitute global struggles to liberate themselves from white rule. Du Bois developed this theme further in the novel *Dark Princess* (1928), which concerns an international group of Asian and African revolutionaries. Du Bois himself visited several Asian countries, such as Manchukuo (a Japanese puppet state in China) and Japan, in 1936, and the People's Republic of China, in 1959, at the invitation of Mao Ze-dong. Japan's victory in the Russo-Japanese War (1904–1905) gave impetus to Japans imperialism and invasion in Asia. However, it had a strong impact not only on Western powers, but also on people of color in Asia, Africa, and the United States. The victory encouraged those who were suffering from racism and Western COLONIAL RULE. When the Japanese proposal to ban "race discrimination" at the Paris Peace Conference in 1919 was rejected, African Americans as well as people in Africa and Asia were discouraged. Between the First and the Second World Wars those eminent blacks who visited East Asia include James Weldon Johnson, secretary of the NAACP, who attended the third conference of the Institute of Pacific Relations in Kyoto in 1929; Heruy Walda-Sellase, the Ethiopian Foreign Minster who, as Emperor Haile Selassie's special envoy, stayed in Japan for two months in 1931 in order to strengthen ties between the two colored independent nations; poet Langston Hughes, who visited Japan and China on his way back from the Soviet Union in 1933; and Du Bois, who stayed a week in Manchukuo followed by two weeks in Japan giving speeches in 1936. Two World Wars had a significant impact on racial consciousness among Africans, people of the African diaspora, and Asians. The rise of Pan-Africanism and Pan-Asianism encouraged the growth of decolonization movements in the 1950s and 1960s. The Afro-Asian Conference held in 1955 in Bandung, Indonesia, on which Richard Wright reported, was to promote solidarity between Africans and Asians. Such trends, in turn, influenced African independence and the civil rights movement in the United States. At the end of the Pacific War, a large number of African-American soldiers took part in the U.S. occupation of Japan and in the Korean War (1950–1953). There were numerous contacts between black soldiers and Japanese and Korean women. Numerous children, born of these unions—especially those who were abandoned by their fathers—suffered enormous hardships, having been rejected by their American fathers and by their Asian communities. After the 1970s, new aspects of black-Asian relations emerged. Most African colonies had gained independence, but were trapped in the Cold War politics. In this context China had political and economic influence on the socialist nations in Africa. On the other hand, there was the tragic expulsion of Asians in UGANDA. In SOUTH AFRICA, black-Asian domestic relations remained tense until the APARTHEID regime collapsed in 1993. Japanese entrepreneurs, in the meanwhile, had been deeply involved in economic assistance to the old regime, enjoying "honorary white" status. In the United States, the civil rights movement ignited the social consciousness of other minority groups, including Asian Americans. As the economic status of Asian Americans rose, however, and newcomers from Asian nations increased, the conflict between the two groups intensified. An example of the conflict could be seen in the Los Angeles riot of 1992. As discussed in this essay, despite occasional tensions, blacks and Asians have actually shared a long, rich history, influencing each other, often in positive ways. At the beginning of the twenty-first century, interactions between Africans or those of African descent and Asians are seen more than ever in the global arena. For this reason, historical studies, as well as studies on current issues in black-Asian relations, become increasingly important. They also provide Africana studies with new and global perspectives.

BIBLIOGRAPHY

Furukawa, Hiromi and Furukawa Tetsushi. *Japanese and African Americans: Historical Aspects of their Relations.* Akashi Shoten, 2004.

Harris, Joseph E. *The African Presence in Asia: Consequences of the East African Slave Trade.* Northwestern University Press, 1971.

Kearney, Reginald. *African American Views of the Japanese: Solidarity or Sedition?* State University of New York Press, 1998.

Snow, Philip. *The Star Raft: Chinas Encounter with Africa.* Weidenfeld and Nicolson, 1988.

FURUKAWA TETSUSHI

Black Consciousness in Africa
Ideology stressing black self-reliance in the fight against apartheid in South Africa.

Unlike more established antiapartheid groups, such as the AFRICAN NATIONAL CONGRESS (ANC), the SOUTH AFRICAN COMMUNIST PARTY (SACP), or the PAN-AFRICANIST CONGRESS (PAC), South Africa's BLACK CONSCIOUSNESS Movement (BCM) was not a single party. It was instead a philosophy, both political and intellectual, that spawned a loose federation of organizations. Drawing inspiration from independence movements throughout Africa, the postcolonial philosophy of négritude, and the Black Power Movement in the United States, Black Consciousness was one of the more powerful influences in the 1976 SOWETO uprisings and in subsequent resistance to SOUTH AFRICA's apartheid system.

For their purposes, Black Consciousness leaders defined *black* to include not only black Africans but also people of Indian or *Coloured* descent. "The way to the future," BCM leader Barney Pityana wrote, "is not through a directionless multiracialism but through a positive unilateral approach." BCM leaders believed that only by working without help from white liberals would black people escape the "slave mentality" spawned by white domination, and achieve the pride and dignity they would ultimately need to end white minority rule. In addition, they called for an economy based on *black communalism*, in which private enterprise would coexist with state-sponsored communal villages.

The Black Consciousness Movement has its roots in the South African Student Organisation (SASO), which was founded in 1968 by Pityana, Steve BIKO, and others. Frustrated by what they saw as the paternalism of white liberals in the National Union of South African Students, these black students sought a movement that would unite only those directly oppressed by apartheid. Although most previous racially exclusive student groups had failed, SASO, which drew support and publicity from the University Christian Movement (itself founded by black students in 1967), sought "not black visibility but real black participation."

To spread its message, SASO established Formation Schools that provided leadership training seminars for black students and solicited their ideas. The avoidance of centralized power or rigid hierarchies was an important part of SASO's philosophy, and no person served more than one year as the organization's president. Nevertheless, Biko was clearly its most important leader. After his term as president, he stayed on as publicity director, speaking and writing about Black Consciousness until his death in 1977 at the hands of South African police.

Many other groups incorporated Black Consciousness into their work. The South African Students' Movement (SASM), founded in Soweto in 1968, operated independently of SASO but shared many of its principles. Black Community Programmes, an organization Biko helped to run, promoted skills training and self-esteem among black teenagers. In 1972 SASO formed the Black Peoples' Convention (BPC) to spread Black Consciousness thinking beyond the student population. The Black Allied Workers' Union, established following the DURBAN strikes of 1972–1973, rejected traditional movement tactics in favor of BCM-inspired training.

But students—including those in secondary school—remained the most active proponents of Black Consciousness, sometimes with tragic consequences. In 1976 police threw tear gas and then opened fire on an SASM-organized demonstration in Soweto against laws mandating teaching in Afrikaans, then considered the language of the white oppressor; three days of rioting followed. Biko, already banned from political action, was arrested repeatedly after the Soweto uprisings and murdered while in police custody in September 1977. Some historians attribute the government's harsh treatment of Biko to its fears about planned cooperation between the BPC and the historically more moderate ANC. Regardless, a month later the South African government banned all BCM-related groups. Although there were attempts to revive the Black Consciousness Movement in exile, internal disagreements doomed such efforts to failure.

See also ANTIAPARTHEID MOVEMENT; APARTHEID; INDIAN COMMUNITIES IN AFRICA.

BIBLIOGRAPHY

Pityana, N. Barney, et al., eds. Bounds of Possibility: The Legacy of Steve Biko & Black Consciousness. Zed Books, 1992.

Woods, Donald. Biko. Henry Holt, 1991.

KATE TUTTLE

Black Orpheus

Literary magazine based in Nigeria.

More than just a periodical, the literary magazine Black Orpheus was a powerful catalyst for artistic awakening throughout West Africa. While the journal Présence Africaine had provided a forum for Francophone Africans since 1947, before Black Orpheus there was almost no acknowledgment of, or market for, literature and the arts in English-speaking West Africa. Founded in 1957 by a German expatriate, Ulli Beier, Black Orpheus

introduced and helped launch the careers of many artists and writers, including Wole SOYINKA, John Pepper CLARK, Gabriel Okara, Dennis BRUTUS, Ama Ata AIDOO, Alex LA GUMA, and Kofi AWOONOR. In addition, Black Orpheus published in English translation several Francophone African writers, such as Aimé CÉSAIRE and Léopold SENGHOR, and the works of visual artists including Valente Malagatana and Ibraham Salahi.

Beier had studied and taught English literature in London before accepting a teaching position in NIGERIA in 1950. There, he often had his Nigerian students compare themes in English texts with traditional YORUBA folk literature. His growing interest in African writers led him to attend the 1956 World Congress of Black Writers in Paris, where he met German scholar Jahnheinz Jahn. Together, they began planning a magazine devoted to new African literature. With support from the Nigerian ministry of education (later augmented by grants from institutions such as the Rockefeller Foundation), they were able to publish their first issue in September 1957.

In its first issue, Black Orpheus proclaimed its editorial mission: to publish works of fiction, poetry, and visual art by Anglophone Africans; to provide English translations of French African works; and to publish works by African American writers. Beier's editorial emphasized that African writers should have African readers—and vice versa. For too long, he wrote, African artists "[have had to] turn to Europe for criticism and encouragement," while African readers could "leave ... school with a thorough knowledge of English literature, but without ever having heard of such great black writers as Léopold Sedar Senghor or Aimé Césaire." Under Beier, Black Orpheus was known for its leanings toward primitivism in its visual arts and social realism in its fiction.

Increasingly frustrated by contentious debates within the African literary world, Beier resigned in 1965. John Pepper Clark and Abiola Irele assumed the editorship of Black Orpheus. An essay by Clark, "The Legacy of Caliban," heralded the magazine's new direction. It emphatically rejected the historic value of pleasing European audiences and critics. According to the writer Peter Benson, Black Orpheus had reached its golden age; the magazine was "controversial, scholarly, imaginative, independent, broad in scope, and influential." Over the next ten years, however, editorial and economic tensions forced Black Orpheus through a series of different editors. There was a brief sponsorship by the University of LAGOS before the eventual demise of the magazine in 1975.

BIBLIOGRAPHY

Benson, Peter. Black Orpheus, Transition, and Modern Cultural Awakening in Africa. University of California Press, 1986.

KATE TUTTLE

Blondy, Alpha

1953–

Popular African reggae singer.

With his eleven albums and worldwide tours, Alpha Blondy has brought an African flavor to the Jamaican-born musical genre of reggae. Although critics admit that Blondy has not yet fulfilled his early goal of becoming the next Bob Marley (probably the best-known reggae artist), they do hail the CÔTE D'IVOIRE singer's passionate lyrics and charismatic performances.

The man born Seydou Kone in Dimbokro, Côte d'Ivoire, was renamed Blondy, a variation on the Dioula word for bandit, by his grandmother, who raised him. Though little is known of his childhood, Blondy says he chose his new first name, Alpha, himself, and that he learned French from reading the Bible (though his grandmother also introduced him to the Muslim holy book, the Qur'an ([Koran]). Expelled from school, reportedly for forming his first reggae band, the Atomic Vibrations, Blondy eventually moved to New York City. There he studied and worked, and continued to learn about reggae, often performing Bob Marley songs at Harlem nightclubs.

When he returned to the Côte d'Ivoire, Blondy began to make a name for himself as one of the boldest singers around, dealing with such controversial subjects as police brutality and race relations. His first album, *Jah Glory* (1983), was a hit throughout West Africa, and with later releases Blondy, who sings in French, English, and Dioula, extended his popularity worldwide. The year 1996 saw the release of a greatest hits album and a new recording of original work. In 2003 Blondy was nominated for a Grammy Award for Best Reggae Album for *Merci*. A number of new albums and a tireless slate of touring keeps Blondy busy. With his insistence on positive, loving images (he says his songs "are all really love songs") and his commitment to social justice, Alpha Blondy is among the world's most popular reggae performers, and one of Africa's biggest recording stars.

KATE TUTTLE

Blue Nile

One of two main tributaries of the Nile River, which originates in Ethiopia.

Known as the Abay (or Abbay or Abbai) in Amharic and as al-Bahr al-Azraq in Arabic, the Blue Nile is purported to originate in a spring in the Ethiopian highlands, a holy site of the ETHIOPIAN ORTHODOX CHURCH. From this spring, the Little Abay descends into Lake Tana. The Abay, or Blue Nile, plunges down the Tis Isat waterfall a short distance below Lake Tana. Just over 350 km (220 mi) farther south, it bends west into the Blue Nile Gorge, which reaches depths of more than 1,000 m (about 3,300

ft). Eventually, it bends northwest into SUDAN, where it joins the White Nile at KHARTOUM to form the NILE RIVER proper. The river's complete course stretches roughly 1,370 km (850 mi). During the flood season (June to September) the Blue Nile provides up to 85 percent of the Nile's total volume, though during the dry season (October to May) the Blue Nile contributes less than 20 percent of the Nile's volume.

Though the Blue Nile is navigable only within Sudan, its water is vital to agriculture for the generation of hydroelectricity. Historically, it also carried nutrient-rich silt from the Ethiopian highlands to Sudan and EGYPT during floods. In 1925 the British completed construction of the Sannar Dam on the Blue Nile to provide water for the Gezira scheme in Sudan, now one of the world's largest irrigation projects, to cultivate cotton for the mills of Lancashire, England. Today, the Rusayris and Sannar Dams generate electricity and together supply enough water to irrigate about 400,000 hectares (about one million acres). The Blue Nile has the potential to generate at least enough electricity for each home in Sudan and Egypt.

Disagreements have arisen between nations over the waters of the Blue Nile. A 1929 agreement with ETHIOPIA negotiated by Egypt's British administration effectively gave Egypt the right to veto any projects on the Blue Nile that affected its access to water. This agreement held until Egypt and Sudan divided the water rights to the Blue Nile among themselves in a 1959 treaty, with most of the water apportioned to Egypt and none to Ethiopia. Ethiopia opposed the treaty, but could do little to assert its rights during more than two decades of civil conflict, drought, and famine.

Because of Ethiopia's poverty and persistent internal strife, Egypt and Sudan have reaped most of the benefits of the Blue Nile's water. During the 1990s, however, Ethiopia began to exploit the river with more than 200 small dams for irrigation and hydroelectricity. Because of Egypt's dependence on water from the Blue Nile, it has threatened war with Ethiopia if Ethiopia invests in larger projects that interfere with Egypt's claims to the Blue Nile's water. This places the Ethiopian government in a delicate situation: Ethiopia expects its population to double in twenty years and desperately needs to develop irrigation and hydroelectric projects to emerge from more than twenty years of devastation. By the late 1990s, rhetoric on both sides had turned toward talk of cooperation, but the threat of violence remains. Interestingly enough, the entire course of the waterway was not successfully navigated until 2004.

See also HUNGER AND FAMINE.

BIBLIOGRAPHY

Fruzzetti, Lina. *Culture and Change along the Blue Nile: Courts, Markets, and Strategies for Development.* Westview Press, 1990.

Wondimneh, Tilahun. *Egypts Imperial Aspirations over Lake Tana and the Blue Nile.* Addis Ababa University, 1979.

ROBERT FAY

Board Games

History of board games in Africa.

Africa is associated with two groups of board games, mancala and draughts. Chess is the first board game on record that has been connected to Africa. In Arab literature, Sa'id bin Jubayr—a scholar, rebel leader, and freed slave from Africa—is said to have played blindfold chess in sixth-century Iraq. Chess reached few Africans on the continent; only ETHIOPIA became part of the early Islamic conquest and still plays its own version of the game. Chess continued north of the SAHARA and conquered Europe instead.

In contrast, mancala games are known to have occupied most parts of Africa since early times. Archaeological finds include boards dating back to the sixth century and earlier, but their use is unrecorded. Written records of European travelers mention mancala rules in the late seventeenth century. Around this time the Atlantic slave trade took mancala to the Caribbean and parts of South America, where it can still be found.

Mancala—also spelled Mankala or Manqala—refers to a group of board games played on rows of holes using a proportionate number of counters. During the game the players—usually two or two teams—take turns in distributing counters around the board. The counters, commonly seeds, shells, or stones, are of equal value and may change ownership during the game. In most cases players start with the contents of a hole at their side of the board. In all mancala variations these contents may be distributed one by one in consecutive holes.

The game of bao, a mancala game that is played on the SWAHILI COAST, has been played at least since the beginning of the nineteenth century at the championship level. It is the most complex mancala game, played on four rows of eight holes with two enlarged holes in the center, and requires intricate rules. The game of wari—also called awèlè, oware, or awari—is dominant in West Africa and the Caribbean, where it has been played at least since the late nineteenth century. This game requires two rows of six holes and has also developed into a championship game. Bao and wari are only two examples of a wide range of mancala games.

Some mancala games are played exclusively by men or during particular ceremonies. Such ceremonies or rituals include weddings, funerals, divination, or ceremonies involving royalty. Certain sculptured boards became prestige gifts and were never intended or used for play. There appears to be no general purpose of mancala other than entertainment, nor are mancala games exclusively African. Mancala games are common across Asia and Africa, although how they arrived there is yet to be determined.

In the nineteenth century draughts games were introduced to Africa. The first variation of draughts dates from around 1500 C.E. and became popular in Great Britain, France, and Central Europe. The British continued to play this version of draughts into the twentieth century. Their game is now referred to as Anglo-Saxon draughts or checkers, as it is known in the United States. The game is characterized by its sixty-four black and white squares with twelve white and twelve black draughtsmen, or checkers, on the board.

In France, the Anglo-Saxon game was replaced, in the eighteenth century, by so-called Polish draughts which had developed in the Netherlands. The playing board counted one hundred black and white squares with twenty pieces on each side. This game of Polish or continental draughts would compete with Anglo-Saxon draughts in the subsequent colonization of the world. The Italians, who had their own version (which was also played on sixty-four squares), took their game to Ethiopia, where it is still played.

From the 1890s onward, the documented history of African draughts has been a history of African players reaching the European continent. The international organization of draughts after World War II also led to the formation of the Confédération Africaine du Jeu de Dames, which organized the World Championships in BAMAKO, MALI in 1980, later followed by DAKAR, SENEGAL in 1984, and Paramaribo, Surinam in 1988. In 1962, Baba Sy from Senegal became the first African world champion, and (grand) masters are now common in several West African countries.

The Anglo-Saxon game checkers had been dominated by Scottish, English, and later American players. Since 1991 Ronald 'Suki' King from Barbados has been world champion in one variation, and in 1994 in the second variation of the Anglo-Saxon game. His success has continued into the twenty-first century.

Other board games in Africa may have reached local fame, such as fanorona in MADAGASCAR, but according to the limited data, they did not travel the continent. Instead, mancala and draughts dominate the minds of African players and those who study African board games.

BIBLIOGRAPHY

Beek, W. E. A. van. *The Fascinating World of Draughts: 50 Years World Draughts Federation.* Shaker Publishing B.V., 1997.

Murray, H. J. R. *A History of Board Games other than Chess.* Oxford University Press, 1952.

Murray, H. J. R. *A History of Chess*, Oxford University Press, 1913.

Stoep, A van der. *A History of Draughts*. Rockanje, 1984.

Voogt, A.J. de. *Mancala Board Games*. British Museum Press, 1997.

A. J. DE VOOGT

Bobo

Ethnic group living predominantly in southern Burkina Faso.

The Bobo were among the earliest settlers of the semiarid savanna region of southwestern BURKINA FASO (formerly Upper Volta). Similarities between the Bobo language and MANDE languages spoken in southern MALI provide linguistic support for the Bobo's oral traditions, which claim that their ancestors migrated from "Mande country," probably between the twelfth and fourteenth centuries C.E. These ancestors are believed to have first founded a village called Tinima, on the plateau east of the Houet River. Other early migrants to the area settled alongside the river, on the site now occupied by the city of BOBO-DIOULASSO. Their descendants established settlements to the north, east, and west of this site.

In the past the Bobo referred to themselves as the sansan, or "the cultivating people." Merchant caravans traveled through Bobo country from at least the sixteenth century onward, but the Bobo themselves participated in the long-distance commerce only peripherally, primarily as suppliers of food for the caravans. The Bobo rejected as well the merchants' Islamic teachings, and instead organized their rituals of ancestor worship around village shrines.

The precolonial political organization of the Bobo was also largely village based. Village elders presided over matters of marriage and inheritance, both of which were (and to a certain extent still are) shaped by the Bobo's *dual descent* kinship system. Rights to land, in other words, are traditionally passed patrilineally (from father to son) while moveable forms of property, such as cattle or cooking pots, were passed matrilineally (from maternal uncle to son, or mother to daughter).

The lack of a centralized state made the Bobo vulnerable to slave raids and conquest in the eighteenth century, especially after the rise of the Dioula KONG empire in the northern part of modern-day CÔTE D'IVOIRE. Many Bobo communities defended themselves by moving closer together; the large size, dense settlement, and fortified housing of many older Bobo villages are architectural legacies of the slave era.

When the French began their conquest of the southern Volta region in the late nineteenth century, they assumed the Bobo peasants were the subjects of the resident Dioula traders. During the early years of COLONIAL RULE, however, unrest in Bobo country demonstrated the peasants' lack of respect for the Dioula "chiefs" appointed to collect taxes and recruit labor. This period also saw rapid cultural changes: the Catholic mission in Bobo-Dioulasso found many converts in Bobo villages just outside the city, while members of the Zara clan, who had already distinguished themselves by their participation in trade and warfare, converted to Islam. After forced labor was abolished in 1946, many Bobo villagers applied their farming skills to commercial crops such as cotton, maize, and vegetables.

Today most rural Bobo continue to earn their livelihoods from farming, often combined with seasonal migrant labor, small-scale trade, or, in the case of women, millet beer-brewing. Many Bobo villages are themselves home to MOSSI migrants from drought-prone provinces to the north. Like most other ethnic groups in Burkina Faso, the Bobo are not an organized force in national politics, but they do play an important role in the municipal government, business, and church communities of Bobo-Dioulasso. Though population estimates vary widely, it is commonly believed that more than 100,000 people consider themselves Bobo.

See also CHRISTIANITY: MISSIONARIES IN AFRICA; ISLAM AND TRADITION: AN INTERPRETATION; KINSHIP AND DESCENT IN AFRICA; SLAVERY IN AFRICA.

BIBLIOGRAPHY

Le Moal, Guy. *Les Bobo: Nature et fonction des masques*. ORSTOM, 1980.

Saul, Mahir. "Matrilineal inheritance and Post-Colonial Prosperity in Southern Bobo Country." *Man* 27 no. 2, 1992.

SUSANNE FREIDBERG

Bobo-Dioulasso, Burkina Faso

Second largest city in Burkino Faso.

The city of Bobo-Dioulasso is located in one of the greener areas of BURKINA FASO, and has long benefited from the fertility of the surrounding countryside. According to the legends of the BOBO people, their ancestors migrated from present-day Mali sometime between the twelfth and fourteenth centuries C.E. and became the first inhabitants of what Bobo folk songs call "the plateau of abundance" in the southern Volta region. Over the following centuries, long-distance traders settled among the Bobo peasants on this plateau and established a community known as Sya on the banks of the Houet River. Located at the crossroads of trans-Saharan and east-west trade routes, Sya was a lively market town by the time European colonization began in the late nineteenth century. French troops, facing fierce resistance from Sya's Zara warriors, conquered the town in 1895. They renamed it Bobo-Dioulasso (in Dioula, "house of the Bobo and the Dioula") and proceeded to build an administrative post and military camp.

In 1934 the completion of a rail line to the port city of ABIDJAN in CÔTE D'IVOIRE attracted French trading firms to Bobo-Dioulasso and spurred increased exports of cotton and food crops, requisitioned from the city's hinterland. Thousands of West African recruits passed through the Bobo-Dioulasso military camp during World War II; in the postwar period, many veterans returned to the city to invest their pensions in trade or agriculture. A palatial central market, built in 1951, testified to the region's booming commerce; wide shady streets radiating out from the city center delineated distinctive neighborhoods, ranging from the labyrinthine old town of Koko to the modern working-class quarter of Accartville. In the years leading up to independence, Bobo-Dioulasso became a stronghold for the RASSEMBLEMENT DÉMOCRATIQUE AFRICAIN (RDA), an anticolonial movement initially backed by the French Communist Party.

OUAGADOUGOU became the national capital of Upper Volta at independence in 1960. As industry and trade as well as government services increasingly concentrated in the capital, Bobo-Dioulasso's economy and infrastructure gradually deteriorated. In the early 1990s, structural adjustment and austerity measures brought factory closures and layoffs, forcing more and more Bobolais into small-scale trade. Yet, despite widespread economic hardship, Bobo-Dioulasso's multiethnic population (435,543 in 2006) supports thriving nightclub, cinema, and drumming scenes. Ringed by gardens and orchards that provision the city's renowned produce markets, Bobo-Dioulasso is a popular vacation destination for West Africans and Europeans alike.

BIBLIOGRAPHY

Roth, Claudia. La séparation des sexes chez les Zara au Burkina Faso. L'Harmattan, 1996.

SUSANNE FREIDBERG

Boganda, Barthélemy

1910–1959

Nationalist leader and hero of the Central African Republic.

Born into a family of subsistence farmers, Barthélemy Boganda attended Catholic mission schools and seminaries in BRAZZAVILLE and YAOUNDÉ. In 1938 he became the first Oubanguian Catholic priest. Sponsored by Catholic missionaries, Boganda was elected to the French National Assembly in 1946. But he soon realized the limits of his influence in France, and left the priesthood and returned to Oubangui-Chari to organize a grassroots movement of small African producers to oppose French colonialism. In 1949 he founded the Movement for the Social Evolution of Black Africa, a quasi-religious political party.

After his arrest for "endangering the peace" and detention for intervening in a local market dispute in 1951,

Boganda became a messianic folk hero and the leading nationalist. The French realized that opposing Boganda would be dangerous and sought to accommodate him. In 1956 Boganda agreed to European representation on election lists in exchange for the financial support of French business leaders. In 1958, with the rush toward independence in much of Francophone Africa, Boganda cautioned that independence for landlocked Oubangui-Chari lacked economic viability. Instead, he called for the federation of Oubangui-Chari with an independent United States of Latin Africa, including all of French Equatorial Africa as well as adjacent Belgian and Portuguese possessions. Such a federation proved unrealistic, however, and Boganda later accepted a constitution covering only Oubangui-Chari as the CENTRAL AFRICAN REPUBLIC (CAR). Once called the "most capable of equatorial political men," Boganda was poised to become the first president of the independent CAR when he was killed in a mysterious plane crash in 1959, just prior to legislative elections. He was succeeded by his close confidant David DACKO.

BIBLIOGRAPHY

Boganda, Barthélemy. Ecrits et discours: Barthélemy Boganda. Harmattan, 1995.

Kalck, Pierre. Barthélemy Boganda, 1910–1959: Elu de Dieu et des Centrafricains. Editions Sepia, 1995.

ERIC YOUNG

Bokassa, Jean-Bédel

1921–1996

Self-proclaimed marshal, emperor, and "apostle" of the Central African Empire, "president-for-life" from 1966 to 1979, and reputed cannibal.

A career soldier who had endured a tragic childhood, Jean-Bédel Bokassa ruled the impoverished Central African Republic with brutal repression, used its revenues for his personal enrichment, and crowned himself emperor. He committed barbarities that caused an international outcry and led to his removal from power.

When Bokassa was six years old, his father, a village chief of the Mbaka people, was murdered. Bokassa became an orphan a week later, when his mother committed suicide. Missionaries raised him until age eighteen when, at the outbreak of World War II, Bokassa joined the French Colonial Army. He participated in the 1944 landings in Provence and later served in Indochina and Algeria, attaining the rank of captain and earning the Legion d'Honneur and the Croix de Guerre. In 1960, after Oubangui-Chari became the independent Central African Republic, Bokassa helped create its army and, in 1964, was given the rank of colonel by President David DACKO, a cousin, who made him the army chief of staff.

In a coup d'état in 1965, Bokassa seized power from Dacko. Over the next eleven years Bokassa governed the republic autocratically with a series of arbitrary decrees and periodic cabinet shuffles, all of which increased his power. Bokassa received military support from France, on which the Central African Republic remained economically dependent. In 1972 Bokassa proclaimed himself president-for-life with the rank of marshal. He ordered the torture and execution of political opponents. Meanwhile, in order to support his lavish lifestyle, he plundered the national economy that was sustained by diamond and uranium exports.

In 1976 Bokassa proclaimed himself Emperor Bokassa I, and renamed the country the Central African Empire. The coronation during the following year, complete with a diamond-studded crown, reportedly cost $200 million, which was largely underwritten by France. He used the occasion to crown his wife empress and to ennoble family members. Bokassa's reign was brief. In 1979, regulations forcing students to purchase school uniforms from a factory owned by the emperor's wife sparked violent demonstrations in the capital. Bokassa's car was stoned and he reacted brutally. Over one hundred imprisoned children, aged eight to sixteen, were massacred. Courts later concluded that Bokassa was personally involved in the killings. Other reports contended that the emperor did not participate directly, but that he later ate some of the children. He claimed innocence, contending that he was a Christian and had a large family himself (fifty-five children reared by seventeen wives). However, it was the International Year of the Child, and foreign governments reacted with sanctions. In September 1979 French troops reinstalled Dacko as president while Bokassa was abroad.

In 1986, after seven years in exile in CÔTE D'IVOIRE and France, during which time he was condemned to death in absentia, Bokassa returned to the Central African Republic. Promptly arrested, Bokassa was sentenced again to death on charges of murder, although he was acquitted of charges of cannibalism. President André Kolingba later pardoned the aging Bokassa and released him from prison in 1993. He died in 1996 at age seventy-five. He received a state funeral, and the state radio described him as "illustrious."

ERIC YOUNG

Bokyi

Ethnic group of West Africa, also known as Boki and Nki.
The Bokyi primarily inhabit Cross River State, NIGERIA and western CAMEROON. They speak a Niger-Congo language and belong to the IBIBIO cultural and linguistic cluster. More than 200,000 people consider themselves Bokyi.

See also LANGUAGES, AFRICAN: AN OVERVIEW.

Bondei

Ethnic group of Tanzania.
The Bondei primarily inhabit northeastern TANZANIA between the Usambara Mountains and the coast. They speak a Bantu language and are closely related to the SHAMBAA people. According to a 2004 estimate, some 124,000 people consider themselves Bondei.

See also BANTU: DISPERSION AND SETTLEMENT.

Bongo

Ethnic group of East Africa, also known as Dor.
The Bongo primarily inhabit northwestern UGANDA and southern SUDAN on the eastern shores of the Albert Nile. They speak a Nilo-Saharan language and belong to the MADI cultural and linguistic group. Estimates of the number of Bongo people vary widely, though the number is usually placed at around 90,000.

See also LANGUAGES, AFRICAN: AN OVERVIEW; NILE RIVER.

Bongo, Omar (Albert-Bernard)
1935–2009
President of Gabon since 1967.
Born in the village of Lewaï in southeastern GABON, Albert-Bernard Bongo was educated in BRAZZAVILLE, REPUBLIC OF THE CONGO. He served in the French air force from 1958 to 1960, the year Gabon became independent of French COLONIAL RULE. Bongo joined the Gabon ministry of foreign affairs in 1960, and in 1962 he was named assistant director of President Léon MBA's cabinet. Later Bongo became his chief of staff and his defense minister. In 1966 Mba, who was terminally ill, created the office of vice president to ensure Bongo's succession. Bongo took office as vice president in 1967. Mba died that same year, and Bongo assumed the presidency.

In 1968 Bongo declared Gabon a single-party state, assuming the post of secretary general of the newly created Gabonese Democratic Party. The sole candidate, Bongo swept the 1973 and 1979 presidential elections. In 1973 Bongo announced his conversion to Islam, changing his first name to Omar. Although Bongo was relatively permissive of dissent within the party, he was less tolerant of outside agitators, as evidenced by his 1982 decision to impose harsh sentences on members of a nonviolent opposition protest group. Bongo encouraged foreign investment, and the stability of the government, combined with Gabon's mineral wealth (primarily petroleum and uranium), succeeded in attracting significant amounts of assistance and investment, particularly from France. Bongo has been accused of financial extravagance, including driving the country into debt in preparation for the 1977 ORGANIZATION OF AFRICAN UNITY (OAU) conference held in Gabon; constructing the massive Trans-Gabon rail system; and building a presidential palace at an estimated cost of $30 million.

In response to a coup plot discovered among the presidential guard in 1989, Bongo agreed to enact sweeping reforms, including the creation of a national senate, decentralization of the budgetary process, and freedom of assembly and press. Bongo officially legalized opposition parties in 1991 and created a transitional government, the Gabonese Social Democratic Grouping. This government oversaw the introduction of a new constitution and the implementation of elections in 1993. Bongo won the elections in 1993 and again in 1998, despite accusations from opposition leaders that the 1998 election process was fraudulent.

See also ISLAM IN AFRICA.

ERIC YOUNG

Book of the Dead
Refers to a large collection of funerary texts of various dates, containing magical formulas, hymns, and prayers believed by the ancient Egyptians to guide and protect the soul (Ka) in its journey into the region of the dead (Amenti).

Egyptians believed that the knowledge of these texts enabled the soul to ward off demons attempting to impede its progress, and to pass the tests set by the forty-two judges in the hall of Osiris, god of the underworld. These texts also indicated that happiness in the afterlife was dependent on the deceased's having led a virtuous life on earth. The earliest religious (funerary) texts known were found cut in hieroglyphs on the walls inside the pyramids of the kings of the Fifth and Sixth Dynasties of the Old Kingdom; these became known as the Pyramid Texts. A famous example is found in the pyramid of Unas (reigned about 2428–2407 B.C.E.), the last king of the Fifth Dynasty. In the first Intermediate Period and in the Middle Kingdom, private individuals had these texts painted on coffins, from which the alternate name Coffin Texts is derived. By the Eighteenth Dynasty the texts were inscribed on papyri placed in the mummy case; these papyri were frequently from 15 to 30 m (50 to 100 ft) long and illustrated in color. This vast collection of mortuary texts has survived in three critical revisions, or recensions: the Heliopolitan Recension, edited by the priests of the College of Anu (Heliopolis), and containing texts in use between the Fifth and the Twelfth Dynasties; the Theban Recension, used from the Eighteenth to the Twenty-second Dynasties; and the Saite Recension, used from the Twenty-sixth Dynasty, about 600 B.C.E., probably to the end of the Ptolemies, 31 B.C.E. The title "Book of the Dead" is misleading; the texts do not form a single connected work and do not belong to one period. Egyptologists have usually given this title to the

last two recensions. Translations of some sections (chapters) were made under various titles; Sir E. A. Wallis Budge made one celebrated English translation of the *Book of the Dead* in 1895.

See also EGYPT, ANCIENT KINGDOM OF.

Bophuthatswana
Former bantustan (black homeland) in South Africa; one of ten territories assigned to the black majority population in the 1950s as part of the South African government's policy of apartheid (racial segregation).

Covering a total area of 44,000 sq km (16,988 sq mi), Bophuthatswana consisted of seven fragments of land scattered throughout Orange Free State, Cape Province, and Transvaal, which were three of the four provinces in SOUTH AFRICA at that time. Bophuthatswana, which means "that which binds the Tswana together," was established as a so-called homeland for the TSWANA people, although it had significant Pedi, Basotho, Shangaan, and Zulu minorities. Bophuthatswana's capital was Mmabatho. The territory also included the towns of Mafikeng, Onverwacht, Phalaborwa, Phuthaditjhaba, Sun City, and Thaba Nchu. In 1994, when South Africa was divided into nine new provinces, most of Bophuthatswana was incorporated into NORTH-WEST PROVINCE; the remaining fragment was included in the province of FREE STATE.

Tswana peoples lived in the region from about the thirteenth or fourteenth century C.E., but they lost most of their land in the nineteenth century to AFRIKANER and British conquest. Shortly after the Union of South Africa (later the Republic of South Africa) was formed in 1910, the white leaders of South Africa began to implement national policies of racial segregation. These policies culminated in the 1950s when the government divided the black majority according to ethnic identity and defined them as citizens of separate ethnic homelands, or bantustans.

The Bantu Homelands Constitution Act of 1971 gave the South African president the power to establish constitutions and legislative assemblies for any of the bantustans. Once a bantustan had a homeland legislature and an executive council and had held a general election, it was considered to be self-governing. Its administrative body could collect taxes and pass laws relating to certain areas, such as schools, hospitals, and transportation, but all of these laws still required the approval of the South African president. The South African government also retained final control over the bantustan's finances. Bophuthatswana was granted self-governing status in 1972.

Five years later Bophuthatswana became the second of the bantustans to achieve so-called independence. In theory, independent bantustans were given complete control over their internal affairs and foreign relations. Some did repeal racially discriminatory laws, but the independence of these bantustans was limited by the fact that the South African government still supplied most of the funding for their budgets and contributed many key civil servants and army officers to the bantustan administrations. Bophuthatswana generated some income through platinum mines, but only 6.6 percent of its land could be farmed, and most citizens of Bophuthatswana continued to seek jobs in other parts of South Africa. No other country besides South Africa recognized the bantustan as an independent country, because to do so implied acceptance of the APARTHEID system.

Although approximately 2.5 million people were defined as citizens of Bophuthatswana, about half that number lived outside the borders of the bantustan. Few black people supported the bantustan system because it meant they were considered primarily citizens of the bantustans instead of citizens of South Africa, even if they had never lived within the bantustans. When a bantustan chose to become independent, its citizens lost their South African citizenship completely. In spite of popular opposition, some black politicians accepted the bantustan system, and the South African government gradually transferred political power to those individuals.

Periodic elections were held in Bophuthatswana, but political power rested in the hands of one party, the Bophuthatswana Democratic Party, founded in 1974. The leader of that party, Lucas Mangope, became president of Bophuthatswana in 1977. In 1988 a military coup staged by members of the Bophuthatswana Defense Force, the bantustan's small army, attempted to overthrow Mangope. The South African government sent in security forces that intervened and restored Mangope to power. He remained president until 1994. On March 7, 1994, Mangope declared that his homeland would not take part in South Africa's first multiracial elections because he opposed the interim constitution that would dissolve the bantustans. The constitution, negotiated by the AFRICAN NATIONAL CONGRESS (ANC) and the former South African government, was scheduled to go into effect at the time of the April 1994 elections. Citizens of Bophuthatswana, eager to vote in these elections, protested Mangope's boycott, and armed white extremists, who opposed the changes occurring in South Africa, came to assist Mangope. Riots broke out and continued for four days, until Mangope agreed to allow participation in the elections. The next day, however, Mangope once again reversed his decision. He was then deposed by the South African government, acting in conjunction with the ANC and the Transitional Executive Council, which was overseeing progress toward the national elections. After the April 1994 elections, Bophuthatswana, along with the other bantustans, was reintegrated into a unified South Africa.

Boran

Ethnic group of East Africa and the Horn of Africa; also known as the Borana.

The Boran primarily inhabit southern ETHIOPIA, northern KENYA, and neighboring southwestern SOMALIA. They speak an Afro-Asiatic language and are one of the OROMO peoples. Approximately 220,000 people consider themselves Boran.

See also LANGUAGES, AFRICAN: AN OVERVIEW.

Bororo

Ethnic group of west Central Africa, also known as the Wodaabe.

The Bororo primarily inhabit the CENTRAL AFRICAN REPUBLIC, CAMEROON, NIGER, NIGERIA, and CHAD. They speak Fulani, a Niger-Congo language, and are a subgroup of the FULANI people. Approximately 200,000 people consider themselves Bororo.

See also LANGUAGES, AFRICAN: AN OVERVIEW.

Botha, Pieter Willem
1916–2006
Afrikaner nationalist, prime minister, and state president of South Africa, who devoted much of his career to upholding apartheid.

Pieter Willem Botha was raised in a militantly nationalistic AFRIKANER family in the EASTERN CAPE. His mother's first husband was killed in the Boer War (1899–1902), in which his father also fought for the Boers. At an early age Botha himself became an Afrikaner nationalist, leaving the University of Orange Free State Law School in 1935 to help found the NATIONAL PARTY. A year later he became public information officer for the party and served on the Sauer Commission, the agency that helped to formulate the National Party's racial program.

In 1948 Botha proved instrumental in helping D. F. Malan and the National Party come to power. That year he won a seat in Parliament, representing the Eastern Cape district of George. As a reward for party loyalty, Botha was appointed to a series of cabinet positions in the apartheid-era governments of Hendrik VERWOERD and Balthazar Johannes VORSTER, including deputy minister of the interior, minister of Coloured affairs, and minister of public works and housing. In these positions Botha maintained allegiance to the government's policies of racial segregation.

In 1966 "P. W." Botha, as he had become known, was appointed defense minister. He used this position to build one of the most formidable military machines in southern Africa. Under Botha the South African Defense Forces (SADF) became an imposing threat to those African neighbors who dared challenge the country's APARTHEID policies. His power was consolidated in 1978 when he was chosen as the country's prime minister.

The initial goals of the Botha regime were to destroy perceived security threats in neighboring countries, incorporate English-speaking whites into the National Party, and exploit class and racial divisions within the ANTIAPARTHEID MOVEMENT. Reform and repression went hand in hand during Botha's tenure. For example, Botha legalized black labor unions in 1973, but at the same time Parliament made it a crime for any white to employ an African who was not registered to work in that city.

By 1983 the growing antiapartheid movement, both at home and abroad, forced Botha to make further reforms. He led the passage of a new constitution granting Indians and Coloureds political representation under a new Tricameral Legislature. Widely viewed as an attempt to weaken the antiapartheid coalition, the move did nothing to stop the massive protests led by the AFRICAN NATIONAL CONGRESS (ANC).

In 1986 Botha convinced Parliament to repeal the ban on multiracial parties, the ban on interracial marriages, and the PASS LAWS. But while he appeared to be dismantling apartheid, he was using the SADF and the South African police to brutally suppress resistance. In 1984 alone, more than 200,000 Africans were arrested for violating pass laws. Between 1980 and 1989 it is estimated that military raids by the SADF on neighboring African countries—including ZAMBIA, BOTSWANA, and ZIMBABWE—took the lives of more than one million Africans, left nearly three million homeless, and caused more than $35 billion worth of damage.

Botha suffered a stroke in 1989 and resigned as party leader shortly thereafter. In August 1989 he lost his post as president after a rebellion in his cabinet. Botha maintained a relatively low profile for a number of years, but his refusal to testify before the country's TRUTH AND RECONCILIATION COMMISSION brought him back into the public eye in 1997. On the subject of human rights violations, he argued that he had made his peace before God and felt no need to appear before what he called a "circus." He was subsequently charged with contempt of court, but his conviction was ultimately overturned by the Cape High Court. It appears that Botha will not be held legally accountable for his role in one of the most brutal political systems of the twentieth century.

ALONFORD JAMES ROBINSON, JR.

Botswana
Landlocked country in southern Africa, bordered by Namibia to the north and west, Zambia and Zimbabwe to the northeast, and South Africa to the southeast.

In many ways, Botswana challenges stereotypical notions about African nations. Since 1970 this former British protectorate has had one of the fastest-growing economies in the world. Spurred by the discovery of vast diamond deposits in the late 1960s, Botswana has swiftly transformed itself from an agrarian society, whose chief export was beef, into an efficiently managed, mineral-based economy. Botswana's economic success has been instrumental in ensuring its equally remarkable political stability. Since independence in 1966, the Botswana Democratic Party has kept its majority in the National Assembly, the country's chief legislative body, despite an open electoral process and the presence of numerous opposition parties. In recent years, however, economic disparities have sparked growing popular discontent. Botswana's mining and cattle economy has produced an ever-widening gap between a wealthy class of ruling TSWANA families and urban elites and a poor, ethnically diverse, and mostly rural population. Another serious threat is HIV/AIDS, which has reached epidemic proportions in Botswana and threatens to undermine the country's economic and social stability.

EARLY HISTORY
Archaeological finds show a human presence dating back many thousands of years in the region now known as Botswana. The earliest inhabitants were most likely the ancestors of the SAN (also known as BUSHMEN), hunter-gatherers who today inhabit the semiarid steppes of southwestern Botswana, and the KHOIKHOI, who probably originated in the north. Scholars believe that by the first century B.C.E., the Khoikhoi adopted cattle herding and gradually spread southward across the eastern savanna. BANTU speakers probably arrived in the region by the first century C.E. They raised cattle, cultivated crops such as sorghum, and had the ability to forge iron tools. By the eighth century C.E., the Bantu-speaking ancestors of the present-day Kgalagadi had settled in eastern Botswana.

The ancestors of the Tswana, today the dominant ethnic group of Botswana, settled in the eleventh or twelfth century on the rolling plains around the Vaal River in what is now the South African province of TRANSVAAL. They tended livestock—mostly cattle—and grew crops such as millet and sorghum. They were seminomadic and did not privately own land but measured wealth in terms of cattle. Clan chiefs maintained their wealth and authority by collecting tribute, and in turn loaned parts of their vast royal herds to peasant farmers for milk and breeding purposes.

Tswana territory extended into parts of present-day eastern Botswana by 1800 but still lay mostly to the south. That changed in the 1820s, during the time of warfare known as the MFECANE (or *difaqane*). The NDEBELE, fleeing Zulu aggression, invaded the Transvaal region at this time and began raiding Tswana and SOTHO settlements. Many Tswana fled into the KALAHARI DESERT, where the inhospitable climate of sparse rainfall and extreme temperature

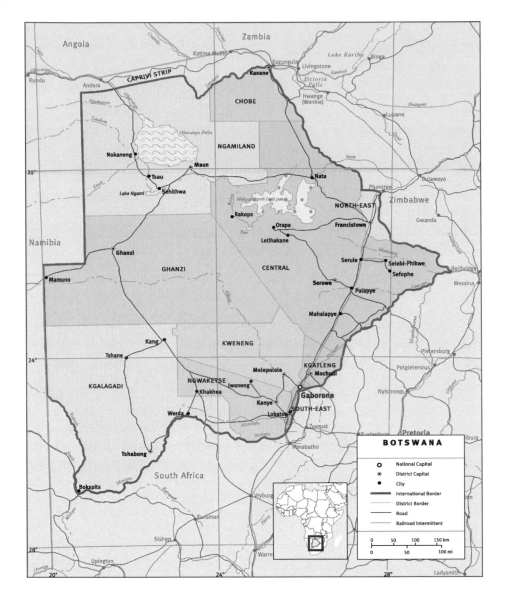

changes deterred the Ndebele from pursuing them further. By the mid-1830s the Ndebele had themselves continued northward into what is now ZIMBABWE. The refugee Tswana clans resettled in the more arable lands near the Limpopo, one of the region's only perennial rivers.

Following the *mfecane*, Tswana culture coalesced around the eight most powerful clans, whose ruling families continue to dominate Botswana politics today. Bitter rivalries among many of the clans prevented them from forming a kingdom, as was the case for many other ethnic groups in southern Africa during this time. The division of the Tswana into rival chiefdoms made them especially vulnerable to incursions by European troops and missionaries, which increased in scale as the British and AFRIKANERS (or Boers) to the south competed to extend their colonial territories further inland.

Of the two European groups, the Boers were the more aggressive, driving the Ndebele from the region. The Boers

believed that their victory gave them rightful claim to all lands formerly ruled by the Ndebele, including, in their estimation, the Tswana territories north of the Limpopo River. By the mid-1840s, Boer commando brigades had begun raiding Tswana towns in an effort to drive the clans from the region. Despite formal appeals by local missionaries, including David Livingstone, for British intervention, the Boer raids continued unchecked over the next forty years.

In 1876 two paramount chiefs, Setshele of the Kwena clan and Khama of the Ngwato, began requesting British protection from the Boers, and in 1885 they finally received it. Although Setshele and Khama had no authority over other Tswana clans and ethnic groups in the region, the British used their request as a justification for claiming the entire territory constituting modern-day Botswana as the British Protectorate of BECHUANALAND. A section of Tswana territory south of the Molopo River was eventually absorbed into the Republic of SOUTH AFRICA.

BOTSWANAN DIAMONDS. Workers inspect rough diamond cuts from workstations in Gaborone, Botswana. The Diamond Trading Company, which opened in Botswana in late 2008, further increased the nation's strength in the diamond trade. (*Themba Hadebe/AP Images*)

BRITISH BECHUANALAND

Although the British claimed humanitarian goals for asserting control over the Tswana, they had purely territorial aims as well. An early goal of the British Empire in Africa was to establish an inland trade route that would link the CAPE COLONY of South Africa with Britain's territories north of the equator. Although Bechuanaland had little material value in terms of known natural resources or arable land, its flat, dry terrain was ideally suited to the construction of wagon roads and railroads. Moreover, the British feared an alliance between the then independent Boer states of Transvaal and Orange Free State to the east and German-controlled South-West Africa (present-day NAMIBIA) to the west on the Atlantic coast. By seizing Bechuanaland, which lay between these two rival groups, the British secured their expansion into the interior.

Economic development of Bechuanaland during the colonial period was, therefore, almost entirely limited to transportation. In 1897 workers completed a railroad across eastern Bechuanaland linking mining sites in the interior of what is now ZIMBABWE to ports along the southern coast. The director of both the mining and railway projects was Cecil John Rhodes, whose British South Africa Company briefly held broad administrative powers over much of the Bechuanaland Protectorate. As South Africa's mining industry expanded, migrant workers from Bechuanaland traveled to South African gold and diamond mines, where they lived in guarded, segregated dormitories and earned a fraction of their white counterparts' wages. Cattle-owning Tswana took advantage of the new rail link to ship cattle for slaughter in the growing cities of South Africa, or even for export to Great Britain.

In 1910 Great Britain unified all its colonies in southern Africa in the Union of South Africa. A proviso in the union charter called for eventual incorporation of all British protectorates, including Bechuanaland. Tswana leaders, who had been allowed to keep many of their political powers in a British system of colonial administration known as indirect rule, successfully prevented this from taking place. However, they could not prevent the British from establishing economic conditions that guaranteed Botswana's dependency on South Africa well into the postcolonial period. The British never installed an infrastructure linking the region to seaports in any country but South Africa. Botswana thus remained heavily dependent on South Africa both for its imports and for what was then its sole export, beef. Economic underdevelopment further guaranteed that, as drought and soil erosion prevented residents from maintaining even subsistence levels of agriculture, Botswana's adult male population would continue to provide a pool of inexpensive labor for South Africa's mines.

Despite these developments, relations between Bechuanaland and the British remained cordial. Many clans, particularly the Ngwato, adopted Christianity, and it was not unusual for clan chiefs and other elites to travel to Great Britain to attend university. One such attendee, the Ngwato heir-apparent Seretse KHAMA, created a furor in 1948 by marrying a white Englishwoman, Ruth Williams. That same year South Africa officially instituted its doctrine of APARTHEID, and the combination of events threatened to totally disrupt relations between the two countries. To appease South African whites, the British barred Khama from returning home to Bechuanaland. Only after he promised to renounce the Ngwato chieftancy did they allow Khama to return in 1956.

Khama considered the loss of the chieftancy a small price to pay. One of the things he had learned from his European schooling was that traditional Tswana political structures were doomed to extinction. Instead, Khama and his allies formed a European-style political party—the Bechuanaland (later Botswana) Democratic Party, or BDP—and campaigned on a nationalist platform to replace the British colonial government with an indigenous one set up along similar lines as a first step toward independence. Self-government came at first in 1961 in the form of a legislative council equally divided between black and white members, despite blacks outnumbering whites in Bechuanaland by a factor of 100. A more egalitarian system of universal adult suffrage swept the BDP into power in 1965, with Khama the prime minister of Bechuanaland. When the country achieved independence on September 30, 1966, Khama became president of the newly formed Republic of Botswana.

INDEPENDENT BOTSWANA

At the time of independence, Botswana was one of the poorest countries on earth. Its prospects appeared limited and its dependency on neighboring South Africa assured, with cattle grazing and subsistence farming as its only economic activities. In addition, over four-fifths of its area was covered by the wastelands of the Kalahari Desert and, farther north, by the vast, economically useless Makgadikgadi Salt Pans and Okavango Swamp.

Botswana's economic salvation came just one year later, in a spectacular form: the discovery of diamonds in the Makgadikgadi Salt Pans near the town of Orapa. De Beers Consolidated Mines of South Africa had been exploring the interior of Botswana for deposits since 1955, but the Orapa site provided the first evidence that such mineral resources existed. By 1971 the Orapa mine was in production, with the Botswanan government receiving 70 percent of the revenues, and efforts had begun in earnest, fueled by international investment, to uncover further diamond sites. The largest of these, at Jwaneng in the Kalahari, opened in 1982. Botswana became the world's largest source of gem-quality diamonds.

The search for diamonds also led to the discovery of other mineral resources in Botswana. Chief among these turned out to be copper-nickel matte, coal, and soda ash. All told, the mining industry in Botswana accounts for more than half the country's GDP and 89 percent of its export revenues. Price fluctuations in the minerals market have not threatened Botswana's phenomenal economic growth, which has averaged 11 percent annually since independence and has not fallen below 4 percent since 1970. This stability derives largely from a series of National Development Plans put forth by the Botswana Democratic Party to cap excessive growth and preserve a substantial foreign exchange reserve.

Despite Botswana's economic prosperity, it remained dependent on South Africa for many of its imports and its overseas exports, nearly all of which still passed through South African ports. Khama and his successor, Dr. Quett MASIRE, therefore maintained a position of diplomatic neutrality toward the apartheid regime and other unstable, white minority–ruled states in the region, such as RHODESIA (later ZIMBABWE) and South-West Africa. Instead, Botswana helped organize the SOUTHERN AFRICAN DEVELOPMENT COMMUNITY (SADC) to coordinate economic cooperation among the "frontline" states—the majority-ruled states of southern Africa bordering states under white minority domination. A 1979 conference of the frontline states in Botswana's capital, GABORONE, initiated a framework for cooperation that formed the basis for the Lusaka Declaration of 1980 on economic cooperation. A 1992 treaty formalized the structures of the SADC.

From independence until the late 1990s, the BDP remained Botswana's ruling political party. The numerous opposition parties, most notably the Marxist Botswana National Front, had little impact on BDP dominance. This was due partly to continued economic prosperity and partly to demography—the Ngwato, the largest of the Tswana clans and accounting for roughly a third of Botswana's population, dominated the BDP. Various indirect political restrictions in an otherwise democratic society, however, also helped to maintain the BDP's hold on power. For example, the BDP controlled Botswana's only daily newspaper, and its authority to grant mining and cattle-grazing rights gave party leaders and their allies near-total control of Botswana's economy. The BDP was strongest in rural areas, where much of the population was dependent on the chiefly classes and the wealthy cattle owners who dominated the party. Opposition to the BDP government centered mainly in the rapidly growing cities, where the educated middle class sought to break the BDP elite's monopoly on power, and where large numbers of impoverished migrants from the countryside faced persistent unemployment. However, the retirement of President Masire, the orderly succession of his vice president, Festus Mogae, to the presidency in 1998, and Mogae's reelection to a five-year term by the National Assembly in 1999 appeared to extend the BDP's firm grip on power.

Despite the continued existence of severe economic inequality and high unemployment, Botswana remained one of postcolonial Africa's few models for multiparty democracy and sustained economic growth during the late 1990s. Recent shifts toward privatization of Botswana's industrial and mining sectors have shown few signs of endangering the country's economic climate. Indeed, South Africa's transition to majority rule has created new economic opportunities for Botswana. South Africa's admission to the SADC in 1994 opened up the possibility of expanded trade and economic cooperation with Botswana's economically powerful southern neighbor.

The specter of AIDS, however, has cast a shadow over Botswana's economic prospects. As of 2003, nearly 40 percent of all Botswanans were infected with the HIV virus—a staggeringly large figure. The government has pursued an aggressive strategy of funding for AIDS treatment and prevention, but many worry that the effort may have come too late. Working in Botswana's favor, however, is its mineral wealth that provides a relatively high standard of living for average Botswanans, who are far more likely than most Africans afflicted by HIV/AIDS to be able to afford the treatment they need.

See also ACQUIRED IMMUNODEFICIENCY SYNDROME IN AFRICA: AN INTERPRETATION; COLONIAL RULE; MINERALS AND MINING IN AFRICA.

ANDREW HERMANN

Botswana (At a Glance)

OFFICIAL NAME:
Republic of Botswana

FORMER NAME:
Bechuanaland

AREA:
600,370 sq km (231,805 sq mi)

LOCATION:
Southern Africa, north of South Africa

CAPITAL:
Gaborone (population 208,411; 2005 estimate)

OTHER MAJOR CITIES:
Francistown (population 113,315), Selebi-Pikwe (49,849), Molepolole (65,570), Kanye (44,716), Serowe (90,000)

POPULATION:
1,639,833 (2006 estimate)

POPULATION DENSITY:
3 persons per sq km (7.8 persons per sq mi)

POPULATION BELOW AGE 15:
35.2 percent (male 329,418; female 318,160)

POPULATION GROWTH RATE:
1.434 percent (2008 estimate)

TOTAL FERTILITY RATE:
2.66 children born per woman (2008 estimate)

LIFE EXPECTANCY AT BIRTH:
Total population: 50.16 years (male 51.28 years; female 49.02 years; 2008 estimate)

INFANT MORTALITY RATE:
44.01 deaths per 1,000 live births (2008 estimate)

LITERACY RATE (AGE 15 AND OVER WHO CAN READ AND WRITE):
Total population: 81.2 percent (male 80.4 percent; female 81.8 percent; 2003 estimate)

EDUCATION:
Most primary schools are supervised by district councils and township authorities and are financed from local government revenues assisted by grants-in-aid from the central government. In the mid-1990s Botswana's primary schools had an annual enrollment of about 301,400, and secondary schools about 99,600; about 4,500 students were enrolled in the University of Botswana in Gaborone.

LANGUAGES:
English is the official language, but most people speak Setswana, a Bantu language.

ETHNIC GROUPS:
The Tswana are the largest ethnic group in Botswana. There are also significant populations of Kalanga and San.

RELIGIONS:
About 85 percent of the population practices indigenous beliefs; the remainder are Christians.

CLIMATE:
The climate of Botswana is semi-arid and subtropical, with warm winters and hot summers. The average annual rainfall varies from about 640 mm (about 25 in) in the north to less than 230 mm (less than 9 in) in the Kalahari Desert.

LAND, PLANTS, AND ANIMALS:
Most of Botswana is a flat to gently rolling tableland; the Kalahari Desert lies in the southwest. Savanna vegetation predominates in most parts of the country. Principal species include acacia, bloodwood, and Rhodesian teak. Wildlife is abundant and includes lions, giraffes, leopards, antelope, elephants, crocodiles, and ostriches.

NATURAL RESOURCES:
Diamonds, copper, nickel, salt, soda ash, potash, asbestos, coal, iron ore, silver

CURRENCY:
The pula

GROSS DOMESTIC PRODUCT (GDP):
$26.04 billion (2007 estimate)

GDP PER CAPITA:
$14,300 (2007 estimate)

GDP REAL GROWTH RATE:
4.8 percent (2007 estimate)

PRIMARY ECONOMIC ACTIVITIES:
The economy has historically been based on cattle raising and crops. Agriculture today provides a livelihood for more than 80 percent of the population but supplies only about 50 percent of food needs and accounts for only 5 percent of GDP. Subsistence farming and cattle raising predominate. Erratic rainfall and poor soils plague the sector. The driving force behind the rapid economic growth of the 1970s and 1980s has been the mining industry. This sector, mostly on the strength of diamonds, has gone from generating 25 percent of GDP in 1980 to over 33 percent in 2003.

PRIMARY CROPS:
Sorghum, maize, millet, pulses, groundnuts (peanuts), beans, cowpeas, sunflower seeds

INDUSTRIES:
Diamonds, copper, nickel, coal, salt, soda ash, potash; livestock processing

PRIMARY EXPORTS:
Diamonds, copper, nickel, meat

PRIMARY IMPORTS:
Foodstuffs, vehicles and transport equipment, textiles, petroleum products

PRIMARY TRADE PARTNERS:
Switzerland, Southern African Customs Union (SACU), United Kingdom, United States

GOVERNMENT:
Botswana is a parliamentary republic. Universal suffrage begins at age 21. The president is elected for a five-year term by the National Assembly, one of the two houses of Botswana's legislature. The president appoints a 10-member cabinet. Botswana's legislative branch consists of the 44-member National Assembly and the 15-member House of Chiefs. The House of Chiefs is a largely advisory body made up of the chiefs of the 8 principal tribes, 4 elected subchiefs, and 3 members selected by the other 12. Major political parties in Botswana include the Botswana Democratic Party (BDP), Botswana National Front (BNF), Botswana People's Party (BPP), and Botswana Independence Party (BIP).

Alonford James Robinson, Jr.

Bouabré, Frédéric-Bruly

1923–

Ivoirian visual artist and mystic.

Not much is known about Frédéric-Bruly Bouabré's early life. He was raised in the Daloa department of western CÔTE D'IVOIRE, and the local KRU culture and community were an important part of his childhood. In 1948, when Bouabré was twenty-four, the as yet undistinguished young man had a celestial vision in DAKAR. According to Bouabré, the heavens opened themselves to him and he understood that he was to use his artistic talent to maintain and share the culture of his people, which is rooted in nature and folklore. After his vision Bouabré considered himself reborn as Cheik Nadro, or "he who does not forget," and has devoted his life to his drawing and other creative projects.

Bouabré's drawings often form a series. They are generally small and rectangular and have a border of narrative text around them. In this regard, many of his drawings strongly resemble traditional African ideograms. The highly representative drawings in a series tell parts of a story and function much like a universal visual language of symbols. Many of the drawings look childlike and simplistic. They are generally done in colored pencil on paper. The artist believes that by using simple, familiar materials and a direct, visual language of icons and symbols, his drawings are accessible to a wide audience. In this way, Bouabré has sought to promote the beauty and commonality of nature and of human experience. Whether they illustrate a traditional Kru folktale, show contemporary life in Côte d'Ivoire, or comment on international politics, Bouabré's drawings are meant to show the similarities among people of the global community.

Bouabré achieved considerable international success in the 1980s and 1990s. His first major international show was the 1989 exhibit *Magiciens de la Terre* in Paris, which attracted worldwide attention for him and other contemporary African artists. Subsequently, his works were shown across Europe as well as in Japan, Mexico, and the United States. Through these international exhibitions, Bouabré has brought his message of global commonality to a truly internation audience. He still lives and works in the city of ABIDJAN.

CHRISTOPHER TINÉ

Boudjedra, Rachids

1941–

Algerian writer who gained a reputation for experimentation with form in his first novel *La repudiation* (1969; The Repudiation), which was surprising and scandalous for its freedom of themes and narrative structure.

Born in 1941 in Aïn Beïda, Algeria, Rachids Boudjedra began to write in French in 1965, and his work led the way for a new generation of Algerian writers. In 1975, his novel *Topographie idéale pour une agression caractérisée* (Ideal Topography for a Specific Aggression) was the first attempt by an Algerian writer at describing the anguish of immigrant Algerian workers in France, exiled in a strange and hostile world. It is the story of an illiterate young Berber who goes to Paris in hope of a better future and is killed by a group of young racists. *Lescargot entêté* (1977; The Stubborn Snail) relates the petty obsessions of a white-collar employee. Elements of Arab culture and language invade Boudjedra's French sentences, acting as harbingers of the author's later works written in Arabic. Fascinated with form, Boudjedra composed *Les 1001 années de la nostalgie* (1979; 1,001 Years of Nostalgia) as a counterpoint to the fifteenth-century collection of Arabian tales—A Thousand and One Nights—with stories borrowed from universal literature and from his own novels interwoven throughout the narrative. The novels that follow *Les 1001 années* deal with Algeria's liberation struggle, which is at the center of most of the creative work by post-independence writers. In 1981, Boudjedra began writing in Arabic with a novel published first in Arabic in Beirut, Lebanon, and then translated by him into French and published in 1982 under the title *Le démantèlement* (The Dismantling). He found that translating a novel was like rewriting it, and from then on, he had others translate his works. He returned to French with a nonfiction work attacking Algeria's Islamists, *FIS de la haine* (1993; The Islamic Salvation Front of Hate). Algeria was thrown into bloody turmoil in 1992 after the government annulled a national election won by the FIS. Writers, journalists, and teachers were killed by the thousands. Other artists and intellectuals fled the country and went into exile, where they were powerless to help their colleagues except by chronicling the country's sorrows through their creative work. Boudjedra was threatened by fundamentalist Islamists and escaped to France. He relates this harrowing experience in *La vie á lendroit* (1997; Life Right Side Up), the story of a man pursued by assassins. Fear and anxiety infuse the story in a unique style that has been described as the "rhetoric of fear." Boudjedra's later works including *La fascination* (2000) and *Funerailles* (2003; Funeral) are more optimistic. Despite Algeria's continued troubles, the mood of *Funerailles* is not mournful and the novel ends on a happy note as the two young protagonists decide to marry.

AMINA AZZA BEKKAT

Boumedienne, Houari

1927–1978

Second president of Algeria and leader in the struggle for Algerian independence.

Houari Boumedienne was born in Clauzel, Algeria. In 1955 he joined the National Liberation Front, known as FRONT

DE LIBÉRATION NATIONALE (FLN), to fight for Algerian independence from French COLONIAL RULE. He rose rapidly as guerrilla commander, becoming the youngest colonel in the FLN two years after he enlisted. In exile by 1960, Boumedienne led the external Algerian armies in TUNISIA and MOROCCO.

After Algeria became independent in 1962, Boumedienne backed exiled leader Ahmed BEN BELLA during the conflict between internal and exiled leaders of the FLN over leadership of the new nation. He accompanied Ben Bella to Algeria, fighting battles with former allies to secure Ben Bella's position as Algeria's first prime minister and president, as well as his own position as vice president and defense minister. In June 1965 Boumedienne engineered a bloodless coup that deposed Ben Bella and secured his own power as the country's leader.

As president, Boumedienne maintained the socialist vision of his predecessors. Remembered mostly for the bold reforms of his Four-Year Plans, Boumedienne initiated an agrarian revolution and a cultural revolution. He nationalized agricultural and industrial enterprises, including French hydrocarbon companies. In 1976 Boumedienne oversaw the creation of the National Charter, which defined a so-called Third World socialist path for the country and a new constitution.

Despite the increased productivity of the Algerian economy, Boumedienne's government faced opposition from student groups, as well as from other revolutionary leaders, such as Ferhat Abbas. Abbas saw the constitution and charter as the president's means of consolidating his own power. Eleven years after his coup, Boumedienne was elected president in an unopposed contest. He died two years later of a rare blood disease.

MARIAN AGUIAR

Bourguiba, Habib ibn Ali
1903–2000
Nationalist leader and first president of Tunisia.

For more than thirty years, Habib ibn Ali Bourguiba guided the nation of TUNISIA through its transformation from French protectorate into independent republic, and then through a period of intense social and political reform. Known as an outspoken, bold man with a wry wit, he is also remembered as a gradualist and a negotiator who used slow-moving tactics to achieve radical ends.

Bourguiba was born in the small village of al-Munastir, but he studied in TUNIS before traveling to France to study law and political science at the Sorbonne in Paris. In 1927 he returned to Tunis, where he became increasingly active in the growing independence movement. He was the cofounder of the newspaper *LAction Tunisienne*, which became a forum for opposition

to the French protectorate. In 1934, dissatisfied with the conservatism of the Destour Party, which was at that time the leading Tunisian rights group, Bourguiba helped found the Neo-Destour Party.

The new organization took center stage in the nationalist struggle by demanding full independence. Under Bourguiba, the Neo-Destour Party garnered broad-based popular support. It is estimated that by 1937 the Neo-Destour Party had 28,000 activists and 49,000 supporters working out of 400 branches. Bourguiba built the group's infrastructure with branches in villages and provisions for replacement leadership in case of emergency. The party waged an intensive campaign using civil disobedience, including a strike in solidarity with nationalist movements in other North African countries. In 1938 the French outlawed the Neo-Destour Party; shortly thereafter, they imprisoned Bourguiba in Vichy, France. He was released four years later when the Germans invaded France, and despite his refusal to promise Tunisian support for the Axis powers, he was allowed to return to Tunisia.

Bourguiba fled to Egypt after the French resumed power following the war. Traveling throughout the Middle East, East Asia, Europe, and the United States for four years, he promoted the cause of Tunisian revolutionaries, who were waging an increasingly violent struggle for independence. He was invited back to Tunisia in 1949, where he engaged intermittently in negotiations with the French. After a period of civil unrest, Bourguiba was arrested once more in 1952 and kept under surveillance, both in and out of prison, for the next two years.

As France prepared to negotiate Tunisian independence, Bourguiba was released to lead the Tunisian delegation. Tunisia won independence in 1956 as a constitutional monarchy. The following year, the bey, or king, was deposed and Bourguiba was elected president of the new republic. Although relations with the former colonial government were strained at first, particularly after a brief armed conflict over French military presence in Bizerte, for the most part Bourguiba maintained Tunisia's position of neutrality with the powers of Europe, the United States, and the Arab world.

As president, Bourguiba immediately initiated modernist reforms that curtailed the impact of traditional Islamic practices in civil society. He promoted women's rights, abolished polygamy, and brought education under state control. In one of his more controversial gestures, Bourguiba advocated breaking the Ramadan fast in order to increase worker productivity. Following a path of moderate socialism, he allocated much of the national budget to education, agriculture, and health while limiting military spending.

Despite Bourguiba's general popularity, his moves to concentrate power raised concerns among some party members. For example, he turned on his minister of planning for initiating an unsuccessful plan to nationalize agricultural production and had the former protégé convicted for treason. During the early 1970s, Bourguiba expelled most of his opponents from what came to be called the Destour Socialist Party, and in 1975, the Tunisian National Assembly (called the Chamber of Deputies since 1981) appointed him President for Life.

Although Bourguiba allowed a considerable amount of freedom for opposition parties in the early years of his tenure, he had become much less tolerant by the 1980s. Following civil unrest beginning in 1984, Bourguiba's administration used mass arrests. These arrests targeted leftist organizations dissatisfied with some of the free-market reforms of his late administration, as well as Islamic organizations opposed to his early social reforms. As Tunisians observed the erratic leadership of Bourguiba, who was by this time well into his eighties, rumors abounded about his deteriorating mental state. In 1987 Prime Minister Zine el-Abidine Ben Ali engineered a bloodless coup to depose him.

After 1987 Bourguiba was kept in close confinement by the government of Tunisia, held up as the symbolic Father of Tunisia but kept out of sight. His disgust with this arrangement was no secret, and on at least one occasion he took the opportunity of a live broadcast to disparage those confining him. He was allowed to return to his native village shortly before his death in 2000 at age ninety-six.

See also AFRICAN SOCIALISM; FEMINISM IN ISLAMIC AFRICA; MARRIAGE, AFRICAN CUSTOMS OF.

MARIAN AGUIAR

Boutros-Ghali, Boutros

1922–
Lawyer, professor, journalist, and diplomat; the first Arab and first African to serve as Secretary General of the United Nations.

Boutros Boutros-Ghali was born to a prominent Coptic Christian family in EGYPT. His grandfather, Boutros Pasha Boutros-Ghali, served as prime minister of Egypt under the British protectorate from 1908 until his assassination in 1910. The younger Boutros-Ghali graduated from the University of Cairo in 1946 with a bachelor's degree, and went on to earn a doctorate in international law in 1949 from the Sorbonne in Paris. Boutros-Ghali pursued postdoctoral work at Columbia University in New York City, and then assumed a post as professor of international law and international affairs at the University of Cairo. He worked as a journalist, writing for the daily Al Ahram. He also held teaching posts at Princeton University in the United States, and at universities in India, Poland, and TANZANIA. In October 1977 Boutros-Ghali left his academic career to serve in the government of Egyptian President Anwar AL-SADAT as a minister of state for foreign affairs. The following month, after Egypt's foreign minister resigned to protest Sadat's intention to hold peace talks with Israel, Boutros-Ghali served as interim foreign minister. He accompanied Sadat on a visit to Jerusalem and later headed the negotiating team that crafted the Camp David Accords with Israel. Boutros-Ghali never became foreign minister, however, because it was a position traditionally reserved for Muslims. Boutros-Ghali went on to build a career as an international statesman. An expert on development issues, he authored studies and articles on the disparity in wealth between rich and poor countries. In addition, Boutros-Ghali negotiated agreements in several African conflicts, and his efforts helped win the prison release of South African leader Nelson Rolihlahla MANDELA. Boutros-Ghali was elected to the position of Secretary General of the United Nations (UN) in November 1991, based on many qualifications: his reputation as a negotiator; his first-name relationship with government officials in the East and the West; his fluency in Arabic, French, and English; and UN members' strong desire for an African in that position. Boutros-Ghali faced a difficult tenure as head of the UN. His term in office began in 1992, when the world was reorganizing politically in the wake of the Cold War. Boutros-Ghali attempted to negotiate several post–Cold War conflicts with limited success. He supported sending UN peacekeeping troops to trouble spots around the globe, including the former Yugoslavia, SOMALIA, and RWANDA. He was, however, outspoken and independent—traits that did not sit well with some member countries, most importantly the United States. Although the majority of member nations supported Boutros-Ghali for reelection to a second five-year term in 1996, the United States, which was dissatisfied with his performance, forced his ouster. Since his tenure at the United Nations, Boutros-Ghali has gone on to sit on a number of boards and organizations. In 2007 he was appointed to head the Egyptian National Council of Human Rights.

ROBERT FAY

Boza

Ethnic group of West Africa; also known as Bozo.

The Boza mostly inhabit the shores of the NIGER and Bani rivers in MALI and NIGER. They speak a MANDE language. Approximately 300,000 people consider themselves Boza.

See also LANGUAGES, AFRICAN: AN OVERVIEW.

Brazza, Pierre Savorgnan de

1852–1905

French-Italian explorer and general commissioner of the Moyen-Congo, present day Republic of the Congo.

After schooling and naval service in France, the Italian-born Pierre Savorgnan de Brazza became a naturalized French citizen in 1874. The following year he led his first official trip to Africa to explore GABON. From 1875 to 1878 he traveled along the Gabon coast and up the Ogooué River to its source, also reaching the Alima River, a tributary of the CONGO RIVER. In 1880, in competition with American journalist and explorer Henry Stanley, Brazza traveled into the Congo River basin interior. There he signed a treaty with leaders of the TÉKÉ people, clearing the way for French control of the northern bank of the Congo River, an area that would be known as the Moyen-Congo. He served as general commissioner of the Moyen-Congo from 1884 to 1898, establishing the town that became BRAZZAVILLE and building the colonial administration. As commissioner Brazza became disenchanted with the exploitive and brutal practices of concessionary companies, and in 1905 was appointed by the French government to investigate them. He died in DAKAR, SENEGAL, on his return from the mission.

See also EXPLORERS IN AFRICA SINCE 1800; CONGO, REPUBLIC OF THE.

ERIC YOUNG

Brazzaville, Republic of the Congo

Capital of the Republic of the Congo, and the country's largest city.

Fighting in 1993 and 1997 between rival Congolese militias twice reduced this picturesque city of wide boulevards and street cafés on the banks of the CONGO RIVER to rubble, destroying many of the buildings that housed its population of more than 900,000. Particularly hard hit were residential neighborhoods such as Bacongo, dominated by the Lari ethnic group, and the MBOCHI- and TÉKÉ-dominated Poto-Poto neighborhood, known for its cathedral, school of art, and writers' community. The city's other districts include the administrative center on the plateau, the Plain commercial district, and the M'Pila industrial zone. According to one 2003 estimate, the city's population had reached some 1.5 million.

Brazzaville, now capital of the REPUBLIC OF THE CONGO, was originally a small Téké settlement known as Nkuma. In 1880 the Tékés' paramount chief ceded Nkuma to the French, who desired access to the interior of the Congo basin via the river and named it in honor of the explorer Pierre Savorgnan de BRAZZA. Although Brazzaville became the capital of FRENCH EQUATORIAL AFRICA in 1903, it was not until the 1930s, when a railway was built from the city to the coast, that the city's population and commercial importance grew. In World War II, when Brazzaville was named the capital of Free France in sub-Saharan Africa, the city's population and infrastructure expanded further. After the war, Brazzaville became the center of the nationalist movement and in 1960 it became the capital of independent Congo. After independence, rural migration to the city continued, seriously straining public services. Urban unemployment reached 50 percent in the 1980s, and strikes, protests, and black-marketeering became common. Even after the 1997 civil war, Brazzaville remains Congo's commercial center and an important port, linked by ferry service to KINSHASA, which is directly across the 24-kilometer (15-mile) -wide river.

See also CONGO, REPUBLIC OF THE; MBOCHI; TÉKÉ.

ERIC YOUNG

Brink, André Philippus

1935–

Afrikaner novelist whose books criticizing apartheid were banned by the South African government.

The son of an AFRIKANER magistrate, André Brink grew up moving from village to village in rural SOUTH AFRICA, each characterized, he says, by "conservative Protestantism . . . generosity and narrow-mindedness." After receiving master's degrees in English and Afrikaans from Potchefstroom University, Brink went to Paris in 1959 to study at the Sorbonne. By his own assessment, the 1960 SHARPEVILLE MASSACRE in South Africa (in which the police killed at least sixty-nine innocent protesters) sparked in him a new political awareness and prompted him to return home in 1961.

Brink began to write fiction while lecturing at Rhodes University. Two novels published in the early 1960s were largely apolitical, but his views on writing changed after he spent 1968 in Paris, where he witnessed student uprisings. Brink came to believe that "in a closed society, the writer has a specific social and moral role to fill." His next novel, *Looking into Darkness* (1973), dealt directly with APARTHEID in its story of a mixed-race actor convicted of killing his white lover. It was the first Afrikaans novel banned by the South African government. Brink wrote his subsequent novels in both Afrikaans and English.

During the 1970s and 1980s, while enduring constant monitoring and harassment by the authorities, Brink published seven more novels: *An Instant in the Wind* (1976), *Rumours of Rain* (1978), *A Dry White Season* (1979), *A Chain of Voices* (1981), *Mapmakers* (1983), *The Wall of the Plague* (1984), and *States of Emergency* (1988). Brink's novels have been translated into more than twenty languages. *A Dry White Season* won both the Martin Luther King Memorial Prize and the French Prix Médicis étranger in 1980, and was made into a movie in 1989.

Brink has also written and directed plays, served as president of the Afrikaans Writers' Guild and as a member of South African PEN, and translated Shakespeare, Henry James, Albert Camus, and other authors into Afrikaans. His later books include *An Act of Terror* (1991), *The First Life of Admastor* (1993), *On the Contrary* (1993), *Imaginings of Sand* (1996), *Reinventing a Continent* (1996), *The Novel: Language and Narrative from Cervantes to Calvino* (1998), and *The Rights of Desire* (2001). He has been nominated for the Nobel Prize three times.

See also ANTIAPARTHEID MOVEMENT; APARTHEID.

KATE TUTTLE

British Central Africa
Former name of Malawi.
See also MALAWI.

British Somaliland
Former name of the northern part of Somalia.
See also SOMALIA.

Brutus, Dennis
1924–
South African poet, teacher, and political activist, whose lyric poetry is structured around a finely wrought tension between the personal and the political.
Born in Salisbury, Southern Rhodesia (now HARARE, ZIMBABWE), Dennis Brutus grew up in SOUTH AFRICA and received his B.A. degree there in 1947 from the University of Fort Hare, in Alice. Brutus taught English and Afrikaans for fourteen years in South African high schools before going on to study law at the University of Witwatersrand. He was a leader in the struggle against racism in sports, and his activity protesting APARTHEID, South Africa's policy of racial segregation, led to his arrest in 1963. Shot while trying to escape, he was then sentenced to eighteen months imprisonment on ROBBEN ISLAND, a high-security facility known for holding antiapartheid political prisoners.

Sirens, Knuckles, Boots, Brutus' first collection of poetry, was published the year he was imprisoned and established him as a gifted poet of tightly crafted political lyrics. While in prison he secretly wrote of his experiences in a series of poems to his wife, later published as *Letters to Martha* (1968). The poems offer powerful descriptions of appallingly brutal conditions and reflect a compassion that avoids any sense of self-pity.

In 1966, with his works banned in South Africa, Brutus left for England on an exit permit that did not allow him to return. He then traveled to the United States, where he was hired as a professor of African literature at Northwestern University. He later held positions at the University of Texas, Swarthmore College, and the University of Pittsburgh.

Brutus brings diverse experiences to his poetry, unifying them through his attention to social injustice. There is great passion, even anger, in some of his lines, but the verse is always restrained and controlled. One sees a clear progression from a somewhat lush, even romantic, tone in his early poems to an increasingly austere precision after the prison experience. Brutus's other collections include *Poems from Algiers* (1970), *A Simple Lust* (1973), *China Poems* (1975), *Salutes and Censures* (1984), *Airs and Tributes* (1989), *Remembering Soweto* (2004), *Leafdrift* (2005), and *Poetry and Protest* (2006).

In 1991 Brutus returned to South Africa, where the government had declared a political amnesty for all exiles. Since the fall of apartheid he has remained active on many other issues, including antiglobalization campaigns and the movement to free death-row inmate Mumia Abu-Jamal. In 2007 Brutus declined induction into the South African Sports Hall of Fame, stating, "Being inducted to a sports hall of fame is an honor under most circumstances. In my case the honor is for helping rid South African sport of racism, making it open to all. So I cannot be party to an event where unapologetic racists are also honored, or to join a hall of fame alongside those who flourished under racist sport."

See also ANTIAPARTHEID MOVEMENT.

Bubi
Ethnic group residing on Equatorial Guinea's Bioko Island.
Although they were among the first inhabitants of Bioko Island, the Bubi have only recently become active in national politics. Archaeologists and linguists believe that ancestors of the Bubi were among the first groups to break from western Bantu, arriving in present-day coastal CAMEROON and GABON around 1500–1000 B.C.E., though unlike many BANTU-speaking groups they did not produce iron. Oral historians date their arrival much later. The Bubi migrated to Fernando Pó, also known as Bioko Island, in four waves beginning around the seventh century C.E. Settling mostly the island's northern coast, they developed four distinct dialects.

The Bubi grew palms and yams on the island's rich volcanic soils, fished, and made pottery and tools. They used small, round pieces of shell as currency. Their monogamous, matrilineal society distinguished primarily between occupational groups, such as hunters, fishers, and farmers, rather than between economic classes. The religion was monotheistic, and based on the worship of fire and other elements.

Several Bubi chiefdoms rose and fell over time, though political authority was generally diffused, and a chief's power was dependent upon the approval of village elders. This changed in the nineteenth century when European merchants, who for years had largely avoided Bioko's rough coastline, began coming ashore, trading European goods for fresh fruits and other foods to sustain the crews while at the sea. As the Bubi chiefdoms competed for trade with the Europeans, small chiefdoms were subsumed by larger ones, and ultimately a supreme chief emerged among the previously disparate chiefdoms. However, their trading relations with Europeans were not always peaceful. King Moka, the Bubi supreme chief during the latter part of the nineteenth century, refused to meet with the Spanish after they colonized the island. In 1907, the Bubi rejected forced-labor laws imposed by the Spanish to increase the productivity of cocoa plantations, and this led to the so-called Bubi war, which was brought under control by Spanish colonial officials three years later. Foreign diseases such as smallpox and syphilis decimated the Bubi, cutting the population to around 12,000 in 1912.

After World War II the Bubi population recovered, and became increasingly integrated with Nigerian workers, who were brought to the island as plantation laborers. Because of their self-imposed isolation, the Bubi played a relatively negligible role in the colonial state and the nationalist movement. Just prior to decolonization, the Bubi sought separation from the mainland of EQUATORIAL GUINEA (known as Mbini, or Rio Muni), but were unsuccessful. A Bubi served briefly as vice president after independence was granted in 1968, but mainland FANG soon marginalized and suppressed prominent Bubi politicians. Only recently have some Bubi groups become more visible opponents of Equatorial Guinea's dictatorial regime, having made several armed attacks on government military outposts since the late 1990s. In 2004 Miguel Abia Biteo Boricó, a Bubi, was elected prime minister but only served until 2006, when he resigned under pressure from the country's president, Teodoro OBIANG NGUEMA MBASOGO.

See also BANTU: DISPERSION AND SETTLEMENT; COLONIAL RULE; DECOLONIZATION IN AFRICA: AN INTERPRETATION; DISEASES, INFECTIOUS, IN AFRICA; ETHNICITY AND IDENTITY IN AFRICA: AN INTERPRETATION.

ERIC YOUNG

Budd, Zola
1966–
South African track and field athlete, known for running barefoot in training and in competition.

Born in Bloemfontein, SOUTH AFRICA, Zola Budd was seventeen years of age in 1984 when she set an unofficial world record for the 5000-meter race with a time of 15 minutes, 1.83 seconds. At that time South Africa was barred from international sport because of its policy of APARTHEID, so Budd adopted British citizenship in order to qualify for the 1984 Olympic Games. This move caused a good deal of controversy because it allowed a white South African athlete to defy the ban and appear in international competitions. At the 1984 Games Budd gained international attention when, in the last lap of the 3000-meter race, American runner Mary Decker-Slaney, the world record-holder in the 3000-meter and the favorite to win, tripped on Budd's foot and fell. Both Budd and Decker-Slaney finished out of the medals. Budd initially received much of the blame for Decker-Slaney's trip, but it was later determined through photographs and video footage that neither runner was at fault.

At the European Cup in London the following year, Budd won the 3000-meter event and set a world record for the 5000-meter distance with a time of 14 minutes, 48.07 seconds. She also won the world cross-country championship in the 1985–1986 season. In 1986 she set a world indoor record for the 3000-meter. During her time in England, however, Budd faced vocal opposition from

BAREFOOT BUDD. South-African-born British athlete Zola Budd holds her lead in a 3,000-meter race on June 29, 1985, in Gateshead, England. (*David Caulkin/AP Images*)

members of the ANTIAPARTHEID MOVEMENT for not publicly declaring herself to be antiapartheid. In 1988 she returned to South Africa, where she married and now lives with her husband and three children. In 1992 she ran with an integrated South African team at the Olympic Games in Barcelona, Spain. After a long period away from the track, Budd returned to competition at age thirty-six when she ran the 2003 London Marathon.

Throughout her career, Budd's trademark has been her barefoot running style. Growing up in a rural background, running barefoot came naturally to her; she was thirteen years old before she received her first pair of running shoes. Despite her success, Budd has suffered numerous injuries, including severe hip and thigh pain as a result of her legs being two different lengths. These problems have been exacerbated by running in bare feet, and in her recent comeback Budd has worn regular training shoes. As of 2008 Budd was living in Myrtle Beach, South Carolina. She took part in the 2008 New York City Marathon.

See also ATHLETES, AFRICAN, ABROAD.

Budjga
Ethnic group of Zimbabwe.
The Budjga (also known as Budga, Budya, and Budja) primarily inhabit northeastern ZIMBABWE. They speak a BANTU language and are one of the SHONA peoples. Approximately 300,000 people consider themselves Budjga.

See also BANTU: DISPERSION AND SETTLEMENT; LANGUAGES, AFRICAN: AN OVERVIEW.

Budu
Ethnic group of the Democratic Republic of the Congo.
The Budu, also known as the Babudu, primarily inhabit the Haute-Zaire region of northeastern Congo, on the western edge of the Ituri Forest. They speak a BANTU language. Approximately 180,000 people consider themselves Budu.

See also BANTU: DISPERSION AND SETTLEMENT; CONGO, DEMOCRATIC REPUBLIC OF THE; ETHNICITY AND IDENTITY IN AFRICA: AN INTERPRETATION; LANGUAGES, AFRICAN: AN OVERVIEW.

Buganda, Early Kingdom of
East African kingdom, founded by the Baganda people, that reached the height of its power during the nineteenth century.
According to legend, the creator of Buganda was Kintu, the "First Man" and "First King," whose wife Nambi created bananas and cattle. Located on the northern shores of LAKE VICTORIA, the Buganda kingdom was initially a tributary of the larger Bunyoro-Kitara state. Between the thirteenth and

sixteenth centuries, Bantu-speakers settled in the region, as did Nilotic-speaking pastoralists migrating from the north. Together these groups became known as the Baganda-speaking Baganda. Located in swamplands, Buganda was an area unattractive to rulers of the more powerful Bunyoro-Kitara kingdom, and thus served as a refuge for political dissidents. While oral tradition names Kintu, the leader of a group of Bantu-speaking immigrants who came in the late fourteenth century, as the first kabaka, or king, other sources claim that a political dissident, Prince Kimera, became the first real king in the fifteenth century.

Buganda monarchs presided over a well-organized hierarchy of patrilineal clan leaders, regional chiefs, and village headmen. Buganda villagers cultivated a variety of crops, but bananas were especially important both as a staple food and for beer. They also kept cattle, a symbol of prosperity. For the monarchy itself, wealth was acquired through raids and the extortion of tribute from weaker neighbors, and used to reward loyal subordinates. Buganda priests and mediums were also important members of society, responsible for guiding the worship of ancestors.

During the seventeenth century, under the reign of Kabaka Katerega (1636–1663), the Buganda kingdom began to expand rapidly, incorporating the Mawokota, Gomba, Butambala, and Singo peoples. At the same time, the Bunyoro-Kitara kingdom was beginning to lose control over its expansive territory, and by the late eighteenth century, its power was dwarfed by that of the imperialistic Buganda.

The political organization of the Baganda marked a radical departure from the hereditary kings of the other kingdoms. While Baganda society was patrilineal, kings were selected matrilineally, effectively preventing fathers from passing power along to their children. Consequently, successions were marked by political upheaval and violence.

Early in the reign of Kabaka MUTESA I (1856–1884), Arab traders visited Buganda in search of slaves and ivory, for which they traded guns and gunpowder. Shortly thereafter, in 1862, the British explorer Captain John Hanning SPEKE had an audience with Mutesa while searching for the source of the NILE. In 1875, Henry Morton Stanley, another British explorer, arranged for the arrival of the Church Missionary Society (CMS). Stanley noted that Mutesa had the ability to organize some 125,000 troops on a military campaign to the east. Mutesa permitted the British missionaries to occupy his court primarily because he hoped their presence would prevent an invasion by EGYPT. Mutesa himself practiced Islam and strictly limited the missionaries' evangelical activities. French Catholic White Fathers also proselytized in Buganda. Ultimately, the religious divisions that became established festered into civil unrest, leading to a religious-based civil war.

When Egypt fell under British control in 1882, the political winds radically changed for Buganda, which had previously used the British as a counterforce against the Egyptians. In 1894 the British began exerting control over Buganda through a combination of military force and diplomacy, establishing Buganda as a protectorate. Although most Baganda chiefs were willing to collaborate, the Kabaka Mwanga, who ruled from 1884 until 1899, was not compliant with the demands of the colonists. The British subsequently deposed the unruly king, enthroned his infant son, and appointed regents to rule in his place. The 1900 Uganda Agreement established ultimate British sovereignty over all of UGANDA while guaranteeing the preservation of the Buganda monarchy. The Buganda kingdom lay at the center of the Uganda Protectorate, with the kabaka's throne located in KAMPALA. The Baganda were afforded special status under British rule; for example, they were granted land rights throughout Uganda at the expense of other ethnic groups.

In 1960 Buganda declared independence, but the British refused to recognize the monarchy's legitimacy. When Uganda became an independent federation in 1963, however, Buganda retained its regional autonomy, and Kabaka Mutesa II became president of the federation. His rule ended three years later, when Milton OBOTE, in the much more powerful position of prime minister, ordered the abolition of the monarchy and an attack on the palace. Mutesa II fled to London, where he remained until his death.

In an attempt to foster Baganda political support, in 1993 the Buganda monarchy was restored by Ugandan president Yoweri MUSEVENI. Ronald Muwenda Mutebbi II took the throne, but the kabaka is no longer a constitutional monarchy and enjoys only a religious and ceremonial role.

Numbering more than a million people, the Baganda remain the single largest ethnic group in Uganda, comprised of some fifty distinct clans. Most are farmers, and bananas and yams are the mainstay of their diet. Although most Baganda identify themselves as Christian, indigenous religious practices remain important, particularly in rural areas.

See also BANTU: DISPERSION AND SETTLEMENT; CHRISTIANITY: MISSIONARIES IN AFRICA; ISLAM IN AFRICA.

ARI NAVE

Builsa
Ethnic group of West Africa.
The Builsa (also known as Builse, Bulse, and Kanjaga) primarily inhabit the Upper West region of GHANA and southern BURKINA FASO. They speak a Niger-Congo language and belong to the GRUSI cultural and linguistic group. Approximately 170,000 people consider themselves Builsa.

See also ETHNICITY AND IDENTITY IN AFRICA: AN INTERPRETATION; LANGUAGES, AFRICAN: AN OVERVIEW.

Bujumbura, Burundi
Capital of Burundi.
Bujumbura is BURUNDI's capital and largest city, with a population of approximately 360,000 and an annual growth rate of 5 percent. Population estimates are difficult, however, because waves of refugees have periodically flooded Bujumbura over the past several years, fleeing violence in the countryside and in neighboring RWANDA. In 1996 the city became a site of violence between Hutu militia and the Tutsi-dominated Burundian army, particularly in the Kamenge suburb. Two years later, some 200 civilians were killed in an attack by Hutu rebels on the city's airport. Occasional armed attacks continue to plague Bujumbura, which remains a very ethnically divided city. Symbolic of the hierarchy of social stratification between ethnic groups, clans, and families that exists throughout Burundi, the national university and the country's elite reside in the eastern hills of Bujumbura. Meanwhile, the crowded lowland suburbs, where public services are few, house the majority of the city's poor.

Originally a small fishing village known as Usumbura, Bujumbura was settled by European traders and missionaries in 1899, when Ruanda-Urundi was a German colony. The town, located on the northern tip of LAKE TANGANYIKA, served as the seat of the German and later the Belgian colonial administrations. Many colonial buildings remain along its wide, palm tree–lined boulevards. In 1962 Bujumbura became the capital and economic hub of independent Burundi after a short, nonviolent nationalist struggle led by political parties. Bujumbura is one of the lakes major ports; food processing, the national brewery, light industry, and the coffee trade dominate the formal economy.

ERIC YOUNG

Bulawayo, Zimbabwe
Second largest city in Zimbabwe.
In the early nineteenth century, the NDEBELE king, Lobengula, established his homestead 5 km (3 mi) south of present-day Bulawayo, on the savanna near the Matsheumlope River. It was first named Gubuluwayo, or place of killing, after Lobengula's army destroyed the army of a nearby chief who refused to submit to his rule. In 1893 Lobengula burned down the town in order to avoid its takeover by European settlers. During the following year the settlers established a new town, Bulawayo, to the north. After the completion of a rail line to SOUTH AFRICA, Bulawayo grew quickly, becoming RHODESIA's principal city until it was gradually eclipsed in the 1930s by Salisbury

(present-day HARARE). According to a 2005 United Nations report, the population of Bulawayo was 676,000.

Bulawayo is laid out on a grid pattern, retaining many of the buildings and wide streets of the colonial era. It has a range of light and heavy industries. Bulawayo is the commercial and transportation hub of southern and western ZIMBABWE, with road and rail links to South Africa, BOTSWANA, and ZAMBIA (via VICTORIA FALLS). The cultural and political center of the Ndebele people, Bulawayo boasts a railway museum, a natural history museum, the Rhodes Matopos National Park, and the Khami Ruins. The city hosts the annual Zimbabwe International Trade Fair.

Recent drought conditions in Bulawayo have diminished water supplies, which has put a strain on public services. Plans are underway to build a water pipeline from the ZAMBEZI RIVER. The city has also worked to improve water delivery services and boost water conservation.

BIBLIOGRAPHY

Jack, Alex. *Bulawayos Changing Skyline, 1893–1980.* Books of Zimbabwe, 1979.

Wolcott, Harry. *The African Beer Gardens of Bulawayo: Integrated Drinking in a Segregated Society.* Rutgers Center of Alcohol Studies, 1974.

ERIC YOUNG

Bulu

Ethnic group of Cameroon.

The Bulu primarily inhabit southern CAMEROON. They speak a BANTU language and belong to the larger BETI cultural and linguistic group. Some 660,000 people consider themselves Bulu, although more than 800,000 speak the language.

See also BANTU: DISPERSION AND SETTLEMENT; ETHNICITY AND IDENTITY IN AFRICA: AN INTERPRETATION; LANGUAGES, AFRICAN: AN OVERVIEW.

Bunu

Ethnic group of Nigeria.

The Bunu, also known as the Kabba, primarily inhabit central NIGERIA, where the NIGER and Benue rivers meet. They speak YORUBA, a Niger-Congo language, and are closely related to other Yoruba peoples. Approximately 200,000 people consider themselves Bunu.

Bura

Ethnic group of Nigeria.

The Bura, also known as Pabir and Babur, primarily inhabit the Borno State of northeastern NIGERIA. They speak an Afro-Asiatic language belonging to the Chadic group. Approximately 250,000 people consider themselves Bura.

See also ETHNICITY AND IDENTITY IN AFRICA: AN INTERPRETATION; LANGUAGES, AFRICAN: AN OVERVIEW.

Burkina Faso

Landlocked West African country bordered by Côte d'Ivoire, Mali, Niger, Benin, Togo, and Ghana.

In 1984 the leaders of Upper Volta changed the name of this former French colony to Burkina Faso, a term combining two of the country's many languages, and meaning "land of upright people." As one of the world's poorest nations, Burkina Faso counts people among its most important resources. Remittances from migrant laborers working in the more affluent CÔTE D'IVOIRE sustain the households of many of the approximately thirteen million citizens in Burkina Faso, 82 percent of whom live in rural areas. This tradition of southward migration became firmly established during the colonial era, when France incorporated the Volta region into its West African empire in order to turn the drought-prone but relatively populous Mossi plateau into a labor reserve. Because the French colonial administration invested little in developing Upper Volta itself, de jure independence in 1960 heralded a new era of de facto dependence on foreign donors, especially France. Steady infusions of aid, however, failed to prevent either the onset of two famines or the overthrow of six governments.

In 1983, flight commander Thomas SANKARA came to power promising an end to both neocolonialism and rural suffering. Although the Burkinabè revolution was cut short by Sankara's assassination in 1987, it did initiate improvements in rural literacy, health, and food security, as well as women's rights. The current regime of Blaise COMPAORÉ has deregulated the economy, mended relations with the West, and pledged a commitment (viewed skeptically by many Burkinabè) to democracy. Burkina Faso is still extremely poor, but it enjoys a reputation for religious and ethnic tolerance, as well as for its rich performing arts traditions.

EARLY HISTORY

Apart from Stone Age axes found in northern Burkina Faso, archaeology provides few clues about the region's first human inhabitants. The ancestors of the LOBI and BOBO peoples were among the earliest agriculturists, settling the savanna west of the Mouhoun (or Black Volta) River perhaps around 1100 C.E. While these lineage-based societies never developed centralized polities, migrants from the DAGOMBA region (in present-day GHANA) founded the MOSSI dynasties on the more arid plateau to the north. The most powerful Mossi kingdom, Ouagadougou, was founded in the late fifteenth century. Nineteen smaller but fairly autonomous Mossi states ruled

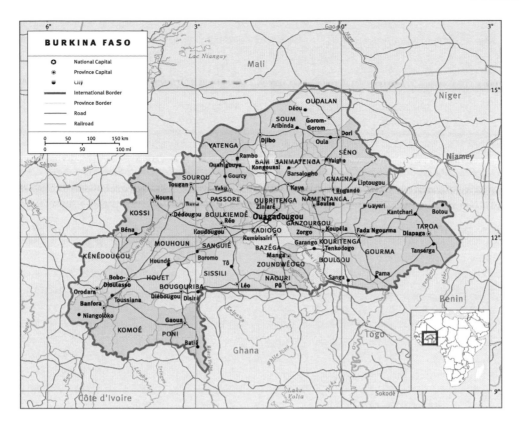

over territories to the north, west, and east, and eventually assimilated many of the neighboring peoples into Mossi society. Both the Mossi and the southern peoples lived primarily from rainy-season agriculture, supplemented during the long dry season by HUNTING, foraging, and in some places fishing. Millet and sorghum were staples throughout the savanna; wetter conditions in the far south supported the production of root crops and, later, rice. In the far north, seasonal rainfall also shaped the migration patterns of Peul (or FULANI) pastoralists.

Situated between the forest and SAHEL ecozones, the Volta region was traversed by caravan traders who dealt in kola, gold, and slaves from the forest regions, salt from the SAHARA, and luxury goods from North Africa. The traders brought weapons and horses to the court of Ouagadougou, but found the most lively markets in southern towns such as Sya (now BOBO-DIOULASSO), where MANDE-speaking Zara merchants had settled amongst the Bobo.

In the sixteenth century, the Mossi expanded northward into the Sahel, where they were rebuffed by the armies of the SONGHAI EMPIRE, led by SUNNI ALI. However, neither Ali nor his successor, ASKIA MUHAMMAD, was able to convince the Ouagadougou king, the *mogho naaba*, to convert to Islam. Although many Mossi traders eventually did convert, the Volta region has remained less Islamized than the rest of the Sahel.

In the eighteenth and nineteenth centuries, SLAVERY became a common practice in the Volta region. Some Mossi kingdoms captured local peoples or bought slaves from other kingdoms to work as agricultural or domestic laborers. These slaves were often allowed to engage in wage-earning activities for themselves, such as cultivating food and raising cattle. At the same time, southern peoples were subjected to slave raids from the KONG empire (northern Côte d'Ivoire). With no armies and few weapons, peoples such as the Bobo lived in large, densely settled villages for protection.

COLONIAL CONQUEST

By the late nineteenth century, Great Britain and France were racing against each other to establish spheres of influence in the West African interior. In 1887 the French explorer Louis Binger visited Ouagadougou during his trip across West Africa. He was unimpressed by the Mossi kingdom, noting that the Mossi cultivated only what they needed in order to subsist, "so that even if there are no paupers in their country, there are virtually no rich men either." Yet the Mossi region was densely populated, and Binger suggested it would make a suitable "labor reserve" for French ventures elsewhere in West Africa. In particular, labor was needed for irrigated cotton production in the fertile but sparsely populated NIGER RIVER basin, which French engineers believed had the potential to become a "new EGYPT."

The Mogho Naaba Wogbo refused Binger's invitation to make his kingdom a French protectorate. The explorer did, however, manage to secure a protectorate agreement from the Ouattara leader of Kong, whose empire by then included much of the southern Volta region. Over the next several years the French conquered regions to the east, west, and north of the Mossi kingdoms, and in 1895 French troops occupied Bobo-Dioulasso, overcoming resistance from the town's Zara warriors. The following year the French defeated Ouagadougou's Mossi army and burned down much of the city. Wogbo escaped and later sought British protection.

COLONIAL RULE

In 1898 France and Great Britain reached an accord, granting France dominion over Upper Volta. The territory was initially designated a military zone, but in 1904 it became part of the colony Haut-Sénégal-Niger, administered from BAMAKO. After their earlier experience with the recalcitrant Wogbo, the French were determined to undermine the authority of the Mossi kingship. When Wogbo's successor Sighiri died in 1905, the French replaced him with a sixteen-year-old *naaba*, who posed little threat to the colonial regime. They also replaced lower-level Mossi chiefs, where necessary, with more compliant appointees, and imposed the indigénat, a legal system that effectively placed all judicial power in the hands of French administrators.

The French could not afford to dismantle the Mossi kingdom or other preexisting authority structures entirely, however. Although French officials were posted to each of the colony's administrative districts (known as *cercles*), they needed chiefs to collect taxes and recruit labor, and thus appointed them to these duties even in regions with no prior tradition of centralized authority. This was the case, for example, in the Bobo-Dioulasso cercle, where appointed Ouattara chiefs were usually unpopular and ineffective, and known for embezzling taxes.

The first quarter of the twentieth century was a period of extreme hardship for the peoples of Upper Volta. Although the French officially ended slavery in 1901, tens of thousands of Voltaics were forced each year to labor in cotton fields and construction sites, while others were conscripted into the military. Such policies, coupled with a punitive system of taxation, provoked popular revolts throughout the colony. These ranged from a 2,000-person anti-tax march in Ouagadougou in 1908 to a series of village revolts west of Bobo-Dioulasso in 1915–1916. Thousands also fled south to the British colony of GOLD COAST, where labor laws were less coercive.

In 1919 the French made Upper Volta a separate colony, in order to better control its people and develop its economy. As in the previous decades, thousands of laborers were forcibly recruited to build an administrative post in the new capital, OUAGADOUGOU, as well as roads and rail lines intended to facilitate the export of cotton—a crop that peasants in many cercles were forced to cultivate. But the French invested little in irrigation, fertilizer, or other agricultural improvements in Upper Volta, since it was still considered primarily a labor reserve for neighboring colonies' projects. Consequently, cotton farming in more arid areas led quickly to soil degradation, especially since many rural households—having lost their most able-bodied members to compulsory labor projects—were too short-handed to tend their land properly. Forced cash-crop cultivation also took time and land away from grain farming, leaving rural areas dangerously vulnerable to food shortages.

This vulnerability became tragically obvious in the late 1920s, when a series of droughts coincided with plunging world prices for cotton and commodities after 1929. Famines in 1926 and 1930 led one French colonial official to warn of demographic collapse. By 1931 Upper Volta was not only famine-stricken but also bankrupt, and in September 1932 the country was dismantled and divided up among neighboring French colonies. Most of the territory went to Côte d'Ivoire, where Voltaic labor was needed for coffee and cocoa plantations as well as for the ABIDJAN-Ouagadougou railway.

The rail line reached Bobo-Dioulasso in 1934, and several European trade firms soon followed. Besides a handful of French administrators and soldiers, most of the town's other European residents were Roman Catholic missionaries known as *Pères Blancs* (White Fathers). As elsewhere in the Volta region, the Bobo mission was hurrying to win converts during a time of rapid Islamization. The Pères Blancs targeted village youth, in particular; they offered catechism classes and staged festivities at the mission, and spoke out openly against forced labor.

When World War II began, more than 10,000 Mossi volunteered for active military service. Some served in Europe or North Africa, but many remained in the Bobo-Dioulasso military camp, or were used for forced labor. Soon after the war ended, the French government agreed to grant its colonies representation in the French National Assembly. Côte d'Ivoire received three seats, and in November 1946 Ivoirian Félix HOUPHOUËT-BOIGNY and two Voltaics, Daniel Ouézzin Coulibaly and Philippe Kaboré—all members of the radical RASSEMBLEMENT DÉMOCRATIQUE AFRICAIN (RDA)—were elected its deputies. In that same year, Mossi chiefs asked France to restore Upper Volta as a separate colony. They were primarily interested in reinstating their own political influence, but France agreed to their request. France was primarily interested in cutting the region off from the anticolonial politics of Houphouët-Boigny and the RDA. The charismatic

Ivoirian was already extremely popular around Bobo-Dioulasso, especially after he convinced the French National Assembly in April 1946 to abolish forced labor.

Upper Volta was reconstituted on September 4, 1947. The RDA remained popular in the southwest, but in the north lost support to Mossi-dominated political parties, such as the conservative Union Voltaique (UV). Over the next decade, growing nationalist movements throughout Africa made DECOLONIZATION inevitable. In Upper Volta, this was a time of relative prosperity; many World War II veterans invested their pensions in commercial agriculture, trade, and transport companies, and both Bobo-Dioulasso and Ouagadougou grew rapidly. Still, political factionalism during the 1950s, combined with the fact that Upper Volta was still landlocked and resource-poor, boded ill for independence.

In 1958, two years after universal suffrage was granted throughout French West Africa, France's African colonies took part in a referendum on whether to become semiautonomous members of the French Community. Upper Volta, like all its neighbors save GUINEA, voted yes. That same year saw the rise to power of Maurice Yaméogo, a Mossi member of the newly formed Parti de Regroupement Africain. After he was elected president of Upper Volta's Council of Ministers, Yaméogo moved to align himself with the now politically moderate RDA and its founder Houphouët-Boigny, who would soon be president of Côte d'Ivoire. A 1959 treaty of economic cooperation between the two leaders indicated that Upper Volta, long the labor reserve of its wealthier neighbor, would continue to depend on Côte d'Ivoire for employment and port access.

Unlike many emerging African leaders, Yaméogo argued that his people were not ready for total independence; as he told one French official in 1959, "We cannot even build matchboxes." By then, however, France was committed to pulling out of all its West African colonies. Upper Volta became independent on August 5, 1960, and Yaméogo became its first president.

INDEPENDENCE

The next two decades confirmed the political omens of the late colonial period. Yaméogo, an authoritarian leader even before independence, moved quickly to undermine the multiparty system and rein in the country's young labor movement. This tactic worked until 1966, when the president's attempts to cut government employees' wages provoked a wave of strikes, followed by a military takeover led by Colonel Sangoulé Lamizana. Military coups subsequently became more the norm than the exception in Upper Volta's politics. Meanwhile, one regime after another failed to invigorate the country's stagnant economy, which remained heavily dependent on exports of cotton and migrant labor, as well as on foreign aid. Despite a sizeable community of international development and relief workers in the capital Ouagadougou, drought-stricken rural northern provinces suffered famines in 1973–1974 and 1984–1985.

Even as political and economic conditions were deteriorating, however, Upper Volta was developing a thriving state-sponsored film industry. Since 1969 the capital has hosted the biennial Festival Panafricain du Cinéma et de la Télévision de Ouagadougou (FESPACO). Ouagadougou has come to be known as the "Cannes of Africa," and Burkinabè filmmakers such as Idrissa OUÉDRAOGO and Gaston Kaboré have won international renown. The state has also actively supported theater festivals, as well as Bobo-Dioulasso's biennial "Bobo Fête," a weeklong event featuring contests and cultural performances of all kinds (including cooking and hairdressing), drawn from traditions throughout the country.

REVOLUTION AND RECTIFICATION

In 1983 drama on the streets of Ouagadougou, not its cinema screens, caught world attention. In the previous year, military officials had overthrown the regime of Saye Zerbo, and established the 120-member ruling Conseil de Salut du Peuple (CSP). A left-wing faction within the CSP, led by the young flight commander Thomas Sankara and his long-time friend Blaise Compaoré had gotten Sankara appointed as prime minister in January 1983. In May the conservative wing of the CSP had Sankara arrested on trumped-up treason charges. Students protested en masse in the capital, and troops led by Compaoré launched a rebellion from the Ghanaian border. On August 4, they marched into Ouagadougou, freed Sankara, and captured the national radio, from where Sankara announced that the Conseil National de la Révolution (CNR) had taken over the country.

Upper Volta had seen many military rulers, but Sankara at age thirty-three was by far the youngest and most revolutionary. He initiated the renaming of the country Burkina Faso, "land of upright people," and was considered by many, both at home and abroad, to be a morally upright leader, though not always a pragmatic one. Once in power, he cut the wages of top civil servants (including himself) and donated all the government's luxury cars to the national lottery, using the proceeds for public spending. He was also an outspoken proponent of women's liberation. He appointed five women to ministerial posts, launched a campaign against FEMALE CIRCUMCISION, and initiated changes in family law. The Sankara government's investments in rural schools, clinics, and agricultural extension services brought modest improvements in living standards, and quite dramatic increases in food production. Sankara's foreign policy, meanwhile, aligned his country squarely with left-wing regimes such as Cuba, LIBYA, and North Korea. He rejected World Bank loan conditions, and promised to "fight against the forces of neo-colonialism and imperialist domination."

Not surprisingly, such rhetoric discouraged foreign investment, just as Sankara's public references to the "big, fat, and gross" bourgeoisie led many Burkinabé merchants and entrepreneurs to take their businesses across the border. More seriously, Sankara's heavy-handedness alienated nearly all the country's traditionally powerful constituencies. Mossi chiefs did not welcome his pledge to destroy rural "feudalism" and "patriarchy," and the president's harsh treatment of critics and striking workers eventually turned even the labor unions against him. Ultimately, however, it was Sankara's own peers—soldiers loyal to his best friend and fellow CNR member Blaise Compaoré—who assassinated him on October 15, 1987. Although Compaoré denied involvement in the murder, he did not hesitate to take power afterward.

Compaoré has ruled Burkina Faso since Sankara's death. He took office pledging to "rectify" the Sankara revolution, and moved immediately to mend rifts with Mossi authorities, the army, the business community, and Western donor nations. His appointed government, the Front Populaire, announced the formation of a new umbrella party, the Organisation pour la Démocratie Populaire/Mouvement du Travail (ODP/MT) in 1989, and a year later it drafted a new constitution, allowing for multiparty elections. However, repression of political dissidents (including many university students) continued, and government control over preelection campaigning and media led opposition parties to boycott the December 1991 presidential elections. Compaoré won easily, but less than a quarter of the population voted.

Since the disputed 1991 elections, political parties in Burkina Faso have proliferated, but the ODP/MT has consistently dominated national elections. Compaoré captured the presidency again in 1998, in an election followed immediately by unrest over the murder of a journalist investigating the death of the president's chauffeur. The killing remains unsolved. A constitutional amendment approved in 2000 lengthened the president's term of office from five to seven years, but limited the president to a single term. These laws, however, were not enough to keep Compaoré from another term in office. He won resoundingly in 2005, securing more than 80 percent of the vote.

Like many other nations in West Africa, Burkina Faso has been caught up in the ongoing violence and civil unrest throughout the region. In the early 2000s Côte d'Ivoire's president, Laurent Gbagbo, initiated a campaign to restrict citizenship in his country, a move that threatened the status of the many Burkinabè immigrants in the country.

After civil war erupted in Côte d'Ivoire in 2002, Gbagbo accused Burkina Faso of supporting the rebels fighting against his government. This dispute led to a yearlong closure of the border between the two countries, which finally reopened in September 2003.

On the economic front, "rectification" brought an end to Marxist-Leninism as an official government ideology. Faced with falling world cotton prices and growing debt, Compaoré agreed to a World Bank STRUCTURAL ADJUSTMENT program in 1991. The accompanying austerity measures—including thousands of layoffs at state-owned factories and fee increases for education and other government services—provoked strikes by students and trade unions. The 1994 devaluation of the West African franc (the CFA) brought further price increases, especially for imported fuel, foodstuffs, and manufactured goods. Economic growth in recent years has been somewhat uneven, but the government's adherence to World Bank reforms has put Burkina Faso near the top of the list of poor nations targeted for debt relief by international donors. The country is also counting on revenue from gold, which has become Burkina Faso's second-largest source of foreign exchange (after cotton) since the Sankara government reopened the long-dormant Poura gold mine in 1984. Foreign mining firms and artisanal gold panners are now working at several different sites around the country, but gold reserves are small and will not last much beyond the year 2000. The government is also attempting to exploit other minerals such as zinc, and to diversify its agricultural exports. Burkina Faso is already Africa's second largest exporter of French green beans (after KENYA), and recent aid programs have secured European markets for sun-dried Burkinabè tomatoes and mangoes.

Despite its status as one of the world's poorest countries, Burkina Faso has in many ways fared better than its wealthier neighbors. It has experienced no debilitating civil wars and is considered by many to be an oasis of ethnic and religious tolerance. Its economy has been competently managed, and rural areas—where approximately 80 percent of the population still lives—have begun to reap the benefits of soil conservation programs dating from the 1980s. In 1998 Burkina Faso hosted the AFRICAN CUP OF NATIONS soccer tournament, Africa's biggest sporting event. Even though the home team lost in the quarterfinals, positive international media coverage of the games' host suggested that the Burkinabè had, at the least, scored a public relations victory.

See also CHRISTIANITY: MISSIONARIES IN AFRICA; CINEMA, AFRICAN; COLONIAL RULE; MINERALS AND MINING IN AFRICA; PASTORALISM; SCRAMBLE FOR AFRICA.

ROANNE EDWARDS AND SUSANNE FREIDBERG

Burkina Faso (At a Glance)

OFFICIAL NAME:
Burkina Faso

FORMER NAME:
Upper Volta

AREA:
274,200 sq km (about 105,869 sq mi)

LOCATION:
Inland West Africa, bordered by Mali, Niger, Benin, Togo, Ghana, and Cote d'Ivoire

CAPITAL:
Ouagadougou (population 1,181,702; 2006 estimate)

OTHER MAJOR CITIES:
Bobo-Dioulasso (population 435,543), Koudougou (131,825) (2006 estimates)

POPULATION:
15,264,735 (2008 estimate)

POPULATION DENSITY:
55.67 persons per sq km (about 144 persons per sq mi)

POPULATION BELOW AGE 15:
46.3 percent (male 3,549,034; female 3,521,684)

POPULATION GROWTH RATE:
3.109 percent (2008 estimate)

TOTAL FERTILITY RATE:
6.34 children born per woman (2008 estimate)

LIFE EXPECTANCY AT BIRTH:
Total population: 52.55 years (male 50.67 years; female 54.49 years; 2008 estimate)

INFANT MORTALITY RATE:
86.02 deaths per 1,000 live births (2008 estimate)

LITERACY RATE (AGE 15 AND OVER WHO CAN READ AND WRITE):
Total population: 21.8 percent (male 29.4 percent; female 15.2 percent; 2003 estimate)

EDUCATION:
Officially compulsory for children aged 7 to 13, but only 35 percent of all children aged 6 to 11 attended school in the early 2000s, and only about 8 percent of those aged 12 to 17. Far fewer girls than boys attend school. In the mid-1990s Burkina Faso's primary schools had an annual enrollment of about 650,195, secondary schools about 116,033, and vocational schools about 8808; about 9452 students were enrolled at the university level.

LANGUAGES:
French is the official language but is not widely spoken outside of cities. More than half the population speaks Moore; the remainder speak a variety of Mande languages.

ETHNIC GROUPS:
Most people belong to two major West African cultural groups, the Voltaic and the Mande. The Voltaic are the most numerous and include the Mossi, who constitute over 40 percent of the population. Other principal ethnic groups are the Fulani, Lobi, Bobo, Sénufo, Gourounsi, Bissa, and Gourmantche.

RELIGIONS:
About 40 percent of the population adhere to indigenous beliefs. About 50 percent are Muslim and 10 percent Christian (mainly Roman Catholic).

CLIMATE:
Semi-arid; the weather is cool and dry from November through March, hot and dry from April through May, and warm and rainy from June through October. Average annual rainfall ranges from 1,000 mm (more than 40 in) in the southwest to less than 250 mm (less than 10 in) in the north. Average temperatures in Ouagadougou vary from 24° C (76° F) in January to 28° C (83° F) in July.

LAND, PLANTS, AND ANIMALS:
Burkina Faso is located on a plateau sloping generally to the south and situated from about 200 to 700 m (about 650 to 2,300 ft) in elevation. The plateau is drained to the south by the Black Volta (Mouhoun), Red Volta (Nazinon), and White Volta (Nakanbe) rivers and to the east by small rivers connecting with the Niger; none are navigable. Most of the country is covered with savanna grasses and small trees. Animals include elephants, hippopotamuses, buffalo, antelope, and crocodiles.

NATURAL RESOURCES:
Mineral resources include manganese and gold as well as small deposits of copper, nickel, bauxite, lead, silver, iron ore, cassiterite (tin ore), and phosphates. Except in the southwest of the country, water is scarce and most of the soils are relatively poor.

CURRENCY:
Communaute Financiere Africaine franc (XOF)

GROSS DOMESTIC PRODUCT (GDP):
$17.41 billion (2007 estimate)

GDP PER CAPITA:
$1,200 (2007 estimate)

GDP REAL GROWTH RATE:
4.2 percent (2007 estimate)

PRIMARY ECONOMIC ACTIVITIES:
Agriculture (32 percent of GDP, 80 percent of employment), livestock, small-scale commerce, gold mining, and migrant labor (approximately 20 percent of the male labor force migrates annually to neighboring countries).

PRIMARY AGRICULTURAL PRODUCTS:
Millet, sorghum, corn, rice, peanuts, shea nuts, sesame, cotton, and livestock

INDUSTRIES:
Cotton lint, beverages, agricultural processing, soap, cigarettes, textiles, and gold

PRIMARY EXPORTS:
Cotton, livestock products, and gold

PRIMARY IMPORTS:
Foodstuffs, petroleum, textiles, iron, steel, metal products, vehicles, electrical equipment, and machinery

PRIMARY TRADE PARTNERS:
European Union (especially France), Cote d'Ivoire, Taiwan, and Thailand

GOVERNMENT:
Parliamentary; nominally a constitutional multiparty democracy. The executive branch is led by President Blaise Compaoré and an appointed 29-member cabinet, which includes Prime Minister Tertius Zongo. A constitutional amendment approved in 2000 changed the president's term of office from five to seven years and limited the president to a single term, although these laws were eventually judged not to apply to the current government. Compaoré went on to a landslide reelection victory in 2005. The legislative branch is the elected 111-member National Assembly, currently dominated by the Congress for Democracy and Progress, or CDP.

Burton, Sir Richard
1821–1890
European adventurer, polyglot, ethnographer, and prolific writer who explored Africa, the Middle East, and Muslim Central Asia.

Sir Richard Burton spoke twenty-five languages and multiple dialects, including Greek, Latin, English, French, Italian, Marathi, Punjab, Arabic, and Hindi. During his travels he observed an enormous range of cultural practices, which he documented in forty-three manuscripts. He also wrote two books of poetry and four volumes of folklore.

Born in Torquay, England, Burton was raised by his English parents primarily in France. He briefly attended Trinity College, Oxford, but was expelled in 1842 for insubordination. He then joined the Bombay army, and served in India (in present-day Pakistan) until 1850. Working as an intelligence officer, Burton learned to impersonate Muslim merchants. His reputation was called into question and his military career cut short, however, when a rival officer spread word that Burton had been investigating homosexual bathhouses in Karachi, failing to divulge that Burton had done so under orders from a senior officer.

After returning to France and writing four books about India, Burton departed in 1853 for CAIRO, disguised as an Afghan Muslim. From Cairo he traveled to Medina, and then on to Mecca, a city forbidden to all non-Muslims. He sketched and described in great detail the mosque and the Ka'bah, the great Muslim holy site, and later documented the journey in *Pilgrimage to El-Medinah and Mecca* (1855).

Immediately afterward Burton traveled to Harar, in the Ch'erch'er Mountains of Somaliland (present-day SOMALIA), a center of Muslim missionary activity and slave trading. He described this risky journey in *First Footsteps in East Africa* (1856).

Later in 1855 Burton set off on an expedition to find the source of the White NILE with John Hanning SPEKE. The party was attacked en route, and Speke was badly hurt. Burton himself was wounded by a javelin piercing through his cheeks, which forced him to return to England. During the next year the two men resumed their search, and this time faced debilitating illnesses. Burton, weak from MALARIA, had to remain in Tabora, while the somewhat healthier Speke continued alone to LAKE VICTORIA, which he declared to be the source of the White Nile. Burton was skeptical of Speke's claim that Lake Victoria was the source of the Nile, a conclusion that Speke based on hearsay rather than firsthand knowledge. Resentful that Speke's "discovery" was celebrated, and unable to procure funds for resuming his own exploration, Burton became increasingly antagonistic toward his old friend.

Burton next traveled to Salt Lake City, Utah, where he conducted research on Mormonism for his book *City of the Saints* (1861). Back in London, he married his long-time love, Isabel Arundell, in 1861—secretly, owing to her Roman Catholic affiliation.

From 1861 until 1864 Burton served as a British consul to Fernando Po, a Spanish-ruled island off the coast of present-day CAMEROON (but a part of EQUATORIAL GUINEA). During his stay, he visited several West African regions, including DAHOMEY (now BENIN). His observations provided material for five more ethnographies. After returning to England, Burton was invited to debate Speke's claims at a meeting of the British Association for the Advancement of Science. While awaiting Speke's arrival, he was informed that Speke had shot himself while hunting, and had died. Burton suspected suicide.

Burton spent four years at his next British consular post in Santos, Brazil. Unhappy and in poor health, he was helped by his wife, who set off for England, where she used her influence to secure him a post in Damascus. He was dismissed in 1871, ostensibly after he tried to protect members of a Muslim sect who wished to convert to Christianity. During the following year he became the consul to Trieste, Italy, where he remained with his wife until his death.

While living in Trieste he published numerous books, attacking Victorian values and detailing taboo topics, from homosexuality to erotica. Despite his translation of the *Kama Sutra of Vatsyayana* and his daring, unconventional essays, he was eventually knighted in 1886. After Burton's death, his wife, fearing that her husband would be depicted as perverted and corrupt, burned virtually his entire collection of journals. Regardless of this historical loss, Burton's remarkable career and his contributions to African ethnography continue to be celebrated.

See also EXPLORERS IN AFRICA SINCE 1800.

ARI NAVE

Burundi
Country located between East and Central Africa, bordered by Rwanda, the Democratic Republic of Congo, and Tanzania.

Nineteenth-century European travelers described the kingdom of Burundi as "a land of almost ideal beauty." Today, the national borders of Burundi, one of Africa's most densely populated countries, remain virtually unchanged, but political turmoil has disfigured its idyllic landscape. Formerly ruled by traditional monarchies, Burundi was colonized by Germany in the late nineteenth century and remained under German and then Belgian administration until its independence in 1962. Just ten years after independence, an abortive coup d'état provoked brutal massacres, claiming the lives of more than 100,000 people. Tens of thousands more have since died, particularly in

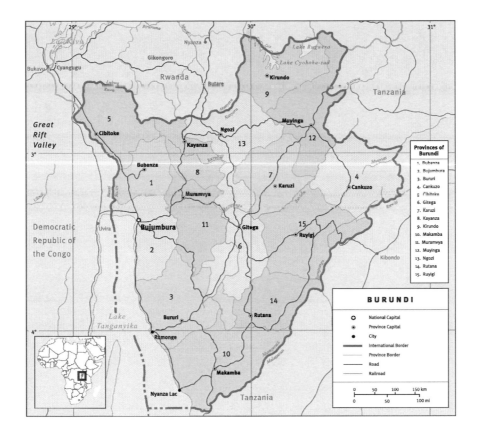

1988 and 1993, in what is usually referred to as "ethnic conflict" between the country's Hutu majority and the 15 percent Tutsi minority. This explanation for Burundi's violence, however, overlooks the long history of cohabitation and intermarriage between these two groups. More fundamentally, it does not do justice to the extraordinarily complex social, economic, and political meanings of ethnic identity in Burundi.

EARLY BURUNDI SOCIETY

There are diverging theories on the origin of the hunter-gatherer TWA, or PYGMY, the first known inhabitants of present-day Burundi. Archaeological evidence indicates the Twa occupied the area beginning around 70,000 B.C.E., whereas linguistic evidence suggests that they migrated to the region from West Africa around 5,000 years ago. Further linguistic evidence reveals that BANTU-speaking cultivators from the lowlands of Central Africa migrated to the mountainous region between Lake Kivu, LAKE TANGANYIKA, and LAKE VICTORIA sometime during the eleventh century. These people took the name baHutu, or Hutu. Pastoralist Hima people (probably from present-day southern ETHIOPIA, though their exact origins are disputed) succeeded them in the mid-sixteenth century, becoming known as the baTutsi, or Tutsi. They established small hillside chiefdoms based on cattle-clientship, in which the Tutsi would give the Hutu cattle as payment for their agricultural labor or surplus crops. Elsewhere the two groups established commercial relationships, again exchanging livestock for food crops. The Tutsi adopted the Hutu language as well as many of their customs, including practices of worshiping ancestors and the belief in the existence of a spiritual life in all living things.

Unlike most other parts of Africa, the kingdom of Burundi developed a national character well before European colonial intervention. In the mid-seventeenth century a Tutsi chief, Ntare, began building this kingdom through conquest. It eventually took the form of several provinces, each ruled by a distinct royal clan: the Batare, Bezi, Batanga, and Bambutsa. Because of succession disputes, by the end of the eighteenth century the king, or *mwami*, Gisabo claimed control over only half the kingdom, which by then covered the approximate area of present-day Burundi. But the system of succession was not clear. In the 1860s the princes, who with their immediate descendants comprised the *ganwa* monarchy, rebelled against the current king, Ntare II.

Burundian society was feudal in character, and its hierarchies extraordinarily complex. The *ganwa* monarchy formed the landholding aristocracy, whose "ethnic" identity as Tutsi was primarily based on their royal status. Socially subordinate to the ganwa were the Banyaruguru Tutsi,

CIVIL WAR IN BURUNDI. Mozambique soldiers disembark a plane at Bujumbura airport in Burundi as part of the ongoing peacekeeping efforts in the continuing civil war between the Tutsi and the Hutu, 2003. (*Aloys Niyoyita/AP Images*)

literally the "people from above," and below them the Hima Tutsi. As in many other parts of Central and East Africa, the pastoralists—in this case the Tutsi—came to dominate the cultivators—the Hutu—through their control of cattle, the primary measure of wealth, as well as through their tradition of warfare. In fact, in the common Kirundi language, Hutu has two meanings, one cultural and the other social, defined as "social subordinate" or "social son." These identities, however, depended on social context: A Tutsi poor in cattle, for example, would be considered a client and a "Hutu" to a wealthier Tutsi patron. The social stratification was complicated by a patrilineal kinship system that divided families between "very good," "good," "rather good," "neither good nor bad," and "bad." Inequality was a source of social cohesion; the poor and weak depended on protection and patronage from the rich and powerful, who in turn relied on clientage ties to legitimate and maintain their status. At the same time, precolonial Burundian society was exceptionally homogeneous culturally, and allowed for considerable social and economic mobility. By acquiring cattle, for example, a Hutu could "become" Tutsi. Intermarriage between cultural ethnic groups, sometimes for status, was common.

Although Burundian society was vertically stratified, the Tutsi were not the political masters of the Hutu. The two groups shared a conception of the Mwami as an absolute monarch whose authority was primarily spiritual, not political. It was the ganwa who ruled the provinces in the name of the Mwami. Meanwhile, the abanyarurimbi, or "those who can judge," either Hutu or Tutsi but not ganwa, controlled the court system. Local disputes were arbitrated by the abashingantache, or "those of the small stick"—posts open to anyone, but typically held by elder Hutu men.

COLONIALISM IN THE HEART OF AFRICA
In the mid-1800s many European explorers and missionaries, including John Hanning SPEKE, Richard Francis BURTON, David Livingstone, and Henry Morton Stanley, traveled through the Burundi kingdom. In the late-nineteenth-century rush to colonize the continent, known as the SCRAMBLE FOR AFRICA, Belgium, Great Britain, and Germany contested possession of Ruanda-Urundi (present-day RWANDA and Burundi, respectively) because the territory lay at the intersection between their respective colonial possessions and at the headwaters of the NILE RIVER. Although the BERLIN CONFERENCE OF 1884–1886 ceded control of Ruanda-Urundi to Germany, the exact boundaries of the colony remained in dispute until the 1910 Kivu-Mfumbiro Conference, attended by Belgium, Great Britain, and Germany. At the time Germany was represented in the area by forty soldiers, a handful of merchants and civil servants, and over 100 missionaries.

Colonization destroyed Burundi's fragile social cohesion and emerging national identity. This occurred largely because European colonial administrators, with help from missionaries, interpreted existing social stratification in terms of rigid ethnic categories, and then allocated political power and material resources accordingly. Upon the defeat of Germany in World War I (1914–1918), the League of Nations transferred control of Ruanda-Urundi to Belgium as a mandate territory. Initially, the Belgian regime concentrated on developing export crop production, achieved through compulsory labor service and crop cultivation. But in 1929 it began to intervene in Burundian political structures, instituting a system of indirect rule by ganwa-izing the colonial civil service. The Belgians considered the *ganwa* not only the traditional and thereby most appropriate rulers, but also a higher race. This pitted the Batare and Bezi clans against each other while marginalizing southern Tutsi. The Belgians also promoted the Mwami Mwambutsa IV as a modernizing ruler, and Catholicism as a moral and religious extension of colonial rule. The colonial education system focused on training the children of the ganwa and Tutsi chiefs, although it also subsidized mission-run schools that focused on universal primary education.

The northern Tutsi's privileged access to education and civil service employment translated into economic advancement at a time when colonial labor policies and taxation were subjecting most other Burundians to severe hardship. As social differentiation hardened into class stratification, tensions between the ganwa and other groups—both southern Tutsi and Hutu—increased. At the same time, generations-old rivalries between the Batare and the Bezi were aggravated by the Belgians' strategy of switching their support from one to the other, depending upon which clan or individual appeared the most reliable and malleable ally. In the 1950s, as the Burundian elite began pushing for self-rule and ultimately for independence, the Belgians settled on supporting Batare Chief Baranyanka and his minor and Batare-dominated nationalist Parti Démocrate Chrétien (PDC) over the more popular and radical Bezi-dominated Union Pour le Progrès National (UPRONA). As the last Belgian resident, or governor, explains: "There was a certain connivance and even a direct complicity between our Authority and the PDC . . . The PDC quickly became the bulwark we hoped to use in order to stop the cancerous metastasis of UPRONA's progress." Not surprisingly, Belgian support for the PDC only further strengthened UPRONA, which was led by the eldest son of Mwami Mwambutsa, the popular Prince Louis RWAGASORE, who identified with the Bezi.

Despite the social tensions fostered by colonialism, the nationalist movement had begun to forge a sense of Burundian unity by the late 1950s. This was shattered by the 1959 Rwandan revolution, in which the majority Hutu peasantry overthrew the Belgian-backed Tutsi aristocracy and took firm control of the nationalist movement, killing many Tutsi in the process. Although the societies in the two Belgian colonies differed significantly, the Rwandan revolution solidified ethnic identities in Burundi. Many Burundian Tutsi feared a similar nightmare, while the Hutu considered it a defining moment in their political aspirations. Adding to the heightened tensions, in October 1961 prime minister–designate Prince Rwagasore was assassinated in a plot approved by the Batare leadership, who feared that the prince and UPRONA would favor the interests of the rival Bezi clan. The simmering discord in Burundi did not prevent the Belgians from implementing a quick withdrawal from the territory.

THE CYCLES OF VIOLENCE IN BURUNDI

On July 1, 1962, Burundi, as part of a short-lived economic federation with Rwanda, became an independent constitutional monarchy. Over the next few years, the new nation's primary political divisions shifted rapidly from the longstanding rivalries between Tutsi clans to unprecedented hostilities between Tutsi and Hutu. Although many observers have blamed colonialism for creating these hostilities, political events of the 1960s were even more directly responsible. Between 1962 and 1965 Mwambi Mwambutsa IV appointed a succession of ineffective prime ministers

and dispute-torn cabinets, while relative parity between Hutu and Tutsi prevailed in the National Assembly. Then, in January 1965, a Tutsi refugee assassinated the Hutu prime minister. In October, Hutu candidates won 70 percent of the new parliamentary seats, but the king appointed a Tutsi prime minister. Although the Hutu had not previously protested the Tutsi's overall political domination, they interpreted this move as an unacceptable shift in the balance of power. It sparked an unsuccessful coup attempt by the few Hutu officers in the Tutsi-dominated army. The army in turn purged all its Hutu and executed approximately 2,000 Hutu politicians and intellectuals. Meanwhile the king fled, and in November 1966 the military officially abolished the monarchy and proclaimed a republic. Army Captain Michel MICOMBERO, a Hima Tutsi from the southern Buriri province, became president.

President Micombero filled his government with southern Tutsi clan members, thereby undermining the power of the ganwa. Many of these supporters were ethnic hardliners who vilified the Hutu masses in speeches and in the media. In response, Hutu soldiers organized a series of unsuccessful coup attempts, culminating in a 1972 uprising among Hutu groups ranging from refugees and guerrillas based in the DEMOCRATIC REPUBLIC OF THE CONGO to schoolteachers, students, and civil servants. As many as 20,000 Tutsi were killed. Micombero retaliated not only by executing the instigators, but also by sending the military and youth groups into the countryside to kill all Hutu "intellectuals," meaning anyone with more than a grade-school education. More than 100,000 Hutu died between April and September 1972, and probably as many fled into neighboring countries. The international community, preoccupied with Vietnam and the reign of terror by Idi AMIN in nearby UGANDA, did not respond. The year of ikiza, or catastrophe, solidified the Hutu people's collective identity as martyrs, historically oppressed and impoverished by an unscrupulous Tutsi elite.

In November 1976 Colonel Jean-Baptiste BAGAZA, also a Tutsi Hima from Buriri, overthrew Micombero in a palace coup. Bagaza's dictatorial government, composed almost exclusively of his fellow clan members, solidified Tutsi hegemony. Bagaza maintained tight control over the military, the single party (UPRONA), and the press. Hutu representation in all branches of the government declined precipitously. Over time, Bagaza's dictatorial rule alienated the military as well as many Tutsi elite, leading to a bloodless coup in 1987 and the installation of Major Pierre BUYOYA as president. Buyoya, also a Hima Tutsi from Buriri, came from a younger generation than his predecessor, and promised "profound change, in the sense of expanded social justice and of real democracy." But the pro-Hutu Party for the Liberation of the Hutu People (PALIPEHUTU) continued to urge Hutu to rise up against the Tutsi, and in August 1988 Burundi again descended into chaos. A local conflict in the north got out of hand and the government responded violently, with the death toll ultimately reaching approximately 20,000.

THE SIMMERING CONFLICT

Poverty and stiff competition for scarce resources have inevitably both contributed to and been aggravated by the ongoing violence. Burundi is one of the most densely populated countries in Africa, and the fact that the vast majority of its people depend on agriculture for their livelihoods has resulted in severe deforestation and land degradation. Income from the only significant export crop, coffee, fluctuates greatly with global market prices, but many farmers are afraid even to cultivate their fields. Sporadic famines have become common. Successive governments, preoccupied with maintaining control through funding the military, have neglected agricultural and infrastructure development projects. Burundi's dilapidated industries, suffering from parts shortages, power outages, and high transportation costs, offer few employment opportunities to residents of BUJUMBURA, the capital and only major city.

In the wake of the 1988 killings, President Buyoya, motivated by personal convictions as well as pressure from the international community, inaugurated a transition to democracy and national reconciliation. By the end of 1990, he had appointed Tutsi and Hutu in roughly equal numbers to UPRONA's central committee. His government had a Hutu prime minister and a constitution guaranteeing basic human rights and multiparty democracy. The Hutu leaders subsequently founded the Front Démocratique du Burundi (FRODEBU), which called for economic justice for the Hutu as well as Hutu political representation proportional to their population majority. In 1993 elections, FRODEBU and its leader Melchior Ndadaye won convincingly and appointed a cabinet that included two-thirds Hutu and one-third Tutsi. Ndadaye also appointed former banker and political moderate Sylvie KINIGI as prime minister, one of the first women to hold that post in Africa. But in October that year, members of the still Tutsi-led army overtook the presidential mansion and killed Ndadaye, putting a bloody end to the reconciliation process. Probably 20,000 Tutsi and 30,000 Hutu lost their lives in the violence that followed in the north of the country.

International condemnation convinced the army to return to their barracks, and the coup leaders fled the country. In January 1994 a moderate Hutu FRODEBU member, Cyprien Ntaryamira, was sworn in as president. In April, Ntaryamira and his Rwandan counterpart Juvénal Habyarimana were en route from United Nations peace negotiations when their plane was shot down under suspicious circumstances, an event that unleashed the Rwandan genocide. Although Burundi itself remained calm, thousands of Burundian Hutu fled to TANZANIA fearing Tutsi attacks. At the same time, Burundi's political parties began to develop militias, in order to both protect their leaders and advance their interests. Ethnic-based parties, in other words, were further nurturing the conditions for civil war.

In September 1994 the moderate parties came to a power-sharing agreement, but extremists on both sides refused to recognize the agreement. Sporadic fighting and atrocities continued throughout the countryside and, increasingly, in the suburbs of Bujumbura. The Hutu hardliners' National Council for the Defense of Democracy (CNDD) waged a terror campaign against the government. In July 1996, as the politicians maneuvered for power in the capital, Buyoya overthrew the elected but ineffective president in a military coup and suspended the constitution. An economic embargo imposed by Burundi's neighbors put pressure on the government and CNDD to negotiate, but the talks stalled.

In 1998 Buyoya and the National Assembly agreed upon a transitional constitution under which Buyoya was formally sworn in as president. In October 2001 the National Assembly adopted a new transitional constitution. This constitution calls for a three-year transitional government that shares power between Hutu and Tutsi parties. Under this scheme, Buyoya remained president for eighteen months with a Hutu vice president. On April 30, 2003, a Hutu, Domitien Ndayizeye, took over as president with a Tutsi vice president, Alphonse Kadege. At the same time, membership in the legislature and the military was carefully balanced between Hutu and Tutsi.

In October 2003 the country's main rebel group, the Forces for the Defense of Democracy, signed a peace treaty with the government. The agreement gave members of the group control of four state ministries as well as 40 percent of the staff and officer positions in the army. Yet despite the agreement, violence continued in parts of the country as a second rebel force, the Forces for National Liberation, continued to fight both the government and the Forces for the Defense of Democracy. In 2004 the United Nations entered the country and assumed a peacekeeping role, and at long last the fighting largely came to an end. A year later, the national constitution was ratified in open elections. Despite these gains, sporadic violence continued throughout the country—much of it at the hands of the opposition Forces for National Liberation—until 2008, when a ceasefire was at last negotiated.

See also ETHNICITY IN BURUNDI: AN INTERPRETATION; PASTORALISM.

ERIC YOUNG

Burundi (At a Glance)

OFFICIAL NAME:
Burundi

AREA:
27,830 sq km (10,750 sq mi)

LOCATION:
Central Africa, bordered by Rwanda, Tanzania, the Democratic Republic of the Congo (formerly Zaire), and Lake Tanganyika

CAPITAL:
Bujumbura (population 908,700; 2004 estimate)

OTHER MAJOR CITY:
Gitega (population 755,900; 2004 estimate)

POPULATION:
8,691,005 (2008 estimate)

POPULATION DENSITY:
312 persons per sq km (about 808 persons per sq mi)

POPULATION BELOW AGE 14:
46.3 percent (male 2,021,320; female 1,998,502)

POPULATION GROWTH RATE:
3.44 percent (2008 estimate)

TOTAL FERTILITY RATE:
6.4 children born per woman (2008 estimate)

LIFE EXPECTANCY AT BIRTH:
Total population: 51.71 years (male 42.54 years; female 43.88 years; 2003 estimate)

INFANT MORTALITY RATE:
60.77 deaths per 1,000 live births (2008 estimate)

LITERACY RATE
Total population: 51.6 percent (male: 50.86 percent; female: 52.6 percent; 2008 estimate)

EDUCATION:
Schooling is free and officially compulsory for children aged 7 through 12. In the early 1990s about 631,039 students annually attended primary schools and about 46,500 attended secondary schools. The University of Burundi (founded in 1960), located in Bujumbura, is the leading institution of higher education; it had an enrollment of about 3,800 in the early 1990s.

LANGUAGES:
Kirundi and French are the official languages. Swahili is spoken along Lake Tanganyika and in the Bujumbura area.

ETHNIC GROUPS:
The chief ethnic groups are the Hutu, a Bantu-speaking people making up about 85 percent of the population, and the Tutsi, a Nilotic-speaking people forming about 14 percent of the total. Since October 1993, hundreds of thousands of refugees have fled Burundi and crossed into Rwanda, Tanzania, and the Democratic Republic of the Congo because of ethnic violence between Hutu and Tutsi factions.

RELIGIONS:
About 67 percent are Christian (62 percent are Catholic, 5 percent are Protestant), 23 percent practice indigenous beliefs, and Muslims constitute 10 percent of the population.

CLIMATE:
Tropical, moderated in most places by altitude. The average annual temperature is 20° C (68° F) on the plateau and 23° C (73° F) in the Great Rift Valley. Dry seasons are from June to August and from December to January.

LAND, PLANTS, AND ANIMALS:
Burundi is mostly a hilly plateau region, with an elevation ranging between 1,400 and 1,800 m (between 4,600 and 5,900 ft). Elevations decrease gradually to the east and southeast. The narrow western margin of the country, bordering the Rusizi River and Lake Tanganyika, lies in the trough of the Great Rift Valley. The main rivers are the Rusizi, the Malagarasi, and the Ruvuvu. Savanna vegetation, a grassland interspersed with trees, predominates in most of the country. Eucalyptus, acacia, and oil palm are the most common trees. Wildlife is diverse: elephants, hippopotamuses, crocodiles, wild boars, leopards, antelope, and flying lemurs are common, as are guinea hens, partridges, ducks, geese, quails, and snipe.

NATURAL RESOURCES:
Mineral resources include nickel, uranium, rare earth oxides, peat, cobalt, copper, platinum (which has not yet been exploited), and vanadium. Current environmental issues facing Burundi include soil erosion because of overgrazing and the expansion of agriculture into marginal lands; deforestation (little forested land remains because of uncontrolled cutting of trees for fuel); and loss of habitat, which threatens wildlife populations.

CURRENCY:
Burundi franc

GROSS DOMESTIC PRODUCT (GDP):
$2.907 billion (2007 estimate)

GDP PER CAPITA:
$300 (2007 estimate)

GDP REAL GROWTH RATE:
3.6 percent (2007 estimate)

PRIMARY ECONOMIC ACTIVITIES:
Subsistence agriculture (54.1 percent of GDP, 93 percent of employment); industry (mining) (16.8 percent of GDP, 1.5 percent of employment); service industries (29.1 percent of GDP, 4 percent of employment)

PRIMARY AGRICULTURAL PRODUCTS:
Coffee, cotton, tea, corn, sorghum, sweet potatoes, bananas, manioc, meat, milk, and hides

INDUSTRIES:
Assembly of light consumer goods such as blankets, shoes, and soap; assembling imported components; construction, food processing

PRIMARY EXPORTS:
Coffee, cotton, hides, tea, sugar

PRIMARY IMPORTS:
Textiles, motor vehicles, flour, and petroleum products

PRIMARY TRADE PARTNERS:
European Union, United States, and Asia

GOVERNMENT:
Republic; a constitutional multiparty democracy. The executive branch has been led by president Pierre Nkurunziza since 2005. A Council of Ministers is appointed by the president. The bicameral legislature consists of the 140-seat Assemblée Nationale (National Assembly), whose members are popularly elected to five-year terms, and the 54-seat Senate. In the most recent legislative elections, held in 2005, the Conseil national pour la défense de la démocratie-Forces pour la défense de la démocratie (CNDD-FDD) won 58 percent of the vote, while the Burundi Democratic Front (FRODEBU) won 21.7 percent and the Unity for National Progress (UPRONA) party received 7.2 percent.

Robert Fay

Busa

Ethnic group of Nigeria.

The Busa, also known as the Busagwe and the Busanse, primarily inhabit northwestern NIGERIA, although some live in northeastern BENIN. They speak a Niger-Congo language and are one of the BARIBA peoples. Though population estimates vary widely, some 20,000 people consider themselves Busa.

See also ETHNICITY AND IDENTITY IN AFRICA: AN INTERPRETATION; LANGUAGES, AFRICAN: AN OVERVIEW.

Busansi

Ethnic group of West Africa.

The Busansi, also known as Bisa, Bissa, Boussansé, Busanga, and Bousanou, primarily inhabit southern BURKINA FASO, northern GHANA, and northern TOGO. They speak a MANDE language. Some 758,000 people consider themselves Busansi.

See also ETHNICITY AND IDENTITY IN AFRICA: AN INTERPRETATION; LANGUAGES, AFRICAN: AN OVERVIEW.

Bushmen

Term, often considered derogatory, used to describe the San, a group of Khoisan-speaking hunter-gatherers who live in the Kalahari Desert.

The first European encounter with the so-called Bushmen of southern Africa came shortly after Dutch colonists established a settlement on the Cape of Good Hope in 1652. The region's NAMA herders told them about primitive, foraging peoples known as the Sonqua, or SAN. In 1660, Dutch soldier Carl Riebeeck led an army mission into the mountainous regions of the Cape, where he reportedly came upon communities of foragers, whom the Europeans later called *Bosjesmen*, or Bushmen.

For nearly two centuries, the Bushmen were vilified by Europeans, who viewed them as "wild creatures" who refused to be civilized. The Dutch *Bosjesman* is in fact derived from the term for bandit or outlaw. European accounts of the time frequently described Bushmen as mischievous bandits, lurking on the peripheries of human settlement. During the seventeenth and eighteenth centuries, these perceptions were used to justify AFRIKANER efforts to exterminate the people they called the "lowest race on earth." Between 1785 and 1795 alone, Afrikaner settlers are reported to have killed at least 2,500 San and taken captive at least another 700. European missionaries were unconcerned with the mass killings because Bushmen were seen as "dogs" whose existence threatened human civilization.

By the mid-nineteenth century, however, European views of Bushmen had changed. Now the Bushman was cast as the "noble savage and hunter," eternally childlike and attuned to nature. Europeans marveled at Bushmen's "timeless existence," and scientists claimed they represented the missing link to primitive society. Archaeological research on rock paintings of hunting scenes in South Africa's mountain ranges provided evidence for the theory that the Bushmen had not changed in thousands of years.

In the twentieth century, the image of the primitive Bushman has been reinforced by photographs, films, and written works. In 1925 the Denver African Expedition catered to American audiences hungry for Tarzan-type images by bribing San people to pose for shots that emphasized their "exotic primitiveness." Later, ethnographic films such as John Marshall's *The Hunter* and written ethnographies such as Marjorie Shostak's *Nisa* supported these ideas by lending a pseudoscientific authority to popular images of the Bushmen.

In the late twentieth century, Western images of the Bushmen, while as far removed as ever from the reality of San life, have become even more commercially valuable. In 1978 Afrikaner film director Jamie Uys struck gold with *The Gods Must Be Crazy*, a popular film that reinforced notions of the happy but primitive Bushmen. In BOTSWANA, the government deliberately propagates the Bushmen myth. In the Central Kalahari Game Reserve, the biggest tourist attraction was once the Bushmen themselves. In 1996, however, the government of Botswana threatened to remove those Bushmen who did not conform to "traditional" Bushmen hunting and gathering techniques and who had acquired cattle herds and other un-Bushmen-like assets. By 2002 the last of the Bushmen had been evicted from the reserve and forcibly resettled in camps and newly built villages.

Supporters of the government's policy argue that the San hunting-and-gathering lifestyle is no longer viable, and point to improvements in the villages over the Bushmen's former nomadic existence. Critics argue that resettlement camps are rife with alcoholism, depression, and a rising incidence of ACQUIRED IMMUNODEFICIENCY SYNDROME (AIDS). They also claim that the Bushmen were not forced off the land for their own good, but rather because the land contains valuable diamond deposits. In 2006 a Botswana court held that the government's actions were an unconstitutional infringement on Bushmen's rights. Though, as of 2009, the Bushmen are legally entitled to return to the reserve, the government of Botswana has thus far not allowed them to do so.

See also KALAHARI DESERT; KHOISAN; ROCK ART, AFRICAN.

BIBLIOGRAPHY

Gordon, Robert J. *The Bushman Myth: The Making of a Namibian Underclass.* Westview Press, 1992.

ELIZABETH HEATH

Busia, Kofi Abrefa

1913–1978

Teacher, author, and former prime minister of Ghana.

Born a member of the royal family of Wenchi, Kofi Abrefa Busia attended the Kumasi Methodist and Mfantsipim Secondary Schools and Wesley College. He received a B.A. degree in politics, philosophy, and economics and then an M.A. degree in social anthropology from the University of Oxford. Busia wrote his doctoral thesis, titled *The Position of the Chief in the Modern Political System of Ashanti*, in 1951. He held teaching positions at the Ghana University College at Legon in the African studies and sociology departments.

Busia left the university to devote himself to politics in 1956. In the fall of 1957, he formed the United Party, composed of different parties in opposition to President KWAME NKRUMAH. He was outspoken in opposition to Nkrumah's government. Busia fled to England, in fear of the increasingly repressive government. In exile, Busia maintained his opposition to the Nkrumah regime and continued teaching and writing, publishing *Urban Churches in Britain* (1956) and *Africa in Search of Democracy* (1967). Returning to GHANA after Nkrumah was removed, Busia participated in the writing of a new constitution. He was elected prime minister in 1969.

Facing very poor economic conditions, Busia expelled foreign workers and imposed new taxes, but his policies failed to stem rising unemployment and inflation. At the end of 1971, Busia devalued the cedi. The resulting massive inflation sparked resistance among the people and the military that led directly to the end of his government. A month later, while out of the country, he was ousted by a coup d'état. He died of a heart attack on August 28, 1978, after living his last years in England.

MARTHA KING

Buthelezi, Mangosutho Gatsha

1928–

South African politician, chief minister of the former bantustan (or black homeland) KwaZulu, and founder of the Inkatha Freedom Party.

Born in what is now the province of KWAZULU-NATAL, Mangosutho Buthelezi is related to the Zulu royal family through his mother, Princess Magogo. He is descended from CETSHWAYO, a Zulu king who ruled in the late 1800s. Buthelezi's father, who was chief of the Buthelezi ethnic group, died when Buthelezi was fourteen years old. Buthelezi's uncle, Maliyamakhanda, was appointed regent to govern the ethnic group until Buthelezi was ready to assume the role of chief.

Buthelezi received his early education at Christian mission schools. He then attended South African Native College (now the University of Fort Hare) in Alice. During college Buthelezi joined the AFRICAN NATIONAL CONGRESS (ANC) Youth League. He was subsequently expelled from college because of his political activities, but in 1951 he received his degree in history and Bantu administration (a discipline designed to train black South Africans for certain government positions) from the University of Natal in Durban. In 1953 Buthelezi returned home and was appointed chief of the Buthelezi ethnic group.

During the 1950s the white South African government divided the black majority population according to ethnic groups and assigned them to separate territories that the government considered to be ethnic homelands. These territories, called bantustans (or black homelands), were part of the government's policy of APARTHEID, or separation of the races. Parts of Zululand became the bantustan of KwaZulu, designated for the Zulu people.

At first Buthelezi opposed this system but then decided to work within it. In 1976 he became the first chief minister of KwaZulu. Also in 1976, he founded the Black Unity Front to promote unity and federation of the bantustans. Buthelezi rejected the idea of full independence for the bantustans, arguing that apartheid could best be fought if the territories remained part of South Africa.

Around this time, Buthelezi reinvigorated a movement called Inkatha. The movement was originally founded as a Zulu cultural organization, but Buthelezi turned it into the political party called the INKATHA FREEDOM PARTY. The party grew rapidly, and it eventually became the dominant party of KwaZulu. Buthelezi attempted to forge the South African Black Alliance in 1978 with other political parties. His political power base remained confined to the Zulu, however, and only a portion of them were his firm supporters.

Tensions mounted between Inkatha and the ANC in the 1980s, after the ANC accused Buthelezi of cooperating with the South African government. Sporadic fighting between supporters of the two parties, carried out mainly in the black townships on the borders of South African cities, began in 1985 and continued in the 1990s, despite a peace agreement signed between the party leaders in September 1991. In 1991 the South African government was forced to admit that it had been supporting Inkatha financially. A 1994 inquiry further revealed that the government's security forces had been providing weapons for Inkatha to use in the township fighting. The government's support for Inkatha was intended to increase political divisions within the black population and to undermine popular support for the ANC.

Buthelezi initially refused to participate in South Africa's first free elections in April 1994, demanding that KwaZulu be granted a certain amount of autonomy and that the Zulu king occupy an official position in the KwaZulu government. KwaZulu, along with the other bantustans, was dissolved at the time of the 1994 elections. He finally took part in the elections, but only after reaching an agreement that recognized the traditional authority of the Zulu king and postponed until after the elections further negotiations about regional autonomy. Buthelezi served as minister of home affairs from 1994 to 2004, when his part in a corruption investigation and a contentious election fight caused him to run afoul of the ANC. He remains president of the Inkatha Freedom Party.

See also SOUTH AFRICA.

Buyoya, Pierre

1949–

Army major and two-time president of Burundi.

Never content to be merely a soldier, Pierre Buyoya has twice seized political power, pledging both times to bring peace and democracy to BURUNDI. Born into a modest Hima Tutsi family in the southern Buriri province, Buyoya received his primary education locally. He then went to Belgium for secondary school, university, and, later, military training. After returning briefly to Burundi in 1975 to command an armored squadron, he received further military training in France, and then joined Burundi's ruling UPRONA party. He was elected to its central committee in 1979. In the mid-1980s Buyoya began openly criticizing President Jean-Baptiste BAGAZA, a former soldier and fellow Tutsi from Buriri, for his hostility toward the Catholic Church. In September 1987, Buyoya led a coup against Bagaza, charging him with corruption, failed economic policy, and constitutional violations.

Upon assuming the presidency, Buyoya suspended the constitution, released political prisoners, and lifted restrictions on the Catholic Church. Buyoya committed his government to healing Burundi's ethnic wounds, but a local conflict escalated and in August 1988 several northern provinces descended into violence in which around 20,000 Burundians died. Afterward, Buyoya appointed a Hutu prime minister, increased the number of Hutu in the cabinet, and established a Commission on National Unity to investigate the massacres and write a charter on national unity. Under pressure from international donors, he also set Burundi on a five-year path toward democratization.

In the 1993 national elections Melchior Ndadaye defeated Buyoya, but the successive civilian governments proved weak and ineffective and were under constant threat from both Hutu and Tutsi militants. Persistent political instability and conflict drew Buyoya back into the political fray. In July 1996 he ousted the elected government in a military coup and suspended the constitution. In September of that year Buyoya restored some political party activity and reconvened the legislature. In mid-1998 Buyoya promulgated a transitional constitution and was formally sworn in as president. Under a new transitional constitution promulgated in November 2001, Buyoya remained president of a power-sharing government that agreed to hand power over to a Hutu president after eighteen months. In May 2003 Buyoya ceded power to his Hutu deputy, Domitien Ndayizeye. Five years later, in 2008, the Peace and Security Council of the African Union chose Buyoya to head a peace mission into CHAD in an attempt to restore relations damaged in no small part by the refugee crisis touched off by the ongoing violence in DARFUR.

See also HUTU AND TUTSI.

ERIC YOUNG

Bwiti

Religious cult based in Cameroon, Equatorial Guinea, and Gabon.

The religious cult of Bwiti is both syncretistic (fusing different belief systems) and multiethnic, and seeks to give its followers privileged knowledge of the world. Bwiti operates as a secret society, but unlike many African secret societies, its core members include both men and women.

Anthropologists believe that the original religious practices revolved around the byer, ancestral skulls, revered by the FANG ethnic group. When European missionaries saw the skulls they became convinced the Fang were cannibals, a myth that the NDOWE, the region's middleman merchants, perpetuated to discourage Europeans from venturing inland for trade. European religions and culture eroded Bwiti rituals and myths until the cult reemerged in the region of CAMEROON, EQUATORIAL GUINEA, and GABON during the late nineteenth century as a reaction to the destruction of African culture.

Although the Bwiti cult once recognized many gods, today, influenced by Christianity, it recognizes few. One of these is the creator god, known as Mebege or Mwanga, depending on the ethnic group. Although some practices and beliefs vary regionally, Bwiti seeks to create "one heartness" among its followers in order to counteract foreign influences. A carved pillar built over a prominent individual's grave signifies a place of worship, and dance plays an important part in many Bwiti ceremonies. Although forbidden by colonial officials and frowned upon by postindependence governments, Bwiti survives through adaptation and secrecy.

See also DANCE IN SUB-SAHARAN AFRICA; RELIGIONS, AFRICAN.

ERIC YOUNG

C

Cabora Bassa

Second largest dam in Africa and one of its largest hydroelectric power stations.

The Cabora Bassa (or Cahora Bassa) Dam is a 2,075-megawatt arch dam on Lake Cabora Bassa, located on the ZAMBEZI RIVER northwest of Tete in MOZAMBIQUE. It stands 171 meters (561 feet) high and is 303 meters (994 feet) wide. The Portuguese colonial government built the dam between 1969 and 1974, partly as an attempt to maintain its rule in Mozambique. The colony's economy needed both irrigation and hydroelectricity, but Portugal also reasoned that supplying SOUTH AFRICA with inexpensive power would encourage that nation to help fight the independence group Front for the Liberation of MOZAMBIQUE (FRELIMO), which opposed the dam's construction. After Mozambique achieved independence in 1975, the FRELIMO-led government refused to maintain the unprofitable dam, and blamed the dam's fiscal woes on the low electricity prices Portugal had set for South Africa.

During Mozambique's seventeen-year-long civil war, Cabora Bassa and associated projects were repeatedly sabotaged. For years, the power station operated at just 1 percent of its capacity because the MOZAMBICAN NATIONAL RESISTANCE (RENAMO) sabotaged key transmission lines. The war ended in 1992, and by the late 1990s the dam had been largely restored. Nevertheless, it remained a debt-ridden project for the Portuguese government, which still held majority ownership of the power station. In early 1998, Mozambique, ZIMBABWE, and South Africa expressed interest in acquiring shares in the dam, and the Portuguese government appeared willing to sell. By 2007 the negotiations had been settled. Mozambique assumed control of the project, with Portugal maintaining a minority interest.

BIBLIOGRAPHY

Ferraz, Bernardo, and Barry Munslow. *Sustainable Development in Mozambique*. Africa World Press, 2000.

Middlemas, Keith. *Cabora Bassa: Engineering and Politics in Southern Africa*. Weidenfeld and Nicolson, 1975.

ROBERT FAY

Cabral, Amílcar

1924–1973

Nationalist leader and political philosopher from Guinea-Bissau.

Amílcar Cabral was born in Bafatá, Portuguese Guinea (today GUINEA-BISSAU). Because both of his parents were from the CAPE VERDE Islands, he automatically received Portuguese citizenship. After earning high marks in elementary school, Cabral attended secondary school in the Cape Verde Islands and then, at the age of twenty-one, the University of Lisbon in Portugal. He graduated with honors, and in 1950 Cabral entered the Portuguese colonial agriculture service and became increasingly active in revolutionary intellectual circles.

Between 1952 and 1954 Cabral conducted the first agricultural survey of Portuguese Guinea. As he gained an extensive knowledge of the land and popular grievances, he helped increase political awareness among his friends, mainly of Cape Verdean descent. Increasingly involved in anti-Portuguese activities, Cabral helped establish a recreation association and other quickly banned organizations before his return to Portugal. In Lisbon, and later in ANGOLA, he met revolutionary leaders from Angola and MOZAMBIQUE, including Agostinho Neto, and secretly became involved in their activities while working as an agronomist.

In 1956 Cabral helped found the Partido Africano da Independencia da Guine e Cabo Verde (PAIGC), which organized labor unions to pressure the Portuguese government to provide a timetable for independence. After Portuguese police killed fifty striking dock workers in Bissau in 1959, Cabral pushed the PAIGC to launch a protracted armed struggle for independence starting in 1963.

Combining Marxism-Leninism, social democracy, republicanism, and a disciplined approach to the study of material production, Cabral's revolutionary thought rested on two basic tenets: (1) that those who accept a moral obligation to resist must actively participate; and (2) that these personal convictions must grow into a broader conception of moral and social renewal. He advocated a revolutionary democracy in which the party would lead the uneducated African peasantry to power through violent struggle. The peasantry, in turn, would elect representative bodies. Cabral's writings also celebrated African culture, a stance that helped him become one of the continent's most renowned nationalist thinkers.

For ten years (1963–1973) Cabral directed the liberation struggle, serving as secretary general of the PAIGC, a role in which he was increasingly resented for authoritarian practices. In addition, people of Cape Verdean descent dominated the movement, while members of mainland ethnic groups were largely excluded from power. Both factors created resentments, and in 1973 political opponents within the PAIGC assassinated Cabral in CONAKRY, GUINEA. His half-brother Luís CABRAL became president of independent Guinea-Bissau in 1974.

ERIC YOUNG

Cabral, Luís

1931–
First president of Guinea-Bissau.

The younger brother of Amílcar CABRAL, Luis de Almeida Cabral was born to Cape Verdean Creole parents in Bissau, Portuguese Guinea (now GUINEA-BISSAU). After a local education and training as an accountant, Cabral worked for a Portuguese firm before joining with his brother to fight and overthrow Portuguese COLONIAL RULE.

In 1956, Luís and Amílcar Cabral helped to found the African Party for the Independence of Guinea and Cape Verde (PAIGC). In 1959, Portuguese colonial authorities killed fifty people in a dock strike that Cabral had helped organize. This led the PAIGC to cancel its policy of nonviolence and forced Cabral's flight to GUINEA. Upon his return in 1961, he helped create and became the secretary general of the National Union of Guinean Workers (UNTG), which backed the PAIGC. With the advent of warfare later that year, Cabral joined guerrilla forces on the borders of the country and assumed increasing responsibility within the PAIGC over the years. By 1965, Cabral was a member of the PAIGC war council, and, in 1970, he became an executive committee member.

Amílcar Cabral, the leader of the PAIGC, was assassinated in 1973, and Luís assumed leadership in his brother's place. When Guinea-Bissau gained independence on September 10, 1974, Luís Cabral assumed the presidency. Cabral introduced a state-led socialist development policy. While he initially espoused democratic principles, Cabral's rule became increasingly repressive over time as economic crises, disagreements among members of the PAIGC, corruption, and inefficiency generated unrest. After a 1980 coup successfully ousted Cabral, João Bernardo VIEIRA assumed power and placed Cabral under house arrest. Investigators uncovered evidence of mass graves containing the bodies of 500 of Cabral's political opponents. A court sentenced Cabral to death. International pressure, however, led to his release in 1981. Cabral went into exile in Cuba and later settled in Lisbon, Portugal. Cabral refused Vieira's subsequent offer to return to Guinea-Bissau on the grounds that Vieira refused to guarantee his safety. In 1999, however, following Vieira's expulsion to Portugal, Cabral at last returned.

Cacheu, Guinea-Bissau
The historic commercial center of present-day Guinea-Bissau.

Shortly after the Portuguese first reached the Cacheu River in 1446, lançados—Portuguese outcasts often married to African women—settled 20 kilometers (12 miles) upriver on the south bank, in the Cacanda region inhabited by Papei, Manjaco, and other peoples. In the sixteenth and seventeenth centuries Cacheu became a center for the trade in slaves from Kaabu and other areas, but relations among the Portuguese, lançados, and Africans were often rocky. Eventually, the Portuguese fortified the settlement, but it remained weak, underfunded, manned by undisciplined soldiers, and subject to frequent raids from nearby African groups. Foreign residents in segregated areas paid tribute to the Cacanda king for the right to stay, and ships anchoring at Cacheu paid him duties.

In the late 1600s, European Portuguese sought to control Cacheu and dominate the slave trade, but both lançados and local Africans resisted. Shortly thereafter Cacheu's importance diminished when the slave trade shifted south and the Portuguese shifted their focus to BISSAU. Cacheu's economy declined further beginning in the 1880s, when a series of punitive colonial pacification campaigns and counterattacks by Africans drove foreign traders away. In 1914 the Portuguese finally crushed all resistance, though by this time the town had become a sleepy backwater. Cacheu's prospects have improved with the recent discovery of phosphate deposits in the area, but political and economic instability have thus far prevented Guinea-Bissau from developing these resources. In 2008 the population of Cacheu was only some 9,800.

See also COLONIAL RULE; GUINEA-BISSAU; KAABU, EARLY KINGDOM OF.

ERIC YOUNG

Caillié, René-Auguste
1799–1838
First European explorer to visit Tombouctou (Timbuktu), and survive.

In 1825 the Paris Société de Géographie offered a prize of 10,000 francs to the first person to visit the legendary city of Tombouctou and return with a description of it. With this challenge they made official an undeclared competition among European EXPLORERS that had already claimed the lives of more than twenty men. Since 1788, explorers had been trying to reach the Sahelian market town, rumored to be the richest in Africa but also one of the most heavily guarded. Only one European, a Scottish explorer named Major Alexander Gordon Laing, had yet entered the fabled city, but he was murdered only days after leaving. However, in 1827 explorer René-Auguste Caillié, born in Mauzé, France, embarked on a journey to Tombouctou that would at last win the prize.

Inspired by the adventures of Daniel Defoe's *Robinson Crusoe* (1719), Caillié had already made two voyages to West Africa and the Caribbean before embarking for Tombouctou. In 1824 he sailed from France to the Senegambia region, where he lived for three years among local people, learning Arabic and Islamic traditions. Disguised as an Arab, Caillié left alone for Tombouctou in April 1827. Beset with difficulties and sickness, it took him almost a year to reach the city, but he was then admitted without problem. What he saw, however, proved extremely disappointing; expecting a metropolis as prosperous and majestic as DJENNÉ, he found Tombouctou to be nothing more than "a mass of ill-looking houses, built of earth." He left after two weeks and joined a trans-Saharan caravan traveling to TANGIER, MOROCCO. From there Caillié departed for France, where after some dispute, he claimed the prize in 1829. He published an account of his trip a year later.

ELIZABETH HEATH

Cairo, Egypt

Capital of Egypt and one of the largest cities in Africa.

Cairo is the industrial, commercial, cultural, and administrative center of EGYPT, and is the Arab League headquarters. Home to a number of universities and many Arabic-language publishing houses, Cairo is considered by many people to be the cultural capital of the Arabic-speaking world. It occupies approximately 453 square kilometers (about 175 square miles) on both banks of the NILE RIVER and includes several of the river's islands. Its architecture, a mixture of the ancient and the modern, reflects its long and rich history.

Although Cairo proper was founded in 969 C.E., the area has been a center of civilization for roughly 5,000 years. The ancient Egyptian capital of Memphis was founded in the fourth millennium B.C.E., approximately twenty-five kilometers (about fourteen miles) south of modern Cairo. Around 2500 B.C.E. construction began on a new Egyptian capital, which later was named

Heliopolis by the Greeks, a short distance to the north, although this city gradually declined in importance over the centuries. The Romans established a military stronghold and commercial center known as Babylon-in-Egypt in the area that is now Cairo's Misr al-Qadimah quarter.

The invasion of Egypt by Islamic Arabs in 641 C.E. sparked the foundation of the city that has become Cairo. The Arab city, known as al-Fustat (roughly, "tent city"), grew from the collection of tents pitched by the Arab army that was besieging Babylon-in-Egypt. Until the Arab invasion, ALEXANDRIA had served as Egypt's capital, but the Arabs established their capital at al-Fustat. In 969 the Fatimids, an Islamic dynasty from modern TUNISIA, founded a new capital al-Qahirah (Cairo). Cairo existed alongside al-Fustat until 1168, when the Fatimids attempted to repel an attack by Christian crusaders by burning al-Fustat. The crusaders were eventually defeated by a Syrian army led by Saladin, who later took control and founded the Ayyubid dynasty in Cairo.

Meanwhile, Cairo had become the center of Egyptian economic, political, and cultural life. In the thirteenth century, the city became the capital of the Mamluks. During their rule the city achieved its greatest prosperity. Indeed, Cairo's grandeur exceeded that of any other city in Africa, Europe, or western Asia. The city became the center of the lucrative east-west spice trade, and was the home of al-Azhar University, the finest Islamic university. The city began to decline, however, after the bubonic plague devastated its population in 1348. Its central economic role disappeared when Portuguese explorer Vasco da Gama opened the route from Europe to the Indian Ocean and ended Cairo's spice trade monopoly.

The Turks of the Ottoman Empire seized the weakened Cairo in 1517, and made the city a provincial capital in its vast empire. Ottoman rule lasted until Napoleon briefly took the city for France in 1798. The Turks returned three years later, and in 1805 appointed Muhammad Ali as the pasha. Muhammad Ali founded a dynasty that ruled Egypt, albeit under increasing British colonial domination. The British occupied Egypt beginning in the 1880s and declared it a protectorate in 1919. Ali's descendants ruled as puppets under British occupation until 1952, when a coup led by Gamal Abdel NASSER established the Egyptian republic, with Cairo its capital.

Today, Cairo remains the commercial and industrial center of Egypt. Tourism plays an important role in the economy. The city has numerous historical and cultural sites to which tourists have been drawn for centuries, including the Blue Mosque, the Egyptian Museum (including the Tutankhamen collection), the Museum of Islamic Arts, the Coptic Museum, the Al Gawhara Palace Museum, and—at nearby Giza—the Great Pyramids and Sphinx. The Citadel, begun by the emperor Saladin in 1176, lies in east Cairo, also the site of the Muhammad Ali Mosque.

The crowded city continues to grow rapidly, with a metropolitan population of well over 17 million. Cairo Metro trains provide an efficient transportation system that averages two million passengers each day. However, unemployment, pollution, and a shortage of decent housing pose numerous problems for the city. Many of Cairo's citizens are rural migrants, with few job skills and little prospect of regular employment. Their growing numbers are straining the city's overburdened infrastructure. In recent years, leaking sewer lines have caused the water table to rise in the city. The waterlogged ground has brought down historical buildings that had been constructed of dried mud bricks. Thus Cairo today presents contradictory images of both squalor and grandeur.

See also COLONIAL RULE; CRUSADES; DISEASE AND AFRICAN HISTORY; EGYPT, ANCIENT KINGDOM OF; ISLAM IN AFRICA; MAMLUK STATE; TOURISM IN AFRICA; URBANISM AND URBANIZATION IN AFRICA.

BIBLIOGRAPHY

Kubiak, Wladyslaw. *Al-Fustat, its Foundation and Early Urban Development.* American University in Cairo Press, 1987.

Lyster, William. *The Citadel of Cairo: A History and Guide.* Palm Press, 1993.

ROBERT FAY

Cameroon

African country on the Gulf of Guinea, bordered by Nigeria, Chad, Central African Republic, Republic of the Congo, Gabon, and Equatorial Guinea.

Cameroon, the country where West and Central Africa meet, is in many ways a microcosm of the continent. Rich in natural resources and ecologically diverse, the mountainous country is home to more than 250 ethnic groups. For centuries, the peoples of Cameroon experienced histories that were dominated by regional dynamics, particularly the transatlantic slave trade and the Christian missionary presence in the south, and the influences of the trans-Saharan slave trade, Islam, and neighboring savannah empires in the north. During most of the colonial period, control of the eastern and western regions of the country were split between two different European powers. Yet unlike much of the rest of postcolonial Africa, Cameroon has forged a strong sense of nationhood, while maintaining relative economic and political stability. Still, Cameroon's state remains far from democratic, and its future stability is far from certain.

EARLY HISTORY

The first inhabitants of what is now Cameroon were various hunter-gatherer PYGMY groups such as the BAKA, who lived in the area in small, nomadic communities as long as 50,000 years ago. Evidence suggests that Bantu-speakers originated in present-day eastern NIGERIA and western Cameroon well before the Early Iron Age, and eventually dispersed across Central, East, and southern Africa, taking with them agriculture, iron working, and unique pottery styles. The NOK people, who lived near the Benue River from around 200 B.C.E. to the fourth century C.E., left rich archaeological evidence of their crafts.

Early farmers found fertile soil on the slopes of the volcanic mountain range that runs north from the coast, and the many rivers of the region supplied fish. The southern forested area, where agrarian peoples lived in small, patrilineal villages that were typically governed by chiefs and councils of elders, saw the gradual emergence of numerous ethnic groups, including the BAKWERI, DUALA, and FANG. In the grasslands and plateaus to the north and west, major dynasties such as TIKAR, Bamenda, Bamum, and BAMILÉKÉ arose. Cultivating yams and bananas, these groups developed extensive trade networks and practiced metalworking, particularly in bronze.

Historians believe that the first foreigner to visit the area was a Carthaginian explorer named Hanno, who recorded sighting the volcanic Cameroon Mountain around 500 B.C.E. In the centuries after his arrival, trade caravans carried gold, salt, and especially slaves from northern Cameroon across the SAHARA to North Africa. Scholars estimate that as many as ten thousand slaves crossed the desert annually, many of them coming from present-day Cameroon. The trans-Saharan and Red Sea slave trade made some societies wealthy; between the tenth and fifteenth centuries, for example, the Sao kingdom flourished in the northern CHARI delta, producing works of pottery, bronze, and copper.

IMPERIALISM AND THE TRANSATLANTIC SLAVE TRADE

Although commerce brought Arab and Islamic influences to northern Cameroon as early as the tenth century, the sixteenth-century invasion of the MASSA people and the subsequent rise of the KOTOKO kingdom broadened the Islamic presence. So too did the immigration of the FULANI people, whose slave-raiding practices caused northerners such as the Bali to flee south into the central highlands. In the 1800s, groups from the center, such as the Fang and BETI, fled toward the coast, where they increasingly came into contact with Europeans.

In 1472 the Portuguese sailor Fernando Pó landed on the nearby island of Mbini, from which he presumably sighted the mainland, but not until some years later did Portuguese

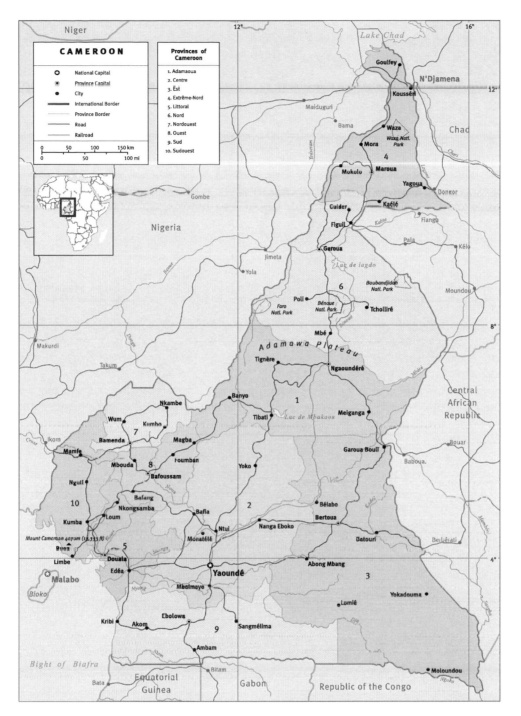

explorers sail into the estuaries. There they found swarms of prawns, and accordingly named the area Rio dos Camarões, or River of Prawns, which the British later Anglicized to Cameroons.

By the sixteenth century, Cameroon had become a major source of slaves for the New World. African middlemen, many of them from the Bimbia and Duala ethnic groups, transported slaves captured in the interior to the coast, where they were shipped to Calabar, the closest European settlement and slave-trading center. In exchange, these middlemen received cloth, liquor, firearms, and other manufactured goods. Supremacy in the trade shifted over time among the Portuguese, Dutch, British, French, and finally the Americans. Trans-Saharan trade declined during this period, though the rise of the Fulani empire, known as the SOKOTO CALIPHATE, in the early nineteenth century brought a resurgence of slave raiding in the north. An empire in the

Lake Chad region established by RABIH AL-ZUBAYR, a slave trader originally from the Nile basin, also revitalized Islam in the area, and pushed more groups south into the Cameroon forests.

The abolition of the transatlantic slave trade in the early 1800s forced African traders to develop commerce in alternative commodities, such as ivory, rubber, and other cash crops. Exports of palm oil and kernels increased significantly at this time, as African farmers expanded production to meet demand in newly industrializing Europe. As cash and credit relations gradually replaced barter, many African merchants and chiefs became indebted to European trading firms.

Christian missionaries, especially from Anglophone countries, were also establishing a presence in Cameroon by the mid-nineteenth century. In 1844 a Jamaican Baptist named Joseph Merrick founded a mission at Bimbia. Other Christian denominations, many of whose missionaries were African American, settled in what became the town of Victoria (today known as Limbe). African converts educated in the early mission schools eventually formed a small Anglophone elite. By 1880 the Anglophone missionary presence, combined with British domination of regional trade, made it seem likely that Great Britain would formally colonize the area. In fact, Germany became Cameroon's first colonizer.

GERMAN, FRENCH, AND BRITISH COLONIALISM

In July 1884, as the European powers at the Berlin Conference agreed to the rules of the division of the African continent, the German explorer and diplomat Gustav Nachtigal signed a treaty with two Duala chiefs. Germany sought to occupy territory before the British and French—who were extensively preoccupied in Nigeria and GABON, respectively—and to break the Duala's monopoly over interior trade. German Kamerun became an exporter of agricultural products such as cocoa, palm, rubber, tea, and tobacco, grown on large German or African-owned estates on the fertile slopes of Mount Cameroon. Africans were recruited, often by force, to work on the plantations, as well as on railway and road construction projects. Thousands died as a result of the harsh working conditions and the spread of disease. Political and economic conditions were somewhat different in the north, where the Germans governed indirectly through Fulani emirs, but also weakened the Fulani's control over regional trade. HAUSA traders from northern Nigeria gained influence over commerce during this period.

The movement of traders and laborers, the spread of Pidgin English, and widespread resistance to colonial rule all fostered the creation of a new collective identity in German Kamerun. Resentful of threats to their trading monopoly, the Duala initially led the resistance to German rule, and were soon joined by the Bafut, Kpe, Bulu, and others. The Germans relied on superior firepower and divide-and-rule tactics to quell a series of uprisings, but many parts of the interior remained outside of effective German control until 1910. In 1914 the colonial government executed two of the most prominent resistors, Chief Rudolph Douala Manga BELL and Martin-Paul SAMBA. Yet even as those living within the newly defined borders of Kamerun began to forge a common identity around the resistance movement, missionaries and the colonial government introduced other, more divisive identities. As well as creating an educated elite, Christian missionaries emphasized distinctions between Christian denominations, traditional (or indigenous) religions, and Muslims. The German colonizers particularly denounced the Muslim Hausa's trade with British Nigeria and their continued use of slave labor.

During World War I Belgian, British, and French colonial armies, including many African troops, invaded German Kamerun. After the war, the League of Nations divided the colony roughly along the axis of the mountains, giving Great Britain control over an eastern slice of the territory (British Cameroons) and granting France the rest (French Cameroun), an area nearly ten times larger. Linguistic and economic differences soon developed between the French and British mandates (renegotiated as Trusteeship Territories after World War II), though both territories' economies depended on agricultural exports such as coffee. British Cameroons ended the use of forced labor in 1918 and left most cash-crop production to small-scale African farmers. In contrast, the French maintained forced-labor laws until the end of World War II, in order to supply labor for large state-owned agricultural estates. Vast differences also existed between the British and French territories in infrastructure, education, and health care. Great Britain invested little in Cameroons and instead made it a marginal province of the colony of Nigeria, run largely by Nigerian civil servants, but France considered Cameroun one of its model colonies. Both the British and French territories, however, concentrated economic development in the fertile south rather than the remote and arid north.

Despite these differences, some sense of common identity still linked British Cameroons and French Cameroun. This was fostered by extensive trade and migration between the two territories—especially after the development of new rail and road links—and the growth of multiethnic urban centers such as DOUALA and YAOUNDÉ. Resentment toward the large numbers of Nigerians recruited to work in labor-scarce regions also helped forge unity among inhabitants of the British and French territories.

NATIONALIST ERA

As elsewhere in Africa, nationalism blossomed in Cameroon after World War II. Nigerian nationalist leaders spoke of uniting southern British Cameroons with Nigeria, but this idea won little support among Cameroonians, who feared Nigerian domination. Meanwhile, for French Cameroun the primary question was the nature of its postindependence relationship with France. The 1944 Brazzaville Conference envisioned France maintaining close relations with Africa, but African agitation for independence continued to escalate. In 1945 a newly created labor union called for strikes in Douala; three years later nationalists formed the socialist Union des Populations du Cameroun (UPC), which called for complete independence as well as reunification of the two Cameroons. Supported primarily by urban workers, students, and the southern-based Bassa and Bamiléké ethnic groups, the UPC responded to French efforts to suppress its organizing with a clandestine sabotage campaign, killing policemen, civil servants, and soldiers, and bombing symbols of colonial rule.

In 1956 France, realizing the inevitability of decolonization, passed the *loi cadre*, which expanded the powers of African assemblies and enlarged the electorate in preparation for independence. Largely in exile or underground, the UPC leadership boycotted the assembly elections, which were instead dominated by the southern and central Démocrates, led by André-Marie Mbida, and the northern Union Camerounaise (UC), led by El Hajj Ahmadou AHIDJO. France supported these more moderate parties, hoping for close relations with an independent Cameroon. Mbida proved to be a cautious nationalist and his transitional government collapsed as Ahidjo and the UC broke from Mbida's governing coalition. In 1958 Ahidjo formed a new government, calling for immediate independence while reassuring France that close economic, cultural, political, and military ties would be maintained. Those ties proved immediately useful to Ahidjo, who depended upon the French military to suppress the guerrilla campaign of the UPC, a conflict that between 1955 and 1962 killed an estimated 600 insurgents, 1,500 government officials and police, and 15,000 civilians.

INDEPENDENCE: STABILITY AND CONTINUITY

On the first day of 1960, the former French colony of Cameroun became the independent Republic of the Cameroon, with Ahidjo as its president. After more than a year in limbo, in February 1961 the people of British Cameroons voted in a United Nations-sponsored referendum on the issue of unification with Nigeria or Cameroon. The north, historically more closely tied to its western neighbor, voted in favor of Nigeria, and the south voted in favor of Cameroon. In October 1961 southern British Cameroons joined the Republic.

President Ahidjo ruled Cameroon for the next twenty-two years. Fearing the divisive potential of ethnic, regional, religious, and linguistic identities, Ahidjo concentrated on building national unity. This he did in part through his broad popular appeal as the "father" of the nation, and in part through his eventual authoritarian control over a single-party state. Ahidjo centralized most decision-making and incorporated previously independent associations representing women, youth, and labor into the sole legal party, the Cameroon National Union (CNU). The police and military suppressed any vestiges of the political opposition, including the moribund UPC, and censored the media. Infrastructure development projects, while intended to foster economic growth and national unity, also helped the government centralize control in the capital city, Yaoundé. In 1972 Ahidjo replaced the federation with a republic.

Ahidjo further solidified his rule by carefully balancing ethnic representation in the cabinet and national assembly, and by dispensing patronage to supporters at all levels of the government bureaucracy, the military, and the business community. He was able to pursue such tactics through his control over the economy and his relations with France, which remained the primary destination for Cameroon's agricultural exports. French businesses, encouraged by a liberal investment code, also invested heavily in the country, particularly in oil exploration, mining, energy, and forestry. Despite poorly planned development projects, Cameroon's economy grew, especially in the late 1970s following the discovery of offshore oil reserves. Meanwhile, the national soccer team, the CAMEROON LIONS, emerged as one of Africa's dominant teams, a position they held into the late 1980s.

In November 1982 Ahidjo handed over power to Paul Biya, the prime minister and his chosen successor. Ahidjo, still head of the CNU, found Biya resistant to his efforts to run the country from behind the scenes. Conflicts between the two men led Ahidjo loyalists in the Republican Guard to mount a bloody uprising, which Biya eventually suppressed. After initial progress toward democratization, Biya reverted to his predecessor's authoritarian style, and came to rely upon Ahidjo's political machinery of patronage to maintain loyalty. Ultimately, Biya built his own political machine by replacing the CNU with the Cameroon People's Democratic Movement and advocating "communal liberalism." Biya claimed that communal liberalism would ultimately include freedom and democracy, but that single-party rule was necessary in the meantime to prevent regional, ethnic, and religious divisions. Widely recognized as corrupt, the Biya regime remained heavily

Cameroon (At a Glance)

FORMER NAME:
French Cameroun and British Cameroon

AREA:
475,440 sq km (183,568 sq mi)

LOCATION:
Coastal West Africa, bordered by Nigeria, Chad, Central African Republic, Republic of the Congo, Gabon, and Equatorial Guinea

CAPITAL:
Yaoundé (population 1,430,000; 2005 estimate)

OTHER MAJOR CITIES:
Douala (population 1,310,400; 2004 estimate), Garoua (490,000; 2005 estimate), Maroua (284,000; 2003 estimate)

POPULATION:
18,467,692 (2008 estimate)

POPULATION DENSITY:
38.84 persons per sq km (about 100 persons per sq mi)

POPULATION BELOW AGE 15:
41.1 percent (male 3,826,232; female 3,757,859; 2008 estimate)

POPULATION GROWTH RATE:
2.218 percent (2008 estimate)

TOTAL FERTILITY RATE:
4.41 children born per woman (2008 estimate)

LIFE EXPECTANCY AT BIRTH:
Total population: 53.03 years (male 52.54 years; female 54.08 years; 2008 estimate)

INFANT MORTALITY RATE:
64.57 deaths per 1,000 live births (2008 estimate)

LITERACY RATE (AGE 15 AND OVER WHO CAN READ AND WRITE):
Total population: 79 percent (male 84.7 percent; female 73.4 percent; 2003 estimate)

EDUCATION:
High rate of school attendance; about 74 percent of children attend primary school; approximately 22 percent of males and 17 percent of females attend secondary school. The University of Yaoundé, established in 1962, has faculties of law, arts, and science. More than 64,500 students are enrolled in institutions of higher education.

LANGUAGES:
French and English are both official languages, but French is more widely used; 24 major African languages are represented in Cameroon.

ETHNIC GROUPS:
Nearly one-third of the population are Cameroon Highlanders (31 percent), one-fifth are Equatorial Bantu (19 percent); some 200 other ethnic groups are represented in the remaining population, of which 11 percent are Kirdi, 10 percent Fulani, 8 percent Northwestern Bantu, 7 percent Eastern Nigritic, and less than 1 percent non-African. The remaining 13 percent are from other African ethnic groups.

RELIGIONS:
About 40 percent of the population adheres to indigenous beliefs; about 40 percent are Christian, and about 20 percent are Muslim.

CLIMATE:
Tropical near the coast, dry inland. Average annual rainfall is about 4,060 mm (about 160 in) along the coast; precipitation in the western mountains is year round, as much as 10,160 mm (400 in) annually; in the north, which has a dry season from October to April, yearly rainfall averages 380 mm (about 15 in). Average temperature along the coast is 25° C (77° F), on the central plateau 21° C (70° F), and in the dry north 32° C (90° F).

LAND, PLANTS, AND ANIMALS:
Cameroon has a dense rain forest along its coastal plain, with mountains in the west, including an active volcano, Mount Cameroon (4,095 m/ 13,435 ft), the highest peak in western Africa. In the center is the Adamawa Plateau, becoming savanna plains in the north. Rivers flowing through Cameroon include the Nyong, Sanaga, Mbéré, Logone, and the Benue, linking up with the Niger River system. Animals include elephants, lions, monkeys, chimpanzees, gorillas, and antelope.

NATURAL RESOURCES:
Timber, petroleum, bauxite, and iron ore

CURRENCY:
The CFA franc

GROSS DOMESTIC PRODUCT (GDP):
$40.24 billion (2007 estimate)

GDP PER CAPITA:
$2,200 (2007 estimate)

GDP REAL GROWTH RATE:
2.7 percent (2007 estimate)

PRIMARY ECONOMIC ACTIVITIES:
Agriculture (43.9 percent of GDP, 70 percent of employment), industry, transport, and other services

PRIMARY AGRICULTURAL PRODUCTS:
Cacao, coffee, tobacco, cotton, bananas, rubber, palm products, sugar cane, plantains, sweet potatoes, cassava, millet, and corn. Livestock raised in the Adamawa Plateau region include cattle, goats, sheep, and pigs.

INDUSTRIES:
Lumber, petroleum production and refining, textiles, food processing, and light consumer goods

PRIMARY EXPORTS:
Petroleum, coffee, cocoa, lumber, aluminum, and cotton

PRIMARY IMPORTS:
Machines and electrical equipment, food, and consumer goods, transport equipment, and petroleum products

PRIMARY TRADE PARTNERS:
European Union (France and Germany), African countries (especially Nigeria), Japan, and the United States

GOVERNMENT:
Cameroon is a unitary republic, under a constitution established in 1972. It has a multiparty regime currently dominated by the government-controlled Cameroon People's Democratic Movement (CPDM). The executive branch is led by the president (currently Paul Biya), who appoints the head of government (currently Prime Minister Ephraim Inoni), a cabinet of federal ministers, and the governors of ten provinces. The legislative branch is the elected unicameral National Assembly.

Barbara Worley

dependent upon France, which operated a military base in Cameroon and consistently vetoed other foreign powers' efforts to pressure Biya for reform.

By 1987, however, Cameroon's oil boom had ended, and government bureaucracy and debt had strained the national budget. Unable to buy political support, Biya faced growing civil unrest. In 1990 the national assembly legalized opposition parties, but Biya's refusal to allow for a new constitution provoked a massive strike throughout the south. Although elections were finally held in 1992, Biya resorted to widespread fraud to defeat the opposition candidate, Anglophone John Ndi of the Social Democratic Front. The government easily put down subsequent riots, and the opposition faded. Even after a devaluation of the currency throughout the West African franc zone, in 1994, sparked sharp price increases, as well as protests in several countries, Cameroon experienced relatively little unrest.

Although a new constitution passed in 1996 provided for local and regional elections, it also gave the executive branch of government broad powers. In elections the following year, no opposition candidate dared challenge Biya's bid for another seven-year term, though recently he has suffered health problems. The economy continued to grow steadily in the late 1990s, with an increase in oil, timber, and coffee exports and the completion of a three-year International Monetary Fund program of structural reforms. However, the troubles plaguing the massive CHAD-Cameroon pipeline, once projected to be the largest infrastructure development in Africa, signaled a significant setback. Expected to add some $540 million to Cameroon's economy, the dam project was instead seriously delayed by a combination of national and international strife, popular opposition, and political opportunism. Relative economic prosperity and strong-arm tactics against opponents have enabled Biya to withstand both international and domestic opposition, and to carry on his predecessor's plan to forge a sense of national unity among Cameroon's ethnic groups, regions, and linguistic blocs.

See also BANTU: DISPERSION AND SETTLEMENT; ISLAM IN AFRICA; SLAVERY IN AFRICA.

ERIC YOUNG

Cameroon Lions
National soccer team of Cameroon and traditionally one of Africa's premier teams.

German colonizers first introduced soccer, known in Africa as football, to CAMEROON around 1880, and the game quickly became popular. Over time Cameroon developed a strong network of professional teams, especially in

YAOUNDÉ and Douala. Many of these teams have won the African Champions Cup, the continental professional league championships.

The Indomitable Lions, Cameroon's national team, have been a major force on the African soccer scene since the 1970s. In 1982 the green, red, and yellow Indomitable Lions reached soccer's World Cup for the first time. The team went on to win the AFRICAN CUP OF NATIONS in 1984 and 1988. The Indomitable Lions' reign peaked in 1990 when they reached the World Cup quarterfinals with passionate play and impressive individual skills. (They were eliminated by one of Cameroon's former colonial powers, Britain.) In the early 1990s the national team was weakened by infighting among players, poor planning and administration, and a lack of funds. It was eliminated quickly in the 1994 World Cup and 1996 African Cup of Nations. Many observers concluded that the Indomitable Lions were a spent force, but in 1998 they returned to top form, qualifying for the World Cup with an unbeaten record in their group and reaching the finals.

Since then the team has achieved numerous triumphs, winning both the African Cup of Nations and the Olympic gold medal in 2000, and the African Cup again in 2002. They qualified for a fifth World Cup appearance in 2002, but were eliminated after the group phase after losing to Germany. The Lions were named African team of the year in 2000; that same year the Confederation of African Football chose the Lions as African team of the century.

Cameroonian soccer stars, seven of whom have been named African Player of the Year, include the legendary Roger Milla, who dazzled fans with his deft ball-handling in the 1990 World Cup and who, at age forty-two, went on to be the oldest scorer in World Cup history; goalkeeper Thomas Nkono; and Jean-Manga Onguene. More recently, forwards Patrick Mboma—the top goal scorer in the 2002 African Cup—and Samuel Eto'o have powered the Lions' rebirth. Many Cameroonian players compete on top-level European, South American, and Asian teams.

ERIC YOUNG

Campbell, Roy
1901–1957
South African poet of European descent.

Born into a prominent Scottish family in Durban, South Africa, Roy Campbell brought to the world of English letters a passionate love for the Africa of his childhood. After attending school in Durban, Campbell left South Africa for Oxford College in England in 1918. Already a writer, Campbell's youthful verses show the influences of Yeats, Wordsworth, and Shelley while featuring rich descriptions of African landscape, wildlife, and indigenous folkways.

Disappointed by Oxford and drifting through the London arts scene, Campbell, who had married in 1922, moved with his wife to a remote cabin in Wales. It was there that he wrote *The Flaming Terrapin* (1924), an epic poem hailed by critics for its energy and exuberance. While dealing with the alienation of the European world following World War I (1914–1918), *The Flaming Terrapin* also introduced readers to Campbell's invocation of African muses. According to literary biographer Peter Alexander, Campbell sought to combine "the intellect of Europe [with] the riotous life of Africa."

Campbell cultivated the image of the rude colonial while in Europe and his poetry can, to modern eyes, appear to exoticize indigenous peoples. Yet he was a fluent speaker of the Zulu language and an advocate of African voting rights as early as 1925. Throughout his life Campbell returned often to SOUTH AFRICA, but never settled there permanently. In all, he published more than twenty volumes of poetry, prose, and translations before his death in a car crash.

See also POETRY, AFRICAN.

KATE TUTTLE

Camus, Albert
1913–1960
French-Algerian writer and philosopher, and winner of the Nobel Prize for Literature in 1957.
Algerian-born Albert Camus was one of France's most famous twentieth-century writers. Although his impoverished boyhood in colonial North Africa led him into left-wing politics as a youth, Camus later became known for his belief in existentialism, a strain of philosophy that argues that human beings are alone in a godless universe and must find meaning without the comfort of religion.

Camus was born in a small town in eastern Algeria. He was only a year old when his father, a farm laborer from France, died in battle in World War I (1914–1918). His mother moved the family to a working-class neighborhood in ALGIERS, where Camus excelled in the local elementary and high schools. As a teenager Camus contracted tuberculosis, a disease that robbed him of his first love, playing soccer, and plagued him his entire life. As a student at the University of Algiers, he studied philosophy, briefly joined the Algerian Communist Party, and acted in a theater troupe that staged plays for working-class audiences.

Camus wrote his thesis on the philosophers Plotinus and Saint AUGUSTINE, but his first two published

collections of essays, *L'Envers et l'endroit* (1937; The Wrong Side and the Right Side) and *Noces* (1939; Nuptials), featured personal meditations on his own family and homeland. In the late 1930s, while remaining active in the theater, he worked as a journalist for the *Alger-Républicain*. He reviewed books by Jean-Paul Sartre and other existentialist writers and wrote articles on a variety of social issues, such as the poverty faced by Muslims in Algeria's Kabylia region.

In 1940 Camus moved to Paris. There he wrote for *Combat*, a left-wing newspaper, and finished his first novel, *L'Étranger* (The Stranger), and a philosophical treatise, *Le Mythe de Sisyphe* (The Myth of Sisyphus), both published in 1942. Both works attracted international attention for their stark yet sympathetic look at the alienation of modern life. In Mersault, the protagonist of *L'Étranger*, Camus created a character so completely exiled from both social convention and his own emotional life that he kills seemingly without reason or remorse—a symbol, critics have noted, for the average person's passive complicity in the face of the social upheaval of the mid-twentieth century.

In his second novel, *La Peste* (1947; The Plague), Camus portrayed a town's reaction to a deadly epidemic. In examining human responses to random evil, Camus began to construct an existentialist argument for human solidarity in the face of an indifferent universe. This strain of moral, rather than ideological, judgment is also evident in his essay "L'Homme révolté" (1951; The Rebel). Its critique of Soviet prisons angered some fellow existentialists, such as Sartre, who were sympathetic to Soviet Marxism. In his last novel, *La Chute* (1956; The Fall), Camus similarly dealt with estrangement and the hope for redemption in community.

When he died at age forty-six in a car accident, Camus left behind his second wife (an early marriage had ended in 1936) and two children. An unfinished novel was published in 1994 as *The First Man*. He had also published two plays and several collections of short stories and essays. "Whatever our personal frailties may be," Camus said of writers while accepting the Nobel Prize in 1957, "the nobility of our calling will always be rooted in two commitments difficult to observe: refusal to lie about what we know and resistance to oppression."

See also LITERATURE, FRENCH-LANGUAGE, IN AFRICA.

KATE TUTTLE

Cape Colony
Dutch and later British colony in southern Africa; now part of South Africa.

See also COLONIAL RULE; SOUTH AFRICA.

Cape Coloured
Term commonly applied to people of mixed ancestry who live in Cape Province of South Africa.

Like the Cape Malay and the Griqua, the Cape Coloured (or simply Coloured) people are part of a larger South African group of mixed African, European, and Asian descent. Their ancestors include slaves brought to the CAPE COLONY from the Far East, MADAGASCAR, and West Africa. The Cape Coloured people are the largest of these groups; they number almost three million and account for nearly 85 percent of the Cape Province population.

Although the term Cape Coloured was not used before the nineteenth century, the processes of intermarriage and assimilation that produced the Coloured social category began in the seventeenth century. Dutch settlers established the Cape Colony in 1652, and they met their need for meat and other foodstuffs by trading with local African populations, such as the pastoral KHOIKHOI. They met their need for labor, however, by importing slaves. Assimilated local Africans and former slaves, as well as the offspring of mixed marriages, came to be known as Coloured. Most people who fell into this category spoke Afrikaans—a variation of Dutch infused with words from African languages—and became members of the Dutch Reformed Church. Many worked as laborers on the farms of Dutch settlers, who came to be known as Afrikaners, or Boers. In 1806 the British assumed control of Cape Colony, and in 1834 they abolished slavery.

Emancipated slaves swelled the colony's Coloured population, and many settled and found work in cities such as CAPE TOWN and Port Elizabeth. This urban, Afrikaner-speaking population came to be known as the "Cape Coloured," a group distinct from black Africans. The Cape Coloureds used this distinction to claim superiority over other African groups and to secure better-paying jobs.

Franchise restrictions began to undermine the political rights of the Cape Coloured population in the late nineteenth century. After British and Afrikaner colonies joined to form the Union of SOUTH AFRICA in 1910, laws such as the Civilized Labour Policy gave whites privileged access to jobs, and segregation policies confounded Cape Coloured aspirations of assimilation. The rights of Coloureds—like those of all other nonwhites—were further undermined after the NATIONAL PARTY (NP) came to power in 1948 and imposed the system of APARTHEID. Although Cape Coloureds' fluency in Afrikaans gave them an advantage over black Africans on the job market, they still suffered under apartheid policies. The 1949 ban on interracial marriages, for example, tore apart hundreds of families. In 1950 the Group Areas Act mandated the relocation of both black and Coloured urban populations. Tens of thousands of Cape Coloureds were forcibly removed from their homes in Cape Town and other cities, and were relocated to overcrowded townships outside the city limits.

Today, the Cape Coloured people have reasserted their unique position in South African society. Even after the injustices of the apartheid era, many Cape Coloured people support the National Party. In general, Cape Coloureds have shown little enthusiasm for the AFRICAN NATIONAL CONGRESS (ANC), despite the party's efforts to win their support. Some Cape Coloureds accuse the ANC of appointing only black South Africans to important political positions.

ELIZABETH HEATH

Cape Town, South Africa
Major city of South Africa.

The present legislative capital of SOUTH AFRICA, Cape Town was also one of the first European colonial settlements in Africa. Located on the WESTERN CAPE some 48 km (30 mi) north of the Cape of Good Hope, modern Cape Town radiates outward from its harbor at Table Bay. With its seacoast nearly abutting the picturesque Table Mountain, Cape Town is widely considered one of the most beautiful cities in the world.

When European ships first landed on the Cape in the mid-seventeenth century, KHOISAN-speaking SAN hunter-gatherers and KHOIKHOI pastoralists had already been living in the region for centuries. Portuguese explorers arrived first, but it was an official of the Dutch East India trading company, Jan Van Riebeeck, who established the settlement that he called De Kaap (the Cape). The company intended to use the site to provision ships traveling between the Netherlands and the Indies; it brought Dutch settlers to build a town and farm the land. By the 1660s the Cape settlement was importing slaves from India, Malaysia, and Madagascar to work the farms.

The early Dutch settlers depended on trade with Khoikhoi pastoralists to supplement their own scarce meat supply, but their efforts to expand onto Khoikhoi grazing lands met with opposition. A combination of European military force and imported diseases (especially the 1713 smallpox epidemic) nearly wiped out the Khoikhoi population. Over the next century, intermarriage between Khoisan speakers, Europeans, and imported slaves created a sizeable mixed-race population, whose descendants came to be known as the CAPE COLOURED people. At the same time, descendants of the early Dutch settlers came to identify themselves as AFRIKANER or Boers. Today, about half of Cape Town's population of 3,497,097 is racially mixed.

By the late eighteenth century, European powers were vying for control over the strategic Cape region. To prevent an English takeover in 1781, the Dutch enlisted French help in building a fort outside their town, which by then had a population of approximately 14,000 people. Cape Town today shows the influence of both Dutch and French architecture and city planning, but in 1806 the town and the surrounding region were taken over by the British.

The nineteenth century saw the incorporation of Cape Town and several of its suburbs, the northward extension of its rail lines, and, in 1834, the emancipation of its slaves. But the opening of the SUEZ CANAL in 1869 eliminated much of the shipping traffic that had long passed through Cape Town's harbor, and soon after the discovery of gold and diamonds in the Afrikaner-held TRANSVAAL region, JOHANNESBURG eclipsed Cape Town in size and wealth. Still, the port city remained an important way station for European and Indian migrants to the Transvaal, and by the early twenty-first century had become South Africa's most populous city.

When British and Afrikaner territories joined to become the Union of South Africa in 1910, Cape Town became its capital. The mining industries spurred industrialization and urbanization throughout South Africa, and during World War II the rapid growth of Cape Town led to the reclamation of 358 acres of formerly submerged land. It was known as the most racially tolerant of South African cities, with less residential segregation than Johannesburg or DURBAN and no racial restrictions on voting in local elections. But in the 1960s and 1970s the NATIONAL PARTY's APARTHEID regime restricted participation in Cape Town elections to whites. It also enforced segregation by bulldozing old neighborhoods and forcibly relocating some 50,000 blacks, Indians, and Coloured people into newly formed townships.

Cape Town's local government unsuccessfully protested the moves, and the city became an important center of the ANTIAPARTHEID MOVEMENT. Since the dismantling of apartheid in the early 1990s, Cape Town's residential segregation is no longer legally enforced but, as in the rest of the country, it has far from disappeared. Cape Town is now one of South Africa's most popular tourist destinations. The city's beaches, mountains, and nearby wine country attract visitors from around the world. The city has also recently become the center of a rapidly expanding mining industry.

See also INDIAN OCEAN SLAVE TRADE; TOURISM IN AFRICA.

BIBLIOGRAPHY

Western, John. Outcast Cape Town. University of California Press, 1996.

KATE TUTTLE

Cape Verde

Small West African country, consisting of ten volcanic islands and five islets off the coast of Senegal.

For more than 400 years, Portugal claimed the rocky, arid islands of Cape Verde. This long history of COLONIAL RULE permanently affected Cape Verdean culture, making the small country seem distinct from other African nations—"more European." But such a view ignores the shared ancestries and political struggles that link the islands to the mainland. Cape Verde is home to a population descended from free people and West African slaves as well as a diverse mix of peoples: Fula, WOLOF, Papeis, BALANTA, BIJAGÓ, Jalofa, Fulupe, Mandingo, MANJACO, Portuguese, Moroccan, Sephardic Jewish, Genoese, Lebanese, Chinese, Dutch, French, English, American, and Brazilian. The children of these settlers and passers-by forged a hybrid culture and language known as Crioulo (Portuguese for Creole), drawing upon the legacies brought to the islands by slavery and colonialism.

PORTUGUESE COLONIZATION AND THE SLAVE TRADE

It is possible that the Cape Verde Islands were visited by Phoenician traders in the fifth or fourth centuries B.C.E., and even more likely that North African sailors in the SALT TRADE passed through during the tenth and eleventh centuries C.E. Fishing folk from the region of modern-day SENEGAL later landed in the area during their expeditions, but the islands were not permanently occupied until the Portuguese took possession of them in the fifteenth century. Exploration and slave trading had brought Portuguese ships past the southern islands for several years before Genoan Antonio de Noli and Portuguese Diogo Afonso claimed them for Portugal in 1455. Although the islands themselves offered limited natural resources, they were strategically located on what were soon to be busy transatlantic trade routes. Having recently settled the Madeira Islands, Portugal next moved to settle Cape Verde, intending to use the islands both as an entrepôt for its merchant ships and a site for producing tropical-climate crops, such as sugar and cotton.

The expansion of the slave trade across the Atlantic Ocean in the sixteenth century soon brought business and settlement to Cape Verde. Portugal made the islands its headquarters for its holdings on the Upper Guinea Coast, and by the sixteenth century was also using the region as a penal colony for convicts and political exiles. The islands were originally governed by the companhia system, a sort of feudal system in which individuals or the church oversaw small plantations where slaves, brought from mainland West Africa, cultivated cotton, sugarcane, and food crops. Early Cape Verdean society enjoyed considerable autonomy from the Portuguese

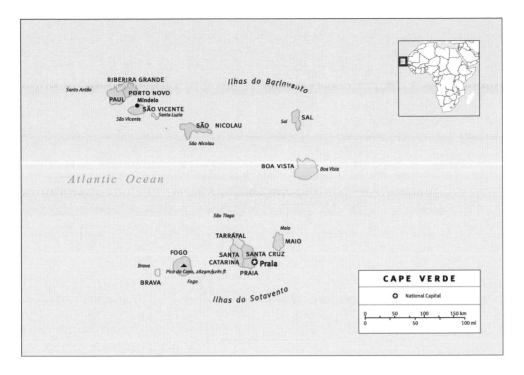

monarchy, making it an attractive base to generations of traders and smugglers.

Despite efforts to develop plantation agriculture, little besides the population grew on the drought-prone islands, and the economy relied heavily on the commerce provided by passing ships, first those traveling to and from West Africa, and later, those crossing the Atlantic. Portugal's merchant ships exchanged rum, cloth, and other commodities for slaves acquired at ports all along the Upper Guinea Coast, and many of the goods and slaves passed at least briefly through Cape Verde. As a result, the islands' ports became targets for plunder by pirate ships sailing under the flags of France, Holland, and England. In 1656 Portugal sent a governor general to oversee more directly the protection and governance of Cape Verde and the Portuguese-controlled Guinea Coast, and to crack down on the smuggling that was eroding Portuguese control over the region's lucrative trades. But with the many free agents operating along the West African coasts—including both "official" European traders and independent smugglers—Portugal had little success controlling trade of slaves or other articles of commerce.

In 1750 the prime minister of Portugal, the marquis of Pombal, declared a trade monopoly for slaves and certain other commodities between Cape Verde, GUINEA, and Brazil. Portugal's goal was to increase and streamline the export of slaves from West Africa to its American colony via Cape Verde, using the forty-one ships of the royal *Campanhia Geral* which the marquis controlled. Some of the slaves routed through the islands were also sold in Britain's North American colonies. Even after the fall of the marquis, Cape Verde remained a favored entrepôt among slave traders—it was closer to the Americas and considered safer than the ports of call on the Africa mainland, which were often controlled by powerful and well-armed African kings and merchants.

Not all African slaves brought to the islands went on to the Americas. Besides working on the cotton, sugar, and coffee plantations, slaves worked as domestic servants, as laborers in the islands' small salt-production enterprises, and as gatherers of plants used for dyes, including orchil and urzella. These dyes were in turn used by slave Wolof spinners and weavers to produce the colorful pano clothes that served as one of the main currencies in the slave trade. In addition, some freed or runaway slaves cultivated land in the hills of the interior.

Over the years, a heterogeneous Creole population developed, comprised of convicts, exiles, Portuguese merchants, social outcasts, and Catholic clerics as well as slaves and migrants from the Upper Guinea Coast. Cape Verdean society made distinctions among the races and the classes, as well as between slaves who lived on the islands and those who simply passed through. At the same time, however, interracial unions between white masters and slave women, who made up more than half of the slave population, created a sizeable mestiço (of indigenous and European descent) population. Over time, this mixed population came to include the children of mixed marriages between renegade traders (lacondos) and their African wives. Some of these traders were Jews fleeing the Spanish Inquisition from the late sixteenth to the mid-seventeenth century, when Portugal was under the rule of the Spanish Crown. Crioulo, a hybrid of Portuguese and various African languages, became the lingua franca of the *mestiços*. Crioulo was also spoken on the Guinea Coast, an indication of the ongoing multiethnic migration and trade between the islands and mainland.

PEASANT FARMING AND MARITIME TRADE

Britain's 1804 edict banning slave trading spelled the end of an era for the local and regional economies, such as Cape Verde's, that had developed around this commerce. Portugal officially abolished its own trade in 1836, though slavers continued to smuggle captives through Cape Verde for decades afterward. Meanwhile, the colony had become an entrepôt for other kinds of commodities from the mainland, including hides, ivory, wax, and dyewoods. With the invention of steam-powered boats, the islands also served as a refueling stop on the transatlantic passage.

The islands supported a growing Creole free peasantry, including manumitted slaves. Farmers cultivated grains, tended banana orchards, and raised livestock, especially goats, but the poor land made subsistence difficult, and a single season of drought often led quickly to famine. Many Cape Verdean farmers sought to bolster their economic security by seeking additional, if low-paid, work as share-croppers or manual day-laborers, but many others signed onto American whaling ships and joined growing expatriate communities in New England.

In the late nineteenth century, even as Europeans were beginning to colonize most of Africa, opposition to Portuguese crown rule was growing in both Cape Verde and GUINEA-BISSAU. In 1886 the Portuguese monarchy sent troops to quell unrest, as did the Portuguese republican government after 1910. A fascist government took control of Portugal in 1926, and wrote colonial policy into the constitution with the Colonial Act of 1933. The government cracked down on communist groups in Portugal who were, among other things, assisting the budding nationalist movements of Portuguese-speaking Africa. Dissidents from Guinea-Bissau and Portugal were sent to Cape Verdean prisons, which were known for their brutal conditions. Nevertheless, anticolonialist and anti-fascist revolts continued to rock Guinea-Bissau, and, to a lesser extent, the Cape Verde islands. In Cape Verde, nationalism found expression in the literary-cultural *Claridade* movement. Using the literary journal *Claridade*, founded in 1936, Cape Verdean intellectuals both on the islands and abroad gave voice to Cape Verdean Crioulo culture. They also wrote critically about the social and economic oppression of Portuguese colonialism.

ANTICOLONIAL RESISTANCE

Many Cape Verdeans opposed the new fascist government as well as the strong-arm Portuguese tactics that had characterized relations with Cape Verde since the late nineteenth century. The colonial government believed it unnecessary to invest in land management and water conservation, and cheap labor made Cape Verde a profitable colony at little expense. Meanwhile, the people of the islands had suffered a series of droughts and bad harvests through the turn of the century. As people died daily from hunger while Portuguese troops landed on the island, Cape Verdeans prepared to revolt.

Fearing a growing nationalist sentiment, Portugal granted Cape Verde the status of overseas province. It also increased police powers in the colonies, and convicts and dissidents were sent to a notorious work camp on the Cape Verde island of São Tiago, where police used torture to quash resistance. Nationalists responded by rallying behind the Partido Africano da Independencia da Guine e Cabo Verde (PAIGC), a party founded in 1956 by Amílcar CABRAL, and staging a series of general strikes. The organization grew and became more militant in 1959, after Portuguese troops massacred striking dockworkers in Bissau. Four years later, PAIGC launched a full-out nationalist war, with fighting concentrated in Guinea-Bissau and clandestine operations based on the islands. Portugal, receiving military and economic assistance from NATO, also used Cape Verde to garrison its troops.

INDEPENDENCE

Following the assassination of Cabral in 1973, the PAIGC intensified attacks against an increasingly weakened Portuguese military, and a year later Guinea-Bissau achieved independence. But the struggle continued with massive protests in Cape Verde. Although Portugal had wished to maintain the islands as an overseas territory, Cape Verde ultimately won independence on July 5, 1975, with PAIGC carrying the popular election. PAIGC leaders in both Cape Verde and Guinea-Bissau at first anticipated the unification of their two countries, but disagreements over socialist strategies as well as resentment about the perceived dominance of Cape Verdeans left the party divided. In 1980, the arrest of Guinea-Bissau president Luís Cabral split the ranks of the PAIGC, and shortly thereafter Pedro Verona Rodriques PIRES, Cape Verde's prime minister and a prominent nationalist, helped found the Partido Africano da Independencia da Cabo Verde (PAICV). Pires moved quickly to silence any potential

Cape Verde (At a Glance)

OFFICIAL NAME:
Republic of Cape Verde

AREA:
4,033 sq km (1,557 sq mi)

LOCATION:
Cape Verde is an archipelago, consisting of ten islands and five islets, in the Atlantic Ocean, due west of the westernmost point of Africa, near Mauritania and Senegal. The windward, or Barlavento, group of islands on the north includes Santo Antão, São Vicente, São Nicolau, Santa Luzia, Sal, and Boa Vista; the leeward, or Sotavento, group on the south includes São Tiago, Brava, Fogo, and Maio.

CAPITAL:
Praia, São Tiago (population 97,900; 2002 estimate)

OTHER MAJOR CITIES:
Mindelo, São Vicente (65,000; 2002 estimate)

POPULATION:
426,998 (2008 estimate)

POPULATION DENSITY:
105.87 people per sq km (about 274 per sq mi)

POPULATION BELOW AGE 15:
31.6 percent (male 77,533; female 76,489; 2003 estimate)

POPULATION GROWTH RATE:
0.595 percent (2008 estimate)

TOTAL FERTILITY RATE:
3.17 children born per woman (2008 estimate)

LIFE EXPECTANCY AT BIRTH:
Total population 71.33 years (male 67.99 years; female 74.76 years; 2008 estimate)

INFANT MORTALITY RATE:
42.55 deaths per 1,000 live births (2008 estimate)

LITERACY RATE (AGE 15 AND OVER WHO CAN READ AND WRITE):
76.6 percent (male 85.8 percent; female 69.2 percent; 2003 estimate)

EDUCATION:
Six years of primary school are compulsory. Almost all (97 percent) of Cape Verdean children attend primary school.

LANGUAGES:
Portuguese is the official language; the national language, however, is *Crioulo*, a Creole based on archaic Portuguese incorporating many African elements.

ETHNIC GROUPS:
More than two-thirds of the people of Creoles, or *mestiãos* (of indigenous and European descent). Nearly all of the remainder are of African ancestry.

RELIGIONS:
Roman Catholicism is the dominant religion, but is often fused with indigenous beliefs.

CLIMATE:
Tropical and dry, showing little variation throughout the year. The average temperature in Praia, the capital, ranges from 20° to 25° C (68° to 77° F) in January and 24° to 28° C (75° to 83° F) in July. Winds are frequent, occasionally carrying clouds of sand from the Sahara in Africa to the east. Precipitation is slight and irregular, and the islands are subject to drought. Average precipitation in Praia is 260 mm (10 in), nearly all of which falls from August through September.

LAND, PLANTS, AND ANIMALS:
The islands are volcanic in origin, and all but three—Sal, Boa Vista, and Maio—are mountainous. The highest point, Pico do Cano (2,829 m/9,281 ft) on Fogo, is also the group's only active volcano. Vegetation is sparse and consists of various shrubs, aloes, and other drought-resistant species. Wildlife is limited and includes lizards, monkeys, wild goats, and a variety of birdlife.

NATURAL RESOURCES:
Cape Verde is located in the midst of rich fishing grounds, although the industry has yet to develop to its potential. Mineral resources are meager and primarily include pozzolana (a volcanic rock used in making cement) and salt. Salt is mined on Sal, Boa Vista, and Maio, with annual production of about 7,000 metric tons.

CURRENCY:
The Cape Verdean escudo

GROSS DOMESTIC PRODUCT (GDP):
$1.603 billion (2007 estimate)

GDP PER CAPITA:
$3,200 (2007 estimate)

GDP REAL GROWTH RATE:
6.9 percent (2007 estimate)

PRIMARY ECONOMIC ACTIVITIES:
Seventy-four percent of the GDP comes from service-oriented industries, including commerce, transport, and public services. Despite scarce arable land and regular drought, 70 percent of the population lives in rural areas, and agriculture accounts for 11 percent of the nation's economic activity. Fish-processing facilities have been constructed in Mindelo, and the government has initiated programs to modernize the fishing fleet. Cape Verde is attempting to capitalize on its strategic location at the crossroads of mid-Atlantic air and sea lanes by expanding airports and port facilities.

PRIMARY AGRICULTURAL PRODUCTS:
Staple crops are maize (corn) and beans, sweet potatoes, coconuts, potatoes, cassava, and dates. Some bananas are grown for export, and sugarcane is raised for the making of rum. Fishing yields yellowfin tuna, skipjack, wahoo (a type of large mackerel), and lobsters.

INDUSTRIES:
Fish processing, salt mining, garments, ship repair, food, and beverages

PRIMARY EXPORTS:
Fish and bananas

PRIMARY IMPORTS:
Foodstuffs, consumer goods, industrial products, and transport equipment

PRIMARY TRADE PARTNERS:
Portugal, Britain, Netherlands, the United States, Germany, France, and Guinea-Bissau

GOVERNMENT:
A new constitution declared in 1992 affirmed Cape Verde as a multiparty democracy, expanding on reforms begun in 1990 that introduced free and popular elections for president and parliament. Legislative power is held by the 79-member National Assembly; members are elected by the voters to five-year terms. The head of state is the president, currently Pedro Pires, also elected to a five-year term. A prime minister, currently Jose Maria Pereira Neves (the latest government having been formed in 2008), is nominated by the assembly and appointed by the president.

Marian Aguiar

political opponents, thus insuring that he enjoyed a long term in office, though with little popular support.

Under Pires, the country followed a socialist path, with programs of nationalization and agrarian reform. Through the 1980s, Cape Verde's close relationship with countries such as the Soviet Union, Cuba, and LIBYA generated opposition from the Cape Verdean diaspora, particularly in the United States. Larger than the resident population of Cape Verde, these communities were not only an important source of economic aid for the homeland, but also an influential voice in Cape Verdean politics. In 1991, in the first multiparty elections since independence, opposition to the PAICV mobilized behind the Movimento para a Democracia (MpD). MpD candidate Antonio Mascarenhas Monteiro was elected president, with an agenda of economic liberalization and human rights. For the next few years, the MpD moved forward with a program of privatization. The party won the majority in a 1995 election, though the PAICV accused the MpD of skewing the elections by buying votes and controlling the media. In 2001 the PAICV returned to power and Pires became president, winning the election by a narrow margin. With aid from the World Bank as well as the European Community (EC)—the largest per capita aid of nearly any nation in the world—Cape Verde has undertaken such infrastructural projects as road development on several islands, as well as electrification and urban development around the city of Praia, São Tiago. The country continues to depend heavily on tourism and foreign investment.

See also CAPE VERDE, ETHNICITY IN; COLONIAL RULE; SLAVERY IN AFRICA.

MARIAN AGUIAR

Cape Verde, Ethnicity in
Historical organization of society and classification of the peoples of Cape Verde.

Like most societies, CAPE VERDE is home to a mixed population that claims ancestry from many different peoples. Some historians characterize Cape Verdeans by their biracial origins—the legacy of Portuguese settlement and the African slave trade. Race has been extremely important in the history of Cape Verde, where the small white population was initially slaveholding and always elite. Yet Cape Verdean society, like that of Brazil, historically had a number of other categories that designated social position and origins as well as race. In addition, as the islands' mestiço (of indigenous and European descent), or mixed, population grew, racial lines became increasingly difficult to draw. Often whiteness or blackness was as much a signifier of class position as it was of blood. Thus, in Cape Verde, to speak of ethnicity is not necessarily to speak only of race.

The Cape Verde islands were visited by Senegalese fishermen before the fifteenth century, but not permanently settled until the Portuguese arrived in 1455. The original inhabitants of the island of São Tiago were Portuguese, Genoese, and Spanish seamen who were granted the land by the Portuguese Crown. These men brought slaves from the West African coast and established a slave trade entrepôt on the arid rocky island. The seafarers were soon joined by settlers and exiles from Portugal.

Early society in Cape Verde recognized a feudalistic hierarchy. The *capitão* were the aristocracy of the islands, holding land grants from the crown and reaping the profits of semiautonomous plantations. They were supported by the noble *fidalgos*, as well as a fighting force of knights, *cavaleiro-fidalgos*, and bureaucrats, *almoxarifes*. Clerics of the Catholic Church also held land titles on the islands. All of these Portuguese elite were considered *brancos* (whites), a designation that ignored the multiracial inheritance of Portugal itself.

By the sixteenth century, Portugal was sending to Cape Verde all those unwanted on Portuguese soil. The *degredados*, or convicts, included petty criminals as well as those charged with civil or political crimes. Degredados, also called *exterminados*, were often used to row galley ships for the Portuguese. By 1548 this group also included Jews fleeing the Inquisition in Portugal. Many of these exiles remained working on the islands even after their sentences expired. Others turned to smuggling goods and became known as lançados, or "those who were thrown out." Operating along the coasts of Cape Verde and Guinea-Bissau, their renegade commerce in slaves and other commodities undermined official Portuguese trade monopolies. The lançados usually took African wives, contributing to the creation of the distinctive Cape Verdean Crioulo (Portuguese for Creole) heritage and culture. The other founders of the Crioulo heritage were those born of the violent legacy of slavery—the biracial children of white masters and black slaves.

From almost the moment of settlement, the Portuguese brought slaves to or through the islands. The Africans who left their mark on Cape Verde included Fulas, Wolofs, Papeis, Balantas, Bijagós, Jalofas, Fulupes, Mandingos, and Manjacos. They were called the pretos (blacks). While most stayed only briefly en route to the Americas, some slaves remained on the islands and worked as domestics or plantation laborers. More than half of the resident slaves were female.

Classification systems and stereotypes institutionalized Cape Verdean racism. Two African groups distinguished for their origins were the WOLOF, whose weavers produced the cloths used as currency in the slave trade, and the Fula, whose women were often designated domestic servants or concubines. A hierarchy developed among the slaves who remained on the island, with the baptized *escravos do confissão* or *ladinos* characterized as the most "civilized" among the Cape Verdean–born slaves, while those born on the African mainland, called *escravos bocais* or *novos*, were portrayed as stupid or raw because of their unfamiliarity with European customs. Freed slaves included the *grumete*, who acted as bodyguards, and the *tangomãos* or *linguas*, who played the indispensable role of translators and middlemen in the slave trade. Skin, hair, nose, and body-type variation were also used to designate racial origins.

By the early seventeenth century, the rapidly growing *mestiço* population was raising fears of African domination among Cape Verde's Portuguese elite. In 1620 the crown sent more degredados, including white female prostitutes, in an unsuccessful campaign to increase the whiteness of the islands' inhabitants. Immigrants from many countries have since settled in Cape Verde, and today the islands are the home to a wide variety of people who claim mixed ancestry. These include Sephardic Jews as well as settlers from Portugal, West Africa, MOROCCO, Genoa, Lebanon, China, the Netherlands, France, England, the United States, and Brazil.

During the period prior to independence, the acknowledgment and celebration of Cape Verdeans' mixed cultural and ancestral heredity became an important political and cultural movement. Although racial identification remains important, the category of race is extraordinarily fluid, making it impossible to define the racial proportions of the national population. Whiteness or blackness can carry the connotation of other markers such as class or education, and it is possible for an individual to become "more white" by moving up in society.

See also ETHNICITY AND IDENTITY IN AFRICA: AN INTERPRETATION; SLAVERY IN AFRICA.

MARIAN AGUIAR

Capitein, Jacobus Elisa
1718?–1747
First African, or person of African descent, ordained as minister in an established Protestant church.

Jacobus Elisa Joannes Capitein was one of the few educated Africans in eighteenth-century Europe. He became a Protestant minister at a time when many Europeans doubted that Africans had souls and thus questioned whether or not they could be converted to Christianity. Capitein was born in West Africa, perhaps in Elmina on the Gold Coast (present-day GHANA), where he was sold into slavery at the age of eight. The man who bought him presented him to a Dutch captain and trader, Jacobus van

Goch, at Elmina. Van Goch named him Jacobus Capitein and took him to the Netherlands in 1728.

Capitein and his owner settled in The Hague, where Capitein learned Dutch. Van Goch acquiesced when Capitein expressed interest in a theological education. Capitein learned Latin, Greek, Hebrew, and biblical Aramaic, and in 1735 he was baptized. In 1737 he won a scholarship to study theology at the University of Leiden.

Capitein explained that he was interested in theology because he wanted "to be able to show his countrymen the way from idolatry to the true worship of God." In his thesis paper he argued that Africans are equal to whites but condoned slavery as a means to convert "heathens." The thesis was published and became very popular among slave and plantation owners because it justified the slave trade. While attending university, Capitein also wrote poems and essays and gave sermons, many of which were published and received significant attention in the Netherlands. Two portraits of him were done and many copies sold. Capitein was upheld as an example of Christianity's universality.

Capitein was ordained upon his graduation in 1742 and appointed chaplain to the European community in Elmina. He attempted to apply his vision for successful missionary work—the use of African languages in teaching, the provision of a separate place of worship for the Africans, daily contact with the Africans, and the training of locals for missionary work. However, his efforts brought few conversions. His work among the Europeans was also unsuccessful—few of the resident Dutch soldiers and slave traders cared to attend church.

Capitein's mission was not only a failure professionally but also personally. His employer, the West India Company, would not permit him to marry an African woman and instead in 1745 sent a white Dutch woman, Antonia Grinderdos, to be his wife. Capitein's financial difficulties further strained this arranged marriage. The company paid him poorly and expected him to supplement his income with private enterprise. His trading initiatives were fruitless. Gradually, Capitein declined physically, emotionally, and financially. Capitein's tragic career provided racists with another reason to believe that blacks should not be members of the church. However, his mastery of European languages and his erudition proved to many Europeans that Africans were their equals.

LEYLA KEOUGH

Caprivi Strip
Strategically important region of Namibia.

In 1890 an Anglo-German agreement ceded to Germany a sliver of land, 500 kilometers (300 miles) long and (at most) 117 kilometers (73 miles) across, located between

ANGOLA, BOTSWANA, and ZAMBIA. It was named the Caprivi Strip after German Chancellor Otto von Bismarck's successor, Count George von Caprivi. At its easternmost tip the Caprivi Strip provides access to the ZAMBEZI RIVER, which Germany sought to use as a link between GERMAN SOUTHWEST AFRICA and GERMAN EAST AFRICA (now TANZANIA). In 1915, after SOUTH AFRICA occupied what is today NAMIBIA, it established a military base on the strip in order to intercept armed nationalists attempting to enter South Africa via Botswana. The western Caprivi has always been sparsely populated, while the east holds approximately three-quarters of the population on its floodplain between the Okavango, Zambezi, and Kwando rivers. A violent secessionist movement spearheaded by the Caprivi Liberation Army took place from 1994 to 1999.

The people who live in the Caprivi Strip include 40,000 Masubia, Mafwe, and San, all closely related to those in the neighboring countries. They are divided into eight clans governed by a representative council. They raise cattle and farm the land, growing maize (corn), sorghum, millet, and other crops.

ERIC YOUNG

Carthage

Ancient city of North Africa founded on the Gulf of Tunis in present-day Tunisia as a Phoenician colony around 800 B.C.E.

For three centuries, from about 500 to 200 B.C.E., Carthage was the capital of a commercial empire that dominated trade in the western Mediterranean. Starting around 250 B.C.E., however, the Carthaginians found themselves increasingly in conflict with the expanding Roman Republic. The Romans, after three ruthless wars of attrition, destroyed the city and scattered its inhabitants. Reestablished by the Romans in later years as a commercial outpost, Carthage languished for centuries after the fall of the empire. Today it is a pleasant suburb of TUNIS, TUNISIA. This article deals primarily with the ancient history of the city and its role, despite its ultimate defeat, in the growth of Roman Africa.

PHOENICIAN COLONIZATION

The Phoenicians were an ancient people who probably emerged from the Arabian peninsula approximately 5,000 years ago. After subduing the indigenous peoples of Syria and Palestine, they established a maritime trading empire at the eastern end of the Mediterranean. Ethnically and culturally a Semitic people, the Phoenicians worshiped a paramount god, Baal, and other minor divinities. They were intelligent and inventive—among other things, they

CARTHAGE CONQUERER. A bust of Scipio Africanus, a military commander who conquered Carthage late in the 3rd century B.C.E. (Bridgeman Art Library International Ltd.)

invented the alphabet. They were also skillful mariners, willing and able to sail where no one else dared. Thus, for example, they did not fear, as the Greeks did, to sail beyond the Straits of Gibraltar. They probably circumnavigated Africa in the sixth century B.C.E. and sailed as far north as Britain, where many Carthaginian coins have been found. Starting as early as 1500 B.C.E., inhabitants of the Phoenician homeland (modern Lebanon and neighboring parts of Israel and Syria) came under pressure from other peoples of the Near East. Slowly but steadily over the next 1,000 years, as their power in their homeland diminished, their "western empire" expanded. Tyre and Sidon, the ancient Phoenician city-states, fell to various enemies, and Greeks challenged their domination of the Mediterranean and its shores. Ever innovative, the Phoenicians shifted their focus from old Phoenicia to Carthage, the "new" city they had founded around 800 B.C.E. on the North African coast.

The founding date is questionable, as are many other Carthaginian dates. Carthaginians were not a literate or artistic people. They used the alphabet to improve business—whereas the Greeks, adopting it in the eighth century B.C.E., used the precious invention not only for business but also to write poetry, history, and philosophy—and they consequently left few records of their achievements and way of life. Although intensely patriotic and fanatic believers in their religion, they were not proselytizers; for the most part they did not try to impose their beliefs or practices on others. Essentially, they wanted to be left alone to do business with the rest of the world. Carthage, the city on the bay, exemplified everything the Phoenicians held dear. Well situated for a maritime nation, it offered anchorage for many ships. Its central Mediterranean location was as close to Europe (at least to Sicily) as any other place on the African coast east of MOROCCO. The distance from Carthage to its colonies in western Sicily is less than 160 kilometers (100 miles) by sea, a distance the swift Carthaginian vessels could sail in a day. This narrow opening between the eastern and western Mediterranean could be patrolled and if necessary closed by a line of warships. The only way around was to pass through the perilous Straits of Messina. In addition to dominating both sides of this narrow gateway, Carthage also exerted control over Malta and other islands in the sea lanes. The high point of the Carthaginian hegemony may have occurred around 400 B.C.E. Carthage founded settlements, which the Greeks called emporia, along the entire coast from the Gulf of Sidra in present-day LIBYA, through present-day TUNISIA and ALGERIA, to the Atlantic coast of Morocco, as well as on all the islands of the western Mediterranean, including the Balearics. Invading ships were sunk when captured, and a large army of Libyan and Nubian mercenaries could march either way from Carthage to counter invasions or put down revolts. The Carthaginian trade continued to flourish, not only by sea but also across the SAHARA Desert. Routes terminating near modern TRIPOLI, LIBYA opened much of sub-Saharan Africa to trade and commerce, especially in gold and precious jewels, for which the Carthaginians exchanged cloth and manufactured articles. At its height the city may have had as many as 500,000 inhabitants, and it was reputed to be the wealthiest city in the Mediterranean world.

PUNIC WARS
The beginning of the end for Carthage came in 264 B.C.E., with the onset of the first Punic War. ("Punic" is derived from a Roman word for Phoenicia.) By that year Rome had acquired control of the entire Italian peninsula and had begun to look both east, toward Greece, and west, toward Carthage. The Romans' first task was to capture the western half of Sicily, which Carthage had used as a fulcrum of its empire. Carthage could not permit the loss of Sicily, and so the war began. It lasted for twenty-five years and was a disaster for Carthage; not only was Sicily lost but also Sardinia, Corsica, Malta, and other islands, together with the monopoly of trade west of Italy. Carthage did not despair. Once before Phoenicians had moved west, from Tyre and Sidon to the coast of Africa; now they could move west again, to present-day Spain. A new empire was rapidly established based on the wealth of Spanish silver mines and trade with the Iberian and Celtic peoples of the region. Again, Rome was concerned and sought any excuse for another armed conflict. The Second Punic War began in 218 B.C.E. and ended in 201. Rome won and Carthage lost. Indeed, Rome's victory laid the foundation for the Roman Empire. But it was a near thing, and victory could have gone the other way. One man made the difference. Hannibal, the son of Hamilcar Barca, leader of the Phoenicians' Spanish empire, inherited the command of the army after his father died and his brother was assassinated. Unlike his predecessors, he believed Rome could be defeated only in its homeland; he therefore determined to invade Italy. The Romans knew he was coming and moved into Gaul to stop his army of some 40,000 infantry, 10,000 cavalry, and fifty elephants. For the first of many times, Hannibal outwitted his opponents and headed for the Alps instead of following the coastal route, as Rome had expected. His passage through the rugged mountains is one of the great feats in military history. The army was harassed by Celtic tribes, who rolled rocks down upon it from the heights. Snow falling on narrow icy paths created perilously slippery conditions. The elephants often fell to their death. Provisions ran short and hundreds starved, while thousands more deserted or were hurt or killed. Reduced to 20,000 men, 6,000 cavalry, and only a few of the war elephants, the army descended into the Po River valley after a journey of five months from Cartagena. A lesser man might have turned tail and gone home. Instead, Hannibal met one Roman army on the Ticino and defeated it, and then overwhelmed a larger force in Lombardy a month later (December 218). Italians began to join the army, which was also augmented by Celtic recruits. Hannibal had hoped that an invasion of Italy might dismember the Roman state, and it seemed as if his hopes might be realized. Hannibal's hopes rose even further the following spring (April 217), when he led his troops south to the Arno and then to (modern) Arezzo and Perugia. In so doing, he trapped a large Roman army on the narrow shore of Lake Trasimeno. Descending from prepared positions in the hills, the invaders pushed

the Romans back, killing thousands and forcing thousands more into the lake, where, encumbered by their armor, they drowned. The site of this famous battle, one of the worst defeats the Romans ever suffered, is near a small town now called Ossaia ("bony"). Even after more than 2,000 years, plows in nearby fields still turn up bone fragments from the ancient encounter. After their defeat at Ossaia, the Roman army was temporarily helpless; the Carthaginians had the chance to enter Rome, little more than 160 kilometers (100 miles) away, but the troops were themselves exhausted and could not take advantage of the opportunity. Meanwhile another Roman army was raised and, unwilling to test Hannibal in another battle, they watched as he wearily followed the river valleys south to Apulia and Campania, where he wasted the country, distributed large amounts of booty, and underwent treatment for wounds he had sustained. Well rested after the winter, Hannibal again outwitted his foes. In the early summer of 216, in a swift maneuver, he seized the army supply depot at Cannae, on the Adriatic coast, and then prepared a trap. The Gauls and the Iberian infantry were drawn up in a line across the plain of Cannae, between the mountains and the sea. On either side were wings of cavalry, not easily visible from the plain. The Roman army, also rested and numerically much superior, attacked the center, which gave way little by little but did not break. Suddenly, without warning, the Libyan and Nubian cavalry circled and attacked from the rear, again annihilating the Romans at Cannae, one of the most famous battles in European history. This great victory had the desired effect, and many Italian regions began to defect from Roman domination. But Hannibal, for reasons that are not clear, did not march on defenseless Rome. Instead, perhaps hoping the peoples of Italy would do his work for him, he spent the winter of 216–215 in Capua. Disappointed, his new allies began to drift away. Fabius, the Roman general, adopted a strategy of never fighting but always threatening, and Hannibal found himself on the defensive for the first time. What is more, he had begun to lose support at home, where a new government of oligarchs, shocked by the expense of the campaign, charged him with misconduct of the war. The rest of the story, after the ambiguous triumph at Cannae, involves a long, slow descent into loss and death, not only for Hannibal but also for his country. The final blow was delivered when still another Roman army, under Scipio Africanus, sailed across the sea and attacked Carthage itself. Hannibal abandoned Italy and rushed to defend his city. He met the Romans at Zama. The losses were terrible—20,000 men and horses and all the elephants, supplies, and provisions. Though he himself escaped, the end had come. Harried from country to country by his enemies, Hannibal lived another twenty years; finally trapped in a small village near the Black Sea, he took poison. The year was 183 B.C.E.

"DELENDA EST CARTHAGO"

Carthage survived even this defeat; a treaty with Rome was signed, and although the treaty's provisions were severe, the city slowly began to prosper again. By 150 B.C.E. it was once more rich and, consequently, influential in African affairs. Cato the Elder, the fierce old conservative who hated all things not Roman, took it as his private crusade to see that Carthage was destroyed once and for all. He repeated the famous phrase "Delenda est Carthago," or "Carthage must be destroyed," on every possible occasion; and he had his way. In 146 B.C.E. the city was besieged, taken, plundered, its inhabitants exiled or enslaved, its wall demolished, its houses and public buildings burned to the ground. The site was dedicated to the infernal gods and, to ensure that it would never again be inhabited, its smoking ruins were sown with salt. Carthage, however, had nine lives; it seemed it could not die. Only twenty-five years later, a Roman colony was established on the site, and in due course New Carthage became the capital of the Roman province of Africa (incorporating present-day Tunisia and eastern ALGERIA) and a favorite vacation spot of the emperors.

See also NORTH AFRICA AND THE GRECO-ROMAN WORLD; NORTH AFRICA, ROMAN RULE OF.

CHARLES VAN DOREN

Casablanca, Morocco

Port city in western Morocco and the nation's most important industrial and commercial center.

Although some sources claim the origins of the coastal city of Casablanca date back to the seventh century, the settlement left few historical traces until it developed as a BERBER town called Anfa in the thirteenth century. In 1468 the Portuguese attacked Anfa, which by then had become the base for a thriving piracy industry. The Portuguese remained a presence in the town they called Casa Branca, or "White House," until an earthquake leveled it in 1755. A series of Moroccan rulers followed, building ramparts that encircled the whitewashed houses and maze of streets. Then called Dar el Beida by the residents, the town became the commercial hub for the regions of Chaouia, Rehamnas, and Tadla, all of which exported goods such as cereals, wool, hides, beeswax, and oil to Europe. During this time, Berbers from the HâHâ region south of Essaouira began moving to what was then still a small town.

Over the next 200 years, Casablanca's mercantile population grew. Spanish grain merchants paved the way for other European traders, who arrived in large numbers after the reigning sultan opened the port to international commerce. By 1907, when the French military occupied MOROCCO, French merchants outnumbered all other Europeans. As Morocco's most active international trade center, Casablanca became the French protectorate's chief port. The French built a modern port and a new city radiating from the Moorish section, which they called the old medina.

Casablanca played a critical role for the Allied forces during World War II (1939–1945). The city was one of three points of the North African invasion. It was also host to the 1943 Casablanca Conference during which United States president Franklin D. Roosevelt and British prime minister Sir Winston Churchill vowed to fight the Axis powers for unconditional surrender.

After the withdrawal of the French in 1956, the city suffered an economic lull, but as an industrializing, strategically located seaport, it soon regained its standing, becoming the commercial capital of Morocco. Casablanca's industries account for more than half of the total industrial production of Morocco and include textiles, electronics, sawmilling, furniture, construction materials, glass, and tobacco products as well as fishing. Exports include cereals, leather, wool, and phosphates. The city, made famous in the West by the film *Casablanca* (1942), also attracts large numbers of tourists, who explore the juxtaposition of old and new quarters.

Casablanca has continued to expand in population to more than 3.8 million inhabitants in 2005. With an urban area that includes some of Morocco's largest slums, elite neighborhoods, and sprawling suburbs, Casablanca is currently Morocco's largest city. In May 2003 Islamic activists launched a series of terrorist attacks that killed forty-five people in Casablanca. Another series of terrorist activities, this one in 2007, saw suicide bombers attacking several sites throughout the city, including a police station and Internet café. Excepting the bombers themselves, however, casualties from the blasts were in the low single-digit figures.

See also COLONIAL RULE; TOURISM IN AFRICA.

MARIAN AGUIAR

Casely-Hayford, Joseph Ephraim
1866–1930
African educator, journalist, lawyer, and politician, and the most prominent African nationalist leader of the 1920s.
Joseph Ephraim Casely-Hayford spent his life working for the advancement of Africans in British West Africa. Born into the coastal elite of the GOLD COAST (present-day

GHANA), Casely-Hayford studied at the Wesleyan Boys High School at Cape Coast and then at Fourah Bay College in SIERRA LEONE. During his early career he was principal of Wesleyan High School in ACCRA and later of Wesleyan High School at Cape Coast. In 1885 Casely-Hayford turned to journalism and wrote for the Western Echo, the Gold Coast Echo, and the Gold Coast Chronicle. Although his career would focus on bringing political change to West Africa, he continued to write for the Gold Coast Leader from 1902 to 1930. In addition, he wrote the novel *Ethiopia Unbound* (1911) and the nonfiction work *Gold Coast Native Institutions* (1903). It was as a politician and activist that Casely-Hayford earned renown. His accomplishments are too many to list fully here. Called to the bar in 1896 after studying in London, Casely-Hayford returned to the Gold Coast to represent the Aborigines' Rights Protection Society in its fight against a British legal initiative that threatened the land tenure system. From 1916 to 1925 Casely-Hayford served as an appointed member of the Gold Coast's Legislative Council. From 1927 until his death in 1930 he was an elected member. He drew inspiration and ideas from a wide range of world leaders, including Mahatma Gandhi, W. E. B. Du Bois, and Marcus Garvey. Perhaps his greatest achievement was his instrumental role in founding the National Congress of British West Africa (NCBWA) in 1920. An early example of Pan-Africanism, this organization brought together nationalists from the British colonies of the GAMBIA, NIGERIA, the Gold Coast, and Sierra Leone. The NCBWA worked unsuccessfully to gain self-rule for these colonies, but set the trend for future political development.

See also PRESS, AFRICAN.

BIBLIOGRAPHY

Casely-Hayford, Joseph Ephraim. Ethiopia Unbound: Studies in Race Emancipation. F. Cass, 1969.

Casely-Hayford, Joseph Ephraim. West African Leadership: Public Speeches Delivered by J. E. Casely Hayford. F. Cass, 1969.

ROBERT FAY

Central African Empire
Name given to Central African Republic by Bokassa for a short spain in the 1970s.

See CENTRAL AFRICAN REPUBLIC.

Central African Republic
Country in central Africa bordered by the Sudan, the Democratic Republic of the Congo, the Republic of the Congo, Cameroon, and Chad.
Located in the middle of the continent, the Central African Republic (CAR) has the potential to be one of Africa's

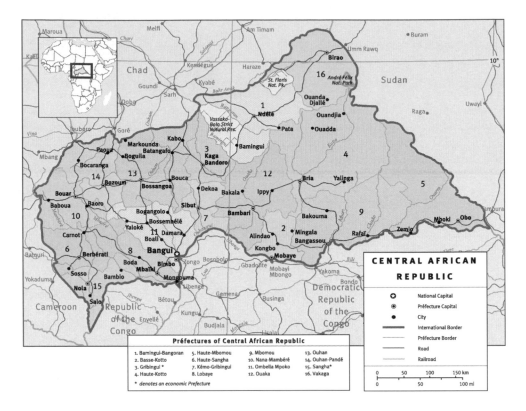

richest countries; during the colonial era, it was known as the "Cinderella of the French Empire." The soil is highly fertile, and the country possesses vast mineral wealth, valuable forests, and an abundance of wildlife for tourism. Although it has a diverse population, the CAR has experienced little ethnic or religious strife. Yet a tragic history has kept the country from fulfilling its potential. The slave trade and French colonialism devastated its population. Since independence, it has suffered a series of repressive and sometimes brutal regimes, and has remained economically and militarily dependent on France. And in recent years, despite efforts toward democratic reform, a number of attempted coups and rebellions have shaken the country. This ongoing violence and unrest make it unlikely that the CAR will soon realize the promise of its natural riches.

GEOGRAPHY AND EARLY HISTORY

A high plateau divides present-day CAR from east to west. The UBANGI RIVER feeds the CONGO RIVER, the CHARI River runs into the Chad Basin, and other minor tributaries feed the NILE RIVER. In the dry north, mountains reach 1,400 m (4,593 ft), while the southern forests experience a perpetual rainy season. The myriad of waterways that crisscross the region created fertile land along fluvial basins.

Archaeological evidence (in the form of polished flint and quartz tools) shows that the migratory Aka PYGMY people, known also as Babinga or Tvides, have fished, hunted, and gathered foodstuffs in the area of the modern-day CAR for at least 8,000 years. Around 2,500 years ago, agricultural peoples settled in the region and cleared the thick brush of the present-day savanna belt to grow millet and sorghum. Arrangements of hundreds of megaliths, many of them several tons in weight, suggest the development of a sophisticated agricultural society.

Linguistic evidence indicates that by the first millennium, speakers of Nilo-Saharan languages had entered the region from the east. At around the same time, speakers of Niger-Congo languages entered the region from the west and opened the forested southern areas to agriculture; gradually, they spread into the central and southeastern savanna areas. One or both of these groups introduced the technology of iron production to the region. Most of the savanna people lived in extended family compounds, with political and social order determined by kinship. As agriculturists, they were dependent upon favorable weather, and droughts created scarcity.

The first evidence of kingdoms in the area dates to the sixteenth century. By this time, three Islamic kingdoms—DARFUR, Wadai, and Bagirmi—had emerged to the north, and eventually extended their rule southward. These kingdoms, particularly Wadai and Bagirmi, carried out raids to capture slaves for the trans-Saharan trade, and people of the northern savanna fled south into the forests.

Meanwhile, in the eastern part of the present-day CAR, an aristocratic caste with origins to the northeast had established kingdoms among the AZANDE people. Newly introduced crops, particularly maize (corn) and cassava, produced agricultural surpluses that supported these states and aristocracies.

SLAVE TRADE IN CENTRAL AFRICA

From the seventeenth century to the nineteenth century, the trans-Saharan and transatlantic slave trades shaped the history of Central Africa. Indeed, there is evidence that slave raiders working in the eastern part of the region also participated in the INDIAN OCEAN SLAVE TRADE. In the mid-seventeenth century, the trans-Saharan slave trade expanded dramatically, with a few thousand or more enslaved people taken annually from the north of the region. At the same time, traders began to send additional slaves to the Atlantic coast and on to the New World. The number of Central Africans involved in the transatlantic slave trade remained relatively small until the late eighteenth century, by which time other areas had become depopulated and demand for slaves had increased. Riverine communities, collectively called the Bobangi or Ubangians, formed extensive commercial networks, trading slaves and ivory for manufactured European goods with the TÉKÉ people on the lower Congo River. Canoes capable of holding at least fifty people plied the rivers, capturing unsuspecting individuals and taking undesirable persons from villages. These slave raiders progressed southward, returning with cloth, jewelry, and guns. As the demand for slaves increased, animosity and violence grew between interior peoples and the raiding riverine traders.

As the transatlantic slave trade declined in the early 1800s, the trans-Saharan and internal African slave trades flourished in the north. Each of the northern kingdoms, including Wadai, Darfur, Bagirmi, and Kanem-Bornu, informally had its own raiding preserve in the region and conducted several raids during the dry season. Fulani slavers from Adamawa in present-day Cameroon conducted raids in the west. As with the transatlantic trade, it is not possible to determine the number of people taken from the area, but the social impact was clearly extensive. Historical enmities, decentralized social structures, and periodic migrations to evade raiding parties made it difficult for the peoples of the region to unify in opposition to the slave traders. Meanwhile, traders depopulated the area, particularly the central and eastern regions. They also brought goods such as salt, sugar, cloth, and tea, created trading posts, and promoted an indigenous merchant class; they took ivory and destroyed the large elephant herds that once roamed the savanna. In

addition, northerners, particularly the Fulani from Adamawa and the Sokoto Caliphate, introduced Islam during slave raids and jihads (holy wars) against the Gbaya and Mbun in the northwest.

The slave trade has marked the history of each of the eight major ethnic groups of the present-day CAR. The BANDA, Gbaya, Mandija, Mbun, and SARA all fell victim to slave raiders. The Mandija and Sara may in fact have entered the region fleeing slave raiders to the north and west. Azande chiefdoms formed alliances with different slave-raiding kingdoms, while the HAUSA and Fulani first entered the region during the eighteenth and nineteenth centuries to obtain slaves for agricultural estates in Adamawa and Sokoto.

In the second half of the nineteenth century, the scale of the trans-Saharan slave trade expanded. In 1879 Rabih al-Zubayr, a military commander and slave trader from the Sudan, settled in the northeast of the present-day CAR. Over the next decade and a half he created an empire by raiding the area for slaves. This empire absorbed the kingdoms of Darfur, Bagirmi, and Kanem-Bornu, as well as most of the Azande chiefdoms, and exported slaves to North Africa and the Middle East. In 1894 Rabih moved his headquarters to the northwest, and left Sultan al-Sanusi in charge of much of his territory in the present-day CAR. Al-Sanusi's domain, based at Ndélé, grew steadily until 1900, when French forces defeated Rabih and moved to incorporate the entire region into their colonial empire.

In 1880, as Rabih and al-Sanusi reigned in the east and north, many Gbaya and Mbun united to resist Fulani dominance in the northwest. A decade later they brought an end to Fulani control over the trade routes from the area. But this was exceptional. For the most part, the slave trade depopulated the region and created animosities among its peoples. Colonialists would soon exploit this discord to their own advantage.

FRENCH COLONIALISM

Located in the remote heart of Africa, the area that is now the CAR saw a relatively late arrival of Europeans and colonialism. At the BERLIN CONFERENCE OF 1884–1885 the European powers had determined the "rules of the game" for the SCRAMBLE FOR AFRICA. A few years later, in 1889, French expeditionary forces established a post on the Ubangi River in the present-day CAR. Paul Crampel's expedition of 1891 and others that followed secured treaties with African chiefs who were hoping to gain protection and advantage over their enemies. In 1894 France declared the area of OUBANGUI-CHARI (the modern-day CAR) a colony. French control of the area was at first tenuous. But in 1898, after the Franco-British confrontation at Fashoda on the Nile River, France sought to occupy Oubangui-Chari militarily in order to control the Chad Basin and unite its Central, West, and North African possessions. In 1900 French-led Algerian, Senegalese, and local troops completed their mission by killing Rabih and defeating his troops near Lake Chad.

Even before the French had fully occupied the region, they set up concessionary companies to exploit its wealth of wild rubber and timber. Holding legal rights over the territories under their concession, seventeen companies controlled more than half the land and subjected their populations to military conscription, taxation, and forced labor as agricultural workers and porters. These practices (as well as company abuses) led to international protests and incited local rebellions, particularly among the Gbaya and Mandija people, between 1909 and 1911. Local resistance forced the French to conquer the area piecemeal—river by river, and valley by valley. Ultimately, the governor general of French Equatorial Africa in BRAZZAVILLE held administrative responsibility for Oubangui-Chari, while poorly trained local administrators, headquartered at BANGUI, exercised authoritarian rule.

Between the 1890s and 1930s, French military aggression and forced labor requirements spread disease throughout the colony's population. Meanwhile, French demands for cash crops and tax payments further undermined the people's ability to feed themselves. Scholars estimate that the region's population dropped by one-third to one-half due to malnutrition and disease during these decades. Between 1928 and 1930, much of the population once again rebelled in the so-called Kongo Wara War, a series of local revolts against forced labor and taxation. In the 1930s, facing widespread economic stagnation in FRENCH EQUATORIAL AFRICA, colonial officials forced the population to grow cotton and coffee for the global market. Alarmed at the decline in the available labor force, the French developed a primary health care system in an effort to control the spread of sleeping sickness. The educational system, however, remained impoverished, and the companies were still controlled by Europeans.

During World War II, as prices rose for cotton, coffee, diamond, and rubber exports, Oubangui-Chari enjoyed economic prosperity. As a result, the French built new roads to facilitate trade. This economic boom began to open the economy to Africans, who entered into commerce, transport, timber, and commercial farming. After the war, French citizenship was extended to all Africans in French colonies, and a 1956 law granted Africans equal voting rights in colonial elections. These events encouraged a proliferation of nationalist political parties in Oubangui-Chari. Most prominent were the Union Oubanguienne and the quasi-religious Movement for the Social Evolution of Black Africa, led by Barthélemy BOGANDA, the first Oubangui Catholic priest and representative to the French National Assembly.

Boganda, recognizing the limits of his influence in France, returned to Oubangui-Chari to organize a grass-roots movement of small African producers to oppose French colonialism. After his arrest and detention by the French, Boganda became a folk hero and, though no longer a priest, was considered a messianic figure and the leading nationalist. Still, the relatively conservative Boganda remained sympathetic to French interests and did not advocate immediate independence. With the rush toward independence in much of Francophone Africa, however, in 1958 Boganda called for independence for Oubangui-Chari. Boganda envisioned Oubangui-Chari not as an independent country, but as part of a larger, more economically viable United States of Latin Africa that would include the present-day states of ANGOLA, Cameroon, both Congos, CHAD, GABON, RWANDA, and BURUNDI. But differences among the nationalist leadership in the various colonies soon made such a federation impossible, and later that year Boganda accepted a constitution covering only Oubangui-Chari, renamed the Central African Republic. Poised to become president of the independent CAR, Boganda was killed in a mysterious airplane crash in 1959, just before legislative elections. The twenty-nine-year-old David DACKO, a family member and close confidant of the popular Boganda, succeeded him.

NEOCOLONIAL INDEPENDENCE
The Central African Republic became independent in August 1960, with Dacko as president. France continued to be intimately involved politically, economically, and militarily in the CAR. The 1958 constitution, which preserved close ties with France, remained in effect, and initially a de facto dual French and Central African administration governed the CAR. Dacko relied heavily on French administrative and military support for his authoritarian rule. He introduced a single-party system in 1962, circumscribed legislative powers, and extended presidential terms to seven years. He was partially successful in securing local control of the economy through limited nationalization, but French corporations continued to control much of the economy. Dacko's greatest success was probably in education—the number of children attending school doubled during his presidency.

With the economy failing due to declining commodity prices, growing corruption, and ill-planned development projects, Dacko was preparing to relinquish power to his military chief of staff when his cousin, Colonel Jean-Bédel BOKASSA, overthrew him on December 31, 1965. Most Central Africans initially welcomed the change. But over the next thirteen years, Bokassa's corrupt, dictatorial, wasteful, and ultimately macabre rule nearly destroyed the country. Bokassa ruled by personal fiat. He dismissed legislators at will, had opponents killed, and allowed only a handful of people to participate in politics.

Like his predecessors, Bokassa was dependent upon French support. Although Bokassa paid his own military well, after a rumored coup plot in 1967 he requested and received French military protection. In 1972 he named himself president-for-life and asserted authority over state-owned enterprises. French corporations retained control of most of the country's diamond exports, timber concessions, agricultural estates, and import-export trade. Bokassa, meanwhile, diverted income from these firms for his own enrichment. In the 1970s, exports to and imports from France accounted for over 60 percent of the country's trade, and almost 90 percent of the CAR's aid came from France. But the country's development came to a standstill as Bokassa pocketed much of the aid, or used it for unnecessary and unsuccessful projects.

After evading several coup attempts, in 1977 the president-for-life crowned himself Emperor Bokassa in an elaborate coronation ceremony modeled after Napoleon's, complete with a diamond-studded crown. The coronation reportedly cost one-third of the government's annual revenue, though France underwrote much of the expense. Bokassa also enthroned several relatives, including his wife as empress, and created an imperial court near his hometown.

The renamed Central African Empire had a short life. A fiscal crisis in mid-1979 forced the government to reduce school loans and withhold payment of government salaries, and student protests and violent demonstrations became common in the streets of Bangui. In September of that year, students protested the requirement that they purchase uniforms from a factory owned by Bokassa's wife. In response, troops massacred more than 100 schoolchildren; according to many accounts, Bokassa himself participated in the slaughter. International outcry ensued, and the French, concluding that Bokassa had outlived his usefulness, sent troops to oust him. They reinstated Dacko as president and backed him financially, though he also remained dependent on the elites who had provided support for Bokassa as well as Dacko's first presidency.

Dacko left the rebuilding of the country to France, and concentrated his efforts on consolidating his power. But student protests, strikes, and occasional attacks on government officials continued, and opposition parties organized. In 1981, under both French and internal pressure, Dacko passed a multiparty constitution and held presidential elections—which were clearly fraudulent, and which he won. Dacko used military force to repress opposition. Giscard d'Estaing's 1981 defeat in France, however, left Dacko without external support. When internal opposition reached new heights, army chief of staff André Kolingba forced Dacko to resign, and declared himself president.

After a brief political honeymoon, a coup attempt surfaced and Kolingba clamped down on opponents of his military regime, especially the popular politician Ange-Félix PATASSÉ. Kolingba increasingly relied on his ethnic kin from the Mbaka region, as well as a select group of corrupt officers within his military committee. To provide a veneer of legitimacy, Kolingba created a new party, the Central African Democratic Assembly, and held single-party elections in 1986. But Kolingba's repressive rule and his enforcement of the economic austerity measures required by foreign lenders sparked strikes and riots in the capital. Facing growing internal unrest and international pressure, in 1993 Kolingba agreed to hold open presidential and legislative elections. Both Kolingba and Dacko ran; however, opposition candidate Patassé and his party, the Movement for the Liberation of the Central African People, won the elections on a platform promising to pay the back salaries of soldiers and civil servants.

But the CAR's disastrous finances made full repayment impossible. Anticipating a loss of influence under civilian government, the military mutinied in May 1996, and Patassé called upon the French to suppress the revolt. Opposition politicians subsequently demanded elections. Unrest continued, and many foreign aid workers left the country. In early 1998, the United Nations sent an all-African peacekeeping force to the CAR to enforce the so-called Bangui Accords of 1997, which called for an armistice and new elections. Patassé was reelected in the 1999 presidential election, which the opposition claimed was rigged. This new term, however, proved short-lived; in March 2003 Patassé was ousted in a coup led by François Bozize, who declared himself president and established a new government. Bozize promised new elections, which were finally held in 2005. Bozize won a relatively small majority of the vote, necessitating a runoff election, which he also won. Despite such small steps, the calamitous history of the "Cinderella" of Africa has continued to unfold around a people who remain poor, despite their country's rich potential.

See also ISLAM IN AFRICA.

ERIC YOUNG

Central African Republic (At a Glance)

FORMER NAME:
Central African Empire

AREA:
622,436 sq km (about 240,323 sq mi)

LOCATION:
Central Africa, north of Democratic Republic of the Congo (formerly Zaire), bordered by Cameroon, Chad, Republic of the Congo, Sudan, and the Democratic Republic of the Congo

CAPITAL:
Bangui (population 652,900; 2002 estimate)

POPULATION:
4,444,330 (2008 estimate)

POPULATION BELOW AGE 15:
41.3 percent (male 922,053; female 911,601; 2008 estimate)

POPULATION GROWTH RATE:
1.509 percent (2008 estimate)

TOTAL FERTILITY RATE:
4.23 children born per woman (2008 estimate)

LIFE EXPECTANCY AT BIRTH:
Total population: 44.22 years (male 44.14 years; female 42.49 years; 2008 estimate)

INFANT MORTALITY RATE:
82.13 deaths per 1,000 live births (2008 estimate)

LITERACY RATE (AGE 15 AND OVER WHO CAN READ AND WRITE):
Total population: 51 percent (males 63.3 percent; female 39.9 percent; 2003 estimate)

EDUCATION:
Officially compulsory; however, only about 43 percent of children in the Central African Republic receive primary education. Secondary and higher education facilities are limited. In the early 1990s about 308,400 pupils annually attended primary schools, and about 47,200 students were enrolled in secondary and technical institutions.

LANGUAGES:
French is the official language, but Sango, an African language, is the most commonly spoken. Many other African languages are also spoken.

ETHNIC GROUPS:
The main ethnic groups of the Central African Republic are the Baya, Banda, Sara, Mandjia, Mboum, and M'Baka.

RELIGIONS:
Approximately 35 percent of the total population follow African religions, 25 percent are Protestant, 25 percent are Roman Catholic, and 15 percent are Muslim. Indigenous beliefs strongly influence the practice of Christianity.

CLIMATE:
Hot and humid; the average annual temperature is about 26° C (about 79° F). Annual rainfall varies from about 1,800 mm (about 70 in) in the Ubangi River valley to about 200 mm (about 8 in) in the semiarid north.

LAND, PLANTS, AND ANIMALS:
The Central African Republic is situated on the northern edge of the Zaire (Congo) River Basin. Most of the land is a plateau that ranges in elevation from about 610 to 790 m (about 2,000 to 2,600 ft). Savanna vegetation covers most of the country except for a dense rain forest in the southwest. Open grassland is found in the extreme north, and a dense rain forest covers a major part of the southwestern area. The country is drained by several major rivers, the Bamingui and Ouham rivers in the north, and the Ubangi, a tributary of the Zaire, in the south. Commercially valuable trees include the sapele mahogany and the obeche. Many species of wildlife are found in the country.

NATURAL RESOURCES:
Although relatively undeveloped, mineral resources include diamonds, uranium, iron ore, gold, lime, zinc, copper, and tin.

CURRENCY:
CFA (Communauté Financière Africaine) franc

GROSS DOMESTIC PRODUCT (GDP):
$3.007 billion (2007 estimate)

GDP PER CAPITA:
$700 (2007 estimate)

GDP REAL GROWTH RATE:
4 percent (2007 estimate)

PRIMARY ECONOMIC ACTIVITIES:
Agriculture (55 percent of GDP, 85 percent of employment), forestry, and mining

PRIMARY CROPS:
Cotton, coffee, tobacco, manioc (tapioca), yams, millet, corn, bananas, and timber

INDUSTRIES:
Diamond mining, sawmills, breweries, textiles, footwear, assembly of bicycles and motorcycles

PRIMARY EXPORTS:
Diamonds, timber, cotton, coffee, and tobacco

PRIMARY IMPORTS:
Food, textiles, petroleum products, machinery, electrical equipment, motor vehicles, chemicals, pharmaceuticals, and consumer goods

PRIMARY TRADE PARTNERS:
European Union, Japan, Cameroon, Cote d'Ivoire, and Kazakhstan

GOVERNMENT:
The Central African Republic is a multiparty republic. The executive branch is headed by a president (Francois Bozize, since seizing power in a coup on March 15, 2003); the Council of Ministers, which the president directs; and the prime minister, appointed by the president. The president, according to the country's constitution, is popularly elected to a six-year term, and Bozize has promised new elections at an unspecified date. Legislative authority is held by the National Assembly, made up of 105 members who are popularly elected to five-year terms. Major political parties include the Central African Democratic Rally and the Movement for the Liberation of the Central African People.

Robert Fay

Césaire, Aimé

1913–2008

Martinican poet, playwright, and political leader, founder of the Négritude movement, and one of the most important black authors writing in French in the twentieth century.

Born in Basse-Pointe, Martinique, the second of six children in a family of relatively modest means, Aimé Césaire grew up with a strong appreciation for French culture. While most young Martinicans heard their bedtime stories in Creole, Césaire's father would read his son French poems by Victor Hugo, which may explain in part Césaire's bias against the Creole language. The family moved to Fort-de-France when Césaire was twelve years old. There Aimé enrolled at the Lycée Schoelcher and met Léon-Gontran Damas, a student from French Guiana. Césaire's exceptional work there led to a scholarship to finish his secondary studies in Paris, France, at the prestigious Lycée Louis-le-Grand. In Paris he met the Senegalese Léopold Sédar SENGHOR, a man whose literary and political itinerary would mirror Césaire's.

Césaire enrolled at the École Normale Supérieure in 1931 and began participating in the vibrant black student life of 1930s Paris. Through his work at *L'Étudiant noir*, a newspaper formed by Senghor and Damas, Césaire met Suzanne Roussy, whom he married in 1937 and who would be one of his principal collaborators at the journal *Tropiques* (published in Martinique from 1941 to 1945). During his years in Paris, Césaire, along with Senghor and Damas, developed the philosophy of Négritude. This ardent assertion of black identity and culture would serve as the guiding principle for Césaire's poetry, plays, and essays.

POLITICAL CAREER

Césaire returned to Martinique permanently in 1939 and, after several years of teaching, turned to politics. His commitment to Communism was tenuous even then, but in 1945 he ran as a Communist candidate for Martinique's *député* (deputy) to France's National Assembly (parliament) and, in a surprising upset, won. Months earlier he had been elected mayor of Fort-de-France, the capital of Martinique; he continuously served in both posts until he retired in 1993. Césaire left the Communist Party in 1956 to form the socialist Parti Progressiste Martiniquais (PPM). He specified his reasons for leaving the Communists in *Lettre à Maurice Thorez* (1956)—in short, that the Communists did not sufficiently address black concerns. It was several years later that Césaire wrote his *Discours sur le colonialisme* (1950; *Discourse on Colonialism*, 1972), an essay denouncing liberal French thinkers for their complicity with colonialism.

Césaire's ability to fuse race consciousness with politics while avoiding the pitfalls of many of his African and Caribbean counterparts has earned him the respect of his contemporaries. As Haitian poet René Depestre characterized Césaire's brand of politics: "If there is one principal reason to praise Césaire ... it is that he managed to limit the scope of Négritude to ethics and aesthetics and avoided building it up into a State ideology or political operation of messianic character. His wisdom allowed all those who recognized themselves in his words to avert the horrors of Papa Doc Duvalier's black totalitarianism." Nonetheless, a younger generation of writers led by Raphaël CONFIANT has attacked what they consider to be Césaire's moderate position on political independence for Martinique and his attachment to French culture.

LITERARY CAREER

While in Paris in the 1930s Césaire began composing what is still considered his most important poetic work, if not the most important work of Francophone literature to date, the *Cahier dun retour au pays natal* (*Notebook of a Return to My Native Land*, 1968). In 1939, the same year he returned to Martinique, Césaire quietly published the first version of this revolutionary poem in a small but respected Parisian journal, *Volontés*. However, it was through a detour of sorts that the poem reached a wider audience. Césaire's writings as editor of the literary journal *Tropiques*, in which he blended the ideas of Négritude with European surrealism, attracted the attention of French writer André Breton, a leader of the surrealistic movement. Breton came across the journal and its creators in 1941 while in Martinique on his way from occupied France to the United States. Several years later, Breton contributed a preface to the 1947 edition of the *Cahier* that propelled the poem, and Césaire, into the literary spotlight.

The *Cahier*, with its neologisms (new words or expressions), historical references, and epic length (1,055 lines), bears the imprint of the nineteenth-century French poet, Lautréamont. The poem begins with a bleak portrait of the geography and psychology of Martinique and passes to an enumeration of the indignities suffered by blacks throughout their history. However, the poem ends on an optimistic note, representing the poet's awakening as well as the triumphant awakening of the black race.

Césaire's first poems written after *Cahier*, *Les Armes miraculeuses* (1946; *The Miraculous Weapons*), contain mythological references and a more restricted range of images—sun, volcano, blood, water, death—that are meant to create meaning through association. The poems, however, still contain traces of the stream of consciousness technique used by surrealist writers. Césaire's next collection of poetry, *Soleil cou-coupé* (1948; *Sun Throat Cut*), begins to move away from the influence of surrealism to engage more purely political concerns. The tension between these two tendencies reaches a crisis point in *Corps perdu* (1950; *Lost Body*). In these poems, Césaire seems torn between a self-contained poetry and the poetry of Négritude, which dictates that the poem address the injustices suffered by the black race. This crisis is resolved in his collection of poems *Ferrements* (1960; *Ironwork*)—published as decolonization was sweeping Africa—that more directly addresses the problems of blacks in an emerging postcolonial world. Césaire's poetic output decreased after the early 1960s, but in 1982 he published a collection entitled *Moi, laminaire . . .*, which American scholar A. James Arnold called "some of Césaire's most moving and mature poetry."

During the interval between *Ferrements* and *Moi, laminaire . . .* Césaire developed a reputation as a talented playwright. He continued his work of raising black consciousness in *La Tragédie du Roi Christophe* (1963; *The Tragedy of King Christophe*, 1969), which presents a model for Caribbean independence in pre-Duvalier Haiti. Two other plays from the same period, *Une saison au Congo* (1966; *A Season in Congo*, 1968) and *Une tempête* (1969; *A Tempest*, 1986), an adaptation of English playwright William Shakespeare's *The Tempest*, pursue Césaire's concerns with colonialism, decolonization, and the dangers of political power. Another collection, *La Poésie*, appeared in 1994. Césaire receded from political life in 2001. He died on 17 April 2008 of heart failure.

Césaire's preeminence in the French-speaking black world was largely the result of his ability to link race consciousness with his poetry and his politics without descending into the racial determinism of which his life-long friend Senghor has been accused. The most striking monument to this ability remains the *Cahier*, a poem that breaks with poetic convention at the same time that it forges a new racial consciousness.

RICHARD WATTS

Cetshwayo
1826?–1884
Last independent Zulu king.

Cetshwayo was the son of Mpande, who was king of the Zulu from 1840 to 1872, and the nephew of SHAKA, who ruled from 1816 until 1828 and greatly expanded the Zulu kingdom. Cetshwayo was raised in the northern part of the Zulu kingdom near present-day Nongoma, SOUTH AFRICA. In 1856 he defeated and killed his half-brother Mbuyazi, whom Mpande had favored as the successor to the throne. After the British colonial forces in the nearby colony of Natal mediated between father and son, Cetshwayo publicly declared his loyalty to Mpande and was ceremonially proclaimed king in 1873.

For a time the British backed Cetshwayo in a land dispute between the Zulu and neighboring AFRIKANERS, white settlers of Dutch origin. The British began to withdraw their support, however, after annexing the Afrikaner territory of the TRANSVAAL in 1877, since they no longer had a need for Zulu allies against the Afrikaners. Beginning in the late 1860s, Cetshwayo had worked to procure arms for his people. He was also determined to preserve the Zulu regimental system, which separated young men from their community at puberty and had them fight as one regiment until they reached marrying age. The regiments proved a highly effective way of controlling the fighting power in the kingdom. Local representatives of the British Empire used Cetshwayo's positions on arms and the regiment system, along with other minor incidents, to justify issuing an ultimatum on December 11, 1878, demanding that Cetshwayo disband his army.

Cetshwayo said he would not attack the British, but he refused to agree to the terms of the ultimatum. War between the British and the Zulu began in January 1879, with the Zulu forces achieving one significant victory over the British at the Battle of Isandlwana. The British defeated the Zulu in other battles, the last being the Battle of Ulundi. Cetshwayo was captured and sent into exile in CAPE TOWN while the British divided his kingdom into thirteen parts.

Cetshwayo went to England in 1882 to plead successfully for his restoration as king. After he returned to Zululand in 1883, a civil war began between Cetshwayo's supporters and those of his main rival, Zibhebhu, who controlled a large part of northern Zululand. Cetshwayo died in 1884. His son, Dinuzulu, succeeded him after a struggle with Zibhebhu.

Chad
Landlocked African country bordered by Libya, Sudan, Central African Republic, Cameroon, Nigeria, and Niger.

Chad's contemporary poverty and ethnic discord have deep historical roots. Beginning in the late first millennium, powerful kingdoms and empires arose in the central SAHEL region. Their power derived in part from their control over the trans-Saharan trade carried by the TOUBOU and Arab pastoralists of the northern desert. The peoples of both the desert and Sahel regions adopted Islam during the Middle Ages. Until the late nineteenth century, the Sahel kingdoms conducted slave raids against the peoples of the south, who lacked states and complex social hierarchies and who maintained traditional religious practices.

French colonialism reversed the traditional dominance of the Islamic northern and central regions. The French

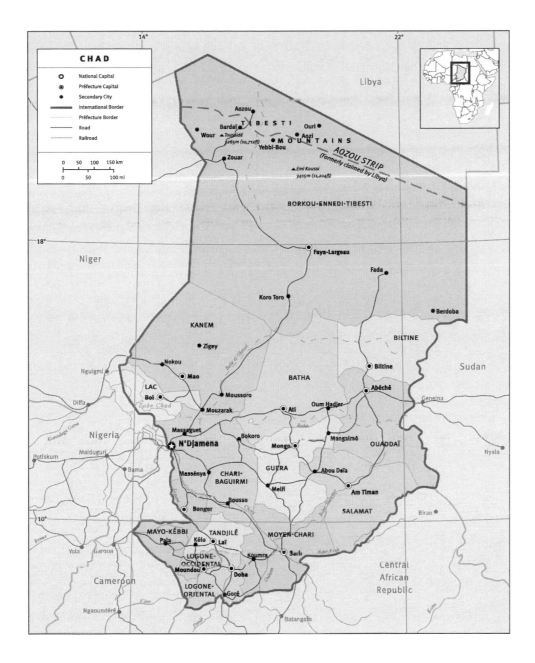

concentrated development in southern Chad because of its greater agricultural capacity, while they disrupted the trans-Saharan trade that had made the northern and central regions powerful and wealthy. As a consequence, southerners, and especially the SARA people, rose through the colonial civil service and dominated Chad's government after independence. Their indifference or hostility toward the peoples of the central and northern regions sparked resentment and, eventually, more than two decades of intermittent civil war. During the 1990s relative peace slowly returned to Chad, as democratic elections took place and the country's war-torn economy gradually recovered. Nevertheless, the country remains one of the poorest in the world, and low-level ethnic conflicts continue, particularly in the south.

GEOGRAPHY AND EARLY HISTORY

Chad's three distinct ecological zones have supported different ethnic groups pursuing a range of different livelihoods. The northern portion is a desert whose inhabitants have traditionally practiced either pastoral nomadism or oasis agriculture. The seasonal grasslands of the middle region, the Sahel, have historically supported livestock herding. The southern section, known as the Sudanese zone, receives a higher rainfall that sustains a savanna environment of grasses, shrubs, and scattered trees.

Large-scale agriculture has been possible only in this southern region.

People have inhabited the region of contemporary Chad for thousands of years. Although the SAHARA occupies much of northern Chad today, this region once enjoyed a less arid environment. AFRICAN ROCK ART discovered at Ennedi plateau, today one of the driest regions of northern Chad, provides the earliest clues about the region's inhabitants. In Ennedi 9,000 years ago, artists left remarkable depictions of local big-game hunting and harpoon fishing. Until perhaps 7,000 years ago a much larger Lake Chad, known as Mega-Chad, covered 336,700 sq km (130,000 sq mi) and stood 55 m (180 ft) above its current level. Over time, however, the region became drier, large numbers of people congregated around the receding shores of Mega-Chad, and by the second millennium B.C.E. local people were farming cereal crops such as millet. Oral histories suggest that an ancient lakeside people, the Sao, the ancestors of present-day Kotoko-speakers along the CHARI and Logone rivers, once dominated much of the region around the lake. Archaeological finds reveal that by the tenth century C.E. the Sao lived in walled cities and engaged in complex artistic practices, including iron and bronze casting using the lost-wax technique. Under the Kanem-Bornu empire, however, the KANEMBU apparently displaced and absorbed the Sao, who disappeared as a distinct ethnic group by the seventeenth century.

EMPIRES OF THE SAHEL

By about the fifth century B.C.E. the development of iron-smelting technology accompanied an increase in agricultural production in the southern savanna zone. By the fifth century C.E., desert peoples first acquired the camel from either North Africa or the Nile Valley. These animals facilitated trans-Saharan trade routes. Commodities such as salt, horses, firearms, and glass beads traveled south, while traders carried ivory and especially slaves north. The appropriation of surplus agricultural goods and the control over this trade gave rise to stratified societies, including the three historic kingdoms of Kanem-Bornu, Wadai, and Bagirmi.

In the ninth century C.E. the Zaghawa, pastoralists of the Ennedi Massif, established a centralized state around Kanem on the northeast shores of Lake Chad. The Kanem empire grew to encompass other groups, including the Toubue (Tubu), of the Tibesti Massif. From the mid-eleventh until the nineteenth century, the Sefuwa, a Kanembu lineage claiming descent from the Zaghawa, ruled the Kanem empire. Trans-Saharan traders brought Islam to Kanem, where it became widespread by the eleventh century.

During the fourteenth century, internal divisions in Kanem allowed Bulala Arabs to oust the Sefuwa from power. The Sefuwa fled to the region of Bornu in present-day NIGERIA, where they regrouped and rapidly established a new powerful kingdom. (After intermarrying with the Sao of Bornu, the Kanembu became known as the KANURI). The Sefuwa recaptured Kanem in the 1500s. The Sefuwa rulers, however, remained in Bornu and allowed the Bulula to continue ruling Kanem as tributaries. At its peak in the 1400s, Kanem-Bornu extended west to the borders of SONGHAI, in the Niger Basin, and north into the Fezzan, in present-day LIBYA. In the following century, however, TUAREG raids caused an increasingly famine-weakened Kanem-Bornu to lose control over the vital trans-Saharan trade routes through Fezzan. Excessive tax collection and internal strife made the empire vulnerable to attacks by the FULANI of the SOKOTO CALIPHATE, which conquered Kanem-Bornu's western provinces. Kanem-Bornu finally fell in 1893 to the army of the infamous Sudanese slave raider, Rabih al-Zubayr.

Far to the east of Kanem-Bornu, near the present-day border with SUDAN, the non-Muslim TUNJUR people founded the Wadai (or Ouadai) kingdom in the sixteenth century. In either 1611 or 1635, MABA people, led by Abd-el-Kerim, mounted a popular revolt and installed an Islamic dynasty. Initially, Wadai was forced to pay tribute to the more powerful neighboring kingdoms of Bornu and DARFUR (in present-day Sudan). But by the eighteenth century Wadai had gained enough strength to assert its sovereignty and carry out raids on Kanem-Bornu. Wadai's wealth derived from its trade in slaves and the tribute it demanded from surrounding chiefdoms. The Wadai sultans organized slave raids over a vast area to the south, including parts of the present-day CENTRAL AFRICAN REPUBLIC. Many of these slaves were marched from Wadai through Darfur to the NILE RIVER. The kingdom experienced frequent turbulent transitions between rulers, particularly during the nineteenth century. In 1835 Darfur took advantage of the instability to conquer Wadai, but in the 1890s the kingdom fell under the control of a proxy of Rabih.

Bagirmi, centered on the city of Massénya just southeast of Bornu, likewise arose during the sixteenth century. For much of their history, however, the kingdom's Barma leadership remained subject to more powerful neighboring kingdoms. Bagirmi also engaged in slave raiding, and specialized in supplying eunuchs to the Ottoman Empire. Despite the adoption of Islam by its rulers, Wadai repeatedly invaded Bagirmi during the seventeenth century on the pretext of reinstating Muslim rule. In fact, the rulers of Bagirmi had refused to pay tribute to Bornu, and Bornu asked Wadai to invade on their behalf. Wadai captured thousands of Barma and other peoples and sold them into slavery. In 1892 Rabih captured Massénya. When the rulers of Bagirmi solicited protection from France, Rabih had Massénya burnt to the ground.

At the end of the nineteenth century Rabih embarked upon a campaign to create a personally ruled empire spanning Central Africa. During the 1880s and 1890s he defeated Wadai and conquered Bagirmi, Adamawa (in present-day CAMEROON), Bornu, and much of the present-day Central African Republic. He set up a capital at Dikwa, south of Lake Chad. The British gave some consideration to recognizing Rabih's sovereignty, but in 1900 they chose instead to partition his territory with France.

EUROPEAN CONQUEST AND COLONIZATION

The French faced fierce resistance from Rabih. After several small skirmishes, Rabih's army faced a large French force in 1900 at the Battle of Kousseri. Rabih was killed and his forces were defeated; the French slowly consolidated their control over the region. In 1910 Chad became a part of FRENCH EQUATORIAL AFRICA. A decade later France instituted a civilian administration for southern Chad. Because of Chad's isolation and political, economic, and strategic unimportance, however, nearly half of all civil service positions were empty at any given time. Indeed, French officials were often assigned to Chad as a punishment.

For several years, the French failed to subdue the Muslim theocracy, the Sanusiya, who had ruled northern Chad and parts of Libya since the late nineteenth century. By 1919, however, the last of the sporadic fighting ceased, and the French exercised hegemony over the region. The northern areas of Chad remained fairly independent of French influence, as long as their inhabitants complied with the slavery ban and did not interfere with French forces. This sparsely populated region, which the French designated the Borkou-Ennedi-Tibesti (BET) Prefecture, remained under the direct jurisdiction, if not the control, of the governor general in BRAZZAVILLE until 1946. In reality, the Sanusiya order continued to have great influence in the north. Thus, Chad was the last territory in Africa that France fully colonized.

The French depended heavily upon soldiers from Chad to combat uprisings in its equatorial holdings. Village chiefs were required to fill quotas for conscripts. France also relied on forced labor to support its colonial effort. When people fled their villages to avoid forced labor or porterage, local collaborators would commonly kidnap women and children or confiscate movable property to coerce the men to work. Alternatively, French forces burned houses and crops to enforce demands for labor. Since the Muslim-dominated north resisted forced labor,

the French concentrated their efforts on the south. Tens of thousands of Chadians labored on the construction of a railroad from Pointe-Noire to Brazzaville, in the present-day REPUBLIC OF THE CONGO, between 1921 and 1936. Sources estimate that perhaps half of the workers died as a direct result of inhumane working conditions.

French colonialism dramatically altered the economy of Chad. The French undermined the centuries-old trans-Saharan trade by regulating and taxing caravan routes, and by building motorable roads that diverted trade to the Atlantic coast. The disruption of the trans-Saharan trade served to impoverish the people of northern Chad.

France also instituted a head tax throughout its colonies after 1901. The French justified the tax as a means to make the colonies "self-sufficient." In fact, the tax served to pay for the salaries of French officials and for the construction of transportation infrastructure primarily benefiting French entrepreneurs. Probably more importantly, the tax forced the peasantry to participate in the cash economy, either by growing cash crops or by working for a wage in French-owned enterprises. Farmers in the fertile south were forced to cultivate cotton to pay their tax. Colonial administrators required them to sell their crop to the French monopoly, Cotonfran, which paid below market value for their crops. Those unfortunates who could not pay often faced severe corporal punishment or imprisonment. The forced adoption of cotton made Chad vulnerable to famine and dependent upon global market prices for the cash crop that continues to dominate its economy. It also undermined traditional society by replacing communal institutions with individual market relations.

French colonialism exacerbated regional disparities. French authorities virtually ignored the arid Muslim north, including the areas of the former Sahel kingdoms that once dominated the region. Meanwhile, inhabitants of the south enjoyed the few advantages of colonial occupation. The most important of these was access to a western education and to low- and mid-level positions in the colonial bureaucracy. By the end of the colonial era, southerners, reversing the historical pattern, dominated the country's economy and politics.

Following World War II, Chad, along with other African colonies, gained limited autonomy as an overseas territory with representation in the French national assembly. The inhabitants were granted citizenship and political parties were legalized. A large number of political parties representing a broad range of interests had formed by the late 1950s. Conservative forces, such as Union Démocratique Tchadienne (UDT), representing French commercial interests and traditional Muslim leaders, advocated the continuation of strong ties with France and respect for traditional authority. In contrast, progressive parties, including the Parti Progressiste Tchadien (PPT) organized by civil servants and labor activists, sought complete independence as well as social and economic reforms. The PPT received its greatest support from the Sara, an ethnic group that dominated the more modern and developed south, while Muslim merchants from the Sahel supported the UDT. After the introduction of universal suffrage in 1956 the PPT gained the lion's share of popular support.

INDEPENDENCE

In a 1958 referendum, Chad's voters chose to form a republic within the French community. PPT leader François TOMBALBAYE won election as prime minister in 1959. Chad declared independence in August 1960 with Tombalbaye as president. In 1962 the autocratic Tombalbaye banned all political parties except the PPT, and Chad became an increasingly corrupt one-party state dominated by the Sara. After demonstrations in the capital, N'DJAMENA, in 1963, Tombalbaye declared a state of emergency and dissolved the National Assembly. When French troops evacuated the BET in 1965, Sara administrators took over and proceeded to alienate the local population with their inefficiency and their often insensitive and sometimes humiliating demands. Discontent and alienation festered, particularly in the Muslim north, until civil disobedience broke out in 1965. The resistance movement coalesced in 1966 into the Front de la libération nationale du Tchad (FROLINAT), operating from a base in Libya. Tombalbaye relied on French assistance to contain the insurgence, which, however, persisted. In the south Tombalbaye also lost support after instituting unpopular economic programs, banning Christian names in an *authenticité* program modeled after MOBUTU SESE SEKO'S ZAIRE (present-day DEMOCRATIC REPUBLIC OF THE CONGO), and making harsh Sara initiation rituals mandatory for non-Muslim Chadians. Meanwhile, during the early 1970s, an increasingly severe drought ravaged Chad. The drought damaged the country's economically vital cotton crop and caused special hardship in the arid, livestock-dependent north.

In 1975, soldiers from the south assassinated Tombalbaye in a coup d'état. A military council, headed by General Félix Malloum, took control of the government. Malloum called for reconciliation with FROLINAT. While one segment of FROLINAT, led by Hissène Habré, joined the Malloum government in 1978, the main body of the rebel force led by Oueddei Goukouni continued to combat government forces. When conflicts between Malloum and Habré deteriorated into armed conflict in 1979, Habré's forces occupied much of N'Djamena and forced Malloum into exile. Meanwhile, FROLINAT forces led by Goukouni also entered the capital and established a fragile

accommodation with Habré. A brutal wave of ethnic killings swept both the north and the south. Remnants of the national army retreated to the south, where southerners established a separate provisional government. With the country in complete disarray, Nigeria, fearful of a compromised border, pressured the Organization of African Unity (OAU) to broker a peace agreement between the warring factions.

The result was the establishment in 1979 of a Gouvernement d'union nationale de transition (GUNT). The GUNT coalition quickly broke down, however, and violence once again shook N'Djamena. Habré fled to the eastern town of Biltine and later to Sudan. Goukouni seized control and immediately looked to Libya for support. In 1980 Libya's head of state, Muammar al-Qaddafi, deployed 15,000 troops into Chad. In 1981 the two leaders called for a political unification of Chad with Libya. France reacted with alarm and maneuvered to force a Libyan withdrawal. Meanwhile, both the United States and France reportedly provided covert backing to Habré.

Habré's Forces armées du nord (FAN) seized N'Djamena, and Habré formed a new government in 1982. Goukouni, who had fled the country, soon returned to the north and regained control of the BET, again with Libyan support. Libya aimed to enforce its claim to the "Aozou strip," a swath of territory in northern Chad. France sent troops in 1983 to prevent Goukouni and the Libyans from moving south of an "interdiction line" between northern and central Chad, and the fighting briefly ceased. Unresolved political and ethnic resentments, however, sparked rebellion in the south. The fighting drove some 25,000 refugees to flee to the Central African Republic. By 1986 the fighting between the troops of Habré, supported by U.S. arms and French troops, and Goukouni, supported by Libyan forces, once again resumed. Habré reclaimed most of the north from Goukouni and the Libyans in 1987. In 1988 Chad and Libya resumed diplomatic relations and agreed to submit their territorial dispute to international mediation. In 1994 Libya accepted the judgment of the International Court of Justice, which rejected Libya's claims to the disputed territory.

Meanwhile, in 1989 a government minister and two senior military officers, including Idriss Déby, led an unsuccessful coup attempt. Déby fled to Sudan. Habré responded by trying to consolidate his power. A 1989 popular referendum approved a new constitution that established a single-party state and awarded Habré another seven-year term as president. In 1990, however, Déby returned from Sudan with 2,000 troops, and Habré fled to Senegal.

Despite promises to institute democratic reforms, Déby initially followed the familiar pattern of ethnic nepotism,

Chad (At a Glance)

AREA:
1,284,000 sq km (495,753 sq mi)

LOCATION:
Central Africa, south of Libya

CAPITAL:
N'Djamena (population 721,000; 2005 estimate)

OTHER MAJOR CITIES:
Sarh (population 108,061), Moundou (142,462) (2008 estimates)

POPULATION:
10,111,337 (2008 estimate)

POPULATION DENSITY:
7.87 persons per sq km (about 20 per sq mi)

POPULATION BELOW AGE 15:
47 percent (male 2,408,638; female 2,346,984; 2008 estimate)

POPULATION GROWTH RATE:
2.195 percent (2008 estimate)

TOTAL FERTILITY RATE:
5.43 children born per woman (2008 estimate)

LIFE EXPECTANCY AT BIRTH:
Total population: 47.43 years (male 46.4 years; female 48.5 years; 2008 estimate)

INFANT MORTALITY RATE:
100.36 deaths per 1,000 live births (2008 estimate)

LITERACY RATE (AGE 15 AND OVER WHO CAN READ AND WRITE IN FRENCH OR ARABIC):
Total population: 47.5 percent (male 56 percent; female 39.3 percent; 2003 estimate)

EDUCATION:
By the early 2000s, 39 percent of children in Chad attended primary school. In the late 1980s there were 3,000 students enrolled at institutions of higher education, including the University of Chad.

LANGUAGES:
French and Arabic are the official languages. Hausa is spoken in the Lake Chad region; Sara and Sango are spoken in the south. More than 100 different languages and dialects are spoken in all.

ETHNIC GROUPS:
The north is inhabited mainly by Muslim peoples, including Arabs, Toubou, Hadjerai, Fulbé, Kotoko, Kanembou, Baguirmi, Boulala, Zaghawa, and Maba. Mostly non-Muslims live in the south: Sara, Ngambaye, Mbaye, Goulaye, Moundang, Moussei, Massa; about 1,000 French citizens live in Chad.

RELIGIONS:
53.1 percent of the population is Muslim, 34 percent is Christian, and 13 percent adhere to traditional beliefs.

CLIMATE:
The Saharan north is hot, dusty, and dry throughout the year. South of the desert there is a hot, dry season from March to July; a rainy season from July to October, with average rainfall 250 to 750 mm (about 10 to 30 in); and a cool, dry season during the remaining months. Rainfall is higher in the south, averaging 1,145 mm (about 45 in).

LAND, PLANTS, AND ANIMALS:
Chad's land-locked terrain is dominated by the low-lying Chad Basin (elevation about 250 m/820 ft), which rises gradually to mountains and plateaus on the north, east, and south. The greatest elevations are reached in the Tibesti massif in the north, with a maximum height of 3,415 m (11,204 ft) at Emi Koussi. The northern half of the republic lies in the Sahara. The only important rivers, the Logone and Chari (Shari), are located in the southwest and flow into Lake Chad. The lake doubles in size during the rainy season.

NATURAL RESOURCES:
Petroleum, uranium, natron, kaolin, and fish

CURRENCY:
The CFA (Communauté Financière Africaine) franc

GROSS DOMESTIC PRODUCT (GDP):
$15.26 billion (2007 estimate)

GDP PER CAPITA:
$1,500 (2007 estimate)

GDP REAL GROWTH RATE:
1.3 percent (2007 estimate)

PRIMARY ECONOMIC ACTIVITIES:
Agriculture (38 percent of GDP; over 80 percent of employment), industry, and services. Chad began to export petroleum in 2004.

PRIMARY AGRICULTURAL PRODUCTS:
Cotton, sorghum, millet, peanuts, rice, potatoes, and manioc (tapioca); cattle, sheep, goats, and camels

INDUSTRIES:
Oil, cotton textiles, meatpacking, beer brewing, natron (sodium carbonate), soap, cigarettes, and construction materials

PRIMARY EXPORTS:
Oil, cotton, cattle, textiles, and fish

PRIMARY IMPORTS:
Machinery and transportation equipment, industrial goods, petroleum products, food-stuffs; textiles, and military equipment

PRIMARY TRADE PARTNERS:
United States, France, Cameroon, Nigeria, Portugal, Germany, and Poland

GOVERNMENT:
Chad is nominally a republic. It is a constitutional multiparty democracy, led by President Lt. Gen. Idriss Déby (since December 1990) and Prime Minister Youssof Saleh Abbas (appointed April 2008). Under the constitution passed in 1996, the legislature consists of the 155-member unicameral National Assembly, first elected in 1997.

Barbara Worley

patronage, and autocratic rule. Nevertheless, in 1991 Déby declared his commitment to eventual democratic rule and permitted the registration of opposition political parties. During the early 1990s Déby's government faced civilian protests against austerity measures, including tax increases, layoffs, and salary reductions for civil servants and members of the military. At the same time, the government deflected a number of attempted coups and armed rebellions, particularly in the south. International human rights organizations criticized the regime for its response to the unrest. A transitional government drafted a constitution in 1994 for a multiparty democracy, and Déby declared an amnesty for political prisoners. A popular referendum approved the draft constitution in 1996, and Déby won the presidency in a multiparty election. After several postponements, Déby's party dominated legislative elections in 1997. Though Déby's defeated opponents claimed electoral fraud, international observers declared the elections free and fair.

In 1998 a rebellion in northern Chad threatened the country's attempts to return to normalcy. A peace agreement was signed in January 2002, calling for the rebels to be reintegrated into Chad's political system, though this and subsequent efforts failed to fully extinguish the violence. Sporadic fighting continued throughout much of the decade, some of it spurred on by Déby's success in removing constitutional barriers to another term as president.

Three decades of continual warfare have left Chad one of the poorest countries in the world. Though the economy has shown recent signs of improvement, a poor transport infrastructure, and continued reliance on cotton and other crops vulnerable to drought has limited the country's potential for prosperity. Ethnic and religious divisions continue to run deep. The government continues to face armed resistance from rebels in the south demanding regional autonomy, and in 1998 Amnesty International charged the government with arbitrarily killing civilians from the south.

See also HUMAN RIGHTS IN AFRICA; ISLAM IN AFRICA; IVORY TRADE; SALT TRADE.

BIBLIOGRAPHY

Azevedo, Mario J., and Emmanuel U. Nnadozie. *Chad: A Nation in Search of Its Future.* Westview Press, 1998.

Bjørkelo, Anders J. *State and Society in Three Sudanic Kingdoms.* Universitetet i Bergen, 1976.

Collelo, Thomas, ed. *Chad, a Country Study.* Government Printing Office, 1990.

Nolutshungu, Sam C. *Limits of Anarchy: Intervention and State Formation in Chad.* University Press of Virginia, 1996.

ARI NAVE

Chagga

Ethnic group of northeastern Tanzania and Kenya.

The third largest ethnic group in TANZANIA, the Chagga, live on the fertile slopes of Mount KILIMANJARO, now one of Tanzania's most prosperous farming regions. The pre-colonial Chagga created an innovative irrigation system that enabled them to transport water 200 meters (650 feet) above river level, which later made it possible for them to grow lucrative crops such as bananas and coffee. During the nineteenth century the Chagga, who lived in scattered villages governed by local chiefs, participated little in the increasingly active East African caravan trades. But under British COLONIAL RULE they became one of the colony's most vocal farming groups. In 1925 the Chagga organized the Kilimanjaro Native Planters Association (later the Kilimanjaro Native Cooperative Union), a marketing organization that became the region's largest seller of coffee during British colonialism. After independence the Chagga continued to prosper, and their cooperative farms were later seen as a model for the *ujamaa*, or family-hood, villages established by Tanzanian president Julius K. NYERERE. Although they are no longer the largest coffee producers in Tanzania, the Chagga continue to be one of the most prosperous groups and have played an influential role in Tanzanian politics. As many as 2 million people consider themselves Chagga.

See also ETHNICITY AND IDENTITY IN AFRICA: AN INTERPRETATION.

ELIZABETH HEATH

Chamba

Ethnic group of West Africa.

The Chamba (also known as Chamba-Daka, Daka, Samba, Tchamba, and Tsamba) primarily inhabit east-central NIGERIA and neighboring CAMEROON. They speak a Niger-Congo language. Approximately 300,000 people consider themselves Chamba.

See also ETHNICITY AND IDENTITY IN AFRICA: AN INTERPRETATION; LANGUAGES, AFRICAN: AN OVERVIEW.

Chamoiseau, Patrick

1953–

Martinican writer whose novels and essays affirm the sociopolitical and cultural status of the French Creole language.

Patrick Chamoiseau was born in Fort-de-France, Martinique and studied law in Paris before becoming a writer. In novels such as *Chronique des sept misères* (1986) and *Solibo magnifique* (1988), Chamoiseau explores the tensions and conflicts that race, class, and language create in Martinique. In his attempt to incorporate elements from oral Creole into his French prose, Chamoiseau has developed a complex rhythmic and lyrical style often filled with ironic humor.

Chamoiseau collaborated with Caribbean writers Raphaël CONFIANT and Jean Bernabé on the essay *Éloge de la Créolité* (1989; *In Praise of Creoleness*, bilingual edition, 1993), one of the most influential theoretical pieces produced in the region in recent times. This essay is an affirmation of a Creole identity influenced by, but also different from the ideas of, Martinican writer and cultural theorist Édouard Glissant. The essay, which is also a manifesto, proclaims the heterogeneous character of the Caribbean and rejects all aspirations to a pure identity. Chamoiseau rejects not only the racist inheritance of French colonialism, but also the nostalgia for pure African roots that some Créolité writers associate with Aimé CÉSAIRE and his Négritude movement.

Chamoiseau's novel *Texaco* (1992) won the prestigious Prix Goncourt, France's most important literary prize, and received wide critical acclaim when it was translated into English in 1997. It tells the story of Marie-Sophie Laborieux, a working-class woman who lives in Texaco, a community outside Fort-de-France named after the neighboring oil tanks. The novel traces her family roots back 150 years, exploring the legacy of slavery, colonialism, and memory interpreted through oral history.

Chamoiseau has also written autobiographical narratives, *Antan d'enfance* (1990) and *Chemin-d'école* (1994), and coauthored, again with Raphael Confiant, *Lettres créoles: Traces antillaises et continentales de la littérature, 1635–1975* (1991). Among his more most recent work is *Creole Folktales* (1997), *School Days* (1998), *Childhood* (1999), *Biblique des derniers gestes* (2002), and *Un dimanche au cachot* (2007). He remains one of the most innovative voices in contemporary Caribbean writing.

VICTOR FIGUEROA

Chari

River in Chad and the Central African Republic.

The 950-kilometer (590-mile) long Chari River drains a 650,000 square kilometer (250,000 square mile) basin in CHAD and the CENTRAL AFRICAN REPUBLIC before it flows into Lake Chad, a drainage basin with no outlet to the sea. The Bamingui River is its true headwater, though the Ouham River provides it with the most water, and a number of other tributaries feed the Chari. At N'DJAMENA the Chari divides into several branches that flow to Lake Chad.

For hundreds of years the Chari was used as a commercial waterway, especially by slave raiders from the north. In 1823, British explorers became the first Europeans to find the river, and in the early twentieth century it became a major transport route for French colonizers. Today, SARA and BANDA people live along the banks of the Chari. River sediments provide fertile soil for foodstuffs as well as cotton, the main export crop, and river fishing supplements local diets. During the summer rainy season, large steam-driven barges navigate the lower 800 kilometers (500 miles) of the river to transport trade goods between N'Djamena, Sarh, and other towns.

ERIC YOUNG

Chewa

Ethnic group of some three million people who live predominantly in Malawi.

The Chewa are the single largest ethnic group in MALAWI, comprising about a quarter of the population. Many Chewa also live in eastern ZAMBIA and northwestern ZIMBABWE. Their ancestors were a splinter group of the Maravi, BANTU speakers who had migrated to the region from Katanga (in the present-day DEMOCRATIC REPUBLIC OF THE CONGO), perhaps in the thirteenth century.

The Chewa broke away from the Maravi confederacy in the eighteenth century, and settled to the west along the Bua, Luangwa, and Dwangwa rivers. Maravi who moved into the interior savanna became the Chipeta ("savanna dwellers"). The remaining Maravi came to be called the Nyanja ("lakeside people"), a large group whose population in Malawi is second in size only to the Chewa. The Chewa language, Chichewa or Chinyanja, is one of Malawi's two national languages, and is spoken by approximately six million people.

In the nineteenth century NGONI groups emigrated north into Chewa territory, fleeing Zulu expansion into their lands. YAO and SWAHILI slave traders also arrived. These more recent immigrants adopted the Chichewa language, and often gained control over Chewa and Nyanja settlements. Politically decentralized, their communities proved vulnerable to slave raiders, and during the height of the INDIAN OCEAN SLAVE TRADE in the late eighteenth and early nineteenth centuries, large numbers of Chewa were captured and sold. But slaves also figured significantly within Chewa society.

Most rural Chewa grow sorghum and maize (corn) as staple food crops, relying on cash crops such as tobacco for income. Hunting and fishing are also important activities. Chewa society has traditionally been relatively egalitarian, and its matrilineal villages are governed by chiefs who rule as much by consensus as through decree. Clan exogamy is the rule; members of the Banda clan, for example, marry Phiri or Mwale. Although traditionally maternal uncles arranged marriages, young men and women today actively court one another. A newlywed man is expected to in engage in bride-service, gardening for his in-laws for two years before receiving a plot of his own.

The Chewa's masked Nyau dances and secret societies—both subjects of considerable ethnographic study—remain vital parts of contemporary Chewa culture. Boys undergo RITES OF PASSAGE in early adolescence to initiate them into the all-male Nyau society. When missionaries arrived in the region in the late nineteenth century, they identified the Nyau dances as pagan rituals that needed to be eliminated. But the dances persisted, expressing not only general discontent with the colonial regime, but also more specific resistance to European cultural incursion and Christian proselytizing. In contemporary Chewa society, Nyau beliefs and Christianity are seen as two distinct worldviews, the former associated with customary rural life, the latter linked to urban lifestyles and the West.

ARI NAVE

Chico Rei

1717–1774

African king, sold into slavery in Brazil during the eighteenth century, who worked to buy his own freedom and then the freedom of his tribe.

In the late seventeenth century, gold was discovered in the area that is now the state of Minas Gerais in Brazil, triggering an inundation of gold prospectors from the surrounding provinces and Portugal. They brought large numbers of African slaves with them to extract the precious metal and began importing slaves from Africa's GOLD COAST (present-day GHANA and the surrounding countries), a region known for its advanced mining activities. By 1720 the city of Ouro Preto had become the center of gold mining in Minas Gerais. This was the destination of the African king Chico Rei and many members of his tribe.

Originally named Galanga, Chico Rei was the king of a small Congolese tribe of some 200 people in what is now the DEMOCRATIC REPUBLIC OF THE CONGO. Around 1740 he and his tribe were taken prisoner by Portuguese slave traders and sold into slavery in Minas Gerais. Before leaving Africa, a Portuguese Catholic priest baptized the captives and gave them new names: Maria for the women, and Francisco for the men. While en route to Brazil, the Portuguese slave traders noticed that many of the slaves looked to Chico Rei for leadership. As a result, King Galanga's name became Chico Rei—Chico being a shortened version of Francisco, and Rei being Portuguese for king.

Many of the members of Chico Rei's tribe, including his wife and some of his children, died during the Middle Passage. When the ship arrived in Brazil, slightly more than a hundred members of Chico Rei's tribe were still alive. They were sold to the owner of the Encardadeira mine near Ouro Preto, in Minas Gerais.

During the eighteenth century in Minas Gerais, slaves often smuggled small amounts of gold out of the mines by hiding it in their hair, between their toes, in their ears, and/or in their mouths. They also took advantage of off-days, which included Sundays and a number of Catholic holidays, to work for themselves and save toward buying their *cartas de alforria* (manumission documents). In this way, over the course of five or six years, members of Chico Rei's tribe accumulated enough gold to purchase their king's freedom. Maintaining their tribal bonds, members of Chico's tribe continued to pool their profits from autonomous work and smuggling and were eventually able to purchase the freedom of the prince, his wife, and then the princess.

At the same time, Chico Rei was working to free the remaining enslaved members of his tribe. After seeking assistance from the black brotherhood Nossa Senhora do Rosário, Chico Rei became owner of a mine. Chico Rei's master sold the Encardadeira mine to him when its production decreased, and little by little, Chico Rei and the liberated members of his tribe collected enough gold to buy the freedom of all of those still enslaved.

While working to free all of his tribe, Chico Rei was also making plans to construct a church for Ouro Preto's black population. Even those slaves who had been converted to Catholicism were generally not allowed to attend worship services at white churches. With the gold extracted from his mine and smuggled contributions from local slaves, Chico Rei built up a fund for the church's construction, which began after Chico Rei secured the approval of colonial officials. The building of the *Igreja Nossa Senhora Santa Efigênia no Alto Cruz* (Our Lady of Saint Efigênia of the High Cross, one of the patron saints of the slaves) lasted some thirty years and involved the artistic collaboration of the famous mulatto sculptor Antônio Francisco "Aleijadinho" Lisboa.

Chico Rei's legacy goes beyond the Church of Santa Efigênia. Some trace the beginnings of the coronation festival known as the *Reisado do Rosário* to Chico Rei. During the eighteenth century, this occasion drew large numbers of free and enslaved blacks and featured regal processions, African music and dance, and, most importantly, the crowning of a black king and queen. Originally held on January 6, the Reisado do Rosário spread throughout Brazil and eventually evolved into the modern-day *congada* celebration.

Chico Rei achieved legendary status among the slaves and earned the respect of the Portuguese slaveholders. Unlike the many slaves who took freedom into their own hands by escaping and joining fugitive slave colonies known as *quilombos*, Chico Rei pursued freedom within the legal constraints by paying for the liberty of each one of his former tribe members, who formed a colony of free blacks. Yet, despite his contributions and uniqueness as a freedom fighter, Chico Rei remains relatively unknown among Afro-Brazilian heroes.

AARON MYERS

Chigumira, Grace

See WOMEN ARTISTS, AFRICAN: AN INTERPRETATION.

Children's Work in Africa

Throughout the world, ecology, culture, politics, and history shape what work is to be done, who performs it and how, and the social meanings ascribed to it, but gender and age tend to organize work most decidedly. In Africa gender and age have greatly influenced children's work across precolonial, colonial, and postcolonial periods. In addition, education and the continuing process of delocalization and integration into a world capitalist economy have affected the everyday experiences of millions of African children.

ETHNOLOGICAL PERSPECTIVES

Children in Africa have been working since the invention of agriculture and the domestication of animals in the neolithic age, but revolutionary changes in technology and demography prove even more important to understanding the social organization of most African societies south of the SAHARA. Livelihood strategies that tie people to resources, land, and each other in great numbers require organizational forms suitable for large kinship groups and territorial concerns. In most cases in Africa, labor is a scarcer resource than land, so competition for prestige focuses less on controlling material resources than on controlling human resources, particularly rights-in-persons acquired by converting prestige goods such as cattle into relations of dependency. In most African societies, the social organization of labor is based on family and kin and the regulation of intergenerational ties. Dependents are usually women, junior males, and children. Children are desired and cherished for the work they begin to do from an early age and for the prestige, social, and spiritual value they confer on kin groups based on hierarchical communal family authority and resource control.

In most African societies south of the Sahara, when children reach the "age of reason" (five to eight years old) they are ready cognitively and socially to learn technical, physical, and intellectual skills. The particular work that children do depends on a society's local ecology, livelihood strategy, context, and culture-specific constellations of gender, age, location, birth order position, family preference, and household divisions of labor. Nonetheless, a shared cultural feature in Africa is that children learn to care for other children while performing domestic chores and productive activities with multivalent purposes and meanings. Tasks are practical yet also teach gender and aged-based adult roles and status expectations, and impart moral and social requirements and rewards of duty and care across households and communities. Children learn early how nurturance and allegiance are organized by principles of descent, affinity, neighborly ties, and religious affiliation. They also learn how support is distributed through dense social networks rooted in the logic and morality of the corporate group. Through work activities in the subsistence sphere, children also develop environmental awareness and knowledge about agricultural production and animal husbandry.

Amid these variations in children's work, two patterns are evident. The first pattern prevails throughout eastern, central, and southern Africa where female-focused systems of subsistence agriculture are both horticultural and intensive, and are practiced by people organized by patrilineal or matrilineal descent. The patrilineal GUSII of KENYA, the Shambala of TANZANIA, and the SHONA of ZIMBABWE are examples, as are the matrilineal Gwembe Tonga of ZAMBIA and Suku of southwestern Democratic Republic of the CONGO. Among the Suku, girls learn domestic work, such as child care and water hauling, from the time they begin to walk and quickly assume horticultural tasks in the cultivation of food crops. Boys tend to ease into their adult agricultural tasks and may also apprentice to blacksmiths, diviners, or curers to acquire socially respected skills. Among the PARE, intensive agriculturists of northeastern Tanzania, girls aged twelve do three-quarters of the agricultural and domestic work of adult women and contribute six to eight hours of work a day, while boys of the same age work only four to six hours a day, primarily in activities valued as productive and not simply domestic. Boys are responsible for land clearing, house building, and other energy- and strength-demanding work crucial to the success of the agricultural enterprise, but their work is episodic while girls' work is regularized, insistent, and time-intensive. Since girls are less easily spared than boys in work activities, it follows that boys have more time for education and other pursuits.

The second pattern widely found centers on groups of patrilineally related men organized into cooperative work groups or age grades. Among West African agriculturists such as the TIV, HAUSA, and YORUBA, work is a critical means of establishing enduring social ties. The exchange of children across families and groups through fostering remains a common social practice among the GONJA of

GHANA, where girls have specific roles and heavy responsibilities in the domestic sphere. In urban regions of northern NIGERIA, children's work enables married Muslim Hausa women to conduct trade while maintaining their prescribed seclusion. They send children to work as intermediaries to run errands, exchange goods, or collect payments. Children contribute to overall household economic strategies while also learning social networks and skills of commerce necessary for adult life. In the urban markets of Senegal, the long tradition of apprenticeship enables boys to learn tailoring, cobbling, and other skilled crafts while girls engage in smaller enterprises, such as marketing produce.

In East Africa, among patrilineal peoples, such as the Jie, TURKANA, and MAASAI, cattle and camels provide the major sources of sustenance. Boys learn animal husbandry skills as early as six and become responsible for tending, managing, and even slaughtering cattle. The twin virtues of possession of superior cattle and military expertise that characterize pastoral societies throughout Africa highlight the value of male roles and statuses. Girls learn to milk, prepare butter, construct houses, and provide a wide range of domestic services from a young age, and they work longer and harder than boys in activities that are time-intensive and time-sensitive.

During the precolonial period, many African societies were connected to extensive networks of trade that linked their communities to wider economies. Generally, however, households and communities were self-sufficient economic units that provided food, housing, and necessities for themselves. The key measure of wealth was the number of dependents one controlled, which meant that access to the means of controlling labor and rights over women, children, and junior men through marriage and other social institutions, was vigorously protected. The principles of age and gender central to the organizational logic of most African societies have far-reaching implications for children's work in colonial and postcolonial, transnational politico-economic systems.

COLONIALISM, CAPITALISM, AND CHILD LABOR

The rules of the game changed when children's multivalent "work" became "labor," a commodity to be exchanged on the market. When Great Britain, France, Germany, Belgium, Spain, Portugal, and briefly Italy, colonized Africa in the late nineteenth century, these countries directed African economies away from domestic need and toward exports. At the same time, Africa became a marketplace for European manufactured goods. These changes offset the costs of colonial rule and established networks of trade and preference that continue in the postcolonial era but strain kinship relations, propel economic individualism, and lead to the feminization of poverty.

African children's agricultural labor during the colonial period helped to subsidize rural households and kept wages low. In male-centered West African agricultural systems, farmers switched from growing food crops for their own use to producing cocoa, palm oil, cotton, peanuts, and rubber for export. Children were important laborers in production of cash crops and were often exchanged across newly constituted national borders, following the centuries-old tradition of fostering children across communities for parenting and care. Africans were forced to labor on the white settler plantations of eastern and southern Africa, where Europeans expropriated the most fertile lands. Where not prohibited by law, African men began to grow cash crops such as coffee, tea, cotton, and sisal to generate incomes and pay taxes. In the areas where female-focused systems prevailed, alienation of women from their customary usufruct land rights of the precolonial period undermined and limited their ability to control resources both within and outside the household. As production shifted from "for use" to "for sale," a "hungry season" appeared, nutritional deficiencies increased, and children's work became even more significant to the survival of households and communities.

White farmers legitimated their demands for child labor in tea production in Southern Rhodesia (present-day Zimbabwe), for example, by explicitly drawing on African models of family privilege and relationship shaped by age, gender, status, and control. Children were expected to labor on plantations for white settlers just as they would on home farms for their fathers. The more child labor increased white farmers' profits, the more farmers sought legal support from the state to use child labor and to control and discipline child laborers. Children received little if any recompense.

Distinct patterns of migrant labor developed in southern and central Africa when men were uprooted from their rural communities to labor in gold, diamond, copper, manganese, and cobalt mines. An "enclave" industry, mining was owned and controlled by foreign companies and operated by foreign technicians using foreign equipment. Boys were important laborers in the mining system. They also became "mine wives" to older male workers separated from their families for much of the year. The contractual arrangement between man and mine wife regulated sexual behavior and delineated domestic activities. Wages circulated in the economy around the mine, which reduced the flow of support back to rural homesteads, exacerbating economic delocalization and the disembedding of production from local supply or control. The men's long absences largely left women to manage the rural sector with only the help of children.

The use of child labor during the colonial period generated profits for capitalists while radically altering the conditions of work. Lineage systems of control began to erode, especially as junior men achieved a modicum of independence from their elders through wage work. But new vulnerabilities in children's life and work experiences were created, setting the stage for some of the modern child labor problems facing the continent.

POSTCOLONIAL AND TRANSNATIONAL CHILD LABOR

The postcolonial era has brought both progress and problems. Though the support of strong families continues to allow many Africans to overcome enormous adversity, the capitalist world economy has adversely affected children's work and lives. After a decade of zero per capita GNP growth in the 1980s, African governments adopted structural adjustment policies (SAPs), crafted by the International Monetary Fund (IMF) and the World Bank, that increased the cost of daily living for all and intensified the vulnerabilities of women and children. After two decades of SAPs, The United Nations describes Africa (in 2002) as the least developed continent in the world with thirty-nine of the world's fifty poorest countries, in per capita economic terms, and the highest proportion of working children.

Increased demand for cash crop exports has caused land consolidation, the creation of landless classes, and the erosion of indigenous knowledge and skill while providing few alternatives. The continuing centrality of female labor in rural work and the domestic domain across much of Africa often precludes the possibility of girls attending school, migrating, or pursuing other life-course trajectories.

In most countries of West and Central Africa, the movement of boys and girls across communities and borders builds on customary practices of child fostering and exchange used to help meet labor needs in agriculture, construction, and the domestic domain. However, child migration, occurring mainly from BENIN, Ghana, Nigeria and TOGO to the Congo, CÔTE D'IVOIRE, EQUATORIAL GUINEA, GABON and, Nigeria (like Benin both a country of origin and a receiving country), has intensified as a response to a market economy that pauperizes formerly self-reliant producers. Today many children have no choice but to labor in quarries, grow cash crops, or serve as domestics, the largest employment category of girls under age sixteen in the world.

Growing numbers of increasingly younger children have appeared in the informal economies of urban Africa. Many children, mostly boys, go alone to towns and cities to find employment and live without their families because opportunities for nutrition and survival are greater. Some

return to areas of origin to visit, remit portions of their earnings, and exchange labor and goods, but many are fending for themselves, usually by laboring in small enterprises in the informal or "shadow economy" in which cash payment prevails, services are rendered under-the-table and off the books, and work goes undocumented in national statistics. Children in urban contexts, or "street children," work as vendors, errand runners, "handshop" operators, stevedores, sex and tourism workers, and artists. Often viewed by governments as problems to be solved by repatriation or rehabilitation, children nonetheless help keep many families and individuals afloat. But since their labor goes unrecorded in national statistics, child laborers are often invisible and have few if any protections. Worse, young girls have been widely trafficked from West Africa, in particular Ghana and Nigeria, to the sex trade in Italy, the Netherlands, and other European countries. Increasing numbers of children engage in prostitution with the full knowledge of their parents or guardians because they feel compelled to make a financial contribution to the household and to care for impoverished parents or other kin. A United Nations report compiled in 2001 holds that across Africa there are some 80 million child workers, a number that the report suggests could increase another 20 million by 2015.

One of the worst child labor problems in Africa today concerns the use of child soldiers. According to a report issued by the Coalition to Stop the Use of Child Soldiers, there are more than 120,000 children under eighteen years of age currently participating in armed conflicts across Africa, some no more than seven or eight years old. The countries most affected by this problem are LIBERIA, SIERRA LEONE, Congo-Brazzaville, the DEMOCRATIC REPUBLIC OF CONGO, ANGOLA, BURUNDI, RWANDA, UGANDA, ETHIOPIA, and SUDAN, the last of which has one of the worst child soldier problems anywhere in the world.

The explosion of child labor in Africa starkly reveals the consequences of the confluence of interests of global capital and the state on individuals and households. Tragically, the strategies people devise to cope with mean conditions end up being used against them: children become a pool of ready, cheap labor that keeps formal economy wages low, so their contributions, while essential, also undermine their capacity to prosper. But an enduring frustration to the efforts of capitalism to privatize, commodify, and profit are relations based on descent, age, gender, and subsistence strategy that continue to embed children in the organizational and moral logics of dense, multivalent social networks. Until the needs of households and communities are addressed, efforts to stop child labor through legislation, regulation, education, or any other means are not likely to succeed.

BIBLIOGRAPGHY

Freund, Bill. *The Making of Contemporary Africa: The Development of African Society since 1800*, 2nd ed. Lynne Rienner, 1998.

Kilbride, Philip, Collette Suda, and Enos Njeru. *Street Children in Kenya.* Bergin and Garvey, 2000.

La Fontaine, J. S., ed. *Sex and Age as Principles of Social Stratification.* Academic Press, 1978.

Moodie, T. Dunbar. *Going for Gold: Men, Mines, and Migration.* University of California Press, 1994.

Van Onselen, Charles. *Chibaro: African Mine Labour in Southern Rhodesia 1900–1933.* Pluto Press, 1976.

KAREN A. PORTER

Chilembwe, John
1870–1915
Nyasaland missionary and nationalist who led a brief revolt against British colonial rule.

Nkologo (John) Chilembwe was born in Sangano, Chiradzulu district, in what is now MALAWI. He received primary schooling at a Presbyterian mission school in Blantyre, then in 1892 went to work as a house servant for the British Baptist missionary Joseph Booth, an advocate for African self-rule. In 1897 Chilembwe traveled with Booth to the United States and attended the Virginia Theological College, a black Baptist seminary, where he became familiar with aspects of the African American experience, such as segregation and racism, and was influenced by such writers as W. E. B. Du Bois.

In 1900 Chilembwe returned to his homeland. By then an ordained Baptist minister, he purchased some forty hectares (ninety-nine acres) of land with the help of African American backers, and built the Providence Industrial Mission (PIM), with the goal of educating and encouraging self-confidence among his people. A number of African American missionaries worked at the mission, which eventually grew to include several primary schools in different parts of the region. Guided by the belief that Africans could use Western knowledge as a tool to achieve their eventual freedom, all PIM schools taught the British classical curriculum.

Chilembwe grew increasingly critical of COLONIAL RULE and the plantation labor system. When World War I broke out and the British began conscripting NYASA men into the King's African Rifles regiment to fight against Germany, a 1914 edition of the *Nyasaland Times* published Chilembwe's angry letter of protest.

Receiving no response from the colonial authorities, Chilembwe organized an armed revolt. Well aware that he would probably die, Chilembwe reportedly felt that his own martyrdom would feed the growth of an independence movement.

NKOLOGO "JOHN" CHILEMBWE (LEFT), C. 1900. (*Prints and Photographs Division, Library of Congress*)

On January 23, 1915, Chilembwe sent 200 of his supporters to attack an estate held by a European colonist who was known for his brutality, and they killed a number of the estate's managers. Within a few days, many of his supporters were caught and imprisoned or killed, while others fled into exile. Chilembwe himself was shot on February 3 while trying to escape to Mozambique.

While the event provoked a Commission of Inquiry, no reforms resulted from the commission's findings. But as Chilembwe predicted, his uprising marked a turning point in NYASALAND's history, destroying the European facade of paternalism and inspiring the development of future nationalist movements.

ARI NAVE

Chiluba, Frederick
1943–
President of Zambia.

Frederick Chiluba was born in Kitwe, NORTHERN RHODESIA (present-day ZAMBIA). The son of BEMBA-speaking miners, Chiluba was too poor to finish school, so he traveled to TANGANYIKA (modern-day TANZANIA) and worked on a plantation. When he returned in 1966, he became involved in the labor movement. While working as a credit officer in an engineering firm, he was elected president of the Building and General Workers' Union in 1971 and president of the Zambian Congress of Trade Unions in 1975.

An outspoken critic of Zambian president Kenneth KAUNDA, in 1990 Chiluba cofounded the Movement for Multiparty Democracy (MMD), a coalition of opposition forces. All opposition parties were illegal at the time, and Chiluba was briefly detained for his role in the MMD. After growing popular unrest convinced the government to register opposition parties, multiparty presidential elections were held in 1991, and Chiluba defeated Kaunda by a wide margin. One of Chiluba's first official acts as president was to lift Kaunda's permanent state of emergency.

After taking office Chiluba faced numerous struggles, including accusations of corruption within his cabinet, popular resistance to the privatization of the state-run economy, the fragmentation of the MMD, and criticism of his handling of ethnic tensions. In addition, Kaunda's party, the United National Independence Party (UNIP), regained popularity. In 1993 Chiluba declared a state of emergency when he discovered the so-called "Zero Option" conspiracy, engineered by UNIP radicals to instigate public discontent and render the country ungovernable. Chiluba revoked the state of emergency two months later, however, after protests from Zambia's Western donor nations.

In 1996 Chiluba's government passed an amendment to the constitution in an effort to undermine the political comeback of Kaunda. The amendment limited presidents to two terms in office and required all presidential candidates to be from families who had lived in Zambia for at least two generations. Kaunda, born of Malawian immigrants, was disqualified on both accounts. Kaunda's UNIP boycotted the 1996 elections, and Chiluba was elected for a second term. In October 1997 Chiluba survived an attempted coup waged by a small contingent of junior officers and soldiers. He stepped down at the end of his term of office in January 2002. The following year, the new government charged Chiluba with sixty-five counts of theft in association with alleged corruption while he was president.

In 2007 Chiluba was convicted by a court in England of stealing nearly $50 million (later increased to about $60 million) during his time as head of government, though thus far Chiluba has refused to recognize the validity of the court's holding. He has suffered from a heart ailment for a number of years, and poor health or the need to seek treatment abroad has frequently delayed or postponed the work of the Zambian courts.

BIBLIOGRAPHY

Ihonvbere, Julius O. *Economic Crisis, Civil Society, and Democratization: The Case of Zambia.* Africa World Press, 1997.

Roberts, Andrew. *A History of Zambia.* Africana Publishing Co., 1976.

ALONFORD JAMES ROBINSON, JR.

Chimurenga Music
Contemporary genre of Zimbabwean protest songs.

During the early 1970s singer-composer Thomas MAPFUMO began to fuse elements of traditional SHONA drumming and mbira (thumb piano) playing with Afro-rock styles to produce chimurenga music. Chimurenga is the Shona word meaning "war" or "struggle." Historically, Shona resistance has had a musical component. For example, during the colonial period chimurenga protest songs welded the call-and-response modality of traditional Shona music to the harmonies and melodies of Christian hymns, imported by missionaries. In the 1970s Thomas Mapfumo continued the tradition of infusing music with political content when he used Shona proverbs to incorporate anticolonial lyrics into a new brand of music. Mapfumo labeled his style chimurenga music.

Chimurenga's subversive messages rallied the people of ZIMBABWE to throw off the yoke of colonial oppression, to take pride in their culture, and ultimately to declare political independence. Mapfumo's first recording, *Shungu Dzinondibaya*, which makes fun of a wealthy man who suddenly loses his fortune, marks an early stage in the development of chimurenga. His 1977 single "Pamuromo Chete," however, popularized chimurenga among disenfranchised Zimbabweans. Colonial authorities subsequently banned his LP *Hokoya* (Watch Out). Following independence in 1980, Mapfumo's lyrics addressed the difficulties of nation building and economic development.

Chimurenga music draws on traditional Shona instruments and Shona musical structures. Chimurenga musicians dampen the strings of the electric guitar to mimic the sounds of the mbira, while the hi-hat and bass drums evoke the sounds of the hosho and the gourd rattle. The music follows both traditional rhythm patterns (*kitsinhira*) and traditional lead melody lines (*kushaura*). The result is a uniquely Zimbabwean form of music, steeped in tradition and transformed by contemporary instrumentation.

In 1983 the Earthworks label introduced Europe to chimurenga music with the release of *Chimurenga Singles*, featuring Mapfumo, and the genre has enjoyed increasing popularity outside of Africa. In 2001 Mapfumo's recording *Chimurenga Explosion* won the Indie Award for Contemporary World Music.

ARI NAVE

Chissano, Joaquim
1939–
Statesman and president of Mozambique.

Born in Malehice, Chibuto District, PORTUGUESE EAST AFRICA (MOZAMBIQUE), Joaquim Chissano enjoyed a privileged youth and an education that enabled him to become a leading member of the Mozambican nationalist movement. He was one of the first black Mozambicans to attend the central high school in LOURENÇO MARQUES (present-day MAPUTO, MOZAMBIQUE). He soon joined the Nucleus of African Secondary Students of Mozambique (NESAM), a nationalist organization of the young elite, and in 1959 became its president. The following year Chissano went to Portugal to study medicine but was forced to leave because of his political activities. He moved to Paris, France, where he helped establish a nationalist student movement among Mozambican exiles.

In 1962 Chissano went to TANZANIA to take part in organizing the FRONT FOR THE LIBERATION OF MOZAMBIQUE (Frente da Libertação de Moçambique, or FRELIMO) and became special assistant to FRELIMO president Eduardo Mondlane. Chissano fought in the war for independence from Portugal but was primarily involved as a trainer in FRELIMO camps in Tanzania and as the movement's chief representative in DAR ES SALAAM, Tanzania. Following the negotiated end to the war in 1974, Chissano headed the transitional government until Mozambique won its full independence on June 25, 1975. Samora MACHEL then became president and Chissano became minister of foreign affairs, a position he held until 1986.

Although Chissano was not a highly visible member of the party, he played a vital role in securing international support for the beleaguered government. While most observers agree that Chissano was uncomfortable with FRELIMO's staunch Marxist-Leninism, he did maintain close relations with the Union of Soviet Socialist Republics and other socialist countries. Chissano also improved ties with the West, securing humanitarian assistance and economic aid from Britain and the United States. He was also the architect of the 1984 Nkomati Accords with SOUTH AFRICA, in which South Africa agreed to stop supporting the insurgent group Mozambican National Resistance (RENAMO) and the Mozambican government agreed to cease its support for the AFRICAN NATIONAL CONGRESS.

After Machel died in an airplane crash in 1986, Chissano became president and head of FRELIMO. He soon proved a far more pragmatic leader than his predecessor. He lifted restrictions on religious freedom, encouraged private enterprise, and showed greater tolerance for traditional chieftains and spiritual beliefs. Initially he maintained Machel's hard-line stance against RENAMO, but in 1988

he began secretly encouraging third-party negotiations. The efforts succeeded and after reaching a peace agreement with RENAMO, Chissano was reelected president in 1994 with 53 percent of the popular vote in national elections, besting RENAMO leader Afonso Dhlakama. Chissano was reelected in December 1999 elections, defeating Dhlakama a second time.

In 2003 Chissano announced that he would not seek a third term as Mozambique's president, a vow he kept, being succeeded by Armando Guebuza. Despite this, Chissano remained active in African affairs. In 2006 he was appointed special U.N. envoy to help solve the conflict between UGANDA and SUDAN. A year later, the Mo Ibrahim Foundation honored Chissano with its first ever Prize for Achievement in African Leadership, carrying with it a $5 million stipend.

BIBLIOGRAPHY

Azevedo, Mario. *Historical Dictionary of Mozambique*. Scarecrow Press, 1991.

Rake, Alan. *Whos Who in Africa: Leaders for the 1990s*. Scarecrow Press, 1992.

ERIC YOUNG

Chokossi
Ethnic group of West Africa; also known as Chakossi, Anoufou, Anufo, and Kyokosi.

The Chokossi primarily inhabit northern TOGO and neighboring northeastern GHANA. They speak a Niger-Congo language and belong to the AKAN cultural and linguistic group. Approximately 100,000 people consider themselves Chokossi.

See also LANGUAGES, AFRICAN: AN OVERVIEW.

Chokwe
Ethnic group of the Democratic Republic of the Congo, Angola, and Zambia; one of the richest trading groups in the Congo basin prior to Belgian colonialism.

Originally seminomadic hunters in the savanna of northeast ANGOLA, the Chokwe migrated to the Congo basin in the early nineteenth century. There, the Chokwe settled in villages and began participating in regional commerce with the neighboring LUNDA. Dealing in ivory and wax, the Chokwe initially exercised little power in the Congo basin, where slave trading brought far higher returns. Nevertheless, the Chokwe traded enough to build up a small armory of flintlock muskets, which would later prove highly valuable.

When the slave trade went into decline in the 1840s, the Chokwe's control over the wax and ivory trades made them one of the richest trading groups in the region. Over the next ten years the demand for wax, which they produced themselves by collecting beeswax from hives in the forest, increased 30 percent in the trading centers of Benguela and LUANDA. Faced with an equally strong international demand for ivory, the Chokwe used their muskets to hunt elephants, eventually helping to decimate the local population. When ivory supplies grew scarce, the Chokwe turned to rubber–tapping.

During the second half of the nineteenth century the Chokwe population increased rapidly, and many migrated north in search of farmland and forests for rubber tapping. As they expanded, they took control of new trade routes and absorbed many smaller ethnic groups in the area between the Kwango River and the Kubango and Kunene rivers. In 1890, however, the military forces of the CONGO FREE STATE, founded by King LEOPOLD II, took control of the region and put an abrupt halt to Chokwe expansion. Today many Chokwe still live in what is now known as the Katanga (or Shaba) region, farming and working in the mining industries, although they are politically overshadowed by the Lunda ethnic group. More than 1.1 million people consider themselves Chokwe.

See also CONGO, DEMOCRATIC REPUBLIC OF THE; IVORY TRADE; ZAMBIA.

BIBLIOGRAPHY

Birmingham, David. *Pre-Colonial African Trade.* Oxford University Press, 1970.

ELIZABETH HEATH

Christianity, African: An Overview

There has been a Christian presence on the African continent for nearly as long as people have considered themselves followers of Jesus Christ. Missionaries and traders have been credited for bringing Christianity to EGYPT and North Africa in the very early days of the Christian movement. Because North Africa was part of the Roman Empire, the politics of Rome had an important bearing on the development of Christianity in Egypt and the Maghreb (comprising present-day LIBYA, TUNISIA, ALGERIA, and MOROCCO). The cosmopolitan city of ALEXANDRIA, EGYPT became one of the most important centers of North African Christianity. The scholarship and teachings of theologians based in urban North Africa, such as Origen, Athanasius, Tertullian, and Saint AUGUSTINE, shaped Christian thought and practice. Alexandria was also a center of Gnostic Christianity, nonorthodox sects dedicated to cultivating secret knowledge of the divine. The initial Egyptian converts to both Gnostic and orthodox sects were residents of cities, and many of them were Jews, Greeks, and Africans; these people were excluded from the Roman ruling elite. Until the early 300s C.E.,

Christians were occasionally persecuted for their beliefs by the Roman government. However, in 331 the emperor made Christianity the religion of the Roman Empire.

From the third century onward, Christianity gradually spread out into the countryside of Egypt and the MAGHREB. As the religion became more popular, it developed practices and attributes that made it distinctive to the region and that influenced Christianity more generally. People worshiped in their local languages, such as Coptic in Egypt, instead of Greek or Latin, the languages of the empire. In Egypt the monastic and hermitic traditions developed and flourished. Through monasteries, Christianity spread to remote rural areas. The Egyptian, Anthony, became a celebrated exemplar of the Christian solitary life and asceticism.

Several theological disputes in North Africa, which divided the church, reinforced the distinctiveness of African Christianity. Egyptian theologians believed that Christ had a single, divine nature. This Monophysite theology deviated from the orthodox (or Dyophysite) belief that Christ had both a divine and a human nature. The orthodox, or Catholic, church eventually declared the Monophysite interpretation a heresy, although it remained an important aspect of Egyptian and other mainly African and Asian traditions of Christianity. During the fourth and fifth centuries, the church in the Maghreb was bitterly divided between the Donatists and orthodox Christians. The Donatist movement venerated the martyrs of early Christianity, and advocated a hard-line interpretation concerning who could be included in the Christian community. Beyond their theological positions, the Donatists viewed themselves as champions of the poor and discouraged obedience to the state. The Donatists were considered heretics by the orthodox. The most able defender of Catholic tradition against the Donatists was Augustine, bishop of Hippo. Although the Monophysite and Donatist disputes may appear abstract, these disputes were important factors in shaping the local character of African Christianity.

NUBIA (in present-day SUDAN) and ETHIOPIA became the other strongholds of Christianity in Africa. Unlike Egypt and the Maghreb, these areas had not been part of the Roman Empire, and thus its imperial politics had little influence on the course of Christianity in these regions. Christianity arrived in Nubia with monks and traders in the fourth or fifth century. Nubian Christians supported a full hierarchy of bishops, priests, and monasteries; a Monophysite form of Christianity became the religion of the kingdoms of Nubia. In the region of modern-day Ethiopia, the leaders of the kingdom of AKSUM converted in the fourth century and likewise adopted Monophysite Christianity. The Aksumite kingdom laid the foundation for the future strong relationship between the Church and state in Ethiopia.

In the 640s C.E., Muslim Arab invaders conquered Egypt with little resistance. The arrival of Islam brought profound, though gradual, changes in the religious environment of the region. Until the tenth century C.E., the majority of Egyptians were Christians. Even after Islam became the religion of the majority, Coptic Christian communities have remained in existence until the present day. In the Maghreb, the relationship between Christianity and the new social and religious order was somewhat different. The Arabs were only able to gain control of this region in the 690s after a series of lengthy sieges. The people of the Maghreb appear to have adopted Islam readily, and the Christian communities were reduced to tiny outposts. In Nubia, the Christian states maintained peaceful relations with their Muslim neighbors from the 650s; for the next several centuries Nubia remained predominantly Christian. Because leaders converted to Islam, however, state support for the church declined, as did the supply of priests. By the sixteenth century, Christianity had disappeared from the Nubian states.

In the region of Ethiopia, Christianity was firmly embedded in the structures of the state and society. After the older kingdom of Aksum declined, successor states emerged in the Ethiopian highlands. In these states the distinctive features and symbols of Ethiopian Christianity emerged. For example, the Ethiopian church emphasized its Old Testament genealogy, the church identified itself with Zion, and Marian devotion was an important aspect of worship. Religious communities of monks and nuns played crucial roles in linking the populace to the church. Monasteries were sites of education and scholarship. Monks featured in the expansion of the Ethiopian culture and state. As the state expanded, the monks established churches in the wake of (or occasionally even ahead of) the conquering armies. Christianity also featured in the diplomacy of the empire; the emperors of the state forged links with the Holy Land. From the early 1400s Ethiopia made contact with European states. During this time the Ethiopian state was engaged in constant skirmishes with the neighboring Muslim states. By the 1500s these conflicts escalated; the Ethiopian state barely managed to prevail—in part, with the aid of Portuguese arms. In the following centuries Ethiopia and its church progressively turned its focus inward.

From the fifteenth century onward, Europeans intensified global exploration, trading, and colonizing activities. Europeans often assumed that as part of their claims on other parts of the world, they bore the responsibility to convert "the heathen" to Christianity. The Portuguese took the initiative in proselytizing as they established trading posts and settlements along the coasts of West, Central, and southern Africa. Initially, missionaries were interested in converting the leaders of the society, a process that had mixed results. Some leaders tolerated the activities of missionaries, while others forbade the missionaries from operating in their polities. In regions of European-African settlement, such as MOZAMBIQUE, CAPE VERDE, and coastal regions of Senegambia (SENEGAL and the GAMBIA), Christianity was the religion of the community.

The kingdom of KONGO was exceptional in the extent to which it adopted Christianity as the religion of the state. Missionaries and lay confraternities, organizations for prayer and social activities, helped popularize Christianity beyond the ruling elite. In the early eighteenth century a young woman named Kimpa Vita (baptized Beatrice) led a popular prophetic movement, called the Antonine movement, which called for the end of endemic warfare and restoration of the monarchy. In different ways, lay confraternities and the Antonine movement illustrated the extent to which Christianity had been integrated into the religious and social life of Kongo.

Between 1500 and 1850 a great deal of the European activity in Africa focused on the transatlantic slave trade. Religious-based opposition to slavery and the slave trade was only intermittent; most Europeans considered slavery compatible with Christianity until well into the nineteenth century. At the same time, however, Christianity became a unifying factor among people of African descent. In Europe and the Americas, people of African descent used the language of Christianity to protest the abuses of slavery. From the 1700s, a handful of West African men, such as Philip Quaque and Jacobus Elisa CAPITEIN, trained as Christian clergymen in Europe and returned to Africa, where they ministered to Europeans and Africans in coastal settlements.

An upsurge of interest in mission Christianity in North America and Europe brought a new wave of Protestant missionaries to Africa in the late eighteenth and early nineteenth centuries. Many of these missionaries were inspired by abolitionist ideals. Some missionaries, such as Johannes van der Kemp in South Africa, extended these principles to the advocacy of Africans' human rights. The settlements of SIERRA LEONE and LIBERIA were founded largely out of abolitionist activism; both regions were important sites of African Christianity. From these settlements, former slaves and people rescued from slave traders (such as Samuel Ajayi CROWTHER) eventually evangelized across West Africa to the Niger Delta (in present-day NIGERIA). Additionally, people of African descent from JAMAICA, the United States, and other parts of the Americas, inspired by the prospect of returning to their ancestral homeland, became missionaries in Africa.

The ways in which Africans responded to Christianity depended on the religious and political environment in which they lived. Although missionaries were important in spreading the religion, many people first heard of Christianity from African catechists and preachers. Sometimes Christianity was mixed with indigenous beliefs, and gained currency even among those people who would not have defined themselves as Christians. African Christians did not always intend to renounce all of their previous alliances and traditions. By contrast, missionaries tended to associate Christian conversion with some degree of "civilization," ranging from monogamy to western-style clothes. The extent to which Christianity required cultural change remained a matter of contention between converts and missionaries. Converts changed the focus of mission Christianity by integrating their own perspectives into the religion. African Christians often emphasized themes deriving from African systems of thought, such as fertility, healing, and the persistence of evil.

In the late nineteenth century, European powers formally colonized much of the continent. The exceptions were Liberia, and Ethiopia, which, in the 1890s, had successfully repelled an Italian invasion. Many western missionaries supported COLONIAL RULE. The number of missionaries increased during this time and the scope of their activities widened. In addition to evangelizing, Roman Catholic and Protestant mission societies often provided social services and resources for Africans, such as schools and hospitals, which the colonial state often did not provide. A small but significant group of Africans used the educational and work opportunities associated with missions as a way to adapt to the new social order. A mission-educated elite, comprised of teachers, nurses, journalists, lawyers, and doctors, exercised an influence far beyond their numbers. Members of this group included some of the most articulate critics of colonialism.

Although many Africans would continue to be associated with mainline Protestant or Roman Catholic missions, in the late nineteenth century and early twentieth century the face of Christianity became much more diverse. New denominations, such as the Jehovah's Witnesses and the Seventh Day Adventists, gained adherents. There were also many African-initiated innovations in Christianity. In West and southern Africa during the 1890s, Christians who were dissatisfied with the racial discrimination in the mission churches broke away to form independent or Ethiopianist churches. Some independent churches emerged out of political disputes; during the 1920s and 1930s, thousands of Christians in Kenya abandoned the mainline Protestant churches and joined independent

churches due to conflicts over education and FEMALE CIRCUMCISION. Many independent churches arose from spiritual calls. During the early 1900s William Wade Harris, a Methodist from Liberia, was inspired to preach by visions he had experienced. He told his listeners that they should be baptized, accept the Bible, reject traditional religion, and attend their nearest church. His South African contemporary, Isaiah Shembe, a healer and a prophet, established the Church of the Nazarites. Independent churches in all of their diversity, such as ALADURA CHURCHES, remain important features of African Christianity. In their hymns, ritual, and liturgy, many independent churches expressly drew upon African traditions and concerns. These concerns were not limited to independent churches. During the twentieth century many Christians in Protestant and Roman Catholic churches attempted to integrate African culture into Christianity. Some missionaries began to rethink their churches' previous enthusiasm for westernization, and emphasized the need to Africanize Christianity. For example, in the mid-twentieth century the Roman Catholic priest, Placide Tempels, and members of his church in Central Africa developed the lay organization, Jamaa. This popular movement emphasized prayer, spirituality, and the African family, and was modeled after indigenous models of social organization. Other lay groups, such as the Legion of Mary and women's prayer societies, not only provided a great deal of vitality within the church, but also were sites in which Africans made the religion their own.

In the years since independence, the leadership of mainline Protestant denominations and the Roman Catholic Church in Africa has gradually become African. There continues, however, to be a considerable foreign missionary presence in Africa. African theologians have participated in the worldwide debates about the Christian response to injustice in society, such as the arguments framed by liberation theologians in Latin America. In southern Africa, Christians opposed to APARTHEID formulated influential theological critiques of racial discrimination. Many Christians have developed theological and practical responses to pressing political and social issues confronting contemporary Africa, such as acquired immunodeficiency syndrome (AIDS), inequality in wealth, poverty, and politicized ethnicity. Other Christians have been deliberately apolitical and have focused on material security or on the afterlife.

The Christian presence in Africa continues to grow. By the early 2000s some 380 million Africans were Christians; a World Council of Churches report estimates that by 2025 this number may well increase to 633 million, representing 67 percent of all Christians in the world. Much of this growth has been fueled by new churches with indigenous cultural roots, such as the Church of the Lord Jesus Christ on Earth of the Prophet Simon Kimbangu. Traditional denominations, however, have also grown significantly. By 2003 the Anglican church in Nigeria, headed by Archbishop Peter Jasper Akinola, was the largest Anglican community in the world. Theologians and religious leaders expect that Africans will play an increasingly important role in shaping the future of the Christian church.

See also ALEXANDRIA AND GRECIAN AFRICA: AN INTERPRETATION; ETHIOPIAN ORTHODOX CHURCH; ISLAM IN AFRICA; ROMAN AFRICA: AN INTERPRETATION.

MODUPE LABODE

Christianity: Independent and Charismatic Churches in Africa

In 1704 a gravely ill Kongolese woman named Dona BEATRICE had a miraculous vision. Saint Anthony appeared to her, calling for the restoration of the Kingdom of KONGO, which had been destroyed through years of internal wars, Portuguese interference, and the slave trade. The young Beatrice was a former nganga marimba, or medium, and her claim to have died and arisen when Saint Anthony "entered her head" was in keeping with patterns of Kongo spirit possession and mediumship. The revelations received by Beatrice and her followers came from the Christian saints alone, however, and the vision her so-called Antonian movement articulated was decidedly nationalist in scope. The Antonians established their headquarters among the ruins of the old capital of São Salvador, next to the abandoned cathedral. They called for the repopulation of the city, the reunification of the Kongo people, and the return of a divinely sanctioned ruler to head a new theocratic Kongo. Beatriz rejected the Capuchin version of church history, insisting that many Catholic saints, including Saint Anthony and Saint Francis, were in fact Kongolese. Moreover, she maintained that Jesus had been born in São Salvador and baptized in the CONGO

INDEPENDENT AND CHARISMATIC CHURCHES IN AFRICA. African American artist Laura James paints primarily biblical themes using iconography found in Ethiopian Christian art, as in this depiction of Simon of Cyrene helping Jesus bear his cross. A similar image can be seen at the Bulawayo Cyrene Mission in Zi. (*Bridgeman Art Library International Ltd.*)

RIVER, and that the Virgin Mary came from the northern province of Nsundi. While Beatriz did not openly denounce the missionaries nor repudiate the authority of the pope, she revised Catholic prayers to emphasize intention over sacraments. She attempted to transform some of her leading followers (known as "Little Anthonys") into an indigenous order of priests (whom she dubbed "Angels") and crowned each one with a cloth headdress made from black *nsanda* bark, which symbolized the dark-skinned peoples of Africa. She also insisted that traditional sacred objects (minkisi), as well as crucifixes, be destroyed and replaced with small metal figurines of Saint Anthony. In 1706 she went so far as to claim that she had conceived a son by the Holy Spirit. Capuchin missionaries convinced the king, Pedro IV, that because the prophetess was supported by one of his rivals, she posed a serious threat, not only to the church but to Pedro's reign as well. She was burned at the stake for heresy in July of that year.

Antonianism is reputedly the earliest documented example of independent Christianity in sub-Saharan Africa. Generally, scholars have applied the label "independent" to those autonomous, African-led denominations and congregations established during the nineteenth and twentieth centuries following the partition of Africa and the widespread colonization of the continent by European powers. Yet the Antonian movement, which developed in one of the most heavily evangelized regions of Sub-Saharan Africa prior to modern times, manifests many of the same general features that characterize later indigenous Christian movements. These features include: 1) a charismatic, visionary founder or founders who disclose God's special dispensation for Africans; 2) insistence on the need for African clergy; 3) the reinterpretation of the gospel according to indigenous beliefs, values, and religiocultural practices; 4) an emphasis on direct communication with God and/or the saints through revelation, prophesy, possession, and dreams; and 5) women's active involvement and leadership. The discussion that follows brings to light each of these features. It will become clear that African independent churches are not exclusively modern phenomena, but part of a centuries-old process of interpretation, adaptation, and indigenization of the gospel.

ETHIOPIAN AND ZIONIST CHURCHES

African independent churches (AICs) numbered more than 7,000 in the 1980s, claiming nearly 15 percent of the Christian population of sub-Saharan Africa, or approximately 32 million members. In an attempt to impose some order on this dynamic and diverse collection of rapidly growing groups, scholars proposed various typologies. While most of these typologies proved artificial and distorting, there is one basic distinction that many outsiders continue to find useful—the distinction between the so-called "Ethiopian" or separatist churches and the "Zionist" or spirit churches.

Ethiopian churches (not to be confused with the ETHIOPIAN ORTHODOX CHURCH) insist upon black leadership and autonomy but do not reject Western liturgies, theologies, or doctrine. Missionary scholar Bengt Sundkler dubbed them Ethiopian after the Ethiopian Church founded in JOHANNESBURG, SOUTH AFRICA in 1892 by ex-Methodists, who, inspired by the black American African Methodist Episcopal Church (AME), rejected mission support and control, invoking Psalm 68:31: "Ethiopia shall soon stretch her hands unto God." Another example of these nineteenth-century separatist movements was largely the result of Bishop Samuel Ajayi CROWTHER's Niger Mission (1841–1891). A freed YORUBA slave and the first African Anglican Bishop, Crowther campaigned all his life for greater self-determination of Africans in Anglican mission churches, and was responsible for converting many people along the NIGER RIVER. The activism of men like Crowther and Lagos Baptist pastor D.B. Vincent Mojola Agbebi affected public sentiment such that, as historian Elizabeth Isichei puts it, "independency was in the air. In 1886 a layman wrote to the *Lagos Observer* exclaiming, '... a revolution must occur in the Episcopalian church. ... We cry aloud complainingly ... and a voice in reply comes to us ringing the word in our ears SECESSION! SECESSION! SECESSION!'"

In 1888 Agbebi joined other leading Baptists in seceding from the American mission to form the Native Baptist Church. Shortly thereafter, the Christian Missionary Society orchestrated the disintegration of Crowther's episcopate by firing most of his African clergy and staff, and replaced the bishop with an Englishman after the former's death in 1891. In anger and protest, the Lagos churches separated from the Anglican Church and established the United Native African Church, while Crowther's congregations in the Niger Delta came together to form a self-supporting African Anglican pastorate.

Like the Ethiopian churches, so-called Zionist or spirit churches insist on African leadership, but they also reject many of the teachings and theologies of the mainline, mission-seeded churches. They call for a thorough indigenization of the gospel in terms of African religious realities and cultural forms. Many churches of this type were founded after the turn of the century by charismatic African prophets, hence they are also known as prophetic churches. Messianic founders such as Isaiah Shembe in the Natal region of SOUTH AFRICA articulated the Old Testament ideal of a Promised Land or Holy City, a Zion that was spiritually ever-present, but also identified with sacred places in Africa. Shembe was an uneducated, itinerant Zulu preacher who gained a reputation as a faith healer and visionary. In 1911 he founded the Nazareth Baptist Church, which integrated features of charismatic Christianity such as baptism in the Spirit and casting out demons, with Zulu dance, music, and ritual, as well as adherence to certain Old Testament laws such as the Saturday sabbath, pork avoidance, and the practice of circumcision and polygyny (the latter two coincide with Zulu custom). Acting on an order from God, Shembe established Ekuphakameni, or "Elevated Place," on a mountainside north of DURBAN, a religious center that has become perhaps the most famous in the African Zion movement. Nazarites see Ekuphakameni as the realization of God's kingdom on earth, and Shembe as a Christlike messiah who brought the promise of God's salvation to the Zulu. Present-day Nazarites continue to gather at Ekuphakameni to sing the more than 200 hymns composed by Shembe and to visit his tomb, where angels and ancestors of the church are also said to reside.

Grace Tshabalala, a leader in another Zionist community in KwaMashu Township, South Africa, once articulated the existential quality of living in Zion. For her, the concept of Zion hinged on her belief in being saved as a Christian, in the here and now. Amid the oppression and poverty of APARTHEID in the 1970s, Tshabalala asserted a realized eschatology: "I have Zion and Zion is my home," Tshabala stated in an interview with the British Broadcasting Corporation. "Whenever I am sick, I have Zion; whenever I am happy, I have Zion. . . . Dead or alive, I am a Zionist." While preaching, Tshabalala felt as if someone were "pumping [her] blood," filling her with "power."

Throughout sub-Saharan Africa, Zionist or spirit congregations can be visually distinguished from mainline and Ethiopian churches by their distinctive style of dress: long gowns of solid colors, especially white, representing purity. Denominational insignia are often sewn across the breast or appliquéd on kerchiefs, turbans, or caps, and colored bars and patches are added to designate rank or religious office. Through appropriating garb originally reserved for the missionary priest or bishop, lay and ordained Africans alike assert their spiritual legitimacy and authority. In some instances, liturgical robes are considered essential to the reception of the Holy Spirit and the exercise of spiritual gifts. A catechist in a Roho (Spirit) church in western KENYA, for example, referred to his gown as his "working tool." Without it, he could not effectively proselytize.

Lively preaching, hymns, and prayers are essential to worship in African spirit churches. The lengthy services generally begin in a formal manner as the pastor leads the congregation through the standard components of the Christian liturgy such as invocation, recitation of the creed, collective confession, and scripture lessons. The officiating pastor may deliver the initial sermon, but in many independent churches, laypeople are also welcome to offer personal testimony and comment on scripture. Preaching and singing complement each other. In many congregations, individuals freely interrupt the preacher to initiate songs whose lyrics highlight the sermon's theme. Hymns may be accompanied by drums, bells, and rattles; some churches condone only vocal music, which is characteristically spontaneous and responsive. Often, as worship progresses, singers increase the tempo, encouraging people to sway or dance. Through song and movement, members create an atmosphere conducive to ecstatic trance and, in some cases, speaking in tongues. Music can therefore open a channel for communication between God and/or the Holy Spirit and the congregation, facilitating the infusion of divine power into the community. Prayer, particularly when led by a charismatic preacher, can have the same effect.

POLITICS PARADING AS RELIGION?
The European administrative officials in African colonies in the late nineteenth and early twentieth centuries were frequently alarmed by the emergence of indigenous Christian movements. They saw African religious leaders as potential threats, subversive schemers who spread discontent and fueled opposition to European authorities, missionaries, and civil administrators alike. One such leader was Simon KIMBANGU, a Baptist catechist who led a healing revival in 1921 in the Belgian Congo. Like Dona Beatrice 200 years earlier, Kimbangu was popularly perceived as a powerful nganga who had risen from the dead. Clutching his prophet's staff, Kimbangu would tremble and shake with the power of the Holy Spirit as he laid hands on those who came to him for healing. Thousands flocked to his village, N'Kamba, which soon became the Holy Jerusalem of the revival. Despite the fact that Kimbangu's movement was primarily religious and therapeutic, Belgian authorities were alarmed by the crowds he attracted. Kimbangu did not openly support separation from the mission churches, nor resistance to the government. However, numerous other bangunza, or prophets, some of whom preached in Kimbangu's name, traveled throughout Lower ZAIRE advocating nonpayment of taxes and foretelling the imminent demise of white rule. In June of 1921, after European settlers complained that workers were leaving their estates in droves to join Kimbangu, the local administration sent soldiers to sack N'Kamba-Jerusalem and had many Baptist deacons and laypeople arrested. Kimbangu was seized but escaped, only to be recaptured in September and condemned to death. His sentence was commuted to life imprisonment; he died in jail in 1951 after serving much of his term in solitary confinement.

Today Kimbanguism is among the largest and most successful examples of African independent Christianity, boasting over four million adherents in the DEMOCRATIC REPUBLIC OF THE CONGO alone. Officially instituted in 1959 as The Church of Jesus Christ on Earth through the Prophet Simon Kimbangu (EJCSK), Kimbanguism gradually made the transition from an underground protest movement to an established church recognized by the international Christian community (the EJCSK was admitted into the World Council of Churches in 1970). Today's Kimbanguists do not encourage spiritual ecstasy or faith healing; they emphatically reject traditional religion and advocate obedience to civil authority. However, they continue to celebrate their martyred founder as the black messiah, who proclaimed God's truth to Africans, just as Christ proclaimed salvation to Israel.

Like other African independent churches with roots in the colonial period, Kimbanguism articulated resistance through religious symbolism, and expressed its religious vision in a political idiom; temporal justice and divine truth were intertwined. Some scholars have been inclined, as were Kimbangu's critics, to see independent Christianity as actual or symbolic political protest "pretending to be religious." However, the advent of national independence throughout most of Africa in the early 1960s did not herald the end of indigenous Christian movements. On the contrary, from 1970 to 1980, the growth rate of independent Christianity far exceeded that of the mainline churches. It soon became clear that monocausal explanations simply could not account for the diversity, richness, and persistence of indigenous Christian movements. AICs speak compellingly to a variety of people, especially the urban poor, creating a sense of community and family that counteracts the alienation resulting from social dislocation and massive migration to the cities. Charismatic and Pentecostal independent churches, with their lively hymns and dance, also provide an opportunity for emotional release, free expression, and a respite from hardship and daily drudgery. Above all, AICs provide access to healing power and spiritual renewal.

THE HOLY SPIRIT IN AFRICAN FORM

African Zionist churches share much in common with charismatic and Pentecostal congregations around the world. They offer, as scholar Rosalind Hackett has observed, a "pragmatic spirituality" centering on "health, spiritual protection, fertility, material well-being and recognition of dualistic theories of sickness and misfortune." It is frequently said that whites brought the Bible, but blacks received the Holy Spirit, and African indigenous congregations are proud of being "strong in the Spirit." The techniques AICs use to cultivate the spirit and the manner in which members articulate their faith have been profoundly shaped by older African religious institutions, practices, and ritual. Founders like Beatrice, Shembe, and Kimbangu, as we have seen, employed traditional methods of mediumship (dreams, trembling and trance, out-of-body journeys to celestial regions) in their ministries and were popularly perceived as diviner-healers. The ALADURA CHURCHES in West Africa integrate aspects of traditional Yoruba domestic shrine design in constructing their worship space to maximize communication with divine forces. Zionists in Natal use staffs to ward off malevolent forces, just as traditional Zulu "heavenheards" used theirs to chase lightning away. In the Lumpa church in MALAWI, central tenets and aspects of spirituality were expressed primarily through symbols and catechetical methods derived from traditional BEMBA initiation rites. By reinvigorating certain aspects of tradition, while emphatically rejecting others, members of AICs create a spirituality that is at once profoundly African and an alternative to past ways.

The ability of independent churches to synthesize the old and the new is particularly apparent when one considers the extent to which women have assumed leadership. Barred from holding office, preaching, or performing sacraments in most mission churches, women figured prominently in the founding of hundreds of AICs. Well-known examples include: Christianah Abiodun, who cofounded the highly successful Cherubim and Seraphim movement in 1955 in NIGERIA with Moses Orimolade; Grace Tani, who established the Church of the Twelve Apostles in GHANA; Marie Lalou, who started the Deima (Holy Water) movement in CÔTE D'IVOIRE; Mai (Mother) Chaza, whose church in ZIMBABWE is named for her; Alice Lenshina, who started the popular Lumpa (Supreme) church in NORTHERN RHODESIA in 1954, but whose members were exiled by the new government in ZAMBIA in 1970; and Gaudencia Aoko, cofounder of the Legio Maria, a Kenyan independent church with Catholic roots. The legacy of women's predominance in spirit-possession religion in many regions of precolonial Africa partly explains why women have been so readily accepted as leading mediums and healers in AICs. In the emergence of the Luo Roho movement in western Kenya, for example, a corps of armed female askeche (soldiers) protected their congregations, incorporating precedents from local cults in which women became possessed by the violent ghosts of slain warriors.

Most of the AICs founded by women are today headed by men; with increased institutionalization, women have, over time, been relegated to largely ceremonial, therapeutic, and supportive roles. There are exceptions to this trend, such as the Communion Church in Kenya, which promotes women priests. Moreover, the existence of parallel men's and women's hierarchies in many AICs such as the Aladura, ensures women some degree of autonomy and control over their own affairs. Although the picture with regard to gender is complex and varied, it can be asserted that AICs continue to provide both men and women the opportunity to renegotiate traditional religious roles, identities, and experience in creative ways as they strive to be agents for God's spirit in the world.

See also AFRICAN RELIGIONS: AN INTERPRETATION; CHRISTIANITY, AFRICAN: AN OVERVIEW.

BIBLIOGRAPHY

Barrett, David B. *Schism and Renewal in Africa: An Analysis of Six Thousand Contemporary Religious Movements.* Oxford University Press, 1968.

Hoehler-Fatton, Cynthia. *Women of Fire and Spirit: History, Faith and Gender in Roho Religion in Western Kenya.* Oxford University Press, 1996.

Jules-Rosette, Benetta, ed. *The New Religions of Africa.* Ablex Publishing, 1979.

Omoyajowo, J. A. *Cherubim and Seraphim: The History of an Independent Church.* Nok, 1982.

Sundkler, Bengt G. *Bantu Prophets in South Africa* 2nd ed. Oxford University Press, 1961 (1948).

Thornton, John K. *The Kongolese Saint Anthony: Dona Beatriz Kimpa Fita and the Antonian Movement, 1694–1706.* Cambridge University Press, 1998.

CYNTHIA HOEHLER-FATTON

Christianity: Missionaries in Africa
Significant factor in religious, cultural, and political change within African societies.

Christianity is an evangelizing religion and, as such, missionaries have been essential to the enterprise from its beginnings. As important as missions and missionaries are to African Christianity, one should not confuse the history of mission Christianity, or the history of missionaries, with the history of Christianity on the African continent. An active Christian community existed in EGYPT from the earliest days of the religion. By the third century C.E., Christian communities had spread throughout North Africa. From these communities, Christianity gradually spread to NUBIA and ETHIOPIA. Monks and priests proselytized to non-Christians; converts evangelized to their friends and families.

European trade and conquest in the fifteenth century brought a new form of missionary activity to Africa. Portuguese, Dutch, and other European traders established small settlements along the coast of Africa to trade in commodities and people, who were sold into the transatlantic slave trade. European governments and trading companies often supported missionary activity by maintaining

that part of their reason for being in Africa was to convert the non-Christian. The case of the Portuguese exemplifies the close relationship between crown and church. In the Treaty of Tordesillas (1494), the pope recognized Portuguese claims to Africa. The crown was also responsible for attempting to convert the indigenous people to Christianity. Much of the missionary effort over the next two and a half centuries was conducted under Portuguese authority. The vast majority of missionaries at this time were Roman Catholic priests; many of them belonged to religious orders such as the Jesuits, Capuchins, and Franciscans.

Missionaries often attempted to convert the ruling elite based on the assumption that if the rulers were converted, the rest of the society would follow. These attempts met with varying degrees of success. Missionaries often alienated potential Christians by their criticism of African customs and their support of the slave trade. It was left to African Christians to generate religious-based critiques of slavery and the slave trade. Rulers were often reluctant to convert to Christianity because conversion often required them to renounce the traditional religions and practices, which were the source of their power and authority. In Ethiopia, the emperor and royalty considered themselves to be in little need of mission activity, because they were already Christians; they saw the Jesuits as a conduit for building alliances with Europeans. In West Africa, Portuguese clergy attempted to proselytize in the early kingdom of Benin and the Warri state, in the Niger delta. In the Mutapa state (in present-day ZIMBABWE), the missionaries met with modest success. Missionaries also worked in Portuguese-African communities in SIERRA LEONE, CAPE VERDE, and ANGOLA. Although some Africans became priests, missionary efforts were often hampered by the short supply of clergy—whether European or African.

One of the few states that adopted Christianity was the kingdom of the KONGO (in present-day Angola, Congo, and the DEMOCRATIC REPUBLIC OF THE CONGO). After encountering the Portuguese in the 1480s, the Kongo king converted to Christianity in 1491, and for the next several centuries the rulers of Kongo were Christian. Christianity initially served as a bridge between Kongo and Portugal, but by the end of the 16th century the relationship had deteriorated and the states were enemies. Part of the conflict arose from the effects of the slave trade in the region. Further, the Kongo state resented the ways in which the Portuguese controlled the supply of clergy and bishops to the region, and the Kongo tried to obtain clergy elsewhere. A Christian presence remained in the region into the 19th century, long after the state had dissolved. In Kongo, as in all areas in which Africans accepted Christianity, the local histories, religion, and politics set the framework in which people gave meaning to the new religion and integrated it into their society.

The Roman Catholic dominance of mission work lasted until the mid-1700s. With few exceptions, Protestants showed little interest in foreign mission work until the late eighteenth century, when a series of revivals helped spark interest in foreign missions among Protestants in the United States, Great Britain, and northern Europe. Church people formed new societies for the promotion of mission work. Clergymen and laymen from all levels of society volunteered to become missionaries. In general, women could go to the mission field only as the wives or other relatives of the male missionary. The number of Roman Catholic priests and nuns increased during the 19th century as orders were founded specifically for mission work.

Many of the missionaries during this time were inspired by humanitarian concerns; they linked the abolition of slavery with their cause. Some missionaries protested against slavery and other abuses to which African people were subjected. Many Western missionaries saw "civilizing" Africans and converting them to Christianity as an extension of humanitarianism. They saw African cultures as degraded and uncivilized, and many missionaries thought that Africans had no religion. Therefore it was part of the missionaries' Christian duty to share the benefits of Western civilization and Christianity with Africans. This perspective meant that missionaries often were dismissive of African cultures and beliefs. In their view, Christianity was linked with Western cultural patterns. Missionaries therefore encouraged converts to adopt Western gender roles and family structure, clothing, literacy, and housing. Christianity was commonly linked with Western patterns of work, agriculture, and consumption. David Livingstone, the Scottish missionary who traveled widely in southern and Central Africa in the mid-nineteenth century, summarized this sentiment when he declared in 1857 that Africa needed "Christianity and Commerce."

Like their predecessors, many missionaries attempted to convert African societies through the rulers, and thus change the entire society. Although relatively few African rulers converted to Christianity in the 19th century, several leaders invited missionaries to work within their polities. MOSHOESHOE of the SOTHO people used missionaries and mission stations as part of his strategy of state building. He used missionaries to negotiate with white settlers in southern Africa, and he also sent his sons to mission schools. In the kingdom of BUGANDA (in present-day UGANDA), the rulers used Protestant and Roman Catholic Christianity, along with Islam and traditional religions, as factors within the complex politics of the state. Although rulers rarely converted to Christianity, other groups of people within society became associated with Christianity. Many of the early converts were somewhat marginal to the established order: young people, refugees, slaves, women. Not all converts were marginal, however. Ntsikana, a councilor to a XHOSA chief, was influential in bringing people to Christianity in SOUTH AFRICA in the early 1800s. He argued that Christianity did not require one to adopt Western culture, and his hymns became important expressions of African Christianity.

The West African colonies of Sierra Leone and LIBERIA were important centers of missionary activity. These colonies were established to provide homes for former slaves and captives; as was the case in other colonies, thriving indigenous communities lived there well before the settlers arrived. A group of British abolitionists, including former slaves, established Sierra Leone in 1792. Liberia was established by the U.S.-based American Colonization Society in the 1820s and became an independent state in 1847. Sierra Leone's development illustrates the complex ways in which Christianity became part of the region's religious landscape. The colony's settlers included people of African descent from Great Britain, Canada, and JAMAICA. Recaptives, Africans who had been captured into slavery but released by the British navy into Sierra Leone, were an important segment of the population. Many settlers were already Christian and they established Christian communities that became a base for further evangelization. Further, some settlers and recaptives became missionaries to other parts of Africa. The most famous of these missionaries was Samuel CROWTHER. Crowther had been captured into slavery as an adolescent and released into Sierra Leone. He converted and became an Anglican minister. Crowther then led a mission of Africans to the Niger delta in 1857. He was ordained a bishop of the Church of England in 1864—the first African Anglican bishop.

Some of the most active promoters of Christian missions were people of African descent from the Americas and Europe. These missionaries thought that Christianity was important to bring to Africa; they often expressed a sense of responsibility to their homeland. From the 1700s through the 1900s, people of African descent from the United States, Canada, and Europe worked as missionaries in Africa. Many of these missionaries were associated with predominately black churches that originated in the United States, such as the African Methodist Episcopal Church (AME), and the National Baptist Convention. Other African American missionaries were associated with predominately white churches.

In the last quarter of the nineteenth century, European powers undertook the rapid partitioning and colonization of Africa, a process often referred to as the SCRAMBLE FOR AFRICA. By 1902, Liberia and Ethiopia were the only independent states on the continent. Western missionaries' reaction to imperialism varied greatly. A few missionaries actively helped European governments defeat African states. Other missionaries protested against abuses associated with colonial governments, but did not question the authority of these governments to colonize Africa. Many missionaries had grown frustrated with the strength of African polities and were convinced that Christianity could advance only when the authority of African states had been destroyed. It appears that most missionaries accepted colonialism and worked within the system. Some colonial governments attempted to forge close links with missionaries; both the Portuguese and Belgian governments privileged missionaries from their nations working in the colonies. Most missionaries and colonial governments worked closely together, although they did not have the same goals and were occasionally in conflict.

Colonial rule opened new opportunities for missionaries. The number of missionaries and mission societies working in Africa increased. Further, from the mid-1800s, most mission societies opened their ranks to single women, and work among African women thus became a higher priority. In addition to the previously established societies, new groups such as the Salvation Army, Seventh-day Adventists, and Jehovah's Witnesses began work in Africa. In addition to evangelizing, many of these missionaries established schools, hospitals, and other institutions.

The number of adherents to Christianity increased steadily during this time. Some people were brought into contact with Christianity through work in the colonial economy, service in the military, or through studying at mission schools. Many people learned of Christianity from African catechists, preachers, friends, or family members. African Christians from areas as diverse as the SUDAN and South Africa acted as missionaries to other African groups. Africans who had been educated in mission schools formed the core of an elite who began some of the earliest challenges to colonialism. The vibrant African Christian community discussed and debated Western missionaries' attitudes toward colonialism, African culture, and civilization. African Christianity developed distinctive features, such as prayer groups, that missionaries could rarely control. African Christians often emphasized aspects of the religion that had special meaning for their situation, such as healing and prophecy.

Missionaries often emphasized the essential equality of all people and claimed that their goal was to establish indigenous, self-standing churches. Many missionaries saw the West as the model for a Christian community, however, and were reluctant to cede authority to Africans.

This reluctance arose from a mix of doubt concerning the leadership capacity of Africans, bigotry, and racism. Western missionaries were often paternalistic in their relationship with African Christians. In practice this meant that there were very few Africans in positions of authority until well into the twentieth century. Those few Africans who had been in leadership positions were often deposed. The fate of the Niger delta mission illustrates this tendency. In the 1890s, white British missionaries took over the leadership of the station that had been established and run by Africans for over three decades.

In some areas, such as South Africa and coastal West Africa, Christians who were distressed with the attitude of missionaries broke away and formed Ethiopian churches. These churches were called Ethiopian in reference to Psalm 68:31:"Princes shall come from Egypt; Ethiopia shall stretch out her hands to God." While these Ethiopian churches often had comparable theologies and practices to mission churches, Africans were in charge. Often Christians who remained in mission churches had the same sort of frustrations with the paternalism of missionaries as did those who formed their own congregations. During this time Africans formed other, prophetic, independent churches, which have often been called Zionist. These independent churches are an important aspect of Christianity but were not always directly related to missions.

Soon after World War II, the European powers recognized that their colonies would eventually become independent. Missionaries in turn acknowledged that the end of colonialism would have an impact on their work. These missionaries began to emphasize developing African leadership in the church hierarchy. This process was somewhat slow; for example, Africans were in the minority among Roman Catholic bishops until the late 1960s. In many cases the number of Western missionaries working in Africa continued to increase. Many mission societies also acknowledged that their work in Africa would have to change, and that the emphasis should be on building a distinctive, African church, instead of modeling the church on a Western form. In 1961 the International Missionary Council merged with the World Council of Churches; this controversial move indicated the extent to which mission churches should be considered an essential part of Christianity and not subordinate to the West. The Second Vatican Council (1962–1965) gave impetus toward creating a church that was more responsive to local needs and concerns.

As African colonies won independence, many missionaries were able to maintain good relations with new governments. The relationship between government and church within independent Africa is a related, but quite distinct, question. In states where the transition to independence was accompanied by violence or civil wars, missionaries tended to keep a low profile. In the southern African states of ZIMBABWE, NAMIBIA, and South Africa, where racial discrimination against the African majority by the white minority was government policy, a few foreign missionaries, such as Michael Scott and Trevor HUDDLESTON, spoke out against these practices.

Independence of African states has not meant the end of mission work. In the 1970s there were some calls by African Christians for a moratorium on foreign missions, so that Africans could gain control of the church. There continues, however, to be a substantial foreign mission presence on the continent. The composition of this group of missionaries has shifted. In a trend dating from the mid-twentieth century, the number of missionaries from North America has increased; most of these missionaries are associated with conservative or fundamentalist evangelical agencies. Generally, the work of missions in postindependence Africa has broadened to include economic and social development, in addition to education and evangelizing.

See also COLONIAL RULE; ISLAM IN AFRICA.

MODUPE LABODE

Chuabo

Ethnic group of Mozambique; also known as the Chwabo and the Maganja.

The Chuabo primarily inhabit the ZAMBEZI RIVER valley in MOZAMBIQUE. They speak a BANTU language and belong to the larger Maravi cultural and linguistic group. Approximately 650,000 people consider themselves Chuabo.

See also BANTU: DISPERSION AND SETTLEMENT.

Cinema, African

Films made by and about Africans.

According to popular legend, cinema was first introduced to Africa in 1896, after a stolen bioscope mysteriously made its way to CAPE TOWN, SOUTH AFRICA. For the next several decades colonial governments effectively delayed the development of an African film industry, but since independence African film directors have struggled to create a viable cinema of their own. Despite ongoing production and distribution problems, they have largely succeeded; African cinema is now internationally recognized. African filmmakers now aspire to reach broader audiences in Africa itself.

COLONIAL-ERA CINEMA

Although Europeans and Americans started to make films in Africa soon after the medium was invented in the 1890s, Africa's colonial regimes restricted Africans' exposure to film and film production until the late 1950s. In British colonies as well as the BELGIAN CONGO (present-day DEMOCRATIC REPUBLIC OF THE CONGO), for example, Africans were forbidden to watch European and American movies. French and Belgian colonial governments controlled the content of all films produced within their borders, and Africans were frequently forbidden from working on film productions. These restrictions reflected the colonial powers' concern about the influence of the cinematic medium on the African population. They assumed that Africans were incapable of distinguishing fact from fiction and would therefore take too seriously films that depicted Europeans and Americans unfavorably. They also feared the possible dissemination of subversive or anticolonial messages through film. Despite these restrictions, some Africans still managed to learn about film and filmmaking. Primarily, they took advantage of colonial efforts to use film as an educational tool. In TANGANYIKA (present-day TANZANIA), for example, the Bantu Educational Cinema Experiment (BECE) was devoted to producing films on hygiene, improved farming methods, and African folktales. Launched in 1935 and sponsored by the colonial office of the British Film Institute, the BECE made films in a variety of East African languages and intended for African audiences. The BECE periodically employed Africans to perform menial tasks, and its supervisor Leslie Alan Notcutt urged that similar cinema projects, also employing Africans, be established throughout British Africa. The subsequent establishments of colonial film units throughout the British colonies provided Africans with one way to acquire filmmaking skills. In the Belgian Congo a similar opportunity emerged for Africans interested in film. In the 1940s the colonial government's Film and Photo Bureau made educational and propaganda films specifically for the African population. In order to reduce costs the bureau employed African workers who were taught the basics of film production. In addition, Africans could acquire cinematic skills at the Congolese Center for Catholic Action Cinema (CCCAC) in Léopoldville (present-day KINSHASA, DEMOCRATIC REPUBLIC OF THE CONGO) or Africa Films in Kivu, both of which were run by Catholic priests. The two companies' films—such as the CCCAC's series Les Palabres de Mboloko, starring an animated antelope— aimed to teach African audiences religious virtues. Both companies offered Africans an opportunity to learn cinematic techniques, but, as in the other colonial experiments, the content and format of the films produced by these groups were severely restricted by the colonial administration. In the French colonies, France's goal of assimilating colonial subjects into French culture provided some aspiring African film directors opportunities to attend film school abroad. One of the first was Senegalese Paulin Vieyra, who graduated from the prestigious l'Institut des hautes études cinématographiques in Paris in 1955. Vieyra later became a well-known film critic and historian. But he and other early Francophone African filmmakers were not permitted to return to Africa to make films. France's 1934 Laval Decree placed strict controls on any filmmaking in its colonies and denied African directors filming permits altogether. By the late 1950s a number of Africans had acquired filmmaking skills, but they still had little autonomy. Instead, African directors were forced to comply with the paternalistic restrictions established by the colonies' production centers, which typically allowed them only to make educational films. Not until decolonization could African film directors begin building a film industry of their own.

FRANCOPHONE FILM PRODUCTION AND THE FEPACI

After independence, film directors in the former French colonies took the lead in African cinema for a number of reasons. Francophone Africa had the largest number of film directors, many of whom had acquired sophisticated techniques from their studies abroad. Consequently, they were best equipped to produce films capable of competing with American and European films for the attention of African audiences. In addition, France offered its former colonies financial and technical support for film production through institutions such as the Consortium audiovisuel international (CAI) and Bureau du cinéma. The first to take advantage of such assistance was Senegalese filmmaker Ousmane SEMBÈNE, whose 1963 *Borom Sarret* is now considered by many historians to be the first African film. During the early years of independence Francophone film directors such as Ousmane Sembène, Moustapha ALASSANE, Gaston Kaboré, Med HONDO, and Timité Bassori not only produced films but also became advocates for African cinema. They identified and denounced the barriers to African film production, such as the European and American distributors' monopoly over African movie theaters (which enabled them to flood the market with foreign films); the lack of production facilities in Africa; and censorship by African governments. In 1969 Francophone directors initiated the founding of the Fédération Panafricaine des Cinéastes (FEPACI), an organization that fought for the political, cultural, and economic liberation of African film. The FEPACI's call for cultural liberation has indeed been heard. During the 1970s and 1980s many African filmmakers, with FEPACI encouragement, rejected sensationalistic Hollywood-style filmmaking in favor of productions about African social problems, politics, and daily life. The FEPACI has also helped to promote African film both in Africa and abroad and is an important supporter of the Festival Panafricain du Cinéma et de la Télévision de Ouagadougou (FESPACO), a biennial film festival held in the capital of BURKINA FASO. Africa's newest generation of Francophone filmmakers, however, has criticized the FEPACI's failure to make African cinema more commercially viable in Africa itself. Filmmakers such as Souleymane CISSÉ and Idrissa OUÉDRAOGO have asserted that the FEPACI tends to promote heavy-handed political films that lack technical sophistication. In order to win broader audiences, they argue, African filmmakers need to improve their techniques and choose plots accessible to rural African audiences.

FILM PRODUCTION OUTSIDE FRANCOPHONE AFRICA

Non-Francophone African film production is relatively limited, except in SOUTH AFRICA. Among the other former British colonies, only NIGERIA has built a sizeable film industry. The growth of cinema in this country was due largely to the efforts of Nigerian film director Ola Balogun. Originally trained in theater, Balogun adapted a number of YORUBA plays for cinema and, between 1972 and 1982, he produced nearly a film a year. Since then, however, Balogun has largely abandoned film for television, which has a wider audience in Nigeria. Other former British colonies with smaller film industries include GHANA (whose industry includes directors Kwaw Ansah and King Ampaw), Tanzania (director Flora M'mbugu Schelling), and ZIMBABWE (directors Ingrid Sinclair and Tsitsi Dangarembgra). In Portuguese-speaking Africa, liberation struggles have been a central theme in films produced since the 1960s. In the early 1970s, for example, French-Guadeloupean film director Sarah Maldoror and Yugoslavian director Dragutin Popovic collaborated with members of three liberation movements—Partido Africano Pela Independencia de Guinè e Cabo Verde (PAIGC) in GUINEA-BISSAU and CAPE VERDE, the Popular Movement for the Liberation of Angola (PMLA) in ANGOLA, and FRONT FOR THE LIBERATION OF MOZAMBIQUE (FRELIMO) in MOZAMBIQUE—to pioneer a form of guerrilla cinema. Maldoror's *Sambizanga* (1972) was the best known of her several films on political struggles in Portuguese-speaking Africa. Mozambique has been known as an innovator in film production since its National Film Institute opened in 1976 and French film directors Jean Rouche and Jean-Luc Godard were invited to teach Africans low-cost film techniques. Years of civil war, however, made filming in this country difficult, and some of its filmmakers now live abroad. Rui Guerra, for example, lives in Brazil, where he is part of the *cinema novo* movement. Elsewhere in Lusophone Africa, Guinea-Bissau's first director, Flora Gomes, released *Mortu Nega* in 1989; Leao Lopes in Cape Verde followed soon afterward with the 1993 release of *Ilheu de Contenda*. In Angola, Zeze Gamboa and Ruy Duarte de Carvalho released several films in the late 1980s and early 1990s.

NORTH AND SOUTH AFRICA

By far the most prolific film industries in Africa today are located in North Africa—particularly in EGYPT, ALGERIA, and TUNISIA—and in South Africa. Nevertheless, both industries have historically been ignored by scholars of African cinema. North African cinema, which is frequently classified with Arab cinema, has generally been disregarded because of the longstanding predominance of commercial interests in the Egyptian film industry, which is one of the oldest on the continent. Egypt produces several hundred films a year, most of them B-grade romances and musicals. Egyptian directors such as Salah Abou Seif, Mohamed Khan, and Youssef Chahine do produce serious films, however, on issues such as Arab identity and the threat of Islamic fundamentalism. Algeria and Tunisia also developed early film industries. Like many other Francophone African countries, they took part in the initial meetings of the FEPACI; in fact they hosted the organization's first two meetings. But by the mid-1970s their participation in FEPACI had waned, and their industries became increasingly dominated by mass-market film makers. Still, a number of Tunisian filmmakers have won international recognition, including Moufida Tlati, Karim Dridi, and Nadia Fares. Algerian director Mohamed Lakhdar-Hamina won a Cannes film festival Palme d'Or prize for his *Chronicle of the Years of Embers* (1976), which is about an Algerian peasant family that fights in the anticolonial war against France. The South African film industry was long ostracized within the world of African cinema because it was dominated by white filmmakers who frequently used film to reinforce racial divisions and perpetuate negative stereotypes about Africans. A few exceptions included directors Donald Swanson, who took an antiapartheid stance in *Jim comes to Jo'burg* (1949) and *Magic Garden* (1961); Zoltan Korda, who adapted the ALAN PATON novel *Cry the Beloved Country* into film in 1951; and Lindi Wilson, whose *Last Supper at Hortsely Street* (1982) documented the forced removals of nonwhite residents in Cape Town's District Six. South Africa's first black director, Gibson Kente, released the antiapartheid film *How Long* in 1976, but until the early 1990s few blacks were able to make films in South Africa. While in exile, South African film directors such as Nana Mahomo, Lionel N'Gakane, and Chris Austen produced a number of movies that have only recently been released in South Africa. Since the end of apartheid several talented film directors have emerged, including Thomas Mogotlane, Brian Tilly, and Oliver Schmitz. Their work has helped break down the former stigma against South African film at international festivals such as FESPACO. In less than forty years African cinema has moved beyond its origins in paternalistic colonial propaganda projects to sophisticated, internationally acclaimed filmmaking. But it has yet to win over the audience African directors most wish to reach—Africans. African filmmakers still face intense competition from European, American, and now Indian film industries, as well as difficulties breaking into the continent's film distribution networks, which are still largely foreign-controlled. Funds are tight for most African film directors, and the political climate in many countries has often precluded free expression. On the other hand, urbanization and the growing number of cinemas in Africa are helping to bring Africans into contact with the medium. International interest in African films, moreover, remains strong; the nomination of the Tanzanian film Maagamizi for a best foreign film Oscar in 2002 further highlighted the success of recent African cinema worldwide. Other breakthroughs—perhaps more of local interest—suggest a broadening of the possibility of film on the continent. In 2008, for example, Manouchka Kelly Labouba became the first woman in Gabon to direct a non-documentary film. In this light Africa's current generation of filmmakers has reason for optimism.

See also DECOLONIZATION IN AFRICA: AN INTERPRETATION.

ELIZABETH HEATH

Cinque, Joseph
1813–1879
African man abducted into slavery who led a rebellion aboard the Spanish slave ship Amistad.

Although Sengbe—pronounced Sin'gway, and later Anglicized as Joseph Cinque—lived for approximately sixty-six years, he is best known for his role in a drama that lasted a little more than three years. Scholars believe that Cinque, who belonged to the MENDE ethnic group, was a married man and father before his abduction. Cinque was born in Sierra Leone and at about the age of twenty-six, he was kidnapped by slave raiders and sold to Portuguese slave traders who took him to Havana, Cuba. There, he and other Africans were resold and put on the AMISTAD. Shortly after leaving Havana harbor, Cinque led a group of slaves who freed themselves and attacked the ship's crew, killing all but two crewmembers. The rebels kept these two alive and ordered them to sail back to Africa. The crewmembers, however, tricked them and sailed north. About two months later, the ship landed on Long Island, New York, where U.S. naval officers arrested the Africans for murder and piracy. The case made Cinque a national celebrity, attracting both praise and condemnation. The proslavery New Orleans Times-Picayune called Cinque a "black piratical murderer," while abolitionists considered him a heroic figure and called him "the Osceola of his race" and a "Hannibal or Othello." Former President of the United States, John Quincy Adams, defended Cinque and the others in court. The U.S. Supreme Court eventually ruled in favor of the Africans and freed them to return to Africa. In November 1841, the thirty-five surviving Africans sailed for Sierra Leone, landing there in January 1842, more than three years after they had been abducted. Little is known of Cinque after his return. Some reports claim that he became a slave trader himself, but there is no documentation of this.

ROBERT FAY

Ciskei
Former bantustan, or Bantu homeland, in South Africa.

One of ten territories assigned to the black majority population of SOUTH AFRICA in the 1950s as part of government's APARTHEID policy, Ciskei, covering 8,495 sq km (3,280 sq mi) between the Keiskamma and Kei rivers in southern South Africa, was one of two so-called homelands set aside for the XHOSA people. The other region was TRANSKEI. Ciskei's capital was Bisho, and the territory also included the towns of Alice, Mdantsane, Middledrift, Peddie, Sada, Whittlesea, and Zwelitsha. In 1994, when South Africa was divided into nine new provinces, Ciskei was incorporated into the province of EASTERN CAPE.

From at least the beginning of the sixteenth century, the region was inhabited primarily by Xhosa-speaking peoples such as the Ndlambe, Nqgika, and MFENGU. These peoples established chiefdoms in the eighteenth century, but in the nineteenth century British colonizers conquered the region in a series of wars. The name Ciskei, which means "this side of the Kei river," was coined by the British to refer to land west of the Kei River. Shortly after the Union of South Africa (later the Republic of South Africa) was formed in 1910, the country's white leaders began to implement national policies of racial segregation. These policies culminated in the 1950s when the South African government divided the black majority according to ethnic identity and defined them as citizens of separate ethnic homelands, or bantustans.

The Bantu Homelands Constitution Act of 1971 gave the South African president the power to establish constitutions and legislative assemblies for any of the bantustans. Once a bantustan had a homeland legislature and an executive council and had held a general election, it was considered to be self-governing. Its administrative body could collect taxes and pass laws relating to certain areas, such as schools, hospitals, and transportation, but all of these laws still required the approval of the South African president. The South African government also retained final control over the bantustan's finances. Ciskei was granted self-governing status in 1972. In 1981 Ciskei achieved nominal independence. In theory, independent bantustans were given complete control over their internal affairs and foreign relations. Some did repeal racially discriminatory laws, but the independence of these bantustans was limited by the fact that the South African government still supplied most of the funding for their budgets and contributed many key civil servants and army officers to the bantustan administrations. Industrial and agricultural development was minimal in Ciskei, and most residents still had to find work in South Africa. Many became migrant workers or commuted several hours each day to jobs outside the bantustan. No other country besides South Africa recognized Ciskei's independence, since recognition would have implied acceptance of the policy of apartheid.

More than two million people were officially Ciskei citizens, but about three-quarters of them lived outside Ciskei in other parts of South Africa. Few black people supported the bantustan system because it meant they were considered primarily citizens of the bantustans instead of citizens of South Africa, even if they had never lived in the bantustans. When a bantustan chose to become independent, its citizens lost their South African citizenship completely. In spite of popular opposition, some black politicians accepted the bantustan system, and the South African government gradually transferred political power to those individuals.

Although Ciskei held periodic elections, power was effectively in the hands of the Ciskei National Independence Party and its leader, Lennox Sebe, who declared himself Ciskei's president-for-life in 1983. A military coup conducted by Ciskei soldiers under Brigadier Oupa Gqozo ousted Sebe in 1990. In March 1994, after several coup attempts, a popular revolt forced Gqozo and the Ciskei government to step down. South Africa's first multiracial elections were scheduled to take place one month later, in April 1994. The Transitional Executive Council, which was overseeing progress toward the national elections, appointed two officials to administer Ciskei temporarily. At the time of the elections, the interim constitution went into effect and dissolved the bantustans. Ciskei was reintegrated into a unified South Africa.

Cissé, Souleymane
1940–
Malian filmmaker; one of the most popular filmmakers in Africa.

Born in Bamako, Mali, Souleymane Cissé became a film devotee as a young child, when his brothers took him to the city's open-air cinemas. By the time he graduated from secondary school, he had already organized a student film group and mastered the skills of a projectionist. In 1962, after seeing a film about Patrice LUMUMBA, former leader of the Republic of the Congo (now the DEMOCRATIC REPUBLIC OF THE CONGO), Cissé decided to become a filmmaker and won a scholarship to the State Institute of Cinematography in Moscow in 1963.

After graduation in 1969, Cissé returned to Mali, where he was hired to make newsreels and documentaries for the Ministry of Information. Three years later he completed his first fiction film, *Cinq jours d'une vie* (1972). This, like all of his subsequent feature films—*Den muso* (The Girl, 1975), *Baara* (Work, 1978), *Finyé* (The Wind, 1982), and *Yeelen* (Brightness, 1987)—won acclaim at international film festivals. Although Cissé's style has been influenced by Soviet social realism and by Italian neorealism, his working conditions have been shaped by the socioeconomic realities familiar to most African filmmakers. "To make a film belongs to the realm of miracle. I have to do everything. I am in turn producer, cameraman and technician. I lend a hand in every area." Despite these constraints, Cissé's productions are praised for their technical sophistication.

His feature films, which portray the conflicts between modernity and tradition through the story of people who have moved from the rural countryside to urban centers, have proven extraordinarily popular in both Africa and France. In fact, *Baara* and *Finyé* were two of the most commercially successful African movies ever on both continents. Among his recent works is *Waati* (1995), in which a South African girl's coming-of-age story evokes all of African history.

In addition to working on his own films, Cissé has been an active member of the FÉDÉRATION PANAFRICAINE DES CINÉASTES and has been leading the effort to increase African film distribution and help new African filmmakers overcome the technical and economic obstacles of their work.

BIBLIOGRAPHY
Stern, Yvan. "Interview: Souleymane Cissé." *Unir Cinema*, Mar./Jun. 1986.

ELIZABETH HEATH

Clapperton, Hugh
1788–1827
Scottish explorer whose account of the region that is now northern Nigeria was the first by a European.
Born in Annan, Scotland, Hugh Clapperton went to sea at the age of thirteen and later became a lieutenant in the Royal Navy. In 1821 the British Colonial Office sent him, along with explorers Walter Oudney and Dixon Denham, on the Bornu Mission to trace the true course of the NIGER RIVER in Africa. They crossed the SAHARA from TRIPOLI, in present-day Libya, and became the first Europeans to see Lake Chad, which Denham set off to explore on his own. From there, Clapperton and Oudney headed west into present-day NIGERIA toward KANO, but Oudney died along the way and Clapperton reached it alone. He then traveled on to Sokoto but, detained by local rulers, was unable to find a guide to take him the 240 km (150 mi) to the Niger. He returned briefly to England before coming back to West Africa in 1825. With British explorer Richard Lemon Lander, Clapperton traveled inland from the BIGHT OF BENIN to the Niger at Bussa and then to Sokoto. Again he was unable to find a guide, this time to help him reach TOMBOUCTOU far upstream (in present-day MALI). After more than a year at Sokoto, Clapperton became ill, reportedly with dysentery, and died in 1827. In an 1830 expedition, Lander succeeded in determining the true course of the Niger, proving Clapperton's theory that it flowed into the Gulf of GUINEA. Clapperton's *Narrative of Travels and Discoveries in Northern and Central Africa in the Years 1822–1823, and 1824* was published in 1828. His second expedition was recounted both in his own *Journal* (1829) and in Lander's *Records of Captain Clapperton's Last Expedition to Africa* (1830).

Clark, John Pepper
1935–
Nigerian poet, dramatist, journalist, and editor.
Born in Kiagbodo, NIGERIA, John Pepper Clark (also known as J. P. Clark-Bekederemo) was raised in the IJAW homeland of southern Nigeria by his maternal grandmother, following his mother's death when he was a baby. At the age of six, his father enrolled Clark in a school in the town of Okrika. After studying at Warri Government College from 1948 to 1954, he studied English at University College in IBADAN where he founded the literary magazine *The Horn*. Clark graduated with honors in 1960.

After a year as a government information officer, Clark became an editorial and features writer for the *Daily Express* in LAGOS. His first play, *Song of a Goat*, a tragedy that drew from Ijaw dramatic traditions, was published in 1961. *Poems*, Clark's first collection of poetry, came out in 1962, the same year he accepted a scholarship to study at Princeton University in New Jersey. Bitterly unhappy in the United States, Clark left school and chronicled his experience in the memoir *America, Their America* (1964).

Back in Nigeria, Clark translated Ijaw epic drama into English, and in 1964 joined the English faculty of Lagos University, where he eventually became a full professor. That same year he published both *A Selection of Poems* and *Three Plays*, which included *Song of a Goat* as well as *The Raft* and *The Masquerade*. Like *Song of a Goat*, the other two plays were lyrical tragedies, written in verse. Another play, *The Ozidi of Atazi* (1966), grew out of Clark's Ijaw research, as did *The Ozidi Saga* (1975).

In 1970 Clark published *Casualties*, a collection of poems written during the Nigerian civil war (1967–1970). Unlike earlier poems, which recalled childhood memories in rhythmic, sensual detail, the verse in *Casualties* was simple and somber. "Show me a house," one poem begins, "where nobody has died/Death is what you cannot undo." Clark, who coedited the literary magazine BLACK ORPHEUS in the late 1960s, has also written scholarly works such as *The Example of Shakespeare* (1970) and *The Hero as Villain* (1978), as well as *A Decade of Tongues: Selected Poems 1958–1968* (1981), *Mandela and Other Poems* (1988), *The Bikoroa Plays: Boats, The Return Home, Full Circle* (1985), and *A Lot From Paradise* (1997). He received the Nigerian National Merit Award in 1991.

See also POETRY, AFRICAN.

Cleopatra

69–30 B.C.E.

Egyptian queen and last ruler of the Macedonian Dynasty of the Ptolemies.

Cleopatra VII was the second daughter of Ptolemy XII Auletes, the king of EGYPT. Although born in Alexandria, Egypt, she was a member of the dynasty of the Ptolemies. Ptolemy Soter, the dynasty's founder, had come from the Greek-speaking region of Macedonia with Alexander the Great and established a kingdom in Egypt after Alexander's death in 323 B.C.E. Upon her father's death, Cleopatra became queen in 51 B.C.E., at the age of eighteen, ruling with her fifteen-year-old brother Ptolemy XIII. Fluent in Egyptian, unlike previous Ptolemies, Cleopatra sought to strengthen her support among Egyptians by claiming she was the daughter of Ra, the Egyptian sun god.

Encouraged by his advisers, Ptolemy XIII exiled Cleopatra and claimed the throne as his own. Cleopatra assembled an army from Syria, but could not assert her claim to the throne until the Roman ruler Julius Caesar arrived. Cleopatra aimed to restore the Ptolemaic Empire, which had once stretched as far as Syria. Realizing Caesar's importance to her struggle, she enlisted his help. The two triumphed in 47 B.C.E. They executed Ptolemy XIII and restored Cleopatra to joint rule with her younger brother, Ptolemy XIV.

During the conflict Caesar and Cleopatra became lovers, out of love or political ambition. When Caesar returned to Rome in 46 B.C.E. Cleopatra went with him. In Rome, Cleopatra gave birth to a son, Caesarion, reputedly Caesar's. She was still in Rome when Caesar was assassinated in 44 B.C.E. Cleopatra then allegedly poisoned her brother, Ptolemy XIV, and returned with little Caesarion to Egypt, where she named him coregent.

Caesar's apparent successor, Mark Antony, met with Cleopatra in 41 B.C.E. The two fell in love, and Antony went with Cleopatra to Egypt, where he treated her as the ruler of an independent nation. In 40 B.C.E., when Antony returned to Rome to marry Octavia, the sister of Octavian (later Caesar Augustus), Antony's rival in Rome, Cleopatra gave birth to twins.

Antony began a campaign against the Parthians in present-day Iran in 36 B.C.E., and Cleopatra joined him at Antioch, where they married. Antony earned the enmity of Rome for this betrayal of Octavia. After his victory against the Parthians Antony returned to Alexandria, where he and Cleopatra plotted the conquest of Rome and the creation of a shared empire with their shared offspring as heirs. Octavian declared war on Antony and Cleopatra. At the Battle of Actium in 31 B.C.E. Octavian's fleet fought the combined forces of Antony and Cleopatra. In the middle of the battle, however, Cleopatra recalled her fleet, and she and Antony sailed for Alexandria. There, she sent a false report of her death to Antony, inducing him to kill himself. She then attempted to form a relationship with Octavian, but failed. Realizing that he intended to parade her in Rome as a spoil of war, she killed herself, either by taking poison or by inducing a poisonous asp to bite her. Shortly afterward Octavian ordered Caesarion killed, and the Ptolemaic Dynasty, which Cleopatra had worked so hard to maintain, ended.

The historical record of Cleopatra's life and death is scant, some say because Roman rulers wanted to erase the memory of her. Scholars have offered differing interpretations of her life and what it signified, but she has continued to capture the imagination of scholars and dramatists.

See also ALEXANDRIA AND GRECIAN AFRICA: AN INTERPRETATION; CLEOPATRA: AN INTERPRETATION; EGYPT, ANCIENT KINGDOM OF.

ROBERT FAY

Cleopatra: An Interpretation

"Cleopatra was an Egyptian woman who made herself into an object of gossip for the whole world," or so Boccaccio, the Renaissance humanist, wanted his readers to believe. But Boccaccio formed his opinion of her from classical Roman writers, and Cleopatra was the enemy of Rome. She was the last pharaoh of Egypt, but when Julius Caesar was assassinated in 44 B.C.E. she was living in great state in Rome. Cleopatra was Caesar's lover and she had a son by him. Twenty years later she would join Mark Antony in his opposition to Octavian (later known as Caesar Augustus).

Together they would make a bid to establish an eastern empire to rival Rome.

Issues of politics and desire are at stake in representing Cleopatra. In her image they are fascinatingly entwined and collapsed into each other, which is one reason why the figure of Cleopatra has survived so strongly as a term in cultural exchange and has been reworked so often. Its power to generate and sustain fantasy is exceptional. More than eroticism is involved: it is a question of the status of the story of Cleopatra as a founding myth in Western culture.

This is not too strong a way to put it. Cleopatra lived and, more important, died at a moment from which our era has often traced its origin. Augustan Rome, with its architecture, law, literature, and history, has been acknowledged as the source of an ideal of civic order. It has been bound together in the Western mind with another watershed, the lifetime of the founder of Christianity. It was the decree of Augustus "that all the world should be enrolled," as the New Testament story reminds us, and that was why Jesus was born in Bethlehem, away from his hometown of Nazareth. Privileged secular texts have supported the same identification. Scholars commenting on Virgil's fourth *Eclogue*, in which he writes of the birth of a new age, once readily saw in it an intuitive acknowledgment that the world was being transformed not only by the rule of Augustus but by the advent of a divine being, Jesus. Milton opens his *Ode on the Morning of Christs Nativity* by affirming this dual identification.

All this would associate Cleopatra only contingently with the moment of origin, but there is reason to connect her with it more intrinsically. It was after the defeat of Cleopatra that Octavian founded his own rule. From the year he broke her power and indirectly brought about her death, in 30 B.C.E., he established a new authority for himself in Rome. To mark it he took a new name, Augustus. It would have been usual to have September, the month of his birth, renamed to match. Instead, he ordered that the month renamed in his honor should be the one in which he brought down Cleopatra, which is why we still call the eighth month August. Other gestures reinforced the implication that the rule of Augustus rested on the defeat of Cleopatra. As pharaoh, Cleopatra had ruled over a North African country where the values and the ways of living were very different from Roman ones: the poets and historians of Augustus reviled her culture and jeered at Egyptian religion, naming Cleopatra herself "the harlot queen."

This leads to the argument that Cleopatra and her story have the weight of an origin myth in Western culture, and used in metaphor, they are specially disposed to illumine the place of women in the social order, particularly African

women. They are charged with the power to generate fantasy as a function of their historical positioning. Stories that account for the status quo are spun out of them. Some versions of Cleopatra made during the Renaissance and the Reformation in Europe were inflected by the moves to subordinate women within the household and within marriage. In these examples the figure is shaped and perceived in relation to current attempts to institute a particular regime of domestic power. Later Cleopatra was shaped by different struggles: around the place of women in intellectual debate in the eighteenth century or the creation of women as dreamers and shoppers in the nineteenth.

By its status as originary myth, the figure of Cleopatra is also aligned with an important component of the individual unconscious. As a female figure, situated at the opening of the constituting narrative of a culture, Cleopatra's meaning in representation inevitably overlaps with the figure of the mother in individual history. Both are found at the beginning of memory itself, at the point of the foundation of identity. The term Cleopatra locates the notion of a woman's body and the notion of authority together. This combination readily maps onto the figure of the mother in the unconscious, the trace of early experience when the mother's power is supreme and her body is the horizon of desire. It is usual to consider the pleasure of Cleopatra's body in terms of the adult sexuality with which it is conventionally associated. It is also helpful to think of it in terms of the multiple desires of the child, which find their satisfaction and their emblem in the mother's body.

This does not mean that Cleopatra has often been represented literally as a mother. Quite the reverse. Not until some twentieth-century works does the fact that Cleopatra actually gave birth to four children receive much attention. When I relate the figure of Cleopatra in representation with the figure of the mother in the unconscious I am addressing the question of desire as Cleopatra has been used to represent it. My point is that by no means all the desires with which Cleopatra is associated in representation are sexual. Historical and political analysis, which expands the local and specific meanings brought into play in images of Cleopatra, also makes it plain that the issue of sexual desire, however variously conceived, does not necessarily govern or orchestrate the way the figure is represented. In Venice, for instance, in the eighteenth century, Tiepolo used the figure of Cleopatra as a sign of Newtonian looking, while in Paris, one hundred years later, it is made both by Gautier and Delacroix into the sign of the revolutionary past, suppressed under the current regime.

There are indeed matters of desire at issue here, though it is not sexual desire that is primarily at stake in these examples. Conflicting attempts to satisfy the desire to understand, to represent, and to interpret appearances animate Tiepolo's usage. In Paris it was the desire to restore the memory of a shared past with its hope for a new political order. These desires are social, and relate to the bonds of the community, its organization, and the exchange of meanings that goes on within it. The figure of Cleopatra has been appropriated in representations as a site where attempts at cultural self-understanding can take place.

In September 1991 the popular American journal *Newsweek* wanted to air some issues associated with Afrocentrism and its reinterpretation of the past. They did it under the heading "Was Cleopatra black?" The front cover showed the head of an Egyptian queen from a temple relief with a bright modern earring fixed to the stone ear. The figure of Cleopatra was invoked to bring into focus the challenge, if not the threat, implied by rethinking Western culture from an African American perspective. The earring hung on it was carefully selected: shaped like a map of Africa and striped with the red, black, and green of Black Nationalism in America, it is one that black Americans can buy and wear today.

This move is in decided contrast with earlier treatments of Cleopatra, where the question of her non-European ethnicity is rarely foregrounded. Notions of the oriental or the exotic were brought into play by Boccaccio during the Renaissance and Gautier in the nineteenth century, for example, but Tiepolo's eighteenth-century Cleopatra is created as a blond Venetian, waited on by blacks. The question "Is Cleopatra black?" is actually formulated and uttered in Cecil B. DeMille's *Cleopatra* (1934), but is put into the mouth of an ingénue, who is ridiculed.

It was not until the nineteenth century that Cleopatra's name began to be associated in art with the question of slavery, and through it, with the question of blackness. When the writer Théophile Gautier and the painter Eugène Delacroix produced their own Cleopatras in Paris in the late 1830s, both represented her in close association with dark-skinned men. For these Frenchmen, working nearly fifty years after the French Revolution, Cleopatra was a reminder of aspirations that had died with the defeat of the revolution— hopes of a reformation of the social order, hopes of new civil rights for all (including women), and plans for the institution of divorce and for the abolition of slavery.

In the United States, where race was a more charged and immediate issue, Cleopatra's image was brought into even closer dialogue with anxieties about slavery. There is a white marble statue of Cleopatra standing in the garden court of the Metropolitan Museum of Art, made by the American sculptor William Wetmore Story. Cleopatra is seated, lost in thought, her right elbow resting on the back of her chair and her right wrist supporting her head. For an early twenty-first-century viewer, there is nothing in her features to suggest any particular racial identity. Since her gown has slipped off her left shoulder, leaving her left breast uncovered, attention is diverted from her face to her torso, particularly her pelvic region, which is emphasized not by nakedness but by the layers of sculpted folds that cover it from direct view. When I learned that, at its first public showing in 1862, reviewers could applaud this image as an accurate sculpture of a *black* woman, such blithe identification of Cleopatra as black by highly cultivated nineteenth-century Americans—the very identification that causes such consternation today—gave me pause. I realized that they must have been picking up special cues about how to read this statue. It was Nathaniel Hawthorne, the American novelist, who provided the answer. Hawthorne knew Story in Rome, when both were living among a community of expatriate Americans. In his novel *The Marble Faun*, Hawthorne included an account of how Story created his Cleopatra, which became famous as a guide to interpreting the statue. According to Henry James, who wrote the first biography of Story, visitors would arrive in the sculptor's studio armed with Hawthorne's novel and read aloud from it as they viewed. The account implies that the sculpture is best understood by traveling down through the surface of Egyptian details and clothing to the body beneath, a body that is described as Nubian, "with a smouldering furnace at its heart."

Hawthorne understood that Story was using Cleopatra to invoke black female sexuality and to hold that sexuality in contempt. According to Hawthorne, Story's statue shows Cleopatra in despair after failing to seduce Octavian: it depicts a black woman's lust rejected by a European man. The image invokes the precedent of Augustus in order to reemphasize a contempt for the alien woman from Africa that he had deliberately fostered so long before. For Americans at least, by 1860 it was apparent that the order of authority that kept women, European men, and slaves in their respective places was under threat. Story's image was arresting in part because it offered a tacit rebuttal of the charges of sexual exploitation laid against white men by showing a black woman as a disappointed seductress. If sexual contact ever did take place between men and their female slaves, the men were not the ones to blame, or so the statue seemed to imply.

Cleopatra seems to be an indispensable term in the way Western civilization, including American democracy, imagines itself. Rewriting her and reframing her story has always accompanied political moves, concerning issues that are rooted not in the historical past at all but in the present. That is how I read the debate over Cleopatra's race that erupted in the American academy in the mid-1990s and was given a wide airing in the media. That argument was conducted in terms of genealogy; Mary Lefkowitz led the classical scholars who insisted, against the counter-arguments of Afrocentrists, that Cleopatra could not have been black. Classicists repeated that Cleopatra was not an Egyptian but a Ptolemy, that is, a member of the Greek dynasty that had been ruling Egypt for the previous 300 years. But "Momma's baby, Poppa's maybe," as we know, it has always been futile to count on paternity, and recent technological advances that have enabled genetic testing have only confirmed this. Many men have been shown not to be the father of children they were supposed to have sired. Over the space of 300 years, who knows what strains have been introduced into a family's genes? In America it used to be said that even one drop of Negro blood made a person black. Maybe we need to ask ourselves why highly intelligent people like these classicists waste their time in pursuing an argument where any proofs must be so lacking in substance.

Afrocentrism is not in essence an intellectual movement, but a form that vernacular Black Nationalism takes in America today. It is not going to be stopped by intellectual arguments. Afrocentrism is charismatic, it is on the street. The argument over the race of Cleopatra, carried out among white people and the intellectuals who define the terms of discussion, is an occasion in which the Afrocentrism of urban blacks can be discredited and brought into contempt. This serves a useful political function, for it discredits their thinking, their culture, and their way of life, very much in the way that the Egyptians were discredited under Augustus. Egypt was a very rich country at that time; just as in the case of antiquity, it is wealth and resources that are at stake in America today. Decisions about who is going to have access to wealth and to resources are being made partly in the name of Cleopatra. Class, as much as race, is the real but unacknowledged stake in these public contests for intellectual authority.

It is no coincidence that the most recent public debates over Afrocentrism took place when the U.S. Congress was in the process of passing bills intended to withdraw economic support from the unemployed, the sick, and welfare mothers. The poorest people in this society, the ones who will be the hardest hit by these changes, are disproportionately black. In the urban ghettos, they are currently facing a new and bleaker deprivation. If we believe it is important to understand our own history rather than simply repeat it, we should note that when the welfare bill was up for discussion, its stringent provisions were justified precisely by reference to culture: contemptuous evocations of the "culture of poverty" and the "culture of dependency." We might almost think of today's "welfare queen" as the latest version of Cleopatra, the woman who has been attacked for over 2,000 years for her independence. Today's Cleopatra rides around in a Cadillac instead of the barge that looked to Enobarbas like a burnished throne. It is mothers, the mothers who might speak on behalf of the poorest of America's children, who are most firmly silenced in the name of Cleopatra today.

See also AFROCENTRICITY; ALEXANDRIA AND GRECIAN AFRICA: AN INTERPRETATION; EGYPT, ANCIENT KINGDOM OF.

BIBLIOGRAPHY

Hamer, Mary. *Signs of Cleopatra: History, Politics, Representation.* Routledge, 1993.

MARY HAMER

Climate of Africa

The precipitation and wind conditions of Africa are shaped by topography, latitudinal position, global wind patterns, and the moderating influence of oceans. Africa's climate, therefore, varies both regionally and over time.

TOPOGRAPHY

Compared to other continents, Africa is flat. Yet since air temperature decreases with elevation by as much as 6.4° C per 1000 m, the continent's few mountainous regions, even those along the equator, can be quite cold. The plateaus and mountains south and east of the CONGO RIVER Basin, which average between 1,000 and 3,000 m in elevation, exemplify the moderating influence that elevation has on direct solar angle. Africa's landscape also differs from other continents by its lack of a major chain of mountains, such as the Rocky Mountains in North America and the Alps in southern Europe, which define distinct climatic regions by fully dividing masses of land. In Africa the discontinuity of mountain ranges and the large unobstructed stretches of land give wind patterns an especially important role in the determination of regional climate.

WINDS

Blowing in patterns shaped by the earth's rotation around its axis and its alignment with the sun, winds tend to converge at the equator in a narrow strip called the intertropical convergence zone (ITCZ). Due to high equatorial temperatures, air in the ITCZ heats and rises, creating the humid, rainy, low-pressure system that typifies equatorial climates. Rising air circulates away from the equator and moves toward the poles, forming a higher, oppositely oriented layer above the ITCZ winds. This higher stratum descends around the Tropics of Cancer and Capricorn, causing high-pressure systems that are dry and windy. The friction caused by these two patterns of air—one atop the other—explains much of the weather between the equator and the Tropics: humidity at one end, dryness at the other, with thunderstorms and variable weather between. The ITCZ moves seasonally as the hemispheres shift in their relative distance from the sun. In the summer of the Northern Hemisphere, the ITCZ moves northward, bringing with it increased rains. In the winter, it dips below the equator while winds sweep the north. Because oceans and mountains affect the motion of the ITCZ, it moves across different regions (even of the same latitude) at different times; likewise, its speed varies from region to region. The ITCZ's passage over East Africa, for example, produces a very short rainy season. Other regions experience bimodal—or twice annual—rains: the first as the ITCZ moves poleward, the second as it returns. The dry winds that originate in the tropical high-pressure systems blow toward the equator and in some places have a great influence on animal life, including that of humans. In the Northern Hemisphere these northeasterly winds originate in Asia, bring little water and much dust, and are called the Harmattan. Although the phenomenon is mirrored in the south, southeasterly winds—which hail from the oceans instead of a dry landmass like Asia—are milder.

LATITUDE

Because Africa straddles the equator symmetrically, meteorological patterns in the Northern Hemisphere roughly mirror those in the Southern Hemisphere. The perennially warm and humid weather in the equator supports rainforests that thin to savannas outside the narrow band of ITCZ humidity. As high-pressure systems arise at the Tropics, savannas dwindle into desert. The SAHARA in the north has its analog in the KALAHARI DESERT and NAMIB DESERT in the south. Africa is the most tropical continent, as the majority of its area falls between the Tropic of Cancer and the Tropic of Capricorn. Accordingly, the sun shines directly, and most of Africa is hot. About 30 percent of the continent experiences temperatures above 38° C, and very few regions, for very short periods of time, experience daytime temperatures that approach freezing. In many other regions the high average temperature leads to high rates of evaporation and can severely limit agriculture.

OCEANS

In addition to tempering the force of southwesterly winds in the Southern Hemisphere, the oceans moderate temperature in much of coastal Africa. Because it takes more heat to raise the temperature of water than it does to raise the temperature of land, the oceans take much longer to change temperature than does land. Furthermore the natural dissipation of heat energy causes warm currents to flow toward the poles and polar currents to flow toward the equator. Coastal temperatures, therefore, tend to be more moderate than temperatures inland, even where other variables, such as latitude and elevation, are equivalent. The moderating effect of water appears in a less dramatic form along the shores of Africa's larger lakes, such as LAKE VICTORIA and LAKE TANGANYIKA.

CLIMATIC ZONES

Roughly speaking, Africa's climatic zones fall into three broad categories: humid equatorial, dry, and humid temperate. Within these zones, altitude and other localized variables produce distinctive regional climates. Humid equatorial climate conditions prevail in West and Central Africa around the equator itself; along the Guinea Coast, in GABON, CAMEROON, DEMOCRATIC REPUBLIC OF THE CONGO, northeastern REPUBLIC OF THE CONGO and surrounding countries; and in East Africa about 5° south of the equator in TANZANIA, MOZAMBIQUE, and MADAGASCAR. Average monthly temperatures remain around 25° C. The regions nearest the equator receive year-round rainfall (the foothills of Cameroon Mountain sometimes receive more than 10,000 mm annually), while those north and south of it experience short dry winters and a lower average annual precipitation. Away from the equator the dry season lengthens, though climate may remain mostly humid. Where the dry seasons are long enough, equatorial regions give way to dry or semi-arid regions. In the north the SAHEL stretches from east to west through MALI, NIGER, CHAD, and SUDAN and borders the Sahara. In the south, a similar region surrounds the Kalahari and fills the interior. Annual rainfall seldom exceeds 500 mm even as temperatures exceed those at the equator, sometimes reaching 45° C. In the deserts themselves, rainfall is even scarcer and temperatures more extreme. Although the daytime temperatures in the desert are high, due to the lack of vegetation and humidity, nights can be extremely cold. In fact, daily temperature fluctuation in arid regions often far exceeds variation in average monthly temperatures. The northern coast and southern tip of Africa diverge from the pattern outlined above, where rainfall diminishes in relation to the region's distance from the equator. Because of oceanic and latitudinal moderation, these regions experience temperate or Mediterranean weather, including dry summers and wet winters. Finally, climate in some parts of the continent is strongly affected by localized topographic or wind conditions. These include the cooler mountainous regions as well as the semi-arid regions in East and Southeast Africa. The latter is explained by the short rainy seasons and the presence of Madagascar, which blocks oceanic winds.

VARIABILITY: PAST, PRESENT, AND FUTURE

The climate of Africa varies cyclically over periods of decades, centuries, and millennia as well as from year to year. For many Africans annual variations both in the timing and duration of the rainy seasons are the most important, because they affect the availability of water for agriculture and livestock. The precise relationships between deforestation, desertification, and drought are debated, but it is clear that recent climate change in Africa reflects human as well as nonhuman causes. Indeed, meteorological records over the last 150 years indicate a cooling and drying trend that can only partially be explained by the impact of humans. Over the long term, Africa's climates have changed dramatically. Since the breakup of Gondwanaland the earth has formed ice caps and Africa has cooled and dried considerably. As recently as 6,000 years ago, the region that is now the Sahara abounded with life—and Nile crocodiles can still be found in oases that lie separated from the river by hundreds of kilometers of inhospitable clime.

See also BIOGEOGRAPHY OF AFRICA; DROUGHT AND DESERTIFICATION; GEOMORPHOLOGY, AFRICAN; NILE RIVER.

BIBLIOGRAPHY

Adams, W. M., A. S. Goudie, and A. R. Orme. The Physical Geography of Africa. Oxford University Press, 1996.

ERIC BENNETT

Clitoridectomy

See FEMALE CIRCUMCISION IN AFRICA.

Clothing in Africa

As elsewhere, clothing in Africa has long served more than one purpose. In addition to satisfying human needs for covering and adornment, textiles and clothing provide media for artistic expression for weavers, dyers, tailors, and clothing designers. For centuries, textiles and garments have been produced both domestically—for household and village community members—and commercially, for bartering or sale. Although the earliest cloth was made primarily of local natural fibers, today's African textiles and clothing incorporate a wide variety of materials and styles.

The precise origin of cloth production in Africa is lost in time, but archaeological findings indicate some of the earliest sites. Drawings of looms can be seen in the tombs of ancient EGYPT, dating back to at least 2000 B.C.E. Archaeologists have found linen remnants in ancient Egypt, as well as fifth-century cotton cloth remnants in Meroe, in northern SUDAN. In West Africa, woven fiber pieces dating back to the ninth century C.E. have been found in NIGERIA, and woven cotton cloth dating to the eleventh century has been recovered in MALI. Evidence of loom use in MAURITANIA dates back to the eleventh century.

CLOTHING IN AFRICA. Models display handwoven Kente clothing from Ghana in a parade celebrating Nairobi's centennial in 1997. The parade included both modern and traditional African clothing. (*Sayyid Azim/AP images*)

TRADITIONS OF CLOTH PRODUCTION AND DESIGN
Bark cloth, or cloth made from tree bark, predates the development of woven textiles in most parts of Africa. Today it is rarely used for day-to-day clothing, but some societies use it for ceremonial costumes. The BAGANDA of UGANDA, for example, make fabric from the inner bark of fig trees, which is worn during ceremonial dances and other occasions when ancestors are being honored. Early clothing in Africa was also made from treated animal hides, furs, and feathers.

Many African societies weave cloth from locally grown cotton. In North Africa and the SAHEL, women also spin and weave camel and sheep wool. Other sources of fiber include the raffia palm in Central and West Africa, jute and flax in West Africa and MADAGASCAR, and silk in Nigeria, Madagascar, and East Africa. All these fibers can be dyed using vegetable and mineral dyes.

The two main kinds of textile looms in Africa are the double-heddle loom, used for narrow strips of cloth, and the single-heddle loom, used for wider pieces. The narrow strips are typically sewn together, then cut into patterns for clothing. The double-heddle loom is generally used only by male weavers, who use it to weave in colored threads and create richly textured fabrics. In addition, weavers in North Africa and in ETHIOPIA also use ground looms, while looms similar to those used in Southeast Asia are found in Madagascar.

Although Africa's weavers produce a wide variety of patterned, colored fabric, they also weave plain cloth. This cloth can either be used "as is" for daily wear around the home, or it can be decorated. Common fabric-decorating techniques include appliqué designs, sewn on in contrasting fabrics; embroidery with brightly colored threads; and dyeing.

Two of the most popular dyeing techniques in Africa are tie and dye, and resist dye. In tie and dye, designs are first tied or stitched into the cloth, using cotton or raffia threads. In resist dye, dyers draw on the cloth using an impermeable substance, such as candle wax or paste made from cassava, a tuber. Artisans then dip the fabrics into solutions typically made from vegetable dyes, which color all but the covered areas. Indigo plants are used for deep blue dyes, while reddish brown dyes are extracted from Kola nuts, the camwood tree, and the redwood tree. Greens, yellows, and blacks are prepared from other sources.

Most designs and motifs used to decorate fabric have names. Many designs are associated with particular plants, animals, events, or proverbs, and are often used in other crafts, such as house painting, carving, and pottery. Others incorporate Arabic script, Roman letters and numerals, or line drawings of contemporary objects, such as bicycles

and cars. Traditional cloth production, in other words, is not only highly varied from place to place but is also influenced by societal and technological change.

In many African societies, men and women are responsible for different stages of cloth production. The gender division of labor, however, varies widely by region, and in many places has changed over time. For example, in Mali, women used to dye bogolanfini mud-cloth, but today young unemployed men in urban areas have taken up this craft. They typically produce lower-quality cloth, which is sold to tourists or exported. Indigo dyeing is women's work among the YORUBA and the SONINKÉ of West Africa, but among the HAUSA, fabric dying is traditionally a men's craft.

Commercial textile and clothing production has a long history in some parts of Africa. In TUNISIA, weavers and dyers as early as the tenth century C.E. organized guilds in order to protect their business. By the fifteenth century, the dyeing pits of KANO, NIGERIA, were renowned as far north as the Mediterranean coast. They are still in operation today. In Kano as in many other precolonial centers of commercial textile production, the city's political elite were among the weavers' and dyers' most important clientele. Royal patronage fostered the development of special luxury cloths. The court of King Njoya of Baumun in present-day CAMEROON, for example, produced especially fine examples of raffia-stitched tie and dye. The ASANTE court in KUMASI, GHANA, supervised the production of silk *kente* cloth (described below).

CLOTHING TRADITIONS ACROSS THE CONTINENT
In North Africa, nomadic pastoralists in mountainous regions weave animal wool into thick cloth for tents, blankets, rugs, and cushions. The mouchtiya is a capelike shawl worn by married women, and like other clothing materials is woven on vertical looms. Across North Africa, both Arab and BERBER influences are apparent in textile designs and clothing styles.

In the highlands of Ethiopia and ERITREA, Amharic and Tigrean women wear kemis, cotton dresses with fitted bodices, long sleeves, and full skirts. The shamma, a light shawl, is thrown over the head and shoulders. A border of woven or embroidered geometric designs highlights the otherwise white cloth. The designs include variations of the cross motif, which is central to the ETHIOPIAN ORTHODOX CHURCH. Men also wear the shamma, as well as shirts and baggy knee-length pants made of the same white cloth. In colder weather, people of this region have traditionally wrapped themselves in a heavy woven blanket (kutta) or cape (bornos). When it rains they don a *wollo*, a cape made from finely woven grass. Farther east in the Horn of Africa, the pleated skirts and tight embroidered trousers and veils worn by Islamic Somali, Harari Oromo, and Argobba women reflect influences from the Indian subcontinent, cultivated over centuries of trade across the Indian Ocean.

Pastoral societies in the lowlands of the Horn of Africa, such as the Boran, make some of their own clothing out of goatskin. The women wear leather or cotton skirts trimmed with beads, metal rings, cowrie shells, and ostrich eggshell beads, and sometimes painted with cow blood. The cotton woven here is multicolored and striped, not unlike the kikoi cloth found along the SWAHILI COAST of East Africa.

In the SAHARA and SAHEL regions of West Africa, TUAREG men wrap their heads in a distinctive blue veil. The indigo-dyed wrap is put on during the initiation ceremonies marking the end of boyhood, and thereafter is rarely removed. The indigo from the veil and accompanying robes rubs off onto the skin, hence the Tuareg's nickname, the "blue men." The Tuareg have traditionally purchased their indigo cloth from Hausa traders in markets along the Sahara's southern edge.

Elsewhere in West Africa, men in many societies weave cotton cloth in long narrow strips, which are then stitched into large pieces. Among the Asante, the men wrap the long piece of cloth around the waist and then loop it over the shoulder, toga-style. Baggy pants that are tight around the lower leg are popular, as are elaborately embroidered, full-length robes. Women across West Africa commonly tie a long wrap around the waist, accompanied by a wide sash, a matching blouse, and a head wrap.

The Yoruba of Nigeria prepare an indigo-dyed cotton called adire eleso. The artists sew finely detailed patterns onto the cloth using raffia or cotton thread, then take the cloth to a dyer, known as an aloro, who, it is said, works under the protection of the Yoruba spirit Iya Mapo. Similar techniques are also used farther west, among the WOLOF, the Soninke, and the MANDINKA, and as far south as the Kasai region in the DEMOCRATIC REPUBLIC OF THE CONGO.

Yoruba women cloth makers, known as aladire, use resist dye methods to make adire eleso. They use cassava paste to paint or stencil repeated abstractions of animals and plants onto the cloth. After dyeing the cloth indigo-blue, they beat it with a wooden stick until it attains a bright glossy sheen. BAMBARA women in Mali also use the resist technique to produce a speckled blue fabric, while Soninke women coat cloth in paste and then run a comb through it, to create a wavelike design after dyeing.

The colors and designs of the adobe architecture found in TOMBOUCTOU and other older cities in Mali are reflected in the Bambara's famous ochre-colored bokolanfini, or mud-cloth fabrics. Women first dye the cloth yellow with a vegetable extract, then carefully paint the cloth with specially prepared mud. After the mud is washed off, the designs appear in yellow against a dark brown background. In the final step, dyers apply bleach to the yellow parts to change them back to the original color.

In Ghana, cloths sewn from narrow cotton strips are either kept white or dyed reddish brown with a dye obtained from the bark of the kuntunkuni tree. The artist then divides the cloth into blocks, and uses stamps made out of calabash shells to decorate the fabric with designs, many of which are associated with proverbs. The finished cloth is worn toga-style by AKAN and EWE men.

Perhaps the most famous fabric produced in Ghana is kente, which was traditionally made by tailors of the Asante court, using European silk acquired first through trans-Saharan trade and later coastal trade. Richly colored and textured fabric, kente was once worn only by Asante royalty, but it has now become an international symbol for Africa. It is worn throughout the African diaspora as an acknowledgment of one's roots on the continent. Outside of Ghana, it is still difficult to find large pieces of high-quality hand-woven kente. But cheap, mass-produced copies of kente designs—often printed rather than woven—are now sold worldwide.

One of the most distinctive textiles produced in Central Africa is raffia cloth. Men weave fibers from the leaves of raffia palm trees into squares that vary in size according to length of the fibers. Tie and dyeing, weaving, cut-pile embroidery, and appliqué are all used to decorate the fabric with geometric designs. The squares are sewn edge to edge into larger pieces, which can be used for dance skirts and for burial cloths. Raffia cloth production has largely died out in more heavily populated areas along the coast, but today the KUBA of the Kasai region continue to weave and decorate raffia cloth for use during funerals.

FOREIGN INFLUENCES

African societies have long incorporated imported materials, textiles, and styles into their own clothing traditions. For centuries, trans-Saharan trade caravans carried cloth back and forth between the city-states of the West African savanna and North Africa. After Europeans began plying Atlantic trade routes around the continent, they too participated in the textile trade. Certain kinds of cloth, in fact, served as currency in West Africa, to be exchanged for slaves or gold. In East Africa, foreign textiles arrived on ships that worked the monsoon trade routes between the Gulf of Arabia, India, and East Asia.

Beginning in the sixteenth century, Portuguese traders frequented the southern African port of Lourenço Marque (now MAPUTO, MOZAMBIQUE), bringing glass beads to exchange for ivory and gold. The NDEBELE people used the beads to decorate leather skirts and cloaks, as well as to make thick hoop necklaces, bracelets, and anklets.

In the late nineteenth century, a new cloth became popular on ZANZIBAR, an island city-state with a long history of transoceanic trade. During the 1870s enterprising Swahili women began to sew brightly colored imported handkerchiefs known as lesos into larger pieces of fabric, which were called kangas. Six lesos were cheaper than one piece of imported fabric of the same size. The textile industries in Manchester, England, and in Holland soon caught on to this new market and began manufacturing similarly sized single cotton pieces that were intended to be sold in pairs. The kangas were worn mainly by women eager to establish their emancipated identity after the abolition of slavery on Zanzibar. They wrapped one kanga around the waist, another around the upper body, and a third around the head and thrown over the shoulder, covering the body in the Muslim fashion. The most popular kangas had proverbs and other sayings printed at the bottom. Kangas are now widely worn in East Africa; most are either produced by domestic industries in KENYA or Tanzania, or imported directly from South or East Asia. Just as at the turn of the century, customers are always in search of new designs and new printed proverbs.

In West Africa, nineteenth-century European traders found large markets for factory-produced wax-printed cloth. The designs of this cloth imitated hand-dyed batik textiles, which the Dutch East India Company began importing from Java in the seventeenth century. West African women wore "dutch wax" wraps (called pagnes in Francophone countries) much like women in East Africa wore kangas.

Today, most independent West African countries' domestic textile industries manufacture cloth decorated with "dutch wax" prints as well as other designs. These factories commonly produce special runs on request, to commemorate holidays or events. Genuine dutch wax cloths are still imported from Europe and are both prestigious and costly. Despite their foreign origin they are widely recognized as African fabrics. A large proportion of both the urban and international trades in dutch wax cloths is controlled by women traders based in West African cities such as LOMÉ, TOGO, LAGOS, NIGERIA, and ABIDJAN, CÔTE D'IVOIRE. The most successful of these traders are known as "Mama Benzis," a reference to their Mercedes Benz cars and other symbols of wealth.

British and Dutch merchants were not the only Europeans who encouraged Africans to adopt new clothing styles during the colonial era. Christian missionaries expected converts to wear modest European-style clothing. During World War I (1914–1918) and World War II (1939–1945), pamphlets used during recruitment campaigns in the colonies featured pictures of soldiers smartly dressed in khaki shorts and shirts. Most colonial-era schools (like many today) required students to wear uniforms, similar to the blouse and skirt (for girls) or shorts (for boys) ensembles worn by European schoolchildren.

CONTEMPORARY TRENDS

Given the association of Western-style dress with the colonial powers, it is hardly surprising that many African anticolonial movements of the 1940s and 1950s made elements of traditional clothing symbolic of their campaign toward independence. Kenya's Jomo KENYATTA wore a beaded *ogut tigo* hat and a beaded leather belt, while Ghana's Kwame Nkrumah encouraged educated nationalists to wear the fugu, a waist-length tunic worn by the common man. At independence, many new republics designed a national dress, intended to unite the diverse peoples within their borders. In the former Democratic Republic of the Congo, Mobutu Sese Seko's *authenticité* campaign urged Zaireans to return to "authentic" African clothing styles.

Contemporary African governments and political leaders still exercise important influences over popular clothing styles. Kangas and kitenges have become wearable billboards, with special-edition designs promoting national health campaigns such as family planning, or celebrating presidential birthdays and national holidays. After Thomas SANKARA came to power in BURKINA FASO in 1983, he declared locally-woven cotton the national fabric and required civil servants to wear it. In southern Africa, men's "Kaunda suits" are named after Kenneth KAUNDA, the former president of ZAMBIA. In SOUTH AFRICA, Mangosutho Gatsha BUTHELEZI, head of the ZULU-dominated INKATHA FREEDOM PARTY, encourages supporters to wear the skins and headdresses of Zulu warriors at public events. Nelson Rolihlahla MANDELA's taste in brightly colored shirts made them fashionable when he served as the country's president from 1994 to 1999.

Economic conditions and changing technologies are also influencing African clothing styles. Currency devaluations carried out under structural adjustment economic reform programs have made imported materials and clothing more expensive, but markets for used clothing ("fripperie" in Francophone countries) remain consistently strong. A significant proportion of the used Western clothing sold in Africa was originally donated to charities in the United States and Europe.

Whether new or secondhand, Western clothing is considered fashionable in contemporary Africa. So, too, are "new traditional" clothes, which mix traditional fabrics and styles with synthetic materials and Western designs. For example, Yoruba weavers of the traditional *aso oke* fabric now incorporate lurex and rayon threads into their fabric. In Mali, tailors use bogolanfini mud-cloth to make European-cut blazers, vests, and caps. Often tailors' customers, especially women, commission outfits using locally bought cloth, but based on imported patterns or designs copied from fashion magazines.

Growing appreciation for handmade African fabrics, both as pieces of art and as materials appropriate for high-fashion clothing, bodes well for the survival of traditional skills. Contemporary artists such as Nike Davis, Senabu Oloyede, and Kekekomo Oladepo of Nigeria use indigo dyed *adire* cloth in tapestries that explore modern themes. In Mali, Pama Sinatoa in DJENNÉ and Ismael Diabaté, and the Groupe Bogolan Kasobane and the Atelier Jamana in Bamako have won renown for their bogolanfini clothes, while Chris Seydou used bogolanfini-inspired textiles in his contemporary clothing styles. In NAIROBI, KENYA, the African Heritage Gallery commissions clothing and jewelry that draws on traditional styles from all over the continent.

See also CHRISTIANITY: MISSIONARIES IN AFRICA; PASTORALISM; SOMALIA.

BIBLIOGRAPHY

Clarke, Duncan. *The Art of African Textiles*. Thunder Bay Press, 1997.
Picton, John, and John Mack. *African Textiles*. Harper & Row, 1989.
Polakoff, Claire. *Into Indigo: African Textiles and Dyeing Techniques*. Anchor Press/Doubleday, 1980.

MUHONJIA KHAMINWA

Coastal Resources in Africa
Natural resources along the African coast and their management.

Relative to other continents, Africa has steep coastlines and few broad coastal plains, beaches, or natural harbors due to its central position in the super-continent Pangaea 225 million years ago. Coastal resources are not only limited, but also unevenly distributed. Approximately one-quarter of Africa's modern states are landlocked and, as a result of the distance from the sea, ancient West African empires used cowrie shells (*Cypraea moneta*) as currency. The continent's geomorphology has affected its human history. Africa's narrow continental shelf of around 15 to 100 kilometers and generally warm water (20 to 25 degrees Centigrade) limit the potential for marine fisheries. Exceptions include nutrient rich areas of colder (9 to 14 degree Centigrade) waters, such as the Benguela Upwelling System off southwestern Africa and the Canary Current coastal upwelling region off West Africa. The Benguela's icy waters and dense fogs create a so-called skeleton coast—shipwrecking conditions alongside the Namib Desert. As elsewhere in the world, improvements

in fishing gear and vessels and increasing numbers of fishers have contributed to degradation of habitat and stagnating fish production. Significant marine resource extraction also comes from European and East Asian factory trawlers operating both legally and illegally in Africa's 200-mile Exclusive Economic Zone, which is difficult to patrol. Other than marine life, the most important coastal resources are hydrocarbons (oil and gas), mangrove forests, diamonds, coral reefs, and commercial products from trees planted in the coastal zone. Cloves, copra, cocoa, gum copal, and palm oil are among the more important tree products. Extraction of oil and diamonds, the most valuable resources, has been highly contested, associated with bloodshed, and has sparked human rights and environmental movements in Africa. Perhaps best known is the effort of Ken SARO-WIWA to inform the world of the effects of multinational oil companies' activities on the Ogoni people and the NIGER RIVER delta in NIGERIA. Population growth is a major driving force in the alteration of the coastal zone, especially since the middle of the twentieth century. Industrial development and urbanization threaten water quality and public health. In many coastal areas, the felling of mangrove stands for construction material and fuel has been associated with the increasing salinity of agricultural lands and nursery ground habitat loss for juvenile shrimp, fish, or oysters. In the 1970s, the tightening of environmental legislation in North America and Western Europe encouraged transnational corporations to seek inexpensive alternatives for waste disposal. Coastal West African people suffered the health consequences of contaminated water supplies until the Basel Convention on the Control of Transboundary Movements of Hazardous Waste and their Disposal (1989) made it more difficult to sell hazardous materials to countries without proper waste management facilities. Inefficient division of responsibility between national, provincial, and local authorities, and a shortage of funds has resulted in inconsistent and often contradictory approaches to coastal zone management, although the 1990s heralded new marine legislation and the development of integrated coastal management plans along East Africa's SWAHILI COAST as well as in SOUTH AFRICA and elsewhere to more effectively monitor and respond to rising coastal populations, water shortage, and other threats. The 1990s also brought more technologically complex approaches to development in Africa. Geographic Information Systems (GIS) databases support coastal planning in such diverse locations as Senegal, South Africa, and from Somalia to Tanzania; however, computer-based management approaches tend to rely heavily on external funds. Coastal tourism in Africa is on the rise, but remains limited. The Red Sea includes of some of the world's best coral reef dive sites, but modest infrastructure, political instability, and concerns over terrorism have kept visitor levels to SUDAN and ERITREA quite low. Similarly, beaches in North Africa do not attract as many visitors as they could due to safety concerns. In East Africa, sea wall construction and removal of natural vegetation is contributing to beach erosion and threatening the nesting sites of marine turtles. Marine parks and reserves have been established for conservation in Africa and generate income from tourism, but parks have had varied success. Some exist more on paper than reality where insufficient funds or their misuse prevent wardens and rangers from effective monitoring and enforcement activities. In several countries, a small but growing aquaculture sector serves the tourist sector and earns much-needed hard currency through exports. In Africa as elsewhere, if the future includes further degradation of coastal resources it may be very difficult for countries to attain their desired economic growth. In addition, the potential long-term effects of global warming and the rise in sea level need to be more fully understood.

BIBLIOGRAPHY

Akyeampong, Emmanuel Kwaku. Between the Sea and the Lagoon: An Eco-Social History of the Anlo in Southeastern Ghana, c. 1850 to Recent Times. Ohio University Press, 2001.

Hauck, Maria, and Merle Sowman, eds. Waves of Change: Coastal and Fisheries Co-Management in South Africa. University of Cape Town Press, 2003.

McClanahan, Timothy R., Charles R. Sheppard, and David O. Obura, eds. Coral Reefs of the Indian Ocean: Their Ecology and Conservation. Oxford University Press, 2000.

HEIDI GLAESEL FRONTANI

Coetzee, J(ohn) M(axwell)

1940–

South African writer, known for his novels set in South Africa during and after apartheid.

"In South Africa there is now too much truth for art to hold," writer John Maxwell Coetzee said of his home country in 1987, "truth by the bucketful, truth that overwhelms and swamps every act of the imagination." These words foreshadowed the coming decade in SOUTH AFRICA, when APARTHEID collapsed and the nation struggled with the truth about its past. Coetzee's remark also provides insight into his own writing, which for more than twenty years has depicted the brutality of apartheid and its psychological effects.

J. M. Coetzee was born in CAPE TOWN, South Africa, into a middle-class family with roots that stretched back to the original Dutch settlers and more recent English immigrants. He received undergraduate degrees in both English and mathematics, as well as a M. A. degree in English from the University of Cape Town. In 1965 he went to the University of Texas at Austin, where he completed a doctorate in linguistics.

Living in the United States during the Vietnam War (1959–1975) provided Coetzee material for his first novel, Dusklands, published in 1974. The work actually contained two novellas, "The Vietnam Project" and "The Narrative of Jacobus Coetzee," which together dealt with the imperialism of both the United States and South Africa. Coetzee followed three years later with the experimental In the Heart of the Country (1977). Written as a series of numbered paragraphs narrated in the first person, present tense, the novel draws the reader inside the mind of a young white woman who, driven mad by her desolate life in rural South Africa, describes killing her father not once, but twice.

Coetzee published his most celebrated novel, Waiting for the Barbarians, in 1980. In the words of critic David Attwell, this work focused on "that moment of suspension when an empire imagines itself besieged and plots a final reckoning with its enemies." Coetzee probed the psychology of both the well-meaning but ultimately complicit rural magistrate and the chilling torturer in dark glasses who has been sent to suppress alleged "barbarian" unrest. Waiting for the Barbarians was published during a time when such figures were all too true to life: the antiapartheid activist Stephen BIKO had died at the hands of his prison torturers three years earlier.

Coetzee's next novel, Life and Times of Michael K (1983), is considered his most political, portraying the brutality of civil war in South Africa through the story of a man named Michael K. Rather than creating a hero, Coetzee created an ambiguous character—a gardener of uncertain race whose life is swept up in the war taking place around him. The work won the Booker Prize, Britain's highest literary award. Foe (1986), a retelling of the story of Robinson Crusoe, developed the metaphor of inarticulation. A character that critic Gayatri Spivak called the "wholly other," Coetzee's Friday is a black man who has had his tongue cut out. Here Coetzee points toward that which is unsaid and unspeakable—a metaphor for the disempowered voices outside of the dominant story of history. Such a theme was particularly relevant in South Africa, where the apartheid government not only controlled the history taught in schools, but censored all other voices of dissent.

The question of authorized voice continues in the Age of Iron (1990). As a woman dies of cancer, she speaks from what Coetzee called "a private death" about the public world of South Africa's townships. Coetzee's next work, The Master of Petersburg (1994), is set in nineteenth-century Russia and retells, with some liberties, the life of Russian novelist Feodor Dostoyevsky. Coetzee published a memoir, Boyhood: Scenes from Provincial Life, in 1997. He won his second Booker Prize for *Disgrace* (1999), a novel about a professor and his grown daughter who struggle to cope with the changing realities of post-apartheid South Africa. In 2003 Coetzee received the Nobel Prize for Literature. He served as a visiting professor of social thought at the University of Chicago until the end of that same year, at which point he retired and relocated to Australia, where he became a citizen. His most recent work includes *Slow Man* (2005), *Diary of a Bad Year* (2007), and a collection of essays titled *Inner Workings: Literary Essays, 2000–2005*.

See also TRUTH AND RECONCILIATION COMMISSION.

MARIAN AGUIAR

Cold War and Africa

Ideological and political confrontation between the United States and the Communist Union of Soviet Socialist Republics (USSR), which lasted from 1945 to 1989 and had major effects on African countries.

During the Cold War both the superpowers, the United States and the USSR, sent large amounts of military aid to Africa, supported undemocratic African governments, and directly and indirectly sponsored wars that led to millions of African deaths through fighting and war-related famines. Although the Cold War was for the most part peaceful in Europe and North America because of the balance of military power between the superpowers, the superpowers fought through proxies in Africa and left deep scars on the continent.

AFRICA AT THE END OF WORLD WAR II

World War II (1939–1945) devastated much of the world but also created opportunities for African people to push for an end to COLONIAL RULE. Thousands of Africans had fought in the war, and many African war veterans felt entitled to the promises of freedom and democracy that had motivated the war effort of the Allies (France, Great Britain, the United States, and other countries). The United Nations (UN), which was founded in the aftermath of the war on the lofty ideals of universal respect for human dignity, supported self-determination (political independence) for colonial territories. The United States, which emerged after World War II as the most powerful country in the world, also stood for self-determination. But the United States remained opposed to apparent Soviet efforts to forcibly control parts of Europe and to exert Communist control over countries in other parts of the world, including Africa. Though the USSR also called for self-determination, it sought to curb the influence of the United States and to limit the spread of capitalism. Leaders of both the USSR and the United States found themselves in the contradictory position of advocating self-determination for

Africa and other parts of the world while at the same time aggressively interfering in the affairs of African countries when it was seen as necessary to stop their superpower rival.

SUPERPOWER RIVALRY IN AFRICAN COUNTRIES

Superpower competition in Africa was motivated primarily by expansion of global political, economic, and military influence. Most European powers granted independence to their African colonies in the late 1950s and 1960s, opening the region to influence by the Soviet Union and the United States. Both superpowers looked to African countries in order to control vast mineral resources, to place military bases in strategic locations, and to increase overall global influence. The motivations of the United States and the USSR did diverge, however. Although the United States and its allies were particularly eager to have access to Africa's mineral resources and to ensure access to strategically placed military bases, the Soviet Union had enough mineral wealth for its own needs and even for export. As a result, the Soviet Union gave ideology and military strategy greater significance than it gave economic objectives in Africa. Despite the difference in motivation, a zero-sum competition—in which a gain for one country is always a loss for the other—became an end in itself. The Cold War rivalry was further complicated by the fact that some African leaders tried to exploit the situation by inviting superpower involvement to counter any advantage gained by their African adversaries in the opposing Cold War camp. The former Portuguese colonies of MOZAMBIQUE and ANGOLA provide examples of this. Both achieved independence in 1975 with Soviet bloc-leaning governments, and both governments were opposed by rebel groups that sided with the West in order to receive military aid from the United States and its allies. Similar diplomatic maneuvers were common across the continent in the second half of the twentieth century. This political competition among Africans themselves provided further opportunities for foreign intervention. China also played a role in the Cold War in Africa, especially in the 1960s and 1970s. Although China and the Soviet Union shared roughly the same Communist objectives, an ideological rivalry emerged between the two powers in the early 1960s. China's diplomatic contact with Africa, which began with the establishment of its first African diplomatic mission in CAIRO, EGYPT, in 1956, was initially based on supporting African revolutionary movements. From the mid-1960s to the 1970s, China's foreign policy focused on competition with the Soviet Union for leadership of poor countries and the Communist world. After the death of Chinese leader Mao Zedong in 1976, China's domestic concerns assumed precedence over rivalry with the Soviet Union in Africa.

MILITARY AID AND MILITARY INTERVENTION

Both the United States and the Soviet Union usually avoided direct military action. More often they provided military aid to African countries—such as weapons, training, and nonlethal equipment such as trucks and uniforms—and built military bases. The United States was a major supplier of arms and military expertise to a number of African states, including ETHIOPIA, GHANA, KENYA, LIBERIA, MOROCCO, SENEGAL, and SOMALIA. The Soviet Union, however, served as the continent's principal arms supplier. Soviet military aid to African countries south of the SAHARA totaled $18.9 billion from 1981 through 1988, as compared with only $1 billion from the United States in the same period. The U.S. had a stronger presence in North Africa, however, as Egypt became second only to Israel as a recipient of American aid, following the 1978 Camp David Accords between Egypt and Israel. About two-thirds of Soviet arms in the mid-1980s went to East Africa, mainly Ethiopia, Somalia, TANZANIA, and UGANDA. Southern and Central Africa came next, receiving 17 percent of Soviet arms, which went mainly to Angola. Soviet deliveries to West Africa, largely GUINEA, MALI, and NIGERIA, totaled about 11 percent. Other recipients included BENIN, REPUBLIC OF THE CONGO, GUINEA, GUINEA-BISSAU, and ZAMBIA. Soviet military involvement in Africa was therefore far more extensive than that of the United States, which preferred to give economic and financial assistance to further its interests rather than provide direct military aid. In a few cases, both the Soviet Union and the United States provided direct support for armed conflicts, creating proxy conflicts between the Communist and anti-Communist worlds. In SOUTH AFRICA, for example, the Soviet Union and its allies provided weapons and training to Umkhonto we Sizwe, the armed wing of the antiapartheid African National Congress (ANC) that operated out of countries bordering South Africa. The ANC was allied with the SOUTH AFRICAN COMMUNIST PARTY, so for much of the Cold War the United States supported the deeply anti-Communist, white-minority government in South Africa. In Angola, the United States provided funding and training for the National Union for Total Independence of Angola (Unita) rebel movement in an effort to topple the Soviet-backed government controlled by the Marxist Popular Movement for the Liberation of Angola (MPLA). The billions of dollars in Cold War military aid had an extraordinary cost. Foreign intervention in Africa's internal conflicts raised the level of violence, cost millions of lives, displaced scores of millions of people within state borders, and forced several million into refuge across the borders. In Angola alone, the

civil war took the lives of more than 500,000 people and forced an estimated 3.6 million to become refugees. Military conflicts inspired or influenced by the Cold War also occurred in CHAD, Ethiopia, Ghana, Guinea-Bissau, Kenya, Mozambique, South-West Africa (now NAMIBIA), Nigeria, RWANDA, Somalia, South Africa, SUDAN, Uganda, and WESTERN SAHARA. Although some of these conflicts might have been easier to resolve without foreign intervention, a lack of intervention might have resulted in an unjust status quo such as the system of APARTHEID in South Africa.

ECONOMIC AND POLITICAL INFLUENCES

Superpower rivalry for economic and political influence in Africa went in tandem with military competition. Both the United States and the Soviet Union tried to build economic and political relationships with African countries that would complement the Cold War military objective of controlling key strategic "choke points." As with the military ties, economic and political ties changed when African regimes shifted their political loyalties. Ethiopia under Mengistu Haile Mariam shifted from the West to the Soviet bloc, for example, and Somalia under Mohamed SIAD BARRE shifted first toward the Soviet bloc and then toward the West. Assistance shifted with the geopolitical tide of alignment. The countries that received the most U. S. economic assistance and political backing included Ethiopia (until the late 1970s), Kenya, LIBERIA, Somalia, Sudan, and Zaire (now DEMOCRATIC REPUBLIC OF THE CONGO). Support usually went to individual leaders who allied themselves with the United States or otherwise followed the capitalist model. These Cold War alliances sometimes meant that the United States would continually reward loyal allies with financial and political support while ignoring rampant corruption and human rights violations. In Zaire, for example, the United States supported the brutal and deeply corrupt regime of MOBUTU SESE SEKO because he was seen as a strong regional ally against Communism. The more common pattern, however, was for the United States to help fund economic development in African countries that supported the United States in the Cold War, even though many of these countries were not democratic. In Kenya, for example, the United States offered economic aid and technical advice that favored free-market reforms and overlooked the sometimes undemocratic policies of the government of Daniel Arap MOI. The Soviet Union, on the other hand, encouraged African countries to follow the socialist model and offered assistance to its ideological and economic allies. The USSR especially favored so-called revolutionary states that promised to work for radical social transformation. In practice, many of these countries were no more democratic or egalitarian than most countries supported by the United States. Countries receiving extensive Soviet support included ALGERIA, Angola, Ethiopia (beginning in the late 1970s), and Mozambique. Somalia and Sudan in the late 1960s and early 1970s also became part of this group of socialist states when they shifted their allegiances to the Soviet Union and its allies. Only two capitalist-oriented states, MOROCCO and Nigeria, received economic assistance from the Soviet Union, which hoped to capitalize on these countries' regional influence. In comparative terms, the United States offered far greater levels of economic assistance than did the Soviet Union. From 1970 to 1976, for example, while the United States provided direct aid totaling $2 billion to sub-Saharan Africa, the Soviet Union provided only $200 million. But neither superpower was very successful in sponsoring sustained successful economic development in its Cold War African allies. On the whole, the embrace of Communism or free-market principles in Africa shifted as priorities changed from liberation to development. Armed anticolonial liberation struggles required military support, which the Soviet bloc readily provided. When many liberation movements won independence for their countries in the 1970s and 1980s, they had to shift their emphasis from military preparedness to economic and social development. Many countries that received Soviet support for their liberation struggles decided to favor socialism after independence, arguing that it could be better adapted to suit the conditions of Africa. Although so-called AFRICAN SOCIALISM differed in some ways from socialism as it was practiced in the USSR, the commonalities fostered cooperation with the Soviet bloc. (Some countries, notably BOTSWANA, CÔTE D'IVOIRE, and Kenya, favored the capitalist model from the start.) But African socialism had few successes, and many avowedly Communist countries embraced a capitalist strategy when the communist model proved a failure. Although the public sector continued to play a major role in the economies of these countries, privatization and the market economy increasingly gained ground and eventually triumphed with the collapse of the Soviet empire and its political and economic ideology.

EFFECTS OF THE COLD WAR
The costs of African conflicts during the Cold War can be estimated in a variety of ways. Loss of lives, including those by war-related famines, is the most obvious. Between 1945 and 1989, African wars related to the Cold War took the lives of about 5.5 million people, mostly civilians. More difficult to assess are economic, social, and cultural losses due to the overall devastation of the country. Civilian populations, especially farmers and other food producers, were often the primary victims. In many countries Cold War conflicts aggravated existing food shortages caused by drought and poverty. In the mid-1980s a massive drought struck much of Africa, and ongoing wars in Angola, Ethiopia, Mozambique, and Sudan transformed the drought into a full-scale famine that took more than one million lives. Cold War-related fighting also caused massive population shifts in Africa, creating an estimated 10 million internally displaced persons (refugees within a country) and about 4.3 million international refugees. In addition, Cold War conflicts also disrupted education and health care and inflicted serious physical and psychological wounds on many of the survivors. The wars also resulted in gross violations of human rights, including, rape, torture, and illegal imprisonment. In some countries the chaos of these wars also led to a breakdown in community ties, cultural integrity, and social cohesiveness. The Cold War also took a toll on many African countries because they spent money on their militaries that might have been better spent on schools, roads, hospitals, clinics, and other badly needed services. Although precise estimates are almost impossible to make, at the peak of the superpower rivalry in the late 1970s annual military spending by African governments averaged about $23 per person. Between 1960 and 1986, military expenditures increased from more than $1 billion to nearly $13 billion. This represented an increase in military spending from 0.9 percent to 3.6 percent of gross domestic product. The dedication of resources to the military meant less money for health care, education, and other important priorities. In the late 1970s, for example, for every 100,000 African people there were 290 soldiers but only 46 doctors. Africa's five largest wars during the 1980s cost around $100 billion. Annual expenditures on weapons rose from $1.2 billion in the period from 1950 to 1952 to about $15 billion by 1979.

LEGACY OF THE COLD WAR
The principal legacy of the Cold War is that it introduced and consolidated a new form of dependency on the African continent. Colonialism had incorporated the continent into a dependency based on the global market economy (which relied on Africa for inexpensive commodities such as coffee) and on European political rivalries. When African countries won independence after World War II, nearly all these countries found themselves in a new dependence based on political and economic rivalry between the two superpowers. Political, economic, and military conflicts in African countries became intensified by the fact that all such conflicts around the world were viewed as part of a larger confrontation between the superpowers. The United States and the Soviet Union did not hesitate to involve African countries in their global contest, often at serious cost to the newly independent African countries.

This meant that many African leaders, rather than seeking legitimacy from their people through representative democracy, relied on authoritarian rule backed by foreign powers. Some countries continue to feel the lingering effects of the Cold War. In Mozambique, for example, hundreds of thousands of land mines laid during Cold War conflicts still littered the countryside in the late 1990s, killing dozens of civilians every year and maiming dozens more. In Angola, the Cold War–inspired civil war raged through the late 1990s, despite international mediation efforts. Hostilities did not formally cease until 2002, after the death of Unita leader Jonas Malheiro SAVIMBI. In most countries, however, the end of the Cold War began to reverse these tendencies toward dependence and excessive military expenditures. With the strategic withdrawal of the superpowers, Africa's problems came to be perceived in a more limited regional context, and responsibility for their solutions was shifted to the Africans themselves. Wider global political conditions continued to affect Africa but with far less searing consequences than during the Cold War. In the view of many analysts, this post–Cold War dynamic challenged all African countries to assume primary responsibility for their own political and economic destiny. In this view, the levels of responsibility can be seen as a pyramid, with the African states themselves at the bottom and with subregional organizations such as the Southern African Development Community (SADC) and the Organization of African Unity (OAU) at the next level. But Africa is an integral part of the global community. This means that at the top of the pyramid—which represents final responsibility for the peace, security, and prosperity of humankind—must be the international community, specifically the United Nations.

Colonial Rule

Policies, problems, and legacies of European colonial rule in Africa, which began in the late nineteenth century and lasted until the 1960s.

European colonization of Africa followed a long history of contact between the two continents. Ancient Egyptian trade in the Mediterranean predates recorded history, and contact between Europe and other parts of North Africa dates back to the Greco-Roman period. Not until the fifteenth century, however, did the Portuguese establish trading posts on the sub-Saharan African shoreline. Although some early ports, such as CAPE TOWN, became permanent settlements, the majority served as little more than entrepôts for the exchange of African and European goods. Over the next 400 years Europeans acquired slaves, gold, ivory, and later agricultural commodities from coastal traders and rulers, but—with the exception of SOUTH AFRICA and a handful of Portuguese holdings—made few attempts to settle or otherwise control the

FRENCH COLONIAL RULE IN CHAD. Charles de Gaulle is greeted by Governor-General Félix Éboué in Chad, a French colony from 1910 to 1960. (*Prints and Photographs Division, Library of Congress*)

interior. By the second half of the nineteenth century, however, rapidly industrializing European economies needed reliable access to natural resources, new markets for their manufactured goods, and new sites for the investment of finance capital. The vast, mineral-rich African continent had the potential to offer all three.

Earlier European conquests of Asia and the New World had demonstrated the risks and costs of colonial occupation, leaving most late-nineteenth-century European rulers initially reluctant to attempt the same in Africa. It would certainly have been easier and cheaper to maintain established trade relations with the African merchants and rulers who, since the abolition of the transatlantic slave trade early in the nineteenth century, had been transporting vast quantities of agricultural commodities—cocoa, peanuts, palm oil—to coastal towns such as PORTO-NOVO and DAKAR. But African middlemen (and women) were not always amenable to the Europeans' terms of trade, and African rulers were in many cases preoccupied by internal power struggles and wars with neighboring states. Equally important, European powers viewed the quickening pace of their own neighbors' trade and exploratory expeditions in Africa—such as Richard BURTON's voyages through East Africa, French expeditions up the

GERMAN COLONIAL RULE IN KAMERUN. Colonial troops outside the German Government Station in Ebolowa, West Africa. (*Prints and Photographs Division, Library of Congress*)

river NIGER, and Heinrich BARTH's travels throughout central and northern Africa—as an indication that preemptive action was necessary, before a rival power established claims to valuable territory.

Thus, during the late nineteenth century SCRAMBLE FOR AFRICA, even leaders with little prior interest in colonization, such as German Chancellor Otto von Bismarck, staked claims to the continent. Meanwhile, Christian missionaries' calls for European intervention to end African slavery and "barbaric" practices (such as human sacrifice in the EARLY KINGDOM OF DAHOMEY) provided a moral rationale for European political and economic ambitions. These ambitions were officially legitimated and negotiated at the BERLIN CONFERENCE OF 1884–1885, when European leaders agreed to partition the African continent into neatly bordered spheres of influence. Rapid conquest and treaty making followed. By 1900, fewer than thirty years after the scramble had started, almost 90 percent of Africa was under European control.

Just as quickly, European powers were confronted with the basic problem of colonial occupation: how to rule effectively and cheaply over a foreign subject population? Although metropolitan governments clearly had to invest in the initial occupation, it was anticipated that colonial administrations would become self-sufficient. In other words, they were expected to establish a system of rule that would generate revenue but not revolt. European colonial powers struggled to find this ideal system for the next half-century.

CONCESSIONARY COMPANIES

One of the earliest approaches to colonial rule in Africa was to delegate the task to one or more "concessionary companies." In German East Africa (present-day mainland TANZANIA), French Equatorial Africa, and the Belgian King Leopold's Congo (later the Belgian Congo, present-day DEMOCRATIC REPUBLIC OF THE CONGO), for example, the metropolitan powers granted private companies large concessions of territory for economic activities such as mining, rubber-tapping, plantation agriculture, and railroad construction. The companies were typically also allowed to set up their own systems of taxation and labor recruitment. Although the concessionary system allowed European governments to occupy and exploit vast regions with a minimum of state financing and personnel, it proved untenable as a long-term solution. Especially in Central Africa, companies' use of forced labor and brutal discipline decimated regional populations, provoked public outrage in Europe, and often generated none of the anticipated profits. By the early twentieth century, most European governments were limiting the powers of the concessionary companies and establishing their own colonial administrations.

DIRECT RULE

Most discussions of colonial rule distinguish between "direct" and "indirect" rule. Although the defining principles of the two forms of rule differed considerably, in practice direct rule administrations—most of which were in French colonies—incorporated elements of indirect rule, especially during the later colonial era.

Under direct rule, colonies were divided into districts administered by European appointees. In FRENCH WEST AFRICA the chief district administrator, the *commandant de cercle*, was responsible for regional tax collection, labor and military recruitment, public works, education, local court cases, and the execution of dictates handed down from the colony's governor. Although Africans staffed the lower levels of the commandant's bureaucracy, most of the top officials were European. The commandant was also expected to maintain public order and discourage offensive or "backward" local customs. Thus direct rule was seen as a means of "civilizing" as well as controlling African populations.

Frequently, regional administrative borders cut through preexisting African politics and ethnic communities. In parts of French West Africa, these borders marked a deliberate policy to divide and weaken militarily powerful groups such as the BAULE and the FON, who for years had resisted foreign occupation. Another part of this policy, at least in the years during and after conquest, was a campaign to dethrone the "great chiefs" of these and other African kingdoms and replace them with more malleable appointees. In general, these traditional authorities were viewed not only as political threats but as obstacles to the "civilizing mission" of direct rule.

Direct rule encountered at least three practical problems. First, European governments lacked the personnel needed to administer their African colonies effectively. Although schools of colonial administration were well established in Europe by the early twentieth century, debilitating diseases and harsh climates discouraged officers from seeking posts in Africa. European colonies often had fewer than one colonial officer for every 22,000 Africans, as was the case in KENYA in 1921. The Belgian Congo had a mere 2,384 officials for an African population of 9.4 million; French West Africa, with an African population of 15 million, employed only 3,660 French personnel.

Second, these administrators were responsible not only for large subject populations, but for vast territories. Travel over long distances was slow and arduous, and communication difficult. As a result, colonial governors had little contact with remote areas, where district administrators often proved incapable or uninterested in carrying out the dictates of their superiors.

Finally, colonial officials' limited knowledge of local languages and customs, combined with their often total lack of legitimacy, undermined their ability to recruit labor, collect taxes, or carry out other administrative duties effectively. In the end, both the "great chiefs" and local village chiefs—both of which had greater legitimacy and more local-level contacts—proved indispensable to the project of colonial administration. For all these reasons, most European powers began to modify their approach to colonial rule in the early twentieth century.

INDIRECT RULE

The alternative method, first adopted by the British, was to rule indirectly through "traditional" African authorities. The logic of indirect rule was first articulated by F. J. D. LUGARD, the high commissioner of the British protectorate of Northern NIGERIA. Based on his observations of the SOKOTO CALIPHATE and the EARLY KINGDOM OF BUGANDA, Lugard recommended that colonial powers take advantage of existing African authority structures. In his book *The Dual Mandate in British Tropical Africa*, Lugard argued that Africans were better off ruled through their own traditional systems and in accordance with the customary laws of their own tribe. Under indirect rule, tribal authorities rather than European personnel would be given responsibility for regional administration and justice. Assumed to represent the highest of Africans' abilities, these kings and chiefs were expected to draw on customary laws to maintain obedience and public order, while also encouraging their subjects to appreciate modern European values.

Lugard emphasized the moral qualities of indirect rule, but it also offered—at least in theory—a number of practical advantages. Foremost, it promised to be cheap: African chiefs could raise the money for their own salaries from their own subjects. Indirect rule also appeared safer and more effective: by co-opting the chiefs' inherited legitimacy, European colonial powers hoped both to improve their ability to carry out routine functions, such as tax collection and labor recruitment, and to avoid large-scale revolts.

Above all, indirect rule assumed the sanctity of the tribe. In much of French West Africa, colonial administrations that had spent years trying to break down tribal authority structures ultimately sought to rehabilitate them. Besides locating and strengthening traditional authorities, colonial administrations endeavored to identify and delineate each tribe's homeland and customs. Often, they called on missionaries and anthropologists for assistance.

Indirect rule worked best in the regions where strong and highly organized states were already in place, like Northern Nigeria, and where the recognized authorities, like the Sokoto caliph, welcomed European collaboration. On the whole, however, erroneous assumptions about the nature of tribal identity, authority, and customary law undermined the effectiveness and ultimately the sustainability of indirect rule.

Fundamental to the logic of indirect rule, for example, was the belief that Africa was comprised of hundreds of mutually exclusive, geographically distinct, and centrally ruled "tribes." In reality, African cultural identities were complex and dynamic. African polities also varied enormously in size and structure, from the hierarchical, multiethnic kingdoms of KONGO, Buganda, and Dahomey and the Sokoto Caliphate, to the loosely federated chieftaincies of the HAYA people, to the village-based chiefdoms and councils of "stateless" peoples such as the Baule in the CÔTE D'IVOIRE, the IGBO of Nigeria, and the NYAMWEZI of Tanzania. Nomadic groups, such as the BERBERS and TUAREGS of West Africa, also confounded European efforts to assign Africans to "tribal homelands."

European colonial officials handled the ambiguities by imposing their own categories and by inventing tribal authority structures where none existed. In 1930 the British administration of Tanganyika (present-day Tanzania) issued the *Native Administration Memorandum on Native Courts*, which defined tribes as "cultural units possessing a common language, a single social system, and an established customary law." Assuming that German colonialism must have destroyed Tanganyika's tribal kingdoms, the British administration grouped disparate communities of SUKUMA people under a centralized chief. In LIBYA the Italian administration randomly divided the BEDOUINS in 1929 and appointed them to tribes and subtribes. In RUANDA-URUNDI the Belgian government assigned Africans passes labeling them as either "Hutu" or "Tutsi," thus creating a rigid distinction between previously contextual identities.

Identifying "authentic" tribal authorities proved no less complicated. Where there was no obvious tribal ruler, colonial administrations summarily appointed one—typically a cooperative village "big man." Some nonhierarchical peoples, such as the Sagara of present-day Tanzania, were placed under the authority of a neighboring kingdom—in their case, the Zaramo—and expected to adopt its language and customs. In Kenya, MAASAI religious leaders were appointed as chiefs, even though they had not previously held administrative responsibilities. In SENEGAL the French, despite concerns about the potential for mass Islamic resistance movements, reinforced the power of the MARABOUTS (or holy men) of the Mourides brotherhood, largely because of their capacity to mobilize large numbers of young disciples for peanut farming.

Even where European colonial powers had no trouble identifying chiefs and kings, they were not always satisfied with them. In Dahomey, the French replaced three "independent-minded" rulers within the first ten years of colonial rule. In Southern Rhodesia (present-day ZIMBABWE) in 1927, the British administration abolished hereditary rights of succession and assumed the power to appoint chiefs, thereby minimizing the chances of chiefly disobedience. Elsewhere, chiefs considered unsuitable were replaced with others deemed more authentic. In southern Upper Volta (present-day BURKINA FASO), for example, the French replaced the KONG Jula they had originally appointed as canton chiefs with members of a local Zara clan (neither, in fact, had a long history of political domination in the region). Colonial administrators' ongoing efforts to find compliant local authorities meant that kings and chiefs enjoyed little job security.

However tenuous their employment, many African rulers were granted unprecedented powers by colonial administrations, often at the expense of preexisting judicial and advisory bodies. In precolonial SWAZILAND, for example, the king's power was checked by both the queen mother and a council composed of royal family members, village headmen, and commoners. Under British rule, women and commoners were excluded from the council, and the king's decisions were subject to approval only by the British administration. In many parts of Africa, chiefs were expected to allocate land and adjudicate local disputes, both responsibilities that had previously often belonged to lineage heads or village councils. Backing up chiefs' new powers was the implicit threat of military force, provided by colonial armies and police.

It soon became clear that this arrangement was susceptible to abuse. As George PADMORE, the Caribbean Pan-Africanist, observed in 1936, "The chief is the law, subject to only one higher authority, the white official stationed in his state as adviser ... No oriental despot ever had greater power than these black tyrants, thanks to the support which they receive from the white officials who quietly keep in the background." Some chiefs took advantage of their powers to collect additional taxes, recruit extra labor for their own plantations, and extract exorbitant tributes and services from their subjects. One German official in Tanganyika, for example, estimated that many chiefs were collecting seven times the required tax, and keeping the surplus. In the 1920s, the British and French attempted to prevent chiefs from taking excessive cuts from local revenue by giving them fixed salaries. In general, however, chiefs known to be corrupt who were otherwise cooperative were usually allowed to remain in office.

Not all chiefs abused their powers, of course, but most found their legitimacy tested by the duties of their office. Collecting taxes, requisitioning crops, recruiting youths for compulsory labor service and military service—only the most gifted leaders managed to carry out these tasks without provoking resentment, rebellion, or flight. In colonial Upper Volta, for example, tens of thousands of MOSSI youths responded to their chiefs' efforts to recruit them for road and agricultural projects by fleeing south to the Gold Coast (present-day GHANA).

Finally, colonial administrations' efforts to impose indirect rule were confounded by the ambiguities of so-called "customary law." Lugard and other administrators assumed each "tribe" possessed a set of stable, universally understood laws. In fact, many African societies' laws were contested and often changing, and the era defined by Europeans as "traditional Africa"—the nineteenth century—was a period of extraordinary upheaval. Shaka Zulu's conquests in southern Africa, the formation of the Sokoto Caliphate in West Africa, the rise of the trading empires of MSIRI and TIPPU TIP in East and Central Africa, and the holy wars of North Africa—all had altered the political landscapes as well as belief systems across the African continent.

Whether or not customary laws were actually very old, most were not written down. As a result, colonial administrators consulted with chiefs, elders, missionaries, and anthropologists, all of whom described customs according to their own views and interests. Chiefs, for example, had an interest in strengthening their own authority to tax and fine subjects, while elders typically benefited from laws that allowed them control over youths and women. Missionaries often argued for the preservation of certain customs (as did anthropologists) but emphasized the injustices of those that interfered with their own evangelical objectives, such as arranged marriages.

Faced with a hodge-podge of often-contradictory accounts, European officials codified those customary laws that seemed most likely to assure their own political, economic, and social objectives. Others they rejected entirely. In Rhodesia, for example, British commissioners were scandalized to learn that NDEBELE women were allowed to marry whom they pleased. Assuming that the group's traditional laws must have been "forgotten or swept away," the colonial commissioner brought in a copy of the Natal Native Code of 1891 (first applied in the Natal colony of present-day South Africa) to teach them how to behave like traditional Ndebele. Colonial administrations outlawed other customs that offended European sensibilities, such as slavery, but were often unable to enforce or uninterested in enforcing their own prohibitions.

Although the institution of customary law helped colonial officials win the cooperation of customary authorities, it did not prevent ongoing challenges to those authorities, especially at the local level. As the expansion of transportation systems and the market economy provided new opportunities for individual mobility and employment, formerly dependent members of rural communities—women and young men, in particular—often contested or simply disregarded the customary laws that dictated to whom they owed labor or who they could marry. Village chiefs and elders found it increasingly difficult to exert control over their own kin members. Especially after World War II, high rates of urban migration placed more and more Africans outside the jurisdiction of customary law and into workplaces and social settings where they participated in growing nationalist movements. The stability that customary law was supposed to provide was fleeting at best.

LEGACIES

By the late 1940s it was clear that colonial rule in Africa could only be sustained at an unduly high cost. As the European powers prepared for DECOLONIZATION, Africans across much of the continent gained voting rights and increased representation in colonial legislatures in the 1950s. Faced with a new generation of African politicians, many of them schooled in socialist thought, chiefs and kings struggled to ensure themselves a role in the postcolonial power structure. Some, such as the kings of Swaziland and MOROCCO, did maintain real authority; but in more radical independent states, government leaders made a concerted effort to limit the powers of chiefs and other customary authorities.

Although scholars debate the extent to which contemporary Africa's political and economic woes can be blamed on colonial rule, it is clear that rigid ethnic categories created during the colonial era have become one of the greatest obstacles to nation-building and regional stability in much of Africa. The fact that the postcolonial state has for many years been one of the only reliable channels of upward mobility in Africa has also undermined the stability and effectiveness of many governments. In addition, postcolonial African states have inherited their predecessors' ambivalence toward customary authorities. Modern African politicians look to village chiefs, spiritual leaders, clan heads, and other such authorities to support their development programs as well as their political campaigns, but cannot always depend on their loyalties. Finally, customary law remains a source of fierce debate, as African states continue to grapple with the problems of defining and legislating modern civil society.

See also ANTHROPOLOGY IN AFRICA; CARTHAGE; DEVELOPMENT IN AFRICA: AN INTERPRETATION; EGYPT, ANCIENT KINGDOM OF; ETHNICITY AND IDENTITY IN AFRICA: AN INTERPRETATION; GOLD TRADE; ISLAM IN AFRICA; IVORY TRADE; MARRIAGE, AFRICAN CUSTOMS OF; PAN-AFRICANISM; SLAVERY IN AFRICA.

ELIZABETH HEATH

Colonialism in Africa

See COLONIAL RULE.

Commodification of African Art: An Interpretation

Before the European colonization of Africa began in the late nineteenth century most African art objects were exchanged locally. Masks, ritual sculpture, and other highly valued objects were circulated by traditional leaders and members of various religious associations and performance groups through local patronage. But to assume that no other exchange of these objects ever occurred is to ignore the obvious routes opened up by war, trade, and diplomacy, often long before the advent of European colonization. The assumption of most art museums and collectors that the movement of African art objects began only in the colonial period is therefore quite wrong. What is undeniably true is that the global market is different from the local and regional one. In the twentieth century this same combination of war, trade, and diplomacy gradually supplanted local patronage as the primary means by which African art circulated. During NIGERIA's civil war (1967–1970) an unprecedented number of artworks were smuggled out of the country and onto the world market. Channels of diplomacy also continue to serve as conduits for exchange. Even though the Africa Reparations Movement in Great Britain wants British museums to return to Nigeria the BENIN BRONZES seized during the British Punitive Expedition of 1897, the Nigerian government continues to give away contemporary versions of the same bronzes as official gifts to various heads of state and institutions around the world. But it is trade—the global market—that has absorbed most postcolonial art production. For every piece of sculpture produced by the typical workshop for local clientele, several more are made for export. This seemingly simple shift in production practices has complex implications. Every artwork, whatever its original inspiration or purpose, takes on the status of a commodity once it moves into a system of exchange. But art museums, as the keepers of high culture, must maintain that artworks and commodities are two different things. To do so, they have imposed their own (sometimes rather peculiar) criteria for differentiating genuine artworks from commodities. One well-known African art museum, for example, declined to collect sculpture that had been carved with imported knives or chisels, since this apparently indicated a commercial tendency. But the tools artists use have little to do with the degree to which their art is commodified. KAMBA sculptors in KENYA are organized into large cooperatives to market their work, but they still use old-fashioned adzes faced with rhinoceros hide. IDOMA sculptors in Nigeria, on the other hand, work exclusively for the local community but use any kind of tool available. Such overly rigid museum selection criteria rarely reflect the way African artists actually work. Yet for the curators of Western collections to claim that they only deal in noncommodities they must, in fact, ignore or downplay the processes by which African art objects become collectible. An Idoma Itrokwu mask, for example, was one kind of thing in the Nigerian village where it was carved in the 1950s and used in mask performances as recently as 1986; it became something quite different after it was acquired by a Swiss collector, who sold it to the French government, who in turn put it on display in a major exhibition in Paris in 1997. What was originally a spirit receptacle and a manifestation of chiefly authority is now an aesthetic object and an artifact representing Idoma culture to a Western audience. While the Musée des Arts Océaniens et Africains can rightly claim that the mask is not presently a commodity—since it is enshrined in its vitrine and now owned collectively by the French public—it clearly had to pass through a commodity phase in the global art market (including its illegal export from Nigeria) in order to get there. As cultural critic Arjun Appadurai has written, a commodity is not really a particular kind of thing but a potential phase in the life of almost anything—from a painting to a saint's relics to a tree or the family pet. The

issue of assigning value and status to an object is further complicated by the fact that the masks, figures, and other pieces identified as "art" by Western collectors did not occupy this privileged sphere in relation to other valued artifacts in the minds of the people who made them. The African makers and owners of these objects did not value them in an abstract aesthetic sense but rather for their visual power and ritual efficacy. Furthermore, the value attached to both ritual objects and utilitarian ones derived from the fact that they successfully performed their intended function. A shrine figure and a water pot were both functional in that sense. This is very different from the determination of value in Western aesthetics, which privileges the nonfunctional object as art but relegates an entity with a clear-cut functional purpose to the category of "craft." A second difference in the process by which art is identified in Africa and in the West is created by the fact that emulation of one artist by another was traditionally an integral part of the African workshop system and an important part of apprenticeship. Precolonial workshops (as well as individual artists outside the workshop system) turned out an established repertory of the forms that their patrons required. The upshot of these two differences in the assignation of artistic merit is that African artists who have not been exposed to Western high-art categories will assign different values to items made by local craftspeople than do the curators of Western museums. The artists will not view the utility of particular forms or the fact that they may be replications of known prototypes as factors in distinguishing between art and craft, artworks and commodities. In an African workshop or cooperative, the meanings assigned to artisanal practices and to the relations between producer-artists and consumer-patrons are often very different from the meanings imagined by faraway collectors. Just as precolonial African art production has been idealized as part of the romantic image of a pristine traditional society, so the art produced in contemporary workshops is frequently seen by the same collectors as commercial and derivative. It is in the workshops and other production sites that differences between African and non-African assumptions about art and commodity are most apparent. In the twentieth century three main artist groups in Africa produced pieces for global as well as local markets: old-fashioned kin-based workshops, cooperatives (which may be founded either by outsiders or members of the community), and experimental, nontraditional workshops (usually supported by external patronage). The Oshogbo artists community in Nigeria and the Tengenenge sculpture workshop in ZIMBABWE are specific examples from the latter group. What the groups produce varies from souvenirs to versions of established traditional genres to new media destined for the

302 COMMODIFICATION OF AFRICAN ART: AN INTERPRETATION

gallery circuit, but most are organized in ways that reflect local patterns of authority and artisanship. The distinction between workshops and cooperatives is sometimes blurred: some contemporary cooperatives are just overgrown local workshops with someone to keep written records of financial transactions. But these cooperatives differ qualitatively from their smaller and more traditional counterparts in terms of relations with their clientele. Most of a typical cooperative's transactions are with middlemen traders and distant, foreign consumers; relatively few involve the artists in an ongoing commitment to supply ritual objects or prestige goods to the community or its leaders. Nonetheless, some workshops and indigenous cooperatives manage to do both. YORUBA family-run workshops in Nigeria are known for maintaining traditional practices, but as demand for shrine sculptures and other objects used in the worship of orishas (the traditional Yoruba spirits) has declined, they have increasingly sought new sources of patronage. In the early 1990s Yoruba workshop sculptors in Oyo State formed a professional association and together rented exhibition space in the state's capital city, IBADAN. The hope was that potential clients would come to see their work and then contact the participating artists. This was clearly an attempt to reach beyond a limited local patronage. It also showed that the artists recognized, pragmatically, that once art is exhibited for sale it takes on a commodity status, which in turn changes the meaning of the relationship between artist and client. It is at the place of sale—be it gallery, kiosk, street corner, or catalog—that the dealer or trader must attempt an accommodation between producer and consumer, African artist and foreign collector. Various strategies come into play. All sellers have a strong interest in making their inventory desirable, which can either be done by appeals to various beliefs held by the buyer—that "authentic" art must be old, for example—or through the introduction of new "stories" that the buyer may not have heard. One art merchant in Nairobi, Kenya, deals in sculpture made by MAKONDE people who have immigrated to TANZANIA from their previous home in MOZAMBIQUE. The merchant exhibits the sculptures under special lighting because he claims the shadows they cast reveal otherwise hidden meanings. These appeals and stories are part of the commodification process, defining what is genuine for audiences far from the source.

See also WOMEN ARTISTS, AFRICAN: AN INTERPRETATION.

SIDNEY KASFIR

Comorians
Ethnic group of the Comoros, also known as the Ngazija.
The Comorians are people of mixed MALAGASY, BANTU, and Arab descent. They speak Comorian (or Ngazija), a Bantu language related to SWAHILI. Approximately 430,000 people consider themselves Comorians.

See also COMOROS.

Comoros
Island nation in the Indian Ocean.
The Comoro Islands consist of an archipelago known for its perfumed crops—vanilla, ylang-ylang, and cloves—and a celebrated past awash in legends of early Jewish settlers and famous buccaneers. More recently, the islands have earned a degree of notoriety as a home for mercenaries. On the four Comoro Islands—Njazidja (also called Grande Comore), Nzwani (Anjouan), Mwali (Mohéli), and Mayotte—Islam is the predominant religion, but the influences of Arabic, African, MALAGASY, and European cultures are apparent both in the language and in daily life. Although the islands are a popular destination for European and South African tourists, they continue to struggle with problems they have faced since independence: low economic growth, scarce land and other resources, and chronic political instability.

EARLY HISTORY
The earliest visitors to the Comoro Islands may have been the Melano-Polynesian immigrants who later settled nearby MADAGASCAR. Some scholars have suggested an early Jewish presence on the islands, based on the fact that many Comorians observe dietary restrictions and behavioral taboos associated with the Saturday Sabbath. The earliest archaeological evidence of widespread occupation dates from the tenth century C.E. East Africans, Persians, and Arabs are thought to have arrived around the thirteenth century, as the trade in GOLD, IVORY, cloth, and other precious items increased between East Africa, Arabia, and India. As Arab traders stopped over on the islands while journeying between Madagascar and East African market towns, such as Kilwa and MOMBASA, the Comoros themselves developed into an entrepôt where goods from Madagascar, including palm cloth, rice, and carved stone vessels, were exchanged for products from the mainland.

Some scholars, however, believe that it was not until after the Portuguese attacked Kilwa in 1506 that large numbers of Persians and Arabs settled permanently in the Comoros, where they developed independent urban centers, ruled by sultans, along the coasts. The Persians of the Comoros maintained close ties through marriage and trading with the SHIRAZI families of Kilwa and ZANZIBAR, who themselves originally migrated from Shiraz, in Persia, during the first millennium. Other sources suggest that the Shirazi migrated from Persia to the Comorian island of Nzwani, only later to disperse to East Africa. Whether the

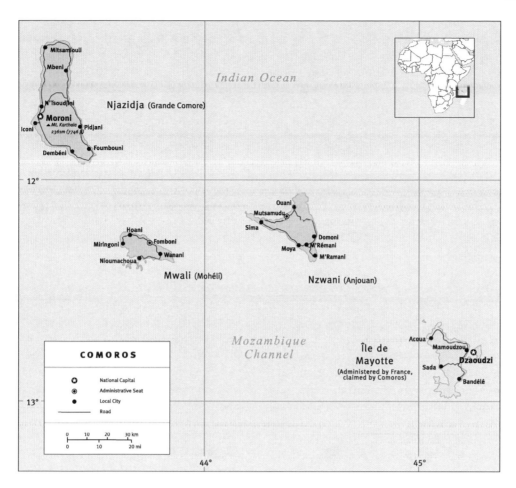

Shirazi were in fact Persian or Arab is debated. Today, the Shirazi remain one of the Comoros' largest ethnic groups.

When Portuguese and, later, other European merchant ships began to call at the Comoros in the sixteenth century, they found the islands controlled by multiple rival chiefdoms, such as Chingoni and Qualey on the island of Mayotte. Strife existed between these coastal sultanates as well as between the sultanates and communities living in the interior. Although the European powers did not at this point establish control over the islands, Dutch, French, and English ships later used them as a staging ground in their struggle against Portuguese domination in the southwest Indian Ocean. They also traded iron for fresh supplies of water and food.

As European navies competed for control over Indian Ocean trade routes, the commerce in luxury goods stimulated the rise of piracy, which reached its height during the seventeenth and eighteenth centuries. The Comoros offered pirates, such as Davy Jones and Captain Kidd, fresh water, a safe haven, and a strategic base for plundering European ships that passed through the Mozambique Channel while traveling to and from India. Comoros towns also provided markets for the pirates' stolen property. During the

eighteenth century, however, European powers increased their military presence in the region. With the French navy established on île de France (present-day MAURITIUS) and English forces based on Nzwani, piracy became riskier.

During the eighteenth and nineteenth centuries, slaves became an increasingly important commodity in the Indian Ocean. French plantations in the colonies of île de France, RÉUNION, and the SEYCHELLES created a tremendous demand for slave labor, much of which came from Madagascar. Arab merchants on the Comoros also sold slaves who had been captured in raids on village communities in the islands' interiors. Although many of the slaves were exported to neighboring islands, Comorian sultans also used slaves on sugar, clove, and sisal plantations.

As demand for slaves rose in the late eighteenth century, conflicts increased between the Comorian sultanates and chiefdoms, as well as between Comorian and Malagasy rulers. In the mid-1790s, a sultan on the island of Nzwani asked his BETSIMISARAKA allies of northeastern Madagascar to raid his rivals in the nearby town of Mutsamundu. The Betsimisaraka went on to attack other Comorian communities, taking slaves as booty. Comorian sultans' desperate appeals to European powers for protection against Malagasy raids were ignored until 1816, when the British government intervened. That year, agents of Robert Farquare, the British governor of Mauritius, successfully pressured the Merina Empire of Madagascar to sign a treaty ending the slave trade. In the 1820s, the Merina Empire overthrew the chief Malagasy raiders—the coastal SAKALAVA—and slave raids on the Comoros and elsewhere ended.

But the Merina-Sakalava rivalry had further implications for the Comoros. In 1828 the sultan of Nzwani, Abdallah, invited the Merina general Ramanataka to settle in the sultan's domain and help defeat his own enemies. Ultimately, Ramanataka established a Merina chiefdom on Nzwani. Not long afterward, the Sakalava leader Andriansouli joined relatives on Mayotte, and soon became one of the island's most powerful figures. Meanwhile, rulers on the island of Njazidja maintained ties to the sultanate of Zanzibar and continued to resist alignment with European powers.

EUROPEAN INTERVENTION AND THE COLONIAL ERA

European colonization of the Comoro Islands came as a result of Anglo-French rivalry in the Indian Ocean. The process was gradual, and occurred somewhat differently on each island. After the British won the Napoleonic Wars and established control of Mauritius in 1810, France looked to the Comoros as a base for preserving its regional influence. On Mayotte, they found a willing collaborator in Andriansouli, who signed a treaty in 1841 that established the island as a French protectorate. Britain responded by opening a consulate in Nzwani—ostensibly to monitor French adherence to antislavery treaties, but also to maintain intelligence of French activity in the region more generally.

Mayotte's local rulers provided French export firms with land to build plantations for the cultivation of sugar, vanilla, coffee, cacao, sisal, and other crops. Because Mayotte had been heavily depopulated by years of slave raids, the French looked to MOZAMBIQUE to supply contract labor. Although sugar production initially dominated Mayotte's economy, many plantations went bankrupt after world market prices fell in the 1890s.

The island of Mwali fell from the control of the Merina ruler Ramanataka when his heir married a Zanzibarian prince. Zanzibar controlled the island during the 1850s, until Merina nobles assumed command. The famous French entrepreneur Joseph François Lambert arrived on Mwali in 1860 armed with a declaration by the Merina queen of Madagascar that granted Lambert complete ownership of the island. Lambert intended to share profits from plantation production with the queen. But the local population resisted, plundering Lambert's house in his absence. The French, meanwhile, sent the navy to reassert Lambert's claims. In 1886 the island became a neglected French protectorate; its local population remained poor and disfranchised in the following decades.

Njazidja remained largely independent of European influence during the nineteenth century, though in 1843 the French secured the right to fell timber and recruit contract laborers from several sultans. The island's two dominant sultanates spent much of the century engaged in an extended conflict. In 1875 the French lent support to the powerful sultan of Bambao, Said Ali. Ali showed his appreciation by providing the French naturalist Léon Humblot with as much land as he desired for plantations, as well as contract laborers. In return, Ali received 10 percent of Humblot's profits. Angry sultans accused Ali of giving away land he did not own. One sultan acquired a German flag, which he had hoisted at Fumboni. In response, in 1883 the French declared the island a protectorate. Despite the occasional presence of the French military, popular uprisings forced Ali to flee the island twice; after the second time, he remained in Réunion until his death. Humblot became ruler of the island in 1892, but his reputation for tyranny and cruelty—children worked as forced laborers on his plantations—led to his removal by the French government four years later.

On the island of Nzwani, the sultan Abdallah established diplomatic ties with the British in 1844, hoping to legitimate his own authority and ward off French imperialism. British entrepreneurs, coming mostly from Mauritius, invested in plantations. They built a primary labor force of Arab-owned slaves, who were hired out as wage laborers, but whose owners confiscated most of their earnings. Abdallah's agreement to bring an end to slavery in 1882 alienated him from his Arab constituents. Unwilling to enact the unpopular law, and indebted to Mauritian bankers, Abdallah initiated political ties with France. The French were quick to use deceit and the threat of force to gain control of Nzwani. By 1887, Abdallah had been stripped of most of his authority, and the French had forced him to abolish slavery. His land was parceled out to French colonists for plantation cultivation.

By 1909 all the islands were French protectorates. Three years later, they became part of the colony of Madagascar, and once-resistant sultans were forced to abdicate to French authority. France invested little in the islands; until World War II, they ranked among the backwaters of the French Empire, and were ruled from neighboring Madagascar. French companies dictated policy much as the sultans had previously, except that profits from cash crop sales were diverted to France. During the 1920 and 1930s, many Comorians emigrated to Madagascar in search of employment. With only one secondary school for all the Comoros, the islands offered few opportunities for advancement. Nor did they produce any significant indigenous political movements during this period.

INDEPENDENCE

During World War II, the British seized the Comoro Islands from Vichy France and handed them over to the Free French government, which later granted the colony greater autonomy as well as representation in the French parliament. In a 1958 popular referendum held within all French possessions, Comorians voted to remain a French territory, though with their own internal administration. Continued economic stagnation and French neglect, along with the death in 1970 of the moderate politician Said Mohammed Cheik, sparked calls for independence. In a 1974 vote the population reversed their initial decision in favor of full independence, with the exception of the inhabitants of Mayotte. As the center of French colonial administration, Mayotte had developed closer ties with Paris while distinguishing itself both linguistically and racially from the Arab-dominated rulers of the other islands of the Comoros. France thus retained control over Mayotte while granting independence to the other islands.

But this plan was unacceptable to the Comorian government. Led by President Ahmed Abdallah, in July 1975 the government unilaterally declared the independence of all the islands, including Mayotte. While the United Nations recognized Comorian independence, however, France refused to relinquish control over Mayotte. Relations between the two nations quickly worsened: France withdrew all support, and the Comorian government nationalized all French possessions. After only one month in office Abdallah was deposed in a coup led by Ali Soilih, with help from the French mercenary Bob Denard. Soilih's socialist government lasted until May 1978, when he in turn was overthrown and killed by Denard's mercenaries. Shortly afterward, Comorians voted to make the country a federal Islamic republic and elected Abdallah president. The mercenaries' continued presence on the islands—many served as Abdallah's bodyguards—resulted in the Comoros' temporary expulsion from the ORGANIZATION OF AFRICAN UNITY (OAU) that same year.

Abdallah reestablished diplomatic relations with France and forged alliances with other Islamic states. In 1979 he declared a single-party state, and over the next few years survived several coup attempts, which were typically followed by crackdowns on the political opposition. As population growth exceeded the agricultural potential of the archipelago's poor soils, the economy continued to decline. The tiny fishing and manufacturing sectors did little to improve the health of the Comorian economy, which lacked the capital needed to improve its infrastructure.

In 1989, as Abdallah prepared to run for a third term as president, he was assassinated by Denard's mercenaries, who then attempted to take direct control of the government. The arrival of French paratroopers, however, forced Denard and his colleagues to flee to SOUTH AFRICA. Supreme Court president Said Mohamed Djohar won subsequent presidential elections, promising economic reforms and a return to multiparty politics. But unrest continued. In 1991 the Supreme Court attempted to dismiss the president for negligence; a year later, Djohar faced a failed coup attempt, as well as strikers protesting International Monetary Fund (IMF) and World Bank austerity measures. The corrupt Djohar regime repeatedly outmaneuvered opposition groups seeking a greater share of political power.

Denard and his merceneries returned to the scene in 1995, invading the Comoros and capturing Djohar. Nine hundred French troops followed, arrested the mercenaries, and sent them to France. With Djohar in Réunion for medical treatment, Prime Minister Mohamed Caabi El Yachroutu stepped in as president. After the 1996 presidential elections, he was replaced by opposition leader Mohamed Taki, and the country adopted a new constitution that embraced Islamic principles. Despite this change in government, the economy remained weak and popular unrest continued.

In 1997 the islands of Nzwani and Mwali announced their intention to secede: in light of the relatively high standard of living enjoyed by Mayotte, they wished to return to French administration. Initially, the French government affirmed its willingness to reincorporate the islands. Later, however, taking a more cautious stance, it urged the OAU to find a peaceful settlement to the conflict. Troops from Moroni unsuccessfully tried to recapture Nzwani by force. In late 1998 Taki died and was succeeded by an interim president. In April 1999, following riots on Njazidja aimed at people from Nzwani, the interim government was overthrown in a military coup. Assoumani Azali, one of the coup leaders, became president. A Transitional National Unity Government (GUNT) was formed on January 20, 2002, following the passage of the new constitution.

GUNT governed until April 2002, when presidential elections were held. Assoumani Azali received 75 percent of the vote. Azali, however, left office in 2006, at which time he was succeeded by the cleric Ahmed Abdallah Mohamed Sambi. On Anjouan, however, President Mohamed Bacar went ahead with his plan to consolidate his own power and in 2007 politically separated the island from the rest of Comoros. Less than a year later, in March 2008, soldiers from Comoros and the African Union landed on Anjouan. The fighting lasted a bit longer than a day. The island was

Comoros (At a Glance)

OFFICIAL NAME:
Union of the Comoros

AREA:
2,170 sq km (838 sq mi)

LOCATION:
A group of three islands, Njazidja, Mwali and Nzwani (formerly known as Grande Comore, Mohéli, and Anjouan, respectively), off the coast of southern Africa in the Mozambique Channel, approximately two-thirds of the way between northern Madagascar and northern Mozambique. These three islands broke from French rule in 1975, while a fourth island, Mayotte, remained a French dependency.

CAPITAL:
Moroni (population 60,200; 2003 estimate)

OTHER MAJOR CITIES:
Domoni (population 191,000), on Nzwani; Fomboni (133,000) on Mwali (2003 estimates)

POPULATION:
731,775 (2008 estimate)

POPULATION DENSITY:
337 persons per sq km (873 per sq mi)

POPULATION BELOW AGE 15:
42.4 percent (male 155,662; female 154,520; 2008 estimate)

POPULATION GROWTH RATE:
2.803 percent (2008 estimate)

TOTAL FERTILITY RATE:
4.9 children born per woman (2008 estimate)

LIFE EXPECTANCY AT BIRTH:
Total population: 63.1 years (male 60.72 years; female 65.55 years; 2008 estimate)

INFANT MORTALITY RATE:
68.58 deaths per 1000 live births (2008 estimate)

LITERACY RATE (AGE 15 AND OVER WHO CAN READ AND WRITE):
Total population: 56.5 percent (male 63.6 percent; female 49.3 percent; 2003 estimate)

EDUCATION:
Many children attend Islamic schools and state education is officially compulsory from age seven to sixteen. Although 75 percent of the school-age group attend primary school, only 25 percent complete secondary schooling.

LANGUAGES:
French and Arabic are the official languages, but most people use one of the island dialects, collectively called Shimasiwa. Shimasiwa dialects are related to Swahili.

ETHNIC GROUPS:
The population formed by successive settlements over at least 1,000 years, including migrations from Madagascar. Residents trace lineage back to Kilwa, Zanzibar, islands off the coast of Tanzania, and even Arabia and the Persian Gulf region. Some citizens descended from slaves from Mozambique. Today no strong ethnic conflicts divide the population; rivalries between the islands are more important than ethnic differences.

RELIGIONS:
Sunni Muslims make up 98 percent of the population, and Roman Catholics form the only significant religious minority.

CLIMATE:
The islands, which lie within the region of the Indian Ocean monsoons, experience the dry season between April and October, with heavy rains and cyclones the rest of the year. Daily temperatures seldom rise above 30° C (85° F), and 5,080 mm (200 in) of rain per year fall on the slopes of Karthala, the site of the heaviest rainfall in Comoros. Despite heavy rainfall, Njazdja retains no water, due to the porous nature of its volcanic rock. Islanders build cisterns to store rainwater for the dry season. In Nzwani, however, streams flow from the mountains throughout the year.

LAND, PLANTS, AND ANIMALS:
All three islands are of volcanic origin and are mountainous. The island shores are rocky, with offshore islets and a steeply sloping seabed. Njazidja has virtually no topsoil, but the volcanic rocks nevertheless support a dense rain forest. The other islands have soils that are rich in minerals and very fertile, providing ideal conditions for the growth of sugar cane, ylang-ylang trees (the blossoms of which are used to make a perfume), vanilla, cloves, and a wide variety of tropical fruits and flowers. A variety of flycatcher called Humblot's flycatcher breeds only on Njazidja. The seas off the Comoros are the home of the famous coelacanth, a fish that was thought to be extinct for millions of years until 1938, when one was caught live.

NATURAL RESOURCES:
Flowers and spices constitute the basic commercial crops and grow readily in the fertile soil of Mwali and Nzwani.

CURRENCY:
The Comorian franc

GROSS DOMESTIC PRODUCT (GDP):
$1.262 billion (2007 estimate)

GDP REAL GROWTH RATE:
−1 percent (2007 estimate)

GDP PER CAPITA:
$1,100 (2007 estimate)

PRIMARY ECONOMIC ACTIVITIES:
Agriculture, including farming, fishing, hunting, and forestry, accounts for 40 percent of GDP and 80 percent of employment; tourism and small industries also contribute to the economy.

PRIMARY CROPS:
Vanilla, ylang-ylang, cloves, perfume oil, copra, and cassava (tapioca)

INDUSTRIES:
Tourism, perfume distillation, textiles, furniture, jewelry, construction materials, and soft drinks

PRIMARY EXPORTS:
Vanilla, ylang-ylang, cloves, perfume oil, and copra

PRIMARY IMPORTS:
Rice and other foodstuffs, petroleum products, cement, and consumer goods

PRIMARY TRADE PARTNERS:
France, South Africa, Singapore, U.S., Kenya, Germany, and Pakistan

GOVERNMENT:
After gaining independence from France in 1975, Comorans suffered a tumultuous two decades of nationalist regimes, mercenary coups, and French intervention. In March 1996 Mohamed Taki Abdulkarim was elected president, in the first democratic elections of Comoros. In 1997 Anjouan and Moheli threatened to secede from the Comoros, prompting a national crisis that appeared to be resolved with the approval of a new constitution in 2001 but would in fact eventually lead to the 2008 invasion of Anjouan by Comoran and African Union soldiers. Under the 2001 constitution, each island in the archipelago elects its own president, and a union president is elected by popular vote to a term of five years. In 2002 Assoumani Azali, who had seized power in a 1999 coup but resigned in 2002 to run in the national presidential election, was elected with 75 percent of the vote. Azali left office in 2006 and was succeeded by Ahmed Abdallah Mohamed Sambi. The federal constitution allows each island to have autonomy in internal matters and to elect its own governor. The legislative branch of government comprises two multiparty houses, a federal assembly and a senate.

Eric Bennett

repatriated, and Bacar fled by speedboat to seek asylum from the French government (which later denied the request, though it refused subsequent extradition requests from Comoros). Elections were held on Anjouan in June 2008.

See also INDIAN OCEAN SLAVE TRADE; UNITED NATIONS IN AFRICA.

ARI NAVE

Compaoré, Blaise
1950–
President of Burkina Faso since 1987.

Compaoré was born in Ziniaré, UPPER VOLTA (present-day BURKINA FASO). He joined the army, completed officers' training school in CAMEROON, and received a commission as second lieutenant in 1975. Compaoré met Thomas SANKARA in 1978 in a paratroop commando class in MOROCCO, where they became close friends. When Sankara seized power in Burkina Faso in 1982 he named Compaoré minister of state to the presidency.

Soon afterwards Compaoré and Sankara developed political and personal differences. Compaoré, fearing that he might be dismissed, led a violent coup in which Sankara and thirteen government officers were executed in October 1987. Declaring himself president, Compaoré disarmed local militias and instituted a program of "rectification," ostensibly designed to resuscitate the nation's socialist revolution. In fact, he began moving Burkina Faso toward a market economy, by privatizing state industries and implementing austerity measures. He also sought to improve relations with Western nations, especially France.

Campaoré formed the Organization for Popular Democracy-Labor Movement (French acronym, ODP-MT) as the new ruling party in April 1989 and pronounced a general amnesty for all political prisoners. In response to public unrest Compaoré resigned his military commission in June 1991 and announced that he would run in multiparty elections as the civilian candidate of the ODP-MT, which would no longer endorse Marxist economic policies, but rather free enterprise. Failed negotiations between the government and opposition groups about the democratic transition process erupted into violent clashes in October 1991, prompting the opposition to withdraw candidates and call for an election boycott. Compaoré, unopposed, won the election with only 22 percent of the electorate participating. He was inaugurated in December 1991 for a seven-year term. In 1998, he was reelected to another seven-year term as president.

In the 1990s Compaoré liberalized the Burkina Faso economy as part of a World Bank structural adjustment plan. Despite these efforts, he still presides over a poor nation that desperately needs international assistance. Although Campaoré's role in the assassination of Sankara has not been forgotten at home, he has sought to build a reputation abroad as a regional peacemaker, by hosting and participating in talks aimed at resolving conflicts in neighboring countries. Despite constitutional challenges to the validity of his run based on a 2000 amendment outlawing more than two terms, Compaoré sought and won a third tenure as president in 2005.

See also STRUCTURAL ADJUSTMENT IN AFRICA.

Conakry, Guinea
Capital of Guinea.

Conakry is on GUINEA's Atlantic coast and is the nation's largest deep-water port. It originally comprised only Tombo Island, but today includes the Los Islands and the tip of Kaloum Peninsula, to which Tombo is connected by a causeway. The climate is tropical; much of the surrounding area is swampland.

The city's name comes from the language spoken by the SOSO ethnic group that has dominated coastal Guinea since the seventeenth century. Conakry was originally a Soso fishing village. The French chose the site for a town in 1880. The town became the capital of FRENCH GUINEA when the French declared Guinea a colony in 1891.

When the country gained independence under Sékou TOURÉ in 1958, Conakry remained its capital, and became increasingly important as a processing and trading center for the iron ore and bauxite mined in the surrounding regions. Today, Conakry is Guinea's main deep-sea port and the site of the country's main international airport. Conakry is also the country's political, cultural, and financial center.

Once the jewel of French colonialism, Conakry suffered immense poverty after independence. Nearly half a century later hunger remains common. Neglect of Guinea's rural economy has driven thousands of Guineans to leave the countryside and seek work in the city. Refugees from wars in neighboring SIERRA LEONE and LIBERIA have also swelled the city's population in recent years. In 2003 more than 40,000 refugees from those two nations lived in Conakry. The city has thus expanded rapidly. Its population in 1970 was estimated at 200,000; today it is about 1.9 million. Such growth has led to a number of problems related to infrastructure and the availability of water and electricity, sparking periodic violence throughout the city. A general strike in 2007 resulted in the deaths of more than one hundred people.

See also COLONIAL RULE; HUNGER AND FAMINE; IRON IN AFRICA; URBANISM AND URBANIZATION IN AFRICA.

BIBLIOGRAPHY

Del Ninno, Carlo. *Welfare and Poverty in Conakry: Assessment and Determinants.* Cornell Food and Nutrition Policy Program Working Paper, 1994.

KATE TUTTLE

Confiant, Raphaël

1951–

Novelist, essayist, and leading figure in the Créolité movement.

Raphaël Confiant was born in Le Lorrain, Martinique. Like many people on the island, Confiant was raised to speak two languages: Creole at home and French in school or at work. Confiant developed an attachment to Creole, the oft-maligned spoken language of his island, and the under-class culture associated with it. With an eye toward gaining acceptance for Creole as a literary language, Confiant wrote his first five novels in this idiom. These works—influenced by authors such as the Haitian Frankétienne (*Dézafi*; 1975) and the Martinican Gilbert Gratiant (*Fab Compè Zicaque*; 1958), who were among the first to write in Creole—present the diversity of Creole culture in Martinique. However, these novels' lack of popular success, resulting in part from a limited Creole-reading audience, convinced Confiant that his subsequent novels should be published in French. But Confiant did not simply give up on Creole. His more widely read and appreciated novels such as *Le nègre et l'amiral* (1988), *Eau de café* (1991), *Commandeur du sucre* (1994), and *Le bassin de Joséphine* (1997) are written in a type of French that is heavily inflected by Creole. Instead of pushing a spoken language (Creole) toward a written form, Confiant has endeavored to make written French more "oral" and therefore more represen-tative of Martinican popular culture.

Confiant's attempts to rehabilitate the Creole language and culture place him in opposition to the most important Martinican writer of the previous generation, Aimé CÉSAIRE. As Confiant asserts in *Éloge de la Créolité* (1989; *In Praise of Creoleness*, bilingual edition, 1993), cowritten with Patrick CHAMOISEAU and Jean Bernabé, and in *Aimé Césaire: Une traversée paradoxale du siècle* (1993), Césaire and the Négritude movement were excessively invested in the struggle between black and white. As a result they over-looked the other peoples that create Martinique's unique cultural identity: the Chinese, Lebanese, East Indian, and other immigrants who have come to the island in the last 150 years as well as the Amerindians who populated the island prior to the arrival of Christopher Columbus.

Confiant's novels reflect the many voices that are obliged to interact in Martinique because of the historical forces that have put them there. Many of the characters in Confiant's novels are products of the racial and cultural intermingling that has occurred in Martinique since slaves first arrived in 1640. The author himself is of Chinese and African descent, a mixture referred to in Martinique as *chabin*. Confiant's preoccupation with racial and cultural diversity in Martinique has been called a form of neo-exoticism by the Guadeloupean critic Willy Alante-Lima, but most critics see Confiant's fiction as indicating a path for moving beyond the black/white opposition that con-cerned most Martinican writers at the middle of this century.

Confiant has remained a prolific writer in the new century. His more recent work includes *Mamzelle dragonfly* (2000), *Nuée ardente* (2002), and *La Panse du Chacal* (2004). He is currently a professor at the Martinique campus of the University of the Antilles and Guiana.

RICHARD WATTS

Congo, Belgian

Former name of Democratic Republic of Congo.

See also CONGO, DEMOCRATIC REPUBLIC OF THE.

Congo, Democratic Republic of the
Largest country in Central Africa, situated on both sides of the equator and bordering nine other countries as well as the Atlantic Ocean.

One of the largest and most ethnically diverse African countries, the Democratic Republic of the Congo (hence-forth Congo) is extremely rich in natural resources, includ-ing diamonds, copper, and gold, as well as the enormous hydroelectric potential of the CONGO RIVER. Historically, however, these resources have benefited only the political and commercial elite. Subjected to one of the most oppres-sive regimes in all of colonial Africa, then to the thirty-two-year rule of MOBUTU SESE SEKO, Congo is now impover-ished and unstable. In 1996 rebel leader Laurent-Désiré KABILA seized power on promises to revitalize and demo-cratize the country. He was unable, however, to withstand a subsequent rebellion backed by armies from RWANDA and UGANDA, and was assassinated in 2001. Though a truce agreement was signed in 2002, the years of fighting and alleged government corruption have seriously undermined Congolese society.

PRECOLONIAL HISTORY
Although relatively little is known about the early history of the Congo, it is believed that the first inhabitants were

PYGMY groups who lived as hunter-gatherers in the rainforests of the northwest. During the first millennium B.C.E. Bantu-speaking peoples migrated from the north and settled throughout the Congo basin. They established agricultural communities and, after contacts with non-Bantu speaking people, herded cattle. Some of these communities were eventually incorporated into relatively centralized states such as the fourteenth-century KONGO at the mouth of the Congo River, and the fifteenth-century LUBA and LUNDA kingdoms to the west of LAKE TANGANYIKA. Other smaller states in the Congo basin area included the Teke, the KUBA, and the CHOKWE.

The first documented contact with Europeans occurred in 1483, when a Portuguese explorer, Diogo Cam (also spelled Cão), sailed into the mouth of the Zaire River (later known as the Congo River) and encountered Kongo villages. Two years later, he took a group of Kongo emissaries back to Portugal. The group returned to Africa in 1491 with priests, soldiers, and European goods. The

emissaries and Portuguese baptized the Kongo king, Nzinga a Nkuwu, and built a Catholic church in the capital. Although Nzinga a Nkuwu later abandoned Catholicism, his son, Nzinga Mbembe (later Afonso), became a devoted Christian. Upon his accession he made Catholicism the state religion.

Subsequent relations between the Portuguese and the Kongo were based on missionary pursuits and trade. Afonso encouraged missionaries to Christianize the Kongo. He also traded slaves and ivory to the Portuguese in exchange for European luxury goods to increase his prestige and authority. The slave trade, however, eventually resulted in the demise of the Kongo kingdom. Kongolese slave raids on neighboring peoples, including the Teke and Kuba, led to retaliation and wars, such as the Jaga War in 1569, that eventually destroyed the Kongo kingdom. Neighboring states such as the Luba and Lunda continued selling slaves and ivory to the Europeans through the late nineteenth century.

THE MARKET PLACE. Congolese traders arrive at market loaded with their wares, c. 1943. (*Prints and Photographs Division, Library of Congress*)

CONGO FREE STATE

In 1874 Anglo American journalist Henry Morton STANLEY was commissioned by the *New York Herald* and *Daily Telegraph* to finish the explorations of David Livingstone, a Scottish missionary who had spent several years mapping the Congo basin. For three years, Stanley explored the Zaire River, returning in 1877 to Europe, where his reports of the region's untapped natural wealth caught the attention of King LEOPOLD II of Belgium. Leopold, keen to extend his personal domain, hired Stanley to return to the Congo

basin to secure treaties with local chiefs and establish contracts necessary to form a commercial monopoly, which would be called the African International Association. Stanley also put hundreds of men, both European and African, to work building a road along the Congo River. Leopold's actions spurred the SCRAMBLE FOR AFRICA, in which other European powers quickly staked claims to other parts of the continent, and then met to formalize their claims at the BERLIN CONFERENCE OF 1884–1885. There, Leopold was recognized as the legitimate authority in the region. In return, he promised to provide European traders and missionaries free access to the territory, which he named the Congo Free State.

Leopold subsequently declared all land not actively occupied or cultivated to be "vacant land" belonging to him and the Free State government. He also appropriated land that was not vacant, which led to violent conflicts between the Free State military, the Force Publique, and the region's powerful traders, TIPPU TIP and MSIRI. Keeping a significant portion of the territory for his own enterprises, Leopold granted vast concessions of land to various companies for mining, rubber-tapping, and railroad construction. Free State companies, including Leopold's, regularly used threats of torture and execution to force Africans to tap rubber or work in the mines. Reporting on the conditions in the rubber tapping regions, Reverend J. B. Murphy wrote that the system of compulsory labor had "reduced people to states of utter despair. Each town in the district is

CONGOLESE DISPLACEMENT, 2008. Displaced residents of Kibumba march 40 km from Goma back to their homes. (*Jerome Delay/AP images*)

forced to bring a certain quantity of rubber to the head-quarters of the commissaire every Sunday. If they will not they are shot down, and their left hands cut off and taken as trophies to the commissaire." Under the Congo Free State, the Congolese population declined by between one-third and one-half due to famine, epidemics, and state-sponsored violence. By 1900 the brutality of the Congo Free State was notorious and international groups pressed for reform, which it haphazardly instituted in 1906. By 1908, however, it was clear that the reforms had been unsuccessful and Leopold, anxious to relieve himself of a burgeoning debt, handed the colony over to the Belgian government, which renamed it the Belgian Congo.

BELGIAN CONGO

Although the new colonial government promised to abolish Leopold's abusive practices, it was also keenly aware that the colony must remain a profitable venture. As a result, the African population saw few real improvements. The government prohibited slave labor but imposed high taxes, which effectively forced adult males to continue working for the rubber and mining companies. In addition, the government required Congolese villagers to spend at least sixty days each year cultivating export crops for the government. It also conscripted thousands to work on large infrastructure projects, such as the building of railroads, and to serve in the Allied forces during World War I and World War II.

Compared to some of the British and French colonial regimes, Belgian colonialism allowed Africans few opportunities in civil service or private trade. It did, however, encourage missionary work in order to "civilize and Christianize" the African peoples. Missionaries did actively convert Africans to Christianity and also built schools that became the primary source of education available to Africans, especially at the secondary and higher levels. Many of the missionary school graduates subsequently became teachers or employees at other mission-run enterprises. They formed an elite class of Africans known as the évolués, many of whom lived in major cities such as Elizabethville and Léopoldville.

In the early 1950s the évolués began petitioning the colonial government for reform, demanding the rights to own land, participate in elections, and serve in public office. The colonial government conceded these demands and permitted Africans to run in local municipal elections in 1957. These changes did not appease growing anticolonial sentiments in the Congo, however, and when the general population broke into riots in 1959 the évolués were the first to demand immediate independence.

The Belgian colonial government was caught off-guard by these demands. Although France and Britain had been discussing decolonization since the early 1950s, the Belgian government did not even consider the possibility until 1956, when Belgian law professor A. A. J. Van Bilsen published "A Thirty Year Plan for the Political Emancipation of Belgian Africa." The riots of 1959, however, forced the government to realize that it had neither the force nor the authority to maintain control. As a result, when it met with African delegates at the Brussels Round Table Conference in 1960, it offered to grant independence within six months, an extraordinarily short time frame. The government encouraged the évolués to form political parties and hold elections, and proposed that Belgian nationals would help smooth the transition by staying in their government and military positions.

In May 1960 the first national elections were held in the Belgian Congo. Nearly forty parties fielded candidates and, after much controversy, a coalition was finally formed between Patrice LUMUMBA's Congolese National Movement and Joseph KASAVUBU's Bakango Alliance, in which Kasavubu was named president and Lumumba was named prime minister. On June 30, 1960, King Baudouin I of Belgium declared the Republic of Congo independent.

EARLY INDEPENDENCE IN THE REPUBLIC OF CONGO

Within a week of independence, however, large-scale chaos erupted. The Force Publique mutinied and violent conflicts broke out between Belgians and Congolese as well as between Congolese ethnic groups fighting over animosities fostered during colonialism. In addition, secessionist movements threatened to break up the republic. On July 11, 1960, Moise-Kapenda TSHOMBE, supported clandestinely by Belgium and the Union Minière mining company, declared Katanga (Shaba) an independent state, and in August, Albert Kalonji declared the independence of South Kasai.

Belgium deployed troops to the Republic of the Congo to protect Belgian citizens, a move quickly interpreted as an attempt to restore Belgian authority. In the face of continuing riots, Lumumba asked the United Nations (UN) for assistance. The UN Security Council authorized a military force, comprised mainly of African troops, to restore order in the Republic of the Congo and oversee the withdrawal of the Belgian troops. The UN troops arrived on July 15, 1960, but when they proved unable to move out the Belgian troops quickly, Lumumba accused the UN of supporting Western imperialists and asked the former Union of Soviet Socialist Republics (U.S.S.R.) for assistance. Dag Hammarskjöld, UN Secretary General, attempted to ameliorate the situation, but died in an airplane crash on his way to negotiate talks in the Republic of the Congo.

Lumumba's action angered President Kasavubu, who fired Lumumba and replaced him with Joseph Ileo. Before Ileo could take office, however, Colonel Joseph Mobutu (later MOBUTU SESE SEKO) seized power through a military coup. Claiming that Lumumba had incited army mutiny, Mobutu ordered the prime minister's arrest. He was killed in January 1961 allegedly after torture by Mobutu's troops. In February 1961 Mobutu returned power to Kasavubu and Ileo.

For the next three years, UN forces and the Congolese military attempted to reunite the fragmented Republic of the Congo. In 1963 Tshombe finally surrendered the Katanga province, and, ironically, was named prime minister in July 1964. A month later the Kasavubu and Tshombe government adopted a new constitution and renamed the country the Democratic Republic of the Congo. Their coalition, however, was short-lived. Taking advantage of widespread civil conflict, Mobutu again seized power in a military coup d'etat and on November 25, 1965, named himself president.

THE MOBUTU ERA
Immensely popular in the early years of his rule, Mobutu centralized and consolidated his power by crushing burgeoning rebellions in outlying provinces and executing dissident politicians. In 1970 he held presidential elections and was elected to a seven-year term. During this term, Mobutu implemented the ideology he called *authenticité* (French for "authenticity"; also called "Mobutuism"), which he used to justify his dictatorial power as well as his economic and social policies. He changed the name of the Democratic Republic of the Congo to ZAIRE and required citizens to Africanize all Christian names and adopt African-style dress. In addition, in an economic policy called Zaireanization, he nationalized foreign businesses, reclaiming the copper and diamond mines in the Shaba region (formerly Katanga), which would become the mainstay of the Zairean economy.

From 1970 until the late 1980s Mobutu built a cult of personality around his presidency, calling himself Citizen-President-Founder and father of the nation. Comparing his role to the patriarchal authority of traditional chiefs, he claimed he had the authentic right to exercise absolute power over his "children," the Zairean people. He used the army, the police, and the Centre National Documentation, an internal spy agency, to enforce his dictates and quell dissent. Mobutu also destroyed political opposition by replacing political parties with one official state party, the Mouvement Populaire de la Révolution (MPR), and making every Zairean a member.

Although Mobutu's policies of *authenticité* and Zaireanization primarily benefited Mobutu and his friends, it also fostered a rich musical scene. Because *authenticité*

forbade certain kinds of foreign music, Zaireans coped with the harshness of daily life by creating their own genres, such as a vibrant music called SOUKOUS that combines modern music with traditional instruments. KINSHASA, which many consider the music capital of Central Africa, became home to musicians such as Franco Luambo Makiadi (known as the king of Zairean music), Wemba, and Abeti Masiniki, and bands such as O.K. Jazz, and Docteur Nico et l'Orchestre African Fiesta. Mobutu also acted as a patron to some of the Zairean musicians and sometimes invited them to play at his palaces.

By the early 1980s Mobutu's government was notorious as a kleptocracy in which public funds were used for private gain, especially for the private gain of the president himself, who diverted vast sums of revenue into his personal bank accounts. Meanwhile, the Zairean economy and infrastructure deteriorated. Mobutu managed to maintain his authority over an increasingly disenchanted populace partly because he portrayed himself as a staunch anti-communist and therefore received generous financial and military support from France and the United States. Although the Western powers hoped their support would not only deter Soviet influence but also stabilize the mineral-rich region of Central Africa, Mobutu in fact aided insurgent movements in neighboring countries such as ANGOLA, CHAD, and SUDAN.

At the end of the Cold War, however, Mobutu's power began to slip. Economic depression due to falling copper prices and unrest among civil servants and military—many of whom had been unpaid for years—forced Mobutu to make concessions to the political opposition. In 1990 he announced the creation of a multiparty democratic system. Although elections were never held, Mobutu agreed to a coalition government with Étienne Tshisekedi. Tshisekedi was fired in less than a month but reinstated in 1992 and served until 1994, when Léon Kengo wa Dondo was appointed prime minister.

Mobutu maintained a low profile in the early 1990s but again became the voice of power in 1994, when he allowed millions of people fleeing civil conflict in RWANDA to take refuge in Zaire and the UN and France urged him to play a role in helping resolve the crisis. This renewed authority, however, was only temporary. Sick with prostate cancer, Mobutu was caught off-guard by an insurrection movement that began in October 1996. During the next six months the Alliance of Democratic Forces for the Liberation of the Congo, a Zairean militia backed by Rwanda, Uganda, and Angola and led by Laurent-Désiré KABILA, rapidly advanced on the capital of Kinshasa. Kabila's forces consisted largely of soldiers from eastern Zaire's small Banyamulenge minority, often known as Tutsi because of their close ethnic ties to the Tutsi of neighboring Rwanda. These forces attacked

Congo, Democratic Republic of the (At a Glance)

FORMER NAME:
Republic of Zaire

AREA:
2,344,885 sq km (905,365 sq mi)

LOCATION:
Central Africa, bordered by Sudan, Angola, Burundi, Central African Republic, Republic of the Congo, Rwanda, Uganda, and Zambia

CAPITAL:
Kinshasa (population 800,000; 2007 estimate)

OTHER MAJOR CITIES:
Lubumbashi (formerly Elisabethville; population 1,074,600; 2002 estimate), Kisangani (formerly Stanleyville; 682,599; 2004 estimate)

POPULATION:
66,514,504 (2008 estimate)

POPULATION DENSITY:
28.36 persons per sq km (about 73.47 per sq mi)

POPULATION BELOW AGE 15:
47.1 percent (male 15,711,817; female 15,594,449; 2008 estimate)

POPULATION GROWTH RATE:
3.236 percent (2008 estimate)

TOTAL FERTILITY RATE:
6.28 children born per woman (2008 estimate)

LIFE EXPECTANCY AT BIRTH:
Total population: 53.98 years (2008 estimate)

INFANT MORTALITY RATE:
83.11 deaths per 1000 live births (2008 estimate)

LITERACY RATE (AGE 15 AND OVER WHO CAN READ AND WRITE IN FRENCH, LINGALA, KINGWANA, OR TSHILUBA):
Total population: 67.2 percent (male 80.9 percent; female 54.1 percent; 2008 estimate)

EDUCATION:
In 2006 about 44 percent of Congolese children attended primary school, and approximately 39 percent of males and 42 percent of females attended secondary school. In the late 1980s approximately 558,000 attended vocational and teacher-training schools.

LANGUAGES:
Although over 200 languages are spoken, French is the official language and the principal business and social language. Four African languages are also widely spoken: Swahili in the east, Kikongo in the area between Kinshasa and the coast, Tshiluba in the south, and Lingala along the Zaire River.

ETHNIC GROUPS:
More than 200 ethnic groups live in the Democratic Republic of the Congo, about 80 percent of which are Bantu-speaking peoples. Sudanese peoples live in the north, and small numbers of Nilotic, Pygmy, and other peoples are present in various areas. The largest single groups are the Kuba, Bakongo (Kongo), and Mongo (all Bantu), and the Mangbetu-Azande (Hamitic). A small number of Europeans live in the Democratic Republic of the Congo.

RELIGIONS:
About 50 percent of the people of the Democratic Republic of the Congo are Roman Catholic, while 20 percent are Protestant and 10 percent are Muslim. Most of the rest adhere to traditional animist beliefs, although syncretic sects, such as Kimbanguism, which combines Christian and traditional elements, likewise have a significant number of followers.

CLIMATE:
Extremely hot and humid except in the upland regions. The average annual temperature is about 27° C (about 80° F) in the low central area, with extremes considerably higher in February, the hottest month. In areas with altitudes above about 1,500 m (about 5,000 ft), the average annual temperature is about 19° C (about 66° F). Average annual rainfall is about 1,520 mm (about 60 in) in the north and 1,270 mm (50 in) in the south.

LAND, PLANTS, AND ANIMALS:
The dominant physical feature of the country is the Zaire (Congo) River basin. This region, constituting the entire central area, is a vast depression that slopes upward on all sides into plateaus and mountain ranges. The highest mountain group in this area is the Mitumba Range, on the country's eastern border. The Ubangi River, chief northern tributary of the Zaire (Congo), rises on the northwestern slopes of this range. In the southeast the basin is fringed by rugged mountain country, sometimes called

the Katanga, or Shaba, Plateau. This region, about 1,220 m (about 4,000 ft) above sea level, contains rich copper fields, uranium, and other mineral deposits.

In the southwest of the Democratic Republic of the Congo the mountain chains are collectively designated the Kwango-Kwilu Plateau. Virtually impenetrable equatorial forests occupy the eastern and northeastern portions of the country. The largest, known variously as the Ituri, Great Congo, Pygmy, and Stanley Forest, extends east from the confluence of the Aruwimi and Zaire (Congo) rivers nearly to Lake Albert, covering some 65,000 sq km (some 25,000 sq mi). In this area, on the Ugandan border, is the Ruwenzori Range, containing the country's highest point, Margherita Peak (5,109 m/ 16,762 ft). Large regions of the Congo Basin consist of savanna land.

Vegetation consists of rubber trees of various species, oil palms, coffee and cotton, banana, coconut palm, and plantain, teak, ebony, African cedar, mahogany, iroko, and redwood trees. Animals include elephants, lions, leopards, chimpanzees, gorillas, giraffes, hippopotamuses, okapis, zebras, wolves, buffaloes, mambas, pythons, crocodiles, parrots, pelicans, flamingos, cuckoos, sunbirds, herons, and spur-winged plovers. Insects include ants, termites, and mosquitoes, including the *Anopheles* mosquito, host of the malaria parasite. Another disease-bearing insect, prevalent in the lowlands, is the South African tsetse fly, disseminator of sleeping sickness.

NATURAL RESOURCES:
Cobalt, copper, gold, cadmium, petroleum, industrial and gem diamonds, silver, zinc, manganese, tin, germanium, uranium, radium, bauxite, iron ore, coal, and hydropower potential

CURRENCY:
The zaire

GROSS DOMESTIC PRODUCT (GDP):
$19.03 billion (2007 estimate)

GDP PER CAPITA:
$300 (2007 estimate)

GDP REAL GROWTH RATE:
7 percent (2007 estimate)

PRIMARY ECONOMIC ACTIVITIES:
Agriculture accounts for 55 percent of the labor force, while 11 percent are employed in industry; services account for another

continued

34 percent of the labor force (2000 estimate). Civil war between 1997 and 2002, which has exerted a death toll estimated at between 2 and 3.5 million people, has severely damaged the economy and threatened foreign investment. In 2002 a cease-fire went into effect which, it is hoped, will lead to a normalization of economic activities.

PRIMARY CROPS:
Coffee, sugar, palm oil, rubber, tea, quinine, cassava (tapioca), palm oil, bananas, root crops, corn, and fruits; wood products

INDUSTRIES:
Mining, mineral processing, consumer products (including textiles, foot-wear, cigarettes, processed foods, and beverages), cement, and diamonds

PRIMARY EXPORTS:
Copper, coffee, diamonds, cobalt, and crude oil

PRIMARY IMPORTS:
Consumer goods, foodstuffs, mining and other machinery, transport equipment, and fuels

PRIMARY TRADE PARTNERS:
United States, Belgium, France, Italy, Finland, South Africa, Nigeria, Kenya, and China

GOVERNMENT:
Following the assassination in January 2001 of President Laurent Désiré Kabila, who led a military coup against Mobutu Sese Seko in 1997, Joseph Kabila (son of the assassinated leader) succeeded to the presidency. The constitution states that the president shall be elected by popular vote to a seven-year term, and that a prime minister shall be elected by the High Council of the Republic. Elections have not been held since 1984. At present, Kabila serves as both chief of state and head of government; a transitional government was established in July 2003 following negotiations with the rebel leaders. Kabila won another term in 2005.

Robert Fay

not only the remnants of Mobutu's army, but also the Hutu refugees whose presence on the border of Rwanda threatened that country's predominantly Tutsi government. Kabila's army was supported by villagers throughout the countryside and faced little resistance from Zairean army troops, who were unwilling to risk their lives for a government that had not paid them for several months. Western powers refused to intervene of behalf of Mobutu. On May 16, 1997, with Kabila's army ready to take control of Kinshasa, the ailing dictator stepped down from power and flew with his family to MOROCCO. Kabila immediately declared himself head of the Democratic Republic of the Congo.

DEMOCRATIC REPUBLIC OF THE CONGO
After taking power, Kabila pledged to revitalize the country, stop corruption, and rebuild the infrastructure, including the mines, which need an estimated $8 billion to resume operation. Denying offices to any politicians or civil servants associated with Mobutu, including the extremely popular Étienne Tshisekedi, Kabila established his government and pledged not to hold elections for at least four years, or however long it took to build the necessary political and social institutions. Kabila's Banyamulenge supporters occupied several prominent positions in his new government.

Originally welcomed as a liberator, Kabila lost some of his popularity soon after taking office. The Congolese were upset by the continued presence of foreign troops, as well as by some of his policies, such as banning pants and short skirts on women. In addition, Kabila faced criticism from the international community, who suspected that his troops were responsible for the disappearance and assumed massacre of thousands of Hutu refugees. Although Kabila did not deny the allegations, during 1997 and 1998 he prevented UN officials from investigating the disappearances.

Meanwhile, Kabila ousted many of his Banyamulenge (or Tutsi) supporters from office and replaced them with members of other Congolese ethnic groups, mainly from Kabila's own home region, Shaba. This shift in ethnic allegiances accompanied a gradual deterioration in relations with Kabila's former allies, Uganda and Tutsi-ruled Rwanda, who accused him of harboring armed rebels opposed to the Rwandan and Ugandan governments in the forested borderlands of the eastern Congo. In mid-1998, Kabila's ousted Banyamulenge supporters, including former foreign minister Bizima Karaba, joined by former supporters of Mobutu and opposition figures such as Arthur Z'Ahidi Ngoma, mounted an armed rebellion against Kabila. The rebels accused Kabila of ethnic discrimination and autocratic misrule. The rebel forces, known as the Congolese Movement for Democracy, quickly took control of parts of the eastern Congo with the assistance of troops from Uganda and Rwanda. Troops from a number of African countries, including Angola, Zimbabwe, and NAMIBIA, came to the aid of Kabila and defeated a rebel offensive on Congo's capital, Kinshasa. Kabila was assassinated in January 2001. His son Joseph Kabila was named president soon thereafter.

The warfare ruined Congo's chances of recovering from decades of economic and political deterioration. More ominously, the participation of other African nations in the conflict threatened to spark a broader regional conflict extending beyond the country's borders. In 2003 the International Rescue Committee (IRC) estimated that 3.3 million people died in eastern Congo between mid-1998 and early 2001 due to violence and starvation, disease, and privation caused by the conflict.

Though Joseph Kabila succeeded in getting Rwandan troops to withdraw from Congolese territory, prompting a truce agreement in 2002, his government continued to face serious challenges. In 2003 a UN report concluded that senior officials linked to Kabila have colluded with Ugandan and Rwandan authorities in selling Congolese resources for their personal benefit; they have denied this charge. The report further indicates that the war was not driven by political goals, as stated, but by economic motives that continue to fuel instability. Kabila won a new term in office in the elections of 2005.

See also COLD WAR AND AFRICA; HUTU AND TUTSI; SLAVERY IN AFRICA.

ELIZABETH HEATH

Congo, Republic of the
Highly urbanized, oil-rich country in Central Africa, bordered by the Democratic Republic of the Congo, the Central African Republic, Cameroon, Gabon, and the Atlantic Ocean.

In the Republic of the Congo (henceforth Congo), regional shifts in population and power have long shaped the country's history. In precolonial times migrations, state formation, and slave trading concentrated population along the coastline and in the river valleys of the south, leaving northern peoples relatively isolated. French colonialism widened regional differences by pouring resources into urbanization and infrastructural development in the south, while drawing military recruits from the less developed north. In the early years of Congo's independence, Communist rhetoric flourished in the south's burgeoning cities— home to vocal intellectuals, students, and workers—but power remained with a military elite from the north. Although some of the country's leaders have since attempted to address the uneven development between north and south, city and countryside, real progress has been slowed by economic crises as well as by the highly militarized nature of national politics. Short-lived political liberalization in the 1990s was brought to an abrupt halt in 1997 by civil war—fought on the streets of the capital, BRAZZAVILLE, until a peace accord signed in 2003 brought an uneasy peace.

EARLY CONGOLESE HISTORY AND IMPERIALISM
The earliest inhabitants of present-day Congo were small communities of forest-dwelling hunter-gatherer PYGMY peoples known as the Binga. Historians believe that Bantu-speaking people migrated to the region from the northeast, around the Lake Chad basin, in the early fifteenth century. Their arrival opened an era of centralized state formation, beginning with the emergence of the KONGO kingdom in present-day ANGOLA, just south of the CONGO RIVER. The Vili split from the Kongo and moved north toward the coast, where they founded the LOANGO kingdom. It became a major slave-trading center, with Dutch, French, Portuguese, and British ships calling at the port, and caravan routes reaching far inland. On the central plateau the TÉKÉ, who are believed to have migrated there during the fifteenth century, established a kingdom known as Tio, and controlled much of the commerce on the Congo River. The transatlantic slave trade ultimately took some thirteen million people from the Congo River basin before its abolition in the early nineteenth century.

Although participation in the slave trade made some of region's kingdoms extraordinarily rich, the raids, warfare, and political rivalries engendered by the trade also contributed to regional instability. In the late seventeenth century the once-mighty Kongo Kingdom collapsed and many of the Kongo migrated north, forcing the Téké further north. At the end of the eighteenth century the MBOCHI migrated south from the western bank of the Congo River and became fishers, boat builders, hunters, and traders in the areas around the Sangha, Likouala, and Oubangui rivers. Over the long term, these patterns of migration, and the Arab slave trade in the north, led to much denser population settlement in the south of present-day Congo than in the north. They also formed the three main ethnic groups that inhabit present-day Congo: the Kongo, including the Vili and Lari subgroups (53 percent of the total population), the Téké (13 percent), and the Mbochi (12 percent).

FRENCH CONCESSIONS, COLONIALISM, AND CONGOLESE NATIONALISM
By the 1780s France had become the major European influence in the region, having established more than seventy trading companies north of the Congo. French missionaries soon followed, though extensive European exploration did not come until 1875, when France

dispatched Pierre Savorgnan de BRAZZA to fortify French claims. Aware that King LEOPOLD II of Belgium already had designs on the Congo River basin, de Brazza negotiated a treaty with the Téké and established a trading post. Competition between France and Belgium in the Congo basin led to the BERLIN CONFERENCE OF 1884–1885, which gave the territory along the river's northern bank to France. France appointed de Brazza commissioner of the Congo—then called Moyen-Congo—and subsequent negotiations between France, Belgium, and Portugal delineated the country's present-day borders.

France exploited Moyen-Congo's resources through a concessionary system, which granted private companies, chartered by the French government, thirty-year

monopolies over vast tracts of land. The concession companies' forced labor regimes not only depleted the region's rubber and ivory supplies but also decimated the population. Thousands of Africans died, and many others fled to the interior. By 1920 international outrage had brought an end to the system, which had, in fact, generated more bankruptcies than profits.

In the early 1930s the French built the Congo-Océan railway from Brazzaville to the deep-water port at Point-Noire, at a cost of 15,000 to 20,000 African lives. Many of the laborers, most of them northerners, eventually settled in the two cities. With the only major railway or port in French Equatorial Africa, which included GABON, CHAD, and OUBANGUI-CHARI (the present-day CENTRAL

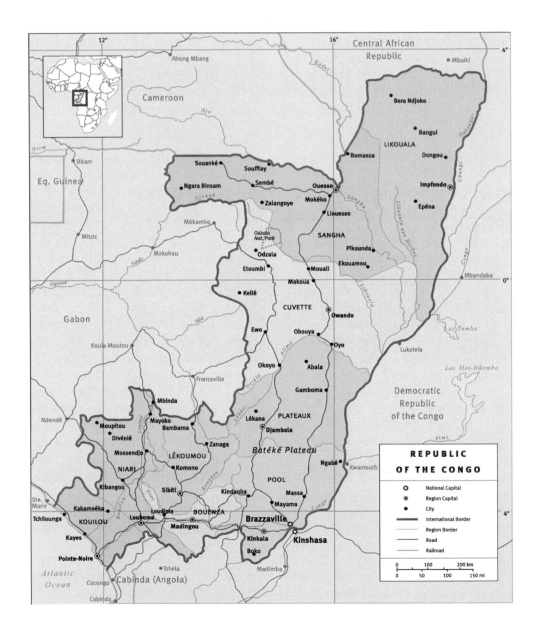

AFRICAN REPUBLIC), Moyen-Congo became the commercial and administrative center of the four territories. The French administration built the most extensive infrastructure as well as the greatest number of schools, courts, and hospitals in Moyen-Congo, particularly in Brazzaville, the capital. Although the colonial government remained strongly centralized—the governor general ruled by decree—educated Africans were employed in the lower levels of the civil service.

During World War II Brazzaville became sub-Saharan Africa's capital of Free France, and Congo became an important source of troops (thousands of Congolese fought in Europe). The expansion of government bureaucracies and urban services during and after the war provoked a second wave of urban migration. Many urban occupations became associated with specific ethnic groups—entrepreneurs and religious leaders, for example, often came from the Lari and Sundi Kongo groups. The French colonial administration contributed to the growing economic and social differentiation between ethnic groups by recruiting northerners, considered more "backward" than southerners, into the military.

At the 1944 Brazzaville Conference, France promised limited self-rule and abolished forced labor. Not surprisingly, nationalism in Moyen-Congo began in the cities. Urban intellectuals and workers together built a strong trade union movement, influenced by French socialists and communists. Members of these groups also founded the Vili-supported Congolese Progressive Party, which sought a gradual progression to self-rule, and the maintenance of strong ties to France and to the Mbochi-dominated African Socialist Movement. The best-known nationalist hero, however, was the evangelical cult leader André MATSOUA, who, despite his death in the late 1930s, was elected in absentia to the French National Assembly in 1945 and 1951.

By the mid-1950s, nationalist movements throughout Africa had made colonialism excessively costly for France and the other European powers. In preparation for decolonization in the Congo, France expanded voting rights in 1956, under the loi cadre, and in 1957 territorial elections were held. Fulbert Youlou, a defrocked Lari priest and founder of the Lari-dominated Democratic Union for the Defense of African Interests, or UDDIA, was elected vice president of the Moyen-Congo's government council. While Youlou was considered pro-French, he enjoyed strong support from fellow Lari as well as from the many Congolese who saw him as Matsoua's political and religious successor. In the 1958 elections, UDDIA victories made Youlou prime minister. When the Congo achieved independence on August 15, 1960, he became president.

POLITICAL ECONOMY OF INDEPENDENCE

Youlou's government, making no secret of its close military and economic ties to France—or of its distaste for radical politics—quickly lost support among Congo's students and workers. As unemployment rates increased and evidence of government corruption accumulated, popular discontent mounted, culminating in widespread demonstrations in August 1963. Youlou was forced to resign, and the military replaced him with the southern Kongolese Alphonse Massemba-Debat.

A former schoolteacher, Massemba-Debat made it his first priority to secure authority over the country's politically influential urban workers, youth, and intelligentsia. He established a single-party state, marginalized conservative opposition, and handed out jobs in the expanding state bureaucracy. He also checked the power of the northern, French-trained military by boosting the role of both the party's National Youth Movement of the Revolution, or JMNR, and the militia Civil Defense Corps, composed primarily of southerners and trained by North Korea and Cuba. Massemba-Debat's nominally socialist economic policies established state-run enterprises and won significant financial support from the Eastern Bloc, but left private industry largely intact. Western investment in the country continued, especially in oil exploration.

Although Massemba-Debat's policies brought neither economic prosperity nor much political support, they did set a precedent for the military regimes that followed his unremarkable term in office. Unpopular among Congolese radicals, conservative business interests, and army officers, he resigned in 1968. After a brief struggle with the JMNR, army captain Marien NGOUABI came to power in August of that year. He established the "vanguard" Congolese Worker's Party, or PCT, proclaimed a "people's republic," and officially adopted scientific socialism. The charismatic Ngouabi incorporated the police and gendarmerie into the military and brought them all under the control of the party. The greatest political implication of the 1968 coup, however, was the power shift to the north. Presidents Youlou and Massemba-Debat had been Bakongo from the south, but Ngouabi and his successors were fully or partially Mbochi from the north, where support for socialist policies was typically stronger. Ngouabi catered to the new power base by implementing reforms more radical than those undertaken by Massemba-Debat, such as nationalizing the main oil company, though many of his policies were more show than substance.

The discovery of oil offshore in 1969 and of phosphate deposits in 1973 led to a brief development boom, outlined in the euphoric three-year (1975–1977) plan, but also to mounting contradictions. International banks loaned generously to the newly oil-rich Congo, allowing the government to pour money into infrastructure projects and social services (especially education), but also accumulate a four-billion-dollar national debt. The nation's leaders, known for their taste for French couture, became even less convincing proponents of socialism than before, and left intact Italian and French corporate control over oil extraction. Except for the main urban centers, the country remained poor and underdeveloped; not until the early 1980s did paved roads reach the Congo's northern regions.

After a 1972 coup attempt, Ngouabi employed the military and security apparatus to crush the youth movement and any other opposition, while at the same time trying to broaden the government's populist appeal. He reestablished the national assembly and the post of prime minister, both of which he had abolished upon coming to power, and promised development projects to the rural population. But moves to cooperate with southern leaders and increase party control over the military alienated many hard-line northern military officers, some of whom were suspected of involvement in Ngouabi's assassination in 1977. Ngouabi was replaced by Brigadier General J. Yhombi-Opango. Known more for his opulent lifestyle than for his ideologies or policies, Yhombi-Opango accomplished little during his two-year term, which ended with a bloodless coup led by Colonel Denis SASSOU-NGUESSO.

Sassou-Nguesso became president with the support of the PCT, the military, the national assembly, and the sole legal trade union. To satisfy radicals and consolidate his rule, Sassou-Nguesso limited the powers of the PCT, expanded the paramilitary forces, promoted more northern Mbochis, and propounded Marxist-Leninist ideologies. He also renewed ties with the East, sending more military personnel to the Soviet Union, Eastern Europe, and Cuba for training, and allowing Cuba to use the Congo to ferry military troops and equipment to the Angolan government, which was then engaged in civil war. Like his predecessors, Sassou-Nguesso came to rely on periodic purges of the top political leadership in which he attempted to eliminate opponents while maintaining at least the façade of an ethnic and regional balance within the government. Yet opposition groups, whether operating underground or from abroad, continued their calls for democracy and an end to "pseudo-socialism."

During a brief economic upturn in the early 1980s Sassou-Nguesso sought to spread some of the wealth to the countryside, and in so doing both slowed urban migration and broadened his rural political base. He initiated rural infrastructural projects and restructured the national assembly to include particular interest groups. But these measures did little to revive an agricultural sector stifled by years of state control. Moreover, generous government spending in both rural and urban areas waned in the mid-1980s, when declining oil revenues forced Sassou-Nguesso to undertake austerity measures as part of a World Bank/IMF structural adjustment program. By then, the civil service employed 73,000 people—one quarter of the labor force—and students had come to expect government jobs upon graduation. Not surprisingly, cuts in wages and education spending sparked strikes and riots in 1985–1986.

In the late 1980s the Congo government privatized, semi-privatized, or closed seventy-six of its 100 state-run industries. It also terminated state monopolies and liberalized investment codes, encouraging investment in mining (copper, gold, lead, potassium, tin, and zinc), secondary industries such as food processing and textiles, and timber. Congo's hardwood forests have since been rapidly logged. But an economy that was still strapped by low oil prices took its toll on the already tenuous legitimacy of the Sassou-Nguesso regime.

Economic liberalization, the loss of support from the disintegrating Eastern Bloc, and pressures from international donor agencies forced quick political liberalization in the Congo. In mid-1990 the PCT, which had a hand in governing as the sole legal party for the previous twenty-two years, abandoned Marxist-Leninism and initiated a transition to multiparty rule. In early 1991 Sassou-Nguesso convened a national conference that, over the next eighteen months, wrote a new constitution, established an interim government, and scheduled elections. In August 1992 southerner Pascal LISSOUBA was elected president and his party won a plurality. Lissouba's party, the Pan-African Union for Social Democracy, or UPADS, joined in a coalition with the PCT, and in attempt at national reconciliation appointed the northerner Yhombi-Opango prime minister. The PCT-UPADS coalition soon fell apart and in 1993 Lissouba called for new elections, which the UPADS won convincingly, over the Lari Bernard Kolélas, and distant third-place Sassou-Nguesso.

Disagreements over legislative elections between Lissouba and Kolélas, who became mayor of Brazzaville, led to open warfare in 1993 between each man's private militias, forces popularly known as the Zulu and the Ninjas, respectively. In May 1997, shortly before scheduled presidential elections, Lissouba's forces tried to disarm members of Sassou-Nguesso's militia (known as the Cobras), claiming they might disrupt campaigning. Clashes between the two forces exploded into civil war in the streets of Brazzaville, killing between 6,000 and 10,000 people and largely destroying the city. In October, with

Congo, Republic of the (At a Glance)

AREA:
342,002 sq km (132,047 sq mi)

LOCATION:
Western Africa, bordering the Atlantic Ocean, Gabon, Cameroon, Central African Republic, and the Democratic Republic of the Congo (formerly Zaire)

CAPITAL:
Brazzaville (population 1.5 million; 2002 estimate)

OTHER MAJOR CITIES:
Pointe-Noire (population 663,400; 2005 estimate)

POPULATION:
3,903,318 (2008 estimate)

POPULATION DENSITY:
11.41 persons per sq km (about 29 per sq mi; 2008 estimate)

POPULATION BELOW AGE 15:
46.1 percent (male 906,345; female 894,568; 2008 estimate)

POPULATION GROWTH RATE:
2.696 percent (2008 estimate)

TOTAL FERTILITY RATE:
5.92 children born per woman (2008 estimate)

LIFE EXPECTANCY AT BIRTH:
Total population: 53.74 years (male 52.52 years, female 55 years; 2008 estimate)

INFANT MORTALITY RATE:
81.29 deaths per 1000 live births (2008 estimate)

LITERACY (AGE 15 AND OVER WHO CAN READ AND WRITE):
Total population: 83.8 percent (male 89.6 percent; female 78.4 percent; 2003 estimate)

EDUCATION:
Free and compulsory for children ages 6 through 12. About 18 percent of boys and 15 percent of girls attend secondary school (2000–2006 estimate).

LANGUAGES:
French is the official language; Lingala and Kikingo are the most widely spoken African languages.

ETHNIC GROUPS:
There are four major ethnic groups: the Bakongo (the major group, accounting for about 50 percent of the total population), the Mboshi, the Sanga, and the Téké, who live in the central region. There are 75 subgroups of these four major groups.

RELIGIONS:
About half the population are Christian, primarily Catholic. Approximately 48 percent follow traditional religious beliefs, and about 2 percent are Muslim.

CLIMATE:
Tropical, with mostly high heat and humidity. While the Mayumbe Mountains experience a long dry season, parts of the Congo Basin receive more than 2,500 mm (more than 100 in) of rainfall annually. Average temperatures in Brazzaville are 26° C (78° F) in January and 23° C (73° F) in July, with an annual rainfall of about 1,500 mm (about 60 in). Temperatures along the coast are slightly cooler.

LAND, PLANTS, AND ANIMALS:
Along the Atlantic coast is a low, treeless plain, which rises inland to the Mayumbe Mountains, an almost completely forested region with an average elevation of about 550 m (about 1,800 ft). In the south central region is the fertile valley of the Niari River. To the north lies the central highlands region, the Batéké Plateau. The plateau is cut by numerous tributaries of the Zaire (Congo) and Ubangi rivers. Dense tropical rain forests cover approximately half of the country and constitute a major natural resource. The principal commercial species are *okoumé* (a mahogany) and *limba* (a hardwood). Savanna vegetation is found in the northeast and the higher plateau areas. Wildlife is diverse and abundant, including antelope, giraffes, cheetahs, crocodiles, and numerous birds and snakes.

NATURAL RESOURCES:
Offshore petroleum potash, gold, iron ore, lead, and copper

CURRENCY:
Communauté Financière Africaine (CFA) franc

GROSS DOMESTIC PRODUCT (GDP):
$12.86 billion (2007 estimate)

GDP PER CAPITA:
$3,400 (2007 estimate)

GDP REAL GROWTH RATE:
−1.6 percent (2007 estimate)

PRIMARY ECONOMIC ACTIVITIES:
Agriculture, handicrafts, oil production, and forestry

PRIMARY CROPS:
Cassava, sugar, rice, corn, peanuts, vegetables, coffee, cocoa, and forest products

INDUSTRIES:
Petroleum extraction, cement kilning, lumbering, brewing, sugar milling, palm oil, soap, and cigarette making

PRIMARY EXPORTS:
Crude oil (90 percent of export revenue), lumber, plywood, sugar, cocoa, coffee, and diamonds

PRIMARY IMPORTS:
Intermediate manufactures, capital equipment, construction materials, foodstuffs, and petroleum products

PRIMARY TRADING PARTNERS:
France, Italy, United States, South Korea, Belgium, Germany, South Africa, China

GOVERNMENT:
A multiparty republican system provides for direct election of the president to a five-year term. Since October 1997 the head of state has been President Denis Sassou-Nguesso, who took office after a coup that toppled President Pascal Lissouba; Sassou-Nguesso was reelected in March 2002. The president appoints the Council of Ministers. A bicameral Parliament includes the Senate and the National Assembly, whose members are elected by popular vote to five-year terms.

Robert Fay

considerable Angolan assistance, Sassou-Nguesso and his Cobras took control of the capital. In an election soon afterward, Sassou-Nguesso became president. He has promised national reconciliation, a return to civilian rule, and a professional military. To revive the war-torn economy and rebuild the capital, the president has liberalized the country's tax codes, and continues to encourage foreign investment and diversification of the export sector. These reforms, however, were hampered when fighting again broke out in 1998. Sassou-Nguesso was reelected in 2002 with 89.4 percent of the vote. A peace accord was brokered in 2003.

BIBLIOGRAPHY

Ballif, Noel. *Le Congo.* Karthala, 1993.

Radu, Michael, and Keith Somerville. *Benin, the Congo and Burkina Faso: Economics, Politics and Society.* Pinter Publishers, 1988.

Vansina, Jan. *The Tio Kingdom of the Middle Congo, 1880–1892.* Oxford University Press, 1973.

ERIC YOUNG

Congo Free State
Former name of the Democratic Republic of Congo.

See also CONGO, DEMOCRATIC REPUBLIC OF THE.

Congo River
Second longest river in Africa.

The Congo River is 4,374 km (2,718 mi) long, and its drainage basin is about 3,457,000 sq km (about 1,335,000 sq mi), covering almost all of the DEMOCRATIC REPUBLIC OF THE CONGO, the Republic of the Congo, the CENTRAL AFRICAN REPUBLIC, eastern ZAMBIA, northern ANGOLA, and parts of BURUNDI and TANZANIA. From its headwaters at the junction of the Lualaba and Luvua rivers, it flows generally north until Boyoma (Stanley) Falls, where it begins to flow generally northeast, then west, and south to its outlet to the Atlantic Ocean at Banana, Republic of the Congo. The river receives an average of 1,500 mm of rain (about 60 in) per year, of which more than 25 percent discharges into the Atlantic Ocean.

The river can be divided into three main regions: the upper Congo, the middle Congo, and the lower Congo. The upper Congo has many tributaries, lakes, waterfalls, and rapids. The middle Congo has seven cataracts known collectively as Boyoma (Stanley) Falls, below which the river becomes navigable. The lower Congo begins where the river divides in two and forms the vast Malebo (Stanley) Pool. The capitals of the Republic of the Congo and the Democratic Republic of the Congo, BRAZZAVILLE and KINSHASA, respectively, face each other on opposite sides of Malebo (Stanley) Pool. The Congo has many tributaries, and its total of approximately 14,500 km (about 9,000 mi) of waterways make it one of the main transportation routes in Central Africa. Especially because the region's road systems have deteriorated during the past three decades, the Congo has become a vital trade artery, supporting a busy traffic in barges as well as smaller boats. The river also has great hydroelectric potential, although this has not been widely exploited. In addition, it is home to numerous fish species and crocodiles.

In 1482, when Portuguese navigator Diogo Cam (also spelled Cão) became the first European to sail up the mouth of the Congo, he met the rulers of the Kingdom of KONGO, marking the beginning of centuries of European slave trading and later colonialism in the region. In the late nineteenth century, Europeans began extensive exploration of the Congo. Scottish explorer and missionary David Livingstone reached the Lualaba River, the Congo's largest tributary, in 1871. In 1876 and 1877, American Henry M. STANLEY traveled from the confluence of the Lualaba and the Congo, descending to its mouth, a journey of about 2,575 km (about 1,600 mi). Not long afterward, author Joseph Conrad published the short story *Heart of Darkness*, loosely based on his observations of the region then under the rule of Belgium's King LEOPOLD II.

More recently, the Congo has witnessed the fall of governments. In May 1997 supporters of former dictator MOBUTU SESE SEKO crossed the river from Kinshasa to Brazzaville, fleeing the army of Laurent-Désiré KABILA. In September 1997, when troops of General Denis SASSOU-NGUESSO ousted then-president of the Republic of Congo, Pascal Lissouba, thousands boarded boats and fled from Brazzaville to Kinshasa.

ROBERT FAY

Conservation in Africa
Allocation and management of natural resources in Africa.
Conservation in Africa, as elsewhere, involves decisions about the allocation and use of resources, including scarce ones, and as such tends to be highly politicized. Many human activities in Africa have had a conservation effect while serving a different primary purpose, such as satisfying human needs or reducing anxieties about society. Pastoralist communities burn grasslands to provide nutrient-rich shoots for their cattle, but these young grasses also support larger numbers of wild herbivores, such as gnu (wildebeest), zebra, impala, antelope, hartebeest, and gazelle. Respecting sacred areas can create "no-take" zones that form biologically diverse "islands" over time, such as the *kaya* forests of KENYA's MIJIKENDA. Indeed, virtually all modern techniques for resource conservation, such as zones of limited or no access, closed seasons, size

restrictions, and limited off-take have been in use for millennia.

Pharaohs in ancient EGYPT set aside lands as hunting preserves to protect diminishing wildlife populations, reducing lands available to common people. Similarly, the colonizers of Africa, especially the British, set aside lands in the late nineteenth and early twentieth centuries for safari hunting. New ideas about wildlife management came with COLONIAL RULE in Africa. Some species, mainly large predators, such as lion, leopard, wild dog, and hyena, were designated pests or vermin, and their populations were greatly reduced to protect colonial ranchers and farmers, especially in Kenya and ZIMBABWE, and throughout British-controlled Africa. Indigenous hunting was often banned at the same time that settler communities were paid for their kills.

Colonial land and labor policies changed the people-environment relationships. Communities became more sedentary, easier to tax and to police, by moving them to indigenous reserves or reservations. Communal and customary land rights were weakened or lost with the increasing privatization of land. Those engaged in PASTORALISM, such as the MAASAI, FULANI, and TUAREG, were settled on ranches or encouraged to use new boreholes and wells along set pathways. In SOUTH AFRICA whites moved indigenous people into bantustans, or homelands. The effect of these mass relocations was to free the most productive lands for use by white settlers and for game parks, and to create overcrowded indigenous areas with a ready supply of labor for new industries. Soil erosion, deforestation, and poor water quality began to plague the newly overcrowded lands.

During the colonial era, the SAHARA expanded into the SAHEL bringing DROUGHT AND DESERTIFICATION. Whereas climatic variation could explain the Sahara's advance, colonial interpretations of environmental change generally involved mismanagement on the part of Africans and a need for corrective conservation measures including forced labor on terracing, irrigation, and other projects. Conservation projects were generally based on best practices for European lands and rarely resulted in environmental improvement.

Conservation during colonial rule rarely included the protection of sacred or totem animals, respecting ancestral grounds, or other socially meaningful activities. Instead resource conservation became associated with fines and imprisonment for hunting, forced relocations without adequate compensation, and the creation of no-take zones for the leisure activities of outsiders. Independent regimes continued top-down, colonial conservation approaches into the 1980s before reevaluating the cost-effectiveness of trying to protect resources from people. Around this time poaching of elephants for the IVORY TRADE and rhinoceros for horn were decimating these populations and generating negative press. Richard LEAKEY, leader of the Kenya Wildlife Service from 1989 to 1994, enforced a controversial but effective shoot-to-kill policy aimed at suspected poachers. Similar approaches to protecting tourism in Africa were used in Zimbabwe, but as in Kenya drew attention to the abuse of HUMAN RIGHTS IN AFRICA.

By the 1990s many countries were looking for more people-friendly approaches to resource management that mixed development and local participation. CAMPFIRE (Communal Areas Management Program for Indigenous Resources) in Zimbabwe is a prime example. Overall, grassroots ENVIRONMENTAL MOVEMENTS IN AFRICA are on the rise, many outside of formally protected areas. Important leaders include Ken SARO-WIWA and Wangari MAATHAI, the latter of whom won the 2004 Nobel Peace Prize for her work in the Green Belt Movement.

Africa is a continent of farmers although, due to its GEOMORPHOLOGY, it has thin, infertile soils relative to other landmasses. Farming communities, such as the ARUSHA, DOGON, HUTU, IRAQW, and KIKUYU, have struggled to maintain soil quality and agricultural output with increasing POPULATION GROWTH IN SUB-SAHARAN AFRICA. The switch, largely during the colonial period from multicropping or intercropping of subsistence crops to monocropping cash crops for export, has accelerated soil erosion and involved the increased use of environmentally harmful pesticides and purchased fertilizer. WARFARE IN AFRICA SINCE INDEPENDENCE has further disrupted the agricultural resource base through the laying of landmines on farms, especially in MOZAMBIQUE and ANGOLA, and the creation of environmental refugees. FOOD IN AFRICA is frequently used as a political weapon and HUNGER AND FAMINE exist in countries that are exporting food. The realities of climate change have only served to exacerbate these problems.

Throughout Africa resource managers face the dilemma of sustainable development—how to meet the needs of current populations without jeopardizing the ability of future generations to meet theirs. Tropical rainforests can provide quick cash through logging, but such activity destroys habitat for primates and other organisms and threatens the way of life of forest people, such as the TWA and other so-called PYGMY groups. How to conserve resources from freshwater to marine and COASTAL RESOURCES to genetic and energy resources is increasingly a concern on a continent with considerable poverty and economic underdevelopment. Conservation was a major discussion topic at the Earth Summit in 2002, in JOHANNESBURG. Many African leaders believe their countries should receive credit for producing less than their global share of acid rain, greenhouse gases, and toxic waste.

Africa contains the second largest contiguous tropical rainforest in the world, the greatest human resources in terms of diversity of languages, more hydroelectric potential (ASWAN HIGH DAM, BLUE NILE, CONGO RIVER, VICTORIA FALLS, ZAMBEZI RIVER, and others) than any other continent, half of the world's flamingo population, all of the world's lemurs, many endangered species, premier protected areas (such as SERENGETI NATIONAL PARK), and the world headquarters for the United Nations Environmental Program in NAIROBI, KENYA. In addition, LAKE MALAWI and LAKE TANGANYIKA of the Great Rift Valley possess high degrees of endemism, that is, species found only in that place. The continent is of prime importance in the global effort to conserve resources.

See also BANTU: DISPERSION AND SETTLEMENT; DROUGHT AND DESERTIFICATION; WILDLIFE MANAGEMENT IN AFRICA.

BIBLIOGRAPHY

Adams, Jonathan S., and Thomas O. McShane. *The Myth of Wild Africa: Conservation without Illusion.* University of California Press, 1996.

Anderson, David, and Richard H. Grove, eds. *Conservation in Africa: Peoples, Policies and Practice.* Cambridge University Press, 1989.

Bonner, Raymond. *At the Hand of Man: Peril and Hope for Africa's Wildlife.* Knopf, 1993.

Carmichael, David L., Jane Hubert, Brian Reeves, and Audhild Schanche, eds. *Sacred Sites, Sacred Places.* Routledge, 1998.

Gibson, Clark C. *Politicians and Poachers: The Political Economy of Wildlife Policy in Africa.* Cambridge University Press, 1999.

Grove, Richard. *Green Imperialism: Colonial Expansion, Tropical Island Edens and the Origins of Environmentalism, 1600–1860.* Cambridge University Press, 1996.

Hulme, David, and Marshall Murphree, eds. *African Wildlife and Livelihoods: The Promise and Performance of Community Conservation.* James Currey, 2001.

Oates, John F. *Myth and Reality in the Rain Forest: How Conservation Strategies Are Failing in West Africa.* University of California Press, 1999.

HEIDI GLAESEL FRONTANI

Constitutional Law in Africa

See LAW IN AFRICA: COLONIAL AND CONTEMPORARY.

Conté, Lansana

1934–2008

President of Guinea since 1984.

Taking power in a nonviolent coup in 1984, Lansana Conté succeeded Sékou TOURÉ, Guinea's first president and the man who led the country's independence movement. While Conté has been criticized for delaying free elections, he is also credited with reversing some of Touré's most glaring excesses.

Conté was born in Dubréka, GUINEA. Although little is known of his childhood, records indicate that he obtained a military education abroad and then returned to Guinea in 1958, just after the independence vote and Touré's installment as president. Having served three years in the French military, Conté joined the Guinean army and by 1975 had become a general. In 1984, a month after Touré's death, Conté and fellow military leader Diarra Traoré successfully staged a bloodless takeover and installed the Military Committee for National Reparation (CMRN). One of Conté's first actions was to free some ninety-seven political prisoners; another was to suspend Guinea's constitution.

A year later Conté weathered an unsuccessful coup attempt by Traoré, then prime minister, and responded by imprisoning at least 200 alleged coup plotters. By 1989 Guinea still had not held free elections, but the country showed signs of recovering from years of economic decline under the autocratic Touré. In particular, Conté's adherence to a World Bank structural adjustment program won approval from western nations such as France, which began to provide aid to Guinea. In 1990 Conté oversaw the writing of a new constitution, and in 1993 he won Guinea's first multiparty election, which outside observers claimed was rigged. After repressing a mutiny in 1996, Conté won reelection to a five-year term in 1998. Opposition leaders rejected Conté's invitation to join the government, claiming that he had not been legally reelected. Despite being slowed by diabetes and heart problems, Conté accepted his party's (Party for Unity and Progress) nomination to run for another term as president in the December 2003 election. He was sworn in during January of the following year.

The last years of Conté's life were tumultuous. He survived a 2005 assassination attempt and was forced to seek treatment abroad for his ailing health on numerous occasions. A 2007 strike in protest of his presidency (and the growing accusations of official corruption coming from both inside and outside the country) turned violent, leading to the deaths of nearly two dozen protestors. On 23 December 2008 Conté died of causes undeclared (though widely assumed to be the result of his long-flagging health). The country was then seized in a coup orchestrated by the Guinean army under the command of Moussa Dadis Camara.

See also STRUCTURAL ADJUSTMENT IN AFRICA.

KATE TUTTLE

Contemporary African Writers in France

The most recent developments in French-language African literature include novels generated by young sub-Saharan African authors living in France. The existence of intellectuals in France from Africa and the African diaspora is certainly not a new phenomenon. Members of the Harlem Renaissance in the 1920s, such as Langston Hughes, Countee Cullen, Claude McKay, Walter White, and Jessie Fauset, were attracted by the myth of France as a land of human equality and liberty. In the 1930s, Léopold SENGHOR, Aimé CÉSAIRE, and Léon Damas founded the Négritude movement, which was organized around the recognition of black people and black aesthetics, and exchanges between the continents. The 1950s and 1960s were a period of continued intense literary activity, with American expatriates like Richard Wright, James Baldwin, and Chester Himes writing in France. Likewise, a number of African expatriates settled in France, often for political reasons. Their literary work reflected upon Africa's future and the conditions necessary for building the newly independent nations. For example, Mongo BETI, during the thirty-three-year period from 1958–1991 when he was away from Cameroon, focused his novels on Africans in Africa. He portrayed a corrupted neocolonial African elite replacing the old colonizers. He was also harshly critical of French intervention in African politics and economy. In the early 1980s, a new generation of African writers, originally from sub-Saharan African countries such as SENEGAL, CAMEROON, GUINEA, CÔTE D'IVOIRE, DEMOCRATIC REPUBLIC OF THE CONGO (formerly Zaire), and the REPUBLIC OF THE CONGO, appeared on the French literary scene. They were mostly rising writers like Cameroonians Simon Njami and J. R. Essomba and the Congolese Daniel Biyaoula; very few of them were well-established writers. One notable exception is the Cameroonian Calixthe Beyala, who has won numerous literary prizes for her eight novels and enjoys spectacular success in France. In parting from the mainstream African novel in French to explore more personal avenues, these men and women are shaping a new literature. Rather than focusing on Africa, their works show a common interest in questions of displacement. They pose new questions about postcolonial identities and cultures. This literature can essentially be characterized along three main lines, corresponding to the direction of the protagonist's gaze. In the first type—what can be called a literature of detachment—the protagonist refuses to look at the continent of Africa and shows a disinterest in Africa and Africans. In Simon Njami's *African Gigolo* (1988), for instance, the protagonist will not confront the lies his life is wrapped in and refuses to invest in any common cause. Philippe Camara's *Discopolis* (1993), focusing on the world of disco and music in the 1970s, is probably the most extreme example of disengagement. In that work there is no mention of race, nor any preoccupation with questions of identity. One might argue that these authors claim first and foremost an individual voice, refusing the implicit plea for African writers to write literature engaged with an African identity. The second type of literature could be called a literature of displacement. In these works, the protagonist directs his or her gaze toward the experience as an African in France. The authors explore such issues as identity and interracial relationships, as well as reflect on notions of hybridity and assimilation into French society. These novels are sometimes critical of the African community in France as well as in Africa. Daniel Biyaoula's *L'Impasse* (1996), for example, presents a harsh criticism of Africans' lifestyle, portraying their infatuation with fashion and appearance. His novel raises issues about beauty criteria and dreams of success, where the West remains the model. Finally, the third type of literature focuses on the experience and dynamics of immigration. The protagonist is no longer merely an individual but is considered as part of the community of African immigrants in Paris. Examples of the literature of immigration are: J. R. Essomba's *Le Paradis du Nord* (1996) and *Le destin volé* (2003), Calixthe Beyala's *Le petit prince de Belleville* (1990), *Maman a un amant* (1992), *Assèze l'Africaine* (1994), and *Les Honneurs perdus* (1996). In this cycle, known as her "Parisian" novels, Beyala was one of the first to give the immigrant community a voice. Using both male and female narrative voices, she contrasts the experience of immigration. She points out the feelings of transparency and vulnerability that accompany men who are labeled immigrants. Women, on the other hand, whether single or married, young or older, are shown in their potential of becoming something new, as they look at immigrating as a dynamic process. Her portrayals of men and women have raised controversy among Africans, particularly on the continent. All of these types of works raise questions of transculturation and adjustment to a multicultural system. Authors like Biyaoula or Beyala look at the interactions between Africans and the French society and how culture flows in not just one direction, but both ways. As a result, the narration lies at the intersection of several layers of gazes and discourses: the Africans looking at the French, the French looking at the Africans, Africans in Paris looking at Africans on the continent. These writers' works raise the question of what it means for postcolonial literature to be written in France. They also call into question the extent to which this literature reflects Africans' concerns, and whether it should still be considered African literature. Whether a literature of detachment, of displacement, or of immigration, this new literature does not look at the past as a source of anchoring. Nor does it hope for a possible return to the motherland. Unlike in the times of Négritude, this is not a movement. Even if the writers sometimes know one another, they do not form a group: they remain individual voices. When asked about their origins, they might answer, "I am an African writer," without specifying Senegalese, Congolese, or Cameroonian. Very rarely will their answer be "French writer." More frequently, they will simply say, "I am a writer," thus indicating their aspirations to a world literature and their conscious participation in a global world.

See also COLONIAL RULE.

ODILE CAZENAVE

Coppolani, Xavier

1830–1905

French colonial leader known as the father of French Mauritania, who was responsible for French control of southern Mauritania.

One of the early proponents of indirect COLONIAL RULE, Xavier Coppolani advocated "peaceful pacification," a policy that employed knowledge of indigenous traditions and social structure to conquer southern Mauritania without warfare. Born in Corsica, Coppolani spent most of his childhood in ALGERIA, where he became familiar with Islam and fluent in Arabic. This background, coupled with his experience in the Algerian Arab Bureau and the French colonial army during the 1890s, made him an ideal candidate to lead the 1902 French campaign into southern Mauritania.

In contrast to the violent colonial conquest waged by the French elsewhere in West Africa, Coppolani proposed a plan to win control of Mauritania by subverting its Moorish social hierarchy. He intended to exploit preexisting rivalries to divide and undermine the powerful *hassan* chiefs, while simultaneously protecting the monastic Moorish groups known as the *zawiya*. Coppolani believed the French could employ the zawiya as colonial agents, thus ruling Mauritania indirectly and inexpensively. Within months of his arrival in Mauritania in late 1902, Coppolani had signed treaties with two major leaders—Cheikh Sidiya Baba and Cheikh Saad Bou—and secured control of valuable land along the north bank of the SENEGAL RIVER Valley.

But Coppolani, arguing that he also needed to win the loyalty of nomadic groups in the Adrar region, convinced the French government to extend his mission northward in late 1904. He immediately encountered the hostility of the Sahrawi religious leader Cheikh Ma Al-Ainin, and soon afterward turned to conventional military means to pacify the Tagant region. In April 1905 Coppolani reached the town of Tidjikja, where, before he was able to launch his next campaign, he was murdered. The French mission in Mauritania subsequently faltered, and the region was not completely colonized until 1913. But the French did adopt some of Coppolani's original plans, including the use of the zawiya as colonial agents.

See also ISLAM IN AFRICA.

ELIZABETH HEATH

Corsairs

Maritime raiders whose activities supported the economic development of several North African coastal cities.

European history books have long portrayed North African corsairs as lawless pirates, looting unsuspecting European merchant vessels and making off with their hard-earned goods. In fact, the corsairs were carrying out government-authorized maritime warfare and plunder, and their activities were common among the many nations operating in the Mediterranean and the North African coastal Atlantic from at least the thirteenth century. The goals of corsair raiding were not simply economic, but also political and sometimes religious. Seafaring nations were forced to make alliances or pay protection money to secure their trading interests. In the aftermath of the CRUSADES, these nations, both Islamic and Christian, often defined friends and enemies according to religion, and used these divisions to justify theft or the capture of slaves.

For centuries, the spoils of these maritime skirmishes fueled the economies of several North African coastal cities. In the thirteenth century, the BERBER Hafsids used profits from commerce raiding to transform TUNIS into a royal capital, complete with schools and mosques. Although many of the later corsair captains claimed Turkish, Greek, or Albanian origins, their ships carried Arab and Berber crews, and the corsairs' histories are intertwined with those of their home ports. Tunis, ALGIERS, and TRIPOLI all owed some allegiance to the Ottoman Empire from the sixteenth century onward, but created powerful city-states that sponsored, or at least housed, corsair activity. In the sixteenth century the city of Algiers was home to the famous Turkish "Barbarossa" brothers, Aruj and Khayr ad-Din. They and their successors invested corsair profits in Algiers and the surrounding countryside. Corsair raids enriched the region around Tripoli from the sixteenth through the nineteenth centuries. In both Algiers and Tripoli, corsair guilds came to exercise considerable political influence over the regional government, especially in matters of commerce and diplomacy.

The twin city of RABAT Salé was another corsair enclave along the Atlantic coast of modern-day MOROCCO. One of the few cities in the region not under Ottoman rule, Rabat's location on a tricky river passage helped Moroccan corsairs evade avenging battleships. Many of the corsair financiers, crews, and profiteers were part of the two separate Andalusian communities that had left southern Spain between 1609 and 1614, fleeing the recriminations of Philip II against politically active Moors. They revived a city around the citadel of Rabat, across the river from the Islamic spiritual center of Salé. Rabat became a bustling commercial center, trading with corsairs from Algiers and other coastal cities.

North African corsair activity did not escape retaliation from more distant maritime powers. Portuguese, Spanish, Dutch, French, British, and finally, American ships tried to capture corsair ships, seize their territories, blockade their ports, or simply blow up their cities. In 1815 the United States Navy attacked Tunis and bombarded Algiers, forcing the cities' leaders to forswear further attacks on American ships. The following year, the British and the Dutch waged a devastating war on the Algiers fleet, leaving the region vulnerable to the French colonial conquest that came fifteen years later.

MARIAN AGUIAR

Côte d'Ivoire

Country in West Africa bordered by Liberia, Guinea, Mali, Burkina Faso, Ghana, and the Atlantic Ocean.

The recent history of Côte d'Ivoire is rife with contradictions. The country that offered some of the most sustained resistance to French colonialism has in the postcolonial era become one of France's most loyal clients. Economic growth and prosperity for elites and foreign investors has come at the price of poverty for large segments of the population. Côte d'Ivoire had only two leaders from 1960 to 1999: Félix Houphouët-Boigny, who led the country from colonial rule through three decades of independence—and his successor, Henri-Konan Bédié. Both helped build a nation of political stability and limited economic prosperity—the "Ivoirian Miracle." At the same time, both maintained a neocolonial dependence on France and blocked effective democratic reforms. Many praised Côte d'Ivoire as a model of political stability until 1999, when Bédié was overthrown in the nation's first military coup.

PRECOLONIAL HISTORY

Unlike many West African countries, little is known about the early history of Côte d'Ivoire. Historians believe that agriculture reached the region before

CÔTE D'IVOIRE MEDICINE. Hundreds of Ivoirians wait in line for vaccinations, c. 1925. (*Bridgeman Art Library International Ltd.*)

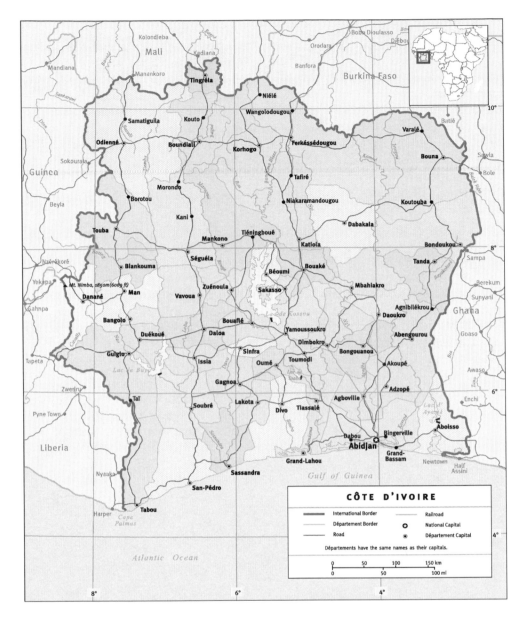

MANDE, KRU, and AKAN groups assimilated much of its population. Fleeing from the MALI EMPIRE and the ASANTE, and searching for gold and KOLA nuts for the trans-Saharan trade, these groups began migrating to the area by the sixteenth century. By the mid-eighteenth century they had established five major kingdoms in the northern, central, and eastern regions: the Kong Kingdom, founded by the Jula and the Senufo; the ABRON KINGDOM; the BAULE Kingdom; and the ANYI Kingdoms of Indénié and Sanwi, all established by different Akan groups. Relying primarily on subsistence agriculture, these kingdoms brought the Saharan trade to the edges of the densely forested south. Nevertheless, the inhabitants of the largely autonomous

forest villages remained essentially isolated from outside influences. Dense woods in the south and a treacherous coastline protected Côte d'Ivoire from inroads by early European explorers, who made only halting contacts before the nineteenth century. The Portuguese briefly landed on the coast during the fifteenth century, and the French founded their first short-lived trading settlement at Assinie during the seventeenth century to trade guns and other European goods for gold and ivory. But inhospitable conditions prevented the establishment of permanent settlements, and thus Côte d'Ivoire largely escaped the horrors of the slave trade. In the 1840s, however, the French, while patrolling the Gulf of Guinea to block the now illegal slave trade, decided to reestablish a foothold in the region of Côte d'Ivoire. In 1842, under orders from the Naval Ministry, Captain Bouët-Willaumez signed treaties with a number of coastal groups. For an annual tribute payment, the French obtained two strategic tracts of land—present-day Assinie and Grand-Bassam—where they built forts and trading posts. As Great Britain acquired large possessions nearby, France attempted to expand in the region and during the next twenty-five years concluded treaties with almost all the major coastal villages. Despite escalating European rivalry in the area, however, defeat in the Franco-Prussian War (1871) forced France to turn its attention away from Africa and back to European affairs. But, hoping to maintain control over the region, France named a merchant, Arthur Verdier, the first resident of Côte d'Ivoire in 1878 and gave him temporary control of Grand-Bassam and other nearby ports. Although Verdier's main interests were commercial ventures along the coast—he built new ports and started a coffee plantation—he also sought to promote France's interests, and in 1887 hired Marcel Treich-Leplène to explore the NIGER RIVER basin and obtain treaties from its inhabitants. At the same time, the French government sent Lieutenant Louis-Gustave Binger into the interior of Côte d'Ivoire. Treich-Leplène and Binger secured treaties with nine major groups, including the Abron and Kong, and when they met up in 1889 they declared the southern region a French protectorate. Subsequent expeditions solidified French claims, and negotiations with Great Britain and Liberia further clarified the boundaries of the French protectorate. (The French repeatedly redefined the northern border until 1947, when they determined its present shape.) In 1893 France declared Côte d'Ivoire a colony.

FRENCH COLONIZATION

France did not secure control of the entire Côte d'Ivoire until 1918. At first, Governor Binger believed that existing treaties and economic incentives would provide all of the leverage necessary to secure French colonial rule, but within months he was proved wrong. Although African leaders had signed treaties giving the French control of their land, poor communication and intentional deception by the French meant that few fully understood the treaties. As a result, French attempts to establish new military and trading posts met hostile resistance and attacks by groups such as the Baule, DAN, BÉTÉ, and Dida. The French military spent years fighting many of these resistance movements. The most famous of these was MANDINKA warrior Samory Touré's long struggle to resist French conquest. Touré, whose empire the French had previously destroyed, rebuilt at Dabakala and began extending his new empire into the

northern part of Côte d'Ivoire. But the French again attacked Touré, ultimately defeating him in 1898.

Although France fought Touré in order to protect the prosperous Baulé, the Baulé not only obstructed that campaign but went on to resist French colonization for nearly twenty years. As the French military moved through Baulé territory on their way to attack Touré, they conscripted Baulé slaves as porters. This action provoked armed attacks by the Baulé and forced the French to retreat and search out another path to Touré. Defeated and distracted by other campaigns, the French made minimal efforts to subdue the empire, but largely ignored the Baulé problem. By 1908, however, the continued resistance of the Baulé and other groups underlined the failure of the French colonial government, which had no control over vast parts of the territory and could not even raise the obligatory "head tax" from the African population. Under pressure from the French government, the newly appointed governor, Gabriel Angoulvant, launched a brutal military campaign he called "pacification" and ordered troops to "seek and destroy" all rebels, their crops, and their homes. For the next seven years, the French colonial army combed the interior of Côte d'Ivoire, killed suspected resistors, and forced local rulers to accept French colonial authority. The results were devastating—the army killed thousands of Africans and subsequent famine caused the death of many more. This ruthless campaign finally secured the entire region for France. In an effort to quell future resistance, the French filled civil service and administrative positions with either African commoners or precolonial rulers who had proved their loyalty to the French. These civil servants received the best the colonial system had to offer Africans—education, political and land rights, and economic security. In contrast, the majority of the African population felt only the burdens of French colonization. Because France had decided that its African colonies must be self-sufficient, the colonial government devised two strategies to generate revenue. First, the government offered to sell land concessions to planters for private plantations. Although the majority of these concessions were sold to white Europeans, some Africans, mainly civil servants in the French colonial administration, also purchased land, and the wealthiest of these planters created a new class of local elites who were vocal in their demands for improved transport and shipping facilities. Second, the government established state mines, lumber, and infrastructure construction projects as well as huge state plantations cultivating export crops, such as cocoa, coffee, and millet. These endeavors suffered from a shortage of labor. Consequently, the colonial government required each adult Ivoirian male to "volunteer" ten days of labor a year for state projects. Many Africans were in fact forced to work more to meet the vast labor requirements of the various projects. Still, a labor shortage persisted, and the government began recruiting workers from Upper Volta (present-day BURKINA FASO), especially from the MOSSI ethnic group. This labor supply ultimately proved so valuable that Côte d'Ivoire annexed the southern part of Upper Volta in order to increase the colony's labor pool. While the labor policy satisfied the needs of the colonial administration, it fostered antagonism and resentment among the African population. These feelings intensified during World War II, when the Nazi-supported Vichy government took over the colonies and not only doubled the forced labor requirement but conscripted laborers for the military. To the detriment of the local populations, the Vichy government also forced Ivoirian farmers to donate large portions of their crops to the military. Ivoirian intellectuals, civil servants, and communists soon joined together in protest and announced their support for Charles de Gaulle's exiled Free French government. In addition, a Baulé planter and local administrator, FÉLIX HOUPHOUËT-BOIGNY, organized a coalition of African planters, called the Syndicat Agricole Africain (SAA), to protest the Vichy government's policies. Although these organizations had little effect on the Vichy government, they did influence de Gaulle, who, in 1944, convened his exiled government and colonial administrators in BRAZZAVILLE to reassess France's relationship with its African colonies. During the conference, the group created a progressive list of postwar colonial reforms, few of which were actually enacted. Nevertheless, the Brazzaville Conference did plant the seeds for decolonization after World War II.

DECOLONIZATION

After the defeat of Germany in 1945, de Gaulle offered France's West African colonies greater political representation and allowed each to elect two delegates to the French Constituent Assembly, one representing the African majority and the other the European minority. Campaigning to end forced labor, Houphouët-Boigny won the African seat for Côte d'Ivoire. When the assembly convened in early 1946, Houphouët-Boigny secured passage of legislation ending the forced labor system—a major victory for the Ivoirian population. This success guaranteed Houphouët-Boigny wide popular support throughout the colony. Upon his return he organized his supporters, including members of the SAA, into a new political party, the Parti Démocratique de la Côte d'Ivoire, or PDCI. In October 1946, he attempted to further increase his political leverage by joining the PDCI with the new multicolony party, the Rassemblement Démocratique Africain (RDA). Led by Houphouët-Boigny and other prominent French West

African leaders, and supported by the French Communist Party, the RDA lobbied for parity between African and French citizens. Although the organization supported widespread reforms, it did not press for decolonization. By 1948, however, the Communist Party had lost its place in the governing coalition, and France faced armed independence movements in North Africa and Indochina. Consequently, the French government began to view the RDA, and by extension Houphouët-Boigny and his PDCI, as a threat. For the next year Houphouët-Boigny and his party members faced harassment and persecution, including arrests. To regain French favor, Houphouët-Boigny decided to break with the Communist Party. By early 1956, he had won French support and become the strongest African advocate of de Gaulle's vision of a French Union (later named the French Community)—a federation of internally self-ruled countries under the executive control of the French president. But because the African population demanded complete independence, Houphouët-Boigny abandoned this plan for limited self-rule. As decolonization became inevitable, Houphouët-Boigny solidified his political power, and in November 1960, only two months after France declared Côte d'Ivoire independent, he was elected president by a landslide.

CÔTE D'IVOIRE UNDER HOUPHOUËT-BOIGNY

During his first three years as president, Houphouët-Boigny built a centralized and highly personalized regime that successfully quelled dissent and political competition. At the same time, armed with French aid and a civil service full of French technocrats, Houphouët-Boigny engineered an economic boom, often called the "Ivoirian Miracle," that helped build his popularity not only in the international financial community but among the Ivoirian population. Meanwhile, rumors of a coup d'état prompted Houphouët-Boigny to further consolidate his power in a "benevolent," authoritarian one-party state. In 1962 an adviser warned him that PDCI members were plotting a coup. Houphouët-Boigny ordered the arrest of more than 125 people, forty-five of whom were convicted and imprisoned. The supposed discovery of another plot in 1963 led Houphouët-Boigny to purge the PDCI of more than 200 dissenters and limit the power of his closest advisers (and potential rivals). At the same time, he began crafting an intricate power system that maintained power by both silencing and co-opting dissenters and by creating a group of loyal politicians who were personally indebted to the president for their positions, prestige, and wealth. Throughout the next two decades, Houphouët-Boigny used this system to monopolize political power. The president controlled access to all government positions, including those in the military, civil service, and local government. At the same

Côte d'Ivoire (At a Glance)

OFFICIAL NAME:
Republic of Côte d'Ivoire

FORMER NAME:
Ivory Coast

AREA:
322,462 sq km (122,503 sq mi)

LOCATION:
Western Africa; borders the North Atlantic Ocean, Ghana, Burkina Faso, Mali, Guinea, and Liberia

CAPITAL:
Yamoussoukro (population 120,000; 1990 estimate) has been the official capital since 1983; however, Abidjan (population 3,427,500; 2002 estimate) is the de facto capital and contains the administrative center. It is also where most foreign governments maintain their official presence.

OTHER MAJOR CITIES:
Bouaké (population 549,800), Daloa (206,200; 2002 estimate), Gagnoa (population 59,500;1986 estimate)

POPULATION:
20,617,068 (2009 estimate)

POPULATION DENSITY:
64 persons per sq km (about 168 persons per sq mi)

POPULATION BELOW AGE 15:
40.6 percent (male 4,215,912 female 4,146,077; 2009 estimate)

POPULATION GROWTH RATE:
2.133 percent (2009 estimate)

TOTAL FERTILITY RATE:
4.12 children born per woman (2009 estimate)

LIFE EXPECTANCY AT BIRTH:
Total population: 55.45 years (male 54.64 years; female 56.28 years; 2009 estimate)

INFANT MORTALITY RATE:
68.06 deaths per 1,000 live births (2009 estimate)

LITERACY RATE (AGE 15 AND OVER WHO CAN READ AND WRITE):
Total population: 50.9 percent (male 57.9 percent; female 43.6 percent; 2003 estimate)

EDUCATION:
Education is free, and primary education is compulsory. A vast television education program was established in the early 1970s that has helped to improve literacy rates. In the early 1990s about 1.5 million students attended primary schools annually and about 423,000 attended secondary and vocational schools. In 2000 about 64 percent of children attended primary schools and 59 percent attended secondary schools, but civil war in 2003 disrupted education in many areas; in 2003 attendance at primary schools had dropped to an estimated 57 percent.

LANGUAGES:
French is the official language and a large percentage of the population uses it, especially for written communication. There are, however, over 60 other languages spoken in Côte d'Ivoire; of these, Dioula is the most widely used.

ETHNIC GROUPS:
The population of Côte d'Ivoire contains over 60 ethnic groups. The largest groups are Baule (23 percent); Bété (18 percent); and Senufo (15 percent). Other groups include Malinke, Agni, Kru, Voltaic, and Mande peoples. There is a significant Lebanese community. A large number of immigrants come from Liberia, Burkina Faso, and Mali.

RELIGIONS:
Between 20 and 30 percent of the population is Christian, between 35 and 40 percent is Muslim, and between 24 and 40 percent adhere to indigenous beliefs. The majority of migrant workers are Muslim (70 percent) and Christian (20 percent).

CLIMATE:
Tropical along the coast, semi-arid in the far north, and varying at the center between forest and savanna. In the southern region temperatures vary between 22° C (72° F) and 32° C (90° F) and there are two rainy seasons, April to July and October to November. In the central part of the country, the temperatures are more extreme, ranging from 12° C (54° F) to 40° C (104° F). Annual rainfall average is 2100 mm (83 in) in coastal Abidjan and 1200 mm (about 48 in) in Bouaké, on the central plain.

LAND, PLANTS, AND ANIMALS:
Côte d'Ivoire is flat with some undulating plains, except for mountains in the northwest region. The north central region has savanna. From the coast to the southern central region there is dense forest containing obeche, mahogany, and iroko. Animals include the jackal, hyena, panther, elephant, chimpanzee, crocodile, and various lizards and venomous snakes.

NATURAL RESOURCES:
Rich, arable soil and forests containing commercially valuable hardwoods. Côte d'Ivoire has mineral deposits of gold, iron ore, manganese ore, diamonds, and petroleum. Hydroelectric plants on the Bia and Bandama rivers provide a significant amount of electricity.

CURRENCY:
The Communauté Financière Africaine (CFA) franc

GROSS DOMESTIC PRODUCT (GDP):
$23.78 billion (2008 estimate)

GDP PER CAPITA:
$1,700 (2008 estimate)

GDP REAL GROWTH RATE:
2.7 percent (2008 estimate)

PRIMARY ECONOMIC ACTIVITIES:
Agriculture (about 68 percent of employment and 29 percent of economy), industry, and commerce

PRIMARY CROPS:
Coffee, cocoa, bananas, corn, rice, manioc, sweet potatoes, sugar, cotton, rubber, and timber

INDUSTRIES:
Foodstuffs, beverages, wood products, oil refining, automobile assembly, textiles, fertilizer, construction materials, and electricity

PRIMARY EXPORTS:
Cocoa, coffee, tropical woods, petroleum, cotton, bananas, palm oil, pineapples, cotton, and fish

PRIMARY IMPORTS:
Food, capital goods, consumer goods, and fuel

PRIMARY TRADE PARTNERS:
France, Netherlands, United States, Mali, Germany, and Italy

GOVERNMENT:
Côte d'Ivoire is a constitutional republic with a multiparty presidential regime. The executive branch is led by President Laurent Gbagbo, who was elected in 2000 after a coup overthrew controversial interim leader Robert Guel, and Prime Minister Seydou Diarra, appointed by the president in January 2003. The legislative branch is the elected 175-member National Assembly, which is currently dominated by President Bédié's party, the Democratic Party of the Côte d'Ivoire.

Elizabeth Heath

time, he maintained popular support and the guise of free speech by holding public forums that offered a chance to speak to him in person. Advertised as an opportunity for constructive dialogue with the receptive and concerned president, these forums were, in fact, nothing more than an opportunity to diffuse popular discontent. Houphouët-Boigny subsequently maintained the appearance of accountability by lavishing inordinate amounts of money and attention on select problems and by scapegoating inadequate government officials, whom he promptly fired and replaced.

A strong economy supported this autocratic system. In 1960 Houphouët-Boigny had inherited one of the most developed economies in West Africa. But the Ivoirian economy remained heavily dependent on the export of crops, particularly coffee, cocoa, pineapples, and bananas. Although pre-independence completion of the Vridi Canal and the ABIDJAN port, one of the largest in West Africa, had helped bolster the economy and raised new revenues, few efforts had been made to promote sustainable economic growth. After independence, Houphouët-Boigny took up this challenge. Having maintained close ties with France since the colonial period, he asked the French government to encourage investment. Foreign investment, coupled with efforts to divert revenues from export crops into other economic sectors, such as manufacturing, helped boost economic growth to an annual rate of 10 to 12 percent during the 1960s. The discovery of oil further stimulated foreign investment, and by the early 1970s agriculture accounted for only 25 percent of the gross domestic product. It seemed that Côte d'Ivoire had successfully engineered sustainable prosperity. But the worldwide recession of the late 1970s and early 1980s undermined the economic progress of Côte d'Ivoire and caused severe problems in Abidjan. The city, until then a focus of investment, had experienced a huge influx of rural villagers seeking stable wages. The sudden economic slowdown caused rampant unemployment, and exacerbated tensions between Abidjan's rich and poor that soon erupted in protests. Demonstrators attacked Houphouët-Boigny's failure to "ivoirianize" the public sector, much of which was still run by French expatriates. At the same time, the recession depressed the price of Côte d'Ivoire's two main exports—cocoa and coffee. The price drop hurt rural farmers and plantation workers, many of them unskilled laborers whose migration from other African countries had been encouraged by Houphouët-Boigny's government. As a result, tensions between Ivoirian and migrant farmers escalated into violence throughout the late 1970s and early 1980s. Meanwhile, decades of exploitation had reduced the southern forest reserves and curtailed profits from another valuable export—hardwood—and exploration proved that the

once-celebrated oil reserves would yield nothing more than a short-lived boom. Rampant inflation and increasingly severe droughts between 1973 and 1985 further exacerbated these problems. At first, Houphouët-Boigny was able to deflect public unrest and criticism onto other government officials. As the situation worsened in the early 1980s, however, he responded to critics by "ivoirianizing" the public sector and decentralizing municipal governments. Nevertheless, the government remained a target of widespread protests, organized by teacher and student unions and opposition groups such as the Ivoirian Popular Front, led by the exiled Laurent Gbagbo. As these continued, Houphouët-Boigny returned to his former policy and dissolved the unions, closed the universities, and arrested the protesters. Facing few serious threats, Houphouët-Boigny had little incentive to change the system that maintained his power and enriched him and his family.

External pressures, however, forced the president to introduce the reforms that internal protests had failed to secure. In the late 1980s the International Monetary Fund and the World Bank pushed Houphouët-Boigny to implement austerity measures that further taxed the impoverished nation and brought new protests. At the same time, foreign supporters began pressing Houphouët-Boigny to open the system to potential successors. In April 1990, Houphouët-Boigny announced the first multiparty elections in Ivoirian history. Disadvantaged by the short notice and encumbered by bureaucratic restrictions, the opposition nevertheless nominated a candidate, Gbagbo, who ran in the presidential election. Although Houphouët-Boigny won with an 81 percent majority, Gbagbo won a seat in the National Assembly in the elections that took place a month later. But electoral reforms failed to bring substantive change to the Houphouët-Boigny system, and the president again sought to quell opposition and dissent.

CONTEMPORARY ISSUES

The need to identify a successor to Houphouët-Boigny soon overshadowed the repressive actions of the Ivoirian government. Already in weak health, in June 1993 Houphouët-Boigny was diagnosed with prostate cancer. He ruled the country from the hospital until his death six months later. Despite expectations of a violent and prolonged power struggle, Henri Konan Bédié succeeded Houphouët-Boigny smoothly. Bédié continued many of the policies of his predecessor. His government refused to implement electoral reforms in the 1995 presidential election, and an opposition boycott tarnished Bédié's victory. Like Houphouët-Boigny, Bédié took measures to silence dissent and criticism. At the same time, he benefited from a healthy economy and made strategic economic concessions to key groups, such as civil servants and rural farmers, in an effort to strengthen the position of the PDCI. With support from France and other foreign donors, the PDCI's system of "one-party democracy" seemed a model of African political stability. Growing unrest in the late 1990s, however, led to Bédié's overthrow in a December 1999 military coup. General Robert Guei, the coup leader, organized October 2000 presidential elections that pitted Guei against Gbagbo. After early voting results showed Guei trailing, Guei dissolved the official election commission and declared himself the winner. A popular uprising swept Guei from power, and Gbagbo declared himself the rightful winner. In the days after the election, at least 200 people died in political violence. Despite his attempts to consolidate power, Gbagbo faced an attempted coup in September 2002. Intense fighting and the suspected covert involvement of Burkina Faso and Liberia caused Gbagbo to request military help from France and from West African allies. In January 2003 rebel leaders were granted ministerial posts in a new unity government, but prospects for civil and economic stabilization were short lived. The rebels refused to disarm, and soon military strikes against them recommenced. A new peace deal was signed in 2007.

See also STRUCTURAL ADJUSTMENT IN AFRICA.

ELIZABETH HEATH

Cotonou, Benin
Largest city, main port, and de facto capital of the People's Republic of Benin.

The commercial and administrative center of BENIN, Cotonou is located on the Nokwe Lagoon on the Gulf of Guinea, about 35 km (22 mi) from PORTO-NOVO, the country's official capital. Originally called Kotuno (FON for "estuary of death") by the Kingdom of DAHOMEY, the MALARIA-ridden area was largely uninhabited until the late nineteenth century. In 1878, however, Dahomey King Ghezo offered it to the French, who were anxious to secure land holdings in West Africa. Soon afterward France asked permission to improve the shallow port, but was denied by Ghezo's successor, Glele. This denial prompted occupation and, eventually, the Franco-Dahomean wars that led to French colonization in 1894.

Under French COLONIAL RULE, Cotonou became the colony's main port. After the completion of the Benin-Niger railroad in the early 1900s, it became the shipping hub for both Dahomey and NIGER. In 1963 the independent Beninese government used development grants to modernize the port. Since then the city has grown rapidly, attracting both international firms and rural migrants. Today, Cotonou is Benin's business headquarters, and home to the main government buildings—the Supreme Court, National Assembly, and Presidential Palace. The city's population was 761,137 in 2006.

Since the colonial era, Cotonou's economy has been supported by the shipping business provided by the port and railroad. It is also home to a number of textile, food-processing, and light-manufacturing plants. Many of Cotonou's residents earn their livelihoods as traders or artisans, or as laborers on the growing city's numerous construction projects. The promise made by former president Mathieu KÉRÉKOU—a government job to every college graduate—became clearly unrealistic during a time of nationwide austerity measures. Although the city has prospered in recent years, unemployment remains high.

ELIZABETH HEATH

Crowther, Samuel Ajayi
1806–1891
First African Anglican bishop.

Samuel Ajayi Crowther was born into a YORUBA family in western NIGERIA. Until his mid-teens, he was raised in traditional Yoruba society. In 1821, however, slave traders raided his home village, kidnapped Crowther, his mother, and sisters, and separated them from each other. Traders then sold Crowther to Portuguese slavers, who in 1822 loaded him onto a slave ship bound for Brazil. Luckily, a British antislavery warship intercepted his captors; they rescued Crowther and took him to FREETOWN, SIERRA LEONE. In Sierra Leone, the Christian Missionary Society (CMS) took Crowther in, and he began attending mission schools. Gifted linguistically, within six months of his arrival Crowther could read and write English. He went by his birth name of Ajayi until 1825, when he was baptized an Anglican and took the name Samuel Crowther after a CMS missionary of the same name. An impressive student, Crowther traveled to England in 1826 to study at a CMS school in London. The following year, he became the first African to graduate from the Fourah Bay Institution (now College) in Sierra Leone. He then began to teach at missionary and government schools in and around Freetown. In 1841 Crowther was selected to accompany the Niger expedition of the Society for the Extinction of the Slave Trade and the Civilisation of Africa, whose intent was to evangelize up the NIGER RIVER. Crowther distinguished himself, and an Anglican priest recommended Crowther for the priesthood. He returned to England to study and was ordained a priest in 1843. The CMS posted Crowther to its Yoruba mission, first at Badagry and, later, his native area of ABEOKUTA, NIGERIA, where he renewed contact with his mother and sister, who had also escaped slavery. Henry Venn, a progressive in the CMS administration, envisioned an indigenous African church, which he hoped Crowther might help build.

Crowther, who had written a Yoruba dictionary and produced a Yoruba translation of the New Testament and the Book of Common Prayer, was a successful evangelist. He preached in Yoruba and won many African converts to Christianity. In 1857 the CMS chose him to head the Niger Mission, and he established missions in Akassa, Onitsha, Lokaja, and Idah. In 1864, consecrated in a ceremony at Canterbury Cathedral as "Bishop of Western Equatorial Africa beyond the Queen's Dominions," Crowther became the first African to hold the title of bishop in the Anglican Church. Despite numerous obstacles, after a few years under Crowther's leadership the Niger Mission boasted 600 converts, 10 priests, and 14 catechists. Despite these successes, Crowther faced opposition, especially among the younger generation of white CMS missionaries, who adhered to the Social Darwinist and racist theories of the day that justified colonialism, and who believed that they were better suited to run the mission than an African such as Crowther. These views doomed Venn's plan for an independent African church. Thus, the CMS forced Crowther to accept a white associate to administer the Niger Mission's finances, and Crowther faced accusations of incompetence. As a final insult, violating established church procedures, the mission's finance committee suspended all of the African priests whom Crowther had ordained. Crowther resigned in protest in 1890. He was making plans for an independent African church when he suffered a massive stroke the following year in Lagos.

BIBLIOGRAPHY

Ajayi, J. F. Ade. *A Patriot to the Core: Samuel Ajayi Crowther*. The Anglican Diocese of Ibadan, 1992.

ROBERT FAY

Crusades
Armed Christian pilgrimages between 1096 and 1291; a joint effort by the Roman Catholic Church and various western European rulers to assert control over the Holy Lands.

From the eleventh to the thirteenth century, successive popes summoned Christians on crusades to seize Jerusalem and the Church of the Holy Sepulcher and defend these lands from infidels (non-Christians). Thousands of Christians took vows to join what they believed was a just and holy war, though arguably their leaders had more interest in controlling the rich markets and trade routes of the East than in converting unbelievers. Many scholars see the Crusades as a precursor to the European wars of conquest in the Americas and parts of Africa two centuries later, wars also justified on religious grounds. Though the Crusades transformed the history and consciousness of western Europe, Islamic rulers at the time were more concerned with Mongol attacks from the east and the Turkish threat to the north than with this localized conflict in Syria and Palestine. The establishment of the Crusader States in otherwise Islamic lands did unite Muslims. The Crusades increased Muslim consciousness of the importance of these lands to Islamic peoples— Muhammad is said to have ascended to heaven in Jerusalem and the Dome of the Rock mosque was built there in his honor. This collaborative opposition to the Franks, as Muslims called the Europeans, helped the Mamluks to rally Muslims behind their Islamic state incorporating EGYPT, Arabia, Syria, and Palestine. The Crusades primarily aimed to capture Jerusalem, but a good number of them also targeted Egypt, the center of the Islamic Empires of the Ayyubids (1169–1250) and the Mamluks (1260–1517), both of which controlled Syria and Palestine. Because Egypt had been a Roman province from 30 B.C.E. to 395 C.E. and also a center of early Christianity, the Europeans felt justified in trying to regain it. Perhaps more importantly, Egypt controlled the rich Indian Ocean trade routes leading to Asia. During this period, Europeans began using religion to justify wars of conquest against Muslim lands more generally—including southern Spain, Portugal, and North Africa. Pope Urban II initiated the First Crusade with a speech delivered in 1095. Seljuk Turks had conquered Syria and Palestine in 1077 and thus gained control of Jerusalem. The pope called for a crusade to liberate the Orthodox Christians of the Holy Lands from their Islamic "oppressors." Many scholars have asserted, however, that Muslims treated this Christian population with respect, and that there is no evidence that the Seljuks ushered in an era of Christian persecution. Some historians believe that the Roman Catholic Church instigated the Crusades in an effort to absorb the Orthodox Church. Others believe that, more often than not, the Crusades were a looting venture. The First Crusade (1096–1099) was the only successful one: Europeans captured Antioch, Jerusalem, Edessa and TRIPOLI. The next few Crusades sought mainly to defend these Crusader States. However, the Muslim ruler of Aleppo, Nuradin, defeated the Second Crusade at Damascus in 1148. Encouraged by this success, Nuradin's lieutenant, Saladin, moved on to conquer Fatimid Egypt. When Saladin captured Jerusalem at the Battle of Hattin in 1187, Europe responded with the Third Crusade, which failed to regain Jerusalem, but captured Acre in 1191. This episode ended when the English King Richard the Lion-Hearted signed a five-year truce with Saladin in 1192, giving Christians access to, though not control of, Jerusalem. The Fourth and Fifth Crusades primarily targeted Egypt; but although they briefly captured Damietta, at the mouth of the NILE RIVER in 1221, their main effect was to send the Byzantine Empire into a terminal decline and establish Venetian dominance in the Mediterranean. The Holy Roman Emperor Frederick II of Germany led the Sixth Crusade. Noted for his sympathy toward Muslims (his entourage included many Moors), Frederick's mission was more diplomatic than military. In 1229 he made a truce with the Egyptians, which left Jerusalem in Christian hands, except for the area of the Dome of the Rock. Louis IX (known as Saint Louis) of France instigated the Seventh and Eighth Crusades. He occupied Damietta in 1249, only to lose it immediately thereafter. In 1268 the Mamluk Sultan Baybars conquered Palestine and Antioch, and in 1291 they took Acre. This European defeat essentially ended the Crusades. Various European powers tried unsuccessfully to revive the Crusades throughout the fourteenth and fifteenth centuries. Although they briefly captured Alexandria in 1365, the fight against the Muslims had shifted to Eastern Europe, where the Ottomans were gaining control, and also to the Iberian Peninsula, which Spanish and Portuguese forces gradually reconquered from the Moors before they embarked on their overseas conquests in the fifteenth century.

See also ALEXANDRIA, EGYPT; ALEXANDRIA AND GRECIAN AFRICA: AN INTERPRETATION; MAMLUK STATE.

LEYLA KEOUGH

Cugoano, Ottobah

ca. 1757–ca. 1803
African abolitionist in Britain who published an autobiographical book arguing against British racism and participation in the transatlantic slave trade.

Ottobah Cugoano was born in Ajumako, GHANA, and was abducted by slave traders in 1770. Horrified by the atrocities he experienced on the Middle Passage voyage, he exclaimed, "Death was more preferable than life, and a plan was concerted amongst us, that we might burn and blow up the ship, and to perish all together in the flames." Though the plan was thwarted, the radicalism that marked the effort remained a theme in Cugoano's life. Cugoano was bought by a white man in the West Indies and in 1772 was taken to England, where he learned to read and write and was baptized. His whereabouts are unknown until 1786, when he and another black man informed the abolitionist lawyer Granville Sharp of the unjust treatment of a slave tied to a mast by his owner. At the time, Cugoano worked for the court painter of the Prince of Wales, a connection he used to plead for abolition in a letter to the prince. Cugoano expressed his abolitionist beliefs in his 1787 book, *Thoughts and Sentiments on the Evil and Wicked Traffic of the Slavery and Commerce of the Human Species.* Though many scholars assert that Cugoano did not write all of the text, according to literary critics Paul Edwards and David Dabydeen the book exhibits "an aggressive and often bitter urgency of tone" that suits what they call Cugoano's "overt and assertive black radicalism." In *Thoughts and Sentiments,* Cugoano used rational and objective methods to advance radical arguments for abolition. Cugoano felt that many slave traders worked in the name of Christianity but sought only personal profit. He cites Protestants as "the most barbarous slaveholders" and likens explorers, slave traders, and their governments to the Antichrist. He equated slaveholders with robbers and believed slave revolts to be a moral duty. Though he did not advocate anarchy, he admonished British law, the monarchy, and parliament for supporting the interests of the elite class involved in the trade, and prophesied divine retribution. In addition, Cugoano refuted secular and Christian claims of African inferiority as well as the assumption that ancient slave practices in Africa justified the trading of Africans. Cugoano proposed the abolition of the slave trade and emancipation of slaves, recommending that the British fleet enforce the ban on the coast of Africa. Maintaining that every British person was responsible for the cruelties of slavery, "unless he speedily riseth up with abhorrence of it in his own judgment, and, to avert evil, declare himself against it," he suggested a day of atonement and fasting for all English people. Cugoano did not believe that the English would abolish slavery any time soon. So he proposed pragmatic improvements, such as humane treatment, the education of slaves in trades and Christianity, and freedom after seven years. Cugoano married an Englishwoman and continued letter-writing campaigns as a member of the Sons of Africa, a black British abolitionist organization. Little is known of his later life, though it is reputed that in 1791 he was working to find skilled laborers among black Loyalists in Canada to journey to SIERRA LEONE.

LEYLA KEOUGH

Customary Law in Africa

See LAW IN AFRICA: COLONIAL AND CONTEMPORARY.

D

Dacko, David
1930–2003
President of the Central African Republic (1960–1965, 1979–1981).

During his first presidency of the CENTRAL AFRICAN REPUBLIC, David Dacko relied on the support of a narrow elite backed by French troops; he repeated this pattern during his brief return to power fourteen years later. The son of a night watchman in Bouchia, OUBANGUI-CHARI (present-day CENTRAL AFRICAN REPUBLIC), Dacko attended local primary and secondary schools and went on to attend classes in neighboring Moyen-Congo, (present-day Republic of the Congo). After his graduation he taught school until he was named a school director in 1955. He became friends with the Central African politician Barthélemy BOGANDA and was elected to the territorial assembly. In the self-governing period prior to independence, Boganda named Dacko minister of agriculture and, later, minister of interior and administrative affairs. When Boganda was killed in an airplane crash, Dacko succeeded him by claiming kin ties to Boganda, despite the constitutional claim of Goumba, the vice president, to succession.

When the Central African Republic became independent in August 1960, Dacko became president. For the next six years he governed the republic as a one-party state. He organized notables from various ethnic groups to support his government in the ruling party, the Movement for the Social Evolution of Black Africa. He maintained close economic and security relations with France, and relied upon French assistance to suppress dissent and opposition movements. French companies dominated the economy in a neocolonialist style, though some small African-owned industries were established in the country. School attendance doubled under Dacko, but the majority of teachers were French.

As events unfolded in the neighboring DEMOCRATIC REPUBLIC OF THE CONGO in 1964, Dacko feared that he would be overthrown by young radicals in the party, and he distanced himself from French neocolonialism in order to avoid this. He began a pseudo-nationalization of the economy, in which he established industrial enterprises, controlled the diamond industry, and reorganized agricultural production. Such moves angered the French, especially the dominant import-export companies, and Dacko moved to resign from power. Before he could resign, however, his army chief of staff, Jean-Bédel BOKASSA, overthrew him on New Year's Eve of 1965.

Dacko spent a decade imprisoned and under house arrest, but in 1976 Emperor Bokassa released him and named Dacko his private counsel. In 1979 Dacko arrived at the presidential palace with French troops, overthrew Bokassa, and announced the end of Bokassa's empire and the restoration of the republic, with himself as president. In 1980 he created the Central African Democratic Union and held elections. Dacko won the elections, but the opposition and public contested them as fraudulent. In governing, Dacko relied on the same small group of notables who had supported him during his previous rule (and who had remained in power under Bokassa), and he relied on the French military for personal protection and for maintaining order.

Dacko faced growing popular unrest in the capital, BANGUI, and withering French support with Giscard d'Estaing's departure from office, he outlawed the two main opposition parties in an attempt to consolidate his power. But under pressure and with little apparent desire to retain the presidency, he yielded power to his chief of staff, André Kolingba, in September 1981. Dacko remained active in the Central African Republic political arena. He received 11 percent of the vote the 1999 presidential election and served as head of the Movement for Democracy and Development party. During a 2003 trip to Cameroon, however, Dacko fell ill and died on 20 November. National radio announced that the cause of death was respiratory problems.

See also CONGO, REPUBLIC OF THE.

ERIC YOUNG

Daddah, Moktar Ould
1924–2003
First president of Mauritania (1961–1978).

Born in Boutilimit in western MAURITANIA into a prominent BERBER family of marabouts (Islamic religious scholars), Moktar Ould Daddah attended an Islamic school at Boutilimit, then the elite Sons of Chiefs' School in Senegal. At that time both Mauritania and SENEGAL were part of the French colony of FRENCH WEST AFRICA. Daddah graduated in 1940 and worked as an interpreter for the French colonial administration, then resumed his education in Paris, completing courses in law and Arabic studies. Mauritania became a French overseas territory in 1946. In 1957, while practicing law in DAKAR, SENEGAL, Daddah was elected to the territorial legislature and appointed to the executive council. In 1958 he was elected secretary-general of the Parti du Regroupement Mauritanien (PRM) and the following year Daddah was elected president of Mauritania's first National Assembly. He served as head of state following full independence in August 1960 and was elected Mauritania's first president in 1961.

Daddah was reelected to three more five-year terms and oversaw Mauritania's transition to a one-party state in 1964, integrating all political parties as part of the PRM. He spearheaded Mauritania's move toward a North African and Arab alliance by severing relations with the United States during the 1967 Arab-Israeli war and securing Mauritania's membership in the Arab League in October 1973. He also declared Arabic the official language of instruction and commerce. These moves were met with resistance by the nation's black African minority. In 1973 Daddah also replaced the French franc with the Mauritanian ouguiya as the official currency.

In 1976 Daddah tried to annex the southern portion of neighboring WESTERN SAHARA. A nationalist group in Western Sahara known as POLISARIO FRONT resisted the occupation of their land and steadily fought back the Mauritanian army. The war, unpopular with Mauritanians of both Arab and African descent, drained the national budget and eventually led to the bloodless military coup that deposed Daddah in July 1978. He was detained and later exiled to France, but was granted amnesty in December 1984, returned to Mauritania and supported opposition politics. Moktar Daddah died in Paris in 2003, and his son, Ahmed Ould Daddah, who has been arrested several times by the government, is currently a major opposition leader in Mauritania.

See also COLONIAL RULE.

Dafi

Ethnic group of West Africa; also known as the Dafing and the Southern Marka.

The Dafi primarily inhabit MALI and BURKINA FASO. They speak a MANDE language. Approximately 200,000 people consider themselves Dafi.

See also LANGUAGES, AFRICAN: AN OVERVIEW.

Dagari

Ethnic group of West Africa; also known as Dagara, Dagaba, and Dagati.

The Dagari inhabit primarily northeastern GHANA and southern BURKINA FASO. They speak a Niger-Congo language and belong to the Molé-Dagbane cultural and linguistic group. Approximately 700,000 people consider themselves Dagari.

See also LANGUAGES, AFRICAN: AN OVERVIEW.

Dagomba

Ethnic group of northeastern Ghana and adjacent parts of Togo; also known as Dagbamba.

The Dagomba speak Dagbane, a language belonging to the Gur subgroup of the Niger-Congo languages. Anthropologists believe that the Dagomba people arose when migrant horsemen, who arrived from the northeast, conquered indigenous Gur speakers around the fourteenth century C.E. These indigenous people farmed grains such as millet, raised cattle, and smelted IRON. They acknowledged the authority of tindamba, or earth priests. The conquerors adopted the language of their subjects, and ruled as an aristocratic caste.

Oral accounts state that a noble warrior, Nyagse, forged the Dagomba into a nation by conquering villages and massacring their priests. Nyagse created a hierarchical state in which power was won by competition but no man could rise higher than his father; therefore, only the sons of the Ya-Na, or paramount chief, could succeed him. A hierarchy of chiefs, all subjects of the Ya-Na, ruled the Dagomba chiefdom, known as Dagbon, but the indigenous tindamba allocated land, played a role in approving the appointment of chiefs, and maintained their spiritual powers.

The expansion of the neighboring Gonja kingdom during the sixteenth century drove the Dagomba out of the western part of their homeland. The Dagomba conquered the KONKOMBA people to the east and built a new capital, Yendi, in the conquered territory. In this region, the Dagomba ruled the Konkomba as overlords. Dagbon prospered by taxing the lucrative trade passing through its territory. HAUSA traders carried kola nuts, gold, and, later, slaves from the forest region to the south. They returned with goods such as salt from the SAHARA and cloth manufactured in the Hausa states. These traders also brought Islam to the Dagomba. The Dagomba aristocracy has largely adopted Islam, but much of the population continued to practice traditional beliefs at the end of the twentieth century. Around 1745 ASANTE conquered Dagbon, which had been weakened by a war of succession. Asante required Dagbon to pay tribute in slaves until 1874, when the British defeated

Asante. Dagbon declared its independence from the weakened Asante kingdom.

In 1896, however, a German force of about 100 destroyed Yendi and defeated a 7,000-man, poorly equipped Dagomba army. In 1899 the British and the Germans split Dagbon between German Togoland and the British Gold Coast. After World War I (1914–1919) the British took control of western Togoland and reunified Dagbon under British administration. The British implemented indirect rule, in which Dagomba chiefs administered local government. This policy perpetuated Dagomba dominance over the Konkomba. The British largely neglected the economic development of Dagbon. To pay the head tax the British imposed, Dagomba had to migrate to the southern Gold Coast to work in mines and on cocoa plantations.

Today the more than 650,000 Dagomba are the largest ethnic group in the Northern Region of GHANA and are the dominant group in the Northern Region's capital, Tamale. Since independence, Dagbon has become known as the "granary of Ghana." Dagomba farmers produce much of the country's millet, maize, yams, and peanuts.

Over the past century, the Dagomba have faced repeated conflict. Following the death of Ya-Na Mahama II in 1954, a succession dispute erupted into violence. The federal government sent troops to Yendi and intervened to decide the succession. Ethnic tension has also plagued northern Ghana. Violence flared between the Dagomba and their Konkomba subjects over land use and ownership in 1914, 1917, the 1940s, and the 1980s. During the 1990s ethnic violence once again racked the region. Twelve people were killed in Tamale in 1994 when police fired on a group of Dagomba who had attacked some Konkomba.

DAVID P. JOHNSON, JR.

Dahomey

See BENIN.

Dahomey, Early Kingdom of

Precolonial West African kingdom located in what is now southern Benin; reached the height of its power and prestige during transatlantic slave trade.

Abomey, the capital of Dahomey, was founded around 1620 by Dogbari, who fled Allada after his brothers fought with one another for control of that kingdom. Dogbari's grandson, Wegbaja, expanded Abomey through military conquest and consolidated it into a powerful state in the middle to late 1600s. Wegbaja's grandson, Agaja, conquered both Allada and Whydah in the 1720s, founding the kingdom of Dahomey with its capital at Abomey. The government of Dahomey was an absolute monarchy with a well-established, centralized state and bureaucracy. Dahomey became heavily involved in the European slave trade, which had begun in earnest a century previous with the arrival of the Dutch.

The rule of Gezu (1818–1858) marked the pinnacle of Dahomey's power and influence. Military victories enabled the kingdom of Dahomey to stop paying its annual tribute to the Oyo empire of what is now NIGERIA. Still, the end of the slave trade in the mid-nineteenth century greatly affected the economic fortunes of Dahomey, forcing it to provide primary products for newly important colonial markets. Its main export, palm oil, never generated the same amount of revenue that the slave trade had yielded. After the French gained control of Porto-Novo, commerce declined. Under the leadership of Glele (1858–1889), Dahomean troops resisted the French occupation; in 1889 the entire French merchant community on the coast was forced to flee into British territory.

Benhazin, Glele's successor, was willing to trade with the French, but only if the French agreed to grant Dahomey unconditional independence. In 1892 the French launched a full-scale offensive against Dahomey. Benhazin surrendered in 1894 and was exiled to Martinique, and the kingdom became the French colony of Dahomey.

Dakar, Senegal

Capital and largest city of Senegal.

Cosmopolitan, hedonistic Dakar has been called the Paris of West Africa. Once the capital of FRENCH WEST AFRICA, Dakar no longer dominates West Africa economically or politically, but it remains an important cultural center. Dakar lies on Cape Verde, near the westernmost point in Africa. Scholars have suggested two origins for the name Dakar. Fugitives from the tyrannical precolonial states of the interior called the Cape Verde Peninsula Deuk Raw (land of refuge), which might have evolved into Dakar. The name could also derive from the WOLOF word for tamarind tree, Dakhar.

Portuguese mariners first arrived along the Cape Verde coast during the mid-fifteenth century. They established a slave-trading post on nearby GORÉE ISLAND, which exported millions of slaves over the next 350 years. By the eighteenth century the French had taken control of Gorée. However, Gorée Island lacked a reliable supply of water, and its inhabitants sought a source of water on the nearby mainland. In the early 1700s the Lebu people occupied the small fishing and farming village of Ndakaru, on the Cape Verde Peninsula, on which Dakar is now built. The French constructed a trading post on the site around 1750.

To protect the merchants who settled there, in 1857 the French established a fort in Dakar. France was extending its control over SENEGAL, and the colonial administration needed a port close to the peanut-growing regions in the interior. In 1862 the French built a breakwater to protect Dakar's port and constructed a modern town on the site. The completion of West Africa's first rail line in, 1885, which ran to Saint-Louis through Senegal's main peanut-growing regions, increased the city's economic importance and caused its population to grow. In 1878 its population was 1,556, which grew to 18,447 by 1904. In 1887 Dakar was named one of the Four Communes of Senegal, and three years later the African residents of the communes, including Dakar, received partial French citizenship rights. In 1902 Dakar became the capital of the vast domain of French West Africa. The completion of a rail line to BAMAKO, far to the east on the NIGER RIVER, transformed Dakar into not only the political center, but also the economic center of much of West Africa.

Dakar was never rigidly segregated, and its residents' status as citizens gave them access to a French education and to French civil service jobs. In time, a French-speaking urban African elite arose, with a strong French outlook and often French ancestry as well.

After Senegal gained its independence in 1960, Dakar became the nation's capital. In addition to government offices, Dakar contains a sizable modern business district, where many international banks, multinational corporations, and international agencies maintain regional headquarters. It also has an international airport with good connections to Europe, North and South America, and many African cities. Furthermore, it is the major port for Senegal and neighboring countries, and has a large agricultural processing industry. Dakar boasts a sizable middle class. Although its living conditions are generally better than those of Senegal's interior, Dakar nevertheless has sprawling shantytowns, often filled with unemployed migrants from the interior. High unemployment, chronic water shortages, and pollution also plague the city, which had a population of about 2.4 million in 2005.

Its beauty, relatively mild climate, and nearby beaches have made Dakar a popular tourist destination. Major sites include Gorée Island, which is now a museum. Other attractions include one of the oldest African art museums on the continent and a thriving nightlife. The French Cultural Center and various nightclubs offer venues for Dakar's lively music scene, which features some of the top African artists, while a number of cinemas offer the latest in Senegalese film. Several markets, including the large Marché Sandaga, offer local crafts and clothing.

See also URBANISM AND URBANIZATION IN AFRICA.

DAVID P. JOHNSON, JR.

Dan

Ethnic group of West Africa who live in northwest Côte d'Ivoire and northeast Liberia.

The Dan language belongs to the Southern (or Peripheral) MANDE branch of the Niger-Congo linguistic family and is closely related to neighboring KWENI (or Gouro). Some scholars believe that the Dan originated in northwestern present-day CÔTE D'IVOIRE. According to this view, MANDINKA expansion drove them to their present homeland in the seventeenth and eighteenth centuries. The Dan consist of two groups. The Daménou, or northern Dan, live in the mountains and cultivate rice. The southern Dan, or Boutyouleuménou, who share a number of cultural features with the neighboring KRU people, hunt collectively and cultivate tubers.

The government of Côte d'Ivoire calls the Dan the Yacouba (or Yakouba). The traditional Dan homeland spans the departments of Man, Biankouma, and Danané in Côte d'Ivoire, as well as Nimba County in neighboring LIBERIA. It is a region of grassy savanna and forested mountains, including the highest point in West Africa, Mount Nimba, with a height of 1,752 m (over 6,700 ft).

In Liberia the Dan, one of the country's eighteen main ethnic groups, are often called Gio, a pejorative term that carries the meaning "slave people" in the Bassa language. The Dan resisted the authority of westernized states based along the coast. The Nimba County town of Tapiple, also called Tapeta, is named for the Dan chief Tapi, who allied with the Liberian government troops that finally subjugated the region in the 1920s. In Côte d'Ivoire, French governor Gabriel Angoulvant suppressed Dan resistance in a series of battles that ended in 1908.

The Dan also resisted the Islam of their northern neighbors and maintained vibrant religious and cultural traditions. They believe in the existence of two gods, one good and the other evil; they also believe that ancestral spirits influence the living. The Dan include male circumcision and female excision in initiation ceremonies. Secret societies remain important. The most powerful of these, the Gor, gives initiates the right to become symbolic leopards and thus impart justice unnoticed. By thrusting a baton between combatants, the Gor have the right to stop war. When one of the brotherhood commits a serious offense, he may be poisoned with crocodile bile.

The Dan excel at dance dramas, with dialogue sung, spoken, or pantomimed. Dance societies often require secret initiations for children as young as two years old. Young girls perform the *Gueu-Gblin* and the *Menton*, while young boys dance the *Gouah*. The Dan also love spectacular acrobatics, which have become tourist attractions, in which men juggle small boys in the air above the point of a knife. Dan music, which features an all-wood drum, is not heavily influenced by European styles and retains much of its spiritual significance. African art collectors prize Dan masks and wall hangings.

In the late 1990s most Dan made a living by growing rice, manioc, coffee, cocoa, and kola nuts. Men also migrated to work on the coast in the logging, palm oil, and tourist industries. In 1998 the Dan numbered around 500,000, with more than 300,000 in Côte d'Ivoire and the remainder across the border in Liberia.

See also BASSA OF LIBERIA; LANGUAGES, AFRICAN: AN OVERVIEW; RITES OF PASSAGE AND TRANSITION; TOURISM IN AFRICA.

DAVID P. JOHNSON, JR.

Danakil
See AFAR.

Dance in Sub-Saharan Africa

African dances are as varied and changing as the communities that create them. Although many types of African dance incorporate spirited, vigorous movement, there are others that are more reserved or stylized. African dances vary widely by region and ethnic community. In addition, there are numerous dances within a given community. African communities traditionally use dance for a variety of social purposes. Dances play a role in religious rituals; they mark rites of passage, including initiations to adulthood and weddings; they form a part of communal ceremonies, including harvest celebrations, funerals, and coronations; and they offer entertainment and recreation in the forms of masquerades, acrobatic dances, and social club dances.

SOUTH AFRICAN DANCE. A group of San women perform a traditional dance during the opening of South Africa's parliament, 2006. (*Obed Zilwa/AP Images*)

TRADITIONAL AFRICAN DANCE FORMS

European explorers of Africa hardly understood either the aesthetics or the meanings of dances in the cultures they sought to scrutinize and conquer. Writers such as Joseph Conrad depicted African dance as an expression of both savagery and aggressiveness. European observers often focused on certain types of African dance that reinforced their stereotypes of blacks as sexualized, warlike peoples. Abandoning these stereotypes, a careful survey reveals extraordinary variety in both the social meanings and aesthetic styles of African dance forms.

Traditionally, dance in Africa occurs collectively in a community setting. It expresses the life of the community more than the mood of an individual or a couple. Dances mark key elements of communal life. For example, dances at agricultural festivals mark the passage of seasons, the successful completion of projects, and the hope for prosperity.

In an annual festival of the Irigwe in NIGERIA, men perform leaps symbolizing the growth of the crops.

Dance does not merely form a part of community life; it represents and reinforces the community itself. Its structures reproduce the organization and the values of the community. For example, dances are often segregated by sex, reinforcing gender identities to children from a young age. Dance often expresses the categories that structure the community, including not only gender but also kinship, age, status, and, especially in modern cities, ethnicity. For example, in the igbin dance of the YORUBA of Nigeria, the order of the performers in the dance reflects their social standing and age, from the king down to the youngest at the gathering. Among the ASANTE of GHANA the king reinforces his authority through a special royal dance, and traditionally he might be judged by his dancing skill. Dance can provide a forum for popular opinion and even satire within political structures: the Ubakala and BAMBARA use dance as a form of criticism and commentary. Spiritual leaders also use dance to symbolize their connection with the world beyond.

Dances provide community recognition for the major events in people's lives. The dances of initiation, or rites of passage, are pervasive throughout Africa and function as moments of definition in an individual's life or sometimes as key opportunities to observe potential marriage partners. Highly energetic dances show off boys' stamina and are considered a means of judging physical health. The learning of the dance often plays an important part in the ritual of the occasion. For example, the girls among the LUNDA of ZAMBIA stay in seclusion practicing their steps before the coming-of-age ritual. Throughout Africa dance is also an integral part of the marking of birth and death. At burial ceremonies the Owo Yoruba perform the igogo, in which young men dance over the grave and pack the earth with stomping movements.

Dance plays a central role in therapy and healing in many parts of Africa. In the West African religious practice of bori, or ajun, women suffering from mental illness are brought to a shrine where they learn a ceremony involving song and dance for three months. This process of learning is as important for the women's therapy as the ceremony itself. The TIV of Nigeria have a dance that expresses the vital life force in the world that combats disease and death. The !Kung SAN of BOTSWANA perform a healing dance that includes both sexes and all ages, the healthy as well as the sick. Possession dance is another form of therapeutic ritual movement. Among the SHONA in ZIMBABWE the mhondoro spirit occupies the bodies of dancers, who move to a rhythm as the ancestors communicate wisdom.

Dance traditionally prepared people for the roles they played in the community. For example, some war dances prepared young men physically and psychologically for war by teaching them discipline and control while getting them into the spirit of battle. Some dances are a form of martial art themselves, such as Nigerian korokoro dances or the Angolan dances from which Brazilian Capoeira is derived.

Dances often tell stories that are part of the oral history of a community. For example, the bamaya dance of Ghana narrates the legend of a man who was hungry and entered the market dressed as a woman in order to steal a chicken. During the dance men play the role of the women in the market, imitating women's hip movements as women call out. Such stories often lie at the heart of a community's identity. The EWE people of TOGO and surrounding countries have created a dance to narrate a tale of the origin and migration of the community. Imitating the movements of a bird with the arms, dancers relate the story of the Ewe who followed the path of a bird when the group migrated from BENIN to the west.

The one unifying aesthetic of African dance is an emphasis upon rhythm, which may be expressed by many different parts of the body or extended outside the body to rattles or costumes. African dances may combine movements of any parts of the body, from the eyes to the toes, and the focus on a certain part of the body might have a particular social significance. The Nigerian Urhobo women perform a dance during which they push their arms back and forth and contract the torso in synchronization with an accelerating rhythm beat by a drum. In CÔTE D'IVOIRE a puberty dance creates a rhythmic percussion through the movement of a body covered in cowrie shells.

Africans often judge the mastery of a dancer by the dancer's skill in representing rhythm. More skillful dancers might express several different rhythms at the same time, for example by maintaining a separate rhythmic movement with each of several different parts of the body. Rhythm frequently forms a dialogue between dancers, musicians, and audience. Typically, the rhythmic dialogue occurs between the dancers and the drums in West Africa and between the dancers and the chorus in East Africa. The call-and-response dynamic found in African traditions all over the world characterizes the rhythmic dialogue among dancers, music, and audience. Unlike many Western forms of art dance, in which musicians and audience maintain a distance from the dance performance, African dance incorporates a call-and-response relationship that creates an interaction between those dancing and those surrounding them. The integration of performance and audience, as well as spatial environment, is one of the most noted aesthetic features of African dance.

Observers describe many of the dances as earth centered, unlike many floating or soaring European ballet forms. Gravity provides an earthward orientation even in those forms in which dancers leap into the air, such as the dances of the KIKUYU of KENYA and the Tutsi of RWANDA.

One of the most remarkable aspects of African dance is its use of the movements of daily life. By raising ordinary gestures to the level of art, these dances show the grace and rhythm of daily activities, from walking to pounding grain to chewing. In the Côte d'Ivoire dance known as ziglibit, stamping feet reproduce the rhythm of the pounding of corn into meal. During the thie bou bien dance of SENEGAL, dancers move their right arms as if they were eating the food that gives the dance its name. The NUPE fishermen of Nigeria perform a dance choreographed to coincide with the motions of throwing a fishing net.

According to the beliefs of many communities, traditional African dancers not only represent a spirit but also embody that spirit during the dance. This is particularly true of the sacred dances involving masquerade. Dancers use a range of masks and costumes to represent spirits, gods, and sacred animals. These masks can be as much as 3.7 m (12 ft) high; sometimes they cover the entire body and sometimes just the face. At funerals and an annual festival, members of the Yoruba Egungun ancestral society perform in elaborate costumes representing anything from village chiefs to animals and spirits as they mediate between the ancestors and the living.

Masquerades take a number of different forms. Some masquerades are representational. For example, many of the pastoralist groups of SUDAN, Kenya, and UGANDA perform dances portraying the cattle upon which their livelihood depends. During one such dance the KARIMOJON imitate the movements of cattle, shaking their heads like bulls or cavorting like young cows. In stilt dances, another variety of masquerade, stilts extend the dancers' bodies by as much as 3 m (10 ft). In the *gue gblin* dance of Côte d'Ivoire, dancers perform an amazing acrobatic stilt dance traditionally understood as a mediation between the ancestors and the living.

Acrobatic dances, such as those performed on stilts, are increasingly popular outside of their original sacred contexts. The SHOPE, the Shangana TONGA, and the SWAZI of southern Africa perform complex dances in which dancers manipulate a long shield and spear with great finesse as they move through a series of athletic kicks. The FULANI acrobats of Senegal, the GAMBIA, and GUINEA perform movements similar to those of American break dancing, such as backspins and head- and handstands.

MODERN AFRICAN DANCE FORMS

Colonialism and nationhood have transformed African society, and new African dance forms have developed in new social contexts. COLONIAL RULE shifted borders, and the cash economy prompted labor migrations. These migrations, often to multiethnic towns, undermined the tight-knit communities so basic to traditional dance, though the art form has survived in rural areas and in connection with traditional ceremonies. At the same time, urban living has given rise to an abundance of new dance forms. Thus modernization in Africa has allowed for some continuity, but it has also encouraged much innovation.

Christian missionaries initially forbade or limited traditional dance among Christian converts for fear of the dance's connection to indigenous religions. In parts of West Africa colonial administrators banned dancing, which they felt might keep workers out too late at night or, worse, stir anticolonial sentiment.

Meanwhile, traditional dance shifted along with its social context. As people traveled during the colonial period, their dances went with them. As a consequence of labor migrations, people from a given ethnic group found themselves next to neighbors with very different dance styles. As rural migrants gathered in cities, for example in SOUTH AFRICA, dance forms gained new significance as markers of ethnic origin and identity. Since the 1940s at the Witwatersrand gold mines, "mine dancers" have competed in teams organized around ethnic origins.

New dance forms expressed nationalism and resistance. One dance of the Zulu in South Africa used rhythmic stomping and slapping of leather boots to express both the meter of work and a march against the oppression of APARTHEID. As a stirring cultural expression, dance could both express tradition and forge a new national identity. During the nationalist period nationalist movements and later governments used dance as a way of expressing a country's identity. With schools such as Mudra-Afrique, founded in 1977 in DAKAR, and events such as the All-Nigeria Festival of Arts, national governments used dance to transcend ethnic identity. Some dance companies, such as Les Ballets Africains in Guinea, the National Dance Company of Senegal, and the National Dance Company of Zimbabwe, gained international renown and represented their new nations abroad.

In recent years modern artistic productions have increasingly drawn on traditional dances. Dance troupes performing on stage have integrated traditional forms with new, improvised themes and forms. The dance theater of the Ori Olokun Company of Ife, Nigeria, for example, created a performance called Alatangana that depicts a traditional myth of the KONO people in Guinea. Dance has influenced several plays by Wole SOYINKA, including *The Lion and the Jewel* (1963), *A Dance of the Forests* (1960), and *Death and the King's Horsemen* (1975).

After World War II (1939–1945) hybrid forms of dance emerged that integrated European and American dance influences. Highlife was the most famous of these forms, synthesizing the European ballroom dance techniques learned by soldiers abroad with traditional dance rhythms and forms. The highlife music and dance rose to popularity in the cities of West Africa during the 1960s, cutting across ethnic boundaries to express a common regional identity derived from the experience of colonialism and urbanization. In southern Africa people danced in discos to the modern African beat of kwela, and in Central and East Africa Congo-beat music gained popularity.

The modern transformation of Africa has thus fostered remarkable creativity and diversity in dance forms. An essential element in everything from improvised traditional performance to ritual coming-of-age ceremonies to the nightlife of dance halls and discos, dance remains a vibrant and changing part of African life.

See also CHRISTIANITY: MISSIONARIES IN AFRICA;
EXPLORERS IN AFRICA SINCE 1800; MASKS AND
MASQUERADES IN AFRICA; MUSIC, AFRICAN; RITES OF
PASSAGE AND TRANSITION.

MARIAN AGUIAR

Dangme
See ADANGBE.

Danquah, Joseph Kwame Kyeretwi Boakye
1895–1965
**Ghanaian scholar, lawyer, and nationalist and the
principal political rival of Kwame Nkrumah.**

J. B. Danquah was one of the founders of the modern state
of GHANA. He cofounded the country's first nationalist
party in 1947. Danquah led the opposition to Kwame
NKRUMAH after Nkrumah became the country's leading
nationalist figure. To silence Danquah, Nkrumah had him
confined to prison, where Danquah died under miserable
conditions.

By birth, Danquah belonged to the royal family of
Akyem Abuakwa, a province of ASANTE. He attended
Basel Mission Schools in Akyem Abuakwa. Subsequently,
he studied in London, England, where he received a law
degree and a Ph.D. in ethics in 1927. Danquah returned to
the then British colony of the GOLD COAST (now Ghana),
where he practiced law privately. In 1931 he founded the
Times of West Africa, which became a leading newspaper.

Danquah's editorial writing led him into politics in
opposition to British colonial repression and exploitation.
During the 1930s he also conducted research on which
he based a controversial claim that the AKAN people (of
present-day Ghana) were descendants of the ancient kingdom of Ghana (in present-day MALI and MAURITANIA).
On the basis of Danquah's work, the Gold Coast was
renamed Ghana when it achieved independence in 1957.
In 1937 he founded the Gold Coast Youth Congress,
through which he intended to unite the Gold Coast
African elite. In 1947 he cofounded the United Gold
Coast Convention (UGCC), whose leadership invited
Nkrumah, then in Britain, to serve as general secretary.

Political differences between the two leaders quickly
emerged. While Danquah preferred working with the
existing elite to find a gradual path to self-governance,
Nkrumah appealed to the masses to support immediate
independence. After the British appointed Danquah,
but not Nkrumah, to a constitutional convention,
Nkrumah left the UGCC to form the Convention
People's Party (CPP), demanding immediate independence. Nkrumah's philosophy resonated with most
Ghanaians, and in 1951, when Nkrumah won election

as prime minister, Danquah assumed his role as leader
of the opposition.

In 1960 Danquah ran for the presidency against
Nkrumah and won just 10 percent of the vote. Nkrumah's
rule became increasingly totalitarian, and Danquah voiced
his opposition to this trend. In 1961 Nkrumah had
Danquah arrested and detained under the Preventive
Detention Act but released him the following year.
Danquah's continued attacks on Nkrumah and his policies
drew Nkrumah's ire anew, and he was jailed once again in
1964. This time, Danquah faced severe prison conditions.
He was chained to the floor and denied meals as well as
medical treatment. He died of a heart attack while detained
in prison as an enemy of the state, but received a hero's
funeral in his hometown.

BIBLIOGRAPHY
Appiah, Joseph. The Man, J. B. Danquah. Academy of Arts and
Sciences, 1974.
Ofosu-Appiah, L. H. The Life and Times of Dr. J. B. Danquah.
Waterville Publishing House, 1974.

ROBERT FAY

Dar es Salaam, Tanzania
Largest city in Tanzania and acting capital of the country.
The administrative, commercial, and manufacturing center
of TANZANIA, Dar es Salaam is located on the East African
coast southwest of ZANZIBAR. Originally a small farming
and fishing village named Mzizima, it began changing
rapidly during the late nineteenth century when the sultan
of Zanzibar, Majid ibn Sa'id, made the town his summer
residence. Attracted by the safe harbor of the neighboring
lagoon, the sultan renamed the town Dar es Salaam (Arabic
for "haven of peace"), constructed a port, and made plans
to move his capital from Zanzibar to the town. But Majid
died before his plans were completed, and his successor,
BARGHASH IBN SA'ID, attempted to control the city from
Zanzibar through alliances with the local Swahili chiefs, or
jumbes.

Although successful for several years, Barghash's
absentee rule collapsed when the German East Africa
Company took possession of the city in 1887. The company
made Dar es Salaam the capital of the German East Africa
Company in 1891 and soon afterward constructed a railroad to carry export crops from the interior to the port city.
Dar es Salaam subsequently became the economic center
of the colony and remained the capital when the British
took over in 1916. In 1972 President Julius K. NYERERE
proposed to move the capital to the more geographically
central town of Dodoma. Nonetheless, Dar es Salaam still
serves as the country's capital and is the largest and most
diverse city in Tanzania. As of 2000 it had a population of

some 2.5 million people, including Africans, Europeans, Asians (particularly Indians), and Arabs.

Since colonial times, Dar es Salaam's economy has been supported by the trading and shipping business brought in by the international port and trans-African railroads. It is also home to an oil refinery and factories that manufacture domestic and export goods such as textiles, clothing, and footwear. In recent years, Dar es Salaam has suffered from inadequate housing and drinking water as well as pollution and crime, all problems exacerbated by the city's rapid population growth and by a sluggish national economy. Municipal officials hope that plans to privatize city services, improve port facilities, and attract foreign investment will improve living conditions and stimulate the economy. In 1999 Dar es Salaam's Kilimanjaro international airport became the first fully privatized airport in Africa.

In 1992 the Sustainable Dar es Salaam Program outlined a plan to involve all sectors of the community with improving city services and city life. Dar es Salaam has seen significant improvement in several areas in recent years as a result of the programs. These include an improvement in waste collection and solid waste management, easing traffic congestion, and relocating street traders to specific market areas. The city has also begun to implement environmental cleanup and recycling programs.

An August 1998 bombing of the United States embassy in Dar es Salaam left nine people dead and some seventy people injured. Previously, East Africa had been considered safe from terrorist attacks, but officials worried that the bombing threatened to deter tourists, a vital source of foreign exchange, from visiting Tanzania. Their fears were not immediately realized, however, as the number of foreign visitors increased by some 20 percent the following year.

See also GERMAN EAST AFRICA.

BIBLIOGRAPHY

Ofcansky, Thomas, and Rodger Yeager. *Historical Dictionary of Tanzania.* Scarecrow Press, 1997.

Sutton, J. E. G. *Dar es Salaam: City, Port, and Region.* Tanzania Society, 1970.

ELIZABETH HEATH

Darfur

Former independent sultanate in western Sudan.

In prehistoric times, the peoples of what is now Darfur were related to those of the Nile Valley (including EGYPT), whose caravans probably reached the region by 2500 B.C.E. According to tradition, the region's first rulers were the Daju. By around 900 C.E., Christianity had spread to the area; by the thirteenth century, however, the region had

FOREIGN SUPPORT FOR DARFUR. A protester in London displays his support for Darfur, 2005. (*Press Association/Edmond Terakopian/AP Images*)

fallen under the domination of the powerful Islamic empire of Kanem-Bornu to the west, and the TUNJUR replaced the Daju as the ruling elite of the region.

The sultanate of Darfur first entered the historical record during the seventeenth century, under Sulayman. Sulayman belonged to the Keira Dynasty, which claimed Arab descent and which removed the Tunjur from power. Except for an interval during the nineteenth century, this dynasty ruled Darfur until 1916. Gradually the Keira merged with the Fur, the agricultural people over whom they ruled. (The state's name, Dar Fur, means "house of the Fur" in Arabic.)

The slave trade figured prominently in both the formation and the expansion of the Darfur Sultanate. Parties from Darfur obtained slaves and IVORY by either raiding or trading with the stateless societies that lay to its south and southwest. Not only did Darfur's rulers export slaves to North Africa and along the "forty days' road," which crossed the desert from Darfur to Egypt, but slaves also served the sultan as soldiers, laborers, and bureaucrats. Sulayman's successors expanded the state. In 1786 Sultan Muhammad Tayrab conquered the province of Kordofan from the Funj Sultanate of Sennar to the east.

In 1821, however, Egyptian forces conquered the Funj Sultanate and wrested Kordofan from Darfur. Traders from KHARTOUM then began to compete in the slave trade with those in Darfur. Turkish-Egyptian forces under Rahma al-Zubayr conquered Darfur in 1874 and overthrew the Keira sultan. In 1885 a Sudanese rebellion under a religious leader called the Mahdi overthrew the Egyptian state, which had come under increasing British influence. In 1898 British forces defeated the Mahdist state and placed it under Anglo-Egyptian administration. Under their policy of indirect rule, the British restored the Darfur Sultanate under Ali Dinar Zakariyya. Ali Dinar played a significant role in an Islamic, anti-Western alliance that formed during World War I. The Anglo-Egyptian government subsequently invaded Darfur, killed Ali Dinar, ended the sultanate, and incorporated Darfur into Sudan. After Sudan attained independence in 1956, Darfur remained under Sudanese rule.

The central Darfur region of Sudan is inhabited largely by Fur farmers; the northernmost section by nomadic camel herders; and the eastern and southern zones by Arab cattle herders. Periods of severe drought since the late 1960s forced the cattle and camel herders to encroach on the rich agricultural land in the central section of Darfur. As competition for access to water and pasture intensified, small-scale raids turned into persistent battles among the different groups. Attempts by successive governments to achieve peace in the region have failed, and the fighting continues.

In February 2003 two rebel groups—the Sudan Liberation Army Movement and the Justice and Equality Movement (with members drawn from the Fur, Masalit, and Zaghawa ethnic groups)—demanded that the Arab-ruled Sudanese government begin to share power and end the economic marginalization of Darfur. The government responded by targeting the civilian populations from which the rebels were drawn.

With support from the Sudanese government, Arab Janjaweed militias forced more than 2.5 million people—mostly farmers—to flee to refugee camps. Some 300,000 have died or been killed, and tens of thousands of homes have been destroyed. It was not until 2006 that the United Nations intervened in any meaningful sense, dispatching more than 20,000 peacekeeping troops to the troubled region. Two years later, prosecutors at the International Criminal Court indicted Sudan's President Omar al-Bashir for crimes against humanity, including several counts of genocide.

BIBLIOGRAPHY

Daly, M. W. Darfur's Sorrow: A History of Destruction and Genocide. Cambridge University Press, 2007.

Kapteijns, Lidwien, and Jay Spaulding. An Islamic Alliance: Ali Dinar and the Sanusiyya, 1906–1916. Northwestern University Press, 1994.

O'Fahey, R. S. State and Society in Dar Fur. Hurst & Co., 1980.

Prunier, Gérard. Darfur: The Ambiguous Genocide. Cornell University Press: 2007.

Steidle, Brian. The Devil Came on Horseback: Bearing Witness to the Genocide in Darfur. Public Affairs, 2007.

ROBERT FAY

De Klerk, Frederik Willem

1936–

President of South Africa from 1989 to 1994, and co-winner of the 1993 Nobel Peace Prize.

F. W. De Klerk was born to an Afrikaner family with a long history of involvement in South African politics. His own political career began during adolescence, when he joined the youth section of the Afrikaner-dominated NATIONAL PARTY.

In 1958 De Klerk received a law degree from Potchefstroom University. He practiced law in Vereeniging from 1961 until 1972, all the while serving as chairman of the local chapter of the National Party. He then abandoned his law career and became a member of Parliament in South Africa. De Klerk rose quickly through the party's rank and file, with appointments to numerous cabinet posts. As a minister he had little patience for antiapartheid protests but was known as a conciliator within the party.

After South African president Pieter Willem BOTHA had a heart attack in 1989, De Klerk became the leader of the National Party. Later that year the ailing Botha resigned, and the Parliament elected De Klerk to replace him. Under Botha, the embattled government had already begun to relax certain APARTHEID restrictions, and De Klerk began his presidency by releasing several jailed senior leaders of the AFRICAN NATIONAL CONGRESS (ANC), though not Nelson MANDELA. In February 1990 De Klerk released Mandela, and the two began negotiations to end white minority rule. Within months, De Klerk had lifted the ban on African political parties. He also lobbied his own party to accept members of all races. In 1993 De Klerk and Mandela together won the Nobel Peace Prize.

In 1994 De Klerk ran as a National Party candidate in the first open elections in South Africa. Although he was returned to Parliament, the ANC had obtained the vast majority of seats, and Nelson Mandela ascended to the presidency. De Klerk joined Mandela's government as second deputy president. In June 1994, De Klerk and other National Party members withdrew from their cabinet posts in order to establish the National Party as a formal opposition party. De Klerk stepped down as leader of the National Party and retired from politics in September 1997.

In 2001 De Klerk's former wife, Marike, was found murdered in her Cape Town rooms. Some time later, a security guard was arrested and convicted of the crime. Following this, De Klerk remained active in politics, although poor health (in 2006 he underwent surgery to remove a tumor from his colon and bypass surgery) sometimes slowed him. He remains much in demand as a public speaker.

ARI NAVE

Decolonization in Africa: An Interpretation
General discussion of the process whereby colonial powers relinquished political authority in Africa to new African states.

The most difficult problem in writing the history of decolonization is the temptation to write it backwards. We know that almost all African colonies eventually became independent states, hence a tendency to relate the triumph of Nationalism, of an African conquest of the colonial state. We know now that the fruits of independence have often turned bitter, hence a temptation to write the history of disappointment, of the continued subordination of Africa to Western powers. Neither the triumphalist history nor the story of frustrated aspirations is sufficient.

If instead of writing history from the present to the past, we watch it run forward, the history of Africa from the 1940s onward opens up to a much wider range of actions, aspirations, and possibilities. We see political movements directed not just at taking over the nation-state, but at revitalizing local belief systems or forging connections among people of African descent all around the world. We see African workers organizing to demand wages equal to those of whites, merchants seeking access to markets alongside European firms, peasants trying to restore harmony to the land. People act together as members of an Islamic brotherhood or as migrants from a particular rural area. Such collectivities are important not simply as they contributed to anticolonial or nationalist movements—even though many of them did—but because they helped reshape people's lives.

A number of scholars would dispense with the concept of decolonization altogether, for some because it never really happened—because Africa remains subordinated to Europe—for others because the term suggests that COLONIAL RULE marched to its own end, rather than being overthrown by people striving to liberate themselves. The term is still useful, as long as one does not read more into it than it deserves. Colonialism may be distinguished from other systems in which a few people ruled over many by the institutions colonial regimes created that explicitly reproduced social difference and inequality. Colonial states drew and redrew distinctions among people under its rule, defining some as natives (in turn, divided into tribes) and others as citizens or Europeans, with different rights and obligations, administered through different agencies. Although states often used similar techniques at home and overseas to command obedience, the ruling fiction in the colonies was difference, while the ruling fiction at home in Europe, at least since the nineteenth century, was the legal and political equality of citizens. Colonial rulers passed laws against intermarriage and tried to prevent whites from "going native," or educated natives from thinking too highly of themselves.

These distinctions became increasingly difficult—and then impossible—to sustain in the period after World War II (1939–1945). Decolonization entailed the transition from empires in which distinction was emphasized to a global system of states in which all states were formally equivalent and in which each regarded its own citizens as *formally* equivalent to one another.

The word *formally* is crucial. The world and its individual states have always been and remain driven by distinctions. Sovereignty allowed African leaders to make certain kinds of claims on world resources, and many became adept at appealing, using a vocabulary of "nation-building" and "development," to rich states' interests in having a world order of states participating in global institutions and markets. Internally, sovereignty also had its uses: sovereign power could be used to reward friends and punish enemies, to forge symbols of national solidarity. The politics of running a state, in short, are not the politics of running a colony.

CRISIS OF COLONIALISM
In 1945 the idea that most of Africa would be divided into independent states within twenty years would have struck most Europeans—and possibly most Africans—as unimaginable. By 1965 it was a fact. Part of understanding this transition is figuring out how the transfer of power became imaginable—in Paris, in ACCRA, in villages in rural Tanganyika (present-day TANZANIA).

Another of the temptations the historian faces is that of making colonialism into more than it was—a solid and unchanging edifice of power. Colonists wanted to believe this, as did anticolonial movements, for it defined their own heroism. Colonialism, in fact, came apart at its cracks, even as colonial regimes tried to remake themselves.

What conquering powers could do best was concentrate forces—to smash African political units one by one, to punish rebellion brutally, and to round up labor or seize resources at certain moments. What they could do least well, try as they did, was to insinuate themselves into the routine exercise of power. In SOUTH AFRICA, ALGERIA, Southern Rhodesia (present-day ZIMBABWE), and parts of other colonies, white settlers both forced indigenous people off their land and provided a surveillance and control over agricultural and mineral production that was impossible elsewhere. When two decades into the colonial period British rulers proclaimed themselves advocates of indirect rule, they were accepting their incapacity either to make Africans into replicas of Europeans or else to turn Africans into the servants of European will. They insisted that keeping African societies in their allegedly timeless integrity had been British policy all along. Actually, this "ethnicization" of Africa—French Africa as well as British—came at a time shortly after World War I (1914–1919) when educated Africans were building associations and political organizations and acting disturbingly like "citizens."

At the very time, in the 1920s, when European powers were pretending that Africans were living within tribal cages, many were deeply involved in boundary-crossing activities: as farmers, opening up new territories; as merchants, exchanging goods from different ecological zones; and as workers, seeking as best they could to obtain cash wages without losing access to land and community. Religious movements were shaping affinities that crossed or expanded lines of language and culture. African intellectuals forged connections throughout the African diaspora and with intellectuals from other colonized regions, while working-class Africans entered into diasporic relations when black sailors and dockworkers from Africa and the Americas met on ships or in ports, and eventually contributed to the rise of the Garvey movement.

The colonialism that collapsed in the 1950s was not the stagnant colonialism of the 1920s or 1930s, but colonialism at its most arrogantly interventionist, its most self-consciously reformist. In the 1920s and 1930s, France and Great Britain rejected efforts from within the colonial establishment for a more vigorous development of African resources. A crisis came with recovery from the 1930s depression, as African workers returned to employers slow to raise wages recently cut, to cities with virtually no social services. The result was a wave of strikes beginning in the British Copperbelt (in present-day ZAMBIA) in 1935, where it spread beyond the mines to engulf entire towns, extending to railroads in the Gold Coast and ports in KENYA, Tanganyika, and elsewhere. The wave struck the British West Indies as well. In London this was seen as an empire-wide threat. More important, it revealed that pretending to keep colonized people in their tribal cages was a failure. The British government decided it had to reclaim the initiative with the Colonial Development and Welfare Act of 1940. This recognized that resources would have to be put into colonies—not just extracted from them—if social peace and colonial initiative were to be restored.

Then came the war—to which Africans contributed their bodies and their labor, and for which they received little. Another strike wave hit British Africa, and this time officials focused specifically on the labor question, partially giving in to wage demands and at last acknowledging the worker as something more than the "detribalized African." In French Africa, parallel developments occurred after the war—in the shadow of major strikes and urban conflicts between 1945 and 1948—and also resulted in a new development initiative.

DEVELOPMENT IN THE SERVICE OF EMPIRE

The international situation had also changed. On the one hand, Europe needed African minerals and crops more than ever. On the other hand, empire became more vulnerable politically. Adolf Hitler gave racist ideologies a bad name, and imperial leaders were at pains to explain why "self-determination" was a useful cry against Nazi conquests but not against imperial domination. Would Africa simply become a zone of heightened extraction, or could imperial powers reconcile expanding production with containing protest and relegitimizing empire internationally? For France and Great Britain, the development idea seemed for a time to offer an answer: their capital and knowledge would both increase output and raise the standard of living of Africans. Development would be the salvation of empire.

In Portuguese Africa, production was expanded within a highly authoritarian system of rule and a highly coercive system of labor recruitment. In Belgian Africa, development meant more power for the already powerful mining companies, which provided services to stabilize workers in their employment. Belgium boasted of health and other services, but it did little to train an elite and less to allow expression, suppressing numerous peasant uprisings, religious movements, strikes, and mutinies.

Modernizing colonialism sharply raised the stakes: the old empire on the cheap was becoming economically and politically impossible, while the expensive empire of the postwar era had yet to prove itself. In fact, the development drive did more to foster demands and disorder than to contain them. And meanwhile, the attempt to legitimize the colonial order was opening cracks in the structure of power, which African political movements quickly pried wider open.

POLITICAL MOBILIZATION IN AFRICA

If one can sense the vulnerability of European powers, one needs to understand the multiple ways in which Africans

Chronology of African Independence State	Date of Independence	Colonial Power	Notes
Ethiopia	Ancient		Italian occupation 1936–1941.
Liberia	July 26, 1847		Private colony 1822–1847. Home for freed American slaves.
South Africa	May 31, 1910	Britain	(Suid Afrika) Union of four colonies, Cape Colony, Natal, Orange River Colony (Orange Vrij Staat), and Transvaal (Zuid Afrikaansche Republiek), the last two of which had been independent Boer republics to May 31, 1902. The Union became republic outside British Commonwealth May 31, 1961.
			White minority rule.
			Unrecognized 'independent' homelands:
			Transkei October 26, 1976
			Bophuthatswana December 6, 1977
			Venda September 13, 1979
			Ciskei December 4, 1981
Egypt	February 28, 1922	Britain	Joined with Syria as United Arab Republic (UAR) from February 1, 1958 to September 28, 1961. Federated with Kingdom of (North) Yemen from March 8, 1958 to December 26, 1961. Name UAR retained by Egypt to September 2, 1961.
Libya	December 24, 1951	Italy	British (Tripolitania and Cyrenaica) and French (Fezzan) administration 1943–1951.
Ethiopia (Ogaden)	February 28, 1955		Italian occupation 1936–1941. British administration 1943–1955.
Sudan	January 1, 1956	Britain & Egypt	Anglo-Egyptian condominium.
Morocco	March 2, 1956	France	(Maroc)
Tunisia	March 20, 1956	France	(Tunisie)
Morocco (part)	October 29, 1956		International zone (Tangiers).
Ghana	March 6, 1957	Britain	(Gold Coast) including British Togoland (UN Trust), part of former German colony of Togo.
Morocco (part)	April 27, 1958	Spain	(Marruecos) Spanish southern zone.
Guinea	October 2, 1958	France	(Guinée Française)
Cameroon	January 1, 1960	France	(Cameroon) UN Trust. Larger part of former German colony of Kamerun.
Togo	April 27, 1960	France	UN Trust. Larger part of former German colony of Togo.
Senegal	June 20, 1960	France	First independent as 'Federation of Mali' with Mali (former French Soudan),
	(August 20, 1960)		Federation dissolved after two months, joined Gambia in Confederation of Senegambia, January 1, 1982, to October 6, 1989.

Chronology of African Independence State	Date of Independence	Colonial Power	Notes
Mali	June 20, 1960 (September 22, 1960)	France	(Soudan Française) Independent initially as 'Federation of Mali' with Senegal, Federation dissolved after two months.
Madagascar	June 26, 1960	France	(Malagasy, Republique Malagache)
Zaire	June 30, 1960	Belgium	Congo Free State (Etat Indépendent du Congo) May 2, 1885, to November 11, 1908 when it became the Belgian Congo (Congo Belge, Belgisch Congo). Name changed from Congo October 27, 1974.
Somalia	July 1, 1960	Italy & Britain	UN Trust, Union of two colonies, Italian and British Somaliland. British Somaliland independent prior to union on June 26, 1960.
Benin	August 1, 1960	France	Name changed from Dahomey November 30, 1975.
Niger	August 3, 1960	France	
Burkina Faso	August 5, 1960	France	Name changed from Upper Volta (Haute Volta) August 4, 1984.
Côte d'Ivoire	August 7, 1960	France	Name changed from Ivory Coast October 15, 1986.
Chad	August 11, 1960	France	(Tchad)
Central African Republic (CAR)	August 13, 1960	France	(Oubangui-Chari, Republique Centrafricaine) Central African Empire from December 4, 1976, to September 20, 1979.
Congo (Brazzavile)	August 15, 1960	France	(Moyen Congo)
Gabon	August 17, 1960	France	
Nigeria	October 1, 1960	Britain	
Mauritania	November 28, 1960	France	(Mauritanie)
Sierra Leone	April 24, 1961	Britain	
Nigeria (British North Cameroon)	June 1, 1961	Britain	UN Trust. Part of former German colony of Kamerun. Plebiscite February 11–12, 1961.
Cameroon (British South Cameroon)	October 1, 1961	Britain	UN Trust. Part of former German colony of Kamerun. Plebiscite February 11–12, 1961. Union with Cameroon as United Republic of Cameroon.
Tanzania	December 9, 1961	Britain	(Tanganyika) UN Trust. Greater part of former German colony of Deutsche Ostafrika. Name changed to Tanzania following union with Zanzibar April 27, 1964.
Burundi	July 1, 1962	Belgium	UN Trust. Ruanda-Urundi, divided at independence, was smaller part of former German, colony of Deutsche Ostafrika.
Rwanda	July 1, 1962	Belgium	UN Trust. Ruanda-Urundi, divided at independence, was smaller part of former German, colony of Deutsche Ostafrika.
Algeria	July 3, 1962	France	(Algérie)

continued

Chronology of African Independence State	Date of Independence	Colonial Power	Notes
Uganda	October 9, 1962	Britain	
Tanzania (Zanzibar)	December 10, 1963	Britain	Union with Tanganyika as Tanzania April 27, 1964.
Kenya	December 12, 1963	Britain	
Malawi	July 6, 1974	Britain	(Nyasaland) Federated with Rhodesia October 1, 1953, to December 31, 1963.
Zambia	October 25, 1964	Britain	(Northern Rhodesia) Federated with Nyasaland and Southern Rhodesia October 1, 1953, to December 31, 1963.
Gambia	February 18, 1965	Britain	Joined with Senegal as Confederation of Senegambia, January 1, 1982, to October 6, 1989.
Botswana	September 30, 1966	Britain	(Bechuanaland)
Lesotho	October 4, 1966	Britain	(Basutoland)
Mauritius	March 12, 1968	Britain	
Swaziland	September 6, 1968	Britain	
Equatorial Guinea	October 12, 1968	Spain	Comprises Rio Muni and Macias Nguema Biyogo (Fernando Poo)
Morocco (Ifni)	June 30, 1969	Spain	(Territorio de Ifni)
Guinea-Bissau	September 10, 1974	Portugal	Guine-Bissau formerly Guine-Portuguesa.
Mozambique	June 25, 1975	Portugal	(Moçambique)
Cape Verde	July 5, 1975	Portugal	(Cabo Verde)
Comoros	July 6, 1975	France	Archipel des Comores. Excluding island of Mayoette which remains a French Overseas Territory (Territoire d'Outre-Mer).
Sã Tomé and Principe	July 12, 1975	Portugal	(St. Thomas and Prince Islands)
Angola	November 11, 1975	Portugal	Includes detached enclave of Cabinda.
Western Sahara	February 28, 1976	Spain	(Rio de Oro and Sequit el Hamra) On Spanish withdrawal seized by Morocco. Occupation disrupted POLISARIO, formed May 10, 1973.
Seychelles	June 26, 1976	Britain	
Djibouti	June 27, 1977	France	(Territoire Française des Afars et des Issas formerly Côte Française des Somalis)
Zimbabwe	April 18, 1980	Britain	(Rhodesia, formerly Southern Rhodesia) Unilateral Declaration of Independence (UDI) in effect from November 11, 1965, to December 12, 1979. Federated with Northern Rhodesia and Nyasaland October 1, 1953, to December 31, 1963.

Chronology of African Independence State	Date of Independence	Colonial Power	Notes
Namibia	March 21, 1990	South Africa	(South West Africa) UN Trust. Former German colony of Deutsche Sudwestafrika.
Eritrea	May 24, 1993	Italy	British administration 1941–1952. Federated with Ethiopia September 11, 1952.
		Ethiopia	Union with Ethiopia November 14, 1962.
African Territories and Islands Not Independent			
Spanish North Africa		Spain	Plazas de Soberania: Ceuta, Islas Chafarinas Melilla, Penon de Velez
			de la Gomera, Penon de Athucemas.
			Small enclaves and islands on the north coast of Morocco.
Madeira		Portugal	(Arquipelago da Madeira)
Canary Islands		Spain	(Islas Canarias)
St Helena with Ascension and Tristan da Cunha		Britain	British Crown Colony
Socotra		Yemen	
Mayotte		France	Island of Comoros Group. Territoire Française d'Outre-Mer.
Réunion		France	Ile de la Réunion, Département d'Outre-Mer (from 1946).
French Indian Ocean Islands		France	Ile Europa, Ille Juan de Nova, Bassas da India, Iles Glorieuses, Tromelin (all near Madagascar).

Source: I. Griffiths, *The Atlas of African Affairs* (1994).

mobilized, and the diverse objectives that they sought. It is too easy to project backwards the struggle for the nation-state, but important to note the way in which African political parties brokered quite diverse movements and aspirations—well enough to create plausible political organizations, not well enough to deepen those connections into a sense of common purpose.

There were struggles to group together chiefdoms into larger units with more influence in the colonial capital, attempts to install younger or more progressive chiefs in place of reactionary ones, efforts of urban migrants to strengthen and expand their communities of origin, and attempts to combat spiritual threats to the health of local communities. These movements used local languages and religious beliefs, and they often involved people literate in English or French who might enhance oral tradition by compiling it in written form. There were Muslim brotherhoods with networks of Koranic schools and leadership

hierarchies across West and North Africa as well as Christian communities and breakaway, sometimes millennial, religious organizations—all bringing people together in other ways. PAN-AFRICANISM in its various forms confronted imperialism on a world scale, insisting that the oppression of people of color demanded a global liberation. South Africans had organized effective labor and strike movements from the 1920s, while Algerian workers—more of whom had jobs in France than in Algerian cities—built a powerful organization of North African workers in France, linked to currents of proletarian internationalism in Europe. It would soon catalyze radical nationalism in Algeria itself.

What was really new after World War II was the possibility of articulating these concepts not simply among people of African descent literate in French and English, but between the elites and wider groupings of people within their respective territories.

Before the war, political parties and other political organizations existed within a number of colonial territories, but most importantly across them—the National Congress of British West Africa and later the West African Students Union notable among these. In North Africa, where European colonization had never eclipsed the merchant or administrative elites of the previous Ottoman Empire, elite movements such as the Young Algerians or Young Tunisians claimed meaningful forms of citizenship. In EGYPT a relatively brief period of formal British rule gave way in 1922 to a restored Egyptian monarchy, besieged by students, commercial elite, and other modernizers, and increasingly by mobilization among workers and peasants, all demanding that the state be truly independent, be truly national, and respond to their needs. Throughout North Africa, Islamic reform movements sought to purify social life and link the region to a broader Islamic world. In the 1940s these movements focused more clearly on demands for political autonomy, but with considerable disagreement over whether this should take place in relation to France or Great Britain, under a monarchy poised between traditionalist and modernizing political movements, or in an explicitly national form.

In South Africa from 1912, the AFRICAN NATIONAL CONGRESS (ANC) drew on Anglo-American traditions of peaceful petition and protest to insist that democracy made sense in Africa too. By World War II, young educated elite throughout Africa were adding a new militancy, linkages to labor movements, and connections to radical anti-imperialists in European and colonial capitals. In French Africa, the Rassemblement Démocratique Africaine organized a wide political movement in 1946, and territorial political parties came under its umbrella.

Social action was necessarily political, and political action invariably had social implications. Yet a labor union was, first of all, a labor union, struggling for better wages and working conditions. In the 1945–1950 strike wave, unions in French Africa turned the government's idea of a single, transoceanic France into demands that all workers within that unit receive the same pay and benefits. Although political leaders saw workers as a constituency, and unions saw political action as useful to their cause, a tension between the idea of solidarity among workers and unity among Africans grew. Similarly, the wide variety of movements among peasants—against the intrusiveness of colonial agricultural projects, over land issues, against below-market prices paid to farmers by colonial crop marketing boards—must be seen in all their specificity, though every success any movement had contributed to a broader sense of empowerment.

It was the genius of men such as Kwame NKRUMAH and Léopold SENGHOR that they could bring together diverse movements and tendencies. They were machine politicians in the best sense of the word. They drew together the poor peasant hemmed in by colonial agricultural policies, the well-off merchant feeling the heavy hand of the European import-export houses, the railway worker facing barriers to advancement, the literate clerk trapped in the racial hierarchy of a bureaucracy, the lawyer espousing constitutional justice into what—for a time at least—was a coherent movement against the injustices of colonial states. Studies of politics in different territories stress that political parties both were constrained by regional and ethnic differences and cut across them, and in any case the affiliations that defined an ethnic group changed in the course of political mobilizations.

The institutions that colonial powers created failed to contain political mobilization, but they often channeled it in certain directions. After World War II, France and Great Britain—but not Portugal and Belgium—sought to open up electoral institutions that would co-opt elite Africans and justify the argument that colonial stewardship was preparing Africans for a democratic, modern future. Limited as these initially were, colonial political institutions defined a game with clear rules. Politics was encouraged when it took the form of electoral campaigns for the legislative body created for each colony, for the local councils, and in the French case the territorial units that elected representatives to the Paris legislature, where they would constitute a numerically small voice in the sovereign body. In NIGERIA or SENEGAL, businessmen, teachers, and trade unionists became the building blocks of early parties. However, in French Equatorial Africa—where a particularly brutal and exploitative form of colonization had been practiced—the electoral system created by the French after 1945 constituted its own political reality, in which politicians turned categories such as urban youth into political units and redrew the boundaries of ethnic affiliations to fit the constituencies they were organizing.

Meanwhile, other forms of political connection—from Pan-Africanism to Muslim brotherhoods—received no such representation, no such encouragement. Indeed, from Sétif (Algeria) in 1945 to MADAGASCAR in 1947 to Central Kenya in 1952 or CAMEROON in 1956 and most notoriously Algeria after 1954, colonial repression was brutal toward movements that strayed beyond quite unclear limits. Yet the interest of Great Britain and France in stopping extremism gave the moderates more room to maneuver. Nkrumah and later Jomo KENYATTA successfully combined enough mass support with enough demonstrated respect for existing economic and political institutions to shed the label of dangerous demagogue for that of responsible moderate. Whether modern national mass movements—as political scientists in the 1960s called them—were all that modern, all that national, or all that mass is a complicated question; the languages and networks of mobilization were indeed diverse and contradictory.

ABANDONING AN EMPIRE: FRENCH AND BRITISH CASES

For all their searching for the moderates with whom to negotiate the evolution of the colonial relationship, Great Britain and France soon became trapped in an expanding spiral of demands: for broadening the franchise, for giving more power to elected legislatures, for making good on promises of equivalent salaries for African workers and agricultural opportunities in rural areas. By insisting that European society and the European standard of living were models for the world, France and Great Britain in fact legitimated a wide range of claims on European budgets.

As early as 1951 or 1952, officials in France and Great Britain were complaining about the results of the development drive: that heavy public expenditure was failing to stimulate private investment, that the inadequate infrastructure was choking on the new supplies coming in, that the lack of trained personnel (African and European) and the strength of African trade unions in ports, mines, and railways were driving up labor costs, and that African societies were stubbornly resisting colonial aspirations to change the way they produced and lived. Ironically, this was the great era of expansion of African exports—the most impressive of the colonial era—when exports of copper, cocoa, and coffee soared. But the act of imagination that had made *development* the watchword of colonialism created its own standards: officials began with an imagined end point—industrialization, European social relations, legislative institutions—rather than with the nature and dynamics of African societies themselves. Nor was the development project doing the political work expected of it: development efforts created more new points of conflict than they resolved. More intensive agriculture by white or black farmers forced tenants off the land—a major cause of the rebellion in Kenya known as Mau Mau—and heavy-handed soil conservation or land consolidation projects led to peasant movements against this disruption of the harmony of relations with nature. Even the heroes of economic growth—prosperous cocoa farmers or owners of transportation fleets—often used their gains to challenge European-owned firms or support political activity critical of colonial rule.

By 1956 or 1957 British and French governments and part of the press were doing something they had not done before: coldly calculating the costs and benefits of empire. Old images that had once justified colonization now appeared in conservative arguments for letting go: Africa as vast, untamed space, inhabited by backward people,

remote from the notions of "the citizen" or of "economic man" that the European elite associated with themselves. The two governments began to think about extricating themselves, a process that was as much an abdication of responsibility for the consequences of their own actions as the devolution of power.

Part of the postwar thinking about development and modernization eased the imaginative transition: development (unlike civilization) was a universal possibility, so that the European elite could expect that Africans would follow a foreordained path that would keep them in close relationship to Europe. But there was an element of cynicism too: an awareness growing out of the experiences of 1945–1955 of the conflict and uncertainty surrounding political and social change, and a desire that African governments, not European ones, be blamed for whatever went wrong.

African politicians had built their power bases within territories defined by the colonial powers. These boundaries and the institutions of state provided the basis for negotiated decolonization, marginalizing other kinds of affinities and aspirations. The recalculation was eased in GHANA by Nkrumah's espousal of his own variant of development, linking him economically to the very forces he criticized as neoimperialist; it was eased in MOROCCO and TUNISIA by relatively coherent political movements willing to open the conservative elite to a measure of nationalism, but not too much. In Egypt, however, NASSER's coup of 1952 threw awry the neocolonial arrangements Great Britain had with the former regime and put in place a symbol of nationalism who influenced other decolonization struggles.

Britain and France had more trouble in colonies with white settlers, both because of the settlers' ability to play racial politics (and to threaten or effect a whites-only form of decolonization) and because of the intensity of social conflicts. It was most difficult of all for France to rethink its empire in Algeria. In this case, a divided French polity was caught between the right's support of an *Algérie française* that denied Muslims full citizenship in their own country and the left's attachment to developing Algeria, while Algerian nationalists themselves fought over strategies and objectives. A brutal colonial war from 1954 to 1962 called into question France's own republican principles. After 1962, newly liberated Algeria was torn by fighting and coups.

DECOLONIZATION IN PORTUGUESE AFRICA

The Portuguese empire does not fit the timing outlined above. As a weak European power, it lacked the confidence that its market power, capital, and technology could shape African evolution when it acted even slightly less colonial. Moreover, Portugal itself was ruled by a dictatorship, and the legitimacy crisis that beset France and England after the war did not apply. Portugal set out to develop MOZAMBIQUE, ANGOLA, and GUINEA-BISSAU, but it was a thoroughly authoritarian version, entailing new waves of white emigration to Africa to take the leading roles in the "modern" sectors. But Portuguese Africa could not escape the ferment and opportunities around it—or the contradictions within. By the mid-1960s in Guinea-Bissau, Angola, and Mozambique, political movements, well aware of the liberation around them, had turned toward armed struggle, using bases in neighboring countries and a wide range of networks and affiliations, although the Portuguese limited their success by manipulating regional rivalries.

The Portuguese government had its own regional connections—with the white regimes of South Africa and, after 1965, Rhodesia (present-day Zimbabwe), which helped with military support as well as economic interaction. The region was caught up in Cold War politics: Soviet support played an important role for nationalist movements FRONT FOR THE LIBERATION OF MOZAMBIQUE (FRELIMO), POPULAR MOVEMENT OF THE LIBERATION OF ANGOLA (MPLA), and African Independence Party (PAIGC)—as well as for the ANC in South Africa, and Zimbabwe African National Union (ZANU) and Zimbabwe African People's Union (ZAPU) in Rhodesia—and the United States quietly helped the South African and Portuguese militaries and some of the anti Communist guerrilla movements they sponsored, even while claiming to oppose racist governments. Portugal's entanglement with its African colonies and the effects of prolonged war came home to Portugal itself. A military coup d'état ended the dictatorship in 1974 and the decision of army and civilian moderates (some of whom knew African leaders from antigovernment networks) brought to an end over 400 years of colonization, in favor of an effort to Europeanize Portugal itself. As with the earlier decolonizations, this one involved an abdication of responsibility for the sins of colonial rule and for the viciousness of the final struggle itself, from the land mines and assassinations to the hasty pullout of Portuguese civil servants and professionals seeking their European future.

WHITE RULE IN SOUTHERN AFRICA

The persistence of white rule in Rhodesia (to 1979) and South Africa (to 1994) has much to do with the ambiguity of the colonial situation there. For most Africans, these were the most colonial of colonial regimes, with a settled white population big enough to staff an effective military and bureaucracy, closely integrated into farms and industries that took control of African labor to ground (or below ground) level. But for many whites, particularly Afrikaans speakers, the sense of possessing the land in which they lived—and of having no home to go back to—was deep

and the willingness to fight to stay strong. But their identification with Africa was not complete. Racial domination was also rooted in a sense of being Western. And social life, especially as white society became relatively prosperous, implied belonging to a global bourgeoisie—of having access to the same commodities, sports events, and travel possibilities as Europeans and North Americans.

Here is where these regimes lost the battle of civilization, Christianity, progress, and democracy, a battle that had begun in the early twentieth century, when the first African national movements began to appropriate the vocabulary of democracy and rule of law. As much as liberation movements in Rhodesia and South Africa drew on affinities and a language of solidarity rooted in the daily lives of different African communities, they also built global networks via churches, labor unions, human rights and antiracist groups, and pan-Africanist organizations—building on ideologies of self-determination and antiracism—to attack the legitimacy and sustainability of racist rule. In the end, the ruling regimes could not maintain unity and ideological coherence, even if for a time they could repress (but not eliminate) armed struggle. The last decolonization, 342 years after the original Dutch intrusion into South Africa, was, remarkably, a negotiated one.

CONSEQUENCES OF DECOLONIZATION

What ended with the decolonizations of 1957–1965, of 1974, of 1979, and of 1994 were the very categories of empire and colony, of white rule. These had been considered normal for centuries; they ceased to be imaginable politically. Decolonization did not end social or political inequality, or the uneven power to determine what kind of policies are discussible. The International Monetary Fund is much better able to make the alleged mismanagement of exchange rates by an African government into an issue demanding correction than an African government is able to make the unavailability of clean water into a question requiring global action.

It would be a mistake either to see colonialism as a phenomenon that could be turned off like a television set—with all problems instantly turned into African problems—or to define a colonial legacy that determined what African polities could do, without considering the openings and closures that occurred during the process of struggle. The anxieties—and the brittle repressiveness—of new African rulers reflected as much their appreciation and fear of the diverse movements they had ridden to power as their inability to confront the divisions in society that colonial regimes had encouraged. Colonial regimes and their successors were gatekeeper states, facing great difficulty routinizing the exercise of power domestically outside of capital cities and commercial or mining centers, and best able to manipulate the interface between their country and the outside world. Their taxation power relied heavily on import-export controls, their patronage on insisting that outside resources pass through them. Their great fear was that social movements would draw on connections independent of the regime. Postcolonial gatekeeper states were more knowledgeable than colonial ones, better able to forge relations of clientelism within their boundaries, but without coercive power coming from outside they were extremely vulnerable to any attempt to contest access to the gate itself. Hence the cycles of coups and military governments that beset Africa shortly after decolonization, as well as the hostility of many governments to the political, intellectual, and cultural autonomy of their citizens.

Great Britain, France, and Belgium and later Portugal never learned how they could adapt state power to working with African societies as they actually were, not as they were imagined to be. In abdicating responsibility for the consequences of their own actions, the decolonizing powers assumed the easier task of judging how Africans carried out the tasks of governance that they themselves had been unable to perform. Such judgments need not be left unchallenged. The history of Africa from the 1940s reveals that many futures have been and can be imagined, that political mobilizations have taken place and can take place on a variety of lines, and that such mobilizations can turn what seemed impossible into an everyday fact. Such an observation applies as much to Africa's future as to its past.

See also AFRIKANER; DEVELOPMENT IN AFRICA: AN INTERPRETATION.

FREDERICK COOPER

Deforo

Ethnic group of West Africa.

The Deforo primarily inhabit southern MALI and northern BURKINA FASO. They speak a Niger-Congo language. Approximately 200,000 people consider themselves Deforo.

See also LANGUAGES, AFRICAN: AN OVERVIEW.

Denakil

See AFAR.

Dendi

Ethnic group of West Africa; also known as Dandawa and Dandi.

The Dendi primarily inhabit BENIN, NIGER, and NIGERIA. They speak Songhai, a Nilo-Saharan language. Though they share cultural practices with other SONGHAI

peoples, they have MANDE origins. Approximately 130,000 people consider themselves Dendi.

See also LANGUAGES, AFRICAN: AN OVERVIEW.

Dengel, Lebna

1496–1540
Ruler of the mainly Christian Ethiopian empire at the time of the Muslim invasion.

Lebna Dengel, who was born in Ethiopia, assumed the throne at the age of twelve, after the death of his father. During his early reign his mother, Helena, served as regent. In 1516 the Muslim sultanate of Adal rebelled against Ethiopian domination, but Lebna Dengel's forces defeated the rebellion. The queen regent, however, feared Muslim expansion, and turned to Portugal for aid. A Portuguese mission arrived in 1520. Some accounts suggest that the emperor sought a relationship with the Portuguese as a means of ending Ethiopia's isolation and acquiring European technology. Others sources, however, imply that Lebna Dengel was unimpressed by the Portuguese visitors, whom he allegedly treated with cool disregard. Sources also disagree about the nature of Lebna Dengel's reign. Some scholars emphasize his devotion to Christianity and claim that his rule was based on justice and mercy, while others assert that he was an arbitrary ruler who alienated the Ethiopian nobility. The latter may be more accurate, for the Adalites rebelled anew in 1527. Led by Ahmad Ibn Ibrahim, also called "Grañ," Arabic for "left-handed," Adalite forces met little resistance. They swept through Ethiopia, destroyed monasteries, and forcibly converted much of the population to Islam. Lebna Dengel fled to a mountaintop monastery at Debra Damo, where he died in 1540. His son, Galawdéwos, defeated Grañ three years later with Portuguese assistance.

BIBLIOGRAPHY

Alvares, Francisco. The Prester John of the Indies: A True Relation of the Lands of the Prester John, Being the Narrative of the Portuguese Embassy to Ethiopia in 1520. Translated by Lord Stanley of Aderley. Revised and edited with additional material by G. F. Beckingham and G. W. B. Huntingford. Cambridge University Press, 1961.

Taddesse, Tamrat. Church and State in Ethiopia, 1270–1527. Clarendon Press, 1972.

ROBERT FAY

Development in Africa: An Interpretation

At the end of four decades of postwar development, the results are so varied that one is tempted to reject the common expression "Third World" when describing all the countries that have been the subject of development policies over these decades. Today, we justifiably oppose a

SEA FARM. A man feeds shrimp at a farm in Eritrea, as part of a project intended to invest in the country's resources and bring more income to its residents, 2000. (*Sayyid Azim/AP Images*)

newly industrialized competitive Third World to a marginalized "Fourth World," to which Africa in its entirety belongs.

GOALS OF DEVELOPMENT

The primary objectives of development policies in Asia, Africa, and Latin America since World War II (or from 1960 for sub-Saharan Africa) were the same, despite the different ideological discourses that accompanied them. Development was a nationalist project, aimed at the rapid modernization and enrichment of society through industrialization. That this goal was so widely shared is easily understood if we recall that in 1945 most of Asia (excluding Japan), much of Latin America, and all of Africa (including SOUTH AFRICA) was rural, nonindustrialized, and governed by either archaic regimes (the landowning oligarchies of the Americas, the monarchies of the Middle East) or colonial ones (Africa, India, Southeast Asia). Beyond their great diversity, nationalist movements in all these regions sought liberation through political independence—a goal proclaimed at the Bandung Conference in 1955—and development through industrialization.

Liberation movements throughout Africa shared this modernist vision, which was by definition a capitalist, bourgeois vision. This does not imply that these movements were inspired, much less led, by a bourgeoisie, in the full sense of the term. An African bourgeoisie scarcely existed—if at all—at independence, and even by the early twenty-first century existed only in an embryonic state. But the ideology of modernization really did exist, and it gave meaning to people's revolt against colonization. It also provided a rationale for "capitalism without capitalists."

Modernization, in other words, was expected to bring the economic and social institutions basic and specific to capitalism: the wage relationship, business management, urbanization, stratified education, a sense of national citizenship. This was expected to occur even though other characteristics of advanced capitalist societies, namely political democracy, were woefully lacking in newly independent Abdel African nations, a lack some argued was justified by the exigencies of catching up rapidly with the economic standards of the industrialized West.

In capitalism without capitalists—that is, without a middle-class business community—the state and its technocrats were to substitute. The radical wings of national liberation movements especially opposed the emergence of such a middle class, suspecting it would pursue its own immediate interests at the expense of longer-term national goals. These radical wings looked instead to the ideologies and methods of the Soviet Union, where the state had already achieved a quite dynamic form of capitalism without capitalists, aimed above all at catching up with the Western world.

Even in countries where radical wings did not come to control the postcolonial government, Soviet-style state-run modernization was the rule rather than the exception. To understand why, it is worth reviewing briefly the historical relationship between the radical or socialist tendencies and the moderates between and within African liberation movements. In some movements the division was frank and clear; in others, it was kept hidden in the interest of presenting a unified front. Some divisions were rooted in class differences among movements' supporters—peasants, laborers, educated intellectuals—while others derived from different movements' sources of political and organizational training (European Communist parties, for example, or trade unions, or churches). In any case, the divide between radical and moderate tendencies grew wider as the two principal colonial powers, England and France, moved toward rapid decolonization.

Africa in 1960 was divided into two blocks: on one side the "Casablanca" group, rallying behind the banners of EGYPT'S GAMAL ABDEL NASSER, ALGERIA'S FRONT DE LIBÉRATION NATIONALE, and GHANA'S KWAME NKRUMAH; on the other, the "Monrovia" group, made up first of the most loyal pupils of Gaullist France and liberal Great Britain (CÔTE D'IVOIRE and KENYA, among others). In the former Belgian Congo (now the DEMOCRATIC REPUBLIC OF THE CONGO), meanwhile, PATRICE LUMUMBA was attached to the first group but major forces in his country sympathized more with the second. When Lumumba became prime minister, moderate forces, with support from Belgium and South Africa, responded by declaring the secession of Katanga and Kasai. It was MOBUTU SESE SEKO who played the reconciliation card and reunited the country. The Congolese example set the stage for further attempts to bring together radical and moderate camps and eventually gradually edge out the former. Emperor Haile Selassie I's genius lay in his understanding that by 1963 it was time to reconcile the Monrovia and Casablanca groups, which he achieved through the creation of the ORGANIZATION OF AFRICAN UNITY in ADDIS ABABA, ETHIOPIA.

The reconciliation created new conditions for pursuing the goals of the Bandung Conference in Africa. All African countries formally showed their support for these goals by becoming members of the Non-Aligned Movement, even if they remained in the lap of the Western powers—even in certain cases under their direct military protection. But by proclaiming their support for the radical nationalism espoused at Bandung, Africa's rulers acquired a certain ability to maneuver. The sanctity of the national development project explains why, despite imperialist pressures from abroad, the initiators of AFRICAN SOCIALISM—Ghana, GUINEA, MALI—were followed by successive generations of radical regimes, such as those in REPUBLIC OF THE CONGO, BENIN, and TANZANIA. It also helps explain the wide margins granted to the nationalist extravagances of dictators at the opposite end of the political spectrum, such as Mobutu.

RESULTS OF DEVELOPMENT

How we assess the results of development obviously depends on how we define development itself, which is an ideological and invariably vague concept. If we consider the criterion used by national liberation movements—that is, of "national construction"—the results are on the whole arguable. The reason is that whereas the development of capitalism in earlier times supported national integration, contemporary globalization instead breaks up societies on the periphery of the world economy. The ideology of the nationalist movements, however, ignored this contradiction, having been enclosed in the bourgeois concept of "making up for a historic backwardness." This ideology assumed that "backwardness" would be overcome through participation in the international division of labor, not through "delinking" from that system. The disintegrating effect of capitalism was more or less dramatic, depending on the specific characters of the precolonial societies. In Africa, where artificial colonial demarcation did not respect the previous history of its peoples, the disintegration wrought by capitalist forces made it possible for ethnicism to survive, despite the efforts of postcolonial ruling classes to get rid of its manifestations. When economic crisis suddenly destroyed the ability of new states to finance transethnic policies, the ruling class itself broke up into fragments which, having

lost their claims to legitimacy based on the achievements of development, then sought new claims, often associated with ethnic loyalties.

If instead we consider socialism as a criterion of development, the results contrast greatly. Of course, it should be understood that socialism here means the kind defined by radical populist ideology. It was a progressive vision, emphasizing maximum social mobility, the reduction of income disparities, a sort of full employment in urban areas—in some ways, it envisioned a poor version of the welfare state. From this viewpoint, the achievements of a country like Tanzania offer a remarkable contrast with those of the former ZAIRE, Côte d'Ivoire, or Kenya, where the most extreme inequalities have persisted for thirty years, both in times of rapid economic growth and subsequently in times of slump.

But the criterion of development that conforms to the logic of capitalist expansion is very different; it is about the ability to be competitive in world markets. From this point of view the results are contrasted to the extreme. The contrast is especially brutal between Asia and Latin America, where many countries have become competitive industrial exporters, and all of Africa, which remains attached to the export of primary products. The former are the new Third World (or what I call the "periphery of tomorrow"), the latter what we now call the Fourth World, which is expected to be marginalized in the new stage of capitalist globalization.

FAILURE OF DEVELOPMENT

The explanation of the failure of Africa as a whole should bring into play all the complexity of the interactions between specific internal conditions and the logic of world capitalist expansion. Because these interactions are too often ignored, current explanations for Africa's failures—both those advanced by economists and by Third World nationalists—remain superficial.

Economists and many other analysts emphasize phenomena that they isolate from the overall logic of the system, like the corruption of Africa's political class, the weakness of its economic base, the backwardness and very low productivity of agriculture, "tribal" fragmentation, and so forth. These explanations inevitably recommend as their solution greater insertion into the world capitalist economy. For this, Africa would need true capitalist businesspeople, it would need to break the self-reliance of the rural community by systematically promoting commercial agriculture, and so on. This reasoning is inadequate because it ignores the overall system in which the proposed reforms would operate. We already know, for example, that truly capitalist agriculture in rural Africa would produce a huge surplus labor population. Given the current state of Africa's economies, this labor could not be employed in industry as it was in nineteenth-century Europe. History does not repeat itself.

Third World nationalists stress other phenomena, no less real, like the fact that world prices for Africa's raw materials are steadily declining. They also justifiably cite the numerous political and even sometimes military interventions of Western powers, which are always hostile to the forces of progressive social change, and which always come to the rescue of reactionary and archaic forces. But these arguments are not structurally linked to the logic of internal conflicts, so they oppose the external to the nation, whose contradictions are overlooked.

My analysis, by contrast, places responsibility for the failure of development in Africa on colonialism and on the neocolonial policies of independent Africa's ruling classes. It also considers the consequences of the geopolitical strategies pursued in Africa by the world's superpowers.

The international division of labor that has created such inequality between the industrialized centers and the non-industrialized peripheries of the world economy dates back to the Industrial Revolution in early-nineteenth-century Europe. The latter's role in this division of labor has been to participate in world trade by exporting products for which they have an advantage based on nature (such as minerals or tropical fruits) rather than on the productivity of labor. Africa was seen to fit this role, as were the other peripheries of Asia and Latin America, which, in terms of their participation in world markets, did not distinguish themselves from Africa until after World War II. One therefore understands why the European powers went on the attack in Africa and then partitioned it among themselves at the BERLIN CONFERENCE OF 1884–1885. Colonization did not involve, as has too often been said, a "wrong" calculation, whose absurdity history would have subsequently demonstrated. Rather, the aim of colonization, for the powers that could afford it, was to acquire a preemptive right over the continent's natural resources.

Once conquered, it was necessary to "develop" Africa. To understand how this was undertaken, we must consider both the logic of world capitalism—what natural resources did the various regions of the continent possess?—and the precolonial history of different African societies. For the purposes of this analysis, we can examine the three different types of colonial economies. The trading economy, first, incorporated the small-scale peasantry into the world tropical-products market by subjecting it to the authority of market monopolies; this made it possible to keep the rewards for peasants' labor to a minimum. Second, southern Africa's mining economies depended on cheap labor from tribal reserves. Laborers were forced to migrate from the inadequate conditions of these reserves, yet their wages, brought back to the reserves, helped sustain traditional subsistence farming and thus helped keep labor cheap. Finally, in regions where the local social conditions did not permit the establishment of a trade-based economy and the mineral resources did not justify the establishment of labor reserves, concessionary companies created economies of pillage, based on taxation and forced labor. The CONGO RIVER basin (split between the colonies of the Belgian Congo and the French Moyen-Congo) belonged to this third category.

Whatever the initial appearances, all the ways colonial Africa was incorporated into the world capitalist economy were later to prove catastrophic for Africans. Colonial development is indeed responsible for the major obstacles that continue to afflict the continent.

First, colonialism delayed by a century any beginnings of an agricultural revolution. In colonial Africa, a surplus could be extracted from peasant labor and from the continent's natural wealth without any investments in modernization (which meant no machines or fertilizer), without genuinely paying for the labor (which was instead sustained by the produce of the peasant farm), and without even maintaining the natural conditions for producing wealth (which meant that soils were farmed to exhaustion, and forests stripped). In the regions where the economy of pillage was practiced, colonial development resulted in particularly acute backwardness.

Simultaneously, colonial development in the context of an unequal international division of labor excluded the formation of any local middle class. On the contrary, each time a middle class began to form, the colonial authorities hastened to suppress it. Therefore, the weakness of Africa's national liberation movements and later its independent states was also a colonial legacy. It was not the product of a pristine but long-gone precolonial Africa (as the ideology of global capitalism would argue, drawing on its usual racist discourse). The critics who blame Africa's problems on its corrupt political middle classes, its lack of economic direction, and its tenacious rural community structures forget that these features of contemporary Africa were all forged between 1880 and 1960.

It is hardly surprising that these features have endured. Suffice it to say that the responsibility of the metropoles was great, because despite all the obstacles of colonial society, liberation movements did produce elites potentially capable of going further—capable, in other words, of exploiting opportunities for getting Africa out of its rut. But when this happened, all effort was made to destroy these opportunities.

To see how Africa's colonizers have ensured its failure, we need only look at the famous Lomé Agreements, which have linked—and continue to link—sub-Saharan Africa to the European Community. These agreements have indeed perpetuated the old division of labor by relegating independent Africa to the production of raw materials even when, during the Bandung period between 1955 and 1975, other Third World regions were embarking on an industrial revolution. These agreements have made Africa lose about thirty years of potential progress during a decisive moment of historic change. Undoubtedly, African ruling classes were partly responsible for the continent's involution, particularly when they joined the neocolonial camp against the aspirations of their own people, whose weaknesses they exploited.

The collusion between the African ruling classes and the global strategies of imperialism is therefore, definitively, the ultimate cause of failure. These collusions were shaped by the geostrategic concerns of the postwar period (1945–1990). Consider the consequences of these geostrategic concerns in the southern part of former Zaire and southern Africa more generally. The entire region, including Katanga province, ZAMBIA, ZIMBABWE, and South Africa, was to the American camp of the Cold War a unique strategic zone, important for its mineral resources (including South Africa's rare minerals and gold) as well as its location, controlling communications between the South Atlantic and the Indian Ocean. The Soviet Union sought to destroy American influence in this zone by forming alliances with African national liberation movements, especially the most radical ones, in ANGOLA, MOZAMBIQUE, Zimbabwe, and South Africa. The Western powers responded by supporting, practically without conditions, the regimes of Mobutu in Zaire, NGWAZI HASTINGS KAMUZU BANDA in MALAWI, JOMO KENYATTA and DANIEL ARAP MOI in Kenya—despite their notorious corruption and their extreme antidemocratic practices—just as they supported the "anticommunist" forces of JONAS MALHEIRO SAVIMBI in Angola, MOZAMBICAN NATIONAL RESISTANCE (RENAMO) in Mozambique, and pressed for a federal compromise in South Africa, even if it was to the detriment of a genuine democratic solution.

Inversely, geostrategic considerations compelled the Western imperialists to support, or at least to tolerate, the initiatives of the middle classes of East Asia, which partly explains at least the success of this region in the period of postwar capitalist expansion.

But today a new leaf has been turned. Anti-Soviet geostrategic concerns are no longer justified. The Bandung era has ended, and new relationships of collusion are being forged between the global powers and countries on the periphery of the world economy. These countries' own economies, however, are now very different from one another, due to the unequal achievements of the Bandung project in Asia, Latin America, and Africa. We can now classify these countries into four groups, according to what they achieved—or failed to achieve—in their attempts to modernize.

SUCCESSFUL INDUSTRIALIZATION:
Countries that are competitive or potentially competitive on global markets fall into this category. This group includes the major industrialized countries of Latin America and East Asia, as well as, potentially, India, Russia, and certain East European countries. Egypt and Algeria could also belong to this group.

UNSUCCESSFUL INDUSTRIALIZATION:
These are countries that one cannot imagine being "competitive." Probably most countries of the Middle East and North Africa belong in this category, as do Nigeria and South Africa. In the future, they could face the destruction of their industrial base, in other words, deindustrialization.

SUCCESSFUL GROWTH:
These countries achieved growth, at least for a brief period, within the old international division of labor, that is, by exporting raw materials. This includes oil-exporting countries (Nigeria, Angola) and countries with copper or other mineral resources, such as Zambia and Congo. It also includes a few exporters of tropical agricultural commodities, such as Côte d'Ivoire, Kenya, and Malawi.

UNSUCCESSFUL GROWTH:
Most countries of sub-Saharan Africa fall into this category, because they failed to achieve growth as raw-material exporters. Their failures were not invariably due to bad policies, but rather in some cases to objective conditions. Ghana, for example, had achieved its potential as a cash crop exporter during the colonial era; independent Côte d'Ivoire's economic "miracle" was simply a matter of that country "catching up" with the colonial achievements elsewhere in West Africa.

The first group lies at the core of the "periphery of tomorrow." Their economies will continue to run on what I call "outputting" industrialization, which in turn will continue to be controlled by the global economic superpowers. These superpowers will maintain control through monopolies in five key areas: high technology, the global financial system, global natural resource access, mass media (and thus public opinion worldwide), and weapons of mass destruction. The second, third, and fourth groups listed above—meaning all of Africa—belong to the next generation's "marginalized periphery." Here is the challenge.

NEW VISIONS AND NEW STRATEGIES

What can be done now? We must take both a medium- and long-term perspective, given the new global framework. Over the long term, Africa must industrialize and must become competitive. But this is still very far off, and to achieve this goal the global system must be reshaped. Third World countries must "delink" from the global economic superpowers in order to create large regional blocs, in the form of a pan-African bloc, a pan-Arab bloc, and so forth. Delinking does not mean autarky, even at the regional level. However, it should allow for regional industrial complementarity. Forming large regional blocs is the only way to mitigate the negative effects of the five aforementioned monopolies. It is the only way to establish negotiated, controlled, and pluriregional interdependency.

More immediately, individual nation-states must fight to achieve popular development—that is, growth for the benefit of the majority. This means building an industrial base capable of supporting an agricultural revolution. It also means transforming the overexploited informal sector into a popular economy that permits workers to negotiate collectively.

Nation-states must protect this popular development from the devastating effects of uncontrolled economic openness. Finally, they must allow for the creation of popular, autonomous political forces. This is the political precondition for popular development, and democratization must be understood in these terms. Third World nation-states must struggle, in other words, not only to build formal democratic systems (with multiparty elections and so forth) but they must also progressively democratize society. This implies, among other things, a transformation of gender relations.

See also COLD WAR AND AFRICA; DECOLONIZATION IN AFRICA: AN INTERPRETATION; ETHNICITY AND IDENTITY IN AFRICA: AN INTERPRETATION; GLOBALIZATION AND AFRICA: AN INTERPRETATION; SCRAMBLE FOR AFRICA.

JESSE RIBOT AND SAMIR AMIN

Diagne, Blaise
1872?–1934
Senegalese statesman, first African deputy to the French National Assembly.

Blaise Diagne was born on Gorée, an island off the capital city of DAKAR, SENEGAL. The son of a cook and a housemaid, he was adopted by a wealthy métis (Afro-French) family when he was very young. The family provided him an exceptional education, first in a Roman Catholic primary school in Senegal and then in a secondary school in France. He returned to Senegal and attended Saint-Louis University, graduating first in his class in 1890. He joined the French Customs Service in 1892 and served until 1914. During his career he was posted throughout the French colonial empire in Africa and South America. These relocations often resulted when his criticisms of oppression and racial discrimination in the colonial system earned him the reputation of a troublemaker. He left the French Customs Service in 1912, after a short leave lecturing in France on French colonial problems.

Diagne returned to Senegal in 1913 and ran for a seat in the French Chamber of Deputies. During his campaign he promised to clarify Senegalese political rights, particularly the right to enlist in the French army, and called for the equalization of the French assimilation policy that benefited métis over Africans. He also campaigned to abolish the head tax, create pensions, and allow Africans the right to organize labor unions. Gathering support among African student groups, civil servants, and Muslims, particularly the MARABOUT from the interior, Diagne defeated a métis incumbent in the 1914 elections and became the first black African to win a seat in the French parliament.

Diagne was seated in parliament only six weeks before the French entered World War I (1914–1918). He immediately proposed a resolution to enlist Senegalese into the French army in exchange for the rights and privileges of full French citizenship. This proposal was made law on October 19, 1915, and Prime Minister Georges Clemenceau asked Diagne to serve as governor-general for military recruitment in French West Africa. Diagne accepted the position and enlisted 60,000 Africans into the French Army.

In 1919 Diagne founded the Republican Socialist Party, the first Western-style sub-Saharan African political party, which soon dominated Senegalese politics. In addition to his own victory in the 1919 election, his party won complete control of the local governments in the four communes of Senegal. Beginning in 1923, however, Diagne's actions alienated many of his African supporters. First he abandoned his demands for the Africanization of the white-dominated Senegalese economy, in exchange for the support of métis and French merchants in Senegal. He was also accused of allowing the French to rig his 1928 reelection to guarantee his victory in return for representation on his councils and party. Finally, in 1930, he defended France's policy of forced labor before the International Labour Organization (ILO) in Geneva, shortly before accepting an appointment as French undersecretary of state for the colonies. During the Great Depression of the 1930s, Diagne negotiated France's first subsidies for African farmers.

BIBLIOGRAPHY

Laguerre, John Gaffar. *Enemies of Empire*. University of the West Indies, 1984.

ELIZABETH HEATH

Dib, Mohammed
1920–2003
Algerian poet and novelist.

"There are times when I should like to meet my death in one of the numerous outrages committed every day; this blood that splashes us, this stench as from a slaughter-house, makes me heave and fills me with horror. Then I suddenly feel such a hunger for life, such a thirst to know what it will be like after, that I am ready to face all the armies and police forces in the world."

In this evocative passage from a short story, Mohammed Dib conveyed not only the brutal trauma of the 1954–1962 Algerian war for decolonization, but also the enduring hope for independent rule.

Dib was born in Tlemcen (now Tilimsen), ALGERIA, to a family of modest means. His father sent him to a French school, a decision that shaped Dib's later choice to write in French. After serving as an interpreter for the Allied army, Dib became a man of many roles: he drew sketches for rug patterns, taught school, worked as a union organizer, and wrote for several newspapers. These jobs exposed Dib to a variety of Algerian characters—the urban poor person, the well-intentioned colonial landholder—many of whom he would later represent in his fictional works.

Dib published his first long poem, "Vega," in 1947, and has always considered himself primarily a poet. His poetry, which includes five published collections, draws on Algerian oral poetic traditions as well as classical Arabic and modern French influences.

Yet Dib is probably best known for his trilogy about the Algerian struggle for self-rule. *La Grand Maison* (1952), *L'Incendie* (1954), and *Le Métier à Tisser* (1957) portray childhood and adolescence in the midst of urban poverty and the oppression of COLONIAL RULE. Critics have noted that the three novels grow progressively more radical in their political stance, mirroring an increasingly militant nationalist struggle (FRONT DE LIBÉRATION NATIONALE). In 1959 Dib was deported for his nationalist leanings, and settled in France.

Like many exiles, Dib looked back to his home country in much of his subsequent work, creating from memory a tangible sense of the Algerian landscape and people. A poetry collection, *Ombre gardienne* (1961), was followed by the novels *Qui se souvient de la mer* (1962), *Cours sur la rive sauvage* (1964), and *La danse du roi* (1968), all of which broke from the realism of his trilogy to incorporate elements more fantastic and psychological. Now in his eighties, Dib continues to write. His recent works include the novel *Comme un bruit d'abeilles* (2001) and the poetry collection *L'enfant-jazz* (1998).

In his short stories, poetry, and novels, Dib has written on the lasting effects of the war on the fighters' psyches; the prominent role of women in the struggle for Algerian independence; the debates about the future of the new nation; and the psychological experience of exile. In almost all of his work, he has explored the universal themes of love and death. As critic François Desplanques says, Dib has sought to portray the history of the conquered, the living dead who "have been crushed by the weight of destiny." Critics characterize his later works as more complicated, merging sections of poetry with poetic prose. But Dib has in fact always incorporated poetic elements into his work—"a progression of kaleidoscopic sensations" representing the sights, smells, and sounds of the war as it passed through the lives and thoughts of the individual.

See also LITERATURE, FRENCH-LANGUAGE, IN AFRICA; POETRY, AFRICAN.

MARIAN AGUIAR

Dida
Ethnic group of Côte d'Ivoire.

The Dida primarily inhabit central coastal CÔTE D'IVOIRE west of ABIDJAN. They speak a Niger-Congo language belonging to the KRU cluster. Approximately 200,000 people consider themselves Dida.

See also LANGUAGES, AFRICAN: AN OVERVIEW.

Digo
Ethnic group of East Africa.

The Digo primarily inhabit northeastern coastal TANZANIA and neighboring KENYA. They speak a Bantu language and belong to the MIJIKENDA cultural and linguistic group. Approximately 400,000 people consider themselves Digo.

See also BANTU: DISPERSION AND SETTLEMENT.

Dingane
1795?–1840
One of the great Southern African Zulu chiefs and the half-brother of the Zulu warrior chief Shaka.

Together with other members of his family, Dingane took part in the assassination of the increasingly despotic Zulu chief SHAKA on September 24, 1828. Dingane subsequently murdered his co-conspirators and became king of Zululand.

As king, Dingane tried to end the ten years of continual war, but to keep the kingdom from splintering he was forced to continue Shaka's repressive policies. In 1837 Dingane was asked for a grant of land by Pieter Retief, one of the leaders of the migration of Boers known as the Great Trek (1835–1843). Fearful of the encroaching Boers, Dingane hedged and asked Retief to show good faith by capturing some cattle which had been stolen by a Tlokwa chief. Retief retrieved the cattle and returned them to Dingane in February 1838. By then the Boer pioneers were already coming over the Drakensburg Mountains with their wagons and cattle, and news reached Dingane of the complete defeat of Mzilikazi, another Zulu chief, by separate Boer forces. Dingane took fright and on February 6, 1838, he invited Retief and his party to a feast of celebration in his kraal (circular compound) where his warriors murdered them. His impis (regiments) then attacked the Boer's camp, killing about 500 people.

The death of Retief and his followers was avenged on December 16, 1838, at the Battle of Blood River when Andries Pretorius, another Great Trek leader, killed 3,000 Zulus with a force of 500 men. After this defeat, some of Dingane's followers broke away and followed his brother Mpande, who collaborated with the Boers to defeat Dingane's forces in 1839. Dingane was overthrown by Mpande in January 1840; he fled to SWAZILAND where he was murdered.

See also SOUTH AFRICA.

Dinka

Largest ethnic group in southern Sudan.

The Dinka people, who number approximately 1.5 million (though estimates vary), are divided into twenty-five subgroups, each of which has its own name. Each once occupied a distinct territory. Each group is further subdivided into a number of lineages based on patrilineal descent (descent through the father's line). The groups were led politically by a chief from a dominant lineage within the group, but his authority depended on general consensus and the cooperation of individuals. The religious authority of each group's spear master (chosen from a second prominent lineage) complemented the primarily secular power of the chiefs. The spear master represented the power of tradition and the authority of the ancestors. Like their NUER neighbors, the Dinka derived their livelihood mainly from cattle raising, though the cultivation of millet, fishing, and hunting were important supplemental activities.

During the eighteenth and nineteenth centuries the Dinka expanded their control over southern SUDAN. The Dinka expansion displaced some Nuer, but the Nuer retreated into the Sudd, a swampy area along the White Nile and its tributaries. The actions of Sudanese and Egyptian slave raiders seriously weakened the various Dinka chieftaincies, but they nevertheless tenaciously resisted both Turco-Egyptian control in the nineteenth century and the British in the twentieth.

A mutiny of southern Sudanese troops in 1955 on the eve of Sudanese independence initiated the Sudanese Civil War. Since the beginning of this conflict, Dinka such as John GARANG DE MABIOR have played a leading role in the civilian and military organizations pressing for greater autonomy or independence for the southern Sudan. The Sudanese Civil War has caused massive population relocations and much suffering among the Dinka, who have endured heavy casualties and famine and have had to seek refuge in the cities of northern Sudan. A treaty to end the fighting was at last signed in 2005, though many Dinka remain scattered throughout Africa and other regions of the world.

See also SUDAN.

ROBERT BAUM

Diop, Alioune
1910–1980
Senegalese writer and editor who became a central figure in the Négritude movement.

Alioune Diop was born in Saint-Louis, SENEGAL, whose inhabitants enjoyed automatic French citizenship during the colonial period. He obtained his secondary education at the Lycée Faidherbe in St.-Louis, and then studied in ALGERIA and at the Sorbonne in Paris. He took a position as professor of classical literature in Paris and represented Senegal in the French senate after World War II (1939–1945). In 1947 Diop founded *Présence Africaine*, perhaps the most influential intellectual journal of its time on anticolonial and emancipatory culture and politics among Africans and peoples of African descent. With frequent contributions from his friend and associate Léopold Sédar SENGHOR, Diop's journal helped foster the Négritude movement, which aimed to promote an African cultural identity and the liberation of the people of Africa and the African diaspora. In 1949 Diop founded Présence Africaine Editions, a leading publishing house for African authors. Diop's journal, though anticolonial in spirit, published the work of notable black politicians, poets, fiction writers, and essayists from Africa, the Caribbean, Europe, and the United States from a variety of ideological perspectives. Although the journal became increasingly political, Diop's own work often focused on the significance of the arts in African culture. A devout Catholic, he also wrote essays critical of the colonial tendencies of some Church organizations. The energetic Diop's contributions to the Négritude movement extended beyond his own publishing ventures. He founded the Société Africaine de Culture (1956) and helped organize several conferences for black writers and artists, including the first and second International Congress of Black Writers and Artists, in Paris (1956), and Rome (1959); the first World Festival of Negro Arts, in Dakar (1966); and the second Festival of Black and African Arts and Culture, in Lagos (1977). Diop left a cultural legacy that continued after his death in 1980. Cultural ministers from the sub-Saharan states established a literary prize in Diop's honor in 1982; the fiftieth anniversary celebration of *Présence Africaine* was held in Paris in 1997; and Présence Africaine Editions remains active under the direction of Yandé Christian Diop, Diop's widow.

BIBLIOGRAPHY

Coats, Geoffrey. "From Whence We Come: Alioune Diop and Saint-Louis, Senegal". *Research in African Literatures* 28, no. 206, 1997.

ROBERT FAY

Diop, Cheikh Anta
1923–1986
Historian, Egyptologist, physicist, linguist, and physical and cultural anthropologist.

Cheikh Anta Diop is regarded as one of the greatest scholars of the twentieth century. A central figure in African-centered scholarship, his intellectual range and work spanned many disciplines. At the 1966 World Festival of the Arts in DAKAR, SENEGAL, Diop shared with the late W. E. B. Du Bois an award as the writer who had exerted the greatest influence on black thought. He is most known for his work to reaffirm the African character of ancient EGYPT through scientific study and to encourage African scholars to use ancient Egypt as a source of valuable paradigms to enrich contemporary African life and contribute to new ways of understanding and improving the world.

Cheikh Anta Diop was born in Diourbel, Senegal, a town that has a long tradition of Muslim scholarship and learning fostered by the Mouride Brotherhood. He began his education at the age of four in Quranic school (a school that emphasized the study of the Quran—the sacred text of Islam). He studied philosophy and mathematics at the University of Dakar, from which he graduated in 1945. He then went to Paris in 1946 to continue his education, enrolling at the University of Paris (the Sorbonne). There he studied a wide range of subjects in the sciences and humanities, including ancient history, archaeology, Egyptology, linguistics, philosophy, and sociology. Two

years later, he published two articles that reflected his early assumption of the role of scholar-activist. They were "The Linguistic Study of Wolof: The Origin of the Wolof Language and Race" and "When Can One Speak of an African Renaissance?" The first of these was published in *Présence Africaine*, a scholarly journal that became the main forum for French-speaking African intellectuals who conducted wide-ranging discussions on pre-independence and post-independence issues in it.

Influenced by the anticolonial philosophy and activities of Aimé CÉSAIRE, the eminent poet, playwright, and essayist from MARTINIQUE, Diop became deeply involved in the African independence movement. He joined the RASSEMBLEMENT DÉMOCRATIQUE AFRICAIN (RDA, or the African Democratic Assembly), the most important pan-African independence organization in the areas of Africa dominated during this time by France. He was one of the founders of the Association of Students of the RDA (AFRDA) and served as its secretary-general from 1950 to 1953. He also wrote articles for its journal, *La Voix de l'Afrique Noire*, among which were "Towards an African Political Ideology" in 1952 and "The Struggle in Africa" in 1953. In addition, he was an organizer of the First Pan-African Students Conference in Paris in 1951.

In 1954 Diop submitted his doctoral dissertation, *Nations Nègres et Culture: de l'Antiquité Nègre Égyptienne aux Problèmes Culturels de l'Afrique Noire d'Aujourd'hui* (Black Nations and Culture: From Black Egyptian Antiquity to the Cultural Problems of Africa Today). Its radical thesis asserted the African character of ancient Egyptian civilization and the cultural unity of Africa. It was not accepted by the university, but was published in 1955 by *Présence Africaine* under the same title. In this seminal work Diop offered an incisive critique of Eurocentric scholarship on ancient Egypt and provided various forms of archaeological, linguistic, anthropological, and historical evidence to prove the African character of ancient Egypt. Moreover, he stressed the importance of the development of national language in the maintenance and expansion of African culture. He also demonstrated the linguistic capacity for scientific discourse of his language, WOLOF, by translating concepts of physics, chemistry, and mathematics, including a discussion of the theory of relativity in it.

During the late 1950s he taught physics and chemistry at the Voltaire and Bernard Lyceums in Paris and studied chemistry and nuclear physics at the Collège de France and the Curie Laboratory. He also established himself as an intellectual of note at the First Congress of Black Writers and Artists, in Paris in 1956, and the Second Congress, in Rome in 1959. At these international gatherings of African intellectuals, Diop presented papers on two of his continuing themes, "The Cultural Contributions and

Perspectives of Africa" and "The Cultural Unity of Africa," respectively.

In 1960, Diop, accompanied by a group of scholars and students to witness the proceedings, returned to the Sorbonne, and successfully defended his dissertation and thus obtained his doctorate. After receiving his doctorate degree, Diop returned to Senegal the same year and was appointed to the French Institute of Black Africa (IFAN), which was later renamed the Fundamental Institute of Black Africa. There he founded the radiocarbon laboratory of Dakar, which specialized in the dating of Africa's oldest archaeological and geological materials. Continuing his scientific work during the 1960s, he published *Le Laboratoire de Radiocarbone de l'IFAN* (1968, The Radiocarbon Laboratory at IFAN) and *Physique Nucléaire et Chronologie Absolue* (1974, Nuclear Physics and Absolute Dating). In these works he discussed IFAN, his scientific work there, and diverse methods of dating archaeological and geological samples, especially those used in research at IFAN.

In 1967 Diop published the seminal study *Antériorité des Civilisations Nègres: Mythe or Vérité Historique*, reaffirming the African origin of civilization and the African character of ancient Egypt. This was republished in 1974 in English as *The African Origin of Civilization: Myth or Reality*.

In 1971 Diop was invited by the United Nations Educational, Scientific and Cultural Organization (UNESCO) to become a member of an international committee charged with the task of writing a survey of African history. As vice-president of the committee, he played a major role in the project, which resulted in the publication of the *UNESCO General History of Africa* (1981–1993), a multivolume, comprehensive history of Africa that became a landmark in Africana studies. He also called a major international colloquium of distinguished Egyptologists on "The Peopling of Ancient Egypt and the Deciphering of the Merotic Script" in 1974 to revisit the question of the African character of Egypt and discuss the work that had been done to decipher one of Africa's oldest scripts, the Merotic script of ancient NUBIA. In the early 1980s Diop became a professor of history at the University of Dakar, which in 1987 was renamed the Cheikh Anta Diop University of Dakar in his honor.

Diop's research findings and theories began to reach an expanded audience in the United States in the 1970s and became a fundamental focus and framework for an emerging Afrocentric scholarship. The publication of James Spady's article "Negritude, Pan-Benegritude and the Diopion Philosophy of History" (1975) and Harun Kofi Wangar's interview with Diop in *Black World*, one of the leading forums for black intellectuals at the time, are considered important early contributions to the introduction and eventual reception of his work as central to the Afrocentric project. Molefi Kete ASANTE, professor of

African American Studies and the founding theorist of AFROCENTRICITY, who defines himself as Diopian in his scholarly approach, argues that Diop's works "turned historiography around and provided the basis for an Afrocentric transformation."

The scope of Diop's legacy, the focus of his life's work, and his meaning to African-centered scholars and thinkers were in great part revealed in his magnum opus *Civilisation ou Barbarie: Anthropologie sans Complaisance* (1981; *Civilization or Barbarism: An Authentic Anthropology*, 1991). In this work he explained that his thrust was not simply to prove the blackness of ancient Egyptians, for that, he argues, had already been proven by the ancients and others before him. His goal instead was to end the Eurocentric falsification of history rooted in imperialist and fascist interests, to contribute to a true history of Africa and humanity and to encourage the use of paradigms from ancient Egypt in the service of modern African people and humanity. Egyptian civilization, he stated, should play in African culture a similar role that Greco-Latin civilization plays in Western culture. For him, the "return to Egypt" by African peoples would serve three basic functions: to reconcile the real history of African civilizations with a true history of humanity; to enable Africa to construct a new body of modern human sciences; and to renew African culture. Renewed and reconstructed in this way, Diop concluded, Africa will be particularly equipped to make its own unique contribution to new and valuable perceptions and practices of humanity.

See also EGYPT, ANCIENT KINGDOM OF; ISLAM IN AFRICA.

Diori, Hamani
1916–1989
First president of Niger.

Born in Soudouré, French West Africa (now NIGER), Hamani Diori was the son of a Djerma public health official in the French colonial administration. Diori attended the distinguished William Ponty Teachers Training College in DAKAR, SENEGAL. At that time, both Niger and Senegal were part of the French colonial territory of French West Africa. Diori worked as a teacher in Niger from 1936 to 1938 and then as a Hausa and Djerma language instructor at the Institute of Overseas Studies in Paris.

In 1946, while working as the headmaster of a school in Niger's capital city of Niamey, Diori cofounded the Parti Progressiste Nigérien (PPN, or Progressive Party of Niger). It was a regional branch of the interterritorial Rassemblement Démocratique Africain (RDA, or African Democratic Rally), the party led by Félix HOUPHOUËT-BOIGNY of CÔTE D'IVOIRE. During the same year, Diori was elected to the French National Assembly. He was defeated in his 1951 reelection bid by his cousin Djibo Bakary. Diori worked as a headmaster until he was elected to the assembly again in 1956 and was chosen to be the deputy speaker. Organizing a powerful coalition of HAUSA, FULANI, and Djerma leaders, including chiefs and traditionalists, in support of Niger's independence referendum, Diori gained French favor. In 1958 he was appointed prime minister. In November 1960, shortly after Niger gained independence, he was elected as Niger's first president and was reelected in 1965 and 1970.

Throughout his presidency, Diori remained in the international spotlight, often serving as a spokesperson for African affairs and as a popular arbitrator in conflicts involving other African nations. Increasingly criticized at home for his negligence in domestic matters, Diori put down a coup in 1964 and narrowly escaped assassination in 1965. Finally, as a result of the corrupt mismanagement of drought-relief funds by members of his administration, Diori was overthrown in a 1974 military coup. He was imprisoned for six years and detained under house arrest for an additional seven years. After his release in 1987, Diori moved to MOROCCO, where he died.

See also HAUSA LANGUAGE.

Diouf, Abdou

1935–
Political leader and president of Senegal.

Abdou Diouf, who served as president of the West African nation of SENEGAL from 1981 to 2000, was born in Louga. He studied in Senegal and France, receiving a degree in law and political science from the University of Paris in 1959 and a diploma from the French Overseas Civil Service School in 1960. Returning to Senegal, Diouf served as director of international technical cooperation, deputy secretary general to the government, and secretary general of the defense ministry in his first two years with the civil service. After joining the Union Progressiste Senegalaise (UPS) in 1961, Diouf quickly became known as the protégé of President Léopold SENGHOR. Between 1961 and 1970 he received appointments to a number of positions. He served as minister of planning and industry from 1968 to 1970. In March 1970 Senghor made Diouf Senegal's prime minister.

Senghor left the presidency in January 1981, naming Diouf as his successor. Later elections kept Diouf in office. Shortly after becoming president, Diouf amended Senegal's constitution to speed the country's transition toward multiparty elections. At the same time, though, he carefully controlled other parties' ability to form coalitions that might be strong enough to challenge his own Socialist party. Later in his presidency, after

demonstrations protesting election results, as well as unrest by students and workers demanding economic reforms, Diouf allowed rival alliances and appointed members of opposition parties to ministerial posts. One success of his presidency came in 1993, when he negotiated a settlement and cease-fire with the Mouvement des Forces Démocratiques de la Casamance (MFDC), an armed separatist movement in Senegal's isolated southern agricultural region. However, the agreement collapsed, and hostilities between MFDC guerrillas and government forces resumed in April 1995. Five years later, the Socialist party was voted out of power and opposition leader Abdoulaye Wade replaced Diouf as president.

In 2003 Diouf became executive secretary of La Francophonie, an internationalist entity whose primary mission includes the advancement of French culture and language around the world, a commitment to human rights, and the promotion of democratic forms of government.

Disease and African History
The impact of diseases on African history.

Many of the most significant pathogens in contemporary Africa have coevolved with their human hosts over millennia. They have competed in an ongoing "arms race," in which human defenses—genetic, environmental, cultural, and pharmaceutical—have been successively overcome by organisms seeking to survive. While selective pressures drive pathogenic organisms to locate and invade human populations, selective pressures also prevent these organisms from becoming too virulent, for an organism that kills off its host too quickly limits its own ability to reproduce. The EBOLA family of viruses may be an example of just such an unsuccessful pathogen.

Up until the last few centuries, humans and diseases such as MALARIA have coexisted and coevolved in Africa in relative equilibrium. Where malaria was endemic, human populations evolved genetic adaptations, such as a high incidence of the allele causing sickle-cell anemia. People also adapted to threats of disease by altering diet, migration, and settlement patterns.

A shift from nomadic foraging to more settled forms of subsistence probably gave rise to the first major period of disequilibrium between humans and their associated pathogens. Viral diseases such as smallpox and measles probably became more prevalent, since dense human settlements provided large reservoirs of never-infected hosts which the pathogens needed to survive. Likewise, densely populated permanent settlements would have increased the occurrence of fecal-oral transmitted diseases, such as dysentery and typhoid.

Another significant period of disequilibrium came when Bantu-speakers began migrating west and south from northern CAMEROON around 3000 B.C.E., carrying with them diseases that contributed to the depopulation of much of the continent's KHOISAN speakers and PYGMY communities. In addition, the Bantu populations inadvertently increased the habitat of disease vectors such as mosquitoes by clearing forest lands for cultivation.

The arrival of Europeans and the subsequent transatlantic slave trade introduced new diseases to the African continent such as smallpox, measles, and syphilis. This trade, as well as the trans-Saharan and Red Sea slave trades, not only caused the disease-related deaths by disease of many captives, but also forced people to flee from slave raids into marginal lands where disease carriers such as the tsetse fly and mosquitoes were prevalent.

Long after Europeans first landed on African shores, vulnerability to diseases such as malaria prevented most Europeans from venturing far inland, except in more temperate regions such as South Africa. Only after the discovery of quinine and other medical advances in the nineteenth century did the widespread European colonization of Africa appear feasible. Once this occurred, however, it brought perhaps the greatest upheaval in African history, resulting in the dispersal of African diseases within the continent, as well as the further spread of non-indigenous pathogens. Africans, particularly in the coastal areas, had long been in contact with foreign explorers, merchants, and missionaries. But the construction of roads, railways, and ports during the colonial era increased human mobility dramatically, exacerbating the spread of disease.

Throughout African human history, diseases have had a significant sociological impact. For example, precolonial populations hard hit by novel diseases often became vulnerable to labor shortages and conquest. In some cases, fictitious kinship (adoption of widows and children) and various forms of servitude helped maintain group size and security, as did the high value placed on large families. In the colonial era, forced labor and taxation demands pushed Africans to migrate great distances to work under conditions of poor sanitation and high population density, such as the mines of the Copperbelt. Tuberculosis epidemics were one result. Where Africans were forced to prioritize cash crops over food crops, such as in the cotton-exporting zones of colonial UPPER VOLTA (now BURKINA FASO), hunger also increased Africans' vulnerability to disease.

Not only did diseases attack Africans directly; they undermined Africans' subsistence as well. In 1890 the cattle virus Rinderpest wiped out East African livestock and wild game, leading tsetse flies to rely more heavily upon human hosts. Although large numbers of Africans died from European diseases, scholars have noted that Africans suffered less than other isolated populations, such as Native Americans, who died in great numbers from diseases brought first by European explorers and colonizers and later by African slaves. The reasons for this relative resistance remain uncertain, although it has been suggested that a longer history of partial exposure to European diseases carried across the trans-Saharan trade routes may have created some degree of immunity in African populations.

Contemporary Africa continues to suffer from several diseases. Deforestation and extreme weather conditions related to global warming, increased urbanization and mobility, and inadequate sanitary and medical services in rural areas and poor urban neighborhoods all contribute to the spread of deadly pathogens, while wars create "climates of disease" in refugee camps and conflict-torn areas. The greatest killers are malaria, diarrhea, and increasingly, acquired immunodeficiency syndrome (AIDS). In 2003 the United Nations reported that one out of every five adults in southern Africa was infected with HIV (the virus that causes AIDS), and that the infection rate in BOTSWANA, LESOTHO, NAMIBIA, and SWAZILAND exceeded 30 percent. The AIDS pandemic has also caused a corresponding increase in tuberculosis (TB), an opportunistic infection that is a leading killer of HIV-infected individuals.

Infectious diseases take millions of African lives each year and divert hundreds of millions of dollars from economic development. The impact of AIDS is especially damaging because the disease kills young adults who are often parents and breadwinners. The disease is expected to orphan between one and two million children in SOUTH AFRICA alone by 2010, and has lowered that country's average life expectancy by an estimated ten to twenty years. One economic report projects that AIDS may cause a 10.8 percent loss in South Africa's workforce by 2005 and a 24.9 percent loss by 2020.

Many of Africa's most common diseases are preventable and/or treatable; unfortunately a low doctor-to-patient ratio and the widespread practice of incorrect self-medication have resulted in the misuse of many medicines, especially antibiotics. The result has been the evolution of drug-resistant strains of bacteria and viruses, including malaria. Immunization campaigns, too, have sometimes generated suspicion; polio vaccinations in northern Nigeria were halted in 2003 after protestors claimed that the vaccines might be intentionally contaminated. Since that time, polio has spread from Nigeria to six countries, including Benin and Cameroon. In early 2004 the World Health Organization (W.H.O.) called an emergency meeting of health ministers from the six African countries where the disease is spreading. The ministers said that they would intensify efforts to immunize 250 million children by the end of the year, reducing by one year the W.H.O.'s goal to eradicate polio by 2005.

Cause for optimism exists in many areas. African governments and the international community have demonstrated increased commitment to public health measures, including the UN's Roll Back Malaria program. The Global Fund to Fight AIDS, Tuberculosis and Malaria has stepped up funding for treatment and prevention of these diseases, as have the World Bank, the U.S. government, and several developing countries. Aggressive intervention campaigns in SENEGAL and UGANDA have contributed to a significant decline in the HIV infection rate in those countries.

See also ACQUIRED IMMUNODEFICIENCY SYNDROME IN AFRICA: AN INTERPRETATION; BANTU: DISPERSION AND SETTLEMENT; DISEASES, INFECTIOUS, IN AFRICA.

ARI NAVE

Diseases, Infectious, in Africa

Like every region of the world, Africa confronts serious infectious diseases. The continent's hot climate and diverse ecosystems create conditions in which tropical pathogens—bacteria, viruses, and parasites—thrive. In addition, European colonialism in the nineteenth century and the more recent stresses of incorporation into the global market economy created social disruptions that greatly exacerbated poverty and increased the spread of disease. Yet popular images of Africa as the source of the most deadly infectious diseases in the world are inaccurate. Bubonic plague and hanta virus originated in Asia, and the most devastating pandemic in history—which took as many as 100 million lives across the globe in 1918—was caused by the influenza virus that most likely originated in the United States.

Indeed, the long history of human evolution in Africa suggests that African populations lived for centuries in a fairly stable equilibrium with infectious pathogens. Diseases such as MALARIA, for example, have coevolved with their human hosts over millennia. For an infectious microbe or parasite to survive, it must not kill its host before it is able to reproduce and spread, particularly if there is no other species to serve as a natural reservoir. For thousands of years, people in Africa and elsewhere lived in fairly small and isolated groups. Particularly deadly viruses and bacteria tended to die out if they killed their hosts too quickly.

The spread of new ways of life, such as settled agriculture and trade, disrupted this equilibrium in Africa (as it did elsewhere), by increasing the size and density of the population and facilitating the spread of infectious diseases. For example, as the agricultural Bantu peoples expanded into central and southern Africa, deforestation enlarged the habitat of mosquitoes and increased the exposure of human populations to malaria. Diseases brought by the Bantu may have facilitated their expansion by killing off PYGMY communities and KHOISAN-speakers who lacked immunity.

The presence of Europeans and South Asians in Africa over the past 1,000 years has generated new risks of infection. Europeans brought diseases little known in Africa, such as measles, smallpox, and syphilis. Although North and West Africans, through centuries of contact, apparently developed partial resistance to these European ailments, the diseases caused many deaths in East and Central Africa in the late nineteenth and early twentieth centuries. The slave trade also spread disease, bringing ailments such as malaria and schistosomiasis to other regions of the world.

Similarly, colonialism affected the spread of infectious disease in Africa. Colonial wars of conquest in the late nineteenth and early twentieth centuries devastated the population in large areas of Africa and left people malnourished and vulnerable to infectious diseases, including those introduced by Europeans. These wars also disrupted the ecological balance by wiping out livestock and expanding the habitat of the tsetse fly, which caused an epidemic of sleeping sickness. Meanwhile, in many regions, head taxes required Africans to labor in mines and urban centers to acquire cash. The loss of labor reduced the ability of colonial populations to feed themselves, and workers' migration facilitated the spread of disease. These early colonialist policies had a devastating impact on African populations: it is estimated that in some regions of Africa, the combination of malnutrition and infectious disease killed between one-third and one-half of the population between 1890 and 1930.

Greater integration into the global market economy, particularly over the past century, has exacerbated health problems by promoting urbanization and migration. Large numbers of Africans live in urban squalor under conditions of poor hygiene where they often lack access to the most basic necessities for healthy living, particularly uncontaminated water. Giardia, typhoid, and cholera are but a few of the more common infectious diseases caused by contaminated food and water supplies. All of these cause diarrhea, arguably the biggest single killer of people in Africa. Diseases such as tuberculosis are particularly difficult to eradicate or even treat adequately in areas that are densely populated and lack health care facilities or qualified physicians.

Development projects have increased the risk of waterborne infectious diseases in contemporary Africa. Flooding from the construction of hydroelectric dams and irrigation projects has dramatically increased the incidence of these diseases, particularly schistosomiasis and Rift Valley fever. For example, after the Daima Dam was built across the Senegal River, some 60 percent of the population developed schistosomiasis. Illnesses such as schistosomiasis, malaria, and ONCHOCERCIASIS (also called river blindness) are tied to water because the mosquitoes, freshwater snails, and black flies that transmit these diseases depend on water supplies to breed.

Thus, political and economic stresses in recent decades have furthered the spread of infectious disease in Africa. Though some diseases, such as EBOLA, receive worldwide attention, more common infections, such as malaria, remain a far greater threat to health and economic development. Malarial infection rates in Africa have quadrupled since the 1960s, and the mortality rate from the disease has also increased. Of the estimated 1.2 million deaths annually worldwide from malaria, 90 percent occur in Africa, where the disease remains the greatest killer of children under age five. (Indeed, in 2003 the WHO reported that malaria killed nearly 3,000 African children every day.)

Though many of Africa's most serious infectious diseases have been known for millennia, scientists have identified thirty new infectious diseases since the mid-1970s, many of which originated in Africa. Without a doubt the most devastating recent disease throughout sub-Saharan Africa is acquired immunodeficiency syndrome (AIDS). By 2003 the disease, caused by the human immunodeficiency virus (HIV), affected one out of every five adults in southern Africa. Because HIV/AIDS damages the body's immune system, those affected by the virus become more susceptible to opportunistic infections such as tuberculosis and pneumonia. AIDS primarily strikes young adults, depriving families of breadwinners and parents. In 2007 it was estimated that some 5.7 million South Africans were living with HIV, with an infection rate among pregnant women of 27.9%.

Given African nations' limited resources, strategies for improving African public health must rely heavily upon education and cost-effective preventive measures. For example, by providing simple filters and information on transmission, in just over ten years the World Health Organization has been able to reduce the incidence of Guinea worm infection from 3.5 million to fewer than 100,000 cases. Likewise the promotion of oral rehydration therapies has saved millions of lives. Disrupting the life cycle of infectious pathogens often proves more effective than expensive drugs, since most infectious diseases, such as malaria, quickly evolve drug-resistant strains. Where possible, vaccination is an effective means of breaking a pathogen's cycle of transmission, but effective immunization programs are expensive. A recent program to combat malaria through the use of medically treated mosquito netting has proven effective in parts of East Africa, but distribution has been disorganized and complicated by lack of training. AIDS education programs focus on simple preventive measures, such as condom use; treatment for HIV-positive patients requires a complex regimen of antiretroviral drugs which until the early 2000s remained prohibitively expensive for African

nations. With a doctor-patient ratio of only one doctor to every 50,000 people, sub-Saharan Africa faces a severe crisis in health care provision; poor health remains widespread.

See also AFRICAN ORIGINS OF HUMANITY; ACQUIRED IMMUNODEFICIENCY SYNDROME IN AFRICA: AN INTERPRETATION; BANTU MIGRATIONS IN SUB-SAHARAN AFRICA; DISEASE AND AFRICAN HISTORY.

BIBLIOGRAPHY

Cox, Francis Edmund Gabriel. *The Wellcome Trust Illustrated History of Tropical Diseases.* The Wellcome Trust, 1996.

Feierman, Steven, and John M. Janzen, eds. *The Social Basis of Health and Healing in Africa.* University of California Press, 1992.

Platt, Anne E. *Infecting Ourselves: How Environmental and Social Disruptions Trigger Disease.* Worldwatch Institute, 1996.

ARI NAVE

Djebar, Assia
1936–
Algerian writer and film director.

Known for her works about women in North Africa's Islamic societies, Assia Djebar is one of a generation of female writers and directors who provide a view of history in which women have a central role. Primary concerns in her work include voice, memory, and language. Although Arabic was the language of her family, Djebar was educated in French because France, which controlled ALGERIA at the time, did not allow the teaching of Arabic. Today she writes in French, striving to make the language her own and not that of her country's colonizers.

Djebar was born Fatima-Zohra Imalayen in Cherchell, a small coastal town west of ALGIERS, ALGERIA, to a schoolteacher father and a mother who died while Djebar was a child. She finished her early studies in Algeria, then became the first Algerian student to be admitted to the prestigious L'école Normale Supérieure de Sèvres in France. In 1957 she earned a degree in history from the Sorbonne in Paris. She went on to teach history at the University of Rabat in Morocco, later studying history in TUNISIA and teaching at the University of Algiers.

Djebar's first novel, *La Soif* (1957; translated as The Mischief, 1958), received both critical and popular attention. It was followed a year later by *Les impatients* (The Impatient Ones), which drew criticism for its eroticism and middle-class values. Two more novels followed: *Les enfants du nouveau monde* (The Children of the New World, 1962) and *Les alouettes naives* (The Innocent Larks, 1962). Djebar also worked in theater, coproducing the play *Rouge l'aube* (Red Dawn, 1960), and wrote poetry that was collected in *Poemes pour l'Algerie heureuse* (Poems for a Happy Algeria, 1969).

Djebar then stopped writing for several years, citing discomfort from writing about subjects too close to her own life—especially in a traditional society where women did not speak of the self. Instead, she concentrated on filmmaking, creating *Walid Garn* (1977), which deals with women's responses to liberation struggles. She then made a controversial feminist film, *La nouba des femmes de Mont Chenoua* (The Festival of the Women of Mount Chenoua, 1979), for Algerian state television. The film weaves together what Djebar called "a polyphony of women's voices." In her next film, *La Zerda et les chants de l'oubli* (Zerda or the Songs of Forgetting, 1982), Djebar superimposed Algerian women's songs over French newsreels of World War I (1914–1918) to document women's participation in the war.

Djebar resumed writing with a collection of stories and an essay, *Femmes d'Alger dans leur appartement* (1980; translated as Women of Algiers in Their Apartment, 1992). Her next novel, *L'amour, la fantasia* (1985; Fantasia: An Algerian Cavalcade, 1985), alternates two women's voices as they explore historical boundaries. With this work, Djebar began challenging the assumption that women's private lives should never become public—the symbolic act of unveiling becomes a recurring theme. *Ombre sultane* (1987; A Sister to Scheherazade, 1989), the second work in a quartet that begins with *L'amour, la fantasia*, alternates narratives from two women, one emancipated and one traditional. *Loin de Medine: filles d'Ismael* (Far From Medina, 1991) addresses questions that Islam and its holy book, the Qu'ran (Koran), pose for women. Djebar's novel *Vaste est la prison* (Vast is the Prison) was published in 1995. The following year she received the Neustadt International Prize for Literature.

Djebar is one of several Algrian writers who have looked to the country's pre-Arabic, pre-Islamic past as a way of interpreting its present multiculturalism. In the novel *Algerian White*, published in 2002, she continued to explore the themes of memory and the links between private and public life. Among her more recent work is *La femme sans sépulture* (2002), *La disparition de la langue française* (2003), and *Nulle part dans la maison de mon père* (2008). In 2005 she was admitted into the Académie Française.

See also FEMINISM IN ISLAMIC AFRICA; LITERATURE, FRENCH-LANGUAGE, IN AFRICA.

Djenné
City in Mali.

Located 400 kilometers (about 250 miles) north-northeast of BAMAKO and 354 kilometers (220 miles) south of TOMBOUCTOU (Timbuktu), Djenné was once a major commercial and intellectual center. Djenné was originally a small fishing village inhabited by the Bozo people,

located near the ancient trading center at DJENNÉ-JENO. In the early thirteenth century, as Djenné-Jeno fell into decline, the SONINKÉ founded a trading town at the present-day Djenné. The town soon became a major market for trade between Tombouctou and the southern forest regions. Trade with Tombouctou followed the Bani and NIGER RIVERS. Djenné provided the desert city with food and cotton as well as gold, ivory, slaves, kola nuts, and spices in exchange for salt and North African goods.

As a trading center, Djenné offered traders security against bandits: the city is completely encircled by the Bani and Niger rivers for nearly half of the year. However, the city's protected location did little to deter conquerors lured by the city's wealth. In the fourteenth century the city was absorbed by the MALI EMPIRE. In 1491, after the fall of Mali, the SONGHAI ruler SUNNI ALI built a naval fleet that allowed him to conquer the city. During the sixteenth century, Djenné fell briefly to Moroccan invaders. The Moroccan soldiers later abandoned the city to the BAMBARA kingdom of Ségu, which occupied it from 1670 to 1810. It was during this period that Djenné became a center of Islamic learning renowned for its distinctive mud-brick mosque. In the nineteenth century, Djenné was conquered by both Cheikou Amadou (who ruined the city's great mosque during the attack) and the religious leader UMAR TAL. In 1893 the French occupied the city; they rebuilt the mosque in 1905. Under French COLONIAL RULE, Djenné lost its commercial importance to nearby Mopti. Today the town is a local trade center for fish, coffee, and kola nuts. It has an estimated population of 21,200.

See also GOLD TRADE; ISLAM IN AFRICA; IVORY TRADE; MALI; SALT TRADE.

BIBLIOGRAPHY

Imperato, Pascal James. *Historical Dictionary of Mali.* Scarecrow Press, 1996.

ELIZABETH HEATH

Djenné-Jeno, Mali
Ancient city whose ruins lie in present-day Mali; also known as Jenné-Jeno and ancient Djenné.

The ruins of a city now known as Djenné-Jeno lie in the central NIGER Valley in MALI approximately 3 km (2 mi) from present-day DJENNÉ. According to archaeological evidence, Djenné-Jeno was founded before the second century B.C.E. It developed into a major trading center before its decline after the eleventh century C.E. and its desertion in the fourteenth century C.E., when urban life and trade shifted to present-day Djenné. At its pinnacle, between 700 and 1000 C.E., the town had a population of at least 10,000 people; it encompassed an area of around 33 hectares (82 acres).

Djenné-Jeno's excavation, begun in 1977, challenged long-held theories about early history in the SAHEL. Prior to the dig, historians believed that before contact with the Arab world around 1000 C.E. through trans-Saharan trade routes, the Sahel borderlands lacked long-distance trading systems, cities, and complex societies. These historians, relying on the ethnocentric chronicles of early Arab travelers, believed that Arabs first introduced complex social structures to the southern populations during the eleventh century. But archaeological evidence from Djenné-Jeno revealed a city that had emerged long before this date. Well before the eleventh century, the population of Djenné-Jeno, including numerous skilled artisans, engaged in considerable long-distance trade. The city, which lacks evidence of the dominant elite who ruled the cities of Europe and the Middle East, may have possessed a relatively egalitarian society governed by various overlapping groups.

The existence of a complex urban society at Djenné-Jeno as early as the fifth century C.E. proves conclusively that cities and complex societies evolved south of the SAHARA independently of influences from North Africa. Recent archaeological finds from the EARLY KINGDOM OF GHANA substantiate the early development of sub-Saharan urbanism. The form of Djenné-Jeno and other recently excavated urban centers, organized loosely in clustered settlements, suggests the development of a unique form of urbanism indigenous to the Sahel and surrounding regions.

ELIZABETH HEATH

Djibouti

A small coastal country in the Horn of Africa bordering Eritrea, Ethiopia, and Somalia.

Djibouti's strategic location on the Strait of Mandeb, where the Red Sea meets the Indian Ocean, has shaped its history. For centuries, the region was a crossroads where the peoples of Africa and the Middle East mingled and traded. In modern times, Djibouti, devoid of significant natural resources, has depended economically on its role as an outlet to the European and Indian Ocean trade for land-locked ETHIOPIA. While Djibouti's arid countryside supports a population of nomadic pastoralists, the country produces only three percent of its required food. The majority of the population lives in the capital of the virtual city-state, DJIBOUTI, DJIBOUTI. The capital's rail connections and free port provide most of the country's income. Because of the economic and military vulnerability of the country, the population moved slowly to sever ties with France, and Djibouti was one of the last African colonies to declare independence. Though Djibouti has a strong commercial sector and one of Africa's best telecommunications infrastructures, much of the population remains

impoverished. And while the country has avoided the warfare that has devastated its neighbors, longstanding ethnic antagonisms continue to divide its population.

EARLY HISTORY
Little is known about the early history of the region. For thousands of years, since the first human populations migrated out of Africa, the area of present-day Djibouti has provided a gateway to the Middle East, just 23 kilometers (14 miles) across the Strait of Mandeb. In prehistoric times, the first speakers of Semitic languages (spoken today in both Ethiopia and the Middle East) passed through the region, as did cultural innovations such as nomadic pastoralism, which still provides a livelihood for many Djiboutians.

Before the rise of Islam, the ancient walled seaport city of Zeila developed just east of present-day Djibouti, in a region then dominated by the Christian kingdom of Abyssinia in the area presently known as Ethiopia. Arab and Persian traders inhabited the city, as did the AFAR (DANAKIL) people, who also populated the countryside. The booming trade in slaves and silver supported the rise of the kingdom of Adal, centered on Zeila. Adal dominated present-day Djibouti and parts of the surrounding region. The earliest written record of its capital, Zeila, comes from the Arab geographer al-Ya'qubi, who noted the prominence of Arab traders when he described the port in 889 C.E.

Zeila was one of the principal points through which Islam came to the Horn of Africa. By the eighth or ninth century, Islam had become firmly established in the coastal communities, although it only had an impact on the population at large after the tenth and eleventh centuries. With the widespread adoption of Islam and improved access to Arabian and Persian markets, Muslim kingdoms such as Adal succeeded in asserting their independence from Christian Abyssinia. During this time, large numbers of Somali ISSAS migrated into southern parts of the region, driving the Afars to the north. From the thirteenth until the sixteenth century, power struggles between the Muslim sultanates and the Christian Abyssinians shook the region, though the area of present-day Djibouti generally remained Muslim. In the late sixteenth century invaders from the West defeated Adal; a number of independent Afar sultanates including Tadjoura, Raheita, and Aussa filled the power vacuum. These sultanates exist to this day, although the sultans have limited political power.

Thus, by the seventeenth century, the traditional cultures and political structures of present-day Djibouti had taken shape. Both the Afars and the Issas are Afroasiatic-speaking pastoralists who share many cultural traditions, social structures, values, and beliefs. The traditional political cultures of the two groups differ, however. The Afars

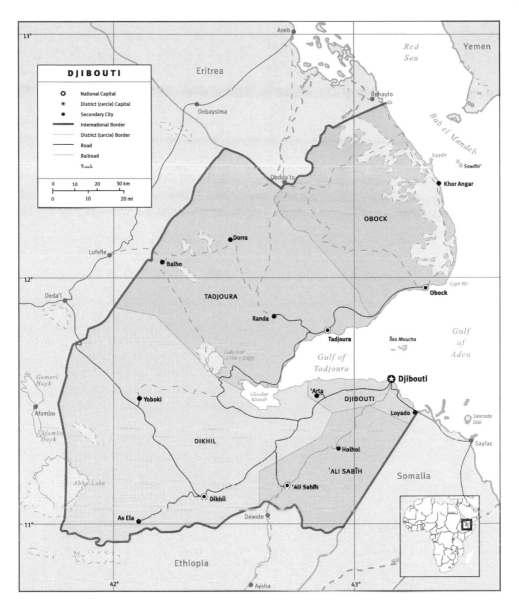

belong to hierarchical chiefdoms divided into noble and common clans. The Issas, in contrast, consist of more egalitarian clans, although they recognize a religious leader, the Ogaz, who resides in Ethiopia. The territory of the Afars extends into neighboring ERITREA and Ethiopia, and that of the Issas extends into Ethiopia and SOMALIA.

Arabs dominated the trade in the Horn of Africa until the nineteenth century. They paid tribute to local Afar and Issa chiefs for passage of their caravans into the interior. By the sixteenth century Portuguese traders began to anchor at ports such as Tadjoura and Obock. These ports exported commodities such as slaves, coffee, and perfume in exchange for firearms, salt, and cloth, which were carried by caravans to inland markets in Ethiopia. The growing trade with Ethiopia attracted the attention of the French,

who also sought control over Indian Ocean commerce. After several exploratory expeditions, the French gained a foothold at Obock in 1862 in exchange for a fee paid to the local sultan. With the opening of the SUEZ CANAL in 1869, the coastal ports on the Strait of Mandeb took on great strategic importance. However, it was not until 1881 that France established a trading company in Obock and sent a small number of colonizers. In 1884 the French concluded a similar agreement with the sultan of Tadjoura.

COLONIAL PERIOD

In 1888 France established the colony of FRENCH SOMALILAND. The French initially chose the port of Obock as its administrative center. When the French decided to develop the colony as a commercial gateway to Ethiopia,

DJIBOUTIAN DEMOCRACY. A ballot is cast in January 2003 as part of Djibouti's first multiparty parliamentary elections since its independence from France in 1997. (*Mahamed Ahmed/AP Images*)

however, they abandoned Obock, since surrounding mountains made it too costly to construct a railroad into the hinterland. In its place they selected Djibouti City because of its easier access to the interior. Djibouti City was named the capital of French Somaliland in 1892. The French governor, Léonce Lagarde, established strong ties with Ethiopia and signed a treaty with Emporer Menelik in 1897 declaring French Somaliland as Ethiopia's trade outlet. In the same year, the French began construction of the rail line. It reached ADDIS ABABA in 1917 and greatly expanded the volume of trade passing through Djibouti City. During this period, many Somalis, including some belonging to non-Issa clans, migrated to French Somaliland for construction work on the railroad, and increasing numbers of Arab merchants settled in the city to take advantage of the growing trade.

French control of the region met with some resistance when Issa and Afar nomads refused to be disarmed or pay taxes. Instances of violence, however, were minimal. France was primarily concerned with the construction of the railroad and the development of Djibouti City and largely ignored the inhabitants of the interior. Under French rule, conflicts between the Afars and the Issas over pasture and cattle were recurrent, and Tadjoura continued to be a center of the illegal trade in Ethiopian slaves who were destined for Arabia and Persia.

In 1935 Italy invaded Ethiopia with an eye on French Somaliland. Unhappy with their dependence on the French rail line, the Italians invested heavily in the construction of a road to Assab, where they built up a port to compete with Djibouti City. When Italy declared war on France in 1940, Italy had some 40,000 troops in Ethiopia, whereas the

Allies had only about 9,000 troops in the region. However, France soon fell to Germany, and in 1940, the fascist Vichy government secured control of French Somaliland. Its actions included the summary execution of literate Somalis as "potential defectors." By 1942, British troops had forced the Italians in Ethiopia to surrender, and after a British blockade of Djibouti City's port, the Vichy French surrendered as well. The Free French, allied with Great Britain, assumed control.

In 1946 France instituted significant changes in the political structure of French Somaliland. It created a representative council that exercised some degree of self-government. The twenty council seats were allocated equally to French nationals and local people. French Somaliland also became an overseas territory, granting the inhabitants French nationality and representation in the French National Assembly. However, in granting equal numbers of seats to Afars, Arabs, and Somalis (including the Issas), the French exacerbated pre-existing ethnic tensions, particularly since these groups' populations in the country were not equal. (The population was roughly 20 percent AFAR, 35 percent Issa, 20 percent non-Issa Somali, 5 percent Arab, and 5 percent French; the remainder are other foreigners.) Armed conflicts broke out between the Gadaboursis and Issas in 1949. The French electoral system classified both of these groups as Somalis and thus permitted them to elect only one representative between them. The election of a Gadaboursi in 1949 left Issas feeling disenfranchised, which provoked an assault on the elected senator. The attack sparked a riot resulting in thirty-eight deaths.

In 1958 France offered each overseas territory the opportunity to decide by popular referendum whether to remain part of the Republic of France or to become completely autonomous states. Over three-quarters of the colony's electorate chose to remain part of the French community as part of the Fifth Republic, in part out of fears of forcible annexation after the unification of British and Italian Somaliland into an independent Somalia. Many also doubted the feasibility of independence for French Somaliland alone, given its lack of natural resources.

Many Issas and other Somalis supported independence and perhaps union with Somalia, while the Afar sought to maintain ties to France, largely in order to avoid Somali domination. Consequently the French strengthened their ties with the Afar community. After Charles de Gaulle's visit to Djibouti City sparked nationalist riots that left several people dead and many wounded, the government scheduled a second referendum on independence in 1967. However, just prior to the referendum, France expelled thousands of ethnic Somalis, labeled alien residents, from the territory. Consequently, even though the Issas, the largest group in the territory, overwhelmingly supported independence, the

Djibouti (At a Glance)

OFFICIAL NAME:
Republic of Djibouti

FORMER NAME:
French Territory of the Afars and Issas; French Somaliland

AREA:
23,000 sq km (14,297 sq mi)

LOCATION:
Eastern Africa; borders the Gulf of Aden, the Red Sea, Eritrea, and Somalia

CAPITAL:
Djibouti (population 542,000; 2002 estimate)

OTHER MAJOR CITIES:
Ali Sabieh (population 13,300; 2003 estimate)

POPULATION:
506,221 (2008 estimate); over the past decade thousands of war refugees from Somalia and Ethiopia have entered the country.

POPULATION DENSITY:
22 persons per sq km (35 persons per sq mi; 2008 estimate)

POPULATION BELOW AGE 15:
43.3 percent (male 110,089; female 109,331; 2008 estimate)

POPULATION GROWTH RATE:
1.945 percent (2008 estimate)

TOTAL FERTILITY RATE:
5.14 children born per woman (2008 estimate)

LIFE EXPECTANCY AT BIRTH:
Total population: 43.31 years (male 41.89 years; female: 44.77 years; 2008 estimate)

INFANT MORTALITY RATE:
93.13 deaths per 1000 live births (2008 estimate)

LITERACY RATE (AGE 15 AND OVER WHO CAN READ AND WRITE):
Total population 67.9 percent (male 78 percent; female 58.4 percent; 2003 estimate)

EDUCATION:
Primary education is free and compulsory for six years, beginning at age six. In 2000, however, less than one third of primary school-aged children attended school. Primary and secondary schools are mostly taught in French, though Islamic teaching has recently been emphasized, due to Saudi Arabia's expressed willingness to subsidize such efforts.

LANGUAGES:
Arabic and French are the official languages; Somali and Afar are also widely spoken.

ETHNIC GROUPS:
Somali 60 percent; Afar 35 percent; French, Arab, Ethiopian, and Italian 5 percent.

RELIGIONS:
94 percent of the population is Muslim, while the remaining 6 percent are Christian.

CLIMATE:
Torrid and dry, although humidity is high in the monsoon season from June to August. The average annual rainfall varies from 210 mm (about 8 in) in December to 400 mm (about 16 in) in June.

LAND, PLANTS, AND ANIMALS:
Djibouti's landscape is extremely varied, ranging from low desert plains in the west and south to mountains in the north. Most of the country is volcanic desert and still geologically active. As rainfall is infrequent, vegetation is minimal. Wildlife includes antelopes, gazelles, hyenas, jackals, and ostriches. Offshore in Djibouti's waters marine life includes tuna, barracuda, and grouper.

NATURAL RESOURCES:
Minerals (including gypsum, mica, amethyst, sulfur); geothermal energy, natural gas; livestock, fish

CURRENCY:
Djiboutian franc

GROSS DOMESTIC PRODUCT (GDP):
$841 million (2007 estimate)

GDP PER CAPITA:
$2,300 (2007 estimate)

GDP REAL GROWTH RATE:
5.2 percent (2007 estimate)

PRIMARY ECONOMIC ACTIVITIES:
The economy is based on the services Djibouti, a strategic port, provides as both a transit port for the region and as an international trans-shipment and refueling center, and to a lesser extent on the railroad to Addis Ababa. As it has few natural resources and little industry, the country depends heavily on foreign aid, particularly from France. Due to scant rainfall, most food must be imported. During the last seven years, due to recession, civil war, and a high population growth rate (including immigrants and refugees), economic growth has evaded Djibouti.

PRIMARY AGRICULTURAL PRODUCTS:
Fruits, vegetables; goats, sheep, and camels

INDUSTRIES:
Small-scale dairy products and mineral-water bottling

PRIMARY EXPORTS:
Hides and skins, coffee, reexports

PRIMARY IMPORTS:
Foods, beverages, transport equipment, chemicals, petroleum products

PRIMARY TRADE PARTNERS:
Somalia, Ethiopia, France, Yemen, China, and Saudi Arabia

GOVERNMENT:
Djibouti became a constitutional republic with a multiparty system by referendum on September 4, 1992. Guerrilla warfare erupted in 1991 due to ethnic tensions between the Afars in the north and the Issa majority in the south. A peace accord in 2001 ended the 10-year Afar uprising. The president, currently Ismail Omar Guellah, is elected by popular vote to a six-year term. A Council of Ministers is responsible to the president. The head of government is currently Prime Minister Dileita Mohamed Dileita. Djibouti's legislative branch is a 65-seat unicameral Chamber of Deputies whose members are elected to serve five-year terms. The dominant political party is the president's party, the People's Progress Assembly (RPP). Other parties include the Front pour la Restauration de l'Unite Democratique (FRUD) and the Democratic National Party (PND).

Marian Aguiar

Afars dominated the referendum, which approved continued association with France. That year, France signaled its alignment with the Afar minority and its opposition to Somali nationalism by renaming French Somaliland the "French Territory of the Afars and the Issas."

The French gradually abandoned their commitment to an Afar-dominated colony. After 1967, Somali immigration had resulted in an increasingly nationalist Somali majority resentful of Afar dominance and potentially sympathetic to unification with Somalia. Meanwhile, the success of Marxist guerrillas in neighboring Ethiopia (home to a large Afar population) sparked French fears that Ethiopia's revolutionary government might absorb the territory. Pressured by both the ORGANIZATION OF AFRICAN UNITY (OAU) and other international agencies, France reluctantly agreed to hold yet another referendum in 1977, in which nearly 95 percent of the population now chose independence. On June 27, 1977, the former French Territory of the Afars and the Issas emerged as the independent Republic of Djibouti.

REPUBLIC OF DJIBOUTI

Hassan GOULED APTIDON, an Issa, became the country's first president. He quickly leaned toward personal rule and in 1979 created a single-party state controlled by his supporters. The Afar formed a clandestine resistance movement, the Front démocratique pour la libération de Djibouti (FDLD). In 1981 and 1987 Gouled was reelected president; he had been the only permitted candidate in these elections. When a bomb exploded in the headquarters of Gouled's party in 1986, over a thousand people were arrested in a draconian crackdown on political dissidents.

Ethnic hostilities only intensified as Gouled's regime increasingly ruled out the possibility of political expression by Afars and others. A militant Afar resistance force of some 3,000 troops organized after 1991 and began to capture much of the north of the country. French diplomats were unable to broker an agreement between Gouled and the insurgent Afars. Under pressure from France and numerous emerging opposition groups, Gouled was forced to schedule another referendum in 1992 to approve a draft constitution that permitted limited multiparty politics. Though voters approved the referendum, most Afars boycotted it and challenged its result. Since the constitution required opposition parties to obtain government approval to run in the December 1992 elections, Gouled was able to eliminate any serious challenge to his power. Not surprisingly, his party won every seat in the national assembly, since the majority of the population had boycotted an election that they viewed as a hoax. Fighting continued. In July 1993 the government mounted a large and successful offensive against the Afar resistance movement.

The Afar insurgents, though greatly weakened, did not surrender. International human rights organizations attacked the Gouled regime for allegedly committing summary executions, detaining people without charge, and harassing the civilian population. Thousands of civilians fled toward the Ethiopian border. In the face of a military impasse, the Afar insurgency movement split, and one faction entered into negotiations with the Gouled government. The negotiations led to a comprehensive treaty in December 1994. The accord provided for a power-sharing agreement based upon ethnic quotas to ensure fair representation, and an amnesty for the Afar insurgents, many of whom ultimately joined Djibouti's armed forces.

Ongoing domestic unrest and heavy military spending damaged Djibouti's economy during the early 1990s. Consequently, the country experienced increasing difficulty servicing its debt, and international lenders demanded that the government increase taxes and cut spending. In 1995, trade unions and teachers held strikes in response to these government austerity measures. Meanwhile, the aging Gouled had to leave the country from December 1995 until February 1996 to seek medical treatment in France. Because Gouled had monopolized power, a destabilizing struggle for succession ensued. Upon his return, he suspended the civil rights of prominent opposition leaders and restated his intention to remain in office until his term expired in 1999. In 1999 presidential elections, Ismail Omar Guellah, Gouled's nephew, won a landslide victory to succeed Gouled as president. While the election was confirmed as legal, opponents claimed that intimidation prevented voters from supporting other candidates.

Twenty-first century Djibouti faces many challenges. Though Afar rebels signed a peace accord with the government in 2001 ending a ten-year uprising, some analysts fear the reemergence of ethnic conflict between the Afars and the Issas. The Afars constitute one-fifth of the population; they are the second largest ethnic group and they dominate the north. One third of Djiboutians, mainly in the south, identify themselves as Issas; they are the single largest ethnic group in the country. The presence of numerous refugees from Ethiopia and illegal aliens from Somalia poses another problem for Djibouti. Estimates vary, but tens of thousands of refugees now reside in Djibouti, where they strain the country's limited agricultural, environmental, and financial resources. In 2003 the United States committed ninety million dollars to Djibouti, making it the largest recipient of U.S. development aid in sub-Saharan Africa. The U.S. considers Djibouti a key ally in its global campaign against terrorism.

See also ISLAM IN AFRICA; PASTORALISM.

BIBLIOGRAPHY

Aboubaker Alwan, Daoud. *Historical Dictionary of Djibouti.* Scarecrow Press, 2000.

Oberlé, Philippe, and Pierre Hugo. *Histoire de Djibouti: des origines à la république.* Presence Africaine, 1985.

Tholomier, Robert. *Djibouti: Pawn of the Horn of Africa.* Scarecrow Press, 1981.

Thompson, Virginia, and Richard Adloff. *Djibouti and the Horn of Africa.* Stanford University Press, 1968.

ARI NAVE

Djibouti, Djibouti
Capital city of the Republic of Djibouti.

The country of DJIBOUTI can almost be considered a city-state. It is the most urbanized country of sub-Saharan Africa and it has only one urban center, Djibouti City. More than three-fourths of the entire country's population lives in the city. AFARS, ISSAS, and other SOMALIS, in addition to a sizable Yemeni Arab population, make Djibouti City their home. A significant number of French and other European expatriates also reside there.

Originally, the French chose the city of Obock, on the opposite side of the Gulf of Tadjoura, as the capital of their Somaliland colony. However, surrounding mountains made the construction of a railway from Obock to the Ethiopian interior too costly. Seeking to expand the volume of trade, the French signed a treaty in 1885 with Issa chiefs enabling the governor, Léonce Lagarde, to establish a new capital on coral reefs that extended from the southern shore of the Gulf of Tadjoura. There, in 1888, the French began to construct the city of Djibouti. In 1892 they designated it the capital of the Côte Française des Somalis (the French Somali Coast), as the territory was then known.

The construction of a railroad and a deep-water port beginning in 1897 created jobs that drew people to the nascent Djibouti City. By 1899 the population had grown to 10,000 people, of whom some 200 were Europeans, primarily on contract to construct the railroad to ADDIS ABABA. In 1900 the population was estimated at 15,000. The railroad tracks extended from Djibouti City to Dire Dawa by 1903, and reached Addis Ababa in 1917. With the completion of the rail line, Djibouti City became the chief outlet for ETHIOPIA's external trade. The volume of trade flowing through the port grew dramatically.

Djibouti City became a center for the arms trade in particular. European merchants would import outdated firearms from Belgium and sell them to Arab traffickers. These weapons were primarily destined for Ethiopia and Arabia. The port lost some significance after the 1930s when the harbor of Aseb (in present-day ERITREA), developed by Italy to reduce Ethiopia's dependence on the port at Djibouti, drew an increasing share of Ethiopia's trade.

Djibouti continues to serve as the main import-export point for products destined for Ethiopia. Its container port serves the only railroad reaching Ethiopia's interior. The modern Ambouli International Airport also handles air freight destined for other parts of Africa. With a stable, market-based currency and reliable satellite- and cable-based telecommunications, a significant banking industry has developed. In addition, the country hosts a French naval base and several thousand French troops. In recent years the United States has used Djibouti City as a base for its military operations against terrorist groups and Iraq.

Surrounded by an arid desert, the city provides some of the only employment opportunities in the country, attracting not only residents from the countryside but also immigrants from neighboring war-torn and impoverished countries. The population of the city tripled, from 124,000 in 1972 to 383,000 in 1995, far outpacing the actual economic opportunities. By 2002, more than 540,000 people lived in Djibouti. The result has been widespread unemployment or underemployment, and the rise of large, squalid shantytowns on the city's outskirts.

This pervasive poverty has promoted a widespread, officially tolerated trade in the drug qat, an Ethiopian green-leaf narcotic, to which many Djiboutians are addicted. To supplement their meager incomes, many of Djibouti's women engage in prostitution, for which French soldiers and transient tradesmen provide a steady demand. Ethnic discord, both between Afars and Somalis and between the dominant Issas and other Somali groups, has also plagued the city, which is largely segregated along ethnic lines.

See also FRENCH SOMALILAND; URBANISM AND URBANIZATION IN AFRICA.

BIBLIOGRAPHY

Tholomier, Robert. *Djibouti: Pawn of the Horn of Africa.* Scarecrow Press, 1981.

Thompson, Virginia, and Richard Adloff. *Djibouti and the Horn of Africa.* Stanford University Press, 1968.

United Nations Economic Commission for Africa. *Socio-Economic Aspects of Poverty (Case Study Djibouti).* United Nations Economic Commission for Africa, 1981.

ARI NAVE

DNA: An Alternative Record of African History

Missing historical identity has always plagued African Americans. In a dramatic protest against this problem, Malcolm Little rejected his American surname and took on X to denote his lost, and seemingly irretrievable, African last name and the genealogy that went with it. He became Malcolm X. The transatlantic slave trade, one of the largest forced migrations of people in history, brought more than ten million Africans to North America, Latin America, and the Caribbean. There, in part because of the loss of the cultural institutions that maintained African oral traditions, most of their descendants—who number now many millions more—have only a vague notion that their origins lay somewhere on the African continent. Malcolm X wrote in his autobiography that the slave trade made it impossible for an African American to ever "know his true family name, or even what tribe he was descended from: the Mandingos, the Wolof, the Serer, the Fula, the Fante, the Ashanti, or others."

Researchers have since tried to recover African American roots by using conventional historical records. Although the records provide useful information about general migration trends, it is unlikely that they can answer the basic question an African American might ask: "Who were my ancestors and where did they live?" The limitations of the historical information are due in part to missing documentation and unrecorded trading of slaves within Africa and the Americas.

Population genetics provides a new approach to filling in the missing historical record. It employs an alternative record of human history, a record based on human genes. Genes are composed of individual segments of the long, coiled molecule called deoxyribonucleic acid (DNA). DNA influences many human characteristics, including physical traits such as eye color. Through recent technological innovations, an individual's particular DNA can be slowly read out like letters on a printed page, creating a genetic surname. By studying the DNA of African ethnic groups such as the MANDINKA and the WOLOF, geneticists may find the missing African "surnames" that could someday link African Americans to their roots in these and other groups.

LIMITATIONS OF THE EXISTING HISTORICAL AND ANTHROPOLOGICAL RECORD

The existing historical evidence provides a starting point for exploring African American ancestry. Records suggest that the transatlantic slave trade, which lasted from the sixteenth to the nineteenth century, forced approximately about eleven to twelve million people to leave Africa. The slave merchants took Africans from trading ports along the western coast of Africa and some of the interior, and from trading ports along the eastern coast in what is now MOZAMBIQUE. Of the millions taken from Africa, about two million died on the voyage across the Atlantic, and about nine million to ten million arrived in the Americas.

Using archival records of slave voyages, the W. E. B. Du Bois Institute for Afro-American Research at Harvard University produced the *Trans-Atlantic Slave Trade Database*, a CD-ROM database that documents about 75 percent of the migration of Africans to the Americas. This historical database reports the general migratory trends of

ethnic groups, identifying the ports involved in the slave trade and showing the relative proportion of slaves taken from each port to the Americas. The database also contains valuable information about age, gender, mortality, and other characteristics of the enslaved Africans.

Although such historical databases expand existing knowledge of the migratory patterns of enslaved Africans, the written records from which they are developed are ultimately incomplete. Records of some voyages have been lost, and many other voyages were not recorded at all. Where records do exist, they sometimes give an incomplete account of the journey and its participants, omitting important details such as the names of individuals and their places of origin.

Construction of a complete historical record is further hobbled because there is very little documentation of the slave trade that took place within the African continent itself. Some of this trade filled a demand for slaves within Africa, but much more of it supplied the transatlantic trade. When the transatlantic trade began in the sixteenth century, slave raiders captured slaves primarily from the edges of the West African coast. But as the commerce continued, slave merchants went progressively deeper and deeper into the African interior to find slaves. Consequently, the enslaved Africans leaving coastal ports for the Americas came from many regions within Africa, a fact that is not revealed in the port-to-port data gathered in the Du Bois Institute database.

Similarly, little is known about the subsequent movement of enslaved Africans within the Americas. Many Africans disembarked in the Caribbean and were later moved to other locations. Since there were so many movements of slaves within the Americas and so few records kept, it is nearly impossible for any living African American to trace his or her genealogy back to a specific place on the African continent.

Some researchers have turned to linguistic and cultural evidence to determine historical relationships between individuals and populations. Although these approaches are useful in studying the diversity on the African continent, they are limited in an African American context. The crux of the problem lies in the irregular patterns in which these traits evolve. A population's language and culture can change dramatically in a single generation and therefore do not always reflect the long-term history of the population. Such was the case in the Atlantic trade and the system of slavery, both of which tended to alter African culture and language in the Americas, often creating new forms.

DNA AS A TOOL FOR HISTORICAL RESEARCH

Incorporating additional information from the genetic record may eventually fill in some of the missing pieces in the historical picture, for the first time allowing African Americans to determine where their ancestors came from. DNA is the primary component of the genetic record. Biologically, it serves as a genetic blueprint, inscribing the structure of the proteins that determine human physical attributes. DNA directs the synthesis of proteins, the vital molecules that serve as building blocks of cells, control chemical reactions, and transport materials to and from cells. Proteins are composed of long chains of amino acids, and DNA provides the biochemical instructions that determine the arrangement of amino acids in a chain. The specific sequence of amino acids dictates the structure and resulting function of each protein. Proteins such as hemoglobin determine the physical traits that humans and other organisms possess. Variations in hemoglobin and other proteins are inherited, influencing physical differences that can be observed.

The genetic blueprint created by DNA provides instructions for attributes shared by all people, such as the presence of hands and feet. DNA also provides instructions for more variable traits specific to individuals, such as eye color. The information carried in human DNA is replicated and passed to offspring through the inheritance of genes. This means that, in addition to serving as a genetic blueprint for human development, DNA functions as a heredity link between generations, very much like a surname that is passed down through a family.

EARLY RESEARCH WITH BLOOD TYPES

Researchers have always been interested in finding ways to identify ancestry. Before they understood the role of DNA and had the tools to study it, they used physical differences such as height, face shape, and skin color to distinguish populations. Although such differences seemed significant to scientists in the eighteenth and nineteenth centuries, later researchers found that these variations were based on fundamentally flawed science and were deeply rooted in the assumption that white Europeans and North Americans were the human ideal. In the early 1900s, scientists began to understand and explore the nature of underlying genetic differences, such as differences in proteins.

Before molecular techniques became available to examine DNA in the 1970s, scientists studied these genetic differences between individuals by looking at protein polymorphisms. A protein polymorphism represents two or more possible variations in a single gene that are found in a population. Geneticists began by identifying specific polymorphisms within ethnic groups and other large populations. With this information, they could then link an individual to that population, even if the individual was far removed from the population by many generations and vast distances.

The first polymorphism in humans was found in 1901 by the Austrian pathologist Karl Landsteiner. He discovered the presence of particular forms of proteins on the surface of blood cells. Landsteiner incorporated these differences into a blood-typing system still used today, in which the letters A, B, and O represent the protein differences found in blood. The proteins found on blood cells are polymorphic because they are determined by a particular gene that appears in various forms throughout a population. The Polish scientists Hanna and Ludwik Hirschfeld were the first to see the potential for using the polymorphisms as tools for historical research. In 1919 the two scientists carried out a worldwide study recording the frequency of A, B, and O blood types among many populations. Most dramatically, Native Americans had almost complete absence of both the A and B blood types. Africans showed a relatively high frequency of the B blood type and a low frequency of the A blood type. Variation within Africa was also uncovered. Higher levels of the A blood type were found in North Africa than in Central Africa, possibly as a result of intermarriage with Europeans and others in the north.

Through global studies of protein polymorphisms, scientists began to realize the power of genetic differences in resolving questions of human history. More precise and more telling genetic differences were soon revealed by identifying certain rare blood conditions in specific populations. Researchers found, for example, that the Duffy-negative blood group was rare in Europeans and Asians but occurred quite frequently in African populations, particularly in MALARIA endemic regions. Another unusual blood condition, the Diego blood group, was found in Native Americans but was absent in Africans and Europeans.

Although the variation in frequencies of these protein polymorphisms is illuminating, differences in protein structure cannot be identified as minutely as differences in DNA composition can be. Only a few blood types exist, and people from genetically distinct populations may share some of the rare blood conditions, such as the Duffy-negative group. Variations in DNA, however, are extremely specific in individuals and in certain populations. Researchers have exploited this fact to pinpoint specific pieces of DNA that would be reliable genealogical markers to match certain individuals to particular ethnic groups.

HOW DNA CREATES GENETIC SURNAMES

Geneticists took advantage of the fact that DNA changes in minute ways over generations. The changes come from two sources: ordinary human cell growth, and the mixing of genetic material during reproduction. Humans, like other living organisms, grow through the division of cells. Each human cell contains within its nucleus coiled strands of DNA, some of which is packaged in genes located on threadlike bodies called chromosomes. Each time the cell divides, the DNA goes through replication, the process of copying the genetic material. Occasionally a copying mistake, or a mutation, arises in the DNA structure during replication. Mutations create polymorphisms—new variant forms—in the DNA. These polymorphisms allow scientists to distinguish individuals' DNA and thus study population history. Human reproduction also leads to variations in DNA through the mixing of the DNA from each parent. In some cases, the mixing of the two sets of DNA leads to subtle alteration of parts of the chromosome, a process known as recombination.

The mutations and recombinations that create the diversity in human populations occur extremely rarely, which is why human evolution is so slow. Both parents contribute nearly identical genetic information, so that virtually every human has the same limbs, internal organs, and other basic traits. (The genetic differences that influence minor variations between humans, such as height, reflect a relatively minuscule divergence in the parents' DNA.) Despite the apparent diversity in the human race, in fact, only a 0.1 percent biological difference exists between humans. Although rare, mutations and recombinations tend to occur at a regular rate. Two populations that are closely related—that is, populations with a recent common ancestor—are likely to have similar haplotypes, and closer relationships increase the likelihood of similarities. (A haplotype is a single permutation of a segment of DNA; haplotypes differ between individuals based on the different composition of polymorphisms along the segment.) Two populations that have a common ancestor further in the past are more likely to have experienced unique mutation and recombination events that produced population-specific polymorphisms and population-specific haplotypes.

The potential for using haplotypes in historical research was first noted in the 1940s by British geneticist Ronald A. Fisher, long before the genetic technology or information became available to analyze haplotypes. Fisher recognized that, in contrast to the protein polymorphisms in blood types or blood conditions, DNA was so massive and complex that the presence of individual haplotypes could conclusively tie individuals to a specific population. In theory, at least, large parts of human history could be reconstructed by tracing the spread of these rare variants through generations and identifying the populations from which they originated. If, for example, an individual haplotype is present only in the MANDINKA, an African American with that haplotype is almost certainly of Mandinka origin.

Later researchers found that applying these insights to African history was quite difficult. On the one hand, Africa is an ideal place to find distinct biological surnames. Geneticists believe that Africa's long history has made it the most genetically diverse continent in the world. Linguistic and cultural analysis reveals that Africa has many hundreds of distinct ethnic groups.

On the other hand, Africa's diverse genetic makeup and its history dating to the origins of the human species mean that the genetic record is extremely mixed up. Population expansions, extensive trade, and migration over time have kept different regions of Africa in constant physical and genetic contact. In addition, slave trading that occurred before the transatlantic slave trade disrupted regional population patterns. Geneticists soon realized that mapping every major population movement and mixture in African history would be impossible.

Instead, researchers decided that if they wanted to find specific genetic markers that could match African Americans to various African communities, they would have to work backwards from the genetic makeup of current populations in Africa. For these purposes, the areas most affected by the slave trade, West Africa and west Central Africa, were marked as the principal regions for genetic study. Of secondary importance were Mozambique and MADAGASCAR in southeastern Africa. Finally, some countries farther into the interior, such as MALI and the CENTRAL AFRICAN REPUBLIC, were also considered to merit study. In each of these parts of Africa, researchers hope to identify genetic material that corresponds to genetic material found in African Americans.

DNA INHERITED FROM ONE PARENT

Combined with the foundation of research into protein polymorphisms, advances in molecular techniques enabled geneticists to look at DNA directly and try to identify specific genetic markers that could tie African Americans to African populations. One important tool was DNA sequencing, a technique for determining the sequence of nucleic acids, a critical structure in DNA. This technique was based largely on the work of British molecular biologist Frederick Sanger, for which he was awarded the Nobel Prize in chemistry in 1980. Another major advance was the development in 1983 of polymerase chain reaction (a technique for making multiple copies of a piece of DNA, usually referred to by the acronym PCR) by the American biochemist Kary Mullis and his associate Fred Faloona. (Based on his work on DNA, Mullis won the 1993 Nobel Prize for chemistry. Mullis shared the prize with British-born Canadian biochemist Michael Smith, but the Nobel committee did not acknowledge Faloona's essential contribution to the PCR technique.) These DNA techniques had many applications, including the potential to uncover several centuries of hidden African American history.

The first DNA-based inquiries focused heavily on uni-parentally inherited DNA—genetic material that is inherited from only one parent. Humans have two copies of DNA, each copy located in the genes found on chromosomes. One chromosome is inherited from the mother and one from the father. However, humans have two regions of DNA that contain only one copy, inherited from one parent. While females have two copies of the X chromosome (the twenty-third chromosome pair), males have one copy of the X chromosome and one copy of the Y chromosome. The Y chromosome is thus passed directly from father to son. Unlike the other chromosomes, it is inherited exclusively through the male line.

Aside from the DNA carried on chromosomes within the nucleus of every cell, humans also carry a small amount of DNA in the mitochondria, specialized regions of the cell outside the nucleus. This DNA is known as mitochondrial DNA (mtDNA). While all humans have mitochondria, mtDNA is inherited from mothers alone because the father's mitochondria are contained in the tail of the sperm, which is lost when the human egg is fertilized.

The promise of research into uniparentally inherited genes was the hope that the mtDNA and Y chromosome would provide two distinct records of male and female genealogy. All humans share an ancient common ancestor for their mtDNA, and all men share a common ancestor for the Y chromosome. Since the time of a common ancestor, mutation has caused the lineages to diverge, developing unique historical records. By studying the variations in mtDNA and the Y chromosome, scientists have developed techniques to independently trace maternal and paternal inheritance of DNA. Additionally, neither mtDNA nor the Y chromosome can undergo recombination, so the only method of genetic diversification is through mutation. This means that changes in both mtDNA and the Y chromosome occur at regular rates, making them ideal for studying large periods of history.

MITOCHONDRIAL DNA

MtDNA is among the most extensively studied regions of the human genome (the complete set of genetic material) and has therefore proved a useful tool in studying African history. In 1987 American geneticist Rebecca Cann, New Zealand geneticist Allan Wilson, and American anthropologist Mark Stoneking, working in Wilson's lab at the University of California at Berkeley, first used mtDNA to resolve the question of human origins and human diversity by locating the origin of humans in Africa and dating it to somewhere between 142,000 and 285,000 years ago. Further mtDNA have been defined for thousands of individuals around the world.

Using these data, researchers produced genealogical trees based on the premise that the number of mutations occurring in the haplotypes of two individuals reflects the closeness of their relationship. If more mutations have occurred that differentiate the two people's haplotypes, there are more generations between them and their common ancestor. Conversely, fewer mutations indicate a closer relationship. Mutations occur at a predictable rate, so geneticists used them to develop genealogical trees. One of the first such mtDNA trees was created by American geneticist Linda Vigilant and her colleagues in 1991. Vigilant's tree contained fourteen African branches that diverged long ago and one branch that was mixed African and non-African. Subsequent studies have confirmed this overall pattern.

The results suggest that all mtDNA haplotypes in modern populations trace back to a common ancestor or "mitochondrial Eve" who lived roughly 140,000 years ago in Africa. Through several subsequent migrations beginning between 80,000 and 120,000 years ago, *Homo sapiens* spread through Asia, Europe, and other parts of the world. Some of the different ethnic groups in Africa may have diverged even earlier.

Vigilant's study, also conducted in Allan Wilson's lab in the early 1990s, demonstrated the geographic specificity of mtDNA types. Individuals shared identical mtDNA haplotypes within populations but not between them, with one intriguing exception. The exception was a shared mtDNA type between a YORUBA (from NIGERIA) and an African American. These two individuals most likely shared a common ancestor that passed this haplotype to them both. If the common ancestor had uniquely Yoruba descendants, this would be the first case of a population specific haplotype identifying descent. While subsequent studies show that maternal gene flow in West Africa has been substantial, rare population-specific haplotypes may exist. Research into mtDNA remains preliminary, however. Although scientists have been able to develop broad genealogical trees and identify some possible connections between Africa and the African diaspora, they have not been able to use this type of research to draw more detailed conclusions about links between African Americans and specific ethnic groups in Africa.

THE Y CHROMOSOME

Since the mid-1980s, attention has turned to the Y chromosome. Studies have established that Y-chromosome haplotypes are often localized to specific geographic regions, making it a useful tool for studying population history. Research on the Y chromosome, like that on mtDNA, has placed human origins in Africa. The ancestral form of the chromosome is most abundant in Africa, with many derived forms present in African populations. Other derived forms later moved out of Africa into Asia and Europe.

The geographical distribution of the Y chromosome indicates that paternal gene flow was restricted by isolation between populations, with geographically closer groups being more genetically similar. Scientists have identified a Y chromosome Alu insertion polymorphism that is specific to Africans, Asians, and Australian aborigines. Furthermore, some of the African ethnic groups are genetically distinct from other groups. The KHOISAN, for example, frequently share a few specific haplotypes, many of which are not found in other populations.

The use of the Y chromosome to study African history to date has been promising. One of the most provocative studies was conducted in the early and mid-1990s by British historian Tudor Parfitt. His research on the traditions and oral history of a small Bantu-speaking population in southern Africa has raised perplexing questions about their ethnic origins. He studied the Lemba, a small ethnic group in northeastern SOUTH AFRICA and other parts of southern Africa. What intrigued Parfitt was the fact that the Lemba look distinctly African, but they practice many Jewish customs, such as circumcision and strict dietary laws. Their oral history proposes that some of the Lemba's ancestors came from "huge towns across the sea," possibly Yemen. These proposed Jewish ancestors are thought to have established ports on the African coast where they interacted heavily with the local population.

In 1996 South African geneticists Amanda Spurdle and Trefor Jenkins used Y-chromosome polymorphisms that distinguish ethnic groups to investigate the infiltration of Jewish culture in the Lemba. The data showed a 53 percent Caucasoid (predominantly Middle Eastern) and 36 percent Negroid Y chromosome contribution in the Lemba. This genetic evidence lent strong support for a Middle Eastern genetic contribution to this South African population but could not distinguish Jewish from other Semitic ancestry. Subsequent research confirmed that the Lemba in fact have historical and genetic ties to Jewish culture, having a significant contribution of a haplotype found that is specific to the kohanim, a lineage of Jewish priests thought to be descendents of the biblical Aaron.

If further studies confirm that no other African groups have a genetic composition similar to the Lemba, this will prove a great feat for the growing field of genetic history. Thus it is important to gain further information about the Y-chromosome haplotypes of other African ethnic groups. By first focusing on the overall genetic architecture of Africa, scientists will have better opportunities to reconstruct history.

POPULATION-SPECIFIC POLYMORPHISMS

In addition to tracing patterns of inheritance of the Y chromosome, geneticists have identified population-specific polymorphisms throughout DNA. Scientists believe that most populations have some isolated and therefore unique mutations. These mutations are probably very rare, occurring in less than 5 percent of the population. If these mutations disrupt the function of important genes, they can manifest themselves as rare population-specific diseases, such as Tay-Sachs disease in Ashkenazi Jews. In most cases, however, the mutations have no noticeable biological impact at all. These harmless mutations serve as useful markers, and their presence can make it possible to find links between people in Africa and the African diaspora.

Although scientists have not yet identified polymorphisms specific to individual African ethnic groups, they have found several population-specific polymorphisms that distinguish broadly between Europeans, Africans, and Native Americans. Scientists have used these markers to investigate African American admixture (the genetic mixing of two different ethnic groups) with Europeans.

In 1992 Indian geneticist Ranajit Chakraborty and colleagues used eighteen African-exclusive polymorphisms and five European-exclusive polymorphisms to measure the extent of African and European genetic admixture. They found that African Americans in the study had 25.2 percent of the European-specific genes under study, with a margin of error of plus or minus 2.7 percent. This figure corresponded with figures found in other studies, including a 1953 study using protein polymorphisms.

In the future, better technology and better information about the human genome may make it possible to scan the DNA of Africans throughout the African continent. This would make it feasible to search for population-specific polymorphisms to identify ethnic groups. These polymorphisms would detect informative microdifferentiation that occurs in populations. Once researchers have constructed this genetic map of the continent, they could then create a database of these population-specific polymorphisms, which would provide a reliable means of identifying descent. Unfortunately, current technological constraints make this approach impractical. The procedure is simply too expensive and time-consuming to use on hundreds and thousands of DNA samples.

COMBINING POLYMORPHISM RESEARCH WITH THE STUDY OF HAPLOTYPES

An alternative approach is to combine techniques relying on polymorphisms with haplotype research. Geneticists search for population-specific haplotypes using previously identified polymorphisms. This approach is more efficient and less expensive than screening for new polymorphisms in DNA. Once polymorphisms have been detected in a given population, inexpensive high-speed methods can be designed to analyze them in large numbers of people. The method is based on the premise that unique recombination events in the history of ethnic groups would create distinguishable haplotypes. Some haplotypes, in other words, can be tracked based on polymorphisms that have already been studied.

One of the few studies using this approach was conducted in 1999 by the American geneticist Pardis Sabeti. She focused on an area of DNA that affects the body's production of phenylalanine hydroxylase (an enzyme involved in protein metabolism). The study demonstrated that African-specific haplotypes can be identified based on polymorphisms present in all human populations. The polymorphisms are found all around the world, but the haplotypes are found only in Africa, so it is likely that the polymorphisms occurred before the divergence and ancient migrations of human populations. The recombination event that created the haplotype thus created a unique African genetic marker. These results demonstrate that haplotypes can, in fact, be seen as genetic surnames with the capacity to identify descent.

The study involved individuals of African descent from Nigeria (from the Yoruba ethnic group), Jamaica, and Maywood, Illinois. It was also designed to test the correlation between historical records and haplotype frequencies. Information from the *Trans-Atlantic Slave Trade Database* suggests that ports from which Nigerians embarked contributed about 45 percent of the Jamaican trade and 4 percent of the United States trade. Based on the historical evidence of these geographic differences, a closer relationship between the Yoruba and Jamaicans than between the Yoruba and African Americans would be expected. In fact the haplotype data showed exactly that, a promising agreement between the historical and genetic record.

In studying haplotype distributions in African populations, scientists are searching for population-specific haplotypes and polymorphisms. These differences are the "holy grail" of ethnic studies that researchers hope to uncover hidden in DNA. The search is likely to be a long one because human DNA contains millions of segments. Ideally the research will find that different regions carry many population-specific polymorphisms and haplotypes that would easily identify ethnic descent.

One marker, on its own, is rarely sufficient to conclusively predict ethnic origins. Alternatively, scientists may find haplotype frequency differences in ethnic groups. Using a combination of genetic markers dramatically increases the statistical power of prediction. As knowledge of the human genome increases, scientists will be able to use an increasing number of independent gene genealogies to infer population histories.

CONCLUSION

In studying Africa, the scientific community has almost exclusively focused its attention on questions of human origins and disease. It is high time that scientists dedicate resources to address African history. The search for regionally specific haplotypes is the search for African American roots. Along the way scientists can learn more about the history of Africa as it is recorded in genes. Researchers have already begun to determine the effect of European admixture on African American descent. Next, they may reveal the historical impact of slavery. The genetic clues may also define the historical relationships between neighboring ethnic groups. Each answer, on its own, is a worthy achievement. By building upon these answers, scientists may one day discover the origins of African Americans.

For Malcolm X, "X symbolized the true African family name that he never could know." For geneticists, the language of X and Y chromosomes represents a new tool for bio-historical investigation. Perhaps one day the chromosomes will help restore the African American family names that have been obscured for centuries.

PARDIS SABETI

Doe, Samuel Kanyon
1951–1990
Liberian military leader and head of state.

Samuel K. Doe, the Liberian leader whose 1980 military coup ushered in seventeen years of violence, corruption, and confusion, left office a casualty of the act that had brought him there ten years earlier—assassination. Doe's ten-year rule was significant not only for what it created but for what it ended: more than a century of single-party rule, and the political domination of Liberia by an Americo-Liberian elite.

Doe was born in Tuzon, LIBERIA. A member of the Krahn ethnic group, he grew up in the Liberian interior. After elementary school he briefly attended a Baptist high school, but soon dropped out. While a soldier, Doe graduated from high school, studied radio and communications, and became an expert sharpshooter. At the time he ascended to the rank of master sergeant in 1979, Doe had no known political affiliation. But his colleagues said that Doe, like many indigenous Liberians, resented the privileged position of Americo-Liberians.

On April 12, 1980, Doe and a band of dissident soldiers overthrew and assassinated the elected president, William Vacanarat Shadrach TUBMAN. Doe, who named himself head of state and commander in chief, publicly shot

Tubman's cabinet members after parading them naked through the capital city of MONROVIA. Despite his reputation for brutality, Doe maintained Liberia's traditionally close ties to the United States, including a state visit in 1982. After future president Charles Ghankay TAYLOR and other rebel leaders launched a civil war in 1989, Doe spent months trapped inside the presidential palace, and was ultimately killed by rebel forces.

KATE TUTTLE

Dogon
Ethnic group of south-central Mali.

According to oral tradition, the Dogon were originally members of the Keita, a MANDE-speaking group from the headwaters of the NIGER RIVER who fled their homes sometime between the tenth and thirteenth centuries because they refused to convert to Islam. The oral tradition may show that the Dogon absorbed Mande-speaking refugees from the centralized Islamic kingdoms of the Niger Basin. However, the Voltaic (or Gur) language of the Dogon suggests a more ancient presence in their present-day homeland in south-central MALI. They inhabit the rugged and isolated Bandiagara escarpment and surrounding regions southwest of the Niger bend. The cliffs at the edge of the escarpment protected the group from outside invaders. Dogon settlements concentrate around isolated pockets of arable land, where they farm millet as a subsistence crop. Traditionally, the Dogon have shared this territory with the pastoral FULANI, who exchanged their dairy products for Dogon grain and produce. Though exact numbers are difficult to come by, today as many as 800,000 people consider themselves Dogon.

The Dogon's rugged and isolated territory left them relatively unaffected by French colonialism and missionary work, though the French did introduce the cultivation of onions as a cash crop during the 1920s. By maintaining their precolonial cultural traditions, the Dogon have attracted the attention of numerous ethnographers, including the French anthropologist Marcel Griaule and the French ethnographic filmmaker Jean Rouche. In recent years, however, the Dogon have increased their participation in the cash economy. Some villages have specialized in traditional crafts and performances in order to attract commercial tourism. Some Dogon have even left their homeland in search of wage labor, particularly in BAMAKO, MALI, and the mines of CÔTE D'IVOIRE. The Dogon have also recently faced animosity from their Fulani neighbors, with whom they compete for scarce mineral resources and mining jobs.

Traditionally, the extended patrilineal family forms the basic social unit of the Dogon, who lack strong centralized authorities. A *hogon*, or headman (traditionally the oldest man in the area), provides spiritual leadership and arbitrates disputes for one or more villages. The hogon performs rituals and safeguards the religious masks for which the Dogon are famous. The power of the hogon, however, is relatively weak; a council of elders holds decision-making power within each village. The Dogon fall into at least four smaller groups: the Dyon, Arou, Onon, and Domno. Like neighboring Mande groups, the Dogon maintain a kind of caste system based on occupation. Farmers rank at the top of the system, while blacksmiths and hunters, who perform "polluting" work, arc lower on the caste scale.

Unlike their Muslim neighbors, most Dogon still practice a traditional religion with a complex mythology. This has received considerable anthropological attention. Dogon cosmology considers every being a combination of complementary opposites; elaborate rituals are necessary to maintain the balance. Ancestor worship is another importance facet of Dogon religion. Members of the Society of Masks perform rituals to guarantee that a person's "life force" will flee from his or her corpse to a future relative of the same lineage. One of the most famous Dogon rituals is the *Sigi*—a series of rituals performed once every sixty years—recorded by filmmaker Jean Rouche. Islamic missionaries, however, have had some success among the Dogon, and approximately 35 percent of the Dogon population are now Muslim.

See also ISLAM IN AFRICA; TOURISM IN AFRICA.

ELIZABETH HEATH

Dogon Art and Architecture
Artwork and buildings of the Dogon people who live in present-day Mali.

Much of DOGON art consists of striking ritual masks made with carved wood and other materials. Dogon architecture conveys symbolic relationships in Dogon society and is considered one of the most distinctive styles in West Africa.

The Dogon live in the rugged yet beautiful Bandiagara escarpment of south central MALI. They migrated to this remote cliff area around the fifteenth century C.E. in part to preserve their cultural beliefs and institutions when the Islamic MALI EMPIRE was at its height. When the Dogon arrived at the Bandiagara escarpment, they found architectural and other remains of earlier civilizations, among these the Toloy (third century to second century B.C.E.) and the Tellem (eleventh century to fifteenth century C.E.). Dogon building, weaving, iron working, and pottery traditions reflect both an interest in these and other earlier regional art forms, and an influence from contemporary regional political and cultural centers such as DJENNÉ and TOMBOUCTOU (Timbuktu).

DOGON ARCHITECTURE

Dogon villages are constructed to resemble a human body. At the "head" of the village is a blacksmith's shop and a *toguna*, a community men's house. The toguna is an open-walled structure with roof supports carved in human shapes, often the female form. Typically, the toguna has eight such supports, with the number representing the first eight Dogon ancestors who sat in a ruling council. Today these ancestors impart wisdom and spiritual knowledge to Dogon elders when they meet in the toguna to discuss village affairs. Across the supports lies a thick, horizontal layer of millet stalks, which provides shade. The layer of millet also recalls the village elders' ongoing concern with community wealth and well being. Following the millet harvest, the roof of the toguna is used as a drying rack for the millet, which is an important crop for the Dogon.

At the "feet" of the village are binu—small, often elaborately decorated temples. The binu are dedicated to nature spirits related to water, healing, and similar concerns. Evergreen plants nearby symbolize the vitality of these spirits throughout the year. The binu, which are molded of earth, have rounded walls, a small central door, and several conical mounds at the top the facade, possibly derived from early family houses in the area. Today, Dogon family residences are rectilinear earthen structures with flat terrace roofs similar to residences of Mande Muslims in the area.

Family residences sit at the "chest" of the village. The ginna, the houses of important families, display a grid of earthen niches across the façade as well as a row of conical mound shrines along the roof line. During annual ceremonies these mound shrines are filled with offerings of white millet, increasing their prominence. The millet-filled mounds draw one's eye both skyward and toward the tall cliffs behind the village, where the dead are placed in caves.

Families store their grain on the upper story of the house, often behind a haar, a small door or shutter. A haar is usually carved with rows of raised-arm figures representing the protective presence of the nommo, the first ancestors. The raised-arm gesture, which is also common to sculptures placed in family shrines, is a reference to prayer and also directs the eyes of worshipers to the sky, from where the nommo are said to have come. The goyo, or granary, recalls myths about the origins of seeds and fire, which is thought of as a piece of the sun. According to Dogon legend, both seeds and fire were taken by a nommo blacksmith bringing civilization to earth. Sculptural portrayals of the nommo often show them with the sexual attributes of both men and women. Their androgny refers to the belief that men and women originally were similar.

DOGON MASKS

Dogon men belong to the Awa mask society. Men both make and perform with their masks at funeral-related rites, as well as at dama celebrations, which end the two year mourning period after the death of an important male elder from the village. A range of mask types is employed to ensure that the nyama (spirit) of the deceased will leave. Maskers represent animals or people that the deceased elder met in life. Animals might include a monkey, a rabbit, a crocodile, an antelope, a ram, or a bird. Humans represented by maskers might include a blacksmith, a healer, a sorcerer, a stranger, or an enemy. The number of masks also indicates the family wealth and social status of the deceased. Together, the maskers symbolize the inhabitants of the Dogon world. Social values are reinforced through negative and positive examples: the monkey mask is a troublemaker, glutton, and thief. The rabbit, in contrast, represents great agility, speed, and stamina.

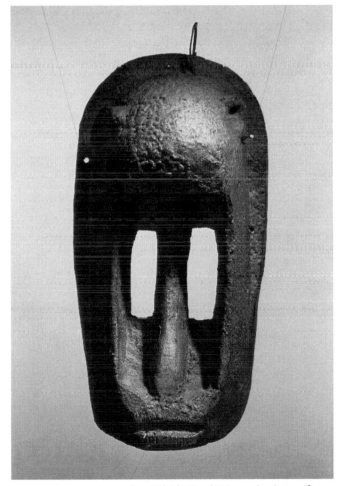

DOGON MASK. A wooden "Black Monkey" mask, dating from 19th century Mali. (*Bridgeman Art Library International Ltd.*)

At the climax of the dama rites, one or more individuals appear wearing Kanaga masks, the unusual abstract shapes of which are said variously to recall crocodiles, birds in flight, and the act of creation (symbolized by the union of heaven and earth). These and other masks also appear during sigui rites (sometimes known as sigi), which are held every sixty years to mark the symbolic death of a whole generation and to recall the first funeral when mask-making was initiated. For each sigui celebration, an enormous serpent-form mask is created. Though too sacred to ever be worn, it is preserved in one of the caves above the village. The number of sigui masks serves as an important historical marker for the number of generations of Dogon who have lived in the area.

See also MASKS AND MASQUERADES IN AFRICA.

BIBLIOGRAPHY

Demott, Barbara. *Dogon Masks: A Structural Study of Form and Meaning.* UMI Research, 1982.

Ezra, Kate. *Art of the Dogon: Selections from the Lester Wunderman Collection.* The Metropolitan Museum, 1988.

Griaule, Marcel. *Conversations With Ogotemmêli: An Introduction to Dogon Religious Ideas.* Oxford University Press, 1965.

Griaule, Marcel, and Germaine Dieterlen. "The Dogon." In *African Worlds,* edited by Daryll Forde. Oxford University Press, 1954.

SUZANNE BLIER

Donatism

Fourth-century North African Christian sect.

In 312 C.E. a group of Christian followers split from the Church of Rome over the controversial election of the bishop Caecilian of CARTHAGE. In the BERBER region of Numidia, now eastern ALGERIA and western TUNISIA, this movement to form a more pure church gathered momentum under the leadership of the charismatic Donatus. It was a populist movement in the face of Roman imperialism: "You come with edicts of emperors," Donatus proclaimed, "we hold nothing in our hands but volumes of scriptures." The Donatists insisted that ministers who dispensed the sacraments be "sinless," and that their church be North Africa-based, comprised of "a small body of the chosen."

Although Emperor Constantine at first confiscated several Donatist churches, creating martyrs of the victims, eventually he tolerated the sect. But Constantine's successors increasingly repressed Donatism, as its following grew to include almost half the Christians in North Africa. In 347, Donatist leaders were exiled; in 411, Rome created laws imposing fines and denying civil rights to all Donatists. The theological scholar SAINT AUGUSTINE, himself a Berber, attacked the Donatists' formation of a separate church, stating that "Heretics, Jews and pagans—they have come to form a unity over against our Unity." In one of Augustine's seminal writings he denied the Donatists' assertion that they could create a pure church on this earth, and argued that the separation of the pure and impure could take place only in the hereafter.

Donatism posed a threat not only to Roman Christian theology; what began as a call for a separate church soon became a movement of Berber resistance against Roman power in North Africa. Donatism has been viewed as a precedent for anti-imperialist and nationalist sentiment, as well as a declaration of Berber identity. Some historians have characterized the Donatists as the urban poor and rural peasants revolting against the landowning class of the Roman church. The Circumcellions, considered an extremist wing of the Donatists, lived in a small peasant community, devoted themselves to martyrs, and attacked landowners with clubs christened "Israel." Women played an active role in this resistance.

Yet other church historians have pointed out that the Donatist leaders were some of the most highly educated Christians in the region. These leaders wrote in Latin, and even the battle cry of the Circumcellions, "Deo Laudes" (Praise God), was in the foreign tongue. Some historians have also argued that the Donatist attacks on Roman landowners were only scattered uprisings, not part of an organized anti-imperialist rebellion.

Nevertheless, many have attributed the decline of Roman influence in North Africa to revolts organized around Donatism. As the region underwent gradual Islamization beginning in the seventh century, Donatism faded, along with much of the early Christian influence in North Africa.

See also CHRISTIANITY, AFRICAN: AN OVERVIEW; ROMAN AFRICA: AN INTERPRETATION.

MARIAN AGUIAR

Dos Santos, José Eduardo

1942–

Angolan political leader and president.

José Eduardo Santos rose to political power in the Central African nation of ANGOLA through the Popular Movement for the Liberation of Angola Party (MPLA). At the age of thirty-seven he became the second president of Angola. Born in Luanda, Santos joined the Marxist MPLA's youth organization as a boy and enlisted in its guerrilla army at the age of nineteen. An MPLA scholarship sent him to the Union of Soviet Socialist Republics (USSR, now Russia and a number of other independent republics) to study from 1963 to 1970. After graduating with degrees in petroleum engineering and radar telecommunications, Santos served as MPLA representative in Yugoslavia and the People's

Republic of the Congo (later known as Zaire, now the DEMOCRATIC REPUBLIC OF THE CONGO) before advancing to the party's central committee in 1974. After Angola achieved independence from Portugal in 1975, Santos held important ministerial posts in the MPLA government. He became president on September 21, 1979, succeeding Agostinho NETO, Angola's first president. Santos moved swiftly to consolidate his power within the government. A political moderate and a pragmatic leader, he replaced those in his administration who wanted to govern strictly according to Communist doctrine with competent administrators and technicians. However, his attempts to build on Neto's economic and political work were unsuccessful because of the continuing civil war between MPLA and the National Union for Total Independence of Angola (UNITA). After Angolan independence, each party had formed a government and claimed to represent the new nation, launching a long-lasting conflict. Each side received aid from foreign powers who saw Angola—and its oil reserves—as strategically important. Santos's government had the support of the USSR, which contributed to the cost of as many as 50,000 troops from the Communist nation of Cuba. UNITA was aided by the United States. UNITA also had the support of SOUTH AFRICA, which controlled South-West Africa (now NAMIBIA), where a black nationalist movement was waging a guerrilla war for independence. In 1975 South Africa sent troops to Angola in support of UNITA's bid to take control of the newly independent country. South Africa invaded again on behalf of UNITA in 1981, 1983, and 1987. South African troops were finally withdrawn from Angola in 1989 as part of the international agreement leading to Namibian independence. The South African invasions helped Santos strengthen his control within MPLA, and he was able to make major economic, diplomatic, and political changes. In August 1987 he announced a major economic recovery plan. Blaming the nation's problems on excessive centralization of socialist planning, corruption, and too much bureaucracy, he proposed to turn some state-run enterprises over to private operators. He also urged banking reforms and other measures to encourage foreign investment. In 1988 he had further changed Angola's economy by opening small businesses to private enterprise and by allowing the first joint ventures with international firms. Angola also affiliated with the International Monetary Fund (IMF) and the International Bank for Reconstruction and Development, known as the World Bank. In foreign policy, Santos met in 1988 with Mikhail Gorbachev, then leader of the USSR, to discuss the removal of Cuban troops from Angola. At that time, South African troops still occupied a portion of southern Angola, but Santos signed the first of a series of agreements that resulted in the withdrawal of all foreign troops from Angola. After South African troops withdrew across the southern border in 1989, Cuban troops left in stages. The last of them had been withdrawn by May 1991. In the political arena, in 1990 the MPLA's Third Party Congress pledged to create a multiparty political system, to study the draft of a new constitution eliminating the central role of the party, and to transform its ideology from Marxism-Leninism to democratic socialism. Dos Santos consistently supported attempts to end Angola's civil war. In May 1991, Portugal, the United States, and the USSR arranged a peace accord that ended the fighting and led to national elections in late 1992. Dos Santos ran for president as the MPLA candidate against Jonas SAVIMBI, the leader of UNITA. Although MPLA won the parliamentary elections and Santos appeared to have won a close victory in the presidential race, the election results became meaningless when UNITA resumed fighting. For the first few months of 1993, it appeared as if Savimbi's forces might achieve through war what they had not gained at the polls. Dos Santos's government, however, got support from UNITA's former allies, the United States and South Africa. In May 1993 the United States government recognized Angola, began pressuring Savimbi to end the war, and, for the first time, made American aid available to the Angolan government. Soon UNITA's offensive had stalled. The Santos government returned to peace negotiations, this time arranged chiefly by the United Nations and African political leaders. A fragile peace was established by the Lusaka Protocol of November 20, 1994, signed in LUSAKA, ZAMBIA, in which Dos Santos was confirmed as president and Savimbi was offered the vice presidency. In February 1995 the United Nations Security Council adopted a resolution establishing a strong international force of 7,000 troops to monitor the cease-fire and ensure that the Lusaka Protocol was enacted. The Lusaka Protocol, however, failed to end the long conflict, and the civil war continued until April of 2002, when the government and UNITA signed another cease-fire. As the UNITA rebels prepared to lay down their weapons, Dos Santos asked the international community for aid to help feed and house thousands of them and their families. In 2001 Dos Santos declared that he might choose to release his hold on political power in Angola and step down from the presidency at the next elections—to be held, he explained, as soon as the country is sufficiently stable. As president and head of the ruling MPLA party, Dos Santos controls the timing of elections and therefore the timing of his withdrawal from power. His announcement, however, turned out to be somewhat premature. Elections are believed to be slated for sometime in 2010, and it is widely suspected that Dos Santos will again run for office.

Douala, Cameroon
Largest city and commercial hub of Cameroon.

The town of Douala first developed on the southeastern shore of the Wouri River estuary in the 1700s as a station for the transatlantic slave trade. Dutch merchants initially dominated the transatlantic trade, but the town was also frequented by ethnic DUALA traders, many of whom acted as middlemen in the human traffic. British influence slowly usurped the Dutch until 1884, when Germany, after signing a treaty with two Duala chiefs, formally colonized CAMEROON. With a good harbor, Douala quickly became the colony's largest trading center, attracting African migrants as well as German and, later, French and British colonists. During World War II (1939–1945), it briefly served as the colonial capital.

Although YAOUNDÉ is now the capital of Cameroon, post independence infrastructure projects have solidified Douala's role as a national and regional economic hub. Today Douala handles approximately 95 percent of the country's foreign trade as well as exports from other countries in Central Africa. Industries include light manufacturing, agricultural processing, and transportation, construction, and engineering services. Douala is also Cameroon's largest city, with a population by 2004 of 1.3 million, having increased from 450,000 in 1976. Social and economic problems have accompanied the city's rapid growth. The Bassa industrial zone, the New Bell commercial area, and the Bonapriso center of official activity have all grown dramatically, creating shortages in public services, especially health and sanitation. Douala has a large population of migrant laborers from the Cameroon interior and neighboring countries; ethnic BAMILÉKÉ run many of the city's businesses.

ERIC YOUNG

Drought and Desertification
Degradation of arid, semiarid, and subhumid land by a combination of human and nonhuman processes.

Ecosystems across the globe are in danger of becoming desertified. Desertification is of particular concern in countries where population growth and economic disadvantage exacerbate ecological instability. Africa has many such countries, especially in the SAHEL region near the southern border of the SAHARA.

Hundreds of qualified people have tried to explain desertification, but no consensus exists because the process invokes questions of sociology, biology, politics, and culture. The history of African desertification has included recurring conflicts between and among peasants, pastoralists, European colonial regimes, intrusive local governments, and international environmental organizations.

DROUGHT IN LESOTHO. A malnourished calf grazes on the sparse remains of Mafeteng's once-verdant land. (*Themba Hadebe/AP Images*)

Often one party will brandish inconclusive scientific data against another, clouding conflicts that were already murky. The social and scientific complexity of desertification leaves more questions than answers. Are "natural" cycles or human abuses the greater culprit?

A careful look at the actual physical processes in arid, semiarid, and subhumid environments helps to clarify the problem. Scientists have isolated three separate states of trauma in such ecosystems: drought, desiccation, and dryland degradation. Only the third state directly involves human-induced environmental distress, but dry-land degradation often arises from desiccation and drought.

DROUGHT
Any dry period that seriously disturbs the normal conditions of an environment is called a drought. However, the term *normal conditions* must be used with care, especially in arid and semiarid environments where droughts may be common occurrences. In fact the peoples inhabiting arid and semiarid regions of Africa have many different means of coping with drought, as do the flora and fauna.

A drought is a dry spell from which an environment can recover—that is, from which an environment incurs little irreversible damage. Although drought most often connotes a lack of rain, one can also occur when rain falls at the wrong time—out of sync with the growing season—or on degraded soil that limits transpiration by plants. Scientists sometimes distinguish between *meteorologic* drought (low rainfall), *hydrologic* drought (low stream flow), and *agricultural* drought (sporadic or ill-timed rains).

DESICCATION
When a prolonged drought causes irreversible damage, the period of trauma is referred to as desiccation. Desiccation

can both eradicate species of flora and fauna and force changes in human livelihoods. Although more destructive than drought, desiccation is just as natural, and decade-long cycles of dryness punctuate Africa's history. Unfortunately, desiccation presents graver challenges to human intervention because it is hard to detect and even harder to ameliorate. Indeed, long-range solutions—if ill-conceived or poorly executed—can lead to dry-land degradation.

DRY-LAND DEGRADATION

When human abuses contribute to the trauma caused by drought and desiccation, the results can be serious and permanent. Geographer Michael Mortimore has suggested the following model. During a drought year animals die and crops fail. Farmers and pastoralists survive by selling assets, including livestock, as well as firewood cut from nearby forests and scrub lands. The next year the rains may return, but if farmers lack manure, their yields are poor and they must cultivate more land, shortening regenerative fallow periods. This strategy can lead to soil exhaustion as well as to conflicts with nearby pastoralists who typically rebuild their herds during post-drought years and may depend on the same land for grazing. Meanwhile economic, environmental, and social problems of dry-land degradation are further exacerbated by rapid population growth.

Some scientists postulate that the damage is even more profound. Land degradation can cause erosion, which, in turn, can cause dust storms. When wind draws dust into the atmosphere, the resulting cloud may inhibit rainfall. Furthermore, defoliated land reflects more solar energy than land with vegetation and thus is often cooler, and land that cools the air above it may also inhibit rainfall. In short, humans can make temporary trauma permanent by causing self-perpetuating processes of environmental change. These particular processes may contribute to desertification because they occur in the zones bordering deserts and can appear to extend the desert further. While the original picture (discussed below) was of an interminably advancing Sahara, more recent models describe pockets of degradation that expand until they join.

Estimates suggest that 34 percent of Africa's surface land is threatened by desertification. At the same time, human populations in the regions most affected have doubled in the past thirty years and continue to increase by 3 percent each year. Desertification has contributed to Sahel countries' inability to produce sufficient food for their populations.

Nor is the problem limited to the Sahel region. Climate-watch agencies have noted that temperature changes along the Atlantic and Indian Oceans are likely to mean decades of drought conditions for the southern part of the continent.

HISTORY OF THE CONTROVERSY

Concerns about the apparent advance of the desert date back to the 1920s and 1930s, a period of unusually low rainfall. The reports of British forester E. P. Stebbing were particularly influential. Compiling evidence from earlier French studies as well as from his expeditions through British and French colonies in Saharan West Africa, Stebbing blamed spreading sand and decreased vegetation on population growth and indigenous farming methods. Stebbing's work established the paradigm of blame that dominated discussions of dry-land degradation for decades. His most conspicuous yet pervasive mistake was to deny natural factors, such as the cyclical variations in rainfall that occur over several years, or even decades.

Along with his observations, Stebbing issued a request that the problem be officially investigated. In 1936 and 1937 the Anglo-French Forestry Commission answered this request and collected data that in large part refuted Stebbing's claims. Nevertheless debate about desertification (a term coined in 1949) continued until wetter conditions returned to the Sahel in the 1950s and colonial scientists turned their attention to other matters.

When drought struck the region in the 1970s, however, the debate was reborn in Stebbing's spirit. United Nations–sponsored quantitative research produced an abundance of alarming but not very accurate data. The Sahara, one study claimed, had advanced about 100 km (60 mi) in seventeen years; soon scientists, legislators, and UN representatives spoke of the Sahara's annual 6-km (4-mi) expansion, a spurious fact.

Although data focused international attention and aid on arid-land environmental problems, it also provided justification for measures to control the populations blamed for desertification. In some countries, governments blamed nomadic herders for overgrazing the savannas. Often they attempted to restrict movement with sedentarization programs that led only to overgrazing and further abuses, exacerbating traditional problems with modern ills. In other cases farmers' practices were held responsible, which also led to wrong-headed correctives: in GUINEA, those who burned brush to clear fields and fertilize soil were nominally subject to the death penalty.

In general these measures were based on very little understanding of the livelihoods of the peoples involved and the circumstances under which their actions may have contributed to overexploitation of local resources. Consequently the measures often failed to reverse environmental degradation. Sedentarization programs had a particularly poor record.

In the 1980s new research incorporating remote sensing and historical data challenged earlier, highly simplified models of desertification. One particularly extensive study conducted by geographers from Lund University in Sweden concluded that "no major changes in vegetation cover and crop productivity was identified, which could not be explained by varying rainfall characteristics." At the Earth Summit in Rio De Janeiro in 1992 and an international Convention to Combat Desertification in 1994, many authorities acknowledged the complexity of the issue and the importance of incorporating local needs and knowledge into antidesertification programs.

CURRENT SOLUTIONS

In the Sahel some efforts to combat desertification at the local level have yielded promising results. In BURKINA FASO, for example, village "land management programs" draw on village labor and expertise to carry out soil and water conservation projects, such as planting trees, constructing microdams, and erecting terraces and soil mounds to limit water runoff and thus soil erosion. Government and donor agencies help by providing funds, fertilizers, and technical assistance. Such programs have in some cases restored the fertility of once "desertified" land. Whether local successes alone can arrest further dry-land degradation, however, remains an open question.

BIBLIOGRAPHY

Adams, W. M., A. S. Goudie, and A. R. Orme. *The Physical Geography of Africa.* Oxford University Press, 1996.

Timberlake, Lloyd. *Africa in Crisis: The Causes, the Cures of Environmental Bankruptcy.* International Institute for Environment and Development, 1985.

ERIC BENNETT

Duala

Ethnic group of southern Cameroon.

The Bantu-speaking Duala migrated to the coastal areas of what is now southern CAMEROON from the CONGO RIVER Basin during the sixteenth century, and were among the first Africans in the region to come into contact with the European merchants who arrived soon thereafter. The Duala became prominent middleman traders, transporting slaves, ivory, and wild rubber from the interior in exchange for cloth, liquor, and firearms. The Europeans welcomed the Duala's entrepreneurial and collaborative spirit.

In 1884 two Duala chiefs signed an annexation agreement with Germany that permitted the Germans to explore and occupy much of the area that is now southern Cameroon. Many Duala sold their land to European settlers, or to BAMILÉKÉ who had migrated south from the highlands to take advantage of the economic growth in and around the thriving port of DOUALA. European missionaries translated the Bible into Duala and used the language in church. Over time, however, German-Duala relations soured as colonial officials tried to break the Duala trading monopoly, and many Duala, among them Chief Rudolph Douala Manga BELL, helped launch the nationalist struggle against COLONIAL RULE. Today, the Duala music, called the *makossa*, and dance are important national symbols that have also won international recognition, and the Duala language has become the region's commercial lingua franca. More than 80,000 people consider themselves Duala.

See also IVORY TRADE.

ERIC YOUNG

Dube, John Langalibalele
1871–1946
South African minister, educator, journalist, and writer who campaigned for the rights of fellow blacks.

John Langalibalele Dube was born near Inanda, Natal (in what is now KWAZULU-NATAL province), in eastern SOUTH AFRICA. Dube studied at Oberlin College, in Oberlin, Ohio, and was ordained a minister before returning to Natal. In 1903 he was one of the founders and the editor of the first Zulu newspaper, *Ilanga lase Natal* (Sun of Natal). In 1909 he founded the Ohlange Institute for Boys and then a school for girls, both near Durban. The same year Dube helped convene a South African Native Convention at Bloemfontein to oppose the "European descent" clause in the draft constitution for the Union (now Republic) of South Africa, which would bar men of color from Parliament.

On January 8, 1912, Dube was elected the first president general of the South African Native National Congress (which later became the AFRICAN NATIONAL CONGRESS). He led the opposition to the 1913 Natives Land Act, which began the process of partitioning land according to race. After heading an unsuccessful delegation to Prime Minister Louis Botha, Dube led a delegation to the British government in London, which was also unsuccessful. Dube described the 1917 Native Administration Bill, which hastened the partition of land, as a policy of extermination. By the 1920s, however, more radical black leaders were denouncing Dube as too conservative.

Although political involvement took up much of his life, Dube also published the first novel in the Zulu language, about the Zulu Chief SHAKA (1930), as well as several other books. In 1936 he received a doctoral degree from the University of South Africa. In 1937 Dube was elected to the Native Representative Council in Natal, where he served until his death.

Durban, South Africa
South African city, formerly Port Natal.
Situated on the EASTERN CAPE of SOUTH AFRICA, Durban is the capital of the KWAZULU-NATAL province and the country's most active seaport. It is surrounded by the Drakensburg Mountain range to the west, the Indian Ocean to the east, and the rolling hills of KwaZulu-Natal to the north and south. Although the area had been visited by European traders and explorers starting in the sixteenth century, its natural harbor was not fully utilized until the British came in 1824. They acquired land through treaties with the Zulu king SHAKA, and named their settlement Port Natal. In 1835 the city's name was changed to Durban, after Sir Benjamin D'Urban, then governor of the Cape Colony.

By 1855 Durban's British colony had begun exploiting the harbor, which continues to export raw materials and manufactured goods from the entire Witwatersrand region. In addition to trade, Durban's economy depended upon the sugar industry; beginning in 1860 large numbers of laborers were imported from India. By the 1950s Durban's population was about evenly divided among Europeans, Indians, and Africans, with a small number of mixed-race people officially designated as "Coloured." As in the rest of South Africa, nonwhites were forcibly relocated to single-race townships during the following decades. In the early 1970s black workers in Durban protested their economic inequality and political oppression with a series of strikes, which led to the founding of several black trade unions.

Since the dismantling of APARTHEID, residential restrictions no longer apply, but the city is still far from integrated. Durban remains an important seaport and the center of the South African sugar industry; another important aspect of the local economy is its popularity as a tourist destination. In 2000 the thirteenth International AIDS Conference was held in Durban, marking the first time that this conference was held in a developing nation. The following year the city hosted the United Nations' World Conference against Racism. As of 2007, the city was home to some 3.5 million people.

See also INDIAN COMMUNITIES IN AFRICA.

BIBLIOGRAPHY
Kuper, Leo, Hilstan Watts, and Ronald Davies. *Durban: A Study in Racial Ecology.* Jonathan Cape, 1958.

KATE TUTTLE

Duruma
Ethnic group of East Africa.
The Duruma primarily inhabit coastal northeastern TANZANIA and adjacent parts of KENYA. They speak a BANTU language and belong to the larger MIJIKENDA (Nyika) cultural and linguistic group. Approximately 180,000 people consider themselves Duruma.

See also ETHNICITY AND IDENTITY IN AFRICA: AN INTERPRETATION; LANGUAGES, AFRICAN: AN OVERVIEW.

Dusé Mohammed Ali
1866?–1945
Early and influential proponent of pan-Africanism.
Although information about Dusé Mohammed Ali's origins is sparse and inexact, Dusé claimed that he was born in Egypt to an Egyptian army officer and a Sudanese mother. In 1876 he was sent to England for an education. As a young man he took up acting and toured the United States and Canada before returning to England in 1898.

Dusé left acting in 1909 for a career as a journalist, publishing articles critical of British racism and imperialism in the *Islamic Review* and the *New Age*, a leading socialist literary journal. In 1911 Dusé published *In the Land of the Pharaohs*, a short anti-imperialist history of Egypt, much of which he was accused of plagiarizing. Nevertheless, the book enjoyed an enthusiastic reception among black intellectuals of the day.

In 1911 Dusé began to publish *African Times and Orient Review*. While the publication failed to gain a large circulation, its wide geographical distribution (subscribers lived in England, West Africa, the United States, the West Indies, and even Japan) meant that Dusé's ideas had a wide influence. He helped shape the ideas of the West Indian pan-Africanist Marcus Garvey, as well as Joseph CASELY-HAYFORD, an activist in the GOLD COAST (present-day GHANA).

In the *Review*, Dusé promoted the investment of capital in West African farming and commercial enterprises, unsuccessfully attempting to convince the British Colonial Office to provide loans. Following World War I (1914–1918), he proposed founding an African bank to help African traders erode the European trading monopoly. The Colonial Office declined to help finance the project, and Dusé could not raise the necessary $5 million himself.

Dusé settled in NIGERIA in 1931, where he became manager and editor of *The Comet*, a popular LAGOS newspaper. By 1933 the paper's circulation had reached 4,000, making it the top-selling weekly in Nigeria.

See also PAN-AFRICANISM.

ROBERT FAY

Dyula

Ethnic group of Côte d'Ivoire, Burkina Faso, Mali, Ghana, and Guinea-Bissau; also known as Jula, Diula, Wangara, and Kangah.

The term Dyula is a MANDE word meaning "itinerant trader" that refers both to the ethnic group and to the occupation for which they are best known. Little is known about the Dyula before the thirteenth century, when they emerged as the main trading class of the ancient MALI EMPIRE. Their Mande language suggests that they originated in the empire's heartland along the upper NIGER RIVER. The Dyula traveled throughout West Africa and traded GOLD, kola nuts (a natural stimulant), salt, and cloth. They played an important role in organizing the production of cloth and, according to some historians, spurred increased production of cloth and other trade goods during the sixteenth and seventeenth centuries. Along with trade goods, the Dyula also helped disseminate the advanced culture of the western SAHEL, including Islam, the dominant religion of the Dyula, as well as Arabic and Sudanic architecture.

Over the centuries most Dyula settled in large market towns, where they had greater trade opportunities. Frequently, this required them to live among other ethnic groups, such as the SENUFO, the MOSSI, and the ABRON, and to accept a second-class "stranger" status among the larger group. Over time Dyula groups became a permanent addition to the surrounding communities, although Dyula traders retained a distinct sense of identity and history through trade connections with other Dyula. During the sixteenth century, however, one group of Dyula traders living among the Senufo along the border of present-day CÔTE D'IVOIRE founded their own kingdom—KONG—that prospered until the late nineteenth century as a hub for trade routes radiating south into the forest and north into the Sahel.

Today, most Dyula still work in commerce, and many still produce textiles for trade. In many regions they continued to dominate long-distance trade in the 1990s. Many of them practice some form of subsistence farming. The Dyula are also known as Islamic scholars. Among some related groups, such as the BAMBARA, it is common for Islamic converts to refer to themselves as Dyula. Most Dyula children attend Koranic schools, and Dyula often view state-sponsored secular education with distrust. Though reliable numbers are difficult to come by, some 300,000 people consider themselves Dyula, though many more speak the language.

See also ETHNICITY AND IDENTITY IN AFRICA: AN INTERPRETATION.

ELIZABETH HEATH

E

East African Community
Regional organization that includes Uganda, Kenya, and Tanzania.

The East African Community (EAC) is modeled in part on the European Economic Community. It was created by the Treaty for East African Cooperation on June 6, 1967, to promote development through economic cooperation among its member states, KENYA, TANZANIA, UGANDA, BURUNDI, and RWANDA. Through the EAC, the member nations work to promote international trade, to create a shared customs union to regulate import and export taxes, and to cooperate in regional development programs. When the EAC was formed, the member states jointly owned the East African Railways Corporation, the East African Airways Corporation, the East African Harbours Corporation, and the East African Ports and Telecommunications Corporation. At that time the EAC was African's most comprehensive regional integration organization. Disputes among the members, however, led to the organization's disintegration in 1977, followed by a long process of dividing its assets and debts. During the 1980s and 1990s, each of the three then-current member nations (Burundi and Rwanda were only added in 2007) experienced economic problems that sparked renewed interest in regional cooperation. In March 1996, the East African Community was revived under the name Commission for East African Cooperation. The new union planned to create a common market and develop an open-border system for member countrie's citizens. It also aimed to establish regional cooperation in transport, communications (such as a digital telecommunications network), trade, industry, investment, customs, energy, tourism, and agriculture. In May 1998 the EAC proposed bringing member states into a still closer union by adopting a single currency—the East African shilling—and by establishing a regional court and legislative assembly with representatives from all of the member countries. A vote on the proposal was scheduled for November 1998, but political problems among the nations caused it to be postponed. Instead, in November 1999 a new treaty formally established the organization under its original name of the East African Community. The treaty also outlined a more modest program of cooperation among the nations. Since that time the EAC has held regular summit meetings and continued to promote regional economic cooperation. It has sponsored seminars to train negotiators in dealing with international financial bodies such as the World Trade Organization, and it has drafted a proposed plan for a regional customs union. The EAC has also played a role in regional infrastructure projects, such as the Lake Victoria Development Programme, begun in 2001 to bring unity to the many environmental laws, resource management programs, and transport systems that involve the lake.

ROBERT FAY

Eastern Cape
Province in southeastern South Africa.

Created in 1994, Eastern Cape covers 169,580 square kilometers (65,475 square miles) and includes the eastern half of the former Cape Province and the former bantustans (black homelands) of CISKEI and TRANSKEI. It is bounded on the south and southeast by the Indian Ocean, on the north by LESOTHO and the provinces of KWAZULU-NATAL and FREE STATE, and on the west by NORTHERN CAPE and WESTERN CAPE provinces. The population of Eastern Cape in 2006 was 6.9 million, most of whom are black Africans. XHOSA is the principal language, but Afrikaans and English are also spoken. The provincial government consists of a premier, an executive council of ten ministers, and a legislature. The provincial assembly and premier are elected for five-year terms, or until the next national election. Political parties are awarded assembly seats based on the percentage of votes each party receives in the province during the national elections. The assembly elects a premier, who then appoints the members of the executive council.

Eastern Cape has a varied topography and climate. Much of the province consists of rolling grasslands, but the northwest section is part of the sparsely vegetated Great Karroo (or Karoo), a large, arid plateau. Extensive forests cover the southern section of the province. A series of mountain ranges runs through the center of Eastern Cape, and the Witteberge Mountains and the Drakensberg Mountains rim the province's northeastern boundary. The Great Fish, the Keiskamma, and the Kei rivers flow through the region. Eastern Cape's coastal area receives abundant rainfall, but the interior is much drier and has had chronic drought problems. The city of East London, located on the coast, receives an average annual rainfall of 900 millimeters (36 inches), while Cradock, in the interior, receives an average annual rainfall of 310 mm (10 in). Most rain falls during the warmer months of October through April. Average temperatures in Eastern Cape range from 18° to 27° C (64° to 80° F) in the summer and from 8° to 20° C (46° to 68° F) in the winter.

Eastern Cape is an agricultural region, producing citrus and other fruits, maize (corn), and sorghum. The province also has cattle and sheep ranches. The leading manufacturing centers, East London and Port Elizabeth, are located on the coast. Port Elizabeth is noted for its automotive industry and its summer resorts. Resorts lie all along the coast of Eastern Cape.

Bisho, the capital of the province, served as the capital of Ciskei after the bantustan became nominally independent in 1981. Other significant cities are Aliwal North, Cradock, East London, Grahamstown, King William's Town, Elizabeth, Queenstown, Uitenhage, and Umtata. The province has four universities: Rhodes University (founded in 1904) in Grahamstown, the University of Transkei (1977) in Umtata, the University of Fort Hare (1916) in Alice, and the University of Port Elizabeth (1964).

Important historical and cultural sites in the province include the home of Olive SCHREINER, a prominent nineteenth-century novelist, in Cradock; the Settlers' National Monument in Grahamstown, which commemorates the contributions of English immigrants to SOUTH AFRICA; Lovedale, a mission school in Alice that was founded in 1841 for the education of black children; and the East London Museum, noted for its natural history collection. Many forts stand throughout the province as reminders of the numerous wars fought between white settlers and black Africans during the nineteenth century. Eastern Cape has two major wildlife reserves: Addo Elephant National Park and Mountain Zebra (Bergkwagga) National Park. Prominent antiapartheid leaders such as Stephen BIKO, Chris HANI, Nelson MANDELA, Govan Archibald Munyelwa MBEKI, Walter SISULU, and Oliver TAMBO were born in what is now Eastern Cape.

Ebira

Ethnic group of Nigeria; also known as Edbira, Egbura, and Igbira.

The Ebira primarily inhabit the Plateau, Bendel, and Kwara states of NIGERIA. They speak a Niger-Congo language and belong to the NUPE cultural and linguistic group. Approximately 1.4 million people consider themselves Ebira.

See also ETHNICITY AND IDENTITY IN AFRICA: AN INTERPRETATION; LANGUAGES, AFRICAN: AN OVERVIEW.

Ebola

Viral disease found primarily in Central Africa and Sudan.

Ebola hemorrhagic fever (EHF) is an infectious viral disease. Identified in 1976, the disease was named after the Ebola River in the DEMOCRATIC REPUBLIC OF THE CONGO (formerly known as ZAIRE), where the first cases were reported. According to the U.S. Centers for Disease Control, four subtypes of the virus have been identified. Ebola-Zaire, Ebola-Sudan, and Ebola-Côte d'Ivoire cause disease in humans. The fourth subtype, Ebola-Reston, has occurred in monkeys but has not been seen in humans.

The Ebola virus is a filovirus, which means that it causes hemorrhagic fever—high temperatures accompanied by bleeding. EHF spreads through direct contact with bodily fluids. Symptoms usually begin within two weeks after infection and consist of muscular pain, headache, and sore throat. As the disease progresses, patients become weak and nauseated. Within days, symptoms expand to inlcude vomiting, diarrhea, and rashes. Severe kidney and liver dysfunction follow and are associated with massive internal hemorrhaging and blood clotting. The disease tends to spread most rapidly in health-care settings, when medical attendants treat infected patients without wearing protective gear or when unsterilized hypodermic needles are used on multiple patients. Ebola-Zaire has been fatal in nearly 90 percent of diagnosed patients, while Ebola-Sudan has a mortality rate of 60 percent. No cure is known for EHF; the health-care response is to try to keep patients alive and and to contain infected persons in order to prevent further spread of the disease.

The life cycle of the Ebola virus is unknown, and researchers have been unable to determine how it first enters the human population. They believe, however, that the first patient in each outbreak becomes infected through contact with an infected animal. After that, the virus is transmitted from person to person. Because EHF quickly kills the majority of both human and monkey hosts, scientists believe that primates are not probably not the natural reservoir of the virus.

The first recognized outbreaks of EHF occurred in 1976 in what was then Zaire and in western SUDAN. Of the more than 550 people infected, 430 died. In 1979 in Sudan, thirty-four people were diagnosed with the virus, and twenty-two of them died. During a 1995 outbreak in Kikwit, in the Democratic Republic of the Congo, about 250 out of 315 infected people died. Outbreaks occurred early in the twenty-first century in UGANDA (2000–2001), GABON (2002), and the REPUBLIC OF THE CONGO (2002 and 2003). A more recent outbreak took place in Uganda in 2008. As is often the case, efforts to stop the spread of the virus were hampered by understaffed and underequipped medical facilities, as well as a generally poorly developed healthcare infrastructure.

Graphic publicity surrounding outbreaks of EHF in the 1990s raised fears of a worldwide epidemic, but the Ebola virus appears to be contained. Outbreaks seem to be self-limiting because hosts die quickly, before they can spread the virus to large numbers of others. For this reason the disease, although deadly, is not considered a large-scale public health risk.

BIBLIOGRAPHY

Morse, Stephen S. *Emerging Viruses*. Oxford University Press, 1993.

Rambhia, Kunal. *After Ebola Outbreak, Uganda Looks Back at Challenges*. University of Pittsburgh Medical Center, Center for Biosecurity, 2008.

Simpson, D. I. H. *Marburg and Ebola Virus Infections: A Guide for Their Diagnosis, Management, and Control*. World Health Organization, 1977.

ARI NAVE

Éboué, Félix
1884–1944
Highest-ranking French colonial administrator of African descent of his time, and a close friend and ally of French general Charles de Gaulle during World War II.

Félix Éboué was born in Cayenne, French Guiana. A very bright child with a nearly photographic memory, he was at the head of his primary school class. He received a French government scholarship to attend high school in Bordeaux, France, where he met René Maran, a Martinican-born Négritude writer. Éboué's passion for learning translated into a passion for politics, as the young man aligned himself with the Socialism of Jean Jaurès, publisher of the left-wing daily, l'Humanité. Éboué finished his secondary studies in 1905 and entered the French Colonial School in 1906 at a time when the colonial vocation was not considered incompatible with socialism.

After completing his studies in 1908, Éboué turned down a coveted position as colonial administrator in MADAGASCAR to take a similar position in the French Congo where he thought he could do more to help the people of his race. He immediately distinguished himself in his style of administration. When collecting taxes and recruiting porters for the rubber companies, Éboué preferred to negotiate and barter with local chiefs than use force to get them to comply, as many of his predecessors had. Éboué was also passionate about the economic development of Africa, believing that the material conditions of the colonial subjects would improve if they devoted more energy to agriculture and less to harvesting rubber. He introduced cotton in the Oubangui-Chari region in 1924, a crop that would become the cornerstone of the economy in FRENCH EQUATORIAL AFRICA.

Éboué's successful development projects and ability to convince hostile indigenous groups to join the French empire by peaceful means allowed him to rise quickly through the ranks of the colonial administration. For his long and arduous work in Africa, he was named secretary general of Martinique in 1932. Éboué brought the same style of leadership to this post that he had employed in Africa and was able to win the support of the local population expeditiously. Just thirty months later, though, he was sent back to Africa, where it was deemed that he could be more effective.

Over the next several years, Éboué spent time in both the Caribbean and Africa in positions of increasing authority. He was serving as governor of CHAD when World War II began in September 1939. The following June, the Germans conquered France and the French government in Vichy signed an armistice with the Nazis. French General Charles de Gaulle formed a government in exile called on the governors of the French colonies to lend their support to his movement. Éboué was the first to do so, and other colonial governors soon followed Éboué's courageous lead. Because of his actions, Éboué was condemned to death in absentia by a Vichy court in 1941, a sentence that was never carried out.

Throughout the war, Éboué provided assistance to de Gaulle's movement at every turn. It was therefore no surprise when, at the end of the war, de Gaulle turned to Éboué to organize the 1944 Brazzaville conference. This conference would redefine the relationship between colonizer and colonized in Africa, giving the colonies more autonomy and beginning the process that would eventually lead to their independence.

Exhausted by the war years in Africa and, in particular, by the complexities of the Brazzaville conference, Éboué requested three months' leave so that he could travel to the Middle East. After passing through the SUDAN, he arrived in CAIRO, EGYPT, where he intended to stay a short while before continuing on to Palestine, Syria, and Lebanon. However, he contracted pneumonia in Cairo, was admitted to the hospital on April 16, 1944, and died one month later. Éboué was mourned by many, especially by de Gaulle, who, in a letter to Éboué's widow, wrote that "Félix Éboué was my friend and nothing can make me forget the man, the companion, the brother in arms that he was to me during the greatest struggle of our time."

See also COLONIAL RULE.

RICHARD WATTS

Economic Community of West African States
Regional organization in West Africa.

Modeled after the European Economic Community, the Economic Community of West African States (ECOWAS) seeks to promote regional development through economic and diplomatic cooperation among its member states. The organization, created by the Treaty of Lagos on May 28, 1975, has fifteen members: BENIN, BURKINA FASO, CAPE VERDE, CÔTE D'IVOIRE, THE GAMBIA, GHANA, GUINEA, GUINEA-BISSAU, LIBERIA, MALI, NIGER, NIGERIA, SENEGAL, SIERRA LEONE, and TOGO. ECOWAS headquarters are located in LAGOS, NIGERIA. Leaders of the member countries meet once each year, but the organization is administered by a council that consists of two representatives from each member state. ECOWAS also oversees a tribunal and five commissions: Trade, Customs, Immigration, Monetary, and Payments; Industry, Agriculture, and Natural Resources; Transport, Communications, and Energy; Social and Cultural Affairs; and Administration and Finance. Among the commissions' goals are the elimination of tariffs and other regional trade barriers and the promotion of open borders for all citizens of the member countries. ECOWAS's original mission was to unite the small national markets of its members to create a regional market large enough to attract investment. For that purpose the member countries planned to eliminate tariffs on each other's goods between 1990 and 2000. Progress toward that goals was hampered by persistent tensions among individual member states and between the English-speaking bloc and the French-speaking bloc. In March 2004, however, ECOWAS announced that its members had agreed to form a common customs union by 2007. Such a union would be a significant step toward building a unified regional economy. Since 1981, the ECOWAS treaty has also included non-aggression and mutual defense agreements. ECOWAS's international defense force is the ECOWAS Military Observer Group (ECOMOG). During the 1990s, ECOMOG intervened in civil wars in Liberia and Sierra Leone. The effectiveness of the force, which is dominated by Nigerian troops, was widely questioned, but eventually it helped to end fighting in both countries. More recently, in 2003 ECOWAS launched ECOMIL in an effort to quell rebel violence during the civil war in Liberia.

ROBERT FAY

Economic Development in Africa
Promotion of economic activity in Africa through means such as education, creation of new businesses, more efficient production, improved financing, and enhanced transportation facilities.

For information on:

General ideas about economic development: See EDUCATION IN AFRICA; GLOBALIZATION AND AFRICA;

AN INTERPRETATION. African self-help economic development: See AFRICAN SOCIALISM; BOTSWANA; SOUTHERN AFRICAN DEVELOPMENT COMMUNITY; ECONOMIC COMMUNITY OF WEST AFRICAN STATES; SOUTH AFRICA; THEATER, AFRICAN. African American projects in Africa: See AFRO-ATLANTIC CULTURE: ON THE LIVE DIALOGUE BETWEEN AFRICA AND THE AMERICAS. Government-to-government programs: See COLD WAR AND AFRICA; DEVELOPMENT; Éboué, Felix; UNITED NATIONS IN AFRICA. Difficulties facing business growth and development: See POPULATION GROWTH IN SUB-SAHARAN AFRICA; EQUATORIAL GUINEA; GABON; KENYA; MALAWI.

Edo
Ethnic group numbering more than a million, living mostly in southern Nigeria.

The Edo people are one of the largest ethnic groups in NIGERIA, though not nearly as dominant as the YORUBA, HAUSA, or IGBO. Yoruba tradition holds that the Edo are an offshoot of the Yoruba. However, today the two group's languages are linguistically distinct, and anthropologists disagree about how closely related the two groups are. The Edo speak a Kwa language, also called Edo. Modern-day Edo descend from inhabitants of the ancient kingdom of Benin, centered in Benin City (not to be confused with the country of BENIN). The kingdom, which was established in the fourteenth century, grew to prominence in the fifteenth century. Much of Benin's power derived from its role in both the transatlantic and African slave trades.

Benin's influence waned in the eighteenth century as the Yoruban states, particularly the Oyo empire, gained power. Then, despite having had profitable and mostly peaceful relations with Portugal, the earliest European power in the area, Benin was ultimately toppled by the British. Benin's last powerful king, Oba Ovonramwen, was forced into exile when the British ended Benin's independence in 1897. After their empire fell, the Edo lived under British rule until Nigeria gained its independence in 1960. Throughout, the position of oba, or king, continued to be recognized by the Edo, although the role no longer carried political power.

In the postcolonial era most Edo have lived in villages and small towns in Nigeria's Bendel State. For the most part they are farmers, cultivating yams, maize (corn), and plantains and raising goats and sheep. While some Edo are Christian or Muslim, many still adhere to traditional religious beliefs. Ancestor worship plays a large role in traditional Edo philosophy. Along with the veneration of ancestors, Edo social structure recognizes age as the primary qualification for leadership, and within the villages, men's work is determined by their generational status.

The Edo are known for intricately carved wooden ram's heads, thought to represent dead patriarchs, that are lovingly guarded by families for generations. The artistry of Edo leather and bronzework is also renowned.

See also BENIN, EARLY KINGDOM OF; COLONIAL RULE; ETHNICITY AND IDENTITY IN AFRICA: AN INTERPRETATION; LANGUAGES, AFRICAN: AN OVERVIEW; OYO, EARLY KINGDOM OF; RELIGIONS, AFRICAN.

Education in Africa

History and status of Western-style schools in Africa.

Much education in Africa follows the Western model of schooling. But although Western-style education predominates, Islamic schools also operate throughout the continent. These schools, known as madrassa, teach followers lessons of the Qur'an (Koran). In some countries, such as MALAWI, Western-style and Qur'anic schools cooperate. In other places, Islamic schooling exists instead of Western schooling.

COLONIAL ORIGINS

European missionaries introduced Western-style education to Africa during the period of COLONIAL RULE. The goal of both Protestant and Catholic churches and missionaries was twofold: to convert Africans to their particular brands of Christianity, and to end slavery. Education in reading, writing, and scripture served both these interests.

But access to education was restricted by the colonial authorities, who also determined what subjects Africans could study and how long their educations would continue. Education was intended to prepare African children for "appropriate" roles. Sons of chiefs had privileged access to schooling, a practice that served both religious and political motives. Before independence, few African children attended school beyond the primary level, and primary education was by no means universal. By 1960, only 25 percent of primary-school-age children were in school, compared with twice that percentage in Latin America and Asia.

EDUCATION AND DEVELOPMENT SINCE INDEPENDENCE

Educational policies in Africa are based on the widely held belief that formal education is necessary for economic and social development. This belief grows out of the fact that in the second half of the twentieth century, Europe and parts of Asia and Latin America developed through industrialization, for which a set of skills, attitudes, and values borrowed from the Western world is considered a necessary first step. Schooling is a means toward this transformation.

The belief that education would bring economic and social benefits to newly independent African countries stimulated governments and citizens to invest in schooling. Many people viewed education as the means to a better life—a perception that was reinforced when educated Africans rose to leadership positions at independence. People came to see education as a reward for citizenship, one of the fruits of independence, and governments regarded it as necessary for building modern, productive economies and for forging national unity. Campaigns to Africanize national civil services by replacing Europeans with newly educated Africans fulfilled both economic goals and popular demands. Apart from its hoped-for economic and political returns, education came to be internationally recognized as a basic human right, like food, shelter, and health. Governments looked to mass education to help fight poverty.

Yet some parts of Africa have criticized Western-modeled education for assuming the importance of modern Western values, calling Western education elitist and neocolonial. But although some countries have experimented with alternatives, such as "Education for Self-Reliance" in TANZANIA and mass adult literacy programs in MOZAMBIQUE, there have been remarkably few efforts to radically restructure educational systems in Africa. Instead, reformers have targeted particular elements of the system, such as curriculum, teaching methods, or teacher training.

In independent Africa, ministries of education became responsible for providing, managing, inspecting, and supporting preprimary, primary, and secondary schools, universities, and colleges, including teacher training colleges as well as vocational, technical, and other training institutions. Education systems inherited from the colonial era were highly centralized, and African governments kept them centralized in order to build a sense of national identity and to ensure control over how education funds were spent. Many governments made education compulsory. The duration of compulsory education varies from eleven years in TUNISIA to four in ANGOLA, with an average of seven.

In the first years of independence, African educational systems expanded tremendously. Primary enrollment rose from 11.8 million in 1960 to 20.9 million in 1970 (not including SOUTH AFRICA and NAMIBIA). Secondary enrollment increased from 793,000 in 1960 to 2.5 million in 1970. Expansion was buoyed by citizens' demand for education and by governments' and organizations' faith that education would bring economic development. Yet although this expansion opened school doors to many groups who had not previously had access to formal education, it was not egalitarian. Most national educational

Literacy Rates in African Countries Country	% Literate (15 and over) Population
Algeria	70
Angola	42.0
Benin	40.9
Botswana	79.8
Burkina Faso	26.6
Burundi	51.6
Cameroon	79
Cape Verde	76.6
Central African Republic	51
Chad	47.5
Comoros	56.5
Congo, Democratic Republic of the	65.5
Congo, Republic of the	83.8
Côte d'Ivoire	50.9
Djibouti	67.9
Egypt	57.7
Equatorial Guinea	85.7
Eritrea	58.6
Ethiopia	42.7
Gabon	63.2
Gambia, The	40.1
Ghana	74.8
Guinea	35.9
Guinea-Bissau	42.4
Kenya	85.1
Lesotho	84.8
Liberia	57.5
Libya	82.6
Madagascar	68.9
Malawi	62.7
Mali	46.4
Mauritania	41.7
Mauritius	85.6
Morocco	51.7
Mozambique	47.8
Namibia	84.0
Niger	17.6

Literacy Rates in African Countries Country	% Literate (15 and over) Population
Nigeria	68.0
Réunion	88.9
Rwanda	64.7
São Tomé and Príncipe	79.3
Senegal	40.2
Seychelles	58
Sierra Leone	31.4
Somalia	37.8
South Africa	86.4
Sudan	61.1
Swaziland	81.6
Tanzania	78.2
Togo	60.9
Tunisia	74.2
Uganda	69.9
Western Sahara	N/A
Zambia	80.6
Zimbabwe	90.7

Source: U.S. Central Intelligence Agency, World Factbook 2003

systems served only about 50 percent of the school-age population, and, like colonial educational systems, they typically favored urban populations.

Overall, Africa's adult literacy rates have improved significantly. Approximately 62.5 percent of all adults were literate in 2003, compared with 27 percent in 1970. After research indicated that educated women have fewer children than uneducated ones, African countries focused on improving female access to education in the 1970s and 1980s. But gender inequality persists in literacy and in other aspects of education. About 71 percent of African men are literate, but only 54 percent of women. The gender gap in sub-Saharan education has, however, gotten smaller since 1980. Almost half of all students in the continent are female—on average, 45.5 percent in primary schools and 44.8 percent in secondary schools. The ratio is higher in some countries and much lower in others.

African educational systems continue to reflect the colonial heritage, particularly in their systems for testing and certifying students and for inspecting schools. Another legacy of the colonial era consisted of different rates of school enrollment in the French-speaking and English-speaking countries. By the 1980s, the former British colonies were approaching full primary-school enrollment, but in the former French colonies only 70 percent of children were receiving at least one year of primary schooling. The gap still exists, with school participation in French-speaking nations generally lagging behind. There are differences in human resources, as well. English-speaking African countries have fewer students per teacher than Francophone nations. The Sahelian countries of GUINEA-BISSAU, SENEGAL, THE GAMBIA, MAURITANIA, MALI, BURKINA FASO, NIGER, and CHAD, most of which are former French colonies, perform less well than the rest of the continent on many education indicators, including public expenditure on education, female enrollment rates, and male and female literacy rates.

EDUCATION REFORM AND ECONOMIC CRISIS

In the 1980s, economic crisis struck much of Africa. Most countries suffered a decline in real per capita income, and living standards fell back to or below 1960 levels. The effects of this setback continue to be felt in education; many African governments have been unable to sustain previous levels of funding. Although countries have continued to build schools to meet the demands of growing populations, inadequate resources have led to a decline in the quality of education.

African governments have turned to external funding to help finance the costs of education. Today it is taken for granted in most African countries that any type of education reform will require foreign aid. Now that most countries have undertaken structural adjustment reform programs that limit government spending on social services such as education, the influence of foreign funding agencies has grown. But although the help is necessary, the increase in outside control over the planning and running of Africa's educational systems simply furthers the continent's dependence and poverty.

Although per capita expenditure on education has declined since the 1980s, African governments still make significant investments in education. Around the turn of the century, countries spent an average of 18 percent of their per capita gross domestic product (GDP) on education. Wide variations existed among countries, however, from a low of 0.4 percent in Kenya in the years 1998 to 2002 to a high of 45.6 percent in Sudan in the years 1993 to 1997. In recent years, most African governments have devoted a larger share of their education budgets to primary and secondary education and a smaller share to higher education. In most African countries, between 80 and 90 percent of the education budget goes toward teacher's salaries, leaving very little for teaching materials—a lack that has contributed to the decline in the quality of schooling.

PLANS AND POLICIES

Approaches to education planning have changed. In the early years of independence, planning was guided by an approach called "social demand." Once governments made education compulsory and created a legal demand for schooling, the term became meaningless. During the 1970s, African governments experimented with "manpower planning," reflecting their view that the future was predictable, and that an education system could be designed to fulfill future labor needs. With the growing influence of financial institutions, such as the International Monetary Fund and the World Bank, over African economic planning, education is increasingly analyzed as an investment. In addition, educational policymaking in Africa makes increasing use of educational research.

Since the economic crises of the 1980s, critics have noted that although African education systems have expanded to serve more students, they have failed to

EDUCATING AFRICAN CHILDREN. English instruction at an Undugu school in Nairobi, Kenya, 2007. (*Sayyid Azim/AP Images*)

bring about higher employment rates, more equitable societies, or better governments. Another source of dissatisfaction is the way in which education reforms and plans are tailored to fit the economic policies set by foreign assistance agencies. The emphasis on efficiency, critics argue, comes at the expense of fairness and accountability to citizens, including students. Such criticisms have led to greater understanding of the complexities of the problems of education. Such negative features of African education systems as high dropout rates and grade repetitions are now being viewed as symptoms of deeper problems that must be better understood if education in Africa is to improve.

In recent years, a number of African countries have made changes in their centralized education systems. There is growing recognition of the need for a wider diversity of voices in making plans and policies for education. Under the old approaches, education planners tended to be separate from the schools where their plans were implemented. The new model of participatory planning, on the other hand, requires planners to be more practical and more closely connected to the schools. The challenge for African governments' education planning units is to move from crisis management to long-term strategic planning.

Education planners in Africa have long held the belief that schooling leads to improvements in individual lives and in national well-being. Today they continue to examine the relationship between education and social and economic change in Africa. This is good news, provided they look for answers to certain key questions: Education for whom? And for what?

One promising development is the emergence of African organizations focused on education. Some are regional research networks, such as the Educational

Research Network for Eastern and Southern Africa (ERNESA) and the Southern African Comparative and History of Education Society (SACHES). The Association for the Development of Education in Africa (ADEA), one of the leading groups, is a partnership between African education ministers and international funding agencies. The Forum for African Women Educationalists (FAWE) has national chapters throughout the continent to promote improvements in the education of girls and women.

See also CHRISTIANITY: MISSIONARIES IN AFRICA; DEVELOPMENT IN AFRICA: AN INTERPRETATION; HUMAN RIGHTS IN AFRICA; STRUCTURAL ADJUSTMENT IN AFRICA.

SUE GRANT LEWIS

Edward, Lake

Lake in east Central Africa; also known as Edward Nyanza.
Lake Edward, located in the DEMOCRATIC REPUBLIC OF THE CONGO and UGANDA, has an area of about 2,150 square kilometers (about 830 square miles) and lies 912 meters (2,990 feet) above sea level. It is connected on the northeast with Lake George (or Lake Dweru) in Uganda, by means of the Kazinga Channel. Lake Edward is fed by the Rutshuru River, a headstream of the White Nile. The lake has only one outlet, the Semliki River, which links it with Lake Albert to the north. High escarpments run along the western shore of the lake and mountains rise on the northwestern shore. The water is brackish with mineral salts. Many fish and crocodiles live in the lake, and waterfowl abound on its shores. The Anglo-American explorer Sir Henry Morton Stanley discovered the lake in 1889. The lake was formerly called Albert Edward Nyanza.

See also GEOMORPHOLOGY, AFRICAN.

Efik

Ethnic group living mostly in Nigeria's Cross River State, numbering approximately two million people.
The Efik speak a Niger-Congo language that shares many characteristics with that spoken by the IBIBIO. While they are historically linked with the Ibibio people, there is much disagreement about the origins of the Efik. Some Ibibio believe the Efik descend from YORUBA or other invaders (the name Efik means "oppressor" in the Ibibio language), but others see them as descended from an Ibibio group. Whatever their historical background, the Efik have long been known as fishers along the Cross River and as traders in Calabar (a name deriving from the Kalabari branch of the neighboring Ijaw ethnic group).

During the seventeenth, eighteenth, and nineteenth centuries the Efik played an important role in the salt and palm oil trades, forming business associations with the Europeans. Contact with Europeans brought CHRISTIANITY to the Efik, and most of them still practice that religion today. Traditional Efik social structure has persisted through the change from a fishing economy to a commercial economy. The heads of households—always male—elect among themselves a ward or village obung, or chief. Many men belong to Ekpe Societies, groups that uphold traditional Efik rituals, adjudicate local disputes, and serve as a kind of informal group government.

In the 1990s the Efik received attention from the West because they value excess weight in women. Many girls still enter the traditional "fattening room" in early adolescence to gain the abundant flesh that the Efik traditionally consider the ultimate in feminine beauty. Some Western observers applaud the Efik for their independence from commercially influenced cultural norms that value extreme thinness in women. Many authorities within NIGERIA, however, have warned them of the health risks associated with obesity.

See also ETHNICITY AND IDENTITY IN AFRICA: AN INTERPRETATION; LANGUAGES, AFRICAN: AN OVERVIEW.

Efutu

Ethnic group of Ghana; also known as Afutu and Fetu.
The Efutu primarily inhabit south-central GHANA and speak a Niger-Congo language. They originally belonged to the Guan cultural and linguistic group, but since the eighteenth century have assimilated with the surrounding FANTE people. Approximately 200,000 people consider themselves Efutu.

See also ETHNICITY AND IDENTITY IN AFRICA: AN INTERPRETATION; LANGUAGES, AFRICAN: AN OVERVIEW.

Egba

Ethnic group of Nigeria.
The Egba primarily inhabit southwestern NIGERIA. They speak YORUBA, a Niger-Congo language, and are one of the Yoruba peoples. Reliable numbers are difficult to come by, but population estimates for the Egba range from 300,000 to some two million.

See also ETHNICITY AND IDENTITY IN AFRICA: AN INTERPRETATION; LANGUAGES, AFRICAN: AN OVERVIEW.

Egypt

The nation in the northeastern corner of Africa, where a land bridge connects the continent with Asia; it borders the Mediterranean Sea to the north, Israel to the northeast, the Red Sea to the east, Sudan to the south, and Libya to the west.

Since ancient times, Egypt's cultural and political significance has extended far beyond its borders. Ancient Egypt, whose pharaohs first came to power nearly 5000 years ago, pioneered one of the world's earliest advanced civilizations. Ancient Egypt served as a crossroads between the Middle East and sub-Saharan Africa, and its culture and people included elements from both neighboring regions. During the Twenty-fifth Dynasty (about 770–657 B.C.E.), black pharaohs from the neighboring kingdom of Kush ruled Egypt, and links of trade and migration have linked Egypt with East and Central Africa since prehistoric times. The ancient Egyptians' distinctive culture, which developed in the fertile NILE RIVER Valley and Delta, surrounded by hostile deserts, provided a model for surrounding peoples, including the Greeks. By the fourth century B.C.E., however, the tide had turned, and Greek-speaking Macedonian invaders conquered Egypt. Repeatedly over the centuries, Egypt has undergone foreign domination and exploitation only to reemerge as a powerful cultural and political center across wide areas of Africa and the Middle East. After three centuries as the center of the powerful Ptolemaic Empire, Egypt was conquered by the Romans, who made it a province of their own empire and appropriated its agricultural surplus to feed Roman soldiers and citizens.

Conquered by Muslim Arab armies during the seventh century C.E., Egypt became the center of the powerful MAMLUK STATE during the thirteenth century. Subdued by the Ottoman Turks during the sixteenth century, Egypt went on to conquer large parts of present-day SUDAN and the Arabian Peninsula under Muhammad Ali after 1805. Virtually a colony of Great Britain by 1900, Egypt emerged as a champion of Arab nationalism under Gamal Abdel NASSER in 1952. Today Egypt's significance revolves around its cultural and political leadership in the Arab world and its important role in Middle Eastern geopolitics.

GREEK AND ROMAN DOMINANCE

In 332 B.C.E., Alexander the Great conquered Egypt. He ended the rule of the pharaohs, which had endured through thirty dynasties for nearly 2600 years before his conquest. Alexander's conquest initiated a period of Hellenic dominance in Egypt that lasted nearly a millennium. In the struggle for power after Alexander's death, Egypt became a separate kingdom under the reign of Ptolemy, who had been one of Alexander's Macedonian guards. The Ptolemaic Dynasty continued for 300 years until the Romans conquered Egypt in 30 B.C.E. and dethroned CLEOPATRA, the last of the Ptolemies. Unlike the Ptolemies, the Romans ruled Egypt from afar, while a heavy Roman military presence enforced the export of Egypt's rich grain to nourish Rome's heartland in (modern) Italy.

By the fourth century C.E. most Egyptians had converted to CHRISTIANITY. The establishment of a new imperial capital at Constantinople marked the beginning of Egypt's Byzantine period (330–640 C.E.). During this time Egyptians adopted the Greek alphabet for writing the Egyptian language, which had until then still been written in demotic, a form of writing based on hieroglyphics. This final form of the Egyptian language is known as Coptic, the language of the Coptic Orthodox Church in Egypt today.

EMERGENCE OF ISLAMIC EGYPT

When the prophet Muhammad united the peoples of Arabia under his leadership in Mecca in about 630 C.E., his Muslim Arab warriors became a potent new force that quickly and easily destroyed the old world order. They forced the Byzantine Empire to retreat north into Anatolia (now part of Turkey), as the Arabs took control of Syria and Egypt, and later North Africa and the Iberian Peninsula. The Arab conqueror of Egypt, Amr ibn al-'As, defeated the Byzantine forces at Heliopolis in 640. In Egypt as elsewhere, non-Muslim subjects had to pay an extra tax. However, the Arabs allowed the overwhelmingly Coptic Christian Egyptians to live freely. Under Ibn al-'As, Egyptians enjoyed a period of relative prosperity, tolerance, and peace.

The Umayyad Dynasty (661–750), however, which ruled Egypt from Syria, began to incorporate Egyptians into Muslim society. Arabic became the official language rather than Coptic or Greek, and the empire promoted a new inclusive Muslim identity rather than an exclusive Arab identity. The empire also allowed the migration of Arabian tribes into Egypt to settle. The conversion of a majority of Egyptians to Islam and the replacement of spoken Egyptian by Arabic, however, took several more centuries to complete.

In the Abbasid period (750–945), power over affairs in Egypt vacillated between the centralized authority of the empire in the Abbasid capital of Baghdad (in modern Iraq) and the local rulers of Egypt, who used Egypt's wealth to raise armies and challenge the authority of Baghdad. During both the Umayyad and the Abbasid eras, the empire used soldier-slaves—often Turkish or Circassian—as an alternative source of military power. They had been bought as young men outside Muslim lands, converted to Islam, trained in the arts of warfare and statecraft, and employed

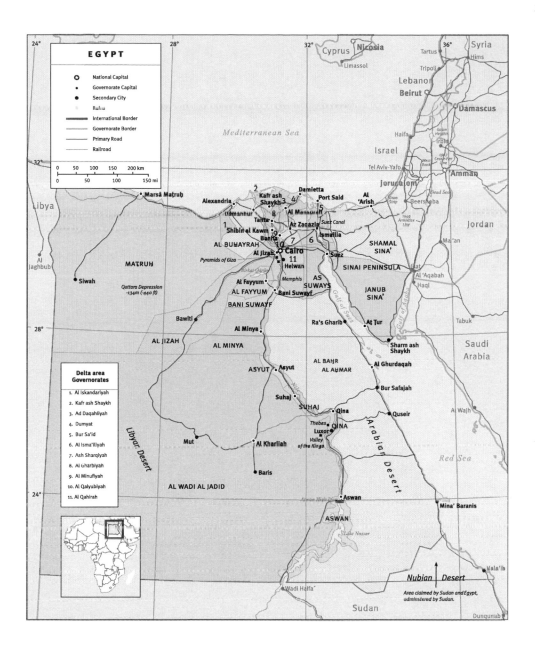

to maintain a loyal military force for the central ruler. These regiments of slaves, rewarded for their loyalty with various favors, became power brokers in Baghdad and often seized power themselves. In 834, Turkish soldier-slaves received the governorship of Egypt in exchange for their military support for the caliph (the Islamic ruler) in Baghdad, and several times Turkish governors became so powerful that they ruled Egypt autonomously. The most famous of these was Ahmad ibn Tulun, who ruled Egypt from 868 to 884.

The next ruling Dynasty was the Fatimids, who belonged to a Shi'ite sect of Islam. They had established a state in present-day TUNISIA, and they set out to challenge the Sunni Muslim Abbasids for control of the Muslim world. Their empire eventually expanded west and east to cover all of North Africa, the Levant, and parts of the Arabian Peninsula. In 969 the Fatimids conquered Egypt and moved their capital there; Egypt became the center of an empire again, rather than a mere province and granary. The Fatimids founded al-Qahira, or modern CAIRO, as their capital. After two centuries of rule, however, the Fatimid Empire began to crumble. In 1169 the Fatimid rulers in Egypt had to call on the forces of their former Sunni enemies in Syria to repulse the European Crusader invaders. The commander of these forces was Salah al-Din al-Ayyubi, known in Western history as Saladin, the leader who expelled the Crusaders from the Middle East. Salah al-Din not only successfully defended

Egypt from the Crusaders, but also replaced the Fatimid ruler and founded a brief Dynasty of his own, known today as the Ayyubids.

The Mamluks quickly succeeded the Ayyubids. The word Mamluk means "owned" in Arabic, and the Mamluks were originally the slave armies of the Ayyubid rulers. In 1250 the Mamluks took power from the ruling Ayyubids and formed their own Dynasty, which was to last formally until 1517. The Mamluk era is divided into two periods, that of the Bahri and that of the Borji Mamluks. In the first period under the Bahri Mamluks, Egypt became the center of the Middle Eastern Islamic world. Controlling the lucrative trade routes connecting the Red Sea (by which ships brought the spices and silks of Asia) and the Mediterranean, the Bahri Mamluks grew rich. The Dynasty supported the arts, and the Bahri era was generally one of great prosperity and cultural development. Under the Borji Mamluks after 1382, however, Egypt, racked by natural disasters and repeated outbreaks of the bubonic plague, entered a period of decline.

Competition among leading Mamluk families further devastated Egypt's ecology and social fabric. The crops the ruling families collected from peasants as tribute or taxes allowed the Mamluks to purchase more slaves and expand their military power, which in turn enabled them to increase their demands on peasants for taxes. However, this practice often forced desperate peasants to abandon settled life and flee into the desert as nomads. In the long run, this overexploitation ruined Egypt's prosperity. Meanwhile, at the end of the fifteenth century, Egypt lost its vital monopoly over trade from the Indian Ocean to the Mediterranean and Europe when the Portuguese began using the sea route around the Cape of Good Hope. As the infighting among the Mamluks increased, their rule became more chaotic and decentralized, and they were unable to face the rising new power of the Middle East, the Ottomans.

The Ottomans were Turkish tribes originally from central Asia who had gradually conquered the Byzantine Empire. At the beginning of the sixteenth century the Ottoman Empire, under Selim the Magnificent, turned its attention to Persia, the Middle East, and North Africa. Ottoman forces arrived in Egypt in 1517. They successfully employed the new military technologies that were sweeping both Europe and the Middle East. The use of powerful firearms had changed the techniques, organization, and cost of warfare and contributed to the rise of larger, more centralized states in the western Atlantic and Mediterranean. The Ottomans exacted taxes and tribute to maximize the flow of wealth back to Istanbul, the new name given to the old Byzantine capital of Constantinople. Once again Egypt had become the granary of a distant

TOURISM. Throughtout much of its modern history, Egypt has enjoyed a robust tourism industry, with travelers from every part of the world eager to see the country's historic landmarks. Photo, c. early 1900s. (*Prints and Photographs Division, Library of Congress*)

empire. However, as time progressed, the Ottoman state relied on the Mamluks to govern Egypt. By the end of direct Ottoman rule in Egypt at the close of the eighteenth century, the Mamluks had once again brought the country to the brink of complete ruin. By 1800 the population of Egypt had declined to between three and five million, whereas in the days of the pharaohs it was estimated at thirty million. In comparison, the population of Egypt was estimated at 74 million in 2003.

MUHAMMAD ALI AND THE EMERGENCE OF MODERN EGYPT

Ottoman power reached its zenith around 1600. Over the next two centuries, rising European powers managed to turn back Ottoman expansion. Napoleon's invasion of Egypt in 1798 shook the Ottoman world. Napoleon attacked Egypt to establish French dominance there and preempt any similar move on the part of the British. His modern armies, supplied with the new weapons of the nascent industrial era in Europe, easily routed the Mamluk forces.

OFFICIAL VISIT. President Jimmy Carter and Egyptian president Anwar Sadat during the latter's visit to Washington, DC, April 1980. Among the most important statesmen in modern Middle-Eastern history, Sadat was the first Arab leader to officially recongnize the state of Israel. (*Prints and Photographs Division, Library of Congress*)

In a pattern that has been repeated to this day, Egypt became a theater of European geopolitical designs. The British aided the Ottoman rulers in ousting the French and reestablishing Ottoman control over Egypt. The British had decided that the Ottoman Empire should serve as a buffer state against Russian expansion. The vulnerable Ottoman Empire gained renewed vitality by virtue of its strategic location between two rival imperialist powers and on the major communications and trade routes with British India and the Far East.

However, local interests disrupted the best-laid imperialist plans. In Egypt Muhammad Ali, the Ottoman military commander sent by Istanbul in 1801 to evacuate the French, had designs of his own. Muhammad Ali recognized the importance of the industrial revolution happening in Europe. He worked to industrialize Egypt and, in particular, to industrialize its military. In order to finance imports of European factories and advisers, the government exported first food grains and later sugar and long-staple cotton. Egypt's resulting military strength allowed it to conquer parts of the Arabian Peninsula during the 1810s and much of present-day Sudan during the 1820s.

Muhammad Ali's regime sought economic as well as military power. It organized Egypt's farms into one large state enterprise run by state administrators. The state also monopolized trade. To maximize state revenues, Muhammad Ali banned Europeans from trade within Egypt. Egypt dealt directly with European traders only at the Mediterranean port of ALEXANDRIA. This trade monopoly angered British and French merchants, and neither London nor Paris looked favorably upon Muhammad Ali's military and economic ambitions. When the British prompted the Ottoman rulers to enforce special trading privileges for European merchants throughout the Ottoman Empire, they forced Muhammad Ali to relinquish his trade monopolies, withdraw his troops from Anatolia, Syria, and the Arabian Peninsula, and reduce the size of his army. In return, in 1841 he received the hereditary title Khedive of Egypt. While still nominally a part of the Ottoman Empire, Egypt became, in fact, a modern Dynasty of Muhammad Ali and his descendants, lasting until 1952.

Muhammad Ali's son, Said, and his grandson, Ismail, continued their forebear's drive for modernization, but their relationship with the European powers differed significantly. Unlike Muhammad Ali, his son and grandson accepted foreign loans and granted concessions to European contractors. Their financial inexperience and the unscrupulousness of international lenders brought financial troubles and eventually the loss of political autonomy.

Said and Ismail vastly expanded the physical infrastructure of Egypt. They commissioned railroads, irrigation schemes, ports, and other communications and transport facilities, but their investments left the Egyptian government deeply indebted. The SUEZ CANAL typified their predicament. The French engineer Ferdinand de Lesseps manipulated the Egyptians into providing the land and labor and borrowing most of the capital for the project, in return for which the Egyptians received almost nothing. The canal was completed in 1869; by 1875 the British government under Prime Minister Benjamin Disraeli had bought the indebted Egyptian government's majority share of stock, and the Egyptians lost control over this vital communications and commercial link, built with Egyptian funds on Egyptian territory.

The increasing contact with Europe also brought new cultural trends. Said and Ismail founded schools to train Egyptian personnel capable of administering the rapidly modernizing economy. Religious thinkers who had always seen Islam as the highest achievement of humanity tried to understand the new precarious position of the Muslim world in relation to European domination. They championed a return to the scriptural roots of Islam. Their call for pan-Islamic resistance to European dominance sparked the first of the modern Islamist cultural movements. The movement spread among the urban elite of the emerging national community of Egypt. At the same time, there were those who attempted to marginalize the influence of religion in daily life and to adopt the more secular attitudes of contemporary Europe.

Debt led to two significant developments: European control of the country and the advent of private property in agricultural land, previously owned by the state. When Egypt began to default on its loans to European bankers, a joint French-British agency intervened in 1876 to oversee government tax collection and the fulfillment of Egypt's

THE SECOND LIBRARY OF ALEXANDRIA. An Egyptian fishing boat sails past the Bibliotheca Alexandrina in 2001, shortly before the library's official opening. (*Amr Nabil/AP Images*)

financial obligations to European bankers. Private property came into being when the government attempted to raise domestic revenue by granting private property rights in exchange for current payment of future taxes. However, Ismail's modernization of the Egyptian military had created an Egyptian officer corps that increasingly resented European encroachment on Egyptian sovereignty. When one of these officers, Ahmad 'Urabi Pasha, led a revolt against the Europeans and their Egyptian allies, the British used the opportunity to begin a military occupation of the country in 1882 that was to last until 1954.

EGYPT UNDER BRITISH DOMINATION

The British exercised increasingly effective control over the affairs of the country, although they allowed the khedive to remain as the nominal ruler of Egypt and left most government offices in the hands of Egyptians. However, a British adviser oversaw each Egyptian government ministry. The British blocked efforts by Egyptian nationalist intellectuals and khedive Abbas Khilmi, who came to the throne in 1892, to resist British rule. In 1898 Egyptian and British forces jointly reconquered Sudan, which had declared its independence in 1885. Meanwhile, the British administration streamlined the Egyptian economy into an efficient agricultural export machine. A new class of wealthy Egyptian landowners supported the British in the development of the cotton and sugar export economy. In 1907, however, these Egyptian landowners began to demand more control over the economy through the establishment of a national bank. This would become part of the institutional basis of modern Egyptian nationalism.

At the onset of World War I (1914–1918), when the Ottoman Empire sided with Germany, the British declared that Egypt no longer belonged to the Ottomans. The British declared Egypt a protectorate in 1914 and ruled through martial law during the war. Though the 1918 Versailles Treaty and the new League of Nations promoted the *concept* of individual nations' right to self-determination, the League actually helped perpetuate European COLONIAL RULE over Africa and Asia. The European victors at Versailles granted a mandate over Egypt to the British. Such paternalism deeply offended Egyptian nationalists, who formed a committee to travel to London and Paris to ask for a seat at the League of Nations and to claim their right to self-determination. In response, British authorities arrested the Egyptian leaders and deported them to the SEYCHELLES. This British act of repression provoked a mass outpouring of nationalist protest and unrest in Egypt. In response, the British backed a 1922 declaration of "independence" that limited Egyptian sovereignty and preserved British control of the military, the Suez Canal, and the Sudan, which they then jointly ruled with Egypt. The British retained this control by exploiting internal political divisions in Egypt, particularly the competing claims of the royal family, who sought to retain a role in Egyptian politics, and the nationalists, who wished sovereignty to lie only with the Egyptian people. The British helped devise a constitution granting extensive powers to the new king (the former sultan), including the power to dismiss the nationalist-dominated Parliament. Thus during the 1920s and 1930s there were frequent dismissals of Parliament and ensuing protests.

Egyptian industrialization and urbanization accelerated during these decades; these processes gave rise to class divisions and mass politics. During the 1930s in particular, new mass organizations contrasted with the more elitist parties that had previously dominated the Parliament. The most significant of the new organizations was the Muslim Brotherhood. It was established in 1928—not by a member of the religious establishment, but by a lay state schoolteacher—in order to spread institutions supporting Muslim morality. The Brotherhood built schools, student associations, and social organizations to aid the poor. Though not formally a political party, the Brotherhood was to become a powerful force in Egyptian society.

At the same time, the currents of Arab nationalism were developing throughout the Arab world. This movement sought first and foremost to overcome European imperialism, but it also held a larger humanist vision combining social equality, rationalist social planning, and cultural modernism. Arab nationalism promised economic progress for the wide segments of society excluded by the elitist economic and political structure of much of the Middle East until then, and it would inspire the coup that deposed Egypt's British client monarchy.

Egypt (At a Glance)

FORMER NAME:
United Arab Republic (with Syria)

OFFICIAL NAME:
Arab Republic of Egypt

AREA:
1,001,450 sq km (about 386,662 sq mi)

LOCATION:
North Africa, on the Mediterranean Sea, bordered by the Gaza Strip, the Red Sea, Sudan, and Libya

CAPITAL:
Cairo (population 16 million; 2006 estimate)

OTHER MAJOR CITIES:
Alexandria (population 4,110,015), Giza 2,681,863), Port Said (570,603), Suez (510,935) (2006 estimates)

POPULATION:
81,713,520 (2008 estimate)

POPULATION DENSITY:
81 persons per sq km (211 per sq mi; 2008 estimate)

POPULATION BELOW AGE 15:
Total population: 31.8 percent (male 13,292,961; female 12,690,711; 2008 estimate)

POPULATION GROWTH RATE:
1.682 percent (2008 estimate)

TOTAL FERTILITY RATE:
2.72 children born per woman (2008 estimate)

LIFE EXPECTANCY AT BIRTH:
Total population: 71.85 years (male 69.3 years; female 74.52 years; 2008 estimate)

INFANT MORTALITY RATE:
28.36 deaths per 1000 live births (2008 estimate)

LITERACY RATE (AGE 15 AND OVER WHO CAN READ AND WRITE):
Total population: 71.4 percent (male 83 percent; female 59.4 percent; 2008 estimate)

EDUCATION:
Compulsory for five years for children between the ages of 6 and 13; 93 percent of primary school-age children were enrolled in school in 2000. Secondary school enrollment was 79 percent that year, including vocational and teacher training schools. About one-fifth of college-age Egyptians attend universities or other institutions of higher education. Egypt has 13 state universities, as well as numerous technical colleges and institutes of art and music.

LANGUAGES:
Arabic is the official language; English and French are also used by educated classes.

ETHNIC GROUPS:
Egyptians, Bedouins, and Berbers of Hamitic descent make up 99 percent of the population, while Greek, Nubian, Armenian, and other European groups (mostly Italian and French) make up the remaining 1 percent.

RELIGIONS:
Muslim, 90 percent; Coptic, 9 percent; Christian and other, 1 percent

CLIMATE:
Hot, dry, and dusty over most of the country; the hot season is from May to September and the cool season from November to March. In the coastal region, average annual temperatures range from a maximum of 37° C (99° F) to a minimum of 14° C (57° F). Wide variations of temperature occur in the deserts, ranging from a maximum of 46° C (114° F) during daylight hours to a minimum of 6° C (42° F) after sunset. During the winter season desert temperatures often drop to 0° C (32° F). The most humid area is along the Mediterranean coast, where the average annual rainfall is about 200 mm (8 in). Precipitation decreases rapidly to the south; Cairo receives on average only about 29 mm (1.1 in) of rain a year, and in many desert locations it may rain only once in several years.

LAND, PLANTS, AND ANIMALS:
Egypt is situated on a desert plateau bisected by the Nile River. Less than one-tenth of the country is settled or under cultivation, principally along the valley and delta of the Nile, in desert oases, and around the Suez Canal. Over 90 percent of the country is desert, including the Libyan Desert west of the Nile, the Arabian Desert in the east, and the Nubian Desert in the south. The Sinai Peninsula consists of sandy desert in the north and rugged mountains in the south. The vegetation of Egypt is confined largely to the Nile Delta, the Nile Valley, and the oases. Wild animals include gazelles, desert foxes, hyenas, jackals, wild asses, boars, jerboas, mongooses, lizards, poisonous snakes, crocodiles, hippopotamuses, and numerous species of birds and insects.

NATURAL RESOURCES:
Petroleum, natural gas, iron ore, phosphates, manganese, limestone, gypsum, talc, asbestos, lead, and zinc.

CURRENCY:
The Egyptian pound

GROSS DOMESTIC PRODUCT (GDP):
$405.4 billion (2007 estimate)

GDP PER CAPITA:
$5,000 (2007 estimate)

GDP REAL GROWTH RATE:
7.1 percent (2007 estimate)

PRIMARY ECONOMIC ACTIVITIES:
Agriculture (32 percent of employment), fishing, oil production, manufacturing, tourism, and other services

PRIMARY AGRICULTURAL PRODUCTS:
Cotton, rice, maize (corn), wheat, beans, fruits, vegetables; cattle, water buffalo, sheep, goats, and fish

INDUSTRIES:
Textiles, food processing, chemicals, petroleum, construction, cement, and metals

PRIMARY EXPORTS:
Crude oil and petroleum products, cotton yarn, raw cotton, textiles, metal products, chemicals, fruits, and vegetables

PRIMARY IMPORTS:
Machinery and equipment, foodstuffs, chemicals, wood products, and fuels

PRIMARY TRADE PARTNERS:
United States and European Union

GOVERNMENT:
Constitutional republic. The executive branch is led by President Mohammed Hosni Mubarak, nominated by the 454-member People's Assembly (last elected in late 2005; the next elections are slated for 2010) and validated by a national, popular referendum. The prime minister (currently Atef Mohammed Abeid) and the Cabinet are appointed by the president. The legislature comprises the 454-seat People's Assembly, currently dominated by Mubarak's National Democratic Party, and the 264-seat Advisory Council, which plays only a consultative role.

Barbara Worley

ARAB NATIONALISM AND POSTCOLONIAL EGYPT

During World War II Egypt played an important role in the Allied war effort; after the war popular demands grew for true political independence from the British, and, more important, for social development. A few very wealthy landowners and industrialists monopolized political and economic power in Egypt. These elites engaged in petty strivings for personal power and ignored the economic and political concerns of the Egyptian people. With popular frustration mounting, the ineptness and defeat of the Egyptian army in the first Arab-Israeli war in 1948 finally triggered the collapse of the old order.

Two political currents were capable of challenging Egypt's entrenched elites: the Muslim Brotherhood and the Arab nationalists. Arab nationalist soldiers, led by Gamal Abdel Nasser, seized the moment in July 1952 and toppled the monarchy in a coup d'état. At first the Brotherhood and the nationalists maintained an uneasy alliance, for though many of their ideals and goals coincided, they had some fundamental philosophical disagreements, particularly around the issue of religion. By 1954 relations between the two groups had soured, and Nasser, who became prime minister in April 1954, began a campaign of repression against the Brotherhood.

Nasser's legitimacy depended on his ability to overcome the social, economic, and political problems that the former regime had been unable to resolve, one of which was the occupation of the Suez Canal zone by British troops. Nasser negotiated a British evacuation in 1954. In 1956 he nationalized the Suez Canal after the United States and the World Bank refused to help finance the ASWAN HIGH DAM. In response, the French, British, and Israelis mounted an attack on Egypt that the Egyptians could not repel. The attack, though successful, provoked a worldwide reaction against what was clearly an imperialist war. Both the United States and the Soviet Union demanded that the attacking forces withdraw. The result was a resounding political victory for Nasser and the Egyptians.

In retaliation for the attack, Nasser confiscated the property of British and French firms operating in Egypt. These initial confiscations were clearly political in nature and not part of an overall economic strategy. However, as the Cold War spurred the superpowers' involvement in the Arab world, Egypt increasingly turned to the Soviet Union, both as a patron and a model. By the early 1960s Egypt was building a state socialist economy. The state undertook extensive industrial development, and, though markets still functioned, the state controlled prices for most products. In agriculture, the state confiscated the land of the very wealthy landowners and leased it to landless peasants; it set up cooperatives to raise agricultural productivity and channeled the surplus into urban industrial investment. The government introduced laws that protected peasants from eviction even when they could not pay rents, and made rental agreements hereditary on both private and state land. All of these measures aimed to improve the livelihoods of the middle and lower income classes upon whose support Nasser relied.

However, Nasser's Arab nationalism suffered a humiliating setback. In 1967 growing tensions between Israel and the Arab nations of Egypt, Jordan, and Syria erupted in the Six-Day War. The Israeli army seized Egypt's Sinai Peninsula and other Arab territories. Following Nasser's death in 1970, his successor, Anwar al-Sadat, decided to reposition Egypt geopolitically by spurning Soviet aid and aligning with the United States. Sadat hoped that U.S. mediation could resolve the conflict with Israel and that U.S. aid would help Egypt to grow economically. As part of this realignment, Sadat traveled to Israel in 1977 at the invitation of Israeli prime minister Menachem Begin to begin peace negotiations. Sadat's perceived betrayal of the Palestinian and Arab nationalist cause sparked outrage in the Arab world, and Arab leaders expelled Egypt from the Arab League.

Sadat turned away from state-led industrialization and moved to liberalize the Egyptian economy. He removed controls that prohibited foreign multinationals from operating in Egypt; he also lessened restrictions on foreign commodities and opened Egyptian markets to multinational competition. Still, the government has been slow to abandon the state-owned industrial structure, and the agricultural laws protecting peasants from eviction were only effectively repealed in 1997. Because of Egypt's strategic importance, the United States has tolerated Egypt's hesitation to privatize and deregulate its economy; it has not forced Egypt to follow a strict structural adjustment program, even though Egypt receives the second-largest share of U.S. foreign aid.

Meanwhile, another force was rising in the Middle East: a reorganized Islam-based (or Islamist) political opposition. Most of the Arab nationalist regimes adopted secularism and socialism. Islamist ideology fundamentally opposed these secular tendencies and the reliance on Western, albeit socialist, visions of modern society. Saudi Arabia and its major Western ally, the United States, had supported and funded the Islamist political opposition during the 1960s and 1970s, and Saudi support for some groups continued into the 1980s and possibly later. The power of the Organization of Petroleum Exporting Countries' (OPEC) oil cartel and the incredible flow of wealth into the Arabian Peninsula after 1973 further shifted power within the Middle East away from the Arab nationalist regimes and toward U.S.-aligned Saudi Arabia and the Gulf States.

In Egypt, Sadat's political maneuvers also fostered the growth of Islamist political movements. Nasser's regime had imprisoned many Islamist political leaders in order to curtail opposition, but this repression, in fact, bred more strident opposition. Sadat attempted to use the Islamist opposition for his own political ambitions by abandoning socialist policies and releasing many of Nasser's political prisoners. Ironically, his attempt to court the Islamists proved deadly for him. The infusion of jail-hardened leadership strengthened many Islamist groups, and they began to mobilize against the Sadat regime after its accommodation with Israel and the United States and its failure to follow an Islamist program. Perceiving a threat to his regime, Sadat arrested 1,300 opposition leaders in September 1981. Angered by the arrests and his rapprochement with Israel, radical Islamists assassinated Sadat the following month.

Egypt under Sadat's successor, President Hosni MUBARAK, has faced increasing pressure from populist Islamist groups who often represent those dissatisfied with the absence of true democracy and the lack of substantial economic progress, particularly among the poor. The regime has faced military attacks by political Islamist groups throughout the nation, and Mubarak has relied primarily upon the military to defend his regime. In 1992 a series of attacks in southern Egypt provoked a large-scale military crackdown. The military failed to suppress the militant opposition completely, and in 1995 attacks resumed, this time at popular tourist sites. Tourism represents one of three main sources of foreign exchange for Egypt, aside from foreign aid; the others are worker remittances and oil. Hence, the attacks on tourist sites aimed to destroy the economy and bring down the regime. The worst such attack, in Luxor in late 1997, showed that the military strategy has not been able to root out such groups.

Under Mubarak the Egyptian regime has undertaken partial democratization, though limited by the fear of religiously inspired opposition groups. Political parties are allowed to operate in Egypt, but only those few approved by the regime. Upon coming to power President Mubarak promised to accept the constitutional limit of two terms; however, during his second term he urged Parliament to amend the constitution so that he could legally remain in power. He is currently the longest-serving leader in Egypt's modern history. The largest Islamist political group is the Muslim Brotherhood, which is still legally prohibited from political work. The Brotherhood represents a moderate form of Islamist opposition, and it exerts its power through participation in other, legal political parties. During the 1990s, Mubarak's continued reliance on the military and his ban on Islamist political opposition threatened his regime's stability, particularly when ordinary Egyptians continued to face economic hardship. The September 11, 2001, terrorist attacks on the U.S. further diminished tourism revenues, adding to Egypt's economic challenges. Citing the lingering economic crisis and political corruption, in 2003 the Muslim Brotherhood and other opposition groups unleashed scathing criticisms of the Mubarak government, the worst criticism the president has faced since taking power. Turning around Egypt's slow economy may depend on the development of a gas export market.

In recent years, Egypt has come under new scrutiny for reported human rights violations, especially those related to the torture of nominal enemy combatants in the so-called War on Terror. A 2008 report from Amnesty International found the entrenchment of governmental powers "that have been used systematically to violate human rights, including prolonged detention without charge, torture and other ill-treatment, restrictions on freedom of speech, association and assembly, and grossly unfair trials before military courts and special emergency courts." To date, however, such criticism has failed to affect any substantial change in Cairo's policy regarding detention and the treatment of prisoners. Meanwhile, terrorism in Egypt—much of it fueled by Islamic extremism—continues to be a problem. A series of attacks in 2005 struck Sharm el-Sheikh—killing eighty-eight people and injuring more than 150 others—as well as Cairo. A year later, several explosions wracked Dahab, a resort city on the Sinai Peninsula, killing two dozen.

Despite this, in the early twenty-first century, Egypt continues to be the cultural center of the Arab world. Egyptian television, videos, and music are seen and heard throughout the Arab world, and intellectuals from throughout the Arabic-speaking world congregate in Egypt, especially Cairo. Egypt plays a leading role in Arab regional politics as well as in international diplomacy. Egypt, or "the mother of the world" in local parlance, thus maintains its role as a vibrant political and cultural center in the modern world, a role it has played repeatedly since ancient times.

See also AFRICAN SOCIALISM; ALEXANDRIA AND GRECIAN AFRICA: AN INTERPRETATION; COLD WAR AND AFRICA; CRUSADES; EGYPT, ANCIENT KINGDOM OF; EGYPTIAN MYTHOLOGY; ISLAM IN AFRICA; KUSH, EARLY KINGDOM OF; LIBYA; SLAVERY IN AFRICA; STRUCTURAL ADJUSTMENT IN AFRICA.

CHARLES SCHMITZ

Egypt, Ancient Kingdom of

Ancient African civilization centered in the Nile Delta and the lower Nile Valley.

The origins of ancient Egyptian civilization, which many regard as one of the fountainheads of Western culture, cannot be established with certainty. Archaeological evidence suggests that early dwellers in the Nile Valley were influenced both by the cultures of the Middle East and by surrounding African cultures. Describing the development of Egyptian civilization, like attempts to identify its intellectual foundations, is largely a process of conjecture based on archaeological discoveries of enduring ruins, tombs, and monuments, many of which contain invaluable specimens of the ancient culture. Inscriptions in hieroglyphs, for instance, have provided priceless data.

The framework for the study of the Dynastic Period of Egyptian history, between the First Dynasty and the Ptolemaic period, relies on the Aegyptiaca of Manetho, a Ptolemaic priest of the third century B.C.E., who organized the country's rulers into thirty dynasties, roughly corresponding to families. General agreement exists on the division of Egyptian history, up to the conquest of Alexander the Great, into Old, Middle, and New kingdoms with intermediate periods, followed by the late and Ptolemaic periods. New evidence and increasingly sophisticated dating techniques, however, have allowed continual refinement of chronology and genealogy.

PREHISTORY AND EARLY DYNASTIC PERIOD

Some 60,000 years ago the NILE RIVER began its yearly inundation of the land along its banks, leaving behind rich alluvial soil. Areas close to the floodplain became attractive as a source of food and water. In time, climatic changes, including periods of aridity, further served to confine human habitation to the Nile Valley, although this was not always true. From the Chalcolithic period (the Copper age, beginning about 4000 B.C.E.) into the early part of the Old Kingdom, people apparently used an extended part of the land.

In the seventh millennium B.C.E., EGYPT was environmentally hospitable, and evidence of settlements from that time has been found in the low desert areas of Upper (southern) Egypt. Remains of similar occupation have been discovered at NUBIAN sites in modern SUDAN. Enough pottery has been found in Upper Egyptian tombs from the fourth millennium B.C.E. (in the Predynastic Period) to establish a relative dating sequence. The Predynastic Period, which ends with the unification of Egypt under one king, is generally subdivided into three parts, each of which refers to a site at which its archaeological materials were found: Badarian, Amratian (Naqada I), and Gerzean (Naqada II and III). Sites in Lower (northern) Egypt (from about 5500 B.C.E.) have yielded datable archaeological material of apparent cultural continuity but no long-term sequences such as those found in Upper Egypt.

Archaeological sources indicate the emergence, by the late Gerzean period (about 3200 B.C.E.), of a dominant political force that was to become the consolidating element in the first united kingdom of ancient Egypt. The earliest known hieroglyphic writing dates from this period, and soon afterwards the names of early rulers began to appear on monuments. This period began with a Zero Dynasty, which had as many as thirteen rulers, ending with Narmer (about 3000 B.C.E.). It was followed by the First and Second dynasties (about 2920–2770 B.C.E.), during which at least seventeen kings ruled the land. Some of the earliest massive mortuary structures (predecessors of the pyramids) were built at Saqqara, Abydos, and elsewhere during the First and Second dynasties.

OLD KINGDOM AND FIRST INTERMEDIATE PERIOD

The Old Kingdom (2575–2134 B.C.E.) spanned nearly five centuries of rule by the Fourth through the Eighth dynasties. The capital was in the north, at Memphis, and the ruling monarchs held absolute power over a strongly unified government. Religion played an important role; in fact, the government had evolved into a theocracy, wherein the pharaohs, as the rulers were called, were both absolute monarchs and, possibly, gods on earth.

The Third Dynasty was the first of the houses that ruled from Memphis. Its second ruler, Zoser (Djoser), who reigned about 2630–2611 B.C.E., emphasized national unity by balancing northern and southern motifs in his mortuary buildings at Saqqara. His architect, Imhotep, used stone blocks rather than traditional mud bricks in the complex there, thus creating the first monumental structure of stone; its central element, the Step Pyramid, was Zoser's tomb. In order to deal with affairs of state and to administer construction projects, the king began to develop an effective bureaucracy. In general, the Third Dynasty marked the beginning of a golden age of cultural freshness and vigor.

The Fourth Dynasty began with King Sneferu, whose building projects included the first true pyramid at Dashur, south of Saqqara. Sneferu, the earliest warrior king for whom extensive documents remain, campaigned in NUBIA (or Kush) and LIBYA and was active in the Sinai. Promoting commerce and mining, he brought prosperity to the kingdom. Sneferu was succeeded by his son Khufu (or Cheops), who built the Great Pyramid at Giza. Although little else is known of his reign, that monument not only attests to his power but also indicates the administrative skills the bureaucracy had gained. Khufu's son Redjedef, who reigned about 2528–2520 B.C.E., introduced the solar element (Ra, or Re) into royal titles and the Egyptian religion. Khafre, (or Chephren), another son of Khufu, succeeded his brother to the throne and built his mortuary complex at Giza. The remaining rulers of the dynasty included Menkaure, or Mycerinus, who reigned about 2490–2472 B.C.E. He is known primarily for the smallest of the three large pyramids at Giza.

Under the Fourth Dynasty, Egyptian civilization reached a peak in its development, and this high level was generally maintained in the Fifth and Sixth dynasties. The splendor of the engineering feats of the pyramids was approximated in every other field of endeavor, including architecture, sculpture, painting, navigation, the industrial arts and sciences, and astronomy. It was during this period astronomers first created a solar calendar based on a year of 365 days. Old Kingdom physicians also displayed a remarkable knowledge of physiology, surgery, the circulatory system of the body, and antiseptics.

Although the Fifth Dynasty maintained prosperity with extensive foreign trade and military incursions into Asia, signs of decreasing royal authority became apparent in the swelling of the bureaucracy and the enhanced power of nonroyal administrators. The last king of the dynasty, Unis, who reigned about 2356–2323 B.C.E., was buried at Saqqara, with a body of religious spells, called Pyramid Texts, carved on the walls of his pyramid chamber. Such texts were also used in the royal tombs of the Sixth Dynasty. Several autobiographical inscriptions of officials under the Sixth Dynasty indicate the decreasing status of the monarchy. Records even indicate a conspiracy against King Pepi I, who reigned about 2395–2360 B.C.E., in which the ruler's wife was involved. It is believed that during the later years of Pepi II, who reigned about 2350–2260 B.C.E., power may have been in the hands of his vizier (chief minister). Central authority over the economy was also diminished by decrees of exemption from taxes. The nomarchs—governors of nomes (districts)—were rapidly becoming individually powerful, as they began to remain in place rather than being periodically transferred to different nomes.

The Seventh Dynasty marked the end of the Old Kingdom and the beginning of the First Intermediate Period. As a consequence of internal strife, the reigns of this and the succeeding Eighth Dynasty are rather obscure. It is clear, however, that both ruled from Memphis and lasted a total of only sixteen years. By this time the powerful nomarchs were in effective control of their districts, and factions in the south and north vied for power. Under the Heracleopolitan Ninth and Tenth dynasties, the nomarchs near Heracleopolis controlled their area and extended their power north to Memphis (and even into the delta) and south to Asyut (Lycopolis). The rival southern nomarchs at THEBES established the Eleventh Dynasty, controlling the area from Abydos to Elephantine, near Syene (present-day Aswan). The early part of this dynasty, the first of the Middle Kingdom, overlapped the last part of the Tenth.

MIDDLE KINGDOM AND SECOND INTERMEDIATE PERIOD

Without one centralized government, the bureaucracy was no longer effective, and nomarchs openly championed regional concerns. Egyptian art became more provincial, and no massive mortuary complexes were built. The religion was also democratized, as commoners claimed prerogatives previously reserved for royalty alone. They could, for instance, use spells derived from the royal Pyramid Texts on the walls of their own coffins or tombs.

Although the Middle Kingdom (2040–1640 B.C.E.) is generally dated to include all of the Eleventh Dynasty, it properly begins with the reunification of the land by Nebhepetre Mentuhotep, who reigned 2061–2010 B.C.E. The early rulers of the dynasty attempted to extend their control from Thebes both northward and southward, but it was left to Mentuhotep to complete the reunification process, sometime after 2047 B.C.E. Mentuhotep ruled for more than fifty years, and despite occasional rebellions, he maintained stability and control over the whole kingdom. He replaced some nomarchs and limited their power, which was still considerable. Thebes was his capital, and his mortuary temple at Dayr al Bahri incorporated both traditional and regional elements; the tomb was separate from the temple, and there was no pyramid.

The reign of the first Twelfth Dynasty king, Amenemhat I, was peaceful. He established a capital near Memphis and, unlike Mentuhotep, de-emphasized Theban ties in favor of national unity. Nevertheless, he gave the important Theban god Amon prominence over other deities. Amenemhat demanded loyalty from the nomarchs, rebuilt the bureaucracy, and educated a staff of scribes and administrators. The literature was predominantly propaganda designed to reinforce the image of the king as a "good shepherd" rather than as an inaccessible god. During the last ten years of his reign, Amenemhat ruled with his son as coregent. *The Story of Sinuhe*, a literary work of the period, implies that the king was assassinated.

Amenemhat's successors continued his programs. His son, Senwosret I, who reigned 1971–1926 B.C.E., built fortresses throughout Nubia (or Kush) and established trade with foreign lands. He sent governors to Palestine and Syria and campaigned against the Libyans in the west. Senwosret II, who reigned 1897–1878 B.C.E., began land reclamation in Al Fayyūm. His successor, Senwosret III, who reigned 1878–1841 B.C.E., had a canal dug at the first cataract of the Nile, formed a standing army (which he used in his campaign against the Nubians), and built new forts on the southern frontier. He divided the administration into three powerful geographic units, each controlled by an official under the vizier, and he no longer recognized provincial nobles. Amenemhat III continued the policies of his predecessors and extended the land reform. A vigorous renaissance of culture took place under the Theban kings. The architecture, art, and jewelry of the period reveal an extraordinary delicacy of design, and the time was considered the golden age of Egyptian literature.

The rulers of the Thirteenth Dynasty—some fifty or more in about 120 years—were weaker than their predecessors, although they were still able to control Nubia and the administration of the central government. During the latter part of their rule, however, their power was challenged not only by the rival Fourteenth Dynasty, which won control over the delta, but also by the Hyksos, a little-known group of people who invaded from western Asia. By the Thirteenth Dynasty there was a large Hyksos population in northern Egypt. As the central government entered a period of decline, their presence made possible an influx of people from coastal Phoenicia (roughly, present-day Lebanon) and Palestine (present-day Israel, Gaza, and the West Bank) and the establishment of a Hyksos Dynasty. This marks the beginning of the Second Intermediate Period, a time of turmoil and disunity that lasted for some 214 years. The Hyksos of the Fifteenth Dynasty ruled from their capital at Avaris in the eastern delta, maintaining control over the middle and northern parts of the country. At the same time, the Sixteenth Dynasty also existed in the delta and Middle Egypt, but it may have been subservient to the Hyksos. More independence was exerted in the south by a third contemporaneous power, the Theban Seventeenth Dynasty, which ruled over the territory between Elephantine and Abydos. The Theban ruler Kamose, who reigned about 1555–1550 B.C.E., battled the Hyksos successfully, but it was his brother, Ahmose I, who finally subdued them, reuniting Egypt.

NEW KINGDOM AND THIRD INTERMEDIATE PERIOD

With the unification of the land and the founding of the Eighteenth Dynasty by Ahmose I, the New Kingdom (1550–1070 B.C.E.) began. Ahmose reestablished the borders, goals, and bureaucracy of the Middle Kingdom and revived its land-reclamation program. He maintained the balance of power between the nomarchs and himself with the support of the military, who were accordingly rewarded. The importance of women in the New Kingdom is illustrated by the high titles and position of the royal wives and mothers.

Once Amenhotep I, who reigned 1525–1504 B.C.E., had full control over his administration—he was coregent for five years—he began to extend Egypt's boundaries in Nubia and Palestine. A major builder at Karnak, Amenhotep, unlike his predecessors, separated his tomb from his mortuary temple; he began the custom of hiding his final resting place. Thutmose I continued the advances of the new Imperial Age and emphasized the preeminence of the god Amon. His tomb was the first in the VALLEY OF THE KINGS. Thutmose II, his son by a minor wife, succeeded him, marrying the royal princess Hatshepsut to strengthen his claim to the throne. He maintained the accomplishments of his predecessors. When he died in 1479 B.C.E., his heir, Thutmose III, was still a child, and so Hatshepsut governed as a regent. Within a year, she had herself crowned pharaoh, and then mother and son ruled jointly. When Thutmose III achieved sole rule upon Hatshepsut's death in 1458 B.C.E., he reconquered Syria and Palestine, which had broken away under joint rule, and then continued to expand his empire. His annals in the temple at Karnak chronicle many of his campaigns. Nearly twenty years after Hatshepsut's death, he ordered the obliteration of her name and images. Amenhotep II, who reigned 1427–1401 B.C.E., and Thutmose IV tried to maintain the Asian conquests in the face of growing threats from the Mitanni and Hittite states of western Asia, but they found it necessary to use negotiations as well as force.

Amenhotep III ruled peacefully for nearly four decades, 1386–1349 B.C.E., and art and architecture flourished during his reign. He maintained the balance of power among Egypt's neighbors by diplomacy. His son and successor, Akhenaton, (Amenhotep IV) was a religious reformer who fought the power of the Amon priesthood. Akhenaton abandoned Thebes for a new capital, Akhetaton, which was built in honor of Aton, the disk of the sun on which his new monotheistic religion centered. The religious revolution was abandoned toward the end of his reign, however, and his son-in-law, Tutankhamen, returned the capital to Thebes. Tutankhamen is known today chiefly for his richly furnished tomb, which was found nearly intact in the Valley of the Kings by the British archaeologists Howard Carter and Lord Carnarvon in 1922. The Eighteenth Dynasty ended with Horemheb, who reigned 1319–1307 B.C.E.

The founder of the Nineteenth Dynasty, Ramses I (1307–1306 B.C.E.), had served his predecessor as vizier and commander of the army. Reigning only two years, he was succeeded by his son, Seti I, who reigned 1306–1290 B.C.E. and led campaigns against Syria, Palestine, the Libyans, and the Hittites. Seti built a sanctuary at Abydos.

Like his father, he favored the delta capital of Pi-Ramesse (now Qantir). One of his sons, Ramses II, succeeded him and reigned for nearly sixty-seven years. Ramses II was responsible for much construction at Luxor and Karnak, and he built the Ramesseum (his funerary temple at Thebes), the rock-cut temples at Abu Simbel, and sanctuaries at Abydos and Memphis. After campaigns against the Hittites, Ramses made a treaty with them and married a Hittite princess. His son Merneptah, who reigned from 1224 to 1214 B.C.E., defeated the Sea Peoples, invaders from the Aegean who swept the Middle East in the thirteenth century B.C.E., and records tell of his desolating Israel. Later rulers had to contend with constant uprisings by subject peoples of the empire.

The second ruler of the Twentieth Dynasty, RAMSES III, had his military victories depicted on the walls of his mortuary complex at Medinet Habu, near Thebes. After his death the New Kingdom declined, chiefly because of the rising power of the priesthood of Amon and the army. One high priest and military commander even had himself depicted in royal regalia.

The Twenty-First through the Twenty-Fifth dynasties are known as the Third Intermediate Period. Kings ruling from Tanis, in the north, vied with a line of high priests, to whom they appear to have been related, from Thebes, in the south. The rulers of the Twenty-First Dynasty may have been partially Libyan in ancestry, and the Twenty-Second Dynasty began with Libyan chieftains as kings. As the Libyan's rule deteriorated, several rivals rose to challenge them. In fact the next two dynasties, the Twenty-Third and Twenty-Fourth, were contemporaneous with part of the Twenty-Second Dynasty, just as the Twenty-Fifth (Kushite) Dynasty effectively controlled much of Egypt during the latter years of the Twenty-Second and the Twenty-Fourth dynasties.

LATE PERIOD

The Twenty-Fifth through the Thirty-First dynasties ruled Egypt during the time that has come to be known as the Late Period. The Kushites ruled from about 767 B.C.E. until they were ousted by the Assyrians (from present-day Iraq) in 671 B.C.E. Egyptian independence was reestablished early in the Twenty-Sixth Dynasty by Psammetichus I. A resurgence of cultural achievement, reminiscent of earlier epochs, reached its height in the Twenty-Sixth Dynasty. When the last Egyptian king was defeated by Persian king Cambyses in 525 B.C.E., the country entered a period of Persian domination under the Twenty-Seventh Dynasty. Egypt reasserted its independence under the Twenty-Eighth and Twenty-Ninth dynasties, but the Thirtieth Dynasty was the last one of Egyptian rulers. The Thirty-

First Dynasty, which is not listed in Manetho's chronology, represented the second Persian domination.

HELLENISTIC AND ROMAN PERIODS

The occupation of Egypt by the forces of Alexander the Great in 332 B.C.E. brought an end to Persian rule. Alexander, who came from Macedonia in present-day Greece, appointed Cleomenes of Naucratis, a Greek resident in Egypt, and his Macedonian general, known later as Ptolemy I, to govern the country. Although two Egyptian governors were named as well, power was clearly in the hands of Ptolemy, who in a few years took absolute control of the country.

Rivalries with other generals, who carved out sections of Alexander's empire after his death in 323 B.C.E., occupied much of Ptolemy's time, but in 305 B.C.E. he assumed the royal title and founded the Ptolemaic Dynasty. Ptolemaic Egypt was one of the great powers of the Hellenistic world, and at various times it extended its rule over parts of Syria, Asia Minor (present-day Turkey), Cyprus, Libya, Phoenicia, and other lands.

Partly because indigenous Egyptian rulers had a reduced role in affairs of state during the Ptolemaic regime, they periodically demonstrated their dissatisfaction by open revolts, all of which were, however, quickly suppressed. In the reign of Ptolemy VI, Egypt became a protectorate under Antiochus IV of Syria, who successfully invaded the country in 169 B.C.E. The Romans, however, forced Antiochus to give up the country, which was then divided between Ptolemy VI and his younger brother, Ptolemy VIII. The latter took full control upon the death of his brother in 145 B.C.E. The succeeding Ptolemies preserved the wealth and status of Egypt while continually losing territory to the Romans. CLEOPATRA was the last great ruler of the Ptolemaic line. In an attempt to maintain Egyptian power she aligned herself with Julius Caesar and, later, Mark Antony, but these moves only postponed the end. After her forces were defeated by Roman legions under Octavian (later Emperor Augustus), Cleopatra committed suicide in 30 B.C.E.

For nearly seven centuries after the death of Cleopatra, the Romans controlled Egypt (except for a short time in the third century C.E., when it came under the power of Queen Zenobia of Palmyra, in present-day Syria). The Romans treated Egypt as a valuable source of wealth and profit and were dependent on its supply of grain to feed their multitudes. Roman Egypt was governed by a prefect, whose duties as commander of the army and official judge were similar to those of the pharaohs of the past. The office, therefore, was one with which the Egyptian population was familiar. Because of the immense power of the prefects, however, their functions were eventually divided under Emperor Justinian, who in the sixth century

C.E. put the army under a separate commander, directly responsible to him.

Egypt in the Roman period was relatively peaceful; its southern boundary at Aswan was only rarely attacked by the Ethiopians. Egypt's population had come under the influence of Greek culture under the Ptolemies, and it included large minorities of Greeks and Jews, as well as other peoples from Asia Minor. The mixture of the cultures did not lead to a homogeneous society, and civil strife was frequent. In 212 C.E., however, Emperor Caracalla granted the entire population citizenship in the Roman Empire.

ALEXANDRIA, the port city on the Mediterranean founded by Alexander the Great, remained the capital as it had been under the Ptolemies. One of the great metropolises of the Roman Empire, it was the center of a thriving commerce between India and Arabia and the Mediterranean countries. It was the home of the great Alexandrian library and museum and had a population of some 300,000 (excluding slaves).

Egypt became an economic mainstay of the Roman Empire not only because of its annual harvest of grain but also for its glass, metal, and other manufactured products. In addition, the Indian Ocean trade brought in spices, perfumes, precious stones, and rare metals from the Red Sea ports. Once part of the empire, Egypt was subject to a variety of taxes as well.

In order to control the people and placate the powerful priesthood, the Roman emperors protected the ancient religion, completed or embellished temples begun under the Ptolemies, and had their own names inscribed on them as pharaohs; the cartouches of several can be found at Isna, Kawn Umbu, Dandara, and Philae. The Egyptian cults of ISIS and Serapis spread throughout the ancient world. Egypt was also an important center of early Christendom and the first center of Christian monasticism. Its Coptic or Monophysite church separated from mainstream Christianity in the fifth century C.E.

During the seventh century the power of the Eastern Roman (Byzantine) Empire was challenged by the Sassanids of Persia, who invaded Egypt in 616. Byzantine forces expelled them again in 628, but soon after, in 641, the country fell to the Arabs, who brought with them a new religion, Islam, and began a new chapter of Egyptian history.

See also ALEXANDRIA AND GRECIAN AFRICA: AN INTERPRETATION; CHRISTIANITY, AFRICAN: AN OVERVIEW; ROMAN AFRICA: AN INTERPRETATION.

Egyptian Mythology

The religious beliefs of the ancient Egyptians were the dominating influence in the development of their culture, although a true religion, in the sense of a unified theological system, never existed among them. The Egyptian faith was based on an unorganized collection of ancient myths, nature worship, and innumerable deities. In the most influential and famous of these myths a divine hierarchy is developed and the creation of the earth is explained.

CREATION

According to the Egyptian account of creation, only the ocean existed at first. Then Ra, the sun, came out of an egg (a flower, in some versions) that appeared on the surface of the water. Ra brought forth four children, the gods Shu and Geb and the goddesses Tefnut and Nut. Shu and Tefnut became the atmosphere. They stood on Geb, who became the earth, and raised up Nut, who became the sky. Ra ruled over all. Geb and Nut later had two sons, Set and Osiris, and two daughters, ISIS and Nephthys. Osiris succeeded Ra as king of the earth, helped by Isis, his sister-wife. Set, however, hated his brother and killed him. Isis then embalmed her husband's body with the help of the god Anubis, who thus became the god of embalming. The powerful charms of Isis resurrected Osiris, who became king of the netherworld, the land of the dead. Horus, who was the son of Osiris and Isis, later defeated Set in a great battle and became king of the earth.

LOCAL GODS

From this myth of creation came the conception of the ennead, a group of nine divinities, and the triad, consisting of a divine father, mother, and son. Every local temple in Egypt possessed its own ennead and triad. The greatest ennead, however, was that of Ra and his children and grandchildren. This group was worshiped at Heliopolis, the center of sun worship. The origin of the local deities is obscure; some of them were taken over from foreign religions, and some were originally the animal gods of prehistoric Africa. Gradually, they were all fused into a complicated religious structure, although comparatively few local divinities became important throughout Egypt. In addition to those already named, the important divinities included the gods Amon, Thoth, Ptah, Khnemu, and Hapi, and the goddesses Hathor, Mut, Neit, and Sekhet. Their importance increased with the political ascendancy of the localities where they were worshiped. For example, the ennead of Memphis was headed by a triad composed of the father Ptah, the mother Sekhet, and the son Imhotep. Therefore, during the Memphite dynasties, Ptah became one of the greatest gods in Egypt. Similarly, when the Theban dynasties ruled Egypt, the ennead of THEBES was given the most importance, headed by the father Amon, the mother Mut, and the son Khonsu. As the religion became more involved, true deities were sometimes confused with human beings who had been glorified after death. Thus, Imhotep, who was originally the chief minister of the Third Dynasty ruler Zoser (Djoser), was later regarded as a demigod. During the Fifth Dynasty the pharaohs began to claim divine ancestry and from that time on were worshiped as sons of Ra. Minor gods, some merely demons, were also given places in local divine hierarchies.

ICONOGRAPHY

The Egyptian gods were represented with human torsos and human or animal heads. Sometimes the animal or bird expressed the characteristics of the god. Ra, for example, had the head of a hawk, and the hawk was sacred to him because of its swift flight across the sky; Hathor, the goddess of love and laughter, was given the head of a cow, which was sacred to her. Anubis was given the head of a jackal because these animals ravaged the desert graves in ancient times. Mut was vulture headed, Thoth was ibis headed, and Ptah was given a human head, although he was occasionally represented as a bull, called Apis. Because of the gods to which they were attached, the sacred animals were venerated, but they were never worshiped until the decadent Twenty-Sixth Dynasty. The gods were also represented by symbols, such as the sun disk and hawk wings that were worn on the headdress of the pharaoh.

SUN WORSHIP

The only important god who was worshiped with consistency was Ra, chief of cosmic deities, from whom early Egyptian kings claimed descent. Beginning with the Middle Kingdom (2040–1640 B.C.E.), Ra worship acquired the status of a state religion, and the god was gradually fused with Amon during the Theban dynasties, becoming the supreme god Amon-Ra. During the Eighteenth Dynasty the pharaoh Amenhotep III renamed the sun god Aton, an ancient term for the physical solar force. Amenhotep's son and successor, Amenhotep IV, instituted a revolution in Egyptian religion by proclaiming Aton the true and only god. He changed his own name to Akhenaton, meaning "He who is devoted to Aton." This first great monotheist was so iconoclastic that he had the plural word *gods* deleted from monuments, and he relentlessly persecuted the priests of Amon. Akhenaton's sun religion failed to survive, although it exerted a great influence on the art and thinking of his time, and Egypt returned to its ancient, labyrinthine polytheism after Akhenaton's death.

BURIAL RITUAL

Burying the dead was of religious concern in Egypt, and Egyptian funerary rituals and equipment eventually became the most elaborate the world has ever known. The Egyptians believed that the vital life force was composed of several psychical elements, of which the most important was the ka. The ka, a duplicate of the body, accompanied the body throughout life and, after death, departed from the body to take its place in the kingdom of the dead. The ka, however, could not exist without the body; every effort had to be made, therefore, to preserve the corpse. Bodies were embalmed and mummified according to a traditional method supposedly begun by Isis, who mummified her husband Osiris. In addition, wood or stone replicas of the body were put into the tomb in the event that the mummy was destroyed. The greater the number of statue-duplicates in his or her tomb, the more chances the dead person had of resurrection. As a final protection, exceedingly elaborate tombs were erected to protect the corpse and its equipment.

After leaving the tomb, the souls of the dead supposedly were beset by innumerable dangers, and the tombs were therefore furnished with a copy of the BOOK OF THE DEAD. Part of this book, a guide to the world of the dead, consists of charms designed to overcome these dangers. After arriving in the kingdom of the dead, the ka was judged by Osiris, the king of the dead, and forty-two demon assistants. The Book of the Dead also contains instructions for proper conduct before these judges. If the judges decided the deceased had been a sinner, the ka was condemned to hunger and thirst or to be torn to pieces by horrible executioners. If the decision was favorable, the ka went to the heavenly realm of the fields of Yaru, where grain grew 3.7 meters (12 feet) high and existence was a glorified version of life on earth. All the necessities for this paradisiacal existence, from furniture to reading matter, were, therefore, put into the tombs. As a payment for the afterlife and his benevolent protection, Osiris required the dead to perform tasks for him, such as working in the grain fields. Even this duty could, however, be obviated by placing small statuettes, called ushabtis, into the tomb to serve as substitutes for the deceased.

See also EGYPT, ANCIENT KINGDOM OF.

Ekiti

Ethnic group of Nigeria.

The Ekiti primarily inhabit Ondo State and Kwara State in western NIGERIA. They speak Yoruba, a Niger-Congo language, and are one of the YORUBA peoples. As many as 1.6 million people consider themselves Ekiti.

See also ETHNICITY AND IDENTITY IN AFRICA: AN INTERPRETATION; LANGUAGES, AFRICAN: AN OVERVIEW.

Ekoi

Ethnic group of western Cameroon and eastern Nigeria known for its unique written script.

Originally hunters and warriors who migrated from the north, today most Ekoi are either farmers, growing yams and palms, or urban workers, especially in NIGERIA's Cross River State. Ekoi society has historically been politically decentralized, with councils of elders governing village affairs. The men's Leopard Society, the Ngbe or Ekpe, also plays a judicial role, while priestesses of the women's Numm Association oversee certain kinds of domestic relations.

Some historians believe that the Ekoi invented Nsibidi, a complex writing system based on signs and pictograms, around the turn of the twentieth century. The term Nsibidi also referred to a secret society of executioners, and the Ngbe's use of the Nsibidi script reinforced the Leopard Society's judicial authority. The script and its symbolic power, along with Ekoi art and dance, all reached the Americas during the transatlantic slave trade. They appear in Cuba, and the Nsibidi script is believed to have influenced the writings of runaway slaves in Guyana and Suriname. Approximately 150,000 people consider themselves Ekoi.

See also ETHNICITY AND IDENTITY IN AFRICA: AN INTERPRETATION; LANGUAGES, AFRICAN: AN OVERVIEW.

ERIC YOUNG

Ekonda

Ethnic group of the Democratic Republic of Congo.

The Ekonda primarily inhabit the Equateur Province of western Congo, also known as Congo-Kinshasa. They speak a BANTU language and belong to the Mongo cultural and linguistic group. Approximately 300,000 people consider themselves Ekonda.

See also ETHNICITY AND IDENTITY IN AFRICA: AN INTERPRETATION; LANGUAGES, AFRICAN: AN OVERVIEW.

Ekwensi, Cyprian

1921–2007

Nigerian novelist, short-story writer, and author of children's literature, who has portrayed the moral and material problems faced by rural West Africans as they migrate to the city.

Born Cyprian Duaka Odiatu Ekwensi in Minna, NIGERIA, Ekwensi began his secondary education at Government College in IBADAN, completing it at Achimota College in present-day GHANA (then called the GOLD COAST) in 1943. In the early 1950s he studied pharmacy at the Chelsea School of Pharmacy in London, England. While working at such jobs as forestry official, teacher, journalist, and broadcasting executive, Ekwensi pursued his writing career. He began by reading his work on a West African radio program. His first published success came with the short novel When Love Whispers (1948). People of the City (1954), a collection of interconnected short stories, chronicles the frantic pace of life in modern LAGOS, Nigeria's commercial capital. The book's critical view of urban existence drew attention within Nigeria and internationally.

From 1957 to 1961 Ekwensi was head of features at the Nigerian Broadcasting Company, and from 1961 to 1967, he was federal director of Information Services. During this period he wrote his most successful novel, Jagua Nana (1961), the story of a vibrant middle-aged prostitute who moves between the corrupt, pleasure-seeking life of the city and the pastoral life of her rural origins. He continued exploring the contrast between the appeal of city life and its corruption in his collection Lokotown and Other Stories (1966). During the Nigerian Civil War (1967–1970) Ekwensi was the director of the Broadcasting Corporation of Biafra, and in 1968 he won the Dag Hammarskjöld International Prize for Literary Merit.

After the war Ekwensi continued to write, reflecting on the war and its aftermath in the novels Survive the Peace (1976) and Divided We Stand (1980). In 1986 he published a sequel to Jagua Nana called Jagua Nana's Daughter. His children's books include The Passport of Mallam Ilia (1960), The Drummer Boy (1960), and Juju Rock (1966). In 2005 Ekwensi was inducted into the Nigerian Academy of Letters. Two years later he published a collection of short stories, Cash on Delivery. It was to be his final work. Ekwensi died on 4 November 2007 at the age of eighty-six.

Eloyi

Ethnic group of Nigeria; also known as the Elowi, Epe, Aho, Eloyi, Afu, and Afao.

The Eloyi inhabit the Benue, Plateau, and Kwara States of NIGERIA. They speak a Niger-Congo language and are related to the larger IDOMA cultural and linguistic group. Approximately 100,000 people identify themselves as Eloyi.

See also ETHNICITY AND IDENTITY IN AFRICA: AN INTERPRETATION; LANGUAGES, AFRICAN: AN OVERVIEW.

Embu

Ethnic group of Kenya.

The Embu primarily inhabit the Eastern Province of KENYA. They speak a BANTU language and are closely related to the KIKUYU people. Approximately 300,000 people consider themselves Embu.

See also ETHNICITY AND IDENTITY IN AFRICA: AN INTERPRETATION; LANGUAGES, AFRICAN: AN OVERVIEW.

Emecheta, Buchi

1944–

Nigerian writer whose novels have focused on the lives of women in her native country, the West African nation of Nigeria.

Florence Onye Buchi Emecheta was born near the city of Lagos, NIGERIA. Both of her parents died when she was young; her father was killed while serving the British army in Burma. After completing a degree at the Methodist girls' high school in Lagos, Emecheta married Sylvester Onwordi at the age of sixteen. The couple moved to London, England, and during the next six years, Emecheta bore five children while supporting the family financially. She began to write during this time, but as she later said in an interview, "The first book I wrote, my husband burnt, and then I found I couldn't write with him around."

Emecheta left her husband in 1966, supporting herself for the next few years by working at the library in the British Museum. She enrolled at the University of London, where she received a degree in sociology in 1974. Her first literary works dealt with her own experiences of poverty, racism, and motherhood, as she described it "The cumulative oppression resulting from being alien, black and female." These reflective, semifictional accounts were first published in the journal New Statesman and later collected into her first novel In the Ditch (1972). She followed this with Second-Class Citizen (1974), which drew on the earlier years of her life and her experience of immigration. Both books dealt with the socioeconomic problems of Africans both in Africa and elsewhere in the world, particularly the oppressions of women.

Emecheta's next novel, The Bride Price (1976), was set in Nigeria in the early 1950s. She told the story of a young IGBO woman who defies tradition by running away with a man descended from a slave caste. The novel portrays a woman limited by Igbo social hierarchies and beliefs, including the belief that if the bride price is not paid, the bride will die in childbirth. The story ends without an answer—Emecheta leaves the reader to imagine whether the traditional prophecy is fulfilled. In The Slave Girl (1977), set in early twentieth-century Nigeria, a young girl is forced into domestic slavery by her brother, then bought from her master by a suitor. Emecheta uses the narrative to illustrate a parallel between slavery and marriage.

Emecheta published her best-known work, The Joys of Motherhood, in 1979. This story, depicting the migrant rural Igbo community in Lagos, spans Nigerian history from the 1930s to independence in 1960. Emecheta focuses on the lives of women who can achieve status only through motherhood—specifically, through their ability to bear sons.

Emecheta's early portrayals of oppressive gender relations created much controversy, especially among her African readers, some of whom thought she had portrayed African men unfairly. Others, especially in the West, held her up as one of Africa's most eloquent "feminists". Yet Emecheta herself has consistently rejected the label feminist. In an interview, she clarified her position, "I do believe in the African kind of feminism. They call it womanism, because, you see, you Europeans don't worry about water, you don't worry about schooling, you are so well off. Now, I buy land, and I say, 'OK, I can't build on it, I have no money, so I give it to some women to start planting.' That is my brand of feminism."

In her later novels, Emecheta addressed a range of sociopolitical issues. Destination Biafra (1982) was, in the author's words, a novel that "needed to be written" about the civil war that wracked Nigeria from 1967 to 1970. Double Yoke (1982) dealt with the moral deterioration of postcolonial Nigeria. The Rape of Shavi (1983), an experimental departure from Emecheta's realist style, was a slightly disguised tale of colonization. Emecheta returned to the theme of the immigrant experience with the novel Gwendolen (1989) (published in the United States as The Family), about a Caribbean immigrant girl who experiences rape and incest. Among her more recent works is Kehinde (1994), a novel. In 2005 she received the Order of the British Empire.

Throughout much of her writing career, Emecheta has taught at various universities. In addition, she founded the publishing company Ogwugwu Afor, which specializes in African literature. She has also published an autobiography, two children's books, and several books for young adults.

BIBLIOGRAPHY

Emecheta, Buchi. Head Above Water. Fontana Paperbacks, 1986.

James, Adeola, ed. In Their Own Voices: African Women Writers Talk. J. Currey, 1990.

MARIAN AGUIAR

Environmental Movements in Africa

Political and social movements organized to address environmental threats to health and livelihood. International conservation groups have focused worldwide attention on the threats to Africa's wildlife and forests. These issues, however, are not necessarily the primary concerns of most environmental movements in Africa itself. Such movements tend to focus instead on threats to local or regional natural resources that are considered crucial to people's health and livelihood. In some regions, people do consider wildlife a vital natural resource, but elsewhere they are more concerned with protecting land and water.

African environmental movements do not necessarily share the priorities of national governments. For example, some governments in wildlife-rich regions of eastern and southern Africa have displaced farming and pastoral communities to create large wildlife reserves, partly to meet the requests of foreign nations that donate aid and partly to encourage wildlife tourism. Another kind of problem seen in all parts of the continent arises when governments are willing to sacrifice environmental well-being to attract foreign investment, to generate economic growth, or to achieve the broad but somewhat vague goal of development. Africa's environmental movements have many different goals, but nearly all of them demand that citizens—particularly groups whose voices have traditionally not been heard—be granted greater control over the uses of national, regional, and local resources. In that sense, environmental movements in Africa are invariably political, as the following cases show.

MOVEMENT FOR THE SURVIVAL OF THE OGONI PEOPLE

The struggle of the Ogoni against pollution and resource destruction by the oil industry in their homeland in southeastern NIGERIA shows how environmental concerns coincide with struggles for self-determination. In 1958, when Nigeria was still under British COLONIAL RULE, Royal Dutch Shell Oil discovered large deposits of petroleum and natural gas in Ogoniland. Shell and the British government—and later, the Nigerian government—exploited these resources. Oil exports have become vital to the Nigerian economy: revenue from oil exports brought in approximately $30 billion between 1958 and the end of the twentieth century, and in some years it has accounted for about 95 percent of Nigeria's export income.

But the oil industry brought severe ecological problems to Ogoniland, an area of 403 square miles (650 square kilometers) on the NIGER RIVER delta. Although Ogoniland is densely populated, its rich land and waterways have traditionally supported the Ogonis' farming and fishing economy. More recently, however, Ogoniland has been nicknamed the Drilling Fields. Some environmental organizations estimate that between 1976 and 1991 the area experienced more than 3,000 oil spills, averaging about 700 barrels each. In addition to spills, gas flares burned twenty-four hours a day, producing incessant noise and causing respiratory problems in nearby Ogoni villages.

Acid rain left farm lands barren; drinking water became polluted; and fish disappeared from nearby rivers.

Moreover, Ogoniland received little of the wealth generated by the oil industry. For years the area had no paved roads, plumbing, or electricity, and schools and health facilities were inadequate. Economic injustice as well as environmental concerns led to the founding of the Movement for the Survival of Ogoni People (MOSOP) in 1990. The group's leaders, including writer and activist Ken SARO-WIWA, tied Ogoniland environmental destruction directly to the Ogonis' lack of political voice in a country where they number about 500,000 among a total population of 154 million in 2004, and where military regimes have done little to protect the rights of minority ethnic groups.

Soon after its founding, MOSOP published the Ogoni Bill of Rights, which called for not only environmental protection and "a fair proportion" of local resources but also religious freedom, the development of Ogoni culture, and above all the political autonomy of the Ogoni people, as "a separate and distinct ethnic nationality" within the Federal Republic of Nigeria. MOSOP's goals clearly went far beyond environmental cleanup.

Some 300,000 Ogonis—60 percent of the ethnic group—gathered on January 4, 1993, in a massive peaceful protest against Shell's activities and the degradation they caused. Shell's complaints about the demonstration drew a decisive response from the Nigerian government, which called in the military three months later to break up a protest against construction of a new pipeline in Ogoniland. According to a 1997 MOSOP account, an estimated 2,000 Ogoni men, women, and children were killed by the Nigerian military. Many were more arrested. Saro-Wiwa and eight other MOSOP activists were charged with murder and convicted in what was widely viewed as a suspect procedure. Saro-Wiwa's hanging in November 1995 provoked international condemnation, but the Nigerian government never recognized the Ogoni claims as legitimate. Although Shell ceased its operations in Ogoniland in 1993 and tried to placate the Ogoni by building schools, hospitals, and roads in the region, it refused to take responsibility for environmental cleanup. As of 2008, however, Shell's continued presence in the region was in grave doubt, with President Yar'Adua suggesting that another company would take over exploration.

GREEN BELT MOVEMENT

Like many environmental efforts in Africa, the Ogoni movement is also a struggle for minority rights. With a slightly different emphasis, the Green Belt Movement in KENYA uses tree-planting campaigns to empower women and to draw connections between environmental and economic impoverishment. Kenyan biologist Wangari MAATHAI founded the Green Belt Movement in 1977, when deforestation was contributing to both soil erosion and rising fuel costs—Kenyan households, like those in many African countries, use wood as their primary fuel source. The tree-planting campaign addressed a widespread problem whose effects are felt particularly by rural women, since it is they who most often walk long distances to collect firewood.

Since its beginning, the Green Belt Movement has employed more than 80,000 people, mostly women, and planted more than fifteen million trees. The women are paid for each tree they plant that survives past three months; as the trees grow, the women can use the fruit, leaves, and branches. With offices now in thirty African countries, the movement promotes organic farming techniques and hosts seminars on environmental management and sustainable development. Founder Maathai emphasizes that the Green Belt Movement not only gives women material benefits but also helps them take control of their environment.

Maathai has not hesitated to speak out publicly on the links between environmental degradation and poverty, and to criticize her own government's environmental and development policies. The response from the Kenyan government has been harsh. Maathai was beaten and jailed after organizing a protest against a proposed office building in Uhuru Park, one of the few remaining green spaces in Kenya's capital city, NAIROBI. Although the government canceled the project, President Daniel arap MOI labeled Maathai "subversive" and evicted the Green Belt Movement from its offices in Nairobi.

LESOTHO HIGHLANDS WATER PROJECT

In southern Africa, the completion of the first phase of a massive water project in early 1998 sparked a protest movement that brought together environmental, church, and civic groups from LESOTHO and SOUTH AFRICA. The Lesotho Highlands Water Project (LHWP) supplies water from Lesotho's Orange River to South Africa's industrialized GAUTENG province, which includes JOHANNESBURG and outlying black townships, such as SOWETO and Alexandra. The protesting groups detailed the LHWP's negative effects on many poor communities in southern Africa—and pointed out that none of these communities had been consulted beforehand. Civic groups in Soweto and Alexandra noted that while black township residents, like other South African taxpayers, had helped pay for the $1.1 billion project, much of the water supply in Gauteng was directed into the swimming pools and gardens of wealthy, predominantly white neighborhoods, and nearly a quarter of it leaked out through poorly maintained pipes. Many needy areas, meanwhile, had no piped water at

all. Protesters argued that additional planned dam construction farther upstream on the Orange River would flood large tracts of farmland and pasture—which are already scarce in Lesotho—and dislocate hundreds of rural households. They also objected that the project would divert Orange River water away from the rural regions of NAMIBIA and possibly damage the area's fisheries.

The protesters appealed to the governments of South Africa and Lesotho as well as the World Bank, requesting that the project be delayed until environmental impact studies had been conducted and the people negatively affected dams had received just compensation. But in June 1998, the World Bank approved a $45 million loan for construction of a second dam, claiming that Lesotho's revenue from the LHWP would pay for resettling and compensating rural communities and that the project would create 40,000 jobs.

Although the endorsement of the World Bank meant that the groups opposed to the project were unlikely to have all (or even many) of their demands met, the opposition to the LHWP reflected the nature of African environmental movements. That opposition had come from a broad base: people from two countries, rural and urban residents alike. Especially since the fall of APARTHEID in South Africa, environmental movements have been expanding across national borders and embracing a far broader range of people and issues. Wildlife conservation may dominate the environmental agendas of some national governments, but the broader environmental justice movements, which call for protecting the environments of people as well as animals, grew rapidly in the 1990s and into the new century and continue to gain strength.

See also DEVELOPMENT IN AFRICA: AN INTERPRETATION; FEMINISM IN AFRICA: AN INTERPRETATION; FORESTRY, PARTICIPATION, AND REPRESENTATION IN AFRICA: AN INTERPRETATION; PASTORALISM; TOURISM IN AFRICA.

ROBERT FAY

Equatorial Guinea

Small country on the coast of Central Africa including both the Bioko Island, just south of Nigeria, and the mainland province of Mbini, lying between Cameroon and Gabon.
Equatorial Guinea is an anomaly in Africa. Due to early migration patterns, a multiethnic society, dominated by the FANG, resides on the mainland, while a single ethnic group, the BUBI, live on Bioko island. Early European imperialism and the transatlantic slave trade exaggerated the differences between the island and mainland. The only

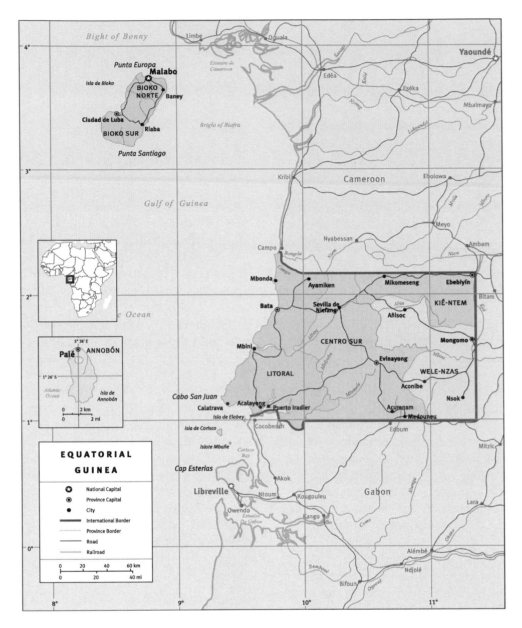

Spanish colony in sub-Saharan Africa, Equatorial Guinea was run by a dictatorial colonial regime, primarily devoted to exploiting the small territory's rich natural resources. The leadership since independence has proven equally undemocratic: for more than three decades two men from the same family have ruled Equatorial Guinea, making use of clan patronage and widespread repression to maintain their rule and their control over the country's wealth. Increasing oil exports in recent years have brought extraordinarily high rates of economic growth (22.1 percent between 1990 and 2000, and 12.4 percent as of 2008), but most of the country's 616,459 citizens have seen few, if any, of the profits.

EARLY HISTORY AND EUROPEAN EXPLORATION

For hundreds of years vast differences existed between the two pieces of present-day Equatorial Guinea. The first inhabitants of the Mbini region (also known as Río Muni) were the Bayele pygmies, though little is known of these people's culture, as it was lost through mixing with other groups. In the second millennium B.C.E. the NDOWE people migrated to the coast of present-day Equatorial Guinea from present-day CAMEROON, splitting off into several related ethnic groups. The Ndowe were followed by the Fang, who are today the country's largest ethnic group, composing 80 percent of the population. Included among the Fang are several cultural subgroup "tribes," or ayong, and within these are several more important familial clans, or ndebot. Common culture and intermarriage united the groups, as Fang custom prohibited marriage within the clan of one's mother. The numerous clans lived in egalitarian villages with no central authority, practicing the shifting cultivation of yucca, peanuts, yams, and malanga on the rich tropical plateau. Leadership depended upon wealth—measured with a currency of spearheads—and charisma. Although conflict between and among the Ndowe and Fang was common, it was limited in scope.

The island of Bioko has a longer history of BANTU-speaking inhabitation, though interpretations of the evidence differ. Archaeologists and linguists believe that the Bioko language cluster was one of the first groups to break from Western Bantu, arriving in present-day GABON probably around 1500–1000 B.C.E., while oral historians date their arrival much later. From there the Bubi migrated to Bioko Island around the seventh century C.E., though unlike many Bantu-speaking groups, they did not produce iron. Several successive societies rose and fell over time, concentrated primarily on the northern coastline. They grew palms on the rich soils of the volcanic islands, fished, and engaged in pottery and toolmaking. Although little is known of the early political and social organization of the Bubi of Bioko, it appears that political authority was diffuse, with the chief's power dependent upon the approval of village elders.

The island's and mainland's early relations with Europeans exaggerated their differences. In 1472 the Portuguese navigator Fernando Pó explored both regions, and named the island after himself. Portugal formally claimed the lands in the 1494 Treaty of Tordesillas with Spain. But attempts to establish sugar plantations on the island were abandoned due to the difficulty of cultivation and access, as natural ports were few. Furthermore, although some European vessels took individual captives, a regular slave trade never developed on Bioko.

By contrast, the Mbini mainland and the nearby islands of Annobón (or Pagalu) and Corsico became important sites for commercial agricultural production, as well as busy markets for slaves and other commodities. In the sixteenth and seventeenth centuries, the islands supplied slave ships bound for PORTUGUESE EAST AFRICA with fresh fruits and cattle. Soon these islands' inhabitants, many of whom had migrated from the mainland and others from Portuguese East Africa (present-day ANGOLA) developed distinctive Creole cultures and languages. On Bioko, meanwhile, Creole culture would not develop until the nineteenth century, when West Africans and slaves who had returned from the Americas were brought to the island by the British. They settled among the Bubi, creating a people that became known as the Ferninandos.

EUROPEAN IMPERIALISM AND SPANISH COLONIALISM

European imperialism and Spanish colonialism exaggerated the economic and cultural differences between Mbini and Bioko, even while uniting the two territories politically. Spain, seeking a dependable base for its slaving operations, purchased Annobón from Portugal in 1777. A year later the Treaty of Pardo provided for Portugal to cede part of the mainland as well as Bioko and other islands, in exchange for lands in Brazil. The Spanish presence remained negligible. Trading stations controlled by the British, Dutch, Portuguese, and Spanish on the islands continued to supply both slaves and provisions to passing merchant ships into the mid-1800s, then switched to provisioning the vessels sent to enforce the British ban on slave trading. British enterprises established and operated palm plantations on Bioko, though when they were unable to compete with other palm-exporting regions, they switched the focus of production to cocoa.

The influx of Europeans brought a host of diseases to the islands and mainland, decimating the indigenous populations. European trade also led to conflicts over access and to the emergence of centralized states. On the mainland, for example, Europeans pushed the Ndowe inland, bringing them into conflict with the Fang, who sought European goods. On Bioko, where the Bubi had long lived without central authorities, control over European trade enabled the Bubi chief Moka to establish a kingdom.

After decades of concentrating its efforts on Cuba and MOROCCO at the expense of Equatorial Guinea, Spain finally laid claim to all of present-day Equatorial Guinea in 1900, at the Treaty of Paris. Four years later, a decree established the colony as a "colony of exploitation," not one of settlement, and it delineated rules concerning land concessions. The colonial administration's top priority was the export of timber and agricultural products, namely cocoa, coffee, and palm oil. Finding labor to produce these crops, however, proved difficult. The administration had relatively few troops or other tools of coercion at its disposal, and local people actively resisted colonial occupation and labor policies. On Bioko, it took Spanish forces until 1910 to defeat King Moko and subsequent Bubi leaders. Colonization proved even more difficult in the forested Mbini interior, where one Fang leader actually captured the governor-general. Not until an all-out pacification campaign in 1926–1927 did the colonial state destroy organized resistance, and put in its place a system of indirect rule, in which administrative dictates were carried out by pliable chiefs. But even then the local labor supplies were insufficient. Instead, the colony turned to importing laborers, including Liberians, Angolans, Mozambicans, and Asians, to work on the cocoa and coffee plantations.

Equatorial Guinea (At a Glance)

OFFICIAL NAME:
Republic of Equatorial Guinea

FORMER NAME:
Spanish Guinea

AREA
28,051 sq km (about 10,831 sq mi)

LOCATION:
Western Africa, bordering the North Atlantic, between Gabon to the south and east and Cameroon to the north. Equatorial Guinea also includes islands off the coast, the largest of which is Bioko.

CAPITAL:
Malabo, on Bioko (population 33,000; 2002 estimate)

POPULATION:
16,459 (2008 estimate); many thousands more are believed to be living abroad, due to the nation's tumultuous political climate.

POPULATION DENSITY:
22 people per sq km (57 per sq mi)

POPULATION BELOW AGE 15:
42 percent (male 131,696; female 127,253; 2008 estimate)

POPULATION GROWTH RATE:
2.732 percent (2008 estimate)

TOTAL FERTILITY RATE:
5.16 children born per woman (2008 estimate)

LIFE EXPECTANCY AT BIRTH:
Total population: 61.23 years (male 60.36 years; female 62.13 years; 2008 estimate)

INFANT MORTALITY RATE:
83.75 deaths per 1000 live births (2008 estimate)

LITERACY RATE (AGE 15 AND OVER WHO CAN READ AND WRITE):
Total population: 85.7 percent (male 93.3 percent; female 78.4 percent; 2003 estimate)

EDUCATION:
Free and compulsory for children between the ages of 6 and 11. Still, more than one-fourth of school-age children do not attend primary school. Only 26 percent attend secondary school. The Spanish National University of Distant Education operates centers for higher education at Malabo and Bata. Some Equatorial Guineans also go abroad (mostly to Spain and France) for a college education.

LANGUAGES:
Spanish and French are the official languages, but Fang, a Bantu language, is most widely spoken.

ETHNIC GROUPS:
Ethnic lines correspond to geographic boundaries, with Bubi and Fernandinos populations on Bioko and a Fang population in Río Muni.

RELIGIONS:
About 90 percent of the people are affiliated with the Roman Catholic church, although traditional beliefs are widely practiced.

CLIMATE:
Tropical; the average annual temperature in Malabo is about 25° C (77° F) and on average more than 2,000 mm (80 in) of rain falls a year. The wettest season is December through February.

LAND, PLANTS, AND ANIMALS:
On the mainland the terrain rolls gently and is heavily forested. The Mbini (formerly Benito) River drains about 60 percent of the land. Bioko has fertile volcanic soil watered by several large streams.

NATURAL RESOURCES:
The rich volcanic soil supports extensive agriculture.

CURRENCY:
CFA (Communauté Financière Africaine) franc

GROSS DOMESTIC PRODUCT (GDP):
$15.54 billion (2007 estimate)

GDP PER CAPITA:
$28,200 (2007 estimate)

GDP REAL GROWTH RATE:
12.4 percent (2007 estimate)

PRIMARY ECONOMIC ACTIVITIES:
Agriculture, petroleum, and forestry

PRIMARY CROPS:
Coffee, tropical hardwood timber, cassava, and sweet potatoes

INDUSTRIES:
Oil, soap, cocoa, yucca, coffee, and seafood processing

PRIMARY EXPORTS:
Petroleum, coffee, cocoa beans, timber

PRIMARY IMPORTS:
Petroleum sector equipment, food, beverages, clothing, machinery

PRIMARY TRADE PARTNERS:
China, Great Britain, Japan, Cote d'Ivoire, Spain, and United States

GOVERNMENT:
Under the 1982 constitution, Equatorial Guinea was a single-party state. This governmental party was named the Democratic Party of Equatorial Guinea in 1987. A new multiparty constitution was approved by public referendum in 1991. It established an 80-member House of Representatives to replace the existing 41-member legislature. Under the constitution, the voters elect a president to a seven-year term and legislators to five-year terms. Teodoro Obiang Nguema Mbasogo has been president since 1979 and was last reelected in 2002.

Eric Bennett

Apart from the plantations, Spain did little to develop the colony's economy or infrastructure. On the mainland, the major town, Bata, consisted of little more than a few shacks. The inhospitable forest made the construction of roads or railways difficult, hindering the forestry industry.

Despite these conditions and a climate conducive to tropical disease, Equatorial Guinea attracted many fortune-seeking European settlers, making it a colony with one of the highest ratios of Europeans to Africans in Africa. Like neighboring Portuguese colonies, Equatorial

Guinea distinguished assimilated (or *emancipado*) and "nonassimilated" Africans, depending upon land ownership and education. But since the colony had few schools, only a small fraction of the African population was able to acquire this status. Even those who did were excluded from political representation.

Although Equatorial Guinea's educated elite were few in number, they were at the forefront of the nationalist movement, which began in the late 1950s under the leadership of Acacio Mane, a Fang activist calling for African teachers' salaries to equal those of Europeans. Mane was denounced by a priest and later executed by Spanish authorities; his martyrdom politicized Equatorial Guineans, and led to the establishment of proindependent parties, namely the National Movement for the Liberation of Equatorial Guinea and the Popular Idea of Equatorial Guinea. Violent repression on the part of colonial officials forced the parties into exile.

Spain, however, was bound by United Nations agreements to prepare Equatorial Guinea for self-rule. It held a referendum on self-determination in the colony in 1963, and municipal and legislative elections the following year. By the time a preindependence constitutional conference was held in 1968 the nationalist movement had fragmented into parties representing Mbini, Bioko, or specific ethnic groups. The constitution created a very strong executive government, modeled after Franco's regime in Spain (and made Bioko and Mbini the two provinces of Equatorial Guinea, though the power soon shifted to Mbini, and especially the Fang and its Esangui clan). In September 1968, Francisco MACÍAS NGUEMA, the Minister of Public Works and a Fang backed by Spanish and French commercial interests, was elected president.

FAMILIAL POLITICS AND UNDERDEVELOPMENT IN INDEPENDENT EQUATORIAL GUINEA

Equatorial Guinea gained its independence on October 12, 1968. Almost immediately the new government faced the anger of 70,000 Nigerian migrant workers prohibited from sending their pay to NIGERIA, due to the ongoing Biafran war. To divert attention, president Macías Nguema began denouncing the Spanish who had remained in Equatorial Guinea, many of whom quickly left. In March 1969 an alleged coup attempt—eyewitnesses claimed it was staged—was followed by a swift government crackdown on the political opposition.

For the next decade Macías Nguema, the self-proclaimed "Unique Miracle," ruled Equatorial Guinea with an iron fist. He used the military youth organization, the Youth in Step with Macías, as well as the presidential bodyguard, which included Cubans and North Koreans, to carry out repression and political killings. In terms of the numbers of deaths relative to the total population, Macías Nguema's regime was even more murderous than Idi AMIN's in UGANDA. Fearing threats to his rule, Macías had thousands of political opponents killed and over 130,000—or one-fourth of the population—fled the country. Because he had no navy of his own, the president banned and destroyed all seagoing vessels (except the presidential "yacht") in order to prevent smuggling, an action that destroyed the fishing industry. During this period the economy collapsed; as foreign workers and the educated elite fled the country, the per capita gross national product (GNP) fell by more than 60 percent within the decade.

Macías went unchallenged until his own security forces turned on the military, killing five members of the National Guard in August 1979. Other Guard officers, military graduates, and relatives of the president gained control of Bioko and Bata. After overcoming intense resistance from presidential loyalists in the interior, those leading the revolt captured, tried, convicted, and executed Macías Nguema for his role in torture, executions, and embezzlement. He was replaced by the nephew who had turned against him, army commander Teodoro Obiang Nguema Mbasogo. On taking power, Teodoro Obiang announced that "for eleven years, politicians have made a mess of everything" and henceforth "the military will oversee everything ... even if there are civilians in the government." The new leadership paid salary arrears to all troops and established a Supreme Military Council to run the country. Many members of the previous regime remained in the government.

In the early 1980s the president brought more civilians into the government, though real power remained in the hands of the Fang-dominated military and president. Obiang's presidential guard, composed of Moroccans, Spaniards, and South Africans, thwarted numerous coup attempts, including an army mutiny in 1985. As opposition groups in exile alerted the international community to events in Equatorial Guinea, Obiang made limited political concessions. In 1987 he created the Democratic Party of Equatorial Guinea, but made membership mandatory. The next year he created a national assembly, but declared himself the head of both the party and the assembly. Legislative elections in July 1988 were lackluster and limited to a few urban centers.

The appearance of political change lured international investment. Having adopted the west and Central Africa CFA franc in 1985, Equatorial Guinea began to develop closer economic ties with France, and soon adopted French as the second official language, after Spanish. French businesses entered the profitable timber, fuel, and fishing sectors. Timber grown on Mbini, especially the softwood okoumé used for making plywood, became the country's leading export, followed by cocoa. The fishing industry, especially in tuna and shellfish, made a slow recovery. Equatorial Guinea has also earned foreign exchange by importing waste, including New York City garbage and toxics from the SOUTH AFRICA–based Anglo-American Company. On Annobón, where the waste is dumped, the prevalence of certain skin diseases is now among the highest in the world.

In the late 1990s foreign investors were showing the greatest interest in Equatorial Guinea's petroleum reserves. Oil was first discovered offshore in the early 1980s, and has now replaced timber as the primary export, accounting for two-thirds of the GNP. But many of the country's other resources—among them gold, iron, thorium, and manganese—remain untapped, and most of its citizens are impoverished. Since the country has gained independence, much of the agricultural sector has been controlled by chiefs, elected by the people, who were responsible for maintaining cocoa and coffee plantations and timber harvests, though most of the revenues have gone to government officials and their companies. The leadership's handling of the economy has resulted in a deteriorating national infrastructure and a deficiency in public services. Equatorial Guinea today has only approximately two hundred miles of paved road. Transportation between the islands and mainland is by air only, because the country possesses only one boat, the presidential yacht.

Most of the wealth generated by the oil boom has gone directly into the hands of Obiang, his family members, and friends within the Esangui clan, leading many observers to question the effectiveness of the country's political reforms. In 1993 Obiang legalized political parties, most of which were controlled by close associates and family members. Violence preceded the legislative, municipal, and presidential elections held in the mid-1990s. In 2002 Obiang was reelected with 97 percent of the vote. The disparity in wealth between rich and poor has led to growing discontentment, manifested in sometimes-violent protests and attacks on Bioko and Annobón islands. Torture and arrests of opponents have remained common and few exiles have accepted the government's offer of amnesty. Many believe that the growth of the oil industry, under the control of American and French companies, will hinder development and political change because the profits within Equatorial Guinea will continue to go mostly to Obiang and the Esangui clan who have controlled Equatorial Guinea for the past few decades.

See also BANTU: DISPERSION AND SETTLEMENT; PYGMY; SLAVERY IN AFRICA; UNITED NATIONS IN AFRICA.

ERIC YOUNG

Equiano, Olaudah
1745?–1797
Former African slave and abolitionist who wrote the first autobiographical slave narrative.

First published in Britain in 1789, The Interesting Narrative of the Life of Olaudah Equiano, or Gustavus Vassa, the African, became a best seller in Equiano's lifetime, with nine English editions and one American as well as translations in Dutch, German, and Russian. Though Ottobah CUGOANO, an African abolitionist in England, had published an autobiographical account in 1787, it was probably heavily edited. Thus, The Interesting Narrative is considered the first autobiography of an African slave written entirely by his own hand. This places Equiano as the founder of the slave narrative, a form central to African American literature. In the book, Equiano describes his abduction in Africa, his enslavement in the West Indies and his manumission in Britain, as well as the legal insecurity and terror faced by enslaved and free West Indian blacks. Equiano's autobiography greatly influenced the rhetorical strategies, content, and presentation of later nineteenth-century slave narratives, such as Frederick Douglass's Narrative of the Life of Frederick Douglass (1845). Equiano was born the son of an IGBO chief in present-day NIGERIA. When he was eleven years old, he and his sister were captured by African traders and sold to Europeans. He was transported to the West Indies, where an Englishman, Michael Pascal, bought Equiano and named him after Swedish hero Gustavus Vassa. Though Equiano at first detested the name, he later used it in most of his writings and became known by it. Equiano served as a seaman with Pascal in the Seven Years' War (1756–1763) in Canada and in the Mediterranean. In 1757 Pascal took Equiano to England, where his honesty and trustworthiness won him friendship and support from many English people. During this formative period, Equiano was educated and converted to Christianity. To Equiano's dismay, in 1763 Pascal sold him to an American, Robert King. By this time, Equiano knew seamanship, hairdressing, wine making, and arithmetic and had become fully literate in the English language. Equiano worked for King as a seaman and trader, once again coming in close contact with the atrocities of the transatlantic slave trade. Even after he bought his freedom in 1766, Equiano elected to remain at sea for several more years. He voyaged to the Arctic as a surgeon's assistant as well as to the Mediterranean as a gentleman's valet, and for a time lived among the Moskito Indians of Nicaragua. Equiano returned to England in 1777 and became active in the abolitionist movement. He brought the massacre of 130 slaves on the ship Zong to the attention of white abolitionist lawyer Granville Sharp, thereby greatly influencing public support for abolition of the slave trade. He also wrote on behalf of abolition and interracial marriages. In 1792 he married Susannah Cullen, a white Englishwoman, with whom he had two daughters. In 1787 Equiano was appointed commissary for stores to a government sponsored expedition to settle freed slaves in SIERRA LEONE. Although at first he was "agreeably surprised that the benevolence of government had adopted the plan of some philanthropic individuals," he soon discovered fraudulence among the organizers. Equiano invited outsiders to view the negligent conditions under which the blacks lived on board the ship after their departure to Sierra Leone was delayed, and he described corrupt procedures to a friend in a letter that was later published. After this, he was dismissed from his post as a "troublemaker." Though demoralized, Equiano returned to England and published his autobiography. He fought unceasingly for abolition as a member of the group the Sons of Africa and in his letter writing and public speaking campaigns until his death.

See also LONDON'S BLACK POOR AND THE SIERRA LEONE SETTLEMENT PLAN.

BIBLIOGRAPHY

Edwards, Paul, ed. *Equiano's Travels*. Heinemann, 1967.
Gates, Henry Louis, Jr., ed. *The Classic Slave Narratives*. New American Library, 1987.

LEYLA KEOUGH

Eritrea

Nation in the Horn of Africa, bordering the Red Sea, Sudan, Ethiopia, and Djibouti.

Eritrea is one of the world's newest nations, and also one of its poorest. Small and drought-prone, it boasts few natural resources. But Eritrea's Red Sea location has a rich cultural history, developed over centuries of migrations and trade, as well as a long history of warfare, fueled largely by the strategic interests of its neighbors and other foreign powers. Compared to other African countries, Eritrea has some of the oldest traditions of Islam and Christianity and one of the shortest experiences of European colonialism: less than fifty years under Italian rule. The region's colonial borders, however, took on new significance as soon as Italy was removed from power and Eritrea was handed over to ETHIOPIA. In the face of Emperor HAILE SELASSIE's despotism, Eritrean nationalism developed quickly and endured through a roughly thirty-year war for independence, ending when Eritrea became Africa's newest nation in 1993. Since then, the country has enjoyed a remarkable political consensus, and most agree that it is a society where ethnic distinctions matter less than differences in religion and lifestyle between the Christian agricultural highlands and the

Islamic pastoral lowlands. Although during the war Eritrean "freedom fighters" never received much outside support, independent Eritrea soon became the darling of the international aid community, lauded for its honest government and economic pragmatism. A renewed conflict with Ethiopia that led to more than two years of fighting threw into doubt Eritrea's future recovery.

FROM ANCIENT TRADE TO COLONIAL DOMINATION
The region now known as Eritrea has a long history of human habitation. Cave paintings in Akele Guzai and Sahel provinces date to 6000 B.C.E. Scholars believe Nilotic-speaking peoples from the forests of southern SUDAN were the earliest inhabitants. They were followed by Cushitic-speaking pastoralists from the desert of northern Sudan and later—probably between 3,500 and 4,000 years ago—Semitic-speaking agriculturalists from the southern Arabian Peninsula (now Yemen). Around 2,500 years ago the arrival of the Semitic-speaking Sabeans, also from Arabia, linked the region to the Sabean's Red Sea and Indian Ocean trade networks. These early Semitic immigrants also brought Judaism to the Horn of Africa.

Trade with EGYPT, Meroe, and the Arabian Peninsula fostered the development of towns and centralized political authority. By the second century C.E., the kingdom of AKSUM dominated a stretch of territory reaching from its highland capital of the same name (now a town in Ethiopia) to the coast. The kingdom exported ivory, slaves, tortoise shell, and rhinoceros horn from the East African interior, and imported textiles, glass and metal goods, and wine. During the mid-fourth century C.E., the Aksum royalty adopted CHRISTIANITY. Ethiopian Orthodox (or Coptic) Christianity eventually became the dominant religion in the highlands, where most of the population practiced sedentary agriculture.

The population in the lowlands was sparser, and the arid conditions favored nomadic pastoralism. By 702 C.E. Arab merchants had brought Islam to the Dahlak Islands, and from there it spread gradually along the coast and through the lowlands, establishing a cultural divide that still exists in Eritrea today. Culturally and spiritually, the coast increasingly looked toward the Arab world. Arabic was the language of scholarship and the window to the outside world. By the early nineteenth century, the TIGRE, the dominant coastal group, had become entirely Muslim. The highlands, however, remained Coptic, one of the oldest organized Christian churches, which spread from Egypt in the first centuries C.E. The mountain people, mostly TIGRINYA, were largely settled agriculturalists.

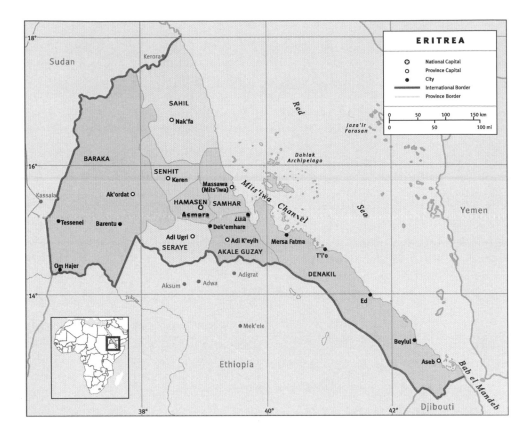

By the sixteenth century foreign powers were jockeying for control over territory in the Horn of Africa. The Portuguese established the first trade posts, followed by the Ottoman Turks, who captured and fortified the port city of MASSAWA in 1557. For more than 300 years control over the territory now called Eritrea was caught up in the imperialistic ambitions of Egypt, Portugal, and later Great Britain and Italy, as well as the neighboring Ethiopian empire. As Europeans rushed to colonize Africa in the late nineteenth century, Italy, despite its previous lack of interest in establishing colonies on the continent, looked to the Horn. The Italian government sought to preempt other colonial powers from carving up all of Africa among them but also hoped to establish settler colonies for dispossessed Italian peasants and to find new markets for Italian goods.

In 1885 Italian troops occupied Massawa. Four years later they occupied ASMARA, which had been ceded to them by the Ethiopian emperor Menelik in exchange for weapons. In 1890 Italy declared colonial control over "Eritrea"—a name taken from the Greek word for the Red Sea. It intended to take over the vast Ethiopian Empire as well, but its troops were soundly defeated by Emperor Menelik's army in 1896. Eritrea's borders, therefore, reflected not a preexisting political or cultural entity but only turn-of-the century military realities.

ITALIAN COLONIAL RULE

Although many Italians did not support their country's colonization campaign—which also included the occupation of SOMALIA and LIBYA—Mussolini would later call Eritrea "the heart of the new Roman Empire." Establishing colonial rule over this part of the "empire" did not come easily, however. The colonial administration expropriated over one-fifth of Eritrea's arable land between 1893 and 1895, in anticipation of massive Italian immigration to the colony. But an armed uprising involving hundreds of Eritreans in late 1894 required two months and thousands of Italian troops to put down, and forced the administration to scale back its plans for Italian resettlement. In 1903 the administration halted land expropriation altogether and began leasing seized lands back to the Eritrean peasantry, in part due to threats of further rebellion.

The Italian emigrants settled mostly in the fertile countryside of the highlands, where they relied on the labor of dispossessed peasants to produce a wide variety of export crops, or in Asmara, Massawa, and the port of Aseb (also known as Assab), where they established trade and manufacturing firms. By the early 1920s coffee, much of it produced on Eritrean peasant farms, had become the colony's largest export. Other major exports included cotton, skins and hides, salt, tobacco, and fresh and canned foodstuffs. Eritrea also supplied Italy with wheat and other grains. Italy's

THE BOMBING OF ERITREA. A bird's-eye view of the aerodrome at Asmara, Eritrea, after an aerial assault from the Royal Air Force of the Middle East command during World War II. (*AP Images*)

search for gold in Eritrea proved largely fruitless, apart from small quantities mined near Asmara. Although reserves of iron ore, lead, and white mica were also found around the capital, these were left largely unexploited. By contrast, Italy invested generously in infrastructure. By 1911 the small colony was spanned by 119 kilometers (approximately 74 miles) of railroads, including one line that twisted and tunneled through the mountainous region between Massawa and Asmara. While the railway as well as an extensive road system facilitated the transport of export crops, Italy never earned a profit from Eritrea, and in fact had to subsidize its colonial administration.

ONE OF THE LONGEST WARS IN HISTORY

In 1935 Italy invaded Ethiopia. For the next six years Eritrea served as Italian base for its East African military campaigns. Thousands of Italians took up residence in Asmara, and industrialization and infrastructure development accelerated. Thousands of conscripted Eritrean soldiers fought for the Italians. In 1941, however, the British demolished their East African defenses and occupied Eritrea. After the war, the British allowed the formation of Eritrean trade unions, publications, and political parties, all of which fostered a growing sense of national identity. For several years, however, Eritrea's political status lay in limbo, as first the Allies and later the United Nations debated its future.

At first most Eritrean Christians favored union with Ethiopia, and Orthodox priests often threatened to excommunicate anyone favoring independence. But Muslims, who feared domination by a Christian state, advocated independent statehood. The proindependence Muslim League was formed in 1946. The following year Woldeab Woldemariam, a labor activist and early advocate of Eritrean independence, helped launch the Christian-dominated Liberal Progressive Party. Bloody clashes between Muslims and Christians occurred repeatedly between 1946 and 1951.

After Haile Selassie heavily lobbied the United States and other leading UN members, the UN voted to federate

Ethiopia and Eritrea in 1951. Over the next ten years Selassie's regime tightened its grip on Eritrea. Factories in Asmara were dismantled and brought to ADDIS ABABA, pushing what was once one of the most industrialized colonies in Africa into poverty. Political dissent was suppressed as the Ethiopian government forced prominent Eritreans into exile, shut down newspapers, and banned trade unions and political parties. In 1958 the Eritrean flag was banned.

Ethiopian repression hit Eritrea's urban and highland populations especially hard, and they responded accordingly. In 1958 underground unions staged a general strike in Asmara and Massawa, and students joined workers in massive protests against the loss of local autonomy. The Ethiopian government reacted immediately. Troops fired on protesters, wounding or killing more than 500. Throughout Eritrea, support for the national government evaporated, and Christians began joining the independence movement.

In 1960 Selassie declared Amharic, the language of Addis Ababa and Ethiopia's largest ethnic group, the official language, and banned other languages from the schools. That same year, Eritrean leaders, including Edris Mohammed Adem, former president of the Eritrean Assembly, met secretly in CAIRO to form the Eritrean Liberation Front (ELF), whose members represented a broad spectrum of society. In September 1961 Eritrean independence advocates battled with police on Mount Adal. Two months later an ELF military campaign in the west marked the beginning of a long and arduous war. Although at first they fought with antiquated Italian rifles, eventually the ELF troops developed into one of Africa's most disciplined military forces. In 1965 the Front established four regional commands. In 1966 Eritrea's future president, Isaias AFWERKI, dropped out of the University of Addis Ababa and joined the ELF, and a Christian-dominated fifth zone was created in the highlands.

Foreign powers soon chose sides in the Eritrean independence struggle. Arab states, sympathetic to appeals by fellow Muslims, were the first to back the ELF, while Israel backed Selassie. Other major powers viewed the conflict in the context of the Cold War, which meant Selassie, a reliable anticommunist, received backing from the United States and Europe. His army became one of the largest and best equipped in Africa. Although the east bloc supported the ELF with rhetoric, it sent little material aid. Socialist countries did train small groups of ELF fighters, however. Afwerki and another leader, Ramadan M. Nur, went to China for training in 1967, and the following year other groups went to Cuba.

As the war intensified, Eritrean refugees streamed into Sudan. The Ethiopian military's tactics of burning villages and killing their inhabitants, rather than intimidating the population into submission, only increased support for independence, even among Christian highlanders who had previously supported Addis Ababa. The ELF, meanwhile, focused on guerrilla tactics, such as blowing up bridges and hijacking airplanes.

Despite success in battle, the rebel movement faced serious internal divisions by the early 1970s. Afwerki and other highlanders eventually split from the Muslim-dominated ELF leadership and formed the Eritrean People's Liberation Front (EPLF). The two groups were soon fighting on different fronts and periodically fought with each other. Although the ELF was initially Christian-dominated, it defined itself as a secular organization. Both groups professed Marxist principles and stated they were fighting not just for political independence but also for revolutionary goals, such as the nationalization of private property.

During the war, women received equality in areas controlled by the EPLF and child marriage was outlawed in 1978. Political and military setbacks ultimately weakened the ELF, and the EPLF emerged as the main independence force. Over the next several years, the Eritrean struggle survived in large part because of its success at mobilizing all possible resources, including popular support in the countryside. One-third of the fighters were women, for example, and they trained and fought alongside men. It also assured Muslim civilians that freedom of religion would be protected. Perhaps most importantly, the EPLF managed to provide the basic rural services that neither the Italians nor Ethiopians had bothered with: it opened 165 schools during the war, educating some 27,000 students. The EPLF also improved rural public health standards by creating a corps of mobile health teams and Italian-trained doctors and establishing a network of pharmacies, laboratories, and village clinics. Many of the facilities were built underground to avoid Ethiopian bomb attacks.

A large proportion of the EPLF's budget for such programs came from abroad. Even before the war, large numbers of Eritreans had migrated to the Persian Gulf, Europe, and North America in search of employment, and now expatriate communities became a key source of monetary support for the rebel movement. Some observers estimate that Eritreans abroad sent back $20 million a month—up to 70 percent of their salaries, in some places—enabling the ELF and EPLF to sustain the war despite in-fighting, drought, military setbacks, and political isolation. The rebels also stole massive amounts of military supplies from the Ethiopian army.

The war's geopolitical alliances changed in 1974, when Haile Selassie was overthrown in a military coup led by MENGISTU Haile Mariam. Like the Eritrean rebel groups, the new Ethiopian regime, known as the Derg, claimed to

Eritrea (At a Glance)

OFFICIAL NAME:
State of Eritrea

FORMER NAME:
Eritrea Autonomous Region in Ethiopia

AREA:
121,320 sq km (46,774 sq mi)

LOCATION:
Northeastern Africa; borders the Red Sea, Djibouti, Ethiopia, and the Sudan and includes the Dahlak Archipelago in the Red Sea

CAPITAL:
Asmara (population 503,000; 2002 estimate)

POPULATION:
5,502,026 (2008 estimate)

POPULATION DENSITY:
45 per sq km (117 per sq mi)

POPULATION BELOW AGE 15:
43 percent (male 1,188,496; female 1,178,520; 2008 estimate)

POPULATION GROWTH RATE:
2.631 percent (2008 estimate)

TOTAL FERTILITY RATE:
4.84 children born per woman (2008 estimate)

LIFE EXPECTANCY AT BIRTH:
61.38 years (male 59.35 years; female 63.46 years; 2008 estimate)

INFANT MORTALITY RATE:
44.32 deaths per 1000 live births (2008 estimate)

LITERACY RATE (AGE 15 AND OVER WHO CAN READ AND WRITE):
Total population: 58.6 percent (male 69.9 percent; female 47.6 percent; 2003 estimate)

EDUCATION:
Few schools functioned during the war of independence that ended in 1993. Officially, seven years of primary education are now compulsory, with lower grades taught in African languages and higher grades in Arabic or English. In 2000, 41 percent of school-age children attended primary school and 22 percent attended secondary school.

LANGUAGES:
The main language groups are Tigrinya, Tigre, Kunama, Hedareb, Afar, Bilien, Saho, Nara, and Rashaida. Arabic is also widely spoken, but English is used in secondary schools and universities.

ETHNIC GROUPS:
Ethnic Tigrinya, 50 percent; Tigre and Kunama, 40 percent; Afar, 4 percent; Saho (Red Sea coast dwellers), 3 percent; other, 3 percent

RELIGIONS:
Muslim, Monophysite creed of the Ethiopian Orthodox church, Roman Catholic, and Protestant

CLIMATE:
The narrow coastal plain receives little rainfall and is extremely hot, with a mean annual temperature of 30° C (86° F). The mean annual temperature in Asmara, located in the plateau highlands, is 16° C (61° F). The plateau receives 400–500 mm (16–20 in) rainfall per year, while the hill country north and west of the core plateau generally receives less. The Denakil depression in the southeast has been the site of some of the highest temperatures recorded on earth, and receives practically no rain.

LAND, PLANTS, AND ANIMALS:
Eritrea's topography consists of four types of land surface. The Red Sea coastal plain widens to include the Denakil Desert in the south. The south central plateau highland is the most agriculturally fertile and densely populated part of the country. To the north of the highlands lie hill country, and to the west lie broad plains. These plains lie to the west of the Baraka River and north of the Setit River. The Mereb (or Gash), the Baraka, and the Anseba flow from the plateau west into Sudan, while the Falkat, Laba, and Alighede flow from the northern highlands to the Red Sea. Off the coast, more than a hundred small islands make up the Dahlak Archipelago.

NATURAL RESOURCES:
Eritrea's resources have supported a largely agricultural way of life. The nation possesses deposits of potash, gold, copper, and zinc, though exploration and exploitation of its mineral resources have been severely hindered by war. The Red Sea is rich in fish, but commercial fishing in Eritrea is also relatively underdeveloped.

CURRENCY:
The nafka

GROSS DOMESTIC PRODUCT (GDP):
$3.619 billion (2007 estimate)

GDP PER CAPITA:
$800 (2007 estimate)

GDP REAL GROWTH RATE:
1.3 percent (2007 estimate)

PRIMARY ECONOMIC ACTIVITIES:
More than 80 percent of the population engage in agriculture that nonetheless produces only a quarter of the total gross domestic product. The country's small industrial sector is still recovering from the devastating war with Ethiopia (1998–2000). Migrant labor is also an important source of income.

PRIMARY CROPS:
Sorghum, lentils, vegetables, maize (corn), cotton, tobacco, coffee, and sisal (for making rope); livestock includes goats; fish

INDUSTRIES:
Food processing, beverages, clothing, and textiles

PRIMARY EXPORTS:
Livestock, sorghum, textiles, food, small manufactures

PRIMARY IMPORTS:
Processed goods, machinery, food, and petroleum products

PRIMARY TRADE PARTNERS:
Sudan, Ethiopia, Italy, Japan, United Arab Emirates, United Kingdom, and Germany

GOVERNMENT:
A decree, announced in May 1993, set up a National Assembly, a president, and a Council of Ministers. Isaias Afwerki was elected by the National Assembly and currently serves as president. The unicameral legislature has 150 members. In addition to the People's Front for Democracy and Justice (formerly the Eritrean People's Liberation Front), other political organizations include the Eritrean Islamic Jihad (EIJ), Eritrean Islamic Salvation (EIS), and Eritrean National Alliance (ENA). The date of any upcoming elections is uncertain.

Marian Aguiar

be Marxist, but it was soon clear that the Derg was concerned less with equality and social change than with maintaining a strong central state. Still, the Soviet Union, China, and Cuba threw their support behind the new Ethiopian Red Army, which launched a massive campaign in 1978 that pushed the rebels northward and out of all the major cities. The Eritrean refugee population in Sudan swelled to 500,000 by 1981. The Ethiopian army under Mengistu purposely targeted food supplies in rebel areas—they burned crops and granaries and slaughtered livestock—so Eritrea was already vulnerable to famine by the time drought struck in 1984. Massive food aid shipments from the West arrived in Addis Ababa, but very little relief reached Eritrea.

In the late 1980s the Eritreans began to regain lost ground and won a number of key battles against the large but poorly trained and increasingly demoralized Ethiopian army. As the Soviet bloc itself began to crumble, the EPLF moderated its Marxist tone and began to collaborate with the growing rebel movements within Ethiopia, such as the Ethiopian People's Revolutionary Democratic Front (EPRDF), led by Meles ZENAWI.

The last major battle of the independence struggle took place on May 19, 1991. The Ethiopian army collapsed at Decamare, outside Asmara, and fled north toward Sudan in a disorganized rout. In the meantime, Ethiopian rebels were approaching Addis Ababa. With the Soviet Union in collapse, the Derg was doomed. On May 21 Mengistu fled into exile in ZIMBABWE, and Zenawi took over as acting president. Recognizing that the EPRDF could not have triumphed without EPLF support, Zenawi agreed to Eritrean independence. Afwerki acted as Eritrea's de facto head of state until a UN-supervised referendum on independence was held in 1993. Ninety-eight percent of the electorate voted yes, and independence was declared on May 24, 1993. Afwerki was formally elected president soon afterward. Elections were tentatively scheduled for 2001 but did not in fact occur.

INDEPENDENT ERITREA

With independence, Eritrea began to rebuild. The war had created a refugee population of at least 750,000, many of whom came streaming back from Sudan soon after the fighting ended. Seventy thousand veterans—many of whom had known no other life beyond the war—also had to be reincorporated into society. One of the government's long-term goals was to rebuild Eritrea's industrial base, but with drought a chronic threat and three-quarters of the country's 2.7 million people dependent on outside food aid, intensifying agricultural production was an immediate priority—as was removal of the land mines still littering the countryside.

During its first years of independence, Eritrea won accolades for its honest government and determination to achieve self-sufficiency. The country has refused loans and aid packages with too many strings attached and has resolved to rebuild the destroyed Massawa-Asmara railroad using only Eritrean labor. The government recruited seventy-year-old former train engineers out of retirement to help restore steam engines from the 1930s. At the same time, Eritrea's once-Marxist government leaders welcomed foreign investment in certain sectors, such as coastal tourism.

Some of the wartime objectives of the EPLF, now renamed People's Front for Democracy and Justice (PDJ), have become government objectives, such as education and legal equality for women, and rural primary health care. It has also pledged to protect religious freedom, though some smaller groups, notably the Jehovah's Witnesses, have complained of persecution. Overall, the sense of national unity forged during the long war has translated into widespread popular support for the government, which at least initially was largely comprised of former fighters. Some outside observers, however, have criticized the PDJ's authoritarian tendencies. The constitution passed in 1997 gave considerable power to the central government but also called for multiparty elections.

Eritrea has had tense relations with its neighbors in recent years. It broke diplomatic relations with Sudan in 1994 over concerns that it was cultivating ISLAMIC FUNDAMENTALISM in border areas. This concern prompted the United States to supply both Eritrea and Ethiopia with military aid. For its part, Sudan has accused the Eritreans of supporting southern Sudanese rebels. In 1996 Eritrea skirmished briefly with both DJIBOUTI over a contested border, and with Yemen over ownership of a collection of small Red Sea Islands.

Perhaps most seriously, armed conflict with Ethiopia erupted again in May 1998. The immediate cause of the fighting was again a disputed border, but tensions over trade issues had been building for months. When Eritrea became independent the two countries had agreed to share Ethiopia's currency (the birr) and Eritrea's port access. These cooperative relations began to deteriorate in 1997, especially after Eritrea introduced its own currency, the nafka. Despite efforts by the United States, the ORGANIZATION OF AFRICAN UNITY, and neighboring African countries to resolve the conflict diplomatically, both sides continued to arm themselves, insisting that nothing less than national sovereignty was at stake. More than 70,000 Ethiopians and Eritreans died in the thirty-month war over the border region, and hundreds of thousands of civilians were forced to flee the area. In December 2000 the UN negotiated a peace treaty to stop the fighting and sent peacekeeping troops to war-torn Eritrea. In April 2002 an international commission settled the border dispute between the two nations. Afwerki's government currently faces the challenge of overcoming high illiteracy and unemployment rates as it seeks to rebuild an economy shattered by Ethiopian invasion.

See also CHRISTIANITY, AFRICAN: AN OVERVIEW; ETHIOPIAN ORTHODOX CHURCH; HUNGER AND FAMINE; ISLAM IN AFRICA; LANGUAGES, AFRICAN: AN OVERVIEW; PASTORALISM; SCRAMBLE FOR AFRICA; UNITED NATIONS IN AFRICA.

DAVID P. JOHNSON, JR.

Ethiopia

Country in the Horn of Africa bordering Eritrea, Djibouti, Somalia, Kenya, and Sudan.

Over 3,000 years ago the Greek poet Homer sang of "the blessed Ethiopians." The English man of letters Samuel Johnson wrote a novel 200 years ago about an Ethiopian prince, in which the philosophers of the country contemplated the mysteries of the universe. In the twentieth century, pan-Africanists, such as W. E. B. Du Bois, saw Ethiopia as the "all-mother of men," an ancient land of immense importance to human history, while the followers of Marcus Garvey dreamed that the children of slaves might return to Africa and live in Ethiopia, a nation that in the biblical Book of Psalms "stretched out her hands unto God." More recently, television and newspapers have depicted Ethiopia in harsh terms as a land of famine, war, and very little else, but the country possesses an extraordinary history, which remains little known outside its borders.

The land now known as Ethiopia witnessed the birth of humanity over 100,000 years ago, and it was home to some of Africa's most ancient and advanced civilizations. Indeed, Ethiopia is one of the oldest nations on earth. For centuries the people of Ethiopia's highlands have maintained a rich cultural legacy, including a literary tradition dating from over 2,000 years ago and a form of CHRISTIANITY dating from the time of the Roman Empire. Over the centuries many of the country's people came to practice Islam, and by the twentieth century, Ethiopia incorporated one of the most ethnically and culturally diverse populations in Africa. From the 1960s to the early 1990s Ethiopia suffered a long economic decline, famine, and civil warfare, first under an autocratic emperor and later under a brutal socialist military government. Though in the late 1990s Ethiopia made progress at overcoming ethnic strife and years of economic mismanagement, it still faces many challenges.

PREHISTORY

Ethiopia was home to some of our earliest human ancestors. Some of the oldest remains of Homo sapiens, dating back about 130,000 years, have been found in the far south, along the Kibish River in the Omo Valley region. Until 1994 the oldest known branch of the human family tree was represented by fossil remains found in 1974 at Hadar, 350 kilometers (217 miles) northeast of the Ethiopian capital, ADDIS ABABA. The famous partial skeleton called "Dinqinesh," or "Lucy," a specimen of Australopithecus afarensis, which dates from between three million and 3.6 million years ago, is exhibited in the National Museum at Addis Ababa. Discoveries of even older hominid remains have now surpassed Australopithecus afarensis. The remains of seventeen individuals, identified as members of a new species, Australopithecus ramidus, have been found at Aramis, on the north side of the Awash Valley, about seventy-five kilometers (forty-seven miles) south of the Hadar region. These new finds take the record in Ethiopia back 4.4 million years, and appear to confirm estimates that the hominid line diverged from that of modern apes between four million and six million years ago.

About 8,000 years ago inhabitants of present-day Ethiopia had begun to practice animal husbandry. The region's people, most likely speaking Cushitic languages, were practicing agriculture 2,000 years ago at the latest. By about 1000 B.C.E. Semitic-speaking peoples had entered the northern highlands, perhaps from southern Arabia. There they probably intermarried with the existing population. These people were the ancestors of today's TIGRE, Tigray, and AMHARA (as well as other, smaller ethnic groups), who speak languages belonging to the Semitic family, which includes Arabic and Hebrew.

EARLY HISTORY

The early history of Ethiopia, whether legendary or confirmed by archaeology, is rich and fascinating. The country's northern borderlands may have been the location of the fabulous land of PUNT (Pwene), known to the ancient Egyptians as a source of luxuries, especially incense, for the courts of the pharaohs. Aromatic resins are still collected in some areas of Tigray Province and ERITREA. The ancient Egyptians called this country "the Land of God" (Taneter).

Between about 800 and 300 B.C.E. a literate and highly developed civilization flourished in the Eritrean and Tigray highlands. Its rulers referred to themselves as the kings or mukarribs of Da'amat and Saba, and may have ruled over parts of south Arabia known as Saba (or Sheba). The title mukarrib indicated something like "federator," and in south Arabia (present-day Yemen) the title referred to the

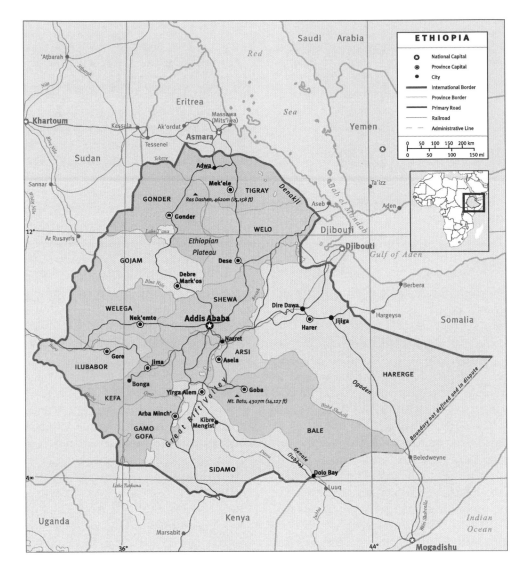

ruler of peoples that were linked by covenant. The people of Da'amat in Ethiopia wrote inscriptions in a language and a script very similar to that found on inscriptions in south Arabia, and presumably the peoples on both sides of the Red Sea shared a common cultural background. Only a few traces of the civilization of Da'amat remain, but they are often spectacular. At Yeha the impressive temple of the god Ilmuqah still stands; it is the most ancient building in Ethiopia. Inscribed altars and some splendid stone sculptures from this period are now on display in the National Museum.

After this period the uplands became the seat of one of the greatest of all the ancient African civilizations; the empire was ruled from its capital city of AKSUM. South Arabian and Aksumite sources, written in the ancient Ethiopian language known as Ge'ez, refer to the so-called Habash people who inhabited the empire. The name of this

people is the basis of the word "Abyssinia," by which Ethiopia has often been known. The name of Ethiopia is taken from a Greek expression meaning "burnt faces." The Greeks applied this term to the Kushite kingdom and black Africa in general. In the fourth century C.E. the kings of Aksum began to use the Greek term (Aithiopia) for their own country when they wrote in Greek. A trilingual inscription of Ezana, the king who converted to Christianity about 340 C.E., employs both names. This is the first known use of the word "Ethiopia" by one of its own rulers to describe part of the modern country. The land was usually called Aksum, after its capital.

According to early church historians such as Rufinus of Aquileia (345?–410 C.E.), a young Syrian named Frumentius brought Christianity to Ethiopia. Around 330 C.E. he was made bishop of Aksum by Athanasius, patriarch of ALEXANDRIA. This established a custom that

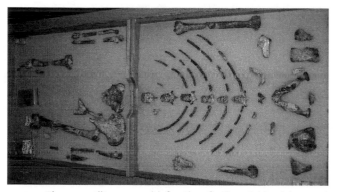

LUCY. The 3.2-million-year-old fossils of a hominid, nicknamed "Lucy," on display at the Ethiopian Natural History Museum in Addis Ababa. (*Les Neuhaus/AP Images*)

continued for over sixteen centuries. Until 1959 the Alexandrian patriarch of the Coptic Church of Egypt appointed the bishops who headed the Ethiopian church. They were always foreign, usually Egyptian.

During the Aksumite period the northern regions of Ethiopia belonged to an international trade network linking the NILE RIVER, the Mediterranean, and the Indian Ocean. Aksum's control over this rich trade provided the basis for its prosperity and cultural achievements. In the sixth century C.E., King Kaleb of Aksum sent a military expedition across the Red Sea to depose the Jewish king Yusuf Asar of Himyar. Even though historical details about the period are relatively meager, objects recovered from excavations indicate a high level of material prosperity, with pottery, architecture, and coinage attesting unique Aksumite styles. By the Aksumite period, the AGAW and other peoples who spoke Cushitic languages had come under the dominance of a ruling class who spoke the Semitic language Ge'ez.

Over a period of seven centuries Aksum firmly left its mark on highland northern Ethiopia. The choice of Christianity, the style of architecture, and the form of kingship were retained even after the city itself ceased to be the political center. The empire first shaped the general cultural heritage of highland Ethiopia, including Christian religion and Semitic language. From every point of view, the Aksumite kingdom was a golden age in Ethiopian history. Its kings erected stone stelae (or pillars) whose height surpassed any other monolithic monuments in the ancient world, and they employed a gold coinage at a time when very few other societies were wealthy or sophisticated enough to do so.

The zenith of Aksum occurred in the sixth century. Soon after, the rise of Islamic power in the Red Sea deprived Aksum of control over the trade that had been its major source of wealth. Its kings were forced to curtail their overseas projects, abandon many of their trading links, and retreat to the highlands. Arab geographers describe an Ethiopian state ruled from a capital called Ku'bar. This Ethiopian Christian kingdom seems to have maintained itself for several centuries, though it was often threatened by expansionist Muslim states to the east and south. Almost nothing is known about it, aside from the occasional remarks in the reports of Arab geographers or in the chronicles of the patriarchs of Alexandria. These chronicles record a disaster that occurred late in the tenth century, when a foreign queen is said to have seized power, killing the reigning *negus*, or king. This incident seems to have been preserved in Ethiopian legends that tell of a queen called Gudit, whom the chronicles blame for destroying Aksum.

In spite of such defeats, the highland kingdom seems to have been able to keep its Christian culture more or less intact. The Zagwe Dynasty, which ruled from about 1137 to 1270, figures in traditional Ethiopian sources as a break in the historical sequence, when a "usurping" dynasty of Agaw origin seized control of the throne. Royal chronicles and accounts of Ethiopian saints provide some information about this period of Ethiopian history. The capital city during this period was Adafa or Roha, which was later named after LALIBELA himself, who is said to have commissioned the city's famous churches, cut from the living rock. The Zagwe kings did not rule over a large area. The limits of Zagwe power seem to have encouraged the Muslims of the coast, who grew strong enough to establish states as far west as present-day Shewa.

The church hierarchy and remnants of the old elite resented Zagwe rule. With the support of the church, the Solomonic Dynasty ousted the Zagwe from power around 1270. Traditional church accounts describe the Solomonic Dynasty as descendants of the "legitimate" rulers, in contrast with the Zagwe "usurpers." In other words, church documents back the new Dynasty's claims of descent from King Solomon of Israel and the QUEEN OF SHEBA through their son Menelik, the legendary first emperor of Ethiopia. In return for the church's support, the Solomonic rulers awarded the Ethiopian church control over vast stretches of land, which gave the church a source of wealth and power that endured until the revolution of 1974. This Dynasty continued into the nineteenth century, and was linked with the family of the last emperor, HAILE SELASSIE. The Dynasty's power was based in the Amhara regions (including Shewa). There seems to have been no real capital. The emperor and his court were perpetually on the move, establishing temporary administration as the need arose. During the dry season, when military campaigns were possible, the capital took the form of a vast but rigidly disciplined city of tents.

THE CAPTURE OF ADDIS ABABA. British soldiers surround a stack of confiscated Italian rifles in the Ethiopian capital of Addis Ababa, shortly after conquering the city in 1941. (*AP Images*)

The founder of this new Dynasty was Yekuno Amlak (1270–1285), and some of his successors were remarkable rulers, who consolidated and extended the kingdom, or made significant contributions to religious and cultural life. During the early years of the Dynasty, royal chronicles give some information about wars with Muslim states such as Ifat, which controlled the area around the Red Sea coast and even some of the highlands of Shewa. For the first time, the Christian kingdom was able to expand toward what are now the southern provinces of Ethiopia. Amda Seyon (1314–1344) even absorbed some Muslim districts, although his empire extracted tribute from more or less autonomous regions instead of imposing direct control. Other emperors campaigned in the north, to gain access to the Red Sea, as well as in the south and the east. Zar'a Ya'qob (1434–1468) controlled a substantial central Ethiopian state in relative tranquility, which allowed the new growth of arts and literature. However, few churches, manuscripts, or paintings survive from this period. Much of the territory and the cultural heritage was soon to be lost, and any further territorial expansion was to remain modest until the late nineteenth century.

INVASIONS AND DISORDER

In the sixteenth century the Portuguese search for a mythical Christian ruler named Prester John led to the Solomonic emperors of Ethiopia. A first envoy, Pero da Covilhão, was sent in 1487. He arrived six years later during the reign of

Eskender, but was never permitted to leave. More envoys arrived in 1508, and in the following year a letter was sent to Portugal with an Ethiopian ambassador, Matthew the Armenian. He finally reached Portugal in 1514, and returned with a Portuguese embassy in 1520. The arrival of the Portuguese embassy enabled one of its members, Francisco Alvares, to write the first detailed description of the country, the only account we have of the medieval kingdom before Muslim incursions destroyed much of its Christian culture.

The great rivals of the Christian emperors were the Muslim rulers of Adal, the region lying east of the Awash River as far as the seacoast, and including Harer. In 1516 the emperor Lebna DENGEL defeated the emir Mahfuz of Adal. Perhaps because of this victory, he neglected to make a military alliance with the Portuguese, but a strong and determined leader soon arose among the Muslims. The imam Ahmad ibn Ibrahim of Harer, known as Grañ ("the left-handed"), won a great victory in 1529, and Muslim armies invaded most of Christian Ethiopia. Lebna Dengel, who had received the Portuguese embassy enthroned in his great pavilion hung with silks and brocades, became a fugitive until his death at Debra Damo in 1540. According to Arabic as well as Ethiopian sources, Muslim forces ransacked and burned churches, monasteries, and treasuries.

This might have been the end of the unique Christian civilization that had flourished in northern and central

Ethiopia since Aksumite times, but the new emperor Galawdewos rescued the state with the aid of Portuguese troops under Cristovão, the son of Vasco da Gama. The decisive factor was the possession of firearms, which the Muslim troops had already acquired in large numbers across the Red Sea. Ahmad Grañ and Cristovão da Gama both lost their lives, but the tide had definitively turned in favor of the Christian state. Christian forces sacked Harer itself, although it survived as the greatest Muslim center in Ethiopia, a trading city in contact with the Red Sea coast and beyond.

After this episode the Solomonic emperors established Christian rule once again over the devastated central regions, but both the Muslim states and the Christian kingdom soon had to defend themselves against a new threat: the Cushitic OROMO peoples. During the sixteenth and seventeenth centuries, Oromo-speaking herdsmen began to migrate from the south, and rapidly became the chief enemies of the Christian state of the north and center. They occupied many parts of what is now Ethiopia, and marriages with Oromo chiefly families meant that some of the Solomonic emperors became part Oromo.

For about a century after their entry into Ethiopian affairs, the Portuguese remained active in the region. Jesuit missionaries attempted to convert the country to Roman Catholicism, with little lasting success. With the accession to the Ethiopian throne of Fasiladas, a firm adherent of the Ethiopian Orthodox church, the Roman Catholic adventure was finished. He expelled the Jesuits in 1632 and made an arrangement with the Turkish authorities at MASSAWA to execute any foreign priest who might attempt to enter the country.

After the expulsion of the Portuguese, Ethiopia was again isolated from European influence. During the following centuries, foreign travelers made occasional visits to the country, which was now ruled from the new capital built at GONDER, north of Lake Tana. Like the Jesuits before them, these visitors recorded their observations of different peoples, plants and animals, political affairs, religious issues, opportunities for trade, and many other features of Ethiopian life. The earlier Gonder period included powerful emperors whose deeds are described in the royal chronicles. Gonder itself is a remarkable testimony to their efforts, the first capital after centuries in which the empire had been governed from tents. The turrets and battlements of its castles still stand, along with some of the forty-four churches that once embellished the city.

In the eighteenth century, however, the power of the central monarchy began to decline. Gonder slowly fell into decay as great provincial lords, largely of Oromo origin, competed to enthrone rival puppet kings. The custom of

exiling male members of the royal family to a remote mountain, to prevent them from plotting against the current emperor, actually provided a reservoir of princes with the required Solomonic blood that provincial lords could recruit in any new attempt to seize power. With the assassination of Iyasu I in 1704, the monarchy became increasingly unstable. After the emperor Iyo'as was murdered in 1769, the empire began to collapse, even though the theory of Solomonic rule remained intact. This chaotic period, known as the "Era of the Princes," continued until the middle of the nineteenth century, with feeble emperors dwelling at Gonder completely at the mercy of the great provincial lords. Some of the emperors lived in such poverty amid the ruins of their palaces that scarcely enough money could be found to provide a decent burial. Only the mystique of their Solomonic descent, or perhaps the need for the great chiefs to have someone to bestow the title of ras (supreme commander), kept the system alive.

PIECEMEAL MODERNIZATION AND THE STRUGGLE AGAINST COLONIALISM

In the middle of the nineteenth century an interloper named Kassa overthrew the power of the provincial lords as well as the old imperial tradition. He eliminated most of his rivals, and restored a strong and united Ethiopia, even subduing Shewa, which had maintained a separate existence under rulers claiming descent from Lebna Dengel. Kassa was crowned in 1855 as Tewodros II, and the genealogists duly found a Solomonic background for him. Recognizing the growing threat of European imperialism, Tewodros attempted to modernize Ethiopia's army and establish a strong central state. To fund this modernization program, he imposed higher taxes on peasants and seized church lands; these actions alienated both the overtaxed peasantry and the country's powerful clergy. Meanwhile, a diplomatic argument with Great Britain led to the Napier expedition in 1868. The British besieged Tewodros at his capital Maqdala, where he committed suicide as British forces overran his defenses. However, even this disaster did not completely destroy the attempts he had made to strengthen and modernize his empire.

As the European world grew more aware of Ethiopia, Yohannes IV and MENELIK II, the two emperors who succeeded Tewodros, fought to retain their independence against Sudanese expansionism and Italian colonialism. Yohannes had been the ruler of Tigray, and emerged victorious from the struggle to fill the vacuum left by the death of Tewodros and the British departure. He thwarted a quest for power by his tributary, the king of Shewa. He failed to keep Italy from acquiring the Red Sea ports of Aseb (1869) and Massawa (1885), but resisted Italian incursions inland. Yohannes died fighting the Sudanese Mahdi, and was succeeded in 1889 by Menelik II of Shewa.

With the Ethiopian treasury drained by ongoing warfare, the new emperor needed peace to establish himself on his throne; this put him in a weak position as he faced the Italians. In 1890 Menelik agreed to the Treaty of Wichale granting Italy control of Eritrea, but the treaty's Italian translation awarded Italy a protectorate over the whole of Ethiopia. After replenishing his treasury, Menelik defeated the Italians at the Battle of Adwa in 1896. This was a unique achievement. Alone among African states, Ethiopia succeeded in retaining independent sovereignty in the face of European colonialism. Even though Menelik lost some territory in Eritrea, he made up for this by his own expansion to the south. Between 1896 and 1906 Ethiopia grew to its present size, as Menelik conquered areas previously ruled by the Oromo or other peoples. Menelik also succeeded in ejecting the last independent Muslim emir from Harer.

Determined to keep his country independent, Menelik used taxes collected from these conquered territories to fund a modernization program. Menelik founded a new capital at Addis Ababa and commissioned Ethiopia's first modern schools and hospitals. Menelik hired foreign advisers and concluded an agreement with a French firm to construct a railroad, completed in 1917, from Addis Ababa to the Indian Ocean port of DJIBOUTI in FRENCH SOMALILAND. During the reign of Menelik, Ethiopia acquired its first modern bank, postage stamps, and a national currency. The first modern roads were constructed, the basis of a telephone and telegraph system installed, and a rudimentary cabinet established. The new transport infrastructure enabled Ethiopia's land-owning elite to export cash crops, primarily coffee, for sale on the global market.

Menelik's grandson Lij Iyasu reigned briefly (1913–1916) after his grandfather's death, but his efforts to give Ethiopia's Muslim population a voice in the government angered the country's Christian elite. A group led by an aristocratic official, Ras Tafari, ousted Lij Iyasu from office and named Menelik's daughter Zawditu as empress, with Ras Tafari as the new regent. Tafari continued attempts to modernize the empire. He abolished slavery and recruited graduates of the new schools to staff a modern civil service. Coffee exports provided revenues for the expansion of Ethiopia's modern infrastructure, and the country's market economy expanded. Tafari kept Europeans from gaining control of Ethiopia's economy, as they had elsewhere in Africa, by requiring at least partial local ownership of all enterprises.

In 1930, upon the death of Zawditu, Tafari was crowned Emperor Haile Selassie I. Coffee exports continued to bankroll his ambitious modernization program. However, his reign faced a crisis in 1935 when Italian troops invaded Ethiopia. The Italian forces won a quick victory, and Italy formally annexed the country the following year. Although there was great international sympathy for Ethiopia, no material assistance was offered, and the fascist occupation lasted for five years. The Italian colonial administration undertook a significant amount of road building and other construction work, and carried out a modern expansion of the capital at Addis Ababa. However, Ethiopian patriot resistance continued in the countryside. Fascist rule collapsed after Italy under Benito Mussolini entered World War II. A combined army of Ethiopian and British troops liberated Ethiopia in 1941. Haile Selassie was restored to the throne, and his country became a founding member of the United Nations.

As the Cold War between the Soviet bloc and the West came to dominate global affairs, Haile Selassie aligned himself with the West. In return, the Western powers awarded Ethiopia the former Italian colony of Eritrea in 1952. With access to Western markets, Ethiopia earned healthy revenues from coffee exports during the 1950s. With Western and, especially, with United States assistance, new hospitals, schools, and roads were built; banking and currency were reorganized; and a national airline was established. Addis Ababa was chosen as the headquarters for both the United Nations Economic Commission for Africa and the ORGANIZATION OF AFRICAN UNITY.

Although the emperor introduced a new constitution in 1955 granting limited rights to the Ethiopian people, the constitution left ultimate power in the emperor's hands. Meanwhile, the emperor failed to respond to calls for further democratization and land reform to end the concentration of the country's land in the hands of the church and aristocracy. Frustrated by the emperor's intransigence, students began to protest and the imperial bodyguard attempted a coup in 1960. Although the aging emperor crushed the opposition and retained his hold on power, his regime lost popular support, and his government faced ongoing rebellion in Eritrea and the Somali borderlands. With the dramatic increase in the price of imported oil in 1973 and a simultaneous drought and famine in northern Ethiopia, Ethiopia's economy collapsed. Demonstrations and strikes in Addis Ababa forced the resignation of government officials in early 1974. Soon thereafter, a military committee, known as the Derg, led by MENGISTU Haile Mariam, seized control of the government and moved to dismantle the entrenched aristocratic power structure for which they blamed the country's ills. On September 12, 1974, the Derg removed the emperor from his throne, and by the end of the year, Mengistu's faction, which was committed to Soviet-style SOCIALISM, had driven moderates from the government.

Ethiopia (At a Glance)

OFFICIAL NAME:
Federal Democratic Republic of Ethiopia

AREA:
1,127,127 sq km (432,300 sq mi)

LOCATION:
Eastern Africa; bounded by Eritrea, Djibouti, Somalia, Kenya, and the Sudan

CAPITAL:
Addis Ababa (population 2.7 million; 2007 estimate)

POPULATION:
82,544,840 (2008 estimate)

POPULATION DENSITY:
73 persons per sq km (190 persons per sq mi)

POPULATION BELOW AGE 15:
46 percent (male 18,922,334; female 19,017,593; 2008 estimate)

POPULATION GROWTH RATE:
3.212 percent (2008 estimate)

TOTAL FERTILITY RATE:
6.17 children born per woman (2008 estimate)

LIFE EXPECTANCY AT BIRTH:
Total population: 54.99 years (male 52.54 years; female 57.51 years; 2008 estimate)

INFANT MORTALITY RATE:
82.64 deaths per 1000 live births (2008 estimate)

LITERACY RATE (AGE 15 AND OVER WHO CAN READ AND WRITE):
Total population: 42.7 percent (male 50.3 percent; female 35.1 percent; 2003 estimate)

EDUCATION:
Education is free and compulsory for children ages 7–13, but regular school facilities are not available to more than half the nation's school-age children. In the early 1990s about 2.8 million students attended primary and secondary schools run by the government and religious groups. In 2000, 47 percent of school-age children attended primary school and 13 percent attended secondary school. Addis Ababa University (1950) has branches in several locations.

LANGUAGES:
Amharic is the official language; Tigrinya, Orominga, Guaraginga, Somali, Arabic, and English are also spoken.

ETHNIC GROUPS:
The Amhara, a highland people partly of Semitic origin, and the related Tigreans constitute about 32 percent of the total population. The Oromo people, living mainly in central and southwestern Ethiopia, constitute about 40 percent of the population. The Shangalla, a people found in the western part of the country from the border of Eritrea to Lake Turkana, constitute about 6 percent of the population. The Somali, who live in the east and southeast, notably in the Ogaden region, are approximately equal in number to the Shangalla. The Denakil inhabit the semidesert plains east of the highlands. The nonindigenous population includes Yemenis, Indians, Armenians, and Greeks.

RELIGIONS:
About 60.8 percent of the people of Ethiopia are Christians, many from the Ethiopian Orthodox Union Church, an autonomous Christian sect headed by a patriarch and closely related to the Coptic church of Egypt. Christianity is predominant in the north; all the southern regions have Muslim majorities, who represent about 32.8 percent of the country's population. The south also contains large numbers of animists. The Falashas, who practice a type of Judaism that probably dates back to contact with early Arabian Jews, were airlifted to Israel in 1991 during Ethiopia's civil war.

CLIMATE:
The principal rainy season occurs between mid-June and September, followed by a dry season that may be interrupted in February or March by a short rainy season. The tropical zone has an average annual temperature of about 27° C (about 80° F) and receives less than about 510 mm (about 20 in) of rain annually. The subtropical zone, which includes most of the highland plateau, has an average temperature of about 22° C (about 72° F) with an annual rainfall ranging from about 510 to 1,530 mm (about 20 to 60 in).

LAND, PLANTS, AND ANIMALS:
The Ethiopian Plateau, a high tableland covering more than half the total area of the country, is split by the Great Rift Valley. In the north, the plateau is cut by many rivers and deep valleys, and capped by mountains in the region surrounding Lake T'ana (the lake in which the Blue Nile rises). The northeastern edges of the plateau are marked by steep escarpments, which drop to the sunbaked coastal plain and the Denakil Desert. Along the western fringe the plateau descends gradually to the desert of Sudan. Along the southern and southwestern limits, the plateau lowers toward Lake Turkana (formerly called Lake Rudolf). The lower areas of the tropical zone have sparse vegetation, but in the valleys and ravines almost every form of African vegetation grows profusely. Afro-alpine vegetation is found on the highest slopes. Giraffes, leopards, hippopotamuses, lions, elephants, antelope, and rhinoceroses are native to most parts of the country. Lynxes, jackals, hyenas, and various species of monkey are also common. Birds of prey include eagles, hawks, and vultures. Herons, parrots, and such game birds as snipe, partridges, teals, pigeons, and bustards are found in abundance. Among the many varieties of insects are locusts and tsetse flies.

NATURAL RESOURCES:
The resources of Ethiopia are primarily agricultural. The plateau area is fertile and largely undeveloped. The wide range of soils, climate, and elevations permits the production of a diversified range of agricultural commodities. A variety of mineral deposits exist; iron, copper, petroleum, salt, potash, gold, and platinum are the principal ones that have been commercially exploited.

CURRENCY:
The birr

GROSS DOMESTIC PRODUCT (GDP):
$56.05 billion (2007 estimate)

GDP PER CAPITA:
$700 (2007 estimate)

GDP REAL GROWTH RATE:
11.1 percent (2007 estimate)

PRIMARY ECONOMIC ACTIVITIES:
The economy of Ethiopia remains heavily dependent on the earnings of the agricultural sector. Participation by most of the people in the monetary economy is limited; much trading is conducted by barter in local markets. Traditional agriculture, including livestock raising, is the most characteristic form of Ethiopian economic activity. Commercial estates, which are run by the government, supply coffee, cotton, sugar, fruit, and vegetables to the nation's processing industries and for export. Coffee is Ethiopia's most important commodity, engaging about one-fourth of the population. A drought in 2002 severely crippled Ethiopia's economy, creating another persisting famine.

PRIMARY AGRICULTURAL PRODUCTS:
Coffee, cotton, sugar, fruit, vegetables, pulses (chickpeas, lentils, haricot beans), oilseeds, and cereal grains; livestock includes cattle, sheep, goats, poultry, and smaller numbers of horses, mules, donkeys, and camels.

continued

INDUSTRIES:
Food processing, beverages, textiles, chemicals, metal processing, and cement

PRIMARY EXPORTS:
Coffee, khat, leather products, and gold

PRIMARY IMPORTS:
Capital goods, food, consumer goods, and fuel

PRIMARY TRADE PARTNERS:
Djibouti, Japan, Saudi Arabia, India, Italy, and United States

GOVERNMENT:
Ethiopia is a federal republic. According to the 1994 constitution, the head of state is the president, currently Girma Wolde-Giorgis who is elected by the legislative body, the House of People's Representatives. A president may not serve more than two six-year terms. The council also nominates a prime minister from among its members, a position currently held by Meles Zenawi, who is the chief executive and heads a Council of Ministers made up of representatives from a coalition of parties constituting a majority in the legislature. The House of People's Representatives consists of 548 directly elected members; at least 20 of these representatives must be members of minority ethnic groups.

Marian Aguiar

THE REVOLUTION AND ITS AFTERMATH

With the old establishment shattered, Mengistu installed a revolutionary socialist government. Abandoning earlier contacts with the United States, he relied on support from the Soviet Union. Several groups challenged revolutionary policies on ideological or ethnic grounds, but Mengistu's regime brutally repressed internal opposition. In 1975, the Ethiopian government carried out a sweeping land reform that seized land from its previous owner and made it the property of the state. This land nationalization eliminated the power base of the land-owning aristocracy and church, which for centuries had relied on the collection of rents from the country's peasantry. Meanwhile, internal unrest, including an ongoing independence struggle in Eritrea, encouraged a Somali invasion in 1975, which the Ethiopian government defeated in 1978 with massive Soviet and Cuban aid. The government nationalized (placed under state ownership) factories, banks, and insurance companies, and in 1984 established a ruling party, the Workers' Party of Ethiopia.

During the 1980s separatist movements in Eritrea and Tigray mounted increasingly successful military campaigns. Meanwhile, the Ethiopian government's land reform and agricultural policies ruined the country's fragile ecological balance, and harvests declined. Government exploitation of the peasantry further hampered both agricultural production and the distribution of food, and in 1984 a grueling famine gripped the country. News of famine brought Ethiopia to the attention of Western media. This publicity resulted in extensive international aid, which emphasized humanitarian relief rather than development. The country thus remained one of the poorest in the world. The Mengistu regime's radical responses to the problems of drought and famine—resettlement and "villagization"—made the situation worse. Resettlement programs involved the relocation of peasants, sometimes forcibly, to uncultivated lands where they often lacked the infrastructure or supplies necessary for successful farming. The government's villagization programs moved peasants from their scattered homesteads to concentrated settlements along roads, supposedly to facilitate the delivery of aid and services, but also to facilitate government surveillance. Both programs further disrupted the country's agriculture and provoked accusations by Ethiopian and foreign observers that dissident groups were being starved deliberately.

In 1988 rebels in Eritrea and Tigre joined forces and successfully fought Ethiopian government troops. Rebels expanded their control over Eritrea and northern Ethiopia during 1989 and 1990. The rebels from Tigray formed alliances with other ethnically based opposition groups to form the Ethiopian People's Revolutionary Democratic Front (EPRDF). By April 1991 all of Eritrea was under the control of the Eritrean People's Liberation Front (EPLF), and the forces of the EPRDF advanced on Addis Ababa. Mengistu fled to exile in ZIMBABWE in May 1991, and his regime collapsed.

The EPRDF established a transitional government with Meles ZENAWI as president in Ethiopia, while the EPLF controlled Eritrea. The EPRDF announced the reorganization of the country as a federal state divided into regions along ethnic lines. The new government promoted this reorganization as a way to acknowledge the country's ethnic diversity, but the reorganization angered many Asmara (the ethnic group that had traditionally dominated Ethiopia), who felt that the plan jeopardized national unity. The EPRDF muzzled the opposition and in 1992 carried out parliamentary elections. In 1993 Eritrea formally declared its independence. The Ethiopian parliament approved a new constitution in 1994 (effective in August 1995), and Meles Zenawi won election as prime minister in 1995. The legislative elections of 2005 were marred by accusations and counteraccusations of fraud and official corruption. Despite this, the country's opposition parties fared relatively well, picking up some two hundred seats in the parliament.

During 1992 and 1993 the transitional government had agreed to a structural adjustment plan that was intended to liberalize the economy. However, the government at first failed to return property seized by the Mengistu regime to private owners. The economy stagnated, and the government's heavy regulation of commerce discouraged agricultural production and food distribution. Once again, in 1994, famine threatened Ethiopia. International assistance saved many lives, and in 1995 the government finally established a process for returning nationalized land to private control. However, this process aroused opposition because it favored supporters of the EPRDF, who were allowed to claim larger allotments of land than families who had received title to land under the regime of Emperor Haile Selassie or Lieutenant Colonel Mengistu. The government also announced controversial plans to privatize its commercial and industrial holdings. The redistribution of land appeared to improve the country's agricultural fortunes: the country enjoyed good harvests in 1996 and 1997. Its overall economy seemed to be recovering from years of government mismanagement. However, ethnic strife and raids carried out by soldiers discharged at the end of Ethiopia's long civil war continued to plague the Oromo and Somali regions in the south and east. In May 1998 a border dispute with neighboring Eritrea erupted into a full-scale war. By the time the UN brokered a peace treaty in December 2000, Ethiopia had spent three billion dollars and had 350,000 of its residents displaced. The end of hostilities and good rainfall led to a brief period of growth. Drought struck again in late 2002, however, creating another persisting famine and crippling the nation's poverty-stricken economy. Malnutrition, malaria, and AIDS currently afflict millions of Ethiopians.

See also ACQUIRED IMMUNODEFICIENCY SYNDROME IN AFRICA: AN INTERPRETATION; AFRICAN ORIGINS OF HUMANITY; AFRICAN SOCIALISM; ANCIENT AFRICAN CIVILIZATIONS; CHRISTIANITY, AFRICAN: AN OVERVIEW; COLD WAR AND AFRICA; DISEASES, INFECTIOUS, IN AFRICA; DROUGHT AND DESERTIFICATION; ETHIOPIAN ORTHODOX CHURCH; HUNGER AND FAMINE; ISLAM IN AFRICA; LANGUAGES, AFRICAN: AN OVERVIEW; STRUCTURAL ADJUSTMENT IN AFRICA; UNITED NATIONS IN AFRICA.

STUART MUNRO-HAY

Ethiopian Jews
Ethnic group that practices Judaism and has migrated in large numbers to Israel since the 1980s.

The East African nation of ETHIOPIA has been home to a Jewish community for many centuries. Outsiders sometimes call the Ethiopian Jews Falasha, which means "moved" or "gone into exile" in the ancient Geez language that was a forerunner to the modern languages of north-central Ethiopia. Today's Ethiopian Jewish community, however, considers the term derogatory and prefers to be called Beta Israel, Hebrew for "House of Israel."

The origins of Judaism in Ethiopia remain a mystery, but it is likely that the community's roots extend back for 2,500 years. Some Beta Israel believe that they are descendants of Menelik, who, according to legend, was the son of King Solomon and the Queen of SHEBA. Others believe the Beta Israel to be the tribe of Dan, one of the ten lost tribes of Israel mentioned in the Bible. Still others trace the group's history to the biblical parting of the Red Sea so that Jews in Egypt could escape into Israel. The Jews of Ethiopia, say these believers, did not cross in time and instead escaped from Egypt by heading south. Some scholars have suggested that the Beta Israel are the descendants of Ethiopians converted by Jews who migrated to Ethiopia about 2,000 years ago from the region of southern Arabia that is now Yemen.

When the Ethiopian kingdom of AKSUM adopted Christianity as its official religion during the fourth century C.E., the Beta Israel were forced to relocate to the mountainous region around Lake Tana. Over the centuries the Beta Israel, numbering in the hundreds of thousands, ruled a powerful state. Beginning around 1400, however, the Solomonic dynasty of Ethiopia gradually subdued them, and in the seventeenth century the Ethiopian emperor finally defeated the Jewish state and seized its people's lands. Most Beta Israel gradually gave up their traditional language, Agaw, and adopted the TIGRINYA or AMHARA language of their neighbors.

Toward the end of the nineteenth century, the Beta Israel suffered from famine, disease, and forcible pressure to convert to Christianity. By 1900, only 60,000 to 70,000 Ethiopian Jews remained. A Polish-born Jew named Dr. Jacques Faitlovitch took up their cause in 1923. He put the Beta Israel in touch with Jewish communities around the world, opened a school for them in ADDIS ABABA, and sent several of them to Jewish schools in Europe. Although Faitlovitch's activities came to a halt during the Italian occupation of Ethiopia, he had achieved something very important. For the first time in modern history, the Beta Israel had some contact with other Jews.

In terms of their religious beliefs, the Beta Israel have always identified themselves as exiles from the land of Israel and believers in the faith of Moses. For almost 2,000 years, however, they were completely isolated from the rest of the Jewish world. They never learned of the Talmud, the codification of Judaism's oral law, or of any of the traditions that arose after biblical times, such as the holiday of Hanukkah. They were so isolated from the rest of the Jewish world that many of them did not know that other Jews still existed, or that the majority of those other Jews were white.

The religious life of the Beta Israel is based on the Torah (the first five books of the Bible), on oral interpretations passed down from generation to generation, and on the community's own holy writings. Some Beta Israel customs are similar to Jewish practices based on oral law and rabbinical literature; others resemble ancient customs practiced by Jews during the biblical and Talmudic periods. Beta Israel villages, usually set apart from neighboring Christian villages, were always situated near a body of water for purposes of ritual bathing and purification. Religious life revolved around the synagogue, called the mesgid or beit makdas.

The Beta Israel have always kept strictly to the kosher diet and observed the Saturday Sabbath as a day of rest. They celebrate all the festivals mentioned in the Torah in addition to those of their own tradition—the timing of holidays is determined by a religious lunar calendar used only by the Beta Israel. A traditional priesthood called the Kohanim are leaders of the community's religious life. During the twentieth century, the Kohanim gained increasing importance as the bearer of the group's traditions. Because the Beta Israel communicate their beliefs and rituals orally rather than in written texts, the expertise of the priests has been vital to keeping the rites alive.

After Ethiopia was liberated from Italian COLONIAL RULE in 1941, the country's laws granted Jews equal rights with the rest of the population. However, equality under the law does not always mean equality in life. The Beta Israel continued to face persecution and discrimination. Along with many other Ethiopian groups, they suffered a great deal under the repressive regime of Mengistu Haile Mariam.

Before the late twentieth century, all but a handful of Beta Israel lived in Ethiopia. In 1984 and 1991, however, the Israeli government arranged two dramatic airlifts—Operation Moses and Operation Solomon—to bring thousands of Ethiopian Jews to Israel. More than 60,000 Beta Israel now live in the state of Israel, whereas a smaller number (perhaps 40,000) remain in Ethiopia, concentrated in the capital of Addis Ababa.

The migration to Israel brought difficulties for the Ethiopians, many of whom were disoriented by the abrupt shift from the rural villages of black Ethiopia to the white, Westernized, and mostly urban society of Israel. Few of them knew Hebrew. Although they are free from the religious persecution they faced in Ethiopia, they now face racism and a daily struggle for integration. This struggle was highlighted in January 1997 when the Beta Israel learned that the Israeli government was automatically discarding blood donated by Ethiopian Jews because of fears of acquired immunodeficiency syndrome (AIDS). The discovery of this racist policy led to a protest by more than 15,000 Ethiopian Jews in Jerusalem and drew widespread publicity.

Most Ethiopian Jews in Israel now live in very poor, segregated towns, with unemployment well above the national average. Surprisingly, the Beta Israel have faced constant challenges to the authenticity of their Jewishness. But on the positive side, the community enjoys greater educational opportunities than ever before in its history, including access to colleges and graduate programs in Israel.

See also ACQUIRED IMMUNODEFICIENCY SYNDROME IN AFRICA: AN INTERPRETATION.

RACHEL ANTELL

Ethiopian Orthodox Church
Formerly the established Christian church of Ethiopia.
The Ethiopian Orthodox Church is a branch of Christianity native to the East African nation of ETHIOPIA, where it has played a central role in the culture of the AMHARA and TIGRE peoples. Although the church no longer wields the power it once held, it continues to have significant influence in Ethiopia.

Scholars are uncertain about the origins of the Ethiopian Orthodox Church. One traditional story states that two brothers from Tyre, in modern Lebanon, Christianized Ethiopia in the fourth century C.E. The brothers—Frumentius (later a saint and Ethiopia's first bishop) and Aedesius—won the support of King Ezana of AKSUM and converted his subjects. Another tradition says that three followers of Jesus— Matthew, Bartholomew, and Andrew—traveled to Ethiopia and spread Christianity, while the New Testament book Acts of the Apostles states that the apostle Philip converted an Ethiopian eunuch. Whatever truth may lie in these traditions, it is likely that Christianity could have reached Ethiopia as early as the first century C.E. through trade connections with the Middle East.

Ethiopia is known to have had contact with the ancient Middle East, particularly with Israel, birthplace of Christianity. The Amhara and Tigre languages of the Ethiopian highlands are Semitic languages, like Hebrew, the language of Israel. Ethiopian legends claim that the biblical King Solomon of Israel fathered a son with the Ethiopian queen Makidda, called the QUEEN OF SHEBA in and human. Instead, the Oriental Orthodox churches insisted that Christ had a single, unified nature simultaneously human and divine. This disagreement led to the separation of the five Oriental Orthodox churches from the Eastern Orthodox churches, the Catholic Church of Rome, and, by extension, the Protestant churches that later broke with the Roman Catholic Church.

The head of the Ethiopian Orthodox Chruch is the archbishop, or abuna (Arabic for "our father"). Until 1951, the patriarch of ALEXANDRIA, EGYPT, appointed the abuna, following a tradition extending back to Saint Frumentius. According to that tradition, Frumentius went to Alexandria to ask the patriarch to send a bishop to Ethiopia, upon which the patriarch made Frumentius the first abuna. A new method of choosing the abuna came into use in 1951. In theory, the Ethiopian clergy now select the abuna, but in reality successive Ethiopian governments have influenced the selection process and chosen some of the candidates. The clergy consists of priests and deacons, whose main functions include celebrating mass and serving as confessors to local families. Debteras are laymen who play music and dance at services; perform wizardry, fortune telling, and astrology; and serve as scribes for the nonliterate.

The practices of the Ethiopian Church can be quite severe. The church requires circumcision for boys as well as the controversial practice of female circumcision. Both clergy and lay members of the congregation are expected to fast, which means that they can eat no breakfast and can eat only vegetables at other meals. Clergy follow a schedule that requires them to fast for 250 days each year, while the laity must fast every Wednesday and Friday and for two months during Lent and the Easter season—a total of 165 days each year. Besides Sunday services, Ethiopian Christians must attend services on holy days. On Sabbath and holy days they cannot perform manual labor. Except for fast days, services begin at six o'clock in the morning and last about three hours. Services for Easter begin Friday and end Sunday at midnight. None but the sick may sit during the services.

The church building centers on the tabot, a replica of the Ark of the Covenant that has been sanctified by a bishop. The faith recognizes the sacraments of baptism, penance, eucharist (or holy communion), marriage, anointing of the sick, and holy orders. Saints, who have been especially empowered by God to intercede on behalf of the faithful who pray to them, figure prominently in Ethiopian Christianity.

The Ethiopian Orthodox Church has a long history of monasticism. There are two main types of monasticism: anchoritism, which consists of solitary meditation and prayer, and cenobitism, or communal life. Many Ethiopian monasteries trace their origins to the so-called

ETHIOPIAN COPTIC ORTHODOXY. A priest blesses gatherered pilgrims at St. Mary's church in Entoto, Ethiopia, 2000. (*Pier Paolo Cito/AP Images*)

the Bible. This son, Menelik, stole the Ark of the Covenant, the symbol of Israel's status as God's chosen people. Thereafter, according to the Ethiopian tradition, Judaism was the state religion until the Ethiopian conversion to Christianity. Certainly Ethiopian Christianity has some similarities to traditional Jewish practices. It emphasizes the dietary laws and rules of circumcision found in the Old Testament of the Bible, and in addition to the Christian Sunday Sabbath, Ethiopian Christians observe the traditional Jewish Saturday Sabbath, as do the ETHIOPIAN JEWS.

The Ethiopian Orthodox Church is one of the Oriental Orthodox churches, a cluster of Christian faiths that includes the Coptic Orthodox Church of EGYPT, the Syrian Orthodox Church, the Armenian Orthodox Church, and the Indian Orthodox Church of Malabar (or Kerala). These churches rejected the conclusion of the 451 Council of Chalcedon that Christ had a dual nature, divine nine monks, said to have come from Syria in the fifth century. Believers claim that the monastic life is the highest stage of Christian life. Devout Ethiopian Christians hope to live their last years as monks or nuns, and many take monastic vows when they enter old age.

The Amhara and Tigre peoples of the northern and central highlands have traditionally been the strongest adherents of Ethiopian Christianity, and the beliefs and customs of the church form an essential part of their traditional culture. Until 1900, the church was the only source for education for Ethiopian children, and that education centered on religion. Church and state were long entwined in Ethiopia. As early as the sixth century C.E. the Aksumite monarchy named the Ethiopian Orthodox Church the state church, and it held that position until 1974. The state financed the church and granted it extensive tracts of land. The vast land holdings of the cenobitic monasteries, and the monasteries' legal jurisdiction over these lands, gave the monastic organizations considerable power. The church lost much of this power in 1974 when the government of Mengistu Haile Mariam nationalized church holdings, or placed them under the ownership of the state. He also stripped the monasteries of legal jurisdiction and disestablished the church, giving it the same status as all other religions.

The modern Ethiopian Orthodox Church has encountered many challenges. It lost its main sources of income when it lost its lands, and with the establishment of modern secular schools it also lost its monopoly on education. It has no modern theological seminaries, and with the church's loss of power and the declining prestige of a traditional religious education, church leaders fear that they will fail to attract enough young men to the priesthood. Church services are in the ancient Ge'ez language, which is no longer spoken in Ethiopia, and many think that the services themselves are antiquated.

Even without government support, however, the church still has influence in Ethiopia, which is why the government insists on approving the clergymen who are appointed to important church offices. The 1991 independence of ERITREA, formerly part of Ethiopia, highlighted the controversial relationship between state and church in Ethiopia. Eritrean leaders insisted on the creation of an Eritrean Orthodox Church separate from the Ethiopian Orthodox Church; the Eritrean church later associated itself with the Coptic Church of Egypt. After Ethiopian bishops protested the separation in letters to the patriarch at Alexandria, the Ethiopian government, wanting to maintain good relations with Eritrea, removed the protesting bishops from their offices and replaced them with candidates it considered more politically acceptable. In 1993, the

Ethiopian government appointed a new abuna who was Egyptian, not Ethiopian, sparking angry popular protest among the church's faithful.

See also CHRISTIANITY, AFRICAN: AN OVERVIEW; FEMALE CIRCUMCISION IN AFRICA.

ROBERT FAY

Ethiopian Theater
Twentieth-century art form that combines local and Western traditions.

During the twentieth century, a new form of theater emerged in the eastern African nation of ETHIOPIA. Fusing local expressive practices with Western performance traditions, Ethiopian theater has been shaped by the shifting political culture of the country. Political authorities have sometimes censored theater and sometimes used it as propaganda, while Ethiopian dramatists have pursued their own goals and sought self-expression.

Theater, as understood in the West, is a fairly new phenomenon in Ethiopia. The first recorded Ethiopian play, a satirical adaptation and translation of the French fables of La Fontaine, was performed before members of the royal court sometime beween 1912 and 1916. Written by Tekle-Hawaryat Tekle-Mariam, it was titled *Yawrewoch Komediya* (Comedy of the Animals). Political censorship, however, banned all dramatic activity following *Yawrewoch Komediya*. Not until HAILE SELASSIE I became emperor in 1930 did theater revive. During the next five years, theater studies began in schools; the first stage was built at a public high school called the Lycée Menelik II in 1934. There was no theater during the Italian military occupation from 1935 to 1940, but when the emperor returned from exile in 1941, theatrical activity was renewed by two groups at opposite ends of the political spectrum: the Hager Fikir (Patriots) Association and the Municipality Theater Company. The latter group produced Ethiopia's first genuinely popular play, Yoftahé Negussé's *Afajeshign* (You Got Me Caught, 1941), which criticized the emperor's handling of the war.

In 1955, the emperor commissioned the building of the 1,400-seat Haile Selassie Theater, later renamed the National Theater. In its early years, the theater was run by Austrians Franz Zulveker and Richard Hager. They staged historical and religious dramas by Ethiopian writers. Among these productions were *David and Orion* (1956) by Prime Minister Mekonnen Endalkachew and the tragedy *Tewodros* (1959) by Girmachew Tekle-Hawaryat. The influence of this early theater is still felt in the naturalism of director and playwright Melaku Ashagre's contemporary work.

In 1960, two highly qualified Ethiopian theater professionals returned from abroad. They were playwright Tsegaye Gebre-Medhin, who came from the Royal Court Theater in London, England, and actor Tesfaye Gessesse, who trained at Northwestern University in Evanston, Illinois. Their arrival moved Ethiopian theater into its contemporary phase. Gebre-Medhin was chosen to run the Municipality Theater Company and also started a short-lived theater school that produced some of Ethiopia's best actors, such as Wegayehu Negatu and Alem-tsehay Wedajo. Negatu and Debebe Eshetu are particularly famous actors from this period. For many people, they epitomize classic Ethiopian acting.

Gebre-Medhin is the best-known Ethiopian playwright both within and outside the country. He has written plays in English, such as the *Oda Oak Oracle*, published in London in 1965 and described by writer Albert Gérard in 1971 as "one of the finest plays to have been written in Africa." Gebre-Medhin has also translated Shakespeare's plays and, writing in the Amharic language, has created learned and poetic dramas that treat Ethiopian political and social history on a large scale.

After Ethiopia's Marxist revolution of 1974, theater was mainly characterized by propaganda and protest productions. It became more popular than ever. Many of the country's theater professionals received training in other Marxist countries, the former Soviet Union and its eastern European satellites. When the University of Addis Ababa established a theater arts department in 1979, classes in performance, playwriting, directing, theater history, and stagecraft expanded the body of available plays and the scope for experimenting with new kinds of theater. This period produced Tsfaye Gessesse's *Teatre Sidada* (When Theater Begins To Crawl), a trio of related plays, as well as productions of works by American and European playwrights.

Some playwrights drew on Ethiopian traditions. For example, Fisseha Belay wrote *Simegn Sintayehu* (I Saw So Much When I Wished, 1985), based on the strategies of rural Ethiopian courtship and Ethiopians' fondness for verbal wit and improvisation. A tendency toward the fantastic, a strong element in traditional Ethiopian storytelling, is the hallmark of director Manyegezawal Endeshaw.

From the late 1970s through the 1980s, Mariam's Marxist government became progressively more repressive toward the arts. At the same time, the involvement of young people in the theater increased through variety shows and political plays that were closely controlled by the government. Theater professionals, unwilling to risk having their plays banned or being imprisoned, tended to avoid controversy and fall back on history plays and translations of foreign classics such as *Hamlet*, *Othello*, and *Oedipus the King*. While this can be seen as a form of self-censorship, such works also involve subtle political allegory.

Ethiopian theater blossomed after the fall of Mengistu's government in 1991. Many private theater companies came into being. Although most were short-lived, some had lasting importance. For example, the Candle Theater Company, founded in 1995 and fueled by a belief in theater as a tool for political and social criticism, obtained its own theater. Another contemporary development was the emergence of theater by Ethiopian writers, directors, and performers living outside Ethiopia, in places like the United States and Great Britain.

See also THEATER, AFRICAN.

Ethiopic Script and Language
The major written and spoken Semitic languages of historical and present-day Ethiopia.

The writing tradition of ETHIOPIA is one of the greatest cultural achievements in Africa. Known as lessâna ge'ez (meaning "the language of the free") or simply as Ge'ez, classical Ethiopic was used in the Aksumite royal inscriptions of the fourth century C.E. It was also used in translations made from Greek, Syriac, Arabic, and other languages; and for a vast body of original Ethiopian literature that includes stories of Christian saints and martyrs, poetry, historical chronicles, and treatises on magic, law, and medicine.

Although it ceased to be spoken by the twelfth or thirteenth century, Ge'ez remained the language of literature and religion. Like Hebrew and Arabic, it is a Semitic language. The modern Semitic languages of Ethiopia—such as TIGRINYA, TIGRE, Amharic (AMHARA), Harari, and Gurage—developed from Ge'ez in a manner comparable to the emergence of Spanish, French, and the other Romance languages from Latin.

Ge'ez is written in a script developed from the South Arabian characters found in inscriptions on both sides of the Red Sea as far back as 3,000 years ago. It consists of twenty-six consonants that can be modified to represent syllables containing any of seven vowels. This produces 182 different characters. Another four characters represent labial consonants, and an additional seven consonants were created for Amharic. With their vowel markings, these consonant signs raise the total to 251 characters. The script is beautiful, and scholars are studying the various styles of Ethiopic calligraphy to help classify and date manuscripts preserved in churches and monasteries.

See also LANGUAGES, AFRICAN: AN OVERVIEW.

Ethnicity and Identity in Africa: An Interpretation

What is ethnicity in Africa? One thing is certain: it is very often misunderstood. Many people, including many contemporary Africans, suppose that in the precolonial period, all Africans lived in groups called "tribes." A "tribe" is thought of as a group of people who are descended from common ancestors and ruled by a hereditary "chief," who share a single culture (including, in particular, language and religion), and live in a well-defined geographical region. Tribal identities are often assumed to be unchanging and ancient.

Many people also suppose that virtually all the contemporary ethnic groups in modern Africa are descended from these kinds of "tribes." While some precolonial African societies, such as some of the small AKAN states of southwestern GHANA and southeastern CÔTE D'IVOIRE, did come close to such a model, most did not. Even where they did approach this model, it was often a quite recent development. So it is usually misleading to speak of modern ethnic groups as "tribes." Nevertheless, many contemporary Africans use the word tribe to talk about their identities, and we cannot understand modern African social and political life unless we understand what they mean by this term.

PRECOLONIAL SOCIAL IDENTITIES

Tribal identities, understood in this way, were not the only nor even the most important of the identities recognized in precolonial Africa. People also belonged to clans or lineages, both groups defined by shared ancestry. (In Islamic North Africa, in fact, the word tribe has most often been used to refer to lineages.) The smallest subgroup of a lineage is a family. Households and extended families were also important sources of identity, as they continue to be today.

In many places people also belonged to age sets, groups of men or women who reached maturity within the same few years. Members of an age set operated together for many social purposes, and their social roles shifted as they passed through different stages of life. Finally, people of different lineages and ages belonged to village communities. Although they might have shared many of their daily life activities with their village neighbors, they often had political loyalties to rulers elsewhere, and connections through trade and secret societies to people in other villages and towns.

One reason that precolonial African's membership in such a variety of groups is often overlooked today is that many of these earlier forms of identity began to lose their power in the colonial period. Village identities became less important as rates of urbanization in Africa increased, especially after World War II. Secret societies were often deliberately targeted for destruction in the colonial period, because they involved rituals and religious beliefs inconsistent with Christianity or European norms of civilization. And age-set membership became less relevant once COLONIAL RULE deprived age sets of their role in community political structures.

ORIGINS OF TRIBAL NAMES

If "tribes" were not the most important forms of identity in precolonial Africa, why do they seem so important now? We must recognize that the ethnic groups of contemporary Africa have a variety of origins. It is often helpful to focus not so much on the history of a group of people and their descendants but on the history of a particular ethnic name, or "ethnonym." Many contemporary African ethnonyms are products of the interaction between the ideas of European colonial officials and anthropologists, on the one hand, and preexisting ways of classifying people in Africa's many precolonial societies, on the other. Typically, ethnonyms fall into one of four categories.

PRECOLONIAL STATES

Probably the easiest modern ethnonyms to explain are those based on the names of precolonial African nations. A few examples include ASANTE in West Africa, BUGANDA in East Africa, and Zulu and SWAZI in southern Africa.

But, as with "tribes," certain standard modern assumptions about kingdoms do not apply. For example, while their kings were, indeed, hereditary, in the sense that they had to have a certain ancestry to become rulers, none of them had a guaranteed rule of succession by, say, an eldest son. In Asante, for example, the king's successor was chosen from the royal family by a group of king makers. If they did not agree, long periods of conflict could ensue, including civil wars.

Another common misassumption is that these nations would share a single language and culture. In each of these states and others like them there was, indeed, a single language of government, which was the language of a dominant ethnic group, and many cultural practices were widely shared. But at the moment of European colonization, many states were undergoing expansion. As a result the king often claimed authority over people who were culturally quite different, including people who spoke completely different languages. Some of these people would have recognized the king's claim to sovereignty over them; others would not. So the boundaries of the king's sway were not well defined: they shrank when a subject people resisted, and they expanded when the king responded by sending out armies to establish (or reestablish) control.

While these states existed before colonization, their development had often been shaped by other kinds of contact with outsiders. The Asante state, for example, acquired significant military technology through trade with the Danes, the Portuguese, and the British, and it taxed commerce between the coast and the Asante hinterland. Long-standing trans-Saharan trade patterns also linked the Asante state to the Islamic societies of North Africa.

Nor were these kingdoms stable, long-established political systems, where people lived according to unchanging customs: SHAKA formed the modern Zulu nation quite rapidly in the early 19th century, drawing on a powerful army and innovative military tactics. His conquest, known as the mfecane, in turn led to the formation of several other southern African states, as skilled leaders such as MOSHOESHOE, founder of the Basotho kingdom, offered vulnerable communities protection in return for tribute and military service. In West Africa, meanwhile, the Asante nation underwent civil wars and constitutional crises of various kinds in the eighteenth and nineteenth centuries.

When European anthropologists and colonial officials arrived in Africa, they were convinced that people there lived in tribes. Some early European explorers referred to the rulers of precolonial states as "kings," the states as "kingdoms" or "countries," and the people as "the Asante," "the Baganda," or "the Zulu." But by the early twentieth century, when these peoples had all been incorporated into the British Empire, it became standard to refer to their rulers as chiefs and the citizens as tribesmen.

There are exceptions to this pattern. The kingdom of ETHIOPIA, where people spoke a number of languages and recognized a variety of religious and cultural traditions, was ruled by a Christian Amhara monarchy. The kingdom's people were never assumed to belong to a single "tribal" group, partly because a Christian emperor fitted easily into existing European ideas about societies, partly because Ethiopians themselves recognized ethnic divisions within the kingdom.

Cultural Groups

A second group of modern ethnonyms refers to groups that have related languages and often share important cultural practices, but were not necessarily ever members of a single political community. The broadest such term in Africa is Bantu, which refers to hundreds of groups in East, Central, and southern Africa who speak related but typically not mutually intelligible languages (though in many of these languages the word for "people" is bantu). The common elements in these languages came from an earlier

"proto-Bantu" language spoken by Central African peoples whose descendants, over centuries, migrated south and east. But there is no reason to think that all modern speakers of Bantu languages share descent from these earlier migrants (just as we would not assume that the reason most people in the United States speak English is that they are descendants of people from England).

In West Africa, the term Akan refers to a number of groups in Ghana and Côte d'Ivoire. Here the similarities are more substantial, since many of the Akan languages are mutually intelligible, and the majority of Akan people—in particular, the Asante, FANTE and Akwapim people—speak one of several main dialects of a language called Twi. Most Akan people also share cultural traits other than language; for example, most are matrilineal, meaning they trace descent through their mothers rather than their fathers.

Another example of a culturally based identity is that of the SWAHILI PEOPLE of coastal East Africa, which is defined partly by their SWAHILI LANGUAGE (a Bantu language much influenced by Arabic), partly by their residence in trading towns, and partly by their connection to Islam. However, many people who speak Kiswahili—which has been used as a trade language for centuries and is now the official government language in TANZANIA—would not claim to be Swahili.

The bonds of language, Islam, and trade are also important elements in the identity of the widely dispersed HAUSA and DYULA peoples of West Africa. Over centuries, participation in long-distance trade led to the establishment of Hausa and Dyula communities in several different parts of West Africa. Leaders of some of these communities established precolonial states, such as the Hausa state of KANO in northern Nigeria, and the Dyula KONG empire in northern Côte d'Ivoire. Today, Hausa and Dyula are the region's two most common African trade languages, and many West African cities have distinct Hausa and Dyula neighborhoods.

Creations of the Colonial Period

Most ethnonyms are derived from African words. But some of these words came to be used in the colonial period to refer to peoples who lived in the same region but had not previously been politically united. Many people in the region of southeastern Nigeria now called Igboland, for example, lived in small towns governed by councils of senior men. Others lived in larger towns with more centralized political systems. These different communities spoke related languages, but they could not necessarily understand one another. They had religious leaders—priests responsible for overseeing rituals and handling problems such as ill health or failed harvests—but no sovereign political leaders whom British colonial officials could easily identify as chiefs. So instead the colonial administration either treated the priests as chiefs, requiring them to assume a new political role, or they appointed so-called "warrant-chiefs" to carry out the duties expected of colonial-era chiefs, such as tax collection. The British also began to consider all the people who spoke this region's related languages as speakers of different dialects of one language called IGBO.

These impositions alone, however, did not create modern Igbo identity. As people from southeastern Nigeria traveled to other parts of the colony to work and trade, they came into contact with people who spoke languages more foreign than the languages spoken by their more immediate neighbors. They also encountered customs more foreign than those practiced by other societies in southeastern Nigeria. So many migrants of this region, based in towns in the north and west of Nigeria, came increasingly to think of themselves as members of a single Igbo "tribe." At the same time, other Nigerians came to regard them as a single "tribe" also. This new identity had tragic consequences later on, when Igbo people in these towns were violently attacked in the period leading up to the Nigerian civil war (1967–1970).

Similar processes occurred in many parts of Africa, as people moved from rural communities to newly expanding urban areas. Whether these were colonial administrative capitals, such as LAGOS and NAIROBI, or mining towns, such as JOHANNESBURG in SOUTH AFRICA, cities became places where people developed new practices and ways of organizing their collective life, based on interpretations of "traditional customs" in the rural areas from which they had come.

Invented Identities

Some ethnonyms lumped together people who had no shared social origins at all. The term Coromanti, for example, often referred in the seventeenth and eighteenth centuries to African slaves in the New World who had all been bought at slave markets in a particular region of the West African coast, in present-day Ghana. Since these and other slave markets typically sold people who came from many different regions of West Africa, this ethnonym imposed on people a completely fictional tribal identity. Because they had been brought together by captors whose language was Akan, these slaves did, however, speak an Akan language; as a result, in the New World, Akan-speaking Coromanti slaves did sometimes join together in slave revolts (as, for example, in a plot discovered in Barbados in 1675).

Similarly, the term Bushmen was used to refer to a very wide range of people, who lived over a vast area of South Africa, ANGOLA, BOTSWANA, and NAMIBIA, even though they certainly had no sense of a shared identity. While these people did mostly speak one of the many KHOISAN languages (which are descended from languages spoken in this region before the

arrival of Bantu speakers), this did not mean they would have understood one another if they had met. But the term has also been used to refer to the Basters in Namibia, who have both European and African ancestry and who speak Afrikaans. In fact, the ethnonym "Bushman" has been used to refer to almost anyone in southern Africa whose appearance is neither that of the typical dark-skinned Bantu speaker nor that of the typical light-skinned European. It has been used, in effect, as if it referred to a "race" that lived in this area before the arrival of Bantu-speaking settlers from the north, and many people have then gone on to assume that this "racial" group had shared culture and traditions.

MODERN ETHNICITY IN AFRICA

As we have seen, then, many African ethnonyms reflect misunderstandings of history. Historians have pointed out that this is true for most modern identities, not only those in Africa. Now-discredited ideas about race have played a central role, for example, in shaping national identities in Europe. The idea of an Anglo-Saxon race, for example, was important in the development of both modern British identity and white American identity in the United States. The fact that these identities are founded on mistaken beliefs does not deprive them of their power to shape people's attitudes and behavior. Many modern Africans identify themselves as Akan or Igbo or Swahili, or members of one of the hundreds of other modern African ethnic groups. Because national politics requires people to collaborate with one another to compete for resources, political leaders often mobilize these ethnic groups to create voting blocs or to organize "sides" in civil conflicts.

Once ethnic identities become politically significant, people who previously thought of themselves as belonging first and foremost to some small local group may decide to identify with a larger, more widely distributed group that seems successful at winning resources. Such considerations help explain why many coastal East African people adopted Swahili identity in the late nineteenth century, and why many people in contemporary Ghana and TOGO have assumed EWE identity. So the size and boundaries of ethnic groups may shift with shifting political fortunes.

Indeed, some anthropologists, such as the Norwegian Frederick Barth, have argued that the very idea of ethnicity exists only where there are boundaries between "us" and "them" within a shared social context. As a result, they say, we can really only speak of ethnicity in the context of many groups, defined by real or imagined shared ancestry, either living together within a single political system or, at least, in regular contact. If that is right, then the boundaries of African colonies and then nations—drawn around people with very different languages, cultures, religions, and traditions—have created an ideal context for the flourishing of ethnicity that we in fact see in modern Africa.

It is not surprising, in this context, that "tribalism" now appears to many people to be one of modern Africa's major problems. For by tribalism people usually mean the *illegitimate* appeal to ethnic loyalty. When people speak of tribalism, they are really assuming that to act on the basis of ethnic loyalty is always wrong. This is because appeals to ethnic loyalty often occur in contexts of national-level competition between an "us" and a "them," and so ethnicity becomes divisive. But, of course, ethnic loyalty (in Africa as elsewhere) can also lead people to do good things for fellow members of their tribe, even when this is not at the expense of others.

The significance of tribalism in Africa can also be exaggerated. Ethnicity is not the basis for political mobilization. Religion, for example, has been important in shaping political loyalties in Nigeria. Islam and Christianity and many other traditional religions are important to people's lives in Nigeria, as, of course, they are in many countries. Islam and Christianity have come to be identified, to some degree, with the political interests of the north and the south of Nigeria respectively, even though many Christians live in the north and about a third of the YORUBA people in the southwest are Muslim. Politics are also shaped by religion in SUDAN where, again, Muslims are concentrated in the north and non-Islamic peoples in the south.

In a different way, professional interests—those of doctors or lawyers or civil servants—and class interests, which join together, say, industrial workers in trade unions, are also important bases of political mobilization. So are the shared interests of peasant farmers of many different ethnic groups, or the interests of the medley of ethnic groups that live together in a particular region of a country. And, increasingly, in the modern world, national interests have become important. Last but by no means least, gender shapes the concerns of Africans as it does of people everywhere, and womens organization's are an extremely important part of the contemporary social and political landscape of Africa. So like the generations before them, contemporary Africans, whether or not they consider themselves members of a "tribe," count many other identities as important.

See also AFRICAN CITY: AN INTERPRETATION; ETHIOPIAN ORTHODOX CHURCH; FEMINISM IN AFRICA: AN INTERPRETATION; RITES OF PASSAGE AND TRANSITION; SWAHILI COAST; URBANISM AND URBANIZATION IN AFRICAN.

KWAME ANTHONY APPIAH

Ethnicity in Burundi: An Interpretation

Contrary to an all too prevalent opinion, BURUNDI, not RWANDA, will go down in history as the site of the first ethnic genocide recorded in postindependence Africa. Between May and December 1972, twenty-two years before the Rwanda holocaust, an abortive Hutu uprising led to the massacre of anywhere from 100,000 to 200,000 of their kinsmen at the hands of an all-Tutsi army. Further outbursts of ethnic violence occurred in 1988 and 1990, albeit on a smaller scale, again primarily aimed at Hutu elements—a sinister prelude to the continuing interethnic killings triggered by the assassination of Prime Minister Melchior Ndadaye, on October 21, 1993, by Tutsi officers.

What gives ethnicity in Burundi its singularly savage edge is not the resurgence of age-old antagonisms between Hutu and Tutsi, but the way in which the concept has been manipulated by urban elite (and the media) to legitimize their claims to power. Hutu and Tutsi are not categories set in stone. As identity markers they have been constantly redefined to serve the purpose of ideologues and politicians. At least two other factors have contributed to invest ethnic divisions with an exceptional potential for violence. One is the relative size of the two principal communities: the Tutsi account for roughly 15 percent of a total population of some 6 million, and the Hutu 85 percent. As in Rwanda, the tension between minority rights and majority rule translates into irreconcilable ethnic claims and counterclaims. For most Tutsi, majority rule means the tyranny of the Hutu majority, and possibly their annihilation as a minority; for the Hutu, democracy means nothing if not the rule of the majority, irrespective of ethnic considerations. Further sharpening the edges of ethnic conflict is the vertical pattern of stratification that has come to characterize Hutu-Tutsi relations, with the Hutu, in most instances, at the bottom of the heap, socially, economically, and politically. If democracy means majority rule, the latter in turn is seen by many Hutu as the only route to social justice.

If much of the history of modern Burundi is a metaphor for ethnic polarization, this is not to suggest that COLONIAL RULE did not play a significant role in the reshaping of collective identities. To take the full measure of these transformations, something must be said of social relations in precolonial Burundi.

HUTU AND TUTSI: THE FALLACY OF PRIMORDIAL ANTAGONISMS

As identity markers, Hutu and Tutsi are not colonial inventions. These labels were part and parcel of the Burundi social landscape centuries before the advent of colonial rule. At no time, however, did they convey anything like the hatreds and inhumanities witnessed since independence. More often than not, occupational and ethnic identities tended to coincide, and because of the symbolic significance attached to cattle ownership, Tutsi pastoralists were held in somewhat greater esteem than the Hutu agriculturalists. Even so, not all Tutsi were on the same footing. To this day, the high-status Tutsi-Banyaruguru ("those who are closer to the Court") are clearly differentiated from the lowly Tutsi-Hima, heavily concentrated in the south. Although as of 1998, the Tutsi-Hima were in control of the army as well as much of the government, they were traditionally viewed with almost undisguised contempt by Hutu and Tutsi alike.

Ethnicity, in short, was by no means the sole determinant of social status; indeed, social rankings within each group—such as between different patrilineages (imiryango)—were far more significant in deciding individual life chances. Clientage relations also afforded opportunities for upward mobility. Patron-client ties ran from top to bottom of the social pyramid, like so many vertical chains of dependency, linking Hutu to Tutsi, Tutsi to Tutsi, Tutsi to princes (ganwa), and princes (as well as Hutu court officials) to king (mwami). It is at this level that the contrast between the complexity of the traditional social system and the present Hutu-Tutsi dichotomy is most apparent; not only did ethnic identities cut across patron-client statuses, but a Tutsi cast in the role of client vis-à-vis a more powerful patron would be referred to as a Hutu. The term Hutu, in other words, has both ethnic and social connotations. Anyone born of a Hutu father is a Hutu, regardless of the mother's identity; and anyone in a subordinate position could be referred to by a superior as a Hutu, here meaning "social son." Thus it is conceivable for someone simultaneously to assume a double social identity as Hutu and Tutsi, a phenomenon known as kwihutura. Conferment of a Tutsi identity for services rendered to a Tutsi patron was a fairly frequent occurrence, thus providing yet another avenue of social mobility.

The real power holders were neither Hutu nor Tutsi but princes, or ganwa, and the fact that they were seen to constitute a distinctive socioethnic category contributed in no small way to defuse tension between Hutu and Tutsi, since neither group was directly involved in succession struggles. In fact, by appealing to both Hutu and Tutsi to strengthen their hand against their rivals, factional struggles among ganwa served to reinforce cross-ethnic solidarities. Thus, writing in 1931, a White Father missionary, Bernard Zuure, concluded that it would be idle to look for differences of attitude and behavior between Hutu and Tutsi, for these, he added, "have become so minimal that one can speak of a common culture."

From a society characterized by highly complex, vertically structured sociopolitical networks, Burundi has now become a greatly simplified—indeed rigidly polarized—social field where Hutu and Tutsi are the only political relevant categories. To grasp fully the significance of this all-encompassing metamorphosis we need to look back to the fundamental changes brought about under the aegis of the colonial state in both Rwanda and Burundi, and in the years immediately following independence.

THE TRANSFORMATION OF ETHNIC IDENTITIES

Colonial rule has significantly reshaped the contours and meaning of ethnic identities, first by ignoring altogether the social rankings inherent in family and clan structures, second by removing from office a number of Hutu chiefs and subchiefs and replacing them with Tutsi elements, and third by investing the concept of ethnicity with normative meanings borrowed from the Hamitic hypothesis, an idea propounded by many missionaries. The aim was to make Burundi society more "legible"—that is, easier to understand—and thus more amenable to administrative efficiency. And what better model of efficiency than Rwanda, where Tutsi-Hutu polarities seemed pleasantly unencumbered by the complexities of criss-crossing social hierarchies and regional subloyalties?

As if to bolster the legitimacy of kingship, the main recipients of Western education were overwhelmingly of Tutsi and princely origins. While the highly skewed pattern of access to schools clearly favored the Tutsi for positions in the colonial administration, the corvée labor, compulsory cultivation, and taxes demanded of the Hutu masses also widened the gap between Hutu and Tutsi.

The emergent restratification of Burundi society not only allowed for efficient economic production and colonial administration, but it was also entirely consistent with the preconceptions underlying the Hamitic view of Hutu-Tutsi relations. Widely perceived as the prototype of the Hamites—described by C. G. Seligman as "pastoral Europeans arriving wave after wave, better armed as well as quicker witted than the dark agricultural Negroes"—for some missionaries the Tutsi were ideally equipped by nature to act as the privileged intermediaries between the European colonizer and the "dark agricultural" Hutu masses.

But if the requirement of administrative legibility made Burundi society look increasingly like its neighbor to the north, Hutu-Tutsi tensions seemed almost nonexistent compared to those in Rwanda in the mid-1950s. When Burundi became independent in 1962, the country was as yet untouched by the demons of mobilized ethnicity; it was still a constitutional monarchy, and the main line of political cleavage was between rival princely families, each claiming the support of Hutu and Tutsi. By then, however, Rwanda had become a Hutu-dominated republic, and Burundi, like UGANDA and the DEMOCRATIC REPUBLIC OF THE CONGO, was hosting tens of thousands of Rwanda's Tutsi refugees. The impact on Burundi has been little short of devastating.

The democratic ideals of the 1959 Hutu revolution in Rwanda eventually became a major pole of attraction for Hutu politicians in Burundi—and a source of permanent revulsion for the Tutsi minority. The projection of the Rwanda situation into Burundi thus lies at the root of the self-fulfilling prophecy. It led many Tutsi in Burundi to anticipate a fate similar to that of their Rwanda kinsmen, should power pass into Hutu hands, and it led not a few Hutu to look to Rwanda as the model polity.

The dominant trend since 1962 has been toward greater social polarization along Hutu-Tutsi lines, culminating with the 1972 carnage and the emergence of a radical, bitterly anti Tutsi movement, the so-called Parti pour l'Emancipation du Peuple Hutu (Palipehutu). That the Palipehutu was born in the refugee campus of TANZANIA is no coincidence. Since the late 1950s refugee flows between Rwanda and Burundi have played a critically important role in intensifying ethnic hatreds, and this is true of both Tutsi and Hutu refugees. Thus a crucial factor in the process of ethnic polarization that followed in the wake of the Rwanda revolution has been the massive exodus of Tutsi refugees into Burundi. Many became actively involved in Burundi politics, casting their lot with the more radical elements of the Tutsi populations. It is noteworthy that Burundi's first Hutu prime minister, Pierre Ngendadumwc, was assassinated in 1965 by a Tutsi refugee from Rwanda, and when the carnage of Hutu began in 1972, many Tutsi refugees volunteered for the predominantly Tutsi army.

THE GENOCIDE

The 1972 bloodbath must be understood in light of the more or less systematic exclusion, from 1965 onward, of Hutu elements from positions of responsibility in the government and the army. In spite of their landslide victory at the polls in 1965, Hutu deputies were denied the right to appoint a government of their choice, which in turn led to the abortive Hutu-instigated coup of October 19, 1965, followed by extensive purges of the army and the gendarmerie and the physical elimination of every Hutu leader of any standing. In the Muramvya province, home of the hardcore Hutu opposition, a brutal repression ensued, causing thousands of casualties among Hutu civilians.

A somewhat similar scenario unfolded seven years later, except this time the repression reached genocidal proportions. On April 19, 1972, a Hutu-led insurgency exploded in the normally peaceful lakeside towns of Nyanza-lac and Rumonge, in the southern tip of the

country. Hundreds if not thousands of Tutsi civilians fell under the blows of the insurgents. The repression began almost instantly. Week after week, month after month, tens of thousands of Hutu men and youngsters—civil servants, teachers, university students, schoolchildren were rounded up and killed by mixed teams of youth groups and soldiers. Their bodies were buried in mass graves throughout the country, while the carnage continued unabated until August. By then almost every educated Hutu was either dead or in exile. The aim, in short, was to eliminate for the foreseeable future any serious threat to Tutsi hegemony. For the next twenty years, the Tutsi minority was able to exercise virtually unfettered control of the army, the government, the civil service, the provincial administration, the university, and the economy. Thus transformed, Burundi became the mirror image of Rwanda.

The impact of the 1972 butchery on ethnic relations was by no means limited to Burundi. In Rwanda a terrible backlash swept through many secondary schools as well as the University of Butare, causing the deaths of hundreds of Tutsi students. It was among exiled Hutu, however, that the genocide's effects on collective representations of ethnicity were most marked: suddenly, the massive inhumanities inflicted on Hutu civilians seemed entirely consistent with the view of Tutsi as Hamitic invaders, whose cunning is surpassed only by their innate cruelty.

HISTORY AND ETHNIC MEMORY

In Burundi as elsewhere, ethnic violence is the product of mobilized ethnicity. It is a recent, urban-based phenomenon. As such, it has little in common with the more fluid, diffuse, negotiable social identities that once characterized traditional societies. Nonetheless, any attempt to make sense of Burundi ethnicity must consider how "ethnic entrepreneurs" have tried to reconstruct the past in order to mobilize support and validate their claims to power.

Illustrative of this phenomenon are the "mythicohistorics" elaborated by Palipehutu leaders in the years immediately following the genocide. In an undated document penned by the late Remi Gahutu, the party's founder and president, the 1972 killings are seen as historically linked to the centuries-old domination of a Hamitic minority, a form of feudal oppression directly related to the "dehumanization of the Hutu serfs." That a small Hamitic minority could have succeeded in imposing its domination on the Hutu majority can only be explained by taking into account the former's consummate skills in the use of ruse and cruelty; the poisoned gift of cows and the "bait of beautiful women" were indeed key ingredients in the strategy employed by the Tutsi to reduce their unsuspecting Hutu hosts into bondage. Much the same story, and worse still, was told to anthropologist Liisa Malkki by Hutu refugees in Tanzania. In order to get food, the Tutsi flatters a Hutu, a cultivator. He says, "I give you my daughter, even two or three cows." Like this. Then the Hutu accepts, seeing a beautiful woman with a long nose and very tall also in stature, elegant if you wish, and who squanders smiles. ... Then this Hutu begins to despise the other Hutu because he is flattered and he boasts about his Tutsi wife.

What emerges from this and many other accounts is an image of the Tutsi as the archetype of the Hamitic "bad guy," whose presence in Burundi has been historically linked to the transformation of Bantu into Hutu, from free people into slaves.

Seldom anywhere (with the exception of Rwanda) has the past been manipulated in more blatant violation of the historical record, and with more obvious political designs: to cast irreparable moral discredit on the Tutsi as a group. In Liisa Malkki's words, the discourse of the Palipehutu, echoed in the stories told by refugees, is not "a description of the past, nor even an evaluation of the past, but a subversive recasting and reinterpreting of it in fundamentally moral terms."

In refutation of the Hamitic caricature projected by Hutu ideologues, Tutsi elite typically argue that ethnicity in Burundi is at best a figment of the Hutu imagination, at worse the despicable offspring of a tribal ideology introduced by the European colonizer. Ethnic differences, they argue, are simply not relevant to an understanding of the country's problems. According to a tract written by Tutsi intellectuals in 1988, the Tutsi have never oppressed the Hutu: "So deep are the strands of social solidarity woven (between Hutu and Tutsi) ... that there are no grounds of objective antagonisms between the two groups."

In the wake of the genocide, two radically opposed forms of ethnic memory emerged: one seeking to project into the procolonial past a conflict situation of recent origins, the other projecting into the present the basic ethnic harmony of traditional Burundi. One version aims to falsify the past to explain recent ethnic killings, the other aims to embellish the past, so as to deny altogether the existence of a fundamental Hutu-Tutsi problem, beyond what was issued from the perverse imagination of the European colonizer.

VIOLENCE AND ETHNICITY: THE INFERNAL DIALECTIC

Contrary to what the foregoing might suggest, not everyone in Burundi succumbed to the siren song of ideological manipulation. Many Hutu saw through the Hamitic delusions of the Palipehutu, and many Tutsi privately scoffed at the posture of ethnic amnesia adopted by some of their kinsmen. But in the sharply polarized arena of postgenocide Burundi, their voice carried little conviction. One of the most tragic consequences of recurrent ethnic violence has been to reduce sharply the political space available to moderates among both Hutu and Tutsi. Indeed, extremists at both ends of the ethnic spectrum—who include members of the army and the militias among Tutsi, and members of the Palipehutu, the FRONT DE LIBÉRATION NATIONALE (Frolinat), the Conseil National pour la Défense de la Démocratie (CNDD) among Hutu—have succeeded in wrecking every attempt at a viable constitutional compromise.

The most dramatic example occurred on October 21, 1993, when the all-Tutsi army undid in a matter of hours all the accomplishments of a carefully engineered four-year transition to democracy. With the assassination of President Melchior Ndadaye by a group of noncommissioned officers, Burundi began a seemingly endless descent into hell—from which it has yet to recover. In his dual capacity as Burundi's first Hutu president and leader of the Front des Démocrates du Burundi (Frodebu)—a party dominated by Hutu moderates, but whose membership included a substantial number of Tutsi—Ndadaye was immensely popular among the Hutu. The news of his death hit the countryside with the force of an earthquake. A grande peur (great fear) seemed to seize the Hutu hillside communities; suddenly images of the 1972 bloodbath reappeared in their minds; Ndadaye's death was the harbinger of a replay of 1972.

In an uncontrolled outburst of collective rage, Hutu peasants turned against their Tutsi neighbors, killing tens of thousands; in one community after another, scores of men, women, and children were hacked to pieces, speared or clubbed to death, or doused with kerosene and burned alive. Equally terrifying was the repression unleashed by the army, causing as many deaths among Hutu as the Hutu had caused among Tutsi. As many as 100,000 people may have died in the course of a carnage in which Hutu and Tutsi finally reached equal status.

This is not the place to explore the causal connection between the events of October 1993 in Burundi and the Rwanda genocide, six months later, except to note that the assassination of Ndadaye greatly strengthened the conviction of Hutu extremists—and not a few moderates—in Rwanda that "the Tutsi simply cannot be trusted." What must be emphasized is the extent to which the Rwanda genocide, once projected back into the Burundi situation, was held up by Tutsi radicals in Burundi as proof of the genocidal intentions of the Hutu as a group. By then, ethnicity and genocide became the two sides of the same conceptual coin, but not without some extraordinary adjustments of historical facts. The discourse of Tutsi extremists, for example, says nothing about the 1972 genocide of Hutu by Tutsi, as if the horrors of 1972 had been obliterated forever from their collective memory.

What is emerging in Burundi are two radically different memories, nurturing different ideologies and political cultures. New traditions are being invented by Hutu and Tutsi designed to strengthen their claims and justify their prejudices. Both as a concept and an empirical referent, ethnicity in Burundi is thus as far removed from its pre-colonial roots as the present ramshackle polity is from the old monarchical order. Whether a meaningful and mutually acceptable compromise can be found—a compromise that could lay the foundation for the reinvention of the state and the redefinition of citizenship in Burundi— remains to be seen. In early 2004, the Forces for National Liberation, the only Hutu rebels still fighting the government, agreed to open talks with President Domitien Ndayizeye. The talks would mean that the Hutus, who have fought for a decade against the political dominance of the Tutsis, were looking for ways to end the violence that killed an estimated 300,000 people. An agreement was at last signed in 2006.

See also HUTU AND TUTSI; PASTORALISM.

RENÉ LEMARCHAND

Ethnicity in Rwanda: An Interpretation
Examination of the historical development of relations between the Hutu and Tutsi peoples of Rwanda.

Who are the HUTU AND TUTSI? This is a question that came into every discussion I had during my visits to RWANDA. While the Hutu opposition had been a target of the 1994 massacre, this was a political matter; the Tutsi had faced true genocide—the attempt to eliminate them as a people. Given this single fact, which illuminates the tragedy of Rwanda for the world at large, I was nonplused to be told over and again by leading people in the Rwandan Patriotic Front (RPF—the Tutsi-dominated ruling party after 1994): "We speak the same language, have the same culture, and live on the same hills; we are the same people." But in casual conversation and out on the street, some of the same individuals would readily identify Hutu and Tutsi individuals. Sometimes they were identified by physical appearance, but in a place like Ntarama in the southern lowlands, where Tutsi made up as many as a third of the population, and where there had been many inter-marriages—a third of the Tutsi daughters were married to Hutu, I was told—this was hardly a reliable method. During the killings, people were asked to produce their identity cards.

Not surprising, one of the issues hotly debated in the Rwandese Alliance for National Unity (RANU), formed by refugees in UGANDA in 1979, was whether the difference between Hutu and Tutsi was one of class or ethnicity. I remembered what I had heard from a Nigerian colleague at a conference organized by the Dakar-based Council for Development of Social Research in Africa (CODESRIA) early in 1995. If he went to a discussion on Rwanda and BURUNDI, he could close his eyes and tell the identity of a speaker from these countries by the twist of their argument: if a person claimed that there were no differences between Hutu and Tutsi, or that the difference was one of class, the speaker was most likely a Tutsi, for a Hutu intellectual was most likely to argue otherwise, that the difference was one between distinct ethnic—or even racial groups.

It is difficult to believe that the Hutu-Tutsi difference is based on class, for both groups are internally differentiated. One finds Hutu and Tutsi in the same class: the Tutsi pastoralists I saw in the southern lowlands were as poor and wretched as the Hutu peasants I met along the way. If the view that there is no difference—or only a class difference—tends to focus on socioeconomic processes, the preoccupation of the ethnic difference per-spective is with the biological and the historicocultural. "If the no difference" view tends to suffer from historical amne-sia—specifically of how power was organized in the preco-lonial Rwandan state—that of "ethnic difference" tends to freeze the history of the Rwandan state at its colonial stage, turning a historical outcome into a primordial difference. If loss of historical memory leads to a tragic political inno-cence, historical fixation leads to a no less tragic pathology. One side overlooks the limits on politics, the other fails to appreciate the possibility of political action. Neither is able to come to grips with the political potential in a given situation.

A careful review of the history of the Rwandan state reveals that Hutu and Tutsi are bipolar identities repro-duced by a form of the state that institutionalized them as such: there cannot be one without the other. In this rela-tionship, first shaped by the precolonial Rwandan state but fully crystallized by the colonial state, Tutsi came to be identified with power and Hutu with subjecthood.

PRECOLONIAL RWANDAN STATE
When I returned from KIGALI, RWANDA, I immersed myself in whatever literature I could find on Rwandan history. I realized that the further back one went, the mistier the historical background. Shrouded in a rich mythology is the question of the origin of the Tutsi. Caught up by the notion that differences and conflicts in human society are the result of racial differences, early European explorers and administrators came up with the Hamitic hypothesis: that the Tutsi were a superior

non-Bantu race who had come from the direction of Ethiopia and conquered indigenous agriculturalists (Hutu) and forest dwellers (TWA). This racist theory was discredited in the heyday of anti-imperial nationalism, but there is still no consensus among historians and anthropologists on the origin of the Tutsi. At least three accounts can be found in the literature.

The first is a dietary explanation of the difference most identified with Walter Rodney; strangely enough, it was standard reading for the RPF cadres in the late 1980s and early 1990s. In his influential work *How Europe Underdeveloped Africa*, Rodney argued that the Twa remained pygmies because "they wandered around in small bands, hunting and digging roots, thereby failing to assure themselves of plentiful or rich food." The Hutu "were more socially advanced than the Twa" because "they did not live entirely on the whims of nature." But, in comparison to the Tutsi, the Hutu remained "short and stocky" because "the quality of their food fell short of the protein-rich Tutsi diet." And so the Tutsi pastoralists, "subsisting on a constantly accessible and rich diet of milk and meat" turned out to be "one of the tallest human groups in the world."

The second explanation accepts the migration theory, that the pastoralists came from outside Rwanda, but argues that their relations with the agriculturalists were peaceful and symbiotic: they exchanged dairy products for garden vegetables. Forcefully put forth by the late Samwiri Karugire, the noted Ugandan historian, it has since been embraced by various political protagonists, including the president of Uganda and many in the leadership of the RPF.

Neither the dietary hypothesis nor the theory of peaceful coexistence is the key to understanding the precolonial period: the nature of the political organized as the Rwandan state. Walter Rodney accepts that "the system of social relations which emerged in Rwanda was more completely hierarchical ... than in most parts of Africa." Similarly, Edward Steinhart, taking inspiration from Samwiri Karugire, concludes with reference to Ankore that "the system of pastoral domination, which had evolved from meagre beginnings in the fifteenth century, had by the early nineteenth century become one of the most rigid and authoritarian systems of political and social exploitation in the intralacustrine region." All scholars are agreed that if there was a system more hierarchical than that in Ankore, it was in Rwanda.

A third explanation has recently been put forth by Archie Mafeje in a book called *The Theory and Ethnography of African Social Formations*. While Mafeje dismisses the Hamitic hypothesis, his work is based on a critical summary of colonial anthropology. Mafeje's starting point is Bunyoro where, "somewhere in the fifteenth century,"

there occurred the "first known processes of political centralization" in the intralacustrine region. In Bunyoro, "the introduction of pastoralism as an elite pursuit must be attributed to ... invaders who, probably, migrated from south-eastern Ethiopia and southern Somalia with their long-horned cattle." But the Chwezi dynasty did not last long in Bunyoro. In a few generations, the Chwezi "were chased out by [B]ito invaders" from the north, moving in a "south-westerly direction where ecological conditions are ideal for cattle-keeping" and "reappeared as conquering [H]ima herders in Ankore, Rwanda, and Burundi." But if the Chwezi disappeared on the way from Bunyoro to Ankore, and reappeared as the Hima in Ankore, the Hima disappeared on the way to Rwanda, where they reappeared as the Tutsi.

Mafeje is at pains to point out that at the outset, Tutsi migration was largely peaceful: "land was plentiful in the areas of migration of the Bahima." Later, though, this seems to have led to forcible conquest and the creation of the Rwandan state: "as the population increased as more [T]utsi kept on entering the country and more land had to be tilled to feed them" and "as cattle were increasing, ... the [H]utu had to move from the most fertile soil." But the very fact that our author has to speak of *disappearance and reappearance* suggests that what is involved here is a stringing together of facts that are otherwise separated by many a historical gap. The result is likely to be as much fiction as fact.

That much of what passed as historical fact in academic circles has to be considered as tentative—if not outright fictional—is becoming clear as postgenocidal sobriety compels a growing number of historians to take seriously the political uses to which their writings have been put, and their readers to question the certainty with which many a claim has been advanced. In the process, several claims that had come to be regarded as sacred cows no longer appear so self-evident: for example, David Newbury questions the long-held assumption that the Hutu were always agriculturalists and the Tutsi pastoralists. He argues that "the people who came to be known as [H]utu had cattle here long before those known as [T]utsi appeared on the scene." Certainly, if Hutu had in fact had a natural aversion to cattle rearing and had always been cultivators, it would have made little sense in the precolonial period to put restrictions on Hutu owning cattle. We must acknowledge that these identifications are less mere facts unrelated to power than historical artifacts created alongside the institutionalized power of the precolonial Rwandan state.

CONSTRUCTING A STATE
This history is important, not because of where the Tutsi and the Hutu originally came from, but because in their

coming together they created certain political institutions that outlived that history and shaped a tragic future. The key political institution forged through their contact was the precolonial Rwandan state. It established a double domination, of a pastoralist aristocracy over a subject peasantry, and of Tutsi over Hutu—and Twa. While the question of the historical origin of the Tutsi is shrouded in mystery, that of the nature of the state they built is not.

The parameters of the cultural complex called Kinyarwanda are much larger than the domain of the present-day state called Rwanda. The disparity between their size was even greater in the precolonial period than it is today. Kinyarwanda is said to have one of the largest groups of speakers of any African language, roughly ten million. Long before the consolidation of the Nyiginya dynasty as the state of Rwanda in what is known as the central court complex, people speaking variants of Kinyarwanda were widely settled in the region. Outside central Rwanda, where the precolonial Rwandan state was based, there are at least two zones that were culturally—but not politically—Kinyarwanda. The first of these is today divided between northern Rwanda and western Uganda, settled by a people known as the Kiga—"the people of the mountains"—who shared the same language but not the same social and political culture as those within the ambit of the Rwandan state. Not only did they have different settlement patterns, clan categories, and marriage forms, but their political life was highly decentralized and community-based, in sharp contrast to the centralized hierarchy of the state of Rwanda. Here there were no Tutsi and no Hutu, at least not until German colonialism integrated part of this area into the Rwandan polity. The cultural difference between what then became northern Rwanda and the rest of the country would later reappear—under the two Hutu republics—as the difference between northern and southern Hutu. The second major cultural zone that lay outside the precolonial state of Rwanda is today divided between western Rwanda and eastern Congo-Kinshasa. These speakers of Kinyarwanda live south and west of Lake Rweru (Edward), and north and south of Lake Kivu, in Congo-Kinshasa. Unlike the Kiga of the north, the Banyabwisha of the west had long accepted delegates from the central court: their social institutions closely resembled those in the central region.

All Banyarwanda spoke Kinyarwanda, the Bantu language originally spoken by the peasant population of Rwanda. Thus we come to the point that the people called Tutsi, and those who came to be called Hutu, spoke the same language, lived on the same hills, and had more or less the same culture, depending on the cultural zones in which they lived. But they had yet to become one people.

I will make my point by contrasting two states that were organized in the intralacustrine region—Rwanda and BUGANDA. Like Buganda, Rwanda was a highly centralized kingdom, with a standing army and an official bureaucracy. But unlike Buganda, the state in Rwanda defined rulers and subjects as belonging to two distinct social groups, pastoralist and agriculturalist, one noble, the other commoner. The kings, considered divine, were all Tutsi; army commanders were all Tutsi. While the entire population was affiliated to the army, there is—once again—no agreement among historians as to whether the warriors were exclusively Tutsi or whether this held true only for an earlier period. Nonetheless, most seem agreed that participation within the army was structured hierarchically. In this context, as Antoine Lema puts it, "the corpse of a Tutsi had more value than that of a Hutu or a Twa ... the Hutu were deprived [of] the right to [a] glorious, honourable, heroic death, since the Tutsi had also social monopoly on that." In the civil bureaucracy, the Mwami of Rwanda appointed and dismissed all chiefs, of which there were three types: the chief of men, who was in charge of recruiting soldiers; the chief of pastures, who ruled over grazing lands; and the chief of landholding, who was in charge of agricultural land and production. The chief of landholding was more likely to be a Hutu, for agriculture was said to be a Hutu calling. In the lower ranks of the administrative hierarchy, non-Tutsi functionaries were more common. There was one institution in precolonial Rwanda that prevented the Tutsi-Hutu distinction from hardening into castelike difference, just as it prevented the formation of a Hutu counterelite that would in time challenge Tutsi domination. This was the rare Hutu who was able to accumulate cattle and rise through the socioeconomic hierarchy could kwihutura—"shed Hutuness"—and achieve the political status of a Tutsi. It is clear that we are talking of a political distinction, one that divided the subject from the nonsubject population, and not a socioeconomic distinction, between exploiters and exploited or rich and poor.

This is why the ruling aristocracy in precolonial Rwanda needs to be understood as both pastoral and Tutsi. The Hutu made up the subject population, while the Tutsi—even when not part of the ruling group—had more of an identification with power and a more privileged relationship to the state. While socioeconomic processes led to class differentiation, particularly among the Tutsi, the political differences created by how the state was organized reflected more than just class differences. It seems to me that the Tutsi developed a political identity—they "formed a distinct social category, marked by marriage and ethnic taboos," says Mafeje—a self-consciousness of being distinguished from the subject population. Thus the mere fact of some physical difference—often the nose, less often the height—could become symbolic of a great political difference. The colonial state built on this political difference, making it the central political artifact around which was constructed the state's local apparatus. As a result, these otherwise incidental physical differences came to bear the weight of an entire history of state formation.

THE COLONIAL STATE

While the Rwandan state clearly lost its independence with colonization, what was not so apparent was that its apparatus actually expanded during the colonial period. The territory it administered reached its widest span under German colonialism, since it was only with German military support—particularly the subjugation in 1912 of the northern districts—that Mwami Musinga was able to enlarge the state's boundaries. The Germans had but five civil and 24 military officers, commissioned and noncommissioned, on Rwandan soil in 1914. They could rule only through the institutional reach of the Tutsi-created state apparatus.

The Germans understood Africa through the optic of late nineteenth-century imperial Europe, which saw humanity as a conglomeration of races that required identification and hierarchical classification. Such was the inspiration behind the new discipline of physical anthropology, whose foot soldiers now began to classify the Tutsi and the Hutu as separate races, one Hamitic and superior, the other Bantu and inferior. But it was the Belgians who, from 1929 to 1933, turned this theory into the very basis of organizing the administrative apparatus of the colonial state. They classified the population into the Tutsi and the Hutu (and the Twa) and issued passes identifying all. Even the relative flexibility of the precolonial period—kwihutura—was removed, and the distinction was frozen into a rigid castelike structure. Indirect rule came to be rule through cooperative elements in the Tutsi oligarchy, those who managed the lowest rungs of the colonial administration that were also the highest rungs of the subordinate but semiautonomous district-level state apparatus.

The reorganization of the precolonial state was highly important. The key shift was in the redefinition of the powers of the state agents called chiefs. The previous trinity of chiefs was abolished and powers that had hitherto been separate and differentiated were fused in a single agent. To quote from René Lemarchand's study of colonial Rwanda, "the old balance of forces between cattle chiefs, land chiefs and army chiefs, which in previous times had served to protect the Hutu peasantry against undue exactions" was abolished. This "concentration of powers in the hands of a single chief, exercising unfettered control over his people, was bound to lead to abuses: not only did it

deprive the Hutu of opportunities to play one chief off against another, but it also eliminated the channels of appeal offered by the previous arrangement." At the same time, most Hutu chiefs on the lower rungs of the colonial administration were dismissed and replaced by those classified as Tutsi. Such institutional change not only augmented state power but made it more despotic in character.

Belgian rule was harsh by any standards. Force was integral to the process of exploitation—particularly forced labor. And the indigenous mask of this brutal foreign domination was the hierarchy of Tutsi chiefs. So severe was Belgian rule, and with such impunity was it translated into practice by the Tutsi chiefs, that hundreds of thousands of Hutu peasants fled into Uganda in the decade after 1928 to take up jobs as migrant laborers in the coffee farms of Buganda. At first, the Belgians found it convenient simply to pass on every demand—say, the upkeep of roads—to customary chiefs so that they used their influence to get the job done, without payment and with a minimum disruption of order. The chiefs also found it convenient to add their own demands to this list of "customary" exactions. The list grew as colonial law made ubureetwa services, a kind of forced labor, incumbent on all Hutu men. Catherine Newbury explains, "The services performed were usually of the most menial kind—collecting and drying firewood for the use of the hill chief's household, serving as night watchman, fetching water, cultivating the hill chief's fields. ... Hutu were not only expected to perform such services without pay, but were often subjected to mistreatment as well." The smaller the chief, the more arbitrary could be the imposition. As one [Catholic] Church observer noted, a *petit* Tutsi chief and his wife "could take almost anything they please—bananas, yams, etc.—and the Hutu must comply lest he be expelled from his fields."

MONEY AND SCHOOLING

But not everything under this political system was hard. There were two broad processes under way—the expansion of a money economy and school-based Western education—that would erode Tutsi economic supremacy while, for a time, leaving intact their political supremacy. The money economy opened up opportunities for enrichment other than through the ownership of cattle, weakening the bonds of pastoral servitude that had been the colonial contract between patron and client. In this context, the expanding school system of the 1940s and 1950s provided the structural basis for the emergence of a Hutu counterelite. School education for children of Hutu families was a church initiative. Admission records of the *Groupe Scolaire* in Astrida (now Butare), a church institution that admitted students from the three Belgian colonies of

Rwanda, Burundi, and the Congo, show that Hutu students were virtually excluded until after the Second World War, but the attitude of the European clergy went through a major shift in the mid-1950s. Postwar newcomers, according to Lemarchand, were likely to come from "le petit clergé"—of "relatively humble social origins," and with a "previous experience of social and political conditions in the French-speaking provinces of Wallonia," they were "more generally disposed to identify with the plight of the Hutu masses."

When the Hutu graduates of the *Group Scolaire* at Astrida entered the job market in the mid-1950s, they found there were few places for an educated Hutu. Literally shut out of jobs in the civil service and the private sector, they turned to the church for opportunities, not just to make a living but also to articulate their major social grievance: the institutionalized exclusion of Hutu from what they saw as a Belgian-supported Tutsi monopoly over all avenues of advancement. With the support of a sympathetic clergy, they took control over church publications—the most important being the Kinyarwanda-language magazine *Kinyamateke*—and began to address those who would listen sympathetically, mainly the Hutu masses below and visiting UN Commissions above.

Though administered by Belgium, Rwanda was a UN trust territory. Under UN tutelage, the process of decolonization unfolded as a series of electoral reforms. Elections set the context in which the Hutu counterelite forged their consciousness against the Tutsi elite. Such a consciousness emerged from the throes of a political contest. Tutsi identity, forged with the creation of the Rwandan state, long preceded Hutu identity. Tutsi consciousness was a consciousness of power while Hutu consciousness would come to be one of lack of power, and of a struggle for power.

The development of a Hutu consciousness was a protracted affair, stretching over the entire span of the colonial period. As late as independence in 1962, the Hutu of the northwestern region insisted on being considered as Kiga like their neighbors in southwestern Uganda—not Hutu. Hutu consciousness developed in phases: before the Second World War, it was a consciousness of subjecthood that transcended all locally anchored identities; in the 1950s it became the consciousness of a people taking power. This shift took place only with the emergence of a Hutu counterelite which, propelled center stage by a series of electoral contests, put forth "Hutu power" as a program for overcoming their identity as a subject people. Branded with a subject identity—Hutu—the counterelite emerging from the ranks of the socially oppressed would hold it up as a badge of pride: Hutu Power! In turning a chain into a weapon, Spartacus-style, in trying to forge an identity for liberation from an emblem of servitude, it was neither the

first nor would it be the last. One only need think of a related example: Black Power!

HUTU POWER AND ITS CONSEQUENCES

The backdrop to these electoral contests was a series of UN decolonization missions that were regularly dispatched to its trust territory after the Second World War. In 1953 elections were held to create advisory councils to state organs, in 1956 the first general election, another in 1959, and the last general elections in 1960 and 1961. This series of elections, and the anticipation of a transfer of power, triggered a chain of events leading, first, to a loosening of the hold of the Tutsi elite on the lower reaches of the state apparatus, and then, to extreme political polarization between the Tutsi and the Hutu—a prelude to an anti-Tutsi pogrom. The shift from indirect to direct elections showed that there was considerable likelihood of a Hutu victory at the polls. There was a clear victory in the 1956 elections of Hutu candidates at the subchief level, where the vote was direct, but not at higher levels, where the vote was indirect.

This was accompanied by an ideological polarization between Tutsi and Hutu, dramatized by two rival documents issued in anticipation of the 1957 UN trusteeship mission. First was *Mise au Point*, a call for an all-Rwandan emancipation issued by the Mwami's High Council, advocating a transfer of power to ease racial tensions between black and white. Within a month followed the *Bahutu Manifesto*, written by Kayibanda and eight other Hutu leaders, all church-affiliated, and a Belgian priest. The difference between the two documents could not have been sharper: independence first, the view of the Tutsi elite, was the claim of the precolonial rulers for a restoration of their prerogatives; democracy before independence, the view of the Hutu counterelite, spelled out its demand for power. One highlighted the racial contradiction in the colony—between white and black—while the other underlined the social contradiction among the colonized.

On October 19, 1959, in anticipation of the next round of elections, and with the blessing of church authorities, a Hutu political party—the Parti du Mouvement de l'Émancipation Hutu (PARMEHUTU)—was created out of the old cultural association, Mouvement Social Muhutu. Almost immediately, there followed confrontations between PARMEHUTU militants and those of the promonarchy Tutsi party, the Union Nationale Rwandaise (UNAR), and Tutsi chiefs in charge of the local state apparatus. These came to a head in and around Gitarama the next month: when news spread that a group of young UNAR militants had attacked the PARMEHUTU leader Dominique Mbonyumutwa, pogroms spread from all over the country. The visiting UN mission of 1960 estimated the killings at 200 but added, "the number may be even higher since the people preferred to bury their dead silently." Some Tutsi chiefs were killed, others were forced to resign. A state of emergency was declared and the country put under the command of Colonel Bem Guy Logiest.

It was in this context that Belgium carried out nothing less than a coup d'état. Arguing that the presence of Tutsi as subchiefs and chiefs "disturbed the public order," Bem Logiest began the replacement of Tutsi chiefs with Hutu, thus shepherding a "revolution" against what had hitherto been the colonial power's own authorities. Half the chiefs and subchiefs on the eve of the 1960 and 1961 general elections were Hutu—and the chiefs had control of the ballot boxes. Without this reconstitution of the local state hierarchy, it is difficult to explain the dramatically different outcome of subsequent elections. Two tendencies gelled around PARMEHUTU and UNAR. In the 1961 election, PARMEHUTU secured 77.4 percent of the popular vote, UNAR 16.8 percent. Independence followed on July 1, 1962: the new government was based on a power-sharing arrangement between PARMEHUTU and UNAR.

Unstable as it was, this power sharing came to an end with the attempt by the Tutsi refugees, who had fled in 1959 to Burundi, to return to power through an invasion called Inyenzi—cockroaches. The response was an organized countrywide killing of prominent Tutsi personalities, who had been previously arrested, and sectors of the Tutsi population: each of the country's ten prefectures was made an emergency zone under the commands of a minister who organized self-defense groups among the Hutu population. It is difficult to know how many were killed. The UN guessed 1,000 to 3,000; the World Council of Churches estimated 10,000 to 14,000. Writing in *Le Monde* on February 6, 1964, Bertrand Russell termed it the most horrible systematic extermination of a people since the Nazi extermination of Jews. No African state except Burundi even raised a voice. The smashing of the counterrevolution, for that is how this pogrom was hailed, eroded any middle ground: the Tutsi who were killed were precisely those who had cut themselves off from the court and from the monarchists, and had hoped for a republican regime in which they could serve.

In the context of this historical account, we can draw the following conclusions:

1) The distinction between Tutsi and Hutu is a sociopolitical distinction. It is not just a colonial creation: created in the precolonial period, the distinction was polarized by the colonial state, and would be inflamed and institutionalized by the postcolonial state.

2) The Tutsi identity crystallized at the time of the formation of the precolonial Rwandan state. It was a self-consciousness of

being in or near power, or simply identifying with power. By contrast, the Hutu identity that gelled later was a self-consciousness of those subject to power. The Hutu identity—and its springboard, the 1959 revolution—cannot be dismissed as simply a sign of backwardness. This identity was limited to the framework of the colonial state, particularly the Tutsi hierarchy of chiefs. It is from this Hutu point of view that 1959 looks like a revolution, and 1994 must look like a counterrevolution.

3) Those who insist that the Hutu and the Tutsi are separate ethnic or cultural groups should ponder one fact: the identity Hutu-Tutsi is bipolar. Neither can exist in isolation. Rwanda's First Republic understood that so long as there is a sociopolitical identity called Tutsi, there will be another called Hutu. So it tried to entrench and keep alive both identities by reenacting the revolution as Hutu power through periodic pogroms, expulsions, and the redistribution of property to its militants in 1959, 1963, and so on. In time, the reenactments borrowed imagery from the French Revolution. Committees of Public Safety posted lists of counterrevolutionaries. In 1972, these were Tutsi who were found in prominent positions in the educational system or the civil service. The pogrom of 1972 gathered in intensity as Hutu refugees were flushed into Rwanda, seeking shelter from a rampaging Tutsi-dominated army in neighboring Burundi. In this context, the minister of defense, Jouvenal Habyarimana, staged a coup d'état, proclaiming that the cultural revolution of 1973 would but complete the social revolution of 1959.

4) The Second Republic tried to bring the permanent revolution that, in reality, was a permanent terror to an end by embedding the identities Hutu and Tutsi in institutions. Habyarimana institutionalized a hierarchical pluralism that he justified as a form of reverse discrimination (affirmative action) that would restore balance to Rwandan society through a system of quotas designed to redress the grievances of a hitherto oppressed majority. The Tutsi would be allowed a subordinate status in civil society, provided they accepted a subject status in political society. In this context, Habyarimana made every attempt to ensure a symbolic Tutsi presence in the state apparatus: in late 1990, there was one Tutsi in a 19-member cabinet, one ambassador, two deputies in a seventy-seat National Assembly, and two members in the sixteen-person central committee of the ruling party, the MRND. Did not the 1959 revolution turn the world that the Hutu knew upside down, but without changing it in other ways? If the corpse of a Tutsi had more value than that of a Hutu in an earlier era, did not the revolution arrive at a point where the corpse of a Tutsi had less dignity than a human corpse? If the upwardly

mobile Hutu could shed his Hutuness (kwihutra) and enter the ranks of power, was not Habyarimana's nominal integration of Tutsi in the state hierarchy, right up to the cabinet, a sort of a kwitutsira?

The allocation of resources and positions within the state was said to reflect the actual numerical weight of the majority and the minority in society so the demographic question became a hot political issue. The Second Republic maintained that the Tutsi constituted no more than 9 percent of the total population of Rwanda—this had the status of a state-sanctioned truth and the figure remained unchanged over decades. Officialdom had little to say about intermarriages between Hutu and Tutsi and the official identity of children of these marriages. Despite centuries of intermarriage, the people of Rwanda were neatly divided into Hutu and Tutsi (or Twa); none were Hutsi.

5) Hutu and Tutsi in Rwanda are more political than cultural identities: when one is power, the other is subject. These bipolar identities are backed up by a form of the state that divides Rwandan society into a permanent majority (Hutu) and a permanent minority (Tutsi). How can Rwanda break out of this notion of the state as a representation of one of two permanently defined parts—one a majority, the other a minority? For any society to continue to exist, democratic competition—whether party-driven or not—presumes the existence of an order based on the consent, not of a majority, but of all. If political competition is not to be destructive of life, all those who participate in it—whether they win or lose—must accept the rules of the game. The creation of a consensus-based political community must precede the adoption of any majority-driven political competition. Failure to learn this lesson will place Rwanda once again in a state of permanent tension. How to move from an order based on conquest to one based on consent is the challenge for Rwanda today.

See also PASTORALISM; PYGMY.

MAHMOOD MAMDANI

Euba, Akin
1935–
Nigerian composer.

Akin Euba of NIGERIA composes classical works that combine elements of European music with the musical traditions of the country's YORUBA people. Throughout his career Euba has worked to create African classical music that is accessible to Africans and non-Africans alike. In his opinion, "the contemporary African composer ... must create music for his own people

and for all people at large and must act as an interpreter between the two."

Born in Lagos, Euba received an extensive musical education at Trinity College of Music in London, at the University of California at Los Angeles, and at the University of Ghana at Legon, where he received his Ph.D. degree in 1974. He has taught at Trinity College in England, at the University of Nigeria at Ife, and the University of Pittsburgh, where he is currently Mellon Professor of African Music. Euba is not only a composer but also a scholar who has published many academic articles on African music.

Most of Euba's earlier music fits into the Western classical or art music tradition. His first major work, a string quartet completed in 1957, is strongly influenced by Hungarian composer Bela Bartók. His 1967 symphonic study *Olurounbi* contains only glancing references to the Yoruba folk tradition. Euba incorporated significantly more African material into his later works. In 1972 his *Dirges* was premiered at the Munich Olympic Games, a tribute to his achievement in synthesizing Western and African musical traditions, and his *Six Yoruba Songs* (1975) for voice and piano are based on original folk songs, with little modification. Euba also composed music for Léopold SENGHOR's poem "Chaka"—an important work that Nigerian literary scholar Abiola Irele believes "comes closest to an original conception of African art music ... [as] the musical material, both in its structure and its instrumentation, is felt to proceed organically from the African musical tradition."

Euba spent the academic year 2000–2001 teaching at Churchill College, University of Cambridge, in England. There he composed *Orunmila's Voices: Songs from the Beginning of Time*, a work for singers, dancers, and a symphony orchestra that was first performed in New Orleans in 2002. Among Euba's more recent works are *Study in African Jazz No. 3* (2002) and *Below Kusumo Falls* (2005), a work for voice, Yoruba dancers, and various instruments. Euba is currently Andrew W. Mellon Professor of Music at the University of Pittsburgh.

See also MUSIC, AFRICAN.

ROANNE EDWARDS

Evora, Cesaria
1941–
Cape Verdean songwriter and singer.

Cesaria Evora was one of seven children in a musical family in Mindelo, a town in the island nation of CAPE VERDE off the West African coast. Musicians in the family included her violinist father, who died when she was a child, and her uncle Francisco Xavier da Cruz, a songwriter whose songs

Evora has recorded. Evora was singing in bars in Mindelo by the age of sixteen.

Evora sings in Criuolo, a Creole derived from Portuguese and African languages. She is most famous for singing *morna*, which roughly translates to "songs of mourning." As with many other kinds of folk music, morna songs are handed down from generation to generation, tracing dominant themes in a people's history. Many morna songs, for example, lament Cape Verdean losses to the Transatlantic Slave Trade and to and emigration. Often accompanied by acoustic guitars, violins, accordions, and cavaquinho, a four-string guitar or ukulele, Evora's vocals have been described as a cross between French singer Edith Piaf and American jazz singer Billie Holiday.

At twenty Evora made a recording for her country's national radio, and it sparked her career. She received offers from bars and nightclubs throughout the ten Cape Verdean islands, soon becoming known as the "queen of morna." Although several tapes of Evora's music traveled to Portugal and the Netherlands, she never performed outside of Cape Verde. Evora once recalled, "I used to sing for tourists and for the ships when they would come here. That's why I always thought that maybe if I made it, people from different countries would love my music." By the 1970s, however, Evora had quit recording and performing, claiming that she was not "making any money."

Evora emerged from retirement in 1985 to contribute two songs to an album of Cape Verdean women's music. Soon thereafter, the Cape Verdean concert promoter Jose da Silva convinced Evora to go to France to record. There she became known as the "barefoot diva" because she regularly performed shoeless. Whether the habit is a symbol of her empathy for Cape Verde's poor women and children (as has been claimed) or simply a personal preference, the nickname became the title of her first album, *La Diva aux Pieds Nus* (1988). After *Distino di Belita* (1990) and *Mar Azul* (1991), Evora had her first international hit at the age of fifty-one with *Miss Perfumado* (1992), which sold 200,000 copies.

Evora toured the United States in 1995 in support of that year's release, *Cesaria Evora*, which was a gold record in France and reached number seven on Portugal's charts. Her popular success has been reinforced by critical and peer recognition. In 1996 *Cesaria Evora* was nominated for a Grammy Award in the United States as best world music album. In addition, at the 1997 KORA All Africa Music Awards, Evora received the Judges Merit Award, best artist from West Africa Award, and best African album. A regular performer at world music festivals, Evora has opened for pop music acts such as Natalie Merchant and counts pop star Madonna as a fan. In 2000 she sang at Carnegie Hall in New York at a jazz festival, sharing the bill with Cassandra Wilson. Among her more recent studio work are *São Vicente di Longe* (2001), *Voz d'Amor* (2003), and *Rogamar* (2006). *Live D'Amor*, recorded in Paris, was released in 2004.

Even after reaching global stardom, Evora has chosen to remain in Cape Verde with her mother and her children and grandchildren (three times divorced, Evora has vowed never to marry again). "I wasn't astonished by Europe," she said, "and I was never that impressed by the speed and grandeur of modern America. I only regret my success has taken so long to achieve."

KATE TUTTLE

Ewe

Ethnic group of coastal West Africa, whose approximately four million members inhabit southeastern Ghana, southern Togo, and adjacent parts of Benin.

The broad Ewe grouping comprises a number of "clans" or ethnic subgroups, all speaking languages of the Niger-Congo family but each with its own history and specific customs. These subgroups include the Anlo of GHANA, and in TOGO the Ouatchi, MINA, ADJA, and so-called Brazilians, a group with diverse origins (including freed slaves) who settled on the coast as traders during the early nineteenth century. The Ewe are the largest ethnic group in Togo, and they dominate the country economically. The Ewe are closely related to the FON of BENIN, but are distinguished by their historical resistance to states such as the Fon-dominated kingdom of Dahomey.

The early history of the Ewe is little known. According to oral tradition, they began a gradual westward migration from Oyo, in the YORUBA region of modern NIGERIA, in the thirteenth century C.E. However, archaeological evidence suggests a longer continuous presence in the Ewe heartland of southern Togo. One theory suggests that this tradition may have arisen during the eighteenth century, when Oyo dominated DAHOMEY and neighboring parts of present-day Togo. Another theory proposes that Yoruba migrants may have at one point achieved cultural hegemony over the indigenous population of the Ewe region.

Oral tradition tells of the Ewe's flight from a brutal seventeenth-century tyrant, King Agokoli of Notsé. This experience may have shaped the Ewe group's long-standing opposition to strong leaders, and hindered state formation. Although the precolonial Anlo Ewe of present-day Ghana formed a regional confederacy of kinship groups, all acknowledging the primacy of a chief priest, most Ewe remained in small local polities. In these polities the power of hereditary chiefs was tempered by the authority of lineage patriarchs, and by local assemblies of male and female elders. Lacking a centralized state, the precolonial Ewe also lacked a strong sense of group identity.

Instead, Ewe territory provided a place of refuge from the neighboring kingdoms of Dahomey and ASANTE. GA- and FANTE-speaking peoples such as the Mina settled among the Ewe as refugees from Asante hegemony, and gradually adopted Ewe language and customs. On the other hand, the Ewe's lack of a strong state structure left them prone to frequent slave raiding from the seventeenth to the nineteenth century.

In addition to sharing a language and certain historical experiences, precolonial Ewe communities were knit together by trade, as market women exchanged fish and imported European goods for the agricultural produce of interior groups. However, European colonial powers partitioned Ewe territory by the end of the nineteenth century between the British in the GOLD COAST (present-day GHANA), the Germans in Togoland, who occupied the Ewe heartland, and the French in Dahomey (present-day BENIN). Paradoxically, the disruption of trade caused by this partition may have sparked the formation of a common Ewe identity.

When British and French mandates further divided the Ewe heartland of southern Togoland, it was primarily the resulting trade disruption that gave rise to the Ewe unification movement after World War I. The movement for the unification of Togoland and all Ewe territories (including those in the Gold Coast) gained momentum after World War II, but the rival colonial powers, fearing a loss of influence in the region, held plebiscites in which non-Ewe Togolese, fearing Ewe domination of a unified Togoland, overwhelmingly opposed unification and outvoted the Ewe minority.

Living near the coast, the Ewe have historically benefited more than their northern neighbors from trade and economic development, and enjoy relatively high rates of literacy. Since the colonial period, they have prospered as owners of cocoa plantations and have played a disproportionately large role in the commerce and civil service of both Togo and Ghana. Especially in Togo, their economic power has earned the resentment of northern ethnic groups such as the KABIYÉ, whose connection to the military regime of General Gnassingbé EYADÉMA has excluded the Ewe from political power in Togo since the days of independence. The Ewe currently lead the opposition to his regime.

See also COLONIAL RULE; DAHOMEY, EARLY KINGDOM OF; LANGUAGES, AFRICAN: AN OVERVIEW; OYO, EARLY KINGDOM OF; POLITICAL MOVEMENTS IN AFRICA; SLAVERY IN AFRICA.

BIBLIOGRAPHY

Greene, Sandra. *Gender, Ethnicity and Social Change on the Upper Slave Coast: A History of the Anlo-Ewe of Ghana.* Heinemann, 1996.

MARK O'MALLEY

Excision

See FEMALE CIRCUMCISION IN AFRICA.

Explorers in Africa before 1500

Foreigners who traveled to sub-Saharan Africa before 1500 to investigate its geography and peoples.

Outsiders have remained in contact with the peoples of Africa since the first modern humans began trickling out of the continent. Desert nomads have crossed the SAHARA and coastal traders have crossed the narrow Strait of Mandeb for thousands of years. From the beginnings of history, the Mediterranean Sea facilitated continuous contact between North Africa and the peoples of Europe and the Middle East. Certainly trade connections existed between EGYPT and the peoples of sub-Saharan Africa by the second millennium B.C.E., and Carthaginians and Asian peoples may have been trading along the coasts of Africa more than 2,000 years ago. However, none of these ancient traders or explorers left written accounts that survive today, so we know little about them and nothing of what they saw during their travels. Our earliest surviving accounts of sub-Saharan Africa come from ancient Greek authors. Herodotus of Halicarnassus wrote extensively about Africa. It was during his travels to Egypt and LIBYA in the middle of the fifth century B.C.E. that Herodotus learned about Africa. He was highly knowledgeable about the NILE RIVER as far south as Gondokoro. Some of his work was based on the travels of the Egyptian pharaoh Necho II, who ruled from about 610 to 595 B.C.E. Early European knowledge of East Africa came from two sources: the Periplus of the Erythraean Sea, written during the first century C.E. by an anonymous Greek trader who lived in Egypt, and Ptolemy's Geography, probably written in the second century C.E. Between 1000 and 1500 C.E., Berber Ibadi traders of North Africa traveled south across the Sahara. Other Arabs and North Africans traveled south of the Sahara on a religious mission to convert sub-Saharan Africans to Islam. Traders from the Arabian Peninsula also made regular journeys to coastal East Africa. Many of these traders settled in coastal communities, where they contributed to the emerging Swahili culture. In the fourteenth century, IBN BATTUTAH, a North African who explored out of curiosity, traveled extensively throughout North Africa, Egypt, and East Africa, and crossed the Sahara to the West African kingdom of MALI, including the city of TOMBOUCTOU. Descriptions of his journeys were published in Rihlah (Travels), which greatly expanded knowledge of African geography in the Muslim and Western worlds. Chinese explorers also traveled to Africa at an early date. Chinese writings include information on East Africa, mainly gathered from Muslim traders, as early as the eighth century C.E. Chinese rulers began sending trading expeditions across the Indian Ocean during the fifteenth century, and two of these expeditions reached the Horn of Africa, one from 1417 to 1419, the other from 1421 to 1422. Fei Hsin, an officer who participated in these voyages, wrote an account of his observations that survives today. By the middle of the fifteenth century, Chinese knowledge of Africa exceeded that of Europeans. Beginning in the fifteenth century, the Portuguese became the first European nation to undertake an extensive investigation of Africa. Prince Henry (later known as Prince Henry the Navigator) spearheaded the explorations. Shortly after 1419, Henry established a research institute to gather information about Africa. Besides his desire for increased trade and for exploration, he was motivated by a dream of forming a Christian union with the legendary Prester John of Africa. In addition, he intended to divert the Muslim-dominated overland GOLD TRADE by sending Portuguese ships to the west coast of Africa. By the 1480s, Africa's west coast was well known to the Portuguese. The Portuguese also sought a greater share of the spice trade, which reached Europe via the Indian Ocean and the Mediterranean Sea. Pedro da Covilhã explored the east coast of Africa during the late 1480s. The knowledge he gathered may have aided the voyage of Vasco da Gama, who in 1497 became the first known European to sail around the Cape of Good Hope to the Indian Ocean. Though Portuguese government officials remained predominantly on the coast, Portuguese clergy, especially the Jesuits, traveled inland to seek converts to Catholicism. Portuguese missionaries reached as far as ANGOLA, the kingdom of Monomotapa (also known as Munhumutapa) in present-day ZIMBABWE, and ETHIOPIA. These Portuguese explorers connected the African coast with Europe and the rest of the world. Their explorations changed the course of African history and paved the way for later explorers. Sadly, they also paved the way for the continent's exploitation and the beginnings of the brutal slave trade.

See also CHRISTIANITY: MISSIONARIES IN AFRICA; EGYPT, ANCIENT KINGDOM OF; EXPLORERS IN AFRICA, 1500 TO 1800; ISLAM IN AFRICA; SWAHILI CIVILIZATION.

BIBLIOGRAPHY

Azzam, Abd al-Rahman. *The Travels of Ibn Battuta.* Hood Books, 1995.

Delpar, Helen ed. *The Discoverers: An Encyclopedia of Explorers and Exploration.* McGraw-Hill, 1980.

ROBERT FAY

Explorers in Africa, 1500 to 1800
Foreigners who traveled to sub-Saharan Africa between 1500 and 1800 to investigate its geography and peoples.

Earlier explorers had essentially finished mapping the African coast by 1514. The interior posed a much more formidable obstacle, however. During the period between 1500 and 1800, Europeans accumulated knowledge intermittently and established few outposts beyond coastal areas. One of the first Europeans to explore inland Africa was Leo Africanus, who was born in Granada, Spain, and lived there until 1492, when Spain expelled all Muslims. He then traveled with his parents to MOROCCO. In about 1507, Leo began traveling around North and Central Africa, where he served as a diplomat. He visited TOMBOUCTOU (Timbuktu) twice. After his second visit there, he traveled to EGYPT via the Bornu kingdom and Lake Chad. He also visited present-day SUDAN twice between 1509 and 1513, and his observations provided the basis for European knowledge of the region until well into the nineteenth century. After his African travels, Leo settled for a time in Rome, Italy, where he published Navigationi et Viaggi (1550), subsequently translated into English as A Geographic Historie of Africa (1600).

The Portuguese exploration of Africa, which began in the fifteenth century, continued in the sixteenth. But their inland explorations remained modest in comparison to their earlier coastal discoveries. The Portuguese António Fernandes explored present-day southern ZIMBABWE, where he visited the gold mines of Monomatapa (or Munhumutapa) between 1511 and 1514. In 1616 Gaspar Bocarro traveled as far as Tete on the ZAMBEZI RIVER. During the late eighteenth century, the Portuguese established bases on the Zambezi, first at Sena, then at Tete, hoping to control trade from these locations. In 1793 Alexandre da Silva Teixeira reached the Luvale people of present-day ZAMBIA. In 1798 Francisco José de Lacerda journeyed from Tete to the court of the Kazembe on Lake Mweru on the southeastern border of present-day Congo-Kinshasa. The Portuguese also gained considerable knowledge about ETHIOPIA, a Christian empire that they initially believed to be the legacy of the legendary Prester John. Francisco Alvarez, a member of a Portuguese embassy to the court of Ethiopian emperor Lebna DENGEL, provided descriptions of Ethiopia that greatly increased European knowledge of that country, as did Jesuits such as Pedro Páez (who also discovered the source of the BLUE NILE) and António Fernandes. In addition, the Frenchman Charles Poncet visited the Ethiopian court at Gonder in about 1699. The travels and discoveries of the Portuguese generated interest among other European nations, which began to send their own expeditions to Africa. Portuguese power gradually declined during the sixteenth and seventeenth centuries, and after 1600, British, Dutch, and French traders began to seize control of Portuguese trading coasts, particularly in West Africa. In 1652 the Dutch established the first permanent European post at the Cape of Good Hope in present-day SOUTH AFRICA. By the early 1700s, Dutch colonists had begun to explore the region's interior. In West Africa, British traders had traveled as far as the Barracuda Falls by 1651, and by 1659 Cornelius Hoges had reached Bambuk in present-day eastern SENEGAL. During the seventeenth century, the French sailed up the SENEGAL RIVER as far as Malam. In 1700 the French established a fort in the region. The British adventurer James Bruce published Travels to Discover the Source of the Nile (1790), which added insight to European knowledge of Africa and also sparked interest in Africa among Europeans, especially in London and Paris. This popularity led to the establishment in London in 1788 of the Association for Promoting the Discovery of the Interior Parts of Africa, also called the African Association. It was this organization that supported James Watt and Matthew Winterbottom in their travels to FOUTA DJALLON and the Rio Nunez in present-day GUINEA. In 1796 Mungo Park traveled up the NIGER RIVER and arrived at Ségou in present-day MALI. In the final twenty-five years of the eighteenth century, travel books dealing with Africa attracted an enthusiastic audience. The nature of exploration would change, however, in the nineteenth century. Although many nineteenth-century explorers came as Christian missionaries, the information they gained on their travels contributed to the colonization of Africa.

See also CHRISTIANITY: MISSIONARIES IN AFRICA; COLONIAL RULE; EXPLORERS IN AFRICA BEFORE 1500; EXPLORERS IN AFRICA SINCE 1800.

ROBERT FAY

Explorers in Africa since 1800

Foreigners who traveled to sub-Saharan Africa after 1800 to investigate its geography and peoples.

Building on the work of earlier explorers, European explorers of Africa after 1800 provided information used by European powers to carry out their colonization of the continent. By crisscrossing the vast continent's interior, nineteenth-century explorers, many of them Christian missionaries, contributed far more to Western knowledge of Africa and its peoples than earlier explorers had. These Europeans discovered that beyond the African coast lay a continent much more hospitable than their legends and myths of the "dark continent" had suggested. European exploration of Africa during the nineteenth century had three main goals: the elimination of the slave trade, the imposition of "legitimate" commerce, and the spread of Christianity among Africans. This new phase of

DR. LIVINGSTONE. Painting by Alonzo Chappel, 1867. (*Prints and Photographs Division, Library of Congress*)

exploration began at the end of the eighteenth century. The Association for the Discovery of the Interior Parts of Africa—founded in 1788 by a small group of wealthy Englishmen and popularly called the African Association—first supported the exploration of North and West Africa. The association funded the efforts by Scotsman Mungo Park to travel to the upper NIGER RIVER during the 1790s. Park discovered that the river flowed eastward, not westward as Leo Africanus had incorrectly asserted in the sixteenth century. Some of the African Association's members convinced the British government that the exploration of Africa was an endeavor worthy of government support, and it was in the employ of the British that Park undertook another—but fatal—expedition in 1805 to chart the course of the Niger. The British government also funded famed explorers Major Dixon Denham and his two fellow travelers, Lieutenant Hugh Clapperton and surgeon Walter Oudney, who crossed the SAHARA after visiting Bornu and Hausland from 1823 to 1825. The brothers John and Richard Lander, who charted the course of the lower Niger in 1830, were funded by the British, as was the German HEINRICH BARTH, who charted the central and western Sudan from 1850 to 1855. The quintessential Christian missionary explorer was perhaps David Livingstone, who in 1841 traveled to South Africa as a member of the London Missionary Society. In 1853 Livingstone traveled from the south to VICTORIA FALLS and from there west to LUANDA. He then turned to the east and found the mouth of the ZAMBEZI RIVER. Livingstone's subsequent book, Missionary Travels and Researches, went through nine editions in England and transformed public opinion of the continent. Britain's Royal Geographical Society formed in 1830 and took the place of the African Association. Unlike its predecessor, it received government funding. Its officers had access to high-placed government officials, and in 1858, it arranged for Livingstone to undertake an expedition up the Zambezi as British consul in charge. After his expedition stalled at the Quebrabasa Falls, Livingstone traveled up the Shire River, attempting to reach the African interior, again without success. He may have taken consolation in the discovery of LAKE MALAWI. Livingstone continued his exploration at his own expense (his travel books had made him a fortune), and he spent his final years, from 1867 to 1873, in the upper reaches of the CONGO. Early in the nineteenth century, France—which had been active in the slave trade and had sent explorers up the SENEGAL in the eighteenth century—contributed little to the exploration of Africa. The only journey of note was undertaken by René CAILLIÉ, who went from Rio Nunez to TOMBOUCTOU and across the Sahara to TANGIER. In contrast to the French, Germans and German speakers contributed much to European knowledge of Africa, many working with British support. German missionaries combed East Africa in their search for converts. Missionaries Johannes Rebmann, Johann Ludwig Krapf, and J. J. Erhardt were the first Europeans to see Mount KILIMANJARO and MOUNT KENYA. Gerhard Rohlfs traveled extensively in the Sahara. Gustav Nachtigal built on the work of Rohlfs. Between 1870 and 1874, Nachtigal explored present-day SUDAN and CHAD. During the SCRAMBLE FOR AFRICA, Nachtigal played a key role in establishing German colonies. Through threats and manipulation, he secured treaties in 1884 with Mlapa III, the chief of Togoville, TOGO, and with the DUALA people of CAMEROON, that provided the basis for German colonial claims to those regions. Later that year, Nachtigal signed a treaty establishing an additional colony in what is currently NAMIBIA.

As European colonial powers completed their conquest of most of the continent during the 1890s and the early twentieth century, their scouts and agents surveyed the territory to be subdued. Mary KINGSLEY, one the few European women to explore the continent, toured the interior of present-day GABON during the 1890s. By about 1914, virtually the entire continent had been surveyed by the representatives of European governments. It is also important to remember that most, if not all, European explorers relied on Africans as soldiers, guides, translators, porters, cooks, and personal servants. Given the possible hazards in Africa—such as hostile animals, Africans seeking to defend themselves against intruders, disabling diseases, and rough terrain—the success of a European explorer's journey depended on the ability and skill of his African employees. Although they faced the same difficulties as their famous employers, their names and personal histories, sadly, are largely lost to us today.

See also CHRISTIANITY: MISSIONARIES IN AFRICA; COLONIAL RULE; EXPLORERS IN AFRICA BEFORE 1500; EXPLORERS IN AFRICA, 1500 TO 1800.

ROBERT FAY

Eyadéma, Gnassingbé
1936–2005
President of Togo.

General Gnassingbé Eyadéma remained in power for decades as president of the West African nation of TOGO. He owes his long tenure as president to two factors—a system of patronage that brought the support of important segments of Togolese society, and personal control over the country's military, which has consistently and often violently repressed political opposition.

According to official sources, Eyadéma was born on December 27, 1936, as Étienne Gnassingbé, to KABIYÉ peasants in Pya, Togo. He completed six years of school before, like other poor young Kabiyé, enlisting in the French army. He enlisted in 1953 and served in FRENCH DAHOMEY (now BENIN), Southeast Asia, ALGERIA, and NIGER. Upon his discharge in 1962, he returned to Togo, as did more than 600 mostly Kabiyé French veterans.

Togo's president, Sylvanus Olympio, refused to enlarge Togo's 150-man army to include these experienced veterans. A group of them, including Gnassingbé, responded by staged West Africa's first military coup in January 1963. During the coup, Gnassingbé killed President Olympio. After the killing, Gnassingbé took "Eyadéma," a Kabiyé word implying courage, as his surname. Eyadéma claims that Olympio was firing a gun while seeking refuge at the gates of the United States embassy, but other accounts suggest that he murdered a defenseless Olympio.

Under Nicolas Grunitzky, chosen by the coup's leaders as Olympio's successor, Eyadéma took charge of an expanded military. When Olympio's political heirs threatened to unseat Grunitzky and bring Olympio's murderers to justice, a military junta seized power in early 1967. Later that year, Eyadéma dismissed the junta, named himself president, and had himself promoted to the rank of general.

When Eyadéma took power, Togo was just beginning large-scale export of phosphate, a chemical compound used in fertilizers and other industrial products. The income from selling phosphate funded a program of political patronage, infrastructural development, and free trade that earned Eyadéma support throughout Togo, particularly among the powerful market women of LOMÉ. Following the example of Zaire's President Mobutu Sese Seko, Eyadéma institutionalized his rule by establishing Togo as a one-party state and building a personality cult around himself. Eyadéma had larger-than-life images of himself placed throughout the country and encouraged people to believe favorable rumors and legends about him. For example, according to an official legend of invincibility, Eyadéma's survival of a plane crash and coup attempts mean that divine powers have saved him.

Patronage, however, gradually turned into financial irresponsibility, and too many positions were given to incompetent friends and supporters. When phosphate revenues declined in the late 1970s, a severe debt crisis forced Eyadéma to cut spending and enact strict economic measures required if the country was to obtain loans from the International Monetary Fund. The president grew increasingly paranoid, withdrawing into a circle of supporters. He also undermined or eliminated potential rivals. The military, overwhelmingly Kabiyé and led by recruits Eyadéma handpicked from his home village of Pya, kept the president in power, subjecting his political opponents to repeated imprisonment, torture, and even murder.

During the 1990s, internal and international pressures forced Eyadéma to allow a more open political process. However, he retained a firm grip on power. The country's military harassed leaders of opposition parties on the eve of elections in 1998 and again in 2003; Eyadéma won both elections. Eyadéma died on 5 February 2005 while "being evacuated for emergency treatment abroad" after suffering a heart attack. He fathered more than one hundred children with numerous women, and at the time of his death Eyadéma was the longest-serving head of state in Africa.

MARK O'MALLEY

F

Fang

Ethnic group of Cameroon, Gabon, and Equatorial Guinea.

The Fang, a BANTU-speaking people, occupy southern CAMEROON, much of mainland EQUATORIAL GUINEA, and northern GABON. They are a dominant group in the region, despite the fact that they are relatively recent migrants. The Fang are also referred to as the Fan or Pahouin. They can be divided into three linguistic groups: the Fang proper, the BULU, and the BETI. Each of these groups can be further divided into several ethnic subgroups. Some 800,000 to 900,000 people consider themselves Fang.

Although scholars originally believed that the Fang came from the upper NILE RIVER, most now agree that they split from other Bantu-speaking groups and migrated to northern Cameroon around the seventh or eighth century. From there they migrated farther southwest to the coastal regions in the nineteenth century. Though the evidence of the exact causes is contested, pressures from other groups, such as the HAUSA, and attempts to flee the trans-Saharan slave trade played a part, as did trade and the belief that the Europeans were rich spirits from the sea. Successful hunters and renowned warriors, the patrilineal Fang pushed such groups as the NDOWE further to the coast and settled in the interior forests as farmers. The large patriarchal clans of polygamous families in the south had little centralized political authority, whereas their counterparts in the north had clan chiefs and were more centralized.

The transatlantic and trans-Saharan slave trades from the sixteenth to the nineteenth century took thousands of Fang from the region as others, such as the Ndowe, acted as middlemen. To secure control over trade in the interior, the Ndowe spread the rumor that the Fang were cannibals, something European missionaries were convinced of when they found skulls in Fang households. In fact, the Fang did not practice cannibalism, but ate of parts of deceased persons in order to gain the deceased person's qualities. Spiritual beliefs, including ancestor worship, also influenced the methods and styles of Fang iron working and wood carving. These trades and crafts were largely destroyed by European influence.

Under Spanish and French COLONIAL RULE, some Fang participated in the IVORY TRADE, while others worked as laborers on cocoa plantations. Many Fang adopted CHRISTIANITY, although syncretistic and more traditional religious sects such as the BWITI became popular. In French-ruled Cameroon and Gabon, the Fang often cooperated with the administration, came to dominate the military and civil service, and consequently received economic and educational benefits. In SPANISH GUINEA, colonial officials favored the BUBI and perpetuated the myth of Fang primitivism. However, many Fang joined the military, which they later used as a power base to control independent Equatorial Guinea. Some Fang resisted outright European intrusion and in 1926 formed the Elarayong movement in Cameroon to create unity within the Fang nation. Most Fang elite were conservative nationalists, preferring a slow transfer of power. Fang politicians have dominated the governments of several countries since independence: Equatorial Guinea, Gabon, and, to a somewhat lesser degree, the more ethnically heterogeneous Cameroon.

See also BANTU MIGRATIONS IN SUB-SAHARAN AFRICA.

BIBLIOGRAPHY

Bureau, Rene. *Bokaye!: Essai sur le Bwiti Fang du Gabon.* L'Harmattan, 1996.
Koumabila-Abougave, Roger. *Les Problèmes de la succession chez les Fang du Gabon de 1843 à 1960.* Université Omar Bongo, 1989.

ERIC YOUNG

Fanon, Frantz

1925–1961

Political philosopher, essayist, psychologist, and revolutionary who developed and promoted theories for the decolonization of Africa.

Born in Fort-de-France on the island of MARTINIQUE into a conventional, bourgeois family, Frantz Fanon grew up with assimilationist values that encouraged him to reject his African heritage. This influence was countered by one of Fanon's high school teachers, Aimé CÉSAIRE, who introduced Fanon to the philosophy of Négritude and taught him to embrace the aspects of self that the colonizer had previously forced him to reject. The encounter with Césaire proved to be a turning point in Fanon's intellectual development. In 1940, following France's capitulation to the Germans in World War II, the part of the French Navy that had declared its allegiance to the collaborationist Vichy regime began the occupation of Martinique. As a result, 5,000 French soldiers commandeered the resources of the island, leaving the resident population to fend for itself. It was in this context that Fanon first experienced the full force of white racism. He experienced similar racial alienation after joining De Gaulle's Free French forces in 1943 and serving with them in ALGERIA. The experiences of the war left Fanon deeply cynical about France's commitment to humanist ideals when it came to its black population. On his return to Martinique, Fanon became involved in politics, helping Césaire win a seat in the French parliament. In 1947, after the death of his father, he went to France to pursue an advanced degree, enrolling in medical school at Lyon University in 1948. While obtaining his degree (he specialized in psychiatry), he continued to read the thinkers to whom Césaire had introduced him: Hegel, Marx, Lenin and, in particular, Sartre. He also formed a student journal, Tam-Tam, that attracted the attention of the editors of Présence Africaine. It was through his connection to this journal that he was able to meet Sartre, who remained Fanon's friend for life. It was also during this time that he began writing Peau noire, masques blancs (1952; Black Skin, White Masks, 1967), a work that took its inspiration from Césaire's protest poetry but brought a psychiatrist's eye to the question of the intellectual and cultural alienation of blacks in a world dominated by whites and white values. Peau noire, masques blancs describes the untenable position of the black bourgeoisie in Martinique who, disdainful of their own race, realize with regret that they cannot become white. Still, Fanon separates himself in this work from the philosophy of Négritude by rejecting the idea of an immutable black essence and by seeking a solution to the problems he describes in a nonracist humanism. In the same year as the publication of this book, Fanon married a white Frenchwoman, Josie Dublé. Fanon has been criticized for marrying a white woman by those who see that act as a betrayal of his own ideals. But as áEmmanuel Hansen points out, Fanon's "writings about the Manichaean world are descriptive and not proscriptive. It is precisely this idea of the black man being sealed in his blackness and the white man being encased in his whiteness that he wanted to avoid." In 1953 Fanon began the African chapter of his life. He assumed the post of chief of staff at the psychiatric hospital in Blida, Algeria, where he treated French soldiers who were suffering the effects of inflicting torture on the local population during the day and surreptitiously treating the Algerian victims of that torture at night. Fanon came to the conclusion that there was no cure for his patients in such a barbaric context. He resigned from the hospital and, after participating in a strike of doctors sympathetic to the National Liberation Front (F.L.N., the group waging war against the French colonizer), was expelled from Algeria. Fanon left for TUNISIA in 1957 to work full time for the F.L.N., writing for its official organ, El Moudjahid. During his time there, he published L'An V de la revolution algerienne (1959), a sociological study of the effects of revolutionary war on the Algerian population. Fanon also began to serve as a diplomat for the F.L.N. and was appointed representative of the Algerian Provisional Government in ACCRA, GHANA, in March 1960. But Fanon's seemingly boundless enthusiasm for the cause of Algerian and, more generally, African liberation was tempered in late 1960 when he learned that he was suffering from leukemia. He was sent to the Soviet Union for treatment, but once there he was encouraged to go to a center for the treatment of leukemia at the National Institute of Health in Bethesda, Maryland. Fanon could not bring himself to travel to the "nation of lynchers," as he put it, and returned to Accra, where he immersed himself in the work of completing Les Damnés de la terre (1961; The Wretched of the Earth, 1967). In this best known of his works, Fanon diagnoses the ills not of a race—as in Black Skin, White Masks—but of a continent under COLONIAL RULE. The cure for the African continent was violence: it was only through violence, he believed, that colonized peoples could free themselves from both the material and the psychological oppression of colonialism. The society that would come on the heels of revolutionary decolonization would be one that would allow Africans and other formerly colonized peoples to acquire what Fanon called an "authentic existence." Shortly prior to his publication of this work (with a preface by Sartre), Fanon had a relapse of his leukemia and was forced to seek treatment in the United Sates. According to the American journalist Joseph Alsop, the Central Intelligence Agency (C.I.A.) arranged for Fanon to be brought to Washington, D.C., where he was kept in a hotel room for eight days prior to being hospitalized. It is impossible to know what transpired during that time, but Fanon's wife has denied that he gave any information to the C.I.A. Fanon died in a Washington, D.C., hospital while reading the proofs of The Wretched of the Earth. A collection of essays by Fanon on the decolonization of Africa, Pour la révolution africaine (1964; Toward the African Revolution, 1969), was published posthumously.

See also DECOLONIZATION IN AFRICA: AN INTERPRETATION; FRONT DE LIBÉRATION NATIONALE.

BIBLIOGRAPHY

Bulhan, Hussein Abdilahi. *Frantz Fanon and the Psychology of Oppression*. Plenum Press, 1985.

Hansen, Emmanuel. *Frantz Fanon: Social and Political Thought*. Ohio State University Press, 1977.

RICHARD WATTS

Fante

Ethnic group of central Ghana.

More than two million people consider themselves Fante, making them one of the larger ethnic groups in GHANA. The Fante are part of the AKAN cultural and linguistic family (along with the ASANTE, Brong, and other groups), and as do other Akan peoples, they speak a language in the Kwa branch of the Niger-Congo language family.

There is some difference of opinion about the origins of the modern Fante. Oral tradition holds that the original Fante immigrated south to their current location from what is now the Brong-Ahafo region of central Ghana. The Fante settled in an area roughly bounded by the Pra and Volta river deltas, living along the coastline and as far as seventy kilometers (forty miles) inland. Although when the Fante arrived is not clear, they were well established there by the time the first Europeans contacted the coast in the late fifteenth century. The Fante probably established themselves through a combination of conquest and inter-marriage with the people already living on the coast, although they remained but one of many groups living in small, independent states. While most Fante made their living as fishers or farmers, some became powerful traders, acting as intermediaries in the GOLD TRADE between the Europeans and the neighboring Asante. The Fante political structure was mostly decentralized, although nominally united under a braffo, or paramount ruler, with a council of elders acting as decision makers and adjudicators of disputes.

Throughout the eighteenth century, the Fante expanded their territory. They conquered some neighboring peoples and made treaties with others in what some historians believe was an attempt to maintain their position as brokers of the transatlantic slave trade. But they could not overcome the powerful Asante, their neighbors to the east, who finally overthrew the Fante in the early nineteenth century.

The Fante regained their independence when the British, their allies in trade for centuries, proclaimed a treaty granting Fante autonomy in 1831. The alliance broke down a few decades later, as the Fante and other groups objected to increasing oppression by the British. They formed the Fante Confederation in 1868, which included the Fante, the Denkyera, and other coastal peoples. Never a stable entity, the Fante Confederation

was declared the GOLD COAST crown colony by the British in 1874.

The Fante are considered one of the more Westernized ethnic groups in West Africa, perhaps because of their long association with the British and other European groups. Most today are Christian. Farming is an important economic activity, especially the cultivation of yams, cassava, and plantains. Some Fante also work in the fishing and timber industries. Probably the best-known modern Fante is United Nations Secretary General Kofi ANNAN.

As with other Akan groups, Fante social structure places primary importance on matrilineal descent (that is, family ties to the mother's side) in terms of kinship and group identity. The various Akan groups commonly believe that all people belong to one of eight mmusua (abusua is the singular term) matrilineal kinship groups, each of which breaks down into several smaller units. Other aspects of an individual's identity, including membership in an asofo, or military association, are inherited through the father's side of the family. Beyond their military purpose, asofo groups also play religious and political roles in Fante society.

See also LANGUAGES, AFRICAN: AN OVERVIEW.

Farah, Nuruddin

1945–

Contemporary writer from Somalia.

Nuruddin Farah was born in Baidoa, SOMALIA. As the son of Aleeli Faduma, a woman considered a master of Somali oral poetry, Farah was born into an artistic tradition of language. Unlike his mother, however, he found his own expression in the foreign tongue of English, on the written page, and in a location far from his home country. With a nonlinear, complicated prose style influenced by Western modernist and contemporary Indian writing as well as by Somali oral tradition, Farah has developed a distinct voice in contemporary English-language African literature.

Farah's education brought him first to the capital city of MOGADISHU, then to England, and finally to Punjab University in Chandigarh, India, where he received his B.A. degree in 1970. By this time, he had already published the novella *Why Die So Soon?* (1965) and written his first novel, *From a Crooked Rib* (1970). Centering on the journey of a woman from her small village to Mogadishu, the novel depicted the different worlds that existed within the nation of Somalia. With his complex treatment of gender, particularly his perceptive representation of female characters, Farah initiated an exploration of female and male identities that would characterize his fictional work.

Meanwhile, events back in Somalia prompted a shift in Farah's focus. In 1969 Mohamed SIAD BARRE staged a coup d'état and established a military dictatorship. In

Farah's next novel, *A Naked Needle* (1976), he grappled with the subject of revolution. Ultimately, the work was unsuccessful in both his own eyes (he prevented the reprinting of the book) and the eyes of the censors, who halted its publication for several years. In 1972 Farah started a fictional series in the newly scripted Somali language, but censorship once again stood in his way.

By this time, it was clear that Farah presented a threat to Barre's regime. While traveling abroad, Farah learned that he would be in danger if he returned to Somalia. He began a life of exile, living at times in other parts of Africa, including NIGERIA, as well as in Europe and the United States. During this time, he taught at several universities and worked as a playwright.

In 1979 Farah returned to the project of portraying dictatorship in a trilogy that he would dub *Variations on the Theme of an African Dictatorship* (1979–1983). *Sweet and Sour Milk* (1979) was followed by *Sardines* (1981) and *Close Sesame* (1983). In this work, Farah grappled with the nature of tyranny. Drawing connections between interpersonal dynamics and the political culture of the state, Farah's trilogy was as much a critique of patriarchy as it was of state totalitarianism.

In perhaps his best-known work, *Maps* (1986), Farah returned to the issue of national identity as he traced a young man's path from his village to the city. A sophisticated work that experimented with shifting narrative voice, *Maps* sifted through layers of selfhood and identity. The second novel in a planned trilogy, *Gifts* (1992), considered the theme of dependency, juxtaposing a love relationship with the politicized context of African economic dependency. In 1998, he won the Neustadt International Prize for Literature for his novel *Secrets*, which explores life in Mogadishu in the period leading up to the civil war that began in 1991. Among Farah's more recent works are *Yesterday, Tomorrow: Voices from the Somali Diaspora* (2000), *Links* (2004), and *Knots* (2007).

See also SOMALI SONGS AND POETRY.

MARIAN AGUIAR

Faye, Safi
1943–
Senegalese film director.

Safi Faye is not only one of the few independent African women film directors, but also one of the few who make ethnographic films, which document cultures. Born near Dakar, Senegal, the daughter of a village chief and businessman of SERER origin, Faye moved to Dakar at the age of nineteen to become a teacher. There she became interested in the uses of film in education and ethnology, the study of ethnic groups and their cultures. Upon meeting

French filmmaker and ethnologist Jean Rouche, Faye embarked on a film career.

Faye acted in Rouche's *Petit à petit ou les lettres persanes* (1968). She learned about Rouche's style of cinéma-vérité, characterized by an unobtrusive camera and spontaneous nonprofessional acting, which influenced her own film work. With Rouche's encouragement she moved to Paris in 1972, enrolling in the École Pratique des Hautes Études to study ethnology and in the Louis Lumière Film School to study film. She completed film school in 1974 and began using film as a way to publish her ongoing research on the Serer. By the time she received her Ph.D., she had produced three films: *Kaddu beykat* (1975), *Fad'jal* (1979), and *Goob na na* (1979).

Faye held several academic positions in Europe while continuing to make ethnographic films. Although much of her work focuses on the Serer ethnic group, she has also produced documentaries for the United Nations and for German and French television stations, filmed in both Europe and Africa. In a 1970s interview she described her methods: "I go talk to the farmers in their village; we discuss their problems and I take notes. Even though I may write a script for my films, I basically leave the peasants free to express themselves in front of a camera and I listen. My films are collective works in which everybody takes an active part." Because the messages communicated by peasants through Faye's work are political, as she intends, government censorship in Africa has prevented most of them from being shown there. However, films such as *Mossane* (1996), which Safi based on a WOLOF legend about a girl whose refusal to accept an arranged marriage dooms her village, are frequently shown in foreign film festivals, such as the annual African Film Festival in New York, New York.

See also CINEMA, AFRICAN.

ELIZABETH HEATH

Fédération Panafricaine des Cinéastes
Organization of African filmmakers.

The Fédération Panafricaine des Cinéastes (FEPACI) is an association of African filmmakers, most of them from the Francophone, or French-speaking, nations of Africa, who are dedicated to developing African film and eliminating colonial influences on it. The FEPACI was born in 1969, when the most prominent and respected filmmakers in Francophone Africa met in ALGIERS, ALGERIA. Recognizing the need for a permanent organization to support and aid African film directors, they created the FEPACI. They outlined two goals: to liberate African cinema from its colonial past and to create a radical new cinema dedicated to the education and politicization of

African film audiences. Since 1970, the FEPACI has been the most influential film group in Africa. It is the organization most responsible for the independence and unity of African film.

ORIGINS OF THE FEPACI

The organization's strength and influence come from the film directors who are its members. The efforts of these directors laid the groundwork for the FEPACI and encouraged other African filmmakers to join the fight for an independent African cinema.

Beginning in the late 1950s, Francophone African directors began to envision an independent African film industry. At this time, however, African filmmakers were not yet permitted to film movies in Africa. Although France, unlike other colonial powers, allowed Africans to enroll in European film schools, in 1934 the colonial government had enacted the Laval Decree to control film production in the African colonies. The French government believed the law would prevent Africans from using movies to promote anticolonial or subversive movements.

Africans were, however, permitted to make films in Europe. The first African film, *Afrique sur scène*, was directed in 1955 by Paulin VIEYRA and colleagues under the name LE GROUPE AFRICAINE DU CINÉMA. Yet Vieyra was dissatisfied with the restrictions placed on African filmmakers. Working with fellow members of the Groupe and with French film professors, Vieyra labored to dismantle the Laval Decree, encouraging Francophone film directors to start planning a future for film in Africa. In 1958, Vieyra published his own views on African cinema in an article titled "Propos sur le cinéma Africain," in which he suggested the eventual creation of a Pan-African film organization.

Following decolonization, Francophone African filmmakers could finally make films in Africa. Soon after, in 1963, the first African film was released—Ousmane SEMBÈNE's *Barom Sarret*—and filmmakers began speaking out against the conditions and policies that hindered their work. Pioneer film directors such as Sembène, Med HONDO, and Timité Bassori denounced the policies of the Bureau du Cinéma, a French organization that provided funding and technical assistance to African film directors.

In 1965, Sembène rejected funding from the Bureau on the grounds that the money was "tainted by paternalism" and that in providing technical assistance to filmmakers the Bureau "used cheap African labor to create a new form of slavery." Hondo and Bassori criticized France for allowing privately owned French film distributors, the Compagnie Africain Cinématographique et Commerciale (COMACICO) and the Société d'Exploitation Cinématographique Africaine (SECMA), to monopolize film distribution in Africa. They

said France effectively used the monopolies to censor African films by preventing them from being distributed and shown. The directors organized a series of meetings: the Colloque de Gène (1965), the Premier Festival Mondial des Arts Nègres de Dakar (1966), and the Table-Ronde de Paris (1967). After these meetings, the directors decided a permanent Pan-African organization was needed to effectively tackle the larger obstacles they faced.

In 1969, at the Festival Panafricain de la Culture in Algiers, African filmmakers created the FEPACI, which was officially inaugurated at the Journées Cinématographiques de Carthage festival the following year. Its goals were to fight for the political, cultural, and economic liberation of African film; to dismantle the Franco-American monopoly on film distribution and exhibition in Africa; and to help African governments create and support national cinemas. The FEPACI was immediately recognized by the Organisation Commune Africaine et Mauritienne (OCAM), the Organization of African Unity (OAU), and UNESCO.

DECADE OF SUCCESSES

In its first five years, the FEPACI did a great deal to support individual filmmakers and build national film associations. By 1975, FEPACI membership included film associations in thirty-nine African nations. Using the money it raised from taxes levied on foreign films, the FEPACI provided financial support and technical expertise to several countries. It helped Upper Volta (now BURKINA FASO) and MALI to nationalize film distribution and exhibition, SENEGAL and BENIN to build national distribution houses, and MADAGASCAR to nationalize its movie theaters. These events forced France to intervene. Afraid that nationalization—placing enterprises under the control of the African governments—indicated a growing anti-French attitude, the French government encouraged French Union Général du Cinéma, a film distributor willing to distribute and show African films, to buy COMACICO and SECMA.

In 1975, the FEPACI organized the Second FEPACI Congress of Algiers to discuss the role of film in the political, economic, and cultural development of Africa. During the Congress, filmmakers realized that they shared a desire for something more than a commercially viable film industry. In the organization report, they established a new goal: to "free the continent from imperialism's economic and ideological domination by politically re-educating the masses . . . and to encourage an African film style, which in its process of decolonization, would also question the images of Africa, challenge the received narrative structure of the dominant cinema, and oppose the sensational and commercial aspect of dominant cinema."

In particular, the FEPACI urged film directors to (1) inspire historical and cultural solidarity within the black world; (2) present the human, social, and cultural realities of Africa; and (3) work for independence and cultural authority in African film. This conference was almost entirely responsible for the political orientation of much African film and for the creation of a uniquely African film form called THIRD CINEMA. The goals expressed at the conference have shaped almost all later sub-Saharan African cinema. They were the top priorities for FEPACI filmmakers between the years of 1975 and 1982.

FEPACI AFTER 1982

After the 1975 Congress, the FEPACI did not meet again until 1982, and many critics believe this gap weakened the organization's effectiveness. Before the decision to convene in 1982, some directors even considered dismantling the FEPACI and creating a new organization. But although some suggested that the organization had outlived its usefulness and that a new one should be created, veteran filmmakers such as Sembène argued for preserving and strengthening the FEPACI. As a result, the 1982 FEPACI Congress in NIAMEY, NIGER, tackled a number of long-unresolved issues. It adopted the "Niamey Manifesto," which affirmed the filmmakers' dedication to the creation of African production and distribution facilities. A group of young filmmakers calling themselves Le Collectif l'Oeil Vert promised to take immediate action to solve economic problems, proposing a cooperative strategy through which African nations would share scarce resources. Finally, the Manifesto proposed a new tax reform plan that would provide revenue to film associations and enable film organizations such as the Consortium Interafricain de Distribution Cinématographique (CIDC) to be self-supporting. But although the FEPACI did achieve some of the goals established in 1982, it had little power to make reforms that required the cooperation of governments, film directors, and film associations. The Manifesto has had only limited success in improving the practical problems faced by African filmmakers.

On the other hand, the FEPACI has done much to shape the political consciousness and educational standards of the African film industry. Since 1982, in fact, this has been the FEPACI's primary focus. The organization's influence is evident in the quality and content of films released in Africa since 1975, many of which are presented at the biannual Festival Panafricain du Cinéma et de la Télévision de Ouagadougou (FESPACO) in Burkina Faso.

See also CINEMA, AFRICAN.

ELIZABETH HEATH

Female Circumcision in Africa

The term female circumcision is commonly used to refer to surgical operations performed in over thirty African, Middle Eastern, and southeast Asian countries, by immigrants from those countries living elsewhere, and by physicians in Europe and the United States between roughly 1850 and 1950. As this geographic and historical range suggests, these operations take place in a wide range of cultural and historical contexts and can have very different meanings and effects. All involve the surgical modification of female genitals in some way, though this may range from relatively minor marking for symbolic purposes to the most radical operation, infibulation. Female circumcision varies widely even within Africa, where it is practiced across a band of the continent that includes parts of MAURITANIA, SENEGAL, GAMBIA, GUINEA-BISSAU, SIERRA LEONE, LIBERIA, MALI, BURKINA FASO, CÔTE D'IVOIRE, GHANA, TOGO, BENIN, NIGER, NIGERIA, CHAD, CAMEROON, CENTRAL AFRICAN REPUBLIC, DEMOCRATIC REPUBLIC OF THE CONGO (formerly ZAIRE), SUDAN, EGYPT, ERITREA, ETHIOPIA, DJIBOUTI, SOMALIA, KENYA, TANZANIA, and UGANDA. The percentage of women circumcised in each country varies considerably (e.g., from 5 to 10 percent in Uganda and 25 to 30 percent in Ghana to 80 percent in the Sudan), as does the kind of surgery practiced, its cultural and personal significance, and its history. Female circumcision is not practiced at all by some communities within this broad area, but it is commonplace in others. Christians, Muslims, and followers of traditional religions all might practice forms of female circumcision. Communities have adopted, abandoned, and modified the practices over time, reflecting ongoing political and religious changes as well as interaction among cultures on the African continent. Female circumcision generally refers to at least three distinct clinical procedures. Clitoridectomy removes all or part of the clitoris and the hood, or prepuce, which covers it. This is sometimes called sunna circumcision, though sunna circumcision might also refer to preputial cutting alone. The name sunna relates the practice to Islamic traditions, though most Muslim scholars and theologians deny Koranic justification for female circumcision. The second type, excision, includes clitoridectomy but also removes some or all of the labia minora; all or part of the labia majora might also be cut. The amount of tissue removed in these two kinds of circumcision varies within these general definitions. The most extreme form of circumcision, infibulation, goes beyond excision. After removing the labia, the sides of the vulva are joined so that scar tissue forms over the vaginal opening, leaving a small gap for urination and menstruation. Infibulation is also called pharaonic circumcision, a name originating in beliefs that the practice was part of ancient Egyptian life. Infibulated women often require surgical opening to allow first intercourse and birthing. In many cases women are reinfibulated after each childbirth. In addition to these three well-recognized types of female circumcision, a fourth is sometimes included. The least severe form (sometimes called mild sunna) involves a symbolic pricking or slight nicking of the clitoris or prepuce. Worldwide, excision and infibulation are the most widely practiced types of female circumcision. In Africa, infibulation is most common primarily in the Horn of Africa. A number of health problems have been attributed as consequences of these operations, but there has been little clear epidemiological research to determine how widespread they actually are in different areas. Immediate risks—all related to conditions under which the procedures are performed and care given after the operations—include infection, shock, excessive bleeding, and urinary retention. Public health education programs often aim first to improve these conditions or to provide training for midwives and traditional surgeons. Long-term health problems are most common with infibulation, but have sometimes been attributed to excision as well. Most of these problems result from heavy scarring and the covering over of vaginal and urinary openings after infibulation: keloid scars, vulvar cysts, retention of urine or menses, painful menstruation, difficulty urinating, and chronic pelvic infections. Heavily scarred women often require surgery before childbirth and may have prolonged and painful labor. Whether and how circumcision affects women's sexuality is much debated. It is important, however, to distinguish between sexual desire, sexual activity, and sexual pleasure. Sexual desire and sexual activity may not diminish with female genital operations. Evidence about sexual feeling and pleasure is variable, difficult to define or measure, and hard to find in the literature. Euro-American opponents of the practices assert that circumcised women feel no sexual pleasure, but a number of African women disagree with these assertions. Studies suggest that the effects vary widely depending on the type of operation performed, prior sexual experience, and other factors. Some African activists also suggest that the emphasis on sexual pleasure in anticircumcision campaigns derives from a recent and primarily Western concept of sexuality. In many places where female circumcision is practiced, the physical operation is but one moment in an elaborate ceremony. For instance, for the Okiek people in KENYA, initiation into adulthood includes circumcision for boys and excision for girls, but the full initiation process continues for several months and involves moral instruction, family and community engagement, and the negotiation of new social relationships.

While the operations are a central initiation trial and create a permanent physical mark of adulthood, initiation cannot be reduced to circumcision or excision alone. In many other societies, initiation does not involve circumcision at all. In every case the purposes and meanings of female circumcision are related to specific cultural understandings of identity, personhood, morality, adulthood, gender, bodily aesthetics, and other important issues. In the Sudan, for instance, female circumcision is seen as enhancing a woman's purity, cleanliness, and beauty. For the KIKUYU people of Kenya, circumcision was the foundation of moral self-mastery for women and men alike, performed as part of initiation into adulthood. The age of those circumcised varies widely according to these cultural understandings. In much of MALI and the SUDAN, for instance, girls are circumcised at six to eight years, while various communities in Kenya and SIERRA LEONE perform the operation in the early teens. For the YORUBA people of NIGERIA, male circumcision and female excision are not related to adulthood initiation, but rather to moral concepts of shame and fertility. They often circumcise their children at just a few days old, much like male circumcision in the United States and Europe. When female circumcision was performed on American and European women, it was done at a much later age than elsewhere in the world and for quite different reasons. In Africa, for example, the operation is usually considered part of a person's social and moral development and so is rarely performed after puberty. In Europe and the United States, however, doctors between roughly 1850 and 1950 regularly prescribed clitoridectomy for adult women as medical treatment for insomnia, sterility, and masturbation (which was defined as an ailment at that time). Many societies practice male but not female circumcision, but the reverse is rare. Where both are practiced, they can only be understood fully in relation to each other. A single word refers to both operations in many African languages, and this correspondence is often central to the way their practitioners understand them. The English translation, "female circumcision," maintains this parallel between male and female genital operations, though anticircumcision activists have criticized the term for being misleading. Both male and female genital operations have engendered long histories of debate and opposition, often centered around cross-cultural disagreements about the meaning and worth of the practices. The value of Jewish male circumcision, for instance, was debated in Rome during the first century C.E. and male circumcision has become a topic of heated opposition in the United States again today. Female circumcision practices have been the subject of international political controversies and abolition campaigns since at least the 1910s. Contemporary campaigns continue the tradition and rhetoric of colonial and missionary opposition and also build on decades of activism within Africa; some early anticircumcision efforts in the Sudan date from the 1860s. Health considerations have consistently been part of the debate, particularly in relation to infibulation. The issues have also been defined at various times in terms of colonialism, neocolonialism, feminism, sexuality, and human rights. In Kenya, for instance, debates about female circumcision began almost as soon as European missionaries arrived. Along with colonial administrators, they made judgments about which local customs violated Christian behavior and sought to discourage them. Campaigns to abolish female circumcision in central Kenya were among these efforts. When the Church of Scotland Mission and segments of the Church Missionary Society tried to prohibit the practice in the 1910s and 1920s, Kikuyu female circumcision became connected with the anticolonial movement and the defense of cultural tradition. Jomo KENYATTA, the future first president of Kenya, was a prominent opponent of colonial attempts to alter Kikuyu custom. Opposition to the colonial campaign to abolish female circumcision provided an impetus for starting independent schools and churches in central Kenya. The Kikuyu circumcision controversy was shaped by church interests and politics in England as well as by events in Kenya itself. It was also related to changing notions of the body and changes in Kikuyu social relations, such as marriage patterns, relations of authority between men and women and between women of different generations, and the waning of ngweko (sexual play between young people). Since 1979 the Kenyan government has conducted several anticircumcision campaigns that were tinged with Christian and colonial overtones. A ban in 1982 had little effect. In 1996 a national organization proposed an alternative initiation ceremony as a substitute. Other countries have their own histories of circumcision debates and policies. International efforts to have female circumcision addressed by the World Health Organization (WHO) in the late 1950s were not effective. In the 1970s, a number of publicity campaigns and publications converged to galvanize international attention. These included articles in African publications, a press conference held in Switzerland before the WHO Assembly in 1977, and publications by Fran Hosken and Mary Daly in the United States. The Inter-African Committee on Traditional Practices affecting the Health of Women and Children was formed in Geneva in 1977. A 1979 WHO seminar in KHARTOUM, SUDAN, helped to make female genital operations a regular topic at international conferences. Anticircumcision activity during this time was also buoyed by the declaration of the United Nations Decade of Women (1975–1985). Since the early 1990s, international debates

about female circumcision have again become increasingly heated and highly politicized. Greater media coverage in the 1990s and publicity over legal cases concerning African immigrants in France and the United States brought the debates to a much wider audience. In the United States, involvement by such well-known figures as novelist Alice Walker also helped to publicize and polarize the debate. A number of African scholars and activists based in the United States (such as Seble Dawit, Salem Mekuria, and Micere Mugo) have been highly critical of the way Walker and others have represented female circumcision in Africa. They argue that Walker and others are engaged in neocolonial depictions that demonize African practitioners, distort the social meanings and contexts involved, portray African women only as victims, ignore decades of activism in Africa, and isolate female circumcision from other issues of women's health, economic status, and education. The growing intensity of these debates became encapsulated in changes in the very terms used between the 1970s and 1990s. In the 1970s, anticircumcision activists increasingly criticized the term *female circumcision*, claiming that it condoned a brutal custom by creating false similarities between male and female circumcision. A more partisan alternative was coined and eventually popularized: female genital mutilation. The new term *mutilation* did not attempt impartial description, but instead judged and condemned the practices through a label that defined them all as intentional mistreatment and disfigurement. Promotion of the new term was part of an escalating anticircumcision campaign that used sensationalism and gory images. As this term became more common, it was shortened to an acronym, FGM. Others reject this term as misrepresenting the intentions of African families, criminalizing parents and relatives, and judging them through Euro-American cultural values. A number of alternative terms came into use in the mid-1990s, seeking more neutral ground: genital surgery, genital operations, genital modification, and body modification. This last term acknowledges broad similarities among such practices as male and female genital surgery, genital/body piercing, and other cosmetic surgery. Attempting to find an appropriate phrase, New York Times reporter Celia Duggers used the term genital cutting in her late-1996 articles, a term she adopted from demographic and health surveys, but one that did not catch on in popular usage. Female circumcision and FGM remain the most common terminology in English. Both female circumcision practices and the arenas of debate have shifted over the years as other circumstances have changed and different constituencies have become involved. Public health education about the potential risks of the operations has increased in most countries where they are practiced. Similarly, an increasing number of female circumcisions are performed in health clinics and hospitals or by specialists who have received some hygienic training. As noted above, alternative rituals have also been proposed in some countries, though it is not clear whether they will be widely adopted. Intense debates continue among African activists about whether a medicalized, minor form of female genital modification should be promoted as an interim substitute for more severe operations. Because African immigrant communities often practice female circumcision, they have brought all these debates to the fore in Europe and the United States, where immigrant populations have grown in recent decades. Sweden, Switzerland, the United Kingdom, and several other European countries passed laws restricting the operations in the 1980s and early 1990s. The United States followed suit in 1997. Contemporary controversies about female circumcision cross a number of social and legal arenas, from family and household relations to international tribunals. The debates involve three interacting arenas:

(1) Home countries, where circumcising practices have traditional standing in some communities; (2) the United States and Europe, which also have a little-remembered history of female genital operations but where female circumcision is now associated particularly with immigrant communities; and (3) international campaigns conducted by international bodies and action groups that seek to intervene in the first two arenas and redefine issues central to particular communities and nations. The social, cultural, and historical contexts of debates vary in each of these arenas and involve many different actors, issues, positions, and perspectives.

The debates cannot be characterized in simple terms; they are not, for example, merely contests of women versus men or Africans versus outsiders. Rather, they now involve national governments and politicians; nongovernmental organizations; churches and religious officials; national and international action groups; the World Health Organization and other international agencies; and journalists—not to mention diverse religious and ethnic communities with different circumcision practices and different histories of involvement in these debates. National, state, and municipal judiciaries and agencies that deal with immigrant communities (e.g., the Immigration and Naturalization Service and Health and Human Services in the United States) also participate in some debates. Within each circumcising community, differences of gender, age, education, religion, and wealth also influence attitudes and positions. For example, in some African settings a Christian mother, her non-Christian husband, his educated brother, and their school-age daughter might disagree about whether the girl should participate with her friends in initiation ceremonies during a school holiday. American media coverage of the legal case of Fauziya Kasinga illustrated just such a range of positions within her own family and community in Togo; Kasinga was granted political asylum in the United States in 1996, citing fear of forced circumcision. Conflicting values and interests are at the crux of the controversy. In the 1980s and 1990s, legal cases dealing with African immigrants in Europe and the United States raised these issues in particularly clear and urgent ways. There is no single, simple answer to the questions and dilemmas raised by genital operations because they are variable practices with different meanings and histories. Decisions about whether and how to maintain, alter, or abolish the operations and associated practices cannot be imposed or legislated overnight, as the long history of the controversy shows, but can only be effective when the many different people directly involved take part. Local support and involvement are essential for any changes in these practices to take place.

See also COLONIAL RULE; FEMINISM IN AFRICA: AN INTERPRETATION; HUMAN RIGHTS IN AFRICA; MARRIAGE, AFRICAN CUSTOMS OF.

BIBLIOGRAPHY

Boddy, Janice. "Womb as Oasis: The Symbolic Context of Pharonic Circumcision in Rural Northern Sudan". *American Ethnologist*, 1982, 9:682–98.

Boyle, Elizabeth H. *Female Genital Cutting: Cultural Conflict in the Global Community*. Johns Hopkins University Press, 2002.

Gruenbaum, Ellen. *The Female Circumcision Controversy: An Anthropological Perspective*. University of Pennsylvania Press, 2001.

Kratz, Corinne A. "Contexts, Controversies, Dilemmas: Teaching Circumcision". In *Great Ideas for Teaching about Africa*. Misty Bastian and Jane Parpart (eds.). Boulder: Lynne Rienner, 1999, 103–118.

Kratz, Corinne A.. "Circumcision Debates and Asylum Cases: Intersecting Arenas, Contested Values, and Tangled Webs". In *Engaging Cultural Differences: The Multicultural Challenge in Liberal Democracies*. Richard A. Shweder, Hazel R. Markus, and Martha Minow (eds.). Russell Sage Foundation, 2002.

Obermeyer, Carla Makhlouf. "Female Genital Surgeries: The Known, the Unknown, and the Unknowable". *Medical Anthropology Quarterly*, 1999, 13:79–106.

Obermeyer, Carla Makhlouf. "The Health Consequences of Female Circumcision: Science, Advocacy, and Standards of Evidence". *Medical Anthropology Quarterly*, 2003, 17:394–412.

Obiora, L. Amede. "Bridges and Barricades: Rethinking Polemics and Intransigence in the Campaign against Female Circumcision". *Case Western Reserve Law Review*, 47 (2):275–378. [This entire special issue is devoted to debates about female circumcision.]

Parker, Melissa. "Rethinking Female Circumcision", *Africa*, 1995, 65:506–24.

Pederson, Susan. "National Bodies, Unspeakable Acts: The Sexual Politics of Colonial Policy-Making". *Journal of Modern History*, 1991, 63:647–680.

Shell-Duncan, Bettina, and Ylva Hernlund (eds.). *Female "Circumcision" in Africa: Culture, Controversy, and Change*. Boulder: Lynne Reinner, 2000.

Thomas, Lynn. "'Ngaitana (I will circumcise myself)': The Gender and Generational Politics of the 1956 Ban on Clitoridectomy in Meru, Kenya". *Gender and History*, 1996, 8: 338–63.

CORINNE KRATZ

Female Writers in English-Speaking Africa
African women who have published works in English.

In many parts of Africa, women have long held primary roles as storytellers, teachers, poets, and oral historians. Yet only since the 1980s has African women's writing garnered significant national and international attention. Schools opened by missionaries during the early colonial period were based on a Western model, prioritizing boys' education over that of girls. These schools in turn became the model for the colonial system of education throughout Africa. Fewer girls than boys have learned to read and write, and the number of women who have been able to study literature at the university level is even lower. Even among educated women, relatively few have had opportunities to pursue careers in writing.

Still, several women were publishing early on in both English and local languages. Early role models, such as Ghanaian playwright Efua Theodora Sutherland, were already publishing in the 1930s. GHANA's Ama Ata AIDOO and SOUTH AFRICA's Bessie HEAD authored numerous short stories and plays during the 1960s, the "boom" period that propelled male writers like Chinua ACHEBE and NGUGI WA THIONG'O to the fore. In 1966 Nigerian author Flora NWAPA wrote *Efuru*, believed to be the first novel published by an African woman in English. In East Africa, by 1960, writers Grace OGOT and Rebeka Njau were already among the first graduates of Makerere College in UGANDA, a center for early East African writing in English. In 1967 Bessie Head followed with *When Rain Clouds Gather*, a novel set in her adopted home of BOTSWANA. If one includes white South African women's writing, the history stretches back much farther to Olive SCHREINER's early feminist writing in the late nineteenth century.

Despite the contributions of these early writers, African women's writing still received little attention. Bessie Head was the only woman published in the important literary journal *Drum* when it flourished in the 1960s. In fact, as Ama Ata Aidoo put it in one lecture, this obscurity "had nothing to do with anything that African women did or failed to do. It had to do with the politics of sex and the politics of the wealthy of this earth who grabbed it and who held it." In the words of Kenyan novelist Asenath Odaga, "The male has always been dominant in Africa; this is their world, the society is theirs." Whether one agrees or disagrees with this statement, it is fairly clear that men's writing has defined the dominant vision of what issues are central to African life.

When African women writers finally began to gain a wide audience, one of their main tasks was to revise literary portrayals of African womanhood. Influential poets of the Négritude Movement in the 1930s, such as Léopold SENGHOR, often portrayed the African woman symbolically, as the essence of the earth and of the physical, and above all as the great mother. Male writers of the next generation, such as Ngugi wa Thiong'o, used the female and mother character in their work to symbolize the nation, or "motherland."

African women writers have presented a very different picture of their societies than men have. Like their male counterparts, African women authors have written about their societies' traditions and the upheaval caused by colonialism and urbanization. But they have also shown the problems that traditions posed for women. For example, in the novel *Efuru*, Flora Nwapa portrayed a small IGBO village much like the one represented by her contemporary Achebe in *Things Fall Apart*. Yet, as critic Jane Bryce points out, while Achebe centered his plot on the conflicts caused by British colonization, Nwapa focused on conflicts within the community itself, particularly on the difficulties faced by a childless woman. Several of Nwapa's novels explore similar themes. Kenyan writer Grace Ogot's novel *The Promised Land* (1966) examines how LUO society places moral pressures on women to make personal sacrifices in order to preserve their families. The novels of Nigerian author Buchi EMECHETA portray the oppression of women through traditional practices, such as the demand for a bride price and the practice of keeping women as domestic slaves. Her best-known work, *The Joys of Motherhood* (1979), shows women trapped in a society that values them primarily as bearers of children and then forces them to deny their own needs once they become mothers. Funmilayo Fakunle examines the oppressiveness of polygamous marriages in novels such as *Chasing the Shadow* (1980).

While African women writers have shared an awareness of patriarchal oppression, their voices and political views have varied widely. For example, as critic Phyllis Pollard has pointed out, Rebeka Njau took a clear stand against the practice of female circumcision in her 1965 novel *The Scar*. Kenyan writers Muthoni Likimani and Charity Waciuma, on the other hand, have portrayed the practice in a negative but more morally ambiguous light. In *They Shall Be Chastised* (1974), Likimani portrays a woman caught between the

LITERARY WOMEN OF AFRICA. South African Nobel Prize-winning author Nadine Gordimer, during a news conference in Mexico, 2006. (*Guillermo Arias/AP Images*)

strictures of traditional practices on the one hand and equally oppressive Christian practices on the other. In *Daughter of Mumbi* (1969), Waciuma places the discussion against the backdrop of the clash of cultures during a period of uprising (MAU MAU REBELLION) declared a state of emergency by the colonial government.

African women writers whose works criticize traditional practices have often been accused of buying into Western value systems. Responding to this charge, Ama Ata Aidoo argued in a lecture that African women have, in fact, long been outspoken: "So, when we say that we are refusing to be overlooked, we are only acting today as daughters and grand-daughters of women who always refused to keep quiet. We haven't learned this from anybody abroad." At the same time, at least some African women writers have acknowledged the need to defend the values of their own societies against Western cultural imperialism. This is one

reason that many prominent African women writers have avoided the feminist label, including Ama Ata Aidoo, Bessie Head, and Buchi Emecheta. In an interview, Emecheta has said: "I do believe in the African kind of feminism. They call it Womanism, because, you see, you Europeans don't worry about water, you don't worry about schooling, you are so well off. Now, I buy land, and I say, 'OK, I can't build on it, I have no money, so I give it to some women to start planting.' That is my brand of feminism." For these women, an African form of feminism is one that takes into account the cultural and material realities of women's lives in Africa.

African women writers have also taken on contemporary political and social issues. The work of poet and playwright Elvania Namukwaya Zirimu, for example, portrayed Uganda, revealing the political and social crises in the 1960s that ultimately led to the ascension of Idi AMIN. One of the main themes of writing has been the changing face of countries like Ghana and NIGERIA following independence. In novels such as *Changes* (1991), Aidoo portrays the difficulties of women in an increasingly Westernized and urbanized Ghana, as they face the responsibilities of maintaining traditional ways as well as the new possibilities of employment and marriage.

In South Africa, both black and white women writers have portrayed life under APARTHEID. Black women began publishing their writing relatively late in South Africa, and even then they faced many obstacles. Miriam TLALI's novel *Muriel at Metropolitan*, the first novel published in South Africa by a black woman writer, was written in 1969 but not published for another five years. Even then, this book about a young black working woman's life was first censored and then banned. In *Amandla* (1980), Tlali went on to portray the politicization of women and children during the 1976 civil unrest in South African townships that culminated in the SOWETO massacre and uprising. Others have contributed to the corpus of South African literature from exile, such as Lauretta Ngcobo, author of *Cross of Gold* (1981), whose work about the tumultuous events in SHARPEVILLE in 1960 was also banned shortly after publication.

As a white South African who has enjoyed greater freedom than many of her country's writers, Nobel Prize-winner Nadine GORDIMER has reached a large international audience with her novels and essays. Chronicling political events from the 1940s to the present, her works paint a vivid picture of "a society whirling, stamping, swaying with the force of revolutionary change." More recently, with such novels as *The House Gun* (1998), Gordimer has continued to illuminate the challenges South Africa faces in the continued violence of the postapartheid context.

South Africa's newest generation of women writers are setting their stories against the backdrop of a rapidly changing society. The impact of education forms an important theme in several works. Tsitsi Dangarengba's *Nervous Conditions* (1989) portrays a young woman who leaves her rural home to live with her uncle in the city and finds herself both alienated from her new world and ultimately unable to return home. South African writers of Indian origin, such as Farida Karodia (*Daughters of the Twilight*, 1986), Jayapraga Reddy (*On the Fringe of Dreamtime*, 1987), Beverley Naidoo (*Chain of Fire*, 1989), and Agnes Sam (*Jesus Is Indian*, 1989), have portrayed life in the Indian community in South Africa.

For the most part, African Anglophone women authors have written in a realist tradition, and their novels are often highly autobiographical and politically engaged in issues of gender and race. Yet more and more African women writers are turning to experimental styles and subjects. Bessie Head's work exploring the nature of madness has provided an early model for nonlinear narratives. South African Zoe Wicomb's *You Can't Get Lost in Cape Town* (1987) has been cited as a multifaceted work that breaks from the single ideological stance that characterized earlier literature committed to mobilization and social change. Women's recent poetic and dramatic contributions have demonstrated the continuing integration and transformation of old and new traditions.

See also COLONIAL RULE; FEMALE CIRCUMCISION IN AFRICA; FEMINISM IN AFRICA: AN INTERPRETATION; FICTION, ENGLISH-LANGUAGE, IN AFRICA; INDIAN COMMUNITIES IN AFRICA; SLAVERY IN AFRICA.

MARIAN AGUIAR

Feminism in Africa: An Interpretation
Female activism and feminist movements in Africa.

In contrast to much of the twentieth century, today we can talk about African feminism because African women themselves do so and because they have quite clear ideas about what they mean when they use the term. Albertina Sisulu, the respected senior woman in the AFRICAN NATIONAL CONGRESS (ANC) of SOUTH AFRICA, and the wife of Walter SISULU, symbolized this new wave of female activism when she joined the women's walkout at the ANC Party Conference in Durban in 1992. The walkout demanded that the ANC commit itself to 33 percent female representation in Parliament and other government positions in the new South Africa to come. This form of feminism in South Africa is but one of many feminisms in Africa. Feminism varies both among the various nations and among different cultural subgroups on the continent. Nevertheless, African women's recognition of something they call "feminism" marks a new political sophistication

borne of their deep engagement with the difficulties and challenges now facing their societies. The emergence of African feminism signals women's desire to play a role in determining the direction of development.

Thus, African feminism is Janus-faced: it looks forward to women's new goals, as well as backward to statuses and roles that women leaders have played in the past. African women are voicing their opinions about the failed elections, military coups, political upheavals, refugee movements, economic recessions, structural adjustment, and other crises that severely affected their lives since the 1980s. They are affirming their own identities while transforming societal notions of gender and familial roles.

African feminism is highly political, and it is a response to African social and political developments rather than an outgrowth of Western feminism. African women know that women and children have borne the brunt of the recent crises, as measured in high child mortality rates, lowered female literacy rates, the continuing confinement of women to agricultural work, and their exclusion from modern, technical, and scientific fields. Many African women (and some African men as well) are committed to correcting these disparities and forging new relationships between state and society, even though Western powers and global institutions still exercise tremendous influence over the economic and political conditions of African states.

Since the United Nations Fourth World Conference on Women, in Beijing, China (September 1995), Western governments and development agencies have urged respect for women's human rights and initiatives for "women's empowerment" in African state policies, although with decidedly mixed results. This Western pressure has provided some support for women's activism. On the other hand, many African politicians viewed Western efforts with suspicion and have questioned the autonomy and legitimacy of women's actions. This controversy has not deterred African women activists. They know this may be their best opportunity to create a place for themselves in national life. Therefore, they are determined that "we will not miss the boat this time around."

DISTINCTIVE FEATURES OF AFRICAN FEMINISM
African feminism differs from Western feminism because it has developed in a different cultural context. Today, African women are seeking to redefine their roles in ways that allow them a new, culturally attuned activism. This is not a totally novel challenge, since there is evidence of gender hierarchy, female subordination, and women's struggles to reshape their statuses and roles within traditional African cultures in earlier historical periods. Gender

ALBERTINA SISULU, 2005. (*Siphiwe Sibeko/AP Images*)

asymmetry and inequality, particularly the distinction between public (political) and private (household) spheres, certainly existed in indigenous African social life. Gender inequality solidified during and following the phases of Islamic expansion and as European conquerors attempted to subdue or ignore female leaders. However, in Africa, female subordination takes intricate forms grounded in traditional African cultures, particularly because it is partially shaped by the "corporate" and "dual-sex" patterns that Africans have maintained through their history. Since culture is not static, new forms of asymmetry and inequality have arisen. Politicians and laypersons alike sometimes present this inequality as customary, but this is a distortion of African history. Women's contemporary activism and their attempts to fashion an African feminist approach to public and private life have emerged in response to these inequities.

The forms of African feminism emerging in various parts of the continent do not grow out of individualism within the context of industrial societies, as did Western feminism. In the West, economic and social trends historically pushed women into more active roles in the economy, and Western feminism has focused on women's struggle for control over reproduction and sexuality. However, African women have had a different experience. African

feminist debates do not focus on theoretical questions, the female body, or sexual identity. Rather, like many of its Third World counterparts, African feminism is distinctly heterosexual, supportive of motherhood, and focused on issues of "bread, butter, culture, and power." The average fertility rate in Africa has stayed around six children per woman, and this reality shapes African women's lives. The practical orientation of African feminism grows out of a cultural heritage of female integration within corporate, agrarian, and family-based societies and a more recent history of political domination and economic exploitation by the West.

In contrast to Western feminism, which emphasizes individual female autonomy, African feminism emphasizes authentic public participation and decision making by women. The issue of African clitoridectomy is one that African women say they themselves should be and are working to resolve—not Western women. African women are now exploring ways to incorporate their own views of women's development into African development policies and the activities of nongovernmental organizations. Since the 1990s women leaders both inside and outside of government have criticized the effects of national policies on women. Political leaders and the military victimized some women for their criticism of social policies: women's demonstrations were disrupted, they were jailed, their markets were burned, and they were forced out of public positions. Nevertheless, African women's experiences of the hardship of economic restructuring and the growing democratization of their societies have pushed them toward greater boldness in voicing their grievances and focusing attention on women's status within their societies.

CULTURAL ROOTS OF AFRICAN FEMINISM
Africans, perhaps more than the peoples of other regions, tend to fuse nature and culture in their traditional conceptions of women's roles. Ali MAZRUI has said that African women have controlled earth, fire, and water—three of the four elements in traditional culture. They have thus held responsibility for preparing food, acquiring fuel for cooking, and tilling the soil, in addition to other productive and reproductive tasks. Although Western observers stereotypically equate women's roles with "nature" and the domestic sphere of family, reproduction, household, and marriage (the private realm), and associate men's roles with "culture" and human complexity in political and economic roles (the public realm), this dichotomy does not hold true in Africa. Most African women combine roles as mothers and as economic contributors. The African feminists of today are—equally—mothers of several children, community participants, and public persons. African

women have always sought to take on politically and economically responsible roles.

Thus, African feminism builds upon a solid tradition of female inclusion in a wide variety of social roles in African cultures. The prevalent Western myth of an African "matriarchy" has no validity here, since women typically do not seek to dominate. Although African women are frequently assertive and strong, the norms of their own societies have usually shaped their roles. These norms situate gender relations within the context of social groupings, such as extended families and secret societies, or encourage what is called dual-sex organization, in which women form their own associations separate from male associations to accomplish their tasks. In some areas, such as West Africa, women's ability to form dual-sex groups in their own interest is highly developed, creating a facade of egalitarianism, while the tradition of separate women's groups is weaker in East and southern Africa. Dual-sex organization was also more firmly rooted in matrilineal areas of West and Central Africa, where descent was traced through women, than in patrilineal areas of East, West, and southern Africa, where men form the core of the family.

Although men generally dominated traditional African societies, women led wars of resistance against foreign powers. The BERBER prophetess Kachina held back the Arab invasion in the eighth century; and the female prophetess Nehanda of ZIMBABWE led her people in resistance to the imperialism of Cecil Rhodes during the late nineteenth century. Queen Mother Yaa ASANTEWA fought against British colonial conquest in the ASANTE kingdom (present-day GHANA). Women who were organized as sisters, wives, market women, and artisans could alter decisions they considered harmful to other women. The early twentieth-century example of the Aba Riots, or Women's War, among the IGBO of NIGERIA demonstrated women's ability to use their associations to protest colonial or community decisions that clashed with women's interests. However, as centralization and statehood emerged, rulers attempted to limit women and control the political process. This type of state bias against women increased during the nineteenth and early twentieth centuries, when colonial regimes attempted to conquer and reshape African societies.

Women have enjoyed representation in social groupings, for example through dual-sex organization, throughout most of African cultural history. This has been advantageous for African women, since they have been able to assume positions allotted to their kin groups within the community. Women could rise to positions of political, religious, or economic prominence if they belonged to prestigious families. Perhaps more consistently than in

any other region of the world, there have been high-status female leaders all across Africa, from ancient Egypt to South Africa, including queens, queen mothers, chiefs, and priestesses. In matrilineal societies, the queen mothers, women chiefs, and priestesses were not feminists, but simply leaders and decision makers. Nevertheless, their leadership did inspire some female activism. Likewise, the dual-sex model is widely scattered across the continent, and often power is balanced between male and female leaders. The dual-sex model assumes its ultimate form in the dual-monarchy of king and queen mother, which exists in many AKAN societies, as well as in SWAZILAND. Women helped to shape the political traditions, charters, and constitutions of traditional African societies that were enshrined in proverbs, oral traditions, and myths of state.

Islamization, colonial conquest, Christianization, economic crisis, and other changes over time have resulted in renegotiation of the traditional social contract. Often this has given rise to gender-biased relations and an attempt to exclude women from political life. Queen Njinga of ANGOLA opposed Portuguese conquest by mobilizing those who supported her right to rule against those who opposed the notion of female leadership. However, in nearly every part of the continent, even in Islamic areas, the preexisting base of female involvement and activism escaped complete destruction, and often unique forms of female resistance emerged. In many countries, African women found ways of linking new practices with older principles of women's participation and activism.

CONTEMPORARY AFRICAN FEMINISM

The crises in African economic and political life have caused serious hardship for women since the 1980s, but this has also generated a new burst of African feminism. Previously, African states were hesitant to discuss women's issues and grievances publicly. However, they were not hesitant to accuse women of subversion or a lack of patriotism when their organizations demonstrated against state policies or when they lobbied international organizations to improve conditions for women. Often, African leaders targeted women when they acted collectively to protest wage cuts or artificially high food prices. Sometimes, governments victimized female merchants and entrepreneurs by charging that these women were hoarding commodities or illegally producing products, and states defamed female aristocrats who offered political opposition.

It is not surprising that the economic arena has generated many defiant responses from African women and feminist organizations. Women are responsible for much of the farm work in Africa, but COLONIAL RULE and the market economy have often isolated women from sources of finance and sometimes damaged their traditional rights to own land. A result has been the concentration of resources in male hands. Women have noted that increasingly, under the pressures of the market economy, their families and lineages have fragmented. Men have divorced or delayed marriages, and men have migrated across borders seeking work in response to resource scarcity at home. During the 1980s and 1990s the International Monetary Fund and World Bank pressured African countries to implement structural adjustment programs that required cuts in health care, social services, and education. These programs harmed women and children disproportionately. But now, African women are refusing to suffer "down on the farm." Much of women's feminist activism in the 2000s is designed to focus state and public attention on the welfare of women and children and to create new economic policies that are beneficial to the entire populace.

Likewise, although African women played important roles in nationalist politics or liberation struggles that brought their countries to independence, very few were chosen as government ministers or diplomats, and most were excluded from leadership positions in political parties. Nevertheless, women in such countries as CÔTE D'IVOIRE and KENYA used their astute knowledge to build women's political organizations that could apply pressure on political parties and begin to hold state politicians accountable to the community. The experiences of women in Côte d'Ivoire, Ghana, Nigeria, Kenya, and South Africa provide us with examples of effective feminist action in the current period of democratization and the struggle against military rule. Only in 2006 did Africa finally realize its first elected female leader, when Ellen Johnson-Sirleaf was voted into office as Liberia's president.

African women today have taken a leadership role in setting new economic and political agendas. One of the legacies of the United Nations Fourth World Conference on Women is that African women are determined to shape the policies of their countries. They have pushed for additional support for girls' education, including training for careers in industrial fields, the sciences, agriculture, or the professions, and for greater gender sensitivity in government and private-sector hiring policies.

Increasingly, African women have led national dialogues about women's human rights. In West and East Africa, and also in Zimbabwe, NAMIBIA, and South Africa, women are stepping up their campaign against sexism and exploitation. African feminists have opposed such practices as early marriage, female genital mutilation, women's exposure to acquired immunodeficiency syndrome (AIDS) through unsafe sex practices, and various forms of medical neglect. In northern Nigeria and Côte d'Ivoire, as well as in South Africa and Kenya, Muslim women have argued that they can be good Muslim wives and mothers even as they pursue professional training, a role in community and regional dialogues, or public office.

African feminists today have fostered a greater awareness of the connections between gender and the political economy of the state by openly discussing the links between the public and private experiences of African women. They have challenged the reluctance to talk about gender conflicts, and they have prompted women to collectively address political actions that affect their lives. African feminists have generated a new model of what feminism is about and new feminist views of civil society, the family, and the state. They have stepped forward to defend their views in international gatherings of policy makers and feminists in the conviction that their approaches will yield more positive results for African local, regional, and national development than will feminist approaches that are imported from Western societies.

See also ACQUIRED IMMUNODEFICIENCY SYNDROME IN AFRICA: AN INTERPRETATION; EGYPT, ANCIENT KINGDOM OF; FEMALE CIRCUMCISION IN AFRICA; FEMALE WRITERS IN ENGLISH-SPEAKING AFRICA; FEMINISM IN ISLAMIC AFRICA; STRUCTURAL ADJUSTMENT IN AFRICA.

GWENDOLYN MIKELL

Feminism in Islamic Africa

Approximately one-third of Africa's population is Islamic, and several African countries identify themselves as Islamic states. Many of the goals of the feminist movement in Islamic Africa are common to feminist movements throughout the world—access to education and the labor market and power in the world of public decision making. But in Islamic Africa, the movement has also responded to the particular problems women face in their own countries, problems shaped by cultural identity and class.

HISTORICAL CONTEXT

The feminist movement in Islamic Africa draws on a rich tradition of women's political participation. In nineteenth-century EGYPT, middle- and upper-class women formed organizations that promoted modernizing projects, such as health-care reform and education for girls. Other women participated in male-dominated political movements, especially the anticolonial resistance of the mid-twentieth century. The contribution of these women to nationalist struggles brought dangers unique to their sex: in ALGERIA, fighters such as Djamila Boupasha, raped by French military police while in custody, suffered sexual brutality during the quest for an independent nation.

Some of the women now considered forerunners of contemporary feminism might not have called themselves feminists. Women's groups and publications frequently took a decidedly conservative stance on such issues as family and child-rearing (as they often still do), but they also provided a forum for women to collectively understand their lives within an Islamic world. According to feminist historian Mervat Hatem, even the bulk of Algerian women's contributions to the liberation struggle, such as nursing, cooking, and hiding weapons, could be seen as an extension and reinvention of women's traditional duties.

After independence, women's organizations in numerous countries, including Egypt, Algeria, and TUNISIA, were often linked to postcolonial governments. Government-funded women's programs provided contraception, literacy training, or classes on domestic budget management, thus serving political and economic agendas as well as feminist ones. Other women's programs, from the 1970s to 1990s, were sponsored by international organizations such as the United Nations or operated as small autonomous collectives. In the last forty years, women throughout much of Islamic Africa have gained the right to work and to vote. In Algeria, women have been elected to the National Assembly; in Egypt, they have entered the civil service as well as several professional fields in significant numbers.

In recent years, Islamic feminists have begun to consider which women have gained from these reforms. Increasingly, they have acknowledged the extent to which class and culture mediate the role of Islam in African women's lives. For example, poor women have always worked outside of the home throughout Islamic Africa, especially in rural areas. In addition, Islamic norms that govern gender relations or women's roles in one location may be entirely foreign to women in another. The religious and social standards applied to urban North Africa women may be unknown to Muslim nomad women in East and West Africa—or to women in the Islamic communities of coastal West Africa, where Muslim women have historically played highly visible roles in urban and regional trade. The priorities of these women have not always been the same as those of Islamic feminist leaders.

FEMINISM AND ISLAM

In recent years, the rise of Islam as a means of asserting national and cultural identity has shaped the feminist discussion taking place within Islamic societies in Africa. Feminists have questioned whether Islamic theology and law are inherently oppressive to women or whether sexism lies in the ways the Qur'an (Koran) and other Islamic texts have traditionally been interpreted by male-dominated institutions ranging from national governments to rural brotherhoods. They have also debated, along with their critics, whether feminism is a Western concept and at odds with an Islamic society.

Most feminists in and beyond Islamic Africa agree that some of the feminist victories of the 1960s through the early 1980s have been eroded since the rise of Islamic fundamentalism in the late 1980s. In Algeria, feminists fought against the Family Code legislation passed in 1984, which counteracted feminist gains concerning such issues as equal inheritance and equal divorce rights. Today, women who stray outside the conservative norms dictating female dress and behavior risk anything from public censure to state persecution to vigilante violence, particularly in Algeria. In response, new feminist groups have sprung up in Egypt, Algeria, MOROCCO, and Tunisia, often working with human rights groups.

Some of these activists argue that Islamic law itself is inherently patriarchal—recognizing only patrilineal succession, in which children inherit titles and property from their fathers. Before the advent of Islam, however, many sub-Saharan societies observed matrilineal succession, in which mothers and their families controlled the inheritance of titles and property. In addition, Islamic law allows fathers to have custody of their children and allows polygamy and unilateral divorce only for men.

Other African feminists argue that Islam and feminism are potentially compatible if interpreted in a profeminist way. According to scholar Mervat Hatem, feminist activists, such as Malak Hifni Nassif and Huda Shaarawi in Egypt and Bechira Mrad in Tunisia, call for a "synthesis" in contemporary Islamic society. They propose a model that would maintain the structure of traditional family life while affirming the value of women's education and employment outside the home.

Still other feminists, such as the Egyptian Nawal El Saadawi, argue that such an ideal ignores the fact that a Muslim woman's public and private lives cannot be separated. In Islamic cultures, the responsibility of maintaining tradition often falls upon women. Through child-rearing, as well as her dress and conduct, a woman is expected to uphold her society's traditional values, both at home and in public. Furthermore, in many nations the norms and values of the private sphere are, in fact, encoded in civic law. Feminists have organized around these personal status laws since the early twentieth century. These national codes, which regulate marriage, family, and spousal relations, effectively legislate the rights of women. For example, even if a woman has a legal right to work or run for office, she may be lawfully restricted from these activities if her husband objects to them. Tunisia is often cited as the most progressive Islamic country because of its relatively liberal personal status laws.

As the rise of Islamic movements has coincided with the ongoing globalization of Western media and culture, debates within the feminist community (and elsewhere) about norms and practices affecting Islamic African women have become increasingly charged. At stake, often, are claims to cultural authenticity. Three of the most controversial issues are the veil, FEMALE CIRCUMCISION, and polygamy.

Since the wearing of a veil in observance of Islamic codes of modesty is relatively rare south of the Sahara, the veil is a subject of debate primarily in North Africa. There, many Islamic women see the veil as a symbol of the oppression of women. In Algeria, women who refuse to wear the veil have been subject to discrimination and, sometimes, violence. But others, including some feminists, value the veil as a form of cultural expression that also enables women to escape unwanted sexual attention.

Female circumcision, the cutting, removal, or closure of female genitalia practiced in numerous North and sub-Saharan African societies—including many non-Islamic ones—has in recent years generated debate well beyond Africa. When Egypt's Health Ministry banned the practice in 1996, conservative religious leaders challenged the ruling, arguing that Islamic law condoned female circumcision. When Egypt's highest court upheld the ban in late 1997, anticircumcision groups worldwide rejoiced. Although feminists within Islamic countries have criticized what they consider a mutilation of women's bodies, not all Muslim women want the practice ended. In Egypt as well as other African countries, the older women who typically perform the circumcision operation often depend on the income it provides, and many mothers continue to have their daughters circumcised in order to assure they will be marriageable. The issue is a complicated one, in which feminists fight to change not only the laws, but social notions of femininity as well.

Polygamy has also been a subject of heated debate. Whether or not a government has banned this age-old practice is often viewed as a key measure of how it treats women generally. Yet African women have various attitudes toward polygamy, depending often on age, class, and culture. For example, one woman might welcome the extra hands and companionship of a co-wife—in rural areas especially, co-wives often share cooking and farming duties—while another might view a new wife as a threat to her own economic security and marriage.

These and other issues have provided material for a wealth of feminist activism, scholarship, and creative work in Islamic Africa. Nawal El Saadawi's now classic text *The Hidden Face of Eve* was a groundbreaking study from Egypt, and writers such as the Moroccan Fatima Mernissi are continuing a tradition of feminist scholarship.

The lives of women in Islamic Africa have been portrayed in the fiction of authors such as Mariama Bâ from SENEGAL and Assia Djabar and Leila Sebbar from Algeria.

See also EDUCATION IN AFRICA; ISLAM AND TRADITION: AN INTERPRETATION.

MARIAN AGUIAR

Fertility and Mortality in Africa

See POPULATION GROWTH IN SUB-SAHARAN AFRICA; URBANISM AND URBANIZATION IN AFRICA.

Fès, Morocco
City in northern Morocco.

According to legend, Fès was founded in the early 800s C.E. by the great sultan Mawlay Idris II as two cities, one BERBER and one Arab, on opposite sides of the river Fâs. This legend draws upon the renown of Idris II as a Berber ruler who brought together the imperial Arab and indigenous Berber cultures and made Fès the capital of the first Moroccan empire. Other accounts hold that Idris I built one city in 789, carving its boundaries into the earth with a silver and gold pickax, and his son founded the twin city across the river nearly twenty years later. Regardless of which account is true, the fact remains that the ruling family located their capital on a commercial crossroads of a main route to the eastern Maghreb and a route to the savanna kingdoms south of the SAHARA. Enriched by trade, early Fès also became a center of Islamic scholarship, especially after the opening of Al Qarawiyin University in 859, the oldest university in North Africa. When Fès came under the rule of the Umayyads dynasty (980–1012), an Islamic Spanish population settled the city on the right bank, and a Tunisian population settled on the left. The Almoravid sultan united these cities in 1069, turning Fès into a major Islamic metropolis. Under the reign of the Marinids (1258–1549) the city flourished, attracting scholars from throughout the Islamic world. The Marinids built the royal palace adjacent to the mosque, importing elements of both the culture of Andalusia (southern Spain) and North African architecture. They also built mellahs, walled compounds, around the city's Jewish quarter, ostensibly to "protect" the Jews but in effect creating a ghetto. After Fès fell to the Sa'dians in 1549, MARRAKECH and Meknès became the chief imperial cities, and the political significance of Fès declined. But the city maintained its status as an important center for religious scholarship as well as for the production of handicrafts such as the fez, a brimless hat worn by many Muslims. By the nineteenth century, many of the citizens of Fès were doing business with European traders and investors. A treaty establishing a French protectorate in

MOROCCO was signed at Fès in 1912. Shortly afterward, the French built a modern district, including an industrial quarter, but left the old city essentially intact. Today, traditional guilds based in the medina, or old city, continue to oversee the production of traditional handicrafts, including pottery, leatherwork, carpets, and richly embroidered cotton and silk textiles. The medina's workshops, bazaars, and mazelike alleys have become popular tourist attractions, and many locals work full-time as guides. Others work in the industrial quarters in oil-processing plants, tanneries, soap factories, and textile and flour mills. Fès is also a marketplace for produce from the surrounding fertile countryside, including beans, olives, grapes, and livestock. As of 2004 the population of the city stood at some 950,000.

See also ISLAM IN AFRICA; JUDAISM IN NORTH AFRICA.

MARIAN AGUIAR

Fiction, English-Language, in Africa
Overview of African literature written in English.

Since the 1960s African literature in English has garnered increasing international attention and literary awards and has made its way into classrooms worldwide. The novels of writers such as Chinua ACHEBE, Wole SOYINKA, Ama Ata AIDOO, Ngugi wa THIONG'O, and Nadine GORDIMER have introduced readers to histories and cultures still poorly understood outside of Africa. In contrast to the ethnographies and travelers' accounts that long shaped the West's images of Africa, literature by African writers portrays diverse, dynamic societies and the complex human relationships within them. It has also helped validate African cultural traditions: in the words of Chinua Achebe, it showed "that African people did not hear of culture for the first time from Europeans; that their societies were not mindless but frequently had a philosophy of great depth and value and beauty, that they had poetry and, above all, they had dignity." This validation was critical to African audiences as well, since colonialism had propagated a myth of cultural inferiority not just abroad but among Africans themselves. But Anglophone African writers have not simply recorded African history and promoted African intellectual and cultural achievements. They have also contributed to world literature many thought-provoking works that are, above all, art.

Any attempt to generalize about African literature, even only about that composed in English, is immediately problematic: Africa is an enormous continent, and its literary movements and individual writers are highly diverse. In addition, much of what is considered African literature has been written by Africans living in the United States or Europe. Author Buchi EMECHETA of NIGERIA, for example, wrote her early novels about a young African woman in England while she herself was living there. These and other works about experiences of exile and immigration could also be considered literature of the diaspora. Africa is not always the primary point of reference even for African writers who remain in their home countries; the works of these authors deal with themes central to literature worldwide, such as identity, alienation, political struggle, romantic love, gender relations, religion, and childhood.

The first Anglophone novel published in Africa by a black African author was *Guanya Pau* (1891) by Liberian J. J. Walters. A graduate of Oberlin College in the United States, Walters was perhaps influenced by the eighteenth-century writings of Africans abroad, including Phillis Wheatley and Olaudah EQUIANO. Thus an early relationship was established between African writing in English and that of the African diaspora.

Given the important role missionaries played in the spread of English, it is not surprising that early Anglophone works grappled with issues of Christianity. Some of these books, such as *Ethiopia Unbound* (1911) by journalist E. Casely-Hayford of GHANA, explored the fraught relationship between African identity and Christianity, providing a model for later nationalist works. Others portrayed Christianity more sympathetically. In his novella *An African Tragedy* (1928), R. R. R. Dhlomo represented urbanization in SOUTH AFRICA as a morally corrupting force.

South African writers in the first half of the twentieth century also used literature to protest racism and economic inequality. One of the earliest works of black South African literature, the *Mafeking Diary: A Black Man's View of a White Man's War* (1900) by Sol T. PLAATJE recounted events during the Boer War. Plaatje's *Native Life in South Africa* (1916) protested the Natives Land Act (1913), a precursor to later APARTHEID laws. In the 1940s, literature by Peter ABRAHAMS and Alan PATON depicted the effects of westernization on traditional ways of life and the extreme poverty of the black urban population. During the SOPHIATOWN Renaissance in the 1940s and 1950s, fiction by writers such as Can Themba gained national recognition in *Drum*, a literary magazine edited by, among others, South African author Es'kia MPHAHLELE. Ironically, despite the prolific nature of black South African protest literature, works by white authors such as Paton reached a far broader audience; white authors were consistently afforded more freedom and opportunities than their black counterparts.

African writers have produced vivid representations of the experience of colonialism. Influenced by the philosophy of Négritude, Anglophone writers gave voice to this historical moment in the company of Francophone authors such as Albert MEMMI, Léopold SENGHOR, and Ousmane SEMBÈNE. Nigeria led the publishing explosion that occurred during and after decolonization with Chinua Achebe's novel *Things Fall Apart* (1958), which is still one of the most famous novels ever written by an African author. It related the history of European colonialism in Africa from the point of view of the colonized. Focusing on an IGBO man's contentious relations with encroaching British administrators and missionaries, Achebe described the social upheavals wrought by colonialism on Igbo village life. Other African novels of this era probed the individual, psychological experience of colonialism. *A Grain of Wheat* (1967), a novel by Ngugi wa Thiong'o of KENYA, centered on events surrounding the MAU MAU REBELLION in the 1950s but drew in stories of individual lives and references to KIKUYU myth. Organizing the novel's plot around individual choices and intimate friendships, Ngugi created a vivid picture of the dilemmas faced by Kenyans waging armed rebellion against the British.

Many African writers attended missionary schools and then European universities, and their writings reflect their own struggles to navigate through a minefield of modern and traditional values. They portray characters torn, for example, between romantic love and obligations to respect their family's marriage arrangements, between the norms learned at school and those learned at home, and between the freedom and opportunities of the city or foreign country and the familiarity and security of the village. Women writers such as Buchi Emecheta and Tsitsi Dangarembga gave voice to the challenges particular to women in postcolonial Africa. In her novel *Changes* (1991), for example, Ghanaian Ama Ata Aidoo explored a woman's difficult decision to leave her polygamous marriage. The psychological narrative work of South African-born Bessie HEAD in *A Question of Power* (1973) used the trauma of a mental breakdown to portray the life of a woman on the margins of society.

Anglophone writers in Africa have challenged postcolonial state power and social hierarchies, often at risk to their own lives. Many authors aimed their barbs at government corruption and violence. In the wake of Nigeria's civil war, for example, Wole Soyinka's play *Madmen and Specialists* (1971) portrayed a cannibalistic genocide. In *The Beautyful Ones Are Not Yet Born* (1968), the Ghanaian novelist Ayi Kwei ARMAH portrayed a society decaying under a corrupt neocolonial state. Like a number of politically engaged writers across Africa, Somali Nuruddin FARAH wrote fiction that offended government authorities, and he was forced into exile by the military regime of Mohamed SIAD BARRE. Undoubtedly inspired by the events in his home country, Farah published *Sweet and Sour Milk* (1979),

the first in a trilogy he titled *Variations on the Theme of an African Dictatorship*. In Nigeria the novel *Sozaboy: A Novel in Rotten English* (1985) by Ken SARO-WIWA exposed the corruption of that nation's military government. Even authors concerned primarily with stylistic experimentation—such as Nigerian author Ben Okri—have continuously engaged the contemporary social and political issues of Africa in their work.

South Africa's apartheid regime lasted long after most African colonial regimes had withdrawn, and it remained a central theme in a wide variety of South African writings. Short stories by Alex La Guma, such as those in the noted collection *A Walk in the Night* (1962), highlighted economic inequalities through vivid portrayals of township poverty. *Muriel at Metropolitan*, a 1979 autobiographical novel by Miriam TLALI, told of a young black educated woman making her way in a divided country. *Waiting for the Barbarians* (1980) by J. M. COETZEE was an unforgettable account of the psychology of domination written from the point of view of a rural magistrate who uncovers his own complicity in oppression. *Burger's Daughter*, a novel by the Nobel Prize winner Nadine Gordimer, portrayed a regime so oppressive that the novel's heroine—a young white woman whose parents have already been jailed for Communist Party ANTIAPARTHEID MOVEMENT activities—is eventually compelled to join the struggle herself.

As writers explored the social and psychological legacies of colonialism and apartheid, they also began to examine the ways in which their own writing related to this history. For some, writing in English became increasingly problematic. Ngugi wa Thiong'o eventually decided to write literature only in Kikuyu because, as he said, "Language carries culture, and culture carries, particularly through orature and literature, the entire body of values by which we perceive ourselves and our place in the world." Achebe, on the other hand, saw English as a necessary tool in building a body of African literature accessible to readers throughout the continent as well as abroad.

Other African authors have experimented with writing styles in order to draw on their own diverse cultural and literary backgrounds. Most but not all the novels about colonialism and independence struggles were written as realist narratives, which made them easily accessible to Western audiences. Yet Africa's own traditions of song, poetry, myth, and allegory incorporate a rich variety of styles and metaphors. Many authors have drawn on elements from these traditions, for example by giving characters mythical names. Some writers, such as Nigerian Amos TUTUOLA, author of *The Palm-Wine Drunkard* (1952), have modeled their writing on oral storytelling traditions. Nigerian Nobel Prize winner Wole Soyinka's fictional works often weave YORUBA mythology into contemporary story lines. Booker Prize-winning Nigerian Ben Okri has developed a style many have compared to magical realism, incorporating both traditional mythic influences and influences of European modernism to explore issues such as urban poverty, bureaucratic corruption, and the exploitation of power by an elite minority.

It is important to realize that the African literature that reaches international audiences represents only a small proportion of the literature actually produced in Africa. Literary critics, elite literary prize committees, and publishing companies together have shaped the canon as we see it. The internationally recognized canon of African literature in English has also been defined in part by historical circumstances. For example, Nigerian and South African writers tend to predominate in anthologies and academic coursework on African Anglophone literature. Their renown reflects the fact that they come from countries with large populations, relatively high literacy rates, and active literary movements and magazines, but their writing should not be assumed to represent the entirety of African Anglophone literature.

See also CHRISTIANITY, AFRICAN: AN OVERVIEW; CHRISTIANITY: MISSIONARIES IN AFRICA; COLONIAL RULE; DECOLONIZATION IN AFRICA: AN INTERPRETATION; FEMALE WRITERS IN ENGLISH-SPEAKING AFRICA; URBANISM AND URBANIZATION IN AFRICA.

MARIAN AGUIAR

Film, African
See CINEMA, AFRICAN.

Fipa
Ethnic group of Malawi, Tanzania, and Zambia.
The Fipa, also known as Wafipa, primarily inhabit the region just east of southern LAKE TANGANYIKA. They speak a BANTU language. Approximately 200,000 people consider themselves Fipa.

See also ETHNICITY AND IDENTITY IN AFRICA: AN INTERPRETATION; LANGUAGES, AFRICAN: AN OVERVIEW; MALAWI; TANZANIA; ZAMBIA.

First, Ruth
1925–1982
South African journalist and opponent of apartheid, the South African government's policy of racial segregation.
Ruth First's parents were immigrant Jews from Lithuania. Born in Johannesburg, First joined the Communist Party of South Africa (later renamed the SOUTH AFRICAN COMMUNIST PARTY) at an early age. As secretary of the

Progressive Youth Council, a communist organization, she approached Nelson MANDELA, one of the founders of the AFRICAN NATIONAL CONGRESS (ANC) Youth League, to ask for affiliation with the group but her request was rejected. She studied social science at the University of the Witwatersrand, in Johannesburg, and was an active supporter of the black miners' strike of 1946. Beginning in 1947 she worked as a journalist. Three newspapers for which she wrote, the Guardian, Clarion, and New Age, were banned by the NATIONAL PARTY government because they were critical of government policies. With activist Reverend Michael Scott, First visited SOUTH-WEST AFRICA (modern-day NAMIBIA) in 1947. As an investigative journalist, she helped reveal the appalling conditions under which blacks were obliged to work. In 1949 she married Joe SLOVO, the Communist Party leader, and they had three daughters. First was arrested in 1956 along with 156 others, including ANC members Mandela and Albert John LUTHULI, on charges of being part of a nationwide conspiracy to commit treason. In the early 1960s she edited the political and literary monthly Fighting Talk and the Transvaal newspaper New Age, which supported the ANC. Following the publication of her book South-West Africa in 1963, First was subject to a banning order, which prohibited the publication in SOUTH AFRICA of anything she wrote. Later that year she was arrested and held in solitary confinement for 117 days under the law that permitted the government to hold people it suspected of dangerous anti-state activities for ninety days without trial, then release and immediately rearrest them. First became a political exile in 1964 and went to Great Britain, where she lectured at Durham University and wrote extensively about South Africa. During that time, she wrote 117 Days (1965) about her experience in solitary confinement. In 1978 she became research director at the Centre for African Studies in MAPUTO, MOZAMBIQUE. In 1982, while in MOZAMBIQUE, she was killed by a letter bomb.

See also ANTIAPARTHEID MOVEMENT; APARTHEID.

Fisheries, African
Important economic activity and source of food for both maritime and inland regions of Africa.
Millions of people in Africa earn their livelihood directly or indirectly from fishing. Due to the scarcity and expense of livestock, fish provide 60 to 75 percent of animal protein consumption in the population's diet in many parts of the continent. Africa's fishing industries are also an important source of export earnings. Globally, marine fishing off the coast of Africa accounts for roughly 5 percent of the world harvest, and inland fishing accounts for approximately 8 percent of the world harvest. Africa's marine fisheries are

generally fully exploited or overexploited. Africa's inland fisheries are generally underexploited, though inland fisheries in KENYA and UGANDA are overexploited, and inland fisheries in DEMOCRATIC REPUBLIC OF THE CONGO, GHANA, MALAWI, TANZANIA, and ZAMBIA are fully exploited.

Africans have relied on fish for their livelihood since ancient times. Our earliest human ancestors in Africa almost certainly depended on fish as part of their diet. Except in arid zones, nearly all African peoples have exploited coastal, lake, and river fisheries. Egyptians have relied on fish from the NILE as a source of protein since ancient times. Dried, smoked, and salted fish are among the oldest trade goods in African history, particularly in arid zones that lack local sources of fish. West African and Sahelian traders have sold fish since at least the fifteenth century.

Historically, Africa's fisherpeople have produced mainly for local and subsistence consumption. To this day, they depend primarily on locally designed technologies and intensive communal and seasonal labor. In both inland and marine fishing communities, fishing equipment typically consists of wood dugout canoes, various designs of traps and nets, and hooks and lines. Since the late 1950s, African fisheries have adopted the use of imported motors, hooks, and synthetic nets and lines, but few use imported vessels.

There is some evidence that commercial fishing was significant by at least the sixteenth century. For instance, the Sorkawa and Bozo, who fished the middle NIGER RIVER, paid taxes to the SONGHAI EMPIRE exclusively in dried fish. However, large-scale maritime commercial fishing and inland fish farming first appeared in Africa during the colonial period.

Today, pollution and overfishing threaten Africa's fisheries. In response to declining catches in both marine and lake fisheries, fishers throughout Africa have resorted to desperate practices such as the use of dynamite and poisons. A 2007 report by the Institute for Security Studies warned that several African nations are in danger of doing permanent damage to their marine environments and wildlife populations. Overfishing not only overexploits the fisheries themselves but also causes severe and irreversible damage to marine and aquatic ecosystems and endangers the future of Africa's fishing industries.

INLAND FISHERIES

Inland fishing plays a tremendous role in Africa. Although maritime fishing has traditionally excluded women, both women and men participate in inland fishing activities. Like coastal fishing, large lake fishing traditionally requires relatively large crews to handle large canoes and nets. Inland fish landings in Africa account for over half of the fish landed annually on the continent. In East Africa, for example, over 95 percent of Kenyan fish landings come from inland fisheries, despite Kenya's coastal reef fishery. While Africa's inland fisheries have not been developed for the international market, development projects have focused on aquaculture techniques to meet local demands.

Africa's major inland fisheries are located in CÔTE D'IVOIRE, REPUBLIC OF THE CONGO, Democratic Republic of the Congo, EGYPT, Ghana, Kenya, MADAGASCAR, NIGERIA, SUDAN, TOGO, and Zambia. Inland fisheries in Africa are mostly in freshwater environments, but coastal brackish waters have always been an important fish source in West Africa, and they are increasingly important in Nigeria and Kenya.

The volume and diversity of fishes in African lakes have declined in the last century due to overfishing and the introduction of exotic species to create new fisheries. For example, Nile perch, introduced to LAKE VICTORIA, probably caused the largest mass extinction of fauna in modern times through competition with indigenous species. Fifty different exotic species have been introduced to Africa's major lakes, most notably Nile perch and various freshwater sardines.

African fish farming exploits more than thirty species of inland fish, particularly various types of tilapia and carp. Public seed production centers supply stocking material. The basic production units for inland fisheries are small, earthen ponds that range in size from 100 to 1,000 square meters (about 330 to 3,280 square feet) (subsistence level to small-scale commercial level). The first attempts at fish farming occurred with the cultivation of trout in Kenya and Madagascar in the 1920s and of tilapia in ZAIRE in 1946. These early aquaculture enterprises generally failed in the 1960s as a result of poor returns, lack of stocking material, drought, and political unrest. The resurgence of freshwater farming in the 1970s and 1980s often accompanied irrigation and dam development projects. Large, privately owned commercial farms exist in Kenya, Malawi, Nigeria, Zambia, and ZIMBABWE and range in size from two to thirty hectares. Some producers use tanks, raceways, and net pens. Small-scale aquaculture is generally a secondary activity to agricultural production, and pond management and labor are usually done by women. In Madagascar, farmers often stock irrigated rice fields with fish. African aquaculture makes use of both organic fertilizer and mineral fertilizers, when affordable.

Medium-sized commercial fleets exist on LAKE VOLTA in Ghana, Lake Chad in CHAD and Nigeria, Lake Nasser in Egypt and Sudan, and Lakes Victoria, Tanganyika, and Malawi in East Africa. These fleets fish primarily for distribution to African countries, though there is a growing market for fresh Nile perch in Europe and the Middle East.

Tanzanian, Kenyan, and Ugandan exporters ship frozen Nile perch products as far as Australia and North America. In 2002 exports of Nile perch fillets from the three nations had a combined total value of $242 million in U.S. dollars. Nile perch products account for 15 percent of Tanzania's foreign-exchange earnings.

MARINE FISHERIES

The richest fisheries on Africa's Atlantic and Mediterranean coasts exist in regions with either a broad continental shelf or cold upwellings and currents. Continental shelf ecosystems generate rich plankton growth, and thus food for an abundance of fish, in three main areas: from TUNISIA to SIERRA LEONE, from Côte d'Ivoire to Togo, and from GABON to the Cape of Good Hope in SOUTH AFRICA. The Canary Current, the Guinea Current, and a permanent upwelling off the coast of SENEGAL furnish nutrient-rich water along the Atlantic coast from MOROCCO to Gabon. Another seasonal upwelling occurs between Côte d'Ivoire and Togo. The cold Benguela Current flows along the southwestern coast of Africa. Productive fishing zones are also associated with the outflow of the CONGO RIVER and an upwelling off the coast of ANGOLA. The main near-surface fisheries along the Atlantic and Mediterranean coasts of Africa yield sardines, sardinella, tuna, and mackerel. The principal deep-sea fisheries contain hake, octopus, grouper, and snapper. Shellfish, crustaceans, and turtles are also fished for local trade and subsistence consumption.

Many of Africa's major Indian Ocean fisheries occur around coral reefs. The most important are those along the coast of MOZAMBIQUE, along the western coast of Madagascar, in the Mozambique Channel, and along the Mascarene Ridge, extending southeast from the SEYCHELLES to MAURITIUS. Near-surface fisheries include tuna and sardine. Major deep-sea fisheries include various reef fishes, sharks, rays, and shrimp.

Africa's traditional and small-scale fishers have to contend with seasonal patterns of fish migration and spawning. In order to sustain year-round incomes from fishing without reliable refrigeration, fishers rely on various traditional methods of processing and preservation, including salting, drying, and smoking. Throughout Africa, fishing communities have independently developed smoking ovens and storage systems. These give fish marketers a means of efficiently distributing their commodity. Fisher migrations are also essential to year-round harvests and profits. The Fante fishers of Ghana, for instance, make short- and long-term migrations from Senegal to CAMEROON to exploit a succession of harvests that follow current and upwelling patterns along the coast of West Africa.

Africa's traditional and small-scale fishing industries rely on labor organized by gender roles and kinship relations. Both women and men participate in near-shore collection of shellfish, crustaceans, and urchins, but only men fish in the deep sea. Several African coastal ethnic groups, such as the EWE of Ghana and Togo and the Swahili of Kenya and Tanzania, enforce cultural and religious restrictions against women setting foot in fishing canoes. Women usually handle the processing and marketing of fish and thus play a dominant role in local fishing economies and communities. Traditional fishing generally relies on communal and familial labor. Particularly in marine fishing, groups of workers are needed to drive fish into nets, to cast and haul large nets, and to paddle and work large canoes. Large hauls of fish also require the cooperation of groups of workers, who need to complete multiple tasks in a brief window of opportunity. Communal labor and relationships between fishers and marketers typically revolve around kinship relations. However, as a result of recent economic restructuring and the environmental degradation of fisheries throughout Africa, these kinds of familial networks are giving way to wage, credit, and contract arrangements among individual fishers, marketers, equipment owners, and laborers.

European and Russian fishing fleets have exploited the fisheries off the Atlantic coast of West Africa for more than a century, though the coastal waters of southern and eastern Africa remained out of reach for most western commercial fishers until recently. Various colonial governments made the first attempts to export marine fish and shellfish from Africa, but on a very small scale. During World War II, a surge in the demand for canned fish coincided with the beginning of catch declines from perennial overfishing in many of the world's fishing grounds. Improvements in fishing technology, particularly of nets and radar equipment, gave western fishing companies a further incentive to expand their operations to distant (often Southern Hemisphere) waters, such as those around the African continent.

Today, European, Russian, North American, and Asian distant water fleets dominate Africa's marine fisheries. Spain and Russia report some of the highest catches of the most valuable species from the east-central Atlantic, though in volume, Moroccan fleets report the highest total catch. Japan, Russia, and South Africa out-catch the well-established, locally owned commercial fleets of NAMIBIA and Angola in the southeast Atlantic. Pakistan and India are the dominant fishers off Africa's Indian Ocean coast, though Japan and France take the highest catches of tuna. These fleets immediately export high-grade species, fresh and frozen, by air or by "over-the-side" deals with courier ships. They freeze and box lower-grade species or process them into meal and oil aboard factory ships. Of the few large-scale commercial processing operations in African ports, most are owned by multinational corporations, such as the Starkist Tuna canning facility in Tema, Ghana.

As part of the structural adjustment plans imposed on many African states in the 1980s, international lenders have encouraged the nontraditional export of fish in coastal states. Ironically, as debt and malnutrition in sub-Saharan Africa have increased in the past decade, so have the exports of nutritionally valuable fish products to the supermarkets, livestock feedlots, and fertilizer factories of the developed world. Per capita consumption of fish in sub-Saharan Africa declined from nine kilograms (twenty pounds) in 1990 to 6.7 kilograms in 1997.

Since 1983, most coastal states have claimed exclusive economic zones (EEZs) over the seas extending 320 kilometers (200 miles) from their coastline. The EEZ is one of the main principles of the United Nations Convention on the Law of the Sea (UNCLOS), intended to promote better management of marine resources through the national privatization of marine space. With the exception of ERITREA, every African state has signed UNCLOS. Many coastal African countries signed UNCLOS hoping to negotiate access fees and other deals for foreign entry into their EEZs. However, given the frontier-like quality of the high seas, access to the EEZs is difficult to enforce for poor African states that cannot afford the necessary high-technology surveillance vessels or military power.

The exploitation of marine fisheries off African coasts has increased substantially since 1980. The reported catch of crustaceans and mollusks in Africa soared from 102,000 metric tons that year to 336,000 metric tons in 1999; the continent's total fish catch rose from 3.5 million metric tons to more than 5.5 million metric tons over the same period. Overexploitation is depleting Africa's fish stocks. Small-scale and commercial marine fishers alike complain of not only reduced numbers of fish, but smaller sizes of fish. Given the poor management practices in both sectors, the future of Africa's marine fisheries is doubtful.

See also MALAWI, LAKE; STRUCTURAL ADJUSTMENT IN AFRICA; SWAHILI PEOPLE; TANGANYIKA, LAKE; VICTORIA, LAKE.

BARBARA WALKER

Fon

Ethnic group of the Republic of Benin whose ancestors built the powerful precolonial Kingdom of Dahomey; also called the Agadja.

Closely related to the Adja and Gun ethnic groups, the Fon were once a part of the Adja Kingdom in Tado (part of present-day TOGO). In the late seventeenth century, however, the Fon broke from the Adja and migrated to Allada. According to Fon legend, the group was forced to leave after Agasu, the son of an Adja princess and a leopard, unsuccessfully attempted to usurp the Adja throne. Agasu and his followers fled to Allada and established their own kingdom, but a later succession struggle forced Agasu's son Dogbari to migrate to Abomey, where he and his Fon subjects established the kingdom of DAHOMEY around 1620.

Dahomey quickly evolved into a highly centralized monarchy, and its large, sophisticated army enabled the Fon to conquer neighboring kingdoms and expand their territory throughout most of southern BENIN. On its conquests the army commonly took captives, who were used as slave labor on the king's plantations or as sacrificial offerings in the annual religious ceremonies held to honor royal ancestors. These ceremonies were also an opportunity for the Dahomey kings to assemble their provincial chiefs and confirm their loyalty.

The Dahomey kingdom expanded during the seventeenth century and the early eighteenth century, reaching its pinnacle during the reign of Agaja (1708–1740). By this time the kingdom stretched from the Abomey plateau to the Atlantic Coast and was well positioned to participate in European trade, particularly the booming transatlantic slave trade. Although some scholars believe the Dahomey intended to end or at least curtail the slave trade, the kingdom became one of West Africa's biggest suppliers of slaves, and it grew heavily dependent on the trade for revenue.

But after 1804, when Great Britain formally prohibited slave trading, Dahomey's rulers were forced to pursue other commodities. They ordered their subjects to produce palm oil and used slaves on their state palm plantations. Despite high European demand for palm oil, however, the Dahomey kings found its production less lucrative than selling slaves and attempted to increase revenue by levying heavy taxes and leasing ports, such as COTONOU and Whydah, to the French. By the late nineteenth century, the French were claiming they had been ceded the land, and when the Dahomey king Glele demanded that France relinquish control of the ports, France took the dispute as an opportunity for conquest. In 1892 the French launched an attack against Glele's successor, Behanzin; two years later they captured him and occupied the kingdom, which subsequently became part of the colony of Dahomey.

The French colonial administration preserved some of the centralized authority structures of the Dahomey kingdom because it found them useful for enacting colonial dictates on the local level. Many of the kingdom's chiefs, almost all Fon, were appointed to the colonial civil service.

As independence neared, the Fon were mobilized by Tometin Justin Ahomadegbe into a political party, the Bloc Populaire Africain. Today, as Benin's single largest ethnic group—numbering somewhat more than 3.5 million—the Fon wield significant political power and were instrumental in the 1991 election of Nicéphore SOGLO, who remained president until 1996. The majority still live in the southern half of the country and are the principal producers of the country's staple crops, including maize and millet.

See also COLONIAL RULE; DAHOMEY, EARLY KINGDOM OF; ETHNICITY AND IDENTITY IN AFRICA: AN INTERPRETATION.

ELIZABETH HEATH

Food in Africa

Patterns of food production and consumption in Africa.

Africa's regional diets and culinary patterns, or foodways, vary on the basis of ecology, culture, class, and other factors. Climate and ecological conditions, for example, determine what food crops and livestock are practical to grow locally. Dietary patterns are also influenced by cultural and religious norms and by a region's history of contact with foreign foodstuffs and cultures through trade, migration, and colonization. Since the 1950s, African foodways have been particularly transformed by urbanization and related changes in women's work and by foreign donations of food aid. Now more than ever, diets vary across class, with the wealthy typically eating not only a greater quantity and variety of foods than the poor but also different foods. This essay discusses some of these variations in African foodways, as well as broad patterns and historical trends. In Africa as in most of the world, most people structure their diets around a relatively small number of starchy or carbohydrate-rich foods. Grains such as millet, sorghum, rice, and maize (corn) and tubers such as yams and cassava (manioc), for example, form the central ingredient of the most common meals in Africa and provide the bulk of the daily caloric intake. These staple starches are traditionally accompanied by protein-rich legumes, such as peas, beans, or peanuts, and by smaller quantities of foods that add both flavor and nutrition, such as vegetables, oils, spices, and meat or fish. These latter foods are often referred to as relishes, condiments, or sauces. Anthropologist and food historian Sidney Mintz calls them "fringe" foods, to emphasize the centrality of the "core" starches. This "core-fringe-legume" pattern of food consumption predominates in Africa, except in pastoral societies, where milk and meat play more central roles.

CORE FOODS

Africa's oldest staple starch crops vary across ecological zones. The major cereal grains—millet, sorghum, and maize—are all common in semi-arid regions. Millet and sorghum, both indigenous to Africa, predominate in the drier regions of the SAHEL and in eastern and southern Africa. Millet can grow in areas where rainfall averages 275 to 400 millimeters (eleven to twenty inches) annually, while sorghum requires between 800 and 1,000 millimeters (thirty to forty inches) of rain annually. Maize, a New World crop first introduced by the Portuguese beginning in the late fifteenth century, is now one of the most widely cultivated food crops in Africa. It can grow in a variety of conditions and be used in many ways, but it is less drought-resistant than either sorghum or millet. Tubers such as cassava, yams, and sweet potatoes, and tree crops such as bananas and plantains (some tree crops are indigenous to Africa and some arrived centuries ago from Asia or the New World) are typically grown in the humid forest ecozones of Central Africa, the Great Lakes region of East Africa, and coastal West Africa. Cassava production in particular has increased in the twentieth century, because while in the field it requires little tending, and it can keep for months underground before harvest. But cassava is low in protein, and in raw form it is toxic.

Most rice in Africa is grown under either lowland (also known as paddy) or upland conditions. In the bend of the NIGER RIVER in West Africa, indigenous African lowland rice production dates back an estimated 3,000 years. Both the rice species and the cultivation methods from this region later crossed the Atlantic with African slaves. Asian paddy rice varieties are also cultivated in areas suitable for irrigation. Upland rice depends on rainfall, not irrigation, and thus grows only in wetter regions. Many rural development projects in Africa since the 1960s have centered on rice production, in part because in comparison to other crops, demand for rice has increased enormously in Africa's cities. Wheat, which favors a cooler and drier climate, grows in relatively few regions. Major areas of production include the highlands of ETHIOPIA and KENYA and certain parts of SUDAN. Barley is a staple-food crop in EGYPT but is not widely cultivated elsewhere. In Ethiopia and ERITREA, teff, an indigenous wheatlike grain, has been a staple-food crop for centuries.

COMMON PREPARATIONS OF CORE FOODS

Compared to the highly varied and often quite elaborate preparations typical of *fringe* foods, the preparations of core starches are fairly simple. One very common dish made of millet, maize, or sorghum is a stiff porridge known in different regions of sub-Saharan Africa as to, putu, pap, nsima, bidia, oshifima, or ugali. Once the grains

FOOD IN NIGERIA. Produce on display in an outdoor market in Lagos, Nigeria, 2005. (*George Osodi/AP Images*)

have been ground into flour—a task women once did by hand but increasingly do in mills—they are mixed with cold water until a thin paste forms. Next the cook mixes in boiling water and stirs continuously until it thickens and then adds more flour until the consistency is so thick that the spoon stands straight up in the pot. This kind of porridge is often consumed communally and typically by hand, with each person scooping out bite-size portions to dip in sauce. Couscous, made from steamed granules of sorghum flour, is a popular dish in North Africa. In Ethiopia and Eritrea, the traditional core of many meals is njera, large puffy pancakes made from teff flour. Like boiled grain dishes, njera and most other baked breads are relatively bland but their accompaniments are often quite spicy. Tubers and starchy tree crops are most commonly boiled, roasted, or fried. Because cassava and some yam varieties contain toxic chemicals, they must be soaked in water for several hours or days before cooking. Once soaked and boiled, cassava and yams, like boiled plantains, are frequently pounded into a thick, heavy paste called fufu (or futu), a popular albeit labor-intensive West African dish. Like porridge dishes, fufu is often eaten communally and by hand and is always accompanied by a soup or stew. Dried, grated cassava, known as gari, is a popular convenience food in coastal West Africa, because it keeps well and can be easily reconstituted with boiling water.

FRINGE FOODS

Although fringe foods typically account for a smaller proportion of caloric intake than the core starches, they are by no means a peripheral part of the diet. Whether served as sauces, soups, spreads, or fillings, dishes made of vegetables, spices, and sometimes animal protein and fat add color, nutrition, and variety to the daily bowls of porridge

or rice. These dishes vary both seasonally and regionally, depending in part on the ingredients available locally. For example, in SENEGAL sauces made with peanuts, one of the country's main crops, are served with rice and occasionally chicken. Farther south in NIGERIA and GHANA, palm oil stew is a more common complement. In KENYA, boiled sukuma wiki, a green similar to spinach, accompanies maize or millet ugali, whereas in Central Africa the greens of potatoes and cassava plants are common sauce ingredients.

Many ingredients found in traditional African fringe dishes reflect foreign influences. The tomato, for example, was brought from the New World by the Portuguese in the sixteenth century and is now cultivated and consumed throughout much of Africa. In coastal East Africa, spices from Asia and the Middle East flavor the sauces served on rice and fish. Similarly, North African cuisines employ many of the ingredients found in other Mediterranean culinary traditions, such as saffron, cinnamon, mint, and chickpeas.

COLONIAL INFLUENCES

European influence on African food habits prior to colonialism was generally limited to the introduction of new crops, such as maize and tomatoes. Colonization led to significant changes both in what foods Africans produced and what foods they had available to purchase. It is important to note that dietary patterns were transformed not only by the introduction of new crops and imported goods, but also by changes in households' use of land, labor, and income. Colonial-era taxes, for example, often forced peasant households to shift at least some of their land away from food crops over to export crops, such as cotton, coffee, and cocoa, which were typically overseen by male household heads. Taxation and compulsory labor service also forced rural men and sometimes women to leave their farms for work on plantations, in mines, and on road and railway projects. In many areas women had to assume greater responsibility for food production and often on more limited land. In one common adaptation to these constraints, women switched from labor-intensive crops such as millet to ones requiring less weeding and other upkeep, such as cassava. In general, as rural households devoted more of their resources to income-earning endeavors, they also began to purchase a larger proportion of their food supplies. Compared to the efforts colonial administrations made to develop export crop production in Africa, most of the time they paid relatively little attention to staple-food crop production. During the First and Second World Wars, however, some colonies made cultivation of certain crops compulsory in order to assure food supplies for the military bases. In the British colonies of

East Africa, for example, peasants in some regions were forced to grow maize, and in the French colony of UPPER VOLTA (now BURKINA FASO), peasants near the military camp in BOBO-DIOULASSO were forced to grow potatoes and peanuts. Imported foods intended for European settlers also made their way into the African diet, as did European foods manufactured in Africa. Initially only a small minority of Africans, mostly the educated urban elite, partook of foreign and costly foods such as bread, pasta, margarine, and soft drinks. In some circles the ability to buy and serve European cuisine became a marker of status, like Western-style clothing. Certain foods, however, eventually became a part of the working-class diet. Men who migrated to urban areas in search of wage labor were among the earliest regular consumers of goods like bread and tea, partly because they were convenient. Migrant laborers also helped introduce these foods to rural regions by bringing them back to their families. Today, regional variations in some popular European foodstuffs reflect the influence of the colonial powers' own cuisines. In the cities of Francophone West Africa, for example, people eat baguettes and drink café au lait, while in the former Italian colonies they eat pasta, and in the former British colonies square bread loaves and tea predominate. Demand for Western-style processed foods is now partially met by domestic production. Bread in Africa is typically made in small or medium-size urban bakeries, while commodities such as instant coffee and margarine are produced in factories owned by multinational corporations. Although these foods are no longer consumed only by an elite few, during times of economic hardship they are too expensive for the vast majority of the population, urban or rural.

FOOD AID

Since independence, food donated or sold on concessional terms by foreign countries—also known as food aid—has transformed both dietary and agricultural production patterns in Africa. Governments of many newly independent African countries willingly accepted food aid because it compensated for their own production shortfalls and ensured that cheap food supplies were available for politically important urban populations. For the United States and the European Union, food aid became a means for disposing of their own agricultural surpluses as well as for establishing African markets for their exports. The United States' Food for Peace Program, for example, granted African and other Third World countries low-interest loans for the purchase of major U.S. agricultural commodities, such as wheat and soybean oil. The U.S. Congress approved the program in 1954 with the explicit aim of

building new overseas markets. It succeeded: countries like Nigeria continued to purchase U.S. wheat even when the aid program was reduced, partly out of the concern to maintain political stability in the cities, where most wheat and other aid foods are consumed. Food aid from the European Union has also helped establish African markets for European goods, such as dried milk products. Although food aid programs were once justified on humanitarian grounds, they have been widely criticized for undermining markets for Africa's domestically produced foodstuffs and for fostering an overdependence on imported foods. Indeed, in 2007 Now Care, a major international charitable organization, set off a firestorm when it announced a boycott of subsidized American foodstuffs. The dangers of African dependency became apparent in many African countries in the 1980s, when austerity measures imposed under World Bank structural adjustment programs drove up prices for import-based foods such as wheat, bread, and milk. The announcement of price increases set off "bread riots" in many African cities.

STREET FOODS

Finally, African food habits have changed along with the patterns and pressures of daily life, especially in the cities. As more and more people—especially women—commute across large cities to work and attend school, midday meals at home have become less practical. Instead, students, marketplace traders, and industrial and office workers rely on so-called street foods for one or more meals daily. Sold from kiosks and carts in cities throughout Africa, street-food fare is eclectic: offerings range from the traditional rice-and-sauce dishes popular among the cities' various African ethnic communities to African "fast foods" like fried plantains and bean fritters to Middle Eastern-style kebabs and European-style sandwiches. For many, street foods are not only more convenient but also more economical than home-prepared meals. Some traditional African dishes require extensive preparation, so when the price of the ingredients and the cooking fuel is factored into the time spent shopping and cooking, it is often cheaper to buy these dishes from street vendors, who prepare them in large quantities. The variety of snacks and meals sold on the streets of African cities reflects an enduring theme in African cuisines: despite the many changes prompted by colonialism, urbanization, aid, and trade, traditional dishes based on locally produced ingredients are still valued. Indeed, because such dishes are now sold in multiethnic cities and eaten by migrants and travelers, they have become familiar far beyond the regions where they were originally developed. Senegalese rice-and-peanut sauce can be found throughout West Africa, for example, and Ethiopian restaurants specializing in njera dishes are common in East African cities such as NAIROBI. Restaurants founded by African immigrants in Europe and the Americas have also popularized these cuisines abroad.

See also BIOGEOGRAPHY OF AFRICA; FISHERIES, AFRICAN; HUNGER AND FAMINE; PASTORALISM; STRUCTURAL ADJUSTMENT IN AFRICA; URBANISM AND URBANIZATION IN AFRICA.

ELIZABETH HEATH

Forestry, Participation, and Representation in Africa: An Interpretation

Participatory development aims to redress the failures and inequities of top-down centralized development strategies. But, what is community participation without representation? Does it redress central control? Does it include community in decision making, resource control, or benefits? Can there even be community participation without some form of locally accountable representation? Community or popular participation is about communities having decision-making powers or control over resources that affect the community as a whole, such as forests and grazing commons or community development. But for such decisions to internalize social and ecological costs or to assure equitable decision making and use, they must be devolved to a body representing and accountable to the community.

Across Africa responsibilities for natural resource management are being devolved to rural communities in the name of decentralization and popular participation. This movement is based on efficiency, equity, and development arguments in which community management is seen to improve performance in each of these spheres. But, a closer look at participation in West African forestry reveals that it is less inclusive than the name implies. In the wooded savannas and forests of the West African SAHEL participatory forestry projects and policies devolve a limited set of responsibilities and benefits to commercially interested, nonrepresentative groups and individuals, as well as to largely unaccountable state and nonstate local authorities. These local authorities are often given only a tangential role in decision making. Community participation, however, requires the devolution of real powers of decision to representative bodies.

This essay explores representation and decision making in so-called participatory forestry projects and policies in four Sahelian countries: BURKINO FASO, MALI, NIGER, and SENEGAL. It examines existing structures of representation in all four countries and then presents two sketches of how representation is integrated into participatory forestry. The essay concludes that participatory forestry does not integrate community representatives even in the few cases where such representatives exist. Without accountable representation, these participatory policies and projects become forms of covert privatization of forest use rights or a modern reproduction of indirect COLONIAL RULE—replete with "participatory corvée" (forced labor). Real participation—in natural resource management as well as other activities which affect community well being—must begin with generalized rural democratization.

EXISTING STRUCTURES OF LOCAL REPRESENTATION

Village chiefs and the rural councils of local state governance structures are frequently taken to represent rural populations in participatory development and natural resource management projects. In the countries of the West African Sahel villages are the most common unit of social aggregation around which local use and management of woodlands is organized both by local populations and by outside agents. Each village, averaging 100 to 500 people, typically has a chief, and some have specialized chiefs overseeing forest use. There are also other poles of authority within villages, such as imams, marabouts, sorcerers, non–village-based pastoral chiefs, griots, heads of certain castes (hunters in Mali) and chiefs of the young (maasamari in Niger). Colonial rulers, however, relied primarily on village chiefs to carry out colonial dictates at the local level. While today these other figures are involved in resource management, most state and outside organizations still privilege chiefs as their primary village interface.

In all four countries most chiefs gain their position through inheritance via a male lineage tracing back to warriors, the founding family of the village, or families chosen by colonial powers to replace antagonistic local leaders. In Senegal and Burkina Faso there are state-sanctioned processes for choosing village chiefs. In Senegal village chiefs (usually the head of the hereditary male line) are elected by heads of households, who are virtually all male. In Burkina Faso each village is divided into committees of youth (men 18 to 50), elders (men over 50), and women (over 18). At national elections, each committee elects its representatives and these representatives constitute a village council. The village council then elects from its members a village council president. All of these processes systematically underrepresent or exclude women, but to a much lesser degree in Burkina Faso, where women have one-third of the village vote.

In Mali, Niger, and Senegal chiefs hold their position for life. They neither represent nor are they systematically accountable to the village as a whole. In Burkina Faso the process for choosing village council presidents appears more accountable, due to regular periodic elections.

Although there are various local mechanisms of account-ability, they are not infallible; some chiefs are despots and others are responsive leaders.

In addition to village chiefs, Burkina Faso, Mali, Niger, and Senegal (like most African countries) have established local units of representative government. In these four cases, the smallest unit of government regroups five to fifty villages, similar in scale to U.S. counties. These local governments have both elected governance bodies, called rural councils, and an appointed central administrator, called a prefect.

In Burkina Faso the rural council is constituted from elected representatives of village committees, who in turn elect a president among themselves. In the other three countries the candidates for rural councils are presented for election by nationally registered political parties. Each party presents a list (or slate) of candidates to fill each council. The list with the majority of votes takes the council and elects a president from among its members. While there is universal suffrage, independent candidates cannot run for election to these councils (nor can any individual or group present lists without a party's endorsement). Since villagers lack the resources to form or even influence national political parties, they are unable to choose their own candidates. Not surprisingly, many villagers therefore feel that rural councils do not represent them, but rather the national parties.

The official role of rural councils in all four countries is to advise and assist the prefect on political and adminis-trative matters. Decisions of the rural councils of local governments must be approved by the prefect. So, even in Burkina Faso, where rural councils are relatively represen-tative of local populations, they are simply not autono-mous decision-making bodies.

PARTICIPATORY FORESTRY POLICIES AND PROJECTS

Given the limitations on existing forms of representa-tion, how do "participatory" policies and projects con-struct local control? Who makes decisions and who benefits? Below are thumbnail sketches of current partici-patory approaches. In Burkina Faso, as in Niger, projects are creating village-level participatory structures, while Mali, like Senegal, is using local government as the basis for participatory forestry.

BURKINA FASO: PARTICIPATION BY COMMITTEE IN NAZINON

Burkina's new participatory forestry laws are modeled on a joint United Nations Development Program and Food and Agricultural Organization project in the forest of Nazinon, thirty miles south of the capital, OUAGADOUGOU. This scheme is based on the creation of village cooperatives, all coordinated by a union, in the area surrounding the forest of Nazinon. In each village the project created a coopera-tive, composed of villagers interested in wood fuel produc-tion, which would then take responsibility for forest management. Each cooperative elected a president, secre-tary, treasurer, and manager. All these officers became members of the General Assembly of the union of Nazinon cooperatives. The union's administrative council, constituted of the cooperative managers and a president elected from the General Assembly, makes daily adminis-trative and business decisions for the union and is respon-sible for surveying the implementation of all laws concerning the union and forest management.

The national Forest Service has set up a technical office for the union, which develops forest management plans in collaboration with the administrative council. Pending approval by the Forest Service, each cooperative's manager is charged with assuring a plan's implementation, under the guidance of the technical office. In addition, an over-arching control committee, composed primarily of national-level government officials as well as a village representative, surveys both the union's and individual cooperatives' accounts.

In general, the new policies place some responsibilities for and powers over wood fuel management into the hands of a group of economically interested indivi-duals—namely, local villagers. But decisions over the man-agement of forests and revenues from forest exploitation are subject to the approval of the Forest Service, which also sets the rules governing where and how production and management take place. The village representative is only one voice among many on the national control committee, which in any case makes no decisions over forest use. In short, little control is devolved to "local" authorities. It stays with the Forest Service and private groups.

MALI: PARTICIPATION THROUGH LOCAL GOVERNMENT

Mali's 1994 forestry laws assign responsibilities for forest management to local government (called Decentralized Territorial Collectives). The new laws give local govern-ments a forested domain within their territorial jurisdic-tion, and the right to protect or conserve part or all of this domain. Any individual or group wishing to cut for wood for commercial use within the forest domain of a local government must organize a rural Wood Management Structure (WMS—Structure Rurale de Gestion de Bois). A WMS can be a cooperative, corporation, association, or any other form of organization recognized by the state. Typically, they are groups of private individuals interested in practicing or investing in commercial woodcutting.

Before a WMS can begin using the forest, the Forest Service must propose a management plan for approval by the local government. This plan includes an annual wood fuel production quota which, according to forestry officials, is to be determined by the "sustainable potential production" of the forested domain in question. The annual quota will be set by an ad hoc commission composed of two WMS representatives, one member of the local government, and one member of the Forest Service. Recognizing the contentious political nature of quota allocation, the new laws also create a ministry-appointed regional commission to resolve conflicts over quota size and distribution. Finally, once a management plan and quota have been established and approved, a WMS pays a forest exploitation tax and receives a cutting permit from the Forest Service.

Mali's new participatory forestry laws, replacing a system in which the Forest Service delivered permits to whom, where, and when it chose, give local governments considerable power over the disposition of forests. Indeed, Mali has developed the most progressive forestry laws in the Sahelian region. Local government representatives can decide to protect the forests by decree or they can control exploitation through approval or rejection of forest management plans. They can also use these powers to control which WMSs can exploit local forests. The Forest Service, however, uses quotas and management plans to maintain control over how much wood can be cut, where, when, and how.

As in Burkina Faso, Mali's local government representative on the quota committee is only one among four members and is not guaranteed a controlling role. Authority over quota allocation on this committee falls to the regional governor, a central government appointee. The Forest Service has also reserved the role of quota dispute resolution for itself, a role better fit for a more neutral body, such as the court system.

In short, in Mali some significant powers have been devolved to local government bodies, but they are weakened by two factors. First, since independent candidates cannot present themselves for local elections, local government is not representative or locally accountable—so these "local" decisions are not necessarily community decisions. Second, jurisdiction over some forests has not been devolved locally, but rather to intermediate-level governance structures, such as Cercles and Regions; many forests, in fact, remain under the control of the central government. Decentralization has also occasionally led to the creation of incompatible or contradictory regulations.

PARTICIPATION BY WHOM IN WHAT?

Who participates in what benefits? The benefits in these cases include income from cutting and/or selling wood fuel and some role in forest decision making. Employment opportunities in woodcutting are important to village communities, since this work has often gone to migrant or urban workers. Integrating local labor increases village income, as do profits from the sale of wood. In Burkina Faso, firewood prices fixed by the minister of commerce keep prices in participatory projects above those received by independent woodcutters. These opportunities and profits go largely to the members of management committees and woodcutting organizations. As membership is self-selected or influenced by foresters and village elites, these are effectively private organizations.

Some benefits from local forestry management are directed at the community as a whole. In Burkina Faso, each cooperative has a fund fed by a firewood tax, part of which is earmarked for village public works projects. In Niger, 10 percent of non-tax revenues from woodfuel sales go to the village chief—this too is ostensibly to benefit the community as a whole.

While some villagers benefit from labor opportunities, local wood fuel sales, and fees collected for community funds, most profit in West African wood fuel markets accrues through access to transport and urban trade. Unfortunately, the national Forest Services have all maintained tight control over transport permits and have refused to help local woodcutters acquire transport or merchant licenses. Villagers in all four countries have expressed their desire to operate in transport and urban sales, but these lucrative trades are currently dominated by urban merchants and truckers. In short, villagers are permitted to "participate" in forest management and use, but only receive a fraction of forest-based profits.

Who participates in decisions? In all four countries, local participatory structures participate in the daily decisions of plan implementation and have some control over the plans. But the rules of cutting and management that they must follow and the quantities they can cut are defined by the Forest Services, based largely on questionable ecological grounds.

The most critical decision, whether forests surrounding a given community will or will not be cut, has been reserved by Forest Services in all cases but Mali. In Mali's new forestry laws, rural councils have the definitive right to protect all or any of their forested domain (although the proportion of forests in the local domain is determined by a national committee). In Burkina Faso, Niger, and Senegal, the Forest Service can grant woodcutting rights to anyone they choose, regardless of local wishes. Moreover, communities in project areas that do not agree to the conditions of "participation," as well as those simply not chosen for projects, have no legal control over the disposition of forest resources: Forest Services can sell the forests out from under them. These local governments and village communities simply do not have the right to say "no" to cutting in surrounding forests sanctioned by the Forest Service. This is hardly "participatory" forestry.

In short, participation amounts to the Forest Services managing forests with the assistance of private groups within local communities, with increased employment and opportunities and profit for these private groups and some income earmarked for community benefit. Critical decisions over forest disposition are only devolved into "local" hands in Mali—but only over limited areas of forest.

ECOLOGY OF CENTRAL CONTROL

Forest Service control of woodcutting may seem to make ecological sense. Indeed, the maintenance of Forest Service control over management plans and quotas is often supported on "technical" ecological grounds—to protect the national good. But the ecological evidence does not support the need for central management. Sahelian vegetation is resilient. What little evidence has been collected indicates robust natural regeneration after woodcutting. Villagers and woodcutters in each country say they return to cut in the same area after five to twelve years; they are not cutting gallery forests. The main human cause of permanent deforestation in this zone is agricultural expansion. But since foresters do not have control over agricultural policy, they instead focus their attention on woodcutting—even if it is not the problem. In any case, wood fuels in this region are not scarce, so micromanagement—to accelerate regeneration—is not necessary.

If central management of forest resources cannot be justified on ecological grounds, why does it persist? National governments, Forest Services, and state agents in all four countries have long profited, both legally and illicitly, from forest control. Forest Services therefore have good reason to argue for continued central control on technical ecological grounds: it helps them maintain a long-standing stake in this lucrative sector. It also happens to attract donor financing. Yet throughout the West African Sahel, much more forest control could be devolved to local communities without threatening the forests.

REPRESENTATION WITH OR WITHOUT PARTICIPATION

Without locally accountable representation the ostensible objectives of participatory approaches are unlikely to be met. There are no guarantees that the social or ecological "externalities" of commercial forestry will be internalized, and there is a great risk that the benefits will not return to the community as a whole.

Devolving control or decision-making powers to non-accountable or nonrepresentative bodies or individuals (such as hereditary or male elite picked chiefs, party picked local councils, cooperatives, village associations, or nongovernmental organizations) is just a new, slightly obscured, form of "privatization" via privatized use rights. It is not devolution to the community as a whole. Rather it gives powers over community resources—and power to profit from them—to community subgroups.

Participation without representation is tantamount to forced labor when it involves responsibilities without choice. By assigning responsibilities in the name of participation, for example, Senegal's new forestry laws give the Forest Service the means to mobilize rural labor. It does so with no checks or balances, creating a potential for what might be dubbed "participatory corvée." Further, when villagers' alternative to participating is the potential loss of forests to outsiders, labor in "participatory" forestry can hardly be considered voluntary.

Further, participation is a modern reproduction of indirect rule when it uses local nonstate authorities to legitimate and carry out state and international organizations' projects, which include but are not limited to environmental management. Like colonial rule, participation can also strengthen and legitimate the nonrepresentative, unaccountable governance structures it relies on. Governments, NGOs and donor agencies involved in participatory approaches must therefore ask themselves if they are unwittingly supporting projects that are actually undermining the ostensible goals of participation. Indeed, by problematizing local representation, these groups could support the emergence of more genuinely democratic rural governance processes.

Conditions for locally accountable representation—for example, local elections that allow independent candidates—are necessary to guarantee generalized rural participation. Such conditions do not guarantee community inclusion; rural elites can always try to manipulate electoral processes as well as elected officials. Nor do such conditions guarantee that local representatives will, in fact, always act accountably. They simply make it a possible outcome of struggle among village classes, castes, and interest groups. Some communities will take advantage of this possibility. Others will not. Unfortunately, given the electoral codes in most of the Sahel, this possibility does not yet exist.

With locally accountable representation, participation becomes meaningful, provided these representatives have powers of decision over valuable resources. In Mali local government has some real powers, but is not representative. In Burkina Faso there is accountable (although gender-biased) representation, but no local decision-making powers. Representation without powers is as much of a farce as powers without representation: popular participation requires both.

See also COASTAL RESOURCES IN AFRICA; CONSERVATION IN AFRICA; FISHERIES, AFRICAN.

JESSE RIBOT

Forros
Dominant Creole population of São Tomé and Príncipe; also known as *filhos da terra*.

Shortly after their discovery in the late fifteenth century, the islands of São Tomé and Príncipe, which lie off the coast of GABON in the Gulf of Guinea, were settled by Portuguese—mostly criminals expelled from their homeland—and African slaves brought there as laborers on the islands' sugar plantations. The first governor of the new colonies—now known as SÃO TOMÉ AND PRÍNCIPE—dictated that each Portuguese convict be given a slave woman as his wife. Their mixed-race children, known as mestiços, occupied a privileged position—some were sent abroad for an education—and were the ancestors of today's forros. Many prospered as traders and later, at the beginning of the coffee and cocoa boom in the nineteenth century, some took over the old sugar plantations to become successful farmers.

By the turn of the century, Portuguese landowners had foreclosed on these lucrative cocoa estates and had driven the forros into a marginal position in the island's plantation economy. During the 1930s, faced with the loss of workers due to laws designed to prevent conscripted African labor, the Portuguese who controlled the colonial government imposed taxes and other legal constraints aimed to force the forros into manual labor on the plantations, work they had historically disdained as beneath them.

It was the middle-class forros, frustrated by their lack of representation in the colonial government and angered at its policies, who initiated the Sãotoméan nationalist movement. Since Portugal granted São Tomé its independence in 1975, forros have dominated the islands. São Tomé's first president, Manuel Pinto da Costa, came from one of the islands' oldest forros families, as did its second president, Miguel Trovoada. Speaking a Portuguese Creole and preserving traditional West African music and dance, the forros are the descendants of the island's earliest inhabitants and consider themselves the only true Sãotoméans. Forros culture, in particular the tchiloli, a ritual theatrical dance, defines Sãotoméan national identity to this day. Approximately 70,000 people consider themselves Forros.

See also COLONIAL RULE; ; DANCE IN SUB-SAHARAN AFRICA.

BIBLIOGRAPHY
Hodges, Tony, and Malyn Newitt. São Tomé and Príncipe: From Plantation Colony to Microstate. Westview Press, 1988.

KATE TUTTLE

Fouta Djallon
Region of Guinea that functioned as an autonomous Islamic state during the nineteenth century.

Now mainly a geographic reference to the central Guinean highlands, Fouta Djallon also refers to an independent state that existed within the borders of present-day GUINEA from the mid-1700s to the late 1800s. The region had been home to the YALUNKA (Jallonke) people since around the eleventh century. The Yalunka, who were mostly farmers, were part of the MANDINKA or Malinke ethnic group. They practiced a traditional religion. In the fifteenth century, members of another ethnic group, the FULANI, began to enter the region peacefully. Starting in the seventeenth century, Fulani people (also known as Fulbe, or Peul) from the Futa Toro empire in the area presently known as SENEGAL began entering the Fouta Djallon, bringing with them the Islamic faith.

The Muslim Fulani gradually conquered the entire Fouta Djallon and, despite their inferior numbers, became the dominant group, using both Yalunka and non-Muslim Fulani as slaves. In addition, the Muslim Fulani built a highly structured religious state, organizing a federation of seven provinces known as diwals under the ultimate control of a head of state known as the alimami. The position of alimami alternated between two leading families, the Alfyas and Soriyas, an arrangement that succeeded for more than one hundred years.

Contact with European traders and colonialists began as early as the 1790s, when British expeditions, based in SIERRA LEONE, began to explore the interior. By the 1830s, historian Winston McGowan says, the French, based in Senegal, started trying to establish connections with Fouta Djallon. This interest was based in part on the area's abundant resources, which included gold, ivory, coffee, rice, and cattle. In addition, Fouta Djallon had a strategic location along the trade route connecting the upper NIGER RIVER basin with the coastline.

By the 1880s, competition between British and French authorities prompted each colonial power to seek an exclusive relationship with the ruling alimamis. In 1881 the alimamis signed an ambiguous treaty with the French. The French held that the document placed Fouta Djallon under French possession or protection, while the alimamis intended it merely as an acknowledgment of friendly relations. In 1893, bowing to pressure from Fouta Djallon, the French offered a new treaty conforming to the alimamis' interpretation.

Despite the diplomatic, administrative, and scholarly prowess of its people, the state of Fouta Djallon began to break down in the 1890s. Internal divisions, particularly between the two dynasties that had long shared power, played a part in this. The constant pressure of negotiations with colonial powers further weakened Fouta Djallon solidarity, as the Fulani disagreed among themselves how much to aid anticolonial efforts, including those of Samory TOURÉ, the Mandinka freedom fighter. The area is still known as the home of Guinea's Fulani people, who continue to practice Islam and raise cattle. The largest city in the region is Labé, which as of 2008 was home to more than 58,000.

See also SLAVERY IN AFRICA.

BIBLIOGRAPHY

Harrison, Christopher. *France and Islam in West Africa, 1860–1960.* Cambridge University Press, 1988.

Fredericks, Frankie

1967–

Namibian sprinter, winner of four Olympic silver medals.

Frankie Fredericks was a talented athlete as a youth, but he never expected to be in the Olympic Games. Until 1990 his country, NAMIBIA, was a colony of SOUTH AFRICA, which had been banned from Olympic competition because of its policy of APARTHEID. Yet Fredericks, who has become one of the world's premiere sprinters, has brought four Olympic medals home to Namibia.

An only child, Fredericks was raised by his mother in Katutura township, just outside the Namibian capital, WINDHOEK. His mother worked several jobs to send Fredericks to private schools, where he excelled in both soccer and academics. In high school he started running track, specializing in sprinting. He won both the 100- and 200-meter races in the South African school championships his senior year. After graduating, Fredericks passed up several college scholarship offers to accept a management training position with the Rossing Uranium Mine Company. The company sponsored Fredericks's education at Brigham Young University in the United States, where he enrolled in 1987.

At Brigham Young, Fredericks earned degrees in computer science and business administration and also became the national collegiate champion in his two sprint events in 1991. When Namibia gained its independence in 1990, the ban on its international competition was lifted, and Fredericks carried the flag for the Namibian team in the 1992 Olympic Games in Barcelona, Spain. He won silver medals in the 100- and 200-meter events.

In international competition leading up to the 1996 Olympic Games, Fredericks not only ended Michael Johnson's unbeaten two-year streak with a personal best of 19.82 seconds in the 200-meter sprint, but he also came within one one-hundredth of a second of breaking the world record in the 100-meter. Fredericks won two silver medals in the Atlanta games, coming in second behind Donovan Bailey in the 100-meter sprint and Johnson in the 200-meter. Fredericks continued to compete into the early twenty-first century, placing second in the mens' 100-meter sprint at an international track-and-field meet in Great Britain in 2003. He retired from active competition in 2004.

See also ATHLETES, AFRICAN, ABROAD.

KATE TUTTLE

Free African Society

Established in the eighteenth century, one of the first African American religious organizations to provide blacks with a place of worship and a place to meet and organize politically.

The Free African Society was founded in Philadelphia, Pennsylvania, by black Methodists Richard Allen and Absalom Jones in 1787. They founded the society in response to a decision by white members of St. George's Methodist Episcopal Church to enforce racial segregation at church services. The society's stated purpose was to enhance the quality of life for African Americans, but its immediate objective was to create a space for African Americans to worship and organize. During its five-year existence, the society was run entirely by African Americans. Although the society was nondenominational, it maintained ties to both the Quakers and the Methodist Church. The society supported the abolitionist movement, opposed proposals for black emigration and colonization, and worked to ameliorate tensions between blacks and whites. As the society grew, it collected regular membership dues, and in Quaker tradition, formed a visiting committee to make sure that all members conformed to the society's strict code of conduct. The society became even more closely associated with Quaker practices when, in November 1789, members voted to begin meetings with fifteen minutes of silent prayer. During the Philadelphia yellow fever epidemic of 1793, the Free African Society suspended activities and society members worked as nurses and undertakers as a gesture of goodwill toward the white community. After the epidemic, members were divided over the question of affiliation with the Quakers and the Methodist Church, and the society dissolved. In 1794, Allen founded the Bethel African Methodist Episcopal Church, the "mother church" of the African Methodist Episcopal Church. In the same year, Jones founded the African Episcopal Church of Saint Thomas.

BIBLIOGRAPHY
Douglass, William. Annals of the First African Church in the United States of America, Now Styled the African Episcopal Church of St. Thomas, Philadelphia. King & Baird, 1862.

ALONFORD JAMES ROBINSON, JR.

Free State

Province in central South Africa, bounded by the Vaal River in the north and the Mohokare (Caledon) and Orange rivers in the south.

Created in 1994, Free State has retained the same boundaries as the Orange Free State, one of the former provinces of SOUTH AFRICA. It covers 129,480 sq km (49,993 sq mi) and includes two former bantustans (or black homelands)—Qwaqwa and one section of BOPHUTHATSWANA. Free State is surrounded by LESOTHO and six other South African provinces.

Free State is located on the High Veld, the large plateau that covers much of the central region of South Africa. The far western part of the province is flat and sparsely vegetated, while in the far east the land rises to the Drakensberg Mountains. The rest of the province consists of rolling plains. Average temperatures range from 16° to 31° C (60° to 88° F) in the summer and from 1° to 18° C (34° to 64° F) in the winter. Average annual rainfall totals 360 mm (14 in) with most of the rain falling in the warmer months, from October to April. The eastern part of the province receives considerably more rain than the western region.

As of 2006 Free State had a population of some 2.9 million. Most of the residents are black Africans. Sesotho and Setswana, two Bantu languages, are the principal languages; Afrikaans, English, and XHOSA are also spoken. The provincial capital and largest city of Free State is Bloemfontein, which is the site of the Appellate Division of the Supreme Court. The main campus of the University of the Orange Free State (1855) is located in Bloemfontein. Other important towns are Virginia, Jagers fontein, Odendaalsrus, and Welkom, all gold mining towns; Kroonstad, Harrismith, and Bethlehem, towns that service the agricultural sector; Sasolburg, which features a massive coal-to-oil conversion plant; and Phuthaditjhaba.

Significant historical sites in the province include the National Women's Memorial in Bloemfontein, which commemorates AFRIKANER women and children who died in concentration camps during the Boer War (1899–1902); the Bloemfontein home of J. B. M. Hertzog, who was prime minister of South Africa from 1924 to 1939; the towns of Bethulie and Philippolis, which were mission stations of the London Missionary Society; and Thaba Nchu (which means "black mountain"), the site of the nineteenth-century mountain fortress of Chief Moroka's Barolong people. Golden Gate Highlands National Park, established in 1963, is in the southeastern part of Free State.

Agriculture is a mainstay of the Free State economy, with many farmers raising sheep and dairy cattle. The leading crop, maize (corn), is mainly grown in the northern part of the province. Cherries and asparagus are produced near the town of Ficksburg, on the southern border with Lesotho. Gold mining, which has been the cornerstone of industrial development in the province since World War II (1939–1945), employs many people. Diamonds, coal, and uranium are also mined in Free State. Free State's provincial government consists of a premier, an executive council of ten ministers, and a legislature. The provincial assembly and premier are elected for five-year terms or until the next national election. Political parties are awarded assembly seats on the basis of the percentage of votes each party receives in the province during the national elections. The assembly elects a premier, who then appoints the members of the executive council.

Freedom Charter

Document written in 1955 by the African National Congress (ANC) and other antiapartheid groups to express their goals for a free South Africa.

After SOUTH AFRICA's NATIONAL PARTY won its second term in power in 1953, Z. K. Matthews, a regional leader of the AFRICAN NATIONAL CONGRESS, proposed a symbolic act of opposition to the National Party's APARTHEID regime. Like many within the ANC, Matthews was uncomfortable with the more militant actions of the ANC Youth League and its founders, Nelson MANDELA, Oliver TAMBO, and others. With government harassment threatening to force the ANC underground, Matthews hoped to reprise the organization's role as the public, national voice opposing apartheid. He called for a national convention "representing all the people of this country irrespective of race or colour, to draw up a Freedom Charter for the democratic South Africa of the future."

On June 25, 1955, more than 3,000 delegates, representing about 200 organizations, met at Kliptown, a multiracial village outside JOHANNESBURG. The intervening two years had been spent planning for the Congress of the People, as it was called, by soliciting the ideas and opinions of average South Africans. Thousands of fliers asking, "If you could make the laws, what would you do?" had been distributed. Armed with the people's wishes, the congress delegates—the majority of whom were members of the ANC, the South African Coloured People's Association, the South African Indian Congress, and a white antiapartheid group called the Congress of Democrats—drafted the Freedom Charter.

The charter affirmed in its preamble that "South Africa belongs to all who live in it, black and white," then set forth ten main propositions, including "The People Shall Govern," "All Shall Be Equal before the Law," and "There Shall Be Peace and Freedom." The charter also called for equality in education, freedom in land ownership, and equal access to jobs and housing. Although some criticized it for its apparent advocacy of socialist economic principles, the Freedom Charter was adopted as the ANC's official platform in 1956. Nearly thirty years later, Nelson Mandela hailed it as "a revolutionary document," one that represented "the people's demands to end the oppression."

KATE TUTTLE

Freetown, Sierra Leone
Capital of Sierra Leone.

Freetown lies near the tip of a mountainous peninsula on the Atlantic coast of SIERRA LEONE. Home to about half a million people before the civil war started in 1991, the city—the largest in Sierra Leone—more than doubled in size by 2006 with a population of 1,070,200 residents. Both African and European cultures have left their imprint on Freetown. The city is the cradle of the KRIO (or Creole) language and culture established by the descendants of freed slaves who intermarried with indigenous people. Freetown was the longest-lasting outpost of British COLONIAL RULE in West Africa. Fourah Bay College, established in 1816, has made Freetown a preeminent center of learning and intellectual life in West Africa for most of the last 200 years.

Freetown was established in 1787. British philanthropists chose the site as a place to send poor black people, mainly freed slaves from Britain, North America, and the Caribbean. In 1808 the town became the capital of the new British Crown Colony of Sierra Leone. The town served as the administrative center for all of Britain's West African possessions until the 1870s and as a headquarters for British naval forces engaged in intercepting the outlawed slave trade. Between 1808 and the 1860s thousands of people who were freed from slave ships settled there. By the 1840s the town was well established as a major center for trade, exporting palm oil, peanuts, gold, and hides. Freetown had excellent access to interior trade routes that were exploited by European, Krio, and other African traders. This trade attracted merchants and laborers from the surrounding area. Minerals—especially diamonds and bauxite—have surpassed agricultural products as the city's main exports since 1930.

During the 1990s, civil war repeatedly devastated Sierra Leone and Freetown. The fighting undermined Sierra Leone's infrastructure, economy, and civil liberties. In 1997 a military coup ousted democratically elected president Ahmad Tejan Kabbah, but on February 14, 1998, Nigerian troops liberated Freetown from the control of the military junta, and Kabbah returned in March to initiate the difficult process of reconstruction.

BIBLIOGRAPHY

Fyfe, Christopher. *Freetown: A Symposium.* University of Sierra Leone, 1968.

French Dahomey
Former name of Benin.
See BENIN.

French Equatorial Africa
Former French colony incorporating the following present-day nations: Chad, the Central African Republic, the Republic of the Congo, and Gabon.

French Guinea
Former name of Guinea.
See GUINEA.

French Somaliland
Former name of Djibouti.
See DJIBOUTI.

French Sudan
Former name of Mali.
See MALI.

French Togoland
Former name of Togo.
See TOGO.

French West Africa
Former French colony incorporating the following present-day nations: Benin, Burkina Faso, Côte d'Ivoire, Guinea, Mali, Mauritania, Niger, and Senegal.

Front de Libération Nationale
Algerian national independence organization.

"The struggle will be long, but the outcome is certain," declared the Front de Libération National (FLN) of ALGERIA in 1954. This proclamation marked the union of diverse nationalist groups—reformist, communist, and Islamicist—in a joint struggle for liberation from COLONIAL RULE. It also marked the beginning of one of Africa's bloodiest wars of independence, a war that drew international attention to Africa's struggle for decolonization. Algerian resistance to French rule dated back to ABD AL-QADIR's revolt in 1837, and nationalist sentiment had grown since the early twentieth century. The FLN broke from more reformist predecessors by declaring as its goal full "national independence through the restoration of the Algerian state, sovereign, democratic, and social, within the framework of the principles of Islam." The organization was prepared for armed struggle to achieve these ends; together with the Armée de Libération (ALN), it launched a brutal military campaign in August 1955. The French retaliated against an FLN-planned massacre in the town of Constantinois with a carnage justified by "collective responsibility." The severity of the French response only served to drive more Algerian groups into the FLN. Political exiles in MOROCCO and TUNISIA planned the struggle, while military units trained in isolated mountain sites. At the Soummam Congress in 1956, the FLN declared itself the sole representative of Algeria and launched an urban guerrilla campaign. Women played a significant role in this campaign—young women passing as French, or older domestic workers, dressed in traditional garments that offered scope for concealment, carried weapons and bombs into restricted French quarters. Soon French police, viewing all city residents as suspects, used brutal methods to eliminate resistance. The war of independence left hundreds of thousands of Algerians and thousands of French dead. The struggle was recorded for the world by FLN political theorist Frantz FANON, a psychiatrist from Martinique, and endorsed by such prominent intellectuals as France's Jean Paul Sartre. International pressure on France increased, and the colonial government finally began to move toward decolonization. After negotiations in 1960, the FLN and France reached the Evian Accords, which gave Algeria political autonomy while preserving some rights for French settlers there. But the French settler vigilante force, the Organisation de l'Armée Secrète (OAS), continued searching out and killing suspected FLN supporters even without the official support of the French government. Finally, a referendum granted full independence to Algeria in July 1962. FLN leader Ahmed BEN BELLA became the country's first prime minister. Following independence, solidarity among nationalists broke down, both within the FLN and among rival nationalist parties. The next year all other parties were banned, and the FLN remained the only legal party in Algeria until 1989.

See also ISLAM IN AFRICA.

MARIAN AGUIAR

Front for the Liberation of Mozambique

Mozambican revolutionary movement and political party.
The Frente da Libertaàão de Moàambique, or FRELIMO, led the movement against Portuguese COLONIAL RULE in the southeastern African nation of MOZAMBIQUE and has ruled the country since independence. FRELIMO formed in 1962 from a coalition of three nationalist organizations: the Mozambican National Democratic Union, the African Union of Independent Mozambique, and the Mozambican African National Union. As Portugal steadfastly opposed the decolonization sweeping the rest of Africa, the party's leaders, including its president, Eduardo Mondlane,

concluded that Mozambique would gain independence only through an armed struggle. FRELIMO launched that struggle in September 1964, supported by China and Eastern European countries that provided military assistance and training. Throughout the decade-long war, the party proclaimed its philosophy of national unity and remained the sole legitimate opposition group. Occasionally, however, FRELIMO experienced internal fragmentation, primarily due to regional differences among members. In 1975, Mozambique became independent under the leadership of Samora MACHEL and the FRELIMO party, which officially became a Marxist-Leninist "vanguard party" in 1977 and continued to uphold the ideals of nationalism and scientific socialism. As the ruling party, FRELIMO wavered between highly centralized administrative policies and efforts to empower the masses through grupos dinamizadores, party groups that would move throughout the country explaining the new political, legal, and social-services systems to the rural population. Most commentators agree that there was little, if any, difference between the party and the state. As with many Marxist parties in Africa, FRELIMO's membership remained small, confined primarily to employees of the state bureaucracy and state-run enterprises. At its Fifth Congress in 1989, FRELIMO dropped Marxist-Leninism. Since that time it has declared itself in favor of political liberalism and promoted a free market economy. Even after the beginning of multiparty electoral politics in 1992, however, FRELIMO retained its political dominance, winning 129 of 250 seats in the newly formed Assembly of the Republic in the 1994 elections.

BIBLIOGRAPHY

Azevedo, Mario Joaquim. *Historical Dictionary of Mozambique.* Scarecrow Press, 1991.

Hall, Margaret, and Tom Young. *Confronting Leviathan: Mozambique since Independence.* Ohio University Press, 1997.

ERIC YOUNG

Fugard, Athol

1932–

South African playwright.

Athol Fugard plays deal with the personal wounds inflicted by the strict policy of racial segregation known as APARTHEID, which was law for many years in his home nation of SOUTH AFRICA. He is best known for his plays *Blood Knot* and *Master Harold . . . and the Boys*, which have brought images of life under apartheid to a wide audience.

Fugard was born near Middleburg, South Africa. The child of an English father and an AFRIKANER mother, Fugard grew up in Port Elizabeth, the Cape Province city where most of his plays are set. He studied philosophy and anthropology at the University of CAPE TOWN, but left school just before graduating to hitchhike the length of Africa. He spent the next two years working on a steamship.

Returning to South Africa in 1956, Fugard married Sheila Meiring, an actress whom he credits for developing his interest in theater. In 1958 he became a clerk for the Fordsburg Native Commissioner's Court. The court handled cases of people accused of violating the PASS LAWS, which were among the many laws restricting Africans' right to live and work where they pleased. Fugard called the job "the ugliest thing I have ever been part of," but it also gave him the intimate view of apartheid's cruelty that became a key element in his work.

By 1959 Fugard had written and produced two plays, No-Good Friday and Nongogo, and he and his wife moved to London to gain theatrical experience. They stayed only a year, returning to South Africa after the SHARPEVILLE MASSACRE in 1960. Fugard's next play, The Blood Knot, opened in 1961 with Fugard and an African actor, Zakes Mokae, playing two mixed-race half brothers confronting the psychological costs of official racism. At the same time Fugard began protesting the official segregation of theater audiences.

In 1967 the South African government seized Fugard's passport and placed him under surveillance. But the harassment did not stop Fugard from collaborating in 1972 with black actor-playwrights John Kani and Winston Ntshona on Sizwe Banzi Is Dead and The Island, each of which was nominated for three Tony Awards. His 1982 play Master Harold . . . and the Boys concerns the relationships between a privileged white boy and his family's black servants.

Considered one of the best playwrights in the English-speaking world, Fugard continues to write and produce plays. He is the author of the plays The Road to Mecca (1985), Playland (1993), Valley Song (1995), and The Captain's Tiger (1998). In Sorrows and Rejoicings (2001), Fugard dealt with issues of race in post-apartheid South Africa. He has also published the novel Tsotsi (1980) and the nonfiction volumes Notebooks 1960–1977 (1983) and Cousins: A Memoir (1998). More recent works include Exits and Entrances (2004), Victory (2007), and Coming Home (2009). Fugard is currently on the faculty at the University of California, San Diego, School of Theatre and Dance.

See also THEATER, AFRICAN.

KATE TUTTLE

Fulani

Pastoral people of West Africa widely dispersed through parts of Senegal, Guinea, Mali, Niger, Nigeria, and Cameroon, with smaller numbers in surrounding countries; also known as Peul, Fula, and Fellata.

The Fulani inhabit a vast territory stretching from SENEGAL on the Atlantic coast to the CENTRAL AFRICAN REPUBLIC to the east. Throughout this region, however, they live side by side with other peoples, and they do not form a majority in any of the countries they inhabit. The Fulani are the only cattle-raising people in West Africa.

The Fulani are the most thoroughly pastoral people of West Africa: more than half of them raise livestock, to varying degrees of exclusivity. Early explorers and researchers noted the cultural and physical differences between the Fulani and neighboring African groups. The Fulani themselves are keenly aware of their distinctive physical appearance: some have relatively fair skin, long hair and aquiline features. The popular image of the Fulani is that they are the cattle keepers of West Africa. However, many Fulani today have adopted settled agricultural or urban livelihoods.

Traditionally, the pastoral Fulani have practiced varying degrees of nomadism. Some have migrated widely in search of water and pasture for their herds, while others have migrated seasonally between summer pasture and a more settled winter existence, which has often included crop cultivation. The Fulani have traditionally exchanged dairy products for cereals and vegetables produced by neighboring agricultural peoples. The Fulani reckon descent patrilineally; lineage groups form the basis for the social organization of the pastoral Fulani. Until the seventeenth century, the highest level of political organization among the pastoral Fulani was the autonomous band with its headman. Although some pastoral Fulani maintain traditional animist beliefs, the majority has adopted Islam.

Scholars believe that the Fulani originated in the grasslands surrounding the valley of the SENEGAL RIVER, in the area known today as Senegal. This belief rests on both historical evidence and the similarities between the Fulani language, Fulfulde (also known as Pulaar, Fula, and Peul), and the languages of the SERER and the WOLOF of Senegal. These languages belong to the West Atlantic group of Niger-Congo languages.

Until the eleventh century, the Fulani practiced a traditional pastoral lifestyle on the western fringes of the ancient kingdom of GHANA. With the fall of Ghana in the eleventh century, a new Islamic state, known as Tekrur, arose in the Senegal valley, and some Fulani for the first time adopted a settled existence. They merged with the settled population to form a Fulfulde-speaking subgroup known as the Tukolor. By the fourteenth century, Fulani groups had begun a gradual migration southward and eastward from their original homeland. By the fifteenth century they had arrived in the FOUTA DJALLON region of present-day GUINEA and in the Macina region of present-day MALI. A century later, pastoral Fulani had reached Hausaland and Bornu in northern present-day NIGERIA. By the eighteenth century the Fulani had taken up herding on the northern grasslands of present-day CAMEROON.

As the Fulani migrated throughout West Africa over the centuries, significant differences emerged among the different groups who considered themselves as Fulani. Most Fulani, known as the Fulani bororo, or "cattle Fulani," maintained a traditional pastoral existence. Others, however, known as the Fulani gida, or "town Fulani," took up a settled existence in the towns of kingdoms such as Mali, SONGHAI, and especially the HAUSA STATES.

Over the centuries, Fulani groups increasingly adopted forms of Islam practiced by neighboring peoples. As they migrated eastward, the rulers of powerful states such as Songhai and the states of Hausaland exacted fees and taxes from both Fulani herdsmen and Fulani merchants living in towns. During the sixteenth century, Fulani began to adopt radical, Sufi-influenced forms of Islam. These included the Qadiriyya and Tijaniyah orders that were carried across the SAHARA by the TUAREG, who had come to dominate the region around TOMBOUCTOU. These Islamic sects maintained the right of believers to rebel against unjust rulers in order to create a society according to Islamic principles.

These Islamic sects inspired reform movements led by Fulani, often with support from neighboring peoples, who advocated jihad, or holy war, to replace rulers perceived as corrupt and greedy with an austere and devout Muslim theocracy. The first Fulani jihad replaced the MANDE rulers of Bondu, in present-day western Mali, with a Fulani theocracy in the late seventeenth century. During the eighteenth century the Fulani established similar theocracies in Fouta Djallon and the Futa Toro region of present-day Senegal. The most famous and powerful of the Fulani theocracies, however, was the SOKOTO CALIPHATE of present-day northern Nigeria. This vast empire arose as the result of a jihad led by a Fulani cleric, USUMAN DAN FODIO, against the Hausa states during the early nineteenth century. Soon thereafter, a Fulani theocracy established control in the Macina region. During the mid-nineteenth century the religiously inspired Fulani and Tukolor, led by UMAR TAL, established a state that controlled most of present-day Mali.

In each of these states, Fulani gida occupied positions of religious and secular leadership. Fulani remain prominent throughout much of this region today. In northern Nigeria the Fulani gida have gradually merged with wealthy Hausa to form an ethnic group sometimes called Hausa-Fulani. This group remains the effective ruling class of northern Nigeria.

There are certain key features common to both Fulani bororo and Fulani gida. The first of these is Fulfulde, the language of the Fulani. Although the basic language is the same throughout West Africa, there are regional dialectal differences, and in all areas the Fulani borrow words from neighboring languages. A second feature common to the Fulani is a common moral and ethical code known as Pulaaku. Though the Fulani's wide geographic dispersal makes it difficult to estimate their population, it is estimated that 10 million to 15 million (if not more) people in West Africa speak Fulfulde.

See also GHANA, EARLY KINGDOM OF; LANGUAGES, AFRICAN: AN OVERVIEW.

YAA POKUA AFRIYIE OPPONG

Fulse

Ethnic group of West Africa; also known as Foulse.

The Fulse primarily inhabit west central BURKINA FASO. They speak a Niger-Congo language and belong to the Grusi cultural and linguistic group. Approximately 100,000 people consider themselves Fulse.

See also LANGUAGES, AFRICAN: AN OVERVIEW.

Fur

Ethnic group of the Sudan with an estimated population of more than one million.

The Fur live mostly in the region of SUDAN called Western Darfur, which is named for the Fur people. People living in the Western Darfur region were probably ethnically related to the peoples of the NILE valley. Egyptian Christian missionaries brought their religion to the area by about 900 C.E. But this early Christian influence was eclipsed by the arrival of Islamic peoples in the twelfth and thirteenth centuries.

History records the existence of the DARFUR state in the early seventeenth century, founded by a man known as Sulayman. A member of the Keira Dynasty, Sulayman was identified as an Arab Muslim. During the early years of Darfur, Islamic rulers used the word Fur to describe the indigenous, non-Islamic inhabitants of the region. A gradual process of intermarriage and religious conversion created a new Fur identity among an Islamic, Afro-Arab population.

Darfur played a prominent role in the African slave trade, making slaves of some of the smaller ethnic groups to the south. Along with the state at Funj, the Darfur state was defeated in the nineteenth century by combined Turkish-Egyptian forces, but it was partially restored by British colonial forces. It was not until just after World War I (1914–1919) that Darfur was completely politically incorporated into Sudan. The split between an Arab-identified, Islamic north and the non-Arab, largely Christian south continued to be a major conflict in Sudan's domestic politics in the twentieth century. For most of the twentieth century, most Fur practiced subsistence farming of millet, tomatoes, and peanuts. Increasingly, they made a living in the cash economy by growing exportable crops such as tobacco and cotton.

G

Ga

Ethnic group of southeastern Ghana.

Indigenous inhabitants of Ghana's coast, the Ga are one of the major ethnic groups of GHANA and the founders of the capital city of ACCRA. They speak a language of the Kwa branch of the Niger-Congo language family and are closely related to the neighboring ADANGBE, who speak a similar language.

Legend states that the Ga people arrived from the east, in a series of land and sea migrations, before the fourteenth century; however, linguistic and archaeological evidence suggests that the ancestors of the Ga occupied their present homeland for more than a thousand years. In the Ga language, the name Ga refers both to the Ga people and to the city of Accra.

Before the arrival of Europeans, the Ga lived in villages along the coast, where they fished, and inland, where they cultivated root crops, oil palms, and plantains. Coastal Ga traded fish with inland Ga for agricultural products. Men fished and raised crops while women dominated trade. Villages were organized by kinship ties. Each village was divided into seven residences, or *akutsei*, which were in turn divided into smaller kinship units, called *we*. Each of the seven *akutsei* had a chief, who wielded limited power. Priests, called *wulomei*, exercised authority over the Ga. Wulomei maintain considerable influence today, even though the Ga are now largely Christian. Village elders also held significant influence.

As a patrilineal society, a Ga individual's social rank and condition usually depended upon his or her father's position. However, girls could inherit property from their mother and married adults often continued to live with their parents, a pattern that still persists. Agricultural and fishing cycles, as well as the forces of nature, held prominent places in Ga worship. Boys underwent ritual circumcision. Funerals were the most elaborate rite of passage.

With the arrival of the Portuguese in the fifteenth century, the trade in gold from the AKAN homeland to the north shifted toward the coast. Subsequently, Akan peoples sought to extend control over the Ga as a means of securing direct access to trade opportunities. Probably in order to defend themselves, the Ga adopted centralized kingships modeled after those of the Akan. Like Akan kingships, the main Ga towns—Accra, Osu, Labadi, Teshi, Nungua, and Tema—each held stools, which symbolized unity and power. Okai Koi, who ruled from about 1610 to 1660, extended his rule over all Ga territory and fought the Akwamu, an Akan people. Okai Koi committed suicide in 1660 after suffering defeat by the Akwamu. By 1680 the Akwamu had incorporated the Ga as a vassal state.

With the construction of several forts in and around Accra beginning in 1650, the Europeans gradually came to dominate the coast. Accra quickly became a major gold-trading and slave-trading center. Many inland Ga moved to the coast for economic opportunities.

As the city of Accra expanded during the colonial era and after independence, increasing numbers of Ga settled in the city and its environs. As a result, the Ga are today one of the most urbanized peoples of West Africa. In the 1990s Ga represented roughly half the population of metropolitan Accra, and Ga was the main everyday language of the city. Many Ga work as laborers, traders, and government officials. Reliable population estimates are difficult to obtain. Some sources place the number of Ga at around 600,000, while others have it as high as 1.6 million.

See also GOLD TRADE; LANGUAGES, AFRICAN: AN OVERVIEW.

DAVID P. JOHNSON, JR.

Gabon

Coastal country in Central Africa, bordered by Equatorial Guinea, Cameroon, and Republic of the Congo.

Densely forested and rich in natural resources, Gabon has one of Africa's strongest economies. Gabon suffered less from the slave trade than other areas along Africa's Atlantic coast. However, French settlers, commercial enterprises, and colonial administrators irreversibly transformed its economy and society in the nineteenth century. The French created a two-tiered society, with a small elite loyal to French political and commercial interests and a poor, disenfranchised, majority. The leaders of independent Gabon have preserved and maintained this division. At the head of Gabon's elite is

497

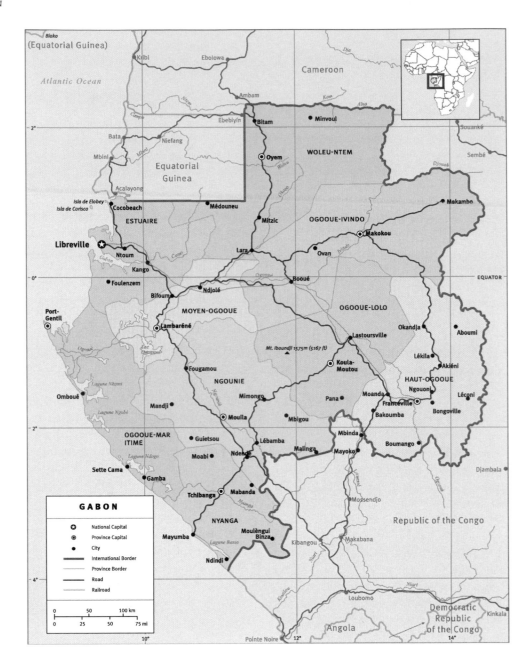

President OMAR BONGO, who has maintained a firm monopoly on power since 1967 and whose tenure in office is now one of the longest of any head of state in the world. Although Bongo's government has made investments in transportation and social services, the country's large oil wealth has primarily benefited Bongo and his clients, while the vast majority of the population remains impoverished.

EARLY HISTORY

For thousands of years, the ancestors of the Babongo people (pygmies) inhabited the tropical rainforest that today covers three-quarters of the area of present-day Gabon. The Babongo hunted chimpanzees, gorillas, and other forest animals and gathered vegetable foods for their livelihood. Most archaeologists believe that Bantu peoples first arrived in the region around 1300 B.C.E. and established small farming communities at the edge of the forest. The Bantu gradually expanded into the surrounding forest. By the seventh century C.E., they acquired iron-making skills and came to dominate the region. Besides hunting and fishing, the Bantu survived by growing yams, bananas, and oil palms.

Extended families and clans provided the foundation of the social structure; ethnic identities were fluid and secondary in importance. Male leaders or "big men" gained prominence through hunting, war, trade, and rituals, and distinguished themselves by the number of their dependents: wives, children, in-laws, servants, slaves, and PYGMY hunters. Women bore and raised children, made pottery, cultivated crops, danced, and performed religious rituals. Bantu peoples used iron for tools, weapons, and jewelry; woven raffia circulated as a form of currency. Over time, clans grouped into scattered villages of a few dozen to several hundred people, located along trade routes such as rivers or footpaths. Most villages held common beliefs in ancestral worship, sorcery, and witchcraft, although these beliefs were often clan-specific in their details; many villages maintained secret societies. The peoples of early Gabon generally lacked state structures, though by the fourteenth century C.E., the kingdom of Loango had extended its rule northward from present-day Congo-Brazzaville along the Gabonese coast.

IMPERIALISM AND FRENCH COLONIALISM

Slavery, international trade, and French colonialism brought profound changes to Gabon. In 1472 the Portuguese first visited the Gabon Estuary, which they named the Gabão, or "hooded cloak," because of its shape. From the late sixteenth through the eighteenth centuries, French, Dutch, and British traders visited the coast and exchanged manufactured goods and salt for slaves and ivory. Local inhabitants rose in opposition to European mercantilism, most spectacularly in 1600 when a group of Ndiwa attacked the Dutch at Corisco Island.

Coastal trade reached its apex in Gabon in the late eighteenth and early nineteenth centuries with the height of the transatlantic slave trade. The coastal MPONGWE and ORUNGU apparently acted as slave brokers. Through trade they acquired the wealth to support an aristocratic elite and to maintain a privileged status in Gabon through the colonial period and down to the present day. However, Gabon never attracted large numbers of slave traders because it had a small population, mostly concentrated in the inaccessible interior. At their height between 1815 and 1830, slave shipments from Gabon did not exceed a few thousand slaves per year.

The French established a colonial presence in Gabon beginning in 1839, partly in an effort to halt the slave trade in West Africa and partly to provide naval protection along the coast for French trading companies. French mercantile vessels suffered regular attacks from the Mpongwe, Orungu, and other coastal peoples who had profited from the slave trade and were angry at France's attempts to abolish it. In 1839 French admiral Edouard Bouët-Willaumez arrived in the Gabon Estuary on his ship, the *Malouine*, and within the next several years had signed treaties with most of the oga, or chiefs, of the estuary and

coast. In the treaty of 1846, for example, France claimed "all the land that seemed appropriate for the creation of military and agricultural establishments" and also set aside land for Roman Catholic missionary activities.

The arrival of the French coincided with an important shift in the ethnic balance of Gabon. The fact that Bouët-Willaumez signed separate treaties with the various oga demonstrates the absence of a political structure uniting the Myènè-speaking clans of the estuary at that time. Meanwhile, the FANG people, who subsequently became the largest ethnic group in Gabon, had begun their migration into the region from the north. To many Fang, the coming of the French fulfilled an ancient Fang legend in which white warriors arrived from the sea.

During the 1840s French, British, and German firms traded along the estuary, where they competed for the ivory and rubber brought from the interior. The French established cotton and sugarcane plantations, but faced a lack of manual labor. In an attempt to solve this problem, in 1849 Bouët-Willaumez settled fifty-two Loangan slaves, who had been taken from a Dutch slave ship, in a site on the Gabonese estuary. On arrival in this new village of LIBREVILLE ("Freetown"), the French granted the slaves their "freedom" and put them to work as wage laborers on the plantations.

The arrival of the Europeans and their values undermined the clan-based societies of the estuary. In the economic sphere, cash transactions replaced bartering, and status increasingly depended on material wealth. Christian missionaries aggressively promoted new ideologies that undermined established patterns of authority. Meanwhile, Europeans were beginning to penetrate the interior: In the 1840s French naval officers explored the hinterland of the estuary, in the 1850s the explorer Paul du Chaillu led expeditions into the northern and southern interior, and other explorers charted the interior over the following decades.

During the 1880s France's interest in Gabon intensified. By this time, the SCRAMBLE FOR AFRICA among the European powers was fully underway. France saw the Gabon region as a source of raw materials, as well as an important gateway to the Congo basin. The trading and military posts France had established in Gabon allowed France to claim the area as part of its sphere of influence at the BERLIN CONFERENCE OF 1884–1885. The underfunded colonial administration divided the territory into parcels and sold development concessions to forty private companies. The companies received trading monopolies granting them exclusive authority over their domains. Employing harsh forced-labor practices, they exploited the rubber and ivory resources aggressively. However, many such companies failed to produce long-term financial returns and went bankrupt.

The concessionary system devastated the Gabonese population. Many people had to abandon subsistence farming. French companies disrupted indigenous trade routes. The companies paid most Africans for their labor in goods or in a currency only used by the concessionary company and made little effort to develop the infrastructure of the regions under their control. This social and economic dislocation resulted in famines and epidemics that killed many thousands of Gabonese. Some Africans resisted forced-labor policies, but company militias dealt swiftly and harshly with any resistance.

In 1910, after the concessionary system had failed to yield profits or to provide an effective basis for administering its African colonies, the French created the federation of FRENCH EQUATORIAL AFRICA, with a capital in BRAZZAVILLE, composed of French Congo (present-day Congo-Brazzaville), OUBANGUI-CHARI (present-day CENTRAL AFRICAN REPUBLIC), CHAD, and Gabon. The French colonial government created a two-tiered social system in Gabon. A small governing elite—mainly composed of wealthy MPONGWE traders and those of dual European and African descent—enjoyed citizenship status. The vast majority of the population were subject to the *indigénat*, an administrative system that imposed upon them an inferior legal and political status accompanied by onerous tax and labor obligations.

With Gabon's ivory and rubber stocks depleted, French colonial administrators neglected the country's development, although during the 1920s timber became an increasingly important export. The French also introduced cocoa and coffee as cash crops. Indigenous Gabonese were forced either to cultivate cash crops such as these or to work for a wage, harvesting timber, in order to pay required taxes.

Many Gabonese opposed French colonialism. In the early 1900s local rebellions were common. The most serious of these was the Fang rebellion in 1903 led by Emane Tole. Indeed, it was not until World War I that French colonial authority encompassed the interior. However, the nascent Gabonese anticolonialist movement in the estuary region was divided between the Mpongwe elite and Fang newcomers who threatened the Mpongwe's privileged status.

During and after World War II, relations between France and its African colonies shifted dramatically. In 1944 Charles de Gaulle organized the Brazzaville Conference as a means to unite the French African possessions against Germany and to initiate greater democracy in the African colonies. The *indigénat* system was abolished in 1946, when Africans received the right to vote. In 1956 the French National Assembly passed a *loi cadre*, or enabling law, that created representative assemblies within the

French colonies and spurred the creation of political parties in Gabon and elsewhere.

The most prominent political figures during this period were the Mpongwe leader Paul Gondjout and the Fang leaders LÉON MBA and Jean-Hilaire Aubame; the latter two had served in the French colonial administration. Mba and Gondjout formed an alliance, supported by the wealthy Mpongwe business community, the coastal Fang elite, and the French timber interests and managed to outmaneuver Aubame and his northern Fang supporters. Few Gabonese pushed for complete independence; in the 1958 referendum the population voted overwhelmingly for continued association with France. However, by 1960 the federation of French Equatorial Africa had effectively disintegrated, and the French sought to grant independence to Gabon.

INDEPENDENT GABON

On August 17, 1960, Gabon became an independent parliamentary republic with Léon Mba serving as prime minister. Mba continued to rely heavily on French civil servants and technicians for administrative support and on the French military for security. In return, Mba assured the French a base for pursuing their interests, which included a steady supply of uranium from Gabonese mines for their nuclear program. Mba worked to consolidate his personal power by removing other leaders such as Gondjout and Aubame from positions of authority. With his encouragement, the National Assembly imposed strict limitations on freedom of speech and political assembly. In 1964 Mba attempted to create a one-party state by dissolving the National Assembly and calling new elections. In response, a group of young army officers overthrew the government in a coup d'état, arrested Mba, and set up a provisional government led by Jean-Hilaire Aubame. A swift military intervention by French paratroopers from Dakar and Brazzaville restored Mba to power. After 1964, opposition to Mba weakened in the face of a permanent French military presence in Libreville. Under Mba's rule, Gabon began extensive exploitation of its mineral resources. French firms provided much of the investment capital for this development, and along with a small Gabonese elite they have reaped most of the benefit. During the early 1960s Gabon began to export both manganese and uranium. Prospecting for petroleum began.

When Mba died in 1967, his handpicked successor Albert-Bernard Bongo (now named Omar Bongo) assumed the presidency. Many Gabonese welcomed Bongo, a TÉKÉ from the southeast. His accession appeared to end Fang-Mpongwe political dominance, and opponents of Mba welcomed Bongo's call for national renewal and his decision to grant amnesty to those who had participated in the

Gabon (At a Glance)

OFFICIAL NAME:
Gabonese Republic

AREA:
267,667 sq km (103,347 sq mi)

LOCATION:
Bounded on the northwest by Equatorial Guinea, on the north by Cameroon, on the east and south by the Republic of the Congo, and on the west by the Atlantic Ocean

CAPITAL:
Libreville (population 578,156; 2005 estimate)

OTHER MAJOR CITIES:
Port-Gentil (population 116,200; 2003 estimate), Masuku (41,300; 2003 estimate)

POPULATION:
1,514,993 (2009 estimate)

POPULATION DENSITY:
6 persons per sq km (about 15 persons per sq mi); over three-quarters of the population lives in cities, and much of the interior is uninhabited.

POPULATION BELOW AGE 15:
42.1 percent (male 320,414; female 318,027; 2009 estimate)

POPULATION GROWTH RATE:
1.934 percent (2009 estimate)

TOTAL FERTILITY RATE:
4.65 children born per woman (2009 estimate)

LIFE EXPECTANCY AT BIRTH:
Total population: 53.11 years (male 52.19 years; female 54.05 years; 2009 estimate)

INFANT MORTALITY RATE:
51.78 deaths per 1000 live births (2009 estimate)

LITERACY RATE (AGE 15 AND OVER WHO CAN READ AND WRITE):
Total population 63.2 percent (male 73.7 percent; female 53.3 percent; 1995 estimate)

EDUCATION:
Schooling is compulsory in Gabon for all children between ages 6 and 16, though not all children in that age group actually attend school. In the early 1990s about 210,000 pupils were annually attending primary schools, and about 56,700 students were enrolled in secondary schools. By 2000, 88 percent of primary school-aged children attended school. The country has technical institutions and teachers colleges, as well as a university, the Université Omar Bongo (founded in 1970).

LANGUAGES:
The official language is French, but many Gabonese speak Bantu languages.

ETHNIC GROUPS:
The ethnic makeup of the Gabonese is diverse. Of the country's approximately 40 ethnic groups, most belong to the Fang, Pounou, Nzeihy, or Téké groupings. Europeans, mostly French, form a small but prominent minority. Pygmies are believed to have been the original inhabitants of the country, but only a few thousand remain.

RELIGIONS:
Between 55 and 75 percent of the population is Christian, primarily Roman Catholic. Most of the remainder, except for a small Islamic community, follow traditional beliefs.

CLIMATE:
Gabon has a hot and humid climate. The temperature varies only slightly throughout the year, hovering around 27° C (80° F). The dry seasons stretch from February to April and October to November. In Libreville the annual rainfall often exceeds 2500 mm (100 in).

LAND, PLANTS, AND ANIMALS:
Coastal lowlands gird the western shores of Gabon. The interior contains a plateau zone that extends over the entire northern and eastern sections of Gabon and part of the south. The Cristal and Chaillu mountains cut across the interior, sending numerous rivers down to the Atlantic. Dense equatorial rain forest covers three-quarters of the country.

NATURAL RESOURCES:
Gabon is rich in mineral resources. Deposits of uranium, manganese, and petroleum dot the country, all of which are being exploited. Large deposits of iron ore, considered among the richest in the world, have also been discovered. Other Gabonese resources include lead and silver ore. Stands of okoume, mahogany, kevazing, and ebony make the forests of Gabon valuable.

CURRENCY:
The CFA (Communauté Financière Africaine) franc

GROSS DOMESTIC PRODUCT (GDP):
$15.91 billion (2008 estimate)

GDP PER CAPITA:
$14,400 (2008 estimate)

GDP REAL GROWTH RATE:
3.6 percent (2008 estimate)

PRIMARY ECONOMIC ACTIVITIES:
Agriculture, forestry, fishing, and mining

PRIMARY CROPS:
Cassava, plantains, sugarcane, yams, and taro

INDUSTRIES:
Food and beverage, textile, lumbering and plywood, cement, petroleum extraction and refining, manganese, uranium, and gold mining

PRIMARY EXPORTS:
Crude oil, timber, manganese, and uranium

PRIMARY IMPORTS:
Foodstuffs, chemical products, construction materials, and machinery

PRIMARY TRADE PARTNERS:
France, African countries, United States, China, and the Netherlands

GOVERNMENT:
Under a constitution adopted in 1991, the voting population elects the president directly for a term of seven years, as well as a 120-member National Assembly. The current president is El Hadj Omar Bongo; Bongo has appointed Jean Eyeghe Ndong as prime minister.

Eric Bennett

1964 coup. Indeed, Bongo carefully co-opted his political opponents by offering them positions in his government. He also consolidated his personal power: he established a single party in 1968 under his control, the Parti Démocratique Gabonais (PDG), and a single trade union within the party.

The rapid growth in oil exports gave Gabon one of the highest per capita incomes in sub-Saharan Africa. The petroleum-based economy, highly dependent on French corporations and technical workers, became a cornerstone of Bongo's rule. Gabon's prosperity allowed the development of a patronage system, whereby Bongo provided a clique of loyal and dependent bureaucrats lucrative government positions, some paying over $200,000 per year. Economic prosperity also enabled the construction of the expensive Transgabonais Railroad from 1974 to 1987. It linked the southeast, with its mineral wealth, to the port at Libreville and served as a potent symbol of national unity. The government also instituted a network of social services such as education and public health.

During the 1980s the Bongo regime faced several significant challenges. In 1981 an opposition group, the Mouvement de Redressement National (MORENA), formed and denounced government corruption, the single-party system, and the economic disparity between rich and poor. The government severely repressed MORENA; its leader, the priest Paul Mba-Abessole, fled to Paris.

Bongo's government faced an even graver challenge when declining oil prices and a weakening U.S. dollar initiated a prolonged economic crisis in 1986. Gabon had difficulty servicing its heavy debt burden, and in the late 1980s international lenders forced Gabon to implement an austerity program. This program had its harshest effects on the middle classes and the impoverished masses. Unemployment rose, and state bureaucrats had their wages slashed. The patronage system that had propped up Bongo's rule collapsed. When the international press exposed the Bongo regime's corrupt and oligarchic nature, widespread popular discontent erupted in strikes and street protests. Meanwhile, Gabon's elite continued to live opulently: one source estimates that 2 percent of the population controlled 80 percent of the country's gross national product.

After the suspicious death of a leading opposition figure, serious riots in Libreville and Port-Gentil led the government to declare a state of emergency and to call upon French troops to intervene. In 1990 Bongo held a national "Conference on Democracy" of government and opposition political figures in an attempt to stem the unrest. Although the publicity leading up to the conference explicitly rejected any discussion of a multiparty system, the conference recommended open elections for a reconstituted National Assembly in September 1990. Bongo's PDG won these elections with a two-seat majority. However, he formed a government of national unity, with one-third of ministerial appointments held by opposition members.

Although significant, Bongo's moves towards more democratic rule proved short-lived. As the 1993 presidential elections approached, opposition candidates found themselves subject to police harassment, and opposition media outlets were silenced. The election results, in which Bongo won 51 percent of the vote, were widely regarded as fraudulent, and rioting erupted in Libreville. In response, in 1994 the PDG and the opposition parties signed an accord that installed a transitional coalition government, revised the electoral code, and scheduled legislative elections for 1996. Divisions in the opposition enabled the PDG to secure a clear victory in these elections. In the December 1998 elections, the president claimed two-thirds of the vote. Bongo again won a large majority of the vote—nearly 80 percent—in the elections of 2005, seizing yet another seven-year term. As Bongo ages and is eventually replaced, the question is whether his authoritarian style will outlast him. Much will surely depend on the influence of Western powers such as France and the United States, who have favored Bongo for creating an apparently stable climate for investment despite the lack of economic and political equality under his regime.

Gabon's abundant natural resources, combined with its small population, have created a strong economy by African standards. Inflation has dropped in recent years due to the government's tight monetary and fiscal policies, while real GDP has continued to grow. Yet Gabon remains heavily dependent on oil exports and the vagaries of the international oil market. The International Monetary Fund (IMF) deemed Gabon's recent performance "broadly satisfactory," but implemented a structural adjustment program in 1995 that required Gabon to diversify and privatize its economy and improve its social services, particularly to the urban poor and the rural population. As Gabon's GDP continues to rise, Gabon has recently taken to calling itself the "Kuwait of Africa." This is an apt comparison, since Gabon, like Kuwait and other Middle Eastern oil economies, is unhealthily dependent on oil and is deeply divided between a small, wealthy elite and a poor majority. About half of the Gabonese population lives in the cities of Libreville and Port-Gentil. Agriculture remains poorly developed. As a result, Gabon relies heavily on food imports; prices of staples such as plantains are three times higher in Libreville than in the neighboring country of CAMEROON. In 2000 and 2001, Gabon signed agreements to reschedule its official debt. The nation's economic progress depends on a strong world economy and Gabonese fiscal adjustments that comply with IMF policies.

The environmental costs of Gabon's state-driven capitalist development have been considerable. Although Gabon still contains some of Africa's densest forests, with up to 80,000 species of plants, they are threatened by powerful and prosperous timber industries. Indeed, one of Gabon's leading exports has been wood and wood products; Gabon's forests have been logged faster than they can recover. Many researchers believe that deforestation sparked the 1995 Gabonese EBOLA outbreak that spread to Congo-Brazzaville. By stressing the forest ecosystem and increasing human exposure to forest animals, deforestation could lead not only to more Ebola outbreaks but also to other new infectious diseases.

See also BANTU subentry on DISPERSION AND SETTLEMENT; CHRISTIANITY subentry on MISSIONARIES IN AFRICA; COLONIAL RULE; DISEASES, INFECTIOUS, IN AFRICA; IVORY TRADE; LOANGO; PYGMY; SLAVERY IN AFRICA; and STRUCTURAL ADJUSTMENT IN AFRICA.

ROANNE EDWARDS

Gaborone, Botswana
Formerly Gaberones, the capital and largest city of Botswana.

Located in southeastern BOTSWANA near the Notwani River, Gaborone was founded in 1890 by Cecil Rhodes' British South Africa Company (BSAC). Originally the site was a fortified white settlement that protected railway and telegraph lines built by the BSAC linking the CAPE COLONY, later a part of SOUTH AFRICA, with the mines of present-day ZIMBABWE. At that time the administrative headquarters of the BECHUANALAND Protectorate (present-day Botswana) was located at Mafeking (now Mafikeng), a small town actually located within the borders of the Cape Colony. As Bechuanaland neared independence in the 1960s, its leaders determined to establish a capital within the country's borders. They chose Gaborone as the site because of its proximity to both the country's main rail line and a water source, the Notwani River. Construction at the site, including a dam on the Notwani, began in 1963. In 1965 the new city was declared the capital of Bechuanaland; one year later it became the capital of independent Botswana. In 1969 the city's name was changed from Gaberones to Gaborone.

Since it was built in the twentieth century to serve a specific purpose, Gaborone is a well-designed, modern capital. Its primary activity remains government administration. There is also a small manufacturing sector within Gaborone, and at the heart of the city is a pedestrian shopping district with hotels and a casino. Noteworthy institutions located in the capital include the Botswana National Museum and Art Gallery, the University of Botswana, and the Botswana Agricultural College. The first medical center in Africa specializing in the treatment of children with HIV/AIDS opened in 2003 at Gaborone's Princess Marina Hospital. During the 1990s the city emerged as a stronghold of the Botswana National Front (BNF). The BNF opposed the Botswana Democratic Party, which has controlled Botswana's national government since its independence. As of 2005 Gaborone has a population of slightly more than 208,000.

ANDREW HERMANN

Gambia
Small country on the far west coast of Africa.

Only a small strip of Atlantic coastline keeps the Republic of Gambia from being completely surrounded by its larger neighbor, SENEGAL. Never more than thirty miles wide, Gambia stretches for more than 300 miles, along both banks of the GAMBIA RIVER and into the center of Senegal. Gambia owes its creation to British economic interests, first in the Transatlantic Slave Trade and then in the coastal trade in agricultural and manufactured commodities. But the British zone of control ended where their boats encountered the Gambia River waterfalls, never reaching into the river basin's natural hinterland. This severely constrained Gambia's economic growth and ultimately shaped its national character. Most ethnic groups of Gambia are found in larger numbers within Senegal and the small nation still struggles to forge a national identity, apart from a shared experience of British COLONIAL RULE. Gambia's peculiar geography illustrates the irrationality of Africa's colonial boundaries and the difficulty of using them as the basis for the creation of nation states in the postcolonial era.

PRECOLONIAL HISTORY
Despite Gambia's small size, it is a country of extraordinary diversity. Located at the frontier between the open savanna to the north and the Guinean forest and wooded savanna to the south, it also represents a cultural frontier between Sudanic cultures and those at the northern limits of the Guinean forest. The Sudanic cultures of the MANDINKA, WOLOF, and Fula were characterized by hereditary caste groupings that determined a member's occupation and potential marriage partners. The Mandinka and Wolof had strong traditions of kingship and centralized authority, and with the exception of the precolonial Wolof, they were markedly patriarchal. The Sudanic peoples' economies were based primarily on millet and sorghum production, artisanry, and long-distance trade. In contrast, the forest-dwelling JOLA, Bainounk, and MANJACO peoples had

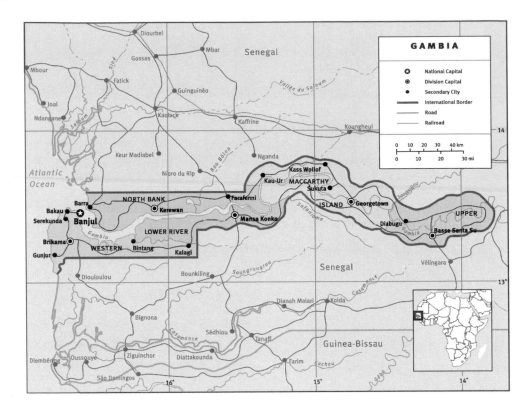

neither occupational castes nor kingly traditions and were generally more open to women's participation in public life. These forest-dwelling communities practiced wet rice agriculture and limited their commerce to local markets. Gambia was one of the areas where an African species of rice (orya glaberimma) was first domesticated more than 2,000 years ago.

Little is known about the first inhabitants of Gambia, but they probably included ancestors of populations that are today known as the Bainounk, Niominka, and Bassari. During the first millennium they built numerous clusters of stone circles that most likely had ritual significance in early Senegambian religion. Beginning in the thirteenth century, Mandinka warriors from the empire of Mali, led by Tiramaghan Keita, conquered much of the Gambia River valley. Many of its indigenous inhabitants embraced a Mandinka ethnic identity, swelling a fairly small group of Mandinka immigrants from MALI into the region's dominant population. Wolof, Serer, and Fula immigrants also entered the area during this period. As the empire of Mali weakened, new Mandinka states emerged along the Gambia River, including Barra, Kombo, Baddibu, and Niumi. The Mandinka empire of Gabou controlled most of the upper river. Although Islam had already been introduced to the area, most people adhered to indigenous forms of religion.

Portuguese travelers first entered the region in 1455. In the sixteenth century, the Portuguese established trading factories along Bintang Creek, a tributary of the Gambia River, where they purchased beeswax, gold, ivory, and slaves from Mandinka and Bainounk merchants. The Duke of Courland established a small trading post in 1661 on an island near the mouth of the river. Two years later the British expelled the Courlanders and established their own fort on the site, which they renamed James Island. In 1681 the French established a trade settlement at Albreda. While the French and British traders pushed the Portuguese out of the region, they tried to expand the area's involvement in the transatlantic slave trade. At its late eighteenth-century peak, approximately 8,000 slaves were sold to European merchants in Gambia each year; in addition, large numbers of people died in warfare or slave raids or while being transported to slave-trading posts along the Gambia River.

After the British abolition of the transatlantic slave trade in 1807, and with the end of the Napoleonic Wars, British interests shifted toward the suppression of the trade by other Europeans and Americans. To achieve that end, in 1816 the British established a new naval base and settlement at the mouth of the Gambia River, on Banjul Island, and named the settlement Bathurst. Its small garrison was charged with curtailing the Gambian slave trade and

Gambia (At a Glance)

OFFICIAL NAME:
Republic of the Gambia

AREA:
11,295 sq km (4,361 sq mi)

LOCATION:
Western Africa; borders the North Atlantic and Senegal

CAPITAL:
Banjul (formerly called Bathurst) (population 418,000; 2002 estimate)

POPULATION:
1,782,893 (2009 estimate)

POPULATION DENSITY:
157 persons per sq km (409 per sq mi)

POPULATION BELOW AGE 15:
Total population: 43.6 percent (male 390,806; female 387,172; 2009 estimate)

POPULATION GROWTH RATE:
2.668 percent (2009 estimate)

TOTAL FERTILITY RATE:
5.04 children born per woman (2009 estimate)

LIFE EXPECTANCY AT BIRTH:
Total population: 55.35 years (male 53.43 years; female 57.34 years; 2009 estimate)

INFANT MORTALITY RATE:
67.33 deaths per 1000 live births (2009 estimate)

LITERACY RATE (AGE 15 AND OVER WHO CAN READ AND WRITE):
Total population: 40.1 percent (male 47.8 percent; female 32.8 percent; 2003 estimate)

EDUCATION:
Primary education in the Gambia is free but not compulsory. In the early 1990s nearly 52 percent of all eligible primary school-aged children attended school, but only 15 percent of all children between the ages of 14 and 20 attended school. By 2000, school attendance had increased; 69 percent of primary school-aged children attended primary school, while secondary schools enrolled 35 percent of eligible children.

LANGUAGES:
English is the official language, but each ethnic group uses its own language. The most common languages are Mandinka, Wolof, and Fulani.

ETHNIC GROUPS:
The population comprises the Mandinka, accounting for 42 percent of the population; the Fulani, who predominate in the eastern part of the country and account for 18 percent of the population; the Wolof, who live mainly in Banjul and the western part of the country; the Jola, who live in the western region; the Serahuli; and a small Aku community.

RELIGIONS:
About 90 percent of the population is Muslim. About 9 percent is Christian, and 1 percent adheres to indigenous beliefs.

CLIMATE:
Subtropical with distinct hot and cool seasons. The temperatures range from 16° C (about 60° F) in the cool season, which lasts from November to May, to 43° C (110° F) in the summer. The rainy season lasts from June to November and the average annual rainfall is about 1020 mm (about 40 in).

LAND, PLANTS, AND ANIMALS:
Almost all of Gambia borders on the Gambia River. The country's land varies between sand and swamp land. Mangroves, oil palm, rubber vine, cedars, and mahogany trees thrive in this environment. Animals include the leopard, wild boar, crocodile, hippopotamus, and several species of antelope. Some game birds, such as the guinea fowl and the sand grouse, are also plentiful.

NATURAL RESOURCES:
Natural resources include the Gambia River, one of Africa's best navigable waterways; fish; and soil suited to growing peanuts.

CURRENCY:
The dalasi

GROSS DOMESTIC PRODUCT (GDP):
$2.64 billion (2008 estimate)

GDP PER CAPITA:
$1,300 (2008 estimate)

GDP REAL GROWTH RATE:
5.5 percent (2008 estimate)

PRIMARY ECONOMIC ACTIVITIES:
Agriculture (75 percent of the population), tourism, commerce, and services

PRIMARY AGRICULTURAL PRODUCTS:
Peanuts, millet, sorghum, rice, maize (corn), cassava (tapioca), palm kernels, and livestock

INDUSTRIES:
Peanut processing, fish and hides, beverages, agricultural machinery assembly, woodworking, metalworking, and clothing

PRIMARY EXPORTS:
Peanuts and peanut products, fish, cotton lint, and palm kernels

PRIMARY IMPORTS:
Foodstuffs, manufactures, raw materials, fuel, machinery, and transport equipment

PRIMARY TRADE PARTNERS:
Great Britain, China, France, Benelux, Brazil, and the Netherlands

GOVERNMENT:
Gambia is a republic under multiparty democratic rule. Following a coup d'état in July 1994, Yahya Jammeh named himself chairman of the Armed Forces Provisional Ruling Council. Bowing to external and internal pressure, Jammeh held elections in September 1996 and was elected to a five-year term with 55.5 percent of the vote. He was reelected in October 2001 and again in 2006. The unicameral National Assembly has 53 seats, of which 48 are elected and 5 are presidential appointees.

Elizabeth Heath

encouraging British commerce along the Gambia River and in coastal Senegambia. The British, however, did little to secure the natural trading hinterland of Gambia, while the French gradually extended control over most of the Senegambia region and its major cash crop, peanuts.

A reason for British reluctance to venture further inland was the fear that any expansion of the colony would entangle them in the considerable political turmoil in the region, caused by the breakdown of the Mandinka-dominated state system in the early nineteenth century. Throughout the latter half of the century, the Soninke-Marabout Wars, fought between followers of Islamic political leaders known as MARABOUTS and followers of an older Mandinka form of leadership, who were called Soninke, had become increasingly violent. Eventually, the British were drawn into these conflicts, but not before the French had occupied much of the surrounding territory, and the power of the Soninke essentially had been destroyed. By the late nineteenth century, Gambia had become predominantly Muslim.

For much of the nineteenth century, Gambia was not even considered a separate colony; from 1821 until 1888, it was administered as a district of SIERRA LEONE. For many years it seemed that it would be only a matter of time before the British ceded its few settlements to the French, who had periodically offered to take them in exchange for their own GABON or CÔTE D'IVOIRE. But the British consistently refused these offers, and after the BERLIN CONFERENCE OF 1884–1885 they were left with a colony in Gambia that extended little more than 24 kilometers (15 miles) in either direction from the riverbanks. In 1889 the French and British agreed on what are now the approximate boundaries of Gambia, leaving the French colony of Senegal with control over many communities that had previously traded through Gambia.

BRITISH COLONIALISM

In 1894 the British proclaimed a protectorate over the interior areas of Gambia, distinguishing it from the colony, which consisted of the town of Bathurst and the Kombo area on the adjacent mainland. In the protectorate, the British established a system of indirect rule, relying on government-appointed chiefs to exercise local authority. In the colony, a limited form of direct rule was established. Because Gambia was small in size, the British invested little in developing its economy. Most Gambians remained in rural areas, cultivating peanuts, millet, sorghum, and rice, though some went to work in the peanut-shelling and peanut-oil factories in Bathurst (now Banjul) or on the docks. Although employment opportunities were limited, the colony attracted migrants fleeing forced labor policies and conscription in French-ruled Senegal.

After World War I (1914–1918), newspaper editor Edward Small and other early nationalists founded Gambia's first labor unions and a Gambian branch of the National Congress of British West Africa, both of which pressed for Gambian economic and political empowerment. During World War II (1939–1945), Senegal was initially allied with the Vichy French, putting British control of Gambia in jeopardy. But in 1943 French West African authorities shifted their allegiance back to the Allies, and the threat to Gambia was removed.

After the war, limited political participation in government was extended to the protectorate. The first political parties, the Democratic Party and the United Party, were formed in 1951, followed the next year by the Muslim Congress Party. In 1959 DAWDA JAWARA, a former colonial veterinary officer, founded the Protectorate People's Party. His party gained a plurality of votes in the 1960 election for the House of Representatives, the first election in which rural voters were fully franchised. In the 1962 elections, Jawara's party, renamed the People's Progressive Party (PPP), won decisively, and Jawara became the chief minister.

INDEPENDENCE

Gambia achieved independence on February 18, 1965, and Jawara was chosen to be the new nation's prime minister. Five years later Gambia became a republic, with Jawara as president. It quickly became apparent that the new republic lacked many things, including experienced administrators who could run the government. Apart from a two-year college for teachers, Gambia had no schools that offered higher education, and its only secondary schools were in the Bathurst-Kombo area. River transport and some all-weather roads facilitated the transportation of peanuts to the processing plants, but little other industry existed. A major source of foreign exchange was the trans-Gambia ferry at Farafenni, which provided a critical link between northern Senegal and the southern Casamance region. Long waits at the ferry helped many merchants on both shores attract Senegalese customers for the low-duty consumer goods available in Gambia. Smuggling between Gambia and Senegal (where tariffs on imports were considerably higher) began in the colonial era and remains a widespread practice.

In the late 1960s, Gambia began to promote its scenic beaches as winter vacation spots for European tourists. British and Scandinavian investors built elaborate hotel complexes in the coastal communities of Bakau and Fajara. By 1975 more than 25,000 tourists, mostly from Sweden and Denmark, visited Gambia each year. Local artisans increased production of batiks, tie-dyes, and other crafts to meet the demand for souvenirs, and Gambian farmers found new markets for their fruits and vegetables in resort restaurants. But most of the tourist industry profits were repatriated to hotel and tour company operators back in Europe. Tourism also created social problems, as the overwhelmingly Muslim Gambians found their streets and beaches invaded by crowds of relatively affluent, scantily-clad vacationers. Some young people, more men than women, went into prostitution, while others sought intimate relationships that would let them pursue greater opportunities in

Europe. The incidence of rapes of tourists and premarital pregnancies among Gambian women also increased.

Aside from the development of a tourist industry, the Jawara government failed to diversify the economy. Close to 85 percent of the population made a living primarily from agriculture, yet peanuts remained the only significant cash crop, and the country continued to be highly dependent on imports of rice and other staple grains. The Sahel drought of the 1970s and subsequent erratic rainfall further undermined rural productivity and economic security.

In 1981 Kukoi Samba Sanyang, a leader in the leftist Movement for Justice in Africa, attempted a coup d'état while President Jawara was away in England. With the aid of Senegalese troops, the coup was suppressed, but not before more than one thousand people had been killed. Part of the cost of this assistance was the creation of a confederation between the two countries, known as Senegambia, which was dominated by Senegal and received little support in Gambia. In 1989 the confederation disbanded and Gambia resumed its status as an independent state, still headed by President Jawara. In 1994 Jawara was overthrown by a group of young military officers led by YAHYA JAMMEH, who then became president of the republic. In 1996, in response to considerable outside pressures, Jammeh held national elections. He was elected president by a small margin, amid accusations that the military government had used intimidation to influence voters.

After seizing power, Jammeh worked to restore international confidence in the Gambian government and to revive the country's tourist industry. He emphasized infrastructure improvements such as the expanding of Yundum airport, the paving of roads, and the building of new schools and hospitals. In October 2001 Jammeh was reelected president in elections that international observers generally endorsed as free and fair. He followed this victory, however, with a crackdown on political dissidents. Jammeh won another elective victory in 2006 amidst suspicions—actual or otherwise—of a brewing military coup.

See also ISLAM IN AFRICA; MALI EMPIRE; SLAVERY IN AFRICA; and TOURISM IN AFRICA.

ROBERT BAUM

Gambia River
One of the longest navigable rivers in West Africa.
The Gambia River flows for 700 miles (1,100 km) from the highlands of FOUTA DJALLON in GUINEA north into SENEGAL, then west through GAMBIA to empty into the Atlantic Ocean. It is navigable for about 200 miles (320 km) as it passes through Gambia, which takes its name from the river. Strong tides and the flat landscape allow saltwater from the Atlantic to reach more than 100 miles

(160 km) upstream. Along the river's saline lower stretch, its banks are covered by mangrove swamps that shelter a variety of fish and shellfish and attract a rich diversity of birds. Some mangrove swamps have been cleared and converted into rice paddies, which must be protected from saltwater by an elaborate system of dikes. Beyond the mangroves, rainy-season floodplains are an important area for swamp rice cultivation. The Gambia River valley was one of three areas where people domesticated African varieties of rice (oryza glaberrima) more than 2,000 years ago; the others were the valleys of the NIGER RIVER and the Casamance River.

Historically, the Gambia River was an important route by which the MANDE people expanded west toward the Atlantic Ocean. After Europeans reached the Atlantic coast, the river became a major trade route for the export of gold and slaves from the western SUDAN, Confederation of SENEGAMBIA, and Casamance areas. But after the colonial powers divided Senegambia into French and British spheres in 1889, the Gambia River, isolated from most of its natural trading hinterland, declined in importance as a West African commercial artery. In 1978 Senegal and Gambia created the Gambia River Development Organization to restore the river's position as one of the most important rivers of West Africa.

ROBERT BAUM

Ganga-Zumba
African king who led the maroon settlement Quilombo dos Palmares in Brazil. Ganga-Zumba died in 1685. He was succeeded by Zumbi.

Garang de Mabior, John
1945–
Rebel leader from southern Sudan.
John Garang de Mabior grew up in a DINKA community in southern SUDAN. In 1970 he joined the Anya-Nya, the military organization waging a war for an independent southern Sudan. After the Addis Ababa Agreement in 1972, which temporarily halted the Sudanese civil war, Garang became deputy director of the military research branch of the Sudanese army. In 1981 he earned a doctorate in agricultural economics from Iowa State University with a dissertation on the agricultural development of southern Sudan. His work with the Sudanese government ended abruptly in 1983 with President Gaafar Muhammad al-Nimeiry's declaration of Islamic law and his dissolution of the southern Sudanese regional assembly.

That same year Garang founded the Sudan People's Liberation Movement (SPLM) and adopted a broader strategy than his Anya-Nya predecessors. He emphasized the cultural diversity of the entire Sudan, not just the north and the south. He advocated a federal system of government to ensure regional autonomy for all cultural minorities. Garang proved adept at generating support among northern Sudanese minorities and among conservative Christian organizations in the West. Both of these groups reacted with concern to what Garang presented as Muslim persecution of a southern Sudanese Christian minority. In fact, most southerners are neither Christian nor Muslim, but followers of religions that are indigenous to the region.

Simultaneously, as commander of the affiliated Sudan People's Liberation Army (SPLA), Garang advocated a military solution in the fight for autonomy and organized a highly effective military organization, primarily in the South. The SPLM and SPLA successfully resisted the Islamic governments of Sudan, though at a considerable cost in military and civilian deaths. Two periods of devastating famine, intensified by the difficulty of delivering food supplies to a war zone, caused a massive rural flight to urban areas of northern and southern Sudan. In July 2002, Garang and Sudanese president Omar Beshir signed a ceasefire agreement and pledged to work toward a peaceful resolution of the civil war. However, the Sudanese government walked out of the peace talks two months later. Finally, in 2005, the SPLA entered into a peace agreement with the government, and Garang ascended to the office of the vice presidency. However, just a few months later, Garang was killed when the helicopter in which he was traveling crashed in southern Sudan.

ROBERT BAUM

Garcia II
Ruler of Kongo at the height of its power and fame, 1641–1661; also known as Nkanga a Lukeni Nzenza Ntumba.
Garcia and his brother Alvaro Nimi a Lukeni a Nzenza Ntumba (later King Alvaro VI, 1636–1641) were descended from AFONSO I, the first Kongo king to embrace Catholicism. In their youth the brothers became close to the Jesuits, who had established themselves in Kongo in 1619. The brothers may have attended the Jesuit college in São Salvador (also known as MBANZA KONGO). Certainly they joined the Congregation of Saint Ignatius, through which they became attached to King Alvaro IV (1631–1635). Both brothers helped to defend the king against the rebellion of Daniel da Silva, Duke of Mbamba, in 1633. Garcia distinguished himself by leading the attack that ultimately killed the rebel duke. As a reward, his brother Alvaro was made Duke of Mbamba and Garcia was appointed Marquis of Kiowa.

When Alvaro IV died, his half-brother, crowned as Alvaro V, sought to remove Garcia and Alvaro Nimi from their offices, and in response the brothers led a rebellion that eventually deposed the king. Electors then chose Alvaro Nimi to be King Álvaro VI and gave Garcia the duchy of Mbamba. From his official position in Mbamba, Garcia

developed close relations with the Dutch merchants who were trading along the Kongo coast. Alvaro VI died suddenly in 1641 and Garcia immediately marched on São Salvador, forcing the electors to make him king. Within a few months, the Dutch had attacked the Portuguese colony of LUANDA and established themselves there. Garcia invited them to visit São Salvador, where they formed an alliance aimed at removing the Portuguese from ANGOLA. A devoted Catholic, Garcia refused Dutch overtures to send Calvinist ministers to Kongo.

With help from the Dutch, Kongo armies reclaimed several territories in the south that had been taken by Portuguese governors during the 1620s and 1630s and greatly expanded Kongo's influence. In 1643, Garcia's armies helped the Dutch force the Portuguese from Kongo territory, although their bases along the Kwanza River remained.

JOHN THORNTON

Gauteng
Province in northeastern South Africa, bounded by Free State Province on the south, Mpumalanga Province on the east, Northern Province on the north, and North-West Province on the west.
Created in 1994 from part of TRANSVAAL, one of the four former South African provinces, Gauteng was named for the SOTHO word meaning "place of gold." Most of the province lies in the High Veld, a plateau of grassy plains that cover much of central South Africa. The Witwatersrand (Afrikaans for "ridge of white waters") is a rocky ridge that extends for about 80 km (50 mi) through the middle of Gauteng and is famous for its rich gold deposits. Average temperatures in Gauteng range from 16° to 32° C (60° to 90° F) in the summer (October to April), and from 6° to 17° C (43° to 63° F) in the winter. Annual rainfall totals 510 mm (20 in), with most of the rain falling in the summer months.

Gauteng is the smallest but most densely populated province in South Africa, with an area of 17,010 sq km (6,568 sq mi) and a population of 9.5 million (2005 estimate). Gauteng has the richest mix of ethnic groups and languages of any province in South Africa. The main black African groups are Zulu, Sotho, PEDI, and TSWANA. Other groups include AFRIKANERS, people of British descent, Italians, Portuguese, and Greeks. Dominating Gauteng is its provincial capital and South Africa's largest city, JOHANNESBURG, founded in 1886 after gold discoveries on the Witwatersrand. South Africa's stock exchange and the headquarters of many corporations are located there. Adjacent to Johannesburg is SOWETO (South-Western Townships), a residential area that began as squatter camps for black laborers. Soweto was developed after World War II as an area designated for blacks under the South African government's former policy of APARTHEID, or racial segregation. Also part of Gauteng Province, to the north of Johannesburg, is PRETORIA, South

Africa's administrative capital and the location of most foreign embassies. Other important cities include Benoni, Brakpan, Germiston, Heidelberg, Krugersdorp, Randburg, Springs, Vanderbijlpark, and Vereeniging.

Universities in Gauteng include two in Johannesburg and three in Pretoria. Johannesburg is the site of Rand Afrikaans University (founded in 1966) and the University of the Witwatersrand (1922). In Pretoria are the University of Pretoria (founded as Transvaal University College in 1908, it became the University of Pretoria in 1930), Vista University (1982), and the University of South Africa (1873). Vista University and the University of South Africa are correspondence schools. Important cultural and historical places include the Voortrekker Monument, a monument completed in 1949 outside Pretoria commemorating the migrations of Afrikaners north from the Cape of Good Hope during the Great Trek in the early 1800s; the Union Buildings in Pretoria, where the president's executive offices are located; the Sterkfontein Caves, near Krugersdorp, where bone fragments of protohumans have been discovered; and the Museum Africa in Johannesburg, which displays exhibits on the history of South Africa.

Gauteng serves as South Africa's commercial, financial, and industrial hub. Most industry is concentrated in the center of the province in what is often called the PWV (Pretoria-Witwatersrand-Vereeniging) triangle. In addition to gold mining, major industries include iron and steel production. Although Gauteng is South Africa's most urbanized province, it also has farming areas that produce maize (corn), vegetables, dairy products, meat, and fruit. Gauteng has two major airports, and an extensive network of roads and railways connects it to the rest of the country.

Gauteng's provincial government consists of a premier, an executive council of ten ministers, and a provincial assembly. The provincial assembly and premier are elected for five-year terms, or until the next national election. Political parties are allocated seats in the assembly based on the percentage of votes each party receives in the province during the national elections. The assembly elects a premier, who then appoints the members of the executive council.

Gay and Lesbian Movements in Africa
See HOMOSEXUALITY IN AFRICA.

Gbari
Ethnic group of Nigeria; also known as Agbari and Gwari.
The Gbari primarily inhabit the Niger State of western NIGERIA. They speak a Niger-Congo language. Some 350,000 people consider themselves Gbari.

See also LANGUAGES, AFRICAN: AN OVERVIEW.

Gbaya
Ethnic group of the western Central African Republic, eastern Cameroon, northern Republic of the Congo, and northwestern Democratic Republic of the Congo.
The Gbaya, who speak a Niger-Congo language, number more than a million, mainly in the west of the CENTRAL AFRICAN REPUBLIC. Fleeing FULANI slave raids and holy wars connected with the founding of the SOKOTO CALIPHATE, the ancestors of the Gbaya migrated to the region from present-day northern CAMEROON and NIGERIA in the early 1800s. They incorporated many of the indigenous inhabitants, creating the six basic subgroups of the Gbaya. Fulani continued to raid the Gbaya region each year to capture slaves for sale, both in the Caliphate and to trans-Saharan caravans.

The traditional Gbaya political organization was decentralized, with village chiefs acting as symbolic leaders and judges rather than political rulers. Only in emergencies were war chiefs temporarily elected, as among the BANDA. In war, age sets insured unity by cutting across clan identities. The clans managed trade with foreigners, marriage arrangements, and religious customs.

French colonizers disrupted these traditions by increasing the powers of village chiefs. They imposed brutal forced labor on many Gbaya, for example on the Congo-Ocean railway. In 1928 the Gbaya initiated the three-year Kongo Wara War against French rule. The French suppressed the rebellion in a "nightmare campaign" that decimated the Gbaya population. However, many Gbaya became nationalist leaders and later figured prominently in political circles.

Today most Gbaya remain rural farmers, growing cassava, corn, peanuts, tobacco, and yams, and supplementing their diet by hunting and fishing. For cash, many Gbaya grow rice or coffee, prospect for diamonds, or work for mining companies.

ERIC YOUNG

Gebrselassie, Haile
1973–
Ethiopian track and field star and Olympic gold medalist.
Haile Gebrselassie was born in Arssi, ETHIOPIA. As a child, he ran barefoot to and from school each day—a round trip of 25 km (15 mi). This was good training for his future career as one of the world's best runners. Like his brother before him, Gebrselassie began running competitively as a teenager. In 1992 he won both the 5000-m and 10,000-m races at the World Junior Championships. The next year, competing against adults for the first time, he won the 10,000-m and finished second in the 5000-m in the World Championships. In 1996 Gebrselassie not only

won the 5000-m event in the World Indoor Championships, he also set an indoor world record, the first Ethiopian to do so. He followed that feat by winning a gold medal in the 10,000-m at the 1996 Olympic Games in Atlanta, Georgia, setting a new Olympic record.

Treated to a victory parade in ADDIS ABABA, ETHIOPIA that was attended by nearly a million people, Gebrselassie became a national hero. In 1997 he set three more world records: in the 5000-m, 10,000-m, and 2-mi races. In 1999 Gebrselassie won the 10,000-m event at the World Championships for the fourth consecutive time, as well as taking gold medals in the 1,500-m and 3,000-m events at the World Indoor Championships. The following year he successfully defended his Olympic gold medal in the 10,000-m race in Sydney, Australia. In 2002 he competed in the marathon for the first time in international competition. Following a perfect 2005 season, in 2006 Gebrselassie smashed the world marathon record by twenty-one seconds, before beating the world record for one-hour runs a year later in the Czech Republic. In 2008, competing in the Berlin Marathon, he set a new world record, bettering his own previous effort. Gebrselassie splits his time between Addis Ababa, where he has a job with the police department, and the Netherlands, where he lives with one of his brothers and continues his training.

KATE TUTTLE

Gedi
East African coastal town founded in the thirteenth century, the ruins of which are now an important historical site in Kenya.

Located 16 km (10 mi) south of Malindi, KENYA, Gedi is something of a mystery. Built on a coral spur, its outer wall encompassed 45 acres. The opulent town proper resided within an inner wall and contained a palace, three pillar tombs, and a great mosque, as well as several smaller mosques and private houses. Lying 6.4 km (4 mi) inland and 3.2 km (2 mi) from a navigable creek, Gedi was undoubtedly influenced by SWAHILI culture but probably did not participate directly in the trade that linked towns along the SWAHILI COAST. Gedi was never mentioned by the Portuguese, who occupied Malindi from 1512 to 1593, nor in any other written record from around the time it was inhabited. Yet the ruins of Gedi show clear evidence of a highly developed and wealthy African civilization.

Archaeological excavations have determined that Gedi was founded in the thirteenth century and was probably rebuilt during the fifteenth century, the height of its prosperity. Gedi was abandoned in the sixteenth century, reoccupied for a short time, and then permanently abandoned in the early seventeenth century.

Many of the construction details indicate that builders considered the comfort and well being of the city's occupants when constructing Gedi. The palace, for example, features sunken courts, the purpose of which was to create a longer shadow and therefore a cooler, more pleasant place to sit. Walls contained pegs for hanging carpets. In private residences walls were thick and roofs were constructed of stamped red earth, also to create a cool living environment. All of the private residences and the palace included partitioned lavatories with washing bowls and bidets, as well as strong rooms adjacent to the owner's bedroom for storing valuables. These rooms had no doorways; instead, one entered via a trapdoor reached by climbing a ladder. Sumps were located throughout the town to hold surface water that would otherwise have compromised the walls of structures.

A few hundred meters from the palace stood the great mosque, built around the middle of the fifteenth century. Constructed of stone, the roof was covered with coral tiles laid in lime concrete. A broad-bladed spear, a traditional Swahili symbol of kingship, was carved into its entranceway. Square niches in which lamps were placed for night prayers were located at intervals around the inside walls. Set in its north wall and framed with a herringbone border was an arched qibla, which showed the direction of Mecca, toward which Muslims are supposed to pray. On the east was a veranda and a court that contained a well, cistern, and lavatory.

Archaeologists puzzle over why Gedi's residents abandoned it, but can offer no definitive answers. Possible reasons for its downfall include a Portuguese or Galla attack, a decrease in water tables that eliminated the water supply, or some sort of epidemic. The ruins were declared a historic monument in 1927 and are open to the public.

BIBLIOGRAPHY

Kirkman, James. *Gedi: The Palace.* Mouton & Co., 1963.

Kirkman, James. *Men and Monuments on the East African Coast.* Lutterworth, 1964.

ROBERT FAY

Geomorphology, African
Physical characteristics of the African continent.

Many of Africa's striking geomorphological features result from the continent's tectonic movement. The science of plate tectonics explores the motion of the earth's outer crust caused by convective currents in a molten substratum called the asthenosphere. Geophysicists believe that Africa once sat at the center of a massive continent, which Austrian scientist Eduard Suess named *Gondwanaland*. About 250 million years ago, Gondwanaland broke into the landmasses of South America, Australia, Antarctica, India, Saudi Arabia, and Africa. Like puzzle pieces, their coastlines seem to line

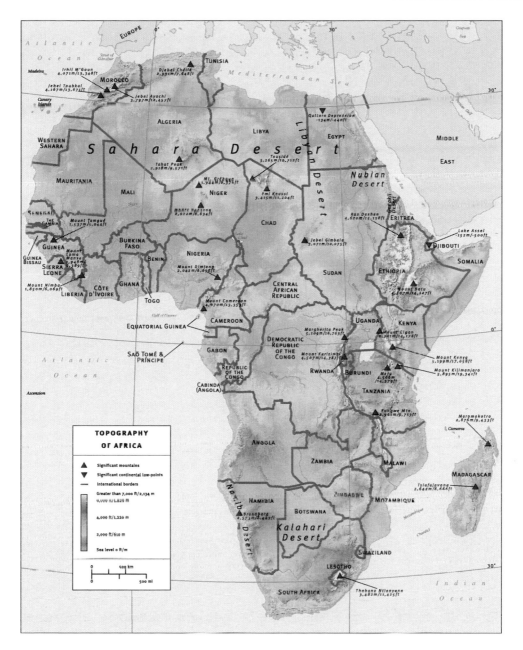

TOPOGRAPHY OF AFRICA

▲ Significant mountains
▼ Significant continental low-points
— International borders

Greater than 7,000 ft/2,134 m
6,000 ft/1,828 m
4,000 ft/1,220 m
2,000 ft/610 m
Sea level 0 ft/m

0   500 km
0   500 mi

up. Geologists have discovered a close correspondence in rock deposits on these landmasses, and paleontologists have found a similar concurrence in the fossil record.

Because the other continents drifted away from Africa, its tectonic history was less cataclysmic than those of other Gondwanaland fragments. Africa bears no fault-block mountains—that is, ranges that have arisen from the collision of tectonic plates. Instead, expansion and rifting characterize its geological history.

Although on average Africa sits 640 m (2,100 ft) above sea level, higher than other continents, its continental shelf—a region of shallow shoreline water—drops off far more quickly than those of many other landmasses. This limits the potential for offshore marine fishing, because shallow-water breeding grounds are small. The lack of natural harbors makes navigation difficult for large ships.

Geographers often divide the African continent in half, drawing a line from northern ANGOLA to northwestern ETHIOPIA to mark its high and low regions. The lowland northern and western sides of the continent average in height from 300 to 460 m (about 990 to 1,510 ft), while the highlands to the south and east average from 1,220 to

Largest Lakes	
Victoria	69,482 sq km (26,828 sq mi)
Tanganyika	33,000 sq km (12,750 sq mi)
Malawi	9,600 sq km (11,430 sq mi)
Chad (wet season)	25,900 sq km (10,000 sq mi)
Chad (dry season)	10,360 sq km (4,000 sq mi)
Turkana	6,400 sq km (2,471 sq mi)
Largest Deserts	
Sahara	9,065,000 sq km (3,500,000 sq mi)
Libyan	1,165,500 sq km (450,000 sq mi)
Kalahari	712,250 sq km (275,000 sq mi)
Nubian	259,000 sq km (100,000 sq mi)
Longest Rivers	
Nile	6,671 km (4,145 mi)
Congo	4,375 km (2,720 mi)
Niger	4,180 km (2,600 mi)
Zambezi	3,540 km (2,200 mi)
Orange	2,173 km (1,350 mi)
Highest Mountains	
Kilimanjaro	5,895 m (19,340 ft)
Batian	5,199 m (17,058 ft)
Margherita	5,109 m (16,762 ft)
Ras Dashen	4,620 m (15,157 ft)

1,520 m (about 4,000 to 5,000 ft). Despite the division, all of sub-Saharan Africa shows a gradual downward slant from east to west.

On the high side of Africa, continental uplifting caused by the breakup of Gondwanaland has given rise to many mountain ranges and highland regions. These include the Great Escarpment, which parallels Africa's southern coast from Angola to southern MOZAMBIQUE; the Cape Fold Mountains and the Drakensburg Mountains in SOUTH AFRICA; the Mitumba Mountains in the DEMOCRATIC REPUBLIC OF THE CONGO; and the highland regions of KENYA and Ethiopia. On the low side of the continent, highland regions in GUINEA, CAMEROON, and the SAHARA break up otherwise flat landscapes.

A system of RIFT VALLEYS adds to the dramatic topography of East Africa. The rift valleys formed when tectonic plates expanded, opening wide and steep chasms that stretch for nearly 7,000 km (4,350 mi), from Jordan through the Red Sea to central Mozambique. Vertical walls reach 900 m (about 3,000 ft) in some places, and the valley width ranges from 32 to 80 km (20 to 50 mi). Lake Tanganyika, Lake Malawi, and Lake Turkana all lie within these valleys. The tectonic forces behind the rift have caused extreme displacements of geological strata, allowing paleontologists and anthropologists access to prehistoric fossil records. Volcanic activity also contributed to the rifting process and created Africa's highest peaks, MOUNT KENYA and Mount KILIMANJARO. Although the change is imperceptible in human time, it is rapid for geologic time. Soon—at least, soon geologically—East Africa will break from the continent, much as MADAGASCAR did in geologically recent times.

VICTORIA FALLS. Mist rises from Victoria Falls, a mile-wide waterfall on the Zambezi River, as the water drops into a 355-foot gorge on the border between Zimbabwe and Zambia. (*Prints and Photographs Division, Library of Congress*)

The rivers of Africa reveal another peculiarity of the continent's geological history. Of the five major rivers—the NILE RIVER, the Orange River, the NIGER RIVER, the CONGO RIVER, and the ZAMBEZI RIVER—the latter three follow odd and circuitous routes before draining into an ocean. Their dramatic changes of direction over long distances suggest that in ages past they drained into landlocked basins rather than into the ocean. Geomorphologists suspect that only with subsequent uplift did these rivers find their way to the coast. The presence of such basins across the continent lends credence to the theory. Broad shallow basin formations in CHAD, SUDAN, and the KALAHARI DESERT serve as the sole repositories for waters from inland rivers.

Because the major rivers of Africa follow twisting routes, they prohibit extensive navigation. Some of the same waterfalls and rapids that prevent their use as transportation, however, hold great potential for hydroelectric power generation.

Although tectonic forces have shaped much of Africa's geomorphology, other processes are also at work. Climate may combine with chemistry to produce dramatic

formations. In Africa's Guinea Savanna regions, inselbergs—solitary, dome-like outcroppings of rock—arise when weather causes some minerals to deteriorate faster than others. Climate also influences soil production: when winds and rain erode rocks, they create the mineral particles that combine with organic material to become soil. Because the so-called parent material from rocks contains the mineral component of soil, rock composition plays an important role in soil fertility.

The slopes of many highland regions, for example, support abundant flora and in some places intensive agriculture, because their volcanic, basaltic bedrock contains high amounts of iron-magnesium minerals. Soil erosion and a phenomenon called leaching, however, prohibit any simple correlation between bedrock and fertility: When water runs downhill or drains into the water table, it often takes mineral content with it. For this reason, the soil on hilly slopes of rain forest is often less rich than the proliferation of plant life might suggest.

The soils of Africa correspond roughly with the biomes that define the BIOGEOGRAPHY OF AFRICA. Oxisols exist throughout 40 percent of the tropical rain forests and contain high amounts of iron and aluminum oxides. Ultisols predominate in subhumid or Guinea Savanna regions. They are often less weathered and thus more fertile than Oxisols, even if they contain less biomass. Altisols, named for their high aluminum content, occur in savanna regions. When well maintained, they can support extensive agriculture. Vertisols abound in subhumid to arid regions. They are rich in minerals, but their high clay content makes them difficult to cultivate. Aridisols of the deserts and the SAHEL, finally, contain little organic material.

See also CLIMATE OF AFRICA.

BIBLIOGRAPHY

Adams, W. M., A. S. Goudie, and A. R. Orme, eds. *The Physical Geography of Africa*. Oxford University Press, 1996.

ERIC BENNETT

Gerima, Haile
1946–
Ethiopian film director, critic, and professor.

Haile Gerima was born in Gondar, ETHIOPIA. As a child, he acted in his father's troupe, performing across Ethiopia. In 1967 Gerima moved to the United States and two years later enrolled in the University of California at Los Angeles drama school. There he became familiar with the ideas of black American leader Malcolm X and wrote plays about slavery and black militancy. After reading the revolutionary theory of THIRD CINEMA, however, Gerima began to experiment with film. Gerima returned to Ethiopia in 1974 to film *Harvest: 3,000 Years*, his first full-length film and the only one of his works to be shot in Africa. Although famine and the recent military overthrow of Emperor Haile Selassie I placed severe restrictions on the film crew, the final result was a sophisticated examination, through the story of a village that finally overthrows its feudal landlord, of the centuries-old oppression of the Ethiopian peasantry. The film was well received on the international film circuit and won the 1976 Oscar Micheaux Award for Best Feature Film from the Black Filmmakers Hall of Fame. Since *Harvest*, the majority of Gerima's film projects have examined problems facing African Americans. Although he is Ethiopia's best-known film director, he has spent most of his career in the United States. In 1976 he released *Bush Mama*, a black-and-white film about the political awakening of a black welfare mother. That same year Gerima joined the faculty of Howard University in Washington, D.C. In 1977 he released a documentary on the court case of the Wilmington Ten—nine African American men and one white woman who were convicted of arson and conspiracy in North Carolina in 1972. A federal appeals court overturned the convictions in 1980. Gerima made the film, titled *Wilmington 10–USA 10,000*, with the help of students at Howard University and volunteers from the local community. In 1982 he finished *Ashes and Embers*, a story about African American veterans of the Vietnam War, and in 1985 he released *After Winter: Sterling Brown*, a documentary about African American poet Sterling Allen Brown. His recent works include *Sankofa* (1994), a film about a fashion model possessed by spirits who take her into the past, *Adwa: An African Victory* (1999), a documentary about the 1896 victory of Ethiopians in the town of Adwa over Italian invaders, and *Teza*, a film about a student who returns to his native Ethiopia only to find it embroiled in a period of political turmoil and violent repression. Although Gerima has lived and worked in the United States since 1969, he maintains close ties with other African film directors. An active member of the Fédération Panafricaine des Cinéastes and the Comité Africain des Cinéastes, Gerima has also coordinated several colloquiums and meetings of African film directors in the United States. In addition, Gerima's own studio, Mypheduh Films, Inc., is one of the leading distributors of films by Africans and African Americans in the United States.

See also FILM, AFRICAN.

ELIZABETH HEATH

German East Africa
Former name for the mainland of present-day Tanzania.
See TANZANIA.

German Southwest Africa
Former name of Namibia.
See NAMIBIA.

Ghana
Coastal West African country bordered by Togo to the east, Burkina Faso to the north, and Côte d'Ivoire to the west.
Known as the GOLD COAST until it achieved independence in 1957, the area that is now Ghana was one of the richest in Africa before its conquest by the British. By the early 1800s the wealthy and powerful ASANTE empire controlled most of the country's modern territory. During the colonial period, Ghanaians led the struggle against British colonialism. As the first European colony south of the Sahara to gain independence, Ghana inspired nationalist movements throughout Africa and the world. Yet despite its wealth and proud traditions, Ghana, like other African countries, has struggled with persistent poverty, mounting debt, and political instability and repression. The AFRICAN SOCIALISM espoused by its independence leader, KWAME NKRUMAH, brought political and economic disaster. In recent years, the country has seen economic recovery and democratization, but a dependence on foreign capital still keeps Ghana from reclaiming its former power and prosperity.

EARLY HISTORY
Archaeological evidence demonstrates a human presence in modern Ghana for at least the past 35,000 years. Agriculture reached the region by 2000 B.C.E., and iron production began by the first century C.E. A mix of PASTORALISM and cereal cultivation has predominated in the northern savanna region, while the cultivation of roots, tubers, and palm tree crops, supplemented by hunting and fishing, has prevailed in the southern forest zone.

Many Ghanaian ethnic groups have traditions of migration from outside the region before the arrival of Europeans. For example, the DAGOMBA supposedly came from the northeast, while both the GA and EWE have traditions of an origin to the east. The name Ghana refers to an ancient empire centered in modern MALI and MAURITANIA whose descendants, according to legend, migrated to modern Ghana after the empire collapsed in the thirteenth century. Archaeological and linguistic evidence suggests, however, that existing groups have continuously inhabited the country for at least 2,000 years. Traditions of migration may refer to relatively small groups of newcomers who achieved hegemony over existing populations.

Traditionally, lineages, or clans, have held land communally and commanded the loyalty of their members. The

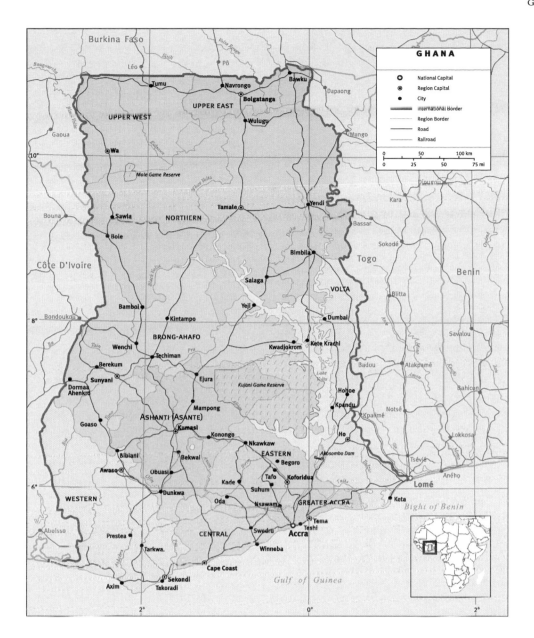

AKAN peoples are matrilineal, while the Ga, the Ewe, and most northern groups are basically patrilineal. By the fourteenth century, Muslim MANDE traders (known also as the DYULA) had arrived in the region to exchange cloth and metal wares from the SAHEL for kola nuts and gold from the Akan, ultimately destined for North Africa. The earliest states in the region, the Akan kingdom of Bono and the northern MAMPRUSI Kingdom, arose during the fourteenth century to control this rich trade.

The arrival of Europeans selling superior weaponry shifted the focus of the Akan gold trade from the Muslim north to the southern coast during the sixteenth century and probably stimulated an Akan expansion toward the coast. Portuguese explorers arrived in 1471 and established

trading posts soon afterward. The Portuguese traded firearms and slaves from other parts of Africa for gold dust. Slaves labored to increase the wealth of the Akan states, and firearms enabled the states to expand. By 1642 the Dutch had displaced the Portuguese from the region, and by 1670 Great Britain and Denmark had established additional coastal trading posts. Because the Dutch, British, and Danes sought slaves to meet a growing demand in the New World colonies, slaves replaced gold as the region's main export, while firearms remained the main import.

The growth of the slave trade provoked wars of conquest. Firearms facilitated the capture of prisoners who could be sold as slaves for more firearms. By the late seventeenth century, the powerful Akan kingdom of Akwamu had conquered the coastal Ga and Ewe, who subsequently adopted Akan state institutions. By the end of the eighteenth century, however, Asante, an Akan empire based in the interior, had conquered Akwamu and parts of the coast, though the coastal Fante (another Akan group) resisted Asante. Asante also conquered large areas of the north, including the kingdoms of Gonja and Dagomba. Conquered regions had to send slaves each year to Asante as tribute. Asante maintained trade connections not only with Europeans on the coast, but also with Muslim regions to the north and northeast. By the eighteenth century, HAUSA traders had taken over the interior trade formerly carried by the Dyula. Their demand for slaves, kola nuts, and other Asante exports helped sustain the empire even after the British banned the coastal slave trade.

On the coast, the slave trade transformed traditional social relations. An indigenous but increasingly westernized merchant class arose, including the "merchant princes" who controlled the slave trade. Merchants organized plantation agriculture and manufacture to provision the slave traders, and a working class developed to provide the necessary labor. An influential "mulatto" stratum arose through the intermarriage of European merchants and local women. Members of this group often had the advantage of a Western education and served as mediators between European merchants and local elites. When European states banned the slave trade, as did Denmark in 1802, Great Britain in 1807, and the Netherlands in 1814, a political economic crisis ensued. Coastal states lost their main source of income and weaponry and became vulnerable to Asante, whose gold exports financed a steady supply of firearms.

GOLD COAST COLONY

Attempting to replace the slave trade with "legitimate trade" in British-manufactured goods, Great Britain increasingly intervened in the affairs of coastal African states. In 1821 the British government assumed control of Gold Coast possessions from the private African Company of Merchants. Because Asante incursions in the coastal region threatened commercial interests, Great Britain initiated the First British-Asante War (1824–1826). A peace treaty in 1831 ended Asante claims to the coast and brought an upswing in trade, missionary activity, and British power on the coast. In 1844 Fante rulers agreed to British legal jurisdiction; in 1850 Great Britain purchased the Danish coastal possessions and established an informal colonial government.

Great Britain's efforts to extend its power and gain control of the gold trade led to the Second British–Asante War (1873–1874). After Great Britain ceded its western coastal possessions in 1867 to the Dutch, who remained

passive allies of Asante, Fante leaders formed the Fante Confederation, with a constitution based on European models, to resist the Dutch and Asante. When the Dutch abandoned their possessions in 1872, the confederation dissolved. In 1874 the British burned the Asante capital of KUMASI, forced Asante to accept a humiliating treaty, and declared the Gold Coast (south of Asante) a crown colony. British victory ended the power and prestige of the Asante state, which suffered a series of crippling succession struggles, while Asante's northern vassals, including Bono, Gonja, and Dagomba, broke away from the empire.

As the Germans and French seized interior regions to the east, north, and west of the Gold Coast in the SCRAMBLE FOR AFRICA, British merchants sought to extend COLONIAL RULE over the interior to protect markets for British goods and exploit the rich Asante gold fields. In 1896, after Asante refused to accept a British protectorate, Great Britain sent an expedition to Kumasi to demand full payment of the reparations stipulated in the 1874 treaty. When the Asante king failed to meet this demand, the British sent him into exile. An Asante noblewoman, YAA ASANTEWA, organized a national struggle to resist British rule in the Third British–Asante War (1900–1901), also known as the Yaa Asantewa War. After heavy losses on both sides, Asante surrendered for the last time and the British exiled Asantewa, along with the entire Asante leadership. Between 1896 and 1910, Great Britain gradually conquered the peoples to the north of Asante, many of them former Asante tributaries. In 1902 the British annexed Asante and the Northern Territories. When Great Britain acquired the western third of German Togoland after World War I as a mandate, the colonial government at ACCRA ruled the entire territory of modern Ghana.

During the 1890s, the British government attempted to claim uncultivated lineage land to lease to British lumber and mining firms. In response, the Aborigines' Rights Protection Society, composed of the coastal elite in alliance with interior chiefs, successfully defended lineage land rights. Thereafter, mining firms were required to secure leases from chiefs and lineage heads, whose wealth and power grew as a consequence. During the colonial period, British firms mined not only gold, but diamonds, manganese, and, beginning in the 1940s, bauxite. British firms also exploited the Gold Coast's forests for timber.

The coastal elite's resistance to land alienation formed part of a larger and less successful effort to resist economic displacement by better-financed European rivals. As foreign competition undermined their commercial strength, members of the coastal elite acquired a western education in mission schools or Great Britain. Increasingly, they found employment as professionals and midlevel civil servants, since British appointees monopolized the top posts.

Ghana (At a Glance)

OFFICIAL NAME:
Republic of Ghana

FORMER NAME:
Gold Coast

AREA:
239,460 sq km (92,099 sq mi)

LOCATION:
Western Africa; borders Togo, Burkina Faso, Côte d'Ivoire, and the Atlantic Ocean

CAPITAL:
Accra (population 1,925,000; 2002 estimate)

OTHER MAJOR CITIES:
Kumasi (population 1,517,000), Sekondi (335,000) (2005 estimates)

POPULATION:
23,832,495 (2009 estimate)

POPULATION DENSITY:
100 persons per sq km (259 per sq mi)

POPULATION BELOW AGE 15:
37.3 percent (male 4,503,331; female 4,393,104; 2009 estimate)

POPULATION GROWTH RATE:
1.882 percent (2009 estimate)

TOTAL FERTILITY RATE:
3.68 children born per woman (2009 estimate)

LIFE EXPECTANCY AT BIRTH:
Total population: 59.85 years (male 58.98 years; female 60.75 years; 2009 estimate)

INFANT MORTALITY RATE:
51.09 deaths per 1000 live births (2009 estimate)

LITERACY RATE (AGE 15 AND OVER WHO CAN READ AND WRITE):
Total population: 74.8 percent (male: 82.7 percent; female: 67.1 percent; 2003 estimate)

EDUCATION:
Primary school and the first three years of secondary school are free and officially compulsory. In the late 1980s nearly 2.3 million children were enrolled in primary schools, and almost 770,000 were enrolled in secondary schools. By 2000, primary school enrolled 58 percent of eligible children and secondary schools enrolled 31 percent of eligible children.

LANGUAGES:
English is the official language of Ghana and is used in schools. There are at least nine other languages used in Ghana, including Akaupem-Twi, Asante-Twi, Dagbani, Dangbe, Ewe, Fanti, Ga, Kasem, and Nzima, which are also used in schools.

ETHNIC GROUPS:
There are at least seven major ethnic groups in Ghana, including the Fante, Asante, Nzima, Ahanta, Ga, Moshi-Dagomba, and Gonja peoples.

RELIGIONS:
About 63 percent of the population is Christian. About 21 percent adhere to indigenous beliefs, and about 16 percent is Muslim.

CLIMATE:
The climate of Ghana is tropical, but temperatures vary with season and elevation. In most areas there are two rainy seasons, from April to July and September to November. In the north, however, one rainy season lasts from April to November. Annual rainfall is 1100 mm (43 in) in the southern areas and 2100 mm (83 in) in the north. The harmattan, a dry desert wind, is felt in the north from December to March and in the south in January. The average annual temperature is 26° C (79° F).

LAND, PLANTS, AND ANIMALS:
Ghana is mostly lowland with a small range of hills on the eastern border. Eastern Ghana also has one of the largest artificial lakes in the world, Lake Volta, which was created from the Volta River by the Akosombo Dam. The vegetation varies from savanna in the northern two-thirds of the country to a tropical forest zone in the south; much of the natural vegetation in central Ghana has been destroyed by land clearing for agriculture. The southern forests include the giant silk cotton, African mahogany, and cedar trees. Animals include the leopard, hyena, buffalo, elephant, wildhog, antelope, and monkey. Ghana has many species of reptiles, including the cobra, python, puff adder, and horned adder.

NATURAL RESOURCES:
Mineral resources include gold, diamonds, manganese ore, and bauxite. Ghana has small deposits of petroleum and natural gas. Forests and access to the ocean are also valuable resources.

CURRENCY:
The Cedi

GROSS DOMESTIC PRODUCT (GDP):
$34.04 billion (2008 estimate)

GDP PER CAPITA:
$1,500 (2008 estimate)

GDP REAL GROWTH RATE:
6.3 percent (2008 estimate)

PRIMARY ECONOMIC ACTIVITIES:
Agriculture (60 percent of employment), manufacturing, and services

PRIMARY CROPS:
Cocoa, rice, coffee, cassava (tapioca), peanuts, maize (corn), shea nuts, bananas, and timber

INDUSTRIES:
Mining, lumbering, light manufacturing, aluminum, and food processing

PRIMARY EXPORTS:
Cocoa, gold, timber, tuna, bauxite, aluminum, manganese ore, and diamonds

PRIMARY IMPORTS:
Petroleum, consumer goods, foods, and capital equipment

PRIMARY TRADE PARTNERS:
United States, United Kingdom, Germany, Netherlands, and Nigeria

GOVERNMENT:
Ghana is a Constitutional democracy. The executive branch is led by President John Evans Atta Mills. The legislative branch is the elected 200-seat National Assembly. Political parties in Ghana include the New Patriotic Party (NPP), the National Convention Party (NCP) and the Every Ghanian Living Everywhere Party (EGLE).

Elizabeth Heath

After European powers banned the slave trade, Gold Coasters sought other commodities to exchange for European manufactures. While Asante could rely on the export of gold until the British conquest, residents of the coastal region turned to the production of cash crops. Until the 1890s, the most important of these was oil palm, tended by indigenous cultivators. By the turn of the century, peasants in Eweland (then largely part of German Togoland), Akwapim, and Asante were turning to the production of Cocoa. By the 1920s, the Gold Coast produced more than half of the world's cocoa.

The cultivation of cocoa further transformed social relations. In Asante and neighboring regions, cocoa production increased the income and power of the chiefs and lineage heads who controlled the land. In the southeast, however, among the Akwapim and Ewe, cocoa production sustained a rural middle class of small farmers, some of them wealthy enough to employ migrant wage laborers. Migrant laborers traveled to the cocoa-growing regions, mainly from the interior Northern Territories and northern TOGO.

The Northern Territories remained largely undeveloped, mostly because its distance from ports made the transport of cash crops uneconomical. Its inhabitants relied primarily on subsistence farming, supplemented by migrant labor in the mines and cocoa groves of the south. British authorities viewed the north as a labor reserve and relied heavily on northern forced labor (until the 1920s) or coerced labor (for which chiefs received a per capita fee) for the operation of mines and the construction of transportation infrastructure. This export of labor probably perpetuated the north's underdevelopment.

The colonial transportation infrastructure facilitated the export of minerals and cash crops. The Gold Coast's first railway connected coastal Sekondi with interior gold-mining districts in 1898 and was extended to Kumasi in 1903. By the 1920s, the network connected Accra with the interior, including cocoa-producing regions. In 1928 workers completed the Gold Coast's first deep-water harbor at Takoradi, and during the 1920s and 1930s the government commissioned new roads in cocoa-growing districts.

A nationalist opposition began to form during the 1920s, when Great Britain introduced indirect rule, delegating local administration to "traditional" authorities. In the Asante region and most of the Northern Territories, where chiefs retained political and economic power, this policy met little opposition. On the coast, however, members of the powerful mercantile and professional class—who had long since displaced "traditional" chiefs as the regional elite—resented their continued exclusion from real power, despite educational and professional qualifications that equaled or exceeded those of British officials. Members of this group, together with representatives from the GAMBIA, SIERRA LEONE, and NIGERIA, founded the National Congress of British West Africa, demanding majority rule. In response to these demands, Great Britain agreed to limited, minority representation for the local elite in the Gold Coast's legislative council.

During the 1940s, the movement toward independence gained momentum. As the Gold Coast suffered economically to support the British war effort, and Gold Coast recruits fought alongside British soldiers in the name of "democracy" and "liberty" denied them at home, many perceived the moral bankruptcy of colonialism. Meanwhile, the successful independence struggles of Ireland, India, and Pakistan inspired Gold Coast nationalists. JOSEPH DANQUAH and other leading nationalists founded the United Gold Coast Convention (UGCC) in 1947 and invited Kwame Nkrumah to lead the group's campaign for representative self-government. When British troops fired on demonstrators in 1948 and riots erupted, the British jailed Nkrumah, Danquah, and other leaders for "incitement."

The young Nkrumah's radical populism proved threatening to the coastal elite and Asante chiefs who dominated the UGCC, however, and when they ousted him in 1949, he founded the Convention People's Party (CPP). The CPP organized workers and farmers for the first time in a mass movement for independence and staged strikes and other actions. British authorities again imprisoned NKRUMAH for "subversion" and "sedition." The British governor convened a committee of the elite, who drew up a new constitution in 1951 providing for internal self-rule and a legislative assembly that reserved large blocks of seats for chiefs and British officials. However, the CPP won an overwhelming majority of elected seats in 1951, and British authorities released Nkrumah from prison to serve as prime minister. In 1954 Nkrumah's government introduced a new constitution providing for direct election by universal suffrage. As prime minister during the mid-1950s, Nkrumah advocated a mixed economy, sought to attract foreign capital, and focused on the modernization of agriculture and rural development.

Nkrumah and the CPP faced increasing internal opposition. The National Liberation Movement (NLM), led by KOFI BUSIA and based in the Asante region, opposed Nkrumah's government in the 1954 elections. The NLM criticized the CPP for its perceived dominance by southerners, its slighting of the Asante region in legislative representation, and its limitations on the powers of chiefs. The NLM pushed for the establishment of a federal state with regional governments, while the CPP advocated a unitary state. Meanwhile, Ewe activists, concentrated in the southern part of the British Togoland mandate, pushed for unification with the Ewe of French Togo.

In separate 1956 plebiscites, however, a majority of British Togoland residents voted for unification with an independent Gold Coast (though a majority in Ewe districts opposed this), and 70 percent of voters in the remainder of the Gold Coast territories voted for independence according to the CPP's unitary (nonfederalist) platform. In

1957 Great Britain granted independence within the British Commonwealth to the Gold Coast, now renamed Ghana.

REPUBLIC OF GHANA

As the first African colony south of the Sahara to gain independence, Ghana became a model and an inspiration for movements throughout the continent seeking an end to colonial rule. Under Nkrumah, Ghana espoused nonalignment. Nkrumah advocated political unification of Africa under his own leadership and played an instrumental role in the creation of the Organization of African Unity (OAU) in 1963.

Domestically, Nkrumah espoused "AFRICAN SOCIALISM." Strong export earnings during the late 1950s provided the basis for nationalization of private firms, the creation of a large parastatal sector, an attempt at industrialization, and infrastructural expansion. Projects completed under Nkrumah's leadership included the large modern port at Tema, expansion of the road and rail network, and Akosombo Dam, which created LAKE VOLTA, the world's largest artificial lake. The dam supplies hydroelectric power to much of Ghana, as well as to neighboring Togo and BENIN. Road construction in the north facilitated the production of food crops for sale in the more urbanized south. The government expanded health and social services, and Ghana became the first African nation south of the Sahara to provide free and compulsory primary education. By the early 1960s, however, a drop in cocoa prices undermined the financial viability of these ambitious programs, while Nkrumah's use of development programs as patronage for often unqualified favorites escalated costs. By the mid-1960s, Ghana's debt threatened its financial stability, and living standards declined.

After independence, Nkrumah moved to suppress opposition. Nkrumah and the CPP drew support mostly from farmers, workers, and market women in the southern coastal region, while the regional elite and their clients, both on the coast and in the interior, opposed the government. Shortly after independence, the Avoidance of Discrimination Act (1957) banned all regional parties. Consequently, the opposition merged to form the United Party, led by Kofi Busia. In 1958 the Emergency Power Act and the Preventive Detention Act gave the government sweeping powers to detain dissidents without trial. Many suffered torture or even death in detention. Meanwhile, Nkrumah assumed increasingly autocratic powers. With the establishment of a republic in 1960, Nkrumah became head of both government and state. Nkrumah assumed sole control of the CPP and banned all opposition within the party. In 1964 the government secured majority approval for a referendum that declared Ghana a one-party state under the CPP.

With opposition to Nkrumah's corrupt and increasingly unpopular government effectively outlawed, a joint military-police junta seized power in a 1966 coup that in Ghana was widely believed to have been backed by the CIA. This junta, known as the National Liberation Council (NLC), suspended Nkrumah's major development projects, released political detainees, investigated official corruption, and proclaimed a market economy. Trade liberalization and reductions in taxes won favor among small proprietors and market women, and chiefs enjoyed the restoration of many powers Nkrumah's government had removed. The NLC's austerity program won it financial assistance from the International Monetary Fund (IMF) and World Bank but caused widespread unemployment and hardship. As strikes escalated in 1968 and 1969, the junta created an assembly to draft a constitution for a return to civilian government.

In a 1969 election from which Nkrumah's supporters were banned, Kofi Busia became prime minister. Backed by a coalition of the southern elite and Akan chiefs, Busia's government continued the NLC's economic conservatism. When another drop in the price of cocoa precipitated a financial crisis in 1971, his government raised prices and interest rates, cut government spending, and devalued the currency. A wave of unrest culminated in Busia's removal from office in a 1972 coup staged by troops unhappy with cuts in military spending.

The new military government, known as the National Redemption Council (NRC) and led by Colonel Acheampong, excluded the leadership of the earlier NLC and reversed many of its policies. The NRC nationalized several private companies in 1972, including the largest gold-mining firm, and declared a moratorium on debt payments, which led the IMF to suspend its credit. The NRC suppressed opposition with a Subversion Decree and a Protective Detention Decree. In 1975 Acheampong transferred power to a new Supreme Military Council (SMC), which excluded his rivals in the NRC. Although the military government enjoyed brief popularity when rising cocoa prices revived the economy in 1972, ongoing economic mismanagement, corruption, rising oil prices, and a persistent drought only deepened Ghana's economic woes in the long run.

In the late 1970s, professionals and students held a series of nationwide strikes to demand an end to military rule. In 1977 the SMC agreed to a transition plan for the establishment of an elected government. When the SMC rigged a referendum in 1978 approving continued military rule, another wave of strikes moved the SMC to replace Acheampong with General Akuffo, who appointed a constitutional assembly and scheduled elections for 1979. On the eve of the 1979 elections, a group of junior officers, led by Flight Lieutenant Jerry John RAWLINGS and backed by popular opinion, overthrew the SMC and formed the Armed Forces Revolutionary Council (AFRC). Elections took place as scheduled, while the AFRC purged state offices of corrupt SMC appointees and executed Acheampong and Akuffo. After three months, the AFRC yielded power to an elected government headed by Hilla Limann.

Limann's government inherited a ruined economy and failed to respond effectively when a drop in cocoa earnings led to rampant inflation and severe food shortages. Corrupt government officials made deals with black market profiteers. The government's popularity plummeted when it responded violently to strikes and demonstrations by workers. By 1981 Ghana was approaching famine and bankruptcy, and Rawlings again led a group of soldiers in a successful coup.

Rawlings, who enjoyed widespread support among workers and the poor, pledged to eliminate corruption and profiteering and to give the masses a voice in the government. Declaring that "bourgeois democracy fosters social inequality," he dissolved parliament, banned parties, established the Provisional National Defense Council (PNDC) in 1982, and appointed civilians, many of them radicals, to head government ministries. He encouraged Revolutionary Defense Committees (RDCs) to assume the powers of local government. By 1983 another drought and a wave of fires had deepened Ghana's economic crisis and again brought the country to the brink of famine. Rawlings became disenchanted with leftist ideology and dismissed his most radical ministers. By 1987, after several coup attempts against Rawlings, his PNDC had consolidated its control over the military and the RDCs.

During the mid-1980s, Rawlings negotiated a structural adjustment plan with the IMF and began a program of austerity and economic reform, including privatization, a reduction in the size of the state sector, renewed investment in infrastructure, and incentives for cocoa producers. His government sought foreign investment in the country's mining sector. By the late 1980s, Ghana's fifteen-year economic decline had been reversed, and both economic output and real income were rising.

But austerity measures provoked protests by workers and students, and Rawlings faced pressure from international donors to implement democratic reforms. In 1988 Ghana held nonpartisan elections for local government, and in 1989 Rawlings promised to restore parliamentary democracy. The government announced a timetable for multiparty elections in 1992, and voters approved a new constitution. Rawlings's National Democratic Congress (NDC), with widespread support in the south and parts of the far north, won a substantial victory over the opposition National Patriotic Party (NPP), which was based in Asante and neighboring regions. Despite alleged irregularities, outside observers judged the election "free and fair."

Democratization has brought new challenges. Critics charged Rawlings with abandoning economic discipline and lavishing patronage on voters. Since the 1992 elections, increased government spending has produced budget deficits. A removal of import controls won the favor of market women but led to a growing trade deficit. However, Rawlings and the NDC won a majority again in 1996 in elections accepted as fair by the NPP, and renewed economic reforms have since attracted increased foreign investment. An improved economic and political climate and the 1997 appointment of a Ghanaian, KOFI ANNAN, to head the United Nations have been sources of pride for many Ghanaians. These developments, along with U.S. President Bill Clinton's historic 1998 visit to Ghana, restored Ghana's prominence among African nations.

Ghana's constitution prohibited Rawlings from running for another term in 2000. In the elections that year John Agyekum Kufour was elected president in a contest regarded as free and fair. This marked the first peaceful transfer of power from one president to another in Ghana's history. Under Kufour, Ghana sought debt relief under the Heavily Indebted Poor Country (HIPC) program. His government's policy goals included tighter monetary and fiscal policies, increased privatization, and improved social services. In the elections of 2008, John Evans Atta Mills of the NDC was elected to the presidency. Mills had served as vice president from 1997 to 2001.

See also COLONIAL RULE; GHANA, EARLY KINGDOM OF; GOLD TRADE; HUNGER AND FAMINE; SLAVERY IN AFRICA; *and* STRUCTURAL ADJUSTMENT IN AFRICA.

BIBLIOGRAPHY

Buah, F. K. *A History of Ghana.* Macmillan, 1998.

Carmichael, John. *African Eldorado: Gold Coast to Ghana.* Duckworth, 1993.

Lambert, Youry. *Ghana: in Search of Stability, 1957–1992.* Praeger, 1993.

Shillington, Kevin. *Ghana and the Rawlings Factor.* Macmillan, 1992.

MARK O'MALLEY

Ghana, Early Kingdom of
Great empire of the western Sudan.

Ancient Ghana was important in the ninth century C.E. when it controlled the Wangara area (between the upper NIGER and SENEGAL rivers), which produced great quantities of gold for trade across the SAHARA. Slaves were also traded with the gold, in return for salt from Teghaza in the desert and cloth from North Africa.

In the eleventh century the kingdom of Ghana was described by the Islamic historian al-Bakri (c.1000). Raised in Muslim Spain, al-Bakri wrote historico-geographical surveys of West African kingdoms and empires in Arabic, albeit from a distance. He never traveled south of the Sahara, but instead contented himself with the reports of trans-Saharan traders and explorers. Nonetheless, Ghana was at the apex of its power during the years al-Bakri performed most of his investigations, and it was he who claimed that it was so rich in gold that dogs there had golden collars, and the ruler of the empire was called "lord of the Gold."

Ghana included what is now western MALI and southeastern MAURITANIA, and its area was probably as large as modern NIGERIA. A strong central government presided in the capital city, which was divided into two parts—a town for the traditional rulers, who were pagans, and a town for the merchants, who were mostly Muslims. Historians believe that the town of KOUMBI SALEH (in what is now Mauritania) was the capital of ancient Ghana in its later years.

The power of the empire declined because of competition from other states in the GOLD TRADE. In about 1076 the ALMORAVID rulers of the Maghreb attacked and destroyed Koumbi Saleh, but the invaders were forced to withdraw and Ghana was able to recover. In about 1203, however, it was defeated by the army of Sumanguru, a leader of the people from the area of Takrur to their west. Sumanguru captured Koumbi Saleh, but soon after he, too, succumbed. He was defeated by an army of Malinke-speaking peoples, and by the end of the thirteenth century the remains of ancient Ghana became part of the empire of ancient Mali. Kwame NKRUMAH renamed the Gold Coast after this illustrious ancient kingdom when it became the first of the British colonies in sub-Saharan Africa to achieve independence in 1957.

See also GHANA.

Ghanaian Coffin Art
Tradition of carving and decorating coffins.

Ghanaian coffin art is the work of the GA people of the southern coast of GHANA and consists of coffins made in the shapes of animals or other objects, carved and decorated to represent and honor the dead. Although Ga funerals have long had an element of spectacle and celebration, the tradition of building representational coffins is recent, dating from to the mid-1900s. The art form developed in the village of Teshi, near Ghana's capital city, ACCRA. The coffins, hand-carved from mahogany or lighter wawa wood and brightly painted, feature animals and other objects that symbolize success, prestige, or other attribute. Animals appropriate for representation—including the hen, bull, lion, fish, and shellfish—come from AKAN proverbs. Symbols may also be related to the dead person's profession, such as a canoe for a fisherman, a truck for a driver, or a saw for a carpenter. Still other coffins, shaped like jet planes or expensive cars, represent the deceased person's prestige in the community.

According to local history, the coffin art tradition may have started with the first fantasy coffin made by Ata Owoo (1904–1976), a carpenter and wood carver in Teshi. Since the end of World War II in 1945, the chief, or mantse, of Teshi has on special occasions ridden in a palanquin carried on the shoulders of the strongest men in the village. In the late 1940s, Teshi's largest and most successful wood shop was that of Owoo, who was commissioned to construct a palanquin in the shape of an eagle for the chief. The chief of a neighboring village, a cocoa farmer, was so impressed by the palanquin that he ordered a similar one for himself in the shape of a cocoa pod. Ata Owoo began the project, but the chief died before he finished the cocoa-pod palanquin, and it was used as the chief's coffin instead.

Ata Owoo later encouraged another local carpenter, Kane Kwei (1922–1992), to pursue the art form. In discussing his work, Kane Kwei emphasized that the forms were not traditional; rather, each piece was a wholly original creation inspired by and intended for the person it would eventually contain. Kane Kwei's coffins were discovered by the international art world in 1973 when a Los Angeles gallery owner visited his workshop in Teshi. She immediately ordered seven coffins for import and resale abroad. The workshop worked night and day to fill the order, with Kane Kwei's cousin and apprentice, Paa Joe (b. 1945) playing a particularly important role. In 1977 Paa Joe left the workshop to open one of his own. For many years the two workshops coexisted in Teshi, each producing about thirty coffins annually. When Kane Kwei died in 1992, Paa Joe designed his coffin. Uncharacteristically plain, it was a simple wooden box with small woodcarvings at each corner: a saw, a hammer, a chisel, and a set square. Paa Joe continues to build his distinctive coffins in Teshi, although at a somewhat slower

COFFIN ART. A pair of craftsmen work on a custom coffin in Accra, Ghana, near a finished coffin built to resemble a fish. These customized coffins often represent the deceased's profession. (*Edward Harris/AP Images*)

pace of ten to fifteen pieces each year. A coffin sells for about what the average person in Teshi makes in a year.

BIBLIOGRAPHY

Soppelsa, Robert T. *A Life Well Lived: Fantasy Coffins of Kane Quaye.* African Arts, 1994.

Secretan, Thierry. *Going into Darkness: Fantastic Coffins from Africa.* Thames and Hudson, 1995.

CHRISTOPHER TINÉ

Giriyama

Ethnic group of Kenya, also known as Giriama and Giryama.

The Giriyama primarily inhabit coastal KENYA. They speak a Bantu language and belong to the Nyika cultural and linguistic group. Approximately 550,000 people consider themselves Giriyama.

See also BANTU *subentry on* DISPERSION AND SETTLEMENT.

Gisu

Ethnic group of Uganda, also known as Bagisu, Gishu, Masaba, and Sokwia.

The Gisu primarily inhabit eastern UGANDA. They speak a Bantu language. Approximately 800,000 people consider themselves Gisu.

See also BANTU *subentry on* DISPERSION AND SETTLEMENT.

Globalization and Africa

See AFRICAN CONDITION IN THE SHADOW OF GLOBALIZATION.

Globalization and Africa: An Interpretation

Africa's encounter with globalization has already spawned two widely-quoted phrases: "When the West catches a cold, Africa gets pneumonia," and "The winds from the east are shaking the palm trees." The first suggests the danger of an era in which Africa integrates into the world economy while remaining a dependent producer of primary commodities. The second evokes the political transformations sparked by Eastern Europe's democratic upheavals. The phrases provide a window into two fiercely contradictory views of globalization's moral impact on African life, but they also contain an assumption that unites contestants on both sides of the ideological divide: that globalization is something that shapes Africa, rather than the other way around.

WHAT IS GLOBALIZATION?

Africa's encounter with globalization is not Africa's contact with the rest of the world—the latter being an almost infinite topic. Globalization is a particular way of defining the current era: as an age characterized by the homogenizing and alienating force of capitalist economic integration. The term has cultural connotations, suggesting, for instance, the rise of an international mass culture powered by new communication technology and the market's penetration into greater spheres of human activity. But it is primarily a way to understand the political economy of the post–Cold War world.

The term finds its antecedents in the work of Adam Smith, who argued that the spread of trade was both inevitable and pacific. In Great Britain, the theory inspired Richard Cobden and John Bright's successful agitation against the Corn Laws in the 1840s. And by the early twentieth century the extraordinary growth of trade and investment between Britain and the rest of Europe, combined with the century-long absence of a continent-wide war, made Smith's idea conventional wisdom. In 1911, to tremendous acclaim, Norman Angell wrote *The Great Illusion*, which argued that the deep economic links between Great Britain and Germany made war between the two nations inconceivable.

The idea found favor once again in the late 1960s and early 1970s. The rise of Germany and Japan led theorists to suggest that economic power was increasingly trumping military power in world affairs. Scholars observed that in the case of the United States' relationship with Western Europe, economic "interdependence" made recourse to arms futile.

Interdependence arguments waned in the 1980s with the revival of the Cold War. But in the years since 1989 it has resurfaced with a vengeance in the form of "globalization." Adherents to the theory believe that the world has grown dramatically more economically integrated in recent decades and that this integration diminishes governments' freedom of action, forcing them toward neoliberal economic policies. Beyond this common framework, globalization is understood differently by those who see it as benign and those who see it as malevolent. Proponents tend to see increased integration as the inevitable result of improved communication technology. Critics attribute it to the coercive power of finance capital or to the hegemony of the United States, a country used to relatively unregulated capitalism. Supporters suggest that because globalization produces an increased demand for free economic information, it breaks down authoritarian political systems and spreads liberal democracy. Critics say that globalization destroys established communities and promotes inequality, thereby paving the way for neofascist ethnic revivals. Following Smith and Angell, proponents argue that globalization increases the costs of conflict between nations, while detractors, following Lenin, suggest that globalization fuels a boundless struggle between capital that leads to war.

AFRICAN INTERSECTIONS

Globalization has changed Africa's relationship to the West. During the Cold War the United States and the Soviet Union aided African governments that mouthed their ideological dogmas and helped them intervene in neighboring conflicts. France and Great Britain may have been motivated more by cultural ties, but they also sought allies that bolstered their position in world affairs. It mattered little what domestic policies client governments pursued, and pro-U.S. and pro-Soviet clients tended toward similar authoritarian political structures. Furthermore, despite U.S. and Soviet rhetoric, neither superpower bothered much with their clients' economic systems. Although pro-Western states like KENYA and MALAWI may have geared their economies somewhat more toward the export of cash crops, both "capitalist" and "communist" African governments tended toward public ownership of key industries, price controls that favored city dwellers over agricultural producers, overvalued currencies, and tariffs that blocked foreign competition in order to encourage domestic industry.

In the current era of capitalist triumph there is no Soviet Union to which aid-dependent African countries can turn; the West is the only source of assistance. And because the United States no longer sees Africa as part of a global struggle that threatens its security, the anticommunist rhetoric that used to elicit aid no longer does. Some aid still flows to countries that are seen as strategically valuable. For instance, America's increased concern over Islamic revivalism and international terrorism has led it to try to isolate SUDAN and to support countries like UGANDA, ETHIOPIA, and ERITREA, which assist the rebels in Sudan's south. To some extent France and the United States also compete for influence, particularly in Central Africa, where France backed MOBUTU SESE SEKO in Zaire (now DEMOCRATIC REPUBLIC OF THE CONGO) and the Hutu-chauvinist MDP government in RWANDA, and the United States supports the regimes that overthrew them.

But geostrategic considerations no longer dominate Western patterns of aid. Globalization advocates often argue that this has "freed" Western donors to lend only to countries that practice democracy and human rights. And there is no doubt that the number of fledgling democracies in Africa has grown since 1989—partly because of popular uprisings inspired by the revolutions in Eastern Europe and partly because dictators lost the funding that secured their rule. The early 1990s saw the first free elections in decades in countries like BENIN, ZAMBIA, MALI, and Malawi. The waning of the Cold War also made it easier for the United States to cut its economic ties to SOUTH AFRICA; and the end of the specter of communist domination helped convince the governing NATIONAL PARTY to enter negotiations with the AFRICAN NATIONAL CONGRESS, which it saw as less threatening without its Soviet ally.

Critics deny that globalization has contributed to African democracy. They point to SOMALIA and LIBERIA, where the end of Cold War funding brought down pro-Western autocrats but where a disengaged West refused to give any new leader the resources to establish control. The result in both places has been anarchic civil war. They also point to ALGERIA, where neoliberal economic reforms may have contributed to the mass unemployment that fueled Islamic extremism. They note that capitalist reforms are often so unpopular that they require government repression to carry them out. And they offer Uganda and GHANA as examples of authoritarian regimes favored by Washington long after the Cold War's end.

The critics are correct that the relationship between globalization and democracy is somewhat beside the point. It is devotion to unregulated capitalism, more than either democracy or strategic advantage, which determines Western treatment of African countries in the age of globalization. U.S. President Bill Clinton designated Ghana and Uganda as the first two stops on his 1998 trip to Africa because they are Africa's most diligent adherents to neoliberal economic orthodoxy. Over the past decade the decline of international communism and the economic success of newly industrialized countries in East Asia have led to a surge of confidence among Western (especially American) elites in the superiority of market-oriented development strategies. As a result, the West increasingly conditions aid on economic deregulation: specifically, the lifting of tariffs against foreign imports, the abolition of purchasing boards that kept prices for agricultural staples artificially low, the privatization of much state-owned industry, the reduction of budget deficits, and the devaluation of currencies to make exports more internationally competitive. These factors led Prime Minister Edouard Balladur in 1994 to force France's former African colonies to accept a 50 percent devaluation of the CFA Franc, the currency guaranteed by the French central bank. The United States-Africa Free Trade Act supported by President Clinton would open some U.S. markets to African goods, if African countries eliminate most government controls on the economy. Supporters argue that countries that have pursued such strategies have seen a rise in economic growth. The increased African acceptance of such policies has even led procapitalist publications like The Economist to declare an end to long-standing Western "Afro-pessimism." Opponents, including relief agencies like Oxfam, argue that such policies reduce government spending on education and health care, thereby increasing poverty, and deny African countries the right to use tariffs to industrialize, relegating them in perpetuity to reliance on the volatile market for primary commodities.

As economic criteria have taken precedence in the globalization era, institutional control of Western aid has also shifted. Governments today are much more likely to take their lending cues from the International Monetary Fund (IMF) and the World Bank, the institutions charged with monitoring economic reforms. During the Cold War, by contrast, the World Bank and IMF more frequently adapted their economic evaluations to the political agendas of Western governments. As a result, African protests against neocolonialism are more apt to center not on American or French military intervention but on the "structural adjustment" policies of the IMF—dubbed by its critics "the Infant Mortality Fund".

The protesters have had difficulty articulating a coherent counteragenda, but two outlines exist. The first rejects capitalist integration as unjust because it denies African governments the right to try to change their subordinate position in the international economy. It envisions global integration of a different kind—led by invigorated international institutions like the United Nations—through which global resources would be redistributed according to state needs. This is not a new idea; it echoes the calls during the 1970s for a new international economic order. But it enjoys much less political support today than it did then, when it was backed by the Soviet bloc and the powerful oil-producing states. Attacks on capitalist integration are also weaker today because the Third World is less united. Many Asian and Latin American countries have since the 1970s developed much stronger economic links to the West—both as exporters of low-end industrialized goods and recipients of foreign investment. Neoliberal governments in places like Chile and South Korea no longer see their countries as sharing a common set of interests with the economically disengaged states of Africa.

The second antiglobalization agenda is not statist international integration, but African regional integration and self-reliance. This idea is not new either. It was advocated in the 1960s by Kwame NKRUMAH, who spoke of a "United States of Africa," and by Julius NYERERE, who furthered the EAST AFRICAN COMMUNITY. The idea has new life in the globalization era because of Africa's decreased relevance to superpower politics—it was Cold War rivalries, for instance, that helped destroy the East African Community in the 1970s. Weary after its Somalia intervention, the United States has even proposed the creation of an African peacekeeping force that would respond to humanitarian crises. One prominent Africanist, Ali MAZRUI, has called for a "new colonialism," in which larger African countries would take control of dysfunctional neighbors until they could effectively govern themselves.

African governments do seem increasingly willing to abandon the ORGANIZATION OF AFRICAN UNITY'S long-cherished principle of noninterference in the internal affairs of neighboring states; many countries, for instance, denounced a 1997 coup in SIERRA LEONE. But Africa still lacks regional hegemons powerful and prestigious enough to replace the Western powers. Postapartheid South Africa has supported regional integration through the SOUTHERN AFRICAN DEVELOPMENT COMMUNITY (SADC), and it has intervened to restore democracy in LESOTHO. In West Africa, NIGERIA leads the long-standing ECOMOG (The Economic Community of West Africa's Military Observation Group) peacekeeping force in Liberia. But Nigeria is too beset by internal troubles to win the confidence of its neighbors. In Central Africa, an alliance of countries led by Uganda and Rwanda toppled former Zaire's Mobutu Sese Seko, believing him to be a force for regional instability. But it is unclear how this political self-reliance could be translated into a strategy for economic development. Since most African states produce the same kinds of goods—primary commodities—they don't complement one another well as trading partners. And except for South Africa, no nation has the capital to invest substantially in its neighbors.

The 1997–1998 economic crisis in East Asia sparked new concerns about the dangers of massive unregulated investment across national borders. Such concerns, combined with protectionist sentiment in the developed world, may lead to new restrictions on global trade and capital flows. Some even see the coming of a post-globalization era. For African critics of globalization, any movement against unfettered capitalism would be welcome. But its impact would be unpredictable. As with the transition from the Cold War to globalization, Africa will feel the effects of a shift to a newly regulated or segmented world economy—but it will not be that shift's author.

See also STRUCTURAL ADJUSTMENT IN AFRICA; UNITED NATIONS IN AFRICA.

PETER BEINART

Gogo

Ethnic group of Tanzania.

The Gogo primarily inhabit TANZANIA's central highlands. While the Gogo speak a Bantu language, they have adapted many of the cultural traits of MAASAI pastoralists. As many as 1.3 million people consider themselves Gogo.

See also BANTU subentry on DISPERSION AND SETTLEMENT.

Gola

Ethnic group of West Africa.

The Gola primarily inhabit western LIBERIA and neighboring SIERRA LEONE. They speak a Niger-Congo language belonging to the Western Atlantic group, although they have borrowed considerably from the neighboring MENDE people. Approximately 200,000 people consider themselves Gola.

See also LANGUAGES, AFRICAN: AN OVERVIEW.

Gold Coast

Former name of Ghana.
See also GHANA.

Gold Trade

Production, trade, and use of gold in Africa from precolonial times to the present.

Gold was an important commodity in precolonial Africa. African rulers valued it as a prestige item in their own land and exported it to overseas markets. The standard gold weights used during the Constantine era of the Roman Empire have been found in West Africa, indicating that gold crossed the SAHARA as early as the fourth century. Around the mid-eighth century, the governor of Ifriqiya (present-day TUNIS) proposed digging wells from southern MOROCCO to the West African savannas to facilitate the transport of gold and slaves.

Although Arab sources suggest that enormous amounts of gold crossed the Sahara before the tenth century, some scholars believe that camel caravans carried a total of only 2,000 to 3,000 kg (4,000 to 7,000 lbs) across the desert during the first millennium C.E. Demand increased in the eleventh century, when the Fatimid caliphate of North Africa sought gold as a means of financing their battles against the Umayyads of Spain and the Abbasids of Baghdad. Other early markets for Africa's gold included the courts of India and the Far East.

Gold deposits in several different regions enriched Africa's precolonial cities and kingdoms. In West Africa, for example, trade in gold from Bure, on the headwaters of the NIGER RIVER, stimulated the rise of the MALI EMPIRE in the thirteenth century. In the fourteenth and fifteenth centuries, the trade in gold in the AKAN region (present-day GHANA) provided revenue for the Bono kingdom. Much of the gold traded in the cities of DJENNÉ and TOMBOUCTU came from Bambuk, just south of the upper SENEGAL RIVER. Gold deposits in Dafina and LOBI were exploited beginning, probably, in the mid-fourteenth century.

Gold was also important to commerce and precolonial state formation in East and Southern Africa. The Arab explorer al-Masudi noted significant gold exports from the MOZAMBIQUE coast in the year 916. The city-state of Mapungubwe, located on the southern banks of the Limpopo River, rose during the tenth century after establishing control over the gold trade. With the demise of Mapungubwe, power shifted south to the kingdom of GREAT ZIMBABWE. Scholars speculate that the founders of Great Zimbabwe owed their wealth to control of the twelfth-century trade in gold from the Save River valley. Skeletons have been discovered at the bottom of narrow, ancient mining shafts in the region. At the peak of the trade, an estimated 1,000 kg (2,204 lb) of gold passed through Great Zimbabwe annually. The port cities of Sofala and, later, Kilwa (in present-day TANZANIA), where much of this gold was destined, flourished from the commerce. After Great Zimbabwe collapsed around 1450, a succession of gold-trading dynasties originated in the region of present-day ZIMBABWE and Mozambique, beginning with Mutapa and Torwa in the fifteenth century and followed by Rozwi in the seventeenth century.

The early years of gold trading and mining were best documented in West Africa. MANDE merchants carried much of the gold from the forest regions to Tombouctou and other savanna towns; they hid gold dust in quills to avoid being robbed. They exchanged the gold for commodities such as SALT, swords, IRON, copper, cloth, silk, and horses. Arab, BERBER, and Jewish traders then carried the gold north across the desert on dromedaries. Numerous dangers existed along the way, as a 1352 account by the Berber explorer IBN BATTUTAH testifies. Sandstorms could disorient navigators, and caravans that were heedless of vital watering holes could perish en route. One such unfortunate camel caravan, dating from the twelfth century, was recently discovered. Two thousand brass bars weighing a total of approximately 907 kg (1 ton) were found among the remains.

Merchants' need to accurately measure quantities of gold led to the use of standardized weights. Arab traders are believed to have brought the first scales and weights to West Africa, where a sophisticated artistic tradition of gold weights later developed, particularly among the Akan. Elsewhere, seeds were routinely used to measure quantities of gold under a standardized system that spread with the Arab trade in gold across the Sahara. In North Africa, mints for coining gold dinars were built in KAIROUAN (TUNISIA) and Fustat (EGYPT) during the eighth century, as gold replaced cowries and iron as the most important medium of exchange.

Little is known about early methods of gold mining. The peoples who actually mined or panned for gold typically did not reveal to traders their exact sources of the valuable mineral. The few existing records portray gold mining as an often arduous and dangerous task. In Bambuk, gold mining was a dry-season activity; men would quarry the ore, from which women would extract the gold. Slaves were often employed to work in the mine shafts, and accidents were probably common, as they have been in more contemporary mines.

After Portuguese sailing ships began to call on ports such as Shama and Elmina (both in present-day Ghana) during the fifteenth century, the West African gold trade gradually began to turn away from the Sahara. The Portuguese acquired some 42,185 kg (93,750 lb) of gold, mostly from Mande traders, during the fifteenth and sixteenth centuries. Much of this gold came from the interior ASANTE region. Other Europeans followed, including French pirates who preyed upon gold-laden ships from as early as 1492. English merchants became increasingly active after the mid-sixteenth century; they were followed by the Dutch. In the nineteenth century, when the British colonized the region that provided so much of the precious metal, they called it the Gold Coast.

Since the late nineteenth century, SOUTH AFRICA has become the continent's greatest producer of gold. It is estimated that half of the world's current gold reserves are located in South Africa. The 1886 discovery of gold in the AFRIKANER-controlled TRANSVAAL region attracted many independent miners as well as large European-owned companies, but only the latter had the heavy machinery needed to exploit deep deposits. After the Boer War (1889–1902), the Transvaal fell under British control. The gold mines there and in the Rand (an area near JOHANNESBURG, which by the 1890s was producing one-fourth of the world's gold) required huge labor forces. Many of the workers migrated from rural areas in South Africa or neighboring colonies, seeking wages to pay colonial taxes. South Africa's gold mines were dangerous and paid whites much higher wages than blacks or coloureds received. But they also became sites of early labor organization and protest.

Gold remains an important commodity for South Africa, but its mining industry faces numerous problems. Because shallow reserves have been exhausted, costly deep mining is now required. The quality of gold ore has declined over time, narrowing profit margins. Furthermore, each year hundreds of miners are killed and thousands are injured in mining accidents.

Since the end of APARTHEID, many of South Africa's largest mining companies, such as the Anglo-American Corporation, have begun to invest in gold exploration and mining in Ghana and other West African countries. For example, they recently spent more than U.S. $300 million to develop the Sadiola mine in Mali. The Gold Fields company, founded by Cecil Rhodes, draws an increasing proportion of its revenue from Ghana's Tarkwa mine. As of 2005 South Africa gold mines accounted for 12 percent of the world's gold discovery, and gold mines generated revenue representing some 18 percent of the country's GDP. The long-dormant gold industry of Burkino Faso has become that nation's second largest source of revenue, after cotton; much of the initial investment capital came from the United States and Canada. Foreign firms are also exploring mining operations in East and Central Africa, in countries such as the REPUBLIC OF THE CONGO and Tanzania.

See also CAPE COLOURED.

ARI NAVE

Golden Stool, The
Sacred symbol of the Asante nation; believed to possess the *sunsum* (soul) of the Asante people.

According to legend, the Golden Stool—sika 'dwa in the AKAN language of the ASANTE—descended from heaven in a cloud of white dust and landed in the lap of Osei Tutu (the first Asante king) in the late 1600s. The king's priest, Okomfo Anokye, proclaimed that henceforth the strength and unity of the Asante people depended upon the safety of the Golden Stool. Drawing upon the Akan tradition of a stool indicating clan leadership, the Golden Stool became the symbol of the united Asante people and legitimized the rule of its possessor. To defend the stool in 1900, the Asante battled the British in the so-called YAA ASANTEWA War. The Asante chose to let the British exile the Asante's last sovereign king, Prempeh I, rather than surrender the stool. Today the Golden Stool is housed in the Asante royal palace in KUMASI, GHANA. The stool leaves the palace for public viewing only in conjunction with the most important ceremonies. Measuring 46 cm (18 in) high, 61 cm (24 in) long, and 30 cm (12 in) wide, the stool never touches the ground; it rests on its own platform or on animal skins. No one is ever allowed to sit on it. When the Asante king is inaugurated, or enstooled, he is lowered over the stool three times without touching it. (Today the Asante king holds limited powers, subject to the government of Ghana.) The Asante are proud that although the British conquered their nation, they never surrendered the stool.

DAVID P. JOHNSON, JR.

Gonder, Ethiopia
Capital of the kingdom of Ethiopia from the seventeenth through the nineteenth century.

The palaces at Gonder remain a mystery. Historians know when they were built, and they know the names of the emperors who founded the capital and adorned it so splendidly. But no one seems to know anything about craftsmen who created a style unknown elsewhere in the country. Ethiopian emperors liked to display their wealth and power by employing foreign experts. Perhaps the palaces incorporate the skills of Italian or Indian masons. Contacts with both countries had increased after the Portuguese had arrived in ETHIOPIA in the sixteenth century. In 1632 the emperor Fasiladas built the first castle at Gonder, then a village near Lake Tana. He may not have intended to create a new capital, but he hoped to find a better residence during the rainy season than the tents of the earlier nomadic court. During the following decades, however, Gonder did become the capital of the empire, and it remained so until the middle of the nineteenth century. It seems that each emperor built his own castle, ignoring those of his ancestors—a custom that may lie in the competitive nature of AMHARA and TIGRINYA society, where young men have traditionally proved their status by surpassing their elders as well as their rivals. The fact that their defensive walls would not have withstood the military technology of the day suggests that they were constructed largely for display. Gonder declined during the chaotic Era of the Princes (1706–1853), when powerful local warlords dominated the emperors who lived among the crumbling palaces. The emperor Tewodros II, whose supremacy ended the anarchy of the Princes, sacked Gonder twice during the 1860s, removing the treasures of its churches. The troops of the Mahdi, the Islamic reformer who founded a state in neighboring SUDAN, also burned the city during the 1880s. Many of the most impressive castles and churches remain, however, along with a charming pavilion known as the Bath of Fasiladas where the festival of Timqat is still celebrated every year to mark the baptism of Christ. Today Gonder is an important regional, economic, and cultural center and the capital of Gonder province. In 2003 the city's population topped 146,000.

See also CHRISTIANITY, AFRICAN: An Overview.

Gonja

Ethnic group of West Africa; also known as Gongya.

The Gonja primarily inhabit northwestern GHANA and northeastern CÔTE D'IVOIRE. They speak a Niger-Congo language and belong to the Guan linguistic group. They established a powerful kingdom during the seventeenth century that was conquered by the ASANTE kingdom during the following century. Today approximately 350,000 people consider themselves Gonja.

See also LANGUAGES, AFRICAN: An Overview.

Gordimer, Nadine

1923–South African novelist, Nobel Prize winner, and outspoken opponent of apartheid.

In a 1965 interview, Nadine Gordimer assessed her political consciousness with a self-scrutiny that characterized much of her political writing: "I have come to the abstractions of politics through the flesh and blood of individual behavior. I didn't know what politics was about until I saw it all happening to people." In her novels and short stories, Gordimer has captured the "flesh and blood of individual

behavior" in minute and sentient detail, chronicling daily life in SOUTH AFRICA under APARTHEID and portraying the human face of resistance.

Gordimer grew up in a small gold-mining town near Johannesburg, South Africa, the daughter of a Lithuanian Jewish father and an English mother. Although she read voraciously as a child, she was removed from school at age ten because of a perceived heart ailment and had little formal schooling. Trailing her mother to afternoon teas, the lively Gordimer spent her time observing and mimicking the people she would later portray so astutely—the "well-meaning" members of white South African society. By age fifteen, when her first story for adults appeared in a journal, Gordimer was already a seasoned writer of children's stories.

A new world opened to Gordimer in 1949 when she began taking courses in Johannesburg at the University of Witwatersrand. There she mixed with musicians, journalists, and writers, for the first time crossing the color line that segregated blacks from whites. As she read the philosophies of Marxism, nationalism, and existentialism, she began to question the social structure of apartheid. She also became involved in the political and cultural movement of the SOPHIATOWN renaissance, which produced the literary journal Drum.

During the same year that she began attending classes in Johannesburg, Gordimer published a book of short stories, Face to Face. Her first novel, The Lying Days (1953), was a loosely autobiographical coming-of-age story. She gained international recognition when her stories were published in the New Yorker magazine during the 1950s. A prominent critic of apartheid and an open supporter of the AFRICAN NATIONAL CONGRESS, Gordimer continued to live in South Africa under apartheid despite the repeated banning of her books. The remarkably prolific writer has published twelve novels and thirteen short story collections.

In the words of critic Stephen Clingman, her writing has represented "the rise to power of the National Party in 1948; the life under apartheid; the political, social and cultural world of the 1950s; the sabotage and resistance of the 1960s, as well as their defeat by the state; the rise of the Black consciousness movement in the 1970s and the Soweto Revolt; the revolution which seemed to have begun by the 1980s." In her well-known novel Burger's Daughter (1979) Gordimer examines the political choices made necessary by the heroine Rosa Burger, the daughter of two communist revolutionaries, who finds herself ultimately unable to opt out of political commitment. Like two of her earlier books, Burger's Daughter was initially banned.

Without compromising her realistic portrayal of the political world, Gordimer also explores the realm of sexuality in works such as the Late Bourgeois World (1966), July's People (1981), and Sport of Nature (1987). Under a political system where the body—skin color, hair texture, facial features—defines identity, she has argued that the political and sexual are inextricable. Her narrative style, influenced by such Russian authors as Ivan Turgenev, links the social, political, and personal. Using the gestures, words, and thoughts of her characters, she portrays "a society whirling, stamping, swaying with the force of revolutionary change."

In numerous essays, collected into four volumes, Gordimer has commented on the politics of writing and the evolution of leftist political action. She has also written on aesthetics and literary criticism and on her own travels around a rapidly changing continent. In her autobiographical essays she probes and scrutinizes the evolution of her own thinking—always with a self-critical gaze at her own position as a white woman.

A self-proclaimed political radical, Gordimer was one of the most visible opponents of apartheid for those outside of South Africa. With a long-established readership abroad, her words have reached a broader audience than most black authors writing on similar issues. Her international reputation, particularly after she won the Nobel Prize for literature in 1991, protected her from some of the reprisals that faced other South African radicals. After receiving the Nobel Prize, Gordimer spoke about the responsibility she felt came with such international prestige: "I have two roles in my life—one as a writer and another one, my commitment to the cause of freedom in South Africa and creating a new post-apartheid culture in South Africa." In her novel *The Pickup* (2001), Gordimer examines the biracial and bicultural relationships that have always been a major part of her work. Among her more recent work is a novel, *Get a Life* (2005), and a collection of short fiction, *Beethoven was One-Sixteenth Black* (2007).

See also BLACK CONSCIOUSNESS IN AFRICA; *and* LITERATURE AND POPULAR RESISTANCE IN SOUTH AFRICA IN THE 1960S.

MARIAN AGUIAR

Gorée Island, Senegal
Island off the coast of Senegal, used as a slave port throughout the transatlantic slave trade.

Settled by southbound Portuguese explorers in the mid-fifteenth century, Gorée Island was first called Palma and served as a port of call for Portuguese ships sailing along the west coast of Africa. Though small, barren and lacking fresh water, the island was of strategic importance to the Portuguese because it was sheltered by the tip of the CAPE VERDE peninsula, had excellent anchorage for large ships, and lay only 4 km (2.5 mi) from the African mainland, at the intersection of several major Atlantic shipping routes. Explorers on their way to Asia around

the southern tip of Africa, including Vasco da Gama and Fernando Po, frequently stopped on the island to pick up supplies and conduct repairs, and as contacts with the mainland developed, the island became a key European outpost to Africa. Because of its strategic value, possession of the island was hotly disputed; in 1588 the Dutch seized it from the Portuguese, renamed it Goede Reede (later corrupted to Gorée) and built two defensive military forts on it. In the next three centuries Gorée changed hands seventeen times, fought over by the Portuguese, the Dutch, the French, and, briefly, the British. The island became increasingly valuable because it offered whoever controlled it a monopoly on the trade in hides, gum, ostrich feathers, wax, gold and, most importantly, slaves. Through Gorée, SENEGAMBIA became one of the most important outlets of the slave trade, supplying at least a third of the captives exported before 1600. By the sixteenth century Gorée had become a bustling port where slaves from the entire region were assembled, examined, and branded before being sent to the Americas. As one of the principal slave ports of the transatlantic slave trade, Gorée was the site of great cruelty, brutality, and violence for nearly three centuries. After the end of the slave trade in the mid-nineteenth century economic activity shifted to the mainland and Gorée declined steadily. It is now a historical tourist attraction administered by the Senegalese government.

See also SENEGAL.

Gouin
Ethnic group of West Africa; also known as the Guin and Kpen.

The Gouin primarily inhabit far northern CÔTE D'IVOIRE and southwestern Burkina Faso. They speak a Niger-Congo language and are closely related to the SENUFO people. Slightly more than 100,000 people consider themselves Gouin.

See also LANGUAGES, AFRICAN: AN OVERVIEW.

Gouled Aptidon, Hassan
1916–2006
President of Djibouti.

Hassan Gouled Aptidon was born to an ISSA family in the village of Garissa, but at age fourteen he left his home to live at a Roman Catholic mission. During his youth he earned a living as a local peddler and as a construction worker.

Gouled began his political career as an activist in the Somali and Danakil Youth Club during the 1940s, where he soon rose to prominence. From 1952 to 1958 he represented French Somaliland (present-day DJIBOUTI) in the

French Senate. He lobbied successfully for continued association with France in a 1958 referendum and represented the overseas territory in the French National Assembly from 1959 to 1967. During this period, France increasingly favored the minority AFAR ethnic group over the more numerous Issa people, fearing Issa allegiance to the Somalis would result in the territory being annexed by the newly independent Somaliland. Angered by French favoritism toward the Afar, Gouled unsuccessfully advocated independence in a second referendum in 1967. In 1972 Gouled became president of the nationalist Ligue Populaire Africaine pour l'Indépendance (LPAI).

The LPAI won broad-based support for independence, and a third referendum in May 1977 endorsed the formation of an independent Republic of Djibouti. In the elections that followed, Gouled became president and his LPAI was swept to power. Initially Gouled sought to create an ethnically representative government. Within a few years, however, the Afar minority began to feel alienated and underrepresented. In 1979 Gouled dismantled the LPAI and outlawed other parties. He created a single-party state and won reelection in 1981 and again in 1987 as the only candidate permitted on the ballot.

During the early 1990s Gouled faced growing popular discontent and an armed Afar rebellion. Attempting to defuse the opposition, he permitted multiparty elections in 1992. However, Gouled chose which opposition groups could contest seats in the election, leading most Djiboutians to boycott the elections. They rejected the results that returned Gouled to power once again.

Organizations such as Amnesty International criticized Gouled's regime severely for terrorizing the civilian population, torturing prisoners, and denying due process, particularly during the Afar insurgency of the early 1990s. At the same time, he won praise for maintaining a stable government despite the conflicts that tore apart the neighboring countries of ETHIOPIA and SOMALIA, where he even helped to broker peace agreements. Near the end of his term in office, the aging Gouled sought to address Afar demands by increasing government representation for the minority group. In 1999, after twenty-two years in power, Gouled resigned and Ismail Omar Guellah, his nephew and handpicked successor, was elected president. Gouled died in the fall of 2006.

ARI NAVE

Goun

Ethnic group of West Africa; also known as Gun.

The Goun primarily inhabit southeastern BENIN. They speak a Niger-Congo language and belong to the ADJA cultural and linguistic group. Approximately 300,000 people consider themselves Goun.

See also LANGUAGES, AFRICAN: AN OVERVIEW.

Gowon, Yakubu
1934–
Soldier, statesman, and former head of the military government of Nigeria.

Former Nigerian president Yakubu Gowon was born in Plateau State, Nigeria. As the country's military ruler from 1966 to 1975, he advocated unity for Nigeria and national reconciliation after the conclusion of the Biafran War. After his ouster in a bloodless coup, Gowon took the role of a senior statesman and continued to work toward regional cooperation in West Africa.

A Christian missionary's son, Gowon was born into the ANGA ethnic group in the Northern Region of Nigeria. He completed secondary school in Zaria, Nigeria, in 1953. Gowon joined the Nigerian army and began his military training in Teshie, GHANA in 1954. In 1955 he moved to Great Britain, where he completed his studies at the Royal Military Academy in Sandhurst the following year.

Gowon served in Ibadan, at the Nigeria-CAMEROON border, and in The Democratic Republic of Congo. He attained the rank of lieutenant colonel by 1963. At the beginning of 1966 he commanded the Second Battalion. As the senior northern officer who survived the January 1966 IGBO-led coup, Gowon was appointed army chief of staff. Northern officers chose him to head the new military government after the northern-led counter-coup of July 1966.

Once in power, Gowon desired a quick return to civilian rule, but Nigeria faced civil conflict. Massacres of Igbos in the north frightened and outraged Nigeria's Igbos, who dominated the Eastern Region. In 1967 Gowon declared a state of emergency and divided Nigeria's four regions into twelve states. This redrawing of internal boundaries effectively put most of Nigeria's lucrative oil fields just outside Igbo territory. Consequently, under Igbo leadership, the Eastern Region seceded in 1967 as the independent state of Biafra.

After the Biafran War in 1970, Gowon sought reconciliation and declared that there would be "no victor and no vanquished." From 1970 to 1975 he implemented policies aimed at reconstruction. He helped establish the National Youth Service Corps (NYSC) and the ECONOMIC COMMUNITY OF WESTERN AFRICAN STATES (ECOWAS). He issued a nine-point transition program by which power would be transferred to a civilian government in 1976.

In July 1975, however, the army overthrew Gowon while he attended a meeting of the ORGANIZATION OF AFRICAN UNITY in KAMPALA, UGANDA. Gowon fled to Great Britain, where he lived in exile and earned a doctorate in political science from Warwick University. He later returned to Nigeria and continued to advocate national reconciliation. After the 1993 military coup, he promoted a peaceful return to democratic rule. During the 1990s, Gowon headed the committee to review the ECOWAS treaty, assumed the post of chairman of the National Oil and Chemicals Marketing Company, headed Nigeria Prays (a religious organization dedicated to social, political, and religious reconciliation in Nigeria), and continued to work with the NYSC. He worked with the Arewa Consultative Forum, a political organization in northern Nigeria. Gowon remains active in politics on the continent, though usually in an unofficial capacity.

ROBERT FAY

Great Zimbabwe

Historic city in southern Africa, established in the eleventh century and flourishing for about 300 years.

At its height Great Zimbabwe dominated much of the present-day country of Zimbabwe. By the end of the fifteenth century the city had declined and had been all but abandoned. Today the stone ruins of Great Zimbabwe, located in south central Zimbabwe, make up a national monument.

HISTORIC STATE

By the eleventh century, Iron Age SHONA-speaking people had established a village on a hilltop near the modern town of Masvingo in south central Zimbabwe. The rulers of this community originally derived their wealth and power from cattle herding. However, during the twelfth century peoples to the north and west discovered and began mining the rich gold vein on the plateau of what is now central Zimbabwe. By the thirteenth century the hilltop village had become a major gold-trading center, located advantageously between the gold-bearing plateau and numerous African and Arab trading posts on the Indian Ocean coast. The village grew into a city and its Shona rulers, profiting from the gold trade, raised a large army to expand their power and built the elaborate stone structures that gave the city its name. Zimbabwe is derived from the Shona phrase dzimba dza mabwe, which means "houses of stone."

By the fourteenth century Great Zimbabwe used its commercial and military power to dominate a state that ranged from the Zambezi River in the north to the Limpopo River in the south and from the fringes of the Kalahari Desert in the west to the Inyanga, Vumba, and Chimanimani mountain ranges in the east. Many other smaller ruins built in the style of Great Zimbabwe are scattered throughout modern Zimbabwe, eastern Botswana, and northern Mozambique, demonstrating the scope of Great Zimbabwe's influence.

Great Zimbabwe had about 10,000 to 20,000 inhabitants shortly before its abrupt decline at the end of the fifteenth century. Historians disagree on the cause of Great Zimbabwe's fall. Many scholars believe that the city's population grew so large that it used up the region's agricultural resources, forcing inhabitants to move away. Another theory is that Great Zimbabwe lost its commercial importance because northern gold-mining regions began transporting gold to the coast by way of the Zambezi River rather than through Great Zimbabwe. By the sixteenth century the city of Great Zimbabwe was almost completely deserted.

RUINS OF THE CITY

In the nineteenth century the ruins of Great Zimbabwe were found and studied by Europeans, who generally refused to believe that black Africans could have built such impressive stone structures. European archaeologists proposed highly improbable theories that an ancient Mediterranean civilization, such as the Egyptians, Phoenicians, Greeks, Hebrews, or Arabs, built Great Zimbabwe. These theories became widely accepted. Even after archaeological research in the early and mid-twentieth century proved that Great Zimbabwe was indeed the work of Iron Age black Africans, the non-African origin of the ruins was taught in many schools in RHODESIA (as Zimbabwe was known in colonial times) until independence in 1980.

The stonework of Great Zimbabwe is remarkable for its precision. Most structures were built with granite blocks so carefully carved that no mortar was required to hold them together. The focal point of Great Zimbabwe is a high granite outcrop that rises steeply above the valley below. On the summit of this outcrop is a set of stone walled enclosures known as the Hill Complex. Scholars believe one of the two large enclosures was a place of worship because it contains plastered altars and carved stone birds, which likely represent the spirits of former rulers. The other large enclosure was a residential area, probably either for the king or for the principal spirit medium, the leading official in the Shona religion.

The ruins of the city of Great Zimbabwe are on the hillside and in the valley beneath the Hill Complex. The city consisted of two parts: the residences of the general population and those of the elite. The general population lived in closely packed mud-and-thatch houses; little is known about the way they lived. A small number of elite people lived inside stone enclosures at the center of the city, in residential areas hidden by high stone walls. These sheltered living quarters testify to the high status and authority of the Great Zimbabwe ruling class.

STONE RUINS. Portuguese traders first encountered the stone ruins of Great Zimbabwe in the sixteenth century. The word Zimbabwe is derived from Shona words meaning "houses of stone" or "venerated house." (*Prints and Photographs Division, Library of Congress*)

The largest of the residential enclosures in the city is known as the Great Enclosure. The Great Enclosure has a complex set of architectural features, including outer walls as high as 10 m (32 ft) and as thick as 5 m (17 ft), and a tall, conical stone tower. Archaeologists have different interpretations of this part of the site. Some believe this was the residence of the king's principal wife, while others argue that it was the king's compound. In the Great Enclosure archaeologists have discovered gold and copper ornaments, as well as fine soapstone bowls and carvings. They have additionally found china, glass beads, and porcelain dating from fourteenth-century China, Persia, and Syria. The presence of such luxury items from so far away demonstrates Great Zimbabwe's valuable connections with traders on the east coast of Africa.

The modern nation of Zimbabwe is named after Great Zimbabwe, and images of the soapstone birds found in the Hill Complex appear on the nation's flag and currency. For today's Zimbabweans, the ruins of Great Zimbabwe are a source not only of income from tourism but also of cultural pride.

Grebo
Ethnic group of West Africa.
The Grebo inhabit primarily southwestern CÔTE D'IVOIRE and southeastern LIBERIA. They speak a language of the KRU group. Approximately 300,000 people consider themselves Grebo.

See also LANGUAGES, AFRICAN: AN OVERVIEW.

Griot
Professional poet-musician and storyteller in West Africa; known for a style of performance, typically accompanied by a string or percussion instrument.

Most griots are found in GAMBIA, MALI, and SENEGAL. Within these countries, griots exist among the MANDINKA (also known as Malinke) peoples, who are West African speakers of related languages in the Mande subfamily. Griots are also found among the FULANI. All of these societies share similar types of social organization and musical styles. The term griot is of French origin and is used in much of West Africa, although in many areas people tend to use equivalent terms from local languages. In some areas people use the related terms dyeli, jali, and gewel, which can be used interchangeably in some contexts. In Mali the Mandinka word denoting a professional musician is dyeli. In Gambia, Mandinka people call a male professional musician jali and a female professional musician jalimuso. Among the WOLOF of Senegal and Gambia, a professional musician is called a gewel. The musical techniques of the griot have influenced various African American musical styles, including

American blues. Parallels to the griot's role as a professional verbal artist, professional poet-musician, and improviser of lyrics can be heard in North American and Caribbean genres such as the blues, Calypso, and Rap.

ROLE IN PRECOLONIAL SOCIETIES

Until the demise of traditional Malian kingships at the end of the nineteenth century, the dyeli played an important role in the social and artistic life of the royal courts, and the noble families were their primary patrons. Mandinka nobility considered it undignified to publicly display emotion through singing, dancing, playing a musical instrument, or in some cases, even by speaking. Therefore, the noble family would retain a dyeli in the household to provide musical and poetic entertainment. The dyeli also played a vital social and ritual role by acting as the public voice of the patron and the whole noble family. In this way a dyeli was as much a verbal specialist as a musician. As a representative for the noble family, the dyeli might help negotiate marriages or sing at weddings, praising important guests and thanking them for gifts. The dyeli also played an important role at the funeral of a noble, praising the deceased and his ancestors. The dyeli attended all significant occasions for the noble's family and assumed responsibility for chronicling the family's history and genealogy. The dyeli often used this in-depth knowledge of the family to sing historical narratives and public praise songs. In other contexts a dyeli might have been called upon to use his musical and verbal prowess to improvise songs that criticized or insulted the patron's enemies. Female dyeli were sometimes present at births, where they could play a role in naming children.

IMPACT OF COLONIAL RULE

European colonialism in the nineteenth and twentieth centuries transformed West Africa, and most of the region's royal courts disappeared. With the demise of royal social and political structures, griots lost their primary source of income. Although caste systems still survive in some places, kingships have been dismantled, forcing modern griots to develop new sources of patronage. A few have been successful at forging international performing careers. Some other griots support themselves by singing genealogy praise songs and historical narratives for important political officials. Some find work as freelance musicians for seasonal celebrations, religious occasions, or important events such as weddings and funerals. Some other griots are forced to rely on a sort of ritualized begging, in which unsuspecting patrons in a public setting are chosen and praised. The patron is then socially obligated to pay the musician, even though they did not request his service and may not be able to afford it.

CONTEMPORARY CASTES

Many societies in West Africa are hierarchically organized into castes—hereditary status groups based on profession, rank, or wealth. Each caste has rights and responsibilities in relation to the others. Griots typically comprise their own special caste or are in a caste with others who have highly specialized skills. Although the specific name for the caste varies from place to place, the griots' musical, social, and ritual responsibilities are generally quite similar. The role of the griot in the Mandinka societies of Mali, for example, is typical of the social role of griots elsewhere. In these cultures, musicians are part of a middle-class caste known as nyamakala, which also includes blacksmiths and leatherworkers. As a group the nyamakala are seen as talented people who have important and valuable skills, though they are sometimes looked down on by members of higher castes.

MUSICAL STYLE

The most common instruments used by griots today are harps, lutes, and xylophones, although there is evidence that some griots in the past used drums. In contemporary Mali a dyeli often accompanies himself on the kora, a hybrid harp-lute with twenty-one strings found only among the Mandinka. Accompaniment may also be provided on the bala (or balo), a type of xylophone found throughout West Africa. In Mali, as in other areas, griots also frequently accompany themselves with plucked lutes. The Wolof gewel typically performs on the xalam, a five-string plucked lute that most experts consider an ancestor of the African American banjo. The Mandinka dyeli uses a similar instrument called the ngoni. Despite the demise of kingships in the late nineteenth and early twentieth centuries, the music of modern griots is deeply rooted in the classical repertoires of songs developed at the royal courts. Contemporary performance contexts have changed, and today performers may incorporate electric instruments. Despite such innovations, narrative styles and processes of musical creation still show strong continuity with core traditional themes of West African music cultures. One of the most important techniques for constructing the instrumental accompaniment to a griot song is the use of repetition, with carefully controlled variation. The foundation for many griot songs consists of an alternation between two chords within a repeating rhythmic structure of two or four measures. The griot will sing precomposed and improvised lyrics over this cycle, while creating subtle variations to the instrumental pattern. During the singing, the instrumental part is subdued and repetitive. In instrumental sections the playing becomes more elaborate. The Mandinka dyeli (in Mali) and Mandinka jali (in Gambia and Guinea), for example, are highly skilled with their instruments and often improvise intricate independent melodies while simultaneously maintaining the underlying rhythmic and harmonic cycle.

NORTH AFRICAN INFLUENCES

Several aspects of griot music, including patterns of melody, demonstrate similarity with styles of Islamic North Africa, reflecting the significant influence of Muslim culture in many West African societies. Griot melodies typically begin on a high pitch, descending to a lower pitch through elaborately ornamented melody lines. The Islamic North African influence is also apparent in the vocal style of many griots, which is often described as nasal or tense. There are also parallels in the social organization of music making between Islamic North Africa and the griot cultures. They share an emphasis on solo performance, although the primary musician may be supported by others. In both North and West Africa, women participate in professional music making mainly as singers, if at all. A griotte (female griot) may excel in singing historical narratives and praise songs. However, control of musical instruments is generally considered a male domain, so men usually provide her accompaniment.

Gronniosaw, James Albert Ukawsaw

1710–1775

African prince sold into slavery whose life story became an influential book.

James Albert Ukawsaw Gronniosaw's idyllic childhood as a prince in the area that is now NIGERIA came to an abrupt end when a merchant persuaded the teenaged Gronniosaw to travel to the Gold Coast (present-day GHANA) and then sold him into American slavery. Years later, in Great Britain, Gronniosaw related his story to a Dutch woman, who wrote and published Narrative of the Remarkable Particulars in the Life of James Albert Ukawsaw Gronniosaw, An African Prince, related by himself (1770). Class-conscious British readers were sympathetic to the story of the victimized African prince; the book was widely read and later influenced the British slave narratives of the authors and abolitionists Olaudah EQUIANO and Ottobah CUGOANO. Gronniosaw was a slave to several Dutch families in colonial New England. His last owner was Theodorus Jacobus Frelinghuysen, a Dutch Reformed minister in New Jersey, who bought Gronniosaw in 1730, taught him Dutch, and presided over his conversion to Christianity. On his deathbed in 1748, Frelinghuysen granted freedom to Gronniosaw. Gronniosaw left to serve in the British Navy

and then moved to London where he became known as James Albert Ukawsaw Gronniosaw. After spending the year of 1762 in the Netherlands, Gronniosaw returned to London to marry a white weaver he had met previously. His minister and friends objected to the marriage not because of the difference in race, but, according to Gronniosaw, "because the person I had fixed on was poor." The Gronniosaw family moved frequently, finding work where they could, but suffering long periods of poverty and deprivation. Shortly after moving his family to Kidderminster, a town whose inhabitants were known for their religiosity, Gronniosaw narrated his life story to a young local woman. She published it in the hope that the sales would profit the Gronniosaws; little is known of their lives after this. The document, however, helped enable the abolitionist battle in England and remains one of the most compelling slave narratives.

BIBLIOGRAPHY

Potkay, Adam, and Sandra Burr, eds. Black Atlantic Writers of the Eighteenth Century. St. Martin's Press, 1995.

LEYLA KEOUGH

Groupe Africain du Cinéma, Le

Group of film students that produced the first film by black Africans and helped end French colonial restrictions on African filmmaking.

In 1955 Paulin VIEYRA, a young Senegalese film director living in Paris, founded a film troupe with three African friends—Manadou Saar, Robert Cristan, and Jacques Melo Keno. Calling themselves Le Groupe Africain du Cinéma, the three filmmakers attempted to direct and shoot the first film by Africans in Africa. Vieyra and his friends petitioned the French government for the right to film an independent movie in SENEGAL. Their petition was rejected, however, under the Laval Decree, a law that restricted the content of films shot in Africa and prohibited Africans from making films in Africa altogether. As a result, Le Groupe Africain du Cinéma remained in Paris, where it shot the first African film, Afrique sur scène, in late 1955. At the same time, the group was determined to have the Laval Decree overturned as a first step toward building an autonomous African film industry. Gathering the support of prominent French film directors and filmmakers, the group again petitioned the French government. The government finally overturned the Laval Decree in 1962. Even after that time, France continued to exert its influence over the Francophone African film world, because few of its former colonies had the funds or the equipment to promote film production independently.

ELIZABETH HEATH

Grusi

Ethnic group of West Africa; also known as Grunsi, Grunshi, Gourounsi, and Gurunsi.

The Grusi primarily inhabit northern GHANA and southern BURKINA FASO. Some Grusi live in TOGO. They speak a Niger-Congo language. Between 600,000 and 700,000 people consider themselves Grusi. The term also refers to a cultural and linguistic grouping that includes the Grusi proper and several related groups, including the BUILSA, the DAGARI, the KASENA, the LILSE, and the SASALA.

See also LANGUAGES, AFRICAN: AN OVERVIEW.

Gude

Ethnic group of West Africa; also known as Cheke, Mapuda, Mubi, the Shede, and the Tchade.

The Gude primarily inhabit eastern NIGERIA. They speak an Afro-Asiatic language in the Chadic group. Nearly 200,000 people consider themselves Gude.

See also LANGUAGES, AFRICAN: AN OVERVIEW.

Guéré

Ethnic group of West Africa; also known as Gewo, Krahn, Kran, and Wé.

The Guéré primarily inhabit western CÔTE D'IVOIRE and neighboring eastern LIBERIA, where they are usually known as the Kran. They speak a Niger-Congo language in the KRU group and are closely related to the WOBÉ people. The Guéré number over 300,000.

See also LANGUAGES, AFRICAN: AN OVERVIEW.

Guèye, Lamine

1891–1968

Influential anticolonialist Senegalese politician who organized the first modern political party in French-speaking Africa.

Born to Senegalese parents in present-day MALI, Guèye fought in France during World War I and remained to study law. Guèye returned to SENEGAL in 1922. The first black lawyer in French-speaking Africa, he was elected mayor of Saint-Louis in 1925. From 1931 to 1934 he served as a magistrate on the island of RÉUNION in the Indian Ocean. In 1935 Guèye, an opponent of French colonialism, assumed leadership of the Parti Socialiste Sénégalais (PSS). He focused on recruiting the educated elite and made the PSS into the first modern political party in French-speaking Africa. In 1936 he affiliated the PSS with the French Socialist Party (SFIO). Guèye promoted Léopold SENGHOR's career, and both men won seats representing Senegal in the French Constituent Assembly in 1945 and 1946. As a member of the Assembly, Guèye helped secure eligibility for French citizenship for all colonial subjects. From 1946 to 1961, Guèye served as the mayor of DAKAR. Rejecting what he saw as Guèye's narrow focus on elite support, Senghor broke with Guèye in 1948 to establish his own party, the Union Progressiste Sénégalaise. This party became Senegal's dominant party and later defeated Guèye and SFIO candidates. Senghor and Guèye reunited in 1958 and sought unsuccessfully to combine French African colonies in an independent federation; they lost to those who sought separate statehood for each colony. When Senegal achieved independence in 1959, Guèye was elected president of the Senegalese National Assembly—an office he held until his death in Dakar in 1968.

Guinea

Coastal West African country bordered by Guinea-Bissau, Senegal, Mali, Côte d'Ivoire, Liberia, and Sierra Leone.

Although today Guinea struggles with persistent poverty, the country possesses agricultural and mineral riches and an equally rich history. In precolonial days the area now known as Guinea was home to several distinct ethnic groups—principally the MANDINKA (or Malinke), FULANI, and SOSO. The region was also the site one of Africa's longest-lasting autonomous Islamic theocracies, known as FOUTA DJALLON. Under French COLONIAL RULE, Guinea was one of the most productive of West African colonies. Its lucrative exports included rubber and bananas. However, French investors and merchants retained most of the wealth those exports produced.

Guinea achieved renown as the first of the French colonies to claim independence, and it served as an example to other African nations seeking autonomy. Guineans voted in 1958 to break ties with France. In the words of Guinea's first president, SÉKOU TOURÉ, Guinea chose "poverty in freedom to opulence in slavery." In fact, poverty has haunted Guinea since independence. Hunger and disease are widespread, literacy levels are low, even by African standards, and the infant mortality rate is among the highest in the world.

EARLY HISTORY

Archaeologists have found evidence of human occupation in present-day Guinea dating back 30,000 years. Artifacts show that inhabitants of the central Guinean savanna were farming cereals such as millet and sorghum by 1000 B.C.E. The people of the southeastern forest region were cultivating yams, oil palms, and vegetables by 100 B.C.E. By around 200 B.C.E. the region's inhabitants were smelting iron. Anthropologists believe that the earliest inhabitants of upper Guinea may have been the ancestors of modern MANDE speakers.

Upper Guinea (the northeastern savanna region) formed part of the heartland of the great Mande empires of GHANA and MALI. The first of these, ancient Ghana,

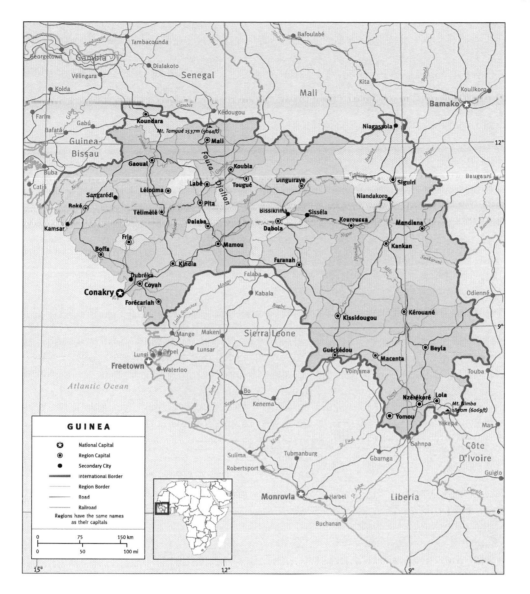

also extended into present-day Mali and MAURITANIA. Ghana achieved its power by controlling trade—in particular, by exacting duties in gold for the transport of salt from northern mines—and it dominated the western savanna from the eighth to the eleventh century. Ghana was supplanted by the MALI EMPIRE, which arose around 1200 C.E. under the leadership of the Mandinka king, Sundiata Keita. Mali also exploited the rise of long-distance trade, including gold and slaves transported across the SAHARA for markets in the north of Africa. The upper Guinea city of Kankan became a center of Islamic scholarship under Mali's rule.

Ancestors of the Baga, Nalu, and Kissi peoples once occupied most of present-day Guinea west and south of the Mande upper Guinea region. However, migrations of

Mande-speaking peoples starting in the tenth century drove the ancestors of the Baga and Nalu toward the coast and the ancestors of the Kissi toward the forests of the southeast. Gradually, the Mande-speaking Soso people came to dominate the Fouta Djallon highlands of central Guinea, while the KPELLE and LOMA moved into the forest region.

Internal divisions caused the slow collapse of the Mali empire beginning in the fourteenth century. Starting in the fifteenth century, a new migration brought Fulani herders to the Fouta Djallon highlands. Although the first Fulani migrants mostly followed traditional religious practices, subsequent waves included Islamic Fulani migrating from areas in present-day Senegal. Islamic Fulani founded Fouta Djallon, an Islamic theocratic state, in the early eighteenth century. Fouta Djallon was a strictly hierarchical society with a ruling class (led by two families from which the alimamies, or leaders, were chosen), artisans, and slaves (mostly consisting of non-Muslim Fulani and non-Fulani inhabitants). To escape this forced servitude, the Soso people who had lived in the region began moving to coastal lower Guinea, where they dominated and gradually absorbed the existing Baga and Nalu populations.

The Soso and other coastal peoples established trade relations with the Portuguese, who first arrived on the coast during the fifteenth century. European powers were attracted to the region's strategic location for trade to the NIGER RIVER Valley. By the eighteenth century the French and English came to dominate the coastal trade. The Europeans traded guns, alcohol, and other products for ivory, gold, and slaves (although the Transatlantic Slave Trade remained relatively small-scale in Guinea). By the early nineteenth century, they had begun to explore the hinterland. The first English expedition inland was in 1816; the French soon followed, with explorations in 1818 and 1827.

Meanwhile, the Fulani maintained a powerful theocratic state in the Fouta Djallon. Their culture of Islamic revival helped spark the rise of the Tukolor empire in the 1840s. Its leader, UMAR TAL, a Fulani-speaking Islamic scholar, ruled over a kingdom that included parts of upper Guinea and the area comprised of present-day SENEGAL and Mali.

COLONIZATION

In the early nineteenth century the French established a trading settlement on the northwest coast as an outpost of their colony in Senegal. In 1849 they declared the coastal region a protectorate, administered from Senegal. They concluded treaties of mutual protection with indigenous leaders and began erecting an administrative structure that eventually included the entire area now known as Guinea. France established three military posts in the region by 1866. At first, the French promoted the cultivation of peanuts, but the humid coastal climate proved unsuitable for this cash crop. During the 1880s the French shifted their focus to the extraction of rubber. On the site of an old Soso fishing village known as CONAKRY, the French founded a town in 1880. In 1891 Conakry became the capital of the newly founded colony of French Guinea.

French colonization, however, met heavy opposition. The Fulani of the Fouta Djallon continued to resist French control. Meanwhile, the Mandinka-dominated region produced one of Guinea's historic heroes: Samory Touré. Touré built an empire covering much of present-day eastern Guinea, southern Mali, and northern Côte d'Ivoire during the 1880s. He fought colonization by the French for nearly twenty years until his defeat in 1898. Although the French defeated Fouta Djallon in 1896 and captured Touré in 1899 in a series of bloody campaigns, isolated resistance movements continued for another twenty years.

Under colonial rule, French commandants headed the colony's administrative districts. Each of these, in turn, oversaw several smaller districts, ruled by indigenous African leaders. The colonial government selected these "chiefs," often from a different ethnic group than the people of their districts, on the basis of their loyalty to the colonial government. As a result, local puppet-chiefs reinforced French rule in Guinea.

Colonial rule also transformed Guinea economically. French laws made former communally held land available for purchase, and France's colonial "head tax" on all Guineans increasingly forced people to supplement traditional subsistence farming with participation in the cash economy. The head tax compelled many Guineans to cultivate cash crops, especially rubber in the coastal and forest zones and peanuts in upper Guinea. During the 1920s, after a collapse in the demand for Guinean rubber, French officials introduced coffee cultivation to the forested highlands. During the 1930s, French investors established banana and pineapple plantations in the country, and the head tax compelled many Guineans to seek menial jobs on these plantations. Meanwhile, educated Guineans found employment in the lower levels of the civil service. For the French, Guinea became a fairly lucrative holding, as its economy shifted from traditional occupations like subsistence farming and craft-production to large-scale farming of peanuts and tropical fruits for export.

INDEPENDENCE MOVEMENT

The French colonial system, increasingly under attack by both French Socialists and the educated elite of Africa, began to loosen after World War II (1939–1945). In 1945 new colonial laws permitted the formation of political parties and trade unions. The growth of unionism in Guinea received added impetus from European communist and socialist parties as well as religious organizations. The Guinean labor movement formed part of a larger Pan-African movement, promoted through regional meetings sponsored by the French Confédération Générale du Travail (CGT).

Fighting a system in which European workers earned three to four times more than indigenous Guineans on the same jobs, the country's communications workers were the first to organize. Sékou Touré, who would become independent Guinea's first president, got his start as the secretary general of the postal workers' union in 1945. The rise in unions such as Touré's occurred alongside similar growth in political parties. In 1946 Touré was instrumental in the formation of the RASSEMBLEMENT DÉMOCRATIQUE AFRICAIN (RDA). He also helped found its Guinean branch,

Guinea (At a Glance)

OFFICIAL NAME:
Republic of Guinea

FORMER NAME:
French Guinea

AREA:
245,857 sq km (94,925 sq mi)

LOCATION:
Guinea is bounded on the north by Guinea-Bissau, Senegal, and Mali, on the east and southeast by Côte d'Ivoire, on the south by Liberia and Sierra Leone, and on the west by the Atlantic Ocean.

CAPITAL:
Conakry (population 1,857,153; 2008 estimate)

OTHER MAJOR CITIES:
Kankan (population 197,108; 2006 estimate)

POPULATION:
10,057,975 (2009 estimate)

POPULATION DENSITY:
41 persons per sq km (106 people per sq mi)

POPULATION BELOW AGE 15:
42.8 percent (male 2,175,852; female 2,128,518; 2009 estimate)

POPULATION GROWTH RATE:
2.572 percent (2009 estimate)

TOTAL FERTILITY RATE:
5.2 children born per woman (2009 estimate)

LIFE EXPECTANCY AT BIRTH (TOTAL):
Total population: 57.09 years (male 55.63 years; female 58.6 years; 2009 estimate)

INFANT MORTALITY RATE:
65.22 deaths per 1000 live births (2009 estimate)

LITERACY RATE (AGE 15 AND OVER WHO CAN READ AND WRITE):
Total population: 29.5 percent (male 42.6 percent; female 18.1 percent; 2003 estimate)

EDUCATION:
Education is free and officially compulsory for all children between the ages of 7 and 13. By 2006, 64 percent of the country's children were completing their full primary education, up from only about 37 percent in the early 1990s. In 2000 primary schools enrolled 47 percent of eligible primary school-aged children and secondary schools enrolled 12 percent of eligible secondary school-aged children. Private schools were nationalized by 1962. The universities at Conakry and Kankan, along with 21 other institutions, provide higher education.

LANGUAGES:
While French is the official language, almost every Guinean speaks one of eight national languages: Malinke, Soso, Fulani, Kissi, Basari, Loma, Koniagi, or Kpelle.

ETHNIC GROUPS:
Peuhl constitute 40 percent of the population, the largest group. Most other Guineans are from the Mande group, either Malinke, in northeastern Guinea, or Soso, in the coastal areas.

RELIGIONS:
About 85 percent of the population practices Islam. Most of the remainder adhere to traditional beliefs. Christians form a small portion of the total population.

CLIMATE:
The dominant factor in the consideration of climatic variation is altitude. Rainfall varies most and temperature varies least in lower Guinea. Rainfall in Conakry averages 4300 mm (about 170 in) in a year, while temperature averages 27° C (81° F). In the mountainous plateau region, less rain falls and the mean temperature is 7° C (13° F) degrees lower. The climate in the highlands is equatorial, with no clearly distinguishable seasons. The rainy season in the remainder of the country occurs from April or May to October or November. In terms of heat, April is the cruelest month; July and August are the wettest.

LAND, PLANTS, AND ANIMALS:
Guinea divides into four major topographic regions. Lower Guinea, the coastal plain, extends in from the coastline. Beyond the plain is middle Guinea, the Fouta Djallon, a mountainous plateau region with an average elevation of 910 m (about 3000 ft). The savannas of Upper Guinea undulate gently, breaking occasionally into rocky outcroppings of some elevation. In the extreme southeast are forested highlands. The vegetation of Guinea includes dense mangrove forests along the coast, sedge in the Fouta Djallon, savanna woodland in upper Guinea, and rain forest in the highlands. Animal life abounds. Snakes and crocodiles are common, as are tropical birds, including parrots. Mammals include leopards, hippopotamuses, wild boars, antelopes, and civets.

NATURAL RESOURCES:
Bauxite ore, iron ore, diamonds, gold, petroleum, uranium, cobalt, nickel, and platinum

CURRENCY:
The Guinea franc

GROSS DOMESTIC PRODUCT (GDP):
$10.44 billion (2008 estimate)

GDP PER CAPITA:
$1,100 (2008 estimate)

GDP REAL GROWTH RATE:
2.9 percent (2008 estimate)

PRIMARY ECONOMIC ACTIVITIES:
Agriculture and mining

PRIMARY CROPS:
Rice, cassava, plantains, vegetables, and citrus fruits

INDUSTRIES:
Bauxite, gold, diamonds; alumina refining; light manufacturing; and agricultural processing industries

PRIMARY EXPORTS:
Bauxite, alumina, diamonds, gold, coffee, pineapples, bananas, and palm kernels

PRIMARY IMPORTS:
Petroleum products, metals, machinery, transport equipment, textiles, and grain

PRIMARY TRADE PARTNERS:
France, Côte d'Ivoire, Belgium, and the United States

GOVERNMENT:
Since 1990 Guinea has made a transition from a one-party, military regime to a multiparty, constitutional civilian system. The new system has a unicameral legislature of 114 seats and universal adult suffrage. Presidential elections were held late in 1993 and again in December 1998; Following the death of President Lansana Conté, a military coup installed Captain Moussa Dadis Camara as president. Shortly thereafter, Camara suspended the country's constitution.

Eric Bennett

the Parti Démocratique de Guinée (PDG). Labor unions functioned not only as effective mobilizers across ethnic group lines; they also served as a training ground for the country's future political leaders.

Strikes in 1950 and 1953 helped mobilize the entire population against the inequities of colonial rule. Even nonunionized workers, according to Touré's account, contributed food aid to striking workers. As Rivière points out, such shared struggles contributed to a growing sense of nationalism among indigenous Guineans. Although they had retained more control over local issues than some other colonized people, Guineans increasingly sought more political autonomy along with more economic fairness. The man at the center of both movements was Touré.

Elected to the national assembly in both 1951 and 1954, Touré was barred from his seat until 1956, when he won office as Conakry's mayor. By then, the Mandinka from upper Guinea had gained a reputation as both a powerful speaker and a shrewd politician. By 1957 he was both vice president of the executive council of Guinea (the national governing body) and the founder of the Union Générale des Travailleurs d'Afrique Noire (UGTAN), a new labor union for Africans under French colonial rule. Immensely popular among the poor and dispossessed of Guinea, Touré effectively quashed rival political parties and by 1958 was the acknowledged leader of Guinean anticolonialism.

France's war with ALGERIA spurred a further liberalization of its colonial policy. French President Charles de Gaulle proposed that the colonies be allowed to choose, by referendum, whether to adopt internal self-rule as part of a Franco-African confederation or to claim complete independence. Led in large part by Touré's inspiring rhetoric—although the PDG conducted no campaign on the matter—Guinea, alone among the French colonies, chose full independence. The vote conducted on September 28, 1958, was 1,134,324 to 56,981.

TOURÉ'S REIGN AND BEYOND

Instantly decried as part of a worldwide communist movement, Guinea's vote for independence sparked a harsh French reaction. De Gaulle recalled French administrators, technical workers, and the French machinery that was crucial to Guinea's modern infrastructure. In addition, France cut off all financial aid to its former colony and left Guinea's economy in danger of total collapse.

Touré assumed office as Guinea's first president shortly after the Republic of Guinea gained independence on October 2, 1958. Drawing from his experience both in building coalitions as a union leader and in neutralizing political opponents, Touré effectively co-opted rival parties into the PDG. His efforts at attracting foreign aid, according to historians, were masterful: Touré emphasized the "positive neutralism"

of Guinea in relation to Cold War allegiances and portrayed Guinea as being punished for personally challenging de Gaulle. Despite the influence of such political theorists as Karl Marx and Ghana's KWAME NKRUMAH, Touré's anticolonialist approach was also strategic and pragmatic. Although he reached out to both eastern and western powers, Touré's anticapitalist stance tended to attract the most aid from the Eastern bloc nations such as the Soviet Union, which helped develop Guinea's potential for the mining of bauxite (the raw material for aluminum production).

Within Guinea, Touré began to centralize authority under an increasingly dictatorial state. According to most historians, the combination of limited economic opportunity and growing political repression led as many as a million Guineans to seek refuge in neighboring states. As his long tenure continued—he would retain the presidency until his death in 1984—Touré faced a series of assassination attempts and coup plots. According to analysts, however, it is difficult to distinguish between the real threats to Touré's power and those manufactured to justify the jailings and executions of his political rivals. By the late 1960s Touré began outlawing opposition parties and labor unions. He had prominent Fulani and Mandinka leaders jailed or executed without trial, on the suspicion that these large ethnic groups could mobilize effective opposition.

By the late 1970s, after years of mismanagement by state-run monopolies and dwindling foreign aid, Guinea's economy had reached a standstill. The population began to demonstrate against Touré's policies. Faced with riots in 1977, Touré prudently launched a series of changes. He traveled widely and approached Western lenders—governmental and private—for help in building a more capitalist economy, and he opened the government monopolies to competition. In addition, he tried to improve relations with Guinea's West African neighbors.

In March 1984 Touré died of a heart attack in a Cleveland, Ohio, hospital. The Guinean government fell into turmoil. On April 3, 1984, the Comité Militaire de Redressement National, a military junta headed by Colonel LANSANA CONTÉ, seized control. At first, Conté, who chose fellow soldier Diarra Traoré as his prime minister, seemed poised to reverse many of Touré's excesses. He freed some ninety-seven political prisoners. At the same time, however, he suspended Guinea's constitution.

As president, Conté changed the country's name back to the Republic of Guinea. Since 1978, under Touré, the official name had been the People's Revolutionary Republic of Guinea. Conté promised a gradual evolution toward a multiparty democracy, with free elections to be held sometime in the future. It wasn't long, however, before opposition to Conté arose. His own prime minister, Traoré, allegedly attempted to overthrow Conté in 1985. Conté jailed and executed several of the alleged plotters. In 1987, perhaps fearing that Touré's supporters would attempt another coup, Conté held secret trials in Conakry and had 60 people sentenced to death for "crimes against the state." Since then, Conté's administration has responded to ongoing protests by imposing limits on free expression, public meetings, and opposition parties. In December 1993 Guinea held the first multiparty elections in the country's history. Conté won the presidency by a slim majority in what observers report was an election rife with fraud.

A violent revolt of at least 2,000 soldiers demanding higher pay in 1996 forced president Conté into hiding. Reports suggest that as many as fifty people died during two days of rioting in Conakry. In an attempt to restore confidence in his ability to improve the financial lot of Guineans, Conté appointed an economist, Sidya Touré, to the office of prime minister in 1996; he served until 1999 when he was replaced by Lamine Sidime.

Neither Conté nor his rivals have found an effective solution to the country's grinding poverty. Guinea remains one of the poorest countries in the world. This poverty persists even though Guinea is the world's second-largest producer of bauxite. The country also has important reserves of iron ore, diamonds, and gold. A structural adjustment plan imposed by foreign lenders in the late 1980s has brought little economic improvement. Though structural adjustment measures have boosted exports of minerals and cash crops, they have also ensured that foreign investors would reap most of the benefits. Associated austerity measures have limited the ability of Guinea's government to invest export earnings in economic development that would benefit the country's population. Instead, Guinea is required to devote much of its export revenue to pay interest on its debt to foreign lenders. The influx of refugees from neighboring SIERRA LEONE and LIBERIA throughout the 1990s put a further strain on Guinea's weak economy. In 2000 and 2001 fighting along the border with Sierra Leone and Liberia exacerbated the refugee crisis. More than 300,000 refugees from those nations flooded into Guinea causing further economic disruption and creating a humanitarian emergency.

In 1998 Conté won reelection to a five-year term amidst reports by the opposition that the election was rigged. Several opposition figures were arrested following the election, including Alpha Conde, leader of the Rally of the Guinean People (RPG). Opposition leaders rejected Conté's invitation to join the government, claiming that Conté had not been legally reelected. Though his health has declined, Conté has taken steps to maintain his hold on power. In 2001, he successfully lobbied to end presidential term limits and to extend the term of office to seven years. In 2003 only one little-known candidate gained certification from Guinea's Supreme Court to oppose Conté in

the December election, virtually assuring the president of another term. Amid accusations of plans to rig the election, voters stayed away from the polls, giving Lansana Conté an easy win. In December 2008, however, Conté died, leading to yet another military coup. The transfer of power was halted and Captain Moussa Dadis Camara of the Guinean army assumed the presidency, at which point he quickly moved to suspend the country's constitution.

See also ANCIENT AFRICAN CIVILIZATIONS; COLD WAR AND AFRICA; GHANA, EARLY KINGDOM OF; ISLAM IN AFRICA; *and* STRUCTURAL ADJUSTMENT IN AFRICA.

BIBLIOGRAPHY

Harrison, Christopher. *France and Islam in West Africa, 1860–1960.* Cambridge University Press, 1988.

Rivière, Claude. *Guinea: The Mobilization of a People.* Cornell University Press, 1977.

Touré, Ahmad Sekou. *Africa on the Move.* Panaf Books, 1979.

KATE TUTTLE

Guinea-Bissau

A small country on the West African coast that lies north of Guinea and south of Senegal.

Guinea-Bissau is one of the poorest countries in the world. Its poverty derives from a long history of slave trading, Portuguese colonial neglect, an eleven-year war for independence, post-independence economic mismanagement, and a lack of natural resources. The small, lineage-based communities of Guinea-Bissau have resisted domination by a series of overlords, including the precolonial kingdom of KAABU, European slave traders, FULANI marauders, Portuguese colonialists, and finally the Cape Verdean elite of the nationalist movement. This strong tradition of resistance has been a unifying theme in Guinea-Bissau's history.

EARLY HISTORY

Archaeologists believe that small groups of hunters, gatherers, and fishing people occupied the region by 9000 B.C.E. A more pronounced migration toward the coast came around 900 C.E., when wars, poverty, and climatic shifts pushed new groups into the region from points further east. They were primarily agriculturists and hunters, though some raised cattle on the eastern savanna. The low alluvial plains and mangrove swamps along the coast and rivers sustained salt extraction and tidal agriculture. Over time chiefdoms proliferated. Lineages held land communally and worshiped local gods in addition to their own ancestors.

The MANDINKA were one of the last groups to arrive in the region. Their kingdom of Kaabu, the region's first real kingdom, emerged in present-day northeastern Guinea-Bissau around 1250, originally as a tributary of the MALI

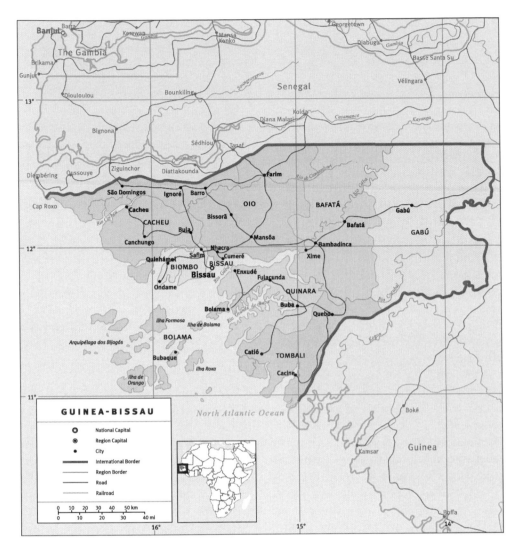

EMPIRE. Kaabu remained powerful for the next six centuries, as it conquered small chiefdoms throughout the region and enslaved their inhabitants. Many groups fled south and west from Kaabu to the coastal lowlands. Others, such as the BALANTA, literally "those who refuse," and the BIJAGÓ of the islands, resisted Kaabu ascendancy and Mandinka dominance. Even when the Balanta were forced to pay tribute to the Mandinka, their adherence to traditional patrilineal succession limited the ability of the Mandinka empire to incorporate them. Kaabu expanded during the late fifteenth and sixteenth centuries, when SONGHAI assaults on the Mali empire, and trade with the Portuguese enabled Kaabu to exercise greater autonomy.

THE SLAVE TRADE AND FOREIGN DOMINATION

In 1446 the Portuguese explorer Nuño Tristão sailed into the Bijagós Archipelago and up some of the rivers, though he died on his return trip. It was not until ten years later that Diogo Gomes returned to Portugal to tell of the "Rivers of GUINEA." The estuaries facilitated trade, and the coastal market town of CACHEU was the commercial center of the region from the late fifteenth to the nineteenth century. At first, the small Portuguese population remained confined to a few coastal settlements, where they paid tribute to local chiefs or kings for the right to stay.

Portuguese and mestiços, or those of indigenous and European descent, traded alcohol, horses, manufactured goods, textiles, and weapons, for copra (coconut flesh, containing the oil), gold, ivory, palm oil, and, increasingly, slaves. Kaabu and other chiefdoms and kingdoms had long been involved in the Arab trans-Saharan slave trade and they simply shifted some of this trade to the Portuguese on the coast. Some groups such as the Balanta, Nalu, Felupe, Manjaco, and others resisted these slave raiding parties. Nevertheless, scholars

GUINEA-BISSAU ART. A pair of carved wooden figurines with horned headpieces and girdles. The figures depict members of the Bidjogo tribe of Guinea-Bissau. (*Private Collection/Bonhams, London, UK/Bridgeman Art Library International Ltd.*)

estimate that from the coming of the Portuguese to the end of the eighteenth century around 600,000 people were sent down the rivers of Guinea to the international slave market. The Portuguese sent slaves to their CAPE VERDE Island territory, where they were put to work on sugar plantations or shipped to the Americas.

As the Transatlantic slave trade shifted further south during the eighteenth century, Portuguese immigrants, mestiços, and Cape Verdeans began establishing larger agricultural estates, or feitorias, along the rivers, and growing peanuts, coffee, sugarcane, and cotton. In the interior, Kaabu, socially stratified and intimately involved in the slave trade, had reached its height, with forty-four provinces providing troops and tribute. When Portugal outlawed the slave trade in 1837, competition in the illicit slave trade increased. Kaabu provincial governors contended for power and control of the trade in intradynastic feuds.

The Islamic Fulani people, who had been subject to heavy Kaabu taxation for generations, eroded the power of the war-torn kingdom through religious conversion and jihads, or holy wars. Often supplied with firearms by the Portuguese, Fulani from the area presently known as Guinea began pushing north in the mid-1800s. The wars between the splintering Kaabu kingdom and the Fulani culminated in 1867 when soldiers loyal to the Fulani marabout (religious leader) Timbo Adbul Khudus forced the surrender of Kaabu, though internal rivalries kept the Fulani from consolidating their rule. However, the fall of Kaabu enabled Portugal to divide the peoples of the region and to rule them through pliable chiefs. In the 1870s and 1880s, Fulani slaves, uncompensated by their Fulani masters for fighting against the Mandinka, revolted. The Portuguese granted the rebellious slaves sanctuary, and in return many of them assisted in Portugal's "pacification" campaigns to subdue the indigenous population.

PORTUGUESE COLONIALISM AND AFRICAN RESISTANCE

When Portugal declared Portuguese Guinea a province in 1879, the Portuguese presence in the region was limited and the Africans, although divided, increasingly resisted. Suffering from tropical diseases and laboring under a lack of funding from colonial authorities on the Cape Verde Islands, the military had thus far failed in its efforts to "pacify" the region. The change in colonial status enabled the Lisbon government to allocate military resources directly to Guinea, which it declared a military district in 1892. But Portuguese pacification campaigns from the 1880s to the 1910s generally remained unsuccessful. The Africans had firearms clandestinely supplied by traders. In addition to these weapons, the Africans used their intimate knowledge of the territories along the rivers in order to hold off the Portuguese military campaigns with ease. In 1908 nearly the whole Portuguese population was forced into the fort at BISSAU. In the 1910s the new republican government in Portugal placed a greater emphasis on crushing African resistance, and the colonial administration succeeded in conquering most of the land, through manipulation and force, and in gaining the support of the Fulani.

Under a fascist dictatorship from the 1920s until 1974, Portugal centralized administrative control over the territory and instituted a harsh system of forced labor and heavy taxation. The Portuguese controlled the administration, and mestiços and Cape Verdeans held over 70 percent of the administrative posts. Appointed regulos, or "chiefs," almost all of whom were Fulani, implemented forced labor on oil palm, rice, and peanut plantations. The lack of capital investment under the Portuguese limited the productivity of these ventures and created the basis for the country's persistent poverty. If they were not on forced-labor plantations, many Africans worked on state-run

Guinea-Bissau (At a Glance)

OFFICIAL NAME:
Republic of Guinea-Bissau

FORMER NAME:

PORTUGUESE GUINEA AREA:
36,120 sq km (about 13,945 sq mi)

LOCATION:
Western Africa; borders the North Atlantic Ocean, between Senegal and Guinea

CAPITAL:
Bissau (population 407,424; 2007 estimate)

POPULATION:
1,533,964 (2009 estimate)

POPULATION DENSITY:
42 persons per sq km (110 persons per sq mi)

POPULATION BELOW AGE 15:
40.8 percent (male 312,253; female 313,609; 2009 estimate)

POPULATION GROWTH RATE:
2.019 percent (2009 estimate)

TOTAL FERTILITY RATE:
4.65 children born per woman (2009 estimate)

LIFE EXPECTANCY AT BIRTH:
Total population: 47.9 years (male 46.07 years; female 49.79 years; 2009 estimate)

INFANT MORTALITY RATE:
99.82 deaths per 1000 live births (2009 estimate)

LITERACY RATE (AGE 15 AND OVER WHO CAN READ AND WRITE):
Total population: 42.4 percent (male 58.1 percent; female 27.4 percent; 2003 estimate)

EDUCATION:
In the late 1980s about 650 primary and secondary schools had a combined annual enrollment of more than 86,100 students. In 1999 secondary schools enrolled 54 percent of eligible school-aged children. The country has several teacher training colleges. Government programs have made progess in lowering the high adult illiteracy rate, which stood at 81 percent in 1980. From 2001 to 2003, however, the nation's school system was paralyzed by a series of teachers' strikes.

LANGUAGES:
The official language is Portuguese, but many people speak Crioulo, which combines Portuguese with African elements.

ETHNIC GROUPS:
The Balanta, Fulani, Malinke, Mandyako, and Pepel constitute the major ethnic groups, while Cape Verdeans form a small but significant minority.

RELIGIONS:
About half of the population follows traditional beliefs; 45 percent are Muslim and 5 percent are Christian.

CLIMATE:
The climate is tropical, with a mean annual temperature of 25° C (77°F). The rainy season lasts from June to November, bringing an average of 1950 mm (about 77 in) of rainfall.

LAND, PLANTS, AND ANIMALS:
Vegetation consists of mangrove and rain forest on the coastal plain and a savanna woodland on the interior plateau.

NATURAL RESOURCES:
Tropical hardwoods, bauxite, phosphate, and petroleum

CURRENCY:
The Communauté Financière Africaine franc (CFAF)

GROSS DOMESTIC PRODUCT (GDP):
$857 million (2008 estimate)

GDP PER CAPITA:
$600 (2008 estimate)

GDP REAL GROWTH RATE:
3.2 percent (2008 estimate)

PRIMARY ECONOMIC ACTIVITIES:
Agriculture and fishing

PRIMARY CROPS:
Cashew nuts, peanuts, rice, maize (corn), beans, cassava (tapioca), and palm kernels

INDUSTRIES:
Agricultural processing and beverages

PRIMARY EXPORTS:
Cashew nuts, palm kernels, peanuts, and fish

PRIMARY IMPORTS:
Foodstuffs, machinery, petroleum products, and transport equipment

PRIMARY TRADE PARTNERS:
China, Uruguay, Thailand, India, Portugal, and Senegal

GOVERNMENT:
A constitution enacted in 1984 vested legislative power in the National People's Assembly. Its 100 members are now chosen by popular vote. A political liberalization program approved in 1991 ended one-party dominance in Guinea-Bissau. By 1994, twelve political parties had been recognized and the first multiparty presidential and legislative elections were held. João Bernardo Vieira was reelected president in 1997 only to face a crisis in June 1998 when a military faction revolted and accused him of corrution. When, according to a peace agreement reached in November 1998 in Abuja, Nigeria, the presidential guard refused to disarm, the military faction attacked on May 8, 1999, toppled Vieira's government and appointed the head of Parliament, Malan Bacai Sanha, as interim president. In February 2000, Kumba Yala took office as president after two rounds of elections. He was ousted in a coup in September 2003. João Bernardo Vieira ascended to the presidency following elections in 2005, but he was assassinated, apparently by elements of the national military. New elections are scheduled for 2009.

Eric Bennett

agricultural estates for wages to pay the high taxes demanded by the colonial state. Other Africans worked as subsistence farmers, producing enough surplus to pay taxes. Through education, employment, land ownership, or military service, Africans could attain the privilege of assimilado status, or Portuguese citizenship with full rights, but few did so. Discriminatory policies as well as attempts to separate ethnic groups and place them under the control of pliable regulos proved ineffective because many Africans remained outside of the colonial state. For example, the Balanta and the Bijagó resisted colonial authority until 1936.

In 1956 AMÍLCAR CABRAL founded the Partido Africano da Independência de Guiné e Cabo Verde (PAIGC). Originally established to advocate peacefully for independence, the party led the nationalist struggle for the next eighteen years. In 1962, three years after Portuguese soldiers killed fifty striking dock workers in Bissau, the PAIGC launched a "people's war" for independence. The southern mangrove swamps and northern forests proved favorable ground for PAIGC guerrillas. Armed with military supplies from Eastern bloc countries, the party effectively controlled two-thirds of the country by 1968, far more than their counterparts the FRONT FOR THE LIBERATION OF MOZAMBIQUE (FRELIMO) and the POPULAR MOVEMENT FOR THE LIBERATION OF ANGOLA (MPLA) would ever control in MOZAMBIQUE or ANGOLA. Even with nearly 50,000 troops, Portugal's counterinsurgency efforts failed. The population, who hated the abuses of Portuguese colonial rule and perceived its weakness, supported the nationalists.

After Cabral's assassination in 1973 by a political opponent, the Cape Verdean ARISTIDES PEREIRA took over the party's leadership. The PAIGC regrouped and was so successful that it made a unilateral declaration of independence in September 1973. One year later, after a coup d'état in Portugal, Lisbon recognized Guinea-Bissau's independence, and the PAIGC took control with LUÍS CABRAL, Amílcar Cabral half-brother, as president.

INDEPENDENCE

The PAIGC, the only legitimate nationalist organization during the independence struggle, was divided between the Cape Verdean–dominated senior ranks and the young soldiers of various ethnic groups from the mainland, especially the Balanta. The party also imposed harsh discipline on soldiers and peasants alike. When Cape Verde became independent in 1975, leaders of both countries anticipated unification, but mainland resentment of mestiço and Cape Verdean domination stood in the way. Meanwhile, the relocation of the party leadership to the capital in Bissau widened the gap between the rural population and party officials, who acquired urban lifestyles and relied on ex-colonial civil servants for technical know-how. As the sole legal party, the PAIGC kept a tight hold on power, and bureaucratic inefficiencies multiplied.

The government tried to revitalize the war-ruined economy through an expansion of state-run agricultural projects and state trading cartels, as it had attempted to do while fighting the independence war, but this was unsuccessful. At the PAIGC's Third Congress in 1977, the state outlined its goal of agricultural and industrial development. The state allowed individuals to own land privately, but state-run trading monopolies would conduct the trade

in their agricultural goods. Furthermore, the central government would control all taxation, large-scale fishing projects, mining, forestry, and industrial development. By 1983 the government realized that state-led development schemes were failing due to corruption, inadequate technical training, and a lack of necessary foreign capital. Guinea-Bissau's dependence on the export of a few cash crops (cashew nuts, peanuts, palm oil) compounded these difficulties, since prices for these crops fluctuated widely and tended to remain low. With the failure of the government's heavy-handed state-centered approach to economic development, the informal economy flourished.

The simmering Cape Verdean/Guinean ethnic differences came to a boil after independence when the government proved authoritarian and inefficient. In 1980 these differences and the marginalization of the mainlander-dominated military led the former vice president and respected guerrilla commander João "Nino" VIEIRA to overthrow Cabral. In the short term, the influence of Cape Verdeans and mestiços declined and the government abandoned its attempt to control the economy; but the government remained authoritarian, and the economic and ethnic problems persisted. In the early 1980s the government demoted prominent Cape Verdeans and mestiços as the Balanta in the military agitated for a greater political role. Historically the Balanta, the largest ethnic group with about 32 percent of the population, were the primary cultivators of Guinea-Bissau's staple crop of rice, but their tradition of dispersed social organization hindered their incorporation into the central government. Balanta discontentment reached its peak in the mid-1980s in the form of a messianic cult and a coup attempt.

The PAIGC sought to consolidate its control through single-party elections in 1984 and 1989. The PAIGC expanded executive powers so that Vieira could squelch the opposition. Corruption pervaded the government. A 1987 structural adjustment program, sponsored by the International Monetary Fund, moved the country away from its centrally planned economy and trade with Eastern bloc countries. Divisions over the program arose within the government, as ministries feared their reduction.

Illegal opposition political parties advocating for democratic reform—many of which were led by émigrés in Portugal or neighboring Guinea—never offered a viable alternative to the supremacy of Vieira and the PAIGC. It was only international pressure and the debate concerning the implementation of the structural adjustment program that led dissenting members of the political elite to convince Vieira in 1990 to move toward political liberalization. In 1991 the PAIGC abolished its political monopoly in Guinea-Bissau; political parties soon proliferated. Nevertheless, in the first multiparty election ever held in Guinea-Bissau, in

1994, Vieira narrowly won the presidency and the PAIGC won 62 of 92 seats in the national assembly.

Guinea-Bissau remained economically stable, but poor. In the late 1990s Guinea-Bissau's inflation stabilized at around 15 percent. It strictly adhered to its structural adjustment program, including cuts in public spending, accelerated privatization, and a restrictive monetary policy. The nation also entered the West African monetary system and adopted the CFA franc. These steps were aimed at alleviating the severe poverty of Guinea-Bissau. Today, primary education is free and compulsory, but there are few secondary schools and no institutions of higher learning, and the illiteracy rate stands at 57 percent. Most of the country's 1.36 million people live in the countryside as subsistence farmers. The main economic activities are small-scale agriculture, forestry, and fishing, though over 50 percent of the country's export earnings come from cashew nuts.

Guinea-Bissau's unexploited reserves of oil have so far caused more problems than benefits. During the mid-1980s, the country's relations with Guinea to the south over offshore oil reserves had to be resolved at the World Court. Beginning in 1989, relations between Guinea-Bissau and SENEGAL also became strained over fishing and oil rights. After Guinea-Bissau agreed to only 15 percent of the oil rights, this disagreement was settled in 1993. The country's bauxite and phosphate reserves also offer prospects for generating revenue, but the high development costs have blocked the use of these resources for economic development. Guinea-Bissau remains one of the ten poorest nations in the world.

Indigenous African religions remain prominent in Guinea-Bissau, and pilgrims from Muslim-dominated Senegal and Guinea visit the country's many oracles and shrines. About half of the population retain indigenous African religions, and about 45 percent follow Islam; a negligible Christian population is growing slowly. Adherence to indigenous African religions is yet another form of the resistance that has characterized the history of Guinea-Bissau's people.

In recent years, Guinea-Bissau has served as a refuge for dissidents, refugees, and pilgrims from neighboring countries. Complicating the dispute between Guinea-Bissau and Senegal over offshore natural resources was the fact that Casamance separatists from Senegal had been using Guinea-Bissau as a sanctuary. In 1993 nearly 20,000 Senegalese fled to Guinea-Bissau to avoid the violence in the Casamance region. In 1998 some units of Guinea-Bissau's armed forces rebelled against the government after President Vieira dismissed army chief General Ansumane Mane on corruption charges. Rebelling officers were accused of smuggling arms to the Casamance separatists. The Senegalese government sent troops to help Vieira end the insurrection. Fighting between rebel troops and soldiers loyal to the government raged off and on through May 1999, when rebel forces, led by Mane, successfully overthrew Vieira. Mane turned power over to PAIGC statesman Malan Bacai Sanha, the speaker of the National People's Assembly, who was declared acting president. Kumba Yalá of the Party of Social Renovation defeated Sanha in presidential elections, held in two rounds, in November 1999 and January 2000. Yalá soon lost popularity for dissolving the parliament and refusing to call new elections. In September 2003 army officers, led by army chief of staff Verissimo Seabra, ousted YalÁ in a coup and set up a transitional government headed by Henrique Pereira Rosa. In the elections of 2005, former president João Bernardo Vieira seized the country's highest office. Three years later, however, Vieira was assassinated by vengeful elements of the Guinea-Bissau military (apparently in retaliation for the murder of General Batista Tagme Na Wai). New elections are scheduled for 2009. In the meantime, Raimundo Pereira of the National Assembly serves as interim president.

See also ISLAM IN AFRICA; SLAVERY IN AFRICA; *and* STRUCTURAL ADJUSTMENT IN AFRICA.

ERIC YOUNG

Guiziga
Ethnic group of West Africa; also known as the Gisiga and the Guizaga.

The Guiziga inhabit primarily northern CAMEROON, southwestern CHAD, and northeastern NIGERIA. They speak an Afro-Asiatic language in the Chadic group. Approximately 100,000 people consider themselves Guiziga.

See also LANGUAGES, AFRICAN: AN OVERVIEW.

Gurage
Ethnic group of Ethiopia; also known as Gerage and Gerawege.

The Gurage primarily inhabit southwestern Shoa Province, ETHIOPIA. They speak a Semitic language in the Afro-Asiatic family. According to a 2007 census, some 1,867,377 people consider themselves Gurage.

See also LANGUAGES, AFRICAN: AN OVERVIEW.

Gurma
Ethnic group of West Africa; also known as Gourmantché.

The Gurma primarily inhabit northeastern GHANA, northern TOGO, and southern BURKINA FASO. They speak a

Niger-Congo language. Over 1 million people consider themselves Gurma. The name Gurma also refers to a cultural and linguistic group comprising a number of related peoples, including the Basari, the BIMOBA, the KONKOMBA, the Gurma proper, and the Pilapila.

See also LANGUAGES, AFRICAN: AN OVERVIEW.

Gusii

Ethnic group of Kenya; also called the Kisii or Kosova.

The Gusii are a Bantu-speaking people who inhabit the hills between Lake Victoria and TANZANIA in western KENYA. They are bordered on the west by the Nilotic-speaking LUO people; on the east and southeast by the Kipsigis and MAASAI; and on the south by the Tende people. They are closely related to the Bantu-speaking KIKUYU, the LUHYA, MERU, Embu, and KAMBA. The Gusii migrated to the Mount Elgon area from what is now UGANDA and then, about 500 years ago, migrated south to the Kano plains, where they practiced a mix of PASTORALISM and agriculture. The expansion of the Luo peoples, beginning around 400 years ago, drove the Gusii to their present location, where they came to rely more heavily on agriculture. During the nineteenth century they fell victim to slave raids carried out by the neighboring Kipsigis.

During their period on the Kano plains, the Gusii lived in individual family units. With their adoption of a settled agricultural lifestyle, however, they began to live in something akin to neighborhoods. Many believe that this clustering led to the establishment of clans. Family heads were still responsible for the day-to-day decisions within the individual family unit. Elders led the clans and resolved disputes, although they did not form a central government. The Gusii remained stateless, and family units enjoyed considerable autonomy.

The Gusii are one of Kenya's most economically diverse and largest ethnic groups, numbering approximately 1.5 million. Their fertile homeland is one of Kenya's most densely populated regions. Gusii farmers grow the subsistence crops of millet, maize (corn), cassava, sorghum, yams, peanuts, and bananas. Pyrethrum and tea are grown as cash crops. In addition, many keep cattle, sheep, goats, chickens, and bees. Gusii crafts are popular, including baskets, pots, and *Kisii* stools, whose seats are decorated with beads, designs, and soapstone carvings.

See also BANTU, *subentry on* DISPERSION AND SETTLEMENT; SLAVERY IN AFRICA.

ROBERT FAY

Gutsa, Tapfuma
1956–
Zimbabwean sculptor.

Tapfuma Gutsa was born in Salisbury, Rhodesia (now Harare, ZIMBABWE). He is one of the best known members of a "second generation" of Zimbabwean stone sculptors. Like members of the "first generation"—sculptors who got their start at the Rhodes National Gallery in the 1960s—Gutsa often draws on themes from SHONA culture. Formally, his pieces reflect his Western art training and the influences of Picasso, Brancusi, and Matisse.

The son of a construction company owner, Gutsa grew up in the capital of colonial Rhodesia (present-day Zimbabwe). He attended the Driefonten Mission School in order to study with a noted sculptor there, Cornelius Manguma. After completing school, Gutsa received the British Council's first grant to Zimbabwe. He used the funds to study at the London School of Art (1982–1985), where he received his diploma in sculpture. In Europe, Gutsa's exposure to Western art traditions pushed him to search for his own style of abstract African art. He freely acknowledges, however, the similarities between his works and Western abstract art. "The Western world has long borrowed from Africa," he writes; "I find no problem borrowing from them."

Gutsa's works range in theme from the political (*The Hidden Agenda*, 1991) to the intimate (*Listening to the Baby Kick*, 1989). Unlike the many Zimbabwean sculptors who work primarily with soapstone, he uses an array of materials, including wood, wire, porcupine quills, and egg shells. His sculptures have been shown in two New York exhibitions as well as in the prestigious Venice Biennale. In 2003 his exhibit, "The Power of the Object/The Object of the Power" opened at the Alliance Française. The exhibit focused on African myths and traditions.

Gutsa lives in Zimbabwe and has twice won the award for overall excellence from his country's National Gallery. In early 2003 he added his voice to those of many Zimbabwean artists condemning political corruption under the regime of President ROBERT MUGABE.

See also ART AND ARCHITECTURE, AFRICAN.

CHRISTOPHER TINÉ

H

Ha

Ethnic group of Tanzania.

The Ha primarily inhabit northwestern TANZANIA. They speak a Bantu language. Approximately 1.5 million people consider themselves Ha.

See also BANTU: DISPERSION AND SETTLEMENT.

Habyarimana, Juvénal

1937?–1994

Military leader and president of Rwanda.

Habyarimana was born in Gisenyi in northern Rwanda into a prominent family of the Hutu ethnic group. He completed one year at Lovanium University (now the University of Kinshasa) Medical School in the former Zaire (now DEMOCRATIC REPUBLIC OF THE CONGO) before joining the army and enrolling in officers' training school in the Rwandan capital of KIGALI. Rising quickly through the ranks, he served in a number of military roles between 1963 and 1973, including national guard chief of staff, commander of the national guard, and minister for the armed forces and police.

Backed by northern military officers, Habyarimana overthrew the civilian government of Grégoire Kayibanda in July 1973 and declared himself president. After creating the National Revolutionary Movement for Development (NRMD) as Rwanda's only legal party in July 1975, he shifted control of many sectors of the government to civilians, while retaining northern Hutu military men in key posts. In single-candidate presidential elections he was returned for five-year terms in 1983 and 1988.

For most of the 1980s, Habyarimana's regime was criticize for its austerity measures, corruption, and the instigation of ethnic tensions. He was faced with pressure from international donors, opposition groups, and international human-rights agencies. Responding to the pressure, Habyarimana initiated a transition to multiparty democracy in July 1990. In October 1990 the Rwandan Patriotic Front (RPF), a rebel army consisting of some moderate Hutu and many rival Tutsi refugees living in UGANDA, invaded northern Rwanda. The invasion sparked a civil war and resulted in thousands of civilian deaths, many at the hands of government security forces. Habyarimana and RPF leaders signed a peace accord in August 1993 but political and ethnic tension remained high. In April 1994, four months after he was installed for a twenty-two-month term as transitional president, Habyarimana was killed when his plane was shot down over Kigali airport. It remains unknown who was responsible for his assassination, which sparked another, even deadlier, wave of ethnic violence.

See also HUTU AND TUTSI.

Hadendowa

Ethnic group of Sudan; also known as the Hadendiwa and the Hendawa.

The Hadendowa primarily inhabit SUDAN and ERITREA between the Atbarah River and the Red Sea. They speak an Afro-Asiatic language belonging to the Cushitic group and are one of the BEJA peoples. Somewhat more than 600,000 people consider themselves Hadendowa.

See also LANGUAGES, AFRICAN: AN OVERVIEW.

Hadza

Ethnic group of Tanzania; also known as the Hadzapi, the Kindiga, and the Tindiga.

The Hadza inhabit primarily the region around Lake Eyasi in TANZANIA. They speak a click language that linguists classify either as Afro-Asiatic or KHOISAN. At the turn of the century, the Hadza were among the few groups in Africa to rely primarily on foraging for their food supply. The Hadza number perhaps as few as 800 people.

See also LANGUAGES, AFRICAN: AN OVERVIEW.

Haile Selassie I

1892–1975

Last emperor of Ethiopia.

Haile Selassie was born Lij Tafari Makonnen in Ejarsa Goro, Ethiopia. His father was Ras (Prince) Makonnen—the governor of Harer Province and a cousin, close friend, and adviser to Emperor Menelik II—and his mother was Yishimabet Ali. Young Tafari received a traditional religious education from Ethiopian Orthodox priests, who also taught him French.

Tafari proved his ability and responsibility in 1905 at the age of thirteen when his father appointed him governor of one of the regions of Harer Province. Upon his father's death the following year, Tafari was summoned to the court of Emperor Menelik, who appointed him the governor of a small province. Tafari set out to modernize the government by instituting a paid civil service, lowering taxes, and creating a court system that recognized the rights of peasants. Menelik rewarded Tafari's success by giving him a larger province to govern in 1908.

Upon Menelik's death in 1913, his grandson Lij Yasu became emperor. Yasu, however, was considered too sympathetic toward Islam, which offended the dominant Amhara Christians. They began to see Tafari as their champion. In 1916 he and his supporters deposed Yasu and installed Menelik's daughter, Zawditu, reputedly Ethiopia's first empress. Tafari assumed the title of ras and served as her regent and heir apparent.

Tafari brought his modernization plan to the national level. In 1919 he created a centralized bureaucracy; two years later he installed the first courts of law. In 1923 he engineered a foreign affairs coup by securing Ethiopia's entry into the League of Nations. By 1928 his support was so strong that he was able to pressure the empress to name him negus (king). Upon Zawditu's death in 1930, Tafari assumed the throne under his baptismal name, Haile Selassie I (Power of the Trinity). The coronation of Tafari, whose Dynasty claimed descent through Lebna Dengel from the biblical King Solomon, inspired followers of Marcus Moziah Garvey in Jamaica to found a new religion, known as Rastafarianism, that idolized the emperor.

In 1931 Selassie introduced Ethiopia's first constitution, which proclaimed all Ethiopians equal under the law and the emperor, and established a parliament with a popularly elected lower house. The emperor still retained the power to overturn any decision that the parliament made. In 1935, however, Italian forces invaded Ethiopia. Although Selassie attempted to rally his forces, they proved no match for the better-equipped Italians. When defeat appeared certain, Selassie gave an impassioned speech before the League of Nations, pleading for help. None came, and in 1936 Selassie fled to exile in Great Britain.

During World War II Selassie helped the British liberate Ethiopia, and in 1941 a joint force of British soldiers and Ethiopian exiles restored Selassie to the throne. He spent much of the next decade rebuilding the country. He expanded Western education, in part by founding the country's first university, improved health care, and expanded the transportation network. Selassie, however, left Ethiopian society—and most notably the feudal

agricultural system—intact. This fact encouraged class distinctions and left many Ethiopians in poverty.

In the 1950s Selassie worked to consolidate his power in outlying areas, and the country's coffee exports created an economic boom that enhanced his popularity for a time. In 1952 Selassie's government annexed the province of Eritrea to provide Ethiopia with an outlet to the sea. In 1960 a group seeking democratic reforms led by students and Selassie's imperial guard staged a coup while the leader was in Brazil. Selassie quickly returned and the coup was put down by Loyalist troops.

After the coup attempt, Selassie, who had spent his life attempting to modernize Ethiopia, adopted a more conservative course. In addition he now focused on foreign policy, ignoring the increasing domestic problems that faced Ethiopia. Selassie commanded great respect throughout Africa as an elder statesman, embraced Pan-Africanism, and sought African unity. To that end, he was instrumental in establishing the Organization of African Unity (OAU), which was later headquartered in Addis Ababa.

Troubles at home, however, demanded Selassie's attention. In 1962 the province of Eritrea sought independence from Ethiopia and Eritrean rebels took up armed struggle. The educated elite, seeking democratic reforms and jobs, began to demonstrate to demand change. A student protest in 1969 ended when soldiers opened fire, killing twenty-three and wounding 157. Continuing economic problems, high unemployment, and famine caused by prolonged drought led Ethiopians to demonstrate for higher wages and against the continuing economic woes. A military contingent led by junior officers deposed Selassie on September 12, 1974, after a gradual, bloodless coup. Selassie stepped down and was held under house arrest until his death on August 27, 1975.

See also ETHIOPIAN ORTHODOX CHURCH.

ROBERT FAY

Hani, Chris
1942–1993
General Secretary of the South African Communist Party; assassinated by right-wing whites.

At the time of his murder Chris Hani (born Martin Thembisile Hani) was second only to Nelson Rolihlahla Mandela among popular antiapartheid activists, and his militant rhetoric made him the favorite of South Africa's disaffected young blacks. His 1993 assassination occurred at the height of the negotiations between the government and antiapartheid organizations and sparked days of rioting and violent government retaliation that threatened to disrupt the negotiating process—results that some felt reflected the assassins' goals. But the crisis instead proved the strength

HANI IS MOURNED. Guards from the African National Congress carry a coffin containing antiapartheid activist Chris Hani, on April 18, 1993. Hani was assasinated by two right-wing opponents a week earlier. *(John Parkin/AP Images)*

of Mandela's leadership, as the African National Congress (ANC) appealed for calm and continued the talks.

Hani, who was born in the bantustan, or "black home-land," of Transkei and graduated from the University of Fort Hare in 1962, was a classics scholar turned freedom fighter. He joined the ANC Youth League in 1957 and in 1962 went into exile to join the ANC's newly formed para-military wing, Umkhonto we Sizwe (Zulu for the "Spear of the Nation," often abbreviated MK). Hani had his first contact with the South African Communist Party (SACP) while working for the South African Congress of Trade Unions in Cape Town in the early 1960s. As a longtime ally of the ANC in the fight against apartheid, the SACP was one of Umkhonto's parent groups and helped secure much of its international support.

Known for his brilliance, energy, and charisma, Hani was drawn to his first military experience from exile as Umkhonto joined the battle against white rule in southern Rhodesia (now Zimbabwe). After serving two years in jail for weapons possession in Botswana, Hani moved to Lesotho, where he recruited and trained troops for sabotage missions into South Africa. He was named to the ANC's executive council in 1975 and selected as Umkhonto chief of staff in 1987. In 1990, after the government released Mandela from prison and reversed the bans on the ANC, SACP, and other groups, Hani returned to South Africa. He moved to Boksburg, a newly interracial suburb of Johannesburg, and called for an end to fighting. Hani's popularity was considered key to the recruitment of young blacks to the SACP, and in 1991 he was elected the party's general secretary, replacing the ailing Joe Slovo. He was a rising star in two major antiapartheid organizations, an important player in negotiations with the government, and commonly seen as a likely successor to Mandela. In April 1993, however, Hani was shot down outside his house by right-wing whites.

Hani's death brought days of mourning, protests, and strikes. At least seven people died in the resulting violence. But Mandela, Slovo, and President F. W. de Klerk called for the talks to continue, and unprecedented cooperation between the two sides served to calm the mourners and to capture the killers. Two men, one a member of the Afrikaner Resistance Movement and the other a former legislator allied with the pro-apartheid Conservative Party, were found guilty of Hani's murder in October 1993 and were sentenced to life in prison.

KATE TUTTLE

Harare, Zimbabwe
Capital of Zimbabwe.

Despite the absence of a port or river access, Harare has become one of Africa's most modern and prosperous cities. In 1890 Rhodesian settlers established what is today Harare at the base of a kopje (small hill) that rises abruptly out of the rolling plain in present-day ZIMBABWE. Originally named Fort Salisbury, for a British member of Parliament, the settlement was proclaimed a municipality in 1897 and a city in 1935. The town slowly became the commercial and political hub of the settler colony, out-pacing the southern town of Bulawayo as it drew on the agricultural productivity of the rich land surrounding the city and the rail link to Beira, Mozambique. As part of the Rhodesian government's racial and land policies, inhabitants were increasingly segregated according to race and class. The division remains today, although unofficially.

At independence, Salisbury's name was changed to Harare to honor the Harari, a SHONA people who inhabited the area before the settlers arrived. At the heart of the city are high-rise office blocks and government buildings. The city's industries and its more than 2.8 million (as of

2006) residents are geographically divided. Light industries are located to the east of the city and heavy industries to the west, including the largest tobacco auction floor in the world. The middle- and lower-income residents live in the southern high-density suburbs, while the upper-income residents live in the northern low-density suburbs. The city grew substantially in the 1980s. By the 1990s it was recording a nearly 7 percent annual population growth as droughts and poverty pushed people from rural areas to the city.

By the early twenty-first century political repression associated with the regime of President ROBERT MUGABE was blamed for increasing city shortages of power, fuel, and consumer goods. Unemployment in the city, estimated at about 30 percent in the 1990s, rose to more than 60 percent, and inflation rose to more than 200 percent. Significant water shortages in 2003 were associated with the city's rapid population growth.

BIBLIOGRAPHY

Macharia, Kinuthia. *Social and Political Dynamics of the Informal Economy in African Cities: Nairobi and Harare*. University of America Press, 1997.

Rakodi, Carole. *Harare: Inheriting a Settler-Colonial City: Change or Continuity*. J. Wiley, 1995.

ERIC YOUNG

Haratine

Social caste in several northwestern African countries consisting of blacks, many of whom are former slaves.

In the northwestern Sahara lands of Mauritania, Morocco, and the Western Sahara, the term haratine (from the Arabic word for "plowmen") refers to a social caste of blacks whose low status is a legacy of slavery in Africa. In recent years, the status of the haratine has become a controversial issue in Mauritania, at times affecting relations with neighboring countries.

Officially, the haratine are black Moors who are either descendents of slaves or former slaves themselves. Although slavery was formally abolished in Mauritania in 1960 and again in 1981, many haratine remain subservient to their former masters. Mauritanian officials have argued that such relationships exist only with the complete agreement of the haratine, but observers from the United Nations and international human rights groups, as well as Mauritanian groups, such as El-Hor and Forces de Liberation Africaine de Mauritanie (FLAM), claim that enslavement of some haratine persists in present-day Mauritania. In addition, they argue that the government, eager to "Arabize" its population, has systematically denied the black haratine opportunities for economic and social advancement.

Most haratine descended from the Bambara, Fulani, Soninké, and Wolof peoples that once inhabited the Western Sahara. Many of these groups fled south into the Senegal River valley when Berber migrants arrived during the third century. Those who remained were enslaved by the Berbers and, centuries later, by the Moors. Under the Moors the haratine eventually adopted Islam, an Arab identity, and the Hassaniya Arabic language. Many of the slaves had been freed before the region came under French Colonial Rule in the early twentieth century. Some gained their freedom under Islamic religious law, which requires masters to free their slaves after five generations. Others gained it through marriage or by running away. Those who remained enslaved gained their freedom—at least technically—under the 1960 constitution.

While some haratine moved to the cities and acquired education and employment, others continue to work for their former masters. Their status is ambiguous. Some, with few opportunities elsewhere, have remained where they can work for food. Others have apparently benefited from staying with their former masters, inheriting land and livestock. But critics believe that many haratine are unaware that slavery was outlawed in Mauritania, and that perhaps 100,000 are still effectively enslaved even though the edict abolishing slavery was reissued in 1981 by Colonel Mohammed Khouna Ould Heydallah. During hearings before the United Nations and the U.S. Congress in 1994 and 1996, haratine representatives recounted tales of slave raids and produced receipts of slave purchases.

Racial tensions erupted into a cross-border crisis in 1989 when Moors, seeking grazing land for their herds, attacked blacks along the Senegal River, and Mauritania expelled large numbers of Senegalese nationals. Such tensions continued to spark sporadic violence throughout the 1990s, but some progress was also made—Colonel Maaouya Ould Sidi Ahmed Taya, for example, supported haratine candidate Fatma Zeina Mint Sbaghou in Mauritania's 1996 parliamentary elections.

BIBLIOGRAPHY

Pazzanita, Anthony. *Historical Dictionary of Mauritania*. Scarecrow Press, 1996.

Stewart, C. C. *Islam and Social Order in Mauritania: A Case Study from the Nineteenth Century*. Clarendon Press, 1973.

ELIZABETH HEATH

Hausa

Ethnic grouping comprising roughly 22 million native speakers of the Hausa language, who live mainly in northern Nigeria and southern Niger.

In addition to those who speak Hausa as their mother tongue, many more use Hausa as a lingua franca in NIGERIA, NIGER, and elsewhere. Recent estimates put the number of Hausa speakers at between 30 and 35 million. Hausa is therefore the most widely spoken language in Nigeria, and the most widely spoken sub-Saharan African language. Hausa speakers include millions of ethnic FULANI.

The Hausa maintain a hierarchy distinguishing among chiefs, officeholders, and commoners. Hereditary occupations also mark distinctions in rank. Hausa society is strongly patrilineal and patriarchal. Hausa men often marry non-Hausa women, and the Hausa thus tend to expand and assimilate outsiders.

The Hausa language belongs to the Chadic branch of the Afro-Asiatic language family. The first Chadic speakers are believed to have cultivated cereals such as millet and sorghum some 6,000 years ago in the vicinity of Lake Chad. Chadic speakers subsequently brought their language and agricultural traditions to present-day Hausaland and merged with existing populations. Their descendants are the present-day Hausa.

The earliest Hausa states probably formed by 1200 C.E. The first towns apparently coalesced around traditional shrines, which attracted pilgrims and became centers for trade. An increase in traffic along the trans-Saharan trade routes to the Hausa towns expanded the commerce in slaves, gold, and kola from the savanna and forest regions to the south. This thriving trade generated wealth that enabled the rulers of these towns to establish states. The seven "true" Hausa states—Biram, Kano, Rano, Katsina, Daura, Zazzau, and Gobir—which the Hausa consider the core of Hausaland, emerged during this period. Arabian horses obtained from trans-Saharan traders enabled the Hausa to raid southern groups for slaves, who provided a valuable source of labor. By the fifteenth century, Kano was one of the most important trading centers in Africa, with a population perhaps approaching 50,000.

Contacts with the neighboring empires of MALI, SONGHAI, and Kanem-Bornu probably brought Islam to the Hausa towns as early as the end of the eleventh century. By the fourteenth century, Islam had been embraced by Hausa leaders and was prevalent through much of the region. Although most Hausa eventually adopted Islam, the Maguzawa, a rural Hausa subgroup, maintained their traditional African beliefs.

At their peak around 1650, the independent Hausa states stretched from the borders of Bornu in present-day northeastern Nigeria to the Niger River, and from the Jos Plateau north to the fringes of the SAHARA. Hausa traders traveled to markets across West Africa, exchanging salt and leather goods from Hausaland for gold and other products of the forest zone. Hausa traders purchased slaves in regions such as Asante and Dahomey even after European powers banned the transatlantic slave trade in the early nineteenth century. Today, a substantial Hausa diaspora persists in countries such as GHANA and CHAD. Hausa communities in West African cities often live in separate districts known as zongos.

In the early nineteenth century, Fulani warriors joined Hausa peasants and merchants under the leadership of Usuman Dan Fodio in a jihad, or holy war, to unite Hausaland under the SOKOTO CALIPHATE. The formerly independent Hausa states became emirates within the caliphate. Initially, Fulani rulers dominated the caliphate. Gradually, however, these Fulani adopted the Hausa language and customs and merged with Hausa elites to form a northern Nigerian ruling class best described as Fulani-Hausa. Under the stable rule of the caliphate, Hausaland prospered during the nineteenth century. Slaves owned by Fulani or Hausa nobles worked the fertile fields of Hausaland and produced a surplus that sustained a substantial number of artisan producers, including weavers, blacksmiths, and leather workers.

During the 1890s, as French troops in present-day Niger began to encroach on Hausaland, British troops conquered the bulk of the Sokoto Caliphate, partly under the premise of stopping the slave trade. Britain replaced the Islamic state as the supreme authority and implemented indirect rule over the region. The colonial administration permitted existing emirs to remain in office as long as they complied with British demands. The British slowly abolished agrarian slavery and encouraged the cultivation of cash crops such as cotton and peanuts.

The precolonial elites of Hausaland not only survived colonialism but have remained powerful since independence. Because they are Nigeria's largest ethnic group, the Hausa have played a dominant role in many of Nigeria's civilian and military governments. Today most Hausa speakers raise food and livestock or cash crops such as millet, sorghum, and peanuts. These farmers live mostly in villages and small towns. Fulani cattle manure provides a primary source of fertilizer. Many Hausa have also migrated to cities such as Kano and Lagos in search of more lucrative wage employment.

See also GOLD TRADE; HAUSA LANGUAGE; ISLAM IN AFRICA; SLAVERY IN AFRICA.

ARI NAVE

Hausa Language
Main language of Niger and the northern parts of Nigeria, commonly spoken in other parts of West Africa where Hausa people have traveled for trade.

Hausa serves as a localized lingua franca—enabling peoples of different languages to communicate with one another. Like Swahili, Hausa features many words of foreign extraction, including English and Arabic words, the latter as the result of Islamic conquests.

Hausa has a rich oral tradition, replete with animal stories, fables, proverbs, and myths. Written literature began about 200 years ago, with the use of the Arabic script (ajami), especially for religious writing. There is much modern writing in Hausa, such as the well-known novels of Alhaji Abubakar Imam, as well as historical and political works. While many modern writings use the Roman alphabet, called boko in Hausa, most religious writing is still done in ajami. Although written poetry in Hausa has been strongly influenced by Arabic traditions, there is also much modern poetry, in the boko script, which is moving away from classical and religious styles.

Oral poetry—often called waka—is a very old tradition of the Hausa people. It is performed with music by professional singing poets, or mawaka. The subjects of poetry may be great men and rulers who pay the poets and performers, but poems may also be about farming, hunting, politics, and wrestling, and sometimes are specially made up for religious and ceremonial occasions. The most important musical instrument used with oral poetry is the talking drum, or kalangu, which can imitate the different tones of the human voice. Stringed instruments such as the molo and garaya also provide music with the poetry.

See also HAUSA; NIGER; NIGERIA.

Hausa States
Former independent states dominated by Hausa-speaking people in West Africa.

Located in what is now southern Niger and northern Nigeria, the Hausa states included Biram, Daura, Gobir, Kano, Katsina, Rano, and Zazzau (sometimes called Zaria). The Hausa states occupied the southern fifth of present-day Niger and an area corresponding roughly to the states of Borno, Kaduna, Kano, and Sokoto in the northern portion of contemporary Nigeria. Since the sixteenth century, the Hausa states have been decisive factors in the cultural, economic, and political history of central West Africa.

According to Hausa legend, the states known as the Hausa Bakwai (Hausa Seven) emerged as distinct Hausa nations. Although the story helped maintain an illusion of ethnic cohesiveness over the centuries, evidence indicates that the Hausa sometimes assimilated non-Hausa people. Fulani herdsmen, for example, were incorporated during the 1800s. The states frequently competed economically and politically after their formation, and as early as the sixteenth century they played a crucial role in the caravan trade across the Sahel (the semiarid region south of the Sahara). Faced with conquest by the British and French in the nineteenth century, the Hausa states became more unified. Since the independence of Niger and Nigeria in 1960, the states have continued to play an important political and economic role, particularly in Nigeria.

EARLY HISTORY
By the end of the first millennium C.E., the Hausa had begun building a centralized state in what is referred to by scholars as Hausaland. The boundaries of Hausaland shifted over the centuries, but at times extended almost to the Niger River to the west, to Lake Chad to the East, to the arid region of Aïr to the north, and to the center of present-day Nigeria to the south.

Prior to the fourteenth century, the Hausa (who are sometimes known as the Habe) lived in societies that consisted of small confederacies, each centered on its own walled community, or birni. Each of these confederacies was governed by a council of notables and chiefs. Much of the subsequent history of this region was shaped by the interaction between two major cultural and political groups. The first group consisted of those who sought to maintain indigenous ritual practices, which were based on a mixture of local traditions and practices brought by early immigrants. The immigrants, the second group, were primarily soldiers from the north and east of the Hausa states who attempted to assert their political power. This led to the development of what social scientists call "dual institutional structures," in which two sets of social and political power existed side by side, often with different leaders. Indigenous priest elders, who claimed ritual ties to the land, were often entrusted with forging agreements between the two structures. In particular, they often had the responsibility of choosing the political leaders and of deposing them in times of military defeats or failing harvests.

Sometime during the fourteenth century, the Wangarawa, traders and clerics of Mande origin, arrived in Hausaland from the west (from parts of what is now Burkina Faso, Mali, and western Niger). The Wangarawa began to promote the emergence of statelike institutional structures, designed primarily to protect their commercial interests. According to some historical sources, the Wangarawa sought to undermine the authority of the priest elders and were primarily responsible for the introduction of Islam in Hausa society. Other sources suggest that rather than coming from the west, Islam was brought to the region by the Kanuri people of Bornu (a kingdom to the east of the Hausa states).

Although scholars disagree about how Islam came to Hausaland, they are in general agreement that while commercial networks rapidly expanded into and around the Hausa states, Islam did not succeed in wrecking the power base of the indigenous religious elites. Instead, a stark contrast developed between urban and rural communities. The urban areas were dominated by a hierarchical Muslim commerce-oriented society. Rural areas, in contrast, were dominated by a more egalitarian social order consisting primarily of subsistence farmers under the leadership of indigenous clan elders. Many of the rural areas had exceptionally dense populations, because the region's high water table and numerous river valleys permitted year-round irrigation. This thriving agricultural sector helped provide food for urban traders and craftspeople.

RISE TO REGIONAL PROMINENCE

By the sixteenth century the Hausa states were playing an important role in local as well as regional trading networks. This prominence was supported by Islam, which maintained ties between dispersed trade settlements and created a sense of shared brotherhood between traders. Hausa capitals became flourishing centers of commerce and craftsmanship. Arab and Berber merchants came from other parts of Africa to buy slaves, leather, ivory, and gold, offering in return manufactured products from Mediterranean regions. Leo Africanus, a North African explorer, wrote of the thriving trade in sixteenth-century Kano, which was by then a powerful capital and one of the most important seats of trade and Muslim scholarship. In his book *Della descrittione dell Africa* (1526; The History and Description of Africa, 1600), Africanus described the city "as filled with civilized handicraft-workers and rich merchants."

The Hausa were at the hub of an important regional network of trade routes, linking the Songhai empire (near the Niger River in what is now Mali) and other polities west of the Hausa regions to distant trading centers. Major trading partners included Bornu, Egypt, and parts of the Maghreb (northwest Africa). The Hausa states reached the peak of their economic and political influence in the eighteenth century. Yet, despite the commercial ascendancy of states such as Katsina (in the northern reaches of what is now the Kaduna state) and later Kano (in what is now the Nigerian state of the same name), the Hausa states were not able to wield much authority outside the walls of their respective capitals. They lacked internal cohesion, and although the walled cities provided much-needed protection for rural villagers in times of war, no Hausa rulers ever managed to impose permanent control over the rest of Hausaland. Until the nineteenth century, the Hausa states remained a loose confederation of partners or rivals, sometimes maintaining cordial relations with one another but more often than not competing for a larger share of the economically critical north-south trade.

FULANI JIHAD

In 1804 Usuman Dan Fodio, a Fulani member of the Qadiriyya (a Muslim brotherhood) and the local head of a clan of Muslim clerics, launched a holy war, or jihad, in an effort to seize control of the Hausa states. This Fulani campaign shook the political, economic, and religious foundations of the Hausa kingdoms and led to the establishment of the Muslim-controlled state known as the Sokoto Caliphate. In his capacity as teacher to the sons of the king of Gobir state (in what is now southeastern Niger), Usuman repeatedly, but unsuccessfully, asked the ruler to implement political and religious reforms. In the end, convinced that peaceful persuasion was useless, Usuman called for political overthrow of the Hausa ruling system.

He soon built an army and won a decisive victory over the state of Gobir. This led to further conquests as his ranks of soldiers swelled with the rapid incorporation of disgruntled Fulani cattle herders wary of paying tribute to abusive Hausa rulers. Regardless of their personal motivations, those who joined the Fulani jihad commonly embraced Usuman's cause to support their own grievances. Usuman and his companions preached against autocracy, political abuse, and social inequities. They aimed to establish a caliphate (Muslim state) that would be governed according to the set of social and religious practices known as the sharia.

Although the Hausa regions of the south easily fell to the Fulani conquerors, Usuman failed to incorporate into his new empire the Hausa-populated regions in what is now northern Niger. Although limited in impact in the north, the jihad had widespread consequences for much of the region. The jihad triggered sizeable migrations as those who opposed the new Fulani order fled to seek refuge in the northern regions. This in turn led to the emergence of new political configurations as rulers in exile recreated independent states on the margins of the Sokoto Caliphate. These included the states of Katsinawa in Maradi and Gobirawa in Tibiri (both to the north of the Hausa states), Zazzawa in Abuja (to the south), and Zango (a district in the emirate of Daurawa).

Some of these kingdoms eventually became tributary states to neighboring states such as Damagaram (east of the Hausa states). Far from constituting clearly defined zones of control, the influence of Sokoto and Damagaram over the region were regularly tested at the margins. Because the caliphate was constantly challenged, Usuman, and later his son Muhammad Bello, had to reinstate imperial authority by periodically sending armies against dissident leaders. Sokoto thus remained a loosely organized empire whose frontiers fluctuated constantly and whose central government only enforced limited authority over tributary states. In 1866 Sokoto lost a major battle against several rebel states. At the turn of the twentieth century, European armies invaded the central Sudan region—the massive area between the Sahara and Central Africa, stretching from the West African coast to the mountains of Ethiopia. By the time the colonizers arrived, the Hausa region's economic influence had already declined significantly. But because of the enduring social and cultural influence of the Fulani on northern Nigeria, the region and its people are sometimes referred to as Hausa-Fulani.

RESISTANCE AND COLONIAL RULE

From 1890 to 1960, Hausaland was divided into two colonies. One came under British rule and in 1914 became known as the Colony and British Protectorate of Nigeria. The other was under French rule as part of French Sudan, which was part of French West Africa. In 1922 this latter portion of French Sudan became the Colonie du Niger (Niger Colony). Instead of dividing a previously united federation, the colonial partition of Hausaland essentially separated Sokoto from its historic northern rivals, thereby ensuring that the Hausa would never achieve political unity. Through the imposition of a colonial boundary over Hausaland, two new identities—Nigerien and Nigerian—were imposed on Hausa populations. Many people welcomed the security afforded by British rule because it signaled an end to their domination by Sokoto or Damagaram.

But the British seizure of control was not entirely peaceful. Despite its waning influence over the rest of Hausaland, the Sokoto Caliphate put up serious resistance to European conquest. The British had to launch major offensives to defeat Fulani armies, and Sokoto did not capitulate until 1903. Following the imposition of peace, northern Nigeria provided the experimental grounds for the implementation of colonial rule by Frederick Lugard, a British soldier who became high commissioner of the protectorate of northern Nigeria in 1900. Lugard established a style of governance known as "indirect rule" that was later implemented in many other British colonies in Africa. Under the policy of indirect rule, the leaders that the British viewed as the traditional, and therefore legitimate, rulers of a people would remain in power, although they were subject to British control. This policy was institutionalized by the "native authorities" system, which established a hierarchy of chiefs under British control.

British administrators were entrusted with the responsibility of advising their African counterparts. The objective was to ensure that Britain ruled in such a manner that these indigenous governments would move progressively toward what the British saw as more modern forms of administration but without unduly interfering with British interpretations of indigenous traditions. Yet, even in northern Nigeria, where the British took extraordinary steps to protect native institutions, such efforts tended to pervert existing structures of authority. Installed as legitimate rulers by the British, the Fulani emirs (Muslim rulers) imposed abusive taxation policies. They soon became little more

than outright dictators, a situation that contrasted sharply with the precolonial era. By the 1920s the emirs' functions pertaining to law, order, and taxation were extended to the control of development programs in agriculture, health, forestry, education, and livestock raising. As a result of the colonial policies that granted exclusive control of these critical sectors, Hausa and Fulani leaders were able to bolster their positions and survive Nigeria's transition to independence and, later, military rule.

French colonial rule in Hausa areas was markedly different. Unlike the British, who consciously tried to adapt colonial rule to indigenous rule, the French sought to centralize control in their colonies. Thus the French administration of Niger was typical of French administration throughout West Africa. In the poor and isolated colony of Niger, administrative chiefs wielded considerably more power over their district than did their British counterpart, and unlike the British, they felt no compunction about stripping local elites of their authority. In contrast to Nigeria, there were no indigenous courts or treasury in Nigerien Hausaland.

SINCE WORLD WAR II

After World War II (1939–1945), the British expanded previously existing representative assemblies in northern Nigeria and encouraged indigenous people to participate in the newly emerging democratic systems of government. But the British did little to unify the budding nation as it moved toward independence in the 1950s. In 1947 the British had divided Nigeria into three regions and by the time independence came in 1960, most political parties focused on controlling regional governments. This divided the country along ethnic and regional lines. Composed mainly of the Islamic Hausa-Fulani, the northern region as a whole remained ethnically, culturally, and economically distinct from southern Nigeria, which included the western region (mostly Yoruba speakers) and the eastern region (mostly Igbo speakers).

These distinctions translated into sharp political divisions between the three regions, and patterns of political recruitment and support followed along ethnic and regional lines. Within the three main parties, the Northern People's Congress (NPC) was represented mostly in the predominantly Hausa-Fulani north, the National Council of Nigeria and the Cameroons (NCNC) was backed primarily in the Igbo east, and the Action Group was mostly supported by Yoruba speakers from the west. Although they kept their interference in the election process to a minimum, the British policies created a political environment favorable to the NPC in northern Nigeria. To the surprise of no one, the conservative Hausa-dominated NPC won the Northern Region in the 1959 elections. Under Nigeria's federal system

HAUSA TRADITIONS. Hausa men in Kano, Nigeria, blow traditional flutes called zunguru during the Muslim festival of Durbar, celebrating the end of Ramadan, 2004. (*George Osodi/AP Images*)

of government, this enabled the NPC to lead a coalition government that controlled the national parliament. In the several decades since independence, the Hausa-Fulani have been quite successful in retaining their political ascendancy at the national level. Two Hausa-speaking northerners, Abubakar Tafawa Balewa and Alhaji Shehu Shagari, have served as heads of state in civilian governments, and others have led military governments.

See also COLONIAL RULE; HAUSA; HAUSA LANGUAGE.

Haya

Ethnic group of northwestern Tanzania.

The ancestors of the Haya first settled on the western shores of Lake Victoria (in present-day Tanzania) during the period of Bantu Expansion. There they established numerous small, loosely affiliated communities, each of which had its own hierarchical political system based on a division between nobles and commoners. The Haya are believed to have been one of the first groups in the region to practice ironworking, a technology that made it possible for them to produce a sophisticated type of pottery, called Urewe ware, around 500 B.C.E. The mainstay of their economy, however, was agriculture. Prior to the nineteenth century, the Haya produced coffee and bananas for trade as well as for brewing banana beer.

During the nineteenth century, many Haya communities formed alliances with the larger and more powerful Buganda kingdom in the hope of securing protection from slave raids by Arab/Swahili traders from the East Coast. Instead of protecting the small Haya communities, however, the Buganda sought to accentuate internal divisions among the various Haya kingdoms as a means of securing new land for themselves. By 1891 the Haya were brought under German Colonial Rule, their groups having been severely weakened and divided. Under German and British rule, the Haya began growing tea and were encouraged to increase coffee production, both of which they processed at local plants. Through efforts to gain influence over coffee prices and agricultural policies in the 1930s, the Haya formed a powerful social and political group, the Buhaya Union. Today, the Haya are the largest coffee producers in Tanzania and, along with the neighboring Chagga, some of the country's most prosperous farmers. Today, some 1.2 million people consider themselves Haya.

See also BANTU: DISPERSION AND SETTLEMENT; BUGANDA, EARLY KINGDOM OF; SLAVERY IN AFRICA.

ELIZABETH HEATH

Head, Bessie

1937–1986

South African author and teacher, and one of the great postwar African novelists.

Bessie Head's writings sound existential themes in unfamiliar terrain, treating topics such as personal and societal alienation, political exile, racial identity, and sexual oppression. She is particularly concerned with describing the institutionalization of evil.

Head was, in effect, an orphan. The child of a white woman and a black man, Head was born in the mental institution in which her mother had been placed in Pietermaritzburg, South Africa. Adopted by a white Afrikaner family when she was very young, she was later returned when her black features revealed themselves. She then lived with a black family, until she moved into an orphanage at the age of thirteen. In a few years she acquired a teaching degree, and taught school in Durban for two years, later leaving that position to work as a journalist for Drum Publications in Johannesburg.

Head became active in politics in the 1960s, eventually joining the Pan-Africanist Congress (PAC), an antiapartheid political party. She married Harold Head in 1961 and had a son. Following several arrests and continual harassment by Afrikaner authorities, Head moved with her son to Botswana where she lived in the village of Serowe, working both as a schoolteacher and an unpaid agricultural worker. Her experiences in political exile were extremely traumatic, provoking a nervous breakdown.

Head's first novel, *When Rain Clouds Gather* (1969), is the only work set in and developed from her experiences in South Africa. Her second novel, *Maru* (1971), addresses the issue of racism among blacks. Head focuses on the Serowe tribal people's abuse of the Masarwa or Bushmen, considered slaves and outcasts within African society. As in Head's other novels, the antiracist sentiments expressed in *Maru* are not intended as a condemnation of the village of Serowe, but more as a broader reflection on the racial prejudices found throughout the world in many different societies. Head's third novel, the largely autobiographical *A Question of Power* (1973), is a portrait of her nervous breakdown, a condition she believes resulted from the ongoing psychological struggles she faced as a woman and a political exile. This novel is often considered a milestone in the development and evolution of African literature, as it is one of the first African novels written from a largely personal and introspective perspective, focusing on the individual as opposed to broader societal issues. Furthermore, as a story written from a woman's perspective, *A Question of Power* gained the attention of feminists, and established Head's reputation as a woman's author, although Head hesitated to embrace the feminist label. Head further established herself as a feminist with her short nonfiction piece *The Collector of Treasures and Other Botswana Village Tales*, a collection of Botswana village stories told from a woman's perspective. These stories are decidedly optimistic and positive in tone, and serve to emphasize the inherent personal and communal strength of women in overcoming male oppressors. Head's major

nonfiction work, *Serowe: Village of the Rainwind* (1981), is a history of Serowe, recorded as a series of interviews.

Health Care in Africa

Overview of primary health care, clinics, and hospitals in Africa.

The health of most of the population in sub-Saharan Africa is in an unstable balance between infectious diseases and poverty. Mortality is high, with the majority of deaths, 66 percent, due to infectious causes, complications of pregnancy and childbirth, and nutritional deficiencies, compared to 30 percent for the world overall. Small gains have been made in life expectancy. A male born in 1978 was expected to live forty-six years, compared to forty-nine years for those born in 1999; the expected life span for females increased from forty-nine to fifty-one years. The total fertility rate, which is the number of children that would be born to a woman if she were to live to the end of her childbearing years, declined from 6.7 in 1978 to 5.4 in 1998 (including a notable drop from 8.1 to 4.5 in KENYA). There is also considerable morbidity from all causes. A survey done in CÔTE D'IVOIRE showed that 20 percent of adults had been sick for a week or more in the last month, with 12 percent inactive for that length of time. Although sub-Saharan Africa has 10 percent of the world's population, it has 24 percent of the total world burden measured in disability-adjusted life years lost.

Another major force, as development occurs, is the shift in the burden of disease away from the infectious diseases and toward human-made problems, such as pollution in the ecosystem from industry and agriculture. The health-care system must also deal with trends of urbanization, sociocultural and political change, and lifestyle changes. Diets now include increasing amounts of fat and sodium, which are both risk factors in heart disease; tobacco and alcohol consumption is rising; and motor vehicle and industrial injuries are increasing. "Diseases of affluence," such as cardiovascular disease, degenerative diseases, and cancer, which currently cause 33 percent of all deaths, will approach the developed world rate of 87 percent as the population ages, further taxing health-care systems.

The ACQUIRED IMMUNODEFICIENCY SYNDROME (AIDS) epidemic is a powerful force in the health of the area. From the first documented cases of AIDS in the mid-1980s, the rate of HIV infection in sub-Saharan Africa climbed to the highest in the world at 3,541 cases per 100,000 people in 1997. Sub-Saharan Africa has 60 percent of all HIV infections in the world, including 81 percent of all infected women and 87 percent of all children. AIDS is also associated with tuberculosis. There have been large increases in the number of reported cases of tuberculosis, and an estimated 20 percent of those people also have HIV.

AIDS is also associated with an increase in the sexually transmitted diseases responsible, in part, for the high rates of maternal morbidity and perinatal mortality. By 2001 parents dying of AIDS had left an estimated 12 million orphaned children throughout Africa. AIDS care is expensive, with a cost per year in Africa estimated (in U.S. dollars) at approximately $800 per person for the latest and most effective medicines. This amount is beyond the resources of most African countries, where the average amount spent per capita on health care is $24. The future impact of AIDS on sub-Saharan Africa is unclear, but it is likely that recent gains in life expectancy and childhood survival will be reversed as many deaths occur, and the rate of population increase will slow. The economic impact, too, will likely be significant.

PRIMARY HEALTH CARE

In the above context of health and disease, primary health care is delivered through four separate systems that are integrated to various degrees. These are the public health-care system, including both the government and nongovernmental organizations; the traditional system; a private for-profit system of Western-style medicine; and programs aimed at specific diseases. The traditional system is the largest of these, with an estimated ratio of one healer to every 350 to 2,000 individuals in the population. In ETHIOPIA in 1986 an estimated 65 to 80 percent of the population used traditional healers such as birth attendants and bone setters, with those from the lower socioeconomic groups the most frequent users. The private for-profit sector is very small and is concentrated in the cities in most countries. In ZAMBIA in 1986 there were only 100 private clinics and 175 private physicians. Some governments are encouraging growth in the private sector, often through deregulation, as one solution to the cost of providing care.

Primary health care, promoted by the World Health Organization (WHO) since 1978, is a philosophy of care underpinned by several principles and consisting of eight technical elements or services that comprise the health delivery package. The guiding principles are equity (where health care is available for all with emphasis on the most vulnerable people), community involvement in the planning and delivery of health care, and intersectoral collaboration between health and other areas such as agriculture and sanitation. The technical elements are health education and promotion, adequate nutrition, safe water and basic sanitation, maternal and child health and family planning, immunization, prevention and control of local diseases, appropriate treatment, and provision of essential drugs.

The basic structure for governments to provide primary health care has been a hierarchical system that focuses on the district, which is a geographic and administrative unit large enough to be representative and small enough to be manageable. The central point is the district hospital, which is the referral center for a number of health centers. They, in turn, are the referral points of health posts and community health workers at the individual village level. Each district hospital refers to regional and central specialty or university hospitals. In 1986 Zambia had three central hospitals, nine provincial hospitals, sixty-eight district hospitals, and 845 rural and urban health centers. Within a defined catchment area, each health center provides curative care and coordinates prevention, promotion, community participation, and intersectoral activities. Recently, reference health centers have developed that also include day surgery, short-term inpatient care, and expanded health promotion and education. The health center is also the training and supervision center for more peripheral substations, dispensaries, and community health workers. Nongovernmental organizations provide primary health care through a parallel system of mission hospitals and clinics, or through specific projects.

The grassroots member of the primary health system is the community health worker, generally recruited from the village as a volunteer or paid through a variety of methods. The community health worker receives basic training in the treatment of common diseases and is the principal link between the village and the formal health-care system. Most villages have a council or committee that administers village affairs, and this group or a subcommittee focuses on health, often in the wider context of economic and social development. This committee is generally responsible for promoting health, identifying community health needs, and making decisions regarding community health activities. The community health worker is accountable to this group. Typical activities at the village level include revolving funds for purchasing medicine, latrine and well installation, and health education.

The amount of funding provided for the system varies. Direct household expenditures for health are the major component of all moneys spent on health care. The government is the next major supplier, with a considerable portion of the funding derived from foreign aid. Some of this funding supports the major programs for specific diseases, but the greater part funds networks of hospitals and clinics, which, for example, in MALAWI provide approximately 30 percent of all primary health-care services. Other funders are industries, such as the mining industry in Zambia, which provides 20 percent of the total funds for the Zambian health system.

The major programs for specific diseases operating in sub-Saharan Africa include the Expanded Program on Immunization (EPI), the Global Malaria Control Strategy, the Onchocerciasis Program in West Africa, and control programs for lymphatic filariasis, schistosomiasis, and other diseases. The emphasis in these programs has moved away from broad environmental control using pesticides toward specific strategies such as the use of bed nets to prevent malaria or mass chemotherapy on an annual basis for onchocerciasis. In other programs economic realities have led to restricting treatment to high-risk groups (e.g., schoolchildren with schistosomiasis) or to integrating programs into the daily activities of the primary health-care system. EPI is regarded as one of the most cost-effective survival programs for children, spending $5 to $10 per child. It uses a variety of approaches to gain population coverage, including mobile teams, fixed facilities allowing integration into the primary health-care system, and mass campaigns. The major portion of the costs of these programs is generally borne by foreign donors. In TANZANIA 65 percent of the fixed-facility portion of the EPI program is funded by this source.

CHANGES IN PRIMARY HEALTH CARE
A major force for change in primary health care has been the economic downturn experienced by many countries. This economic downturn affected both gross national products and the amount of foreign aid available. In thirty-seven African countries, real expenditure dropped an average of 5 percent in the social area, 11 percent in production, and 22 percent in infrastructure. The extent of the indebtedness of many countries led the World Bank to introduce Structural Adjustment Programs (SAPs) in the mid-1980s as a condition of further borrowing. SAPs restructured economies by increasing production, particularly for export, and decreasing imports and public spending. The net effect on the health-care system has been cuts in expenditure, the introduction of user fees, and policies to allow private-sector development. The reduction in expenditure on health, combined with other factors such as the emergence of AIDS, an increased frequency of natural and human-made disasters, the emergence of drug-resistant diseases, and the increase in chronic conditions has resulted in declining health status, especially among the most vulnerable people.

To cover the gap between costs and income, user fees have been introduced for a variety of services, such as drugs and outpatient visits. The impact of these fees on patterns of access and use has been variable but tends to negatively affect low-income users. The additional funds may only increase the total money allocated to health by about 20 to 25 percent, but they provide an important funding source at the facility level if collected effectively. Various kinds of revolving funds have been tried; in revolving drug programs, for example, users' payments for drugs are used

to purchase more drugs. Other options include insurance schemes, either through the private sector, in national programs as in NIGERIA, or in compulsory programs such as the Kenya National Hospital Insurance Fund. There are also community financing options, such as the Bamako Initiative, which was launched in 1987 to improve essential drug provision and utilization and to improve community health centers through cost recovery.

Another change has resulted from concerns about the sustainability of health-care services. In October 1994 the World Bank estimated the cost of providing a basic package of health care at $13 per capita in sub-Saharan Africa. Countries spending less per capita need outside aid to provide basic services, and indeed this is the case in many countries. Donor investment in the past has focused on developing new projects, often with a short-term perspective, resulting in the donor agency dominating resource allocation decisions by an individual country's ministry of health. The expectation has been that the recipient country will assume the recurrent costs of these projects once donor funding ceases, a situation often beyond the country's resources. In some cases, however, such as GHANA, the relative strength of the ministry of health has allowed a shift toward capacity building and long-term development. Donor assistance provides management, technical, and budget support. The end result should be a more sustainable health-care system. In what is likely to become a trend in sub-Saharan Africa, Ghana is also considering reversing the traditional focus in which government funds the hospitals and donors fund primary health care, in the hope of increasing local ownership of primary health care. There have also been attempts by donors to influence reform in health-care systems by using nonproject assistance to improve planning, resource allocation, and administration. Examples include development of hospital accounting systems in NIGER or support of decentralization in Nigeria.

A number of attempts have been made to improve services in primary health care. In the administrative area the major trend has been to decentralize planning, budgeting, training, and data collecting by shifting these functions to the district level. Financial control has, however, proven more difficult to decentralize. In UGANDA, for example, only 15 percent of spending on primary health care is controlled at the district level. WHO has played a major role through its Strengthening District Health Systems initiative, aimed at developing district health-management teams. The purpose of these teams is to strengthen district-level administration in the areas of planning, resource allocation, and management. Policy issues such as gender inequalities in health priorities and the equitable delivery of services, particularly to the most destitute, are challenges both nationally and at the district level. In March 1996 the United Nations launched the Special Initiative on Africa, which is a ten-year plan to address health development as one of several key areas of development in Africa.

In the clinical area of primary health care, several strategies have been tried to improve the quality of care. These include developing essential drug lists for health centers, using standard treatment protocols for common conditions like pneumonia, and training and integrating traditional healers into the health services. The latter has been most successful with the upgrading of traditional birth attendants. In addition, related services, both curative and educational, have been combined in comprehensive packages. For example, maternal health care has been linked with child health care, family planning, and AIDS prevention, so that the person is exposed on one visit to as many relevant services as possible. Attempts are being made to integrate appropriate elements of disease-specific programs into primary health care as well. Education about bed-net use to prevent malaria and condom-distribution programs to prevent AIDS are examples of programs available at health centers that complement community-based programs.

Other innovations based on the tenets of primary care are intersectoral collaboration and community participation. Collaboration with other sectors is very complex and is often part of larger changes in societies. In the least developed countries the focus generally is on infectious disease control, water safety, and sanitation. In many health centers one member of the team is responsible for development and educational activities in these areas. Community participation ranges from educating the community about local health problems to actively involving the community in determining health priorities, allocating resources, and facilitating development. Village health committees are often the focus of these activities that collaborate with the local health center. Change can be at the household or community level and requires persistent effort over time to be successful. A major shift in primary health care is away from curative programs based in the health center and toward educational and preventative programs at the community level. These can range from mass immunization programs to selective screening and treatment of specific high-risk groups. Community distribution of condoms and educational events are examples of the ways AIDS prevention occurs at this level.

In reality, primary health care works through a complex interplay between national and local health priorities and resources balanced against changing disease patterns, mortality, and morbidity. Lack of adequate administrative structures and problems with the distribution and supply of essential equipment and drugs all affect the quality and consistency of primary health care in sub-Saharan Africa. Nevertheless, despite these problems, substantial gains have been made over the last two decades in the overall health of the population.

HOSPITALS AND CLINICS

The complexity of the history of the development of hospitals, health centers, and clinics in Africa is well illustrated by those countries that had a protracted and difficult period of serial colonizations. For example, SUDAN's medical and health services started from a base of ancient Arab, Egyptian, and African traditional health practices. The regime of the Turco-Egyptian administration (1820–1885) established military hospitals that treated dysentery, malaria, smallpox, and venereal diseases. Arab and French doctors initially brought Western medicine to Sudan, but it had little impact on the population. The Anglo-Egyptian condominium established an organized medical service with British senior army officers seconded to the Egyptian Army Medical Corps. Syrian medical graduates from Beirut were added, and British civilian doctors, including some from the Wellcome Research Laboratory, arrived. By 1904 there were seven hospitals; by 1924 there were nineteen, with fifty-five dispensaries. The Sudan Medical Service existed from 1924 to 1948, and the number of expatriate and Sudanese doctors and medical assistants began to rise. A rural network of health centers started in 1944, and the Ministry of Health was established in 1948. In 1956 Sudan became an independent state and a member of WHO; by that time there were forty-nine hospitals, more than 300 dispensaries, and twenty health centers.

Medical missions also played a role. They originated in the mid-1800s with Roman Catholic missionaries and were spread by the Church Missionary Society, the American Mission, and the Sudan Interim Mission. Over the years these missions and their hospitals suffered great setbacks, and in 1962 all missionaries were expelled from southern Sudan.

Many countries in Africa have a similar complex evolution of hospitals. The DEMOCRATIC REPUBLIC OF THE CONGO (DRC) started with the uniquely exploitative CONGO FREE STATE (a private empire) and then was a colony until 1960. Although the Belgians claimed that their medical service was outstanding in colonial Africa and had conquered human sleeping sickness, the paternalistic and hierarchical system came in for considerable criticism.

The role of medical missions and the hospitals and clinics they established in most African countries has been regarded variously. It has been seen by some as totally constructive, providing caring, scientifically correct medicine in many countries, but it has also been evaluated as the cutting edge of colonialism: coercive, serving the interests of capitalism, paternalistic, and destructive of traditional norms and values. The missions regarded their medical work as continuing Christ's healing work and assisting in evangelization of the heathen. But in most countries—for example, Uganda and Tanzania—the importance of medical missions and their hospitals is firmly established. Mengo Hospital, established by Sir Albert Cook in the kingdom of Buganda, and Masasi Hospital and the Kilimanjaro Christian Medical Centre in Tanzania have made tremendous contributions. These contributions come through the excellence of their work, the trained and expert human resources they have produced, and their advocacy for the care of women and children and the control of communicable disease and malnutrition.

CATEGORIES OF HOSPITALS AND CLINICS

In sub-Saharan Africa standard terms for various health facilities have been gradually and generally adopted. In the early days of independence, there were many versions of hospitals, dispensaries, clinics, and occasionally health centers. With WHO's rising influence over national ministries of health, increased international movement, and the fading of racial discrimination in most countries, health services and referral systems have become more uniform.

The hospitals came to be considered within a hierarchy of health units often classified by their place in a referral chain, with increasing range of expertise and services. Previously these institutions were ranked according to cost, staffing, size, expertise, and centrality, from largest and most complex to smallest, simplest, and most peripheral. With the slow acceptance of the primary health-care approach after 1978, the orientation has changed so the periphery is now the most important level, in rhetoric if not in resource allocation. The present levels in the hierarchy of primary health care are listed below.

- Community-based health care, with perhaps a village or community health post.
- Small clinic or small health center, or dispensary, with or without mobile visiting points.
- Health center—possibly a community health center—with more facilities and expertise, perhaps supervising several small clinics, and with a mobile clinic and outreach services. (The difference between a mobile clinic and outreach is that the former has a special team of workers and goes on a circuit to several places, perhaps over several days, whereas the latter is more local and members of staff take services to places on the periphery of their catchment area.)

- Hospital that serves as the referral point for a group of units. This could be a district or subdistrict government hospital or a mission hospital.
- Larger referral hospital with more specialist services, such as a regional hospital or larger mission hospital serving several districts.
- National referral hospital, with larger referral capacity and a full spectrum of specialist care, and more training responsibility.

CLINICS OR DISPENSARIES

Clinics are the first level of care for perhaps the bulk of Africa's population. They are usually staffed by medical auxiliaries or enrolled or staff nurses, who have lower entry qualifications and shorter training periods than professional nurses. In some cases they are involved in community-based health-care activities, providing support to health workers who may be employed at a health post within the community. Tanzania, for example, has a large network of these clinics that assist community-based health workers in "ujamaa villages" (collective villages) within their territories. The clinics supervise community-based growth monitoring and provide immunization, prenatal care, and family planning on a monthly basis. The smaller units, such as clinics and health centers, brought family planning to Africa. Small clinics in Tanzania have three staff members: a maternal and child health aide, a medical aide, and a health assistant. They cover a spectrum of maternal and child health work, outpatient care for common complaints, referral of serious cases to the next level of health facilities, and environmental work done with community involvement. This category of health unit, being the most numerous and found mostly in rural areas, where the majority live, does the greatest amount of preventive and promotional work.

Being the most peripheral, and serving especially isolated communities, these units have experienced the greatest destruction in civil wars. MOZAMBIQUE, ANGOLA, LIBERIA, SOMALIA, and ETHIOPIA have had many of these small units and their dedicated staffs wiped out. In some areas of Mozambique, staff members were especially targeted for kidnapping.

HEALTH CENTERS

Health centers are the most important facilities for promoting health, providing early treatment of disease, lowering death rates, and improving nutrition. They are of different sizes, depending on the staff forming the team and the size of the catchment area. The political, social, and economic factors that historically determined the relationship between hospitals and rural health centers is well illustrated in SOUTH AFRICA, where racial policies of exploitation developed a system of migrant black labor for the mines and created impoverished, overcrowded rural areas that became bantustans. Large areas had poor health services, and the black population had high mortality from largely preventable diseases. After World War II (1939–1945), medical assistants were to be trained to serve in rural areas, but this plan aroused opposition from doctors, and in the end insufficient numbers were trained to serve the large rural areas. A community health center was developed by Sidney and Emily Kark at Pholela, a rural area in Natal, which later became the model for about fifty centers established in the late 1940s. The Institute of Family and Community Health, established under Sidney Kark in Durban, became a teaching focus for the new faculty of medicine for black students. Government support waned, however, and most of the staff left these health centers and emigrated to start what later became known as community-oriented primary health care in other countries, such as Uganda and Kenya.

Some of the bigger health centers in Africa have registered nurses, community nurses, and medical assistants. Urban centers have one or more doctors, but rural ones seldom have this level of expertise. These centers aim not only to achieve a high level of patient care but also to improve the health of a population in a more or less defined catchment area, such as a division or a ward for which vital and other epidemiological statistics can be established. These data guide interventions by a team of health workers, including some who live in and are responsible for specific localities. These health centers have a few maternity and holding beds, and radiological, laboratory, and dental facilities. The field staff is trained to improve environmental sanitation and water supply, and perhaps to improve agriculture and kitchen gardens. Some workers may be assigned to improve women's skills in health and child care. Referral links are established with hospitals. These community-oriented health centers can provide the whole spectrum of health promotion, disease prevention, early diagnosis, and treatment and rehabilitation.

In Kenya, with assistance from the U.S. Agency for International Development (USAID), a number of large regional training health centers were set up to train teams for health centers. A team consists of nurses, medical assistants, and environmental health officers. Such a team provides services for a defined geographical area and supervises a number of smaller clinics; together they form a health unit. The team is trained in community diagnosis and in improving the health of the whole population, not just of the sick people who come to the center. After these rural training health centers were formed, the basic training of nurses changed and a cadre of enrolled community

nurses was trained, which made it necessary to construct small health centers with accommodations for trainees.

Teaching health centers often have been attached, with donor support, to university faculties of medicine, and some form the basis of large research projects. Kasangati Health Centre was developed with funds from the Rockefeller Foundation for training and research in community health at Makerere Medical School in Uganda. The Danfa Project with the Danfa Health Centre opened in 1970 with assistance from USAID and with linkage between the UCLA School of Public Health and the Department of Community Health, University of Ghana Medical School. The objectives were to train health staff to work as a team to handle community problems with local participation and to strengthen operations research and institutional capacity. The Rockefeller Foundation, the Liverpool School of Tropical Medicine, and the medical school of Ibadan University (Nigeria) had earlier set up a rural health teaching center at Igbo-Ora in 1963. By training cohorts of doctors, these centers influenced the further development of health centers in their countries, and the scientific papers they generated influenced services in neighboring countries.

HOSPITALS

The most important hospitals since primary health care approach began in 1978 are the district hospitals, usually situated in the small urban centers of predominantly rural districts with populations varying from 250,000 to 800,000. They were at first under the control of medical superintendents who often were also district medical health officers—a difficult combination with two different perspectives and conflicting time demands. In several countries the district health office is now separate from the hospital, although this officer, who is often (but not necessarily) a doctor, still must have close links with the hospital for obtaining health information and for budgeting purposes. In LESOTHO, health districts are based on hospitals (sometimes mission), and in Tanzania, district hospitals can be mission hospitals with government subsidies and staff. The day of the 100-bed hospital with one overworked doctor is nearly over except in countries such as Malawi—where there may be no doctor, only a well-trained medical assistant in charge.

An increasing proportion of rural hospitals, both government and nongovernment, have several doctors, often with some degree of specialization acquired in practice if not at the postgraduate level. One doctor may have management skills and be the medical superintendent, another may have a flair for surgery, and others may be competent in anesthesia, pediatrics, or obstetrics. This staff may be supplemented by newly graduated doctors or medical students who come from developed countries for short periods to get an orientation in "third world medicine." Although doctors receive much attention, the services of small hospitals in Africa largely depend on medical auxiliaries such as medical assistants or clinical officers, and nurses or nurse practitioners. Nurses in hospitals are at different levels of training. Registered professional nurses belong to an association and register with a nursing council that acts as the watchdog of standards and ethics. Staff nurses or enrolled nurses have lower entry requirements, shorter training, and lower pay. There are also nursing assistants or nurse aides who are trained on the job and have even lower levels of basic education and pay. These are the backbone of many impoverished church hospitals—in fact, many are staffed by nuns who are professional nurses or doctors and are supported by the church.

Small district hospitals overcome the lack of expert specialist staff in other ways. Some develop radio links with national or regional hospitals so they can get advice. A nongovernmental organization, the African Medical and Research Foundation, which is based in NAIROBI, KENYA, and has offices in Uganda and Tanzania, set up a network of radio links with many hospitals in the three countries. Since it also runs the Flying Doctor Service, it can send specialists or air rescue teams to fetch critically ill patients to hospitals in Nairobi for specialist care. It also has surgeons and physicians who visit mission or government district hospitals to perform surgery (such as plastic surgery for cleft palates) and train the local doctors. Another service needed is repair and maintenance of equipment. Government specialists based in regional (provincial) hospitals in many countries provide a visiting service to small hospitals or large health centers. The special services most often provided are ophthalmology, psychiatry, orthopedic rehabilitation, dentistry, tuberculosis diagnosis and treatment, or epidemic investigation.

The district hospital, as a focal point of the district health system, has changed in several countries. Often located in a small town, it does not always have the community relationship that a health center can have. The supervisory health management team for the district is often based in a separate office that collects health information from the outlying areas (after it has been analyzed and used locally, one hopes). The hospital is a center to which difficult cases are referred for diagnosis or management. In some countries, such as Kenya, it is also the center for continuing education of district staff.

Poorer countries have experienced deteriorating conditions in first- and second-level hospitals as recession and economic reforms have reduced funds, drugs, and staff. Buildings and equipment deteriorate not only through lack of maintenance and availability of spares

but also through overuse. Wards designed for eight patients now hold twenty-four (on the floor, under and between beds, and two in a bed). Toilets become blocked and water may be insufficient. Hospitals designed in the 1960s and 1970s now have to provide for a population that had doubled by the 1980s and 1990s. In much of tropical Africa the small hospitals are battling to deal with great numbers of preventable diseases: chloroquine-resistant complicated malaria, infected and bleeding abortions, measles with complications, pelvic inflammatory disease, AIDS with tuberculosis, pregnancy with severe anemia, severe malnutrition, and diarrhea with dehydration. Hence the importance of increasing the number of health centers is apparent. Some of the other useful work hospitals do is in the delivery of high-risk maternity cases (some of which need cesarean section or vacuum extraction) and in management of trauma and surgical and medical emergencies.

The regional or provincial hospitals have become increasingly better staffed with specialists as faculties of medicine in most countries have embarked on postgraduate training. All the major specialties—internal medicine, gynecology and obstetrics, surgery, pediatrics, and psychiatry—are now represented. Supporting them are radiographers (seldom radiologists), laboratory technologists (seldom a pathologist), physiotherapists, and occupational therapists. Management skills often lag behind, so that poor organization, budgeting, maintenance, and financial control have led to low staff morale and patient dissatisfaction. Hence, in many countries it is not unusual to find patients preferring to be referred to large private or church hospitals. Like district or local authority hospitals, these bigger hospitals rely on nurses and medical auxiliaries to do most of the work in the wards and in the general outpatient departments.

In the Republic of South Africa, Baragwanath Hospital, serving the densely populated "African townships" in metropolitan Johannesburg, had to train nurses in primary health care—actually primary medical care—making them nurse practitioners able to diagnose and manage the common complaints coming to the outpatient departments. This had been the practice in large hospitals in eastern and Central Africa, where medical assistants or clinical officers see most outpatients, and doctors see the patients whom assistants or officers refer. Clinical officers in these countries are able to take specialized courses in ophthalmology, orthopedic work, operating theater techniques, intensive care, pediatrics, and psychiatry. These courses are also available for nurses in the more southerly countries (South Africa, Botswana, Lesotho, Swaziland), where there is no category of medical assistant or clinical officer; however, Lesotho has nurse practitioners, and

South Africa and Namibia now have primary health-care nurses. In the latter two countries, returned political exiles who qualified as medical assistants in other countries are having problems being placed.

The last category of government medical care institution is the national teaching and referral hospital. Many of these are now parastatal institutions. Examples that should be mentioned are Groote Schuur Hospital (South Africa), Kenyatta National Hospital (Kenya), Mulago Hospital (Uganda), Lusaka University Teaching Hospital (Zambia), Ibadan University Teaching Hospital (Nigeria), Mama Yerno in Kinshasa (DRC), and teaching hospitals in Côte d'Ivoire, Senegal, and Ghana. These large hospitals often use a large proportion of the national health budget and employ a large percentage of the nation's doctors and professional nurses.

The direct impact of large national hospitals on national health is negligible for the country; analyses usually show that only a small proportion of cases come from beyond the city, district, or region in which they are situated. Their indirect impact on health is considered to be through training and research, and advocacy for improved national health services. Training is, however, in a high-technology setting with excellent diagnostic and other equipment, and the doctors they produce are often reluctant to work in remote, underequipped district hospitals. Research may be for international acclaim rather than for impact on national priorities. Groote Schuur Hospital in South Africa was the site of the world's first heart transplant—for an old man—while thousands of children died from preventable diseases. Advocacy emerging from these hospitals is usually for more hospital beds and more trauma units, rather than for preventive measures. Countries becoming independent or changing from an apartheid government usually have had to take firm measures to put a brake on these hospitals' virtual monopoly of the budget and their absorption of the bulk of trained human resources. Examples are ZIMBABWE, where Pararinyatwa Hospital in Harare had to be changed from elite to less costly accommodation, and Tanzania, where a policy swing led to more investment in clinics and health centers. NAMIBIA's carefully documented changes to decentralize and move specialists to more densely populated, less endowed regions have been studied by South Africa, which faces this problem as much as the DRC, Kenya, or Uganda. This change in priority from large hospitals serving a few to more decentralized smaller units serving the majority depends on the ideological orientation of the government.

A rapidly growing category of hospital is the private commercial hospital. The more famous of these attract the ailing politicians of the less developed countries in Africa. The Republic of South Africa and the city of Nairobi perhaps have the most publicized private services. These hospitals are efficiently run as business enterprises, and their fees are such that only the wealthy or the insured can use their high-technology services. Senior civil servants with government health coverage use them extensively, so that a large part of government health expenditure is enriching the private sector.

With deterioration and overcrowding of many government referral hospitals (such as Kamuzu Central Hospital, Malawi; Kenyatta Hospital, Kenya; and Mulago Hospital, Uganda), many patients prefer to go to a smaller private hospital (mission or commercial). There is thus a rapidly increasing number of small private hospitals in most towns where patients can get their prescribed drugs and be cared for by a skilled doctor and nursing staff—at a cost greater than people can really afford but less than that of the big private hospital. These hospitals are not as overcrowded and corrupt as the major national hospitals in countries with economic problems. Corruption may be evident in situations in which patients have to pay extra to see a doctor, to receive all the drugs needed, or to get onto a waiting list. In some countries patients argue that in the end it is cheaper to go to a private hospital.

In a few countries having many mission hospitals, the hospitals have come together to form an association, as with the Private Hospital Association of Malawi (PHAM). This association has an officer in the Ministry of Health so that training activities and subsidies can be coordinated. These associations bring together Catholic, Protestant, and other health services. In eastern Africa the Aga Khan (also known as Ismaili) Health Services makes a considerable contribution to hospital and primary health care services.

Specialized hospitals serve particular classes of patients and, hence, usually provide care of a higher standard with more expert staff and special equipment and drugs. The most important are mental hospitals, tuberculosis or infectious-disease hospitals, and hospitals related to endemic disease research (e.g., trypanosomiasis or leprosy). Two famous hospitals at opposite ends of Africa are the Red Cross Paediatric Hospital in CAPE TOWN, SOUTH AFRICA, and the Fistula Hospital in ADDIS ABABA, ETHIOPIA. The latter deals with the common and difficult problem of vesico-vaginal fistula in women, resulting largely from the local infibulation type of clitoridectomy.

In Africa, where wars are recurrent and where military regimes come and go, large amounts of state funds go to the armed forces. Besides the obvious trauma surgery required by soldiers, army medical services and hospitals may also serve the troops' families. However, this area of expenditure is seldom open to public scrutiny. The South

RURAL AFRICAN HEALTH CARE. A lack of transportation infrastructure in Malawi forces health care worker Anna Kalinda to ride her bicycle to a patient's home in the Monkey Bay district, 2006. (*Tsvangirayi Mukwazhi/AP Images*)

African army, the most advanced in Africa, has very well-trained doctors (specialist and general) and paramedics, and on occasion uses them in emergencies or epidemics affecting the civilian population. Rural mission hospitals play a role in liberation movements. In Zimbabwe and in northern Namibia, they had always supplied most of the medical care to the tribal and more densely populated peripheral areas. Thus they began caring for communities and fighters identified with the liberation forces.

If one has to summarize the achievement of hospitals in Africa, it probably lies in completing the curative end of the spectrum of care and the chain of referral, thus forming one important component of the primary health care approach. In addition, hospitals have provided training in technical skills and in attitudes of caring at an individual level (less often at the family or community level). Many of them have greatly furthered knowledge and the ability to manage illness, even if not always in ways that can be applied across the nation. Perhaps they have made their greatest contribution in the management of complicated malaria and childbirth, acute children's diseases, and trauma. As transport and electronic communication improve, hospitals will be reached by a larger proportion of an increasingly demanding and urbanized population. With demographic and epidemiological transition, the proportion of old people is increasing, and chronic cardiovascular and respiratory conditions are becoming more common. With increased emphasis on health centers and preventive measures, those who require more specialized care need access to hospitals. Decentralization or improved transport will become increasingly essential. The emphasis will change as geriatric beds exceed pediatric beds—a situation that is emerging in this century in most of Africa.

Clinics and health centers, on the other hand, are the facilities that have immunized children, taught mothers about essential health care such as oral rehydration and nutrition, and made scientific family planning available so that women can control their fertility. On a national level, control of fertility will reduce high birthrates and change the demographic pattern to one more consistent with development and economic growth.

See also ACQUIRED IMMUNODEFICIENCY SYNDROME IN AFRICA: AN INTERPRETATION; DISEASE AND AFRICAN HISTORY; DISEASES, INFECTIOUS, IN AFRICA; STRUCTURAL ADJUSTMENT IN AFRICA.

"Health Care: Primary Health Care by Michael Stephenson and Health Care:" Hospitals and Clinics by F. J. Bennett. Used by permission of Charles Scribner's Sons, an imprint

PHELOPHEPA TRAIN. Patients in Kirkwood, South Africa, wait in line for assistance from volunteer health care workers on the Phelophepa Train, whose name means "Good Clean Health." The train brings doctors, dentists, optometrists, psychologists, and health educators to remote areas of South Africa. (*Denis Farrell/AP Images*)

of Macmillan Library Reference USA, from *Encyclopedia of Africa South of the Sahara*, John Middleton, Editor in Chief, Vol. 2, pp. 288–299. Copyright 1997, Charles Scribner's Sons. Updated by *Encarta Africana* staff by permission of Charles Scribner's Sons.

BIBLIOGRAPHY

Amonoo, Lartson R., G. J. Ebrahim, H. J. Lovel, and J. P. Ranken. *District Health Care: Challenges for Planning, Organisation, and Evaluation in Developing Countries*. Macmillan, 1984.

Bayourni, Ahmed. *The History of the Sudan Health Services*. Kenya Literature Bureau, 1979.

Feierman, Steven, and John M. Janzen, eds. *The Social Basis of Health and Healing in Africa*. University of California Press, 1992.

Heggenhoughen, Kris, Patrick Vaughan, Eustace P. Y. Muhondwa, and J. Rutabanzibwa-Ngaiza. *Community Health Workers: The Tanzanian Experience*. Oxford University Press, 1987.

Kark, Sidney L., and Guy W. Steuart. *A Practice of Social Medicine: A South African Team's Experiences in Different African Communities*. E & S Livingstone, 1962.

Lyons, Maryinez. *The Colonial Disease: A Social History of Sleeping Sickness in Northern Zaire, 1900–1940*. Cambridge University Press, 1992.

Rohde, Jon, Meera Chatterjee, and David Morley. *Reaching Health for All*. Oxford University Press, 1993.

Hehe

Ethnic group of Tanzania.

The Hehe primarily inhabit south-central Tanzania. They speak a Bantu language. Approximately 750,000 people consider themselves Hehe.

See also BANTU: DISPERSION AND SETTLEMENT.

Herero

Ethnic group of Namibia and Botswana that suffered greatly from German colonialism.

The Herero, who now call themselves Ovaherero, are thought to have arrived on the central plateau of NAMIBIA during the sixteenth century, migrating with other Bantu-speaking peoples from the area around LAKE VICTORIA. Some of these migrants settled in the northern Kaokoveld and became known as the Himba, while the rest continued south into east-central Namibia. Politically decentralized, the seminomadic Herero recognized both matrilineal and patrilineal descent and inheritance systems. Like the Sotho, to whom they are probably distantly related, the Herero placed great cultural and economic value on cattle, and still do today. Although women's agricultural produce provides much of their food supply, men's cattle herds are an important measure of wealth, especially in marriage and religious rituals.

During the 1800s European missionaries began to live among the Herero, and many Herero women adopted long, European-style dresses and turban-like hats. Around the same time, competition for grazing land—especially after a drought in 1829 to 1830—led to conflicts between the Herero and their neighbors to the south, the Oorlam. The Herero usually found themselves on the defensive until 1863, when the Herero, led by Maherero and armed with German-supplied weapons, launched a year-long "Freedom War."

The colonization of Namibia by Germany led to new clashes and, ultimately, the near destruction of the Herero. In early 1904 SAMUEL MAHERERO called upon Herero to attack German farms and outposts, on the ground that German settlers had stolen these lands. Maherero specifically ordered that women, children, Englishmen, and Afrikaner people be spared, a policy that the Herero followed. Although initially outnumbered, the Germans brought in reinforcements until their well-equipped army was double the size of the Herero's 10,000-troop force. After the Battle of Waterberg in August of 1904, the defeated Herero sought peace. But the peace accord meant little, as the Germans essentially sought to exterminate the Herero in what historians have called one of the bloodiest of all colonial wars. In three years the Herero population was reduced from 80,000 to 15,000. Their cattle herds decimated, many survivors fled to Bechuanaland, today known as Botswana.

The Herero who remained behind found themselves pushed onto a Herero "homeland" after South Africa occupied German South-West Africa in 1915. Soon afterward the elder chiefs formed the Herero Council. The council would later play an important antigovernment role, repeatedly petitioning the United Nations for South African withdrawal. Although many Herero also joined the nationalist South-West African National Union in the 1960s, the Herero Council itself was more conservative and ultimately endorsed the "internal settlement" arrangements proposed by South Africa, rather than the total independence demanded by the more radical nationalist group, the SOUTH WEST AFRICA PEOPLES ORGANIZATION, or SWAPO. In part this stance reflected the Herero leaders' fears of OVAMBO dominance in an independent Namibia. Today many Herero, especially the Himba, see themselves as discriminated against by the SWAPO- and Ovambo-dominated government, and in elections they have been more likely to support the opposition Democratic Turnhalle Alliance. The Herero now number around 240,000.

See also BANTU: DISPERSION AND SETTLEMENT; CHRISTIANITY: MISSIONARIES IN AFRICA; PASTORALISM.

ERIC YOUNG

History, African
Record of trends and events in Africa's past.
For information on

Development of humankind in Africa: See AFRICAN ORIGINS OF HUMANITY; HOW AFRICA BECAME BLACK: AN INTERPRETATION; LEAKEY, Louis; LEAKEY, MARY DOUGLAS NICHOL. History of early African civilizations: See ANCIENT AFRICAN CIVILIZATIONS. Specific African civilizations: See AKSUM; BANTU: DISPERSION AND SETTLEMENT; BENIN, EARLY KINGDOM OF; BUGANDA, EARLY KINGDOM OF; DAHOMEY, EARLY KINGDOM OF; EGYPT, ANCIENT KINGDOM OF; GEDI; GHANA, EARLY KINGDOM OF; KAABU, EARLY KINGDOM OF; KASANJE; KUSH, EARLY KINGDOM OF; LOANGO; OYO, EARLY KINGDOM OF. Creation of colonial empires: See COLONIAL RULE; EXPLORERS IN AFRICAN BEFORE 1500; EXPLORERS IN AFRICA, 1500 TO 1800; EXPLORERS IN AFRICA SINCE 1800; SCRAMBLE FOR AFRICA. End of colonialism and history since independence: See COLD WAR AND AFRICA.

HIV in Africa
See ACQUIRED IMMUNODEFICIENCY SYNDROME IN AFRICA: AN INTERPRETATION.

Hlengwe
Ethnic group of southern Africa; also known as Bahlengwe and Hlengue.
The Hlengwe primarily inhabit southwestern MOZAMBIQUE, northeastern SOUTH AFRICA, and southeastern ZIMBABWE. They speak a BANTU language and belong to the TSONGA cultural and linguistic group. Approximately 1.4 million people consider themselves Hlengwe.

See also BANTU: DISPERSION AND SETTLEMENT; ETHNICITY AND IDENTITY IN AFRICA: AN INTERPRETATION; LANGUAGES, AFRICAN: AN OVERVIEW.

Holy Spirit Movement
Insurgent group in Uganda since the 1980s.
The Holy Spirit Movement, later known as the Lord's Resistance Army (LRA), the United Democratic Christian Movement (UDCM), and the Uganda People's Democratic Christian Army, blended religion with political opposition

in the eastern African nation of Uganda beginning in the mid-1980s.

The Holy Spirit Movement was founded in 1986 by Alice Auma, an Acholi woman from the oppressed northern region of Uganda. She claimed to have received spiritual orders to fight evil—namely, the government. Taking the name Alice Lakwena, she recruited people to her cause, promising that her magical powers would protect them against bullets. Lakwena's message appealed to many ethnic Acholi who, because of their association with the military forces of former president Milton Obote, had suffered abuse from the regime of Idi Amin during the 1970s and vengeance from the military forces of Yoweri Museveni, who came to power in 1986. To Lakwena's followers, who referred to her as laor (messenger) or nebbi (prophet), her movement offered both spiritual renewal and, on a more secular level, the opportunity for retribution.

The Holy Spirit Movement's attempts at sabotage and guerrilla warfare in the Acholi district rarely succeeded, but the movement itself maintained momentum. In October 1987, however, Lakwena took her followers farther afield, to Busoga, where they suffered a devastating military defeat. Lakwena escaped to Kenya but was captured and imprisoned. Most of her followers surrendered when Museveni instituted an amnesty program. However, Joseph Kony, claiming kinship to Lakwena, continued her resistance, although he did not claim prophetic powers as she had done. Supported by arms shipments from Sudan, the rebels, now known as the Lord's Resistance Army (LRA), stepped up their terrorist campaign after 1993. When his following began to dwindle, Kony kidnapped thousands of Acholi children and indoctrinated them into his army; they soon made up the bulk of his guerrilla force. After an LRA attack on civilians in March 1998, government forces killed some sixty of the rebels, and Kony fled to Sudan.

ARI NAVE

Homosexuality in Africa

Sexual relations between people of the same sex in Africa.
Homosexuality is found throughout the African continent, as it is found throughout the world. Homosexuality in Africa is sometimes associated with important rituals such as initiation (coming-of-age) ceremonies, but often it is simply a part of everyday life. Homosexuality is controversial in Africa. Although many African leaders claim that homosexuality was brought to Africa from other parts of the world, most scholars believe that homosexuality has long been a part of various African cultures.

OVERVIEW
The term homosexuality refers to sexual relations between people of the same sex—that is, between men or between women. Thus homosexuality is also referred to as "same-sex relations." Men who engage in these relations are known as gay men or homosexuals, and women are known as lesbians. Bisexuals are people who have sexual relations with both men and women, and people who dress as the opposite sex (known as cross-dressers) are also referred to as transvestites. Transsexuals are people who have surgery in order to transform their bodies and their official identities from male to female or vice versa. People who are "cross genders"—that is, dress, behave, or want to assume the identity of the opposite sex without surgery—increasingly refer to themselves as "transgendered" people. The term sexual minorities is used to refer to people in all of these different categories. However, people in Africa do not necessarily refer to themselves as homosexuals, gay men, or lesbians. Instead, they use local terms for talking about particular identities that may involve same-sex relations, often in conjunction with cross-dressing and work. For example, mashoga in East African Swahili-speaking societies (including parts of coastal KENYA and TANZANIA) are biological men who sometimes dress like women and do women's work by cooking food or preparing women's wedding celebrations. The mashoga are sometimes known by women's names, and they have sex with other men. The oldest evidence of same-sex relations is found in southern Africa, where 2,000-year-old rock paintings depict men having sexual relations with men. There are at least seventy documented words in various African languages for men or women who engage in homosexual relations. There are also a variety of ways that African societies have historically tolerated or even celebrated the people who engaged in these practices. Some royal courts, such as those in the nineteenth-century kingdoms of Dahomey (in what is now BENIN) and Buganda (in what is now UGANDA), institutionalized certain forms of same-sex relations. In Africa, as in the West, beginning in the twentieth century homosexuality became the basis of a political movement centering on the social identity of the sexual minorities, or lesbian, gay, bisexual, and transgendered people.

FACTORS AFFECTING LEGAL AND SOCIAL STATUS
There are three main factors that affect the current legal status and physical safety of sexual minorities in Africa. The first is legal restrictions found in contemporary law. These are often based on varying interpretations of Islamic law, known as the sharia, and on laws retained from British, French, and Portuguese colonial penal codes. The second factor affecting the status of sexual minorities in

Africa is religious practices and traditions, which provide a social context that may suppress or support homosexuality. These include traditional religions, CHRISTIANITY, and ISLAM. The third factor affecting the treatment of sexual minorities is the presence of civil unrest or warfare. In both ALGERIA and in the central Great Lakes region (in east Central Africa), for example, ethnic, political, and sexual minorities have been targets of human rights abuses, including sexual assault, torture, rape, and murder. By the end of the twentieth century, a variety of groups in Africa proclaimed a proud and positive identity as gay men and lesbians. In the 1990s gay social and political groups emerged in CÔTE D'IVOIRE, Kenya, NAMIBIA, NIGERIA, SOUTH AFRICA, and ZIMBABWE, generally in response to government persecution of sexual minorities. Indeed, in 1994 South Africa became the first country in the world to provide constitutional protection for the civil rights of lesbians and gay men.

AIDS AND HOMOSEXUALITY

In Africa, ACQUIRED IMMUNODEFICIENCY SYNDROME (AIDS) is not usually associated with homosexuals or homosexuality. This is largely because in Africa the main mode of transmission for the human immunodeficiency virus (HIV), the virus that causes AIDS, is through heterosexual contact. The only exceptions are in some urban areas with visible homosexual populations, particularly in southern Africa. In many of these cities gays and lesbians have organized to educate communities and to care for people with HIV and AIDS. These public health efforts sometimes lead to a backlash against AIDS education and to increased persecution of sexual minorities. For example, in 1998 the leaders of an AIDS education organization in Kisumu, a city in western Kenya, faced government hostility and were forced to shut down their organization because of rumors that the leaders were gay.

HISTORICAL EVIDENCE IN NORTH AFRICA

American scholars Stephen Murray and Will Roscoe provide a comprehensive overview of homosexuality in North Africa in their work *Islamic Homosexualities* (1997). They argue that before the twentieth century, North Africa contained some of the most visible and well-documented traditions of homosexuality in the world. During pre-Islamic times, the Roman emperor Constantine allegedly exterminated an entire class of "effeminate priests" in ALEXANDRIA, EGYPT. A specific genre of Arabic poetry describing the virtues of men loving young boys emerged in the cosmopolitan, literate civilizations that flourished in medieval times. There is also some evidence of female homosexuality in classical Arabic poetry, although relatively few of these manuscripts have survived. Homosexuality was

an integral part of the social and political order in North Africa under the Mamluks, who ruled the area from the thirteenth century until the late eighteenth century. Certain warrior groups, comprised of slave and foreign soldiers, were known for widespread same-sex relations with boys. At that time, Christian boys were also sold in Europe and then transported to EGYPT for sex work. In CAIRO, EGYPT, cross-dressing men known as chauel or khawal entertained audiences by dancing and singing. Cross-dressed entertainers such as these performed throughout the Islamic world, suggesting that the role may be related to pre-Islamic religious roles. More recent reports indicate that same-sex relations were common in the twentieth century among groups living in western Egypt. The Siwa Oasis (in northwestern Egypt) was mentioned by early-twentieth-century travelers as a place where male same-sex relations were quite common. There, a warrior group historically gave bridewealth (a reverse dowry) for young boys in marriage, although this practice was outlawed by the 1940s. Although rumors abound about extensive female same-sex relations within the harems of North Africa, there are no accounts known to have originated with the women themselves.

CONTEMPORARY LEGAL STATUS: NORTH AFRICA

In North Africa, same-sex relations for men and women are legal only in EGYPT, though gay men in that country have occasionally been prosecuted as Satanists. Homosexuality is illegal in all other countries, with punishments ranging from three months to five years of imprisonment. In some North African countries, officials turn a blind eye to violence against homosexuals, unofficially encouraging their persecution. The worst situation for gay men and lesbians is in Algeria, where the militant Islamic resistance movement began targeting homosexuals for assassination in the late 1990s, along with intellectuals and feminists. The legal status of sexual minorities in North Africa demonstrates how Islamic law, or the shariah, can be interpreted in radically different ways. The legal codes of most North African countries are influenced by the sharia, and sharia prescriptions also have powerful effects through religious and cultural organizations. In Egypt in 1997, a fatwa, or religious decision, upheld the right of individuals to undergo surgery to become transsexuals and thus be accepted as legal members of the opposite sex. In contrast, in 1993 a Tunisian court denied a request for a change of civil status by a transsexual, effectively denying transsexuals the right to change their sexual and social identity. Both of these decisions were based on different interpretations of the sharia.

HISTORICAL EVIDENCE IN WEST AFRICA

In West Africa there is extensive historical evidence of homosexuality. There is also evidence of flexible gender

568 HOMOSEXUALITY IN AFRICA

systems that allowed women to become "men" and vice versa. Religious rituals and the court societies of some of the great kingdoms provided two important contexts for these practices. In the eighteenth- and nineteenth-century ASANTE court (in what is now GHANA), male slaves served as concubines. They dressed like women and were killed when their masters died. In the eighteenth- and nineteenth-century kingdom of Dahomey, eunuchs (castrated men), known as royal wives, played important roles in court society, alongside female soldiers. The women soldiers who made up these troops believed that they had transformed themselves into men and sang songs ridiculing the male soldiers they defeated for being "women." According to the beliefs of the Dagari (who live in what is now BURKINA FASO), homosexual men are gay because they are able to mediate between the spirit and human worlds. The Yan daudu are a male homosexual group found among the HAUSA of Nigeria. These men are associated with certain religious cults and have created a vibrant subculture within contemporary society. Yan daudu engage in erotic and emotional relationships with other men, whom they refer to as their saurayi (boyfriend) or miji (husband). Marriage between women is also found among several different groups in West Africa, although scholars have long debated whether these relationships involve sexual relationships between the female husband and her wife. For example, in some traditions a woman can "become" a man, and thus marry a wife or wives, by participating in specific rituals. This was the case during the mid-twentieth century in the kingdom of Dahomey and among some IGBO groups in Nigeria. A woman-to-woman marriage provides the female husband with economic power and independence from men. She controls the work done for the family by her wife. Although anthropologists have long denied that any sexual activity takes place in these socially sanctioned marriages, they have also typically failed to ask the women involved about the relationships. Initiation ceremonies are another important arena for same-sex activity in West Africa. Historically, these ceremonies, which focused on teaching pubescent boys and girls how to grow up to become adults, involved explicit sexual lessons.

CONTEMPORARY LEGAL STATUS: WEST AFRICA

In many West African countries, the status of sexual minorities and the legality of same-sex relations is not known. This is the case in Côte d'Ivoire, GAMBIA, GUINEA-BISSAU, and NIGER. Several countries, including GUINEA, LIBERIA, Benin, and MALI, outlaw same-sex relations. In TOGO the punishment can include fines and up to three years of imprisonment. In other countries it is clear that colonial laws and contemporary religious beliefs influence the legal status of sexual minorities. For example, Nigeria criminalizes same-sex relations between men, mandating imprisonment terms of three to fourteen years for these "crimes against the order of nature." (In some areas of the country, the penalty is death or caning.) The same terminology is found in Kenyan and Ugandan legal statutes—a direct result of the British colonial law found in Britain's East and West African colonies. In CAPE VERDE, the laws punishing homosexuality as an "act against nature" are based in the Portuguese Penal Code of 1866. In Ghana, there were reports in the early 1990s of the imprisonment and torture of several gay men and the exile of others. Although same-sex relations among women are rarely mentioned in West African legal statutes, violent attacks against lesbian feminists have been documented in Nigeria. In 1994 four lesbians were raped at a women's center in Calabar (in southeastern Nigeria), where they had sought refuge. Contemporary Islamic movements have also led to stricter laws against homosexuality. In 1983 MAURITANIA—where Islam is the state religion—enacted a penal code that identified homosexuality as a hadd offense, or an act interpreted as being against the divine will of God. Same-sex relations thus became punishable by death. In at least three West African countries—Côte d'Ivoire, Ghana, and Nigeria—associations were established to advocate for rights for sexual minorities. In Ghana, the Afro Lesbian and Gay Club was organized to fight laws used to persecute gay men and lesbians. In Nigeria, the Gentleman's Alliance held the first national conference for gay rights in 1991. The motion picture Woubi Chéri (1998) documents the establishment of the Association of Ivory Coast Transvestites (AICT) in the late 1990s. This group was formed to provide a social and political venue for transvestites, their boyfriends, and other gay men and lesbians.

HISTORICAL EVIDENCE IN EAST AFRICA

In precolonial and early-twentieth-century East Africa, there are several different instances in which male priests in traditional religions are known to have dressed as women, and sometimes to have married other men. Among the Meru and Kikuyu of Kenya, the local term for these priests was mugawe. Among the HUTU AND TUTSI peoples of BURUNDI and RWANDA, the terms were iki-hindu and ikimaze. Religious roles for cross-dressing men were also found in the kingdom of Bunyoro in Uganda. The kingdoms of eighteenth- and nineteenth-century East Africa were also a site of institutionalized same-sex relations. The Bunyoro kingdom included homosexual priests. Among the Maale people of ETHIOPIA, men who cross-dressed, performed women's work, and had sex with other men were known as ashtime. Reports indicate that the ashtime were protected by the king. In Buganda, young men served in the royal court and provided sexual pleasure for male visitors and elites. In 1866 King Mwanga ordered all of the pages in his court killed because they had converted to Christianity and subsequently refused to have sex with him and other men. These young men became known as the Namugongo martyrs, and a church was dedicated to them and consecrated by Pope Paul VI in 1969. Same-sex relations also occurred during initiation rituals for boys and girls in East Africa. Maasai boys in Kenya and Tanzania could cross-dress during their initiation. This was also the case with NANDI boys in Kenya. KAGURU girls in Tanzania were reported to engage in same-sex relations during their initiation rituals. Contemporary East African cultures also include homosexual practices. Among some AMHARA people of Ethiopia, there are two distinct categories: wándar-wárád, which translates literally as "male-female," and wándawánde, which translates as "mannish woman." The Teso peoples of Uganda are also reported to have a category for men who dress as women. Among SWAHILI PEOPLES in Kenya and Tanzania, weddings are a time of raucous sexual joking and demonstrations. Women, in particular, show girls how to provide pleasure during sexual relations. The Swahili also have a term, Wasagaji, for women who have sex with other women. A Wasagaji is typically a married or divorced woman who has an intimate emotional and erotic relationship with another woman. In precolonial and early-twentieth-century East Africa, marriage between women has been noted among fourteen different ethnic groups, including the DINKA, Kikuyu, KIPSIGI, Kisii, Kuria, LUO, Nandi, and NUER. These types of marriages are most commonly described as an economic arrangement. Wealthy women exchanged goods for a "wife," her work for the household, and any children she might bear, regardless of the impregnator's identity.

CONTEMPORARY LEGAL STATUS: EAST AFRICA

In several of the former British colonies of East Africa (including Kenya, Tanzania, and Uganda) sexual relations between men are explicitly illegal. British colonial law in East Africa, like that in West Africa, described homosexuality as a "crime against the order of nature." Today, the maximum punishment in Uganda is life imprisonment. In Kenya and Tanzania, the penalty is up to fourteen years in prison. In SOMALIA, law mandates up to three years of imprisonment, but punishment can also include police surveillance to ensure that the "crime" is not committed again. Ethiopia is the only country in East Africa that explicitly prohibits same-sex relations between both men and women. The penalty can range from three to ten years of imprisonment. In other countries, including MADAGASCAR and Rwanda, there is no specific mention of homosexuality in the legal

codes. In COMOROS and ERITREA homosexuality is legal. However, in 1995 two gay men from Eritrea were granted asylum in the United States, based on persecution in their home country. This fact seems to indicate that even where homosexuality is legal the violation of human rights of sexual minorities can and does occur.

HISTORICAL EVIDENCE IN CENTRAL AFRICA

As early as the sixteenth century, there were reports of cross-dressing priests in the kingdom of Congo (in what is now the DEMOCRATIC REPUBLIC OF THE CONGO, or DRC, and ANGOLA). In 1732 French missionary Jean Baptiste Labat described the role of the Ganga-Ya-Chibanda, a male priest who wore women's clothing, was in charge of sacrifices, and was known as "grandmother." In late nineteenth- and early-twentieth-century CAMEROON, German ethnographer Günther Tessman described homosexuality as a "national custom" among the Bafia people. Same-sex relations were attributed, in part, to strict rules that prohibited young men and women from having social or sexual contact before marriage. Same-sex relations were also described as a logical extension of intimate friendships among adults. The debate over whether same-sex relations were indigenous to the AZANDE peoples (in what is now southwestern SUDAN, CENTRAL AFRICAN REPUBLIC, and the DRC) dates back to the 1920s. The debate itself highlights the difficulties that Westerners had in trying to understand local African traditions. Within the hierarchical Azande state, royal families ruled various groupings of chiefdoms. Evidence indicates that same-sex relations were institutionalized by the state. Royal men married young men by giving a boy's parents a spear in exchange for the boy. Warriors also married boys by giving bridewealth to their parents, thereafter calling the parents "mother-in-law" and "father-in-law." When the boys grew up and themselves became warriors, they were given gifts by their husbands and in turn married other boys. These rituals were remembered but no longer practiced in the 1930s. Same-sex relations were also reported in the 1930s among Nkundó women in what is now the DRC. This type of relation, known as yaikyá bonsango, was reported to take place among co-wives of a polygynous household (household in which a man has more than one wife).

CONTEMPORARY LEGAL STATUS: CENTRAL AFRICA

The legal status of sexual minorities in Central Africa is largely unknown. Same-sex behaviors are explicitly criminalized in only one country, Cameroon. There the punishment ranges from six months to five years in prison, along with fines. Several countries have recently legalized homosexuality. This is the case in the Central African Republic, CHAD, and

GABON. In the REPUBLIC OF THE CONGO, where same-sex relations are not explicitly criminalized, the government does not acknowledge the existence of homosexuality. Although the statutes of the DRC that cover crimes against family life—including assault, rape, and assaults on minors—do not explicitly criminalize same-sex behaviors, they could be used to target or simply penalize homosexuals.

HISTORICAL EVIDENCE IN SOUTHERN AFRICA

Scholars have long documented homosexual relations in southern Africa, particularly between men in military detachments. In Zulu king SHAKA's famous warrior impis (armies) of the mid-nineteenth century, for example, young men were encouraged to engage in homosexual sex. This was not only a means of controlling their sexual urges in an environment devoid of women: It also created intimacy and loyalty among the warriors. Anthropologists have also examined the Mummy-Baby relationships in LESOTHO, where older women, whose husbands are migrant workers in the mines of South Africa, take younger women as their spouses. Modjadji, the Rain Queen of the Lovedu in the Northern Province of South Africa, is a female hereditary leader who keeps as many as forty wives. In southern Africa, same-sex oriented women are often considered traditional healers (sangomas or inyangas). Not only is their difference seen as something that gives them a special connection to the supernatural; their healer status also means they need not get married. This allows them to live independent lives as unattached women. Perhaps less surprising, there is also ample history of homosexual activity in the region's urban areas. In the Coloured community of Western Cape Province, there is a tradition of moffies (transvestites) that goes back to the early nineteenth century. In addition, marriages between men have been common among migrant laborers in South African cities since the late nineteenth century. In South African townships today, homosexual men are either injonga (butch, or masculine) or skesana (femme, or feminine), and these roles are considered fixed and unchangeable. Often, too, homosexuals are seen as freaks or supernatural beings with both male and female organs. In South Africa homosexuals are often known, pejoratively, as stabane.

CONTEMPORARY LEGAL STATUS: SOUTHERN AFRICA

Homosexuals face legal restrictions throughout southern Africa, except in South Africa, which outlawed discrimination on the basis of sexual orientation in its 1994 interim constitution (later adopted in the 1996 final constitution). The constitution was subsequently used to fight inequality in labor legislation, in medical aid and pension plans, in immigration law, in adoption policies, and even in the recognition of same-sex partnerships. At his inaugural address in CAPE TOWN in 1994, South African president Nelson MANDELA himself stated that discrimination on the basis of sexual orientation would not be tolerated. As a result of this policy, South Africa is gaining a reputation as a gay mecca in Africa, and there are burgeoning communities of gays and lesbians in JOHANNESBURG and Cape Town. In the early 2000s, homosexual couples have increasingly gained equal rights. In September 2002, for example, South Africa's Constitutional Court ruled that same-sex couples may jointly adopt children. Spurred on by the South African experience, gay people in southern African countries such as BOTSWANA, NAMIBIA, SWAZILAND, and Zimbabwe have begun lobbying for gay rights. But in stark contrast to the situation in South Africa, these countries have responded with clampdowns and repression, and in every case churches have been a bulwark against gay activism. Homosexuality has remained illegal in all southern African countries except South Africa. For example, the president of the Swaziland League of Churches, Isaac Dhlamini, declared in 1997 that "[homosexuals] hate God. According to the Bible, these are the people who were thrown into the dustbin. The Bible says they should be killed." In Namibia in 1996, the country's president, Sam NUJOMA, told a women's conference that homosexuals had no place in the country, spurring the formation of a gay group, the Rainbow Project, the following year. An official statement from the ruling SOUTH WEST AFRICA PEOPLE'S ORGANIZATION (SWAPO) called on Namibians to "totally uproot homosexuality as a practise" and to "revitalize our inherent culture and its moral values which we have inherited for many centuries from our forefathers. We should not risk our people being identified with foreign immoral values."

OUTLOOK

Homosexuality is controversial in Africa today, as it is in the West. The controversy in Africa is largely due to the legacy of colonial attitudes toward same-sex relations and to certain Christian and Muslim religious doctrines. The political and economic instability of some governments also makes sexual minorities an easy target for politicians to use to distract people from lingering problems. Although Daniel Arap MOI, former president of Kenya, and President Robert MUGABE of Zimbabwe both denounced homosexuality as a Western perversion, many scholars assert that it is homophobia and the political persecution of homosexuals that have been imported from abroad and enthusiastically endorsed by African politicians. Throughout Africa, there is a remarkable range of opinions and attitudes toward homosexuality. Although Christian religious leaders are often the most vocal in condemning homosexuality, Bishop Desmond

GAY PRIDE IN SOUTH AFRICA. A group of lesbians celebrates Gay Pride Day in Soweto, South Africa. In contrast to other African states, South Africa has outlawed discrimination based on sexual orientation and has become the continent's gay mecca. (*Denis Farrell/AP Images*)

TUTU of South Africa has openly supported the rights of sexual minorities. Similarly, in many communities that have long-standing traditions of a particular role or identity that includes same-sex relations, individuals can live rich and productive lives, although there may be some stigma attached to them. The rise of social and political organizations for sexual minorities throughout Africa reflects an international movement to recognize the human rights of sexual minorities. The trend also indicates the widespread accessibility of Western mainstream and gay culture, from music videos to American soap operas. The increasing availability of films, television programs, and the Internet has greatly facilitated this trend, and it is reflected in the adoption of international gay symbols by some of the groups, including the Rainbow Coalition in Namibia. In the future, lesbian, gay, bisexual, transgendered, and traditional sexual minorities in Africa may increasingly find themselves in the forefront of political struggles over human rights and democracy. This relatively recent development highlights the fact that the African continent continues to be a complex and vibrant meeting ground for different peoples, traditions, and beliefs about the world.

See also ACQUIRED IMMUNODEFICIENCY SYNDROME IN AFRICA: AN INTERPRETATION; BUGANDA, EARLY KINGDOM OF; CHRISTIANITY, AFRICAN: AN OVERVIEW; DAHOMEY, EARLY KINGDOM OF; ISLAM IN AFRICA; MAMLUK STATE.

DEBORAH AMORY

MARK GEVISSER

Hondo, Abid Mohamed Medoun (Med)
1936–
Expatriate Mauritanian film director whose films focus on the experiences of Africans abroad.

The son of farmers, Med Hondo was raised in the Atar region of MAURITANIA on the edge of the SAHARA. At 18 he left home to attend cooking school in MOROCCO, after which he went to work as a chef in France. It was in France that he became interested in the performing arts.

Hondo began his artistic career by acting for French theater companies. Frustrated by the roles they offered him, he soon formed a theater ensemble with the aim of producing plays that expressed feelings common among Africans in Europe: exile and estrangement. To earn extra income, he also took parts in movies and television. Through this work he became fascinated with film and taught himself to use a movie camera. In early 1969 Hondo directed his first short film. By the end of the year he completed his first full-length feature, *Soleil O.* It was well received on the international film festival circuit, including the Cannes Film Festival in France, the Locarno

Film Festival in Switzerland, and the Festival Panafricain du Cinéma et de la Télévision de Ouagadougou (FESPACO) in BURKINA FASO.

Since 1969 Hondo has released five feature films, including *Les Bicots-nègres, vos voisins* (1973), the musical *West Indies*, and *Sarraounia* (1986). Hondo's movies explore conditions of exile and alienation, often examining the case of African expatriates working in France, as in *Soleil O* and *Les Bicots-nègres, vos voisins*, or the problems of colonization, as in *West Indies*. Through his films, Hondo hopes to raise the consciousness of his audiences, particularly French audiences. He has said: "I decided to make films to bring some Black faces to the lily-white French screens. . . . For three centuries, a whole people has been led to believe that it was superior and such an ideology has not been eradicated in spite of the independence of African countries. People should be educated about the richness of the African heritage and the discrimination faced by immigrants in France. I hope my films explain Africa and the crucial and burning issues faced by Black people in Africa and abroad." Although Hondo's films have been critically acclaimed at film festivals, their general distribution has been severely limited by censorship in Africa and, in some cases, France.

Hondo is a prominent member of the FÉDÉRATION PANAFRICAINE DES CINÉASTES (FEPACI), Comité Africain des Cinéastes (CAC), and the West African Film Corporation, in which he has done much to promote African cinema, particularly the production and international distribution of African films. Hondo brings a rare point of view to these organizations as one of the few African directors who works solely outside of Africa.

In addition to his recent work on short films and documentaries, Hondo directed the feature film *Watani, un monde sans mal* (1998), in which a black street sweeper and a white banker lose their respective jobs on the same day in Paris. The film attracted controversy when Hondo criticized its restricted rating, which the French ratings board blamed on its violence. The director, however, insisted that this violence was integral to the film's depiction of immigrant life in contemporary France.

In 2000 Harvard University awarded Hondo the Genevieve McMillan and Reba Stewart Fellowship for Distinguished Filmmaking. Among Hondo's projects is his appearance in the film *Antilles-sur-Seine* (2001), in which he stars as the mayor of a seaside town who resists the ruthless business interests that want to promote tourism. His more recent projects include *La Guerre de*

2,000 ans (2001), a play by Kateb Yacine, and the film *Fatima, l'Algérienne dé Dakar* (2004).

See also CINEMA, AFRICAN.

BIBLIOGRAPHY
Ranvaud, Don. "Interview with Med Hondo." *Framework*, Spring 1978.

ELIZABETH HEATH

Honwana, Luís Bernardo
1942–
Mozambican writer who was the first African writing in Portuguese to have a book-length literary work published in English.

Luís Honwana was born in Lourenço Marques (now MAPUTO, MOZAMBIQUE), although his family was living in Moamba, about 55 kilometers (34 miles) northwest of Lourenço Marques. His given name was Luís Augusto Bernardo Manuel, but he later adopted the ancestral surname of Honwana. Luís was one of several children born to Raúl Bernardo Manuel (Honwana) and Naly Jeremias Nhaca. Although they were members of the RONGA ethnic group, Honwana's parents were assimilated Africans with special status under the Portuguese colonial regime.

Honwana spent the first seventeen years of his life in Moamba, where his father worked as an interpreter. In 1959 he went to live with relatives in Lourenço Marques, where he attended high school and began a career in journalism. He threw himself into the intellectual and cultural life of the city and while still in his teens published his first short story, appropriately titled "Despertar" (Awakening), in a Lourenço Marques newspaper. A number of established writers living in Lourenço Marques—including the well-known poet José Craveirinha—were so impressed with Honwana's story that they encouraged him to continue writing.

With the support of Craveirinha and influential members of Lourenço Marques's liberal European intelligentsia, the young Honwana was inspired to publish stories in the literary sections of local newspapers. In 1964 seven of Honwana's stories were brought together in a volume titled *Nós Matamos o Cão Tinhoso*. This slim volume, later published in English as *We Killed Mangy-Dog & Other Mozambique Stories* (1969), became an instant and enduring success. The title story, set in Moamba, captures the social, cultural, and emotional juxtapositions between the colonizer and the colonized through the eyes of adolescent black, white, mixed-race, and East Indian children.

The same year that his book was published in Lourenço Marques, Portuguese authorities imprisoned Howana after accusing him of supporting the pro-independence FRONT FOR THE LIBERATION OF MOZAMBIQUE (FRELIMO). Upon his release from prison in 1967, Honwana, although under constant police surveillance, was able to resume his career as a journalist. In 1970 he was awarded a scholarship to study law at the University of Lisbon, in Portugal. Portuguese authorities constantly monitored every aspect of Honwana's life, and in 1972 he dropped out of the law program and fled to Paris with his wife Suzette. Eventually, they found their way to Tanzania to join up with FRELIMO, which maintained its headquarters-in-exile in the Tanzanian capital of DAR ES SALAAM.

When independence came in 1975, Honwana returned to Mozambique, where he was named chief of staff in President Samora Machel's office. Subsequently, Honwana became the minister of culture for the FRELIMO government. In the 1990s Honwana moved to SOUTH AFRICA, where he serves as regional director of the UNITED NATIONS Educational, Scientific, Cultural Organization (UNESCO) in Pretoria. Although Honwana has published only one book, it has already solidly established his reputation among leading African writers from former Portuguese colonies.

See also LITERATURE, PORTUGUESE-LANGUAGE, IN AFRICA; UNITED NATIONS IN AFRICA.

Hottentot

Pejorative term used by Europeans in South Africa to describe pastoralists who speak Khoi, a clicking language.
The first Europeans to encounter the cattle-herding people who later became known as Hottentots were the Portuguese explorers Bartolomeu Dias and Vasco Da Gama, who stopped at the Cape of Good Hope in the fifteenth century. They and later European explorers and traders bartered tobacco and other goods for the pastoralists' livestock. It was at some point during these early stops that European travelers adopted the term Hottentot to describe the pastoralists, who referred to themselves as KHOIKHOI or Kwena. Hottentot is derived from an old Dutch expression hotteren-totteren, which means to stammer or stutter; presumably the name was given in reference to the Khoikhoi's language, Khoi, which is made up of implosive consonants frequently called clicks.

Europeans came to associate the term Hottentot with savagery and barbarism during the seventeenth and eighteenth centuries, when Dutch settlers on the Cape often clashed with the Khoikhoi over land and cattle. Frequently, the Dutch pressured the Khoikhoi to sell more cattle than they wanted to, and both sides accused the other of stealing livestock. In 1659 and 1673 these conflicts erupted into wars that eventually forced the Khoikhoi to accept Dutch sovereignty.

The term Hottentot also came to be associated with particular physical types and cultural practices, which Europeans considered exotic and uncivilized. In particular, Europeans were repulsed by the Khoikhoi custom of mixing red pigment with rendered seal fat and applying the mixture to their skin. Europeans were also shocked by what they viewed as the oversized buttocks and genitalia of Khoikhoi women. These characteristics supported Europeans' belief that the Hottentot were "oversexed" and degraded.

In the nineteenth century, European images of the Hottentot were further reinforced by traveling exhibitions. The most famous of these was an 1810 pay-per-view exhibit in London of the Hottentot Venus—a caged South African SAN woman named Saartjie Baartman. After her death in 1815, Baartman's body was examined by Swiss anatomist Georges Cuvier, who later published a report of the autopsy. This report also became the basis for the Hottentot entry in his 1827 book, The Animal Kingdom, which claimed to give scientific evidence of the Hottentots' filthy and disgusting nature.

Today the term Hottentot is occasionally used by white South Africans to identify Africans who trace their ancestry to the original Khoikhoi inhabitants. In general, however, the term has fallen into disuse and the term Khoikhoi is more acceptable. Today, some 55,000 people consider themselves Khoikhoi.

See also PASTORALISM SOUTH AFRICA.

ELIZABETH HEATH

Houphouët-Boigny, Félix
1905?–1993
Physician, politician, and president of Côte d'Ivoire from 1960 to 1993.
Félix Houphouët-Boigny was the first president of the CÔTE D'IVOIRE. Many people credit his political acumen and skillful leadership for the achievement of stability and economic prosperity in the country. Born in Yamoussoukro, the son of a BAULE chief, Houphouët-Boigny attended the prestigious École Normale William Ponty and the École de Médicine et de Pharmacie, both in DAKAR, SENEGAL. After graduating in 1925, he practiced medicine and, at the same time, ran a coffee plantation. In 1940 he was appointed the canton chief of his family's home district; he subsequently turned his attention to politics, especially as they affected the Baule coffee farmers. Confronted by the racist policies of the colonial government, Houphouët-Boigny organized fellow planters into the Syndicat Agricole Africain (SAA) to protest the colonial administration's race-based crop prices and use of forced labor, which only benefited European farmers. Although the SAA itself made little progress, it did provide Houphouët-Boigny with the backing necessary to take these concerns before the French Constituent Assembly, where he represented the newly formed Parti Démocratique de la Côte d'Ivoire (PDCI). In 1946 the

assembly voted in favor of Houphouët-Boigny's bill to outlaw the forced labor system in all of France's colonies—a victory that guaranteed him popular support throughout FRENCH WEST AFRICA for years to come. That same year Houphouët-Boigny joined with African assembly members from neighboring colonies to form the RASSEMBLEMENT DÉMOCRATIQUE AFRICAIN (RDA). Although the party had the initial backing of the French Communist Party, Houphouët-Boigny was afraid to alienate French President Charles de Gaulle and conservative planter interests at home, so he cut ties with the Communist Party in 1950. His support for de Gaulle's vision of a federal community in French West Africa won him a series of influential administrative posts, ranging from mayor of Abidjan to cabinet minister in France. But ever the shrewd politician, Houphouët-Boigny stopped advocating limited self-rule as soon as it became apparent that Ivoirians would accept nothing less than complete independence. When independence came in 1960, Houphouët-Boigny was easily elected president. Over the next three decades Houphouët-Boigny ruled the Côte d'Ivoire as his personal kingdom. The country was technically a democracy; the one-party government held regular legislative and presidential elections. But Houphouët-Boigny used a combination of charisma, patronage, and low-key repression—primarily the jailing of dissident party members—to quell any serious opposition. At the same time, he maintained the appearance of accountability by holding public forums and allowing citizens to voice complaints. He would then choose a number of problems on which to lavish money, while blaming government officials for not having addressed the problems earlier. A strong economy was central to Houphouët-Boigny's popularity. During the first two decades of independence, the "Ivoirian Miracle" owed much to the stable world markets for Côte d'Ivoire's two principal export crops, cocoa and coffee. Foreign investment, drawn by Houphouët-Boigny's free market policies, also contributed to economic growth, as did continued aid from the French government. A worldwide recession in the late 1970s and early 1980s, however, weakened both the economy and Houphouët-Boigny's popular support. Although the president was initially able to deflect criticism onto other officials, he was eventually pressured by opposition leaders and international donors to hold multiparty elections. The international donors, especially, were concerned about the health of the elderly president, and the possibility of the government's instability after his death. Houphouët-Boigny held multiparty elections in 1990 and won them, but even after being diagnosed with prostate cancer in June 1993 he refused to name

his successor. He died on December 10, 1993—the thirty-third anniversary of the Côte d'Ivoire's independence—and was buried in his hometown of Yamoussoukro.

See also COLONIAL RULE; POLITICAL MOVEMENTS IN AFRICA.

BIBLIOGRAPHY

Amondji, Marcel. *Félix Houphouët et la Côte d'Ivoire: L'envers d'une légende.* Karthala, 1984.

ELIZABETH HEATH

How Africa Became Black: An Interpretation
This article discusses the massive population movements in Africa during the past 2,000 years as well as the racial diversity found on the continent.

Despite all I had read about Africa, my first impressions upon being there were overwhelming. As I walked the streets of WINDHOEK, the capital of newly independent NAMIBIA, I saw black HERERO people and black OVAMBO; I saw NAMA, a group quite unlike the blacks in appearance. I saw whites, descendants of recent European immigrants, and outside Windhoek I saw the last of the formerly widespread Kalahari BUSHMEN struggling for survival. These people were no longer pictures in a textbook; they were living humans, right in front of me. But what most surprised me was a street sign on one of downtown Windhoek's main roads. It read "Goering Street." Surely, I thought, no country could be so dominated by unrepentant Nazis that it would name a street after Hermann Goering, the notorious head of the Luftwaffe. As it turned out, the street actually commemorates Hermann's father, Heinrich, founding Reichskommissar of the German colony of SOUTH-WEST AFRICA, which would later be renamed Namibia. But Heinrich is no less a problematic figure than his son: his legacy includes one of the most vicious attacks ever carried out by European colonists on Africans, Germany's 1904 war of extermination against the Herero. Today, while events in neighboring SOUTH AFRICA command the world's attention, Namibia, too, struggles to deal with its colonial history and establish a multiracial society. Namibia illustrated for me how inseparable Africa's past is from its present. Most Americans think of indigenous Africans as black and of white Africans as recent intruders; and when they think of Africa's racial history they think of European colonialism and slave trading. But very different types of peoples occupied much of Africa until as recently as a few thousand years ago. Even before the arrival of white colonialists, the continent harbored five of what many consider to be the world's six major divisions of humanity, the so-called human races, three of which are native to Africa. To this day nearly 30 percent of the world's languages are spoken only in Africa. No other continent even approaches this human diversity, and no other continent can rival Africa in the complexity of its human past. The diversity of Africa's peoples results from its diverse geography and long prehistory. Africa is the only continent to extend from the northern to the southern temperate zone; it encompasses some of the world's driest deserts, largest tropical rain forests, and highest equatorial mountains. Humans have lived in Africa far longer than anywhere else: our remote ancestors originated there some seven million years ago. With so much time, Africa's peoples have woven a complex, fascinating story of human interaction, a story that includes two of the most dramatic population movements of the past 5,000 years: the Bantu expansion and the Indonesian colonization of MADAGASCAR. All those interactions are now tangled up in politics because the details of who arrived where before whom are shaping Africa today. How did the five divisions of humanity in Africa get to be where they are today? Why did blacks come to be so widespread, instead of one or more of the four other groups whose existence Americans tend to forget? How can we ever hope to wrest the answers to these questions from Africa's past without written evidence of the sort that taught us about the spread of the Roman Empire? African prehistory is a detective story on a grand scale, still only partly solved. Clues can be derived from the present: from the peoples living today in Africa, the languages they speak, and their plant crops and domestic animals. Clues can also be dug up from the past, from the bones and artifacts of long-dead peoples. By examining these clues one at a time and then combining all of them, we can begin to reconstruct who moved where at what time in Africa, and what let them move—with enormous consequences for the modern continent. The Africa encountered by the first European explorers in the fifteenth century was already home to five human races: blacks, whites, Pygmies, KHOISAN, and Asians. The only race not found in Africa is the aboriginal Australians and their relatives. Now, I know that classifying people into arbitrary races is stereotyping. Each of these groups is actually very diverse, and lumping people as different as the Zulu, MAASAI, and IGBO under the single heading blacks ignores the differences between them. So does lumping Africa's Egyptians and Berbers with each other and with Europe's Swedes under the single heading whites. The divisions between blacks, whites, and the other major groups are arbitrary anyway because each group shades into the others. All the human groups on Earth have mated with humans of every other group they have encountered. Nevertheless, recognizing these major groups and calling them by these inexact names is a shorthand that makes it easier to

understand history. By analogy, it is also useful to divide classical music into periods like baroque, classical, and "romantic," even though each period is diverse and shades into other periods. By the time European colonialists arrived, most of Africa's major population movements had already taken place. Blacks occupied the largest area, from the southern Sahara to most of sub-Saharan Africa. The ancestors of most African Americans came from Africa's western coastal zone, but similar peoples occupied East Africa as well, north to the SUDAN and south to the southeast coast of South Africa. They were mostly farmers or herders, as were the native African whites, who occupied Africa's northern coastal zone and the northern SAHARA. (Few of those northern Africans—the Egyptians, Libyans, and Moroccans, for instance—would be confused with a blond, blue-eyed Swede, but they are often considered white because they have lighter skin and straighter hair than the peoples to the south.) At the same time, the Pygmies were already living in groups widely scattered through the Central African rain forest. Although they were traditionally hunter-gatherers, they also traded with or worked for neighboring black farmers. Like their neighbors, the Pygmies are dark-skinned and have tightly curled hair, but that hair is more thickly distributed over their body and face. They also are much smaller and have more prominent foreheads, eyes, and teeth. The Khoisan are perhaps the group least familiar to Americans today. In the 1400s they were actually two groups, found over much of southern Africa: large-statured Khoi herders, pejoratively known as Hottentots, and smaller San hunter-gatherers, pejoratively called Bushmen. Most of the Khoi populations no longer exist; European colonists shot, displaced, or infected many of them, and the survivors interbred with Europeans. Though the SAN hunter-gatherers were similarly shot, displaced, and infected, a dwindling number managed to preserve their distinctness in Namibian desert areas unsuitable for agriculture. (They are the people depicted some years ago in the widely seen 1981 film The Gods Must Be Crazy.) The Khoisan today look quite unlike African blacks: they have light brown skin sometimes described as yellow, and their hair is even more tightly coiled. Of these population distributions, that of North Africa's whites is the least surprising because physically similar peoples live in adjacent areas of the Middle East and Europe. Throughout recorded history people have been moving back and forth between Europe, the Middle East, and North Africa. But the puzzling placements of blacks, Pygmies, and Khoisan hint at past population upheavals. Today there are just 200,000 Pygmies scattered amid 120 million blacks. This fragmentation suggests that Pygmy hunters lived throughout the equatorial forests until they were displaced and isolated into small groups by the arrival of black farmers. Similarly, the Khoisan area of southern Africa is surprisingly small for a people so distinct in anatomy and language. Could the Khoisan as well have been originally more widespread until their more northerly populations were somehow eliminated? Perhaps the greatest puzzle, however, involves the island of Madagascar, which lies just 450 kilometers (250 miles) off the coast of southeastern Africa, much closer to Africa than to any other continent. In Madagascar the fifth African race is found. Madagascar's people prove to be a mixture of two elements: African blacks and—surprisingly, given the separation seemingly dictated by the whole expanse of the Indian Ocean—Southeast Asians, specifically Indonesians. As it happens, the language of the MALAGASY people is very close to the Malanyan language spoken on the Indonesian island of Borneo, over 6,000 kilometers (4,000 miles) away. No one even remotely resembling the Borneans lives within thousands of miles of Madagascar. These Indonesians, their language, and their modified culture were already established on Madagascar by the time it was first visited by Europeans in 1500. To me this is the single most astonishing fact of human geography in the whole world. It is as if Columbus, on reaching Cuba, had found it occupied by blue-eyed, towheaded Scandinavians speaking a language close to Swedish, even though the nearby North American continent was inhabited by Indians speaking Indian languages. How on earth could prehistoric people of Borneo, presumably voyaging in boats without maps or compasses, have ended up in Madagascar? The case of Madagascar shows how peoples' languages, as well as their physical appearance, can yield important clues to their origins. Similarly, there is much to be learned from African languages that cannot be gleaned from African faces. In 1963 the mind-boggling complexities of Africa's 1,500 languages were simplified by the great linguist Joseph Greenberg of Stanford. Greenberg recognized that all those languages can be divided into just four broad families. And, because languages of a given language family tend to be spoken by distinct peoples, in Africa there are some rough correspondences between the language families and the anatomically defined human groups. For instance, Nilo-Saharan and Niger-Congo speakers are black, and Khoisan speakers are Khoisan. Afro-Asiatic languages, however, are spoken by a variety of both whites and blacks. The language of Madagascar belongs to yet another, non-African category, the Austronesian language family. What about the Pygmies? The Pygmies are the only one of Africa's five races that lacks a distinct language: each band of Pygmies speaks the language of its neighboring black farmers. If you compare a given language as spoken by Pygmies with the same language as spoken by blacks, however, the Pygmy version contains unique words and, sometimes,

distinctive sounds. That makes sense, of course: originally the Pygmies, living in a place as distinctive as the equatorial African rain forest, must have been sufficiently isolated to develop their own language family. Today, however, those languages' disappearance and the Pygmies' highly fragmented distribution both suggest that the Pygmy homeland was engulfed by invading black farmers. The remaining small bands of Pygmies adopted the invaders' languages, with only traces of their original languages surviving in a few words and sounds. The distribution of Khoisan languages testifies to an even more dramatic engulfing. Those languages are famously unique—they use clicks as consonants. All the existing Khoisan languages are confined to southern Africa, with two exceptions: the click-laden HADZA and Sandawe languages spoken in TANZANIA, some 2,400 kilometers (1,500 miles) from their nearest linguistic kin. In addition, clicks have made it into a few of the Niger-Congo languages of southern Africa, such as Zulu and XHOSA (which is the language of Nelson Mandela). Clicks or Khoisan words also appear in two Afro-Asiatic languages spoken by blacks in Kenya, stranded even farther from the Khoisan peoples of today than are the Hadza and Sandawe speakers of Tanzania. All this suggests that Khoisan languages and peoples formerly extended far north into Africa until the Khoisan, like the Pygmies, were engulfed by the blacks, leaving behind only a linguistic legacy to testify to their former presence. Perhaps the most important discovery from linguistic sleuthing, however, involves the Niger-Congo language family, which today is spread all over West Africa and most of subequatorial Africa. Its current enormous range seems to give no clue as to precisely where the family originated. However, Greenberg has pointed out that the Bantu languages of subequatorial Africa, once thought to be their own language family, are actually a subfamily of the Niger-Congo language family. (Technically they are a sub-sub-sub-sub-sub-sub-sub-sub-subfamily.) These Bantu languages today account for nearly half of the 1,032 Niger-Congo languages, and Bantu speakers account for more than half (nearly 200 million) of the Niger-Congo speakers. Yet all 494 Bantu languages are so similar to one another that they have been facetiously described as 494 dialects of a single language. There are some 170 other such Niger-Congo subfamilies, most of which are crammed into West Africa, a small fraction of the entire Niger-Congo range. Even the most distinctive Bantu languages, as well as the Niger-Congo languages most closely related to Bantu, are concentrated there, in a tiny area of CAMEROON and adjacent east and central NIGERIA. From Greenberg's evidence it seems obvious that the Niger-Congo language family arose in West Africa, while the Bantu subfamily arose at the east end of that range, in

Cameroon and Nigeria, and then spread out over most of subequatorial Africa. That spread must have begun sufficiently long ago that the ancestral Bantu language had time to split into 494 daughter languages, but nevertheless recently enough that all those daughter languages are still very similar to one another. Since all Niger-Congo speakers—including the Bantu speakers—are black, it would be nearly impossible to infer who migrated in which direction just from the evidence of physical anthropology. To make this type of linguistic reasoning clear, let me give you an example: geographic origins of the English language. Today the largest number of people whose first language is English live in North America, with others scattered over the globe in Great Britain, Australia, New Zealand, and other countries. If we knew nothing else about language distribution and history, we might have guessed that the English language arose in North America and was carried overseas by colonists. But we know better: we know that each of those countries has its own English dialect and that all those English dialects make up just one subgroup of the Germanic language family. The other subgroups—the various Scandinavian, German, and Dutch languages—are crammed into northwestern Europe. Frisian, the Germanic language most closely related to English, is stuck in a tiny coastal area of Holland and western Germany. Hence a linguist would immediately deduce—correctly—that the English language arose on the northwestern coast of Europe and spread around the world from there. Essentially the same reasoning tells us that the nearly 200 million Bantu-speaking people now flung over much of the map of Africa arose in Cameroon and Nigeria. Thus linguistics tells us not only that the Pygmies and the Khoisan, who formerly ranged widely over the continent, were engulfed by blacks; it also tells us that the blacks who did the engulfing were Bantu speakers. But what it cannot tell us is what allowed the Bantu speakers to displace the Pygmies and Khoisan. To answer that question we need to look at a different type of surviving evidence, that of domesticated plants and animals. This evidence is so crucial because farming and herding yield far more calories per acre than do hunting wild animals or gathering wild plants. As a result, population densities of farmers and herders are typically at least ten times those of hunter-gatherers. That is not to say that farmers are happier, healthier, or in any way superior to hunter-gatherers. They are, however, more numerous. And that alone is enough to allow them to kill or displace the hunter-gatherers. In addition, human diseases such as smallpox and measles developed from diseases plaguing domestic animals. The farmers eventually become resistant to those diseases, but hunter-gatherers do not have the opportunity. So when hunter-gatherers first come into contact with

farmers, they tend to die in droves from the farmers' diseases. Finally, only in a farming society—with its stored food surpluses and concentrated villages—do people have the chance to specialize, to become full-time metalworkers, soldiers, kings, and bureaucrats. Hence the farmers, and not the hunter-gatherers, are the ones who develop swords and guns, standing armies, and political organization. Add that to their sheer numbers and their germs, and it is easy to see how the farmers in Africa were able to push the hunter-gatherers aside. But where in Africa did domesticated plants and animals first appear? What peoples, by accident of their geographic location, inherited those plants and animals and thereby the means to engulf their geographically less-endowed neighbors? When Europeans reached sub-Saharan Africa in the 1400s, Africans were growing five sets of crops. The first set was grown only in North Africa, extending as far as the highlands of ETHIOPIA. North Africa's rain falls mostly in the winter months—the region enjoys a Mediterranean climate—so all its original crops are adapted to germinating and growing with winter rains. Archaeological evidence tells us that such crops—wheat, barley, peas, beans, and grapes, to name a few—were first domesticated in the Middle East around 10,000 years ago. So it makes sense that they would have spread into climatically similar and adjacent areas of North Africa, laying the foundation for the rise of ancient Egyptian civilization. Indeed, these crops are familiar to us precisely because they also spread into climatically similar and adjacent areas of Europe—and from there to America and Australia—and became some of the staple crops of temperate-zone agriculture around the world. There is little rain and little agriculture in the Sahara, but just south of the desert, in the SAHEL zone, the rain returns. The Sahel rains, however, fail in the summer. So even if winter-rain-adapted Middle Eastern crops could somehow have crossed the Sahara, it would still have been hard to grow them in the summer-rain Sahel zone. Instead, here the Europeans found the second and third sets of African crops, both of which are adapted to summer rains and the area's less variable day length. Set number two is made up of plants whose ancestors were widely distributed from west to east across the Sahel zone and were probably domesticated there as well. They include sorghum and pearl millet, which became the staple cereals of much of sub-Saharan Africa, as well as cotton, sesame, watermelon, and black-eyed peas. Sorghum proved so valuable that it is now grown in hot, dry areas on all the continents. The wild ancestors of the third set of African crops are found only in Ethiopia and were probably domesticated there. Indeed, most of them are still grown only there: few Americans have ever tasted Ethiopia's finger millet beer, its oily noog, its narcotic chat, or its national bread, which is made from a tiny-seeded cereal called teff. But we all have the ancient Ethiopian farmers to thank for the domestication of a plant we know exceedingly well: the coffee plant, which remained confined to Ethiopia until it caught on in Arabia and then spread around the globe. The fourth set of African crops was domesticated from wild ancestors in the wet climate of West Africa. Some of them, including African rice, have remained virtually confined there; others, such as African yams, eventually spread throughout much of sub-Saharan Africa. Two, the oil palm and the kola nut, spread to other continents. West Africans were chewing the caffeine-containing kola nut as a stimulant long before the Coca-Cola Company enticed Americans to drink its extracts. The plants in the last batch of African crops are also adapted to wet climates. Bananas, Asian yams, and taro were widespread in sub-Saharan Africa when the Europeans arrived, and Asian rice was well established on the coast of East Africa. But these crops did not come from Africa. They came from Southeast Asia, and their presence in Africa would be astonishing if the presence of Indonesians in Madagascar had not already alerted us to Africa's prehistoric Asian connection. All four indigenous groups of crops—from North Africa, the Sahel, Ethiopia, and West Africa—came from north of the equator. No wonder the Niger-Congo speakers, people who also came from north of the equator, were able to displace Africa's equatorial Pygmies and sub-equatorial Khoisan peoples. The Khoisan and the Pygmies were not unsuited for the farming life; it was just that southern Africa's wild plants were unsuitable for domestication. Even the Bantu and the white farmers, heirs to thousands of years of farming experience, have rarely been able to develop southern Africa's native plants into food crops. Because there are so few of them, summarizing Africa's domesticated animal species is much easier than summarizing its plants. The list does not include even one of the big wild mammals for which Africa is famous—its zebras and wildebeests, its rhinos and hippos, its giraffes and Cape buffalo. The wild ancestors of domestic cattle, pigs, dogs, and house cats were native to North Africa but also to western Asia, so we cannot be sure where they were first domesticated. The rest of Africa's domestic mammals must have been domesticated somewhere else because their wild ancestors occur only in Eurasia. Africa's sheep and goats were domesticated in western Asia, its chickens in Southeast Asia, its horses in southern Russia, and its camels probably in Arabia. The one exception is the donkey, which is widely believed to have been domesticated in North Africa. Many of Africa's food staples and domesticated animals thus had to travel a long way from their point of origin, both inside and outside Africa. Some people were just luckier than others,

inheriting suites of domesticable wild plant and animal species. We have to suspect that some of the lucky Africans parlayed their advantage into an engulfing of their neighbors. But all the evidence I have presented thus far—evidence from modern human and language distributions and from modern crops and domestic animals—is only an indirect means to reconstruct the past. To get direct evidence about who was living where when, and what they were eating or growing, we need to turn to archaeology and the things it turns up: the bones of people and their domestic animals, the remains of the pottery and the stone and iron tools they made, and the remains of the buildings they constructed. This evidence can help explain at least some of the mystery of Madagascar. Archaeologists exploring the island report that Indonesians arrived before 800 C.E., possibly as early as 300, and in a full-fledged expedition: the earliest human settlements on Madagascar include the remains of iron tools, livestock, and crops. This was no small canoe load of fishers blown off course. Clues to how this expedition came about can be found in an ancient book of sailors' directions, the Periplus of the Erythraean Sea, which was written by an anonymous merchant living in Egypt around 100 C.E. The merchant describes an already thriving sea trade connecting India and Egypt with the coast of East Africa. When Islam began to spread after the beginning of the ninth century, Indian Ocean trade became well documented archaeologically by copious quantities of Middle Eastern and occasionally even Chinese products such as pottery, glass, and porcelain found in East African coastal settlements. The traders waited for favorable winds to let them cross the Indian Ocean directly between East Africa and India. But the sea trade was equally vigorous from India eastward, to Indonesia. Perhaps the Indonesian colonists of Madagascar reached India by that route, then fell in with the westward trade route to East Africa, where they joined with Africans and discovered Madagascar. The union of Indonesians and East Africans appears to live on today in Madagascar's basically Indonesian language, which contains loan words from coastal Kenyan Bantu languages. But there is a problem: there are no corresponding Indonesian loan words in Kenyan languages. Indeed, there are few Indonesian traces in East Africa besides some musical instruments, such as the xylophone and the zither, and the Indonesian crops discussed earlier. Is it possible that the Indonesians, instead of taking the easier route to Madagascar via India and East Africa, somehow—incredibly—sailed straight across the Indian Ocean, discovered Madagascar, and only later got plugged into East African trade routes? We still do not know the answer. The same sorts of archaeological evidence found in Madagascar can be found on the African continent itself. In some cases they can help prove hypotheses that the other evidence could never fully resolve. For instance, linguistic and population distribution evidence merely suggests that the Khoisan were once widespread in the drier parts of subequatorial Africa. But archaeologists in ZAMBIA, to the north of the modern Khoisan range, have in fact found skulls of people resembling the modern Khoisan, as well as stone tools resembling those the Khoisan peoples were making in southern Africa when the Europeans arrived. There are, of course, cases in which archaeology cannot help. We assume from indirect evidence that Pygmies were once widespread in the wet rain forest of Central Africa, but it is difficult for archaeologists to test this assumption: although they have found artifacts to show that people were there, they have yet to discover ancient human skeletons. Archaeology also helps us determine the actual dates and places for the rise of farming and herding in Africa, which is the key to understanding how one group of people was able to conquer the whole continent. Any reader steeped in the history of Western civilization would be forgiven for assuming that African food production began in ancient Egypt's Nile Valley, land of pharaohs and pyramids. After all, by 3000 B.C.E., Egypt was undoubtedly the site of Africa's most complex society. Yet the earliest evidence for food production in Africa comes not from the Nile Valley but from, believe it or not, the Sahara. Archaeologists are able to say this because they have become expert at identifying and dating plants from remains as fragmentary as charred seeds recognizable only under a microscope. Although today much of the Sahara is so dry that it cannot even support grass, archaeologists have found evidence that between 9000 and 4000 B.C.E. the Sahara was more humid; there were numerous lakes, and the desert teemed with game. The Saharans tended cattle and made pottery, then began to keep sheep and goats; they may even have started to domesticate sorghum and millet. This Saharan PASTORALISM began well before food production got its start in Egypt, in 5200 B.C.E. when a full package of western Asian winter crops and livestock arrived. Farming then spread to West Africa and Ethiopia. By around 2500 B.C.E. cattle herders had already crossed the modern border of Ethiopia into northern Kenya. Linguistics offers another way to date the arrival of crops: by comparing words for crops in related modern languages that diverged from each other at various times in the past. It thus becomes clear, for instance, that the people who were domesticating sorghum and millet in the Sahara thousands of years ago spoke languages ancestral to modern Nilo-Saharan languages. Similarly, the people who first domesticated the wet-country crops of West Africa spoke languages ancestral to the modern Niger-Congo languages. The people who spoke ancestral Afro-Asiatic languages were certainly involved in the introduction of Middle Eastern crops into North Africa and may have been responsible for the domestication of

crops native to Ethiopia. Analyzing the names of crops leaves us with evidence that there were at least three ancestral languages spoken in Africa thousands of years ago: ancestral Nilo-Saharan, Niger-Congo, and Afro-Asiatic. And other linguistic evidence points to an ancestral Khoisan language (that evidence, however, does not come from crop names, since the ancestral Khoisan people didn't domesticate any crops). Surely, since Africa harbors 1,500 languages today, it was big enough to harbor more than four ancestral languages in the past. But all those other languages must have disappeared, either because the peoples speaking them lost their original languages, as the Pygmies did, or because the peoples themselves disappeared. Pulling archaeology and linguistics together, we conclude that these four language families survived because of a historical accident: the ancestral speakers of Nilo-Saharan, Niger-Congo, and Afro-Asiatic languages happened to be living at the right place and time to acquire domestic plants and animals, which allowed them to multiply and either replace other peoples or impose their language upon them. The few modern Khoisan speakers survived mainly because they were isolated in areas of southern Africa, places where it was impossible for the invading Bantu-speaking farmers to grow their crops. When did the Bantu expansion actually begin? Linguistic evidence tells us that the expansion of ancestral Bantu farmers from West Africa's inland savanna south into its wetter coastal forest may have started as early as 3000 B.C.E. Words still widespread in all Bantu languages also tell us that the Bantu already had cattle and wet-climate crops such as yams, though they did not have metal and they were not farming full-time. Indeed, they were still fishing, hunting, and gathering. They also managed to lose all of the few cattle they had to diseases borne by tsetse flies in the forest. But as they spread into the Congo Basin's equatorial forest zone, they began to clear gardens and increase in number. That is when they began to engulf the Pygmy hunter-gatherers living on the forest's edge and push them into the forest itself. Soon after 1000 B.C.E. the Bantu emerged from the east side of the forest into the more open country of East Africa's RIFT VALLEY and Great Lakes. Here they encountered a melting pot of Afro-Asiatic and Nilo-Saharan-speaking farmers and herders, probably blacks like themselves, who were growing millet and sorghum and raising livestock in the drier areas. They also ran into the Khoisan hunter-gatherers. But the Bantu prevailed because they carried with them the wet-climate crops they had inherited from their West African homeland. They were able to farm forested areas of East Africa that were too moist for their previous occupants. By the last centuries B.C.E., the advancing Bantu had reached the East African coast. In East Africa the Bantu began to acquire millet and sorghum, along with the Nilo-Saharan names for those crops. They also reacquired cattle, a gift from their Nilo-Saharan and Afro-Asiatic black neighbors. And they began to make iron, which had just begun to be smelted in Africa's Sahel zone. The addition of iron tools to wet-climate crops created a military-industrial package that proved unstoppable in sub-equatorial Africa. In East Africa the Bantu still had to compete with numerous Nilo-Saharan and Afro-Asiatic Iron Age farmers, but to the south lay 3,000 kilometers (2,000 miles) of country with only Khoisan hunter-gatherers in the way. The Khoisan had neither iron nor crops. It was no contest. Within a few centuries, in one of the swiftest colonizing advances of recent prehistory, Bantu farmers swept all the way to Natal on the east coast of what is now South Africa. Of course, it is easy to trivialize what was undoubtedly a rapid and dramatic expansion, and to picture all the Khoisan being instantly steamrollered out of existence by onrushing Bantu hordes. In reality, things were more complicated. The Khoisan peoples of southern Africa had acquired sheep a few centuries ahead of the Bantu advance. The first Bantu pioneers were probably few in number and selected wet-forest areas suitable for their yam agriculture, leapfrogging over drier areas, which they left to Khoisan herders and hunter-gatherers. Trading and marriage relationships were undoubtedly established between the two groups, given that they were occupying adjacent habitats; such relationships continue today between Pygmy hunter-gatherers and Bantu farmers. Only gradually, as the Bantu multiplied and incorporated cattle and dry-climate cereals into their economy, did they fill in the leapfrogged areas. The result, however, was undeniable. Bantu farmers came to occupy most of the former Khoisan realm. The Khoisan legacy was reduced to a few clicks in scattered non-Khoisan languages, some buried skulls and stone tools, and the Khoisan-like appearance of many southern African Bantu peoples. What actually happened to all those vanished Khoisan populations? We do not know. All we can say for sure is that where Khoisan peoples had lived for perhaps tens of thousands of years there are now Bantu. In modern times, when steel-toting white farmers collided with stone-tool-using hunter-gatherers of aboriginal Australia and Native American California, the hunter-gatherers were rapidly eliminated: men were killed or enslaved, women were appropriated as wives, and both sexes were infected with epidemics of the farmers' diseases. This could easily have happened in Africa. Of course, some Khoisan survived; they live today in southern African areas unsuitable for Bantu agriculture. The southernmost Bantu people, the Xhosa, stopped at the Great Fish River on South Africa's southern coast, 800 kilometers (500 miles) east of CAPE TOWN. It is not that the Cape itself is too dry for agriculture: it is the breadbasket of modern South Africa.

But the Cape has a Mediterranean climate—it has winter rains—and the Bantu grew summer-rain crops. In 1652, when the Dutch arrived at Cape Town with their winter-rain crops of Middle Eastern origin, the Xhosa had still not spread beyond the Great Fish River. That seemingly small detail of plant geography had and continues to have enormous political consequences. Once the Dutch managed to kill, infect, or drive off the Cape's Khoisan population, they began to claim that since the whites had occupied the Cape before the Bantu, they had prior rights to it. Of course, they had not worried much about the prior rights of the Cape Khoisan whom they dispossessed. But the truth was that the Dutch settlers in 1652 had to contend only with a sparse population of Khoisan herders instead of a dense population of iron-equipped Bantu farmers. In 1779, when whites finally spread east to encounter the Xhosa at the Great Fish River, a period of desperate fighting began. Even though the Europeans were able to supply troops from their secure base at the Cape, it took nine wars and 100 years for their armies, advancing at an average rate of barely a couple kilometers per year, to subdue the Xhosa. They might not have succeeded in establishing themselves at all if the first few Dutch ships arriving at the Cape had faced such fierce resistance. Thus the agony of modern South Africa stems at least in part from a geographic accident. The homeland of the Cape Khoisan happened to contain no wild plants suitable for domestication; the Bantu happened to inherit summer-rain crops from their ancestors of 5,000 years ago; and Europeans happened to inherit winter-rain crops from their ancestors of nearly 10,000 years ago. Just as I was reminded by the sign Goering Street in the capital of newly independent Namibia, Africa's past has stamped itself deeply on Africa's present. Reprinted with permission of Discover magazine.

See also BANTU: DISPERSION AND SETTLEMENT; BANTU MIGRATIONS IN SUB-SAHARAN AFRICA; COLONIAL RULE; DISEASE AND AFRICAN HISTORY; ETHNICITY AND IDENTITY IN AFRICA: AN INTERPRETATION; IRON IN AFRICA; LANGUAGES, AFRICAN: AN OVERVIEW; PYGMY.

JARED DIAMOND

Huddleston, Trevor
1913–1998
British Anglican priest renowned for his opposition to apartheid, the South African government's rigid policy (now abolished) of racial separation.

Trevor Huddleston was ordained a priest in 1937 and entered the Community of the Resurrection Anglican order before being sent to South Africa in 1943. As deacon of the Anglican Missions of Sophiatown and then Orlando (outside of Johannesburg), Huddleston witnessed and protested against the injustices of apartheid. When the Native Resettlement Act of 1954 called for the destruction of Sophiatown to make way for a white suburb, he became chairperson of the Western Areas Protest Committee to support the blacks in defense of their homes. Despite his actions, Sophiatown was bulldozed in 1955 and the black residents were relocated to the black township of Soweto. Huddleston recorded the plight of Sophiatown in his 1956 book *Naught for Your Comfort*, a condemnation of South Africa's policy of persecution. He also worked with the African National Congress (ANC) to help bring about the Freedom Charter (the ANC's guiding statement of principles). Huddleston was later recalled to Great Britain, where he worked to focus international attention on the antiapartheid movement.

Huddleston served as bishop of Masasi in Tanzania from 1960 to 1968; bishop suffragan (bishop of a diocese within an archdiocese) of Stepney in London from 1968 to 1978; and both bishop of Mauritius and archbishop of the Indian Ocean from 1978 to 1983. He was vice president of the British Anti-Apartheid Movement from 1969 to 1981 and became chairman of the International Defense and Aid Fund for Southern Africa in 1983. He became founding patron of Action for Southern Africa in 1994. His work for social justice earned him a United Nations Gold Medal in 1982.

When Huddleston died in 1998, world leaders eulogized him as a hero. "If you could say that anybody single-handedly made apartheid a world issue then that person was Trevor Huddleston," stated South African Archbisop Desmond Tutu. President Nelson Mandela declared that "his memory will live in the hearts of our people."

See also CHRISTIANITY: MISSIONARIES IN AFRICA.

Human Rights in Africa
Overview of the history and status of the human rights movement in Africa.

The term human rights has been problematic in Africa since the mid-twentieth century, in both concept and reality. The phrase was coined after World War II in response to the atrocities committed against European Jews in the Holocaust. However, when the United Nations adopted the Universal Declaration of Human Rights in 1948, nearly all of Africa was under COLONIAL RULE, which meant that Africans were unable to participate in the drafting of the document that has defined human rights for the world. Ironically, although colonialism in Africa entailed a comprehensive catalogue of human rights violations, Africa was excluded from the process of integrating human rights into international law.

HUMAN RIGHTS IN PAN-AFRICAN TREATY LAW
The human rights paradigm of the Universal Declaration is state-centered: the nation-state is recognized as the greatest guarantor of human rights as well as the greatest threat to them. Before Africa could fit into this paradigm, modern African states had to be born. Most of them, under the banner of the right to self-determination, came into being in the 1960s. African leaders and scholars recognized early the power and potential value of a Pan-African treaty incorporating international human rights law. But they also saw the differences between the communitarian and collectivist nature of African societies and the more individualistic societies of the West. An African human rights treaty would have to go beyond the Universal Declaration to reflect individuals as right-holders enmeshed in communities, with collective rights and specific duties to others. In 1961, a year that many African states gained their independence, a conference on the rule of law took place in LAGOS, NIGERIA. The final document of this conference, known as the Law of Lagos, contains the first formal reference to a possible African convention, or agreement, on human rights. This convention would follow the model developed in Europe, the Americas, and the United Nations, and would include a tribunal to monitor and enforce its provisions.

As soon as the term human rights came into use, however, it became a battleground in the Cold War between the capitalist nations of the West and the socialist or communist bloc of states led by the Soviet Union. The debate over human rights within Africa echoed some of the themes of the Cold War. Many of the great leaders of African independence movements, such as Senegal's Léopold SENGHOR, Tanzania's Julius NYERERE, and Ghana's Kwame Nkrumah, were socialists. For them, the West's vision of "rights" (traced back to the American and French Revolutions) was suspect because of its historical coexistence with colonialism; it was also limited by its focus on civil and political guarantees. Further, African leaders were well aware of Western hypocrisy on the subject of human rights, knowing that even the most basic of these guarantees had been denied to black Americans before the Civil Rights Movement in the United States in the 1960s. "Rights" were an essential part of the rhetoric of independence in Africa, but in the decades after independence, African leaders generally emphasized economic and social rights—that is, economic development and self-sufficiency—over the civil and political rights to which most of the Universal Declaration is devoted.

But the idea of an African human rights treaty persisted, and was given new life with a colloquium on human rights and development, held in 1978 in DAKAR, SENEGAL. The first complete draft of the African Charter of Human and Peoples' Rights was finished by the end of 1979. In 1980–1981 the justice ministers of the ORGANIZATION OF AFRICAN UNITY (OAU) member states met in BANJUL, GAMBIA, to approve the official version of the African Charter, also called the Banjul Charter. This draft was adopted by the OAU Assembly of Heads of State in Government in June 1981.

The African Charter reflects the political consciousness of African intellectuals, giving prominence to communitarianism, collective identities, individual duties, and economic development. It contains substantial economic and social rights provisions, such as the right to education and health care. The rights of a people to self-determination and control over their natural resources and environment are also included. The individual duties mentioned in the African Charter include the duties to take care of one's parents, to avoid committing treasonous acts, and to promote the spirit of African unity.

The African Charter, which went into effect in 1986, had been ratified by more than fifty countries by the beginning of the twenty-first century. It established the African Commission on Human and Peoples' Rights as a monitoring and enforcement body. The African Commission is composed of eleven independent African human rights experts who are elected by the OAU summit; it meets twice a year and is headquartered in Banjul. The Commission has two primary activities: to promote the rights specified in the charter by examining reports submitted every two years by the countries, and to protect those rights by hearing cases brought by individuals and nongovernmental organizations (NGOs) against the states. The African Commission got off to a slow start but has become a major focus for human rights activities across the continent. Due in part to the active involvement of NGOs, the Commission has been able to undertake a wide range of activities not specified in the charter. For example, it has held seminars and conferences and commissioned special reports on issues such as extrajudicial executions, prisons and detention conditions, and the status of African women.

The 1998 OAU summit meeting, held in OUAGADOUGOU, BURKINA FASO, approved an optional protocol to the African Charter that would establish an African Court of Human and Peoples' Rights. The court is intended to solve some of the Commission's problems, such as lack of respect from states' parties. However, the court will be sure to face some of the same difficulties, including insufficient material and financial resources.

AFRICA'S HUMAN RIGHTS RECORD

Despite the progress made in creating a formal structure of African human rights law, the actual record of human rights in Africa has been grim. Violations fall into several general categories, touching nearly every aspect of Africans' daily lives. Tragically, the human rights violations associated with the most widespread and terrible suffering are those least responsive to international legal provisions and protections. Many of these violations are linked to the legacies of colonialism: in other words, to the ethnic relations, political boundaries, and patterns of state power that were created under colonial rule.

One category of violations concerns civil and political rights. The African Charter, nodding to tradition, begins with these rights: to political participation, association, freedom of speech, as well as freedom from arbitrary detention and right to fair trial. The most outstanding example of comprehensive violation of these rights and the social misery that resulted was South Africa under APARTHEID—an oppressive, institutionalized system that not only condoned, but enforced, racial discrimination. Elsewhere in sub-Saharan Africa, most countries became one-party states with independence, and a single man headed those parties. Many of these leaders, not without justification, argued that one-party rule was needed to build modern nation-states out of the ethnically diverse territories left by colonialism and to achieve rapid economic development on the model of African socialism. They also argued that a one-party system embodied traditional, consensual African patterns of governance.

Whatever their philosophical justifications, most one-party states became highly repressive of civil and political rights. Opposition political parties and press freedom were unknown under even respected leaders, such as Nkrumah and Jomo KENYATTA of Kenya. In the worst cases, dictators such as Idi AMIN of Uganda, Jean-Bédel BOKASSA of the CENTRAL AFRICAN REPUBLIC, Macías Nguema of EQUATORIAL GUINEA, Kamuzu BANDA of MALAWI, Daniel Arap MOI of Kenya, and MOBUTU SESE SEKO of the former ZAIRE—to name only a few—brutally suppressed opposition, targeted specific ethnic groups for persecution, and ordered massacres. Of the countries that have not been ruled for long periods by a single figure, many have suffered through a succession of coups d'état and military governments. Nigeria, for example, has been governed by the military for almost all of its post-independence history.

The need to build unity among an ethnically diverse population has served as a justification for political dictatorship, but too often the lack of democratic process, combined with pervasive discrimination, increases the likelihood of civil strife as one ethnic group monopolizes state power and systematically excludes others. In Sudan, national unity seems a dim hope as the state, dominated by Muslim Arab northerners, wages a long-running war with southern black populations, who practice Christianity and traditional religions. That civil war has already cost hundreds of thousands of lives. An analogous conflict in Mauritania in the late 1980s drove tens of thousands of black Mauritanians over the southern border to Senegal. National unity is also a distant goal in Rwanda and Burundi, where tensions between the HUTU AND TUTSI peoples deepened during the colonial era. After independence, those tensions produced recurrent massacres in both countries, including the 1994 Rwandan genocide.

The effectiveness of the OAU and the African Commission in combating violations of civil and political rights has been limited by African states' reluctance to criticize one another. This contrasts with Europe, where the system of human rights law was shaped and given stature by a number of prominent state-against-state cases. Together, the many nondemocratic states in Africa have impeded the implementation of the African Charter. In addition, even now that the Charter is in force and the commission has been established, Africa's human rights system suffers from the inadequate funding provided by the OAU. The Commission's sessions, for example, originally lasted fourteen days but were cut to ten days by the OAU. The OAU also pays the salary of only one lawyer in the Secretariat.

Another problem is that the human rights violations common in civil conflict are particularly difficult for international law to handle. A system of treaty law relies upon state action to define punishable violations. Although widespread violations of the right to life are common in wars—as are incidents of torture, rape, mass displacement of populations, and destruction of property—assigning blame to either side may be nearly impossible. This task belongs in a "political" realm that international law must shun in order to preserve its legitimacy. International human rights law thus has not proven effective in situations of massive civil unrest. Because remarkably few wars in Africa have been fought between recognized states, the humanitarian law that governs such "official" conflicts has offered relatively little protection.

Another category of human rights abuses can be characterized as "customary" or "traditional" practices. The best-known example is female genital mutilation, also called FEMALE CIRCUMCISION. Other traditional practices that many consider human rights violations include the levirate (in which a widow is required to marry one of her brothers-in-law) and the giving or selling of young children to religious leaders, a practice

known as trikosi in Ghana. SLAVERY IN AFRICA also persists in some forms, particularly in Mauritania and Sudan. These practices, while not as devastating to the entire society as civic strife or systematic oppression, resist abolition by law because they do not involve actions of the state. Such traditions are typically long-standing and sometimes grounded in religious beliefs. Even when governments are willing to publicly oppose them, it is difficult to force an end to them by legal means.

The African Charter itself is deliberately ambiguous on customary practices, requiring only that African states preserve positive African traditional values. The determination of which African values are positive and which are not is left for the African Commission to interpret. A great deal will depend on the cases brought before the commission, and the arguments put forth by each side. It is unlikely that the commission would accept practices such as female circumcision or trikosi as positive, but to declare them outright violations of the African Charter would be highly controversial, especially if these practices involve no direct state action. The African human rights system will probably not be the forum where these issues are addressed.

A third category of violations concerns economic and social rights. The inclusion of these rights in the African Charter demonstrates their importance, in light of enduring poverty in Africa. But regional treaties have proven relatively to be ineffective remedies for economic ills. One difficulty is the lack of direct state action in such violations—the extent to which a government is responsible for its nation's poverty cannot be measured. Another problem is that there are no objective standards for measuring the extent of economic and social rights violations. Finally, African states often truly lack the financial resources needed to improve social services, such as health care and education. As a result, the African Charter's articles on economic and social rights have meant little in practice. Only recently has the Charter begun to form the basis of some lawsuits that may result in concrete standards, at least for specific situations.

One development during the years since the drafting of the African Charter has been the general recognition of the interdependence of rights. In other words, the political oppression that has long plagued many African countries is now recognized as one of the factors contributing to the continent's failure to achieve greater economic success. Even financial institutions such as the World Bank and the International Monetary Fund, while they are loathe to speak of economic rights, can no longer overlook the clear relation between transparency and efficiency. They now speak of the need for good governance, a euphemism for respect of civil and political rights.

HUMAN RIGHTS AND INTERNATIONAL SECURITY. The United Nations Security Council votes in favor of a permanent, mandatory arms embargo against South Africa on November 4, 1977. (*AP Images*)

FUTURE OF HUMAN RIGHTS IN AFRICA

A wave of democratization swept Africa in the early 1990s. The most dramatic example was South Africa, where the post-apartheid government committed itself to guaranteeing the human rights of the population. While democratic revolutions may have stalled in many other countries, a new momentum in African civil society promises to be the best guarantor of rights. Nongovernmental organizations have sprung up everywhere, dealing with the whole range of civil and political rights, combating traditional practices, and advocating for development. While not all of these organizations articulate their mission in terms of human rights, they have been vital to the development and support of the African regional system, and to human rights and development work at the national level. Not only have NGOs provided staff for the Commission's Secretariat and suggestions for its programs, but the overwhelming majority of complainants bringing human rights cases to the courts are NGOs. The majority of observers at the Commission's sessions are also representatives of NGOs, whose participation has had a distinct influence on the growth of the human rights system. NGOs are also intervening in nearly every issue at the national level by publicizing, litigating, and lobbying in support of human rights. If African states eventually fulfill the role of guarantor of human rights, it will be because of active prodding from NGOs.

Intergovernmental bodies also offer reason for hope. The African Commission has grown more efficient in its administration and bolder in implementing its mission, handing down decisions against Nigeria, Malawi, Chad, and Cameroon, among others. It has taken missions to Mauritania, Senegal, Sudan, and Nigeria. Governments have recently shown more interest in the Commission's work and become more cooperative. The OAU itself has begun to treat human rights as a priority, at least in rhetoric, and to incorporate them into peace accords.

The human rights situation in Africa remains grim —especially in the cases of widespread violations caused by civil wars. A 2007 report by the U.S. State Department documents a seemingly endless litany of human rights abuses, either at the behest of the state or under an umbrella of state indifference or impotence. Still, there are signs that the combined pressures from NGOs, regional bodies such as the African Commission, and forces outside the continent will together help bring about positive changes in the behavior of governments and in society itself. The definition of human rights will remain fluid and subject to debate, but Africa may yet use its innovative treaty provisions and distinctive philosophy of rights to make a global contribution.

JULIA HARRINGTON

Hunde

Ethnic group of the Democratic Republic of the Congo.

The Hunde primarily inhabit the Kivu Province of the east central DEMOCRATIC REPUBLIC OF THE CONGO (DRC). Other Hunde live in RWANDA and in southwestern UGANDA. They speak a BANTU language and belong to the larger Kivu cultural and linguistic cluster. Approximately 200,000 people consider themselves Hunde.

See also BANTU: DISPERSION AND SETTLEMENT; CONGO, DEMOCRATIC REPUBLIC OF THE; ETHNICITY AND IDENTITY IN DISPERSIONAFRICA: AN INTERPRETATION; LANGUAGES, AFRICAN: AN OVERVIEW.

Hunger and Famine

Conditions of severe and potentially life-threatening food deprivation.

Famine struck Africa several times during the twentieth century, and famine and hunger continued to threaten parts of the continent in the twenty-first. While graphic media coverage and celebrity appeals have helped to raise international awareness of African famines since the 1970s, it has done less well at explaining why famines persist, how they occur, and how they differ from the equally critical—and perhaps more serious—problem of chronic hunger. Many African peoples are vulnerable to food deprivation, despite the numerous "coping strategies" they have long employed in order to survive in harsh and unpredictable environments.

HUNGER

According to the United Nations Food and Agricultural Organization (FAO), the average African consumes 2,300 kcal/day, significantly less than the global average of 2,700 kcal/day. In the late 1990s, the FAO estimated that 316 million Africans, or approximately 35 percent of the continent's total population, were chronically undernourished. Although hunger in Africa is hardly a new phenomenon, it now occurs in a world that has enough food to feed all its citizens. Moreover, while Africa's population is growing rapidly, there remains ample fertile land for growing food. Hunger, therefore, reflects not the absolute scarcity of food but rather people's lack of access to the resources—whether at the individual, household, community, or national level—needed to produce or purchase adequate food supplies. "Bluntly stated," said a 2003 FAO report, "the problem is not so much a lack of food as a lack of political will." A World Food Program report released the same year seconded this assessment, noting that hunger in Africa was simply "overwhelming the system," both the national

instruments of relief and those of continental and international NGOs.

The reasons people cannot obtain enough food are rooted in historical patterns of inequality. These patterns include the inequalities between Africa and its former colonizers or contemporary financiers, and between Africa's rich and poor. Inequality can also exist among members of the same household—food and the resources needed to obtain it, such as land and income, are often unevenly distributed between men and women, old and young. Whatever the reasons for food deprivation, when the result is malnutrition the damage can be long-lasting. Malnutrition makes people more susceptible to many diseases, including malaria, rickets, anemia, pellagra, and perhaps ACQUIRED IMMUNODEFICIENCY SYNDROME (AIDS). Malnourished children suffer stunted growth and, often, learning problems. Malnourished adults have less energy to work. Over the long term, inadequate nourishment can cast communities into a vicious cycle of sickness, underproduction, and poverty.

The 2003 FAO report concluded that hunger was worsening in many countries, particularly in sub-Saharan Africa. Although the number of undernourished people declined in some countries, such as Mozambique, during the second half of the 1990s, other nations, among them Nigeria, saw the number of malnourished climb. The report noted that the problem was especially severe in countries torn by war, such as Liberia and the DEMOCRATIC REPUBLIC OF CONGO. The FAO estimated that 75 percent of people in the Democratic Republic of Congo were undernourished in the period 1999–2001. BURUNDI was close behind with 70 percent. There and in other countries in West and Central Africa, war had brought food production almost to a standstill. A different problem has hurt food production in southern Africa. The spread of AIDS has killed or weakened many citizens, causing some families to lose their breadwinners or even to abandon their fields.

FAMINE

Famine is commonly defined as "acute starvation associated with a sharp increase in mortality." This seemingly straightforward definition, however, fails to answer the much more complicated question of why people reach the point of starvation. Contrary to popular media coverage of the issue, famine in Africa is not an abrupt event. Nor is it the immediate, inevitable outcome of DROUGHT AND DESERTIFICATION or other climatic misfortunes. Rather, research on the history of famine shows that several factors typically contribute to a society's or region's vulnerability to starvation, and that some of the causes of famine have changed significantly over the past century.

In a famine, the first victims are mostly children, followed by men; women's greater biological stamina makes them most likely to survive prolonged food deprivation. The primary cause of death is not starvation itself, but diseases such as diarrheal infection and malaria. Famine not only increases mortality or death rate but also decreases fertility—and thus birthrates. Famine is typically rural rather than urban, because for Africa's leaders—from the era of COLONIAL RULE to the present—food security in politically influential cities has almost always taken priority over rural areas. Although famines are truly devastating, the reported mortality rates from contemporary African famines are notoriously inaccurate, partly because it is difficult to collect information and partly because international agencies exaggerate figures in order to emphasize the need for donor support.

An important feature of famine is that it typically strikes only after people have exhausted a range of strategies intended to compensate for unpredictable climatic, economic, or political downturns. The nature and effectiveness of these coping strategies have been transformed by the environmental, demographic, and political-economic changes in Africa during the past century. For example, rural communities in arid and semiarid regions have long cultivated drought-resistant crops, such as millet, sorghum, and cassava, with the goal of producing a surplus that will last through several months of dry weather. Although this remains a desirable strategy for many rural dwellers, environmental degradation in some areas has reduced yields. Even more significant has been the need to produce cash crops such as cotton, a change that has caused farmers to depend more and more on markets for basic food supplies. When drought leads to crop failure, farmers may have little or no money to buy food, and this happens just at the moment that grain prices are skyrocketing. Under such conditions, rural dwellers might seek income elsewhere: through wage labor or the sale of household assets such as family heirlooms, furniture, or livestock. But such strategies are unlikely to work in severely impoverished regions, and selling assets can make people more vulnerable to future famine—if households, for example, are left without draft animals or transport.

Cultivating far-ranging social relations is another time-honored coping strategy. When famine threatens, rural dwellers often ask their urban relatives for money, food, employment, or temporary foster care of children. Entire families may migrate to cities, neighboring countries, or, if necessary, relief camps. Abandoning home and field, however, tends to be a last-ditch strategy. By the time people migrate, they may have already severely cut back on their daily food intake.

Africa's nomadic livestock herders were among the hardest hit by twentieth-century famines. Historically, they survived in austere environments by migrating seasonally between grazing lands and by developing commercial and patronage relationships with farming communities. In the past several decades, however, new obstacles, such as national borders, fenced-off land, and expanding agricultural settlements, have increasingly restricted seasonal movements. This in turn has provoked conflicts between nomads and surrounding communities, as well as between nomads and the national governments that control food aid. Since the 1960s, declining rainfall in arid regions such as the Sahel has also restricted nomads' migratory range.

As the experience of many nomads indicates, the descent into famine depends a great deal on politics. During the colonial period, improved infrastructures and agricultural technologies should have improved food security, but colonial governments' high taxes, crop requisitions, forced-labor policies, and overall lack of accountability all increased vulnerability to famine in many regions. One example is the French colony of UPPER VOLTA (now BURKINA FASO). Rural households forced to grow cotton suffered severe famine in the early 1930s after rains failed and cotton prices fell with the worldwide commodities market collapse that marked the beginning of the Great Depression.

One reason famine still occurs in the early twentieth century is that many independent African governments have shown as little accountability to the people as their colonial predecessors. Some famines have occurred on the heels of governments' failure to respond to warning signs; this was the case in ZIMBABWE in 1991–1992, when famine accompanied a drought. Other famines have resulted from draconian government efforts to control and extract revenue from rural populations. Famine in Ethiopia in the mid-1980s, for example, was caused not only by drought but also by burdensome government crop requisitions and massive forced relocation schemes in the country's northern regions. In such instances, the lack of basic democratic institutions made it possible for famine's warning signs to go unheeded, both within and beyond the country in question. As the economist Amartya Sen has noted, " . . . in the terrible history of famines in the world, it is hard to find a case in which famine has occurred in a country with a free press and an active opposition within a democratic system."

Some of the worst contemporary African famines have resulted from wartime sieges. During the 1967–1970 Nigerian civil war, the federal government of Nigeria blocked all food shipments to Biafra, leading to widespread starvation. In 1993, siege brought famine to parts of war-torn ANGOLA. And in SUDAN's long-running civil war, the northern-based government has used its control over food shipments to weaken insurgents in the south.

International food aid agencies, despite their seemingly apolitical humanitarian appeal, invariably complicate the political picture. Sometimes food relief lets negligent governments off the hook; sometimes it even sustains repressive regimes. Ethiopia again offers a prime example. In the late 1970s and 1980s, the military regime of Mengistu Haile Mariam received huge quantities of food aid to fight a famine it had helped create. Yet 90 percent of international aid went to Mengistu's followers, while only 10 percent reached equally famine-stricken rebels. The famine—and the aid—strengthened Mengistu's grip on the country. On the other hand, some countries that experienced dire famine in the mid-1980s have made significant gains in food security, despite the chronic threat of drought. Burkina Faso is one example; ERITREA is another. In both cases, specific measures such as soil and water conservation programs in villages have helped increase agricultural productivity in drought-prone areas, although they have not ended dependence on imported food aid. But past famines have also made food security a potent political issue, one that these countries' leaders cannot easily ignore. Success in combating hunger and famine in Africa will ultimately depend partly on technical advances, partly on sustained economic growth, but also on the recognition, both in Africa and abroad, that food security is a basic right.

ERIC BENNETT

Hunkanrin, Louis
1886–1964
Journalist, educator, and early nationalist in French West Africa.

Louis Hunkanrin was born in Porto-Novo, Dahomey (present-day Benin). One of the earliest critics of French colonialism in Dahomey, Hunkanrin spent most of his adult life imprisoned for challenging colonial policies and attempting to win new respect and rights for Africans in French West Africa. A descendant of the royal family of Porto-Novo, Hunkanrin received an exceptional early education and matriculated at the École Normale in Senegal, where he graduated with a teaching degree in 1904. Immediately afterward he accepted a teaching position at a public school in Whydah and began vocalizing his criticism of France's arbitrary colonial policies.

Hunkanrin was dismissed from the school in 1909 after a series of disputes with the headmaster. He subsequently accepted a job at the Compagnie Française de l'Afrique Occidentale (C.F.A.O.), but in 1912 he was fired, tried, and convicted for insulting and threatening his superior. He was sent to prison in Dakar, where he became friends with Blaise Diagne and refined his critique of French Colonial Rule.

Hunkanrin returned to Dahomey in 1914. In articles written for local journals he railed against the racism and oppression of French colonialism. He also urged Africans to educate themselves; education, he claimed, was the only way for Africans to acquire equality with the French. Although he did not actually call for decolonization, the French colonial administration still considered him a threat. Hunkanrin consequently spent the next four years in hiding, traveling between Dahomey, Nigeria, and Senegal. He came out of hiding in 1918 after Diagne arranged for him to volunteer for military service in World War I, but his service was marred by a string of disputes that eventually resulted in a court-martial in 1921. Hunkanrin later severed ties with Diagne, who he claimed was taking monetary bribes to lure Africans into the military. Hunkanrin returned to Dahomey in December 1921 and spent the next two years in prison for forgery. While in jail, he helped organize the 1923 anticolonial demonstrations in Porto-Novo. The French administration then sent Hunkanrin into forced exile in Mauritania. Although he returned to Dahomey in 1933, he spent most of the next twenty-three years in jail, during which he was exiled to the French Sudan for challenging the Vichy government and supporting Charles de Gaulle's Free France campaign. He was finally released from jail after Dahomean independence in 1960. He died four years later, at which time the Dahomean government posthumously awarded him the title "Grand Officier de l'Ordre National du Dahomey."

ELIZABETH HEATH

Hunting in Africa
Killing of game for subsistence and exchange.
Hunting has been an integral part of the foraging strategies that Africans, like others, have used since the beginnings of human existence. Indeed, many scholars have suggested that hunting provided a basis for human reciprocity and cooperation. By coordinating strategies and sharing the spoils of the hunt, Africans were able to hunt even the largest game animals on the savanna effectively and reliably. Indeed, contemporary hunting and gathering (or foraging) societies continue to be among the most egalitarian. A 1987 estimate suggested that only about 270,000 people continued to depend upon hunting as a mainstay of their economy. All of these people rely heavily on the gathering of plant foods as well. Although meat rarely surpasses gathered nuts and roots as a source of calories among foragers, foraging communities highly value game. A great many more Africans, such as the Barabaig pastoralists of TANZANIA, hunt to supplement their diets and to acquire valuable animal products such as skins. For others, hunting is a rite of passage. For

example, the male MAASAI initiate traditionally must kill a lion to prove his manhood. After about the fifth millennium B.C.E., the practice of cultivating cereal and root crops began to spread across Africa. By the first millennium B.C.E., large numbers of Bantu speakers began to disperse east and south through the forests of Central Africa from their homeland in present-day CAMEROON. They grew yams and other root crops and later adopted the cereals grown by peoples of the SAHEL. As agriculturists brought more land under cultivation, they pushed hunters into marginal environments undesirable for gardening. Today the remaining foraging populations in Africa are located in rain forests of the Congo Basin, arid areas of southern Africa, and scrub forests of Tanzania and KENYA. The Binga, the TWA, the Mbuti, the KHOIKHOI, the HADZA, and the Okiek are six prominent groups that continue to follow traditional hunting practices in significant numbers. In all these groups, men are the principal hunters, particularly when the hunted animals are large. Women tend to capture smaller animals or participate in big game hunts as beaters, driving quarry into nets by beating the forest undergrowth. Women generally also provide most of the gathered plant foods. Contrary to the stereotype that foraging societies lack complex social organizations, all of these groups traditionally rely on a complex set of relationships, based on kinship ties, for allocating access to resources such as hunting terrains, and for distributing meat and other animal products. The majority of contemporary African hunters, about 200,000, inhabit the Congo Basin. These include the Binga, the Twa, and the Mbuti peoples. These foraging forest dwellers continue to follow traditional hunting techniques that are well adapted to the forest ecology. Bands rotate among regularly used camps where thirty to sixty people remain for several weeks at a time. Within these camps they prepare nets, bows, arrows, and spears. Through trade with neighboring Bantu-speaking farmers they acquire iron, which they frequently shape into arrowheads. Among these groups, successful hunting is a sign of prestige. Traditionally in some of these groups, men must slay a large animal to earn the right to marry. Few Khoikhoi speakers today continue to forage for a living; most have taken up PASTORALISM or farm labor. Those who still hunt tend to seek large animals such as gemsbok and eland, which figure prominently in Khoikhoi religious beliefs. They are permitted to hunt on natural reserves, but only using traditional methods, and they are forbidden to hunt elephants, giraffe, and other endangered animals. They use a number of different hunting techniques. Small groups of two or more men often spend several days tracking larger animals such as kudu, springbok, and duiker, which they shoot with a slow-acting poisoned arrow. Khoikhoi hunters use traps and snares to catch smaller animals, including birds, rodents, and tortoises. They often use a knobkerrie, a type of short club, to kill trapped animals. They use long flexible poles to skewer burrowing animals such as the springhare. On occasion, all the men from one or two bands (200 to 300 people) will drive large herds between fallen tree trunks and into pitfall traps that are three meters deep. These hunters also frequently employ horses and dogs to help spear large animals. As with other groups, the owner widely distributes meat from large kills. In some Khoikhoi groups the first to sink an arrow into the animal is the owner; in other groups, the person who shaped the arrow is the principal owner, whether or not the arrowsmith participated in the hunt. By exchanging arrows with many people, a man increases his chances of getting enough meat for his family. The Hadza are foragers who inhabit the area around Lake Eyasi, Tanzania. Their language uses click sounds similar to those of the Khoikhoi people, and many anthropologists suspect that these peoples are distantly related. Unlike the Khoikhoi, the Hadza do not trap small animals, but concentrate almost solely on hunting large game. The sexual division of labor is more distinct among the Hadza and the social stratification greater. Accomplished hunters enjoy considerable prestige and influence. The Okiek live primarily in the Mau forest of Kenya, where they use dog packs to hunt animals such as the giant forest hog. Although during the twentieth century most Okiek abandoned full-time hunting in favor of pastoralism or agriculture, many continue to hunt to supplement their diets. Scholars have often drawn conclusions about prehistoric African hunters from surviving foraging communities. Although contemporary foragers may provide clues to early subsistence strategies, their social structures and cultures differ widely. Consequently, they do not offer a good basis for generalizations about foraging societies. Nor is hunting an inherently primitive means of subsistence, as it is sometimes depicted. Researchers have found that foragers work less hard and in many ways have a higher standard of living than small-scale cultivators. However, hunting and gathering can support only relatively low population densities. Therefore, some scholars believe that population pressures forced people to abandon foraging for agriculture, at the cost of much leisure time.

See also ANTHROPOLOGY IN AFRICA; BANTU: DISPERSION AND SETTLEMENT; KINSHIP AND DESCENT IN AFRICA; RITES OF PASSAGE AND TRANSITION; WILDLIFE MANAGEMENT IN AFRICA.

ARI NAVE

Hutu and Tutsi
Groups living primarily in Rwanda and Burundi.

Most reference sources on RWANDA and BURUNDI estimate that both countries' national populations are approximately 85 percent Hutu, 14 percent Tutsi, and one percent TWA. Although these terms are commonly believed to refer to distinct ethnic groups, the people known as Hutu and Tutsi have lived in the same region and under the political authorities for centuries. They have intermarried, speak the same language, and share many cultural practices. According to historical, linguistic, and cultural definitions of ethnicity, in other words, the Hutu and Tutsi are not distinct groups. Historically, the more important differences have been occupational and political: the agricultural people of this region have traditionally identified themselves as Hutu, while the Tutsi were traditionally the cattle-owning political elite. Even these categories were not immutable, however, at least not until European colonial rulers began using rigid tribal identities to define Africans' access to education, employment, and other resources. Following decolonization, violent civil conflicts in both Rwanda and Burundi further polarized Hutu and Tutsi populations. More recently, however, after 2006, hostilities between the two groups appear to have cooled somewhat, though the possibility that violence will recommence is ever present.

See also ETHNICITY AND IDENTITY IN AFRICA: AN INTERPRETATION; ETHNICITY IN BURUNDI: AN INTERPRETATION; ETHNICITY IN RWANDA: AN INTERPRETATION.

SUSANNE FREIDBERG

I

Ibadan, Nigeria

City with more than three million residents, Ibadan is the capital of the Oyo state in southwestern Nigeria.

Ibadan's development predates written history, though its modern composition traces back to wars between the YORUBA kingdoms during the 1820s, after which victorious armies of the Oyo, IFE, and IJEBU settled on the site. Scholars and traders brought Islam to the city in the mid-nineteenth century, and missionaries brought CHRISTIANITY a few decades later. In 1893 Ibadan fell under British COLONIAL RULE, and by 1912 railroads linked the city both to LAGOS in the south and KANO in the north.

Local industries include brewing, canning, publishing, tobacco processing, and the manufacture of furniture and automobiles. Yoruba handicrafts, such as blacksmithing and ceramics, as well as weaving, spinning, and dyeing, retain important roles in the economy. These wares, along with locally produced food, are sold in Ibadan's numerous markets. As in many other Yoruba towns, most of the city's residents have traditionally made a living from farming. Today this is less common; farmers usually supplement their agricultural income with trade or artisanal work.

Ibadan University, founded in 1948, was NIGERIA's first institution of higher learning. Although national economic troubles have undermined the university's world-class reputation, it continues to earn Ibadan the status of Nigeria's intellectual center. The Agodi Gardens, the Ibadan University Zoo, two stadiums, a technical institute, three institutes of agricultural research, and a branch of the National Archives all bolster Ibadan's reputation as cultural hub of the nation.

As of 2006, Ibadan had a population of 2,550,593.

See also ISLAM IN AFRICA; OYO, EARLY KINGDOM OF.

ERIC BENNETT

Ibibio

Ethnic group of the Cross Rivers State in southeastern Nigeria.

The Ibibio number about five million people. Ibibio-carved masks are renowned for their artistry. Many of the Ibibio support themselves by growing yams and cassava or by producing palm oil products for export. Others fish, typically in dugout canoes.

There are many small subgroups within the larger Ibibio family, including the ANANG, Andoni-Ibeno, Eket, and Enyong. The Ibibio are closely associated historically, socially, and linguistically with the EFIK ethnic group. Some anthropologists believe the Efik to belong to the Ibibio family. Others argue that although the Efik speak a variant of the Ibibio language, the Efik people have a distinct ethnic identity. Within the region inhabited by both the Ibibio and the Efik, identity as either Efik or Ibibio is tinged with historical resentment by the Ibibio, who sometimes refer to the Efik as "the oppressors."

Ibibio social structure is decentralized. Each village is led by its council of elders. Most men—and many women—belong to secret societies that honor traditional rituals and religious practices. Both boys and girls are circumcised at adolescence.

See also ETHNICITY AND IDENTITY IN AFRICA: AN INTERPRETATION; LANGUAGES, AFRICAN: AN OVERVIEW; *and* NIGERIA.

Ibn Battutah

1304–1368

Medieval North African jurist whose Saharan travels resulted in one of the most valuable early commentaries on African cultures.

Like the majority of North Africans, Ibn Battutah (whose full name was Abu 'Abd Allah Muhammad ibn'Abd Allah al-Lawati at-Tanji ibn Battutah) was ethnic Berber, and his family traced its ancestry to the nomadic Luwata ethnic group originating in Cyrenaica west of the Nile Delta. Born into the Muslim religious elite in Tangier, Morocco, he would have received a classical literary education in addition to rigorous studies in Islam.

Ibn Battutah wrote poetry in addition to traveling across Africa, Arabia, Asia Minor, India, and China. Most important of his works are his descriptions of the life and culture of peoples of the Niger Basin and Central Sahara, among the earliest and by far the most detailed. After Ibn Battutah returned from his voyages he recounted his observations to Ibn Juzayy, who recorded and edited them at Fès, in Morocco.

At the age of twenty-one, Ibn Battutah set out on a pilgrimage across North Africa to Mecca, an obligation expected of Muslims who can afford it. En route, he visited Damascus and traveled throughout Syria to the borders of Asia Minor before joining the Muslim pilgrim caravan heading to Mecca, where he spent three years. He then made a visit to trading towns along the coast of East Africa, and returned to Mecca, after which he decided to go to India.

The Islamic brotherhood provided support for Ibn Battutah in his travels, supplying food and lodging as he moved from city to city throughout Asia Minor. He traveled across the Black Sea, visited Constantinople, and journeyed across the steppes of Central Asia. Wherever he traveled, rulers and wealthy people bestowed gifts on him, including many horses. He became quite rich and had many admirers. In India, the Sultan was so fond of Ibn Battutah that he appointed him judge, a Malachite qadi, in Delhi, and later asked him to lead a royal envoy to the powerful Mongol Emperor of China. A series of mishaps, however, left him separated from his ships and destitute for many months on the coast of Malabar. From there he sailed to the Maldive Islands, where he was again appointed judge. But after only a year there Ibn Battutah's curiosity took him in 1345 to see the "footprint of Adam" in Ceylon, where he climbed Adam's Peak.

After further journeys in Southeast Asia, Ibn Battutah finally visited China. He made the long journey home, after many years away from Morocco, returning through Sumatra, Malabar, Oman, Baghdad, Cairo, and Tunis, reaching Fès in 1349. He briefly contemplated taking part in the Crusades, and traveled to Grenada, Spain, in Andalusia.

It was toward the end of Ibn Battutah's travels that he undertook what was probably his most adventurous journey, across the Sahara to visit the peoples living along the bend of the Niger River. For three years, from 1352 to 1354, Ibn Battutah traveled by camel on ancient caravan routes from oasis to oasis, and through major market towns. He stayed for months at a time with rulers in the kingdoms of Mali and Songhai, as well as with Tuareg pastoralists living in the Niger River basin.

Ibn Battutah's description of the Sultan of Mali at court is an excellent example of his keen eye for detail. "On certain days the sultan holds audiences in the palace yard, where there is a platform under a tree . . . It is carpeted with silk and has cushions placed on it . . . The sultan comes out of a door in a corner of the palace, carrying a bow in his hand and a quiver on his back. On his head he has a golden skullcap . . . His usual dress is a velvety red tunic . . . The sultan is preceded by his musicians, who carry gold and silver guimbris [two stringed guitars]. . . ."

Ibn Battutah is the only traveler known to have visited all the Muslim-ruled lands of medieval times. He is estimated to have traveled up to 75,000 miles in all, and his observations are renowned for their detail, credibility, and color.

See also ISLAM IN AFRICA.

BIBLIOGRAPHY

Gibb, H. A. R. *Ibn Battuta, Travels in Asia and Africa 1325–1354.* G. Routledge and Sons, Ltd., 1939.

BARBARA WORLEY

Ibn Khaldun
1332–1406
Fourteenth-century North African scholar, considered one of the greatest Arab historians.

Ibn Khaldun wrote a monumental history of North Africa, the *Kitab al-Ibar.* But his most significant contribution, in the eyes of many contemporary scholars, is the *Muqaddimah,* perhaps the first systematic philosophical study of history and society. Ibn Khaldun was born in Tunis in the region of TUNISIA to a family that for centuries had played a prominent political role in Andalusia, or southern Spain, before fleeing to North Africa to escape the Christian reconquest. As a young man he received a formal education in the Qur'an (Koran), Arabic poetry and Islamic law, preparing him for a life among the ruling class of North Africa. In 1349 both his mother and father died as the black plague ravaged Tunis. As a young married man, Ibn Khaldun joined the royal court in Tunis, and later in Fès, MOROCCO. After a rebellion upset the court, he was accused of treason and imprisoned. This was the first of several times Ibn Khaldun would be ensnared in the intrigues of fourteenth-century court life, where dynasties rose and fell and intellectuals competed for royal favor. He was released after the sultan's death, and went into exile in Muslim-held Granada, where he worked as a diplomat. He also developed a close but contentious relationship with Granada's prime minister and scholar, Ibn al-Khatib. The two men's eventual falling-out, followed by another accusation of treason, forced Ibn Khaldun to flee once again. After years of negotiating the treacherous waters of dynastic service in the Maghreb, mostly as a diplomat and tax collector among the BERBER confederacies, around 1375 Ibn Khaldun sought refuge at a Sufi shrine. He resigned from his royal duties and moved with his family into seclusion in a small town in ALGERIA. For the next four years he wrote *Muqaddimah,* which not only recounted the history of the region's Berbers and Arabs, but also outlined a method for the historical study of society. According to many historians the work was a masterpiece, as well as the first study of its kind. It foreshadowed contemporary sociology by arguing that societies are held together by 'asabiyah (social cohesion), a characteristic that exists in everything from kinship relations to dynasties, and which may be amplified by the unifying force of religion. While he was working on *Muqaddimah*, Ibn Khaldun began his history of North Africa, *Kitab al-ibar* (Universal History). He continued writing after he returned to Tunis, but soon afterward he fell out of favor with the powerful imam, or religious leader, of the city's mosque. In 1382 he began a pilgrimage to Mecca. He stopped in the city of CAIRO, and remained there under the patronage of EGYPT's Mamluk ruler. Tragically, his family died in a shipwreck en route to join him. While in Cairo, Ibn Khaldun continued writing his massive history, taught at the famous Islamic university al-Azhar, became a grand Maliki judge, and once again became embroiled in dynastic politics. In his remaining years Ibn Khaldun traveled further through the Arab world, whose history he recorded for posterity. Finally he made his way to Mecca. In 1400 he traveled with Cairo's new sultan to the besieged city of Damascus, where the armies of the Tatar ruler Tamerlane had taken possession. Ibn Khaldun's reputation preceded him, and he enjoyed a hospitality not afforded to the conquered masses outside the camp's gates. After presenting the conqueror with a written history of North Africa, Ibn Khaldun returned to Cairo, where he lived until his death six years later.

See also ISLAM IN AFRICA; MAMLUK STATE.

MARIAN AGUIAR

Ibrahim, Abdullah

1934–
Prominent South African jazz pianist.

Born in CAPE TOWN, SOUTH AFRICA, Adolphus Brand (also known as Dollar Brand and Adolphus Johannes Brand) began studying piano as a young child. As a teenager in Cape Town he earned the nickname "Dollar" because he always carried United States currency to purchase the latest jazz albums from American sailors. His formidable musical talent soon landed him a spot in the Shantytown Sextet, a band strongly influenced by the American mainstream jazz trend toward leaner groups after the demise of the big-band sound. The Shantytown Sextet played in a style called bebop mbaqanga. In 1959 Brand, together with Hugh Masekela and Kippie Moeketsi, formed the Jazz Epistles, a group that won the jazz competition at the first Castle Larger Festival, held in JOHANNESBURG in 1961.

In 1962, shortly after marrying the singer Sathima Bea Benjamin, Dollar Brand and the other members of the Jazz Epistles fled the oppressive APARTHEID policies of South Africa to settle in Zurich, Switzerland. There he caught the eye of Duke Ellington, who was on tour. Ellington introduced Brand to the American jazz scene, arranging for the South African musician to record an album and to play at the Newport Jazz Festival on several occasions.

In 1968 Brand converted to Islam, changed his name to Abdullah Ibrahim, and returned to South Africa a world-famous musician. Of the more than forty albums he recorded, his 1974 album *Mannenburg* is considered his seminal work, drawing on both the slow-tempo marabi South African style and American jazz elements. In 1976 Ibrahim fled apartheid oppression once again and settled in New York, where he formed the band Ekaya. During the 1980s Ibrahim broadened his range to include orchestral music. He wrote an opera, *Kalahari Liberation*, which was well received in Europe, and also performed with the Munich Radio Philharmonic.

With the erosion of apartheid in the early 1990s, Ibrahim returned to play music in South Africa. He remains one of the most respected musicians in contemporary jazz, voted top jazz pianist by *Downbeat* magazine for three consecutive years during the 1990s. He resides in Cape Town, where he has established a music school, the M7 Academy. His recent projects include an album with the German radio NDR Big Band. In 2006 he founded the Cape Town Jazz Orchestra. His most recent recordings include *African Magic* (2002) and *Senzo* (2008).

See also ISLAM IN AFRICA; MUSIC, AFRICAN.

ARI NAVE

Idoma
Ethnic group of Nigeria.

The Idoma primarily inhabit Benue State of southeastern NIGERIA and speak a Niger-Congo language. They are an ethnic group of roughly 600,000 people.

See also ETHNICITY AND IDENTITY IN AFRICA: AN INTERPRETATION; LANGUAGES, AFRICAN: AN OVERVIEW.

Idris I
1890–1983
Emir of independent Libya and a leader of the struggle for decolonization from Italy.

Sidi Muhammad Idris as-Sanusi was born in al-Joghboub, Libya, the son of Sayyid al-Mahdi, leader of the Sanusi, a powerful Islamic religious order. As heir to his father's position, Idris became the de facto ruler of the Libyan region of Cyrenaica, where the Sanusi order was based. Soon after he assumed leadership at the age of twenty-two, Idris began negotiations with Italy for recognition of an emirate in Cyrenaica. In 1920, in return for a promise that Cyrenaicans would lay down their arms, Italy acknowledged Idris as the autonomous Sanusi emir of several oases. Many nationalists from both Tripolitania and

Cyrenaica subsequently regarded Idris as the leader of the independence movement.

During World War II, Idris risked reprisal from Italy by allying with Great Britain. Following the Allied victory, he was installed as emir of Cyrenaica. Libyan support for the monarchy was in no way complete—some nationalists in Tripolitania sought a republic, or simply opposed a Cyrenaican-dominated state, and some Cyrenaicans wanted autonomy. Nevertheless, under the constitution of October 1951, Idris was declared emir of Libya. Due to continuing disagreement over the choice of a capital city, however, Idris was forced to establish two royal cities in two regions.

After the discovery of oil in Libya, Idris continued to cultivate strong trade and military ties with the West and authorized the construction of a giant oil pipeline. By the late 1960s, Idris faced growing unrest over his alliances and priorities from a movement of young pan-Arab republicans, led by Muammar al-Qaddafi. Perhaps sensing the changing tide, Idris left the country in June 1969 for a long medical stay in Turkey. On September 1, 1969, a group of soldiers deposed the emir in his absence. Although Idris ultimately accepted the coup and handed over power peacefully, he was later tried in absentia and sentenced to death. Idris continued to live in exile in Egypt until his death in 1983.

See also COLONIAL RULE; ISLAM IN AFRICA.

MARIAN AGUIAR

Ife

Ethnic group of West Africa.

The Ife primarily inhabit southwestern NIGERIA, although Ife populations can also be found in western BENIN. They speak Yoruba, a Niger-Congo language, and are one of the YORUBA peoples. Approximately one million people consider themselves Ife.

See also ETHNICITY AND IDENTITY IN AFRICA: AN INTERPRETATION; LANGUAGES, AFRICAN: AN OVERVIEW.

Ife, Art of the Early Kingdom of
Sculpture and pottery of the early kingdom that is present-day Nigeria.

The art of the early Ife kingdom, sometimes known as Ile-Ife, is unusual because unlike most other precolonial African sculpture, which was made of wood, early Ife art was made from metal, terra-cotta (baked clay), and other durable materials. The use of these materials means that today there is a strong historical record of the artistic traditions of Ife, which are among the most famous in West Africa.

IFE ARTWORKS. A terracotta scuplture of a Yoruba queen's head. This sculpture from Ita Yemoo in the Ife kingdom (modern-day Nigeria) dates from the 12th or 13th century. (National Commission for Museums and Monuments, Ife, Nigeria/Heini Schneebeli/Bridgeman Art Library International Ltd.)

Ife was an ancient city-state and capital of the Yoruba peoples of Nigeria. The ancient town still stands in southwestern Nigeria today, and it remains an important artistic and cultural center in the region, as it was from the eleventh to the fifteenth century C.E. When Leo Frobenius, a German traveler, first visited Ife in the early twentieth century, he was so impressed with the sophistication of the kingdom's artworks that he claimed to have discovered the mythic lost Atlantis, the fabled lost Greek civilization. Archaeological evidence revealed, however, that the art found at Ife was produced by African artists and patrons, and was not of European or Mediterranean origin.

The most famous Ife artworks are a series of human heads and figures. Made either from terra-cotta or copper alloys, these spectacular sculptures display a remarkable degree of naturalism that sets them apart from many other art forms in Africa, including much of the more recent Yoruba sculpture. Most Ife sculptures represent men and women of striking, idealized beauty. Other works are distinctive because they display individuals suffering from various congenital conditions or diseases such as dwarfism (which causes people to grow to less than normal height) or elephantiasis (which causes parts of the body to swell to enormous proportions). These figures seem to be connected to shrines associated with healing.

Many works of art from Ife are related to royalty. Notable among these is a life-size mask cast of pure copper. The mask is associated with the city's third ruler, Obalufon II. The ancient Ife throne, which was used for the coronation of Ife kings, was referred to as the throne of Obalufon. Fashioned by hand from hard quartz, the upper and lower sections of the throne are joined by a handle that resembles an elephant trunk. The throne is now in the British Museum in London.

A series of copper-alloy heads also appear to have been associated with Obalufon. These heads have holes around the hairline, presumably for the attachment of a beaded crown. This beaded crown may have inspired those worn by Yoruba monarchs in more recent history. Some of these heads bear distinctive scarification marks—often a series of long thin vertical lines—possibly representing different branches of the royal family. It was once thought that these heads were created in conjunction with funerals for the long succession of Ife rulers. But this theory has been ruled out because all the copper-alloy heads appear to have been made around the same time by a very few select artists. More likely they were used in ceremonies to legitimate the coronations of the various Yoruba kings having allegiance to Ife. Today Obalufon is honored in the Yoruba area as the god of metal-casters, and crowns and sculptures of metal are an important feature of Obalufon shrines.

Ancient shrines and historic sites around the city underscore its long-standing importance as a sacred site. Floors made with potsherds thought to have been part of old temple courtyards—as well as the sheer number of these bits of old pottery—offer evidence of the value placed on art by early residents. The potsherds have also helped scholars to date art works found nearby. Terra-cotta urns were unearthed in the twentieth century behind the Alafin (main palace) in what appears to have been a royal cemetery dating to around the twelfth century C.E. The urns have beautifully sculpted lids, some shaped to resemble animals such as elephants and rams. Some of the urns are decorated with stylized jewels.

See also ART AND ARCHITECTURE, AFRICAN.

Igala

Ethnic group of Nigeria; also known as Igara.
The Igala primarily inhabit Benue and Kogi states in southeastern NIGERIA. They speak a Niger-Congo language and are closely related to the IDOMA people. Approximately two million people consider themselves Igala.

See also ETHNICITY AND IDENTITY IN AFRICA: AN INTERPRETATION; LANGUAGES, AFRICAN: AN OVERVIEW.

Igbo

One of the major ethnic groups in Nigeria, with roughly 17 to 20 million Igbos concentrated in the southeastern part of the country.
Belonging to the Kwa subgroup of the Niger-Congo linguistic family, scholars believe the Igbo language separated from related languages such as YORUBA, IGALA, IDOMA, and EDO several thousand years ago. There are some thirty Igbo dialects, which vary in their mutual intelligibility; Owerri Igbo and Onitsha Igbo are the most widely understood "standard" dialects. The traditional Igbo homeland lies on both sides of the lower NIGER RIVER, though most Igbo live to the east of the Niger between the Niger Delta and the Benue Valley. Igboland is one of Africa's most densely populated regions. Although Igbo speakers fall into over a dozen subgroups, they share a common culture and have lived in the same area for thousands of years.

The Igbo have a long history of cultural achievement. Traditionally, the Igbo have excelled at metalwork, weaving, and woodcarving. Excavations at the village of Igbo-Ukwu have unearthed sophisticated cast bronze artifacts and textiles dating from the ninth century. Since ancient times, the Igbo have traded craft goods and agricultural products. Traditional Igbo religion varied regionally, but generally included a belief in an afterlife and reincarnation, sacrifice, and spirit and ancestor worship. The Igbo performed elaborate ceremonies marking funerals and other life passages.

Unlike some of their neighbors, the Igbo never developed a centralized monarchy. Chiefs or kings with limited powers ruled the villages of a few subgroups, such as the Nri, the Onitsha Igbo, and groups to the west of the Niger. Until the colonial era, however, most Igbo lived in autonomous, fairly democratic villages, where a complex structure of kinship ties, secret societies, professional organizations, oracles, and religious leaders regulated village society. This mix of overlapping institutions gave most Igbo some decision-making power and prevented any single person from gaining too much power.

Europeans arrived in the late fifteenth century, and by the late seventeenth century the area became a major center for the slave trade. Many Igbo, especially those living along the Niger River, became traders who sold captives from the interior, including both interior Igbo and members of other ethnic groups. The British (and their North American colonists) played a key role in this trade during the 1700s. Igboland exported large quantities of palm oil after the British suppressed the slave trade in the early 1800s. The British wanted to encourage what they called "legitimate trade" in products, such as palm oil, needed in British manufacturing. Later in the century, the British sought to establish effective control over Igboland, and the decentralized Igbo could not resist British advances. In 1885 the British established the Oil Rivers Protectorate, named for Igboland's abundant palm oil. By the 1890s the British had occupied the area. They imposed indirect rule in 1900 by appointing African warrant officers, who frequently lacked any standing in the Igbo communities they were supposed to oversee.

The decentralization and cultural openness of the Igbo made them prime targets for missionaries. Today most Igbo are Christian, and they have a high literacy rate. From the colonial period onward, the Igbo produced disproportionate numbers of civil servants and military officers. Educated Igbo thus played a central role in the struggle for Nigerian independence. NIGERIA's first president, NNAMDI AZIKIWE, was an Igbo. When the country achieved independence in 1960 thousands of Igbo moved to cities all over Nigeria to work as civil servants and administrators. Members of other groups, especially in the north, came to resent the perceived Igbo dominance.

Rising ethnic tensions followed the discovery in the mid-1960s that Nigeria had large oil reserves, mostly in or near Igboland. Many Igbo feared that plans to redraw the boundaries of Nigeria's internal administrative divisions would reduce their political clout and deprive them of revenue by placing the main oil-producing regions in divisions outside Igbo control. In 1966, following protests that the presidential election had been rigged, a group of Igbo military officers staged a coup. A countercoup by northern officers followed, along with a massacre of Igbo living in the north. In 1967 the military governor of the eastern region, Lieutenant Colonel Ojukwu, declared the independent state of BIAFRA, dominated by the Igbo. Nigerian forces quickly forced the Biafran troops to withdraw to a small territory in Igboland, where hundreds of thousands of Igbo starved before Biafra surrendered to Nigerian troops in 1970.

The central government was largely magnanimous in victory. They failed to take reprisals against the Igbo and allowed Ojukwu to return from exile. While ethnic tensions remain, the Igbo are again integrated into Nigerian society. They play an important role in the oil-producing economy based in the cities of the southeast, though Igbo reside in cities throughout Nigeria. Several of Nigeria's leading writers are Igbo, including Chinua Achebe, CYPRIAN EKWENSI, and Nkem Nwankwo.

See also CHRISTIANITY: MISSIONARIES IN AFRICA; COLONIAL RULE; ETHNICITY AND IDENTITY IN AFRICA: AN INTERPRETATION and LANGUAGES, AFRICAN: AN OVERVIEW.

DAVID P. JOHNSON, JR.

Igede

Ethnic group of Nigeria; also known as Egede and Igedde.
The Igede primarily inhabit Benue State in southeastern NIGERIA. They speak a Niger-Congo language and are closely related to the IDOMA people. Approximately 300,000 people consider themselves Igede.

See also ETHNICITY AND IDENTITY IN AFRICA: AN INTERPRETATION; LANGUAGES, AFRICAN: AN OVERVIEW.

Ihetu, Dick ("Tiger")
1929–1971
Nigerian professional boxer.
Known as Dick Tiger, Ihetu won boxing crowns as both a middleweight and a light-heavyweight. Born in Nigeria, little is known of his childhood, but records show he began his professional career in 1952, compiling a record of sixteen wins, one loss over the next four years. A strong counterpuncher, Ihetu was known for his left hook. In 1956 he moved to England, where his career at first faltered—he won five and lost four bouts in his first year there. But he soon regained his form, winning thirteen out of fifteen fights over the next two years, and becoming the British Commonwealth middleweight title-holder along the way.

Ihetu first fought in the United States in 1959, and by 1962 had won the World Boxing Association middleweight title by defeating American Gene Fullmer in fifteen rounds. He twice defended the title against Fullmer in 1963, fighting in Las Vegas and in Ibadan, Nigeria. In December 1963, however, he lost the title to Joey Giardello, an American boxer. Two years later Ihetu defeated Giardello to regain his title, but lost it again in 1966. Now fighting as a light middleweight, Ihetu won the WBA title for that weight class (which comprises fighters from 160 to 175 pounds) in December 1966, successfully defending it until May 1968, when the thirty-seven-year-old Ihetu was knocked out for the first time in his career. He won his next three fights, but retired in 1970 with a final record of sixty-one wins (twenty-six by knockout), seventeen losses, and three draws. He died the following year.

See also ATHLETES, AFRICAN, ABROAD.

KATE TUTTLE

Ijaw

Ethnic group of the Niger Delta in Nigeria; also known as Ijo.
Living in a region covered with mangrove swamps and frequently flooded fields, the Ijaw have for centuries combined fishing and agriculture as their main economic activities. According to Ijaw legend, all Ijaw descend from a common ancestor who arrived in the NIGER Delta in the fifteenth century. Many anthropologists believe, however, that the Ijaw are made up of formerly autonomous village groups who may have lived in the area longer than any other local ethnic group. Their language is distinct from those of their neighbors.

In addition to fishing, farming, and collecting palm oil, the Ijaw manufactured salt by leaching it from seawater that flowed into the Niger River delta. During the African SALT TRADE the Ijaw developed experience as traders. They later used these trading skills, becoming influential brokers in the transatlantic slave trade. European demand also created a vast market for palm oil, and some Ijaw traders built vast fortunes from the trade. Economic and regional pressures forged a sense of identity among the Ijaw people, uniting formerly autonomous villages behind such larger communities as Calabar, Bonny, and Nemke. To some extent, traders replaced kings as Ijaw leaders, and even some former slaves gained prominence.

During the mid-twentieth century, life changed drastically for the Ijaw. The discovery of natural gas and oil in their land brought the Ijaw, with the rest of NIGERIA, into contact with multinational corporations. Oil brought some new jobs to the delta region; however, its inhabitants felt increasingly oppressed by the oil companies and the destruction of the local fishing economy that came with petroleum production. In the late 1990s and early 2000s some of the Ijaw, especially young people, openly revolted against major oil companies and sabotaged oil operations in order to take back resources that they viewed as their birthright. Population figures for the Ijaw vary widely, though it is possible that as many as 15 million people belong to that group.

See also ETHNICITY AND IDENTITY IN AFRICA: AN INTERPRETATION; LANGUAGES, AFRICAN: AN OVERVIEW.

Ijebu

Ethnic group of Nigeria.
The Ijebu primarily inhabit Ogun State, southwestern NIGERIA. They speak Yoruba, a Niger-Congo language, and are one of the YORUBA peoples. Though exact population figures are hard to come by, it appears that well more than 800,000 people consider themselves Ijebu.

See also ETHNICITY AND IDENTITY IN AFRICA: AN INTERPRETATION; LANGUAGES, AFRICAN: AN OVERVIEW.

Imam, Ayesha Mje-Tei

Contemporary Nigerian human rights activist and educator.
Ayesha Mje-Tei Imam has won international recognition for her work in support of human rights in Africa, especially the rights of women who live in Islamic nations. Although much of her work has concerned her native country of Nigeria, Imam has contributed to research and to human-rights, pro-democracy, and gender-awareness programs in a number of other countries as well.

Imam studied in England, receiving a bachelor of science degree in sociology from the Polytechnic of North London in 1980. Seven years later she received a master of science degree in the same subject from Ahmadu Bello University in Zaria, Nigeria. Imam went on to earn a doctor of philosophy degree in social anthropology from the School of African and Asian Studies of the University of Brighton, England.

While pursuing her educational goals during the 1980s, Imam also began her work as a teacher and activist. In 1984, working with the Council for the Development of Social Science in Africa in Dakar, Senegal, she directed a program that developed two-month courses on gender issues for young African social scientists. The following year she advised the Institute for Economic Development and Planning (IDEP) of the United Nations on the role of gender in economic development. Through these activities, Imam gained threefold recognition—as a scholar of women's roles and gender-related issues in African society, as an educator working to teach others about those roles and issues, and an advocate for women's rights.

Of special interest to Imam is the status of women in northern Nigeria and other parts of Africa where Muslim law often limits their roles and rights. In 1992 she became an officer of an international network called Women Living Under Muslim Laws. She oversaw studies on women and the law in twenty-six countries in Africa, Asia, and the Middle East, and helped train local groups in thirteen countries. Imam has also been closely involved with several other advocacy groups for women's rights. She organized Women in Nigeria (WIN), the country's first feminist organization, and she is the founder and director of BAOBAB, a volunteer group that works to protect women's rights as they are shaped by tradition and also by the law, both civil and religious.

Imam and BAOBAB have led campaigns against conservative forms of shari'a (traditional Islamic law) that they feel discriminate against women. In several Nigerian legal cases that have received international publicity—cases involving women threatened under shari'a with extreme punishments, such as death by stoning for sexual relations outside marriage—Imam has spoken out for women's rights, risking angry reactions from conservative Muslims. In 2002 she won the John Humphrey Human Rights Award for her work with BAOBAB. Now living and working in the United States, Imam plans to publish some of the research she has done on women's rights and the law.

REBECCA STEFOFF

Imbangala
Militant sect that originated in the central highlands of Angola; also known as Isinde and Jaga.

The Imabangala, a militant sect that emerged in the late sixteenth century, was responsible for considerable social disruption throughout the region that is present-day Angola. The term kimbangala (singular form Imbangala) is of uncertain origin, but possibly refers to the walled enclosure of their military camps. According to the earliest accounts, Imbangala originated in the kingdom of Bembe, an important but little known state in modern-day Bié Province in Angola. When first encountered by Europeans around 1600, the Imbangala were engaged in constant raiding and warfare—several armed bands, possibly with little connection among them save a recognition of a similar lifestyle, that lived primarily by what they could capture.

Imbangala raided communities, harvesting crops and depleting palm groves to make palm wine. They killed wantonly, but took adolescent children into their bands to increase their numbers. According to tradition, the Imbangala did not permit babies among their numbers, and would kill infants, relying on forced recruitment of children as their primary method of replacing members and enlarging the group. These children were inducted into the band through a series of brutal rituals designed to inculcate fear and ultimately loyalty in them. Once fully integrated into the band, any member could rise to the highest positions on the basis of military-style promotions. The Imbangala also practiced ritual cannibalism, in part as a tactic to instill terror within their own group and among those they planned to fight, and in part as a sort of antireligious strategy in which they embraced practices that were considered witchcraft or evil by others.

At first, the Imbangala operated in the region south of the Kwanza River, although as early as 1600 they sometimes sold their captives to Portuguese slave traders from the colony of Angola. Around 1615, however, Angolan governor Bento Banha Cardoso invited several bands to come north of the Kwanza to fight as mercenaries in the Portuguese army. The bands that came, especially that from Kasanje, contributed greatly to Portuguese military success in their wars against Ndongo. But the Imbangala bands were too destructive to be reliable allies and within a few years some bands, such as the Kalandula, Kaza, and Kasanje, were raiding more or less independently. Over the course of the next thirty-five years—from 1622 to 1657—the stable powers of the region either destroyed the bands or integrated them into their own armies as regularly deployed troops. Kasanje, which remained independent, formed its own kingdom in the valley of the Kwango River.

Imbangala bands remained active for a longer period south of the Kwanza, where they were still a part of the scene in the eighteenth century. Even there, however, they largely abandoned the nomadic, pillaging lifestyle of their predecessors and became stable if often predatory polities in the central highlands.

JOHN THORNTON

Indian Communities in Africa
South Asian immigrants and their descendants in East Africa and South Africa.

In 1972 IDI AMIN, the dictator of UGANDA, ordered the immediate expulsion of Asians—as people of Indian or South Asian descent—from his country. Amin's policy with regard to Asians was harsher than those of other African nations, but it played on tensions that exist elsewhere on the continent. It also raised questions about the future social, economic, and political roles of Asians in the African countries where they already had long histories. Besides Uganda, these countries include MAURITIUS, KENYA, TANZANIA, MALAWI, SOUTH AFRICA, and ZAMBIA.

EAST AFRICA
Although South Asians had been trading with people on the east coast of Africa since the first millennium B.C.E., British Colonial Rule transformed the relationship between these trading partners and their respective continents. The areas of India controlled by the British East India Company during the nineteenth century provided a source of labor for the exploration and colonization of East Africa and Mauritius. In 1815 the British in Mauritius began importing Indian convicts to rear silkworms. After 1834 they imported indentured labor for road building and plantation work.

After the British Imperial East African Company was granted its royal charter in 1888, it encouraged Indian immigration to East Africa, primarily to provide indentured labor for railway construction. Most of the immigrants were poor younger sons from middle castes, or peasants released from land debts in their home villages. Many came from agricultural parts of the Indian regions of Uttar Pradesh, Bihar, and Madras. According to Indian colonial law, forty women were recruited for every hundred men in order to provide at least some semblance of a stable immigrant society. For the most part, these Indians did not permanently settle in East Africa; only about one-fourth of them stayed beyond their term of service. The permanent South Asian community was made up of the traders, artisans, and professionals who arrived after the establishment of the indentured settlements, particularly after World War I ended in 1918. They were Hindus, Muslims, Sikhs, and Christians, primarily from Gujarati- and Punjabi-speaking areas, as well as from Konkani-speaking Goa.

Indians came to occupy the middle level of a three-tiered hierarchy in British colonial Africa—below white settlers and above Africans. In general, Indians enjoyed fewer restrictions on property ownership than Africans and better access to the resources needed for commercial enterprises, such as bank credit. Consequently, greater numbers of Indians were able to establish themselves as shop owners, hoteliers, commercial farmers, and export merchants. Although the economic mobility available to this group did not immediately provoke anti-Indian sentiment amongst Africans, it did set the stage for later tensions.

By the early twentieth century, white settlers and Africans alike were beginning to resent the Indian communities' control over important sectors of the economy. There were social tensions as well. Indians were accused of discriminating against non-Indians. In fact, the Indian community was itself not homogeneous, and caste, religious, and language identities regulated relationships within it just as race sometimes restricted relations outside it. To shift the balance of economic power, settlers successfully pressured for immigration regulations. The 1915 Crown Lands Ordinance, for example, restricted Indians from owning land in Kenya's fertile highland regions. Despite such measures, another wave of Indian immigration to East Africa began in the 1920s, this time bringing accountants, teachers, technicians, and other professionals. The Asian population in East Africa swelled from approximately 34,000 in 1915 to 105,000 by 1939.

Indians were already beginning to organize in East Africa, inspired in part by anticolonial resistance in India. The East African Indian National Congress, formed in 1914, demanded equal rights and, later, compensation for Indians' service in World War I. East African nationalist movements drew not only on the example of the successful anticolonial movement in India, which secured independence in 1947, but also on the active participation of some Indians in East Africa's nationalist organizations. Indians also defended African interests when, as members of colonial legislatures, they represented Africans in the years before blacks won direct representation in government.

In 1959, Ugandan businessman Augustine Kamya led the first major anti-Asian boycott. In addition to the boycott, vandals targeted Asian traders, and Africans who defied the boycotts were also subject to violence. Asians faced a series of official and unofficial discriminatory policies throughout East Africa in the 1960s. Tanzania began nationalizing banking and trade firms in the 1960s and later effectively took over Asian businesses by seizing all rented buildings above a certain value. As a result, the country's Asian population dropped from 88,700 in 1961 to 52,000 in 1971. In Kenya, where in 1967 the government started restricting immigration as well as noncitizens' access to trade and work permits, the Asian population dropped from 176,613 in 1962 to approximately 105,000 in 1982. In Malawi, Asians' land was confiscated, and noncitizens were deported; in 1968, Zambian president Kenneth KAUNDA banned noncitizens' businesses in both rural and urban areas. The most severe discrimination was in Uganda, where President Milton OBOTE's nationalization scheme and restrictions on work permits drove down the Asian population by 35 percent between independence and 1971. That year Kaunda was overthrown by Amin, who ordered all Asians to leave the country within ninety days. Citizens and residents of Asian origin fled in terror from Uganda, forfeiting their properties and savings. The Indians who left East Africa relocated in many places, but primarily Britain and India. In 1990 the Ugandan government under President Yoweri MUSEVENI offered repatriation and compensation for Asian exiles. Several hundred families have since returned to Uganda.

SOUTH AFRICA
The history of Indians in South Africa is different from that of Indians in East Africa, both because of the concentration of Indians in the Natal region of South Africa and because of Indians' participation in the The Dutch Cape Colony, founded in 1652 in the southern part of modern-day South Africa, which imported slaves from the Dutch East Indian empire as well as from other parts of Africa until the early nineteenth century. Great Britain took over the colony in 1806 and outlawed slavery in 1834. After that time, European colonialists in southern Africa recruited indentured laborers from many parts of Asia, but particularly from India. The eastern province of Natal, especially the city of Durban, became a center for the Indian community in South Africa. Indians worked on sugar plantations and road and railway projects, in mines, and as domestics in British and Afrikaner homes. As in East Africa, many of the immigrants were from rural regions of Uttar Pradesh

and Bihar, but a good portion also came from Tamil and Telugu-speaking areas. More than 150,000 indentured workers arrived in Natal between 1860 and 1911.

Few laws protected indentured workers against exploitation by recruiters and employers. After 1875, however, legal reforms in Natal improved the rights of indentured laborers who completed their five-year terms of service, encouraging more Indians to settle permanently. The colony's whites viewed the increasing Indian population with apprehension—in the words of a London journalist, they feared the colony "might soon be submerged in dusky waters." A Natal government commission recommended deportation, or, if that was not possible, segregation. The 1891 Immigration Act banned land grants to former indentured laborers, eliminating one incentive planters had used to maintain a stable work force. Four years later the government imposed a tax on indentured and ex-indentured laborers and their families. Yet even as these measures encouraged indentured laborers to return to India, the population of "passenger Indians"—those who paid their own way from India or Mauritius—increased. This group included large-scale merchants, many of them Gujarati Muslims, as well as small traders, artisans, preachers, and teachers. The result was that by 1904, Indians outnumbered whites in Natal. When Natal outlawed indentured labor in 1911, the decision was influenced equally by concern in British India about labor shortages and the exploitation of Indians, and by resistance to further Indian immigration on the part of South African settlers.

In the Afrikaner South Africa Republic, also known as the TRANSVAAL, Indians could not become citizens or own property. When the British took over the Afrikaner states, they effectively maintained racial segregation in urban areas. Segregation, taxes, and the South African government's refusal to recognize anything but Christian marriages inspired the passive resistance campaign led by the Indian lawyer Mohandas Gandhi. Based in Durban, Gandhi had been teaching the satyagraha, a philosophy of nonviolent resistance, since 1894, when he became the first secretary of the Natal Indian Congress (NIC). The growing momentum of Gandhi's movement exploded in 1913 with strikes by Indian workers as well as defiance of discriminatory laws. The movement ultimately caused the government to retract the tax and acknowledge Hindu and Muslim marriages.

The push for segregation and deportation of South African Asians to India—euphemistically termed repatriation, even though it would involve the forcible expulsion of people from their native land—continued. In 1914 the South African government began to offer free passage to Indians returning to India and, later, added payments as an extra incentive. The 1924 Class Areas Bill and 1925 Areas

Reservation Bill, forerunners of later segregation laws, had the admitted aim of reducing the Indian population in Natal through the threat of segregation. Citing the ultimate goal of pushing Indians out of South Africa, politicians who sponsored such acts as the 1932 Transvaal Asiatic Land Tenure Act—which limited Indian trading by preventing Indians from acquiring property outside designated areas—introduced permanently the principle of statutory segregation. Despite this act, Natal's Indian community continued to grow.

The tensions between Indians and white traders, as well as poor Afrikaners, helped propel the National Party to power in 1948. The National Party government's 1950 Group Areas Act was one of many laws that enforced racial segregation. In Durban alone, the act forced 75,000 Indians to relocate and give up valuable land outside the city. The National Party eased its pressure for deportation, however. Some historians have argued that it did so because it wanted the black population to turn its opposition against the Indians instead of against the white government. Those who advance this theory point to Indian-African race riots in Durban in 1949 as evidence that the tactic worked.

Overall, however, political solidarity between Indians and Africans increased between the 1920s and the 1950s. Important Indian groups during this period included the NIC and the countrywide South African Indian Congress (founded in 1919). The NIC became an organizing model for the African National Congress (ANC). Both Indian organizations had links to high-profile Coloured (of mixed African and European heritage) and African activists such as Abdurrahman of the African Peoples' Organization, Bantu Professor D. D. T. Jabavu, and ANC leader Reverend John L. Dube.

As the Indian community grew from its immigrant roots, it took on more of an urban character, and contact between Indian and black workers increased, particularly in the labor movement. Indian leaders such as Dr. Yusuf Dadoo and Nana Sita publicly supported the ANC, and activists such as Ahmed Kathrada were imprisoned for their activism to promote racial justice. In the 1970s the NIC, which had been defunct for several years, joined the ANC in mobilizing young Indians into political action against apartheid. Indian activists and lawyers filled gaps in the antiapartheid struggle left by exiled or imprisoned ANC leaders. Later they played a more direct role in the United Democratic Front, an antiapartheid alliance formed in 1983. In addition, India's government aided the ANC and appealed to the United Nations about Indians' mistreatment in South Africa. India was the first nation to cut ties with South Africa over the issue of apartheid.

Compared to South Africa's black population, however, South Africa's Indians enjoyed relative freedom, particularly after the National Party began easing restrictions in order to win the support of the Indians. During the late 1960s and 1970s, Indians were granted limited representation within the government and allowed to take middle-management, manufacturing, and service jobs that were prohibited to blacks.

In post-apartheid South Africa as in East Africa, the economic successes of Indians have caused tension. Polls in 1994 showed that the majority of Indian voters, a group that had previously supported the ANC, now leaned toward the National Party. This conservative shift has been attributed to an Indian fear of losing economic power to the growing black business class. Other analyses point out that it might take some time to overcome the legacy of apartheid—a system that not only separated groups by race but fostered conflict between them. Today, more than 1.1 million Indians make their homes in South Africa.

MARIAN AGUIAR

Indian Ocean Slave Trade

Forced movement of people under bondage across the Indian Ocean.

The Indian Ocean slave trade is to a certain extent a misnomer, as it subsumes two historically and geographically distinct trades that shared only the body of water they crossed. For more than 1,000 years, Arab traders transported African slaves across the Indian Ocean to the Arabian Peninsula, the Persian Gulf, and Asia. Centuries later they were joined by European slave traders who brought large numbers of Africans to the Mascarenes and other Indian Ocean islands, as well as to the Americas. Because the early Arab traders left few surviving records, it is difficult to estimate how many Africans they took across the Indian Ocean as slaves. It is likely, however, that the number would be comparable to the seven to ten million Africans shipped across the Atlantic, though over a much longer period of time.

ARAB SLAVE TRADE

The earliest Arab traders probably voyaged to the east coast of Africa on dhows, small sailing ships developed during the first millennium B.C.E. Unlike the slave traders who crossed the Atlantic centuries later, Arab slave merchants were predominantly small dealers who transported fewer than one hundred slaves at a time, and usually also traded in other commodities, such as ivory, spices, and leather.

The first direct evidence of a sizable Indian Ocean slave trade dates to the seventh century C.E., when large numbers of East African male slaves labored on the plantations of the Abbasid Caliphate, in Mesopotamia. Slaves exported by Arab traders to southwest Asia, India, Indonesia, and China worked mainly as soldiers, concubines, and household servants. But African slaves were engaged in diverse occupations—in Bahrein and Lingeh, for example, they dove for pearls. Although legally they were assigned the status of chattel, Muslim law accorded slaves basic human rights. Thus, many slaves attained relatively high social status as concubines and bureaucrats, while others worked under harsh conditions and periodically rebelled. In the late ninth century, for example, tens of thousands of African slaves in Abbasid revolted.

The Arab Indian Ocean slave trade subsequently went into decline for several centuries, as Arab and Asian demand for slaves was eclipsed by a demand for other African commodities such as gold and ivory. It increased again in the late seventeenth century to meet a growing demand for labor on date plantations in Oman and, later, the sugar plantations on the Mascarene Island colonies. Large slave markets developed in Zanzibar and Pemba where, at the height of the trade, as many as 15,000 to 20,000 slaves passed through annually. The slave trade became so significant that in 1840 the Sultan of Oman moved his seat of power to Zanzibar. In the East African interior, peoples such as the Nyamwezi, Ngoni, Yao, and Makua raided neighboring communities and sold their captives to Arab caravans, often in exchange for firearms. In addition to the many East African slaves sent to the distant shores of Arabia and the Persian Gulf, others remained as laborers on Arab plantations in East Africa, such as the Omani clove farms on Zanzibar.

Long after European countries outlawed the transatlantic slave trade in the early nineteenth century, Arab dhows continued to disembark from Zanzibar, Mombasa, and other depots, little hindered by the British fleet that patrolled the Indian Ocean seeking to enforce the prohibition on slaving.

EUROPEAN SLAVE TRADE

European slave-traders began operating in the Indian Ocean during the seventeenth century, when the settlement of the Mascarene Islands increased the demand for cheap labor. Some East African slaves during this period were shipped around the Cape of Good Hope and across the Atlantic to Caribbean colonies such as Saint-Domingue (present-day Haiti). During the eighteenth and nineteenth centuries, more and more East African slaves were sent to the Indian Ocean island colonies, such as Île de France (in Mauritius), and Réunion. Although the vast majority of slaves ultimately would labor in the sugarcane fields, initially slaves built the islands' colonial infrastructures and cleared fields of rocks.

As the British attempted to impose controls on the West African slave trade at the beginning of the nineteenth century, European slavers grew to rely upon East African markets to supply their ships. Mozambican slaves were primarily destined for Brazil and Cuba. At the height of the Indian Ocean slave trade to European colonies, as many as 15,000 slaves from Mozambique alone were exported annually. Similar numbers flowed through Zanzibar as well. The Indian Ocean slave trade did not, however, consist entirely of exports from the African mainland; in addition to slaves taken from Madagascar, the Mascarene Islands also imported slaves from India and Malaysia.

Although the slave trade was formally abolished after Britain took possession of Mauritius in 1810, slavery remained an integral part of the economy until 1835. British agents signed a treaty with Radama, the Merina king of Madagascar, to eliminate Madagascar as a principal source of slaves in the Indian Ocean. But the Merina court did not have complete control over Madagascar, nor was it entirely invested in the abolition of slavery. The independent Sakalava kingdom of Madagascar continued to route East African and Comorian slaves though Madagascar before shipping them to Mauritius under a "free labour emigration scheme." Likewise, French traders shipped slaves from Mozambique to the many islands of the Seychelles, and then introduced them "legally" to Mauritius as slaves that existed before the ban on the trade and property of French estate owners. Zanzibar and Kilwa also remained active export centers until the 1870s.

IMPACT ON EAST AFRICAN SOCIETIES
The Indian Ocean slave trade provided one route for the introduction of Islam to East Africa, and it had many other lasting social consequences as well. Particularly as the slave trade escalated from the seventeenth through the nineteenth centuries, large regions of eastern, southern, and Central Africa suffered social disruption and depopulation. Although slavery had existed within Africa for centuries, typically it was not a commercial enterprise but rather a means of extending kinship relations and increasing social status. External demand for slaves resulted in forced migrations; weaker groups fled from slave raiders pursuing the accumulation of wealth and power made possible by the new market-based trade. While raiders traded slaves for rifles and ammunition, violence spread across the East African interior, as the missionary David Livingstone observed when he visited the Lake Nyasa region in the mid-nineteenth century. Not long afterward, the need to abolish slavery and "pacify" the region became one of the primary justifications for the European colonization of East Africa.

See also INDIAN COMMUNITIES IN AFRICA; ISLAM IN AFRICA; SLAVERY IN AFRICA.

ARI NAVE

Inkatha Freedom Party
South African political party based in the KwaZulu-Natal province.
The Inkatha Freedom Party was originally formed as a Zulu cultural association, but for years it has been one of South Africa's most controversial political forces. Its leader, Mangosutho Gatsha Buthelezi, was at one time a member of the African National Congress (ANC) but has become one of the ANC's most formidable rivals. Today, despite the widespread opinion that Buthelezi commands a corrupt and undemocratic—and strictly ethnocentric—organization, Inkatha remains the dominant party in KwaZulu-Natal province.

Inkatha, the political party, has its roots in Inkatha Ya Ka Zulu (Zulu National Movement), a cultural organization founded in 1928. In 1974, some twenty years after South Africa's apartheid government designated bantustans, or "Bantu homelands," for all the nation's major African ethnic groups, Buthelezi renewed Inkatha as Inkatha ye Nkululeko Ye Sizwe (National Cultural Liberation Movement). KwaZulu, like the other homelands, was partly self-governed, but Bantustan ministers were regarded as puppets of the national government. Most observers believe that Buthelezi revived Inkatha to undermine the Zulu King Goodwill Zwelithini, his only rival for power in KwaZulu.

Buthelezi, who had spoken out openly against apartheid, nonetheless supported the bantustan system. He also emphasized that Inkatha, unlike many black South African political organizations, was pro-capitalist. Although Buthelezi has often reminded audiences of his close ties with Nelson Mandela, throughout the 1970s Inkatha criticized the ANC's support of student protests and presented itself as an alternative movement. Its less ideologically militant stance, stressing cooperation with the existing regime, made Inkatha palatable to South African whites as well as to western governments. Following the Soweto uprising in 1976, Buthelezi's cooperation with the South African police in forming anti-militant vigilante groups confirmed the suspicions of critics, especially within the Black Consciousness Movement, who had branded him a government puppet.

The ANC officially broke with Inkatha in 1980, after Buthelezi leaked details of private meetings with exiled ANC leaders. The two organizations soon became bitter enemies. Never as large or as powerful as the ANC, Inkatha dropped its initially nonviolent stance; throughout the 1980s, armed Buthelezi supporters carried out strikes against ANC and United Democratic Front (UDF) supporters. Inkatha was reportedly responsible for dozens of assassinations at ANC funerals.

In 1990 Inkatha became an official political party, the Inkatha Freedom Party. A year later, reports emerged that

Inkatha had received past support from the South African Security Police and Military Intelligence forces. Buthelezi, seeking a sovereign Zulu state, nearly forced a delay in the 1994 elections with Inkatha demonstrations and rioting. At the last minute he allowed his name to be placed on the ballot as a candidate for president in the national elections. Inkatha won 10.5 percent of the national vote and forty-three legislative seats. Buthelezi was named minister of home affairs, but he and other representatives of Inkatha demanded more autonomy for the KwaZulu-Natal than the ANC-dominated government was prepared to allow. In April 1995, Inkatha members withdrew from the parliament. They remained absent when the country's new constitution was ratified in May 1996 but rejoined the government later that year and have held seats in the legislature ever since. Buthelezi continued to head Inkatha in the early years of the twenty-first century.

KATE TUTTLE

Iramba
Ethnic group of Tanzania; also known as Anilamba.

The Iramba, who speak a BANTU language, primarily inhabit central TANZANIA. Nearly 800,000 people consider themselves Iramba.

See also BANTU: DISPERSION AND SETTLEMENT; ETHNICITY AND IDENTITY IN AFRICA: AN INTERPRETATION; LANGUAGES, AFRICAN: AN OVERVIEW.

Iraqw
Ethnic group of central Tanzania.

According to oral history, the ancestors of the Iraqw migrated to their present location from Mesopotamia (modern-day Iraq). During this journey, the group developed a unique language that incorporated aspects of Cushitic, Nilotic, KHOISAN, and BANTU languages. At least three different groups split from the main group; one of these, the present-day Iraqw, traveled down the Great Rift Valley and into the Mbulu and Hanang district of TANZANIA. There they settled in scattered, locally governed villages, raised cattle and goats, and cultivated subsistence crops.

During the nineteenth century, the Iraqw avoided contact with merchants, missionaries, and other Europeans. Under German and British COLONIAL RULE, however, the Iraqw were forced to begin cultivating commercial crops, such as millet and maize. After independence the Iraqw attempted to reestablish their precolonial autonomy and resented intrusions by the Tanzanian government, especially attempts by President JULIUS K. NYERERE to relocate them into collectivized villages. In recent years, however, the Iraqw have grown more receptive to government development projects as well as to commercial agriculture. Today, some 500,000 people consider themselves Iraqw.

See also ETHNICITY AND IDENTITY IN AFRICA: AN INTERPRETATION; LANGUAGES, AFRICAN: AN OVERVIEW.

ELIZABETH HEATH

Iron in Africa
Political, economic, and demographic history of the metal's influence on the continent.

Iron, a strong yet malleable metal, can be shaped into the tools used in agriculture, hunting, forest-clearing, conquest, and construction. Iron facilitated the rise of Africa's early centralized states. Early in the twentieth century, scholars painted a succinct picture of the diffusion of ironworking from North Africa across the Sahara. The arrival of iron tools was thought to explain the rapid adoption of agriculture and the subsequent rapid Bantu dispersion across sub-Saharan Africa. However, recent linguistic studies, combined with new archaeological discoveries, suggest that the initial wave of Bantu expansion occurred before the dawn of the Iron Age.

HISTORY OF METAL USE

Naturally occurring metals such as gold, silver, and copper were probably used for ornamental purposes since about the eighth millennium B.C.E. Most metal is found in ores, however, and must be heated, or smelted, to remove the impurities. Iron smelting is a particularly complex process that experts believe was discovered only a few times in the course of human history, or, perhaps, only once. Copper smelting first appeared in West Asia in the fourth millennium B.C.E. The earliest evidence of the more difficult process of iron smelting is found among the Hittites of West Asia and dates from the second millennium B.C.E.

It is generally believed that the use of metals diffused from West Asia to North Africa and that iron smelting was introduced during the seventh century B.C.E. to Egypt by Greeks and Assyrians and to Carthage by the Phoenicians. Egyptians were already using naturally occurring copper by the fifth millennium B.C.E. and were smelting copper by the following millennium. Copper became an important trade item and the standard against which other objects were weighed. Bronze—copper mixed with tin—is found to be present in Egypt as early as the third millennium B.C.E., and iron objects, probably imported, appeared around 1400 B.C.E. Traditionally, two avenues of diffusion have been suggested to explain the spread of iron smelting from North Africa to sub-Saharan Africa: along the Nile River from Egypt, and across the trans-Saharan trade route from Carthage.

DIFFUSION FROM EGYPT
When the iron-wielding Assyrians attacked Egypt in 670 B.C.E., the Egyptian rulers fled south to Nubia, establishing the city of Meroe (in present-day Sudan) as their capital. Ironworking sites discovered at Meroe have yielded dates between the third and sixth century B.C.E. Contemporaneous iron slag has also been found at Aksum (in Ethiopia). However, the data are insufficient to prove that these sites represent a diffusion of smelting practices along the Nile. Archaeological excavations in southern Sudan have not produced evidence of iron smelting before 500 C.E.

TRANS-SAHARAN DIFFUSION
A second theory traces the diffusion of iron smelting across the Sahara. Phoenicians brought ironworking technology to North Africa from the area of Lebanon when they established the city of Carthage (in present-day Tunisia) during the ninth century B.C.E. Some scholars believe Phoenician ironworking techniques diffused across the Sahara along established trade routes and were adopted by Bantu-speaking populations in West Africa. In the past, archaeologists supported the theory of iron diffusion across the Sahara by pointing out the lack of an indigenous copper industry in Africa before iron appeared, as many experts believed that the production of copper and its related alloys is a prerequisite to the production of iron. However, recent findings have established the existence of annealed copper at Sekkiret and Agades, Niger, dating to the second millennium B.C.E. Equally ancient evidence of copper working has also been found at Akjouj in Mauritania. This copper industry may have been a local invention or a product of cultural diffusion.

Several findings in West Africa support the claim of diffusion across the Sahara. Furnaces or other evidence of ironworking that date from the seventh to the fourth century B.C.E. have been found at sites in Niger, Nigeria, Cameroon, Democratic Republic of the Congo, and Gabon. Thus, iron smelting appears in West Africa at about the same time that it is believed to have reached North Africa. However, a furnace from the ninth century B.C.E. found at Do Dimmi, Niger, suggests that ironworking in West Africa may have predated the arrival of the Phoenicians. But the evidence remains inconclusive given that carbon dating, the method used to determine the age of the furnaces, provides only approximate information.

INDEPENDENT INVENTION?
Evidence of early ironworking has also been found in East Africa. For example, smelting furnaces in Rwanda and northwestern Tanzania have been dated to the ninth century B.C.E. Most sites, however, such as Urwew, near Lake Victoria, date between 300 B.C.E. and 200 C.E. The scarcity of archaeological evidence, combined with the uncertainty of carbon dating during this era, makes it difficult to reconstruct with any certainty the exact origins of copper or iron smelting. The use of metals may have diffused from Egypt and North Africa, or it may have arisen independently, or both.

Scholars have noted that at least three distinct kinds of iron-smelting furnaces are found in Africa: bowl furnaces, low-shaft furnaces, and high-shaft furnaces. Early bowl furnaces are found throughout eastern and southern Africa. The more common low-shaft furnaces are present from West to southeastern Africa. A few later-dating high-shaft furnaces have also been found in West Africa, Lake Tanganyika, Lake Malawi, and along the Zambezi River. The distribution of furnaces gives few clues to the origin and development of ironworking technologies on the continent. Several furnaces do, however, show remarkable innovations in the shafts, bellows, and tuyeres (the nozzles) used to increase the temperature, allowing the iron bloom to reach higher carbon levels, thus effectively producing steel. Although the origins of ironworking in sub-Saharan Africa remain unclear, it is known that iron smelting was firmly established among Bantu speakers in West Africa by the first half of the last millennium B.C.E.

BANTU DISPERSION AND SETTLEMENT
Ironworking is associated with the spread of Bantu speakers eastward and southward beginning in the first millennium B.C.E. Numerous iron furnaces, dating from between the sixth and the first century B.C.E., have been found along this migration route. Iron-smelting furnaces dating to the third or fourth century C.E. have also been found at KwaZulu-Natal and are viewed as markers of this migration. The importance of iron tools in fueling this rapid migration, however, is still debated.

CULTURE OF METALLURGY
The importance of iron is depicted in many myths and folktales, such as Yoruba stories of Ogun, the god of iron, and the widespread depictions of African blacksmith-kings. The Italian explorer Cavazzi published a book in 1687 depicting the Ngongo king laboring at a furnace while musicians play. In many societies, such as that of the Montagnard of North Cameroon, ironsmiths form distinct

castes and pass on their specialized knowledge from generation to generation. Smiths are often identified with mystical powers, and the molding of the iron bloom is interpreted as a creative, transformative process, laden with symbolism and associated with rituals and taboos. Among the Barongo of Tanzania, for example, the furnace is depicted as a womb and the iron as the offspring, and the slag by-product is equated with a placenta. Contemporary smiths continue to produce iron products, particularly ceremonial items, such as axes. Indigenous smelting became increasingly rare after large amounts of iron products were imported during colonial times. Today, a number of African countries have their own iron industries, and some, such as Liberia and Mauritania, are major iron exporters.

See also BANTU: DISPERSION AND SETTLEMENT; BANTU MIGRATIONS IN SUB-SAHARAN AFRICA; EGYPT, ANCIENT KINGDOM OF.

ARI NAVE

Isis
Goddess of fertility and motherhood in Egyptian mythology.
According to the Egyptian belief, Isis was the daughter of the god Keb ("Earth") and the goddess Nut ("Sky"), the sister-wife of Osiris, judge of the dead, and mother of Horus, god of day. After the end of the Late Period in the fourth century B.C.E., the center of Isis worship, which was then reaching its greatest peak, was on Philae, an island in the Nile River, where a great temple was built to her during the thirtieth dynasty. Ancient stories described Isis as having great magical skill, and she was represented as human in form though she was frequently described as wearing the horns of a cow. Her personality was believed to resemble that of Athor, or Hathor, the goddess of love and gaiety.

The cult of Isis spread from Alexandria throughout the Hellenistic world after the fourth century B.C.E. It appeared in Greece in combination with the cults of Horus, her son, and Serapis, the Greek name for Osiris. The Greek historian Herodotus identified Isis with Demeter, the Greek goddess of earth, agriculture, and fertility. The tripartite cult of Isis, Horus, and Serapis was later introduced (86 B.C.E.) into Rome in the consulship of Lucius Cornelius Sulla and became one of the most popular branches of Roman religion. It later received a bad reputation through the licentiousness of some of its priestly rites, and subsequent consuls made efforts to suppress or limit Isis worship. The cult died out in Rome after the institution of Christianity, and the last remaining Egyptian temples to Isis were closed in the middle of the sixth century C.E.

See also EGYPT, ANCIENT KINGDOM OF; EGYPTIAN MYTHOLOGY.

Islam and Tradition: An Interpretation
The person who laid down the principle of tradition as an important part of the Muslim heritage was al-Shá'fí (d. 820), the great Muslim lawyer of Cairo. He believed that the community was central to maintaining tradition. Community for al-Shá'fí meant a group of recognized leaders and experts who use their knowledge to agree on something that affects public and personal life. Al-Shá'fí believed that such agreements carried the weight of truth, for in his view it was impossible for the community to agree in error. Error, he said, arose from separation, and not from collective decision making. For al-Shá'fí, then, a living community was responsible for maintaining sound tradition.

However, al-Shá'fí was not just interested in tradition simply for the sake of protecting community interests. Rather, he defended the community because he saw it as necessary to preserving the tradition of the Prophet Muhammad. That tradition, called the sunnah, or custom of the Prophet, forms the superstructure of Muslim law, religion, ethics, education, worship, and devotion, and al-Shá'fí was largely responsible for making it the foundation of mainstream Islam. His book on the subject, called the Risálah, not only brought together the knowledge of a lawyer and a collector of tradition but it also brought about a major reform by streamlining local and regional deviations in the interpretation of scripture and law. Al-Shá'fí simply soared in his steady drive to secure the authority of tradition for a Muslim community in serious danger of breaking up. He did this by setting up clear rules to uphold the authority of the sunnah. We may summarize these rules as follows:

- The Prophet enjoys a special status (wahy) as God's approved messenger. The Prophet's sunnah, therefore, has lying upon it the seal of divine approval.
- The sunnah of the Prophet and the Qur'an (Koran), as the book of revelation, are always in agreement.
- Therefore, conflict between the sunnah and the Qur'an cannot happen.
- The sunnah can replace the Qur'an if the Qur'an has nothing to say on any subject. But even if the Qur'an has something to say, the sunnah can still provide complementary explanations.

Al-Shá'fí thus established the rule that no one was allowed to ignore tradition in Islam. He gave encouragement and a sense of unity to Muslims who were scattered in many different places and observing many different customs. Now everyone could agree on what Muslims should do, and why.

Yet by making tradition so important, al-Shá'fí opened the door for people to fabricate stories about the Prophet, stories that even the most careful of scholars could not

AL-AZHAR. Human figures are dwarfed by the massive entrance of the al-Azhar mosque in Cairo, Egypt, c. late 19th century. (*Prints and Photographs Division, Library of Congress*)

control entirely. For example, one story, or hadíth, claimed that the Prophet said, "Whatever is said and found to be beautiful, it can be attributed to me," the sort of catch-all statement that is welcomed by the scrupulous and unscrupulous alike. In response, Muslim experts tried to organize the stories so that they could be included in official handbooks and collections. However, we must stress that such collections, called hadíth collections (ahadíth), were not simply ornamental, their words borrowed by people to decorate an idea they liked. They were used to allow Muslims to overcome differences among themselves. It was for the sake of that sense of unity that many of the handbooks allowed sound or holy stories about the Prophet to exist alongside weak or even dubious ones. So these handbooks became an important resource for preserving Muslim unity across centuries and cultures.

Al-Sháʿfí's success in establishing tradition enabled Muslims to make changes in their religious practices without losing touch with the past. In effect, al-Sháʿfí created

ISLAMIC RITUALS. A Muslim worshipper performs a ritual cleansing before prayers, 1872. (*Prints and Photographs Division, Library of Congress*)

the idea of a living tradition, which allowed Islam to enter new cultures and societies outside the Arab heartland. That was how Islam came to Africa, where Muslims followed the advice of al-Shá'fí and another Muslim scholar, Imám Málik (d. 796) of Medina. Both scholars emphasized the importance of traditions about the Prophet. However, Imám Málik was more interested in what Muslims in Medina were actually practicing, while al-Shá'fí looked for rules that Muslims everywhere should follow. For example, Imám Málik would begin his account by saying something like, "This is the agreed on way of doing things among us," or "according to the way things are done among us," while al-Shá'fí surveyed the world of Muslims and pointed out contradictions in local practice and custom. Nevertheless, their approaches were complementary, and both stressed the central importance of the Prophet's sunnah.

SUPPORTERS AND CHALLENGERS

We must now consider the pressures and challenges that tradition faces in Muslim communities. It is natural that as Muslim traders and strangers entered African societies—first in North Africa, then in East and West—they would be wary of mixing freely with their non-Muslim hosts. As a result, these early Muslims lived in secluded quarters, making only occasional and necessary trading

forays. The Muslim ritual code imposes restrictions of food, dress, and calendrical observance: it prohibits pork, strangled meat, and alcoholic beverages; forbids exposure of certain parts of the body at worship; and calls for observance of the Friday sabbath, the Prophet's birthday, and the two Islamic festivals of fasting and pilgrimage. In time, Muslims' observance of the ritual code left a marked impression on neighboring populations in Africa, and an attentive ruler would be quick to draw on that appeal to keep in step with his people. Some rulers converted at this stage, but only halfway—enough to explore the potential of the new religion, while still enjoying the demonstrated advantages of the old. A shrewd ruler would take care not to step too far ahead of his people as a convert to an unknown or distrusted religion, nor lag behind as a resister of a growing faith. Some rulers, in order to hedge their bets, would thus pledge their children to the different religions in their realm.

Such calculations in the conversion process introduced novel ideas and practices into Islam, creating what the upholders of Muslim tradition call "a state between two states." They are referring to an indecisiveness they find objectionable, because it creates excuses for people who are ill informed or ill intentioned. But it was in this state that the once-secluded communities of traders and strangers broadened, and took in the half-hearted and the compromising. Eventually scholars would object to compromises of Muslim tradition and call for reform. But by this time, enough teachers and lawyers would have been trained, and enough people would have converted to Islam, to make successful reform reasonably certain.

Those who want to uphold the Muslim tradition face the challenge of reconciling the rules of religion with the experiences of life. If they want to change and reform Muslim practice, they will have to determine if their own societies' Muslims agree with them. They cannot take single-handed action simply because they think they know better than others what is right and wrong. So Muslim defenders of tradition have had to walk a narrow line between what the lawyers find in the rule books and what ordinary Muslims do in real life.

AFRICAN DIMENSION

Let us consider more concretely how Islam spread and became established in Africa, in light of the tension between the authority of tradition and the effects of practice.

When Islam first appeared in African societies, people were intrigued, curious, puzzled, perhaps even bewildered. But they were seldom hostile, in part because of the novelty, and in part because of the small numbers involved. The welcome Muslims thus received allowed them to flourish as minority communities. They usually established themselves along important trade routes, where their usefulness to their non-Muslim hosts was assured. In time these Muslim merchant communities grew in size and influence, attracting converts from the local population. Yet these converts continued to practice their old religions, because they saw no conflict with the new religion. It was only with time that Islam gently broke away from the old religions, but even then many converts continued to observe local customs.

However, as knowledge of Muslim tradition increased and practice became less lax and better informed, some Muslims began to demand reform and a genuine break with the old customs. It typically took several generations for this reform phase to emerge, if it emerged at all. Reformers called attention to rules of faith and practice and called for sanctions against those guilty of mixing Islam and African customs. These sanctions were to be found in Muslim scripture, law, and tradition. Only occasionally did reformist movements lead to jihád, or "holy war." Reform was normally undertaken peacefully, such as when a charismatic Qur'anic schoolteacher or a holy person appeared in the land, and offered the community instruction for their uninitiated children. The children, once initiated into Islam, would be better informed than the older generation, and they would raise the standards of observance and conduct. By the time the next generation arrived, knowledge of religion and rules would have been generally improved. Some people would then decide to go to Mecca, the pilgrimage site in Saudi Arabia Muslims visit every year. While in Mecca pilgrims are introduced to other Muslims from all over the world, and that experience helps to strengthen the Muslim tradition back home.

Eventually, important Muslim visitors would begin to visit the community. Their coming would demonstrate the worldwide nature of Islam, and upon their departure they would leave behind some religious objects, such as an illuminated manuscript of the Qur'an, a legal manual, handsomely bound volumes of the Prophet's sunnah, an embroidered turban or prayer rug, a picture of the Ka'ba (though never of the Prophet), some prayer beads, a silk gown, and so on. Eventually a ruler would emerge in the community who would undertake the pilgrimage, and return in triumph for having visited the holy city of Mecca. His personal example would inspire respect for Islam and give it a high political profile.

What is most interesting about the historical spread and consolidation of the Muslim tradition in Africa is not what happened when the rule books were first introduced nor what happened after reforms succeeded, but rather what happened in between, because it was then that African societies took Islam and adapted it to their own traditions. Islam emerged from that adaptation clearly marked by Africa, and also with clear proof that Africans had much to contribute to Islam. So Africa provided another element in the relationship between Islam and tradition.

Let us look at how this adaptation took place. Muslims, for example, are required to pray five times a day and to fast once a year during the month of Ramadan. The five daily prayers, including the congregation worship on the Friday sabbath, define the Islamic week. The fast of Ramadan is determined by the Islamic annual calendar, which is a lunar calendar, and thus approximately three weeks shorter than the solar calendar. So festivals of the Muslim calendar occur at a different time each year. The five daily prayers thus introduce a regular, daily habit in local Muslim observance, while the Ramadan fast breaks with the seasonal solar cycle and its agricultural customs and ceremonies. The members of peasant communities who converted to Islam would often find themselves absorbing Muslim feasts into a time period previously devoted to their agricultural solar festivals. They typically continued to observe these festivals, but added Islamic content. For example, they would observe a new year's harvest thanksgiving at the customary time of the year but would make a tithe in compliance with the requirements of Islam.

Conversion to Islam was eased in other ways as well. For example, people would retain the local names of the old rituals marking the new year, rain, harvest, and so forth, but they would observe these occasions with prayers and rites based on the Qur'an and sunnah. If we take a long-range view, we may say that Islam undermines the old customs and will in time overthrow them. On the other hand, if we take a medium-term view, we may say that the old customs will co-opt Islam, as people adapt it in line with their own interests. Thus in Africa dreams, dream interpretation, healing, and amulets belong as much to the Muslim religious tradition as they do to indigenous religious practice. We should not, therefore, draw too sharp a line between the two traditions.

ASSERTING THE PRIMACY OF TRADITION

The achievement of the Muslim "founding fathers," such as al-Shá'fí and Imám Málik, has given reform-minded Muslims the incentive to safeguard the Muslim tradition from harmful compromise. In Africa one such person was the Nigerian *shaykh* Usuman dan Fodio (1754–1817), who reformed Muslim practice through the strict application of Muslim law and tradition. Yet he was not opposed to using African ways to achieve reform. Accordingly he used special dream techniques, called salát al-istikhárah, to authorize his followers to take action. In his own account he speaks of how, in 1794, at the significant age of forty, the need for reform ripened into a command and an obligation, with dreams and visions steadying his resolve and clarifying his goals. "When I reached forty years, five months and some days, God drew me to him, and I found the Lord of djinns and men, our Lord Muhammad. ... With him were the Companions, and the prophets, and the saints. Then they welcomed me, and sat me down in their midst. Then the Saviour of djinns and men, our Lord Abd al-Qadir al-Jilani, brought a green robe embroidered with the words, 'There is no god but God; Muhammad is the Messenger of God' ... and a turban embroidered with the words, 'He is God, the One' ... the Lord Abd al-Qadir al-Jilani ... said, 'Dress him and enturban him, and name him with a name that shall be attributed exclusively to him.' He sat me down, and clothed me and enturbaned me. Then he addressed me as 'Imam of the saints' and commanded me to do what is approved of and forbade me to do what is disapproved of; and he girded me with the Sword of Truth, to unsheath it against the enemies of God. Then they commanded me ... and at the same time gave me leave to make this litany that is written upon my ribs widely known, and promised me that whoever adhered to it, God would intercede for every one of his disciples."

The authority to reform the Muslim tradition was thus obtained. As a result, Usuman dan Fodio decided to confront the compromising Muslims and their corrupt political leaders. Three years later, in 1797, we find the shaykh firmly set on the course of reform, and preparing to arm his followers for jihád. He commanded that this preparation for jihád was a sunnah, an order found in the tradition of the Prophet himself. During the months of preparation, the shaykh used prayer to inspire his disciples. His brother, Abdalláh dan Fodio, wrote that the shaykh "began to pray to God that He should show him the greatness of Islam in this country of the Sudan, and he set this to verse in his vernacular ode, al-Qádiriyya ("The Qadirite Ode"), and I put it into Arabic in verses." The shaykh coupled this experience with a decision to emigrate from his home in the Hausa state of Gobir to Gudu. It was at that moment that he chose to launch his movement. He intended it to be an act of political defiance: the people of Gobir had been hostile to him and his disciples, and so he denounced them as infidels and enemies of God. Usuman dan Fodio insisted on the territorial passage, the hijrah, as a condition of sound faith, and combined it with a call for personal sacrifice: "O brethren, it is incumbent upon you to emigrate from the lands of unbelief to the lands of Islam that you may attain Paradise and be companions of your ancestor Abraham, and your Prophet Muhammad, on account of the Prophet's saying, 'Whoever flees with his religion from one land to another, be it [merely the distance of] the span of a hand, will attain to Paradise and be the companion of Abraham and His Prophet Muhammad.'"

This denunciation of the political leaders in northern Nigeria was not a call for Muslims to retreat into prayer cells. The shaykh and his followers intended no flight from the world; they merely wanted to conquer it in order to change it. Religious discipline for them helped to safeguard sound tradition from compromise and error, and to warn the faithful that they should always be on guard against giving in to the world.

But Muslim African leaders have also used less harsh methods to correct falling standards. In the Fouta Djallon region of Guinea, for example, some local religious leaders in the late nineteenth century organized revival-type meetings that drew together numerous communities and taught them how to maintain proper standards. The centerpiece of these revival meetings was a form of devotion called "repeated prayer." The people repeated a litany about the tradition of the Prophet. The devotions were held in village congregations called missidi, and the discontented peasants, freed slaves, and poor people who attended were taught special prayers that were intended to inspire them. People came out of their prayers motivated to change the world by replacing those in power with people of their persuasion. They wanted change because they felt the leaders of the day had abandoned the truth and followed their own ideas. However, the French colonial authorities feared

these revivals might make the people revolt, and so sent troops to close down the main congregation at Diawia. That action frightened the other congregations, and people abandoned their farms and scattered. In this way the French proceeded to suppress Muslim religious activity in their colonies. They were determined that Muslims should become loyal subjects of the colonial empire, but Muslims instead became antagonized by Colonial Rule.

CONCLUSION

The leaders of the Muslim community have long recognized that the Muslim tradition will weaken unless they take steps to teach it to their children and support schools and teachers who can do that well. That is why many teachers and educators have taken responsibility for Islam, becoming active in Muslim communities as leaders of a unified, living tradition.

See also AFRICAN RELIGIONS: AN INTERPRETATION; ISLAM IN AFRICA; SOKOTO CALIPHATE.

LAMINE SANNEH

Islam in Africa
Expression of Islam in Africa, and the role of Africans in the spread and practice of the religion.
For information on

African Islamic political leaders: See ABD AL-QADIR; BELLO, AHMADU; IDRIS I. African Islamic scholars: See ABD ALLAH IBN YASIN; AHMAD BABA. Beliefs and traditions of Islam: See ISLAM AND TRADITION: AN INTERPRETATION. Specific aspects of Islam. See FEMINISM IN ISLAMIC AFRICA; ISLAMIC FUNDAMENTALISM: AN INTERPRETATION; ISLAMIC SALVATION FRONT; MARABOUT.

Islamic Fundamentalism: An Interpretation

Although Islamic fundamentalist movements have attracted much attention since the success of the Iranian Revolution of 1979—and, increasingly, since the terrorist attacks on the United States in 2001 and the wars in Afghanistan and Iraq that followed—they are not new nor have they ever been prevalent among Islamic societies. When they do emerge, these movements are more symptomatic of profound societal crises than a direct outcome of Islamic political and legal thought as such, or a common feature of all Islamic societies. But fundamentalism, as defined below, is not the only possible response because societies react differently to similar crises; and a history of fundamentalist response does not necessarily lead to the recurrence of the phenomenon. For example, there are more Muslims in sub-Saharan Africa

than in the Middle East—twice as many, if one includes North Africa. Moreover, the Sudanic belt of Sub-Saharan Africa experienced strong fundamentalist movements in the eighteenth and nineteenth centuries. Yet, there is little indication of fundamentalism in this part of Africa at present, except in Sudan and northern Nigeria, though the region as a whole faces similar crises to those that have prompted fundamentalist responses in North Africa and elsewhere in the Muslim world.

Islamic fundamentalism everywhere can be seen as an expression of the right of Muslim peoples to political, religious, or cultural self-determination. That is, Islamic fundamentalists claim to represent the free choice of their communities, whether in terms of demands for the strict application of shari'a (Islamic law as a comprehensive way of life) by the state (when Muslims are the majority) or through voluntary compliance in social relations and personal lifestyle (when Muslims are the minority). Much of the debate about Islamic fundamentalism tends to focus on the possibility or desirability of assertions of Islamic identity and self-determination in the abstract, with little attention to the underlying causes and dynamics of this phenomenon in the specific context of particular societies. For example, given the ideological orientation and political practice of fundamentalist groups in a variety of settings, it is pertinent to ask whether this approach is a legitimate means of realizing the right to self-determination in the modern context. A more basic question is whether fundamentalism is consistent with its own claims of exclusive representation of Islamic identity, political system, and legal order.

DEFINING OR IDENTIFYING ISLAMIC FUNDAMENTALISM

There is much debate about the appropriateness of using the term fundamentalism, as a product of Western Christian experience, to describe various religiopolitical movements in the presumably very different context of Islamic societies. This term was coined in the United States in the early decades of the twentieth century to refer to a Protestant group who published a series of twelve pamphlets between 1910 and 1912 under the title The Fundamentals: A Testimony to the Truth. But the origin of the term should not preclude its application to movements in the Islamic, Jewish, Hindu, or another religious tradition, if they share the same salient features and important traits.

The defining characteristic of the American Protestant fundamentalist movement was firm, principled, and militant opposition to the inroads that modernism, liberalism, and higher biblical criticism were making into the Protestant churches, and the supposedly Bible-based culture of the United States at large. That movement called for the defense of a certain form of inherited religiosity that is based on the literal and categorical belief in, and understanding of, the fundamentals of the Protestant faith. Islamic fundamentalists hold sufficiently similar beliefs in relation to Islam and the Qur'an (Koran) to justify using the term *fundamentalism* to identify these movements. Moreover, Islamic movements in North Africa and the Middle East do use the corresponding Arabic terms (*Usuli/Usuliyya*) to describe themselves and their beliefs, and not simply as a matter of recent translation of the American term. The call to affirm and implement the "fundamentals" of the faith, as distinguished from its incidentals, is an established and recurrent theme in Islamic theological and political discourse, as can be seen from the title of the book by al-Ashari (d. 935): *al-Ibanah 'an Usul al-Diyanah (The Elucidation of the Fundamentals of the Religion)*. Other scholars who emphasized this theme in their work include al-Ghazzali (d. 1111), ibn Taymiya (d. 1328), and ibn Abdel Wahhab (d. 1787).

Like their Christian counterparts, Islamic fundamentalists view themselves as the moral guardians and saviors of their societies, which they condemn for their apostasy, godlessness, moral depravity, and social decadence. They see Islamic history as one of decline and fall, to be rectified at their hands to achieve complete restoration and fulfillment of the divine design for all of humanity. Islamic fundamentalists also share a profound mistrust of all notions of human progress—gradual evolution or historical development—as antithetical to divine action and intervention in the world. As the select few, they see themselves as entrusted with discovering and implementing the will of God through the literal reading of the Qur'an, which they hold to be manifestly clear, unambiguous, and categorical, irrespective of the contingencies of time and place. Upholding the absolute sovereignty of God on earth, which they alone can discern and implement, Islamic fundamentalists reject the separation of Islam and state, and the sovereignty of the people. To them the state is simply an instrument for implementing the will of God, as expressed in the Qur'an; it does not exist for the people, as defined by secular constitutional instruments.

FUNDAMENTALISM IN ISLAMIC HISTORY

The Islamic legitimacy of the state has always been a cause of conflict and civil war since the death of the Prophet Muhammad in 632. For the majority of Muslims, the reign of the first four caliphs of Medina, western Arabia (namely, Abu Bakr, Umar, Uthman, and Ali), is generally accepted as an ideal Islamic state and community, but Shiite Muslims regard the first three of the Medina caliphs as illegitimate usurpers of the position to which only Ali (the Prophet's cousin) and his descendants from Fatima (the Prophet's only surviving child) were entitled.

Throughout his reign as the fourth caliph (656–661), Ali was locked in bitter civil war against the Umayyad clan and other factions, including some of his own supporters, know as al-Kawarij (secessionists), who condemned him for accepting mediation with the Umayyad. Following Ali's assassination by one of the al-Khawarij in 661, the Umayyad clan established a monarchy—contrary to shari'a principles—that ruled the expanding Muslim empire from Damascus, Syria, until 750. The Abbasid (descendants of the Prophet's uncle) launched their successful challenge to the Umayyad dynasty in the name of Islamic legitimacy, but the Abbasid state (750–1258) was also a monarchy that ruled from Baghdad, Iraq, more in accordance with political expediency than shari'a principles. The same was true of the other states of various sizes and duration that ruled Islamic societies ever since: from Spain, North and West Africa, Central Asia to India, including the Ottoman Empire, which was finally abolished in 1923–1924.

The tension between Islamic legitimacy and political expediency was usually mediated during different phases of history through mutual accommodation between al-umara (rulers) and al-ulama (scholars of shari'a) whereby the former acknowledged the theoretical supremacy of shari'a and the latter conceded the practical political authority of the rulers. Occasionally, some rulers professed commitment to more rigorous implementation of shari'a, as happened during the early Abbasid Dynasty, the Ibadi Khariji kingdom of Tlemsen, MOROCCO (761–909), Almoravid in Morocco and Spain (1056–1147), and the Ismaili Shia Fatimate Dynasty in parts of North Africa (969–1171). It is difficult to assess the scope and efficacy of those episodes of shari'a application because of the lack of independent and sufficiently detailed historical sources. But it is reasonable to assume that the decentralized nature of the state and administration of justice in the past would not have permitted a systematic and comprehensive application of shari'a as demanded by Islamic fundamentalists in the modern context.

The basic difficulty that has frustrated efforts to establish an Islamic state that would effectively implement shari'a has been the lack of political and legal institutions to ensure compliance by the state. While the Ulama were supposed to be the guardians of shari'a, they had no resort except appealing to the moral and religious sentiments of the rulers. Another factor was that the Ulama were too concerned with safeguarding the unity of their Muslim communities, and the maintenance of peace and public order, to press their demands forcefully on rulers, especially in times of internal strife and external threat. The few scholars who expressly addressed constitutional and legal matters in their writings, like al-Mawardi (d. 1058) in al-Ahkam al-Sultaniya (Principles of Government), and Ibn Taymiya in al-Siyasa al-Shariiya (Islamic Public Policy), confined themselves to elaborations of what ought to happen, in the form of advice to the ruler, rather than demands for application of shari'a as an obligation of the state.

Most of Islamic history can therefore be seen as a record of aspirations to an ideal state that would faithfully and impartially implement shari'a as a total way of life—aspirations that were frustrated by the realities of political expediency and security concerns. When the balance tilted too much in favor of the latter considerations, however, the intensity of demands for the application of shari'a would rise, usually in the form of a local or regional fundamentalist movement.

The most recent incidence of such fundamentalist resurgence prior to the present cycle initially began in dispersed places that gradually influenced one another, culminated in regional campaigns to establish Islamic states. Early examples of jihad movements in West Africa include those of Nasir al-Din in MAURITANIA (1673–1677), Malik Dauda Sy in SENEGAMBIA (1690s), and Ibrahim Musa, who was also known as Karamoko Alfa (d. 1751) in FOUTA DJALLON. This movement eventually succeeded in setting up an Islamic state in 1776 under the leadership of Ibrahim Sori. The most successful and influential jihad movement in the central Sudanic belt is that initiated by USUMAN DAN FODIO (1754–1817) who began his mission in 1774, achieved significant military success by 1808, and went on to control most of what is now northern NIGERIA and northern CAMEROON by 1830. This movement, known as the Sokoto Caliphate, spread to parts of southern Nigeria and CHAD, as well as influencing other jihads in Senegambia to the west. Other jihad movements in the region include that of Umar Tal (d. 1864) in the west, and Muhammad Ahmed "al-Mahdi" (d. 1885) along the NILE RIVER valley in the east.

These and other jihad movements of the Sudanic belt of Africa varied greatly in their scope, intensity, and consequences. Some movements lasted for several decades and succeeded in establishing centralized and effective Islamic states in parts of present-day Nigeria, the Volta region, CÔTE D'IVOIRE and GUINEA, while others were more in the nature of religious revivals, with little political or military success. Many jihad movements were uprisings of Muslim religious teachers and their followers against local military or landowning elites. The Islamic orientation of these movements also varied, as Islam was more of a mobilizing force than a religiopolitical program to some of them. Others, like that of Umar and Samory Touré (d. 1900), forbade dancing and the use of tobacco, alcohol and charms, prohibited pagan ceremonies and the worship of idols, and appointed Muslim scholars to enforce shari'a even in non-Muslim areas under their control.

While usually driven by local political, economic, and security considerations, these jihad movements were also

confronting the initial stages of European colonialism throughout the region. Like earlier cycles of Islamic fundamentalism, these African movements emerged in the context of societal crisis due to a combination of internal and external factors. Despite the recent history of jihad movements, there is little indication of fundamentalist resurgence in postcolonial Sub-Saharan Africa except in Sudan, along the Nile valley, and northern Nigeria by the end of the twentieth century. However, these societies may still produce fundamentalist movements in response to the present crisis, as an expression of their collective right to self-determination.

FUNDAMENTALISM AS SELF-DETERMINATION IN THE MODERN CONTEXT

Whatever may be the potential for resurgence of Islamic fundamentalism anywhere in the world today, it is clear that the internal and external contexts within which claims of Islamic identity and self-determination are made today are radically different from the way they used to be in the precolonial era. All Islamic societies are now constituted into nation-states that are part of a global political and economic system. They are members of the United Nations and subject to international law, including universal human rights standards, some of which are binding as customary international law even if the state is not party to relevant treaties. None of these nation-states is religiously homogeneous, politically insulated, or economically independent from the non-Muslim world. Even ostensibly purely Islamic and rich countries like Saudi Arabia are in fact vulnerable to economic, security, technological, or other forms of dependency on non-Muslim parts of the world.

In this light, it is clear that the right to self-determination cannot mean that a people are completely free to do as they please in their own country. Whether legally as a matter of national constitutional law or international law in relation to other states, or because of pragmatic political and economic realities, the right of one people or group to self-determination is limited by the right of other peoples or groups to their own self-determination as well. It is neither legally permissible nor practically possible for a group of Muslims to force non-Muslims or fellow Muslims to accept and implement a specific view of shari'a whether as a matter of state policy or informal communal practice. Any attempt to force one's own views on others in the name of self-determination is itself a negation of that right as basis of the claim in the first place.

If and to the extent that Islamic fundamentalists usurp the right of other Muslims to express their views about the nature and implications of Islamic identity, or the desirability of enforcing traditional formulations of shari'a, that cannot constitute legitimate exercise of the right to self-determination. Similarly, fundamentalist understandings of Islam and shari'a that would violate the human rights of women, religious minorities, or any other individuals or groups cannot be allowed in the name of self-determination. But if fundamentalists are simply claiming the right to political participation and freedom of belief and expression and so forth, with due regard to the rights of others, then it is wrong to deny them that right simply because one strongly disagrees with their views.

Despite the repeated failure of fundamentalist projects in the recent experiences of Islamic societies, some of them may still experience such responses to internal crisis or external threat. That should be seen as part of the struggle of these societies to develop and implement a positive and humane understanding of their right to self-determination, as each society will have to negotiate these issues for itself and within its own specific context.

See also ALCOHOL IN AFRICA; COLONIAL RULE; FEMINISM IN ISLAMIC AFRICA; ISLAM AND TRADITION: AN INTERPRETATION; ISLAM IN AFRICA; UNITED NATIONS IN AFRICA.

BIBLIOGRAPHY

Al-Azm, Sadik J. "Islamic Fundamentalism Reconsidered: A Critical Outline of Problems, Ideas and Approaches," Part I, in *South Asia Bulletin*, Vol. XIII, No. 1 & 2 (1993), pp. 93–121; Part II, in *South Asia Bulletin*, Vol. XIV, No. 1 (1994), pp. 73–98.

Esposito, John L. *Islam: The Straight Path*. Exp. ed. Oxford University Press, 1992.

Esposito, John L. ed. *The Oxford History of Islam*. Oxford University Press, 2003.

Hoveyda, Ferydoun. *The Broken Crescent: The 'Threat' of Militant Islamic Fundamentalism*. Praeger, 1998.

Jansen, Johannes J. G. *The Neglected Duty: The Creed of Sadat's Assassins and Islamic Resurgence in the Middle East*. Macmillan, 1986.

Lapidus, Ira M. *A History of Islamic Societies*. Cambridge University Press, 1988.

Levtzion, Nehemia, and Pouwels, Randall L. (eds.). *The History of Islam in Africa*. Ohio University Center Press, 2000.

Sayyed Ahmed, Rifa'at. *The Armed Prophet: The Rejectionists, and The Armed Prophet: The Revolutionaries*. Riad al-Rayyes Books, 1991.

Westerlund, David, and Rosander, Eva Evers (eds.). *African Islam and Islam in Africa: Encounters between Sufis and Islamists*. Hurst & Company, 1997.

ABDULLAHI AHMED AN-NA'IM

Islamic Salvation Front

Outlawed political party in Algeria that advocates the establishment of an Islamic state.

Islam has been an important presence in Algeria since the seventh century, and during the twentieth century, Islamic groups played a critical role in the struggle against French Colonial Rule. The movement for an Islamic state in Algeria dates from this struggle, gaining momentum after 1978, when Iranians revolted against the shah and established the Islamic Republic of Iran. In the 1980s the Islamic Salvation Front (Front Islamique du Salut, or FIS) led the call for an Islamic state in Algeria.

University professor Abassi Madani and political leader Ali Benhadj founded the FIS in the capital city of Algiers at a time of widespread popular unrest, food shortages, high unemployment, and growing anti-Western sentiment. Criticized for censoring political opposition, the ruling Front de Libération Nationale legalized the FIS in 1989. The FIS, which was critical of the West and advocated a return to Islamic values, attracted many Algrians who were displeased with the situation in their country, especially unemployed and alienated youth.

The FIS employed "Islamic police" to ensure that people followed Islamic codes of behavior. The anti-Western sentiments of the FIS extended to members of the international press corps, and the group was suspected of sponsoring the murders of foreign journalists. Women activists and intellectuals who spoke out against the establishment of a conservative Islamic state also risked reprisal from the powerful group. Actions attributed to the organization have been difficult to verify. The movement, dubbed "Islamic fundamentalism" in the West, extends beyond official FIS actions. Some violent acts attributed to the FIS may actually have been committed by offshoot or rival groups, or by FIS members acting independently of the organization.

Dissent within the party itself emerged between the followers of Madani and the more militant followers of Benhadj, who called for a pan-Islamic republic. Nevertheless, the success of the FIS in the municipal elections of June 1990, when the party won 850 of 1,541 council seats, left no doubt about the popular appeal of the party. After the start of the next set of elections in December, the FIS accused the ruling party of fixing votes and demanded a presidential and parliamentary election. Violence erupted throughout the country, and Madani threatened a holy war against the state. In June 1991 both Madani and Benhadj were arrested.

Even without its leaders, the party continued to gain power; in the first round of elections in 1992, the FIS won 188 of 232 seats. But after the military-led High Council of State seized control from President Chadli Benjedid, the new government outlawed the FIS and arrested its remaining leaders, interning some in a notorious desert concentration camp. During the period that followed, violent protests and guerrilla attacks by FIS followers, including the bombing of the Algiers airport in 1992, were countered by equally extreme military crackdowns. Since 1992 other militant Islamic groups have stepped into the void left by the FIS, which is now officially in exile. The FIS, meanwhile, has officially distanced itself from these groups, and in 1997 the leadership in exile called for all sides to lay down their arms and end the violence. By the early twenty-first century, Benhadj and Madani had been released from prison but the FIS is still banned in Algeria.

See also ISLAM IN AFRICA; ISLAMIC FUNDAMENTALISM: AN INTERPRETATION.

MARIAN AGUIAR

Isoko
Ethnic group of Nigeria; also known as Biotu, Igabo, and Urhobo.
The Isoko primarily inhabit Delta State in southern NIGERIA. They speak a Niger-Congo language and are closely related to the neighboring EDO people. Some 750,000 people consider themselves Isoko.

See also ETHNICITY AND IDENTITY IN AFRICA: AN INTERPRETATION; LANGUAGES, AFRICAN: AN OVERVIEW.

Issa
Ethnic group of the Horn of Africa; also known as Esa.
The Issa primarily inhabit southern DJIBOUTI, northern SOMALIA, and Harer Province, ETHIOPIA. They speak Somali, an Afro-Asiatic language in the Cushitic group, and are considered part of the Dir clan of the Somali people. More than 400,000 people consider themselves Issa.

See also ETHNICITY AND IDENTITY IN AFRICA: AN INTERPRETATION; LANGUAGES, AFRICAN: AN OVERVIEW.

Iteso
Ethnic group of East Africa; also known as Elgumi, Teso, and Wamia.
The Iteso primarily inhabit northeastern UGANDA and western KENYA. They speak a Nilo-Saharan language. Approximately 1.5 million people consider themselves Iteso. They are the second-largest ethnic group in Uganda after the BAGANDA.

See also ETHNICITY AND IDENTITY IN AFRICA: AN INTERPRETATION; LANGUAGES, AFRICAN: AN OVERVIEW.

Itsekiri
Ethnic group of Nigeria; also known as Chekiri, Irhobo, Iwere, Shekiri, and Warri.
The Itsekiri primarily inhabit Delta State in southern NIGERIA. They speak a Niger-Congo language and are closely related to the EDO people, although today many speak YORUBA. Some 450,000 people consider themselves Itsekiri.

See also ETHNICITY AND IDENTITY IN AFRICA: AN INTERPRETATION; LANGUAGES, AFRICAN: AN OVERVIEW.

Ittu
Ethnic group of Ethiopia; also known as the Itu.
The Ittu live mainly around Harer, ETHIOPIA. They speak Oromo, an Afro-Asiatic language, and are one of the Oromo peoples. Approximately 5 million people consider themselves Ittu.

See also ETHNICITY AND IDENTITY IN AFRICA: AN INTERPRETATION; LANGUAGES, AFRICAN: AN OVERVIEW.

Ivory Trade
One of Africa's oldest, most lucrative, and now most controversial export trades.
Ivory is a form of dentin obtained mainly from elephant tusks. It is excellent for carving and is admired for its creamy color, smooth texture, and hardness. Long a symbol of luxury, it was used for furniture inlay, book covers, birdcages, brooches, scabbards, figurines, and boxes in ancient Egypt, Assyria, Crete, Greece, Italy, China, India, and Japan. Craftworkers in Benin were well known for their skill at carving masks, statuettes, caskets, jewelry, bells, and rattles. Because ivory has been highly sought, the ivory trade has historically been lucrative. In the late twentieth century, however, declining African elephant populations, attributed to poachers, brought controversy to the trade.

Ancient Egyptians from the Sixth Dynasty (2323–2291 B.C.E.) onward used ivory extensively, obtaining most of their supply from the region of present-day Sudan. The Romans in North Africa kept up a brisk trade in ivory following the demise of the Egyptian Empire. After Rome's decline, China and India became the largest importers of African ivory.

As Arab Islamic dynasties spread across much of North Africa in the seventh and eighth centuries, they established trade relations with peoples south of the Sahara. Towns such as Koumbi Saleh, Tombouctou, and Gao became commercial centers where tusks were exchanged for salt, silk, copper, gold, and swords. European demand for ivory was sparked during the Crusades. Initially, ivory was exported to Europe primarily from North Africa, but in the late fifteenth century Portuguese merchant vessels began trading European goods for ivory along the coasts of West and Central Africa.

Ivory also became an important trade commodity along East Africa's Swahili Coast, which stretches from Somalia to Mozambique. From at least the fifteenth century, Swahili merchants exported ivory to India after obtaining

IVORY HARVEST. Ethiopian men at an ivory warehouse, c. 1900. (*Giraudon/The Bridgeman Art Library*)

it from inland peoples, such as the Kamba of modern Kenya, the Nyamwezi of Tanzania, the Yao of Mozambique, and the Bisa of Zambia. In the mid-nineteenth century, the Omani rulers of Zanzibar sent trading caravans into the East African interior. These merchant caravans also traded in slaves, and in fact used slave labor to carry elephant tusks from the African interior to the coast.

One of the most famous Swahili traders was Tippu Tip, a native of Zanzibar who established an inland trading empire that stretched from Zanzibar to the Lualaba River in the modern Democratic Republic of the Congo. In the nineteenth century the trade expanded further with the coming of European settlers and adventurers, many of whom subsidized their hunting expeditions by selling ivory and trophies in Europe.

At the same time, industrial revolutions in Europe and the United States drove demand for ivory to unprecedented heights, supplementing the eastern demand. By the late 1800s Great Britain and the United States imported more than 1.5 million tons of ivory per year to be used for combs, piano keys, billiard balls, and fans. This frenzy for ivory in the late nineteenth century devastated Africa's elephant populations.

European colonial-era restrictions on hunting by Africans—intended to force Africans into wage labor and preserve elephant populations for European safari hunters—slowed the ivory trade. By the 1930s, however, ivory exports rose again. In the 1970s booming Asian economies fueled international demand, which, because of the advent of automatic weapons, was easily met.

Between 1979 and 1989 the African elephant population declined from approximately 1.3 million to approximately 625,000, and ivory had doubled in price, from around U.S. $60 per kilogram (about U.S.$132 per pound) to between U.S.$120 and U.S.$300 per kilogram (about U.S.$264 to U.S.$660 per pound). In October 1989 the nations composing the Convention on International Trade in Endangered Species of Wild Fauna and Flora (CITES), responding to pressure from U.S. and European environmentalist and animal welfare lobbies, agreed to a complete ban on the ivory trade.

Many disagreed with the ban, however, citing the uneven distribution of elephants in Africa. For instance, in Kenya elephant populations were as low as 19,000, mostly because of poaching, but in Botswana, Namibia, Zimbabwe, and South Africa, effective conservation programs resulted in elephant herds so large that they were damaging wild vegetation as well as farmers' fields. In these countries, elephant herds had to be culled regularly. The ivory from these culled animals represented an important potential source of income for these countries' governments. Not surprisingly, they protested the ban, arguing that they were being penalized for sound resource management.

In 1997 CITES partially lifted the ivory trade ban, allowing Botswana, Namibia, and Zimbabwe to sell their excess ivory stocks to Japan. Since the ban was lifted, critics have claimed that poaching has increased significantly throughout Africa. A 2003 report from the conservation group World Wildlife Fund, for example, alleged that 4,000 kilograms of illegal ivory was on public display in Nigeria, Côte d'Ivoire, and Senegal.

See also EGYPT, ANCIENT KINGDOM OF; GOLD TRADE; HUNTING IN AFRICA; NORTH AFRICA, ROMAN RULE OF; SAFARI HUNTING; SALT TRADE; WILDLIFE MANAGEMENT IN AFRICA.

BIBLIOGRAPHY

Sugg, Ike, and Urs Kreuter. *Elephants and Ivory: Lessons from the Trade Ban.* Institute of Economic Affairs, 1994.

Wilson, Derek, and Peter Ayerst. *White Gold: The Story of African Ivory.* William Heinemann, 1976.

ROBERT FAY

Iwa

Ethnic group of Zambia; also known as Awiwa and Mashukulumbwe.

The Iwa primarily inhabit northeastern ZAMBIA. They speak Mambwe, a BANTU language. Approximately 300,000 people consider themselves Iwa.

See also BANTU: DISPERSION AND SETTLEMENT; ETHNICITY AND IDENTITY IN AFRICA: AN INTERPRETATION; LANGUAGES, AFRICAN: AN OVERVIEW.

Iyasu I

One of the great warrior emperors of Ethiopia; also known as Iyasus the Great.

Iyasu was the son of Emperor Johannes I and grandson of Emperor Fasiladas. He came to the throne in 1682, at a time of decline in imperial power that had begun during his grandfather's reign. Through his brilliance as a military leader, Iyasu temporarily halted the trend of decline, reestablishing control over rebellious vassals and conquering areas to the south of his domain. In addition to his military and political exploits, Iyasu was a patron of arts and letters and sponsored buildings in the city of Gonder. He also attempted to settle doctrinal differences within Ethiopia's Coptic Church, but without long-lasting success. Iyasu was deposed by his son Takla Haymanot in 1706 and assassinated. A series of ineffectual emperors followed Iyasu until the middle of the nineteenth century. During this period, imperial power declined and the empire lost territory.

J

Jagas

Term used to refer to a group of invaders who entered the kingdom of Kongo in the 1500s.

The term Jagas was first used in the late sixteenth century to name of a group of invaders who entered the kingdom of Kongo from the east in 1568, and was later widely used in West Central Africa before the twentieth century. It probably derives from the Kikongo verb *yaka*, meaning "to grab, take, or hold," and became *Jagas* when the Portuguese settled in the region.

Since the seventeenth century there have been attempts by European writers to connect all pillaging groups with cannibalistic tendencies to a single source. This "history" has included such diverse groups as the Sumbas (late-sixteenth-century invaders in the region that is present-day Sierra Leone), the Oromo (in Ethiopia and Somalia), and the Zumbas (in Malawi, Mozambique, and Tanzania). Modern scholars believe that the term originally described a way of life rather than a particular ethnic group characterized by raiding, pillaging, and often cannibalism. The term *Jaga*, however, was also used in seventeenth-century Kongo to describe other vagabond and rootless people, even if they were neither violent nor destructive.

Originally applied to the raiders of 1568, and other raiding groups, especially those from the north side of the Congo River who attacked Kongo frequently in the mid-seventeenth century, the term was later used to refer to those who supported pretender kings in regional civil wars. Modern traditions from the eastern part of the old kingdom of Kongo speak of wars with the "Yakas" in the indefinite past. The inhabitants of the Niari Valley in present-day Republic of the Congo, are often called Yaka, and there was a Yaka kingdom in the middle Kwango Valley in the seventeenth century, whose past may have been linked to these earlier rootless people.

The invasion of Kongo in 1568 marked a severe crisis for the kingdom, and may have been facilitated by a variety of internal disagreements as well, including popular discontent, dynastic rivalries, or commercial interests. King Alvaro I (1568–1578) was forced to flee the kingdom and take refuge on an island in the Congo River, and the capital city was sacked and looted. Alvaro appealed to Portugal for assistance, and was forced to allow the Portuguese to establish their colony in Angola in return for that help. Portuguese troops helped defeat the Jagas and remained in Kongo until 1575.

The Portuguese colonists in Angola used the term *Jaga* to refer to the Imbangala, a similarly rootless group of raiders originating in the Umbundu-speaking central highlands of Angola. This latter group was famous for fighting alongside the Portuguese as they built the colony of Angola in the early to mid-1600s.

Jameson, Sir Leander Starr

Nineteenth-century British administrator of the lands comprising present-day Zimbabwe.

See also Rhodes, Cecil.

Jammeh, Yahya

1965–

President of Gambia.

Yahya Jammeh was raised in a Jola Muslim community in the western part of GAMBIA. In 1984, a year after graduating from high school, he enlisted in the Gambian army, where he gradually rose through the ranks to become lieutenant. In 1994, after leading the coup that ousted President Sir Dawda Jawara, Jammeh promoted himself to captain and made himself head of state. He led a group of Gambian soldiers, who had recently served in West African peacekeeping efforts in Liberia under the auspices of the ECONOMIC COMMUNITY OF WEST AFRICAN STATES (ECOWAS) and who had not received their back pay. In July 1994, after installing a five-member Armed Forces Provisional Ruling Council, Jammeh declared himself chairman, suspended the constitution, and banned all political activity. Jammeh immediately announced his intention to return Gambia to civilian rule "as soon as we have set things right." The young president created five civilian commissions of inquiry to investigate corruption charges and recover stolen government funds, detained and questioned many prominent businessmen and government officials (most of whom were later released), and installed a joint civilian-military government.

Despite its declarations supporting freedom of expression, the Jammeh regime has been criticized by international human rights groups for harassing and imprisoning journalists, and for detaining dissidents for lengthy periods without trial. In 2008 he demanded that all gays and lesbians leave the country and threatened to impose lethal penalties upon those who remained. These penalties, he boasted, would rival the draconian punishments meted out by the regime in Iran. On the other hand, Jammeh has support among some Gambians for his campaign to suppress a growing sex industry associated with European tourism, and to restore a sense of pride and modesty among Gambian women. He has banned, for example, the importation of all skin lighteners and hair straighteners, products frequently used by Gambian prostitutes. Having survived two attempted coups, in November 1994, and again in January 1995, Jammeh gave in to pressure from Western donor nations and announced in early 1996 that Gambia would hold open elections in October that year. They were held on schedule and Jammeh was elected president of the republic with more than 55 percent of the vote. In October 2001 Jammeh was reelected in presidential elections that were generally endorsed as free and fair by international observers. Nevertheless his opponents continue to claim that his administration incites intolerance among the country's majority Muslim and minority Christian populations, and prohibits freedom of the press. Expectations that Jammeh would face significant opposition in the 2006 presidential election were somewhat overstated, and he was easily reelected. In 2006 he survived what was reportedly a brewing military coup.

See also HUMAN RIGHTS IN AFRICA; TOURISM IN AFRICA.

ROBERT BAUM

Jarbah
Island off the southeast coast of Tunisia; also known as Djerba.

Legend has it that the island of Jarbah was the land of the lotus-eaters portrayed in Homer's Odyssey—a land where the sailors ate enchanted fruit and forgot everything but the beauty around them. Historians believe that the Jewish community on the island dates back to 500 B.C.E. Archaeological evidence shows that Carthaginians occupied this flat, fertile island in the Mediterranean Sea. Romans followed and named it Meninx. In 655 C.E., Arabs conquered the island, which they loosely ruled as part of the province of Ifriqiya (present-day TUNISIA and eastern ALGERIA).The island became a center for the Kharijites, an Islamic sect popular among the many BERBER inhabitants. By the eleventh century, the Hafsid dynasty ruled Jarbah from TUNIS. The island's strategic

location in the Mediterranean made it desirable to many different states. In 1284 the Spanish Aragones captured Jarbah; for the next four centuries control of Jarbah would pass between Hafsid, Spanish, and Sicilian-Norman rule. As the Hafsid empire waned in the sixteenth century, the struggle for control of the island revived between the Islamic and Christian forces. First the Muslim corsair Darghut took the island, but then the Spanish staged a brutal conquest in 1560, seizing the Mediterranean prize.

Only a few years later the Ottoman Empire took possession of Jarbah, initiating a rule that would last over 300 years. Over 300 mosques still remain on the island; the Ottomans constructed most of them during this time. Residents on the island cultivated the olive and date orchards for which the island became famous. By the nineteenth century, these agricultural pursuits had replaced corsair activity as the focus of the island's economy, supplemented by a fishing and artisan industry. When the French claimed Tunisia as a protectorate in 1881, they also took Jarbah. Since Tunisian independence in 1960, Jarbah has been a major tourist attraction, and the government of Tunisia has built large hotels and an international airport to cater to the European visitors who flock to the beaches.

The ancient Jewish community on the island has maintained a continuous presence through centuries of different rule, and Jarbah is home to a sizable Jewish population. Relations between local Arabs and Jews have been peaceful for the most part. However, in April 2002 a Tunisian driver exploded a truckload of natural gas outside the island's main synagogue, killing fifteen people. The driver was suspected of having connections to the international terrorist group Al-Qaeda.

See also CARTHAGE; CORSAIRS; JEWISH COMMUNITIES IN NORTH AFRICA.

MARIAN AGUIAR

Jawara, Sir Dawda Kairaba
1924–
First prime minister and first president of Gambia.

Dawda Kairaba Jawara was born in Barajally, a small Mandinka community on the upper GAMBIA RIVER. The son of a Muslim merchant-farmer, he attended an elementary school in Bathurst that combined Islamic and Western education. After a brief stint working at the Royal Victoria Hospital in Bathurst, he attended Achimota College in the GOLD COAST (present-day GHANA), and later studied veterinary surgery at the University of Glasgow. In 1954 he returned home and began work as a government veterinarian. The following year he became a Christian, took the name David, and married Augusta Mahoney, the daughter of a prominent

Sierra Leonean in Bathurst. They had five children before divorcing in 1967.

Appointed the colony's principal veterinary officer in 1957, Jawara resigned two years later to enter politics. In 1959 he became one of the founders of the People's Progressive Party. The following year he was elected to the Gambian House of Representatives, and in 1962 became minister of education and chief minister, succeeding his rival Pierre S. N'Jie. His accession to the chief executive office marked the rise of the interior districts of the protectorate, dominated by Mandinka and Fula Muslims, and the decline of the urban, multiethnic groups of the coastal areas, which had dominated Gambian political life throughout the colonial period.

After Gambia gained independence in 1965, Jawara was chosen prime minister; he also returned to his Islamic faith and to his Muslim name, Dawda. The following year he was knighted by Queen Elizabeth II. When The Gambia became a republic in 1970, Jawara was elected as president, and went on to be reelected in 1977 and 1982. In 1981, however, a coup attempt while he was out of the country—undertaken by members of the left-wing Movement for Justice in Africa—required the intervention of the Senegalese army. Shortly thereafter Jawara decided, despite little Gambian support, to join Gambia with Senegal in 1982 in a loose confederation of which he became vice president. Abdou Diouf, the president of Senegal, became president of the Senegambian confederation. Jawara retained political authority in Gambia throughout the period of confederation and returned to the presidency after its dissolution, in 1989. In 1992 he won reelection to his fifth presidential term. Two years later, young officers of the Gambian military, led by Yahya JAMMEH, overthrew Jawara's government and took control of the country. Jawara fled to Britain where he lived in exile until 2002, when he returned to Gambia after Jammeh granted him unconditional amnesty. More recently, he has taken part in political affairs elsewhere on the continent, traveling to Nigeria in 2007 as part of the Economic Community of West African States' mission to assess that nation's readiness to hold fair elections.

See also ISLAM IN AFRICA.

ROBERT BAUM

Jewish Communities in North Africa

Communities of Jews who settled in North Africa during a series of migrations beginning before the Roman conquest of the region.

Until the 1960s, North Africa was home to one of the largest Jewish populations in the world. EGYPT figures prominently in the Torah, which records a Jewish presence in Egypt as early as the second millennium B.C.E. In the sixth century B.C.E., the time of the first Jewish dispersion,

Jews again sought refuge in Egypt, and it is believed that they accompanied Phoenician settlers to western coastal North Africa. Since then, Jewish communities have continuously inhabited the region now comprised of Egypt, LIBYA, TUNISIA, ALGERIA, and MOROCCO. The Muslims who conquered North Africa, beginning in the seventh century, found Jewish, as well as Christian and traditional, communities among the Berber and Egyptian-speaking populations. Under early Muslim rule, Jews were granted a special status as "People of the Book," and Islamic law allowed them to own land, administer justice within their communities, and practice their religion. Under Muslim rule, Jews sometimes enjoyed tolerance, though at other times they faced violent anti-Semitism.

When the Islamic dynasties of the ALMORAVIDS and ALMOHADS conquered the region of southern Spain known as Andalusia, North African Jewish communities established ties to their fellow Jews in Spain. From the fourteenth to the seventeenth centuries, these Spanish Jews, who were known as Sephardim and spoke a Judeo-Spanish dialect called Ladino, fled the terror of the Spanish Inquisition and the forced conversions of the Christian reconquest. Many settled in North Africa.

Although these immigrants settled throughout the Maghreb and Egypt, particularly large Sephardic communities settled in Oran, Algeria, and in northern and coastal Morocco. They flocked to cities; in Morocco, they lived in walled ghettos called mellahs. In some places, such as Tunisia, the first wave of Sephardic Jews integrated with existing Jewish communities. But many of the new immigrants were from a privileged background in Spain, and their cosmopolitan ways, their wealth, and their Judeo-Spanish language set them apart from existing Jewish communities. Wielding considerable influence in the trading centers of North Africa, they often occupied a higher social position than their counterparts who spoke Judeo-Arabic or Judeo-Berber languages. Throughout North Africa, Sephardic Jews prospered as merchants, middlemen, and diplomats, and some even occupied prominent positions within Islamic dynasties. Arabic- and Berber-speaking Jews generally worked as artisans, tradesmen, jewelry-makers, or small-scale farmers, harvesting fruits and vegetables.

With the sixteenth-century conquest of much of North Africa by the Ottoman Empire, Jews in Algeria, Tunisia, Libya, and Egypt faced special taxes and discrimination. Once again, however, the relative privilege of different Jewish groups split their communities along lines of origin. For example, the Tunisian Grana, a cosmopolitan group of Jews who arrived from Livorno, Italy, in the late seventeenth century, often served as agents and middlemen for the Turkish Corsairs. Jews from Eastern Europe, as well as some from other parts of the Ottoman Empire,

JEWISH COMMUNITIES IN ZIMBABWE. Rabbi Ambros Makuwaza conducts a Rosh Hashana service at Rusape's Jewish Tabernacle in Zimbabwe, 1996. (*Denis Farrell/AP Images*)

settled in Egypt, where they established prosperous communities in CAIRO and Tanta.

By the nineteenth century, some Jewish communities were involved in the expanding trade with European powers. Their links with commercial interests might be one reason colonized Jews at first enjoyed a relatively privileged position compared to their Islamic counterparts. In Algeria, where their population numbered 30,000 at the time of French colonization, Jews were even granted French citizenship in 1870—a move that generated anti-Semitic violence by French settlers and Muslims in cities around the country. During World War II (1939–1945), however, the rights Jews had gained disappeared when the Axis powers held forth in North Africa. Many Jews under the Vichy government were interred and forced into labor camps.

Jewish communities split over the issue of decolonization—in the words of Tunisian writer Albert Memmi, "The Jewish population identified as much with the colonizers as with the colonized." Despite this, many Jews took part in liberation struggles, and nationalist organizations such as the Algerian Front de Libération Nationale (FLN) promised tolerance under independent rule. Yet the tide turned against Jews as nationalist struggles took on an increasingly Muslim character, and many Jews either sided with the colonial governments or fled North Africa.

In Egypt, where a large Jewish community included those who had left Palestine during World War I (1914–1918), tensions increased with the rise of Zionism and Islamic nationalism. During the 1950s and 1960s, in several North African states promoting an Islamic identity, Jews lost civil rights, and many of their places of worship were pillaged or seized. Numerous Jews left Egypt after the 1956 Suez War, and those who remained were imprisoned by the government in concentration camps during the 1967 Arab-Israeli war. Throughout North Africa, anti-Semitic violence increased after this war, and most Jews left for Europe, Israel, or the Americas. Today, there are still Jews living in North Africa, but the communities are small and scattered. Somewhat more recent communities, also small, have taken shape in such countries as CÔTE D'IVOIRE, GHANA, and ZIMBABWE, among others.

BIBLIOGRAPHY

Hirschberg, H. Z. *A History of the Jews in North Africa.* Brill, 1981.

MARIAN AGUIAR

Johannesburg, South Africa
City in northeastern South Africa.

One of the largest cities in southern Africa, Johannesburg's population is slightly more than 3.8 million (2007 estimate). Its area, around 800 sq km (310 sq mi), consists of not only the city itself but also more than 400 suburbs, as well as the townships where nonwhites were forced to live under the government's policy of APARTHEID.

Situated on the Witwatersrand mountain range, the Johannesburg area was home only to scattered TSWANA settlements before 1886, when the discovery of gold deposits spurred the rapid immigration of speculators and diggers from other parts of southern Africa as well as from Europe. Within a decade, Johannesburg had grown from a mining camp into an industrialized city of some 100,000 people, an estimated three-quarters of whom worked in the mines. For many years far more men than women migrated to Johannesburg, and many of them lived in workers' hostels. During and after World War II (1939–1945), booming industrial growth spurred another wave of urban migration and the growth of Sophiatown and other shantytowns. By this time, some of SOUTH AFRICA's largest labor unions were well established in Johannesburg.

After the NATIONAL PARTY began imposing apartheid policies in 1948, many of the Johannesburg shantytowns were destroyed, and blacks were relocated either to rural *bantustans* or to newly created townships outside the city. These areas were poorly serviced and soon became extremely crowded, often with as many as ten people sharing one room. The largest township, Soweto (with a current population estimated at between 2 and 4 million people), was the site of a 1976 police massacre of peacefully protesting schoolchildren. Other townships housed the Asian and "coloured" populations.

Since the dismantling of apartheid in the early 1990s, Johannesburg has become increasingly racially integrated. Great income inequality persists, and most of the city's black residents still live in Soweto, while the wealthy suburbs remain predominantly white. In addition, the freedom to move within the country has brought more job-seeking migrants to Johannesburg, straining already crowded conditions. Crime and pollution have become major problems in Soweto and other poor areas.

Johannesburg is now the capital of Gauteng, the richest of South Africa's nine provinces. The city is home not only to the mining industry but to the national stock exchange, a wide range of manufacturing industries, the international airport, and the University of Witwatersrand. Since 1994 the African National Congress has dominated Johannesburg's elected metropolitan council; some 32 percent of the council seats are held by women.

BIBLIOGRAPHY

Thompson, Leonard. *A History of South Africa.* Yale University Press, 1995.

KATE TUTTLE

Jola

Ethnic group of Senegal, The Gambia, and Guinea-Bissau.
The Jola, now numbering more than 1 million people, are the major ethnic group of the lower Casamance region of SENEGAL and are a significant minority group in THE GAMBIA and GUINEA-BISSAU. Reflecting the irrationality of the partition of Africa, national boundaries often bisect Jola villages or separate the villages from their rice paddies. Described by agronomists as the best wet-rice farmers in West Africa, Jola farmers regularly produced substantial food surpluses until the frequent droughts of the last thirty years. Traditionally they have not formed states, but have lived in communities governed by village councils and groups of elders, without formal political authorities. Since 1981 they have been one of the principal ethnic groups involved in the Casamance regional movement to secede from Senegal, a movement that has become particularly violent in recent years.

The name Jola is a relatively recent one, first applied to the people we know as Jola in the nineteenth century by Wolof sailors in response to French administrators' questions about the ethnicity of the people they encountered along the Casamance River. The Portuguese name for Jola, Floup, has been used to refer to the group since the beginning of the sixteenth century. Oral traditions suggest that the Jola or Floup originated in the coastal areas of central and northern Guinea-Bissau. They expanded to the north and west at the expense of the Bainounk, the earliest known inhabitants of the Casamance, many of whom were assimilated into various Jola communities. In the sixteenth century a substantial Jola kingdom, ruled by the Mansa Floup, dominated the southern Jola areas in Casamance and Guinea-Bissau. The growth in the slave trade destabilized this state, and the Jola assumed the stateless political organization that has characterized them ever since. Jola captives were sold into the transatlantic slave trade as early as 1500 and were taken initially to Spanish and Portuguese colonies off the coast of Africa, such as the Cape Verde Islands, and to Latin America. As the British became active in the slave trade in the seventeenth century, they took Jola captives to the Carolinas and Georgia, where they taught British settlers how to grow rice.

The French occupied most of the Jola lands in the nineteenth century, though the British occupied small areas in the northwest and the Portuguese occupied the southern Jola areas. Each colony practiced a different form of colonialism, and the Jola sought to minimize the disruption to their communities by migrating across colonial borders to avoid such burdens as military conscription, forced labor, and taxation. All three colonial powers found the Jola difficult to govern, reluctant to pay taxes, and often ready to resist. In 1942 a prophetic movement, led by a woman named Alinesitoué Diatta, contributed to open resistance to the pro-Nazi Vichy French government. She was arrested and charged with the crime of resisting colonial initiatives and causing embarrassment to the colonial administration. She died of starvation after a year of exile.

Since independence, many Jola have felt that the central government has neglected the Casamance region, separated from the rest of Senegal by The Gambia, and that the overwhelmingly Muslim peoples of northern Senegal have looked down on their adherence to traditional religion and Christianity (though some Jola profess Islam). This frustration finally led to open resistance beginning in 1981. Mass arrests by the Senegalese government and attacks by the guerrilla rebels on opponents of secession have both contributed to the escalating level of violence. The persistent drought that has affected Senegal since the 1960s, together with STRUCTURAL ADJUSTMENT policies and consequent economic austerity since 1980, have also caused discontent among the Jola and generated support for rebel forces. In The Gambia, however, a Jola junior officer, Yahya JAMMEH, became head of state after a military coup in 1995 and was recently elected president of The Gambia.

See also ISLAM IN AFRICA.

ROBERT BAUM

Judaism in North Africa
See JEWISH COMMUNITIES IN NORTH AFRICA.

Jugnauth, Anerood
1930–
Prime minister of Mauritius from 1982 to 1995, and since 2000.
Born into a family of Hindu planters in Palma, Mauritius, Anerood Jugnauth began his political career shortly after completing legal studies in Great Britain. Running as a candidate for the Independent Forward Bloc (IFB), he won a seat in the legislative assembly during the 1963 general elections. In 1966 Jugnauth attended the Constitutional Conference in London, primarily to ensure adequate Hindu representation in the future government of independent Mauritius. He shortly thereafter was appointed minister of state for development. In 1967 newly elected prime minister Seewoosagur Ramgoolam appointed Jugnauth minister of labor. But disagreements with the prime minister soon caused Jugnauth to resign, and he returned to law as a magistrate.

In 1971 Jugnauth reentered politics as a member of the newly formed Mouvement Militant Mauricien (MMM), a progressive socialist party founded by Franco-Mauritian Paul Bérenger. With many MMM leaders imprisoned during a government crackdown on the opposition, Jugnauth was able to quickly establish himself as an indispensable party asset, rising in the ranks to become party president in 1974. Winning a seat in parliament in 1976, Jugnauth became leader of the opposition.

The MMM won a crushing victory during the 1982 general elections; its candidates won all sixty elective seats. To ensure support from the Hindu community, Jugnauth, a Hindu himself, was appointed prime minister, while Bérenger became minister of finance. Conflicts between the two quickly arose over Bérenger's determination to maintain structural adjustment economic austerity measures and to make Creole the official language. Jugnauth was forced to leave the MMM and subsequently formed a new political party, the Mouvement Socialiste Militant (MSM).

In the 1983 elections, Jugnauth's MSM party allied with two others to push the MMM from power. Jugnauth upheld the economic reforms he had previously opposed and his administration presided over unprecedented economic growth and industrialization, making Mauritius one of the wealthiest countries of sub-Saharan Africa by the 1990s.

Jugnauth's regime was criticized, however, as both corrupt and undemocratic. In 1983 four members of the Mauritian Legislative Assembly, traveling under diplomatic passports, were arrested in an Amsterdam airport for smuggling 20 kilograms (44 pounds) of heroin. A Mauritian commission of inquiry later implicated several other legislators in drug trafficking. The same legislation also authorized press censorship with Jugnauth's support. Despite accusations of corruption, Jugnauth won the 1987 elections.

Over the next two years, Jugnauth survived two assassination attempts. In 1995 the electorate, tired of corruption allegations and hungry for new leadership, voted overwhelmingly for Navin Ramgoolam, son of the late prime minister, ending Jugnauth's thirteen-year tenure. In September 2000, however, a MSM-MMM coalition swept legislative elections, and Jugnauth became prime minister once again. Now in his seventies, he remains in office, having been overwhelmingly re-elected in September 2008.

ARI NAVE

Juju
Musical genre originating among Nigerian pop musicians, which emphasizes speechlike layers of polyrhythmic drumming, a broad range of rhythmic guitar patterns, and lyrics underscoring traditional Yoruba social values.
Juju music is an internationally popular musical expression growing out of a tradition of West African guitar-based popular music. The meaning of the term juju is unknown, though some historians have linked it to the sounds of a tambourine. It emerged in the 1930s in southwestern Nigeria, where local Yoruba musicians began casually making music in bars (palm-wine shacks) with transient laborers and descendants of freed slaves from the Caribbean and South America. The musicians played

guitars and banjos, sometimes supplemented by hand-held percussion instruments. Although early lyrics often drew on Yoruba folk sayings, juju songs later came to express thinly veiled anticolonial sentiments.

The first commercially available recordings appeared as 78s in the 1930s by musicians like Tunde King and Julius O. Araba. These recordings proved influential to Nigerian musicians after World War II (1939–1945). The compact disc compilation titled *Juju Roots: 1930s–1950s* clearly reveals the nature of the genre's evolution. Juju recordings from the 1940s and 1950s express a forcefully driving music with heavy emphasis on multiple, interlocking layers of poly-rhythmic percussion intersected by electric guitar lines. In addition to a variety of hand-held percussion instruments (shakers, bells, rattles), the traditional Yoruba pressure drum (also called talking drum, or *gangan* in Yoruba) was incorporated. The talking drum is a two-headed drum capable of producing a wide range of pitch variations imitating to some degree the tonal contours of spoken Yoruba. The instrument offers an ongoing parallel "commentary" to what a juju vocalist would sing, an ironic counterpoint or complementary expansion. The introduction of electrified guitars introduced a new spectrum of coloristic effects and rhythmic patterns, all at a volume capable of filling a large dance hall or concert arena.

The first major innovator in this heavily percussive and electrified style was I. K. Dairo. His bands, originally the Morning Star Orchestra and, later, the more famous Blue Spots, added accordion fills to complex guitar and drum-driven instrumental patterns. Song lyrics, tapping ancient Yoruba folkloric sources, began to comment sharply on social issues faced by increasingly cosmopolitan and wes-ternized urban audiences. By the 1970s Dairo had become the first juju musician to attract international audiences. From the 1980s to the present, Commander Ebenezer Obey and King Sunny Ade have developed individual styles, building on the Dairo legacy. Obey's guitar playing has synthesized African American blues and rock styles with juju. Ade has introduced the pedal steel guitar, pre-viously associated with American country music, to juju, along with songs extending to a half hour or longer. Both artists use sophisticated recording studio technology to create atmospheric electronic effects, furthering juju's evolution.

See also MUSIC, AFRICAN.

BIBLIOGRAPHY

Waterman, Christopher A. *Juju: A Social History and Ethnography of an African Popular Music.* University of Chicago Press, 1990.

K

Kaabu, Early Kingdom of

Historical kingdom centered in northeastern Guinea-Bissau.

Founded by Tiramakhan Traoré, a general of the MALI EMPIRE, the MANDINKA kingdom of Kaabu ruled the area that is presently known as northeastern GUINEA-BISSAU and southeastern SENEGAL from 1250 to 1867. For six centuries, Kaabu dominated small chiefdoms throughout the region and enslaved their inhabitants. Initially the kingdom remained a dependency of Mali. Kaabu expanded slowly; many groups fled to the coastal lowlands while others resisted Mandinka dominance. The kingdom was an important source of salt, gold, and slaves for Mali. The kingdom was socially stratified, with royal succession by matrilineal descent. In the late fifteenth and early sixteenth centuries, Songhai assaults on Mali enabled Kaabu to assert its independence. At the same time, the Portuguese and other European slave traders demanded an increasing volume of slaves for the transatlantic slave trade. Kaabu expanded considerably through warfare that was intended to capture slaves for export. At its height, the Kaabu kingdom included forty-four provinces that were providing troops and tribute.

When Portugal outlawed the slave trade in 1837, competition in the illicit slave trade increased. Kaabu provincial governors competed internally in intradynastic feuds that weakened the kingdom. The Islamic FULANI people, subject to heavy Kaabu taxation for generations, began to subvert the weakened kingdom through religious conversion and holy wars. Wars between Kaabu and the Fulani reached their apex in 1867 at the Kaabu capital, Kansala, when the Fulani Muslim religious leader Timbo Adbul Khudus and 12,000 soldiers forced Kaabu's final surrender.

See also GOLD TRADE; SALT TRADE.

ERIC YOUNG

Kabila, Laurent-Désiré

1939?–2001

African military leader and president of the Democratic Republic of the Congo from 1997 to 2001.

In 1997 Laurent-Désiré Kabila received international attention when he led a seven-month rebellion in ZAIRE (now the DEMOCRATIC REPUBLIC OF THE CONGO) that toppled longtime dictator MOBUTU SESE SEKO. Kabila's rapid rise to power followed nearly three decades of opposition to the regime of Mobutu. Laurent Kabila was born into the LUBA ethnic group in the mineral-rich province of Katanga in 1939. Little is known about his childhood. He attended university in France, where he studied political philosophy and became a Marxist, and in DAR ES SALAAM, TANZANIA, where he befriended Yoweri MUSEVENI, the future president of UGANDA. He returned to the BELGIAN CONGO shortly before it achieved independence (as the Congo) in 1960. Upon his return, Kabila became a member of the North Katanga Assembly and a staunch supporter of Congo's first prime minister, Patrice LUMUMBA. After Lumumba's murder in 1961, Kabila and other Lumumba supporters fled to the Congolese borderlands, where they began organizing against the government. In 1964 Kabila's rebel group received financial backing from Russia, China, and Cuba and staged an insurrection in the eastern provinces of the Congo. The rebellion briefly established a separatist state near Kisangani. In early 1965 Argentine revolutionary Che Guevara came to assist the rebellion, but quickly became frustrated with Kabila's leadership and left soon afterward. Later that year, the Congolese army, led by Joseph Mobutu (later Mobutu Sese Seko), ended the rebellion. Mobutu seized control of the Congo in late 1965. In 1967 Kabila cofounded the People's Revolutionary Party (PRP), a leftist rebel group that launched sporadic attacks against Mobutu and his regime. The group received funding from China and also supported itself by exporting gold and ivory. In the 1970s the PRP established a small socialist state in the South Kivu province of Congo (by then renamed Zaire) near LAKE TANGANYIKA. In 1975 Kabila and the PRP gained international notoriety when the group kidnapped three American students and a Dutch researcher from the nearby Gombe Stream Research Center founded by Jane Goodall. The PRP held the hostages for sixty-seven days but released them unharmed after the PRP received an unspecified ransom. Two years later, Mobutu's troops finally forced the PRP to abandon their mountain stronghold, and the rebel group fled into nearby TANZANIA. Kabila spent much of the 1980s in Tanzania, where he lived in relative obscurity. He sold gold mined in eastern Zaire in Dar es Salaam. At some point between 1980 and 1996 he developed ties with Museveni, president of Uganda, and Paul KAGAME, the Rwandan leader. Kabila disappeared in 1988, and many of his associates believed him dead. Kabila returned to public view in 1996, after Mobutu's government attempted to expel hundreds of Banyamulenge rebels (closely related to the Tutsi of neighboring BURUNDI and RWANDA). The rebels resisted, and Kagame recruited Kabila to lead a rebellion against Mobutu's regime. Later that year, Kabila united Banyamulenge and other guerrilla groups into the Alliance of Democratic Forces for the Liberation of Congo-Zaire (AFDL) and vowed to overthrow Mobutu. The group enjoyed instant support among the disillusioned and impoverished Zairean population and, in town after town, Kabila's troops easily defeated Mobutu's army. In May 1997 Kabila and his army approached KINSHASA, the country's capital. The cancer-stricken Mobutu fled, and Kabila's troops marched triumphantly into the city, where he renamed the country the Democratic Republic of the Congo and declared himself president on May 17. After taking control of the Congo, Kabila had a mixed record. At first, he was extremely popular among the Congolese, who applauded his promises to rebuild and revitalize the Congo and to end the rampant corruption that terrorized the citizenry and contributed to the country's decay. When Kabila imposed restrictions on civil liberties and political activity, however, he lost much of his initial popularity. Citizens complained that they had more freedom during the last years of Mobutu's regime and accused Kabila of nepotism and promoting only his own ethnic group, the Luba. Kabila faced international criticism as well for failing to hold democratic elections, for limiting free speech, and for arresting and threatening opposition groups. He was also criticized for thwarting a United Nations investigation into the disappearance of more than 100,000 Rwandan Hutu refugees, who may have been massacred by Kabila's largely Banyamulenge troops. By late 2000 Kabila's government faced serious threats from rebel forces that were gaining strength in the Congo. Kabila was assassinated in January 2001. His son, Joseph Kabila, succeeded to the presidency.

See also GOLD TRADE; HUTU AND TUTSI; IVORY TRADE; POLITICAL MOVEMENTS IN AFRICA; UNITED NATIONS IN AFRICA.

ELIZABETH HEATH

REBEL TROOP INSPECTION. Zairian rebel leader Laurent Kabila at Goma airport, 1997 (*Remy de la Mauviniere/AP Images*)

Kabiyé

Ethnic group of northern and central Togo and adjacent parts of Benin, numbering perhaps as many as 700,000, including closely related subgroups such as the Logba and Losso, who speak mutually intelligible dialects; also known as Kabre or Cabrai.

Broadly defined, the Kabiyé are the second largest ethnic group in TOGO, after the EWE. They dominate the country's military, and since General Gnassingbé Eyadéma, an ethnic Kabiyé, seized power in 1967, they have dominated the government as well.

Researchers believe that the Kabiyé, who call themselves "Lanmba," and related groups such as the Logba once occupied a broad band of territory across northern Togo and BENIN. However, during the seventeenth and eighteenth centuries KONKOMBA, fleeing conquest by the Dagomba of modern northern GHANA, displaced the Kabiyé from their western territories. Meanwhile, Bariba fleeing the expanding kingdom of Dahomey drove them out of modern Benin. By the early eighteenth century, the Kabiyé were concentrated in the densely populated La Kara region of Togo where they live today. During the eighteenth and early nineteenth centuries, the Kabiyé fell victim to slave raids carried out by the Bariba for their Dahomean overlords.

Most Kabiyé raise Millet, peanuts, Yams, and other crops for subsistence. They build stone terraces to prevent erosion on their rocky hillside fields and have a reputation as hard workers. Traditionally, Kabiyé men also worked as blacksmiths, and Kabiyé women sold metal wares and agricultural produce to neighboring groups.

Until the late nineteenth century most Kabiyé groups lacked political structures beyond patrilineal descent groups and strong age-grade societies, though the Logba appointed officials to arbitrate disputes. A centralized chieftainship with limited powers emerged among the Kabiyé during the 1860s. The German colonial administration strengthened the powers of the Kabiyé chief.

The Kabiyé resisted German occupation but in 1897 were forced to surrender. The Germans relied heavily on Kabiyé forced labor to build railways and other infrastructure. They established valuable teak and mango plantations on the denuded slopes of La Kara. After World War I (1914–1919), the French forcibly relocated many Kabiyé from this crowded region to relatively underpopulated regions of central Togo, and a voluntary southward migration of Kabiyé farmers has continued to this day. During the colonial period, many Kabiyé men migrated seasonally to work in the cocoa plantations of southern Togo and the GOLD COAST (today Ghana), and others, including Eyadéma, enlisted in the French military.

Under French and German colonial rule, the Kabiyé north experienced little development. The region suffered persistent poverty, and many Kabiyé grew to resent the relative wealth of southerners such as the Ewe. Since 1967, however, many Ewe and other non-Kabiyé have come to resent Kabiyé domination of Togo's military and government.

See also SLAVERY IN AFRICA.

Kabwe, Zambia

Mining town in central Zambia.

Known as Broken Hill before ZAMBIA gained independence in 1964, the town of Kabwe grew around Broken Hill Mine, opened in 1902, an important source of zinc, vanadium, sulfuric acid, and lead ores. The mine prompted construction of the region's first railroad, which passed through LUSAKA on its route to present-day ZIMBABWE. The railroad was extended north into the Copperbelt region soon thereafter. In 1924 a hydroelectric dam was built over the Mulungushi River to the southeast. Following the construction of major trunk roads after the turn of the century, small numbers of European colonizers began to settle the region surrounding Broken Hill in order to grow maize and tobacco. The earlier inhabitants were displaced and forced to work as miners or tenant farmers. Migrants from a variety of ethnic groups arrived seeking employment; the town began to grow rapidly by 1927, when copper mining reached full production. By 2003 the town's population reached an estimated 219,000.

ARI NAVE

Kabylia

Berber region in eastern Algeria and the site of an important uprising against French colonialism.

By the late nineteenth century, the Berber people who lived and farmed in the mountain region of eastern Algeria had enjoyed centuries of local governance. Even during the more than 250 years of rule by the Islamic Ottoman empire based in Turkey, Kabylia villages largely governed themselves, with decisions made by assemblies of adult men based on a fusion of local tradition and Islamic law. But as the French moved into the region in the 1850s, leaders, such as Bu Baghla and, later, Lalla Fatima, led the Kabylia in a struggle to resist conquest. Although they were unable to stop French forces, the spirit of resistance endured, culminating in the Great Revolt of 1871–1872, when leader Muhammad al-Hajj al-Muqrani proclaimed a jihad, or holy war, against the Christian invaders. About 150,000 Kabylias joined the rebellion, which spread toward Algiers. The French responded with military action, killing al-Muqrani and capturing his successor. Afterward, the

French seized large tracts of fertile land, paving the way for colonial expansion.

Kabylia is still known for its fierce independence. One of the most militant regions in the war against Colonial Rule (from 1954 to 1962), it is now home to many of Algeria's nationalist political and cultural leaders. After independence, the Kabylias revolted against the efforts of new president Ahmed Ben Bella to centralize power. Since the 1980s, they have been active in national politics, opposing Arabization laws and policies and promoting Berber rights. In recent years, the Algerian government has kept a close eye on Kabylia as a possible center of activity for the al-Qaeda terrorist network.

MARIAN AGUIAR

Kadalie, Clements
1896–1951
South African trade union leader of the 1920s.

Born in Nyasaland (in what is now MALAWI), Clements Kadalie emigrated to CAPE TOWN, SOUTH AFRICA, where he became the most important black trade union leader of his day. In 1919 he assisted a strike of black dockers and later that year formed the Industrial and Commercial Union (ICU), originally consisting of twenty-four black and mixed race dockworkers. Kadalie became the national secretary of the ICU, which he reorganized in 1921 as he consolidated his influence in Cape Province. He tried to present the ICU as no more than a trade union and did not attempt to compete in political terms with the African National Congress (ANC). He opposed the harsh handling by Prime Minister Jan Smuts of the 1922 miners' strike on the Witwatersrand, and he threw the support of the ICU behind the Nationalist-Labour Party of James Hertzog in the 1924 elections.

The Nationalist-Labour Party was victorious, but Kadalie found that the new government was even more reactionary than that of Smuts. As a result of this experience, he became increasingly anti-white and overtly political. By 1927 the ICU claimed more than 100,000 members and had become the largest black movement and South African trade union of the time. He moved the ICU headquarters to JOHANNESBURG in 1927, but no white unions or organizations would enter into relations with the ICU except for the Communist Party. Kadalie faced growing opposition from Communists and radicals within the ICU after the failure of several regional strikes and his reluctance to lead a nationwide strike. Although Kadalie expelled all Communists from the movement, his influence began to decline. He went to Geneva, Switzerland, in 1927 and then on to Great Britain in hopes of receiving international recognition of the ICU. When he returned to South Africa he found his position in the ICU had been undermined. A split developed and in 1929 Kadalie resigned. The ICU became less effective and broke apart in 1933. Nevertheless, it provided a model for later mass movements. Kadalie remained active in small local unions until his death.

Kagame, Paul
1957–Commander of the Rwandan Patriotic Front (RPF); president of Rwanda since 2000.

In July 1994 Paul Kagame led the guerrilla Rwandan Patriotic Front (RPF) to power in RWANDA, overthrowing a government whose members had participated in a genocide that killed an estimated one million people. Kagame quickly became the foremost figure in Rwandan politics and in 2000 was elected president of the nation. Kagame was born in southern Rwanda, but in 1959 a HUTU revolution in the Belgian colony of Rwanda forced into exile thousands of TUTSI, including two-year-old Kagame and his family. Kagame grew up in a refugee camp in western UGANDA, where he attended school. As a young man he joined the rebel army of Yoweri MUSEVENI to fight against the dictatorship of Milton OBOTE in Uganda. Museveni took power in 1986 and Kagame was awarded the post of chief of military intelligence. A year later Kagame and about 8,000 other Uganda-based Tutsi founded the RPF guerrilla army with financial and military support from Museveni.

In 1990 Kagame was taking military courses in Fort Leavenworth, Kansas, when the RPF invaded Rwanda. When the RPF's leader was killed, Kagame flew back to take over. In 1993 the RPF and the government of Rwandan president Juvénal HABYARIMANA signed a peace accord calling for a transition to multiparty democracy and the repatriation of Rwandan Tutsi refugees. In April 1994, however, Habyarimana's plane was shot down over KIGALI, the capital of Rwanda. His government immediately blamed the RPF (responsibility for the fatal crash was still undetermined years later), and Hutu militias began retaliating. Over the next several weeks hundreds of thousands of Tutsi and Hutu moderates were killed by the militias, the Rwandan army, and civilians following orders. The RPF resumed its war against the government in mid-April. Due partly to the chaos caused by the genocide and partly to Kagame's skilled military leadership, the RPF advanced quickly on the capital. At the same time more than 1.5 million Hutu fled the country. By the time the RPF took control of the government in early July, Kagame's leadership role was universally acknowledged. The RPF demonstrated Kagame's pledge to reunite Rwanda by appointing as president and prime minister two Hutus: Pasteur Bizimungu and Faustin Twagiramungu, respectively. Kagame, as vice president and defense minister, remained widely regarded as Rwanda's de facto leader. His disciplined and pragmatic governance won quick praise in the West, but many Rwandan Hutu resented the predominance of Tutsi in the army and cabinet; numerous figures in these organizations were, like Kagame, from Uganda. Kagame's support of Laurent-Désiré KABILA's 1996–1997 rebellion against MOBUTU SESE SEKO in the former ZAIRE, now the Democratic Republic of the Congo (DRC), led to accusations that Rwandan forces committed atrocities against Hutu refugees in the DRC. Although postgenocide Rwanda depended heavily on foreign aid, Kagame did not hesitate to criticize or defy the West on issues concerning his own country's recovery. From the beginning he insisted that reconciliation between Hutu and Tutsi could occur only if those guilty of genocide were brought to justice, and in 1998 he defended his government's executions of the first convicted criminals. In April 2000 legislators and government ministers elected Kagame president of Rwanda. He received eighty-one of eighty-six possible votes in the special election. Under Kagame, the human rights situation in Rwanda has come under nearly constant criticism and scrutiny from various international watchdog organizations. In 2006 the United States offered only a lukewarm appraisal of the human rights condition in Rwanda on a variety of fronts.

See also HUTU AND TUTSI; POLITICAL MOVEMENTS IN AFRICA.

LEYLA KEOUGH

Kaguru

Ethnic group of Tanzania; also known as the Kagulu.
The Kaguru inhabit the highlands of northeastern TANZANIA. They speak a Bantu language. Approximately 250,000 people consider themselves Kaguru.

See also BANTU: DISPERSION AND SETTLEMENT.

Kagwa, Apolo
1869–1927
Prime minister of Buganda from 1889 to 1926.
Born in Busoga, Apolo Kagwa was originally a slave and worked as a page for Kabaka MUTESA I (the king of BUGANDA). During this time many Muslim and Christian missionaries were arriving in Buganda. Although Kagwa initially practiced Islam, he was later baptized in the Anglican Church.

After Mutesa's death in 1884, religious civil war broke out in Buganda. Mutesa's successor, Mwanga II, purged many Christians from the Buganda court, but Kagwa survived. By 1887 he was commanding Buganda's royal guards. A year later, Mwanga was overthrown; Kagwa fled to the neighboring Ankole kingdom. In 1890 Kagwa

returned to lead the Christian Party and help reinstate Mwanga, who in turn made Kagwa the katikiro, or prime minister. In this position Kagwa welcomed both the Church Missionary Society and the British East Africa Company, and signed the treaty making Buganda a British protectorate in 1894. When Mwanga rebelled against the British three years later, Kagwa helped to overthrow him. The king's infant son, Daudi Chwa, became the new kabaka, but Kagwa, as one of Chwa's three regents, effectively ruled Buganda for nearly two decades.

The British rewarded Kagwa's collaboration by promising to assure Protestant hegemony in Buganda, and by granting Buganda considerable autonomy within the protectorate. Kagwa also received a vast tract of valuable land for his personal use. In 1905 the British knighted him.

After Chwa came of age in 1914, Kagwa came into increasing conflict with the new kabaka. His efforts to preserve Bugandan sovereignty also undermined his formerly friendly relations with the British. Ultimately Kagwa was forced to resign in 1926 after he challenged the British colonial administration's practice of dealing directly with Baganda chiefs, rather than with him. He died a year later, reportedly after a fall.

Kagwa wrote extensively in Lugandan. His books on the history and culture of the Buganda kingdom are considered important early works of modern African historiography.

ARI NAVE

Kahina
575?–702?
Berber priestess who led a campaign of resistance against Arab movement into North Africa in the seventh century.
In the seventh century, the Arabs arrived in the land they called Ifriqiya, in present-day TUNISIA, bringing Islam and seeking gold. The Jarawa Berbers in the Aurès Mountains became the main force halting their progress through North Africa. This group was known for their military prowess, and although they offered nominal allegiance to the Byzantine Empire, they in fact ruled their own land. Their chief was the Kahina, a woman who, some said, was more than a hundred years old and had two sons of two fathers, one Greek and one BERBER. She might have been a Christian or a Jew, and some historians have attributed her resistance to religious fervor. Or she might have simply been a strong ruler who would rather burn down her own kingdom than let it fall into the hands of an outside force. There is little historical documentation of the Kahina's life, although she appears frequently in the legend and literature of the Berbers, the Arabs, and the Europeans—all groups that came to have a stake in the rich Mediterranean region.

In Arabic literature, the Kahina appears as an Amazon, charging fiercely into battle with her long hair streaming behind. European writers depicted her as a romantic figure who fought heroically but in vain against marauding Islamic imperialists. All the stories tell how the Kahina, a traditional Berber prophetess, used divination to lead the Jarawa Berbers against the invaders. The Arab leader Hassan first reached the Aurès after defeating the Berber leader Kosaila in 686. The Kahina met the Arabs on the banks of the river Meskiana, after ordering the destruction of her own capital Baghaya so it could not be taken. She and the Jarawa were victorious and subsequently pursued the retreating Arabs to the town of Gabès, in present-day Tunisia. There the Arabs suffered such a defeat that they halted their advance for the next five years.

While the Arabs built the city of Tunis, the Kahina ruled the adjacent land in an uneasy stalemate. Stories tell how she adopted an Arab captive during this time, a handsome man of remarkable nobility and bravery, and symbolically gave him her milk, making him her third son. She had a vision of the Arab future triumph and of her sons granted a place of honor among the enemy. Before the Kahina faced the Arabs a final time, she sent the three sons to swear allegiance to Hassan.

The Kahina then destroyed her kingdom rather than let the Arabs take it. But as she burned fields, cut down trees, and destroyed towns, she alienated her own people. When the Arabs attacked again, now bolstered by reinforcements from the East, they met a Berber force weakened by divisions. Hassan killed and took the head of the 127-year-old Kahina at the well that now bears her name, fulfilling her final prophecy of her defeat.

BIBLIOGRAPHY

Norris, H. T. *The Berbers in Arabic Literature*. Longman, 1982.
Sweetman, David. *Women Leaders in African History*. Heinemann, 1984.

MARIAN AGUIAR

Kairouan, Tunisia

Tunisian city and the first permanent Arab settlement in North Africa.

Founded in 670 C.E. by the Arab Uqba ibn Nafi on behalf of the Damascus-based Umayyad dynasty, the Tunisian city of Kairouan (armed stronghold) was the vanguard of Arab conquest and the cradle of Islam in North Africa. From this first permanent settlement, Arab armies asserted control over the region they called Ifriqiya, a region which comprises present-day TUNISIA and eastern ALGERIA.

The location of Kairouan, halfway between the coast and the mountains, revealed that the Arabs had objectives different from those of all previous foreign conquerors. Unlike the Phoenicians and the Romans, who had ruled from cities such as CARTHAGE along the coast, the Umayyads placed their provincial capital inland. The strategy revealed their ambition to control autonomous Berber regions that had escaped the control of Carthage and Rome, and to convert the inhabitants to Islam.

For more than a century, Berber confederacies responded to growing Arab power by targeting Kairouan. In 683 they seized the city. After a long campaign against the militant Berbers, led by the "warrior queen" Kahina, the Arabs retook Kairouan in 691. The Berbers who continued to plague the city did not necessarily oppose Islamic rule—many belonged to the Kharijite sect of ISLAM—but they did oppose the rule of the Umayyad dynasty.

As the capital of the ninth-century Aghlabid dynasty, Kairouan grew in grandeur. The Aghlabids built the Mosque of the Three Doors (866) and Kairouan became a site of holy pilgrimage. With a series of public works, including a system for the storage and distribution of water, Kairouan metamorphosed from a military outpost to a cosmopolitan city. These projects, along with a lavish court, cost a great deal, and the Aghlabids imposed heavy taxes on the citizens of Kairouan. The city thrived economically under Aghlabid rule, however, as a center for trade along the routes across the Sahara and to the Middle East.

The subsequent Fatimid dynasty ruled from both Kairouan and coastal Mahdiyya. When they moved their capital to EGYPT, the Zirids, the Fatimid's vassals in Kairouan, faced an economic crisis as trade routes shifted away from the city into the region controlled by the Almoravids. Kairouan's crises contributed to a chain of events that transformed the entire Maghreb. In 1049 the Zirids broke with the Fatimid dynasty, and in retaliation, the Fatimids instigated, or at least did not stop, the Banu Hilal and Banu Sulaim invasion of Ifriqiya and the surrounding regions. The Banu Hilal sacked Kairouan in 1057, and their migration Arabized the hinterlands of the Maghreb. Kairouan would never again be a royal city or the center of the Tunisian political world.

Today, stone walls surround the old city, where low, whitewashed houses stand near ancient mosques. A thriving artisan trade includes rug making, coppersmithing, and shoemaking. The city maintains its status as a religious center; it is considered the fourth most important holy city in the Islamic world and in 2009 the Islamic Educational Scientific and Cultural Organization named the city the Islamic Cultural Capital. Because of this status, in the 1960s Kairouan was the site of demonstrations against the secular reforms of Habib Bourguiba, and today the city is at the heart of Tunisia's pro-Islamic movements. Kairouan's population, as of 2003, was some 150,000.

See also NORTH AFRICA, ROMAN RULE OF.

MARIAN AGUIAR

Kakwa

Eastern Sudanic-speaking ethnic group inhabiting a region that includes southern Sudan, northeastern Uganda, and northwestern parts of the Democratic Republic of the Congo.

According to oral tradition, the Kakwa migrated from East Africa into the southern SUDAN and then south into present-day UGANDA and the DEMOCRATIC REPUBLIC OF THE CONGO, where they settled among and intermarried with the MADI, BARI, and Lotuke peoples. On the eve of European colonialism in the late nineteenth-century the Kakwa homeland was incorporated into Equitoria, a territory controlled by the Egyptian Khedive Isma'il until 1889. The following year, much of the area became part of the Ugandan Protectorate.

Currently, approximately 100,000 Kakwa live in Uganda, while another 40,000 live in Sudan and 20,000 reside in the Democratic Republic of the Congo. Kakwa villages have traditionally been organized around a core of related men and their wives, and governed by councils of elders. Rural Kakwa depend primarily on agriculture for subsistence and income—corn, millet, and cassava are among their staple crops—but also raise cattle, which are valued as markers of prestige. Fishing is a significant economic activity for those Kakwa who live near the NILE. Many Kakwa observe the Islamic faith and follow the Malakite school of Islamic law.

Although the Kakwa are a relatively small minority in Uganda, comprising an estimated 1 percent of the total population, the ethnic group became well known when Idi Amin, a Kakwa by his father, became the Ugandan head of state after leading a coup to oust MILTON OBOTE.

Kakwa in Sudan were among the members of Anya Nya, an insurgent group in Sudan's first civil war (1956–1972). As Obote's army chief and, later, as Uganda's president, Idi AMIN supplied Israeli arms to Anya Nya. As president, Amin also recruited many Ugandan Kakwa into the armed forces and began to exterminate ACHOLI and LANGO soldiers, who had previously dominated the military. When Amin was ousted in 1979, many Kakwa fled to Sudan to escape Acholi and Lango retribution; many also later allied themselves with YOWERI MUSEVENI in opposing Obote's second regime.

ARI NAVE

Kalahari Desert

Semi-arid region in southern Africa inhabited by the Khoikhoi peoples.

Covering an area of approximately 260,000 sq km (about 100,000 sq mi), the Kalahari Desert spans southern BOTSWANA, eastern NAMIBIA, and northern SOUTH AFRICA. Although it is not actually a desert (it is classified as a "thirstland"), the Kalahari is an arid region covered by grasses and brush, although tubers and bulbous plants grow there. Except for the Boteti River, the region is fed with no surface water; thus Kalahari wildlife, which includes wildebeest, zebra, eland, giraffe, and elephant, must rely on waterholes.

Largely unsuitable for agriculture, the Kalahari was long inhabited only by the KHOIKHOI and SAN peoples (often referred to as BUSHMEN), who lived by hunting, foraging, and raising livestock. But parts of the Kalahari have now been turned into national parks and game reserves. These have provided some employment for the desert's longtime residents, but have also restricted access to their former hunting territory.

See also BIOGEOGRAPHY OF AFRICA; TOURISM IN AFRICA; WILDLIFE MANAGEMENT IN AFRICA.

BIBLIOGRAPHY

Main, Michael. *Kalahari: Life's Variety in Dune and Delta.* Southern Book Publishers, 1987.

Thomas, David S. G. *The Kalahari Environment.* Cambridge University Press, 1991.

ROBERT FAY

Kalanga

Ethnic group of southern Africa; also known as Bakalanga and Kalaka.

The Kalanga primarily inhabit northeastern BOTSWANA and western ZIMBABWE. Others live in MOZAMBIQUE. They speak a BANTU language and are closely related to the SHONA people. Approximately 400,000 people consider themselves Kalanga.

[*See also* BANTU, *subentry on* DISPERSION AND SETTLEMENT.]

Kalenjin

Collection of ethnic groups in Kenya.

The term Kalenjin did not traditionally refer to a single ethnic group. Instead, it encompassed several peoples of the RIFT VALLEY who spoke Southern Nilotic languages and were known to outsiders as "the Nandi-speaking peoples." These groups, who also share many cultural traits, forged a common identity in the years following World War

II (1939–1945) in anticipation of Kenyan independence. Today, approximately 3 million people consider themselves Kalenjin. Groups that compose the Kalenjin include the KIPSIGI, the NANDI, the TUGEN, the KEYO, the POKOT, the Marakwet, the Sabaot, and the Terik.

The origins of the Kalenjin remain uncertain, but some scholars believe that ancestors of the Kalenjin migrated from Ethiopia, arriving in the Mount Elgon area around the sixteenth century. The territorial expansion of the MAASAI in the eighteenth century pushed the Kalenjin into the area where they now predominate, between the Rift Valley and LAKE VICTORIA. Kalenjin myth names Misri, or EGYPT, as their place of origin; customary Kalenjin religious beliefs, based on sun worship, refer to the ancient Egyptian god Asiis.

Kalenjin peoples have traditionally practiced nomadic PASTORALISM, but many today, especially among the highland-dwelling Kipsigis and Nandi, are farmers. It is not uncommon for members of the same family to live in close proximity to one another yet practice different livelihoods. Staple food crops include millet, maize, beans, peas, and cassava; in the highlands, tea is an important cash crop. Nomadic pastoral Kalenjin peoples include the Tugen, Keyo, Marakwet, and Pokot, but even sedentary farming Kalenjin often keep cattle.

Kalenjin society is divided into patrilineal clans (ortinuek) as well as into male and female age groupings. Circumcision for both sexes has traditionally signified the passage to adulthood. Politically decentralized, in precolonial times both nomadic and sedentary Kalenjin peoples vested decision-making responsibility in local councils of elders.

The Kalenjin unified in order to more effectively represent their interests to the British colonial government. Today they account for a smaller percentage of the Kenyan population than either the KIKUYU or the LUO. Nevertheless, they hold considerable political influence, largely because KENYA's president, DANIEL ARAP MOI—himself a Kalenjin—has promoted their interests at the expense of larger groups, especially the Kikuyu.

See also FEMALE CIRCUMCISION IN AFRICA; and RITES OF PASSAGE AND TRANSITION.

ROBERT FAY

Kamba
Ethnic group in Kenya.
The Kamba are a central BANTU-speaking people closely related to the neighboring KIKUYU. Before they migrated to their present location in the Ukamba Highlands, according to tradition, the Kamba resided around Mount KILIMANJARO in TANZANIA. Although the majority of

the Kamba practice Christianity, approximately 40 percent still practice the traditional Kamba religion, which is similar to that of the Kikuyu. Traditional Kamba believed in a supreme god, Ngai, and in aimu, or ancestral spirits.

The Kamba traditionally live in extended families on separate homesteads, each with its own agricultural plot. Several such homesteads make up an utui, which roughly translates to "village" and includes a common grazing area. The Kamba hold and inherit land patrilineally. The main political division in traditional Kamba society is the mbai, or "clan." The society historically has been organized by age grades, although this practice lost importance during the colonial period.

Although they mainly grow maize, millet, and sorghum today, many Kamba maintain a pastoral tradition and keep livestock. Trade has historically been an important element to the Kamba economy. Long-distance trade with SWAHILI traders along KENYA's coast was fruitful, especially because of the Kamba access to IVORY. Today, Kamba craft products such as woodcarvings, calabashes, and woven baskets remain in demand both locally and internationally. In recent years, because of overpopulation and soil erosion, large numbers of Kamba have migrated to NAIROBI and other urban areas to find work. As many as 4 million people consider themselves Kamba.

ROBERT FAY

Kamberi
Ethnic group of Nigeria; also known as the Kambari.
The Kamberi primarily inhabit western and northwestern NIGERIA. They speak a Niger-Congo language. Approximately 100,000 people consider themselves Kamberi.

See also LANGUAGES, AFRICAN: AN OVERVIEW.

Kampala, Uganda
Capital and largest city of Uganda.
Originally a settlement scattered across seven hills on the northern shore of LAKE VICTORIA, Kampala has grown into a city that spans nearly fifty hills and houses more than 1.2 million people (as of 2002). The original settlement was known as Mengo, and during the nineteenth century it served as the royal seat for the BUGANDA kabaka, or king. English explorers such as Sir Richard Francis BURTON came to the Buganda court at Mengo in 1862 and entered into diplomatic relations with Kabaka MUTESA I shortly thereafter. In 1890, seeking to establish British control over the source of the NILE RIVER, Captain FREDERICK LUGARD built a fort for the Imperial British East African Company on a hill near

Mengo that was known as Kampala to the Bagandans, and as Fort Hill to the British. Four years later Great Britain formally claimed possession of the region. Eventually, the town around the fort grew to encompass Mengo, and Kampala became Uganda's largest town, as well as its center for commerce and communication.

Along with Jinja, Kampala grew to become a major industrial center with factories processing agricultural commodities, particularly sugar and cotton, and light manufacturing plants producing consumer goods. By the 1930s a sewage and plumbing system had been constructed, and several roads had been surfaced. When Uganda achieved independence in 1962, Kampala became the political capital.

Although Kampala's infrastructure deteriorated during the conflict-torn regimes of MILTON OBOTE and Idi AMIN, transportation and communication services have improved in recent years. Port Bell, a few miles to the south of the city, services the shipping industry along Lake Victoria. The city is also connected by major railroad lines to port facilities at MOMBASA, KENYA.

Many of the hills of Kampala are crowned by cathedrals, churches, and mosques. Lugard's fort, now a barrack, remains a hilltop landmark, as do Mulago Hospital and Makerere University. Elevation is also a marker of class; prosperous neighborhoods line the hilltops, while shantytowns dot the valleys. Extensive suburbs surround the city. In 2002 Kampala was the scene of a massive demonstration by the BAGANDA, the country's largest tribe. Bagandans, who make up a quarter of the population, were marching to demand a new federal constitution that recognizes their kingdom as a semi-autonomous state.

ARI NAVE

Kana

Ethnic group of Nigeria; also known as Khana and Ogoni.
The Kana primarily inhabit River State in southeastern NIGERIA. They speak a Niger-Congo language and are closely related to the IBIBIO people. Approximately 300,000 people consider themselves Kana.

See also LANGUAGES, AFRICAN: AN OVERVIEW.

Kanembu

Ethnic group of Chad.
The Kanembu primarily inhabit the northern shores of Lake Chad. They speak a Nilo-Saharan language and are closely related to the KANURI people. Approximately 650,000 people consider themselves Kanembu.

See also LANGUAGES, AFRICAN: AN OVERVIEW.

Kano, Alhaji Aminu
1920–1983
Teacher and radical politician.
Alhaji Aminu Kano was born in Kano, northern Nigeria, to a FULANI family of Islamic scholars. As a youth he studied Arabic and English as well as HAUSA, and became familiar with the Qur'an (Koran). Kano attended Kaduna College from 1937 to 1942 and then went abroad, studying at the University of London from 1946 to 1948.

When he returned to Nigeria, Kano worked as a teacher and associated with other members of the young, foreign-educated elite who wished to reform northern Nigeria's class structure. He was one of the founding members of the Northern People's Congress (NPC) in 1949, but the next year, frustrated by the conservatism of the NPC, he broke off and founded the more overtly anti-colonial Northern Elements Progressive Union (NEPU). In 1959, with the support of the NEPU, Kano was elected to the Nigerian House of Representatives. Kano remained at the head of his party until 1966, when the party was banned after a failed coup attempt.

During the Biafran War (from 1967 to 1971), Kano served the military government as the federal commissioner for communications and later as the federal commissioner for health. In the late 1970s, as Nigeria prepared for a return to civilian rule, Kano participated in the assembly that finalized the new constitution. When the ban on party politics was lifted in 1978, Kano founded the socialist People's Redemption Party, and ran for president on its ticket. Although he lost, the party secured governorships of Kano and Kaduna states.

Kano died in 1983 as the Second Republic was coming to an end. Enhancing his political legacy, he had written one book in English, *Politics and Administration in Post War Nigeria*, as well as some plays, songs, and poetry, all written in Hausa.

BIBLIOGRAPHY
Feinstein, Alan. *African Revolutionary: The Life and Times of Nigeria's Aminu Kano*. Lynne Reinner, 1987.

ERIC BENNETT

Kano, Nigeria
Also called Kano City, Kano is a large city in northern Nigeria that serves as the capital of Kano State.
In the tenth century C.E., Bayajidda Abuyazid, said to be an exiled prince from Baghdad, founded seven HAUSA city-states, of which Kano was one. Prehistoric stone tools discovered on the site, however, suggest that the city's actual history extends much further into the past. Scholars from the ancient empire of Mali brought Islam to Kano in the 1340s, and the city achieved great prosperity

during the rule of Muhammad Rumfa (1463–1499). Walls built during that period still surround the old quarter of the city, and Rumfa's palace, located next to NIGERIA's largest mosque, now serves as the emir's palace.

For centuries Kano was an important market town on trans-Saharan caravan routes. Kola and other products from the forested coastal areas of West Africa changed hands in Kano's market, as did Saharan SALT, luxury goods from North Africa and Europe, and slaves. Kano's resident Hausa artisans also manufactured textiles as well as leather and metal goods for both long-distance and local commerce, while nearby villages produced most of the city's food supply. After the FULANI conquest of Hausaland in the early nineteenth century, Kano became the capital of an emirate within the SOKOTO CALIPHATE. In the twentieth century, Kano has retained a vital role in the regional economy, but through different means. Today the primary crop is peanuts, which are consumed locally and exported. The tanning and decoration of hides and skins, however, remains a major economic activity.

Most contemporary residents still claim to be Hausa, though sizeable populations of FULANI and Abagagyawa also reside in Kano. The city has six major districts: Fagge, the Syrian Quarters and the adjoining Commercial Township, Sabon Gari, the Nassarawa, Bompai, and the original, walled area. These districts divide further into approximately 100 small neighborhoods (unguwa), each of which centers on a mosque and a market. Two hills, Dalla and Goron Dutse, dominate the oldest part of Kano. At their bases, water collects in pools that provide most of the clay used in constructing homes.

Kano is still a center of old-style textile making and leather- and metalworking. But it also hosts food industries, such as meat-processing, canning, bottling, and the production of peanut and vegetable oils; light manufacturing, such as modern textiles, knit fabrics, plastics, pharmaceuticals, and furniture; and heavy industries, such as steel-rolling and the production of chemicals, automobiles, and asbestos. In addition, Kano remains a hub of transport—highways converge upon the city, railroads run to NGURU, LAGOS, and Port Harcourt, and the airport services major international flights.

Kano is also home to numerous schools and institutes, including Kano State Institute for Higher Education, an Arabic law school, Bayero University, a state polytechnic college, a commercial school, an agricultural research institute that focuses on peanuts, two libraries, and several teacher-training institutes.

In 2001 Muslim demonstrations against the United States led to destructive riots in Kano that left more than 200 dead and 17,000 displaced. Most of the violence was targeted at Christians of the IGBO and YORUBA ethnic groups who control much of the city's commerce. More violence erupted following the contested local elections of 2007. As many as thirty people were killed in the chaos.

See also ISLAM IN AFRICA; MALI EMPIRE; *and* SALT TRADE.

ERIC BENNETT

Kanuri

Ethnic group of Nigeria, Niger, Chad, and Cameroon; also known as Beriberi in some areas.

The Kanuri, dispersed throughout four countries around Lake Chad, once ruled the powerful and centralized kingdom of Bornu. They speak a Nilo-Saharan language, which anthropologists believe originated in what is today the SAHARA, before climatic changes that occurred about 5,000 years ago made the region dry and inhospitable. Kanuri oral histories, however, like those of many other Muslim groups in western Africa, claim that the group originated in Yemen. According to legend, their ancestor, Sayf, founded the Kanem kingdom (in present-day CHAD). His family, the Sefuwa dynasty, would control Kanem and its successor, Bornu, for over a thousand years.

By 1000 C.E., Kanem, dominated by the KANEMBU people, was renowned throughout the Islamic world for its prosperity and trade connections. A regular stop for many trans-Saharan trade caravans, the capital city was also a popular resting point for Muslims who were traveling across the continent on the pilgrimage to Mecca. Beginning in the mid-thirteenth century, however, a series of disputes over succession ravaged the kingdom and made it susceptible to outside invaders. After several attacks, a rival group from the north called the Bulala invaded the kingdom in the fourteenth century and usurped power from the Sefuwa dynasty.

The majority of the Kanembu fled from the invaders and established a new kingdom southwest of Lake Chad in Bornu. Here the Kanembu intermarried with indigenous Sao and KOTOKO people to form the ethnic group known as the Kanuri. Bornu eventually recaptured Kanem and conquered surrounding regions. At its peak in the sixteenth century, the Bornu empire stretched from KANO in present-day NIGERIA around Lake Chad and north into the Fezzan of present-day LIBYA. Bornu's rulers traded SALT from their lucrative mines at Bilma for GOLD and military equipment from the nearby HAUSA. In addition, they imposed heavy taxes on their subjects. These revenues supported the jihads (holy wars), that Bornu's kings, like many other West African rulers, launched during the sixteenth and seventeenth centuries to subdue the "heathen" groups living outside their territory and to acquire slaves. Bornu also conducted campaigns against neighboring kingdoms. The kingdom imported firearms from North Africa, and one ruler, Idris Aloma, even hired Turkish mercenaries to train his army—a strategic move that enabled Bornu to defeat SONGHAI in the mid-seventeenth century.

Bornu's military expansion, however, sapped the kingdom's power. The constant military campaigns impoverished the Kanuri and caused popular discontent. In an effort to regain popular support, Bornu's rulers limited military action to slave raids, and made the empire a center of Islamic learning. This decision, however, eventually contributed to Bornu's downfall. As rival armies continued to improve, Bornu became an easy target. During the nineteenth century, Bornu lost its western Hausa territories to the SOKOTO CALIPHATE, and a Bornu tributary, the Damagaram kingdom based in Zinder in present-day NIGER, declared its independence from Bornu. In 1897 the kingdom finally fell to an invader from the east, RABIH AL-ZUBAYR. By 1900, however, the French took control of much of the area and killed Rabih.

Three different European powers—Great Britain, France, and Germany—divided the Bornu empire between four different colonies—Nigeria, Niger, Chad, and CAMEROON. (Great Britain and France divided the German territory after World War II.) The British and French disrupted the profitable trans-Saharan trade, subjecting the Kanuri to the colonial economy. Further, colonization divided the once-united Kanuri, although today most inhabit an area in northeastern Nigeria around the city of Maiduguri. The Kanuri now earn their income predominantly through commerce and agriculture. They produce guinea corn, millet, peanuts, and cotton, and they raise cattle. Today, some 4 million people consider themselves Kanuri.

See also ETHNICITY AND IDENTITY IN AFRICA: AN INTERPRETATION; ISLAM IN AFRICA; LANGUAGES, AFRICAN: AN OVERVIEW; and SLAVERY IN AFRICA.

ELIZABETH HEATH

Kaonde

Ethnic group of south central Africa; also known as Bakaonde, Kaundi, and Kunda.

The Kaonde primarily inhabit the North West Province of ZAMBIA and southeastern DEMOCRATIC REPUBLIC OF THE CONGO. They speak a BANTU language and are closely related to the neighboring BEMBA and LUBA peoples. Some 330,000 people consider themselves Kaonde.

See also ETHNICITY AND IDENTITY IN AFRICA: AN INTERPRETATION and LANGUAGES, AFRICAN: AN OVERVIEW.

Karaboro

Ethnic group of West Africa; also known as Karakora.

The Karaboro primarily inhabit northern CÔTE D'IVOIRE and southwestern BURKINA FASO. They speak a Niger-Congo language and are closely related to the SENUFO people. Approximately 100,000 people consider themselves Karaboro.

See also ETHNICITY AND IDENTITY IN AFRICA: AN INTERPRETATION; and LANGUAGES, AFRICAN: AN OVERVIEW.

Karimojon

Ethnic group of East Africa; also known as the Karamojong.

The Karimojon primarily inhabit northeastern UGANDA and neighboring parts of KENYA and SUDAN. They speak a Nilo-Saharan language. Approximately 500,000 people consider themselves Karimojon.

See also ETHNICITY AND IDENTITY IN AFRICA: AN INTERPRETATION; and LANGUAGES, AFRICAN: AN OVERVIEW.

Kasanje

Kingdom in Angola that emerged in the mid-1600s.

Located along the banks of the Kwango River, Kasanje formed in the mid-1630s when the Imbangala band led by Kasanje Kalunga ka Kinguri chose the location as a permanent habitation. Kasanje's band is first known in 1617 when it and several other Imbangala bands came from the central highlands of Angola across the Kwanza River at the invitation of the Portuguese governor of Angola, Luis Mendes de Vasconcelos. Kasanje served with the Portuguese during their campaigns against Ndongo in 1618 and 1619, but soon left Portuguese service to engage in independent raiding. Kasanje's raids devastated Ndongo, and their removal was a key issue in the negotiations between Ndongo and Portugal in 1622. Nevertheless, Kasanje continued to migrate frequently and raid widely in the region between the Lucala River and the Kwango, both north and south of the Kwanza River, including incursions as far north as the southern parts of the kingdom of Kongo in 1628 and 1829. Njinga Mbandi, Ndongo's queen, joined Kasanje's band briefly in 1629, following her expulsion from her capital on the island of Kindonga and her forced acceptance of a humiliating position as Kasanje's wife. When Njinga broke with Kasanje a few years later, the two polities became bitter rivals and remained so from then on.

Kasanje settled in the province of Ngangela near the Kwanza around 1635, and in 1639 accepted overtures of peace from the Portuguese government of Angola. The alliance thus formed became an important part of Portuguese policy in the eastern section of their domain. When the Dutch took over Luanda in 1641, the Portuguese government renewed the alliance and promoted Kasanje's attack on Njinga's army as a way to reduce pressure on their forces during the war. After the Portuguese restoration in 1648, Kasanje Kalunga ka Kinguri renewed the relationship that had been strengthened during the war years.

Around 1650 Ngonga a Mbande, a Mbundu captured at Dambi a Kitala in Ndongo when he was only a child and adopted by Kasanje Kalunga ka Kinguri, overthrew his patron and took power, naming himself Kasanje ka Kinguri. He maintained a vigorous policy of raiding that extended north along the Kwango and west along the Kwanza for considerable distances. He sought a closer alliance with Portugal, fearing Njinga's rapprochement might endanger him, and received a Portuguese mission in 1655 that included a priest, who eventually persuaded him to be baptized as Pascoal Rodrigues Machado two years later. Christianity was never accepted there, however, except by resident Portuguese merchants. The Portuguese made him a general in their armed forces.

Because the Kasanje often captured slaves during their raiding expeditions, the Portuguese court attracted merchants who settled there, and through diplomatic negotiations, became subject to the oversight of a capitão mor who regulated their affairs at the market. The capitão mor served as a permanent representative of the Portuguese government and sought to persuade Kasanje to form closer alliances.

Kasanje actively fought wars against Njinga in the 1660s and south of the Kwanza, eventually expanding into territory bordering the central highlands, where it developed a long-term rivalry with Muzumbo a Kalunga, the mightiest of the late seventeenth-century powers in the region. In the 1670s Kasanje made commercial contact with the emerging Lunda empire and became an important broker of slaves from the deeper interior to Angola. When Kasanje ka Kinguri died, around 1679, interventions by Matamba on behalf of a pretender resulted in the death of Kitamba kia Kaita Pascal Machado, his first elected successor, and the eventual elevation of Kinguri kia Kasanje.

For much of the eighteenth century Kasanje's history is obscure. In the middle of the century there were large and continuous wars associated with a rearrangement of power in the Kwango valley, including challenges to Matamba's authority from the north and the disruption of Kasanje's trade relations with Portugal. In 1754 the king declared that no Europeans or their agents could even see the Kwango River, let along cross it, as Lunda's power emerged and

became a richer source for the slave trade. Portuguese diplomatic attempts to improve the situation failed, and in 1767 Lunda forces arrived, sparking major battles with Kasanje. The Portuguese refused to aid their allies in this war, however, claiming that they had blocked trade and were thus rebels. The following year, however, they sent support to quell a rebellion led by his second-in-command.

In the 1830s Portugal sought to expand its power and influence in the region. It raided the Kasanje market in 1836, and established the presidio of Duque de Braganza on the Lukala River, on the road to Kasanje, two years later. In 1850 Portugal attempted to bring Kasanje under its control by sending an expedition to break Kasanje's control over regional trade. The several expeditions launched between 1850 and 1862, however, were met with determined resistance by Mbumba a Kinguri, who prevented any permanent occupation or the installation of an effective puppet. In the final campaign Kasanje's forces compelled the Portuguese to withdraw, and even though Mbumba a Kinguri formally accepted vassalage to Portugal, he remained independent.

When Mbumba a Kinguri died, in 1873, the country split into warring factions related to the radical changes in wealth and power engendered by the new commerce, in which wax and ivory replaced slaves as the region's most important exports. These new conditions favored local rulers over the central market, and the Kasanje ruling house split into three segments, each controlling a different part of the country. The problems engendered by this loss of authority greatly facilitated the final conquest of the country by the Portuguese in 1895–1901.

JOHN THORNTON

Kasavubu, Joseph
1910?–1969
First president of the Republic of the Congo (now the Democratic Republic of the Congo), and former president of the Bakongo Alliance.

Joseph Kasavubu was born near Tsehla, Belgian Congo. Originally trained as a Catholic priest, Kasavubu dropped out of seminary in 1940 and soon entered the colonial civil service. While a civil servant, Kasavubu joined several KONGO cultural societies, many of which advocated the eventual reunification of the Kongo kingdom. In 1955 he was elected president of the Bakongo Alliance (Abako), a cultural society with political leanings, and he soon transformed the group into a serious political party advocating Kongo autonomy.

Abako's development coincided with the burgeoning independence movement and, as it was one of the few organized political parties and the dominant party in the city of Léopoldville (now KINSHASA), Kasavubu soon became a key political leader. In the 1957 local elections, Kasavubu was elected mayor of a section of Léopoldville. Although he was arrested in 1959 after riots broke out in Léopoldville, he was soon reinstated.

In January 1960 Kasavubu participated in the Round Table Conference on Belgian Congo independence in Brussels, Belgium. Soon afterward, the Belgians nominated Kasavubu to be president of the new Republic of the Congo and named Patrice LUMUMBA prime minister. This, however, soon proved to be an uneasy alliance because of their vastly different political visions. Kasavubu hoped for a federal structure that might grant the Kongo population some autonomy, while Lumumba wanted a strong unitary state. This coalition was further strained by the chaos that erupted after independence. Although Kasavubu and Lumumba formally split in September 1960, both were unseated by a military coup led by MOBUTU SESE SEKO.

Kasavubu was reinstated in February 1961 and remained president until 1965. During this time, he stabilized his position by deflecting difficult decisions to the prime minister. In 1965, Kasavubu was removed in a second coup d'etat by Mobutu Sese Seko and retired from politics.

See also CONGO, DEMOCRATIC REPUBLIC OF THE.

BIBLIOGRAPHY

Lemarchand, René. *Political Awakenings in the Belgian Congo.* University of California Press, 1964.

Young, Crawford. *Politics in the Congo: Decolonization and Independence.* Princeton University Press, 1965.

ELIZABETH HEATH

Kasena

Ethnic group of West Africa; also known as Kassena.

The Kasena primarily inhabit northern GHANA and southern BURKINA FASO. They speak a Niger-Congo language and belong to the GRUSI cultural and linguistic group. Approximately 300,000 people consider themselves Kasena.

See also ETHNICITY AND IDENTITY IN AFRICA: AN INTERPRETATION; and LANGUAGES, AFRICAN: AN OVERVIEW.

Kateb, Yacine

1929–1989

Algerian novelist, poet, and playwright whose most famous work, Nedjma, is considered the starting point of North African (or Maghreb) literature in French.

Yacine Kateb was born in 1929 in Condé Smendou, a small village in eastern ALGERIA that was under French rule at that time. His family was highly educated and imbued with a strong sense of Algerian history and culture. His mother introduced Kateb to theater and poetry and he later referred to her as "a theater unto herself." As a young boy, he attended a Qur'anic school and then was sent to a French language school within the colonial education system or "dans la gueule du loup" (in the wolf's mouth), as he described it.

He was later expelled from that secondary school, which was in Setif, after participating in a demonstration by Algerian nationalists on May 8, 1945, to celebrate the end of World War II. They paraded through the streets of the city, carrying a new flag and claiming independence for Algeria. The French rulers cracked down on the demonstrators, killing thousands and forever changing the relationship between the two communities. According to French historian Benjamin Stora, the French army killed around 50,000 people that day. Kateb was arrested, but freed several months later. While in prison, he began writing poetry, inspired in part by his mother, who, believing him to have been killed, had a mental breakdown and was institutionalized for many years. The imprisonment was a crucial time for the writer, and for the country, which established an independence struggle nine years later.

From 1948 to 1951 Kateb worked as a journalist at *Alger Républicain.* He also published poems in literary reviews including *Forge, Simoun, Soleil,* and *Terrasses.* In 1951, he traveled to France, where he settled in Paris for a long period of exile. In 1954, he published *Le Cadavre encerclé* (written in 1953; The Enclosed Corpse) in the review *Esprit.* While in Paris, he met the famous German playwright Bertold Brecht and read and wrote prodigiously. William Faulkner and James Joyce were among his favorite authors.

When *Nedjma* was published in Paris in 1956, it was compared to Faulkner's *The Sound and the Fury* for its discontinuous chronology, multiple narrative voices, and unusual concentric structure. The figure of Nedjma, a mysterious spirit woman, and the themes in the novel of traditional Algerian history, legends, and tribal allegiance form the crux of Kateb's literary production. Nedjma, a name that means "star" in Arabic, is also the name of the author's cousin, whom he adored. He himself said that his creative work was in effect only one continuous piece: "Je crois bien en effet que je suis l'homme d'un seul livre" (I believe that I am a man of only one book). Another novel, *Le Cercle des représailles* (The Circle of Reprisals), published in 1959, and a collection of plays, *Le Polygone étoilé* (The Starry Polygon), published in 1966, dealt with many of the same themes and characters as *Nedjma.*

Algeria achieved independence in 1962 and Kateb returned there in 1970, remaining until his death in 1989, from leukemia. Once back in his homeland, he stopped writing in French and began writing plays in the vernacular languages of Arabic and Berber (now called Tamazigh). His collected works, published after his death, continue to influence Algerian and North African literature.

AMINA AZZA BEKKAT

Kaunda, Kenneth
1924–
President of Zambia from independence in 1964 until 1991.

The eighth child of migrants from MALAWI, Kenneth Kaunda adopted the language of the BEMBA people among whom he was raised. His parents were both teachers, and Kaunda followed in their footsteps as a teacher and headmaster from 1944 to 1947.

His political career began with involvement in the Northern Rhodesia African Congress. He was elected secretary in 1950 and rose quickly through the ranks. In 1953 he was elected secretary-general of the organization, which was renamed the African National Congress (ANC). Within a few months, his call for civil disobedience in opposition to the white-ruled Central African Federation led to his arrest. In 1955 he was again arrested and this time imprisoned. In 1957 Kaunda traveled to England under the auspices of the Labour Party to study the parliamentary system. He returned to Northern Rhodesia in 1958. Disillusioned with the moderate stance of the ANC leader, HARRY NKUMBULA, Kaunda broke away and founded the Zambian African National Congress (ZANC). The colonial administration banned the ZANC in 1959 and imprisoned Kaunda.

Shortly after his release in 1960, Kaunda was elected president of the newly formed United National Independence Party (UNIP). Kaunda ran for a seat in the legislative assembly as a UNIP candidate during the 1962 elections. Kaunda took a ministerial post and established himself as the most powerful African in the government. In the face of civil disobedience organized by Kaunda and other nationalists, the British government finally acquiesced to demands for independence, and abolished the federation in 1963. In the 1964 elections, UNIP's sweeping victory won Kaunda the office of prime minister.

Zambia finally received independence on October 24, 1964, with Kaunda as president. Kaunda faced numerous obstacles, including ethnic partisanship that erupted in violence during the 1968 elections. Intolerant of opposition, Kaunda banned all political parties but UNIP in 1972 and made Zambia a one-party state. His policies, including nationalization of the copper industry and reliance on food subsidies for the poor, made Zambia increasingly dependent on revenues from copper exports. As president of a Front Line State, a country bordering the nations that were still under minority rule and subject to sanctions, Kaunda had to balance a commitment to majority rule against

DIPLOMATIC RELATIONS. British Prime Minister Margaret Thatcher dances with Zambian President Kenneth Kaunda at the Lusaka Press Club annual awards dinner, 1979. (*AP Images*)

Zambia's continued vulnerability to economic sabotage and military attack. Kaunda served as the chairman of the Organization of African Unity (OAU) from 1970 to 1971, and again from 1987 to 1988.

By the mid-1980s the Kaunda regime had lost public support. With corrupt government officials at the helm and a failing economy, calls for a return to multiparty politics increased. Eventually, Kaunda yielded and called for multiparty elections in 1991, in which FREDERICK CHILUBA's Movement for Multiparty Democracy (MMD) defeated Kaunda's UNIP. In 1993 Kaunda announced plans for retirement from political life; however, during the following year he returned to challenge the MMD in the upcoming elections. In response, Chiluba instituted constitutional amendments barring Kaunda from running by requiring that the candidates' parents be Zambian. The

UNIP and other opposition parties boycotted the 1996 elections, and Chiluba consequently won reelection.

In August 1997, Kaunda suffered bullet wounds when police opened fire on his car. He charged the government with attempted assassination, and though evidence indicated that senior police officers had ordered his shooting, the government denied his charges. In October 1997, a group of drunken soldiers attempted a coup. Kaunda was accused of plotting the coup and was detained, despite a lack of evidence. He served as leader of the UNIP until 2000, when he announced his retirement from politics.

After retiring, Kaunda established the Kenneth Kaunda Children of Africa Foundation as part of his campaign to fight the spread of AIDS on the continent. He is also working to reduce poverty in Africa. Kaunda has been awarded honorary doctorates of law and other honorary degrees from universities throughout the world. Currently, Kaunda is involved in a number of charitable organizations and serves as Chair of the Kenyan Olympic Committee.

See also ACQUIRED IMMUNODEFICIENCY SYNDROME IN AFRICA: AN INTERPRETATION and POLITICAL MOVEMENTS IN AFRICA.

ARI NAVE

Kavango
Ethnic group of northeastern Namibia, northern Botswana, and southern Angola.

The Kavango people are descendants of groups of ethnic OVAMBO who split from that society during the seventeenth century and settled in the northeast of what is today NAMIBIA, in the floodplain and on the islands of the Okavango River. Known as Kavangoland, this area has a high seasonal rainfall, and the river's silt deposits make for rich and arable soil. The riverine environment also supports a variety of hardwood, nut, and fruit tree species. Papyrus growing in blackwater pools produce leaves used for mats and thatch.

Organized into matrilineal, small-scale states, the Kavango complemented farming and cattle herding with iron smelting and trade. Slavery among the Kavango was common. They raided neighbors for slaves, used enslavement as a form of criminal punishment, and used slaves in trade. This trade was exacerbated by the expansion of the transatlantic slave trade into the area. Because the Kavango were geographically isolated and generally unfriendly toward visiting missionaries, they had limited contact with Europeans until Portuguese traders began arriving in Kavangoland in the mid-1800s.

Eventually a few missions established themselves in the region and provided what little education was available during German colonialism and South African occupation.

In addition to dividing Kavangoland, the colonial administrations of ANGOLA, BECHUANALAND, and SOUTH-WEST AFRICA introduced taxation and European legal statutes, especially concerning the ownership of land that had previously been communal. In 1973 SOUTH AFRICA granted Kavangoland self-governing status with an administrative and commercial center at Rundu. In contemporary NAMIBIA, the Kavango number some 140,000, and they are materially poor; hardwood timber and carvings are their most valuable exports.

See also BOTSWANA; ETHNICITY AND IDENTITY IN AFRICA: AN INTERPRETATION; CHRISTIANITY subentry MISSIONARIES IN AFRICA; and SLAVERY IN AFRICA.

ERIC YOUNG

Keino, Kipchogo
1940–
Kenyan long-distance runner.

Kipchogo Keino was the first of KENYA's world-class distance runners to make his mark on the world sports scene. He won gold and silver medals at both the 1968 and 1972 Olympic Games, set long-standing world records in both the 5000- and 3000-meter races, and inspired a generation of Kenyan track and field athletes. Keino, an ethnic NANDI, was born in Kipsamo, Kenya. He was orphaned at the age of two and raised by his grandmother. His first racing success came in 1962, when he set a national record for the mile. In 1964, while working as a physical fitness instructor for a police academy, Keino participated in his first Olympic Games, where he finished fifth in the 5000-meter race. The following year he broke world records in both of his main events, the 3000- and 5000-meter races. Sports analysts believe Keino's training on Kenya's mountainous terrain was one reason for his success in the next Olympic Games in 1968, which were held at Mexico City. There he won gold in the 1500-meter race and silver in the 5000-meter race, and led a Kenyan team that garnered a total of eight Olympic medals. In 1972 Keino repeated his two-medal performance, winning gold in the 3000-meter steeplechase and silver in the 1500. Soon runners worldwide were imitating his high-altitude training methods. In 1996 Keino was named coach of Kenya's national track team. He now chairs the National Olympic Committee of Kenya and operates a training center for African athletes. Keino is renowned not only for his stellar track career, but also for his personal beneficence. Since 1964 he and his wife, Phyllis, have taken over 400 orphans and homeless children into their home. For this humanitarian work, the American magazine Sports Illustrated named Keino one of its Sportsmen of the Year in 1987. Keino recently added a modern primary school to his home in western Kenya, now called the Kip Keino Ophanage and Training Center. In 2003 the International Fair Play Committee awarded the Willi Daume Trophy to Keino and his school. He also operates a tea farm and a sporting goods store. He has received a number of honorary degrees, including one from the University of Bristol.

KATE TUTTLE

Keita, Modibo
1915–1977
Former president of Mali.

The first president of MALI, Modibo Keita is often blamed for the economic problems that have afflicted the country since independence. A descendant of the MANDINKA lineage that once ruled the ancient Mali kingdom (MALI EMPIRE), Keita originally trained to be a schoolteacher. After his graduation from the William Ponty School in DAKAR, SENEGAL, Keita taught school, but soon abandoned teaching for politics.

In 1945 Keita co-founded the Bloc Soudanais, a political party with socialist leanings. A year later the party joined the RASSEMBLEMENT DÉMOCRATIQUE AFRICAIN (RDA)—a multi-colony political party founded by Félix HOUPHOUËT-BOIGNY of CÔTE D'IVOIRE—to form the Union Soudanaise-RDA (US-RDA). As the US-RDA candidate, Keita won election to the territorial assembly of FRENCH SUDAN (present-day Mali) in 1948, the French chamber of deputies in 1956, and the territorial assembly in 1957. Keita sought to build a state, the Mali Federation, incorporating several Francophone West African territories and linking French Sudan to the sea. In 1958 he was elected president of the Federation (initially comprising French Sudan and SENEGAL). However, Houphouët-Boigny opposed the Federation, and Léopold Sédar SENGHOR withdrew Senegal from the Federation in 1960. Keita subsequently became president of an independent Mali Republic.

Mali inherited a weak, overwhelmingly agricultural economy from French COLONIAL RULE; Keita's strict anticolonialist and socialist policies only added to the country's economic difficulties. At first, Keita severed relations with France and pulled Mali out of the French-dominated Communauté Financière Africaine (CFA) franc zone. With the support of communist countries, Keita nationalized Mali's banks, transportation, and public services and established village cooperatives. In addition, he imposed trade restrictions and tariffs that drove trade underground and depleted the national budget. Mali's economy rapidly deteriorated, and, against the wishes of his advisers, Keita negotiated Mali's readmission to the CFA in 1967.

Keita, however, placated his advisers with a series of political reforms styled after Mao Zedong's Cultural Revolution in China. He replaced the national legislature with a committee of radical supporters. He created a militant youth organization, the Popular Militia, to repress popular opposition. He also began purges of the government and military. In retaliation, army officers led by Lieutenant Moussa TRAORÉ removed Keita in 1968 in a military coup d'état. Traoré imprisoned Keita, who died in custody on May 16, 1977.

BIBLIOGRAPHY

Imperato, Pascal James. *Mali: A Search for Direction.* Westview Press, 1989.

Snyder, F. G. *One-Party Government in Mali.* Yale University Press, 1965.

ELIZABETH HEATH

Keita, Seydou
1921–2001
African photographer.

Seydou Keita was born in the French Sudan (present-day MALI) and lived his entire life in his hometown of BAMAKO. There, from 1945 to 1977, he created photographic portraits of thousands of locals and visitors. His work comprehensively documents the changing styles and social mores of urban West Africa during the decades when Mali underwent the transition from French colony to independent nation.

As an adolescent, Keita learned carpentry and embarked on a career as a cabinetmaker. In 1945, however, when an uncle returned from SENEGAL with a six-by-nine inch Kodak box camera, Keita fell in love with photography and quickly learned its fundamentals. At the time there were few photographers in Bamako, but Keita learned to develop and print from French expatriate Pierre Garnier, who ran a studio and photo-supply shop. After practicing the basics on family and friends, he studied more advanced techniques under photographer and anti-colonial campaigner Mountaga Kouyaté, who eventually loaned his darkroom to Keita.

Keita soon became Bamako's preeminent portrait photographer. In 1949 he opened his own studio and began using five-by-seven inch and thirteen-by-eight inch formats. Although color film had become available, it had to be sent to France for developing, and in any case Keita preferred the aesthetics as well as the ease of black-and-white film. By word of mouth his patronage grew quickly, and he settled into a schedule of shooting during the day, developing at night, and spotting negatives early in the morning, before customers returned for their photographs.

The business provided enough income that Keita could afford to buy automobiles and support his growing family.

He hired his old carpentry apprentices to recruit subjects at the train station, and, indeed, Bamako's status as a crossroads city greatly helped Keita's business. Many travelers from BURKINA FASO, the Ivory Coast (present day CÔTE D'IVOIRE), and NIGER stopped in Bamako en route to other parts of West Africa. As Keita's reputation grew, many visited the city solely to be photographed by him. Among Bamakois, a Keita portrait became a necessary acquisition for those who aspired to be cosmopolitan.

The photographs themselves reflected this interest in status. Keita stocked his studio with European goods to use as props, such as fountain pens, plastic flowers, a radio, and a telephone. He also kept three suits, along with hats, ties, and shoes, for men who wished to assume a modern look. Although many women continued to pose in African robes, they often donned Western-style accessories, and they too chose radios, mopeds, and cars as background scenery.

After Mali gained independence in 1960, Keita was appointed state photographer. Soon afterward, however, the socialist government demanded he close down private operations; his studio was subsequently burglarized. Keita continued working, however, now for the state, until his retirement in 1977. His photographs for the Military Committee for National Liberation (CMLN)—of leaders, state events, and official visits—remained for a time inaccessible to the public.

French photographer Françoise Huguier claimed to have "discovered" Keita during a trip to Mali in the 1980s. While getting his camera fixed at a local photo shop, Huguier heard stories of a famous Bamako photographer who had ceased practice in the 1970s. Huguier looked up Keita, who showed him numerous boxes of well-preserved negatives. These archives, which Keita had tended meticulously, comprised a stunning record of Bamako's emergence into modernity.

In the 1990s Keita's work appeared in exhibitions in Paris, London, Copenhagen, Birmingham, Arles, and Rouen. French art collector André Magnin did much to promote Keita, editing as well as contributing text to a book of his prints. In 1995 Editions Lux Modernis, a Paris company, published a CD-ROM of his work, and in 1996 the National Museum of African Art in Washington, D.C., presented his first United States retrospective. Keita died in Paris on November 22, 2001, two weeks before the opening of a show of his works at Sean Kelly Gallery in New York.

Critics acclaim Keita's work for its beautiful composition and detail as well as its epochal content. Some of his best photographs contrast the pattern of a backdrop with the pattern of a dress or shirt. Typical of Keita's work is an angled subject, such as a person leaning from the vertical axis of the shot. Also common are portraits that feature both customary forms of body ornamentation—scarification, piercings, and women's elaborately braided hairstyles—and Western fashions. Keita's simple, striking compositions captured the advent of modernity.

See also PHOTOGRAPHY, AFRICAN.

ERIC BENNETT

Kela

Ethnic group of the Democratic Republic of the Congo; also known as the Bakela.

The Kela primarily inhabit the Kasai-Oriental region of the central DEMOCRATIC REPUBLIC OF THE CONGO. They speak a BANTU language. Approximately 200,000 people consider themselves Kela.

See also ETHNICITY AND IDENTITY IN AFRICA: AN INTERPRETATION; LANGUAGES, AFRICAN: AN OVERVIEW.

Kenya

East African nation with some of the world's earliest evidence of human ancestry.

Kenya is on the Indian Ocean coast of eastern Africa, bordered by ETHIOPIA, TANZANIA, SOMALIA, and UGANDA. Fringed by coral beaches, crowned by MOUNT KENYA, and cut through by the majestic RIFT VALLEY, Kenya's physical landscape is among the most beautiful and varied in Africa. It is a landscape made familiar to many in the West through novels, Hollywood films, and the country's well-developed tourist industry. But safari tours in Kenya's national parks provide little more than a glimpse of a country that has one of the world's longest histories of human habitation and an enormously diverse—and often divided—society.

British colonialism helped turn cultural differences into ethnic animosities, and it established a lasting gap between the land-rich and the land-poor. Rights to the fertile land in central Kenya, in fact, were at the heart of a bloody anticolonial uprising—the so-called MAU MAU REBELLION—and after independence, export crops produced on that land contributed to the young nation's economic prosperity. But years of economic mismanagement, corruption, and political repression, especially after President DANIEL ARAP MOI came to power in 1978, dimmed Kenya's early promise. With a population estimated at 31.6 million in 2003, Kenya is burdened with massive foreign debt, a failing infrastructure, accusations of widespread human rights abuses, continuing ethnic tensions, and a high rate of HIV/AIDS.

PREHISTORY AND EARLY HISTORY

Millions of years ago, early hominids, or humanlike beings, evolved in the East African region now known as Kenya. Archaeological digs in the Rift Valley and around LAKE TURKANA, Kannapoi, and Allia Bay have uncovered remains of distant human ancestors, such as *Australopithecus anamensis* and *Australopithecus boisei*, as well as of more recent and direct human ancestors, including *Homo habilis* and *Homo erectus*. The latter are believed to be about 1.8 million years old. Archaeological research in Kenya's Malewa Gorge has also uncovered evidence of Stone Age toolmaking, dated at 238,000 B.C.E.

The earliest known human societies in the East African interior were speakers of the Khoisan languages. They inhabited the savanna, forests, and lakeshores, using sophisticated stone tools to hunt, forage, and fish. Approximately five thousand years ago, speakers of Cushitic languages migrated south from ETHIOPIA and settled in the Rift Valley. These people cultivated dryland crops such as sorghum and millet and kept herds of sheep, goats, and cattle. Approximately three thousand years ago, BANTU-speaking farmers migrated east from the rainforests of Central Africa to settle around LAKE VICTORIA.

The drier climate of East Africa, combined with interaction with their Cushitic neighbors, led the Bantu speakers to take up grain farming and PASTORALISM, or animal herding. Bantu-speaking communities expanded and spread rapidly, displacing or absorbing surrounding peoples. By about the fourth century C.E., Bantu-speaking communities had reached the Indian Ocean in the east and ZAMBIA in the south.

Other early migrants to Kenya included Nilotic-speaking herders from the SUDAN, who migrated in waves between one and two thousand years ago, and the Eastern Cushitic-speaking ancestors of the pastoral OROMO and SOMALI peoples, who moved south from Ethiopia into northern Kenya around 1000 B.C.E. Eventually Bantu-speaking peoples, such as the Kikuyu and Kamba, occupied much of central and southern Kenya. Nilotic-speaking KALENJIN peoples predominated in western Kenya, Nilotic-speaking TURKANA lived as nomads in the arid north, and the closely related MAASAI herded cattle in the fertile Rift Valley. Kenya's ecological diversity encouraged the development of distinctive regional economies and cultures.

For centuries, political organization in the Kenyan interior remained decentralized. Most trade occurred either locally, between farmers and herders, or between groups in Kenya's diverse ecological zones. Food, SALT, iron tools, and pottery were the primary goods traded among inland peoples. IVORY made its way through networks of traders to the coast, where it was exported.

Although the history of the East African or SWAHILI COAST is generally better documented than that of the interior, patterns of early coastal settlement are not entirely known. Hunters and gatherers were probably the first inhabitants of the coast, later joined at some point by Cushitic-speaking herders. The pastoral Oromo and Somali peoples in the coastal region are believed to be descendants of these groups. Finally, Bantu-speaking peoples migrated to the coast during the Iron Age.

They were primarily farmers and fishers, but they also hunted, kept livestock, and engaged in regional trade. After merchants from the Arabian peninsula began trading and settling along the African coast, the regional economy turned increasingly toward long-distance and sea-based trade. According to a second-century C.E. Greek text called *Periplus of the Erythraean Sea*, this trade dates back at least two thousand years.

Generations of intermarriage between coastal Africans and Arabs produced the SWAHILI PEOPLE, who had a distinctive culture. They were among the first East African Muslims—a mosque excavated at Shanga, a settlement in the Lamu Archipelago, dates to the eight century C.E.—and they created numerous independent coastal city-states. Ocean commerce in high-value goods such as RHINOCEROS horn, tortoise shell, ivory, GOLD, and slaves contributed to the prosperity of cities such as MOMBASA, Malindi, LAMU, and PATE during what Swahili history calls the "golden age," between the twelfth and eighteenth centuries.

The largest Swahili cities competed for domination of the coastal and sea trades. At the end of the fifteenth century, Malindi's power was waning and Mombasa's was rising. Then the arrival of Portuguese explorer Vasco da Gama began a new era of power struggles along the coast. The Portuguese, seeking to control Indian Ocean trade routes, allied with the Swahili dynasty in Malindi to take over Mombasa, which resisted Portuguese rule until 1529.

Portuguese efforts to tax the Swahili city-states led to repeated revolts. In 1593, the Portuguese built the formidable Fort Jesus at the entrance of Mombasa harbor, where its ruins still stand. The ruler of the Arabian state of Oman finally drove the Portuguese out of Mombasa in 1660, but the Portuguese held onto the fort until 1699. Although the Portuguese had few lasting effects on Swahili culture during their two-century-long occupation of the Kenyan coastline, they did introduce the American crops cassava, maize (corn), and tomatoes, which have since become part of both coastal and interior cuisines.

OMAN

Oman's victory over the Portuguese signaled growing Omani interest in East African trade, but Oman did not gain control of Kenya's coast. Instead, Mombasa's Mazrui clan, who claimed descent from Omani settlers, took control of the city after the Portuguese were driven out. They extended their influence through an alliance with the rulers of Pate, at that time the most powerful city-state in the Lamu Archipelago, but their allied forces were defeated by soldiers from Lamu in the early nineteenth century. The Mazrui were deposed, and many were later driven out of Mombasa by the Omani sultan SAYYID SA'ID IBN SULTAN, who claimed all of the Swahili city-states north of Cape Delgado between 1820 and 1830.

After 1840, the sultan oversaw his East African trade empire from the capital he established in ZANZIBAR. With a large navy and support from the British, he was able both to rule the coast and develop inland trade routes. These caravan routes opened the East African interior not only to Swahili traders, but to Europeans as well. Exports of ivory, slaves, and hides, as well as cloves, sesame, and other crops produced on coastal plantations, helped revive the economies of Swahili communities that had been in decline since the arrival of the Portuguese.

EUROPEAN COLONIZATION

Meanwhile, European powers had begun competing for control over the East African mainland. In the so-called SCRAMBLE FOR AFRICA, Germany claimed the mainland across from ZANZIBAR, which led the British to claim the region directly to the north. In Berlin in 1886 the two countries agreed on the boundary between their territories, and the following year they met to determine the sultan of Oman's holdings. They granted him all of the islands along the coast as well as a strip of coastline extending ten miles (sixteen kilometers) inland; in the British territory, this extended as far north as the mouth of the Tana River. In 1888 the Imperial British East Africa Company obtained royal permission to undertake economic development in East Africa north of Mount KILIMANJARO. Although the region had few natural resources other than fertile land, the British wanted to secure their interests both on the coast and in the BUGANDA kingdom around the headwaters of the NILE RIVER.

The British East Africa Company proved ineffective, however, and in 1895 it lost its territory to the British government, which declared it a protectorate. That same year, Great Britain signed a treaty with the sultan that gave it control of the coast in exchange for yearly payments. The transfer of power sparked a nine-month rebellion along the coast, beginning in Mombasa—the so-called Mazrui rebellion. The Swahili Mazrui clan took part in the rebellion, but so did others, including the Mijikenda people. The British later transferred administration of the coast to

the sultan of Oman, an arrangement that continued until Kenyan independence in 1963.

Great Britain's initial goals in the East Africa Protectorate were to make it economically self-sufficient and to build a railway from Mombasa to Lake Victoria. For the latter task the British recruited not only African workers but also indentured laborers from India. Many of the Indian laborers remained in Kenya afterward, becoming merchants in the towns that arose along the railway, which reached NAIROBI in 1899 and was completed in 1901. In 1907 the British moved their administrative capital from Mombasa to the more centrally located Nairobi, a former railroad depot.

The completion of the railway, combined with the addition of Uganda's fertile eastern province to the East African Protectorate in 1902, spurred increased European and Indian settlement in Kenya. The railway also let the British bring in the troops needed to suppress resistance in several different parts of the interior. Between 1900 and 1908, the British troops put down uprisings among the Nandi, Embu, GUSII, KIPSIGI, Bakusu, and Kabras peoples.

From the beginning, Kenya's white settlers enjoyed government representation and support far out of proportion to their numbers. The all-white Legislative Council, established in 1906, gave settlers a voice in colonial affairs. Even more important, the colonial government set aside Kenya's fertile highlands for settler farms. To create what became known as the "White Highlands," the government declared pastures and fallow farmland to be unoccupied, making them available for white settlers. Only Africans working on settler farms could use land in the highlands, and they were subject to abrupt evictions. At the same time, the government forced hundreds of thousands of Africans into crowded "native reserves," where farmland was often too poor and too scarce for households to support themselves.

Colonial rule in Kenya depended on defining and dividing "tribes." The government assigned Africans to reserve lands according to what tribe they claimed to belong to, and it appointed chiefs as tribal authorities. Many of Kenya's ethnic groups had not historically recognized political powers higher than their village councils or clan elders, however, and Britain's attempt to rule indirectly through traditional authorities was, in many cases, not traditional at all. The British also drew on ethnic stereotypes to create a colonial division of labor: the Kikuyu, for example, were considered suitable for lower-level civil service, while the Maasai were preferred for police and military service.

One of the appointed chiefs' main responsibilities was to recruit labor. The Native Authority Ordinance of 1912 authorized chiefs to recruit their tribal subjects for up to two months of compulsory labor, either on public works projects or for a private employer, typically a white farmer. The Native Registration Act of 1915 helped prevent laborers from fleeing by requiring all African adult males to carry identification whenever they left the native reserves. During World War I (1914–1918), approximately 195,000 black Kenyans were recruited to help as porters; an estimated 50,000 of them died from poor treatment. Another 10,000 served as soldiers.

The colonial government also used taxation to force Africans into wage labor. Men and women alike worked on the coffee and tea plantations of white settlers, while men predominated in the wage labor forces of Nairobi and Mombasa. Although some women also migrated to the cities—beer-brewing and prostitution were among the few income-earning options open to them—those who remained in rural areas often had to assume greater responsibility for farming.

The government of the protectorate based its plans for economic self-sufficiency on export crops such as coffee and tea that were produced by white settlers. By 1915 the settlers had not proven to be very productive farmers, but still the Colonial Office extended their land leases from ninety-nine to 999 years. Kenya's new governor, Major General Sir Edward Northey, encouraged British soldiers to settle in the colony, seizing an additional 12,810 acres (5,186 hectares) of land from native Kenyan peoples. In 1921, the East African Protectorate became a Crown colony named Kenya.

The World War I era saw the emergence of African political protest in Kenya. This protest was urban, led largely by the mission-educated elite, and moderate in tone. Its leaders, such as HARRY THUKU of the Kikuyu Central Association, objected to colonial land and labor policies and called for unity among tribes. The colonial government arrested Thuku in 1922, but not before his speeches had inspired a young mission-educated man named JOMO KENYATTA.

Kenya's Indians also began to pressure the colonial government for reforms. By the mid-colonial period, many Indians had established shops and other small businesses, but they objected to the urban segregation policies that barred both Indians and Africans from living in certain neighborhoods. They also protested limits on Indian immigration. In 1923 the colonial government granted five seats on the Legislative Council to Indians, also agreeing to loosen segregation and immigrant restrictions. The highlands, however, remained reserved for whites. Meanwhile, the European settlers pushed, with little success, for greater independence from the British Crown.

Excluded from the colony's political institutions and from most of the social services available to Europeans and Asians, many educated Africans put their energies into self-help associations, such as the Kavirondo Taxpayers' and Welfare Association and the Kikuyu Central Association (KCA). Although these were initially established to provide social services, they later became some of the driving forces of Kenyan nationalism.

During World War II (1939–1945), Kenya was mobilized against the threat of an Italian invasion from Somaliland. Mombasa and Nairobi grew rapidly as laborers poured in, seeking work on the docks or in industry. Labor unions began to flex their muscles—strikes rocked Mombasa in 1939 and again near the end of the war. In the countryside, the forced-labor policies used to secure workers for European farms spurred protest. Although the administration had used the invasion threat as an excuse to ban African political activity, it attempted to calm the unrest by agreeing to modest wage increases for urban workers. The administration also nominated Eliud Mathu, a politically prominent school principal, to an unofficial seat on the Legislative Council in October 1944. Africans gained an additional three seats (all unofficial) the following year.

Mathu was supported by a group of Nairobi activists called the Kenya African Study Union (KASU). Their name was purposefully nonpolitical, but their goals—among them, the return of settlers' land to Africans—were not. Still, KASU remained a small, elite organization until Jomo Kenyatta, by then a KCA leader, returned from university studies in Great Britain and became its president. Renamed the Kenya African Union, the group grew rapidly, attracting members from all socioeconomic groups. Its leadership was divided, however, between militant nationalists who wanted immediate independence and land handovers, and moderates like Kenyatta, who were willing to work for gradual independence through constitutional reform.

By the early 1950s, rising violence among Kenyans led the British to fear a general uprising. They suspected Kenyatta as the ringleader, and although he denied any involvement, in October of 1952 he and approximately one hundred other activists were arrested and jailed. The administration then declared a colony-wide state of emergency, which sparked the Kikuyu-dominated uprising known as the Mau Mau Rebellion. Support for the uprising in Nairobi was quickly crushed; afterward, many of its organizers hid in the forests around the capital city. The Mau Mau Rebellion was mainly aimed at the British, but its forces also attacked Africans who were loyal to Great Britain. By the end of the fighting in 1956, the British had detained more than 80,000 Kenyans. More than 12,000 Africans and 100 Europeans had died. Great Britain won

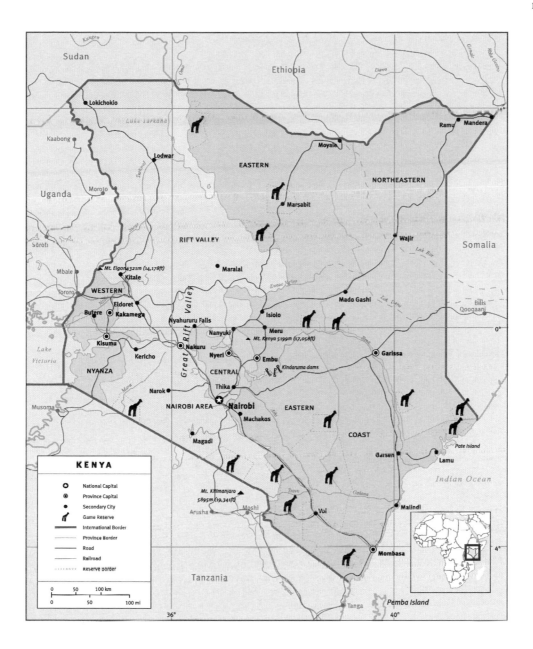

militarily but lost faith in its future as a colonial power in East Africa. It agreed to grant Kenya its independence.

The state of emergency ended in January 1960, and a delegation of Africans, including TOM MBOYA and Jomo Kenyatta, traveled to London to negotiate a transitional constitution for Kenya. Completed by February 1961, the constitution gave Africans the majority of seats in the legislative council and made political parties legal. Soon afterward, African council members formed the Kenya African National Union (KANU).

KANU candidates won a majority in the legislative council in 1961 but refused to form a government while Kenyatta remained in prison. Released in August of that year,

Kenyatta became president of KANU. In general elections in May of 1963, KANU was the overwhelming victor. Kenyatta became prime minister at Kenyan independence on December 12, 1963. One year later, Kenya officially became a republic, with Kenyatta as its president.

POSTCOLONIAL DEVELOPMENT AND NATIONHOOD
Kenya's first independent government was moderate. Kenyatta favored free-market economic policies and close ties with the West. He set in motion a plan for land distribution in which the government purchased European-owned farms and settled landless Africans on them. During the first ten years of independence,

Kenya (At a Glance)

OFFICIAL NAME:
Republic of Kenya

FORMER NAME:
British East Africa

AREA:
582,646 sq km (224,960 sq mi)

LOCATION:
Eastern Africa, bordering the Indian Ocean, between Somalia and Tanzania; bordered by Ethiopia, Somalia, Sudan, and Tanzania

CAPITAL:
Nairobi (population 3,138,295; 2009 estimate)

OTHER MAJOR CITIES:
Mombasa (population 712,600; 2003 estimate), Kisumu (population 275,100; 2003 estimate), and Nakuru (population 333,800; 2003 estimate)

POPULATION:
39,002,772 (2009 estimate)

POPULATION DENSITY:
66.94 persons per sq km (174 persons per sq mi; 2009 estimate)

POPULATION BELOW AGE 15:
42.3 percent (male 8,300,393, female 8,181,898; 2009 estimate)

POPULATION GROWTH RATE:
2.69 percent (2009 estimate)

TOTAL FERTILITY RATE:
4.56 children born per woman (2009 estimate)

LIFE EXPECTANCY AT BIRTH:
Total population: 57.86 years (male 57.49, female 58.24; 2009 estimate)

INFANT MORTALITY RATE:
54.7 deaths per 1,000 live births (2009 estimate)

LITERACY RATE (AGE 15 AND OVER WHO CAN READ AND WRITE):
Total population: 85.1 percent (male 90.6 percent, female 79.7 percent; 2003 estimate)

EDUCATION:
Although the first eight years of school are compulsory, in 2000 the average schooling of adults was only 4.2 years. Also in 2000, about 68.5 percent of eligible pupils were enrolled in primary school and 23 percent in secondary school. For the years 1998–2002, 71.2 percent of elementary-school pupils reached grade five.

LANGUAGES:
Swahili and English are official languages, although Kikuyu and Luo are also widely spoken. Nearly all Kenyan ethnic groups have distinct languages.

ETHNIC GROUPS:
The largest of Kenya's many African ethnic groups are the Kikuyu, Luhya, Luo, Kalenjin, Kamba, Kisii, and Meru. Asians, Europeans, and Arabs make up 1 percent of the country's population (2003 estimate).

RELIGIONS:
About 45 percent Protestant, 33 percent Catholic, and 10 percent Muslim. Another 10 percent of Kenyans follow traditional religions (2003 estimate).

CLIMATE:
Kenya is divided into two almost equal parts by the equator. The region north of the equator is hot and receives comparatively little rain. The southern region falls into three meteorological zones. The coast is humid with an average annual temperature ranging from about 24° C (about 76° F) in June and July to about 28° C (about 82° F) in February, March, and April; the highlands are relatively temperate; and the Lake Victoria region is tropical.

LAND, PLANTS, AND ANIMALS:
Kenya covers several well-defined geographical and climate zones extending from the Indian Ocean coast upward to lofty mountain ranges that reach elevations of more than 3,050 m (10,000 ft) above sea level. From a low coastal strip the terrain rises gradually to a broad, arid plateau that covers the largest portion of the country. The region west of the plateau contains great volcanic mountain chains; the principal peak is Mount Kenya (5,199 m/17,058 ft). The southern and southeastern portions of the country are heavily forested, and in the west, the immense depression of the Great Rift Valley is rimmed by steep cliffs. The chief rivers of Kenya are the Tana and Galana (known as the Athi in its upper course). Besides a small portion of Lake Victoria, Kenya contains almost all of Lake Turkana (formerly called Lake Rudolf).
Coastal forests contain palm, mangrove, teak, copal, and sandalwood trees. Forests of baobab, euphorbia, and acacia trees cover the lowlands to an elevation of approximately 915 m (approximately 3000 ft). Extensive tracts of savanna (grassland), with scattered groves of acacia and papyrus, cover the terrain from about 915 to 2,745 m (about 3,000 to 9,000 ft). The principal species in the dense rain forest of the eastern and southeastern mountain slopes are camphor and bamboo. The alpine zone (above about 3,350 m/11,000 ft) contains large senecios and lobelias. Major animal species include the giraffe, elephant, rhinoceros, zebra, lion, other large cats, birds, and reptiles.

CURRENCY:
The Kenyan shilling

GROSS DOMESTIC PRODUCT (GDP):
$31.42 billion (2008 estimate)

GDP PER CAPITA:
$1,600 (2008 estimate)

GDP REAL GROWTH RATE:
2.2 percent (2008 estimate)

PRIMARY ECONOMIC ACTIVITIES:
Agriculture, small-scale mining and manufacturing, and tourism

PRIMARY AGRICULTURAL PRODUCTS:
Tea, coffee, corn, wheat, sugarcane, fruit, vegetables, dairy products, beef, pork, poultry, eggs

INDUSTRIES:
Small-scale consumer goods (plastic, furniture, batteries, textiles, soap, cigarettes, flour); processing agricultural products; oil refining; cement; tourism

PRIMARY EXPORTS:
Tea, coffee, petroleum products, canned pineapple, hides and skins, sisal, soda ash, and pyrethrum extract (used in insecticides)

PRIMARY IMPORTS:
Crude petroleum, industrial machinery, motor vehicles, iron, steel, agricultural implements, pharmaceuticals, and fertilizer

PRIMARY TRADE PARTNERS:
United Kingdom, Uganda, United Arab Emirates, Tanzania, Japan, India, Germany

GOVERNMENT:
Kenya has a modified one-party parliamentary form of government. Executive authority is exercised by a president, elected for a five-year term by popular vote. Mwai Kibaki took office as president in 2002. However, a power-sharing agreement was reached after the violence following the controversial and highly suspect 2007 election. A vice president and a cabinet are appointed by the president from members of the National Assembly, the legislative branch of government. The assembly consists of 210 directly elected members, the attorney general, the speaker, 12 members nominated by the president. Major political parties include the National Rainbow Coalition (NARC), the Forum for the Restoration of Democracy (FORD), and the Kenya African National Union (KANU).

Robert Fay

approximately 150,000 landless people were given about 640,000 acres (259,000 hectares) of land. The pace of government reform, however, was unsatisfactory to some more militant KANU members. By 1965, the party was divided into two broad camps. Tom Mboya led the conservative wing, while OGINGA ODINGA, a fellow Luo and Kenya's vice president since 1964, led the radical wing. In 1966 Odinga and many of his supporters left KANU and formed the Kenya People's Union (KPU). Kenyatta responded by broadening the government's power to censor and detain critics. He also merged the two legislative bodies into one. Minister of Home Affairs Daniel arap Moi became the new vice president.

In July 1969, Mboya was assassinated in Nairobi by a Kikuyu man, aggravating tensions between the Luo and the numerically and politically dominant Kikuyu. Luo demonstrations in the western town of Kisumu gave Kenyatta an excuse to ban the KPU and place Odinga under house arrest, without charges, until 1971.

Throughout the 1970s, the aged Kenyatta grew more reclusive and took more rule into his own hands. But high prices paid around the world for Kenya's tea and coffee exports, along with a thriving tourist industry, brought relative prosperity and helped ensure the president's reelection to a third five-year term in 1974. Kenyatta died in office in August of 1978. Vice president Moi succeeded Kenyatta despite opposition led by Kenyatta's nephew, Njoroge Mungai.

Moi, an ethnic Kalenjin, made no immediate moves to end Kikuyu political dominance. For his administration he took the motto Nyayo, Swahili for "footsteps," indicating his wish to follow in Kenyatta's path. A year later, however, he banned ethnic associations and began giving former Kikuyu properties to his Kalenjin supporters. In 1982, discontented air force officials attempted a coup d'état against Moi. They failed, and Moi reorganized the armed forces and outlawed all political parties except KANU. Over the next several years, Moi tightened his hold on power by replacing Kikuyu in his administration with fellow Kalenjin and eliminating press freedoms. Critics claim that he also encouraged ethnic violence to divide his opposition.

By the early 1990s, Kenya had lost its reputation as one of Africa's most stable and prosperous countries. Pressure from foreign aid donors forced Moi to hold multiparty elections in 1992. He was elected then and again in 1997, although opponents claimed that both elections were rigged. His regime did little to improve its record of corruption, ethnic favoritism, and human rights abuses. Before and after the 1997 elections, towns on the coast and in the Kikuyu regions—centers of opposition to Moi—were violently attacked by what many believe were Moi's Kalenjin henchmen. Some 1997 presidential

candidates had campaigned for an end to "tribalism," but in April of 1998, the human rights organization Amnesty International warned that ethnic tensions had made Kenya a "powder keg waiting to explode."

Kenya's open-door investment policies promoted diversified agricultural exports—for example, Kenyan coffee, fresh-cut flowers, and green beans are known throughout Europe. Overall, though, the economy suffered not only from widely acknowledged government corruption but also from mounting debt and a crumbling infrastructure. Heavy rains associated with the 1997–1998 El Niño weather patterns inflicted especially severe damage on the road system, lengthening the five-hour trip from Mombasa to Nairobi to two days. Political instability also hurt Kenya's tourist industry, one of the country's primary sources of foreign exchange.

The 2002 elections appeared to open a new era in Kenyan political life. Mwai Kibaki, the candidate of the multiethnic National Rainbow Coalition, became president after campaigning on promises to crack down on corruption and to promote tribal unity. Such hopes, however, were short-lived. After Kibaki appeared to win reelection in the elections of 2007, suspicions of vote tampering and other irregularities touched off protests in the country that led to widespread violence and the deaths of some 1,500 Kenyans. Shortly thereafter, the United Nations brokered a power-sharing agreement in which Kibaki's Orange Democratic Movement-Kenya (ODM) party rival Raila Odinga joined the new unity government.

See also BANTU, subentry on DISPERSION AND SETTLEMENT; HUMAN RIGHTS IN AFRICA; and INDIAN COMMUNITIES IN AFRICA.

ROBERT FAY

Kenyatta, Jomo
1894?–1978
First prime minister and first president of Kenya.

Jomo Kenyatta was born in Ichaweri, British East Africa (now KENYA), and his life spanned almost the entire period of British COLONIAL RULE in the area that is now Kenya. Raised in the countryside near MOUNT KENYA and educated at a Church of Scotland mission school, Kenyatta became a leading member of the generation of African elites who rose in protest of oppressive colonial policies. Kenyatta's political career began in 1922 when, while working as a civil servant in NAIROBI, he joined the East African Association (EAA), a short-lived KIKUYU organization led by Harry THUKU that was formed to regain stolen African lands from white settlers.

Pressure from the colonial administration forced the EAA to disband in 1925 and reform as the Kikuyu Central

Association (KCA). In 1928 Kenyatta became the KCA's general secretary and the editor of its journal, *Muiguithania* (the Reconciler). *Muiguithania* publicized and gathered support for the KCA's demands, which included the return of confiscated land to Africans, improved social services, African representation on Kenya's Legislative Council, the repeal of hut taxes, and noninterference in Kikuyu customs, such as polygamy. The KCA also opposed a British proposal for "closer union" among the colonies of Kenya, UGANDA, and TANGANYIKA.

When Kenyatta traveled to England to protest the proposal (which the British government ultimately dismissed), his speeches and publications won increased support for Kenyan reform among members of Britain's Labour Party. Kenyatta spent 1931 to 1946 away from Kenya, a time of intellectual ferment for him. Kenyatta continued his activism, and he attended classes at Moscow State University and received a degree in anthropology from the London School of Economics. His thesis, *Facing Mount Kenya*, a study of traditional Kikuyu customs and beliefs, became a bestseller in England after its publication and is still considered an anthropological classic. In addition, Kenyatta helped organize the 1945 Pan-African Congress in Manchester.

Kenyatta found a radically different Kenya when he returned after World War II (1939–1945). The colonial government had banned the KCA, and in response, nationalist members of the organization had formed the Kenya African Union (KAU), a multiethnic, pro-independence organization, of which Kenyatta became president in 1947. Growing anticolonial militancy in Kenya erupted into the 1952–1956 MAU MAU REBELLION. Mau Mau, a Kikuyu secret society that drew members from the KAU and other organizations, was committed to armed struggle to oust the British. Although Kenyatta was excluded from Mau Mau and, under pressure from the colonial government, had denounced its activities, the government arrested him and some 150 other nationalists on October 21, 1952. In 1953 he was tried and convicted of "managing the Mau Mau terrorist organization" and sentenced to seven years in prison. Although Mau Mau failed militarily, it brought international attention and criticism to the colonial government's brutal crackdown—which cost more than 12,000 African lives—and pushed Great Britain to accelerate its plans for Kenyan independence. In 1960 the KAU was renamed the Kenya African National Union (KANU), and Kenyatta, still in prison, was elected its president.

After his release, Kenyatta helped negotiate the terms of Kenya's independence at the London Conference in 1962. KANU won pre-independence elections in May 1963, and on independence day—December 12, 1963—Kenyatta

JOMO KENYATTA. Jomo Kenyatta, leader of the Kenya African National Union, speaks in Nairobi in 1962, shortly before being elected Prime Minister of Kenya. (*AP Images*)

became the country's first prime minister. The following year Kenya became a republic and Kenyatta its president, an office he held until his death in 1978.

Under his motto Harambee ("pulling together"), Kenyatta sought to unite Kenya and build a stable nation. He outlawed Kenya's sole opposition party in 1969, but also attempted to overcome ethnic divisions, appointing members of various ethnic groups to key government posts. He maintained friendly relations with Western nations, encouraged a free-market economy, and promoted foreign investment and TOURISM, all of which helped the economy to grow five-fold between 1971 and 1981. Although most of the generated wealth was concentrated in the hands of a few—namely Kenyatta, his family, and their close associates—the president faced little opposition during his time in office.

ROBERT FAY

Kérékou, Mathieu
1933
President of Benin from 1972 to 1991, and since 1996.
Born in Kouarfa in what was then DAHOMEY (part of FRENCH WEST AFRICA), Kérékou attended schools in MALI and SENEGAL before enrolling in the French army and attending Fréjus Officers School in France. In 1961 he was commissioned second lieutenant in the Dahomean army, serving as aide-de-camp (military assistant) to President Hubert Maga (1961–1963). Kérékou was a close adviser to his cousin Colonel Iropa Maurice Kouandete and played an important role in Kouandete's 1967 overthrow of the Christophe Soglo military regime. After a series of attempted military coups and mounting chaos among civilian leaders in the early 1970s, Kérékou (then a major) seized power on 26 October 1972. He dismissed most senior army officers, imprisoned all three former presidents (who were eventually released in 1984), and established a government staffed entirely by army officers under the age of forty. Kérékou proclaimed Marxism-Leninism the official ideology of the state and changed the country's name from Dahomey to BENIN in 1975. In 1979 he held elections, nominally converting Benin to civilian rule, while ensuring his own power base. Kérékou changed his name to Ahmed in 1980, but remained widely known as Mathieu. Kérékou's policies of nationalization and government expansion remained in effect until the early 1980s, when economic woes and resulting internal strife forced him to agree to reforms, including privatization and reduction of government. He abandoned Marxism-Leninism in 1989, and in March 1991, faced with both international and domestic pressure, Kérékou allowed free elections. Defeated by NICÉPHORE SOGLO, he publicly apologized for the abuses of his regime and received amnesty from the new

government. He remained active in politics and after Soglo failed to revitalize Benin's economy in his first five-year term. Kérékou was reelected president in March 1996. He then liberalized Benin's economy and secured economic assistance from the International Monetary Fund (IMF). Kérékou was reelected to another five-year team in March 2001. The national constitution, however, prevented him from seeking a third term. Kérékou left office in 2006.

See also POLITICAL MOVEMENTS IN AFRICA.

Kerere
Ethnic group of Tanzania; also known as Kerewe.
The Kerere primarily inhabit northern TANZANIA, just south of LAKE VICTORIA. Others live on Ukerewe Island in Lake Victoria itself. They speak a BANTU language. Approximately 100,000 people consider themselves Kerere.

See also ETHNICITY AND IDENTITY IN AFRICA: AN INTERPRETATION; and LANGUAGES, AFRICAN: AN OVERVIEW.

Keyo
Ethnic group of Kenya; also known as Elgeyo and Keiyu.
The Keyo primarily inhabit the western shores of the Kerio River in northwestern KENYA. They speak a Nilo-Saharan language and are related to the KALENJIN people. Approximately 200,000 people consider themselves Keyo.

See also ETHNICITY AND IDENTITY IN AFRICA: AN INTERPRETATION; and LANGUAGES, AFRICAN: AN OVERVIEW.

Khaled Hadj Brahim
1960–
Algerian singer considered the most prominent star of the contemporary North African music style Rai.
Khaled Hadj Brahim was born and raised in Oran, a cosmopolitan port city with a rich musical tradition. By age ten he was playing the harmonica, bass, guitar, and accordion, and with his first single "La Route de Lycée" (The Road to School; 1974), recorded at age fourteen, he emerged as an underground sensation on the Algerian pop scene. He took the name "Cheb," or "young," Khaled, to mark himself as part of a youth culture ready to change ALGERIA.

During the late 1970s and 1980s Khaled reworked Rai, an improvisational folk music that emerged from the bars and bordellos of Oran during the 1920s. Holding on to the sounds of the traditional instruments, and the outspoken, often sexually provocative lyrics, Khaled added the Western sounds of drum machines, synthesizers, and electric guitars. The new Rai, which means "opinion" in Arabic, appealed to youths disenchanted with traditional romantic lyrics that had little to do with their lives. Rai spread throughout North Africa, where over 60 percent of the war-ravaged population was under twenty-five, and the fame of Khaled, "the King of Rai," spread with it.

Khaled's music was censored in Algeria until 1983, when the government relaxed controls on popular culture in an effort to undermine growing support for Islamic fundamentalism. Conservative Islamic leaders saw Khaled's music as corrupting and declared a fatwa, or religious decree, pronouncing a death sentence against him. In 1990 he bargained the profits for his record *Kutche* for a visa, and fled to France.

Since his move to Europe, Khaled has once again updated the sound of Rai, this time incorporating African American jazz saxophone improvisations and hip-hop "scratching," as well as other transcultural sounds, including Asian string arrangements, found in "world beat" music. His lyrics have also evolved, and now include the experiences of the North African diaspora.

By the mid-1990s Khaled was a well known pop figure in North Africa, the Middle East, South Asia, and Europe: his single "Aicha" sold more than 1.5 million copies and went gold in Europe. With his songs featured in the popular American films *Killing Zoe* (1994) and *The Fifth Element* (1997), he also won recognition in North America. Among his recent studio albums are *Ya-Rayi* (2004), *Anajit Anajit* (2006), and *La Liberté* (2008). Khaled continues to tour and record new music.

See also ISLAM IN AFRICA; ISLAMIC FUNDAMENTALISM: AN INTERPRETATION; *and* MUSIC, NORTH AFRICAN.

BIBLIOGRAPHY

Cullman, Brian. "Cheb Khaled & the Politics of Pleasure." *Antaeus* (Fall 1993).

MARIAN AGUIAR

Khama III

1837?–1923

Chief of the Bamangwato (Ngwato) clan of the Tswana people in Bechuanaland (present-day Botswana), who ensured that his people came under the protection of the British.

Known as Knainas (Khama the Good), Khama was baptized a Christian in 1860. In 1872 he attempted to seize the chieftainship from his father, Sekgoma I, because Sekgoma opposed Christianity, but he was forced into exile. Three years later, however, Khama overthrew his father and became chief of the Bamangwato. Khama was a reformer who embraced the new European values that were spreading through the region at this time. He abolished a number of old tribal customs that he considered anti-Christian, including circumcision, rainmaking, and bride-wealth (payment made by the groom to the bride's family). He also allowed the London Missionary Society to establish a mission on his territory. Khama was opposed to AFRIKANER attempts to expand into BECHUANALAND from the independent Boer state of the TRANSVAAL, and in 1876 he asked for British protection.

In 1885 Khama welcomed British general Charles Warren, who established the Bechuanaland Protectorate. In 1890 Khama assisted British colonialist Cecil RHODES when Rhodes took a group of pioneer settlers north into what became SOUTHERN RHODESIA (modern ZIMBABWE). When the NDEBELE under King Lobengula rose against the white settlers in 1893, Khama led some of his own troops against them in support of the settlers. However, he opposed a plan, devised by Rhodes, to have Bechuanaland taken over by Rhodes's British South Africa Company. In 1895, accompanied by two senior Tswana chiefs, Khama went to London and successfully petitioned that Bechuanaland remain a British protectorate and not come under the control of the settlers. Although he retained substantial powers for himself, he was obliged to surrender a strip of his land for the construction of a railway.

See also COLONIAL RULE.

Khama, Seretse

1921–1980

First president of Botswana.

Born in Serowe of royal parents, Seretse Khama inherited the title of chief of the Ngwato (Bamangwato) people, who make up more than one-third of the population of BOTSWANA. When he violated the color bar by marrying a white woman in 1948, British authorities banished him from the country (1950) and deposed him as chief (1952). Allowed to return in 1956, he founded the Botswana Democratic Party in 1962. Three years later, campaigning on a multiracial platform, the party was swept to power and Khama became prime minister. He was elected president in 1966 and was knighted the same year. Khama died in office.

Khartoum, Sudan

Capital city and commercial center of Sudan, located at the confluence of the White Nile and the Blue Nile Rivers.

A city of more than 2 million inhabitants in 2005, Khartoum is the center of SUDAN's largest urban agglomeration, including the larger city and Islamic center of Omdurman and the slightly smaller industrial city of Khartoum North. This urban region has absorbed approximately 1,800,000 refugees since the resumption of the Sudanese civil war in 1983; the urban region's population now totals more than 8 million.

In the 1820s, when Uthman Bey's army occupied the region on behalf of the Ottoman regime in Egypt (known in Sudan as the Turkiyya), Khartoum was a small farming village. Recognizing its strategic importance at the most important river junction in northeast Africa, Uthman built a fort there and made it his administrative center. In 1829 Muhammad Ali, Viceroy of Egypt, designated it as the capital of the Egyptian Sudan. After the opening of the White Nile to riverine commerce, Khartoum became an important center for the slave and ivory trades. In 1885 the Mahdi's defeat of the Egyptian forces and the death of General Gordon at the battle of Khartoum marked the end of the Turkiyya administration of the Sudan. The Mahdi destroyed the city and moved the capital across the river to Omdurman, which remained the capital until 1898.

When Horatio Kitchener led a British and Egyptian army to overthrow the Mahdist state in 1898, he rebuilt Khartoum and made it the capital of Anglo-Egyptian Sudan. Upon independence in 1956 Khartoum became capital of the Republic of the Sudan. Under COLONIAL RULE Gordon College, the first institution of higher education in Sudan, was established at Khartoum. During the 1950s it became part of the University of Khartoum. Khartoum sits at the hub of Sudan's road and rail network and, together with Omdurman and Khartoum North, serves as the cultural, financial, and industrial center of the country.

In August 1998, after car bombings at U.S. embassies in Kenya and Tanzania killed 224 and injured more than 4,000, the United States bombed a pharmaceutical plant in Khartoum, alleging that the factory was manufacturing chemical weapons and was linked to Osama bin Laden, who was believed responsible for the embassy attacks. Arms specialists later determined that no chemical weapons were made at that plant. Plans were made to rebuild the factory. More recently, fighting broke out in the city when a rebel group from Darfur attempted, unsuccessfully, to overthrow the national government.

See also BLUE NILE.

ROBERT BAUM

Khayr ad-Din
?–1546
Sixteenth-century corsair and Ottoman regent of the Maghreb, also called Barbarossa or Red Beard.

Though some histories remember the man whose birth name was Khidr as Khayr ad-Din, the name was actually a title first held by Khidr's brother, Aruj. The Turkish brothers are believed to have been born on the island of Lesbos or Mytilene. They gained a reputation for their prowess as CORSAIRS preying on the commerce of the sixteenth-century Mediterranean Sea. A legendary figure, Khayr ad-Din captured the imagination of both Western and Eastern writers for centuries after his death. Also known as Red Beard the Pirate, he has been the subject of such works as the eighteenth-century play *Barbarossa*.

Historians have debated the motives behind the brothers' intervention in North Africa. Whether they saw the potential for profit and power, or they came to the assistance of fellow believers, in 1511 Khidr and Aruj landed in ALGIERS to overthrow Spanish rule. Although the Spanish did not hold the city militarily, they controlled the port from the occupied island of Peñon. Muslim and Christian forces contested the city for the next four years, until the brothers finally prevailed. Aruj pursued the Spanish to the city of TLEMCEN in 1517 and left his younger brother and lieutenant, Khidr, in his place as leader of Algiers. Aruj succeeded in taking Tlemcen, but was killed a year later by the Spanish.

Khidr assumed the title Khayr ad-Din, and sought the backing of the powerful Ottoman Empire. Khayr ad-Din pledged loyalty to the Ottomans in exchange for military assistance and the title of regent of the MAGHREB. He and his successors created a strong corsair state around the city of Algiers. They built mosques and the now famous white-washed military fortification, the Casbah. Under Khayr ad-Din, Algiers became a stronghold for Mediterranean corsair activity.

Khayr ad-Din enjoyed relative autonomy from the distant Ottoman Empire, yet he and his successors greatly expanded Ottoman authority in North Africa. They brought other parts of what is now ALGERIA under nominal Ottoman rule, although their expansion encountered resistance in the east: As the Ottomans pushed up against the border of the Tunisian-based Hafsid empire, the Hafsids responded by attacking Algiers in 1534. By then the admiral of the Ottoman fleet, Khayr ad-Din retaliated by taking TUNIS and its environs. He held Tunis for only a year, until the Spanish Hapsburgs restored the Hafsids to power. Khayr ad-Din faced Europeans again in the 1538 Battle of Prevenza, in which he defeated the naval forces of Hapsburg emperor Karl V. As a result of his victory, North African corsairs and the Ottoman Empire held the eastern Mediterranean. Ultimately, Khayr ad-Din's successors expanded Ottoman rule from the base that he had established in Algeria into areas now known as TUNISIA and LIBYA.

See also ISLAM IN AFRICA.

MARIAN AGUIAR

Khoikhoi

Ethnic cluster of southern Africa; also known as Khoekhoe, Namaqua, Khoi, and pejoratively as Hottentot.
The Khoikhoi consists of KHOISAN-speaking pastoral groups, including the NAMA. The Khoikoi live mainly in NAMIBIA and SOUTH AFRICA. Traditionally they have based their livelihood on cattle herding and foraging.

Khoikhoi pastoralists were engaged in both foraging and cattle raising in northern BOTSWANA over one thousand years ago. Over the centuries, they slowly migrated south to the Cape region in present-day western South Africa. When Europeans arrived in the mid-seventeenth century, they displaced the Khoikhoi population from their homeland in the Cape. Dutch settlers referred pejoratively to the Khoikhoi as HOTTENTOTS. Smallpox, introduced by the Europeans, decimated the Khoikhoi, who lacked natural resistance. The survivors either withdrew to marginal areas, mainly in present-day Namibia, or merged with other groups to form the CAPE COLOURED people. Some AFRIKANER settlers intermarried with Khoikhoi, forming a new ethnic group called Baster (Bastards), Afrikaner-speaking Christians who currently number about 30,000.

Today, the surviving Khoikhoi mostly live in arid districts of Namibia, where they continue to raise sheep and goats. Wage labor, however, earns the lion's share of income. More than 100,000 people consider themselves Khoikhoi.

See also DISEASE AND AFRICAN HISTORY; ETHNICITY AND IDENTITY IN AFRICA: AN INTERPRETATION; HOTTENTOT; *and* LANGUAGES, AFRICAN: AN OVERVIEW.

ARI NAVE

Khoisan

Family of languages spoken primarily in southern Africa.
Khoisan languages, known for their click consonants, are spoken by both SAN foragers, pejoratively called BUSHMEN, and KHOIKHOI pastoralists, often called HOTTENTOTS. The term refers collectively both to these groups and to the languages they speak. There are three distinct and mutually unintelligible Khoisan languages: Zhu, Khoi, and Qui. In ancient times, Khoisan speakers are thought to have occupied most of southern and even East Africa, but the BANTU expansion either absorbed or displaced most of them, particularly during the past 2,000 years. Today the remaining Khoisan speakers, numbering somewhat over 200,000, live almost entirely in NAMIBIA and BOTSWANA.

Khoisan is not the only African language family to contain click sounds. The NGUNI languages are Bantu languages in southern Africa that have absorbed click phonemes from Khoikhoi and San populations. In addition, the Hadza and Sandawe foragers of TANZANIA speak languages that use clicks. Many linguists classify these languages as Afro-Asiatic. However, other scholars believe that these groups are both linguistically and genetically related, though fairly remotely, to the Khoisan, after thousands of years of separation.

Although language is often used as a proxy for genetic relationships, there are clear cases where the two do not coincide. Khoisan and Bantu speakers have intermarried for centuries and often cannot be regarded as genetically distinct. Despite these ambiguities, Bantu and Khoisan continue to be used frequently as racial terms.

See also ETHNICITY AND IDENTITY IN AFRICA: AN INTERPRETATION; HOTTENTOT; *and* LANGUAGES, AFRICAN: AN OVERVIEW.

ARI NAVE

Kidjo, Angélique

1960–

Beninese singer and bandleader.
With music that blends African and Western influences, Angélique Kidjo has become a crossover star, winning worldwide popularity, as well as a role model for women and girls in her native BENIN. Kidjo was born in Cotonou, Benin, as one of nine children in a musical family. She remembers her older siblings singing folkloric Beninese songs as part of the Kidjo Brothers Band, in addition to songs by American rock and roll stars. When Kidjo began making her own music, she was influenced both by the West African rhythms of her homeland and by the American soul and pop music she heard on the radio. As a solo singer, she developed a local following by the late 1970s.

Rather than stay in Benin, where she faced pressures to perform propaganda for the communist government, in 1983 Kidjo moved to Paris and studied jazz and opera. She quickly became involved in a Parisian musical scene bursting with expatriate Africans. The cross-cultural influences of jazz, gospel, funk, hip-hop, and Western pop music are evident in *Logozo* (1991), Kidjo's first hit album. Two earlier albums, *Pretty* and *Parakou*, had limited success; she followed *Logozo* with *Ayé* (1994), *Fifa* (1996), *Oremi* (1998), and *Black Ivory Soul* (2002). "Agolo," a song from *Ayé*, was nominated for a Grammy Award. With lyrics in FON, Mina, YORUBA, and Swahili, as well as French and English, Kidjo sings about love, religion, motherhood (she has a daughter, Naima), and social issues. Among her recent albums are *Oyaya!* (2004) And *Djin Djin* (2007).

Kidjo is a strong, charismatic performer, and she disputes the notion that, as an African woman, she should restrict herself to African material or project an "exotic" character. Yet her cultural roots run deep, from the influence of her childhood religion, vodou, to her frequent trips home to Benin, which she visits to "breathe the air of the country, to see my people, my mother, and pay respect to my ancestors." Kidjo continues to perform live and to record new music.

See also MUSIC, AFRICAN.

KATE TUTTLE

Kiga

Ethnic group of East Africa; also known as the Chiga and the Ciga.

The Kiga primarily inhabit northern RWANDA and southern UGANDA. They speak Kinyarwanda, a BANTU language, and are closely related to the HUTU, of whom they are sometimes considered a subgroup. Approximately 200,000 people consider themselves Kiga.

See also ETHNICITY AND IDENTITY IN AFRICA: AN INTERPRETATION; ETHNICITY IN RWANDA: AN INTERPRETATION; and LANGUAGES, AFRICAN: AN OVERVIEW.

Kigali, Rwanda

Capital, economic center, and largest city in Rwanda.

Spread over four hills beside the Ruganwa River in the central Rwandan highlands, Kigali is the only large city in this mostly rural nation. Kigali boasts an international airport, a technical college, and a modern business district. Kigali is a center for coffee and tea exports, as well as a mining and manufacturing hub. The city is making a slow comeback after suffering greatly during the 1994 Rwandan civil war.

In the late fifteenth century the Tutsi kingdom of RWANDA occupied Kigali, which was a trade site for caravans traveling as far as the Indian Ocean. Kigali later became a colonial economic center under the German East Africa Company from 1899 to 1916. After Germany's defeat in World War I (1914–1918), the League of Nations granted Belgium a mandate to administer Rwanda as part of the territory of Ruanda-Urundi in 1923, and Kigali became a Belgian administrative center. The Belgians established mining operations near Kigali during the 1930s, and revenue from the mines contributed to the city's growth. The city had picturesque streets lined with flowering trees. In 1962 Rwanda gained its independence and Kigali became the nation's capital.

The 1994 Rwandan civil war devastated Kigali. A series of massacres took place in the city, and one-third of the population were killed or fled. During the late 1990s displaced residents and other Rwandans uprooted by unrest congregated in Kigali. In 1995 Kigali had a population of 286,000, most of them returned refugees However, segregation has increasingly divided the HUTU AND TUTSI residents of Kigali, and tensions between the two groups threaten to undermine the city's political and economic recovery. By 2005 the population had risen to more than 850,000, but large numbers of Kigali's residents still live in dreary slums and have few or no opportunities for employment. In recent years, a program of micro-loans—small loans to individual entrepreneurs rather than to large companies or directly to the state itself—has provided some hope of economic recovery for Kigali.

See also ETHNICITY IN RWANDA: AN INTERPRETATION.

Kikuyu

Ethnic group of Kenya.

The Kikuyu are the most populous—and most politically and economically powerful—ethnic group of modern-day KENYA. More than 5 million people consider themselves Kikuyu. An agricultural people who speak Kikuyu, a BANTU language, they have traditionally occupied the fertile highland areas between MOUNT KENYA and the Kenyan capital of NAIROBI. Although they probably migrated to this area from the northeast around 1500 C.E., Kikuyu origin myths claim that their first ancestors, Gikuyu and his wife Mumbi, were given Kikuyuland by the god Ngai, who is believed to reside on Mount Kenya.

The Kikuyu are divided into nine clans, or mihiriga, which are in turn divided into sub-clans. The mbari, a residential group of families all descended from a common paternal ancestor, has historically been the most important landholding unit in Kikuyu society. The muramati, generally the first son of the first wife of his father, determines land distribution, though he has no greater rights to land than his brothers. Age and sex have also figured importantly in Kikuyu social organization. Groups of boys and girls are initiated into separate "generation sets" that in the past defined which generation of adults held political authority.

Land has long been vital to Kikuyu livelihoods. Precolonial Kikuyu societies practiced hoe cultivation, raising crops such as sorghum, Millet, beans, peas, and yams. Land also holds important spiritual meaning. In his book *Facing Mount Kenya* (1938), Jomo Kenyatta, Kenya's first president and himself a Kikuyu, wrote of the land's spiritual impact on his people: "Communion with the spirits is perpetuated through contact with the soil in which the ancestors of the tribe lie buried."

Because the Kikuyu's land includes some of the best farmland in East Africa, they were not the only ones to appreciate its value. After British COLONIAL RULE was established in the late nineteenth century, colonial land policies displaced many Kikuyu to make way for European settlers. This created a class of Kikuyu wage laborers who lived in overcrowded tribal reserves and worked on European plantations or migrated to urban areas in the hope of finding other menial work.

In the 1920s this displacement of the Kikuyu inspired the first political protest against colonial rule. Such organizations as the Kikuyu Central Association were formed in an effort to regain confiscated Kikuyu lands. Later they came to protest other issues, including Christian missionaries' efforts to discourage traditional Kikuyu religious practices, such as polygamy and clitoridectomy (FEMALE CIRCUMCISION IN AFRICA). Following World War II, many dispossessed Kikuyu joined the MAU MAU REBELLION, a violent anticolonial revolt that cost more than 12,000 African lives, but succeeded in hastening an end to British rule.

Although Kenyatta's official slogan was *Harambee*, meaning "all pull together," he favored his fellow Kikuyu, who developed into an economic elite during his presidency. Many of them became large landowners in the highlands. When Kenyatta died in 1978, his successor, DANIEL ARAP MOI, began to favor members of his own ethnic group, the KALENJIN. Gradually, this new favoritism eroded some of the privilege the Kikuyu had enjoyed.

As Moi's regime became increasingly repressive in the 1980s and 1990s, the Kikuyu once again formed one of the largest factions calling for an end to authoritarian rule. However, the government-controlled media managed to keep the opposition divided, in part by appealing to other ethnic groups' fears that Kikuyu political domination could come at their expense. In the December 1997 presidential election, the Democratic Party candidate Mwai Kibaki, an ethnic Kikuyu, finished second to Moi but won few non-Kikuyu votes. Five years later, Kibaki won the presidency as the head of a multiethnic party.

See also ETHNICITY AND IDENTITY IN AFRICA: AN INTERPRETATION; KINSHIP AND DESCENT IN AFRICA; *and* LANGUAGES, AFRICAN: AN OVERVIEW.

ROBERT FAY

Kilimanjaro
Highest mountain in Africa.

Called Kilema Kyaro ("that which makes the journey impossible") by the local CHAGGA people, Mount Kilimanjaro is located in northeastern TANZANIA, near the border with KENYA. Kilimanjaro is a dormant volcano, its two peaks standing about eleven kilometers (about seven miles) apart, connected by a broad ridge. Kibo, the higher peak, rises to 5,895 meters (19,341 feet) above sea level, and the summit of Mawensi is 5,149 meters (16,893 feet) above sea level. Although Kilimanjaro lies three degrees south of the equator, an ice cap covers the crater of Kibo year-round; this ice cap is pierced by several small craters. Whether the recent reduction in the size of the ice cap can be attributed to climate change remains a subject of some debate among scientists.

Kilimanjaro has a number of different vegetation zones on its steep slopes, ascending through tropical rain forests at its base, and including moorlands, alpine meadows, and alpine desert. Chagga farmers grow coffee and plantains on the lower slopes of Kilimanjaro. The mountain was successfully scaled for the first time in 1889 by German geographer Hans Meyer and Austrian mountain climber Ludwig Purtscheller. In recent years, Kilimanjaro has become a highly popular destination for recreational hikers and mountain climbers, and an important source of revenue for the Tanzanian government.

See also GEOMORPHOLOGY, AFRICAN.

Printed in the USA/Agawam, MA
February 16, 2011

556665.022